WOODWORKER VOLUME 86
Index

12 monthly copies January 1982-December 1982

 Model & Allied Publications, Argus Books Ltd.

Woodworker 1982

AUTHOR INDEX

SUBJECT INDEX

ADVERTISERS' INDEX

Published by
Model & Allied Publications
Argus Books Ltd.,
Wolsey House, Wolsey Road,
Hemel Hempstead, Herts.

Model & Allied Publications Ltd.
First Published 1982

Printed in Great Britain

Woodworker

THE MAGAZINE FOR THE CRAFTSMAN

JANUARY 1982 Vol. 86 No. 1058 ISSN 0043-776X

Front cover: Modern reproductions of Renaissance racketts by Barbara Stanley and Graham Lyndon-Jones, St Albans. *(Photo: John Cuerden)* See also Early Music exhibition details pp20-23.

Editorial	Polly Curds	
Advertisement Manager	Glyn Crole-Rees	
Advertisement Director } MAP Leisure	Michael Merrifield	MEMBER OF THE AUDIT
Managing Director } Division	Gavin Doyle	BUREAU OF CIRCULATIONS

SUBSCRIPTION DEPARTMENT: Remittances to MODEL AND ALLIED PUBLICATIONS, PO Box 35, Hemel Hempstead, Herts HP1 1EE. Price per copy 95p includes p&p. Subscription queries: Tel: Hemel Hempstead 51740. Subscription rate, including index, £11.90 per annum; overseas sterling £12.90; $29.00 US for overseas dollar subscribers. Second class postage paid in the US at New York, New York. *Distribution* to North American hobby and craft stores, museums and bookshops by Bill Dean Books Ltd, 166-41 Powells Cove Boulevard, Post Office Box 69, Whitestone, New York 11357, USA. Tel: 1-212-767-6632. *Distribution* to news stand sales by Eastern News Distribution Inc, 111 Eighth Avenue, New York, NY10011, USA. Tel: 1-212-255-5620.

WOODWORKER is printed in Great Britain by H. E. Warne Ltd, East Hill, St Austell, Cornwall PL25 4TN for the proprietor and publisher Model & Allied Publications Ltd (a member of the Argus Press Group). Trade sales by Argus Press Sales & Distribution Ltd, 12-18 Paul Street, London EC2A 4JS. WOODWORKER (ISSN 0043-776X) is published on the 3rd Friday of the month.

Model & Allied Publications Ltd

PO Box 35, Bridge Street, Hemel Hempstead, Herts HP1 1EE. Telephone: Hemel Hempstead (0442) 41221.

THE WRONG BOARD

George Nakashima is a woodworker and architectural designer from Seattle, Washington, USA. He has written a book called *The Soul of a Tree* which is beautifully produced and contains in its 221 pages many fascinating illustrations – superb pencil sketches and black and white and colour pictures of trees, furniture, rooms and all sorts of objects in wood.

Much of the text is devoted to the author's search for the meaning of life and therefore those whose interests are practical rather than philosophical may perhaps find the going a little hard at times.

Nevertheless, there is much of value to be distilled from the pages. For example: The selection of furniture parts is always most important. Of the roughly 10 000 boards available in the warehouse, the perfect choice must be made for each part of each board. Sometimes five or 10 years pass before a board is selected for use... The grain of the wood must relate closely to its function. The abutment of the edge of one board to an adjoining board can mean the success or failure of a piece. There must be harmony, grace and rhythm. It is so easy to place the wrong board...

There is so much individuality in these boards. Some are of great distinction and nobility, others plain and common, still others of such poor aspect that they must be relegated to the scrap pile. Each species of wood has its own strong personality... Roots, too, have strong personalities, especially where they meet the tree's trunk, producing fantastic richness of graining. Roots must be used in a precise and exact way. They may be cut round or square or oval. Or they may be left entirely natural, or 'free'.

Quite often the shape, size, texture and the extravagances of graining dictate the design and function of an object.

The author comments that furniture should be lived with and not treated as something 'overly precious.' A certain amount of scratching adds character to a piece. 'To me,' he says, 'there is nothing quite so uninteresting as a shining, perfectly smooth surface that looks as though it has never been used.'

On the subject of craftwork George Nakashima is encouraging. 'There is a pride evident today in work well done. Many strive to create and to create well... To the advantage of craftsmen, the modern commercial system has produced its own built-in difficulties. The costs to a large manufacturer of mass-selling small objects are now so high, involving so many middlemen, that it is possible for craftsmen to build a better product and sell it for less by direct contact with the buyer. This helps in some measure to explain the resurgence of the craft movement.

'The maker of fine wood furniture reaches out into hundreds of lives, listens to voices and shares in the lives of so many people, giving and receiving.'

The Soul of a Tree (ISBN 87011-482-4) is published by Kodansha International Ltd and distributed by Prentice-Hall International, 66 Wood Lane End, Hemel Hempstead HP2 4RG. The price is £23.95.

Woodworker Annual Vol 85 (1981)

Available early January the *Annual* runs to nearly 900 pages and includes context and advertisement index. Published by Argus Books Ltd, Argus House, St James Road, Watford, Herts., at £9.95 it comprises the 12 monthly issues of WOODWORKER magazine for 1981 within hard covers.

If Grandad could see me now -he'd be proud of me and Kity

" Isn't it amazing how some woodworkers still use old-fashioned methods? They wouldn't dream of drawing water from a well, travelling to work on horseback or cooking on an open fire and yet their woodworking belongs to the Dark Ages. Mind you – I ought not to criticize them: I used to be the same. I was proud to work like my grandfather did and I believed the results would be better if I did everything by hand. It never occurred to me that my grandfather and his father before him did everything by hand because they had no alternative. Anyhow, I soon found out how wrong I had been when I started using the Kity combination. I obtained better results in a fraction of the time and with little physical effort.

The Kity combination is ideal for the modern craftsman and I am just one of hundreds of satisfied users. Why don't you join us?''
Read on for details of this superb combination.

Kity offers you Circular Saws, Bandsaws, Planer Thicknessers, Spindle Moulders and Slot Mortisers, along with a complete range of accessories, motors and floor stands. Each machine can be independent or part of a combination for example:
You can start your workshop with a circular

saw, motor and stand. After a few months you can mount your saw on the large table and drive any other machine from your existing motor. You can then continue to add machines until you have a fully equipped workshop. This is a unique flexibility, that will benefit the professional and the amateur woodworker alike. Using a mixture of Kity independent and combination machines, you can build a workshop that exactly suits your requirements.

You do not have to purchase one complete unit that costs a lot of money and may be a compromise in size or difficult to use. With Kity you do not have a lot of complicated attachments, nor do you have to swing the machine into different positions or use a special tool. Simply slip the belt from one machine to the next.

The Circular Saw 617
This is the heart of most workshops. The Kity machine has a cast and machined, tilting work table; a rise/fall arbor with hand wheel control; it accepts blades up to 9″ in diameter giving a 3⅛″ depth of cut; and is capable of running at two speeds; 3400 rpm and 7000 rpm. It is powered by a 1½ H.P. motor with No Volt Thermal Overload Starter. You will have no

difficulty in cutting any wood based mater from melamine faced chipboard to Africa hardwoods.
Accessories included in the price are the m guide with repeat cut stop, and wobble wa for grooving. The machine is guarded to comply with international standards.

The Planer Thicknessers 535, 635, 636
Kity manufacture three 'under and over' planer/thicknessers, a 10″ × 6″, 8″ × 6″ an 6″ × 4″.
Each machine is available with stand and motor and can be used as an independent or will fit as part of the combination.
Each machine has cast tables and a twin k cutter block and is of the 'under and over' type.
The thicknesser is power fed with an adjus thicknessing table giving true results along whole length of the timber, this is usually difficult to achieve with the 'over fed' clan type thicknesser. The 636 and 635 both ha unusual long (40″) surfacing tables ideal fo straightening a twist in a plank of timber.

Spindle Moulders 626/627

The Spindle Moulder is a versatile and powerful tool. It does a totally different job to a router, although the system is similar. For example:

The 626 & 627 are capable of making large rebates 1¼" × 1¼" in hundreds of feet of timber. They will also produce moulding, deep grooves, tongue and groove joints, V-joints, tenons, profiles and counter profiles, all with effortless power.

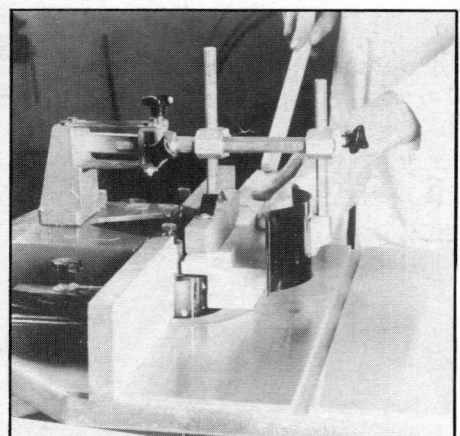

The 626 has a standard adjustable fence with the capability of positioning the cutting tools over a 4" vertical range. The 627 has the same specifications but with individual micro adjustable fences. Both machines have cutting speeds of 7000 rpm, and are guarded to full international standards.

The 625 Slot Mortiser

The only machine in the whole range that is *not* available as an independent machine.

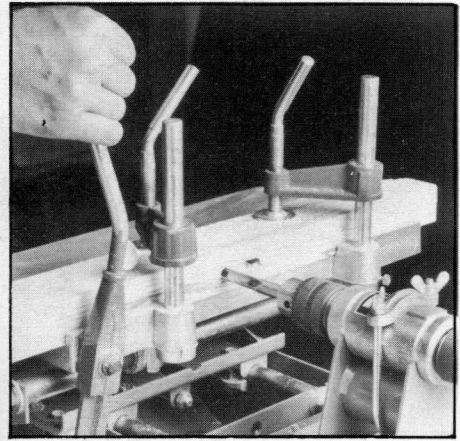

Working from the 700 table it will provide a ½" slot, up to 5" long and 4" deep. An excellent machine for motice joint production.

The 612 Bandsaw

Kity make an all steel, two wheel, Bandsaw with a 5½" depth of cut and an 11½" throat. It will accept blades from ¼" for tight turns to ⅞" for deep cutting and planking of timber. Unlike 'Plastic' Bandsaws the steel construction of the Kity machine allows you to set a high blade tension. This enables you to cut fast and in a straight line through hardwood and knots with a maximum depth of 5½", 'Like a hot knife through butter'.

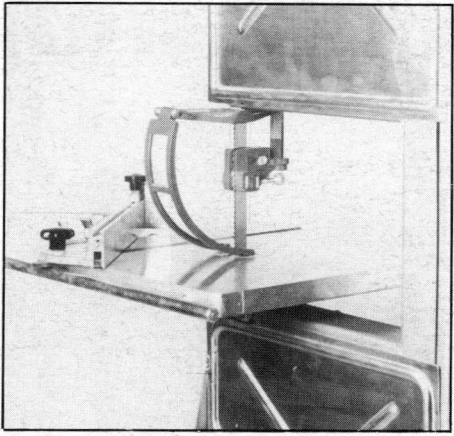

Service and Support

All manufacturers claim to provide a service. We can demonstrate ours BEFORE you purchase your machine.

Kity Information

As a Kity user, every few months you will receive an 'in house' newsletter printed exclusively for you. It includes other Kity users' practical ideas as to how to make more use of your Kity machines, plus information on new accessories, competitions and many other interesting ideas.

Kity Plan Sheets

These are issued for a nominal charge exclusively to Kity users and titles include, 'basic joints', 'carpentry work bench' and 'fitted kitchens'. These practical plan sheets include cutting lists and complete manufacturing instructions on the relevant subject, and a new title is issued every 3 to 4 months.

Stockist Training

Most manufacturers ask for a large order when appointing a new stockist plus a continual minimum yearly quota. This is not the case with Kity. We expect all our stockists to attend our product training courses, which enables the stockist to offer the best technical advice when you make your purchase, without the pressure to 'sell' minimum quantities. In the long term we will have far less service problems if you have chosen the right machine for the job, through correct advice.

Instructions on machines

Many service problems arise because machines are incorrectly assembled or adjusted, or are used far beyond their capabilities. Each Kity machine has comprehensive instructions to ensure you have the knowlege to use the machine correctly.

For work requiring precision and reliability, and for results you can trust use KITY machinery.
Remember – KITY turns men into craftsmen.

Two Year Guarantee
Should there be a problem with your machine we will make every effort to repair or replace as necessary at no cost to yourself, during the first two years of use.

KITY UNITED KINGDOM

For more information about this and many more Kity products, please fill in this coupon and return.

NAME ....

ADDRESS ....

....

.... TEL............WW1

Kity U.K., Sizer's Court, Henshaw Lane, Yeadon, Leeds LS19 7DP. Tel. (0532) 509110. Telex: 557920

for the serious craftsman

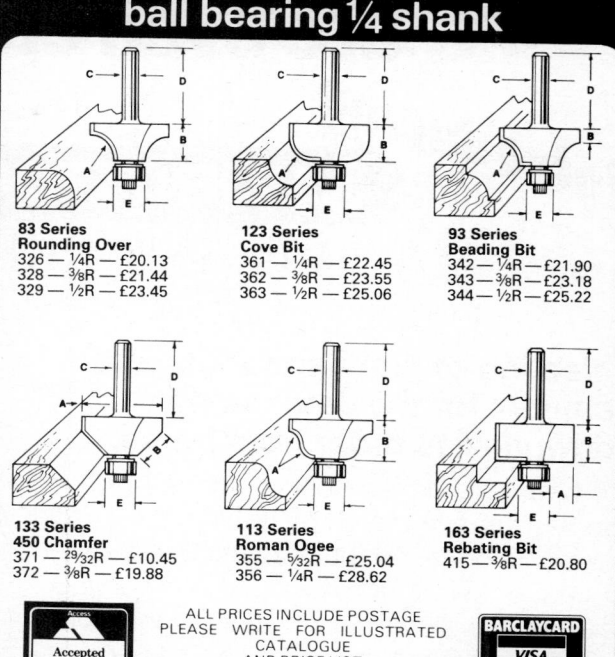

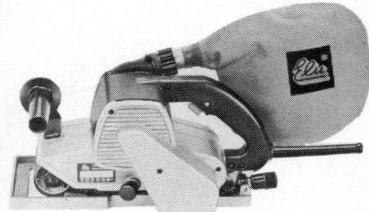

Now, good tools from the name you know are even easier to choose

Introducing

SARJENTS TOOLS
WOODWORKING CATALOGUE

A selection of fine hand tools and machinery for the demanding woodworker to order from home.

Up to now, ordering by post or phone from our wide range has been impeded by the lack of a good, well laid-out catalogue. All that has changed; looking through the new Sarjents Tools Woodworking Catalogue, the discerning craftsman will find a range of the highest quality hand tools and machines that are a pleasure to use.

The emphasis is on quality throughout – both in content and presentation. 100 big (12″ × 8″) pages show the products in full colour photographs, and the text not only carries detailed descriptions, but also many hints and tips as well. And to make life really easy, the prices shown are the prices you pay; there is no extra for V.A.T., postage or packing.

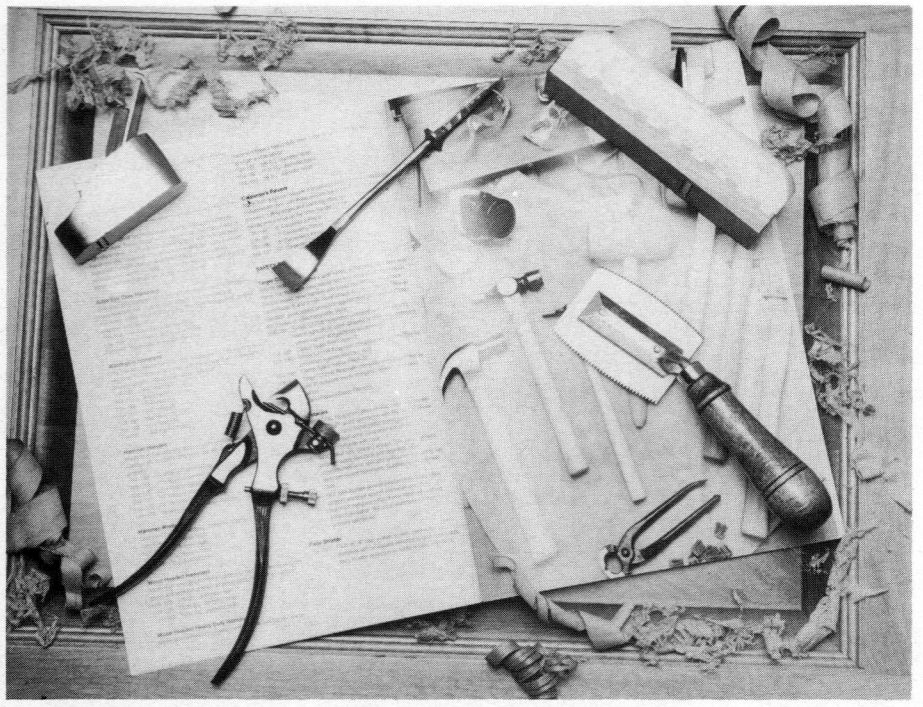

For your copy of this super catalogue, please send a cheque or postal order for £1 to:

SARJENTS TOOLS

Dept. W.W.,
Oxford Road,
Reading.
Or write or phone
(0734) 586522
with your Access or
Barclaycard/VISA number.

Overseas readers are advised to send £3.00 (in sterling currency or sterling bank draft only please) to the same. Airmail (not Europe) £5.50.

Prices quoted are those prevailing at press date and are subject to alteration due to economic conditions.

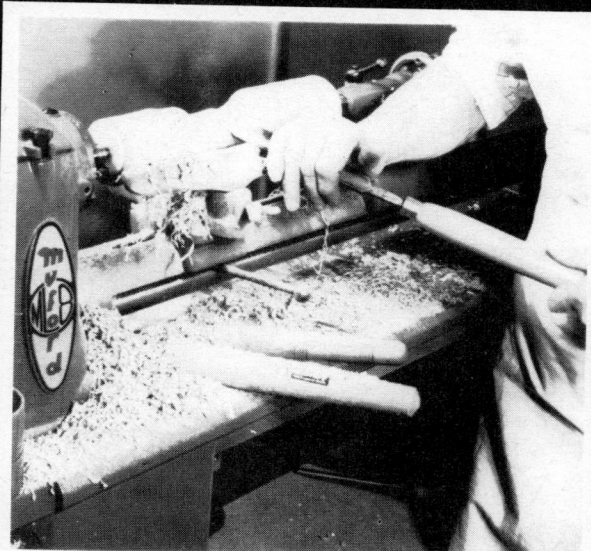

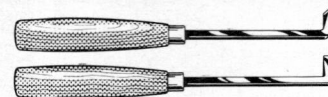

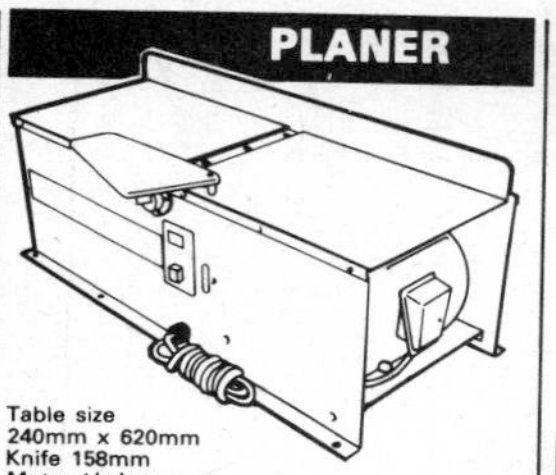

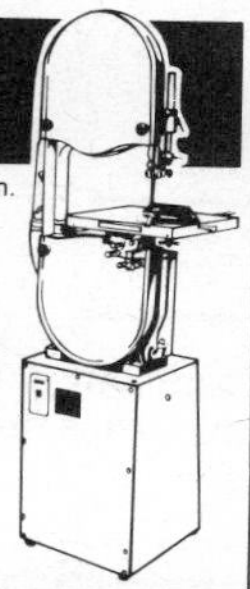

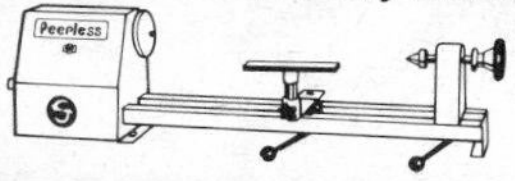

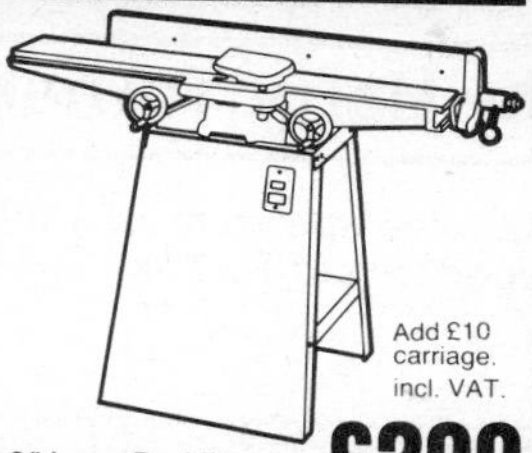

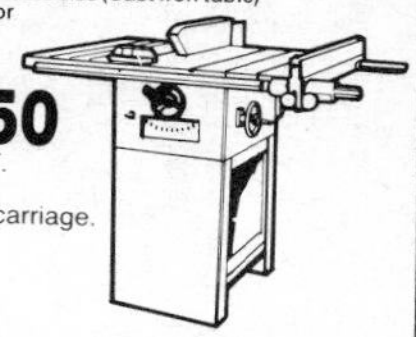

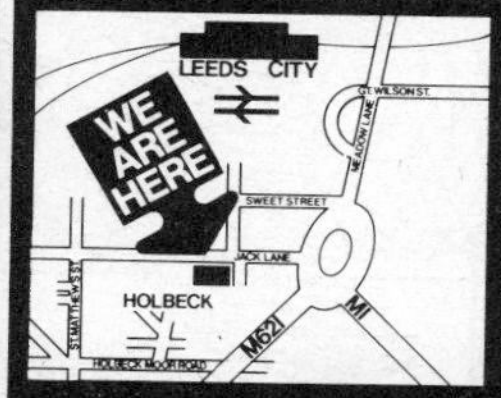

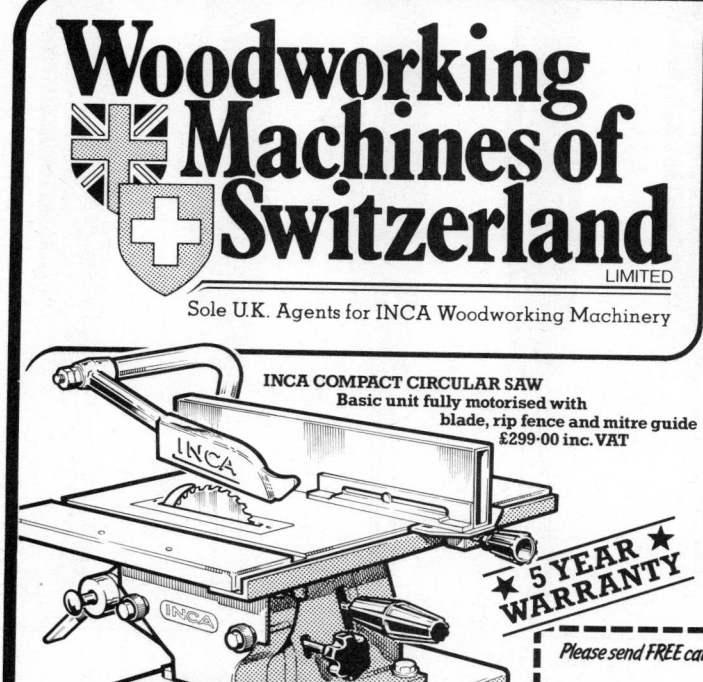

FIGURE & DECORATIVE CARVING 1

by Harry Turner

The title of this series covers a wide spectrum of work but part 1 is the beginner's approach: How to start? What wood to use? The tools and how to use them? And such like questions.

The fish (Fig. 1) is a first project. Obtain a piece of plywood 300 × 150mm (12 × 6in.) and paint one side with two coats of white emulsion. Divide into squares as shown using a pencil and apply two coats of polyurethane matt varnish. Also get two packs of Plasticine of one colour and some modelling tools.

You may wonder what all this has to do with carving. The answer is: start modelling without worry, by working in contour, judging depths and observing shadow effect on ultimate detail, and allowing correction of mistakes by adding to or taking away.

Lighting is important. An Anglepoise-type lamp or even a table lamp placed at one side of the work gives excellent cast shadow effect.

The fish should be modelled from Fig. 1. On completion you will have a like-for-like pattern to work from instead of a drawing which you would have to transform into three dimensions. It is not essential to model every detail such as scales and fin fluting. What is needed is the form of the fish. (The Plasticine will be used in further projects.)

If this first work gives you a sense of achievement in a non-permanent material, what is better than having the work enhanced by the grain, the colour and finish of a beautiful permanent material such as wood? It can then be handled or displayed to advantage, or given as a present. What can be more personal?

As to the wood to suit the project, you may have a piece set aside but if not you could use lime, oak, pear, chestnut, elm, meranti. This last is knot-free and carves well so is suitable for beginners to relief carving. A piece 300 × 150 × 50 or 38mm (12 × 6 × 2 or 1½in.) would suit your Plasticine model.

For beginners the many profiles of carving tools can be rather confusing and Fig. 2 shows a boxed set suitable for most early needs. The tools are 150mm (6in.) long which is a handy size for close working. With experience of the use of carving tools and knowledge of the function that each performs you can with confidence go on to the other profiles.

Fig. 3 shows items such as a beech mallet; gouge slip; oil stone; oil can; rifflers; and wood rasp. You also need Carborundum sheets for finish sanding. There are various rifflers (tools for finishing the awkward places) though the three illustrated are sufficient for beginners' needs. The Carborundum sheets can also be cut into strips and 'pencil rolled' for

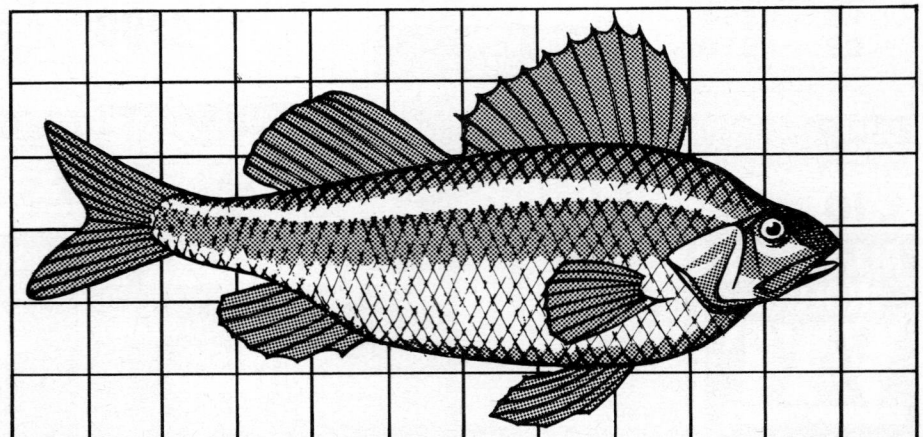

Fig. 1

Fig. 2

finishing awkward places. The wood rasp (medium tooth) can be used to achieve a smooth background to the fish carving. However, you can leave the gouge marks in a 'wavy line' effect to simulate water if you wish to have such a background.

In Fig. 4 an attempt is made to show the technique of handling gouges and chisels. Control of the tools is essential if you are to avoid incorrect cutting or splitting-off important detail. Do remember to keep your hands behind the cutting edge of the tool

you are using.

Fig. 4 (a) shows the left hand acting as anchor with right hand to apply pressure and control; this helps straight or circular cutting across the grain. Fig. 4 (b) is as (a) but for shorter more controlled cuts. Fig. 4 (c) shows the technique for vertical cuts or lightly marking lines or curves using the mallet. Fig. 4 (d) is similar to (a) but shows that more hand pressure can be applied by pressing the weight of the body against the right hand. Fig. 4 (e) is the technique for

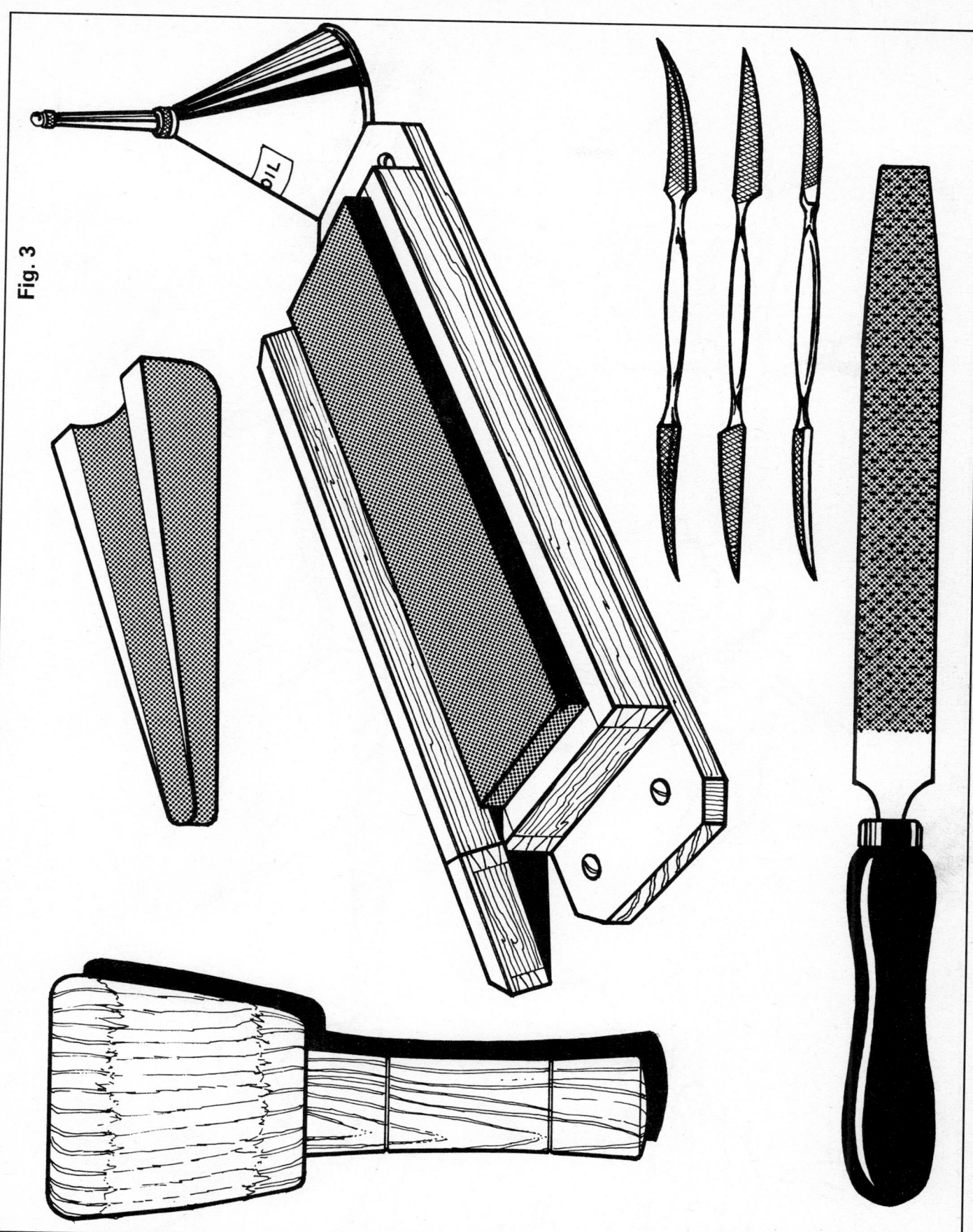

Fig. 3

horizontal heavy cutting or light paring using the mallet. Fig. 4 (f) indicates hewing surplus wood in large shavings using the mallet as at the start of the work.

The various stages from initial drawing to finished carving are shown in Fig. 5. Sequ-

ence of working is: plane and finish the wood to a fine surface; put masking tape round the four thin edges; apply two coats of white emulsion paint to the top (or design surface); rule squares with pencil; score these lines with marking knife and a square.

Draw in design in pencil (erasure and correction can be done as the squared lines have been scored); alternatively apply and secure a design drawing over carbon paper and trace on to the surface. Then apply two coats of polyurethane matt varnish with a

Fig. 4

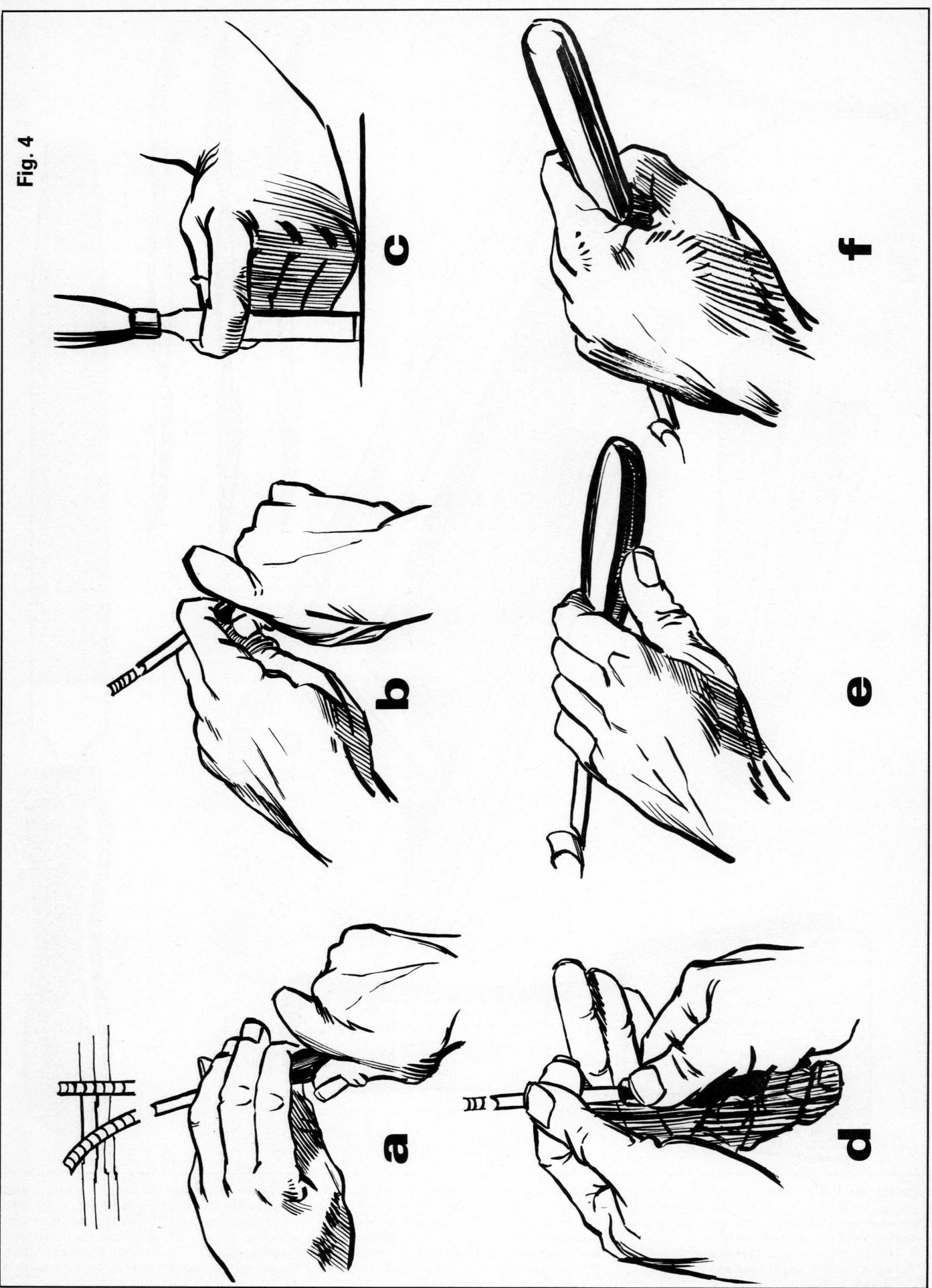

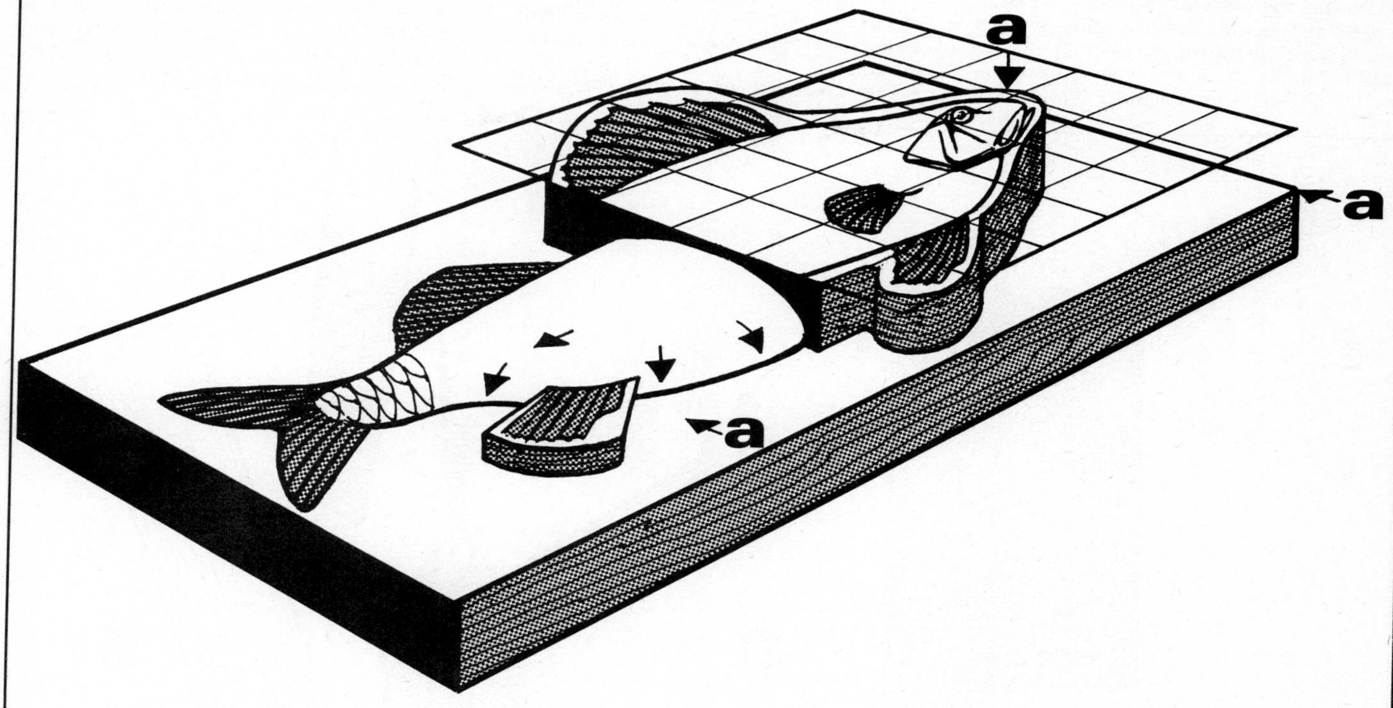

Fig. 5

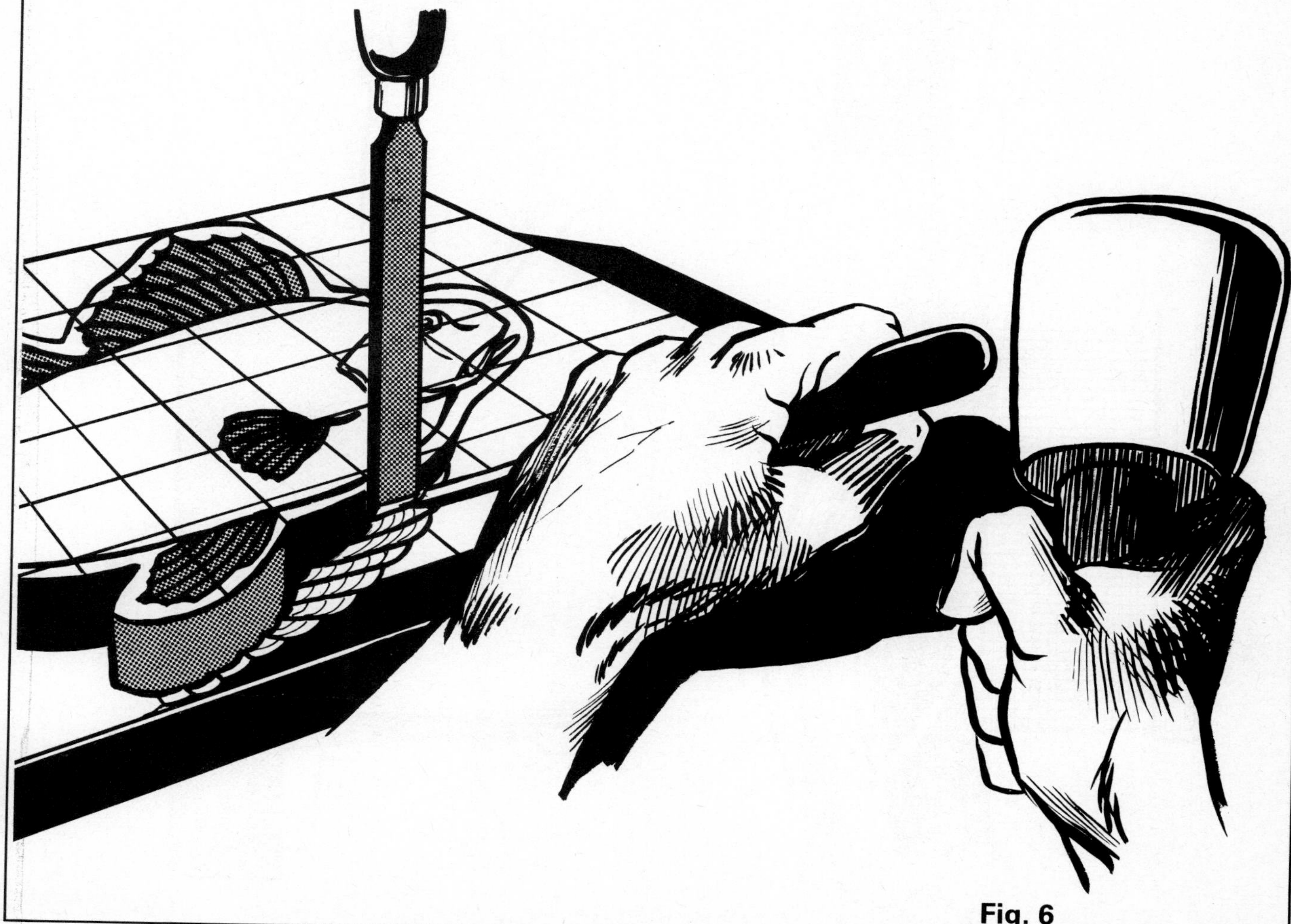

Fig. 6

(text continued from p.11)

soft brush; this fixes the design and prevents smudging or wearing during carving.

Define the cutting depth by gauging a line round the edges of the wood.

Using a flat chisel and mallet cut downwards – clear of the design – then with a gouge and flat chisel cut horizontally across the grain (Fig. 6). It is easier to 'nibble away' at the wood than to try cutting straight across in the horizontal plane when there is a tendency for the wood to split or skid with the chisel.

The roughly-chiselled edge clear of the design can then be carefully chiselled to the required contour. Half-height pieces such as the fin in the foreground can be cut down to the appropriate level (Fig. 7). This is followed by rounding and tapering with chisel cuts in the direction indicated by the four arrows on the body of the fish.

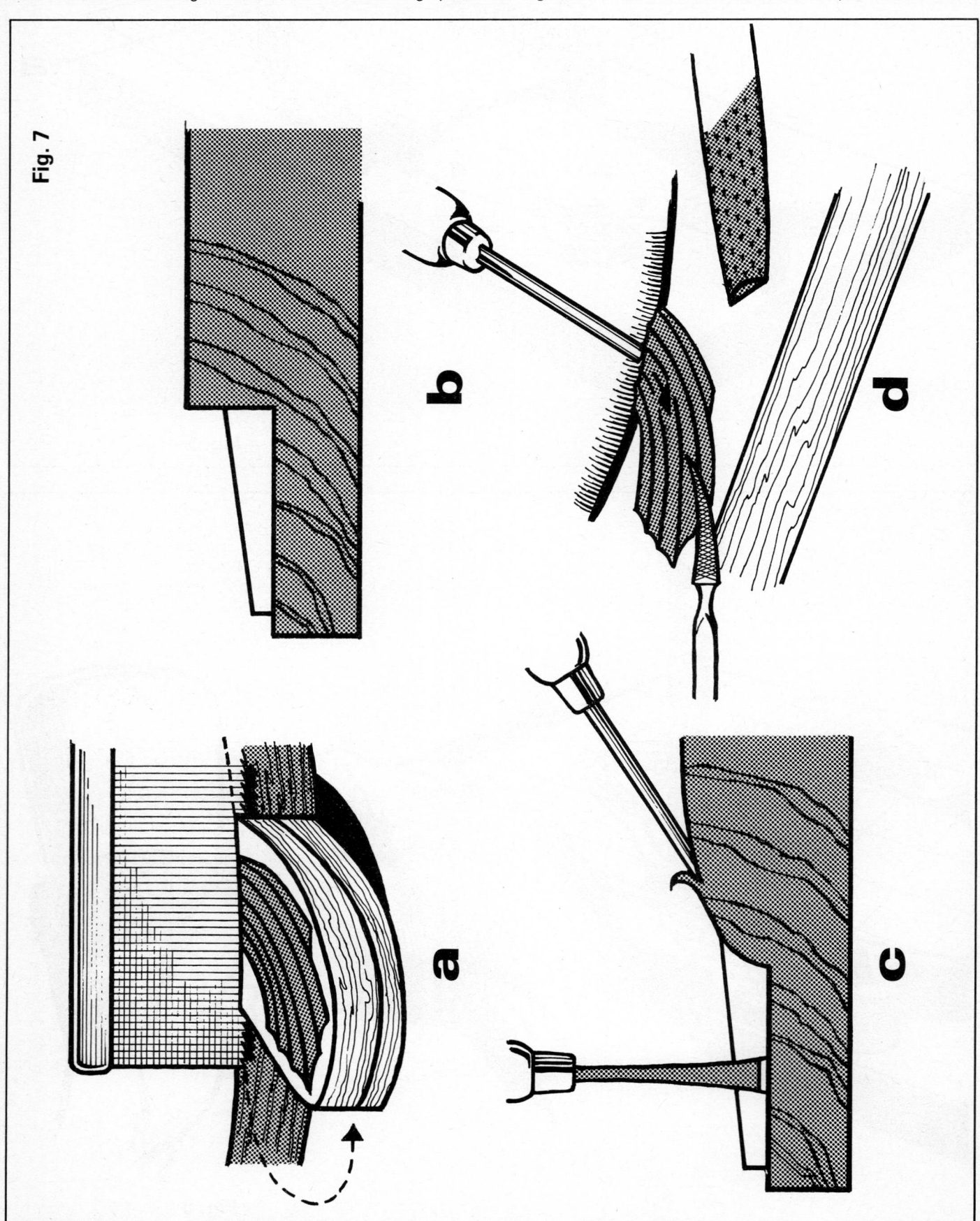

Fig. 7

DESIGN EDUCATION IN NORWAY & DENMARK

In April and May 1981 Ian M. Barker, principal lecturer at the School of Art & Design Furniture & Timber of Bucks College of Higher Education, High Wycombe, visited Norway and Denmark to study the education of designers and craftsmen in the furniture industries.

Mr Barker, who had been awarded a Bowen scolarship by the Worshipful Company of Furniture Makers of the city of London, reports that both countries devote more resources to fewer students. This creates competition between students and must help to raise their standards. However, it follows that a large number of those employed in the furniture industries have little chance of developing their talents further.

He points out that the system of loans to students as opposed to grants must increase the motivation of students. Again, however, to leave college in Norway or Denmark owing the equivalent of £10 000 or more must be a daunting prospect and may discourage many from applying in the first place.

The emphasis on drawing and art in the design colleges must be to their advantages and Mr Barker believes design courses in this country should follow this pattern. He found that the Norwegian furniture factories were well equipped and placed great importance on their designers. 'An interesting comparison with British firms, particularly the smaller ones,' he comments.

Establishment of the state Craft College at Oslo underlines the Norwegian's concern at preserving the traditional craft skills. 'An area which I believe is a serious omission in the British system,' adds Mr Barker.

This college is organised into a number of departments: traditional cabinetmaking, traditional upholstery, clockmaking; and others. Mr Barker reports: 'The overall impression is one of space and a very high level of equipment available to student use. Each craft is catered for by a three-year full-time course (except traditional upholstery which is a one-year course).

'In the current year the college had received 150 applications for 36 places on the cabinetmaking course; standards are therefore high. At the end of the first year only the top 12 students are allowed to progress to the second year; competition between students is very noticeable.

'The majority of the cabinet work was being constructed in pine. All timber was stored indoors and the use of humidifiers was extensive. Dust-extraction plants were located inside and used a filtering system to re-circulate the warm air. All buildings are, of course, double-glazed.

'Each student has his or her own workbench with an extensive set of hand tools. All designs were traditional and I was very impressed with the standard of work being produced.

'I understood that until the early part of 1981 anyone wishing to start in business as a cabinetmaker must have obtained his craft certificate from the craft college and also to have successfully passed examinations in business administration. With these two certificates he could register himself as a craftsman able to take on commissions. I understand the rules have been relaxed to some extent but was unable to establish the precise nature of the changes.'

The state Technical College at Oslo has a furniture department with a one-year postgraduate-level course in furniture production which caters for 10-12 students. The syllabus content of the course revealed a distinct similarity to the diploma course in furniture production and managment at High Wycombe.

The college staff is also responsible for operating the Norwegian furniture control system which monitors the products of the country's furniture industry.

Manufacturers wishing to mark their products with the furniture control Norway mark must first submit to inspection and approval and must undertake to meet all the quality requirements of furniture control Norway. Furniture control is responsible for testing and approving each new model. The technical and other tests are extremely thorough. 'It was like having the Furniture Industry Research Association (FIRA) located in the college at High Wycombe,' observes Mr Barker.

He also visited several furniture factories. 'They were proud of the certificates issued by the furniture testing department of the state Technical College and these were reproduced in their catalogues.'

In Denmark Mr Barker went to the Skolen fur Brugskunst at Copenhagen. It is financed and adminstered by the government and of the five departments one is furniture design. Total student number in this department was 40. Applications for the course are high and students are selected by a series of tests which last for a week. In addition they have to submit portfolios showing samples of their work. As with the colleges in Norway, there is great emphasis on drawing and painting and thereafter almost two years is devoted to the study of chair design.

Mr Barker did not have travelling time to visit other colleges in Denmark but he was able to go to furniture factories and noted that there were no apprentices or learners as in Britain. He was also 'greatly impressed' by the Scandinavian Furniture Fair held at Copenhagen and by the superb ranges at the Illums Bolighus furniture store in the Danish capital.

Below: Ian M. Barker of Buckinghamshire College of Higher Education receiving his award from Lucian Ercolani DSO DFC, chairman of Ercol Furniture Ltd and immediate past Master of the Worshipful Company of Furniture Makers.

The saw designed to give you _perfect_ results in modern materials

NOT JUST FOR PROFESSIONALS

Advanced production systems bring this precision tool within your reach. For little more than the cost of a light pressed steel sawbench, you can enjoy the accuracy and precision of the TGS171.

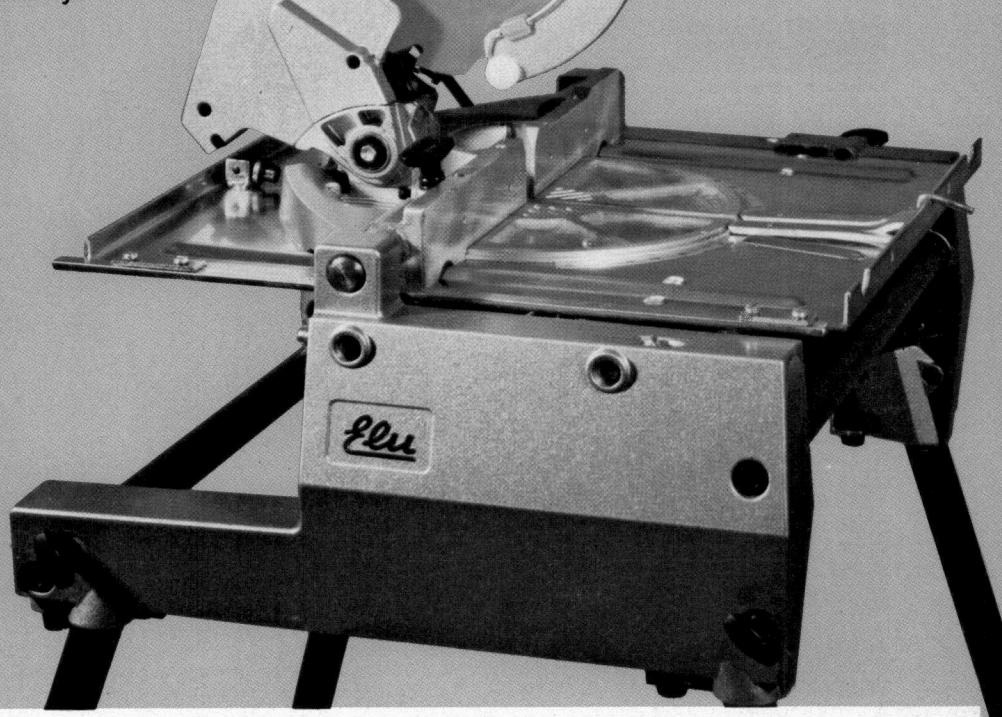

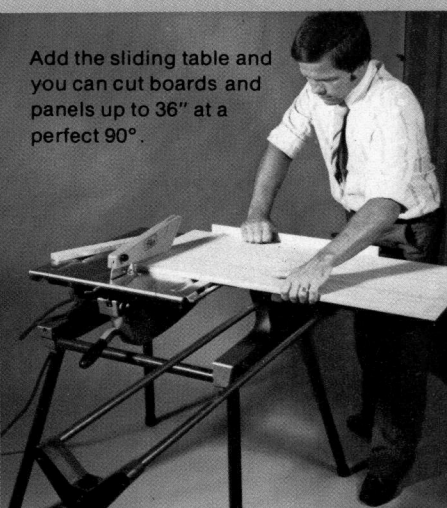

Add the sliding table and you can cut boards and panels up to 36" at a perfect 90°.

Versatility

Simply pull the plunge table locking lever, and the overhead mitre cutting saw swivels through 180° to become a conventional bench saw.

A sawbench......... A simple flip over..... A perfect Mitre saw.

Stability

Wide bearing point of pivot, precision ground for stability.

Whether you need to cut delicate veneered boards for cabinet building or even alloy extrusions for mitred frames, the new TGS171 has been developed to give the performance and consistent accuracy you want.

Further Information
Elu have a nationwide network of over 200 authorised distributors. Contact us today for your **FREE** fully illustrated colour brochure and full list of authorised Elu dealers.

Superb Accuracy

Positive locking at any precise angle between square and 45°.

Elu Machinery Ltd.

310-312 Dallow Road, Luton, Bedfordshire. LU1 1SS

Tel: (0582) 425001 Telex: 825540

Barrie smiles a lot these days because he's saving himself money.

Barrie smiles a lot these days because he's saving himself money.
Recently Barrie and Lynne Goddard of Bottesford, near Scunthorpe, decided to improve their kitchen. Their dream was to have solid oak fronts; easy clean work tops; concealed lighting; extractor fan; tiles for walls and floors; quality sink, taps and fittings – a really luxurious project. The going rate for the job from a professional contractor was around £5,000. However, with Kity machinery to help him, Barrie built their dream kitchen for just £2,000 – now you can see why he smiles a lot!

Here is his shopping list:
8 cubes well seasoned oak
8 sheets 8' × 4' white laminated chip board
29 solid brass handles
20 pairs flush hinges
24 sq. ft. laminated, leather finish, worktop
19 sq. yds. ceramic wall and floor tiles
Stainless steel sink, taps and fittings
Oven and hob units, light fittings and fan
Stain, polish, paint, screws and glues.

His method:
Read and study carefully Kity plan sheets on kitchen layout and construction details, e.g. joints, rebates and mouldings. Plan carefully and make the fullest use of Kity machinery.

Ideas can now become reality.
At some time or other most of us have had to scrap excellent creative ideas because we could not afford to call in the professionals and we did not have sufficient expertise to carry them out ourselves. Kity has gone a long way towards removing this frustration by supplying illustrated instruction sheets which explain, step by step, the simple machine techniques needed to transform ideas into superb reality.

K5 international woodworker

Special price £559 (+ VAT £83·85)

Common base for all functions.
The K5 has units for separate machine functions mounted on a common base and driven by a centrally mounted power unit – the K5 motor. You have all the versatility of separately mounted machines, any change of operation becomes simplicity itself. Just connect the belt to the machine you want to use, adjusting the tension easily by means of a simple, quick release lever. Without losing your pre-set adjustments, you can change from one function to another in a matter of seconds. Continuity of work is thus assured.

Engineering specification

Circular saw.
180mm (7") blade normally fitted but will accept a 200mm (8") blade giving a 57mm (2¼") depth of cut. 2 speeds, 3750 for normal wood and 6200 r.p.m. for laminated boards. Complete with rip fence, mitre guide, repeat cut length stop, wobble washers for grooving, tilting table 0.45°.

Surface planer.
700mm (27½") long × 200mm (8") wide cast bed. Maximum planing width 150mm (6"). Adjustable 90° – 45° fence for bevel planing. Dynamically balanced cutter block rotating at 11,400 cuts per minute.

Thickness planer.
Fully automatic feed, 7.5m (24') per minute. Maximum capacity 100mm (4") deep, 150mm (6") wide. Anti kick-back fingers, calibrated scale.

Spindle moulder.
6400 rpm shaft speed. 45mm (1¾") vertical adjustment. Capable of taking 25mm (1") × 25mm (1") rebate in one pass. Accepts both French moulding profiles and white hill type blocks.

Slot mortiser.
Rise/fall table with 100mm (4") of adjustment. Maximum bit diameter 12mm (½"). Produces accurate mortises, also horizontal boring for perfect dowel joints.

2 year guarantee.
When you buy a K5, you will be protected against all manufacturing defects (parts and labour) for the first two years after purchase, no matter how hard you work your machine.

If you have a dream project you'd like to build, write today for more details. You can soon have a smile like Barrie's.

KITY UNITED KINGDOM

For more information about this and many more Kity products, please fill in this coupon and return.

NAME ....

ADDRESS ....

....

.... TEL .... WWI

Kity U.K., Sizer's Court, Henshaw Lane, Yeadon, Leeds LS19 7DP. Tel. (0532) 509110. Telex: 557920

Prices quoted are those prevailing at press date and are subject to alteration due to economic conditions.

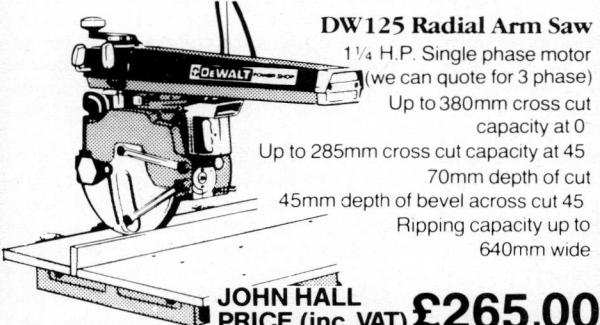

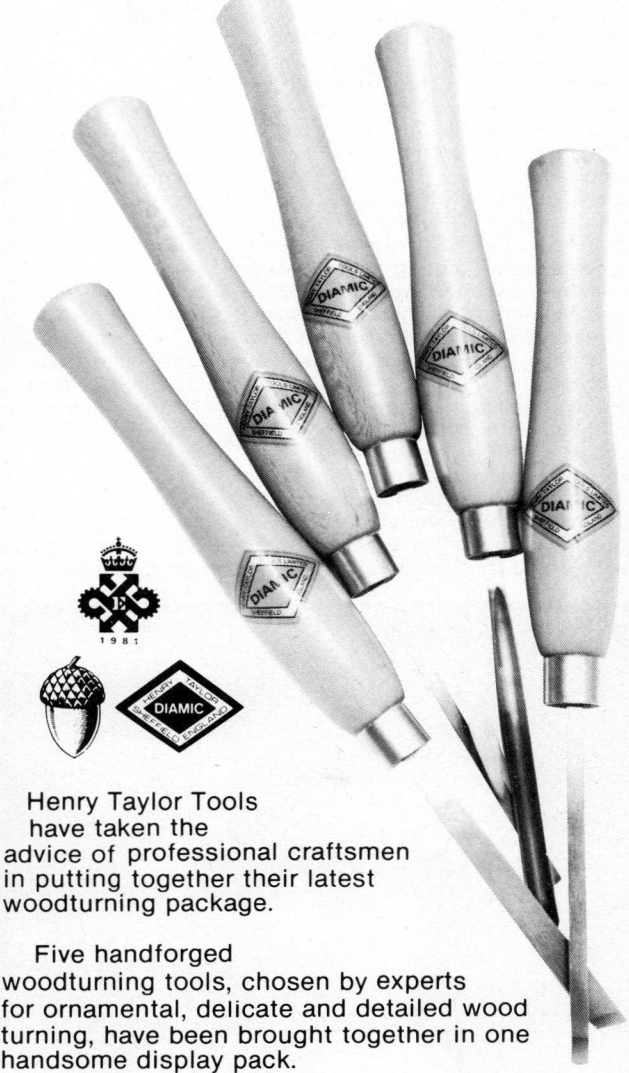

MAKE A JOYFUL NOISE

WOODWORKER visits the Early Musical Instruments exhibition
photography JOHN CUERDEN

The fifth London exhibition of Early Musical Instruments was held from 1-3 October at the New Horticultural Hall, Westminster in association with the Early Musical Instrument Makers Association whose committee along with Richard Wood and Malcolm Greenhalgh of the Early Music Shop were responsible for the production and organisation of yet another memorable occasion.

The work of the Early Musical Instrument Makers Association is centred on supporting professional makers of fine musical instruments and ensuring that working together they can supply the musical needs of their customers. 'Early music' now spans 8 centuries of musical activity since it is no longer limited to the period Dowland to early Haydn.

The range of instruments available at this year's show was arguably the most comprehensive anywhere for the performance of early music; a rewarding experience both tonally in the recitals which took place in the upstairs recital room and aesthetically in the craftsmanship and beauty shown by the pieces on display and for sale.

Stand 86 was occupied by the department of Musical Instrument Technology of the London College of Furniture. Their department now offers full-time courses in the making of harpsichords, clavichords, virginals, lutes, viols, guitars, violins, violas, cellos, early woodwind, pianos and electronic musical instruments.

Full-time courses each lasting 4 years provide a thorough training in a chosen specialised field backed by a number of important subsidiary subjects such as science, acoustics, history of music and instrumental classes. There are also part-time courses in violin, woodwind and fretted instrument making.

At the other end of the learning and making musical instrument scale Oxford University Press were promoting *This Merry Company* by Alison and Michael Bagenal. Suitable for children of 9-12 years

A young Early Music enthusiast tries her hand on a children's harpsichord, made for his daughter by John Rawson of Clerkenwell, London.

old the scheme consists of pupils' books centring around 3 medieval plays, a medieval castle and Christmas with a teacher's book and cassettes instructing in music, dance and costume. Full details are given for making 3 musical instruments, a psaltery, a stringed dulcimer and nakers.

Michael and Alison Bagenal also supply kits and plans for children to make simple harps. These are available from their home address in Godmanchester, Huntingdon.

The city of Cambridge appears to be a favourite place for early music — four musical instrument makers and repairers live and work within one mile of each other and the city centre. . . Daniel Bangham (woodwind), Anna Brock (violin), Trevor Beckerleg (harpsichord) and Mark Stevenson (harpsichord). Trevor was on stand 51; he started his first workshop in 1964 and has done restoration work, notably for the Raymond Russell collection in Edinburgh, the Fitzwilliam museum and Cambridge University Faculty of Music. He displayed a two-manual harpsichord in English walnut with keys in bone and ebony; a wing spinet based on a spinet of c.1690 and a single

Fritz Heller of Aachen, West Germany playing his Grosser Bock, an early bagpipe, on which both chanter and drone terminate in animal horns.

Erin Headley of Philomel, a London based Early Music group, demonstrates her lirone, made by John Pringle, of London.

manual harpsichord. Mark Stevenson was on stand 15, he has been building keyboard instruments since 1961 and moved to Cambridge from London in 1966. He builds traditional instruments in traditional timbers with the help of 4 assistants and showed a French 2-manual harpsichord and an English wing spinet in walnut after Thomas Hitchcock.

Ipswich, Suffolk is the home of Donald Garrod (see WOODWORKER December 1981, April, June August, October 1973, January 1974). Donald made his first harpsichord in the early 50s and always uses solid locally grown timber except for his sound boards which are of spruce. His inspiration comes from early English and Italian models and he had some fine examples on show.

Readers of WOODWORKER may remember the cover picture and article on Ian Tucker of Manningtree, Essex (WOODWORKER October 1980). He and his wife Anne are both harpsichord makers and restorers and have now been joined in their workshop by Roger Murray. They place their emphasis on producing a tone true to type, a reliable action and a good quality finish. Every part of the instrument is hand-made in their workshop and they also provide certain parts for professional and amateur makers — jacks of pear or apple, keyboards in lime (unless otherwise stated), soundboard painting in egg tempera with traditional pigments.

Ian Harwood was to found on stand 116; he claims to be among the longest-established instrument makers working in Britain having made his first lute in Cam-

bridge in 1956. He set up a full-time workshop in Oxford in 1958 and over the years between then and 1972 made other plucked instruments, mainly citterns, bandoras and vihuelas. After various diversions such as curator of early keyboard instruments at Fenton House, Hampstead, he is now settled in Sussex and specialises in Italian Renaissance viols of figure of eight shape without soundpost or bass bar. He also makes treble lutes, citterns and bandoras and Renaissance bows. He proposes to add small treble and bass viols of English pattern to his repertoire plus a 'treble violin'.

Dominic and Richard Shann of Glan y Gors workshop, Deiniolen, Gwynedd, make viols and harpsichords and virginals respectively. Dominic's viols follow the work of John Rose and Henry Jaye while Richard makes to the designs of Jan Ruckers.

Stefan Beck was born to a woodworking environment in Germany in 1944, his father's and mother's families were cabinetmakers. Stefan has a workshop in Berlin and is the first woodwind maker to make the crumhorn type after 1 MILLA (Vienna) to any tuning and pitch required, both as a diatonic or chromatic instrument. There were many other makers and many famous names at the exhibition but no exhibition of

The stand of Alison and Michael Bagenal, of Godmanchester, Huntingdon, who specialise in instruments and Early Music for young children to play.

Flemish style harpsichord after Ruckers, by Robert Goble & Son, Headington, Oxford.

this type would be complete without the raw materials and the tools of the trade.

These were supplied by North Heigham Sawmills who had a comprehensive selection from their vast range of timbers; Instrument Making Tools of Bradford showed a range of tools, finishes, materials and sundries; David Carroll of Touchstone Tonewoods, Reigate (a regular advertiser in WOODWORKER) had a large selection of tools, tonewoods, finishes and accessories including assorted sizes of ebony offcuts.

The Early Music Shop, Bradford, is essentially a mail order house covering the entire spectrum of early instruments and sheet music. They had on display their simple crumhorn kits available in four sizes (soprano, alto in F, tenor and bass) needing minimal skill to complete; the body is already bored and decorative collar turnings are turned; the wood used is sycamore. Their other kit on sale was the hypothetical Glastonbury pipe... an alto windcap instrument with a chromatic compass of f—b'. Robert Longstaff of Woking had his usual display of plans, kits, parts and materials, John Storrs was showing a selection of his keyboard instruments and kits; details of his courses were also available. Timber, plans, a complete range of accessories and kits for home construction of harps were shown by Michael Saunders of Letton, Hereford (another regular advertiser in WOODWORKER). Heckscher & Co of Bayham St, London exhibited parts and materials including harpsichord jacks, eg. their new classical jack in pearwood, turning tools, tuning pins, hinges and specialist books.

Some of the exhibitors are included in *Modern Harpsichord Makers — portraits of nineteen British craftsmen and their work —* by John Paul published at the end of September by Victor Gollancz Ltd, 14 Henrietta St, London WC2E 8QJ at £15.50 (ISBN 0 575 02985 4).

These include Arnold Dolmetsch; Malcolm Rose who has a small workshop in Mayfield, Sussex specialising in French and Italian work; Robert Goble & Son whose workshops are at Headington, Oxford; David Law of High Wycombe who until recently ran the Department of Musical Instrument Technology at the London College of Furniture and now undertakes restoration work and accepts orders for single and two-manual harpsichords and virginals; John Rawson who shares his Clerkenwell workshop with restorer Miles Hellon; Mark Stevenson, the scientifically-minded craftsman from Cambridge and Trevor Beckerleg also from Cambridge; Donald Garrod; (all mentioned above) and Morley Galleries who have been makers since before 1816. This year is their centenary year at Lewisham, the site of their present workshops.

An enjoyable show and one to be revisited in two years' time to again try the instruments, talk to the craftsmen and absorb the 'early' atmosphere.

MAKING MUSICAL INSTRUMENTS — 6-15 APRIL AT WEST DEAN COLLEGE, WEST DEAN, CHICHESTER

The aim of the course is to give craftsmen, teachers of all kinds, lecturers and educational advisers who may have little or no experience, the opportunity to make musical instruments of varying degrees of complexity from simple percussion and melodic instruments to sophisticated instruments like the lute, celtic harp, spinet, viola da gamba and Renaissance woodwind.

Tuition and practical activities take place in large, fully equipped workshops. The music making will be a secondary element of the course, but basic tuition is offered on many of the instruments being made. Materials are available at the College and can be purchased during the course. Costs range between £6-£90 plus, depending on the complexity and the size of the instrument.

For further details, including cost of the 9 day course, write to Peter Sarginson, Principal, West Dean College, West Dean, Chichester, West Sussex PO18 0QZ.

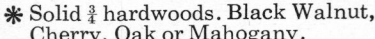
 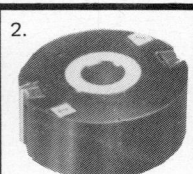 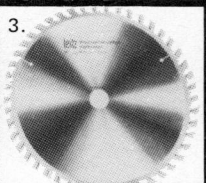
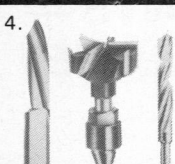  

DRYING YOUR TIMBER

7

In subsequent articles W. H. Brown FIWSc will be discussing the preparation of a drying or conditioning room or small chamber. Here he considers the intermediate stage of drying timber which is critical for a number of reasons.

We mentioned in part 6 (WOODWORKER for October 1981) that once fibre saturation point (FSP) was reached, ie from 25 to 30% m.c., wood being dried would attempt to shrink. We also said that moisture movement through the wood might be impeded by infiltrates or growths such as tyloses plugging some of the pores. Furthermore, after FSP was reached, the pits in the element walls became less permeable due to the tori being drawn toward the primary wall.

In practical terms this means that a stage is reached in the drying of wood where a gradient of moisture is initiated, extending from the relatively wet core to the relatively dry outer skin. This gradient is not a true parabolic curve but in sinuous form, meandering through the thickness of the wood, the thicker the wood the greater the undulations. In other words, part of the bulk of each piece has reached FSP in advance of the remainder.

This intermediate stage of drying is critical for a number of reasons. It will be noted that two things are happening to the wood at this stage. Firstly, parts of it (below FSP) are trying to shrink but are being held back by the remainder of the wood above FSP. Secondly, since the tori becomes aspirated and tends to block the pits once FSP is reached, liquid water is being converted to vapour which is having greater difficulty in moving through the pits.

The wood reacts by becoming stressed in tension in the outer zones of the wood that are attempting to shrink, with the inner zones (as yet unable to shrink) balancing the structure by forming a compression stress. Under good drying conditions, as the inner zones dry further so that all the wood is below FSP, the stresses reverse with compression in the outer zones and tension lower down (Fig. 1).

These as described are natural drying stresses and are of no great significance. But should the drying conditions, ie temperature and humidity of the air and its circulation, mean that removal of moisture from the wood is sporadic, or the surfaces dry-out too far in advance of the inner wood, the wood surfaces become set in tension. This is a condition known as casehardening.

Casehardening can be relatively mild or severe. However, this does not become apparent until sawing or other means of conversion relieves some of the stress. When this happens (and particularly when such wood is resawn, say, by deep cutting) the sawn pieces cup easily or otherwise warp because of a compression stress on

one face and an irreversible tension set on the outer face.

With conventional methods of kiln-drying it is possible to take sample slotted discs (Fig. 2) from the wood towards the end of the drying run; then if the prongs indicate severe stresses in the wood to revert to what is called equalising and conditioning in order to reduce the stresses to a very minimum.

This is part and parcel of the technique of kiln-drying and ought to be followed every-time: unfortunately this is by no means the case.

We said earlier that the normal drying of timber produced stresses which were to an extent acceptable. Anyone who has worked in wood mills will know that quite often, loads of resawn wood, say, intended for drawer sides and left in the warm shop overnight will, the following morning, show the top pieces to have curled or cupped.

If these pieces are turned they will flatten themselves in a few hours, which actually is the wood's response to air changes causing reversal of the stresses. If, however, the wood is badly casehardened then the wood

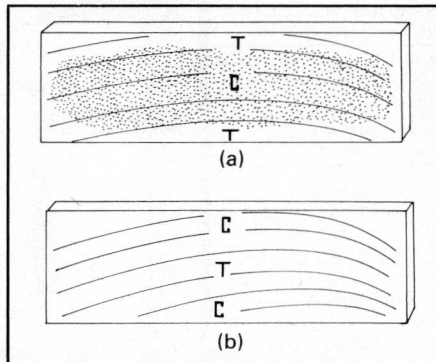

Fig. 1 End grain sections; (a) of partially-dried wood (b) of uniformly-dried wood. In (a) only the outer zones are below FSP and have taken on a tension stress with compression in the wetter core. In (b) the wood is now all below FSP. The tension has been relieved by shrinkage at mid-thickness and stresses have reversed.

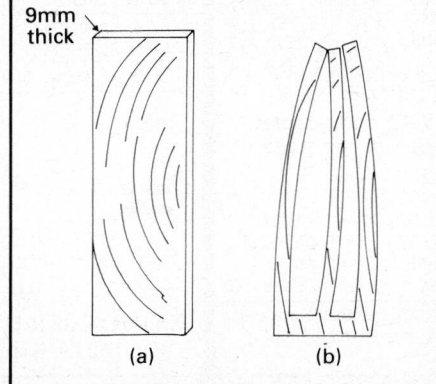

Fig. 2 An end grain wafer about 9mm thick taken from the full width of a sample board (a) may appear stress-free but after slotting-out (b) if the wafer is left in a warm room for a couple of hours or less, the prongs will react and if badly casehardened will then turn inwards.

will cup, quite often as it comes from the saw but it will not easily resume its flatness except by trueing-up on the overhand planer. This of course will reduce its desired thickness.

It should not be assumed that this type of drying applies only to wood that is artificially dried, ie by conventional kiln or by a dehumidifier placed in an enclosed area. It applies to all methods of removing moisture from wood by means of air changes.

The only difference between these methods and air-drying, followed by further drying in a warm room or workshop, is that in the former methods there is adequate control of the air conditions while in the latter there is not.

This is why it is important for the small wood user who wants to season his wood in the garden or other restricted place to bear in mind the following: some wood species dry more quickly and easily than others to the extent that the degree of exposure of the wood in question (and particularly the wide faces of boards and the ends of logs) to the drying elements of wind and sun, and the restraining influence of rain and mist, is usually of greater importance than the time taken in air seasoning. If bad stress patterns are initiated early on, say by the use of very thick sticks to separate the pieces; or the pieces receive too much dry, high wind, there might not be much evidence of this when the wood is removed for conversion and further drying but it will react later to sawing and other machining.

We have on various occasions in our replies to letters sent to Question Box, recommended that green or very wet wood placed in the open air to dry should be wetted from time to time. We have suggested use of the garden hose or even buckets of water during very dry spells, or if the outsides of the pieces appear to be drying-out quickly.

This may seem drastic. But once the outer skin of a piece of wood has reached FSP it is extremely difficult to put moisture back short term. The idea, and especially with thick pieces of wood, is to keep the outside moist for as long as possible during the first two or three months of drying.

Naturally, if the wood is initially exposed during the winter months, then much depends on whether there is any significant drying taking place during that time. Under those conditions wetting could well be required the following March if drying winds prevail, or a little later when the sun gets warmer.

Drying your timber

We are asked to point out that the word 'humidifiers' on p691 of WOODWORKER for October should in fact be dehumidifiers. The last sentence then reads: This applies to dehumidifiers also where if a range of thicknesses and types of timber are likely to be dried, they benefit from the inclusion of a humidistat as well as a thermostat.

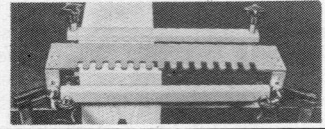
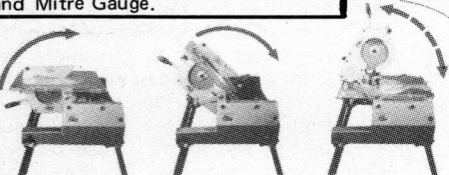

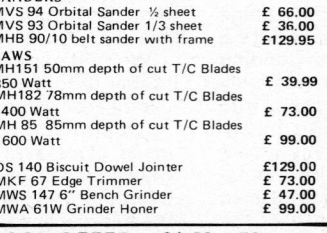
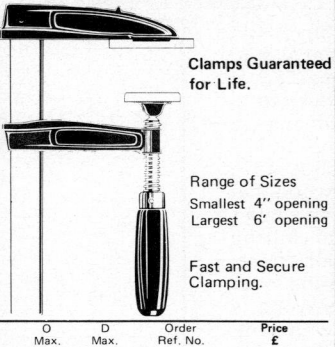
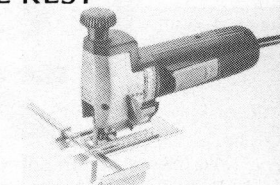

Prices quoted are those prevailing at press date and are
subject to alteration due to economic conditions.

TIMBER *TIMBER* *timber*

The stronger the wind the tougher the trees

Catalogues and price lists arrive on the editorial desk with dependable regularity but it was a rare treat to receive the autumn 1981 catalogue and price list from John Boddy and Son (Timber) Ltd. The company, who advertise on our wood suppliers pages, was founded in 1935 by John Boddy, the present chairman. It was founded as a boat building company and following difficulties in obtaining sawn larch, John Boddy installed his own saw. The last 30 years has seen the company run as a sawmillers and timber merchants.

Six years ago after spending all his early working life in the timber trade concerned with veneers, joinery and hardwoods Frank Boddy joined his father, as managing director of the firm, utilising the skills learnt in larger multicorporate concerns.

Together with the help of their 48 employees they have established the sawmill with 2 log bandmills and various re-saws processing 4500 cu ft of timber per week. They also have 4 kilns, one being the first of the Westair high temperature kilns. This, together with 20 000 sq ft of kiln-dried storage area, enables the firm to hold extensive stocks of British hardwood, in kiln-dried, air-dried and fresh-sawn form, available ex-stock.

They specialise in oak, ash, elm, sycamore, sweet chestnut, yew, cherry, beech and lime and such exotics as pear, apple, acacia, walnut, figured sycamore and brown oak for use in the furniture and joinery trades.

They are also able to offer large dimension oak and elm for building and dock work, but more particularly for restoration work in historic buildings and period homes.

Although the majority of their business is to the timber, furniture and joinery trades, they are receiving an ever-increasing demand from the cabinetmaker and woodworking craftsman for supplies of relatively small quantities of British hardwood.

Many timber merchants simply cannot handle this type of order. John Boddy and Son can. Their most recent venture is the setting up of a yard sales office where visitors may come and inspect stocks, select and take away their precise requirements. Many of their older stocks are being cleared at attractive prices to launch this venture.

A personal service is given to visitors/customers who can choose from the stock of over 20 000 cu ft of kiln-dried timber and 15 000 cu ft of air-dried timber. It is also possible to select from stocks of round logs which may be converted and kilned to individual requirements.

Open Monday to Friday 8 am to 5 pm, Saturday 8 am to 12 noon, J. Boddy and Son also encourage trips from colleges and schools in order that students may appreciate British timber and the various processes involved in bringing the timber to a dry usable condition.

The catalogue produced by the company is clear, concise, of excellent quality, colour coded for easy reference: yellow for definitions of terms (some are listed here to help

SOME USEFUL DEFINITIONS

SUPER FEET, BOARD MEASURE
This is a square face measure. Foot super means square foot. The super feet of a board is calculated by

$$\frac{\text{length in feet} \times \text{width in inches}}{12}$$

$$\text{For example } \frac{18\,\text{ft} \times 15\text{in.}}{12} = 22\tfrac{1}{2} \text{ super ft}$$

To obtain the cubic content of the board the super feet is then divided for example.

22½ super ft 1¼in. thickness
22½ ÷ 9.60 = 2.34 cu ft

The following divisors are used for calculating the cubic content of the various thicknesses of boards.

½in.	÷	24	1½in.	÷	8	3¼in. ÷ 3.69
¼in.	÷	16	1⅝in.	÷	7.38	3½in. ÷ 3.43
⅝in.	÷	19.20	2in.	÷	6	3¾in. ÷ 3.20
⅞in.	÷	13.72	2⅛in.	÷	5.65	4in. ÷ 3
1in.	÷	12	2¼in.	÷	5.33	4½in. ÷ 2.67
1⅛in.	÷	10.67	2½in.	÷	4.80	5in. ÷ 2.40
1¼in.	÷	9.60	2⅝in.	÷	4.57	6in. ÷ 2
1⅜in.	÷	8.73	3in.	÷	4	7in. ÷ 1.71

FOOT RUN
A term used when measuring timber per foot length.
To calculate the cubic content from foot run

$$\frac{\text{Length in feet} \times \text{width in inches} \times \text{thickness in inches}}{144}$$

$$\text{For example } \frac{24\,\text{foot run} \times 16\text{in.} \times 1\text{in.}}{144} = 2.67 \text{ cu ft}$$

CONVERSIONS
Cubic feet into cubic metres × 0.028317
Cubic metres into cubic feet × 35.3147

TYPES OF MEASUREMENT
H M = per cubic foot, sawn through and through and/or with one square edge on Round Hoppus Measure.
S F M = per cubic foot, sawn through and through and/or with one square edge on Super Feet Board Measure.
S E = per cubic foot, sawn square edged. Foot run or Super Feet Board Measure.

KILN DRIED
Timber sawn from the round log, then usually air dried for a period of time prior to being kiln dried. Kiln dried timber is supplied at an average moisture content of 12½% to 15%.

AIR DRIED
Timber sawn from the round log and put into stick for a period of time.

FRESH SAWN
Timber sawn from the round log and supplied fresh off the saw.

THROUGH and THROUGH or UNEDGED or WANEY EDGE
The term used when converting logs by parallel cuts the full depth of the log. Giving boards with the wane and sapwood on both edges.

ONE SQUARE EDGE
Boards which have wane and sapwood on one edge and a square edge on the other.

the not too knowledgeable prospective buyer), blue for kiln-dried stock, green for air-dried stock and brown for fresh-sawn, plus a detailed map showing the location of the premises. Attention should also be drawn to the stocking of a relatively inexpensive product — upholstery quality hardwood — which at J. Boddy and Son receives the same care and attention in sticking and stacking as their first quality material. The timber is sawn mainly with one square edge and the logs used are a mixture of butt lengths and good second lengths yielding a good quality of timber at a higher standard than that usually associated with upholstery work.

Selected oak beams are held in stock specifically for conversion into beams and braces. One of J. Boddy's most recent contracts for oak beams was the supply of timbers for the replacement, due to death watch beetle attack, of the whole of the north nave aisle roof of York Minster. The largest of these beams being 24ft × 12in. × 12in. These together with a large number of smaller section timbers, amount to approximately 800 cu ft of oak beams.

An excellent service by the firm is to offer storage facilities for customers' stocks.

SQUARE EDGED or SQUARES

Boards with square edges to all sides.

END REARED

This is the term used for stacking timber on its end after conversion from the log. Timbers such as sycamore if sticked directly off the saw, will produce stick marks. This process eliminates the problem.

ROUND HOPPUS MEASURE

This is a measurement system for round logs. The length is taken to the nearest 6 in. and the quarter girth measured at the middle of the log, round the circumference, to the nearest ¼in. quarter girth.
The cubic content of the log is then calculated.

$$\frac{\text{Length} \times (\text{Quarter girth})^2}{144}$$

For example a log 14 ft long × 16¾ in. quarter girth
$$\frac{14 \times (16\frac{3}{4})^2}{144} = 27.28 \text{ cu ft}$$

The name Hoppus is that of the author of the Hoppus Timber Measurement System.

Fresh-sawn timber is put into stick after conversion at 35p per cu ft (present price), then stored free of charge with fire insurance cover for up to 12 months. End rearing is at 35p per cu ft. (present price).

John Boddy and Son (Timber) Ltd., Riverside Sawmills, Boroughbridge YO5 9LJ. Phone Boroughbridge (09012) 2370.

workpieces

The real thing

'It is surprising how many people are carrying out restoration work or even building new vehicles. Indeed, many have progressed from making models to the real thing,' writes J. B. Pearce, hon secretary of the Model Horse-Drawn Vehicles Club in his *Newsletter no. 53*.

His remarks are prompted by 'another outstanding book from J. A. Allen' *The Restoration of Carriages* by George Isles. It covers every aspect of the work involved. Step-by-step instructions are given and some of the methods of the last century are dealt with in conjunction with modern materials and techniques. The book is priced at £15 and the reference no. is ISBN 0-85131-366-3.

The *Newsletter* also describes a collection of farm machinery comprising more than 1000 items including hand tools as well as the big exhibits like threshing boxes and farm carts. Previously housed at Burton Constable hall the collection has been given to the Yorkshire Museum of Farming which is due to open this year at Murton near York.

Bigger than we think

It is reported that the bowmen of England in Tudor times were bigger than we think. Longbows recovered from the wreck of the *Mary Rose* warship which sank in Portsmouth harbour in 1545 have been subjected to materials testing.

Initial results indicate that the original draw strength of the bows could have exceeded 100lb. All the bows so far recovered are between 1.84 and 2.06m long, suggesting that the bowmen must have been well over 6ft tall — and very muscular — to use them effectively.

The salvaged bows are of close-grained yew, probably imported from Spain or Italy. Samples from one of the better-preserved bows showed that though the sapwood had disappeared after 436 years under water the heartwood was in perfect condition.

Auction prices

At a three-day auction sale conducted by the James Abbott Partnership at Dunmow, Essex, in September, a Wadkin Bursgreen planer/thicknesser realised £1050; Wadkin Bursgreen type PP dimension saw and accessories £1525; Wadkin Bursgreen BZB bandsaw £500; Wadkin Bursgreen AGS 10in. tilting arbor sawbench £625; Interwood type OFL router £1275.

Sheets 8 × 4ft teak-faced ply 15mm thick made £24 each while 10 sheets of miscellaneous ply went for £75. Five lots of 12mm single teak-faced ply 5 × 4ft, each lot comprising a single sheet made £17 per lot. A quantity of opepe realised £60.

Sjöberg benches

The Swedish firm of Ab Bröderna Sjöberg, Box 420, S—551 16 Jönköping, which manufactures the well-known Sjöberg workbenches, is now represented in UK by Scan Marketing Ltd, Elstow Storage Depot, Kempston Hardwick, Beds (0234 741960). Details of the benches currently available can be had from Scan Marketing.

Training schemes

Pilot schemes to give unemployed youngsters experience and training in building and construction skills, including carpentry and joinery, have been introduced by the Construction Industry Training Board (CITB). They are being run by the board under the manpower services commission youth opportunities programme.

Courses consist of periods of college training with on-site experience. Entry is open, as with other YOP courses, to youngsters between 16-17 who have been unemployed for six weeks.

Further details can be had from CITB, 5 St Clement's Lane, London WC2A 2HA.

Sharper now

Peter Scaife writes: For years I seem to have had my saws sharpened by amateurs. A panel saw has come back set to cut in a long curve; another giving an impossibly wide kerf; a dovetail saw with fangs where there should have been teeth.

Now a saw-sharpening service operated by Hunt & Ford, Handford Road, Ipswich, has altered all this; five of my hand saws (the firm does circular saws too) sharpened as if they were new.

What is more – and this seems incredible in this day and age – Hunt & Ford has someone who knows the difference between setting for ripping and crosscutting!

Quality assurance

'The attainment of quality is a priority today,' says British Standards Institution (BSI). A reputation for quality is a commercial necessity; as a marketing aspect, quality assurance cannot be ignored. For the specifier and purchaser a thorough knowledge of quality assurance methods and procedures is essential for the assessment of supplies and crucial where contractual commitments exist.

BSI has published *Quality Assurance – BSI Handbook 22* containing the full text of seven British Standards dealing with specific aspects of quality assurance.

Quality assurance is defined as embracing all activities and functions concerned with the attainment of quality. Quality assurance includes the determination and assessment of quality. That there is a good deal more to the subject than may be thought is evident from the handbook which runs to over 240 pages with diagrams.

The publication costs £75 (£37.50 to BSI subscribers) and a prospectus is available from Sales Department (Dept M), Newton House, 101 Pentonville Road, London N1 9ND.

workpieces

Miniaturists form society

The Society of Miniature Artisans has been formed to promote professional British miniaturists and encourage standards of workmanship. There are membership and associate membership grades (£25 a year for the former and £5 a year for the latter). President is Denis Hillman, vice-president Stuart King, chairman Michael Tong, secretary Mrs M. R. Tong.

Registered office is at 62 Kiln Ride, Wokingham RG11 3PH, and further details are available from the secretary at that address.

Safety seminar

Health and safety matters were discussed at a seminar in Coventry organised by Woodworking Machinery Dealers Association. Speakers were J. M. Ruscoe of the factory inspectorate, E. Curtis from the Machine Tool Industry Research Association and A. Kaye of Dominion Machinery Ltd.

Mr Ruscoe outlined the current legislation on industrial health and safety while Mr Curtis explained the development of codes of practice with particular reference to safety regulations in EEC countries. Mr Kaye reported how his company attempted to advise users of machines on the obligation to provide adequate guarding.

One of the problems considered at the seminar was the varying interpretations of WMR by different factory inspectors. It was agreed that some form of certification by manufacturers relating to the safety of their machines would be a progressive step.

Another seminar is being organised by WMDA at the Hemel Hempstead Post House on 21 January. Particulars can be had from the association's office at 31a Hill Avenue, Amersham HP6 5BX.

New brochure

The latest catalogue from Craft Supplies, Millers Dale, Buxton, Derbyshire has a host of small items within its pages for use in making up all those last minute Christmas and New Year presents.

To mention but a selection from the range is enough to whet the appetite; the woodturner in particular will find the fittings to match all his or her offcuts and small pieces of timber. For example: grinder mechanisms for salt/pepper mills, nutmeg and coffee grinders, glassware to set into flat wooden tiles to form hors d'oeuvre sets, cheese tiles and domes, gemstone inserts for the ideal finish to those small boxes you always intended to complete.

If you have turned something larger in the container theme perhaps Craft Supplies' range of plastics liners (used in the food and pharmaceutical industry) would fit to turn them into tobacco jars, herb jars or cosmetic containers all with hygienic liners.

Sheffield-made cutler blanks are available for your personalised wooden handles, in your favourite wood, as sets of cutlery for a special present or as one-off items like jam spoons or pickle forks.

Slimline digital clock movements fit neatly and attractively into a shallow 1¼in. recess to add prestige to a desk set or the top of a box. Three designs of brass candle holders are also available.

All this plus the usual mix of machinery, jigs and chucks usually associated with the company. Craft Supplies claim to be specialists in woodturning tools and supplies.

They carry the universally known 6-in-1 chuck and their catalogue devotes a full page to operating instructions plus details of optional extras. Other chucks listed are the spigot chuck, handy collet chuck and independent pin chuck.

Finishing materials include stoppings, thinners, sealers, french polish, craft-eeze, beeswax/carnauba, stains, teak oils and grain fillers.

There are many other items including books, in particular books on woodturning, within the 48 pages of the catalogue. Dated Autumn 1981 it costs £1.00. Its back cover is aimed at overseas customers and gives handy postal information to help estimate mailing costs and insurance details when ordering from countries other than UK.

B & D catalogue

The Black & Decker consumer products catalogue is a 40-page book printed in full colour with a cover price of 50p. A number of new items are included. For woodworkers these include more hammer and reversing drills; portable power plane; routers; workbenches; electric paint stripper; bandsaw and planer; belt sander; chainsaws; and attachments such as drill guide and bench-mounted sanding and sharpening device.

Furniture fittings

The furniture fittings catalogue and handbook for 1982 issued by Woodfit Ltd, Whittle Low Mill, Chorley, Preston PR6 7HB, runs to 148 pages and carries a cover price of 40p. In addition to fittings it lists furniture finishes, cabinet lighting, adhesives, furniture plans and books as well as the standard ranges. Over 900 items are included.

Tools by post

Portable power tools, static machinery and accessories as well as a wide variety of hand tools are listed in the new edition of Sarjents Tools *Woodworking Catalogue*. Some of the hand tools are new to this country. Illustrations are in full colour and descriptions often include hints on the care and use of the tools.

The catalogue is available from Sarjents Tools, Oxford Road, Reading, at £1. The company, established in 1849, is also located at Oxford and Swindon, and points out that though for many years craftsmen and tradesmen have travelled miles to these branches, introduction of the catalogue will facilitate ordering from the wide range of items stocked.

From New England

The 1982 catalogue issued by Woodcraft Supply Corp, 313 Montvale Avenue, Woburn, Massachusetts 01888, US, runs to 112 pages and includes a big section of books on woodworking and associated subjects. Many illustrations of tools are in colour. Woodcraft also operates a gift voucher scheme.

Ornamental turners

Publications on the subject of ornamental turning are listed in the Society of Ornamental Turners *Bulletin no. 65* (September 1981). There are also pictures and a description of the Hartley lathe now in possession of the society. The lathe was devised and made by William Hartley of Manchester prior to 1873 and after many ups and downs of fortune it has been restored to working condition.

Editor of the *Bulletin* is J. F. R. Ince, Wangfield House, Curdridge, Southampton SO3 2DA. Hon secretary of the society is W. A. Bourne, 2 Parry Drive, Rustington, Littlehampton BN16 2QY.

Royce and the joiner

In July 1981 WOODWORKER made reference to restoration of a 1932 Rolls-Royce motor involving use of solid walnut for the internal facia panels.

From Derby, A. Crosby sends an interesting reference to the great man of the company, Sir Henry Royce himself. For health reasons Royce had to move from the midlands to the south coast and for many years directed the affairs of Rolls-Royce from his house at West Wittering near Chichester, Sussex.

Mr Crosby's late father, a joiner of exceptional skill, was sent by his firm in Derby to carry out repairs and renovation work at Royce's house. Sir Henry was not a man to compliment another's work lightly, as Mr Crosby rightly points out, so praise from Royce was praise indeed.

Sir Henry's letter to Mr Crosby's father is dated May 27 (?) 1923 and reads: 'I would like to express my gratitude to you for the excellent work you have done at this house.

'Thanks to the fine timber and machining and the prompt and careful attention the work has received from the Ford & Weston firm who so kindly sent you, the two oak floors and wainscotting and the six windows and linings etc have with your skill and energy resulted in a very great improvement in this old house.

'Naturally I am pleased the work is now finished but we shall miss your cheery presence.

'Thanking you also for your many helpful and sound suggestions and for so accurately taking the many necessary dimensions.'

The letter is signed 'Yours very truly, H. A. Royce.'

Mr Crosby in his covering letter to WOODWORKER comments: 'The letter is a testimony both to an old-time craftsman and to one of England's great engineers who took time to say "thank you" to a workman for a job well done. How many leading industrialists of today would do this I wonder?'

Small machines tooling

Hobby brand tooling for spindle moulders and universals which comprises profile cutters, groovers, rebating heads and cutter heads is illustrated and described in a four-language (English, German, Spanish, French) catalogue available from Leicester Wood Technique Ltd, Hothorpe House, Main Street, Theddingworth, Lutterworth LE17 6QY.

THE WORLD'S TIMBER TREES

In no. 23 of his series (October 1981), C W Bond FIWSc described one of the world's most valuable timbers, Honduras or Central American mahogany. This month he deals with the original Cuban or 'Spanish' mahogany. It was introduced early in the 18th century and revolutionised furniture making under Chippendale, Heppelwhite and other master craftsmen.

CUBAN MAHOGANY: 24

Swietenia mahagoni. mahagoni — from an old name for the tree, *mogano* or *m'ogan-wo,* used widely with various spelling modifications by those concerned with extraction through earlier years. Was it first used by the African slaves? Meliaceae.

This is the original mahogany first exported to England early in the 18th century and seized upon by woodworkers who soon discovered its response to hand tools and hence their pleasure in artistic constructions. The tree grows throughout the Caribbean islands except Trinidad.

It is worthwhile for a craftsman to keep a discerning eye for any pieces of this wood, since you never know when and where prime material may reveal itself. Demolition work warrants investigation in view of this possibility alone; and items of old furniture are always worthy of close inspection.

Perhaps a thoughtful word of advice will be excused. *Never underestimate the man you are talking to.* Many years ago I spotted a large table in a musty junk shop. Carelessly shuffling through the doorway I asked the unkempt old dealer what he wanted 'for that old table.' The answer, in a thrilled and excited and confidential whisper was: 'Ah! That's a piece of the real old genuine ma'ogany. Can't let it go for less than.....' Inflation advises me against publishing the price but, though high, the deal was a bargain all right!

Below right: Cross section ×3·3 as seen with a ×10 hand lens. Below: Cross section ×10

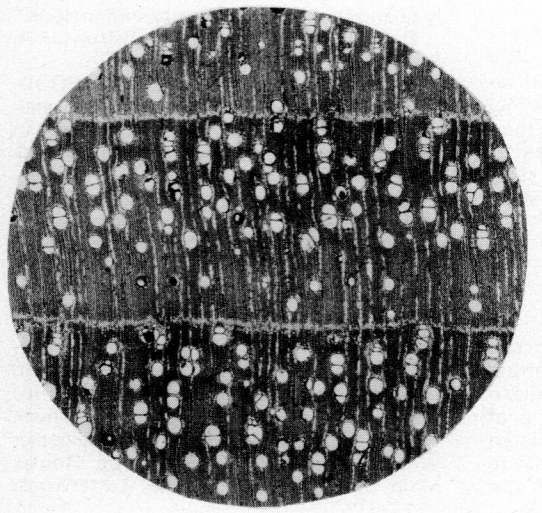

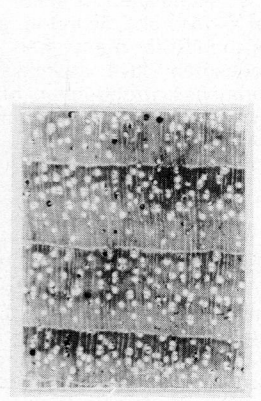

Swietenia mahagoni
Drawn from material in the Forest Herbarium, University of Oxford. Acknowledgements to the Curator

The wood is considerably harder and heavier than that of *S. macrophylla,* much deeper and richer in colour and distinctive in general character. A whitish deposit is frequent in the vessels.

The photomicrograph shows a seasonal 'terminal' line of parenchyma cells, but this is often less well-marked. The vessels appear slightly smaller and somewhat more numerous than in *S. macrophylla,* but variation is evident in both species.

5 cm

MOORFIELD PROTECTIVE GARMENTS

A COMPLETE RANGE FOR ALL PRACTICAL PURPOSES

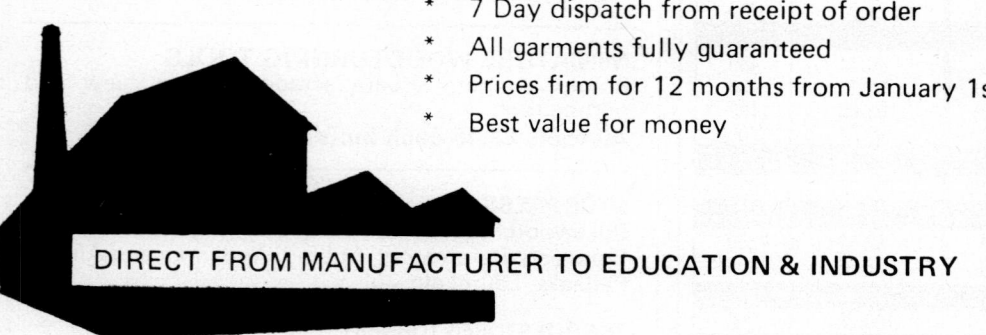

* 7 Day dispatch from receipt of order
* All garments fully guaranteed
* Prices firm for 12 months from January 1st
* Best value for money

DIRECT FROM MANUFACTURER TO EDUCATION & INDUSTRY

for brochure and price list contact:--

MOORFIELDS APRONS DIVISION
PERSEVERANCE MILL · OLIVE LANE · DARWEN · LANCS · BB3 3DS · Tel: 0254-74131-2-3

Guild of Woodworkers

Following the success of the two-day seminar on skills and profit-making held at Salisbury last June in co-operation with the Council for Small Industries in Rural Areas (CoSIRA), the guild has arranged a further series of two-day seminars on the same subject.

The first will be held at the Lord Hill hotel, Abbey Foregate, Shrewsbury, on Wednesday and Thursday 24 and 25 February. It will also include a short visit to Shrewsbury Technical College on 25 February. The second will be at the Pottergate Course & Conference Centre, 83-5 Pottergate, Norwich, on Wednesday and Thursday 28 and 29 April. The fee for each seminar is £50 plus £7.50 VAT (total £57.50) which includes tuition, papers and lecture material, morning coffee, lunch and tea in the afternoon. Accommodation is not included but arrangements can be made on request.

Subjects will include business principles; business skills; marketing; production utilisation; financial control; budgets; tax; planning for growth and much more. The programme is carefully tailored to meet the requirements of those who contemplate starting their own businesses or who have recently set up in the woodworking sector.

The instructors are CoSIRA officers all of whom have much practical experience in small business operation and each seminar allows time for discussion and exchange of views. As reported in WOODWORKER for September last year: 'It (the seminar at Salisbury) was all done in a practical way and with good humour, informality and quick-fire question-and-answer technique.' One member said afterwards: 'Its all a matter of commonsense really but I did not realise it until now. The seminar has certainly opened my eyes.'

The whole purpose of being in business is to make a profit. At the Salisbury seminar, John Matthews (CoSIRA senior production management officer) said: 'If you want to make £10 000 a year you've got to make £1 every 10 minutes, so when you are on your own you can't afford to just stand around.'

Further details can be had from the administrator, Guild of Woodworkers, PO Box 35, Bridge Street, Hemel Hempstead HP1 1EE, or complete the reservation form below. If you wish to make a provisional reservation please mark the form 'provisional'. Note that a cancellation charge of half the fee will be made unless the cancellation is received in writing 14 days prior to the date of each seminar. Transfer will, however, be accepted up to the day before each seminar.

Cheques/postal orders should be crossed and made payable to M.A.P. Ltd.

SEMINARS: SKILLS AND PROFIT-MAKING

Guild of Woodworkers – Council for Small Industries in Rural Areas

To: Administrator
Guild of Woodworkers
PO Box 35
Bridge Street
Hemel Hempstead HP1 1EE

Date ....

Please reserve a place for me on the seminar to be held
on 24-25 February 1982 at Lord Hill Hotel, Abbey Foregate, Shrewsbury,
on 28-29 April 1982 at the Pottergate Course & Conference Centre, 83-5 Pottergate, Norwich.
(Tick which seminar you wish to attend).

I enclose cheque/postal order for £57.50 in payment of seminar tuition fee, papers and lecture material, refreshments and lunch.

I contemplate starting my own business
I am already trading on my own account
(Tick whichever applies).

Please reserve accommodation for me at a guest house,
hotel,
bed & breakfast

(Tick whichever applies)

I understand that accommodation is not included in the seminar fee and I will pay for my accommodation direct.

Name .... BLOCK CAPITALS

Address in full ....

....

Telephone number ....

Signed ....

Membership number ....

Attention is drawn to the cancellation charge of half the fee unless the cancellation is received in writing 14 days prior to the date of each seminar.

TEAR OFF AND POST IMMEDIATELY TOGETHER WITH REMITTANCE

Letters

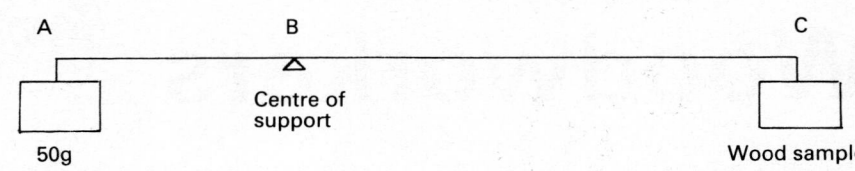

A   B   C

Centre of support

50g   Wood sample

From: I. Lauder, Brisbane, Australia
Dear Sir

It is a pleasure to receive WOODWORKER by ASP. On 21 July I received August 1981 issue and I am writing to indicate an error in the method adopted by J. K. W. Wheatley for determining the m.c. of wood (p506).

If the 300mm blade from an adjustable square were weightless, this error would not exist. As this is not so the method of calculation by Mr Wheatley is incorrect. The calculation by W. H. Brown (also on p506) is incorrect too.

It is possible to calculate the weight of water which has been lost by the sample by the method adopted by Mr Wheatley but it is necessary to know the exact weight of the blade and the weight/mm must be constant.

The centre of gravity of the portion AB of the blade is at the mid-point of AB and correspondingly for BC. By use of the equation:

$$50 \times \text{length of AB} + \text{weight of AB} \times \frac{\text{length of AB}}{2}$$

$$= \text{wt of wood} \times \text{length of BC} + \text{wt of BC} \times \frac{\text{length of BC}}{2}$$

the m.c. may ultimately be derived.

The method is not recommended. Mr Wheatley could easily make a simple kind of chemical balance which would have a much better accuracy than 1/10oz = 2.8g. The beam should be made as light as possible (aluminium) and the lengths AB and BC should be equal. Weights could be made out of aluminium wire. From the density of aluminium (2.702g/cu cm) and the diameter, the length may be calculated for any chosen weight. For small weights use small-diameter wire.

I would also like to comment on the reply to W. Robinson's query in Question Box for July 1981 (p461). The main constituents of air are nitrogen and oxygen in the ratio 4:1. The nitrogen molecule, the oxygen molecule, the water molecule (the smallest particles of these substances in air) have masses in the ratio 28:32:18.

If some of the oxygen and nitrogen molecules in air at a *uniform temperature* are replaced by water molecules, as occurs in a drying process, the air becomes less dense and would therefore rise. The exit vents would need to be higher than the wood being dried.

Yours faithfully, **I. Lauder**

From: Paul R. Harper, Flint, Clwyd
Dear Sir

May I come to the aid of J. K. W. Wheatley and W. H. Brown (WOODWORKER for August 1981 p506) in rectifying an error in basic physics which both contributors seem to have made in calculating the m.c. of a sample of oak.

Mr Wheatley's method has many inaccuracies which Mr Brown points out, but their error is in not accounting for the weight of the steel blade used as the balance beam. If the beam is, as stated, uniform then its centre of gravity corresponds to its geometric centre; and when the fulcrum is placed directly under it the weight of the blade does not act to over-balance the beam in either direction.

However, when re-weighing the correspondent shifted the fulcrum from the centre of gravity of the beam, so now its weight does act to one side of the fulcrum producing a turning effect or moment.

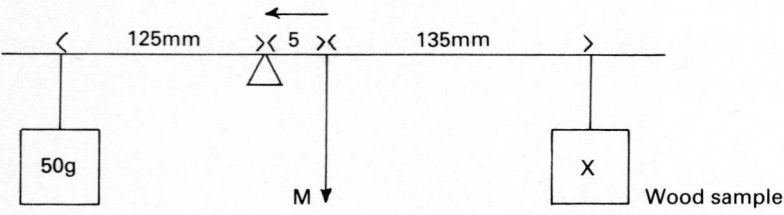

125mm   5   135mm

50g   M   X   Wood sample

If Mr Wheatley wishes to persist with this method he will need to find the weight of the blade (M) and put its value into the following formula to find the unknown weight of the wood (X): $50 \times 125 = 5 \times M + 135 \times X$.

Many woodworkers would like to know the approximate m.c. of their wood but do not have access to sophisticated balances or Protimeters. I wonder if the following method could prove useful. I have not used it to find the m.c. of wood but my experiments suggest it is feasible. It has the advantages that it does not depend on the uniformity of the balance beam and it requires no knowledge of the weight of the beam nor even of the sample of wood itself:

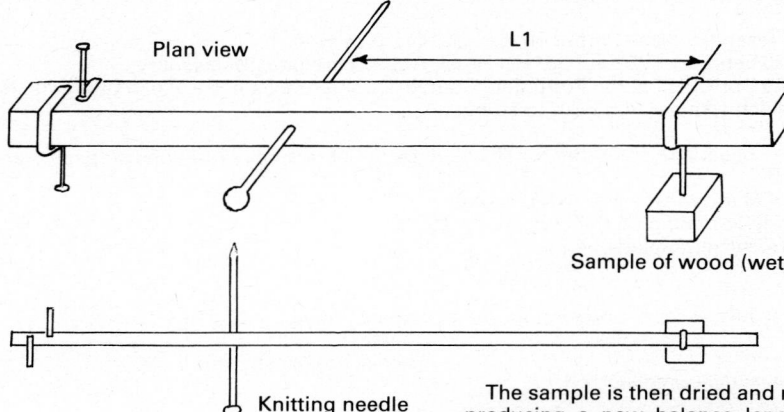

Plan view

L1

Sample of wood (wet)

Knitting needle

Take a wooden lath about 1m in length and drill a hole through the lath at a point about 20cm along from one end and slightly above the centre line. A knitting needle is passed through the hole to act as a fulcrum. The wet sample of wood is suspended by cotton about 60cm from the fulcrum and the beam balanced by clamping two fretwork clamps (or similar clamps without movable parts, such as tomray bars) to the other side of the beam.

To avoid the beam tilting sideways and to gain maximum sensitivity the clamps should be identical and arranged symmetrically around the beam. When the beam is balanced horizontally the distance of the sample from the fulcrum (L1) is measured.

The sample is then dried and re-weighed producing a new balance length L2, the clamps not being moved in the interim. The percentage m.c. can then be calculated by substitution in the following formula:

$$\% \text{ m.c.} = \frac{L2 - L1}{L1} \times 100$$

Yours faithfully, **Paul R. Harper**

W. H. Brown writes: I would comment briefly on the letters from I. Lauder, Brisbane; and Paul Harper, Flint, in regard to m.c. calculations. In the industrial drying of timber the universally accepted method is based on the oven-dry weight; there is another method, ie that of distillation which is quicker and more accurate than the former method but has never been used commercially for various reasons which include a fire risk.

The reference to accuracy should be noted because only by extracting all the moisture from the wood can its amount be truly assessed; and by the oven-dry method there are a few variables likely to be present, eg more resin or gum in one sample as opposed to another, hasty re-

moval of the sample from the oven before it has dried out thoroughly and so on.

However, in a commercial sense proper adherence to the method is acceptable. In a non-commercial sense the most important factor in drying or seasoning wood is to ensure its quality is not spoiled by careless handling; the final acceptable degree of moisture is often related to local circumstances. For instance, where usable wood spends a long time in the workshop because working time is limited perhaps to evenings and weekends.

In my comments regarding an experimental method of taking m.c. (letter from J. Wheatley in August 1981 WOODWORKER) I said that up to a point it was unimportant how m.c. was assessed, provided the method was adhered to and was based on results which satisfied the work. It was quite obvious that the experiment in question did not meet these requirements due to variable factors and particularly to the cutting of the sample to suit the system; this would produce serious errors in assessment alone.

I did not refer to the weight of the beam (blade) used although, of course, it was relevant. But to do so would have been to confuse the issue further, for if a beam is to be properly balanced there is also the necessity to introduce a suspension point as frictionless as possible, and the fact that the further out of balance the less stable the beam becomes.

It must be understood that in lots of cases a proper sample taken from the full width of a thick board can be relatively heavy, so any form of balance must take this into account. As I have said previously a 1g weight is a tiny amount, but if accuracy is essential then weights must be properly assessed.

I would also reply to a further comment made by Mr Lauder on the question of moisture and air. His remark that air that has been made less dense by the introduction of water molecules would rise is valid but is out of context with the reply we gave W. Robinson (WOODWORKER for July 1981, p461) which we pointed out was merely 'food for thought'.

It was not possible to give the information requested firstly because it was involved and required suitable space, and secondly because we had already decided to give proper details in a full-length article.

In the fifth paragraph of our reply we spoke of the need for moisture-laden air to be vented off; this is the air to which Mr Lauder refers and it would certainly tend to rise and, in many circumstances, would need to be vented-off (as opposed to fresh air ventilation) at a relatively high level.

Our main concern, however, was in wet air, and there is a difference although the term is perhaps not strictly correct. In a home-made drying chamber there would be certain factors needing attention; water vapour would tend to rise but it could condense at dew point. For example, air that held, say, 4 grains of moisture/cu ft might, if its temperature was reduced by the cooling effect of ventilation, now only hold 3 grains of moisture with 1 grain condensing out as precipitation. This is what we termed wet air and this certainly tends to fall in a sluggish atmosphere. It is a well-established fact that timber stacked in the open air to dry is frequently less dry at the lower levels of the stack; and it is sometimes the practice to build a space up through the centre of the stack to act as a

chimney that will encourage an upward draught.

However, to digress slightly, it is part of the design procedure for squash courts to arrange a sensible air flow from the rear of the floor area to vents built into the top of the playing wall, ie diagonally upwards. If this lower ventilation is impeded in any way (and it can happen) the very high perspiration rate of the players may be converted into serious damp problems at the lower levels of walls and at floor level, generally as unsightly black mould growths with the top levels remaining clean.

This simile can serve to illustrate the internal conditions of a home-made drying chamber. One of the problems with custom-built drying kilns is in the air and heat tightness of doors and it is not unreasonable to assume that in a home-made drying chamber there could be quite a lot of moist air vented out from around the door frame, especially at the top. But if there were additional vents placed low down on the opposite side to the door, the air flow would be encouraged to adopt a similar pattern to that of a squash court.

Obviously that is not the whole answer, but it will be seen that if heating is introduced, say, from just a few light bulbs, the moisture extracted from the wood will certainly migrate upwards initially until the vented-off air is replaced by cooler air when a problem of condensation at the lower levels might occur.

From: Peter Copestake, Colne, Lancs
Dear Sir

I cannot help wondering what will happen when Hugh Blogg (WOODWORKER for August 1981 p526) realises how much leverage he can exert on a poor harmless screw by using his screwdriver horizontally (see my sketch).

However, while the rest of us are using our tools in the manner for which they were devised (if you wanted more power the answer certainly would be a fatter handle), perhaps Mr Blogg should study motoring magazines for a while. He would discover that rally drivers and speedway riders apply 'opposite lock' to counteract the oversteer produced by the sliding back wheels which would otherwise cause them to come off the inside of the bend.

The technique is referred to as 'steering into the skid' when more restrained and less skilled drivers find their back wheels have lost their grip on an icy bend.

Yours faithfully, **Peter Copestake**

From: P. J. Knott, Swindon, Wilts
Dear Sir

I cannot let Hugh Blogg's remarks (p526 of the August 1981 issue) pass without comment. Maximum effect is achieved if all

the driver force is applied at right angles to the slot, parallel with the flat and preferably near the ends of the slot.

Taking Mr Blogg's explanation towards its logical limit exposes his error. The driver forces are now split into the useful tangential turning forces T and the 'in-line' forces W — at best wasted, and more probably causing the blade to rise up out of the slot and damage it. This last effect can only be counteracted by heavy downward pressure, and how wasteful that is!

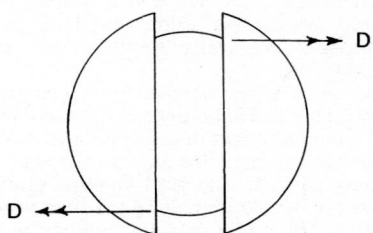

His 'spanner' explanation applies only if the screw is welded to the driver or, for example, when using a brace and driver bit. How much better to keep screw and driver in line to maximise the useful turning force.

I believe the advantages of a long driver are more easily explained:
(a) A driver that is offset at an angle to the screw tends to slip out and does not use its force to maximum effect on the screw.
(b) We are anatomically unable to keep driver and screw in line; we displace the handle sideways; and the more we strain the more we wobble.
(c) For a given sideways displacement, a shorter driver means a larger offset angle; the wobble has less effect at the far end of a longer driver.
(d) Therefore with a long driver we can apply more force before it starts to slip

out, and more of the applied force acts in an efficient direction on the screw head.

More list — less twist
In line? — that's fine.

Incidentally, I like the idea of gaining an advantage from the 'springiness' of a long driver — we have all experienced this effect I'm sure. But I have a nasty feeling it is more psychological than real. The actual twist in a few inches of driver steel would probably be quite imperceptible.

Yours faithfully, **Peter Knott**

Work by the schools: CHANCELLOR'S

At Chancellor's School, Brookmans Park, near Hatfield, 150 11-16 year-old boys are doing woodwork under the tuition of Maurice L. W. Halls, Head of the crafts department.

Mr Halls firmly believes that mastery of hand tools and hand processes is an essential foundation for the development of skills. The exhibition of his pupils' work at the school early in July 1981 showed that the boys are developing along the right lines.

WOODWORKER was also pleased to see a good display of joinery items such as step-ladders, sawhorses and tool carriers, in addition to the furniture and turnery pieces. The furniture was mostly in chestnut and elm.

In the six years he has been at Chancellor's Mr Halls has been encouraging pupils to appreciate the raw material, especially the home-grown hardwoods, and to realise the importance of conditioning and storage. Outside the workshop he has around 80cu ft of chestnut in-stick purchased from a local mill. Apart from the cost advantage of air-drying at the school, the stock is an important part of the educational scheme.

A teacher for 34 years Mr Halls trained at Shoreditch College when it was in Pitfield Street, London. Later he taught at schools in east and central Africa.

Left: dinner wagon in English chestnut by Graham Deans; kitchen stool in chestnut by Graham Bice; laminated lamp in mahogany and chestnut by Gavin Young. All 5th year students.

Left: Elliptical table in English chestnut by Sean Beaman, 4th year student.

Below: Examples of the range of 4th and 5th year work achieved at Chancellor's school.

Left: Coffee table by Grahan Deans, chairs by Michael Coleman and Darren Payne, all in chestnut. All three pupils are in their 5th year.

Left: Three more chestnut items, round table to **WOODWORKER** design by Steven Mardle, slab end stool/tables by Martin Bray and David Ladbury, 5th year pupils.

Left: Square plant pot stand by Neil Neighton (5th year), centre plant stand by Sean Beaman (4th year), plant stand on right by David Bennett (5th year) and magazine rack by Stephen Sulley (4th year) all in chestnut.

Right: steps by Graham Bice, Martin Page and Adam Beardon, sawing stools by Mark Matthews, mallet and shoulder plane by Graham Deans, tool boxes by John Model and table by Darrel Mileson all 5th year students.

PUZZLERS' WORLD

R. W. Grant offers a selection of puzzles ranging from simple assemblies to hideously complicated ones.

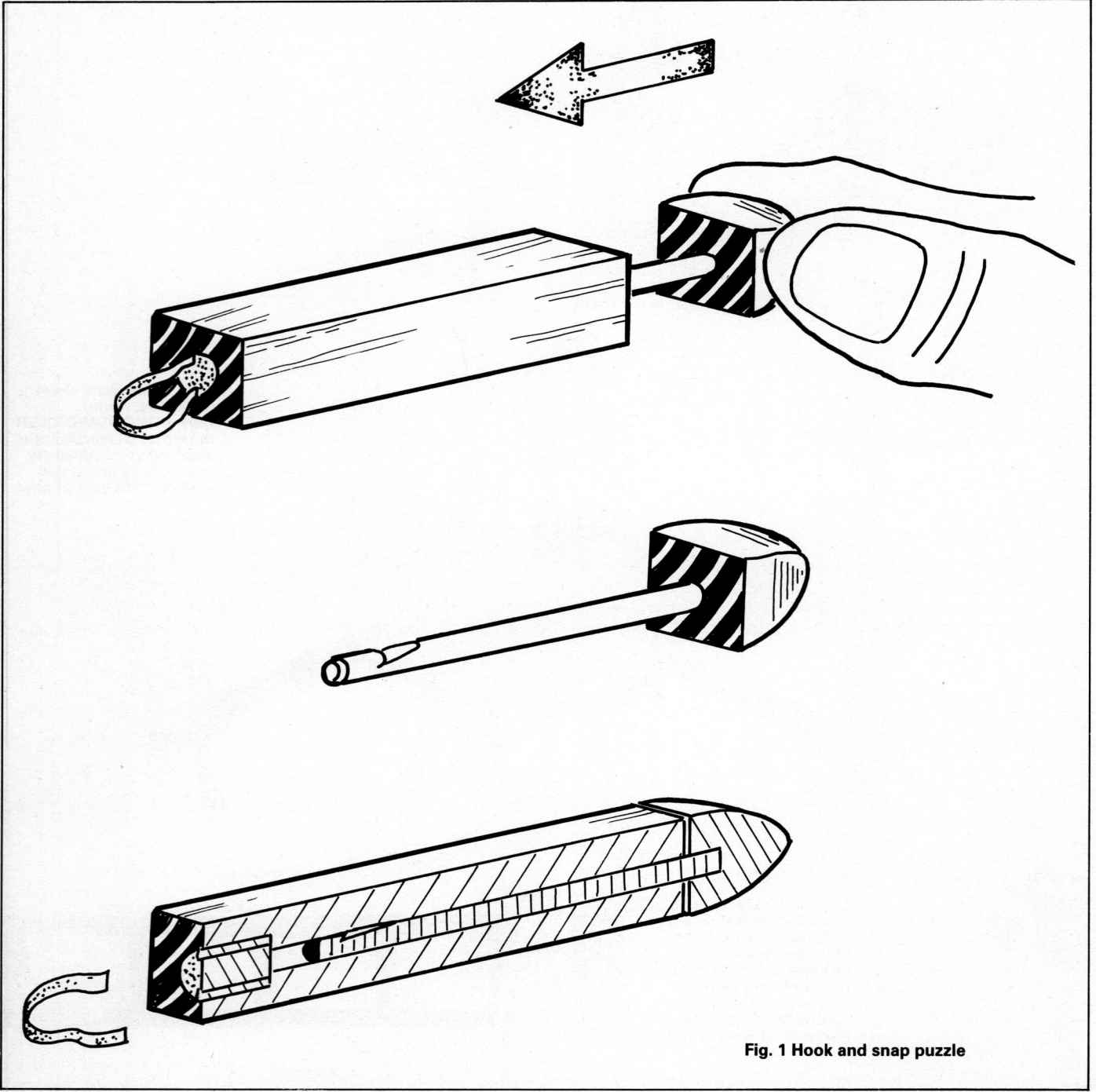

Fig. 1 Hook and snap puzzle

Twelfth night marks the end of the Christmas and New Year festivities but there are a lot of dark evenings ahead and fireside amusements might make a pleasing alternative to the ever-present TV. Here R. W. Grant offers a selection of puzzles ranging from simple assemblies to hideously complicated ones that will tax the most nimble brain.

He says: 'They are not only interesting in themselves but provide excellent examples for you to demonstrate your prowess as a craftsman. A hardwood (beech is ideal) should be selected for the manufacture of these puzzles. Absolute accuracy in marking-out and cutting is essential.'

His drawings show the construction.

The hook and snap (Fig. 1) is probably more of a trick than a puzzle but in the hands of a dextrous operator it can be totally mystifying. By showing your audience the handle piece and explaining that the hook at the bottom has to catch the loop of a rubber band inside the barrel piece (clear evidence

of which can be seen by the other end of the rubber band sticking out of the bottom), proceed to insert the handle piece and fish about making several 'plunges' and twists to loop the band.

Then perhaps with a sigh of satisfaction, draw the handle back a short way and show how it snaps back into place when released. Offer the puzzle to your victim and see if your success can be repeated.

Eventually, to preserve friendship, you may have to explain how it is done. Of

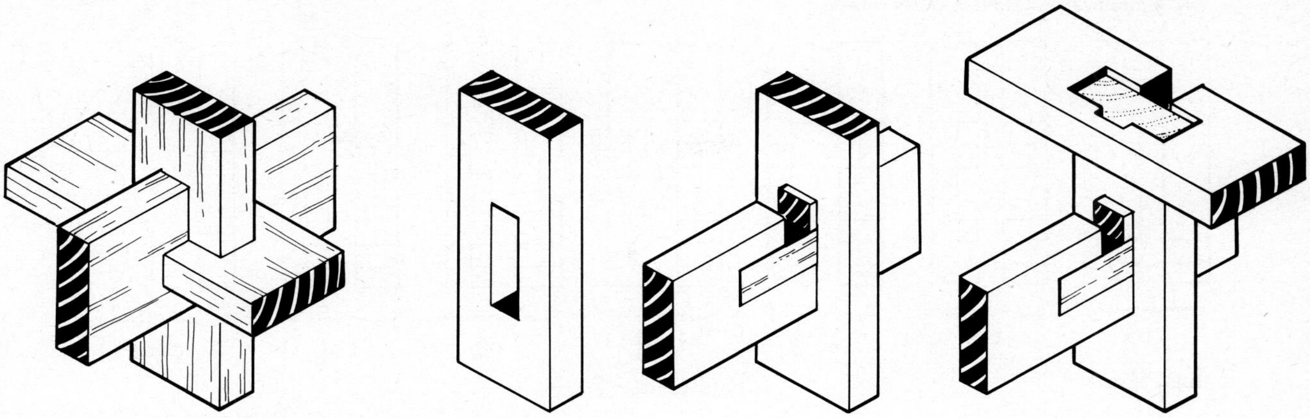

Fig. 2 The completed puzzle

Fig. 2 The completed puzzle

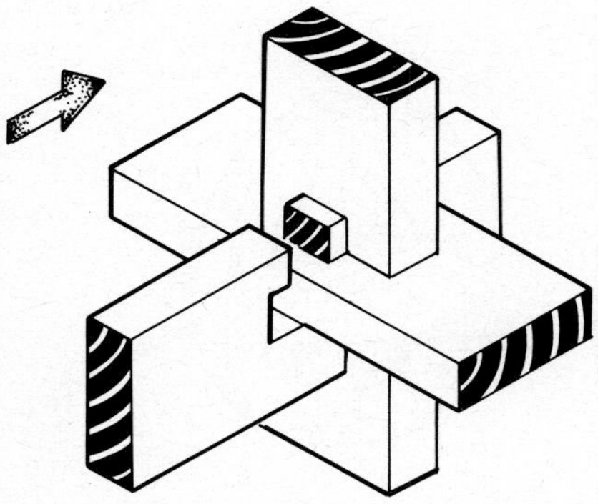

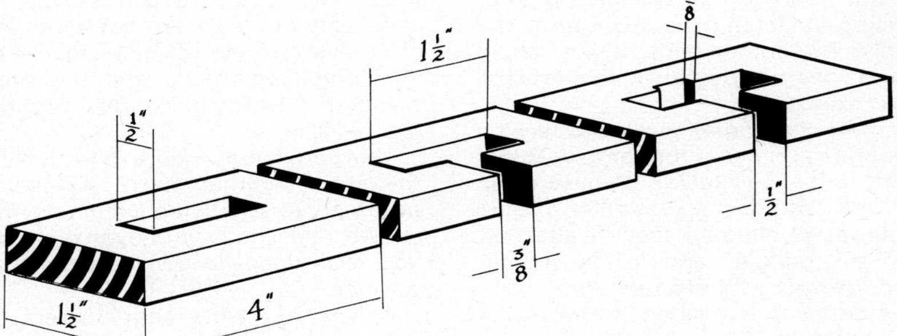

Fig. 2a Sizes for the three pieces

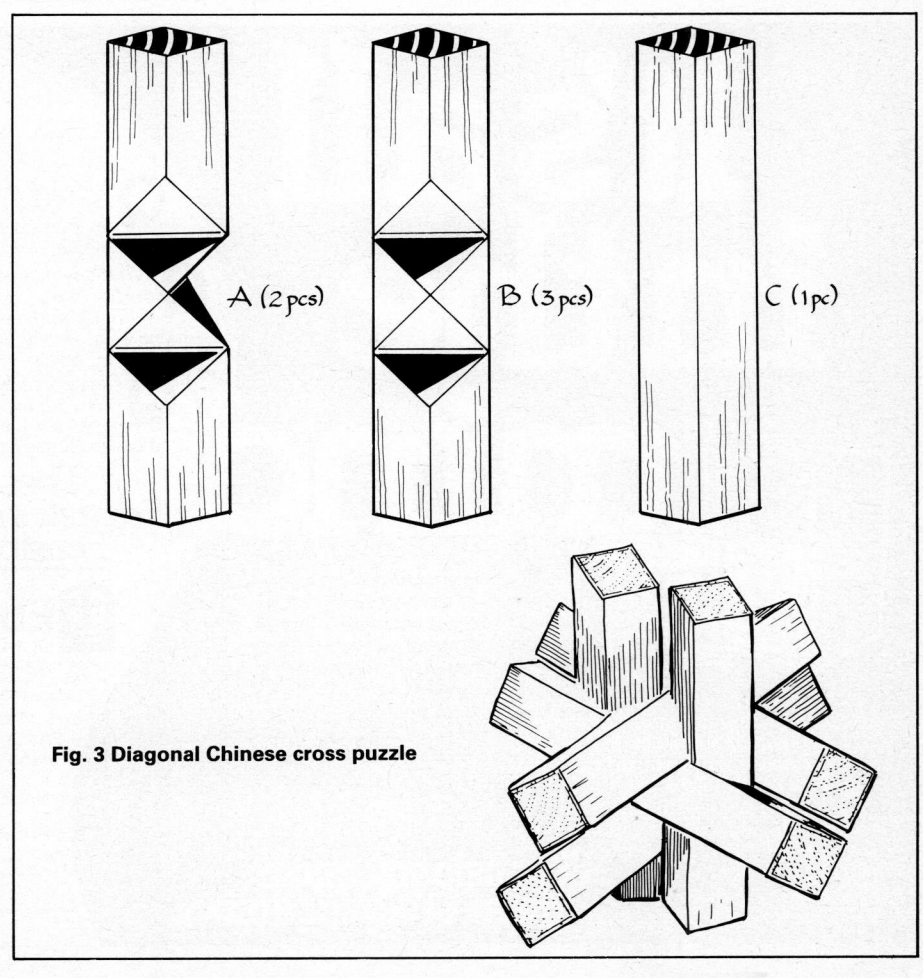

Fig. 3 Diagonal Chinese cross puzzle

A (2 pcs)

B (3 pcs)

C (1 pc)

course there is no loop inside the barrel and the realistic snap-back into place is achieved by squeezing the specially-shaped knob between thumb and forefinger making it shoot forwards.

The piece is easy enough to make. A 3in. length of beech ¾in. square should be bored through to take a ¼in. diameter dowel. At one end counterbore with a ⅜in. drill and insert a plug that has two saw kerfs and a loop of rubber band fixed into it. A spot of adhesive will hold all in place.

Take a ⅝in. length of the same material and fix the ¼in. dowel to it. This should not 'bottom' in the plug and should have a chisel knick in it (rather like a crochet hook). The sectional drawing (Fig. 1) shows the general assembly. The knob should be carefully shaped like a square dome so that the grip can be obtained. Finish the piece with a hard lacquer to withstand handling.

The mortising puzzle (Fig. 2) is a more conventional piece. It is simple to make and comparatively easy to solve although in its completed form looks to be an impossibility.

Prepare three pieces of wood each 4in. long, 1½in. wide and ½in. thick. Chop a 1½ × ½in. mortise in each piece. Two of the pieces need to be further cut as shown. The whole can then be assembled (and dismantled) as shown in the sequence of drawings (Fig. 2a).

Of greater complexity is the diagonal Chinese cross puzzle (Fig. 3). Prepare six pieces 3in. long and ¾in. square. Saw and pare them as shown in the diagrams, ie two pieces like A, three pieces like B and one piece like C. Piece C is a plain length and acts as the key piece.

No doubt you will have fun making this

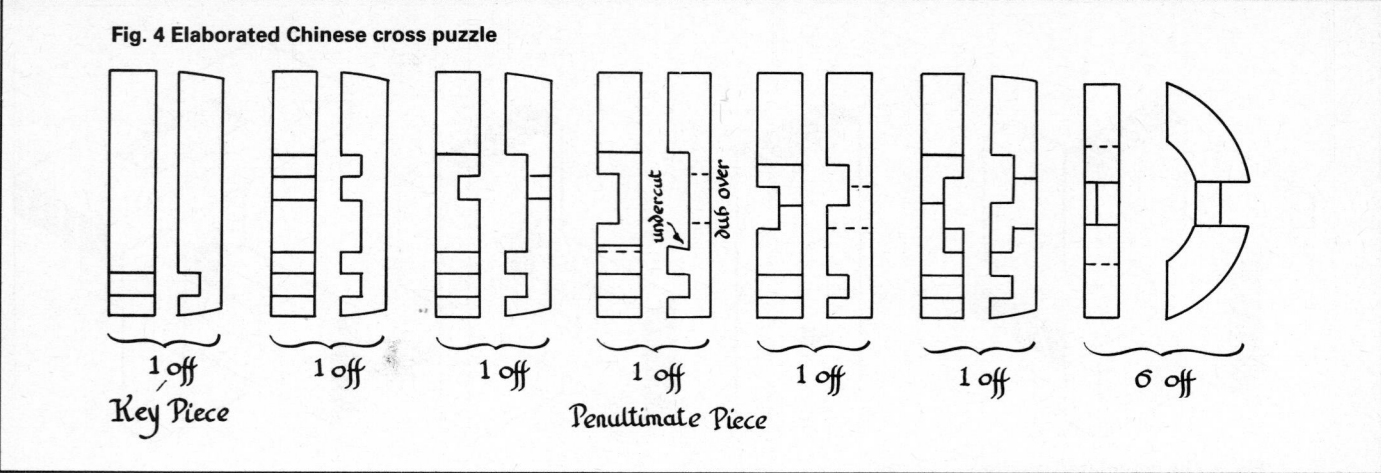

Fig. 4 Elaborated Chinese cross puzzle

undercut *dub over*

⌣ 1 off ⌣ 1 off ⌣ 1 off ⌣ 1 off ⌣ 1 off ⌣ 1 off ⌣ 6 off

Key Piece *Penultimate Piece*

puzzle but perhaps you will gain greater satisfaction in finding the solution to the assembly. The author adds: 'I can assure you that it does go together, as shown in my freehand sketch.'

Your most challenging piece may well be the elaborated Chinese cross puzzle. This is a variant of the well-known Chinese cross puzzle and includes six annular pieces linking the arms, although they are attached only in the middles and locate slightly above or below their true equators.

Some deftness is needed to make this puzzle. Although 2¾in. lengths of ½in. square beech were used in the original the sizes could be enlarged, bearing in mind that the interlocking notches are multiples, halves or quarters of the section.

Fig. 4 shows each constituent piece in

both front and side elevations and the notch at the bottom of each arm carries an annular piece. The freehand sketch (Fig. 4a) shows the completed puzzle and indicates the position of the key piece which is slipped in last of all.

The penultimate piece effectively locks the arms together and it will be found necessary to slightly undercut one notch as shown and lightly dub-over one edge as you will need to twist the piece into position.

Before you write angry letters to the editor after hours of struggling to assemble the puzzle, you may like to know that this piece faces the key piece in an upright position with its annular arm at the bottom when held in the same aspect as the assembly sketch.

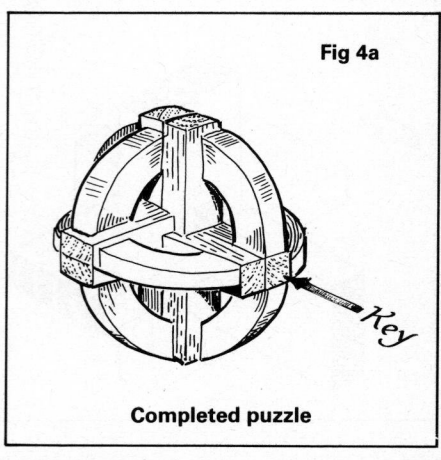

Fig 4a

Key

Completed puzzle

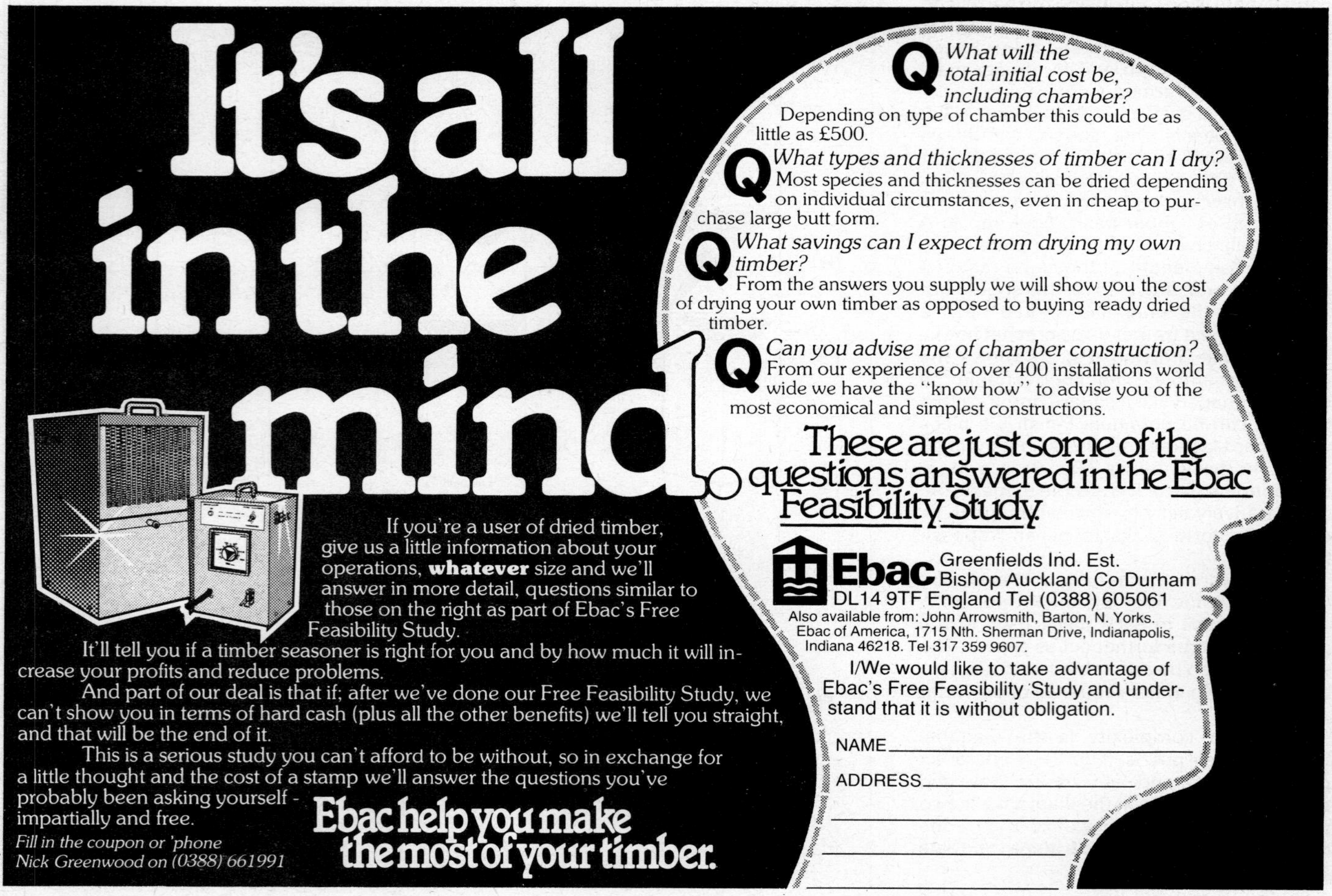

Send for Your NEW COWELLS Catalogue TODAY!

COWELLS 1982 CATALOGUE

We have just printed our new catalogue for 1982 which is packed with photos and information on machines, tools and accessories, model steam engines, technical books, clocks and lots more exciting constructional projects.

Some of the machines are shown for the first time, proving once again that the **Cowell Collection** is getting bigger and better each year.

Send for your **free** copy.

Write or call

Cowell Engineering Limited

Rackheath, Norwich, England, NR13 6LF.
Phone (0603) 720141.   Telex 97256.

United States Sales:
Cowells Incorporated, P.O. Box 427, 226 East Adele Court, Villa Park, Illinois, 60181.
Phone (312) 833–4405.   Telex 72–1586.

MAKE MINE MING

Ming style furniture

The arts of China, Korea and Japan, although clearly related, are the products of distinct and independent cultural traditions. China, with an unbroken artistic heritage reaching back some 7000 years to the Neolithic period, has been the principal source of influence and inspiration in Far Eastern art. The Far Eastern gallery at the Victoria and Albert museum, South Kensington, London SW7, displays in broadly chronological sequence only the finest examples of the arts of Far Eastern countries from the museum's collections. The Chinese section begins with the pre-Christian era and proceeds in a clockwise direction to conclude with the decorative

Above: Armchair in huang hua li, 18th century Ming donated to the Victoria and Albert museum by Sir John Addis KCMG. *(photo: Courtesy Victoria and Albert museum)* (Material for this article taken from one of a series of V&A broadsheets and *China Pictorial.*)

arts of the Ch'ing dynasty. Even in these early but immensely sophisticated objects the intricate, often abstract, decoration illustrates those formal qualities in design which are such a fundamental and enduring feature of the arts of China. The Chinese section concludes with the magnificent and unique carved red lacquer throne of the Emperor Ch'ien-lung (1736-95).

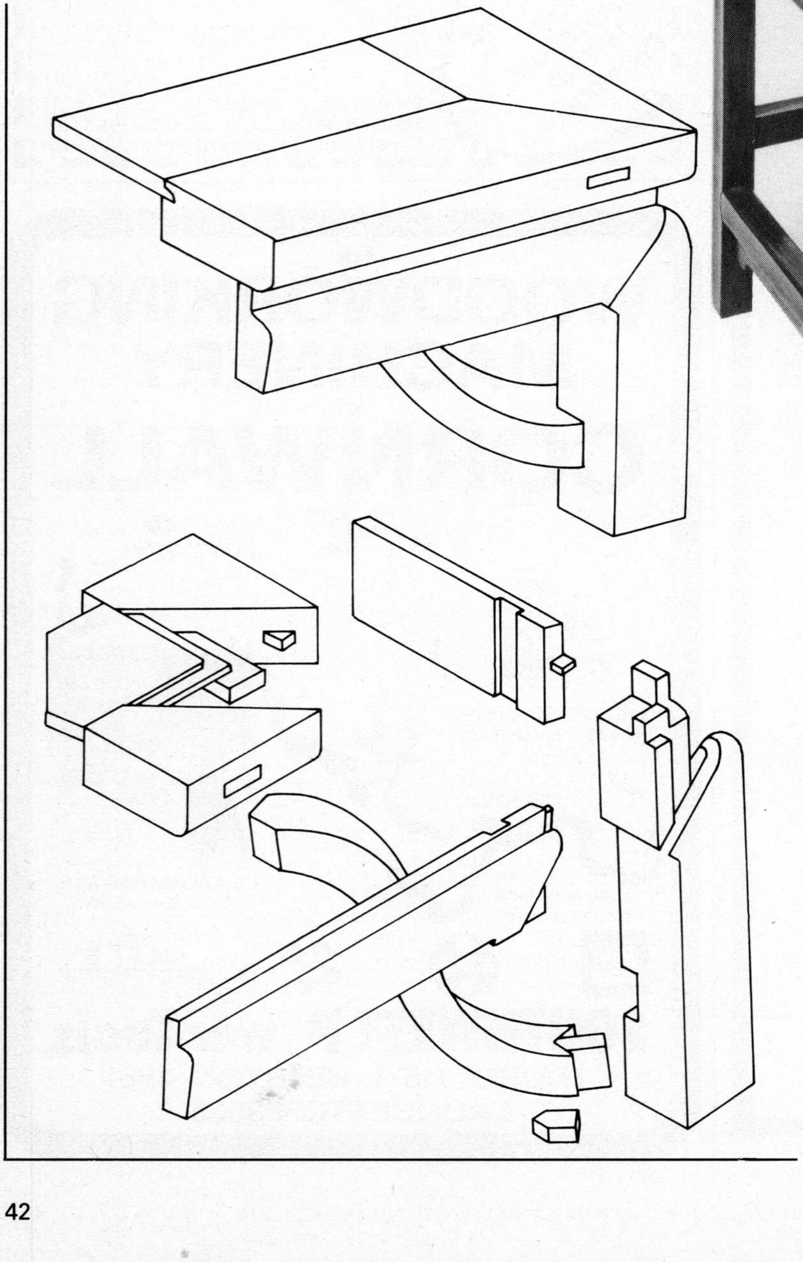

Other pieces in the Chinese section include the Bodhisattva Kuan-Yin in carved wood painted and gilt on gesso, Sung dynasty (13th century). In this representation of the Bodhisattva the figure sits in the *mahārāja-līla*, or Royal Ease, pose on a rocky outcrop which symbolises the deity's island home and her traditional role as protector of the sea. The fluent but ornate style, bejewelled pendants and rippling draperies, providing a rich and decorative effect, are characteristic features of Chinese Buddhist sculptures of the Sung dynasty.

Right and opposite left: outline sketches show examples of mortise and tenon jointing Chinese style. (Acknowledgements to China Pictorial)

Also of great interest is the carved red lacquer imperial table from the Ming dynasty (reign of Hsüan-tê 1426-35). Carved on the top surface with a design of five-clawed dragons and phoenixes among lotus scrolls, this red lacquer table was made for the use of the early Ming court; and is today unique of its kind. The facing edges of the three drawers are also carved with dragons and phoenixes, traditionally emblems of the Emperor and Empress respectively; the side and rear panels and legs bear designs of lotus, peony, chrysanthemum and cherry. The underside of the table is lacquered black and on the inside of the rear apron is an incised and gilt six-character mark of the Emperor Hsüan-tê.

Stories of master craftsman Lu Ban building spectacular towers and pavilions with linked terraces and upturned eaves are told throughout China. The woodworking trade in ancient China centred around house construction and furniture making. The latter took its cues from the former. The round legs and supports of a chair for instance appear to have been modelled after the columns and beams of a wooden structure. Over the centuries a uniquely Chinese tradition of cabinetmaking gradually evolved.

Chinese furniture making attained its peak of development during the early part of the Ming dynasty (1368-1644). Ming hardwood furniture still enjoys a high prestige today.

Furniture does not only have the functions of utility, comfort and beauty, it also fills up space and sets it off. Ming furniture combines art and function organically and distinguishes by its elegance and simplicity of form. Ming furniture is mostly made of choice wood — mainly *Ormosia henryi* (also known as Hung Tou, the red bean tree, rich red, hard and heavy, beautifully marked and esteemed for cabinetmaking of a high quality); red sandal (also hard, heavy and durable with similar properties to those of teak, it has an interlocked grain and medium fine texture, difficult to work with, it polishes well . . . a variety of *Pterocarpus*); and mahogany — all used for their hardness, fine grain and glossy surface. The component parts of Ming furniture are delicate with small cross sections. They are usually put together neatly being joined by an intricate but ultimately simple mortise and tenon system, unique to China. The excellent quality of the timbers chosen and the sturdy frames enable the pieces to last hundreds of years without rotting, being worm-eaten or loosening at the joints.

Ming furniture is distinguished by its simple form, few but concentrated decorations, elegant yet dignified appearance. The lines are simple and modest. The overall length, width and height of a piece and its integral parts are kept in strict rational proportions. The back and arms of a chair, for example, must be in conformity with the length and curve of the human body so that it imparts a feeling of comfort. Groove work is a common practice for decoration. The plain contour lends beauty to the piece by breaking the monotony of the surface. The elaborately worked line, the interesting design and method of decoration have definite associations with Chinese painting, calligraphy and seal engraving.

The excellence of Ming furniture had much to do with the state of the economy at the time. The development of water-borne communications in China in the early 15th century led to the growth of foreign trade. The import of foreign timber and the transport of wood from the south to the north provided material for the manufacture of hardwood furniture. It was a time too when handicrafts were well developed. The iron parts of woodworking tools were carbonised — something which provided favourable technical conditions for hardwood processing.

During the Ming dynasty, in the closing period of feudal society, high officials and rich merchants settled in such prosperous cities as Suzhou, Yangzhou and Beijing (Peking). As a result of the growth of important private residences, furniture was in great demand as an important part of the interior furnishings. Tang Yin (1470-1522), Wen Zhengming (1490-1559) and Don Qichang (1555-1636) scholars and artists brought their skills to the art of furniture making, adding inscriptions or paintings to pieces of furniture and thus bringing an extra dimension to the craft.

Ming furniture can be seen as a maturation of Tang and Song furnishings. In earliest times people generally sat cross legged on the floor in a plainly furnished room. By 770-221BC only *ji* (a short table used as an arm rest) *an* (a general purpose table) beds and shelves were made, to be followed later by chests, cupboards and divans. By the Sui and Tang period (690-1279) people had formed the habit of sitting with their legs hanging down, so chairs, stools and tall tables made their appearance. By the Song dynasty (960-1279) the mode of life in towns and cities had changed so much that chairs, tables and other items of furniture were now widespread.

In the 6th century, the influence of Chinese furniture spread to Japan and Korea and to certain western European countries in the 18th century.

Above right: Altar table in rosewood, an example of 16-17th century Ming furniture. Below: A 17th century Chinese side table. Both pieces in the Far Eastern gallery at the Victoria and Albert museum. *(photos: Courtesy Victoria and Albert museum)*

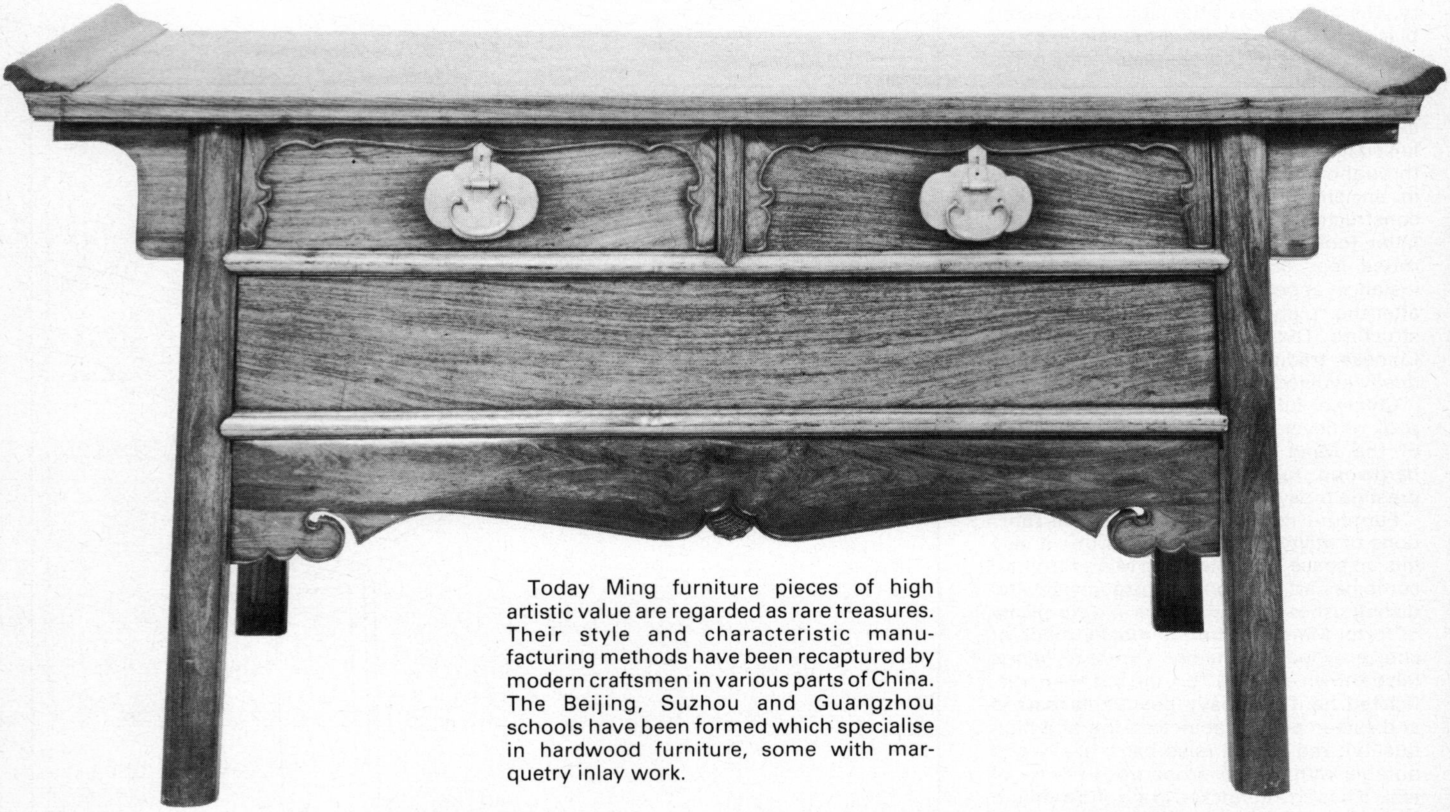

Today Ming furniture pieces of high artistic value are regarded as rare treasures. Their style and characteristic manufacturing methods have been recaptured by modern craftsmen in various parts of China. The Beijing, Suzhou and Guangzhou schools have been formed which specialise in hardwood furniture, some with marquetry inlay work.

EXCELLENCE IN WOODWORKING

Woodworkers from all parts of the east coast of America and several countries, including Britain, attended the first Excellence in Woodworking East show at Madison Square Garden, New York, 11-13 September. Woodworking seminars on wood properties, jointing, finishes and finishing, attracted capacity audiences. Exhibitors demonstrated machines and tools and several book publishers and magazines were present including WOODWORKER. The picture shows Russ Zimmerman from Vermont (see WOODWORKER October 1981 p671) gathering an audience of interested people. Over 7000 attended the show.

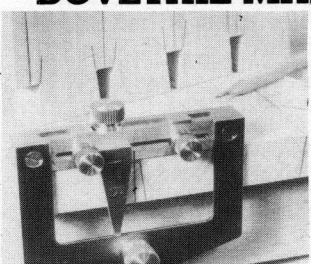
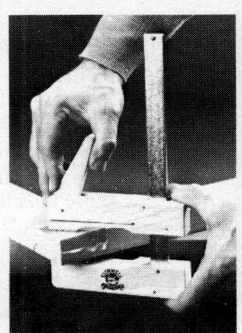

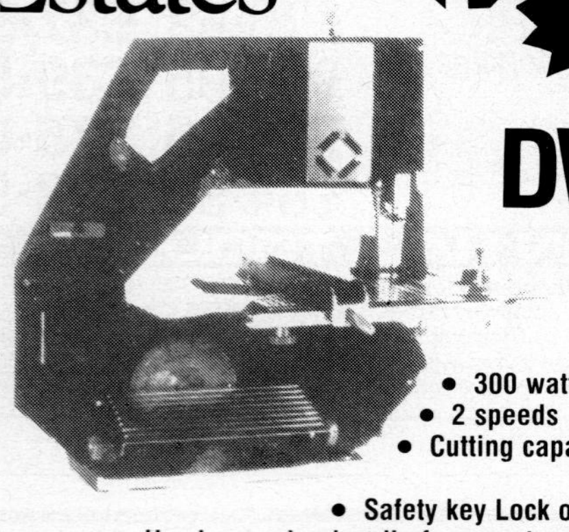

BOOK REVIEWS

Straight forward carpentry

F. E. Sherlock, lecturer in woodwork at Tottenham College of Technology, has revised the book entitled *Carpentry* by Charles Hayward (editor of WOODWORKER until the late 60s) first printed in 1939. This 1981 third edition of the book, a Hodder & Stoughton paperback at £1.50 (ISBN 0-340-27112-4), contains tools, their use and care, joints and their applications, workshop practice, outdoor woodwork, small items (boxes, breakfast flap, high stool, tiled tray, bathroom cabinet and hi-fi unit) designs for furniture and power tools.

It is a practical guide to all aspects of carpentry for the diy beginner and enthusiast. **P.C.**

Carpentry in construction

With most technical books written in America and eventually published in UK, usually it becomes necessary for the reader to adapt many of the techniques described to fit our practices, although recognising and accepting the expertise evident in the text.

Frequently this tends to devalue the book's authority as a standard work of reference which is always a pity, bearing in mind the time and effort that has gone into its preparation.

To some extent this can be said of *Carpentry Fundamentals* (Glenn Baker and Rex Miller) from McGraw-Hill Book Co, except that if the true definition of the adjective fundamental is considered, ie 'of affecting, or serving, as a base or foundation' then, irrespective of American trade terms, the general purpose of the book, that of demonstrating the best carpentry methods to employ in construction projects, has been achieved and can provide a basis of knowledge satisfactory to students, apprentices and to anyone interested in wood use.

Usually this type of book tends to assume a measure of practical experience on the part of the reader in relation to basic techniques. Here the text is organised in such a way as to permit the fairly experienced reader to press on from one chapter to the next, while the inexperienced is encouraged to pause and consider a series of study questions at the end of each chapter before reading on.

There are 25 questions to the first chapter alone including: Why would a carpenter need a nail set? What's the difference between a try square and a bevel? How is a coping saw used? Elementary if you like, but essential. The general text, divided into 17 chapters, is concerned with house construction and all that it implies, from site preparation and laying the foundations, to building and installing roofs, doors, interior trim and so on, right through to construction for solar heating.

The text is supported by easy-to-follow line drawings, diagrams and photographs and contains a host of ideas and information on carpentry which is universal and not bound by building codes and regulations which, although similar in basic requirements, usually differ from one country to another in their deemed to satisfy provisions.

A minor criticism I would make is on the overall lack of introduction of wood chipboard into the text, since apart from its suggested use as a subfloor it is not mentioned. Plywood, quite rightly, is reasonably well covered, but not chipboard.

Throughout Europe, chipboard of various types and densities is used in construction work for many economic applications and especially for fully-floating floors, roof and wall linings and sheathing, and for built-in fitments. It is well represented in ISO standards, particularly BSS and German DIN; I feel even a few examples in the text would have been to advantage.

However, there is something for everyone in the book and it could prove valuable to the average householder since much of the text is applicable to maintenance, remodelling and improvement of existing buildings. *Carpentry Fundamentals* (ISBN 0-07 003361-7) runs to 517 pages and costs £11.50 (hardback). The publisher is at Shoppenhangers Road, Maidenhead SL6 2QL. **W.H.B.**

Wood is precious

As the publisher of this, the 4th book of James Krenov's work, states 'Krenov speaks to everyone who appreciates the special beauty and grace that only human hands can fashion'. *James Krenov – Worker in Wood* (ISBN 0-442-26336-8) published by Van Nostrand Reinhold Co Ltd, Molly Millars Lane, Wokingham RG11 2PY at £15.00 (cloth) is a penetrating look at the creations of an artist-craftsman who has maintained his distinctiveness in an assembly-line age.

Krenov has said that for him woodworking is 'a way of living rather than a way of making a living'. That sentiment comes through in the book, which is large format and sensitively illustrated; it is a guided tour in picture form to the work of an artist at his peak of perfection. There are over 100 black and white photographs and 47 in full colour; the text by James Krenov gives a unique insight into the harmony within the man and with his work. Effort, skill and patience lie behind the excellent photography of Bengt Carlén who again captures the precision, delicacy and subtle strength of each exquisite piece. The photographs reveal intricate grain detail, satin-smooth finish and meticulously executed joints. They show Krenov's willingness to let the wood dictate the finished form.

This is a book about the closeness of a craftsman to his work; personal expression, gentleness, clarity and intimacy and a sense of love and well being are all here. Krenov's message is a simple and poetic one, it starts with a respect for wood, it has a respect also for tools and it believes in an intuitive feel for what is right.

Each piece, mainly cabinets, cases and tables, within the book is lovingly described in detail and the reader is carried along in the quickening enthusiasm of the craftsman as he explores and develops each idea.

'Some ideas,' says Krenov talking of a writing table in Italian walnut, 'simply impose themselves, there is no design or originality involved. When I write I twist to the left – a straight edged table is not ideal... A plank of wonderful Italian walnut, had the curve and the taper that said "Here it is".'

Most of his work is fairly small, partly because his shop is small and because he has a tendency toward detailed work. The largest object in the book is barely six feet tall – a cabinet showcase in doussie and lemon wood. Other treasures include a cabinet in Andaman padouk, a wall cabinet in English brown oak (with 2 drawers for fun, from Swedish chestnut kept for nearly 20 years), a wall cabinet in spalted maple, a table for a Chinese horse in East Indian rosewood and Indian laurel. There are others, but these are my favourites.

Krenov believes a sense of caring is essential, he is primarily concerned with the *way* the work is being done, not the *how* of technique, rather the *why* of attitude.

As Craig McArt says in his foreword 'transcending the craftsmanship one senses the spirit and soul of an extraordinary man.'

I have been lucky enough to see some of James Krenov's work at first hand; one day I hope to have the good fortune to meet the sensitive man whose will of mind matches the skill of his hands. **P.C.**

Trade secrets revealed

If wood finishing doesn't sound adventurous to you let the master craftsman George Frank share the secrets and stories of his lifetime in Paris and New York with you. *88 Rue de Charonne: Adventures in Wood Finishing* published by the Taunton Press, 52 Church Hill Rd, Box 355, Newtown CT 06470 at $9.95 (ISBN 0 918804 06 X) has it all. George Frank knows wood finishing as few others know it. His book is about his experiments, trials and errors, successes and failures. He speaks as a friend not as a scholar, about his life from his birth in 1903 in Hungary, where he trained as a cabinet-maker and later earned a diploma as a master of wood colouring from the Technological Institute of Budapest; through his life in Paris, as a foreman at Jansen, in his own shop (88 Rue de Charonne) and in New York from 1940 to his retirement from the trade in 1973.

This is not a 'finishing manual' this is a lifetime of experience, a panoply of anecdotes, a treasurehouse of technical information all told as stories that instruct rather than stories for stories' sake. It is a collection of techniques and ideas from the basics of shop lighting to recipes for dyes and stains.

There are only two reasons for finishing wood — to protect it and to embellish it. George Frank has spent his life learning, inventing and improvising ways and means of finishing wood. Read this book and you will feel a part of that life, you will learn a great deal and enjoy the absorption of new facts. The stories are colourful, the author is a born raconteur. As he himself concludes 'take over readers, and make out of the trade of wood finishing a skill, a science and art'. *Adventures in Wood Finishing* will wet your appetite for more practice of the polishing craft if nothing else. Its a marvellous read too even for the non-woodworker. **P.C.**

Suppliers

KILN DRIED Acacia, Ash, Cherry, Elm, Lime, Yew etc. Rustic wood slices. Telephone: (0222) 861584. I-K

VENEERS, all types. SAE List—S. Gould (Veneers), 342 Uxbridge Road, W12. Tel: 01-743 8561. T/C

DRIED HARDWOODS for crafts and hobbies. Yew, Beech, Elm, Ash, Oak Alder etc. Boards or offcuts. Birmingham area. Earlswood 2823. I-K

EXOTIC WOODS, Cocobolo, Ebony, Lemonwood, Kingwood, Madagascar Rosewood, Partridgewood, Indian Rosewood, Satinwood, Walnut, and many others. Chart, Telephone: Reading (0734) 695336. J

WELL SEASONED HARDWOODS. Discs. 4" to 16" dia. ½" to 3½" thick. Various Hardwoods all sizes. No reasonable offer refused. View. Telephone: Maidstone 43872. J

CORNISH WOODCRAFT
Suppliers of English & Foreign Hardwoods

We can supply all your hardwood requirements both bulk (cubic foot orders and *sizes cut to your specifications.*

A few examples from our lists are as follows:

Cubic Measure
S. American Mahogany .... from **£7.50**
Teak .... from **£24.00**
English Oak .... from **£22.00**
Yew .... from **£19.00**

Many more species stocked, write/phone for lists/quotations

CORNISH WOODCRAFT,
NEWBRIDGE, PENZANCE. Tel: (0736) 788291
Nationwide Delivery   *We accept Barclaycard & Access*

YORKSHIRE HARDWOODS
KILN DRIED HARDWOOD FOR CRAFTSMEN

We specialize in English Oak and can supply anything from long waney edged boards up to 36" wide to small turning blanks. We will cut and machine to your exact requirements ☎

Yorkshire Hardwoods Limited
Pocklington Grange,
Bielby Lane, Pocklington, York YO4 2NT

Pocklington
075 92-2870

ENGLISH OAK FOR SALE

1" KILN DRIED OAK (9-10% M.C.) 1" AND 2" PART AIR-DRIED OAK. *Timber can be supplied machined.*

HEART OF ENGLAND TIMBER
Paul Newey, Woodcote, Snitterfield, Stratford-on-Avon CV37 0JH. Tel: Stratford (0789) 731323 Day, 731417 Evening.

VENEERS
SHORT AND FULL LEAVES
In all popular timbers. Send S.A.E. for FREE price list or 55p for samples of 12 pieces 4" × 3" to:
ELLIOTT BROS.
Four Winds, Moorwoods Lane, Dore
All letters to PO Box No. 6, Glossop, Derby. *Reg. No. 2064782*

For best results when buying or selling use the CLASSIFIED COLUMNS — Telephone: Valerie Tester, (0442) 41221, Ext. 266

SEASONED HARDWOOD
(12% M/C + or − 1%)

HARDWOODS FOR TURNING

Bowl or spindle blanks 2"-3"-4" in Brazilian Mahogany, African Mahogany, Teak, Iroko, Sapele, Beech, Ash, Oak, Sycamore. Good stock of Cabinet Makers Timbers for the serious craftsman. Ask us to price your requirements.

SEASONED HARDWOOD TIMBER COMPANY

Unit 2, 156 High Street, Arlesey, Beds. SG15 6RP
Phone Hitchin 732800 - 732039
Open Mon-Fri 9am-5pm Sat 1pm

VENEERS, inlay bandings, stringing and marquetry panels. Large selection.
Mail order and callers welcome. S.A.E. for list.
R. AARONSON (VENEERS) LTD
45 Redchurch St., London E2.
Tel: 01-739 3107

HAVE **ENGLISH YEW**
(Will Haggle)

1000 cu ft — Come and choose from wide variety of sizes. Well Seasoned. Loads of Offcuts. Schools supplied.
Callers made welcome anytime.
"The more the cheaper"
W. Pearson, ASHLEY MOOR HALL, ORLETON, Nr. LUDLOW, SHROPSHIRE.
Tel: Yarpole 236

ACACIA, ASH, CHESTNUT, MAPLE, OAK, YEW, SYCAMORE, WALNUT.
Fresh Sawn, Air Dry or Kilned. Machining Available.
William and Penny Garvey,
Furniture Makers,
Leyhill, Payhembury, Honiton.
Tel: Broadhembury (040 484) 430.

Rustic Woodslices
For House Signs, Wall Plaques, etc., seasoned hardwoods. Sawn obliquely with Bark on, up to 30" long **£2.00** each or three for **£5.00**. Post Free.
A. CRACKNELL
2 ORFORD ROAD, BROMESWELL, WOODBRIDGE, SUFFOLK.

GREEN TIMBER CONVERTED ON SITE

Timber felled, kilning facilities available, green timber for sale. Countrywide service.
Telephone: Shrewsbury (0743) 66702

ENGLISH HARDWOODS

Oak, Ash, Sycamore, Beech etc. Air & Kiln dried
All sizes in stock
HOGHTON TIMBER
HIGHER WALTON TRADING ESTATE
PRESTON, LANCS.
Tel: Preston 36193

LET "WOODWORKER"

work for you by advertising your timber supplies within these pages.

For further details telephone

Valerie Tester (0442) 41221 Ext. 266

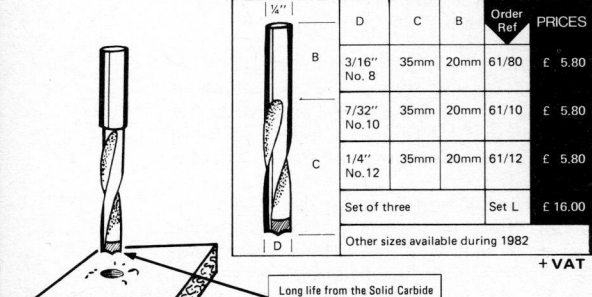
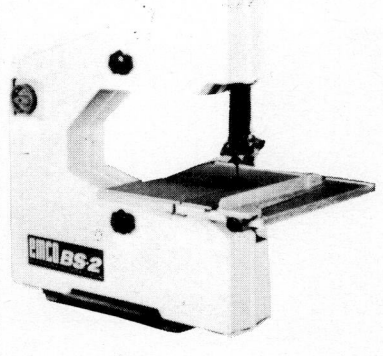

SPECIAL QUALITIES

One of his old students pays tribute to Peter van der Waals's special qualities as a furniture designer

For 28 years until his retirement in 1977, Charles W. Shute was adviser in design and technology for Oxford city schools. As a student of Loughborough college he was tutored in design by Peter van der Waals and formed a friendship which lasted until Waals's death in 1937.

Following the publication in WOODWORKER for August 1981 of I. G. Cleaver's appreciation of Waals's life and work, the editor invited Mr Shute to record some of his personal memories of Peter van der Waals.

He writes: When Peter van der Waals died in 1937 there ended for me an association that had lasted only a few years but, flowering at an impressionable period of my life, has left many happy and grateful memories of this gifted but humble man.

As it is best to lead up to these memories in chronological order, I ought first to explain that I had travelled some little way along the path of craftsmanship before our first meeting. My grandfather had been a respected village carpenter and admiration — perhaps envy — of what he could do, kindled the first spark in my youthful ambition.

Almost as soon as I was fit to be alone on a bicycle (and conditions in the early 1930s were in everyway safer than they are to-day) it became my hobby to cycle round the lovely lanes of my native Gloucestershire visiting the workshops of rural craftsmen. Many there were in those days and if their special skills varied from carpentry, they still bore a kinship with my grandfather as practical men who were part of the village as well as living in it.

But schooldays with their academic timetables took their toll of the hours available for these workshop visits. However, I was very fortunate in attending Prince Henry's grammar school at Evesham, where woodwork was pursued to an advanced level under the capable leadership of Henry J. Hall, an enthusiastic craftsman as well as a competent teacher.

Some readers will be young enough to need reminding that craft tuition of this order was quite an exception in the days about which I am writing. We did not have a GCE with its O-level and A-level and the issue of certificates for single subjects. Instead, there was the school certificate and the higher certificate. In the first a certificate was only issued on reaching a sufficient standard in five subjects from three groups at one and the same examination. In the second it was by specialisation in one group of allied subjects supported by at least one subsidiary subject. The important point is that woodwork or metalwork, along with art and music, could not *contribute* to the gaining of a certificate, though competence in these group IV subjects, (as they were called), was always recorded on a certificate otherwise gained.

Small wonder then that schools in the main concentrated on 'useful' subjects and neglected the arts and crafts. And my good fortune in attending the school I did was enhanced by my obtaining, along with two fellow students, a distinction standard. Mine took me on to Loughborough college.

It was in my final year at Loughborough that fortune again smiled: I was lucky enough to be tutored in design by Peter van der Waals. Physically, he was a man of ample proportions; years of benchwork had endowed him with big, powerful hands that looked quite out of proportion to the 2in. stump of pencil he seemed to prefer to a long one. Yet the dexterity with which he used it for his sketches served only to emphasise the incongruity, the combination providing a visual memory-fixer.

Waals was in his mid-60s when he travelled up in his little black Ford 8 from Chalford near Stroud, Gloucestershire, to spend a couple of days each fortnight at Loughborough, converting us students to the Cotswold style of design.

Previous to his appointment as adviser in design we had been largely left to our own ideas about design. All too unwittingly we accepted the prevailing commercial standards without realising these represented an attempt to provide economical, mass-produced necessities suited to the financial stringencies under which most potential setters-up of first homes had to content in those difficult years.

Peter Waals and I continued our association after my Loughborough days, and I was privileged to visit his Chalford workshop until shortly before his death. It was on one of these visits that I gazed in amazement at a solid ebony wardrobe under construction and wondered however it would reach its ultimate destination!

Following my wartime service I was appointed lecturer in woodwork and metalwork at Weymouth teacher training college, and while there regularly accompanied my students on visits to another distinguished designer and craftsman — Edward Barnsley, whose workshops are at Froxfield near Petersfield in Hampshire.

He paid return visits to Weymouth, and many happy hours we spent together discussing all aspects of craftwork. A modest man of philosophical outlook, his expertise in his subject is remarkable. Our friendship of some 30 years, with mutual visits, continues to this day though, of course, between Petersfield and Oxford, for I left Weymouth in 1949.

In that year I moved to become adviser in design and technology for Oxford city schools for the next 28 years until my retirement in 1977. By this time I had established my home near Woodstock and built a workshop which I ultimately equipped with machine tools chosen in the light of my varied experience from the range of EMCO equipment. These machines reliably perform to the accuracy I demand of them — and make my retirement the fulfilment of a lifetime's preparation.

The heading photo shows me with a recently completed bow-fronted sidetable in quarter-sawn English oak. If I can no more than wish that Peter van der Waals could be here to see that his inspiration and encouragement have not been wasted effort, I can at least be truly thankful that my own continued good health is the paramount blessing that has made all these things possible.

Left: Advanced handicraft students work 1948-49; above 1947-48, Weymouth Training College exhibitions.

Revitalisation of files

In Question Box (July 1981) P. Wareham of Darlington asked for advice on revitalisation of files.

Peter Walmsley from Preston, Lancs, recommends this method: 1 Clean file by boiling in a 10% caustic soda and water solution; dry well. 2 Place file in enamel or glass dish and leave all areas of file as free as possible (support file on wire). 3 Cover file with water and *slowly* add sulphuric acid up to 25% by volume; a fine file should be left in the solution for 5min, a coarse file for 10min. 4 Remove file from dish, wash it well in water and household soda to neutralise the acid.

Mr Walmsley makes the point that the acid must be added to the water *very slowly to avoid a dangerous and violent eruption.* It should also be remembered that caustic soda is a dangerous substance. Wearing of protective clothing and eye protection while carrying out the operation is essential.

Another reader, Clifford G. Green, who has carried out a considerable amount of investigation into the cleaning and restoring of metals, writes: 'There are two acids that can be used: hydrochloric and orthophosphoric. The first is used at about 50% concentration and the second at 30% concentration. I prefer the second as a phosphated finish is developed which is rust-resistant.

'The actual operation is quite simple. The file is first cleaned with a wire brush and degreased by immersing in a solvent such as trichloroethylene. Benzene or carbon tetrachloride for degreasing are not recommended as they are now considered carcinogens and highly flammable as well as anaesthetic.

'When the solvent has evaporated the file is placed in acid until the teeth are nice and sharp again. This can take several hours depending on how blunt the file has become. It can be removed from the acid bath from time to time, washed-off and the teeth examined. Finally a thorough rinsing is necessary to remove all traces of acid and it should then be washed in alcohol or acetone. Drying in a warm oven is also an advantage.

'If acid is purchased in concentrated form it can be diluted by *adding to* distilled water: 50 parts of hydrochloric to 50 parts of distilled water; 30 parts of orthophosphoric to 70 parts of distilled water. *Acid must be added to water, stirring all the time.* Face and hands must be protected, all containers clearly labelled and all harmful substances kept in a safe place away from child access.

'To avoid the necessity of large volumes of acid, tall and narrow vessels are required. For example, pvc piping of suitable bore can have a wide-base plastics cap bonded on with epoxy resin adhesive but screw caps from coffee jars are ideal. Hydrogen gas will be evolved so there must be no naked flames and no smoking while the operation is being performed. The acid bath will rapidly turn black but all the while the gas is being given off it will be doing its job.'

B. H. Read of Spondon has sent photocopies of pages from an 1884 publication *Workshop Receipts* by F. Spon. This gives an acid method (one part nitric, three parts sulphuric, seven parts water and milk of lime as a neutralising agent; the final finish recommended is olive oil and turpentine in equal parts and a brushing over with powdered coke!)

The other method quoted by Spon is galvanic. The file is first cleaned with hot water and soda, then placed in connection with the positive pole of a battery, in a bath composed of 40 parts of sulphuric, 80 parts of nitric and 1000 parts of water. The negative pole is formed of a copper spiral surrounding the file but not touching it. The coil terminates in a wire which rises towards the surface. When the file has been 10min in the bath it is taken out, washed and dried.

Mr Read comments: 'I haven't tried either method but as a chemist would warn readers to mix the acid into the water, not the other way round. Incidentally, washing soda could be substituted for milk of lime in the first method.'

From Bexleyheath Charles D. Cliffe gives the acid method: The file should first be cleaned by brushing with a wire brush or file card. Then it is immersed in dilute sulphuric acid contained in a glass or earthenware dish. The acid dissolves a small quantity of the steel and thereby increases the cutting power of the teeth.

The file should be removed from the acid and examined at three or four hour intervals to see how the revitalisation is progressing. When sufficient metal has been eaten away the file is taken out of the acid and well washed in hot water. Finally it is immersed in a bath of ammonia or washing soda to prevent rusting.

A solution of one part of sulphuric acid to eight or 10 parts of water should be satisfactory. When making the solution always add the acid to the water in small quantities and slowly. *Never add the water to the acid. Do be careful and wear protective clothing.*

We would emphasise what readers have said about safety precautions and the wearing of protective clothing and the storage of harmful substances.

Finishing plywood
From: A. N. Waller, Lower Lydbrook

I am having difficulty in finishing birch-faced ply which does not seem to absorb polyurethane. Any advice will be welcome.

We are a little puzzled by your reference to difficulty of absorbence of polyurethane into birch-faced plywood. Birch is a permeable wood and in general sometimes causes problems because a particular finish has been absorbed patchily.

On the other hand, polyurethane varnish depends not on absorbency into the substrate but on polymerisation onto the surface. This means that unless sufficient is applied firstly to act as a seal and secondly as a finish, its true function is impaired. In other words if you cannot get polyurethane to be absorbed by the wood, then this is to the good and you ought really to get a good finish.

The Finnish Plywood Development Association, Broadmead House, 21, Panton Street, London SW1Y 4DR, recommends that the wood be clear-sealed, followed by

two coats of clear polyurethane and rubbing down each coat with fine wire wool, then rubbing in a wax polish. The FPDA also says that a pleasing effect is obtained by using a technique often employed in Finland of mixing a little white pigment with the sealer. The original whiteness of the birch face is preserved and a tough clear-sealing coat is then applied for protection.

Whatever class of finish you require it is essential first of all to seal the surface to reduce absorbency.

Ramin doors
From: T. Dixon, Worksop, Notts

I have bought some ramin-framed doors with ply panels. These have been fixed to a ramin-framed wardrobe in a bedroom facing east.

Because of lack of time I found it necessary to give a coat of cellulose grain filler which I thought would keep the timber clean until I could get down to finishing the doors.

When applying the cellulose the panels went slightly darker in colour and after about six weeks they have gone much darker. Is there any method I can adopt to return the panels to the ramin colour of the frames?

We doubt very much if there is a satisfactory way in which you could restore the original colour of the panels; bleaching would make the matter worse and sanding would seem to be out of the question. Even if by chance the original appearance was restored we are fairly certain that without introducing a stain there would still be a contrast between the panels and frame.

We say this because of probable natural colour differences and also grain differences between the solid wood and the veneer of the plywood. Ramin as a commercial timber is produced by the botanical species *Gonystylus macrophyllum* which grows in Sarawak, the principal exporting area. Furthermore, because of certain natural characteristics of the species, the wood is sawn as far as possible on the quarter, that is to say it now presents a wide face which is radially cut and a little more compact than if tangentially cut.

If the same species is peeled for veneer then its surface is midway between radial and tangential and accordingly the grain is more open.

If a material such as a filler or, say, a varnish is applied to both types of wood, the veneer will accept more and tend to darken in consequence.

However, the matter as a rule is not as straightforward as this. Ramin also grows in Malaysia but here there are three species, ie *G. affinis*; *G. confusus* and *G. macrophyllum*, collectively sold either as ramin telur (the Sarawak name) or as melawis. Since most SE Asian plywood is produced in Malaysia, it is highly probable that melawis/ramin plywood would contain three types of veneer, each with a slight colour variation. There is no assurance, though, that your panels are melawis/ramin because other species somewhat similar to ramin are frequently used, eg one of the dipterocarps such as white seraya or white and yellow meranti.

Even slight differences in colour become enhanced under the application of liquids. Clear finishing on light-coloured hardwood and plywood in combination is not very satisfactory as a rule and usually colour matching by staining is essential.

This gong with carved supports inlaid with silver wire is of Chinese origin and dates from the early part of the last century. (*Photo H.W. Gates.*) **This month sees the start of a series of articles on figure and decorative carving.**

Renovating joints
From: J. Cotter, Farnham, Surrey

I have a number of old chairs and other pieces needing renovation. Some of the joints are loose and others quite firm. I know from experience that quite a lot of force will be needed to dismantle the frames so that these can be fully re-glued and clamped; and that there is a danger of damaging the pieces by levering with chisels or tapping with mallets. Can you advise please?

Chairs are probably the most widely abused pieces of furniture. Apart from being stood on, they often have to bear the intolerable strain of people leaning back at such an angle that the front legs are lifted off the floor. The strain at the joint where the side rails meet the back legs (usually a dowelled joint) is so great that eventually the joint fails.

Where both joints are loose the remedy is straightforward. With a block of wood to spread the blows of the mallet, the joints are carefully tapped apart. All traces of old glue are cleaned-off and broken dowels drilled out.

New dowels, with a saw kerf along their length to allow surplus glue to escape, are prepared. The joints are glued, assembled and cramped, care being taken that the frame is out of winding.

Unfortunately all repairs are not so easy. It may be that both joints are not loose and it has to be decided whether a repair can be effected without disturbing a perfectly sound joint. If this can be avoided by springing apart the loose joint, so much the better.

The old glue is cleaned-off, new glue worked in to the dowel holes or mortises and on the meeting faces. Then the joint is assembled and cramped until the glue has set.

Where such a course is not possible and access can only be had by parting a sound joint, the task must be approached carefully. A properly glued joint is stronger than the wood and if the joint is hammered apart it will not part at the join but will split a piece off the leg. The resulting mess will be far worse than the original trouble.

As the pieces which you are repairing are old, it is most probable that they have been glued with scotch glue. In these circumstances the old glue is softened by soaking a rag in hot water and applying it to the joint. The work is not flooded. Just sufficient hot water is used to penetrate the joint to soften the glue and allow the joint to be tapped apart. All traces of old glue are scraped away and the wood allowed to dry thoroughly before being re-glued.

Because the shape of a chair frame is rarely square or rectangular, but more often that of a trapezium, or even circular, it will be necessary to cut specially-shaped softening blocks. When the cramps are applied they will then pull the joints together and not bruise the corners of the legs or distort the framework.

As in most occupations, the advice to leave well alone is very sound and as little disturbance as possible should be the aim.

Distortion
From: M. Foden, Southport

I turned a small box the lid of which is made from two discs of lime with laburnum branch inlay (grain horizontal in finished turning). When completed the lid fitted the box perfectly and the whole was finished and left for 48hr before a coat of shellac sanding sealer was applied. When dry a further coat was applied (all this with lid on the box). When the second coat had dried the lid was removed. When replaced it did not fit.

The inside of the lid was also treated with shellac in case it was 'out of balance' but this did not help. The joint is only about ½mm out, or less, but there is a see-saw action due to the poor fit. Could this be due to the moisture in the sealer? I would be grateful for your advice. Incidentally, the wood used was received kiln-dried two years ago and has been in my workshop since. The finished box has remained in the same environment.

Although lime is a softish, mild textured, straight-grained wood, it does have a tendency to distort during the drying process. This means that although a piece of dried wood may be flat it could contain a residual stress, even a mild one, to the extent that once part of the bulk was removed by machining the wood could 'pull' due to the relieving of the stress.

The amount of distortion you mention, ie 0.5mm or less would be typical of this sort of movement and largely to be expected. The amount approximates very roughly to movement that corresponds to a 1% m.c. change. In other words if your wood at, say, 12% m.c. dried to 11% m.c. (an amount over which there is little control, generally speaking) the movement would be directional to the stress and might result in the type of slight distortion you are experiencing.

However, we think that while this has contributed to the distortion, it has been encouraged by slight imbalance of the lid due to the laburnum branch inlay and the shellac sealer. In effect, additional material was applied to the outside of the lid which meant that when it was removed the first time after sealing the outside, the sealer pulled the wood slightly out of true in the direction dictated by the residual stress.

The wood would tend to take on a permanent set and no amount of sealer now applied to the inner surface of the lid would restore its original shape. The bottom half of the bowl did not respond in quite the same way because there was more restraint to movement offered by the slightly thicker material and the absence of the inlay.

The sustained very close fitting of wooden lids to items such as bowls and small barrels as a rule can only be achieved by introducing a rubber seal somewhere into the construction because of the hygroscopic nature of wood substance.

So far as your present problem is concerned we suggest increasing the depth of the 1/16in. rebate in the bottom section and bonding a thin rubber or baize strip to the vertical wall. This ought to take up the slightly distorted lid and encourage it to seat more precisely.

In future items we suggest you seal the lid at least on both sides simultaneously using polyurethane rather than shellac. We do not think the shellac introduced unwanted moisture to the wood but it does produce a rather rigid-type coating by comparison with the more elastic-type film of polyurethane.

QUESTION BOX

Acid finish
From: B. R. Drage, Wooditon, Peterborough

Can you please tell me how to identify the acid finish (or German finish)? Is it possible to restore the polish with a 50% meths-50% polish mixture?

There are several processes in french polishing. In the early stage of applying a good body of polish to the wood, a small quantity of raw linseed oil on the face of the polishing rubber acts as a lubricant and prevents it from sticking. Ultimately this oil has to be removed and the shellac surface burnished to bring it perfectly smooth, clear and brilliant.

This is achieved with a clean rubber containing meths only and the rubber is worked in straight sweeps along the grain. This spiriting-off lifts out the oil (traces can soon be seen on the rubber's rag covering) and produces a brilliant finish.

The German method was used to give their pianos an absolutely flawless finish. There is no test which can be applied to a polished surface to identify whether it has been finished by the German method or not, except to say that it generally produced a superior result. The difference lies in the final stage.

Having bodied the surface so that the grain is completely full, a rag dipped in dilute sulphuric acid (one part acid to 12 parts of water) is wiped all over the work. The solution is then rubbed well in with the palm of the hand until the entire surface is uniformly smeary. The palm of the hand is dusted with Vienna chalk from a pounce bag and a little chalk at a time is rubbed into the work with the hand.

The film of the solution will disappear and as dusting and rubbing continues the surface will be dry and bright without a trace of oil. The solution lifts out the oil and the rubbing of chalk with the hand burnishes the shellac to a perfectly smooth, brilliant finish. All traces of Vienna chalk are then removed with a chamois leather.

Should an acid-finished surface be scratched or damaged so that re-polishing becomes necessary, there is no particular difficulty. The work is rubbed-down with fine wire wool to remove the scratches and give a uniformly matt appearance. After a thorough dusting-off repolishing is commenced with a mixture of half polish and half meths.

The advantage of starting with thinned polish is that the new polish takes more readily to the old. Bodying can be continued with full-strength polish until a good body is obtained. The polish is then gradually diluted until the spiriting stage is reached when finishing can be either by spiriting-off or the acid finish. The latter method is not recommended for beginners because unless the grain is perfectly filled, a deposit of Vienna chalk will show in the open pores.

Incidentally, when making the solution the acid must be added slowly to the water; it is dangerous if done the other way round.

QUESTION BOX

Lamp bases
From: Frank Penty, Masham, Yorks

When drying timber in a kiln does it dry best in a moist or dry atmosphere? In a dry atmosphere the insulation may be better and the heat loss less.

I wish to decorate lamp bases with coloured wood and want to put on two or three concentric pieces of colour using dowelling. Would it be best to glue the pieces?

With regard to your question as to the state of the atmosphere in the kiln-drying of timber. In conventional kiln-drying, the air is moist initially in the run, say at 80-90% RH, either by virtue of moisture extracted from the wood and allowed to circulate in the air of the kiln; or by wet steam injected into the kiln.

The RH is progressively reduced, however, in step with reductions in m.c. of the wood, until in the final stages of drying the air is fairly dry, say at 30% RH. Excessive moisture is vented-off generally automatically. As to your second question we are not clear how you propose to construct your lamp bases, but from the point of view of colouring certain sections for them to show through after machining, we do not think this is feasible.

Penetration of liquids through the side grain of wood is invariably slight and would generally be machined-out and you would be back to bare wood again. The normal practice, say in a turned standard where different coloured wood is required to show through, is to use the natural colour of contrasting woods, eg whitish sycamore or holly and perhaps mahogany to give a white and red effect.

There are various wood dyes on the market, and there are aniline dyes in colours such as red, blue, green, yellow etc. which can be made-up to suit. We demur from suggesting this latter use since the substances are exceptionally powerful and must be used with caution.

To try to colour the separate wood parts after machining, is likely to prove difficult because of the liability of the dye to creep. We cannot think of a satisfactory alternative to the use of natural colour wood which would give the effect we think you are seeking. We think, too, the parts would best be glued together.

Burr wood
From: R. C. Maguire, Laurencekirk

I have come across a huge burr of what appears to be ash. It is roughly spherical, with the original trunk passing through the middle. The whole thing is nearly 4ft in diameter.

I am thinking of using it in thin sections for furniture making and in large pieces for turning. Can you kindly advise on the practicality of this and how to cut the burr, dry it and finish it?

The wood of burrs is the most difficult, and often well-nigh impossible, material to use generally because of its severely contorted grain arranged round hundreds of tiny pith centres of adventitious buds. It is not practicable to consider the wood in any form other than as veneer. (Turnery may be produced, but the finish is not smooth from the tool and it is prone to checking and splitting.)

In the production of veneer from burrs, the wood must first be steamed to soften it and after this the veneer is produced by slicing. Because of its nature there is a special technique for laying burr veneer and that is the insistence on applying a cross-band veneer, usually of mahogany, between the surface of the substrate and the burr.

It will be appreciated that any form of movement, however slight, in the substrate will allow checking of the burr; hence the supporting influence of the crossband. For that reason plywood is invariably used as a substrate and the crossband is applied in one of two ways: If the length of the burr veneer, ie the made-up panel, runs in the same direction as the grain of the top veneer of the plywood then the crossband veneer is applied horizontally to these. If the burr is set at right angles to the plywood veneer then the crossband is applied diagonally.

In passing, we must mention that the reverse side of any panel must be made up in the same way in order to give a balanced construction. Finishing of burrs requires much filling and it is probable that a wax finish is best.

Mixed timbers
From: M. C. Carr, Wolverhampton

I have acquired over the years quite a lot of red-coloured wood which appears to be of various species such as the so-called African 'walnut'; and possibly African or American mahogany; odoko; and sapele. Can you please tell me whether it is structurally sound to mix these woods in the same piece of furniture.

As to the structural aspects of mixing red-coloured hardwood in furniture we would remark that the problem is more likely to be one of matching for colour rather than of strength. Structural soundness in furniture is of course important but, generally speaking, the avoidance of palpably weak pieces of wood such as those containing brittleheart or cross-grained 'thunder shakes' is the main criterion on which to base structural suitability.

American mahogany, ie *Swietenia* spp. but in this case specifically from Belize (Honduras) has general strength properties higher than one would expect for a timber of its weight. At one time it was the premier wood for making aeroplane propellers and most of the red timbers used as alternatives to Honduras mahogany for other purposes are usually compared to that wood in terms of strength.

Brazilian mahogany, presently the principal one from that area, is a little stronger as are most other red woods such as sapele and red meranti. Utile is about the same as *Swietenia* as are the medium-weight species of African mahogany, with lighter-weight types a little weaker and the heavier types stronger.

Years ago it was often the practice to substitute birch for mahogany in furniture feet because it stood up to hard knocks better, while the back sweeps used for chair legs were bandsawn from specially selected stock because of the weak area of relatively cross-grain near the base of the leg, the timber frequently being weak in shear. However, we would say that given dry stock the general run of red hardwood can be mixed, all other factors being equal.

Oak for flooring
From: D. N. Harding, Orpington

I have a number of pieces of well-seasoned oak about 1 × 3½in. wide and mostly either 18 or 36 in. in length. I would like to make strips for flooring to lay over existing boards. Would it be feasible to have these pieces of oak sliced into thinner strips about ¼in. thick?

We doubt if it would be feasible to slice the oak for several reasons. Firstly, the boards are probably too thin to be dogged (fixed) to the slicer; this normally takes ¾in. or more of wood with the knife only working above this. Secondly, it is usually impracticable to slice oak at ¼in. (6mm) thickness because due to the pressure exerted and the wedge-like action of the knife oak tends to fracture, often badly, in the vicinity of the large rays.

It is more usual in veneer production to keep the thickness of sliced oak down to 0.8mm and not entirely for economic reasons; if the thickness is increased above this the fracture tendency also increases.

It would seem the only feasible way in which to produce thin sections is to resaw the wood. The smallest saw kerf you could reasonably expect would be about ³⁄₃₂in. and, therefore, if two deep cuts were made (to produce three pieces) this would take ³⁄₁₆in. leaving ¹³⁄₁₆in. of wood, or three boards each ¼in. full.

These, however, would be unplaned and no doubt variable in actual thickness with the edges as originally sawn. If you have sufficient material three ex 1in., we suggest you ask a local firm of precision woodworkers to not only do the deep cutting but to run the wood through a moulding machine set to clean-up the face with a hit-and-miss finish on the reverse, finishing the width, say, at 3³⁄₈in. The resultant pieces ought to be about ³⁄₁₆in. thick.

With wood overlay flooring a subfloor is essential. In other words, hardboard ⅛in. thick, or cheap, C-quality or packing-case grade 3mm plywood is first pinned over the existing floor with the overlay flooring applied to this. Under these conditions a very thin pedestrian wood surface wears well in domestic situations.

QUESTION BOX JANUARY 1982

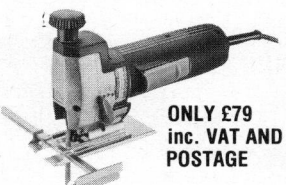
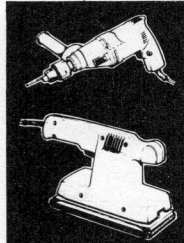
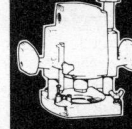
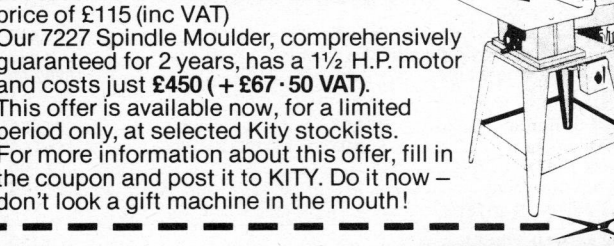

Robland universal

Specification of the five-operation Robland universal models K210 and K260 has been upgraded in both constructional and safety aspects.

The upgrading provides ground-finish castiron tables, castiron support for mortise table, 9in. diameter TCT blade, extra-long fence on sliding table serving saw and spindle moulder, the fence being adjustable to any angle between 90 and 45° and fitted with a repetition stop.

Safety features include spindle moulder fence with independent fine-screw adjustment of both faces plus top and side pressure pad. There is also a captive swing-away guard and chip deflector for use when thicknessing; this covers cutter block and feed rollers and deflects the chips on to the floor in front of the machine.

The Robland has triple motor drive system to saw, planer and spindle moulder, with planer block, saw and spindle bearings 'sealed for life.' Control of the motors is by a selection switch having isolation and cutout safeguards; a second cut-out switch is located adjacent to the mortiser unit and away from the main

Bill Conroy, woodworking sales executive of Startrite, demonstrates the improved universal woodworker to representatives of the press.

switch panel. Electrical and working parts are housed in the heavy-gauge steel plate cabinet base.

When working with the spindle moulder a set of Tiger cutting tools is available for use. The set includes a 3¾in. diameter cutter block complete with nine pairs of shaped cutters and two pairs of saw segments for accurate grooving. All these are contained in a polished hardwood box. A set of five mortise miller bits is also available to complete the standard tooling items required to use every machine function.

Made in Belgium to meet the requirements of Startrite Machine Tool Co Ltd, 625 Princes Road, Dartford DA2 6EH (0322 28538 & 77634), the Robland specification is as given in the table on this page (see left below):

Optional equipment such as sawblades, planer knives etc are available as are individual machines like the Robland planer/thicknesser SD310 and spindle moulder T30; and Inca planer/thicknesser AF190M and bandsaws AF186F and AF186FM.

Startrite says that due to the popularity of the Robland universal and the use of high-volume production technology, it has been possible to improve the specification without increasing the price which is listed at £1360 for model K210 (415V 3-phase); and £1445 (240V 1-phase). Model K260 is respectively £1540 and £1632. Prices are ex-works and do not include VAT.

Robin Sloane, Woodford Green, Essex, has recently acquired a Robland K260 for his workshop. Inset is the Tiger cutterhead set.

ROBLAND SPECIFICATION

	K210 mm	in.	K260 mm	in.
Surface planer				
Table size	210×1225	8¼×48	260×1225	10¼×48
Cutterblock speed	6000 rpm		6000 rpm	
Cutterblock diameter	60	2⁵⁄₁₆	60	2⁵⁄₁₆
No. of cutters	2		2	
Motor	2 hp		3 hp (2 hp single phase)	
Thicknesser				
Table size	210×440	8¼×17¼	260×440	10¼×17¼
Max planing thickness	155	6	155	6
Feed speed	6m/min	20ft/min	6m/min	20ft/min
Saw				
Table size	825×420	32½×16½	825×420	32½×16½
Spindle diameter		1		1
Max saw diameter	230	9	230	9
Blade above table	85	3¼	85	3¼
Saw speed	3250 rpm		3250 rpm	
Motor	2 hp (1¼ hp single phase)		2 hp (1¼ hp single phase)	
Sliding table				
Table size	370×240	14½×9½	370×240	14½×9½
Stroke for sawing max crosscut	450	17¾	450	17¾
Spindle moulder				
Spindle diameter		1¼		1¼
Rise and fall	110	4¼	110	4¼
Speed	6000 rpm		6000 rpm	
Motor	2 hp		3 hp (2hp single phase)	
Mortiser				
Table size	160×350	6¼×13¾	160×350	6¼×13¾
Longitudinal stroke	130	5	130	5
Traverse stroke	130	5	130	5
Vertical adjustment	80	3⅛	80	3⅛
Chuck capacity	0-16	0-⅝	0-16	0-⅝
Overall dimensions	1650×1225	65×48	1700×1225	67×48
Net weight	270kg	595lb	300kg	660lb

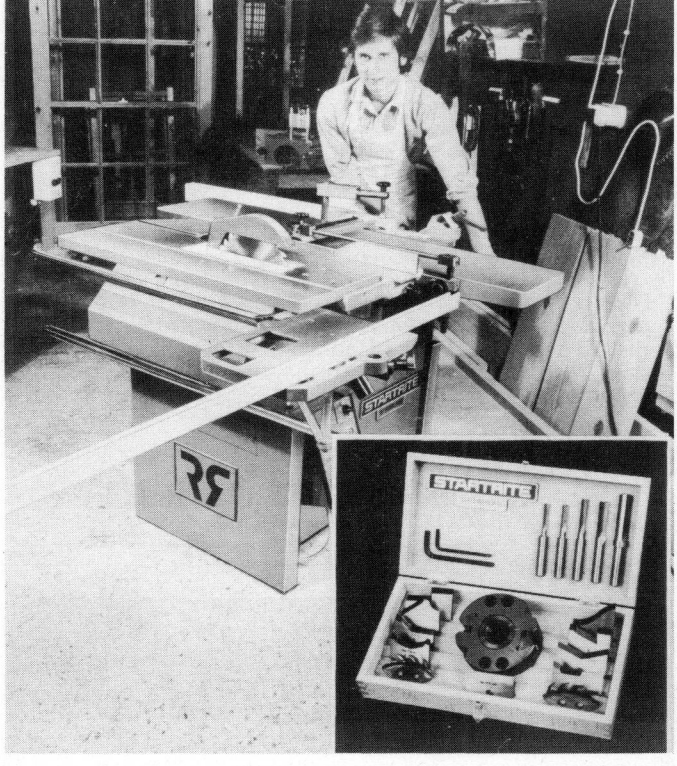

For modellers

Hardwood for modellers and makers of miniatures is imported from the US under the Midwest brand name by Chart Hobby Distributors Ltd, 648 High Road, North Finchley, London N12 0LN (01-445 6531). The hardwood (mahogany, walnut and lime) is selected, cut and sanded and comes in a variety of sizes. There are also mouldings and scribed sheets as well as conventional strip and sheet.

Further details and names of stockists can be had from Chart Hobby Distributors at the address given.

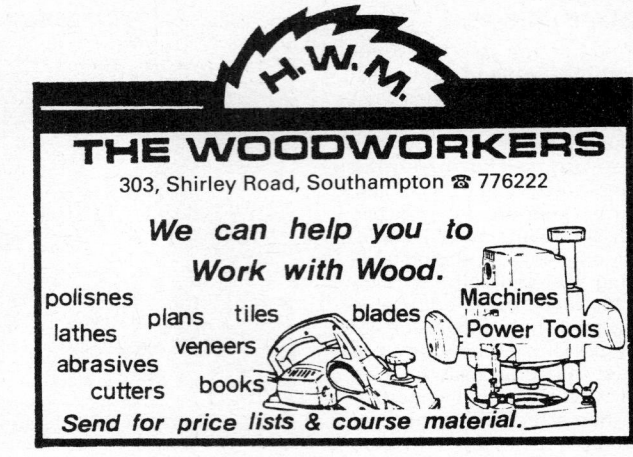

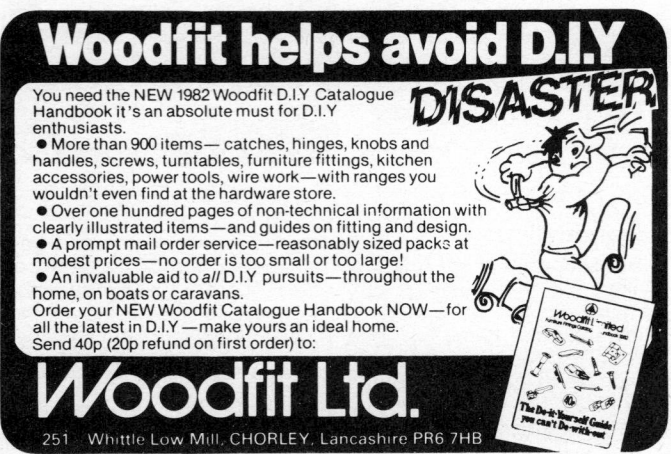

DREMEL DELUXE MOTO-SHOP

Cuts wood up to 1¾" thick,
Light metal, tile etc.,
45° table tilt

No 577
220 Volt

A 15" Combination Scroll Saw/Workshop. Blade can be faced sideways for long cutting. Power takeoff for sanding, polishing and flexible drive. Supplied complete with flexible shaft and accessories.
List Price £89.05, *OFFER PRICE* **£74.00**
Carriage free (UK)

POWER TOOLS ETC

Cat No.		M.R.P.	Our Price
2525	Craftsman Router Crafter	£84.95	£41.00
746-2	Craftsman 1hp heavy duty router	£94.45	£70.80
743-2	Craftsman 1½hp super router with dust bag	£110.00	£80.00
2571	Craftsman 12" dovetail kit	£59.50	£44.50
096-2	Craftsman 7½" circular saw, 2⅛hp	£94.45	£70.80
26269	Craftsman Trim-a-Form Router Attachment	£45.95	£33.00
25444	Craftsman Heavy Duty Router/Jigsaw Table	£55.95	£42.00
2509	Dremel Moto-Tool Kit with 35 accessories	£51.15	£43.00
358	Dremel Variable Speed Moto-Tool	£50.45	£42.50
359	Dremel Variable Speed Moto-Tool Kit with 35 accessories	£63.05	£52.50
284	Dremel Moto Tool Woodcarver's Kit	£65.00	£55.00
292	Dremel engraver	£13.70	£11.50
96H	Skil power plane, 480 watt	£80.39	£67.00
98H	Skil power plane, carbide blades, 1030 watt	£107.99	£83.00
1474H	Skil ½" reversing hammer drill, 500 watt	£67.74	£55.00
574U	Skil 7¼" circular saw, 1000 watt	£62.10	£52.00
1490H	Skil 4½" bench grinder, 36 and 60 grit stones	£50.03	£41.50
400-E	Bosch ½" variable speed hammer drill, 400 watt	£49.00	£37.00
450-2E	Bosch ½" variable speed hammer drill, 450 watt	£68.50	£54.00
620-2E	Bosch ½" variable speed hammer drill, 620 watt	£82.50	£67.00
S33	Bosch 6" circular saw attachment	£21.50	£18.00
PST50E	Bosch variable speed jigsaw	£45.50	£37.00
PSS230	Bosch orbital sander	£39.50	£30.00
PSP250	Bosch spray gun set	£48.50	£41.50
PKS46	Bosch 6" circular saw	£57.50	£45.00
S9	Bosch saw table for PKS46 saw	£39.95	£33.50
PKS65	Bosch 7½" circular saw	£89.50	£69.00
S10	Bosch saw table for PKS65 saw	£49.95	£42.00
POF50	Bosch plunging router with 1 router bit	£55.50	£44.00
S7	Bosch milling stand	£44.50	£38.00
S8	Bosch routing bench for above	£19.95	£16.95
S2	Bosch drill stand	£19.95	£16.95
S18	Bosch lathe kit	£56.25	£47.80
1130	Barrus universal drill stand	£41.98	£32.50
1120	Barrus shaper table for above	£18.11	£14.40

BOSCH INDUSTRIAL

SB4502	Bosch 2 speed impact drill with free tool handy & 750 rawlplugs	£89.13	£69.00
1179	Bosch ½" 2 speed impact drill	£113.85	£89.00
1287-1	Bosch orbital sander with induction motor	£113.85	£89.00
PWS6000	Bosch 7" angle sander/grinder	£89.70	70.00
1577	Bosch orbital action jigsaw in metal case	£110.40	£85.50
1578	Bosch orbital action jigsaw, variable speed	£122.48	£96.00
P400	Bosch power plane, 75mm planing width	£112.13	£87.00

HAND TOOLS

781000	Jet Clamp	£10.35	£9.00
04	Record 2" blade smoothing plane	£21.62	£16.50
311	Record 3 in 1 plane	£33.35	£28.25
050C	Record combination plane, 18 blade	£60.38	£51.00
020C	Record circular plane	£50.60	£43.00
405	Record multi plane, 24 blade	£149.50	£127.00
52E	Record Q.R. woodwork vice, 7"	£42.09	£35.75
130	Record cramp heads	£9.78	£8.25
145	Record bench holdfast 6⅞" opening	£16.50	£14.00
146	Record bench holdfast 7⅝" opening	£22.60	£19.20
140	Record corner cramp 2" capacity	£8.05	£6.80
148	Record dowelling jig	£29.33	£24.00
M1160	Marples draw knife	£16.50	£14.00
M2400	Marples 12" bow saw	£17.83	£15.00
M1002	Marples set of 8 turning tools	£51.41	£43.50
M60	Marples set of 12 carving tools	£73.37	£62.00
M60A	Marples set of 6 carving tools	£41.40	£35.00
M444/S5	Marples set of 5 blue chip chisels	£22.37	£18.50
M260	Marples set of 5 wood sculpture tools	£37.49	£31.75
13-052	Stanley plough plane, 10 blade	£35.65	£29.95
13-050	Stanley combination plane, 18 blade	£54.50	£45.95
5½	Stanley 15" jack plane	£25.60	£21.00
7	Stanley 22" jointer/try plane	£32.20	£26.95
71	Stanley hand router, 3 blade	£21.30	£17.95
TS	Henry Taylor superflute turning gouge	£21.28	£18.40

All prices include VAT. Carriage free on orders over £20 (UK Mainland)
Henry Taylor and Marples Woodcarving and Turning Tools in stock
BENMAIL, 48 Station Road, St. Georges, Weston-s-Mare, Avon BS22 0XL
Tel: 0934 24385 *We close Thursdays*

JUST PUBLISHED!
EVERYTHING YOU EVER WANTED TO KNOW ABOUT SUPPLIERS, COURSES & ASSOCIATIONS

POPULAR CRAFTS' GUIDE TO GOOD CRAFT SUPPLIERS

£1.00

Featuring
Equipment
Craft Suppliers
Craft Courses
Guilds
Associations

M.A.P. LEISURE PUBLICATION

Where can I buy a batik Tjanting? Who stocks plain white china for china painting? Can you tell me where I can get tiny hinges for egg decorating? Where in London can I buy an enamelling kiln? Is there anywhere that I can buy the tools for carving leather? Do you know of a supplier of wood for miniature furniture making? Does anyone supply stained glass tools? I am opening a craft shop — how do I find wholesale suppliers? Is there a weekend course on lacemaking? Where can I go to learn weaving? Please put me in touch with a glass engraving guild? What tools do I need to start jewellery making? Can I start pottery at home? Please advise me on how to make money from my craft?

All these questions and much much more are answered in:
THE POPULAR CRAFTS GUIDE TO GOOD CRAFT SUPPLIERS.
Send for your copy today!

Sales Office, Popular Crafts, 13/35 Bridge St., Hemel Hempstead, HP1 1EE
Please rush me *Popular Crafts Guide to Good Craft Suppliers.*
I enclose P.O./Cheque for £1.25 (£1 plus 25p p+p).

Name ....

Address ....

....

LINCOLNSHIRE

LINCOLN   Tel. 0522 36168/9
R & S TOOLS (LINCOLN)
LIMITED
BEEVER STREET LN6 7AD
Open: Mon-Fri 8.30 a.m.-5 p.m.
Sat 9.00 p.m.-12.00 p.m.
H.P.W.WM.D.CS.A.BC.

LINCOLN   Tel. 0522 30199/
WOODWISE LIMITED   39871 or
121 HIGH STREET   0522 68428
& 06077 5777/5288
(after hours) ★
Open: Mon-Sat 9 a.m.-5.30 p.m.
P.W.WM.D.A.BC.

LONDON

ACTON   Tel. 01-992 4835
A MILLS (ACTON) LTD   ★
32/36 CHURCHFIELD ROAD
W3 6ED
Open: Mon-Fri 9.00 a.m.-5.00 p.m.
Closed Saturday
H.P.W.WM.

HANWELL   Tel. 01-567 2922
G. D. CLEGG & SONS
83 Uxbridge Road, W7 3ST
Open: Monday to Friday
9.00 a.m.-6.00 p.m.
Saturday 9.00 a.m.-5.30 p.m.
H.P.W.WM.D.

LONDON   Tel. 01-636 7475
BUCK & RYAN LIMITED
101 TOTTENHAM COURT ROAD
W1P 0DY
Open: Mon-Fri 8.30 a.m.-5.30 p.m.
Saturday 8.30 a.m.-1.00 p.m.
H.P.W.WM.D.A.

LONDON   Tel. 01-739 7126
CECIL W. TYZACK   ★
79-81 KINGSLAND ROAD
SHOREDITCH
Open: Mon-Fri 8.45 a.m.-5.15 p.m.
Saturday 9 a.m.-12 noon
H.P.W.WM.D.A.BC.

WOOLWICH   Tel. 01-854 7767/8
A. D. SKILLMAN & SONS LTD
108-109 WOOLWICH HIGH ST
SE18 6DW
Open: Mon-Sat 8.30 a.m.-to 5.30 p.m.
Half Day Thursday
H.P.W.CS.A.

MERSEYSIDE

LIVERPOOL   Tel. 051-263 1359
TAYLOR BROS (LIVERPOOL) LTD
5/9 PRESCOTT STREET
Open: Monday to Friday
8.30 a.m.-5.30 p.m.
H.P.W.WM.D.A.BC.

MIDDLESEX

HARROW   Tel. 01-863 9462
ALLIED HARDWARE   ★
219 STATION ROAD
Open: Monday-Saturday
9.00 a.m.-6.00 p.m.
H.P.A.

NORTH HARROW Tel. 01-863 2492
WILLIAMS TECHNICAL SERVICES ★
36 STATION ROAD
Open: Mon-Fri 8 a.m.-5.30 p.m.
Wed 8 a.m.-1 p.m.,
Sat 9 a.m.-5.30 p.m.
H.P.W.WM.D.A.

NORFOLK

NORWICH   Tel. 0603 898695
NORFOLK SAW SERVICES
DOG LAND, HORSFORD
Open: Monday to Friday
8.00 a.m.-5.00 p.m.
Saturday 8.00 a.m.-12.00 p.m.
H.P.W.WM.D.CS.A.

NORFOLK

NORWICH   Tel. 0603 400933
WESTGATES WOODWORKING   Tx.
MACHINERY, JUPITER ROAD   975412
OFF MILE CROSS LANE
Open: 9 a.m.-5 p.m. weekdays
9 a.m.-12 a.m. Sat.
P.W.WM.D.

NORTHAMPTONSHIRE

RUSHDEN   Tel. 093-34 56424
PETER CRISP LIMITED   ★
7 HIGH STREET
Open: Monday to Saturday
8.30 a.m.-5.30 p.m.
Thursday 8.30 a.m.-1.00 p.m.
H.P.W.D.BC.

NORTHUMBERLAND

BLYTH   Tel. (06706) 69279
ALLAN McNAIR WOODCRAFT   ★
69-71 PLESSEY ROAD
Open: Monday to Saturday
9 a.m.-5 p.m.
H.W.WM.D.T.CS.A.BC.

NOTTINGHAMSHIRE

NOTTINGHAM   Tel. (0602) 225979
POOLEWOOD   (06077) 5777
EQUIPMENT LTD
5a HOLLY LANE, CHILLWELL
Open: Mon-Fri 9 a.m.-5.30 p.m.
Sat. 9 a.m. to 12.30 p.m.
P.W.WM.D.CS.A.BC.

NOTTINGHAM   Tel. 0602 811889
THE WOODCUTTER
5 TUDOR SQUARE
WEST BRIDGFORD
Open: Tues-Sat 9 a.m.-5.30 p.m.
Fri 9 a.m.-7.30 p.m. Closed Mon.
H.P.W.WM.D.T.CS.A.

OXFORDSHIRE

BICESTER   Tel. (08692) 4156/
WOODMEN   3218/3219
104 CHURCHILL ROAD
Open: Monday-Saturday
9 a.m.-5.30 p.m.
P.W.WM.D.A.BC.

OXFORD   Tel. (0865) 45118/9
SARJENT'S TOOL   ★
STORES LTD
150 COWLEY ROAD
Open: Monday to Saturday
8.30 a.m.-5.30 p.m.
H.P.W.WM.D.A.BC.

STAFFORDSHIRE

TAMWORTH   Tel. 0827-56188
MATTHEWS BROTHERS LTD
KETTLEBROOK ROAD
Open: Mon.-Sat. 8.30am-6.00pm
Demonstrations Sunday mornings
by appointment only
H.P.W.WM.D.T.CS.A.BC.

SUFFOLK

BURY ST. EDMUNDS   Tel.
TOOLS & THINGS   0284 62022
21 CHURCHGATE   ★
Open: Monday to Saturday
9.00 a.m.-5.30 p.m.
H.P.W.WM.D.A.BC.

IPSWICH   Tel. 0473 86216
FOX WOODWORKING   ★
'STEBBINGS' BACK LANE
WASHBROOK
Open: Tues. Fri. 9.00am-5.30pm
Sat. 9.00am-12 noon
H.P.W.WM.D.A.B.C.

SURREY

CARSHALTON BEECHES   Tel.
SURREY WOOD   01-642 6636
MACHINE SALES LTD   ★
56A BANSTEAD ROAD
Open: Tues-Fri 9.30 am-6.00 pm
Saturday 9.30 am-2.00 pm
P.W.WM.D.BC.CS.

SURREY

CROYDON   Tel. 01-688 5513
L. H. TURTLE LTD   ★
6-12 PARK STREET
Open: Monday to Saturday
8.30 a.m.-5.30 p.m.
H.P.W.WM.D.A.

GUILDFORD   Tel. 0483 61125
MESSINGERS FOR TOOLS
14-18 CHERTSEY STREET
Open: Tuesday to Saturday
8.30 a.m.-5.30 p.m.
Closed all day Monday
H.P.W.D.BC.

SUSSEX

WORTHING   Tel. 0903 38739
W. HOSKING (TOOLS &
MACHINERY)
96a MONTAGUE STREET
Open: Mon-Sat 8.30am-5.30pm
Wednesday 8.30am-1.00pm
H.P.W.WM.D.CS.A.BC.

WEST MIDLANDS

WEST BROMWICH   Tel: 021-
CONWAY SAW &   533 5461/2
SUPPLY LTD   ★
SWAN LANE
Open: 8 a.m.-6 p.m. Mon-Fri
9 a.m.-1 p.m. Saturday
P.W.WM.D.CS.BC.

WILTSHIRE

SWINDON   Tel. (0793) 31361
SARJENT'S TOOL STORES LTD ★
64 FLEET STREET
Open: Monday to Saturday
8.30 a.m.-5.30 p.m.
H.P.W.WM.D.A.BC

YORKSHIRE

BRADFORD   Tel. 0274 560699
STEENWISE LIMITED   ★
LIMEFIELD MILL,
WOOD STREET, CROSSFLATS
BINGLEY
Open: Mon to Fri 9 a.m.-5 p.m.
H.P.W.WM.D.T.CS.A.BC.

HALIFAX   Tel. 0422 884075/
TIMBERLITE LTD   884788/33575
VICTORIA BUILDINGS   ★
LUDDENDEN FOOT
Open: Monday to Friday
Saturday 9.00 a.m.-5.00 p.m.
H.P.W.WM.D.CS.A.BC.

HARROGATE   Tel. 0423 66245/
MULTI-TOOLS   55328 ★
158 KINGS ROAD
Open: Monday to Saturday
8.30 a.m.-6.00 p.m.
H.P.W.WM.D.A.BC.

HUDDERSFIELD   Tel. (0484)
NEVILLE M. OLDHAM   641219/(0484)
UNIT 1 DAYLE ST. WORKS   42777
DAYLE STREET, LONGWOOD   ★
Open: Mon-Fri 9.00am- 5.30pm
Saturday 9.30am-12.00pm
P.W.WM.D.A.BC.

LEEDS   Tel. 0532 790507
GEORGE SPENCE & SONS LTD
WELLINGTON ROAD   ★
Open: Monday to Friday
8.30 a.m.-5.30 p.m.
Saturday 9.00 a.m.-5.00 p.m.
H.P.W.WM.D.T.A.

SHEFFIELD   Tel. 0742-441012
GREGORY & TAYLOR LTD
WORKSOP ROAD
Open: 8.30 a.m.-5.30 p.m.
Monday-Friday
8.30 a.m.-12.30 p.m. Sat.
H.P.W.WM.D.

YORKSHIRE

SHEFFIELD   Tel. 0742-24659
GRAHAM OXLEY'S SHOWROOM ★
BRIDGE STREET
Open: Monday to Friday
9.00 a.m.-5.30 p.m.
Saturday 8.30 a.m.-12.30 p.m.
H.W.D.A.BC.

SCOTLAND

EDINBURGH   Tel. 031-337
SCOTSPAN   7788/665 3121
195 BALGREEN ROAD
Open: Monday to Friday
9.00 a.m.-3.00 p.m.
P.W.WM.D.A.

N. IRELAND

Co. ANTRIM   Tel. 0266 6384
GEORGE GARDINER
49 BALLYMONEY STREET
BALLYMENA
Open: Mon-Fri 8.30am-5.30pm
Wednesday 8.30am-1.00pm
H.P.W.D.A.BC.

Co. DOWN Tel. (0247) 819800 (day)
NEWTOWNARDS   812506 (night)
NORLYN MACHINERY, UNIT 10
Malcolmson Ind. Est., 80 Bangor Road
Open: Mon-Fri 9.30am-5.30pm
or any other time by request
H.P.W.WM.D.A.BC.

S. IRELAND

COUNTY KILKENNY   Tel.
WOODMEN   (0409) 5460
CASHEL HOUSE   ★
KELLS ROAD, KILKENNY
Open: Monday to Saturday
9.00 a.m.-5.30 p.m.
P.W.WM.D.A.BC.

WALES

BRITON FERRY   Tel. (0639)
WOODMEN   820803/4
49 NEATH ROAD   ★
Open: Monday to Saturday
9.00 a.m.-5.30 p.m.
P.W.WM.D.A.BC.

CARDIFF   Tel. (0222) 373007
JOHN HALL TOOLS LIMITED   ★
22 CHURCHILL WAY
Open: Monday to Saturday
9.00 a.m.-5.30 p.m.
H.P.W.WM.D.A.BC.

CARDIFF   Tel. (0222) 30831
F. W. MORGAN   & 25562
(CANTON) LTD., 129-133
COWBRIDGE RD EAST,
CANTON, CARDIFF
Mon-Sat 8-5 Sun. 9.30-12.30
H.P.T.CS.A.BC.

CARDIFF   Tel. (0222) 36519/
WOODMEN   373793/35221
43 CRWYS ROAD   ★
Open: Monday to Saturday
9.00 a.m.-5.30 p.m.

CARMARTHEN   Tel. 0267 7219
DO-IT-YOURSELF SUPPLY   ★
BLUE STREET, DYFED
Open: Monday to Saturday
9.00 a.m.-5.30 p.m.
Thursday 9.00 a.m.-1.00 p.m.
H.P.W.WM.D.T.CS.A.BC.

**YOU CAN BUY WITH
CONFIDENCE FROM THE
SHOPS IN THIS
SHOP GUIDE**

*★Shops offering a mail
order service are denoted by
an asterisk*

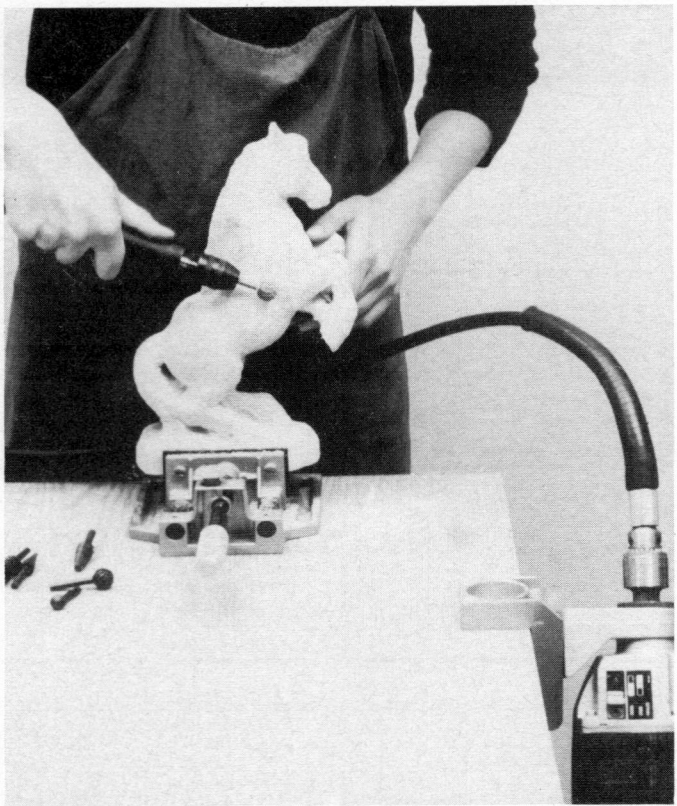

Flexible shaft and drill stand

To fit any power tool the Wolfcraft Super Duty flexible shaft is introduced by PTS Tool Specialists Ltd, PO Box 242, Henley Street, Camp Hill, Birmingham (021-772 4370). It is 51in. (1300mm) long and fitted with ⁵⁄₁₆in. (8mm) chuck. Suitable for right-hand rotation only it can operate at drill speeds from 1000-6000rpm. It is fitted with ballbearings.

The flexible shaft complements the Wolfcraft sanding, brushing, polishing, drilling, milling and rasping accessories.

Wolfcraft Super Duty flexible shaft fits any power tool states PTS Tool Specialists.

Another introduction is a drillstand said to accommodate any UK, continental or US power tool with ¼-⅜in. (6.3-9.5mm) chuck. It has hexagonal column, rack-and-pinion feed mechanism of the drillstand, adjustable micro-scale depth control and adjustable depth stop. For tools with ½in. (12.7mm) chuck an adaptor spindle (part no. 4955) is available.

The stand is 18in. (450mm) high, maximum travel is 9½in. (240mm) and the table is 6½ × 7½in. (170 × 190mm).

Noise control

Teleslide noise-control enclosure is said to have reduced an emitted noise level of 102-103dB(A) to 85-86dB(A) on a moulder installed at the Swansea factory cf Remploy Ltd, the government-supported company which provides employment for the severely disabled.

The Teleslide modular system has been developed by the Noise Control Centre (Melton Mowbray) Ltd, Saxby Road, Melton Mowbray LE13 1BP (0664 67316). It can be modified to suit specific requirements.

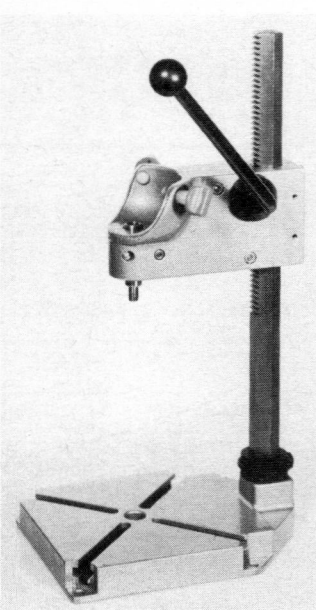

The heavy-duty drillstand from Wolfcraft features a rigid hexagonal column and a rack and pinion feed mechanism for control in use.

Hand tools

Several own-brand items are included in the ranges from Roger's, 47 Walsworth Road, Hitchin SG4 9SU (0362 4177). For example, socket paring chisels up to 1½in., hand-forged and highly polished; veneer hammers individually made in selected hardwood; shoulder plane reproduction of the type made at the turn of the century by Alex Mathieson, bronze body with rosewood centre and available with 1⅜in. irons in either tool steel or HSS.

Other additions are beech spokeshaves with 2in. blades; Japanese-made chisels having ebony handles and laminated steel blades ¼-1½in. with the backs hollow-ground; Arrow carving tools from Switzerland (initially fish-tail gouges but the range is being expanded); two styles of carver's hooks; and Swedish-made whittling and bench knives with laminated steel blades.

In the Conover range from US are thread boxes (woodscrew sets) in kilned maple with ½, ¾ and 1in. (bottoming) taps and a sharpening stone. There are also palm planes (smooth, scrub and beading) the bodies of which are 2¼in. long. Rebating as well as standard irons are available, with a toothing iron for the scrub planes. Scraper planes with 2¼ and 4in. bodies are introduced; spare blades are available.

Two other tools from Conover are a bit brace reproduction to antique pattern but fitted with a modern chuck; and a blind nailer for hiding nail holes.

Roger's also offers combination hard and soft Arkansas stones in cedar box; this is in addition to the individual stones.

Lathe

Design changes and modifications to the 17 × 37 lathe increase its flexibility, according to manufacturer Tyme Machines (Bristol) Ltd, Unit 3, Halls Road, Kingswood, Bristol (0272 601770).

Modifications include streamlining of the headstock, tailstock and chisel rest. The main headstock shaft has a location diameter to ensure all accessories run true. A 150mm faceplate, driving centre, hardened and ground running centre and woodscrew chuck set (1½-2¾in. capacity) are provided with the lathe which is complete with ½hp motor mounted at the rear and no-volt overload switch, all wired and ready to plug-in.

Bowl turning up to 17in. diameter is standard because of the gap bed design. Maximum length between centres is 37in.

Further details are available on application.

Percussion drills

Six models, one of which has left and right revolutions, are introduced by AEG-Telefunken, 217 Bath Road, Slough SL1 4AW (Slough 872101). Though intended for industrial users, the company states that the SB2-401 and SB2-501 are within home users' price bracket.

The six models are from 400 to 900W and include four with electronic variable speed control; all but SB2E-901 are in 110 or 240V. Prices, exclusive of VAT, are from £39 to £125. Further information can be had from AEG-Telefunken at the Slough address.

Planer knives

Spearplane Super Economy thin planing knives are available in the full range of standard sizes and lengths, states Spear & Jackson (Industrial) Ltd, Aetna Works, Savile Street, Sheffield S4 7UR (0742 20202). The company points out that these knives are specifically designed for use on softwood in place of the traditional HSS knives.

Made from a specially heat-treated low-cost alloy steel the new range is claimed to offer a considerable saving in costs to the operator. Super Economy knives complement the existing HSS range from Spear & Jackson.

Chainsaw

The Stihl 011AV chainsaw weighs just over 9lb and is powered by a two-stroke petrol engine developing 1.9hp at the drive sprocket at 7500rpm. It is equipped with guidebar lengths of 12, 14 or 16in. and incorporates anti-vibration system, patented chain-arresting mechanism, double-switch throttle, safety chain, chain-catching bolt and other features.

Manufactured in W Germany it is distributed by Andreas Stihl Ltd, Stihl House, Goldsworth Park Industrial Estate, Woking GU21 3BA (048 62 20222), which gives the retail price as from £149 with availability from the 600 Stihl service centres in UK.

Two-blades saw

From Cintride Ltd, Ashford Road Works, Bakewell DE4 1GL (0629 812513), comes its version of a padsaw having 7in. blade which can be replaced with one of similar length for cutting metal. Complete with the two blades and plastics handle the Wood 'n' Metal saw, as it is called, retails at £1.40. Replacement blades of either type cost 40p each. Overall length of the saw is approximately 11¼in.

FOR SALE

460 WOODWORKER MAGAZINES 1930-1981 including 24 complete years. £20.00 o.n.o. the lot. Buyer collects. Telephone: (0954) 81036. (Cambridgeshire). J

6-IN-1 UNIVERSAL CHUCK for Major Coronet, only used four times £28. No longer needed by present owner. Telephone: 01-977 8917 J

WOODWORKER Magazine—bound volumes from 1939 to 1951. Packed with useful information. A bargain at £10.00 each. Telephone Leeds 498956. J

RECORD 405 MULTI-PLANE immaculate £65. Old silver verge watch in pair case £135. Coxtie Green 72892 (Essex). J

CORONET MINOR WOODLATHE 36" between centres, with sawbench fitted. Good condition. £270.00. Telephone: Cadnam (Nr. Southampton) 3700. J

CARVING TOOLS. Addis and Marples. Used professionally 40 years. Excellent condition. Offers or exchange turning tools. Telephone: Southport 41005. J

DeWALT 110 RADIAL ARMSAW heavy duty with moulding block and cutters, drum sander, disc sander and jigsaw. £350. Sharpenset with two additional stones and planer knife, grinding attachment. £150. Tel: Harpenden 61282. J

MYFORD ML8 LATHE, bench mounted. 3-in-1 chuck; 3 jaw chuck. Excellent condition £250. Leek 371744. J

STANLEY 55 MULTI-PURPOSE PLANE, boxed, mint condition with instruction booklet £85. Telephone: Dartford (0322) 77079 (Evenings). J

CORONET MINOR woodturning lathe. Stand. End-turning rest. £150 ono. Other attachments if required. Old "Woodworker" magazines. Telephone: 061-437 3696. J

ROYAL 10" saw bench tilting arbor, rise and fall, ¾hp motor, r.p.m.2350, single phase, starter good condition £125. Telephone: 01-542 3009 (Surrey). J

CORONET MAJOR WOOD LATHE, with saw table, mortiser, spindle moulder and many other extras. As new £650. Also old, but solid, bandsaw £120. Telephone Temple Cloud (0761) 52788. J

EBAC Mini Timber Dryer, unused. £300 ono. Telephone: Glos (0451) 31049. J

"ROYAL" tilting arbor 10" dia. sawbench on maker's stand, complete with ¾hp single-phase motor and push button starter. Cast iron table, fitted with precision ground steel extension table to right of sawblade, permitting saw to fence dimension of 24". This machine is in excellent condition £250. One "Wolf" ES14 chisel mortising machine, complete with 600 watts industrial drill. Very little used and in excellent condition. £80. Swingler, 10 Elsworthy Road, London NW3. Telephone: 01-586 0085. J

LACE BOBBIN. Woodturning blanks. Exotic and unusual hardwoods. S.A.E. list or 50 blanks of 25 woods £6.20 inclusive. Box No. 497 (Walsall), c/o Woodworker Magazine, 35 Bridge Street, Hemel Hempstead, Herts HP1 1EE. J-K

WELSH SLATE oil stones for sale at very competitive prices. Send S.A.E. for details: INIGO JONES & Co. Ltd., Groeslon, Caernarfon, Gwynedd. Tel: 0286-830242. F-R

FOR ALL SUPPLIES
FOR THE

Craft of Enamelling

ON METAL

Including
LEAD-FREE ENAMELS

PLEASE SEND 2 × 10p STAMPS FOR FREE CATALOGUE, PRICE LIST AND WORKING INSTRUCTIONS

W. G. BALL LTD.

ENAMEL MANUFACTURERS

Dept. W. LONGTON
STOKE-ON-TRENT
ST3 1JW

R & S TOOLS (LINCOLN) LTD.

BEEVOR STREET, LINCOLN. Tel: Lincoln 0522 36168/9

Why pay more when you can get up to 25% discount off most leading makes of power tools and hand tools?

Stockists of:

ELECTRIC POWER TOOLS:
AEG—ELU—BOSCH—MAKITA—SUPER STORK—SKIL WOLF—METABO—WADKIN—KANGO

WOODWORKING MACHINES
DEWALT—MULTICO—SEDGWICK—WADKIN—STARTRITE

SAWBLADES
SANDVIK—TEX—MICOR—FIRTH—BROWN

HAND TOOLS
ALL LEADING MAKES OF BUILDING AND ENGINEERING TOOLS

ABRASIVES
ENGLISH—TEX—KLINGSPOR—UNIVERSAL GRINDING WHEELS

Up to 30% off most leading brands of coated abrasive

TCT CIRCULAR SAW BLADES
Contact us for the best price.

For the first time ever we can now offer an A.E.G. Drill of industrial quality at D.I.Y. price – £44.85 (inc. V.A.T.). Carriage extra.
Access & Barclaycard welcome.

SOLE AGENTS FOR SWIFTSURE CUTTING & CUTTING DISCS
FOR YOUR QUOTATION—PLEASE PHONE BETWEEN 8.30 am and 5 pm

VISIT BARRIE IRONS NEW SHOWROOM

and see our stock of ELU, BOSCH, DE WALT STARTRITE and other leading makes, all at discount prices at

81 Uxbridge Road, Stanmore, Middx.

Tel: 01-954-0181

FINAL PRICE SLASH
ELU-DE WALT

Before buying phone
Machine Sales & Services (Bournemouth) Ltd.,
0202 527781 or 527780
WE CAN PROVE WE ARE CHEAPER!
E. G. DW 30 – £140

ORNAMENTAL LATHE BY BONSALE

Marsh & Co., various Cutting Frames, Epicycloid Gearing, Good Tool Box and Accessories.
Best Offer around £1,000.
Telephone: (0451) 31049
Evenings only 6-7 pm.

HAND CARVED
'Adam Style' motifs in Mahogany — Example 10" × 5" centre lamp and two side pieces — £25.00
Send S.A.E. for details and quotation. Your own design quoted for if required.
SAM NICHOLSON
22 Lisnagarvey Drive,
Lisburn, Co. Antrim,
N. Ireland. Phone Lisburn 3510

TOOLS TO TREASURE

Adzes, Drawknives, and other high quality tools for the Woodcraftsman, including a fine selection of "Pax" Hand and Panel Saws.
EXPORT ENQUIRIES WELCOME
CATALOGUE 45p
CORBET TOOLS DEPT. WW/1
224 Puxton Drive,
Kidderminster, Worcs.

CORONET INTERNATIONAL WOODWORKER

Universal Woodworking Machine, infinite variations of speed from 800 rpm to 4,000 rpm with tilting arbor saw. Many attachments which include sawing, planing, rebating, thicknessing, moulding, mortising, sanding, turning.
£1,000.00
Telephone 01-542 6655 or 0734 732091 Evenings. Illustrated literature available.

WORKSHOP EQUIPMENT

PLANERS 6", 9" planers/thicknessers, 12" × 7", 9" × 6", 12" × 7", sawbenches, 10", 12", combination woodworkers. British made. Particulars, send stamp. Dodd Machine Tools Ltd., South Woodham, Chelmsford. Tel: 320 691. C-N

MACHINERY. A comprehensive range of new/used machinery. Check our prices, e.g. HMO 10"×5½" planer/thicknesser £325. HF30 spindle moulder £328. 12" tilt arbour sawbench 2hp motor £121. Shopsmith MK5 home workshop £782. Morso mitring machine £437, (including V.A.T.). See these machines and Ryobi industrial small tools demonstrated at Woodman Woodworking Machinery Co. (Sign of the Axe), Little Malgraves Hall, Lower Dunton Road, Bulphan, Nr. Upminster, Essex. Tel: (0268) 415511 or (0702) 331729. I-U

FRETSAW BLADES, Marquetry saw blades, Whetstones. Details and prices Lea Blade Sales, 16 Barclay, Hertford Heath, Herts. JK

WASHITA & ARKANSAS whetstones now readily available from importer. Large selection, SAE for list. C. Rufino, Manor House, South Clifton, Newark, Notts. T/C

CIRCULAR AND BAND SAW BLADES for all applications from: A. A. Smith of Lancing Ltd., Churchill Industrial Estate, Lancing, Sussex. Tel: 09063-4474 (24 Hours). I-O

Prices quoted are those prevailing at press date and are subject to alteration due to economic conditions.

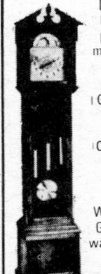

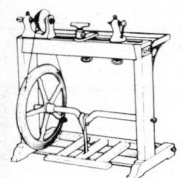

CRAFT/ANTIQUE/ SECOND-HAND TOOLS

OLD WOODWORKING TOOLS, Norris planes. Mitre planes. Brass and Ebony Mortice gauges, and any unusual tools. Top prices paid by Private collector. Please ring Mr. Lowe 0530 34581 evenings. IJK

OLD AND NEW complete toolkit or individual tools wanted. Carpenters, joiners, coopers tools. D. Loftus, 14 Hounslow Rd., Whitton, Middlesex. Tel: 01 898 4586. E-K

WOODCARVING STUDENT requires carving tools. Mr. Chavasse, 5 New Row, Tanyard Lane, Steyning, Sussex BN4 3RN or Telephone: Steyning 812952 (after 8pm). J

£300 MINIMUM OFFERED for unusual Ultamatum braces in good condition for my own collection. Also wanted Spiers, Norris or any other equivalent quality planes and tools. Can call anywhere. Reg Eaton, High Street, Heacham, Kings Lynn, Norfolk (0485) 70067. H-J

LARGE MAHOGANY LINED fitted tool chest for sale. Offers invited. For details telephone: (0474) 63160. J

MARTIN ANTIQUES always have an interesting selection of old woodworking tools. Callers only 2-5 daily at 36 St. Stephen St., Edinburgh. G-R

MULTI PLANES Stanley 13050 £25. Lewin plus extra blades £45. Both excellent condition. Telephone: 01-607 8420. J

WANTED

GOOD QUALITY WOOD LATHE. Must be 40/42 inches between centres, single phase and floor mounted. Leek 371744. J

WOODTURNER REQUIRES any 4"-6" thick timber suitable for conversion to squares for table lamp production. Yew, Pine, Cedar of Lebanon, Ash and unusual hardwoods particularly required. Must be well seasoned. Box No. 499 (Avon), c/o Woodworker Magazine, 35 Bridge Street, Hemel Hempstead, Herts. J

CLASSIFIED
Telephone Valerie Tester (0442) 41221 Ext. 266

STARTRITE TABLESAW either TA/SP.165 or TA/SP.175 with sliding table if possible. Also wanted, Startrite 352 bandsaw. Private buyer will pay cash for top condition machines. Telephone Dave Binnington 01-385 5363 (evenings). I-J

WANTED to buy Coronet Major wood lathe with accessories 1 PH electrics. Could collect. Tel: 04866 4464. HIJ

MARPLES ULTAMATUM or Ultamatum type braces, Norris planes, gunmetal planes, mitre planes, or any unusual tools. Private collector will pay top prices. Please ring Mr. Lowe, Coalville (0530) 34581, evenings. G-J

RATES
20p per word, minimum £3.00. Box Nos £1.25 extra.
Semi-display s.c.c. £4.00 (min £10.00)

GENERAL

SOLID BRASS DOOR, cabinet and window fittings, in period and modern designs. Full colour catalogue illustrates over 300 different items. Send 50p (refundable with first order) to: Classic Brass (Dept. WW2), West Road, Westcliff on Sea, Essex. I-N

TEACH WOODWORK IN AMERICA for summer '82. Hundreds of Woodwork enthusiasts needed by BUNACAMP as counsellors in U.S. children's summer camps. Over 12,000 BUNACAMPers have enjoyed the most unforgettable rewarding summer of their lives. 8 sunny weeks, hard, fun work, then up to 6 weeks holiday. Flight, work visa papers, job, board, lodging all provided. $200-$230 salary. Contact Tim Wilkins, BUNACAMP, 58 Berners Street, London W1P 3AE. Telephone: 01-580 9458. J-M

1/12th SCALE BRASS HARDWARE
Period handles, hinges, grille
S.A.E. for list
MARGARET VARNEY (MINIATURES)
10 Hardays Lane,
West Haddon, Northampton

BUSINESS OPPORTUNITY

EXCELLENT OPPORTUNITY to start a part/full time business with minimum capital and risk. Essentials are a good outbuilding or garage, telephone and a little capital which you should recover within 6 months. For initial discussion please write to Box No. 498, c/o Woodworker Magazine, 35 Bridge Street, Hemel Hempstead, Herts. J

BUSINESS FOR SALE

A GENUINE SALE OF A SUCCESSFUL HOME BASED MAIL ORDER VENEER/HANDICRAFT BUSINESS. We offer a catalogue, strong list of established customers, and reasonable stocks for a wise investment. Perfect for part or full time working, or as a retirement or hobby business. For full details apply to Miss A. J. Jones, 9 Arksey Place, Leeds 12. J

PROFESSIONAL SERVICES

TAXATION ACCOUNTANT & BUSINESS CONSULTANT; for the self-employed and starting businesses. Why worry about TAX and business regulations? Get organised, seek help. Telephone: (SE London) 01-699 3039/01-274 1256. J-O

Classified advertising in WOODWORKER brings quick results. An advertisement in these columns is cheaper than you think. For further details contact VALERIE TESTER now on (0442) 41221, Ext. 266.

Classified Advertisements

From:

....

....

....

I enclose remittance value.......................to cover ....

Insertions under the heading:

WORKSHOP EQUIPMENT ☐   BOOKS & PUBLICATIONS ☐

COURSES ☐   PLANS ☐

CRAFT/ANTIQUE/SECOND-HAND TOOLS ☐   MATERIALS ☐   FOR SALE ☐

WANTED ☐   SERVICES ☐

MUSICAL INSTRUMENTS ☐   WOOD SUPPLIERS ☐

To: **Valerie Tester**
WOODWORKER

CLASSIFIED ADVERTISEMENT DEPT.
PO BOX 35, BRIDGE STREET,
HEMEL HEMPSTEAD, HERTS HP1 1EE

★ **Lineage rate 20p per word. Minimum charge £3.00**

★ **Semi display single column cm = £4.00 (Minimum £10.00)**

★ **Box numbers £1.25 extra**

Name and address if to appear must be paid for

BLOCK CAPITALS PLEASE

Prices quoted are those prevailing at press date and are subject to alteration due to economic conditions.

THE MAGAZINE FOR THE CRAFTSMAN

FEBRUARY 1982 Vol. 86 No. 1059 ISSN 0043-776X

Front cover: A composite of the winners from the Woodworker show. Guitar by B. Meadows, Lewisham, (best of class, musical instruments), dance fantasy by A. Axon, Bexley (first, figure carving section) and lakeside tableau by E. Smith, Warlingham (first, relief carving section). *Photos by Bill Gates.* Show report pp80-97.

	Editorial	Polly Curds
Advertisement Manager		Glyn Crole-Rees
Advertisement Director ⎫	MAP Leisure	Michael Merrifield
Managing Director ⎭	Division	Gavin Doyle

MEMBER OF THE AUDIT BUREAU OF CIRCULATIONS

SUBSCRIPTION DEPARTMENT: Remittances to MODEL AND ALLIED PUBLICATIONS, PO Box 35, Hemel Hempstead, Herts HP1 1EE. Price per copy 95p includes p&p. Subscription queries: Tel: Hemel Hempstead 51740. Subscription rate, including index, £11.90 per annum; overseas sterling £12.90; $29.00 US for overseas dollar subscribers. Second class postage paid in US at New York, New York. *Distribution* to North American hobby and craft stores, museums and bookshops by Bill Dean Books Ltd, 166-41 Powells Cove Boulevard, Post Office Box 69, Whitestone, New York 11357, USA. Tel: 1-212-767-6632. *Distribution* to news stand sales by Eastern News Distribution Inc, 111 Eight Avenue, New York, NY10011, USA. Tel: 1-212-255-5620.

WOODWORKER is printed in Great Britain by H. E. Warne Ltd, East Hill, St Austell, Cornwall PL25 4TN for the proprietor and publisher Model & Allied Publications Ltd (a member of the Argus Press Group). Trade sales by Argus Press Sales & Distribution Ltd, 12-18 Paul Street, London EC2A 4JS. WOODWORKER (ISSN 0043-776X) is published on the 3rd Friday of the month.

Model & Allied Publications Ltd

PO Box 35, Bridge Street, Hemel Hempstead, Herts HP1 1EE. Telephone: Hemel Hempstead (0442) 41221.

THE 'FEEL' OF THE THING

Woodworker Show 1981 bucked the trend of many exhibitions. More people came and more business was done by the trade stands. There were more entries in the competition classes and, overall, standards of craftsmanship were higher. Reports by the judges (printed elsewhere in this issue) make interesting reading and their comments are well worth study.

The judges are rightly critical and expect the highest standards of design and execution. We would particularly direct attention to their remarks on the subject of finish. For example 'the pins which secured some of the mouldings still showing'; 'liberally applied high-gloss finish masked the character and beauty of the woods employed'; 'not so well finished'; 'lacked true understanding of the "feel" of the thing'; 'inappropriate inlay'; and so on.

It also seems that some entrants did not comply with what one judge described as 'the very basic rules' – or misinterpreted the rules. The organiser of Woodworker Show endeavours to keep the rules as simple as possible for obvious reasons but if entrants are not sure in their own minds on any matter, the organiser will be pleased to help. Of course entrants must appreciate that the organiser cannot act as a grand jury and present a true bill. The judges at Woodworker Show are unfettered — and the petty jury is not packed!

For the record the attendance at last year's Show numbered 12 867 over the five-day period, an increase of 2433 on the 1980 figure. As G. D. L. R. Home, managing director of Model & Allied Publications Ltd (proprietor of WOODWORKER), said: 'In these difficult times of recession it is very encouraging indeed to be able to knock-up such an excellent result, not only for M.A.P. Ltd but for the woodworking business as a whole. There is no doubt that the business has benefitted enormously from trade done during the Show.'

Judges at the 1981 Show were: Cabinet-making – H. G. Triggs, John Price, Christopher Simpson. Woodcarving – Ashley Iles, T. A. Woolhouse. John Sainsbury. Woodturning – Ray Key, Jack Hill, E. A. Doulton. Musical instruments – Ieuan Owen, Roger Rose. Marquetry and inlay – C. H. Good, Norman Martyr, G. F. Barnett. Toys and miniatures – John Gould, Stuart King. Model horse-drawn vehicles – John Thompson, A. J. Lown. Junior entries – C. W. Bond, Keith Riseborough. Clocks – R. W. Grant, Martin P. Bulger.

No entries were received for the carpentry and joinery class.

The proprietor of WOODWORKER and organiser of Woodworker Show express sincere thanks to all the judges for their careful assessments of the entries in all classes and for their helpful comments both in relation to the entries and in matters of organisation.

The organiser hopes that many of the suggestions made will be incorporated in this year's Show which is scheduled for 19-24 October (Tuesday-Sunday inclusive) at the RHS New Hall, London SW1.

Those wishing to reserve stand space in the trade sections should get in touch with Mary White (exhibition organiser) at PO Box 35, Bridge Street, Hemel Hempstead HP1 1EE (0442 41221). Early reservation is advised.

Guild of Woodworkers

First-aid

On 1 July 1982 fresh regulations covering medical first-aid and applying to virtually all workpeople will come into force. A code of practice and guidance notes are to be issued by the HSC explaining what employers will have to do to comply with the regulations. These will apply to work covered by the Health & Safety at Work etc Act 1974 and orders.

SI 1981 no. 917: *The Health & Safety (First-Aid) Regulations 1981* (ISBN 011 0169174) is the relevant document; available from HMSO or through booksellers at £1.10 plus postage.

Course on finishing

Two-day courses on finishing are being arranged for guild members on 1-2 March and 8-9 March 1982 at the Hudson hall, rear of 40 Bean Road, Bexleyheath, Kent. The course starts at 10.00am and will end about 4.30pm each day with an hour (12.30-1.30pm) for lunch. Refreshments can be obtained at a nearby pub.

The course will be restricted to six to permit individual instruction to be given under the following headings: materials; preparation of surfaces; staining (water and spirit); filling and making fillers; bodying-up; spiriting-off; acid and eggshell finishes repolishing; waxing.

Cost of the two-day course is £31.60 for each member inc. VAT. This does not include cost of lunch.

Annual subscriptions

Guild of Woodworkers is now entering its eighth year. It is divided into two classes of membership: individual craftsmen and trading craftsmen, the latter class including all commercial interests involved in wood processing, woodworking and allied activities. Individual craftsmen and trading craftsmen in UK and throughout the world are eligible to belong to the guild.

Among the services and facilities which are the essence of guild activities are: programmes of evening, one-day and weekend instructional courses, seminars and meetings at moderate cost; visits to museums and buildings noteworthy for their collections of furniture and other objects in wood, or for their constructional use of timber and timber-based products; special guild features in WOODWORKER; visits to timber yards and sawmills; arrangements for reduced subscriptions to certain national organisations; special facilities in relation to the insurance of tools and equipment; preferential admission charges to exhibitions organised by Model & Allied Publications Ltd; special prices for plans published by Model & Allied Publications Ltd.

Annual subscription rates are as follows: individual craftsmen £3.00; trading craftsmen £6.00 (equivalent currency for those in both classes outside UK). There is a registration fee of £1.50 (equivalent currency for those outside UK) payable by new subscribers in both classes but this registration fee is waived in respect of those who are already members.

Individual craftsmen and trading craftsmen receive an indenture, personal identification card and wallet. It should be noted that the indenture and identification card remain the property of Model & Allied Publications Ltd and are to be surrendered on termination of payment of annual subscription.

Copyright of the indenture, certificate, the guild badge and all other promotional material made available to members of Guild of Woodworkers, is retained by MAP Ltd.

Tool Insurance

In April 1980 WOODWORKER p219, we announced an insurance scheme to cover members' woodworking tools and machinery had been arranged at an average cost of 2½% of total value. (Subject to variation in certain high-risk areas.) In May 1981 WOODWORKER p302 we announced that several members had asked if the total amount of £500 could be increased to a figure more closely related to current values.

We are now able to announce that improved facilities are available. Members may now insure their tools and machinery for £500 (premium £5.00 per annum) or £1000 (£12.50 per annum). The underwriters still require an excess of £10 to obviate a large number of small claims. Other exceptions are wear and tear, electrical and mechanical breakdown, gradual deterioration and losses due to climatic conditions. The success of an 'all risks' policy depends on maximum support. Forms and details from: The Administrator, Guild of Woodworkers, PO Box 35, Bridge Street, Hemel Hempstead, HP1 1EE.

TWO-DAY NON-RESIDENTIAL COURSE ON FINISHING

To: Administrator
Guild of Woodworkers
PO Box 35, Bridge Street
Hemel Hempstead HP1 1EE

Date.....................................

Please reserve a place for me on the above course to be held on 1-2 March 1982 and/or 8-9 March 1982 at Bean Road, Bexleyheath. I enclose cheque/postal order for £31.60 inclusive of VAT in payment of course fee. (Strike out dates which are inapplicable).

Name ....

Address in full ....   BLOCK CAPITALS

....

....

Telephone number ....

Signed ....

Membership number ....

TEAR OFF AND POST IMMEDIATELY TO GUILD OF WOODWORKERS TOGETHER WITH REMITTANCE

A cancellation charge of half the fee will be made unless the cancellation is received in writing 14 days prior to the date of the course. Transfer will be accepted up to the day before the course.

Following the success of the two-day seminar on skills and profit-making held at Salisbury last June in co-operation with the Council for Small Industries in Rural Areas (CoSIRA), the guild has arranged a further series of two-day seminars on the same subject.

Subjects will include business principles; business skills; marketing; production utilisation; financial control; budgets; tax; planning for growth and much more. The programme is carefully tailored to meet the requirements of those who contemplate starting their own businesses or who have recently set up in the woodworking sector.

Further details can be had from the administrator, Guild of Woodworkers, PO Box 35, Bridge Street, Hemel Hempstead HP1 1EE, or complete the reservation form below. Cheques/postal orders should be crossed, payable to M.A.P. Ltd.

Provisional programme for the seminar on maximising the profits of your business to be held at the Lord Hill hotel, Shrewsbury, on 24th/25th February 1982.

Wednesday, 24th February

9.30 – 9.45 a.m.	Arrival and registration
9.45 – 10.00	Questionnaire
10.00 – 10.30	Business principles I, II and III
10.30 – 10.45	Coffee
10.45 – 11.15	Business principles I, II and III
11.15 – 12.15 p.m.	Checking out your business idea — your market and how you reach it
12.15 – 1.30	Lunch
1.30 – 2.45	Your skills, quality and utilisation
2.45 – 3.15	Financial control
3.15 – 3.30	Tea
3.30 – 4.00	Financial control
4.00 – 4.30	Film
4.30 – 5.00	Discussion and summary

Thursday, 25th February

9.00 – 9.30 a.m.	Marketing — you and your customer
9.30 – 10.00	Marketing — selling
10.00 – 10.15	Coffee
10.15 – 12.15 p.m.	Visit to Shrewsbury College
12.15 – 1.30	Lunch
1.30 – 2.00	How to trade — your business organisation
2.00 – 2.30	Case study – syndicates
2.30 – 3.00	Case study — reports by syndicates
3.00 – 3.15	Tea
3.15 – 4.00	You and your staff
4.00 – 4.30	Review and summary

SEMINARS: SKILLS AND PROFIT-MAKING

Guild of Woodworkers – Council for Small Industries in Rural Areas

To: Administrator
Guild of Woodworkers
PO Box 35
Bridge Street
Hemel Hempstead HP1 1EE

Date ....

Please reserve a place for me on the seminar to be held
on 24-25 February 1982 at Lord Hill Hotel, Abbey Foregate, Shrewsbury,
on 28-29 April 1982 at the Pottergate Course & Conference Centre, 83-5 Pottergate, Norwich.
(Tick which seminar you wish to attend).

I enclose cheque/postal order for £57.50 in payment of seminar tuition fee, papers and lecture material, refreshments and lunch.

I contemplate starting my own business
I am already trading on my own account
(Tick whichever applies).

Please reserve accommodation for me at a guest house,
hotel,
bed & breakfast
(Tick whichever applies)

I understand that accommodation is not included in the seminar fee and I will pay for my accommodation direct.

Name .... BLOCK CAPITALS

Address in full ....

....

Telephone number ....

Signed ....

Membership number ....

Attention is drawn to the cancellation charge of half the fee unless the cancellation is received in writing 14 days prior to the date of each seminar.

TEAR OFF AND POST IMMEDIATELY TOGETHER WITH REMITTANCE

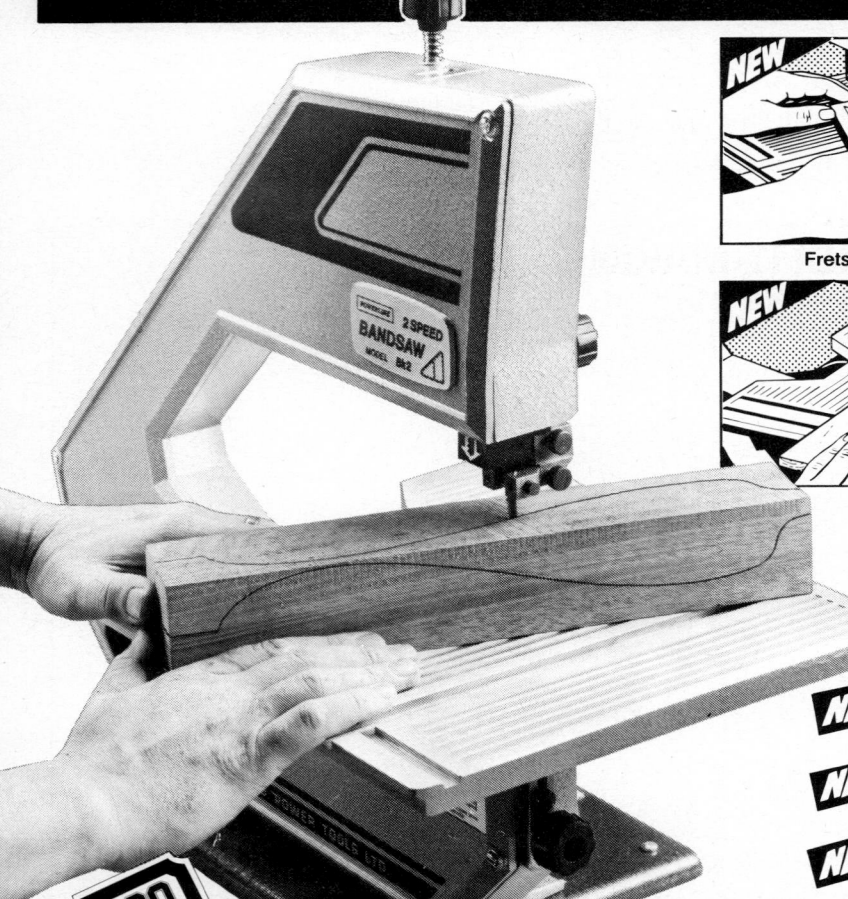

Prices quoted are those prevailing at press date and are subject to alteration due to economic conditions.

HERE ARE THE STOCKISTS....

AVON
Membery Bladwell Ltd. Tel: 0225 27661
Pan Tools Tel: 0272 664717
Avon Tool Centre Tel: 0272 298947
Gardiner & Son Ltd. Tel: 0272 20011
Philpott & Cowlin Ltd. Tel: 0272 668431
Woodberry Chilcott & Co. Ltd. Tel: 0272 770407

BEDFORDSHIRE
Cooks of Bedford Tel: 0234 52932
Gibbs & Dandy Ltd.
Tel: 0234 63131/0582 63421/0582 21233
Golding & Co. Ltd. Tel: 0234 52321
Gelmic Partners Ltd. Tel: 0582 31371

BERKSHIRE
Southern Sail Planes Tel: 0488 71399
House of Toomer Tel: 0635 42100
Sarjents Tool Stores Tel: 0734 586 522
Rabbitt & Son Ltd. Tel: 0753 23302/0753 23281
Tunes Engineering Supplies Ltd. Tel: 0753 22371/2
Frank Bush Ltd. Tel: 075 35 63837

BUCKINGHAMSHIRE
Jones & Cox Tel: 0296 88154
A. Pollard & Son Tel: 0908 75221
Isaac Lord Ltd. Tel: 0494 22221
Saffetts Tel: 024 04 2176
F. E. Chipperfield Ltd. Tel: 0908 73133
Odells Hardware Ltd. Tel: 0908 562146
Gardiner & Son, High Wycombe.

CAMBRIDGESHIRE
D. Mackay Tel: 0223 63132
E.J. Piggott Tel: 0223 352641
Porta Power (Hire or Buy) Tel: 0223 47386
Williams Distributors Tel: 0733 64252

CHESHIRE
Thomas & Willis Homecrafts Ltd. Tel: 0606 74879
Lawton Tools Ltd. Tel: 093 67 3336
Vicmores Ltd. Tel: 061-480 8623
C.J. Bent & Son Ltd. Tel: 0925 35466
Robert Kelly & Son Ltd. Tel: 051-709 5342
G. Tunstall Tel: 0270 21488
Blackshaw Bros. Ltd. Tel: 0625 22063

CLEVELAND
Charles Dickens Tools Tel: 0429 73134
Cleveland (DIY) Tel: 0642 219766
Kayes (Middlesbrough) Ltd. Tel: 0642 247972
The Building & Hardware Centre Tel: 0642 453861

CORNWALL
W.K. Bartlett Tel: 0326 313824
Northwest Power Tools Tel: 0326 54961
Liskeard Engineering Ltd., Liskeard.
Conway Supplies Tel: 0637 32516
Parkers of Penzance Tel: 0736 3882
Toolserv, St. Austell.
South West Power Tools Ltd., Launceston.

DERBYSHIRE
Kirby & Son Tel: 0246 70131
Bennetts Limited Tel: 0332 44261
Derby Co-op Society Ltd. Tel: 0332 40230
Hazlehursts Tel: 0332 41862

CUMBRIA
Burrows Tel: 0229 25412
Underwoods Ltd. Tel: 0229 20218
J. Albright Ltd. Tel: 0229 52029

DEVON
Styles & Brown Tel: 0297 33656
North Devon Tools Ltd. Tel: 02372 3513
Edwards & Drage Ltd. Tel: 0392 50761
The Handyman Tel: 039 55 3816
Wippell Bros. & Power Ltd. Tel: 0392 75048
John Wride & Co. Ltd. Tel: 0392 73936
Trago Mills Ltd. Tel: 062 682 461
F.T.B. Lawson Ltd. Tel: 0752 665363
John Hall Tools Ltd. Tel: 0752 705141
Totem Timber Ltd. Tel: 0752 266390
Westward Building Services Tel: 0752 330303
Power Tool Centre Tel: 08842 4108
Supersales Tel: 0803 862737
M.J. Dickson & Sons, Woodbury Salterton.
West Country Tool Co. Tel: 0626 6751/2
Wrides Tel: 0752 266179
A.R. Church Tel: 0364 52292

DORSET
Humphries Tool Stores Tel: 0308 22354
Castle & Son Ltd. Tel: 0202 484844
Megeet Machine Tools Tel: 0202 746011
Geo. Spiller, Sherbourne.
Bert Bolton Timber, Bridport.

DURHAM
King & Co. Ltd., Chester-le-Street.
Percy Stevenson & Son Tel: 0385 53511

ESSEX
Stewart & Co. Tel: 01-594 3535
Price & Woods Tel: 0277 220359
W.L. Cook Ltd., Chadwell Heath.
Corbin & Frost Tel: 0245 67333
George Farmer Tel: 0206 72930

ESSEX (Cont.)
F.G. Lang Ltd. Tel: 0375 4901
Southern Discount Stores
01-478 3738/0702 330309
Marshall & Parsons Tel: 0702 74867
G.A. Dunball Tel: 0708 24721

GLOUCESTERSHIRE
Sharpe & Fisher Ltd. Tel: 0242 21477
C. Gillman & Sons Ltd. Tel: 0285 3220
Fast Tools Ltd. Tel: 0452 29671
Jason Hire Tools Ltd. Tel: 0452 35010
Merrylees Pugh & Co. Ltd. Tel: 0452 24093
Merrylees Ltd., Stroud.

GUERNSEY
Channel Island Auto Spares Tel: Guernsey 23444
Leale Ltd. Tel: 0481 24774
Wholesale Supplies Tel: Guernsey 26573
Norman Piette Ltd. Tel: Guernsey 45801

HAMPSHIRE
Stephens & Johnson Tel: 0252 22345
Hampshire Bolt & Tool Supplies Tel: 0256 29781
Techno Trade Ltd. Tel: 0329 232495
Technosales Ltd., Farnborough.
Streets Tel: 0705 471516
T.J. Tools Tel: 0705 27431
Barron's Tools Tel: 0703 773343
John Hall Tools Ltd. Tel: 048 92 5277
S.E. Borrow Tel: 07014 4444

HEREFORD/WORCESTER
Hobbs of Ledbury Ltd. Tel: 0531 2976
Phillip Morris Tel: 0432 69501
Pen Tools Ltd. Tel: 0432 3018
W.E. Timmis & Son Tel: 0562 2392
Underwoods Tel: 0905 21454
Asperman Limited Tel: 06845 61167

HERTFORDSHIRE
Maslens Sales Ltd., Bishop's Stortford.
Charles Creig, Cheshunt.
T. Brooker & Son Ltd.
Tel: 0462 4501/046 26 6094
Roger's DIY Tel: 0462 4177
Chas. Love & Son Ltd., Knebworth.
Chiswick Supplies Tel: 0763 60493
S. Gomm Ltd. Tel: 0727 53236
Hobco Tool Co. Ltd. Tel: 0727 63311
Viva Tools Tel: 0727 61331
E.N. Mole & Co. Ltd. Tel: 0923 22648
Trident Machine Tools Ltd. Tel: 0923 34211
J. Simble & Son Tel: 0923 26052
Pond Tool Co. Tel: 070 73 27272
Homecare Centre Tel: 0923 48434

HUMBERSIDE
Pottage Bros. Tel: 0482 881395
Peter Tice Tel: 0377 43650
E.J. Elvin Tel: 0482 20586
T.S. Kaye & Son Tel: 0482 20731
J.H. Robinson Tel: 0482 27637
Waddington Tools Ltd. Tel: 0482 29356

JERSEY
The Iron Stores Tel: Jersey 23551
Jersey Tool Supplies Tel: Jersey 24520
B.G. Romeril Co. Ltd. Tel: Jersey (0534) 77788

KENT
Ashford Tool Centre Tel: 0233 23010
John Parker & Co. Ltd. Tel: 0227 66899
Alan G. Smith Ltd.
Tel: 0634 407824/0474 66817/0622 52286/
0634 44067/0795 75546
E. Jones & Son Tel: 0622 52286
J.N. Tool Sales Tel: 0843 585206
George Higgins Tel: 01-300 3161
A.E. King (Tools) Ltd. Tel: 01-300 7359
Bearstead Tool Supplies Tel: 0795 76400
Webbs Limited
Tel: 0795 24141/058 06 2132
S.E. Haward & Co. Tel: 0892 22224
Parry & Son Ltd. Tel: 0959 73777

LANCASHIRE
Atlas Trading Co. Tel: 061-330 3061
R.L. Jepson Ltd. Tel: 0245 59123
Mercer & Sons Tel: 0254 52701
J. Ardron & Son
Tel: 0254 21203/0253 36282
Chadwicks Tel: 0254 32559
Geo. W. Forbes Ltd. Tel: 0253 45225
Brabbin & Rudd Ltd.
Tel: 0204 21171/0942 42933
Sutcliffe Tools Tel: 0282 24308
T.W. Tyson Ltd. Tel: 061-764 4935
Wilcock & Sons Tel: 02572 2135
T. Grubb Ltd. Tel: 0524 63522
The Lile Tool Shop Tel: 0524 2886
J.H. Williamson Tel: 061-624 5441
Frank Warren Ltd. Tel: 061-624 1377
F.S. Newlands Tel: 0695 75377
Speedwell Tool Co. Ltd. Tel: 0772 52957
William Moore Ltd. Tel: 0772 796446
Robert Kelly & Co. Ltd. Tel: 0744 58672
Entwistle & Joynt Ltd. Tel: 0942 43081
G & V Meadow Tel: 045 752109
Seymour Wilson & Co. Ltd. Tel: 061-330 1553

LINCOLNSHIRE
Carr & Son Tel: 0205 64581
Hutson's Tel: 0205 62107
Collards Tel: 0476 3159
Smiths Tools Tel: 0476 4066
Jackson Shipley Ltd. Tel: 0522 30303
Musgraves Tel: 0522 27088
J.A. Arnold, 58-60 Lumley Road, Skegness.
J.E. Draper Ltd. Tel: 0754 3206

LEICESTERSHIRE
Randalls Tel: 0530 32433
Roy Startin Tel: 0455 43254
Charles Corts Tel: 0455 632004
A.K. Davey Tel: 0455 634288
Bettinsons Tel: 0533 832580
A. Oldham & Sons Ltd. Tel: 0533 58954
Pillar Eng. Supplies Tel: 0533 20401
Sankey Corts Tel: 0533 544666
Welford Ironmongers Tel: 0533 707018
H. Adey & Sons Ltd. Tel: 0509 212922
Loughborough DIY Tel: 0509 61451
H.E. Morgan Tel: 0509 212379
Tylers Tel: 0509 212560
Middleton Mail Order Tel: 0858 63502
Hiregiene Tel: 0664 4951

GREATER LONDON
G.T.R. Electric Tool Repair Tel: 07842 54396
A.E.A. Edwards Ltd., Eastcote.
Richardsons Ltd.
Tel: 01-890 4399/01-890 9946
Masterfix DIY Tel: 089 56 36776
Williams Tech. Services Ltd. Tel: 01-863 2492
A. Copley Ltd. Tel: 01-574 1313
K.R. Tools Tel: 0784 61225
W.A. Powell & Son Tel: 01-997 2181
Majacks Ltd., Uxbridge.
S.E. Borrow, Waterlooville.

W. LONDON
Geo. Buck Tel: 01-631 4191
Buck & Ryan Ltd. Tel: 01-636 7475
Burgess & Galar Ltd. Tel: 01-437 4989
Gould Hopkins & Purvis Tel: 01-437 3544
Selfridges Ltd. Tel: 01-629 1234
Dyno Electric Ltd., Acton.
A. Mills Ltd. Tel: 01-992 4835
Standard Wallpaper Co. Ltd., High Road, W.4.
Kays of Ealing Tel: 01-567 2387
G.D. Clegg Tel: 01-567 2922
Electrobuild Tools Ltd. Tel: 01-743 9892
Channon Tel: 01-242 8045

N. LONDON
E. Amette & Co. Tel: 01-837 3433
Heward & Dean Ltd. Tel: 01-800 3443
J.H. Martin & Son Ltd. Tel: 01-888 1147
H. Glickman Tel: 01-808 3308
S.G. Lee & Son Tel: 01-808 3267
Croydills Tel: 01-727 9360
Thomas Bros. Ltd. Tel: 01-272 2764
Tuck & Norris Tel: 01-889 4309
Flairline Supplies Ltd. Tel: 01-450 4844
R.P.M. Motor Acc. Ltd. Tel: 01-203 4407
Tool Supplies Ltd. Tel: 01-459 0043
Harrow Tool Co. Tel: 01-969 8237

S. LONDON
Miller, Childs & Zola Ltd. Tel: 01-928 6704
B. Stevenson Ltd., Boro' High Street, S.E.1.
Parker & Co. Ltd. Tel: 01-698 1445
A.D. Skillman & Son Tel: 01-854 7767
W. Hobby Ltd. Tel: 01-761 0428
I. Grizzard Tel: 01-385 5109
A. Gatto & Son Tel: 01-874 2671
John Hall Tools Tel: 01-542 6644

E. LONDON
C.W. Tyzack Ltd.
Tel: 01-739 7126/2630/8301
Clarkes Compressors Tel: 01-986 8231
C. Pattman & Co. Ltd. Tel: 01-472 4811/2
A.W. Phillips & Son Ltd. Tel: 01-472 0435
G.H. Chappell Ltd. (M/c Tools) Tel: 01-539 3500
Fred Blake (Metals) Ltd. Tel: 01-552 1221
J. Russell Eng. Supplies (Limehouse) Ltd.
Tel: 01-987 1423
Alexander Collins, Leytonstone Road, E.15.
Parry & Son Ltd. Tel: 01-739 9422
Houndsditch Warehouse Co. Ltd. Tel: 01-283 3131

GREATER MANCHESTER
Engineering Supplies Tel: 061-445 6570
Joseph Gleave & Sons Ltd. Tel: 061-236 1840
E.C. Hopkins Ltd. Tel: 061-834 7142
Robert Kelly & Co. Ltd. Tel: 061-832 9920
Timms for Tools Tel: 061-789 3764

MERSEYSIDE
R. Bernard Tel: 051-652 3136
Robert Kelly & Co. Ltd.
Tel: 051-709 5341/0744 58672
Taylor Bros. Ltd.
Tel: 051-263 1359/0704 32905
H.M. Hampson Tel: 0744 22271

NORFOLK
A.T. Johnson Tel: 0366 33407
Fakenham Hardware Stores Ltd. Tel: 0328 2044
Coopers (Gt. Yarmouth) Ltd. Tel: 0495 57539
Plowright, Pratt & Harbage Ltd., Kings Lynn.
R. Edmunds & Son Tel: 069 24 2113
Leach & Son (Norfolk) Ltd. Tel: 0603 20225

NORTHAMPTONSHIRE
T. Cunnington Tel: 05366 3160
Burtons Tel: 0536 2137
Dalkeith Ironmongers Tel: 0536 3761
Midland Power Tools Tel: 0604 33056
Rowland Hill Tel: 0604 38814
Peter Crisp Tel: 09334 56424
J. Rowlatt & Sons Ltd. Tel: 0933 222179

NORTHERN IRELAND
Hewitt & Robinson Tel: 08462 76161
Fobel DIY Centre, Portadown.
Lockes Tool Centre Tel: 0762 32546
Benny B Stuart Tel: 0365 4172
Duffs, Ballygawley.
General Merchants (Dungannon) Ltd. Tel: 08687 22469
Stockdales Tel: 066254 206

NOTTINGHAMSHIRE
Cromwell Tools Tel: 0602 223311
J & H Lacey Tel: 06076 5155
Blaker & Beely Tel: 0623 25667
Hameyer Copeland Tel: 0623 23340
B. Jephson (Mansfield) Ltd. Tel: 0623 26364
D. Arundel & Co. Tel: 0636 2382
C. Hall & Sons Ltd. Tel: 0602 46823
H. Hopkinson Tel: 0602 50377
Nottingham Co-op Society Ltd. Tel: 0602 581601
Pools Tools Tel: 0602 51212
Barry Jephson Tel: 062385 2812
R.A. Morgan, Worksop.
Charles Manson Tel: 0909 564021

OXFORDSHIRE
Hoods Limited Tel: 0295 2875
G.E. Dean & Son Ltd. Tel: 086 92 2463
Cotswold Hardware Factors Ltd. Tel: 0865 772582
Hopkins of Cowley Tel: 0865 778127
Selfridges Tel: 0865 44991
P.S. Whitman & Co., Wallingford.

SCOTLAND
James Syme & Co. Ltd., Falkirk.
Watt & Dewar Ltd. Tel: 0383 2416
Andrew Hutt Ltd. Tel: 0592 51057
Thomson Bros. Ltd. Tel: 0592 60055
Gibb's Tool Market Tel: 0224 51714
Hendersons (Schoolhill) Ltd. Tel: 0224 25543
Ken Kennedy Ltd. Tel: 0224 571603
Wm. McCormack Tel: 0343 2294
Duncan Forbes, Inverurie.
McDonalds Hardware Tel: 0349 2180
Inverness Tool Distributors Ltd.
Murrays Tool Stores
Tel: 031-229 1577/031-337 1400/031-667 3571
John Wilkinson (M&T) Ltd. Tel: 031-554 1641
Powercraft Ltd. Tel: 0292 68908
N.S. Catani Tel: 041-779 3311
E.C. Conroy Ltd. Tel: 041-429 0420
Crockett (The Ironmongers) Ltd. Tel: 041-332 1041
Colin M Grant Ltd. Tel: 041-336 8741
Wm. Young (Kilmarnock) Ltd. Tel: 0563 22408
George Coghill Tel: 041-889 2645
C.G. Oldfield Ltd. Tel: 041-889 4285
George Stephen Ltd. Tel: 0382 21246
Garvie & Syme Ltd. Tel: 0738 20601
Wm. Hume & Co. Ltd. Tel: 0738 26173

SHROPSHIRE
Herbert Tucker Tel: 0952 810002
Abbey Hardware Tel: 0743 3930
R.B. Richards & Sons Tel: 0743 52931/53225
Hughes & Holmes Tel: 0952 586171

SOMERSET
Somerset Hire Services, Street.
Morrison Tool Co. Tel: 0823 3224
Servu of Yeovil Tel: 02013 3191

STAFFORDSHIRE
Harlow's Tel: 0283 68148
Jones & Clark Tel: 0283 67881/2
Charles Linford Ltd.
Tel: 05435 3118/3618
Skinner & Son Tel: 0538 383315
Skinner (Ironmongers)
Bickleys Tel: 0782 616576
The Handiman Tel: 0785 52707
Jaton Tel: 0782 262441
Granthorne Timber Tel: 0782 88601

SUFFOLK
Andrews & Plumpton Tel: 0284 3967
Ridley & Hooper Ltd. Tel: 0284 2864
Tools & Things Tel: 0284 62022
Martin & Newby Tel: 0473 54447
R.J. Bryce & Co., Lowestoft.

SURREY
Dalfords (London) Ltd. Tel: 093 28 66841
Turtles Tel: 01-688 5513
V. Messinger & Son Ltd. Tel: 0483 61125
Kingston Tools Ltd. Tel: 01-546 4634
Thames Tools Tel: 01-979 7272

EAST SUSSEX
Aird & Co. Tel: 0273 27191
County Tools Tel: 0273 686091
G.H. Elliott Tel: 0273 63478
Thorcraft Tel: 0424 3072
Louis G. Ford Ltd. Tel: 0273 71261
County Hardware Tel: 0323 894783

WEST SUSSEX
A. Olby & Son Ltd. Tel: 0243 3100
S. Hammond & Son Tel: 04446 3244
David Messam Tel: 0243 787829
Crawley Tools Tel: 0293 24011
W. Hoskins Tel: 0903 38793

TYNE AND WEAR
Ian Gloag DIY Stores Tel: 0670 4878
Henry Osborn Ltd. Tel: 0632 23881
Pringles Tel: 0632 72365
G.T. Robson Tel: 0632 520202
Handimans Tel: 06706 2953

WALES
Lightfoots Tel: 0745 31564
Thomas Nicholas Ltd. Tel: 05542 3181
Bridgend Ironmongery Ltd. Tel: 0656 56151
Tool Centre (F.J. Nuttall)
Tel: 0873 6329/063 33 5771
J.S. Harrison & Son Tel: 0495 303215
Handiman Tel: 049 55 2796
James Payne Tel: 0492 76705
Pontypridd Builders Supply Tel: 0443 404341
Buck & Hickman Ltd. Tel: 0222 594812
John Hall Tools Ltd.
Tel: 0222 22242/0222 22246
Ryall & Walters Tel: 0222 31367
Woodmen Ltd. Tel: 0222 36519
Swansea Timber & Plywood Tel: 0792 55680
Kittle Hardware Tel: 044 18 2508

WARWICKSHIRE
Home Handiman Tel: 0789 2450
Alberts (Leamington) Ltd. Tel: 0926 23043
A.H. Russell (DIY Centre) Tel: 0926 22940
H.C. Porter Tel: 0203 382564
H.S. Gare Tel: 888 4216
Moores Handicrafts Tel: 888 4065
E. Lacey & Son Ltd. Tel: 0789 292670
A.B. Wylie Tel: 0926 42470

WEST MIDLANDS
Paintain Tools Tel: 021-706 5545
W. Pond & Co. Ltd. Tel: 021-236 6871
W.H. Price Tel: 021-359 4282
Stirchley Tools & Ironmongery Tel: 021-458 1593
Thomas Sutton Tel: 021-236 7139
Bobs Models Ltd. Tel: 021-772 4917
Webb's Power Tools Ltd. Tel: 021-495 1561
Matterson, Huxley & Watson Tel: 0203 24081
H.E. Phillips Tel: 0203 27091
Gordon Richards Tools Tel: 0203 26034
H. Case (Hardware) Ltd. Tel: 0384 69922
The Tool Shed Tel: 0384 62862
H.L. Owen Tel: 021-705 1058
John Smallman Tel: 038 482 5641
G.J. Dodd Tel: 021-354 2045
Hughes & Holmes Ltd.
021-557 7174/0922 25266/0902 773851
James Lister & Son Ltd. Tel: 021-553 2411
Howard Lugg Tel: 021-556 1551
Edward Parry Ltd. Tel: 0902 773851

WILTSHIRE
C.M.A. (Calne) Ltd. Tel: 0249 812864
Sarjents Tool Stores Ltd. Tel: 0793 31361

SOUTH YORKSHIRE
David New Tools Tel: 0302 60412
C. Denham (Rotherham) Ltd. Tel: 0709 2236
Turner Hire & Sales Tel: 0709 73725
J.T. Chadwick Ltd. Tel: 0742 28702
Gregory Taylor Ltd. Tel: 0742 41012
K.W. Hawley (Tools) Ltd. Tel: 0742 77121
Heeley Tools Tel: 0742 52491

NORTH YORKSHIRE
Bedale Hardware & Building Tel: 0677 3593
The Harrogate DIY Centre Tel: 0423 67938
Northallerton Hardware Tel: 0609 4289
Rodbers of Richmond Ltd. Tel: 0748 2491
Sagars Ltd. Tel: 0723 60770
Barnitts Ltd. Tel: 0904 25601

WEST YORKSHIRE
Dixon Hall & Co. Ltd. Tel: 0924 476166
H. Ellis & Sons Tel: 0274 24989
Thomas Wright Ltd. Tel: 0274 663471
Charles Watson Ltd. Tel: 0422 63056
James Wilson & Co. Tel: 0422 53935
Gregory & Sutcliffe Ltd. Tel: 0484 40311
Timothy Wood Ltd. Tel: 0484 32101
R.W. Morten Ltd. Tel: 0943 609131
John V. Laycock Ltd. Tel: 0535 602299
Geo. Spence & Sons Ltd. Tel: 0532 709507
D.B. Keighley Machinery Ltd. Tel: 0532 574736
G.M. Eastwood Ltd. Tel: 0924 73588

Simple Reliable

There's a lot of talk these days about revolutionary, highly sophisticated woodworking machinery – the new, low cost, over complicated little wonders that do almost everything – providing of course you're a keen engineering student with more than a lot of time on your hands.

Well – no one ever said Kity machines were sophisticated or revolutionary – and we're proud of it – in fact we designed and built them to be simple, reliable and easy to use. You don't have to change your woodworking methods or be an engineer, Kity simply adds power and precision to develop your own skills – and sometimes even your bank balance.

Recently Barrie and Lynne Goddard of Bottesford, near Scunthorpe, decided to improve their kitchen. The going rate for the job, from a professional contractor, was around £5,000; however with Kity machinery to help him, Barrie built their dream kitchen for just £2,000.

Ideas can now become reality

All of us at some time have had to scrap excellent creative ideas because we couldn't afford to bring in the professionals and didn't have sufficient expertise to carry them out ourselves. The simplicity of Kity machinery has gone a long way towards removing this frustration and our illustrated instruction sheets will explain step by step the machine techniques needed to transform your ideas into superb reality.

Common base for all functions.

The K5 has units for separate machine functions mounted on a common base and driven by a centrally mounted power unit – the K5 motor. You have all the versatility of separately mounted machines, any change of operation becomes simplicity itself. Just connect the belt to the machine you want to use, adjusting the tension easily by means of a simple, quick release lever. Without losing your pre-set adjustments, you can change from one function to another in a matter of seconds. Continuity of work is thus assured.

K5 international woodworker

– complete power workshop for only **£559**
(plus VAT. £83.85)

Engineering specification

Circular saw.
180mm (7″) blade normally fitted but will accept a 200mm (8″) blade giving a 57mm (2¼″) depth of cut. 2 speeds, 3750 for normal wood and 6200 r.p.m. for laminated boards. Complete with rip fence, mitre guide, repeat cut length stop, wobble washers for grooving, tilting table 0.45°.

Surface planer.
700mm (27½″) long × 200mm (8″) wide cast bed. Maximum planing width 150mm (6″). Adjustable 90° – 45° fence for bevel planing. Dynamically balanced cutter block rotating at 11,400 cuts per minute.

Thickness planer.
Fully automatic feed, 7.5m (24′) per minute. Maximum capacity 100mm (4″) deep, 150mm (6″) wide. Anti kick-back fingers, calibrated scale.

Spindle moulder
6400 rpm shaft speed. 45mm (1¾″) vertical adjustment. Capable of taking 25mm (1″) × 25mm (1″) rebate in one pass. Accepts both French moulding profiles and white hill type blocks.

Slot mortiser
Rise/fall table with 100mm (4″) of adjustment.

Maximum bit diameter 12mm (½″). Produces accurate mortises, also horizontal boring for perfect dowel joints.

2 year guarantee

When you buy a K5, you will be protected against all manufacturing defects (parts and labour) for the first two years after purchase, no matter how hard you work your machine.

The Kity Heavy Duty Range

Arthur is a highly skilled, traditional craftsman who uses the Kity Heavy Duty Range, ideal machinery for the busy modern craftsmen. By purchasing a mixture of independent and combination machines he built a superb workshop that exactly suited his requirements and his pocket. Arthur says... "It's amazing how some woodworkers still use old fashioned methods that belong in the Dark Ages. Mind you – I ought not to criticize them I used to be the same, I was proud to work like my Grandfather did and I believed the results would be better if everything was done by hand. It never occurred to me he had no alternative – and in any case, I always thought machines were complicated and some how difficult to use. Anyhow, I soon found out how wrong I was when I started using Kity machinery. I got better results in a fraction of the time and with very little physical effort. There's no doubt in my mind that Kity machinery is simple and very easy to use – and sure, it makes makes me money."

Kity offers you Heavy Duty Circular Saws, Bandsaws, Planer Thicknessers, Spindle Moulders and Slot Mortisers, along with a complete range of accessories, motors and floor stands. Each machine can be independent or part of a combination for example: you can start your workshop with a circular saw. With Kity you don't have a lot of complicated attachments, nor do you have to swing the machine into different positions or use a special tool. Simply slip the belt from one machine to the next.

The Circular Saw 617

This is the heart of most workshops. The Kity machine has a cast and machined, tilting work table; a rise/fall arbor with hand wheel control; it accepts blades up to 9″ in diameter giving a 3⅛″

Prices quoted are those prevailing at press date and are subject to alteration due to economic conditions.

and ^(very) easy to use

depth of cut; and is capable of running at two speeds; 3400 rpm and 7000 rpm. It is powered by a 1½ H.P. motor with No Volt Thermal Overload Starter. You will have no difficulty in cutting any wood based material, from melamine faced chipboard to African hardwoods.

Accessories included in the price are the mitre-guide with repeat cut stop, and wobble washers for grooving. The machine is guarded to comply with international standards.

The Planer Thicknessers 535, 635, 636

Kity manufacture three 'under and over' planer/thicknessers, a 10″ × 6″, 8″ × 6″ and a 6″ × 4″.

Each machine is available with stand and motor and can be used as an independent unit or will fit as part of the combination.

Each machine has cast tables and a twin knife cutter block and is of the 'under and over' type. The thicknesser is power fed with an adjustable thicknessing table giving true results along the whole length of the timber; this is usually difficult to achieve with the 'over fed' clamp type thicknesser. The 636 and 635 both have unusually long (40″) surfacing tables ideal for straightening a twist in a plank of timber.

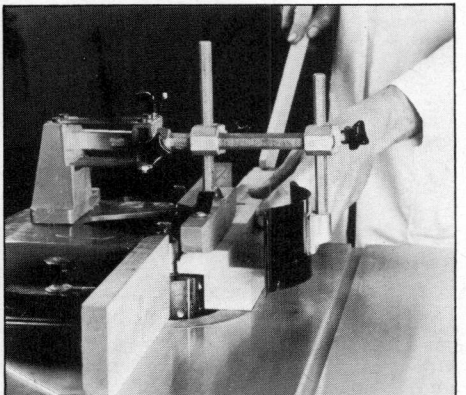

Spindle Moulders 626/627

The Spindle Moulder is a versatile and powerful tool. It does a totally different job to a router, although the system is similar. For example: — The 626 and 627 are capable of making large rebates 1¼″ × 1¼″ in hundreds of feet of timber. They will also produce moulding, deep grooves, tongue and groove joints, V-joints, tenons, profiles and counter profiles.

The 626 has a standard adjustable fence with the capability of positioning the cutting tools over a 4″ vertical range. The 627 has the same specifications but with individual micro adjustable fences. Both machines have cutting speeds of 7000 rpm, and are guarded to full international standards.

The 625 Slot Mortiser

The only machine in the whole range that is *not* available as an independent machine.

Working from the 700 table it will provide a ½″ slot, up to 5″ long and 4″ deep. An excellent machine for mortise joint production.

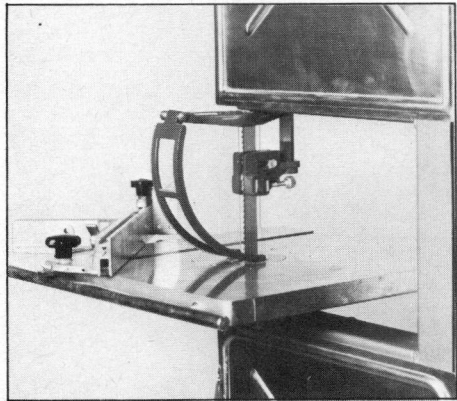

The 612 Bandsaw

Kity make an all steel, two wheel, Bandsaw with a 5½″ depth of cut and an 11½″ throat. It will accept blades from ¼″ for tight turns to ⅞″ for deep cutting and planking of timber. Unlike 'Plastic' Bandsaws the steel construction of the Kity machine allows you to set a high blade tension. This enables you to cut fast and in a straight line through hardwood and knots with a maximum depth of 5½″.

Kity Plan Sheets

These are issued for a nominal charge exclusively to Kity users and titles include, fitted kitchens and furniture. These practical plan sheets include cutting lists and complete manufacturing instructions on the relevant subject.

Nation-wide Service

Kity have 150 fully trained stockists throughout the U.K. and they provide a service second to none – there'll be one near you, ask for a demonstration, before you buy.

If you have a dream project you want to build or if you're a busy craftsman then you need Kity – simple, reliable and easy to use machinery.

Instructions on machines

Each Kity machine has comprehensive instructions to ensure you have the knowledge to use the machine correctly.

2 year Guarantee

Woodworker Show

STAND 74

END OF HALL

The urge to have a go

Above: W. C. Ross who had ten entries in the carving classes was a centre of interest as he carved a Waterloo piece during the show. Below: The Record Ridgway stand in the lecture theatre provided a wealth of information on the sharpening and maintenance of tools. *(Photos H. C. King)*

H. C. King reporting on Woodworker Show 1981 comments: 'Visitors were entertained, educated, convinced that it is all worthwhile. They were presented with displays, demonstrations and inspiration. They had opportunities to buy and to discuss their wants and problems – and lots more.'

The word Show is variously defined as 'to inspire'; 'to teach or demonstrate'; 'to prove'; 'a display of abilities'; and 'a display of excellence'. Woodworker Show 1981 fulfilled all those definitions admirably as I found during the two happy and interesting days I spent at the event. The reputation of previous Shows had obviously been noised abroad as, I am informed by the organiser, visitors during the six days this year totalled nearly 13 000, an increase of 22% over 1980.

Among the visitors were three generations of woodworkers as well as a number of novices, the latter anxious to learn about the craft. The many very experienced woodworkers were ever ready to give advice and urge others to have a go. Interested spectators were there too being, I am sure, more than interested before they left.

A good percentage of visitors were ladies not only admiring the competition entries, but visiting the trade stands. There they were even urging their menfolk to spend money! However, one lady hearing a salesman extolling to her husband the virtues and the many uses of a power drill, commented: 'Very nice, but can it clear up the mess he makes?'

Whatever their urge to see the rest of the Show, most of the visitors went straight to the displays of competition entries. What an education and inspiration to see the work of other people including some by ladies, and to compare or, more often, to contrast it with our own efforts. There was certainly no drop in quality or variety in this year's entry of 172 pieces.

In the cabinetmaking class P. J. Bennett's chest-of-drawers decorated with a rose pattern marquetry was a superb achievement and fully merited first prize and the Robbins rose bowl. It was in the white and looked lovely as it was. The judges gave the same marks to Brian Bostock's magnificent lady's table-mounted workbox. This entry was in yew and rosewood, and the two woods had been used very cleverly to give a striking effect. The workmanship, too, was of extremely high calibre. Mr Bennett and Mr Bostock share the top award in consequence.

The woodcarving classes produced 40 entries and in general the quality matched up to the quantity. In the architectural carving section a precise, crisply-carved ash scroll, with the legend 'Home Sweet Home' won first prize and the Henry Taylor award for Ralph Fellows.

One of W. C. Ross's 10 entries, his panel 'Household Cavalry', was placed second. This was a realistic relief plaque with an amazing amount of detail but carved with a minimum of tools. In the figure carving section (14 entries) 'Dance Fantasy' by A. Axon was a masterpiece. It was full of movement and beautifully carved. From a very wide range of subjects, N. K. Lamb's 'Gorilla' was no surprise. Its excellent carving, its portrayal of strength and its anatomical perfection won for him the second prize. 'Lakeside Tableau' in the relief carving section was a beautiful symbolic work on the title's theme of flowers, a bird etc. The carving and the interpretation were both so good that it won first prize for E. Smith. A close second was R. J. Smith's wall plaque.

Woodturning classes produced 41 entries and a first-rate display of turning to prove to visitors just what can be done on the lathe. Out of that collection, by far the best was a yew fruit bowl made from six smaller bowls. With it T. A. Marsh won first prize in the segmental turning section and the Henry Taylor award. The small bowls had been cut in half vertically and used around a central turned base to form scalloped sides of a large bowl. The turning and assembling were well-nigh perfect. The same worker continued in the prize list by taking a second with his yew fruit bowl with rosewood and sycamore lines.

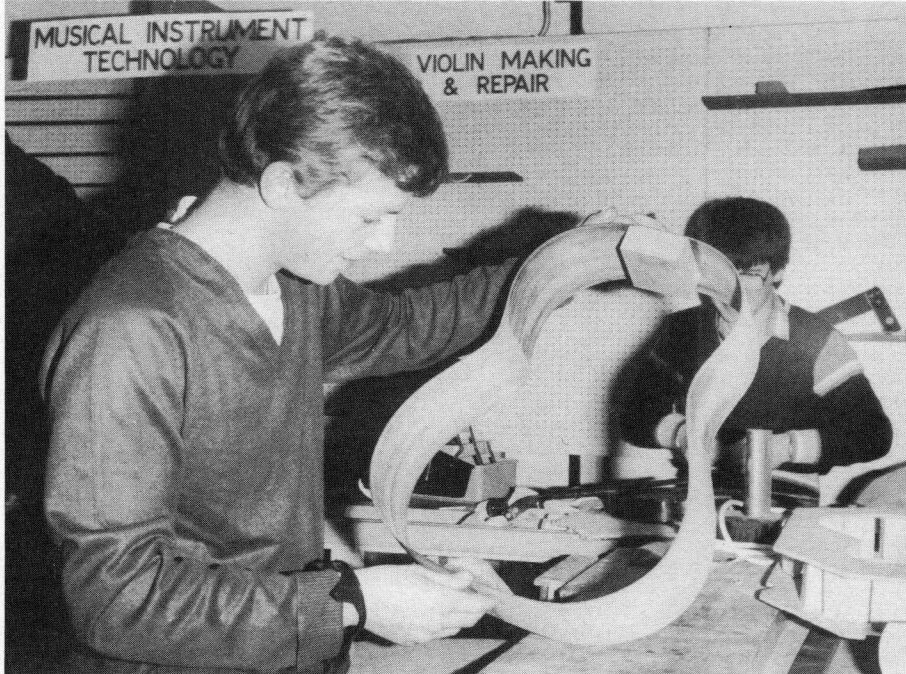

For spindle turning R. Wilson had made a lovely set of lace bobbins with which he won first prize. The second place was given to J. Milsom for an unusual yet very pleasing 'family' of turned sculptures. T. A. Marsh continued his successes by winning first and second prizes for faceplate turning. His dish of yew topped the list and an American black walnut fruit stand came second. Altogether Mr Marsh scored four prizes and the best of the class award. Is this a record?

In the musical instrument classes no wind instruments were entered but out of the 10 submissions in the stringed section, B. Meadows won first prize and the Woodworker challenge cup with a beautiful acoustic jazz guitar. G. B. Britten took second place with his violin inlaid with ebony and ivory. Visitors had no opportunity to hear them played and I wondered to what extent the inlaying on the violin affected the tone.

Above: Throughout the show Merton Technical College gave demonstrations of the making and repair of musical instruments. (Photo H. C. King)

Junior staff on the Roger's stand demonstrate the ease of use and safety of a Burgess bandsaw. (Photo H. C. King)

Marquetry and inlay classes offered some wonderful work. The World of Wood cup and first prize went to F. Taylor for 'Cable Car', a masterpiece of the art, while 'Woodcutters' was a worthy second for W. A. Spinks. 'Relativity' by J. E. M. Limpus showed skilful use of the grain of the wood.

In the class for miniature marquetry pictures there were only two entries but the winning piece was a little gem entitled 'Market Place, St Albans' by F. Taylor. The pictorial or geometric decorative veneering or parquetry section had only four entries from two workers. The section title took so long to read that perhaps there was no time left to produce other entries? One of O. D. Standen's three submissions (circular rosewood box) was placed first. It was decorated with an intricate design excellently done in exotics.

The toy class was topped by R. Cummings with a well-designed and skilfully-made rocking horse with which he also won the Brian Bowman trophy. On the strength of his success, he is now making rocking-horses on a professional basis.

Some wonderful work was to be seen in the model horse-drawn vehicle class. In spite of strong competition, N. M. Foxall's Oxfordshire waggon gained a worthy first place and the John Thompson trophy, and T. J. Spires took second also with an Oxfordshire waggon. One of the judges in this class was A. J. Lown, persistent winner of prizes and trophies at previous Shows. He had been asked to display some of his work as examples of perfection.

The junior class was very interesting and ranged through several branches of woodwork. D. A. Smith had made a first-rate jewellery box in walnut with which he won the first prize and the Woodworker challenge cup. A pleasing and well-made tripod table scored second place for R. J. Vinall, last year's class winner.

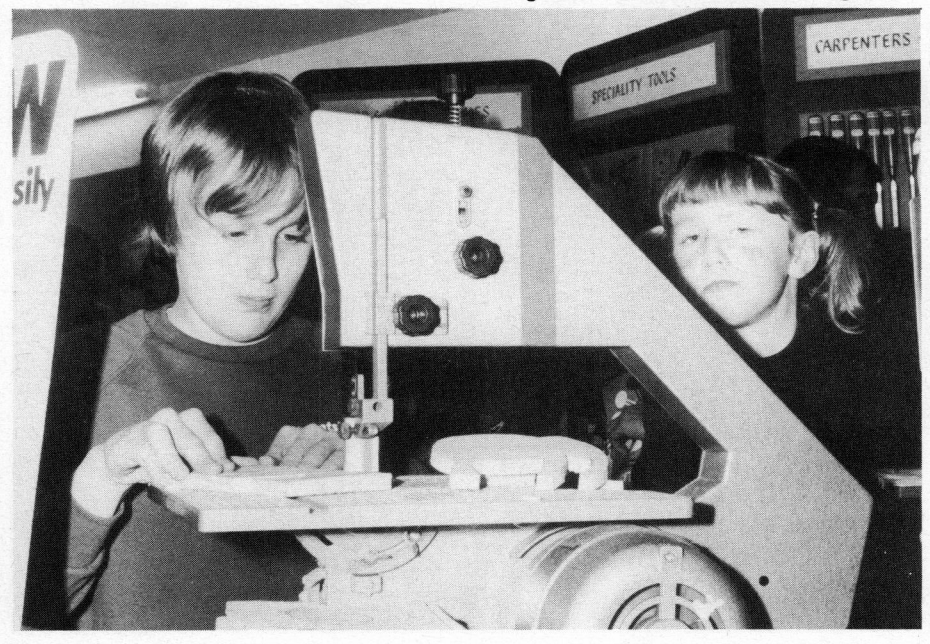

Of the longcase clocks, M. Sullivan's Vienna clock was a masterpiece of construction and finish – a lovely piece and worthy of the first prize. M. Lund won the second prize in this class with his mahogany wall clock. The same worker also won a first and the Woodworker challenge cup in the bracket clock class. His entry, surmounted by twin eagles expertly carved, was a most outstanding case.

Although the Ashley Iles-WOODWORKER International carving competition is separate from the Show classes, the entries were on display. Ashley Iles gave a Westminster set of 18 carving tools valued at £80 as the prize. The theme for the competition was 'Four Legs'. M. Lund was the winner with his beautifully detailed carving of a dog. The posture and anatomy of the animal were extremely good. The second place was

Daily draw winners

In the Nobex-a-day-free, the draw organised at the Show by C. D. Monninger Ltd, Overbury Road, London N15 6RJ, the following received prizes of Nobex mitre saws: J. Hobbs, Draycott, Derbyshire; M. Fielding, Gressenhall, Norfolk; M. Hunt, London W11; P. Greenall, Hayes, Kent; J. H. Davey, Newlyn, Cornwall; R. W. Bond, Harold Hill, Essex.

The draw was made at 4.30pm on the Monninger stand each day.

taken by C. Yeagan from San Diego, California, with his 'Female Centaur'.

Before doing the rounds of the trade stands it was well worth while seeing W. C. Ross, one of the carving winners, demonstrating his technique of carving with a minimum of tools. On the stands, too, there were several novel items. One junior and two very juvenile 'assistants' were boldly badged 'technical advisers'. Two of them

Craft show

One of the biggest specialist craft exhibitions to be held in the midlands will be the Model, Craft & Country Show, at the Royal Agricultural Society of England ground, Stoneleigh, Warwickshire, on 22 and 23 May. Within the Show will be a woodworking display in the Tate & Lyle hall.

The Show is a multi-purpose event for the entire family. Each hall will feature a different aspect of various crafts and model-making.

Visitors will be able to choose the halls they want to visit and select the many demonstrations of woodworking and specialist crafts taking place throughout the RASE complex.

The Model, Craft & Country Show is a joint venture by the Royal Agricultural Society of England and Model & Allied Publications Ltd which publishes WOODWORKER and a large number of modelling and craft magazines.

The Show at Stoneleigh will be supported by a programme of lectures and films on many aspects of woodworking and craft activities.

Car parking is free and entry is £2 for adults and £1 for children and OAPs — members of Guild of Woodworkers qualify for concessionary rates. There are restaurants and snackbars and, of course, the Stoneleigh ground is ideal for picnics.

were demonstrating a bandsaw quite competently. On the same stand more of Ian Norbury's fine carvings were displayed. These are a range of characters from *Alice in Wonderland*. Ian is from the White Knight Gallery, Cheltenham.

There were more timber and veneer firms at the 1981 Show. E. C. Young had a very good display in the lecture area. I remember the high-quality of the material when I

Above: The Jabberwock by Ian Norbury of the White Knight Gallery, Cheltenham (Photo Gloucester Photographic Agency). Below: General view (Photo Bill Gates)

bought from the firm half a century ago. The Timber Purchasing Pool offered a valuable service by buying in bulk and selling in small quantities to members of the pool. Aaronson showed a magnificent array of veneers.

For the professional and semi-professional there were machines galore while other firms catered for the home workshop. Hand tools were there in hundreds. Neither were finishes forgotten. One stand had a full range of everything one could wish for in the way of stains, fillers and polishes. Charles Greville had a spark-

ling display of clock movements and fittings.

There were many machinery stands. Woodmen showed its popular Luna W59, Hitachi the new U210 and Emco the D85 lathe with full copying facilities. Kity had a full range of machines as did Sumaco. The latter created a great deal of interest with its Gamma router. Alan Holtham was there with lathes, tools and timber. The range of trade stands indicated how wide is the readership of WOODWORKER in craft circles both professional and amateur, and in woodworking business too.

The lecture theatre upstairs was a popular educational centre. Record Ridgeway concentrated on tool maintenance and did it very well with demonstrations, frequent lectures and a video programme. Merton Technical College put on a demonstration of muscial instrument making and repair. Rycotewood College showed what its students could do while Shrewsbury College offered a display of photographs of work.

Clock kits

Classic Clocks (Clerkenwell) Ltd, Jerusalem Passage, St Johns Square, London EC1V 4JP, showed clock movement kits for assembly. The movements come in two forms: one having all components fully machined, polished and lacquered ready to assemble. The other requiring some filing of the plates and polishing and lacquering to be done by the buyer. For the simpler types of movement, kits of materials and drawings are available.

Skeleton clock kit, fully machined, requiring no special skills for assembly, from Classic Clocks.

Kits include a single-fusee version for bracket or wall clock, a skeleton movement, one for a long caseclock and a Congreve rolling-ball type. All kits are from antique designs. An associate firm offers kits of wood and mouldings to make cases in black walnut.

Trade reaction

Trade exhibitors reported satisfactory business at the 1981 Show. One maker of hand tools said his orders were up by about 40% on the 1980 event; another supplier of equipment had done more than £4000-worth of business. 'A significant increase,' was the comment of John Farrar, managing director of Rawdon Machine Sales Ltd, Yeadon, Leeds, which imports Kity woodworking machinery. 'We had two stands at the Show,' said Mr Farrar and our sales were the best for the past three years. Not only did we sell – on the Saturday alone over 20 of the K5 International Power Workshops were purchased – but we took a large number of inquiries from which we confidently expect further sales.'

Above and left: joint winners of the Robbins rose bowl for cabinetmaking, chest by P. J. Bennett and needlework box and table by Brian Bostock. (Photos Bill Gates)

Results of Competitions

WA1 (Cabinetmaking-furniture) joint 1st and Robbins rose bowl (chest of drawers with rose pattern marquetry base open William and Mary design) P. J. Bennett, Chislehurst (lady's workbox on a table in yew and rosewood), B. L. Bostock, London; 3rd equal (carved spinning stool in mahogany) A. K. Broderick, Bedford (carved oak chest), F. N. Snowden, Chelmsford.

WB1 (Woodcarving-architectural) 1st and Henry Taylor award (scroll carved from ash Home sweet home) R. G. Fellows, Dudley; 2nd (carved panel-Household Cavalry) W. C. Ross, London; 3rd (carved fire surround in pine) R. W. Holman, Sevenoaks.

WB2 (Woodcarving-figure carving) 1st (dance fantasy) A. Axon, Bexley; 2nd (gorilla) N. K. Lamb, Oxford; 3rd (old tramp) A. F. Flanaghan, Leicester.

WB3 (Woodcarving-relief) 1st (Lakeside tableau) E. Smith, Warlingham; 2nd (wall plaque) R. J. K. Smith, Fleet; 3rd (brute strength) E. C. McGuire, East Malling.

WC1 (Woodturning-spindle turning) 1st (set of lace bobbins) R. Wilson, Gravesend; 2nd (examples of turned sculpture-family group) J. Milsom, Honiton; 3rd (pair of candlesticks) D. White, West Drayton.

WC2 (Woodturning-faceplate turning) 1st (dish made of yew) T. A. Marsh, Brighton; 2nd (American black walnut fruit stand) T. A. Marsh, Brighton; 3rd (large circular box on centre stem) R. G. Fellows, Dudley.

WC3 (Woodturning-segmental turning) 1st and Henry Taylor award (yew fruit bowl made from six smaller bowls) T. A. Marsh, Brighton; 2nd (yew fruit bowl made with rosewood and sycamore lines) T. A. Marsh, Brighton; 3rd (circular urn with lid) R. G. Fellows, Dudley.

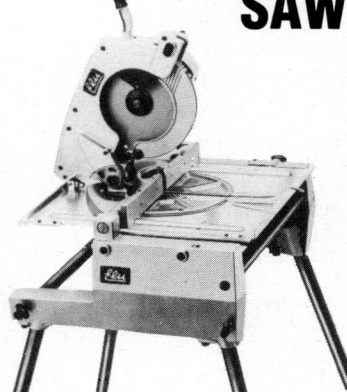

WD2 (Musical instruments-string) 1st and Woodworker challenge cup (acoustic jazz guitar) B. Meadows, Lewisham; 2nd (violin inlaid with ivory and ebony) D. G. Britten, Northampton; 3rd (guitar, steel string acoustic) N. J. Clarke, Stevenage.

WD3 (Musical instruments-accessories) 1st (viola bow) J. H. Maw, Denham.

WE1 (Marquetry and inlay) 1st and World of Wood cup (The cable car) F. Taylor, St Albans; 2nd (The Woodcutters) W. A. Spinks, Worcester Park; 3rd (Relativity) J. E. M. Limpus, Esher.

WE2 (Marquetry and inlay-miniature) 1st (Market Place, St Albans) F. Taylor, St Albans.

WE4 (Marquetry and inlay-pictorial or geometric decorative veneering or parquetry) 1st (circular rosewood box) O. D. Standen, Beckenham.

WF (Toys and miniatures) 1st and Brian Bowman trophy (rocking horse) R. Cummings, Liverpool.

WG1 (Model horse drawn vehicles – farm cart or waggon or agricultural implement, drawn by horses or for industrial purposes such as brewer's dray) 1st and John Thompson trophy (Oxfordshire waggon) N. M. Foxall, Oxford; 2nd (Oxfordshire waggon) T. J. Spires, Maldon; VHC (South Lincolnshire waggon) B. J. Smith, Colchester; HC (log waggon) W. A. Rothwell, Southport; C (Devon chest waggon circ. 1891) A. W. Martin, Worcester.

Below: W. C. Ross carved this panel of the Household Cavalry which won second prize in the architectural section of the carving classes. Right: this table won a second prize in the junior section for R. J. Vinall (*Photos Bill Gates*).

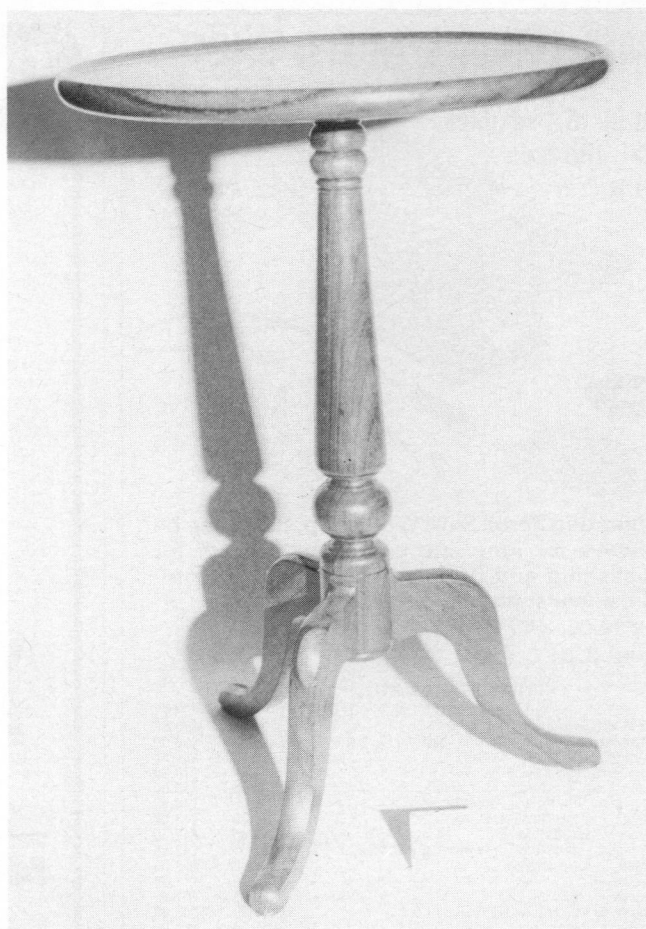

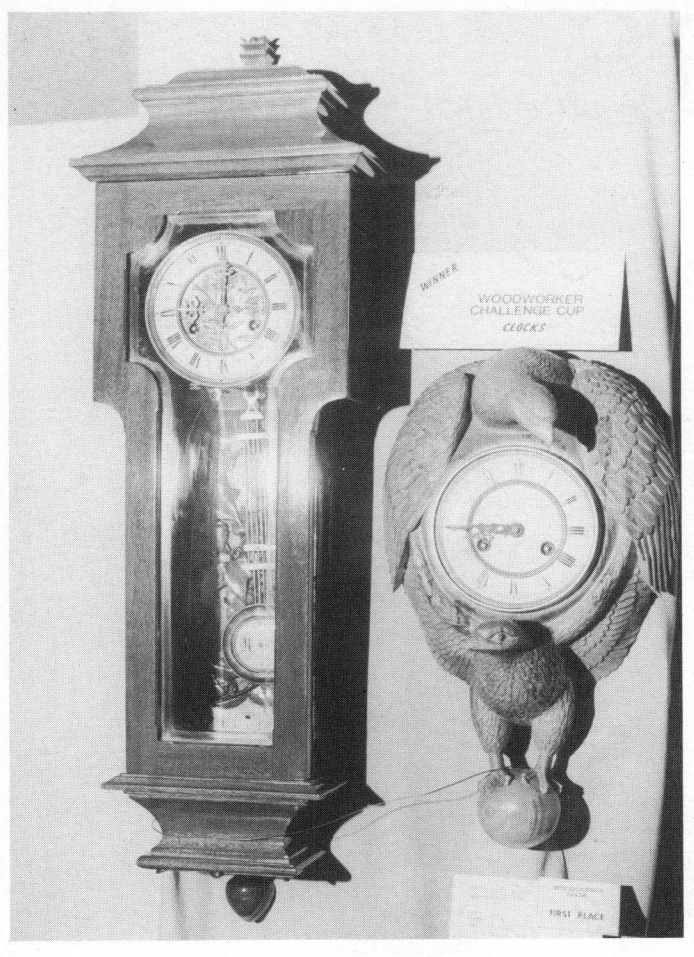

Above left: two of the clocks entered in this year's competition including Mr Lund's winning entry. Above right: Ralph Fellows won the Henry Taylor award and first in the woodcarving section with this immaculate incised scroll. (Photos Bill Gates)

Right: Matt Sullivan's clock that took the first prize in the longcase section of the clock competition. (Photo Bill Gates)

FOUR LEGS

▶ **2**

◀ **7**

◀ **8**

◀**11**

▼**12**

9
▶

10▼

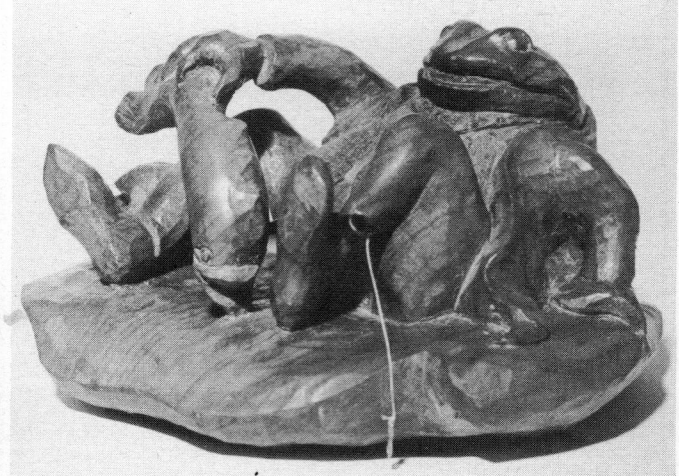

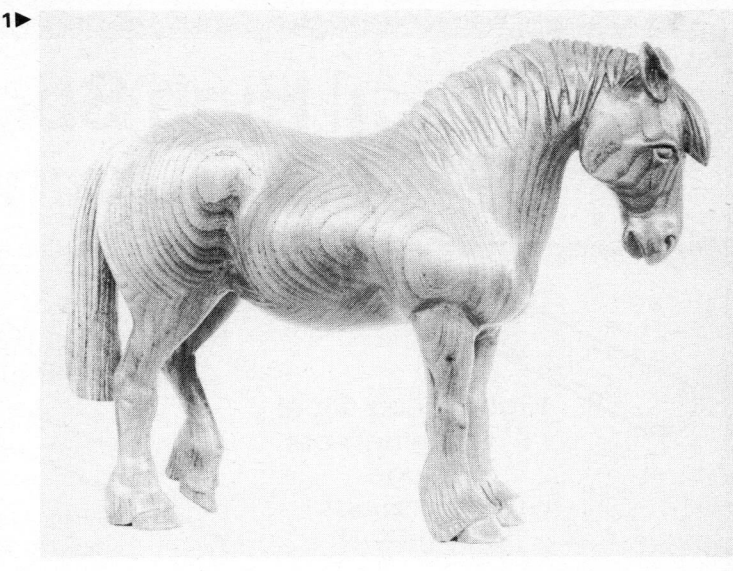

1▶

◀3

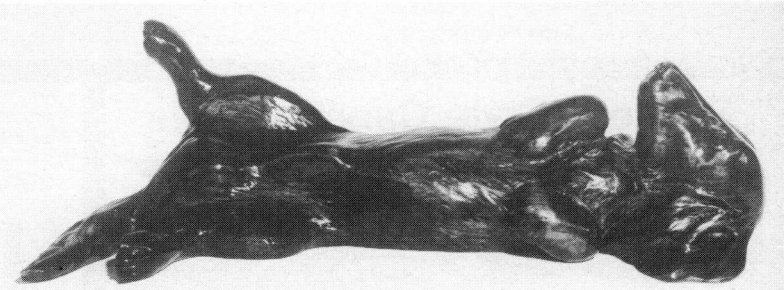

◀4

5▲

▼6

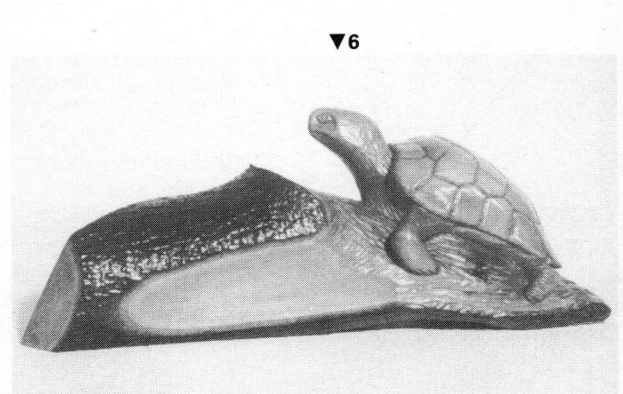

13▶

ASHLEY ILES/WOODWORKER
INTERNATIONAL CARVING COMPETITION

Winners: 1st (No. 2) Dog by M. Lund, Welling, Kent; 2nd (No. 3) Female centaur by C. Yeagan, San Diego, California US; 3rd (No. 8) Dragon by R. Riddell, Harworth, S. Yorks; 4th (No. 1) Suffolk punch by R. L. Smith, Allestree, Derby.

▼14

Pictured here:
1. By R. L. Smith, Allestree 2. By M. Lund, Welling 3. By C. Yeagan, San Diego 4. By D. R. Saunders, West Malling 5. By A. L. B. Mayer, Kidderminster 6. By F. Dickinson, Wigan 7. By R. L. Smith, Allestree 8. By R. Riddell, Harworth 9. By B. Quinn, Sunderland 10. By L. Spillman, Surlingham 11. By J. Arlow, Lessingham 12. By H. Petrie, Manchester 13. By G. Rockey, Portsmouth 14. By J. R. Davis, Liphook.

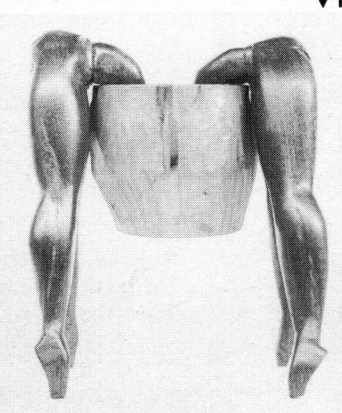

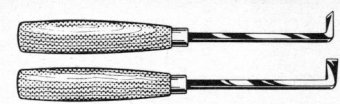

90   Prices quoted are those prevailing at press date and are subject to alteration due to economic conditions.   Woodworker, February 1982

WG2 (Model horse drawn vehicle-caravan, coach used for public transport) VHC (hansom cab) G. G. Jannetta, Dunkirk.

WH (Junior section) 1st and Woodworker challenge cup (jewellery box in walnut) D. A. Smith, Portslade; 2nd (tripod table) R. J. Vinall, Barnehurst; 3rd (cask in rosewood) D. A. Smith, Portslade; HC (baluster back Windsor armchair) C. E. Stewart, Chinnor; (hi-fi cabinet) J. G. Mansfield, Bourne End; (maghogany armchair) P. Ballard, Kings Langley; (oak chest) G. C. C. Mallinson, Henley on Thames; (marquetry picture) T. Hollings, Seaford; (bowl of eggs) M. Green, Seaford.

WJ1 (Clocks-longcase) 1st (Vienna clock) M. Sullivan, Ballybunion; 2nd (mahogany wall clock) M. Lund, Welling; 3rd (longcase clock) C. W. Reynolds, Bognor Regis.

WJ2 (Clocks-bracket) 1st and Woodworker challenge cup (carved clock case in the form of twin eagles) M. Lund, Welling; 2nd (ebonised bracket clock) R. S. Wadsworth, Widnes; 3rd (bracket clock) I. D. White, London.

Ashley Iles/Woodworker international carving competition, 4 legs. 1st (dog) M. Lund, Welling; 2nd (female centaur) C. Yeagan, San Diego; 3rd (dragon) R. Riddell, Harworth; 4th (Suffolk punch) R. L. Smith, Derby.

Above: The shoemaker entered by C. Williams in the marquetry and inlay classes. *(Photo Bill Gates)*

Below: T. A. Marsh holding his yew bowl which won the Henry Taylor award and first in the woodturning classes.

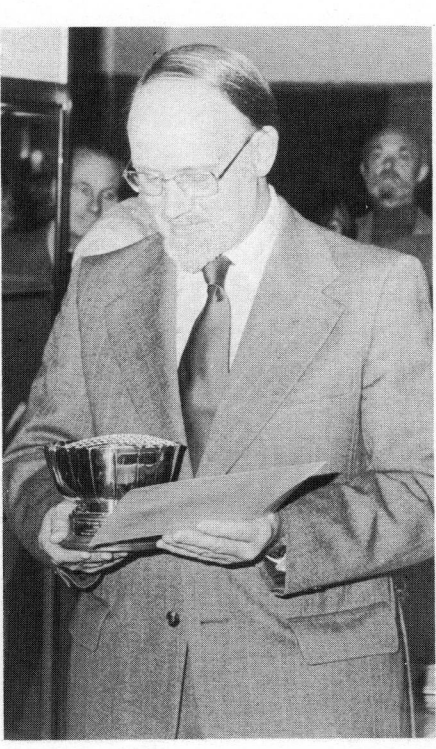

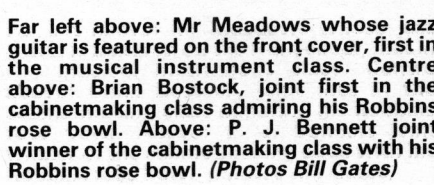

Far left above: Mr Meadows whose jazz guitar is featured on the front cover, first in the musical instrument class. Centre above: Brian Bostock, joint first in the cabinetmaking class admiring his Robbins rose bowl. Above: P. J. Bennett joint winner of the cabinetmaking class with his Robbins rose bowl. *(Photos Bill Gates)*

WF — Toys and miniatures

How do we judge a toy boat against tumbling clowns or a suite of miniature furniture against a tiny set of chessmen? Are we to be tactful or truthful? But of course we must be honest and therefore we have to express disappointment. First on account of the small number of entries and second on account of the careless way in which the specified scale of 1/12 had been interpreted. Miniature chess sets and boards seemed a popular theme but two of the entries would have scaled-up having 6in. squares.

In fact, only two entries were anywhere near the 1/12 scale and neither was consi-dered sufficiently meritorious to be awarded a prize.

The toy class also suffered from misinterpretation of the simple rules. A toy is a plaything. Unfortunately therefore a nicely designed and beautifully finished nursery mirror and nursery clock and also a cribbage board had to be eliminated. Only one award was made and this for an excellent rocking horse.

It was a pity that through non-compliance with the very basic rules of each class a number of creditable entries lost the chance of being placed among the winners.

Exhibitions department report

Newcomers to this year's Woodworker Show included a number of timber suppliers, who were constantly obliged to return to their premises for further stock to meet the very buoyant demand.

a WIDE CHOICE helps you make a WISE CHOICE

Here are some MACHINES & TOOLS we normally have available
from stock at POPULAR prices

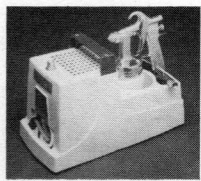

BURGESS S.R.122 Diaphragm Compressor Sprayer. 14 psi. with pressure feed gun.

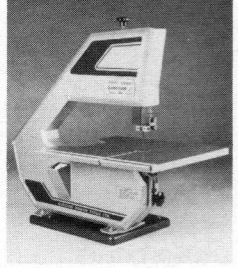

BURGESS B.K.2 Band Saw 2 speed. Max: cut 1" thick × 12" wide or 3' × 10".

MYFORD ML8A Woodturning Lathe. 30" between centres with rear turning attachment.

ELU MWA61W Grinder/Honer. 125mm dia: wheel, leather honing belt & grinding clamp guide. 0.35 hp.

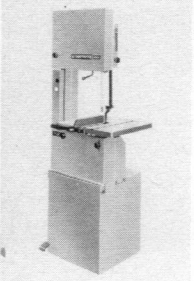

STARTRITE 352 Band Saw. 2 speed. Max: cut 11.8" thick × 13.7" wide. 1 hp.

ELU 055 Combi Bench. Can be fitted with portable circular saw or router. Snip-Off attachment available.

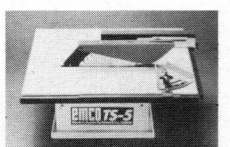

EMCO TS-5 Circular Saw. Max: cut 55mm thick, tilting table. Sanding & Combing accs: available. 1.20 hp.

MULTICO Type M Chisel Mortiser. Takes ¼"-1" Chisels. Can be used as drilling machine. ¾ hp.

STARTRITE-INCA AF.190M Planer-Thicknesser. Planes up to 10¼" wide. Thicknessing up to 6¼". 1¼ hp.

PLEASE NAME THE ITEMS THAT INTEREST YOU WHEN ASKING FOR DETAILS AND OUR SPECIAL PRICE LISTS.

EMCO-STAR Multi-Purpose Machine. Combines Circular, Band, Jig & Fret Saws. Belt & Disc Sanders. 2 speed. 0.5/0.7 hp. Planer-Thicknesser & Lathe attachments can be fitted.

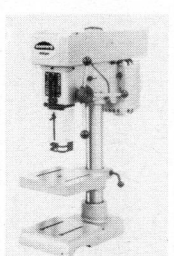

STARTRITE S.P.50 Bench Drill. ½" Chuck. 5 speeds. ½ hp. 5 Ball Bearings. Floor type available.

KITY Combination Set. Circular saw, spindle moulder, planer-thicknesser, mortiser & grinders on table with 1½ hp. motor.

STANLEY 268 Heavy Duty Router. Takes ¼" & ⅜" shank cutters. All ball bearings. 1½ hp.

ELU MFF 80/00 Planer/Rabbetter. 80mm wide TCT. blades. 650 watts. Inversion stand available.

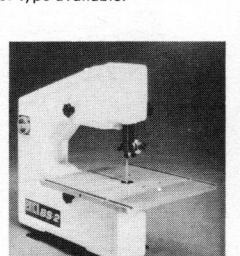

EMCO BS.2. Band Saw for wood, metal or plastic. 3 speed. Max: cut 145mm thick × 360mm wide. 370 watts.

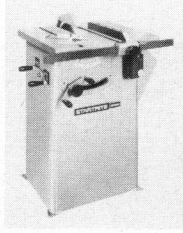

STARTRITE TA/SP.145 Saw Bench. Max: cut 3⅛" deep. Tilt arbor. 1 hp.

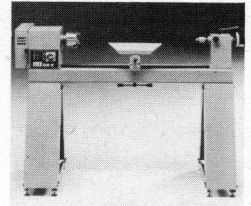

EMCO DB.5. Wood Turning Lathe. 1000mm between centres, 200mm centre height. 4 speeds. ¾ hp. Copying attachment available.

KITY 7227 Spindle Moulder. 20mm dia: spindle. Takes cutters in slot or block. 6200 rpm. 1½ hp. on stand.

L.H. Turtle Ltd.
6-12 Park Street,
Croydon, Surrey. CR0 1YE.

Turtle's TOOLS CROYDON MACHINERY

BARCLAYCARD VISA

Open 6 days per week 8.30-5.30

Established
1894
01-688-5513

Prices quoted are those prevailing at press date and are subject to alteration due to economic conditions.

Bigger Show this year

The scope and interest of this year's Woodworker Show is being considerably extended. In addition to occupying the Royal Horticultural Society's New Hall, London SW1, the Show will also have the Old Hall which is just a few minutes' walk away.

In the Old Hall the lecture and educational sections of the Show will be greatly expanded. It is planned that the Colleges will have more space to display many more examples of the best of their students' work. There will be additional space for demonstrations by craftsmen and women of woodworking and allied activities such as upholstery and rush and cane seating.

Facilities will be available for individual craftsmen and small businesses to show their products being made, as well as displayed in finished form. The date of the Show — 19-24 October inclusive — will present a first-class opportunity to catch the start of the Christmas gift-buying period.

In addition to the lecture and educational sections, demonstrations by craftsmen and the craft business stands, there will be further space in the Old Hall for trade exhibitors.

Admission charges to Woodworker Show will, of course, cover both the New and the Old Halls.

For details of the larger Woodworker Show 1982 contact Mary White, M.A.P Ltd, exhibitions department, PO Box 35, Bridge Street, Hemel Hempstead HP1 1EE, or telephone Hemel Hempstead 41221.

Above: A delighted Mr Cummings receives his Brian Bowman challenge trophy for the best toy entered in the show, from Mrs Doyle, wife of the managing director. Left: Gordon Stokes presents Maurice Lund with his tool voucher on winning the Ashley Iles/Woodworker carving competition. (Photos Bill Gates)

Below: John Tiranti presenting Ralph Fellows with his Henry Taylor award for the best entry in the woodcarving classes of this year's show (Photo Bill Gates)

WC — Woodturning

The standard of entries in this class covered a wide range. Some entries lost marks on points of design while in others good turning was spoiled by poor finishing. In each sub-class the best entries were very good indeed and the judges had little difficulty in reaching a unanimous agreement on a small group from which the final three were chosen.

Placing these into 1st, 2nd and 3rd order proved to be more difficult however, as they were so close together in quality.

Evidence of good craftsmanship was a main criterion in making the final choice, with consideration being given equally to traditional and contemporary design.

WB — Woodcarving

The overall standard was good but we would like to see a larger and more representative number of entries — and more from overseas. Three-dimensional work gave us much thought and, indeed, some difference of opinion. The entries were lively with considerable movement and expression. But we feel that a closer study of the human and animal forms might have improved a number of entries and given a greater degree of perfection.

Entrants must avoid the use of colour. Wood is the most beautiful of the raw materials which a craftsman can handle; it needs no colour adding. And the very strong grain in some woods may actually detract from the beauty of the carving.

The architectural class was dominated by one man — one or two seemed to have been works of long-standing and had in one or two instances been repaired and added to. The incised lettering of Ralph Fellows was as fine as we have seen at Woodworker Show.

The Ashley Iles international award once again gave us problems of decision since the entries (fewer in number than in 1980) were so good. The first prize went to a superb piece of carving (one of the judges would like to have bought this).

We would advise entrants to read the rules (general conditions of entry as published in WOODWORKER) and observe them strictly. Judges have to; there are often problems of rejection which the adjudicators have reluctantly to accept.

WA — Cabinetmaking

We have been pleased to again see a good overall response displaying a wide field of application and interest, mostly in techniques. These ranged from a small box with simple inlay quite well-made and finished to a semi-carved sculptured flower stand which was perfection in its making and finish. However we criticised the piece for some aesthetic and functional errors. Between those two were ranged some very good and obviously painstaking entries of work, mostly with a traditional design basis.

Somewhat noticeable was a slight decline in entries of a contemporary design character. Consideration of use, eye-appeal and current materials are of equal importance to perfection of making. It was particularly pleasant when opening the cabinet of two entries to be met with the aromatic smell of ceder. It is these details which ultimately help to affect the judges' decision: the overall impression, looking for perfection in all aspects.

To discuss briefly the work of the joint winners: The yew work-box on stand (B. L. Bostock) had very simple lines, was extremely functional and the disguised locking mechanism worked well. The whole piece was excellently crafted in making and finish.

We debated for some time the merit of this entry against the other joint winner (the marquetry chest by P. Bennett). This piece had obviously taken many hours of precise, painstaking marquetry cutting which was, moreover, excellently done and very well displayed on a carcase of equal quality.

Both entries equated in their various merits, and the judges therefore decided to split the award.

Above: This year the John Thompson trophy for model horse-drawn vehicles was won by N. M. Foxall, seen here being congratulated by Gavin Doyle (managing director MAP leisure division) and Mrs Doyle. *(Photo Bill Gates)*

WG — Horse-drawn vehicles

The judges were faced with an unusual situation in glass WG1 (farm waggons etc) in which the two entries which stood out from the rest for workmanship and finish were both models of the same Oxfordshire waggon. (Incidentally, the plans for this waggon drawn by John Thompson are listed in *Woodworker Planbook.*)

In the event it was the model built by W. M. Foxall which took first prize. The workmanship could not be faulted and the finish was in excellent taste, with matt varnish on the oak and beech and the metal parts blackened.

T. J. Spires took second prize with his version of the Oxfordshire waggon, also displaying fine workmanship, but perhaps not quite so well finished.

Several other models were worthy of commendation but the number of entries was down on last year. This was partly because Arthur Lown, a consistent prize-winner at previous Woodworker Shows, was a judge in 1981 and thus could not enter. However, he had loaned several models for display; these together with an impressive display of timber-handing vehicles on loan from Eric Horne, ensured that the craft of the model wheelwright was well represented.

Above: D.A. Smith of Portslade whose jewellery box in walnut was judged the winner of the junior section *(Photo Bill Gates)* Left: Hilary Wilson tried out a Kity planer and thicknesser. She is a bride to be with lots of projects in view! *(Photo H. C. King)*

Quality or price?

Swiss precision engineering and highly efficient production techniques together give INCA the edge for quality and value for money.

You won't find a more versatile and reliable range of woodworking equipment.

Price for price, quality for quality, you need the best. It pays to invest in INCA.

INCA solves the problem!

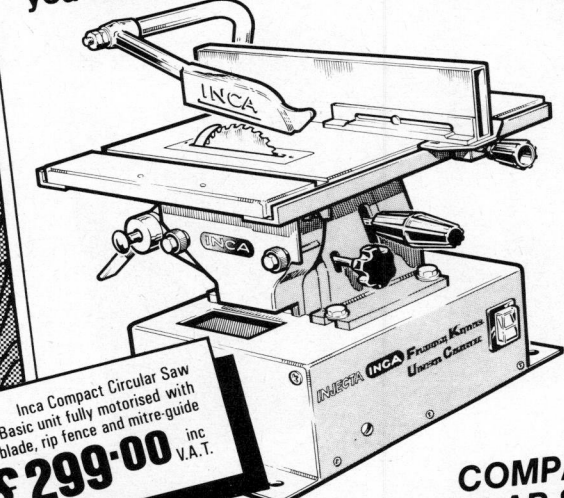

Inca Compact Circular Saw Basic unit fully motorised with blade, rip fence and mitre-guide

£299·00 inc V.A.T.

COMPACT UNIVERSAL CIRCULAR SAW

The 'Compact' is easy and safe to use, has a wide range of functions, yet weighs only 25kg.

This incredibly accurate machine is precision built to give years of pleasure to the amateur cabinet maker.

Full range of accessories include:
- Micro Adjuster for rip fence making cutting adjustment of 0.1mm possible.
- Tenoning Jig—indespensable for making a series of tenons and grooves.
- Comb Jointing Device—produce the perfect comb joint quickly and easily.
- Dado Blades (Grooving Cutters). 6 widths available. Wobble washers standard with saw.
- Moulding Head and Cutters—for safe spindle moulding cutters have soft metal core and hard steel cutting edge. Suva protecting device holds workpiece down and at the same time presses it against rip fence.
- Mortising Table for precision drilling, boring and slot mortising.
- 3 Jaw Chuck—special taper fit design for drills and slot mortice bits.
- Sanding Disc and Drum—for use in chuck or on flexible driving shaft.
- Saw Blades—many different types available.

INCA BANDSAW

- Precision built 10" bandsaw with all essential parts in pressure cast alloy. Ideal for wood, non-ferrous metals and plastics.
- Professional blade tracking control and accurate tilt table (45° one way) dove tailed for optional mitre guide.
- Separate saw blade micro adjusting screw guides and thrust rollers fitted above and below table.
- Blade tension indicator and moveable brush on lower wheel to remove sawdust.
- Standard equipment includes rip fence and depth stop.
- Optional extras include 8 different blades, sanding attachment, fret saw with special guides to allow 3mm minimum radius. Micro-adjuster for rip fence giving accuracy of 0.1mm.
- Unmotorised version available for 'v' belt or electric drill power.

Basic unit, fully motorised **£279·00** inc V.A.T.

Basic unit, unmotorised **£169·00** inc V.A.T.

THE COMPLETE INCA RANGE INCLUDES:
- Inca Multi-Purpose Circular Saw
- Inca Combined Jointer-Planer/Automatic Feed Thicknesser
- Inca Bandsaw
- Inca Spindle Moulder
- Inca Benches and Work Stands
- Inca Major Circular Saw
- Inca Jointer-Planer
- Inca Rabbeting Planer
- Inca Blades / Cutters
- Inca Woodworking Project Plans

Woodworking Machines of Switzerland LIMITED

Sole U.K. Agents for INCA Woodworking Machinery.

Now, good tools from the name you know are even easier to choose

Introducing

SARJENTS TOOLS

WOODWORKING CATALOGUE

A selection of fine hand tools and machinery for the demanding woodworker to order from home.

Up to now, ordering by post or phone from our wide range has been impeded by the lack of a good, well laid-out catalogue. All that has changed; looking through the new Sarjents Tools Woodworking Catalogue, the discerning craftsman will find a range of the highest quality hand tools and machines that are a pleasure to use.

The emphasis is on quality throughout – both in content and presentation. 100 big (12″ × 8″) pages show the products in full colour photographs, and the text not only carries detailed descriptions, but also many hints and tips as well. And to make life really easy, the prices shown are the prices you pay; there is no extra for V.A.T., postage or packing.

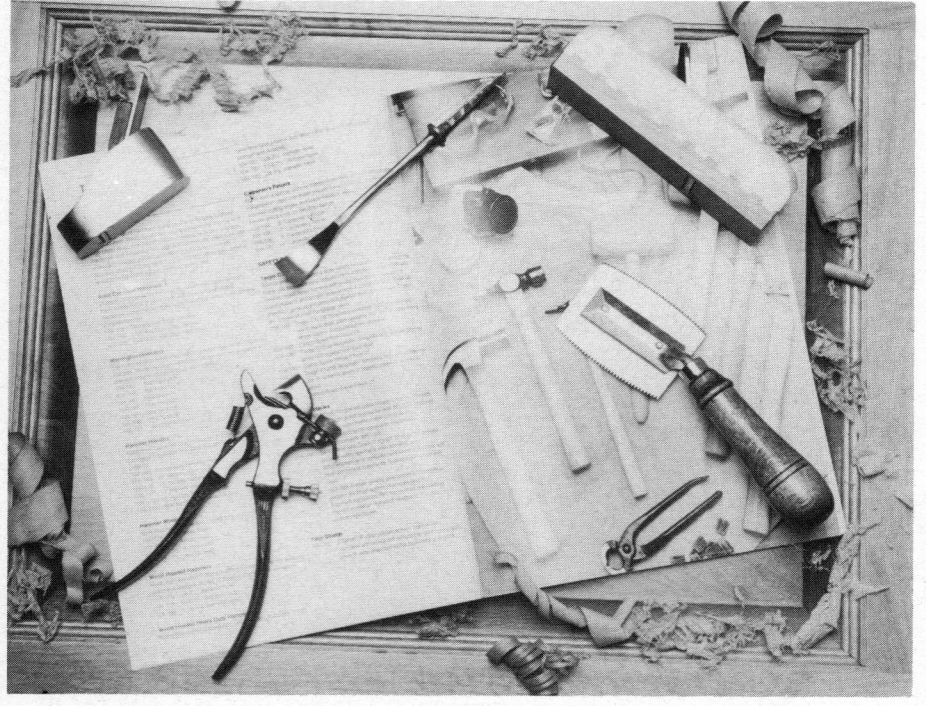

For your copy of this super catalogue, please send a cheque or postal order for £1 to:

SARJENTS TOOLS

Dept. W.W.,
Oxford Road,
Reading.
Or write or phone
(0734) 586522
with your Access or
Barclaycard/VISA number.

Overseas readers are advised to send £3.00 (in sterling currency or sterling bank draft only please) to the same. Airmail (not Europe) £5.50.

Prices quoted are those prevailing at press date and are subject to alteration due to economic conditions.

WJ — Clocks

The judges in this class submitted individual reports. One reads as follows: Of the three exhibits in the bracket clocks section the carved clock by M. Lund stood out clearly as the winner. Mr Lund's near faultless carving and original design was a joy to examine. The finish on all other clocks varied from reasonable to abysmal.

The varied designs made it a very interesting section although closer inspection revealed some poor finishing, like the pins which secured some of the mouldings still showing; varnish applied like icing on a cake — and just as thick.

The longcase Vienna clock was a brave attempt to escape from traditional lines but was thwarted by the use of a piece of elm fit only for the fire.

There was some very skilful marquetry work in evidence on J. Herbert's half-scale longcase clock. The winning longcase clock in mahogany by M. Sullivan overcame admirably some difficult design features and well-rewarded his long journey from Ballybunion on the west coast of Ireland.

The other judge comments: I observed a general and pleasing increase in the number and quality of the pieces entered in the two classes of 1981. Perhaps, however, at future Shows there might be a third class of entry for those who wish to employ the Vienna movement in their pieces. It was somewhat difficult to judge the three pieces of this kind entered and mixed in with the longcase or grandfather clocks.

Designs and constructions attempted were more ambitious than in 1980 and these included carving, domed hoods, split turnings and marquetry doors.

However, it was sad to see good and varied work marred by some very poor finishing. In most cases the liberally applied high-gloss finish masked the character and beauty of the woods employed. With the honourable exception of R. Wadsworth's ebonised bracket clock, the overall effect was one of unsubtlety and vulgarity.

With such traditional-looking things as bracket and longcase clocks what better than to emulate the time-honoured finishes? Such things were never cheap and were always prized and revered. Any measure that cheapens them should surely be avoided.

WD — Musical instruments

Unfortunately, there were no entries in WD1 (any woodwind instrument) but, under the circumstances, we were in agreement that the viola bow (by J. H. Maw) was of such high quality as to merit a 1st prize in, perhaps, a third category (WD3 — Essential Musical Instruments Accessories).

As for WD2 (any string instrument) we were unanimous over the prize winners.

In our assessments we kept the following criteria in mind: 1 Quality of craftsmanship. 2 Appropriate use of materials. 3 Evidence of an understanding of the way in which musical instruments function (the 'feel' of the thing). 4 Overall aesthetic appeal.

There were five guitars, all of a very good standard of craftsmanship, the 1st prize winner being quite outstanding in all respects according to the above criteria.

More attention needed to be given to some aspects of the remaining guitars, eg the correct setting-up of the instrument in order to make it playable. In one instance the actual string length, a technical matter, was quite at fault. On another there was inappropriate inlay to the detriment of the instrument. In some instances the finish suffered.

Of the two violins, the Hellier copy quite naturally merited an award. We were able to place it second. The maker of this instrument deserves high praise for his work.

The other violin was a very good first effort at violin making. The tone was good and it 'spoke' easily. This maker deserves encouragement in spite of the fact that we were unable to give a placing. The bowed psaltery and the balalaika were quite well made but lacked evidence of a true understanding of the 'feel' of the thing; and in no way approached the overall standard of work required to accomplish the winning instruments. Nevertheless, these makers should be encouraged.

As for the miniature violin and bow in case this was exquisite in its own right. Unfortunately, we were unable to place the entry in the category of musical instruments.

Above: Maurice Lund receiving his cup for the clocks section of the show from Mr and Mrs Doyle. His carved twin eagles clock was much admired. Below: F. Taylor of St Albans with the World of Wood cup he won in the marquetry section. *(Photos Bill Gates)*

WH — Junior class

We have been very impressed with the high standard of work in the Junior class. It was most difficult to segregate and to place the items in any sort of order of merit. The standard of finish was most commendable and, after all, the well-finished article must be well-made or flaws will soon show through the polished surface.

Another difficulty is the variation inherent in all species of timber. The beauty of wood is evident in the simplest example but we have been particularly impressed with a tripod table in padauk and a turned item in rosewood, two of the world's most outstanding timbers. But that in itself by no means reduces the effect of old favourites like oak and elm.

We repeat, it was most encouraging to see so many examples well-constructed and well-finished, it was difficult indeed to make any judgment between one and another.

The number of exhibits was somewhat down on the 1980 entry and if we have any regrets at all it is in the rather limited number of examples. We look forward to more this year!

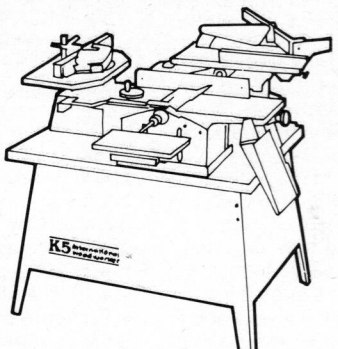
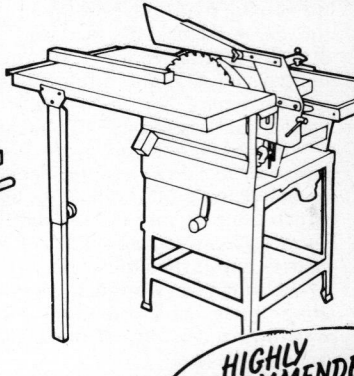
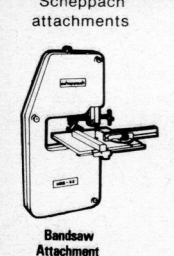
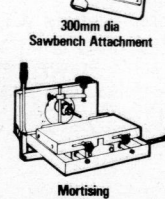
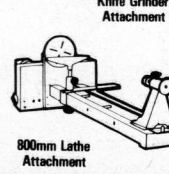
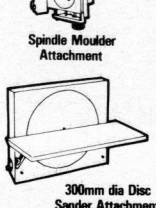
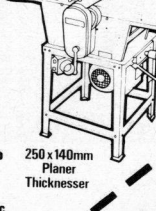

ELU Power Tools, lowest UK prices?

ELU HEAVY DUTY ROUTERS
MOF 98 Router including free cutter **£105.00 + £3 p & p**

65mm depth of plunge, 2.2 HP 22,000 rpm fitted with ½ collett, side fence, 30mm. guide bush and holder, spanners

MOF 31 including free cutter **£85.00 + £3 p & p** 1 - 7 HP

MOF 96 ROUTER including 6 cutters **Only £69.95 + £3 p & p**

50mm depth of plunge 24,000 rpm, 600 Watt motor fitted with ¼ collett and complete with side fence, guide rods, guide bush and two HSS cutters and spanners. Full instructions

ROUTER ACCESSORY KIT (for MOF 96) £39.99 + £3.00 p&p

Comprising: Router table complete with legs and clamps for vertical and horizontal moulding, spring loaded suva guard, copying follower with wooden suva guard, fine adjusters trammel bar

ELU ROUTER TABLE   ONLY £69.99
Suitable for use with the MOF 96, 69, 77, 98, 31 Routers. Standard Equipment: Table Top, 4 Steel Legs, Push Button N.V. Starter, Moulding Fence, Top Suva Guard, Router Fitting Kit and Insert Plate.

ONLY £65.99 ELU STANDARD SAW TABLE for MH 182 and 155 Saws Table Top, 4 Steel Legs, Push Button N.V. Starter, Rip Fence, Riving Knife and Guard, Fitting Kit for Saw. 2 Insert Plates.

ONLY £89.99 ELU SAW TABLE + SNIP OFF ARM AND MITRE GAUGE Details as Standard Saw Table + Snip Off Arm, with fitting kit and Mitre Gauge.

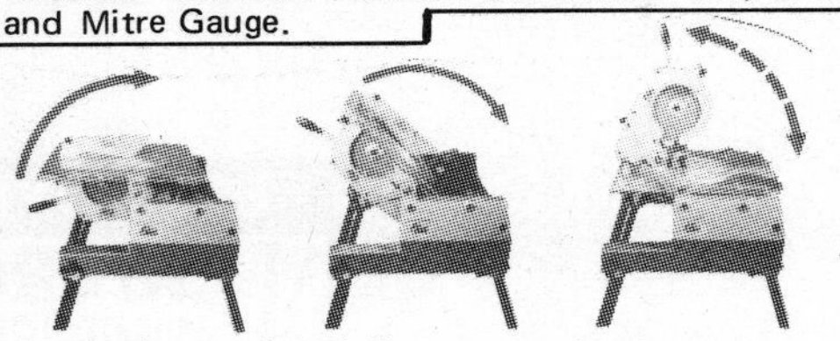

A sawbench . . . . . . A simple flip over . . . . . . A perfect Mitre saw.

The saw designed to give you perfect results in modern materials

Versatility *Simply pull the plunge table locking lever, and the overhead mitre cutting saw swivels through 180° to become a conventional bench saw.*
Add the sliding table and you can cut boards and panels up to 36" at a perfect 90°.
Whether you need to cut delicate veneered boards for cabinet building or even alloy extrusions for mitred frames, the new TGS 171 has been developed to give you the performance and consistent accuracy you want.

TGS 171 SPECIAL PRICE £229.95 LIMITED STOCK including wood set. Aluminium set in place of Wood set **£35.00 extra**

DOVETAIL KIT
£42.50 + £3.00 p&p
ELU DOVETAIL KIT for use with 96 Router, takes boards up to 12" wide complete with instructions and T/C Dovetail Cutter

ST 142/1 2 speed JIG SAW £63.00 + £3.00 p&p
60mm depth of cut 2150/2800 strokes/min 4 setting orbital movement. Universal blade fitting. 450 Watt motor complete with metal case and side fence

MFF 80/10 PLANER £66.50 + £3.00 p&p

☆ **NEW 850 WATT NOW IN STOCK** ☆
80mm planing width 0-2.5mm depth of cut, up to 22mm rebating depth 220V. 12,000 rpm FITTED WITH T/C BLADES complete in steel case with spare blades, side fence, bevel fence and dust bag

---

LIMITED OFFER
AUTOGRAPHED COPIES OF 2 WOODWORKING BOOKS

Techniques of Routing
By: Jim Phillips

The first ever book printed in the UK devoted to the craft of routing.
140 pages packed full of know-how, with numerous illustrations to support it.
Published by Northwood Publications

£4.50 plus 80p postage and packing

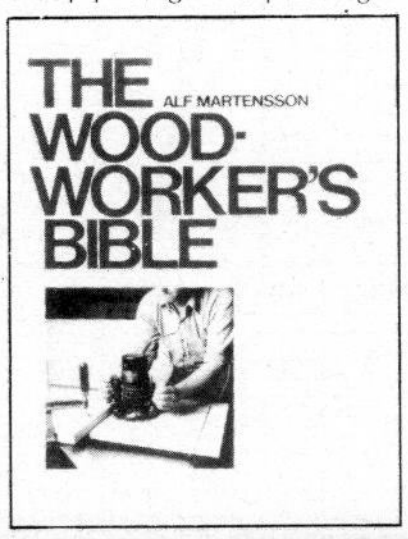

THE WOODWORKER'S BIBLE

THE WOODWORKERS BIBLE
By Alf Martensson

The Woodworker's Bible is a complete guide to the equipment and techniques you will need to set up and run a workshop and serves as both a reference book and workshop manual for professional and amateur craftsmen in wood.
Published by Pitman Publishing
£7.95   £1.60 p & p.

ELU MHB 90/10 BELT SANDER AND FRAME	**£129.95**
MVS 47	**£75.00**
MVS 94	**£68.00**
MVS 91	**£82.00**
ST 142/1	**£66.00**
MKF 67	**£73.00**
MH 151 SAW	**£42.00**
MH 182 SAW	**£73.00**
MH 85	**£99.00**
MWS 147 6" GRINDER	**£45.00**
MWA 61W GRINDER HONER	**£90.00**
DS 140/10 BISCUIT JOINTER/ GROOVER	**£129.95**

BOSCH POWER TOOLS   DRILL HAMMER ACTION
320 RLE Reversing Screwdriver	£ 34.95
350 - 2	£ 24.95
450 - 2	* £ 46.95
450 - 2E	* £ 52.95
600 - 2	* £ 58.95
620 - 2E	* £ 64.95
* ATTACHMENTS	
S 2 DRILL STAND	£ 16.95
S 7 MILLING STAND	£ 37.95
S 18 LATHE KIT	£ 48.95
S 40 DRILL BIT SHARPENER	£ 16.95
S 48 BENCH STAND	£ 7.95
POF 50 320 WATT Plunge ROUTER	£ 39.99
PST 50 E 350 WATT variable speed jig saw	£ 35.95
PWS 115 4½ Angle grinder 400 WATT	£ 49.95
IMPACT DRILLS/ROTARY HAMMERS	
SB 4502 2 speed impact drill ½ chuck, 5/8 (masonry)	£ 68.95
1179 2 speed ¾ (masonry) ½ chuck	£ 88.95
1174 2 speed spade grip 1" (masonry) 5/8 chuck	£118.95
1578 ELECTRONIC JIG SAW, top handle	£ 95.95

Fantastic Offer on **STANLEY** *ROUTER CUTTER SETS*
Choose any set for only £22.50 including VAT and postage.

BW3	BW4	BW5	BW6	BW7
LIST PRICE £28 85 + VAT	LIST PRICE £27 80 + VAT	LIST PRICE £33 95 + VAT	LIST PRICE £27 35 + VAT	LIST PRICE £34 50 + VAT
1-³/₁₆" STRAIGHT	1-¼" STRAIGHT	1-³/₈" STRAIGHT	1-½" STRAIGHT	1-¼" STRAIGHT
1-³/₈" CORE BOX	1-³/₁₆" VEIN	1-¼" BEAD	1-¼" CORE BOX	1-VEE GROOVE
1- CHAMFER	1-³/₈" ROUND	1-⁹/₃₂" DOVETAIL	1-¼" ROUND	1-¼" PANEL
1-³/₈" REBATE	1-³/₈" COVE	1-¹³/₁₆" OGEE	1-¼" COVE	1-³/₈" STRAIGHT (TC)

HOLZ-HER More Technology - Greater Safety!

FREE GIFT! Send 40p stamps for full details of the new HOLZ-HER SAWS and your FREE GIFT.

The new HOLZ-HER portable circular saws offer you numerous of advantages:

- 3 different safety systems with inner or outer pivoting guards, or the »plunge« principle. That's something quite unique
- Powerful motors with high overload capability and optimum speeds.
- The motors are »turbine« cooled with low-noise ventilation systems and stand up to high continuous loading.
- The grips are positioned exactly at the centre of gravity and ensure working without fatique. Extra grips facilitate accurate and safe guidance of the saws.
- The cutting depth and bevel adjustment have two support mountings. The saw remains torsion-free, even with a high contact pressure.

- HOLZ-HER portable circular saws are provided with sturdy sole plates made of zinc galvanized steel.
- The precise line-of-cut indicator and cutting width markers add to the practical ease of operation.
- The adjustable precision rip fences are particularly stable and can be used as desired on the right or on the left of the soleplate.
- TC-tipped sawblades are standard equipment on HOLZ-HER portable circular saws.
- The chip ejection is equipped as standard with an adapter for connection to any desired extractor system; a chip bag can also be attached.

- HOLZ-HER portable circular saws surpass all – even inter-national – safety require-ments. Thus you are protected from electric shock even if an electric cable is accidentally cut into.
- HOLZ-HER portable circular saws have riving knives that can be adjusted in a quick and simple way. World first: for the »e« types it is no longer necessary to take off the riving knife before plunge-cutting.
- The saws feature a HOLZ-HER slipping clutch for protection of the gears.
- The switch can only be operated with the safety catch released. This prevents accidental switching on of the machine.

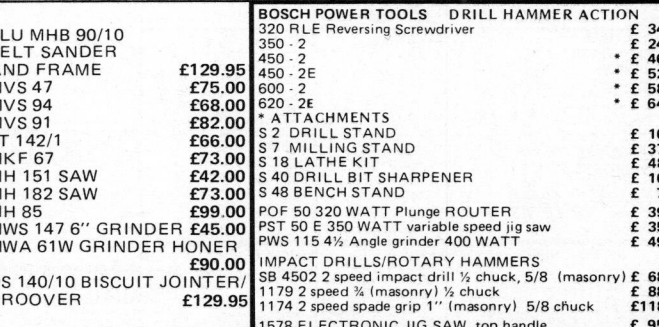

£119.95   £106.95   £95.95   £86.95   £91.50   £91.50

Trade name	t55a	t65a	t65i	t65e	t85i	t85e
Type	2115	2116	2117	2119	2118	2120
Guard safety system	Exterior pivoting guard	Exterior pivoting guard	Interior pivoting guard	Plunge principle	Interior pivoting guard	Plunge principle
Depth of cut	55 mm	65 mm	65 mm	65 mm	85 mm	85 mm
Sawblade dia.	170 mm	190 mm	190 mm	190 mm	230 mm	230 mm
Bevel cutting	0 – 45°	0 – 45°	0 – 45°	0 – 45°	0 – 45°	0 – 45°
Power input	1200 W	1400 W	1400 W	1400 W	1700 W	1700 W
Power output	1020 W	1180 W	1180 W	1180 W	1260 W	1260 W
Idling speed	5000 rpm	5000 rpm	5000 rpm	5000 rpm	5000 rpm	5000 rpm
Machine weight	5.8 kg	6.3 kg	6.2 kg	7.0 kg	6.5 kg	7.5 kg

Send large 20p s.a.e. for the **NEW '82 TREND CUTTER WALL CHART**

THATCHER'S POWER TOOL CENTRE
W. Thatcher & Son Ltd., Est. 1934

W. Thatcher & Son Ltd., 221A Kilburn High Road, London NW6 7JL (First floor above Travel Agency)

☎ 01-624 5146   CLOSED WEDNESDAYS

All prices are inclusive of VAT and carriage unless otherwise stated.

As we are now trading as a Mail Order outlet, we are unable to accept personal callers unless by prior appointment.

FULL CASH REFUND UNDERTAKEN (LESS CARRIAGE COST) ON ANY ORDER SUPPLIED BY US IF YOU ARE NOT COMPLETELY SATISFIED.

Please send 50p stamps for full Brochures and Price Lists.

A SUCCESSFUL D.I.Y. YEAR TO OUR MANY SATISFIED CUSTOMERS

Prices quoted are those prevailing at press date and are subject to alteration due to economic conditions.

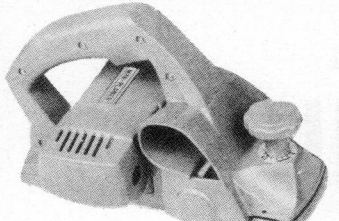 **RYOBI INDUSTRIAL POWER**

PLANER
L-120N ☐92mm

- Compact, Lightweight — (7.3 lbs) and easy to handle.
- Excellent machined surface at a high speed of 15,000 rpm.
- Chamfering can be done with ease.
- Ryobi's unique blade replacement mechanism with quick and easy change.
- Easy blade re-sharpening with optional attachment.

CAPACITIES

Planing	Depth	1 mm (³⁄₆₄")
Planing	Width	92 mm (3-⅝")
Rabbeting	Depth	6 mm (¼")

PRICE ONLY
£64.03

BELT SANDER
B-7075 ☐75mm

- Compact design but powerful motor.
- Large front handle for better control.
- Can be used as bench sander for small pieces and craftsman's job, simply turning upside down.
- Longer wide base plate for stable and efficient sanding.
- Simple belt replacement only by uprighting tension lever.

STANDARD ACCESSORIES
Abrasive Belt 3" × 21"
Dust Bag

PRICE ONLY
£105.52

PLUNGE ROUTER
PRICE ONLY £106.15
R-500 ☐13mm

- Versatile applications — rounding, flushing, chamfering, trimming and dovetailing with wide range of accessories.
- Rated for continuous production use.
- Exclusive design allows bit to be clearly visible when cutting.
- All ball bearing construction.
- Plunge depth is set by simple thumb action.
- Stopper block can be adjusted for three different cutting levels.

STANDARD ACCESSORIES
Guide holder, Straight guide, Roller attachment, Template guide, Bit adapters, Spanners, Router bit.
Suitable for ¼", ⅜" and ½" shank router bits

IMPACT DRILL
PD-1920 ☐19mm
2 SPEED

- Percussion and rotary drilling plus two speed.
- Compact, lightweight.
- Auxiliary handle can be positioned in free direction for convenience of operator
- 550 watt motor
- ½" Chuck.

PRICE ONLY
£70.76

STANDARD ACCESSORIES
Chuck key, Auxiliary handle, Stopper pole.

DRILLING CAPACITIES

Wood	30mm (1-³⁄₁₆")
Steel	13mm (½")
Masonry	19mm (¾")

ALL THE ABOVE PRICES INCLUDE VAT.

BENSON & CO. (Droyslden) LTD.
164 Plymouth Grove, Chorlton-on-Medlock, Manchester M13 0AF
Telephone: 061-273 2067/8

ALL ABOVE CARRIAGE FREE

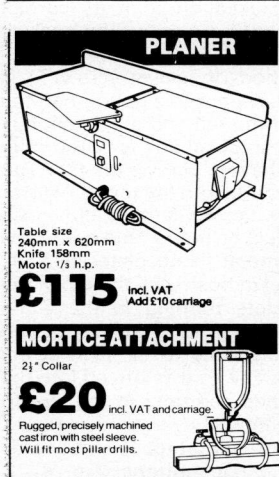
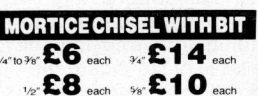

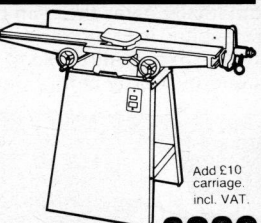

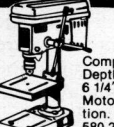

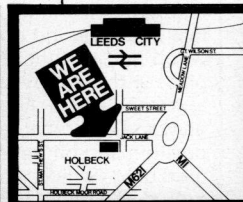
---

workpieces

America at play

Toys from the Detroit Antique Toy museum at the Bethnal Green museum of Childhood until 28 February, sponsored by the Detroit Historical Society. Bethnal Green museum is in Cambridge Heath Road, London E2 9PA; open 10.00 to 6.00 Monday to Thursday and Saturday, closed Fridays, open Sundays 2.30 to 6.00, admission free (next to Bethnal Green underground station).

Craft fairs

Southern Craft Fair, the Assembly Rooms, Alton, 26, 27 March; the Town Hall, Petersfield, 4, 5 June; the Haslemere Hall, Haslemere, 3, 4 September. If you are interested in taking part in any of these fairs write with sae to Southern Craft Fairs, 33 Westbourne Road, North End, Portsmouth, Hants, or phone (0705) 698449.

Elu has moved

Elu Machinery Ltd is now at 310-12 Dallow Road, Luton LU1 1SS. Telephone is 0582 425001 and telex 825540. Expansion of business has brought about the move from the previous premises at Borehamwood, Herts.

Exhibition

Eurocucina (European kitchen furniture fair), Milan, Italy, from 26 February to 1 March.

Show down on the Lleyn

Cabinetmaker Joe Worthington was born in Llanbedrog and now lives in the village of Dinas on the Lleyn peninsula in North Wales. His natural liking for wood as a creative material and his ability as a craftsman are shown in the wide range of hand-made products and woodturnery he sells at Lleyn Woodcrafts.

His range includes model field guns (the house speciality), rocking horses, tea pot stands, tops and whips, lovespoons, wall clocks, milking stools, solitaire, wine tables and bowls. Lleyn Woodcrafts is at Highgate, Dinas, (phone. Tudweiliog 321).

Timber in small lots

A little over a year ago D. P. L. Antill established Yorkshire Hardwoods Ltd with the express object of supplying small quantities of good-quality hardwood to joiners, cabinetmakers and other craftsmen.

Mr Antill tells WOODWORKER: 'We decided to specialise in English oak partly because of its universal appeal and partly because it seemed to be the most difficult to obtain; this may be because it is one of the more difficult species to dry.'

Yorkshire Hardwoods is at Pocklington Grange, Pocklington, York YO4 2NT, about half a mile off the main road from York to Market Weighton. Here the company air and kiln-dries its timber for supply as waney-edged boards or dimensioned stock to customers throughout the country. Most orders are for quantities of 5cu ft or less though larger quantities are available.

'We have been encouraged by customers' reaction,' says Mr Antill. 'Some who have been in the trade all their lives tell us that the quality is as good as they have ever seen. We have had many repeat orders.'

WOODWORKER understands that the company intends to offer other kiln-dried hardwood in the near future.

Stock sheet

From R. B. Brett of North Heigham Sawmills, Paddock Street, Norwich NR2 4TW, comes a nine-page stock list with prices and delivery charges as well as charges for selected or quarter sawn boards and planing and deep sawing. A wide range of home-grown and foreign woods are available.

Guide to suppliers

Popular Crafts' Guide to Good Craft Suppliers compiled by Lynnette Fogden and Evelyn Barrett, published by Model & Allied Publications Ltd, ISSN 0144-2937 special edition, is available from book shops at £1.00 or direct from the publishers at PO Box 35, Bridge Street, Hemel Hempstead, HP1 1EE, at £1.25. The guide is based upon the fact that most craft/leisure items are fairly bulky so a list of local stockists is invaluable, even though the dedicated specialist will travel quite a distance to obtain his supplies.

It is divided into six main sections: a list of craft suppliers and a list of craft courses, both arranged in county order; a subject list of guilds and associations and a county by county list of regional guilds plus two indices — one to suppliers and one to courses, both arranged alphabetically under subjects. Three short articles and several useful advertisement pages complete the guide. WOODWORKER readers will find interest in the sections covering miniature furniture, pyrography, caning and rushing, marquetry, picture-framing and woodcarving.

Spooning

Born in Birmingham in 1939, John Thompson is a commercial artist turned wooden spoon maker. He uses holly, yew, laburnum, oak, birch, elm, lilac and fruitwoods.

In the green wood he turns a shape containing two basic spoon forms, then cuts this lengthwise, carves the two bowls, dries them over a stove for two days, shapes and finally gives them an oil finish.

He has exhibited in France and the US and at the British Craft Centre *Wood & Silver* show in London shortly before Christmas.

TAKE A HINT
by Charles Cliffe

Fitting solid wooden tops to tables, cabinets, sideboards and such like is not difficult. But it must be remembered that no matter how well seasoned wood may be it moves with changes of temperature and humidity. This is most noticeable when furniture is brought from a non-centrally heated house into a centrally-heated one and previously free-running drawers now tend to bind, doors may warp and table tops twist. As Charles Cliffe points out, allowance for movement has to be made when securing wooden tops to the framework below, otherwise there is a danger of the top splitting.

Pocket-screwing (Fig. 1) is a common method of securing tops. A ⅜in. hole is drilled into the rim to a depth of about halfway to admit a screwdriver. A smaller hole to accommodate the shank of the screw is then drilled through. The top is placed upside down on the bench, the underframing placed on it in its correct position and screws are put in the pockets and screwed home.

Another method of pocket screwing is shown in Fig. 2. A pocket is gouged on the inner surface of the rail and a hole slightly larger than the screw shank is bored obliquely through the rail. Screws are then run through the rails and into the top as before.

But where a wide top is fitted allowance for shrinkage must be made. One method is to use slotted metal fixing plates (Fig. 3). The plates are let in flush with the top of the rim with the slots running in the same direction across the grain. Plate (A) is used at the ends while plate (B) is used at the sides of the top. The screws driven into the top are positioned centrally in the slot to permit full movement.

A better way of fitting tops to sideboards and tables is to use buttons (Fig. 4). A rectangular block of wood is rebated to fit into a corresponding groove cut into the top inner face of the table or sideboard rim (Fig. 5). The button is drilled and countersunk to take the fixing screw. If the buttons are fitted at 6 in. intervals they will hold the top quite securely while allowing for movement.

Where a thin plywood top has to be fitted there may be insufficient thickness to screw through the rails without the point of the screw showing a bump. In this case an alternative fixing is used. This relies on the fact that plywood does not move like solid wood and can therefore be fixed firmly in place without provision for movement.

As shown in Fig. 6 the edges of the plywood are rebated, the top is glued into position and pinned through the rebates. A moulding which fits the rebate is then mitred and glued in position.

FITTING TOPS

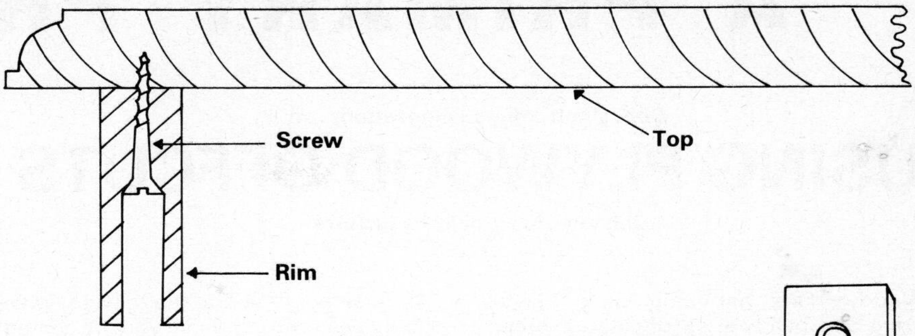

Screw

Top

Rim

Fig. 1 (Right) Rim pocket-screwed to top.

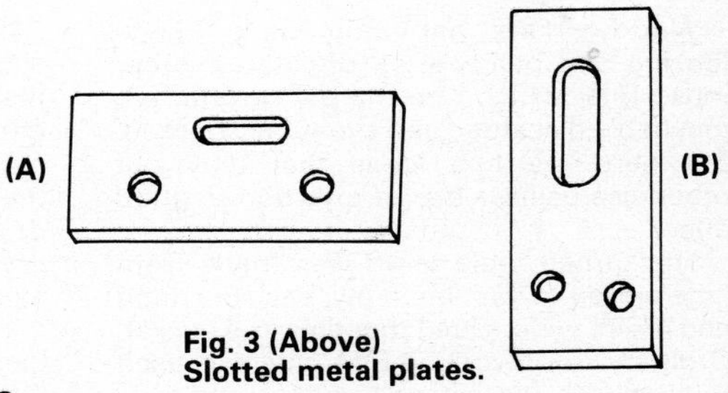

(A)   (B)

Fig. 3 (Above) Slotted metal plates.

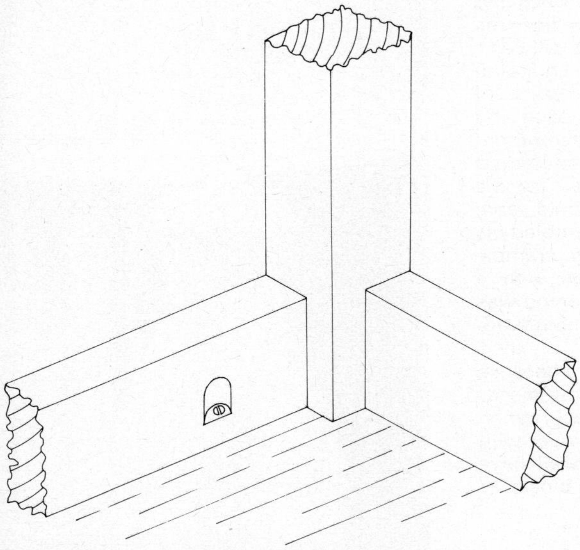

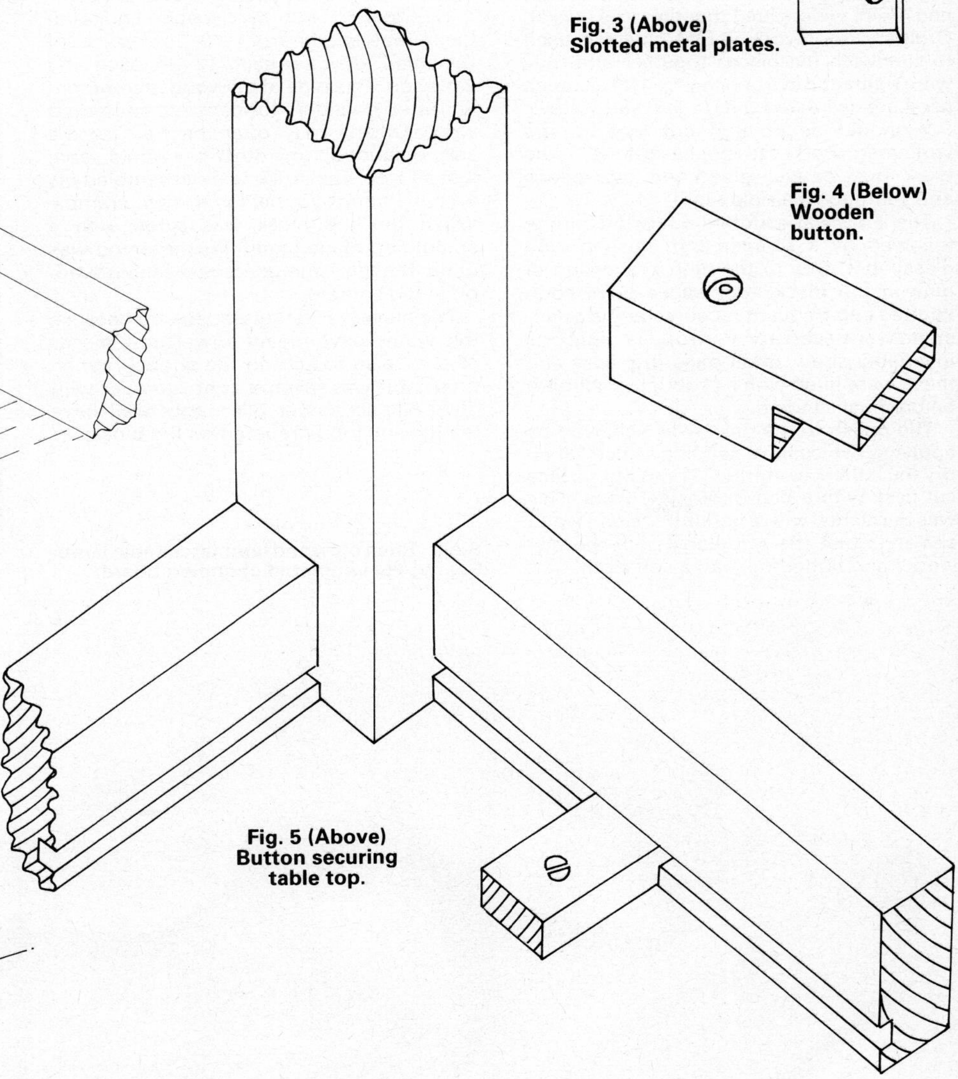

Fig. 4 (Below) Wooden button.

Fig. 2 (Above) Pocket gouged on inner face of rim and screw run obliquely into table top.

Fig. 5 (Above) Button securing table top.

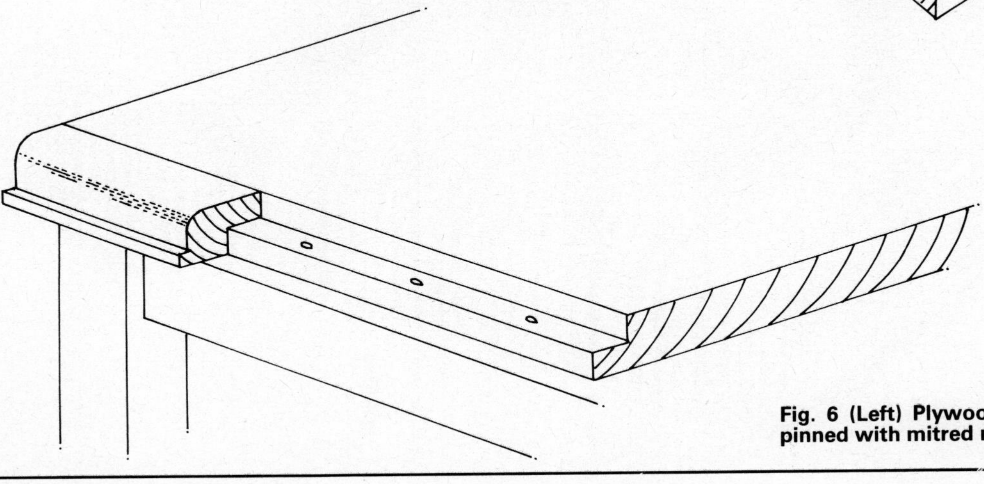

Fig. 6 (Left) Plywood top rebated, glued and pinned with mitred moulding.

A PRIMARY PROJECT

Bob Grant offers suggestions on

USING PLYWOOD OFFCUTS

John Peacock took the pictures

Woodworkers habitually save likely-looking and handy-sized offcuts for other jobs. Bits which are hardly useful are inevitably discarded and eventually burned. But here are two ideas that may put otherwise useless bits of plywood to good effect.

The turned table lamp was made from nine pieces of ½in. birch ply, each 8in. long and 4½in. wide, glued together as a packet. Ordinary woodworking PVA glue was used to sandwich the pieces together and they were tightened in a bench vice with as much pressure as I dared put on the lead screw!

It should be pointed out that turning laminated work can be hazardous – the work must be well glued and low speeds and sharp tools employed.

The lamp was roughed-out with a gouge followed by a scraper and finished with glasspaper. Due to the high proportion of glue in the block, tool edges were soon blunted and frequent recourse to the grindstone was necessary. Plywood laminations invariably show small gaps in places and these were filled with a proprietary stopper before final sanding.

The polish to the piece was achieved by applying two coats of sanding sealer. When dry the lathe was started up and the surface cut back with a pad of 00 steel wool. This was burnished with a handful of clean wood shavings (not the scrapings from the plywood) and buffed-up with a soft cloth.

A final point about the design which should be borne in mind if you are contemplating making a similar lamp: The annular effect will only be apparent when the outline of the job departs from the axis of the block. In other words, a straight-sided drum would show only tightly packed end grain. The greater the sweep away from the axis the more dramatic the effect will be.

The sturdy and serviceable chopping block was made from 10 1in. strips of Canadian plywood each 12½in. long and 2in. wide. This type of plywood is commonly used by builders for concrete shuttering work. Offcuts may often be had for the asking although any other ply would serve just as well. The strips were assembled (as with the lamp) but held with sash cramps. When dry the block was trued with a smoothing plane (again resharpening was quite frequent) and generously chamfered-off at the corners.

The block was not glasspapered because this would have meant unwelcome pieces of grit being lodged in the surface. When finished it was given a light rub over with olive oil; any other oils might well have tainted any food prepared on the block.

**Right: Birch plywood laminated table lamp.
Below: Ply laminated chopping board.**

HEAD FOR A POTTERS WHEEL

In WOODWORKER for August 1981 details were given for making a potters wheel designed by J. A. Dabell and P. R. Cave. In response to requests we give here information which the authors have supplied for making a wheel head.

This wheel head is of a type used by traditional Japanese potters. It is simply a round wooden block attached to the crank by means of a threaded metal flange.

The flange is made by welding a 20mm nut to a piece of 10mm plate (Fig.1). If the thread on your crank is too long to allow the shoulder to reach the face of the nut, run a drill (17.5mm) and tap (20mm) through the plate to allow plenty of clearance. The flange can then be mounted in the lathe on a mandrel and turned up. Drill and countersink the three screw holes, paint the flange with Hammerite and it is ready to be attached to the wheel head.

We chose iroko (Chlorophora excelsa) for the head itself because of its durability, stability and comparative cheapness. Despite these favourable properties we decided to do a belt and braces job by laminating the head out of 10mm strips and alternating the heart sides (Fig. 2). Because iroko is diffuse porous the growth rings are normally difficult to see with the naked eye. This slows the gluing-up process.

To overcome this several chalk lines are struck across the timber before it is sawn into strips, enabling a method of 'chalk up – chalk down' to be adopted ensuring that all the strips are in their correct places (Fig. 2).

Once glued-up with Cascamite that which was to be the back was planed true and the circular recess was routed out to accommodate the flange (Fig. 1). If this recess is likely to cause undue problems, there is no reason why the flange should not be screwed on to the back of the block.

The block can be roughly sawn round and mounted in the lathe on a mandrel to be turned true. The mandrel can be the threaded part of the crank itself (Potters Wheel, August issue) if you have not got round to welding it up yet, or a smaller one made up for the job.

Turning the head in this way ensures that it will run true to the crank, and you can also turn in some shallow concentric circles to help with initial centering of the clay (Fig. 3).

Since the wheel-head will be used in exceptionally wet conditions, it needs to be sealed well. It does not, however, want to be a glass finish, as the clay will tend not to adhere.

To get over this cut the sealant (exterior grade polyurethane) with thinners to about 50/50. The extra thinners will act as a carrier and get better penetration. The next coat can have more polish added and so on until you have built up protection in the wood itself.

Finally, flat the surface off with fine glasspaper or steel wool to provide a key for the clay.

MATERIALS LIST
1 20mm nut
1 piece BM steel 75mm dia × 10mm
6.5m × 50mm × 10mm iroko (for 250mm dia wheel head)
8.5m × 50mm × 10mm iroko (for 300mm dia wheel head)
3 No. 1¼in. × No. 12 countersunk steel screws

1.

2.

3.

AWARDS
TO YOUNG CRAFTSMEN

Another of the very worthwhile services provided by the Council for Small Industries in Rural Areas (CoSIRA) is the new entrant training scheme (NETS) for young craftsmen usually in the 16-19 age group who have served a probationary period of three months with an employer.

Training is for a period of three years and trainees attend four one-week courses each year at the CoSIRA workshops at Salisbury. Each year also the council's training officers visit trainees at their places of employment to ensure that the training programme is being carried out in accordance with the syllabus issued by CoSIRA.

Presentation of NETS certificates and awards were made on 24 September at the Salisbury offices of CoSIRA by H. F. W. Cory JP, a director of the council and chairman of its Wiltshire small industries committee. He was accompanied by W. F. Nesbitt, chief advisory officer of CoSIRA.

Mr Cory told the trainees: 'You have all worked with application and goodwill and this is a great credit to you and to your instructors. You and your employers are the gainers because the standards set by the council are of a high order and the council has great pleasure in handing on the skills of its instructors to the craftsmen and craftswomen in rural industries.'

Above: Carl Mapes, best entry in the CoSIRA NETS furniture making course for 1981. Carl is employed by R. Fyson of Lechlade, Glos.

Presentations were made to the following: Carl Mapes (employed by R. Fyson, Lechlade); Martyn Richards (employed by G. B. Spicer & Sons, Pontesbury) (furniture making leading to furniture restoration). M. Northcott (Devon); J. Bretherton (Wilts); K. Catherick (Kent); M. Ching (Dorset); R. Davies (Devon); G. Denton (Warwicks); M. Lewis (Berks); C. Northover (Norfolk); P. Reading (Northants); A. Wright (Devon) (thatching).

D. Wrigglesworth (Oxon); P. Glanville (Devon); Helen Watkins (Glos); Molly Claridge (Berks); D. Busk (Hereford & Worcs) (saddlery and leatherwork). D. Hawes (Norfolk); N. Collett (Suffolk & Northumberland); M. K. Bland (Essex); G. O. Jones (Somerset) (forgework).

Details of CoSIRA new entrant training scheme can be had from the council at 141 Castle Street, Salisbury SP1 3TB.

Left: Martyn Richards receiving his certificate for successfully completing the CoSIRA NETS course in furniture making. Martyn is employed by G. B. Spicer & Sons, Pontesbury, Salop.

The **NEW** EMCO REX 2000 offers all the basic woodworking operations in one compact machine, requiring the minimum of space and giving the maximum of power to make all your woodworking projects a pleasure.

Project yourself into the year 2000 with an EMCO REX 2000 machining centre.

Moulding with the EMCO REX 2000
Quiet running and smooth surfaces are ensured due to playfree moulding spindle manufactured in vibration free cast iron. Full transmission of power by stable v belt drive, adjustable stop for longitudinal and cross moulding ensures quick and safe setting of moulding depth, two working speeds of 4000 and 6000 RPM.

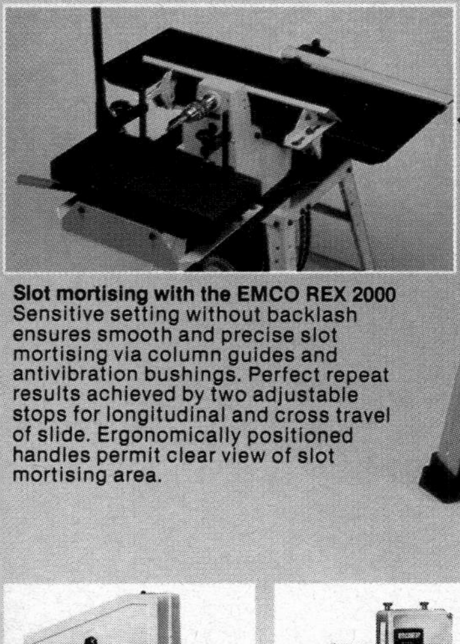

Slot mortising with the EMCO REX 2000
Sensitive setting without backlash ensures smooth and precise slot mortising via column guides and antivibration bushings. Perfect repeat results achieved by two adjustable stops for longitudinal and cross travel of slide. Ergonomically positioned handles permit clear view of slot mortising area.

Sawing and sanding with the EMCO REX 2000
The large size tilting table allows cutting of bulky work pieces. The 10 inch saw blade gives a big 3 inch depth of cut (6″ by double cut). Exact and quick adjustment of the cutting depth is reached with the conveniently located operating handwheel. The sanding disc ensures smooth accurate surfaces all the time.

Planing and Thicknessing with the EMCO REX 2000
Big capacity of 10″ x 6″, 3mm depth of cut with automatic feed. Easy action rise and fall of thicknessing table with metric and imperial scales. Tilting fence up to 45°. SAFE all danger spots fully guarded.

The EMCO REX 2000

The EMCO REX 2000 machining centre is the product of 25 years development by top Austrian designers. There are over 80,000 EMCO Woodworking machines in service throughout the world. The EMCO Rex 2000 will pay for itself in the first major project. It can handle a job for which you would need five single purpose machines. You don't need to shuttle back and forth between several machines. What's more, you will save space, a corner of your garage or cellar will do. Built on the modular principle, having purchased the planer thicknesser as the basic power unit the other attachments can be bought separately.

On the subject of safety your safety is worth more than the standards require. For example the attachments are driven separately from the planer shaft, this makes a mistake impossible. When it comes to accessories, things like an effective circular saw guard, a safety cutter head or a safety hold down device are a matter of course for us.

All EMCO machines are fully guaranteed.

These are other machines in the Fabulous EMCO range from EME.

BS2 BANDSAW
A 3 speed bandsaw for wood, metal and plastic. 14.3″ throat by 5-7″ depth of cut allows cutting of large work pieces. Ease of operation ensures exact and clean cuts, long-lasting durability.

EMCO STAR
A single machine and yet a complete workshop. Six woodworking operations: band sawing, circular sawing, fret sawing, jig sawing, belt sanding, disc sanding and with the comprehensive EMCO accessory range the machine will perform 16 major woodworking operations.

EMCO DB5 WOOD-TURNING LATHE
Fitted with all the technical details of a modern wood turning lathe including torsion resistant steel construction heavy duty spindle, 4 ideally stepped speeds, heavy duty machine bed, practical and stable tool rest, mechanical and electrical safety devices,

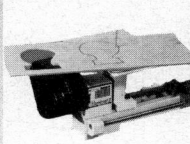
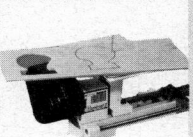

EMCO UNIMAT 3 LATHE
A woodworking and metalworking lathe in miniature. The woodworking operations are turning, jig sawing, fret sawing, circular sawing, moulding. The metal working operations are turning, facing, taper turning, threadcutting, centre drilling, polishing, grinding and milling.

EME

BEC
THE ELLIOTT GROUP

EME LIMITED
BEC HOUSE
VICTORIA ROAD
LONDON NW10 6NY
TELEPHONE: 01-965 4050

EME LTD.
(Northern Branch)
18 Sidcup Road,
Roundthorne
Industrial Estate,
Wythenshawe,
Manchester 23,
Tel: 061-945 2382

EME LTD.
(Scottish Branch)
The Machine Tool Centre,
Law Place,
Nerston,
East Kilbride G74 4QL
Tel: (03552) 48221
Telex: 777319

This elegant piece which is only 2ft 2in. × 15 × 11in. overall, features a bowed front with framed and slatted doors. Readers wishing to attempt this job should refer to the accompanying scale drawings and the description given here.

Great attention is always paid in Mr Barnsley's Froxfield workshops to the selection of materials for each job and dominant features in the grain are always placed symmetrically to preserve the balance and harmony of the design.

The slatted doors for instance would have been obtained from deeped stock opened out to provide two matching panels. These panels would then have been ripped into slats and carefully numbered for re-assembly later on. The slats by the way, are a neat constructional solution to making curved doors.

The carcase is constructed of a top secret lap dovetailed to the sides with shelves dovetail housed in and the bottom is lap dovetailed. An adjustable half shelf is provided in the cupboard. The back framing has a central muntin dividing two cedar of Lebanon panels and the whole sub-assembly is rebated into the back of the carcase and secured with raised-head screws.

The drawer front is cut from the solid and inlaid with 1/16in. sycamore line set some 3/32in. from the edge. The drawer pull is dovetailed into the top edge of the drawer front and is screwed and pelleted in. The projection of the drawer pull is allowed to 'die' away at the ends to blend in with the face of the drawer.

Cedar is specified for the drawer bottom, as for the back, because this wood has an aromatic scent which sweetens what would otherwise be a stale volume of air. Quartered oak is preferred for the drawer sides because of its inherent stability and hard-wearing qualities.

The bowed doors have an unusual design feature. The top mortise and tenons at the meeting edges are reversed from the usual practice in order to preserve the visual continuity of the top rails. The sycamore inlay lines which 'tie' each door frame are set 3/32in. from the inner edge and the shoulder lines of the corner joints are mitred to provide visual continuity again (as shown in the accompanying sketch).

The door slats are held by tongued and grooved joints and these are not glued. The butt line between each slat is emphasised by rounding over the edges; the shutting stiles on the doors are butted in order that either door may be opened. These are secured by magnetic catches.

Doors and drawer are set back 1/16in. from the carcase which has all arrises radiused over. The brass hinges for the doors are cleaned-up and decorated as described in WOODWORKER for August 1981 pp510-11.

The underframe is mortised and tenoned together and the shoulders are mitred as shown to avoid short grain at the blending of the serpentine curve. The side rails are profiled to emphasise the stability of the structure. Wooden buttons are used to secure the underframe to the carcase, suitably slotted to allow for movement.

A waxed finish would look well on this piece, although nowadays a spray lacquer is frequently applied to the jobs coming from the Froxfield workshops.

BEDSIDE CUPBOARD

Design by Edward Barnsley

Described and illustrated by R. W. Grant DLC FRSA MSIAD

Cutting list

Net sizes given
Dimensions in inches

No.	Description	L	W	T	Material
	Carcase				
1	Top	16	ex 11	5/8	Mahogany
1	Bottom	16	ex 11	5/8	Mahogany
2	Shelves	16	ex 11	5/8	Mahogany
2	Sides	21	10	5/8	Mahogany
1	Half shelf	14	7	5/8	Quartered oak
	Back				
1	Top rail	14½	1	5/8	Mahogany
1	Bottom rail	14½	1½	5/8	Mahogany
2	Stiles	21	1 3/8	5/8	Mahogany
1	Muntin	21	1½	5/8	Mahogany
2	Panels	20½	7	¼	Cedar
	Doors				
2	Top rails	6½	1¼	ex 2	Mahogany
2	Bottom rails	6½	1½	ex 2	Mahogany
2	Hanging stiles	13	1 3/8	5/8	Mahogany
2	Shutting stiles	13	1 1/8	5/8	Mahogany
2	Panels to cut slats	11	6	5/8	Mahogany
	Drawer				
1	Front	14	4	ex 2	Mahogany
1	Back	14	3	¼	Quartered oak
2	Sides	9½	4	¼	Quartered oak
1	Bottom	14	9¾	¼	Cedar
	Underframe				
4	Legs	4	1¾	1¾	Mahogany
2	Rails	14½	2½	¾	Mahogany
2	Side rails	10	2½	¾	Mahogany
4	Brass butt hinges	1½			
2	Magnetic catches				

Fixing buttons to underframe and handles to suit. 1/16in. sycamore lines for doors and drawer.

PREVIOUS ARTICLES IN THIS SERIES OF DESIGNS BY EDWARD BARNSLEY

1. **UPHOLSTERED STOOL WOODWORKER NOVEMBER 1980 pp718-720**

2. **OCTAGONAL DRESSING TABLE MIRROR WOODWORKER MARCH 1981 pp162-163**

3. **CIGAR BOX IN INDIAN ROSEWOOD WOODWORKER JUNE 1981 pp376-377**

4. **WALL FITMENT WOODWORKER AUGUST 1981 pp510-511**

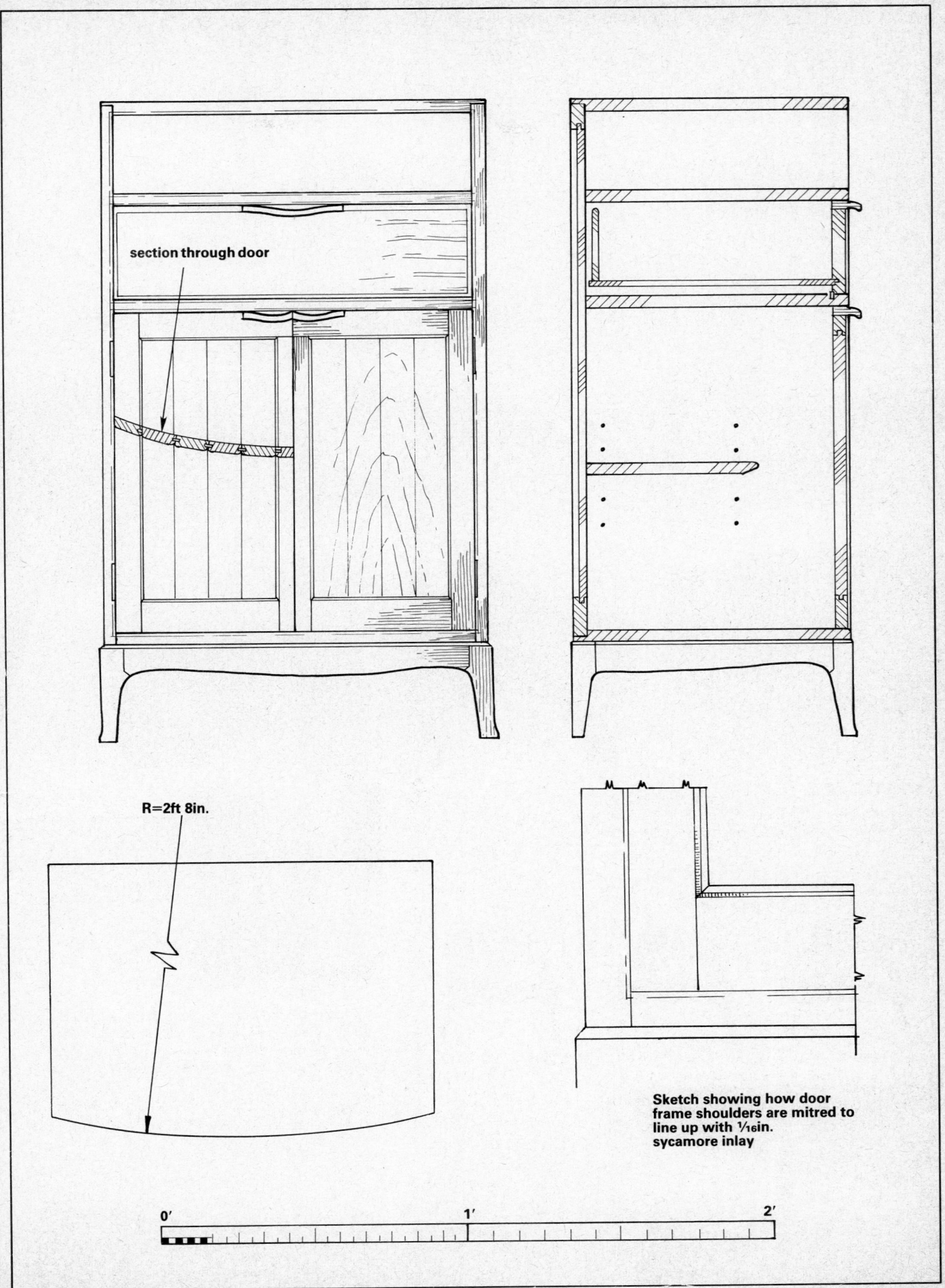

section through door

R=2ft 8in.

Sketch showing how door
frame shoulders are mitred to
line up with 1/16in.
sycamore inlay

0'   1'   2'

The saw designed to give you __perfect__ results in modern materials

NOT JUST FOR PROFESSIONALS

Advanced production systems bring this precision tool within your reach. For little more than the cost of a light pressed steel sawbench, you can enjoy the accuracy and precision of the TGS171.

Add the sliding table and you can cut boards and panels up to 36″ at a perfect 90°.

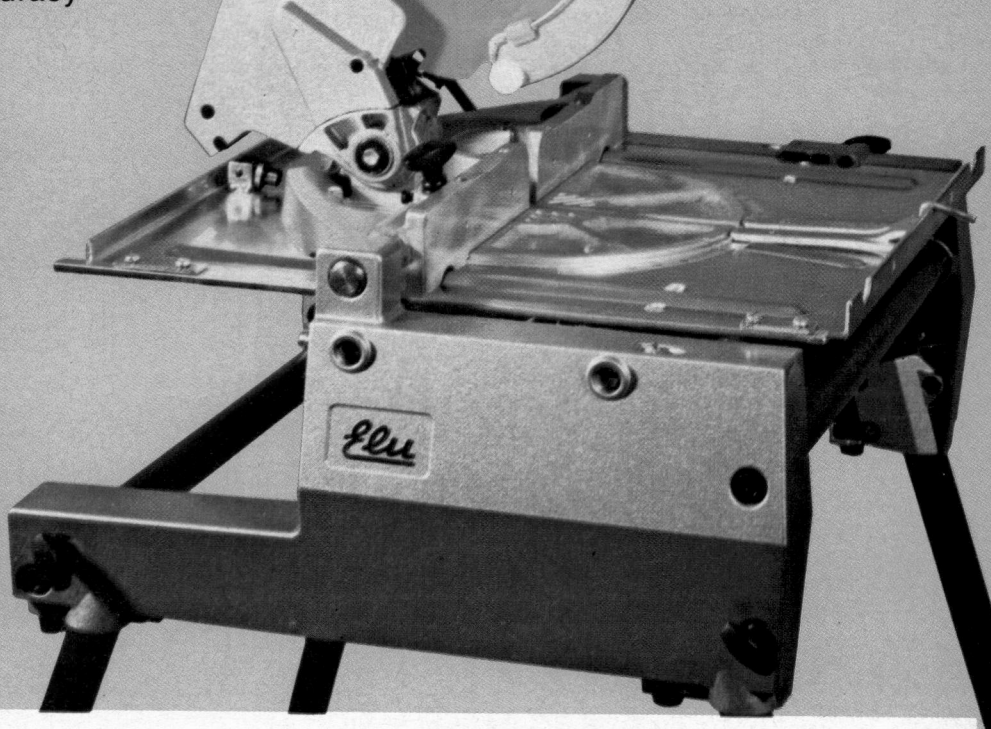

Versatility

Simply pull the plunge table locking lever, and the overhead mitre cutting saw swivels through 180° to become a conventional bench saw.

A sawbench.........A simple flip over.....A perfect Mitre saw.

Stability

Wide bearing point of pivot, precision ground for stability.

Whether you need to cut delicate veneered boards for cabinet building or even alloy extrusions for mitred frames, the new TGS171 has been developed to give the performance and consistent accuracy you want.

Further Information
Elu have a nationwide network of over 200 authorised distributors. Contact us today for your **FREE** fully illustrated colour brochure and full list of authorised Elu dealers.

Superb Accuracy

Positive locking at any precise angle between square and 45°.

Elu Machinery Ltd.

310-312 Dallow Road, Luton, Bedfordshire. LU1 1SS

Tel: (0582) 425001 Telex: 825540

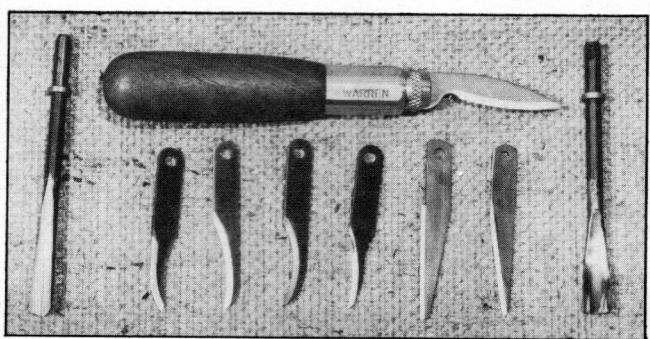

 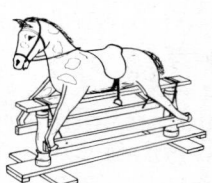  

Prices quoted are those prevailing at press date and are subject to alteration due to economic conditions.

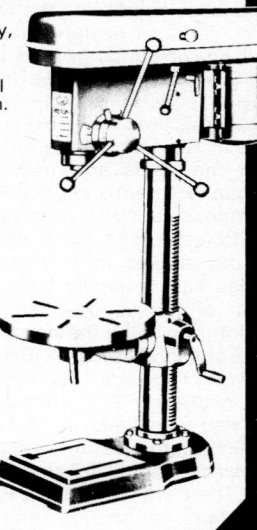

'Out of the whinnying green stable
On to the fields of praise'

In the November 1981 issue of WOOD-WORKER pp742—743, Bob Grant gave readers an insight into the work of Lucinda Leech, furniture designer and maker whose working surroundings are some old stables and a coach house. Now in early 1982 we provide readers with a glimpse into another stable. This time the venue is not Oxford but London N8, just off the old drovers' road from the fields and market gardens of Enfield, Waltham and Cheshunt en route to the markets of north London.

In October 1979, Brian Bostock acquired the old stables in Fairfax Mews. These stables had originally been the overnight home of horses destined for the horse auction ring (now the home of the Harringay Conservative club). Between October 1979 and February 1980 a lot of hard work was necessary to turn the old hay loft (reached by a ladder) and the ground floor stabling, into useful, workable premises which now enjoy a light industrial classification. There was no electricity, no stairs, no insulation, no heating, no... The list was endless.

Now it is a comfortable workshop in which a workforce of 4 (4.6 to be exact) manages to harmoniously live and work together in a relatively quiet atmosphere (only broken when necessary by the sound of small power tools; the talk of men mainly absorbed in their work or the ring of the door bell and telephone).

Bostock Woodcraft Ltd offer the 'best of both worlds – the designs of today made with the care and quality of yesterday.' As one of their advertising leaflets says 'we do not print the grain of mahogany or teak on vast sheets of chipboard... we do not mould you a chair of short lived and dangerously inflammable plastics... our drawers are not extruded from pvc.' They do, however, have boards of seasoned hardwood, oak, walnut, elm, yew, exotic timbers, utile, mahogany; their workbenches have dovetail saws, planes and chisels.

A variety of high quality furniture is made by traditional handmaking methods; made with skill to a high standard of design and finish from quality timbers personally selected to the customer's own requirements.

Complete schemes of interior design are undertaken for domestic and commercial applications, picture framing and antique restoration are also offered, plus certain turned items and smaller woodcraft in good quality hardwood.

Working in reverse order – the latest and youngest fulltime member of Brian's staff is David Withers. David trained at the London College of Furniture. His simulation project in furniture restoration was the subject of an article in WOODWORKER (November 1981 pp750-752) and one on oyster veneering in the same issue (p781). David came to Bostock Woodcraft at the end of the college year in 1981. His skills have already been appreciated and utilised and his first major piece was a gate-leg table. David and Brian hope to work together on design and cabinetmaking in the future thus broadening the scope of the workshop and bringing a new dimension to the creative talents of the firm.

Above: the yew and rosewood needlework box that won for Brian Bostock joint first prize in the cabinetmaking section of the 1981 WOODWORKER SHOW.

In June 1981 Brian's brother Derek joined the firm as sales manager of the other facet of the enterprise, the Craft-Equip side. Derek is responsible for the development, organisation and planning of this side of the business. He also handles the PR side of the company and initiates many of the sales and orders usually being the one to 'leg' the

product around the various possible retail outlets. Derek had an engineering training but it is his skills as a personnel manager of an electrical company that now come fully into their own.

When you are offering trade quality items in diy pack/kit form and quantity a vast percentage of one's time is spent in assembling those packs. It is no use receiving via mail order a stool kit to find you only have three cabriole legs or a tapestry frame without its mahogany tightening nuts.

This area then is one that Derek handles methodically and efficiently. No one is perfect and mistakes do happen... in such a

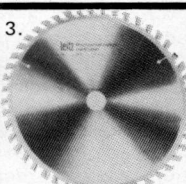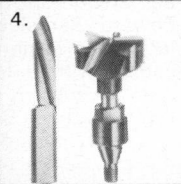

case the brothers have gone out of their way to personally rectify the fault, believing that a firm is responsible for its products whether they are ordered in ones, tens or hundreds.

In March 1980, a month after trading started at the mews premises Leslie Delaforce joined the company. Though only a 'Monday and Tuesday' man, Leslie slips into a slot every Monday morning with his 'mini production line' side of the business. He is the sort of person who has retired and therefore works harder than ever before, often seen in the craft of woodworking.

Of Hugenot extraction, Leslie is an experienced and well qualified man; a fascinating person to speak to; his eyes twinkle as he tells of his many activities. Trained originally as a pattern maker, followed by a spell as instructor at the Ministry of Labour and National Service (The Manpower Services Board) Leslie was until his retirement a lecturer in design and drawing at the technical college in Southgate.

He is currently spending time (when not at Bostock Woodcraft) illustrating a textbook to be published next year by McDonald & Evans, written by Keith Parsley, concerning technology for the new technical education courses. A versatile craftsman indeed, Leslie has designed and made the jigs needed for the production of the spoon display racks and lace bobbin winders they are currently making and marketing. At the recent ICHF held at Wembley Conference Centre the firm introduced these and other lacemaking items and significantly the bobbin winders now have the approval of the English Lace School and the Lace Guild. The Embroiderers Guild is also interested in items and equipment for canvas work.

Another once a week member of the BW team is Bill Davis. A retired woodmachinist, Bill comes to the workshop each Thursday and prepares timber for the following week's work. He says he thoroughly enjoys his 'day out' – certainly he arrives singing and joking and is still just as happy at the end of the day. The firm would be the poorer without Bill in the team.

Which brings one to the head of the firm, the driving force – the man holding the reins (to carry the stable analogy a little further) Brian Bostock himself.

Brian was born in the 30s in Leicestershire and after a traditional schooling was accepted by the teachers' training department of Loughborough college, not on the teachers' course, which was largely full of mature students being retrained (after the war) under government handicrafts schemes; but on a parallel course in cabinetmaking.

This was still the period of Cotswold orientated craftsmen at Loughborough, particularly through the principal lecturer Frank Ockenden and Cecil Gough, the latter an ex-Gordon Russell workshops man. Edward Barnsley CBE was the visiting lecturer in design. Brian's was a five year course with a local education authority grant to support him initially (£44 a year). While a student Brian took his intermediate and final City and Guilds exams in cabinetmaking. He is a 'first prize' medallist, one of the highest awards in cabinetmaking. He is too modest about his achievement. 'I was in the right place and atmosphere at the right time,' he says. Possibly true but without ability nought is achieved. Beside the medal he received a prize of £5 – a princely sum which he lavished on a copy of *Modern Cabinetwork Furniture and Fitments,* otherwise known as Wells & Hooper – a cabinetmakers' bible that he still treasures and uses. After this five years Brian joined the forces and trained as a field engineer in the RE. No doubt the joists and quality of his workshops' constructional joinery owe much to the early practice gained on Bailey bridges.

Brian wanted a job as a furniture designer; typically he did not sit around waiting for a job to fall into his lap. He worked for six weeks with Robson of Newcastle, as a furniture restorer. One of the pieces that passed through his hands was a games table belonging to the Duke of Northumberland. This was in the shape of a 5ft diameter roulette wheel with yes/no alternating around the circumference rather than the red/black and numbers of the conventional wheel. Several years later when visiting Alnwick Castle as a tourist Brian was able to point the table out to his wife. It was still as grand as he remembered it to be.

He found his design job in Sunderland and worked for a year with a firm producing

basic kitchen furniture, handwork was little or nil since machine production runs were used to mass produce on a modest scale. The Suez crisis loomed, petrol went on ration and the long journeys previously undertaken with vans carrying a small amount of finished furniture and a lot of wasted air space became impossible.

Brian redesigned and the factory foremen rejigged the whole range for manufacture in KD form. Some 260 pieces could now be carried per van in this KD state and with a bench on the tailboard the cabinets etc were assembled in the town of delivery often in the local carpark.

A year later he was back in the Arts and Crafts movement atmosphere and the Cotswold tradition; back that is at Loughborough – now the Loughborough Training College – as their staff production officer – half his time, he says, was spent instructing in cabinetmaking and wood machining and the other half running the workshops and making furniture. There are, therefore, many pieces of furniture in offices and in the library with Brian's name on them.

Life at Loughborough was idyllic from 1957-1960, the college life suited the Bostocks. Brian's wife Linda was lecturing in mathematics for engineering students as they brought up their family and then came to that turning point in a career where you have to decide to move or you stay and put it off for ever.

They moved, to the London County Council (now the GLC) – Brian became buyer and designer of furniture mainly for education. For nine years (until 1969) he was responsible exclusively for furniture; and bought for schools and colleges, offices and residential homes. The law courts at Croydon are furnished to his designs. Equipping the Crystal Palace National Recreation Centre was a major challenge since it included retractable seating and changing room lockers on a large scale, furnishing of the hostel, buying all manner of equipment even to the spring boards of the Olympic size swimming pool. In the late 60s now a senior technical officer in furniture purchasing, he was part of the team working on London's South Bank schemes, he had a hand in furnishing the Festival Hall, the Queen Elizabeth Hall and the Hayward gallery. (Architect for the GLC at that time was Sir Hubert Bennett).

Health reasons forced Brian's early retirement in 1979 and so we are now back to the start of Bostock Woodcraft in Fairfax Mews.

Brian also has some outworkers – part of the .6 of his workforce – turners and other craftsmen who take some of the pressure when production is heavy, who complete certain orders to assembly stage and who generally, for the most part, fit in on a freelance basis when and where needed. One of these is Geoff Bullimore who won the musical instrument section (stringed instruments) at the 1980 WOODWORKER SHOW with his excellent guitar. Geoff has made a Cuban mahogany table with boxwood and ebony inlay to a commissioned design of Brian's. Here we see the firm following the old traditions of master designer and craftsman with apprentices or staff carrying out the actual work to the required specifications.

Left: the nest of tables that Brian designed and now forms one of his commissioned lines. Detail shown over the page.

Brian has made some splendid church furniture, the latest works are two processional crosses. His book of commissions includes chairs, sideboards, presentation boxes and caskets, a chart table for a Trinity House pilot, nests of tables, dressing tables, wardrobes. A range of traditional English oak furniture (dresser, table, chairs) and stools, benches and tables in pine are offered. In a range of smaller craft items spoon display racks are regularly made as are steak knives and forks with handles of rosewood, teak, elm, mahogany, holly and/or yew, also toilet mirrors, both round and oval in oak and mahogany.

An early recent commission was to make a writing table for a lady (who had spent much of her working life in the far east) to suit her precise requirements but also to fit into an Oriental atmosphere. A piece with the curved inturned feet of the Ming dynasty was made for her; it certainly does not look out of place. Another recent commission was for the Worshipful Company of Gardeners – a poors box – designed to be passed person to person it needed handgrips and ease of entry for both notes and coins. As a perfect complement to the livery company Brian used 12 English woods to make this attractive item.

His latest, a most exciting commission, has been the display presentation case to hold a crystal vase given by the Directors of Hudson's Bay, London to the Soviet State Fur Company on the occasion of fifty years of trading. This was presented in Moscow in October. The box lined in red velvet and covered by blue leather, has ebony inserts at all the edges and a macassar ebony

plinth. The hinged doors are lined with mirrors tinted copper-bronze, the hinges and handle are of brass, a magnificent setting for exquisite crystal.

One of the latest pieces – a rosewood and yew needlework box was entered in the cabinetmaking section of the 1981 WOODWORKER SHOW. It was awarded joint first prize in the cabinetmaking section.

WOODWORKER was pleased to visit Brian and discuss his work. His venture is growing, his skills and those of his craftsmen are obvious in their work and the way they handle their tools; theirs is no rate race; life can be a struggle for a small firm but they are artisans practising their art and craft, they will succeed. We look to more beautiful objects leaving his stable in the future 'on to the fields of praise' indeed.

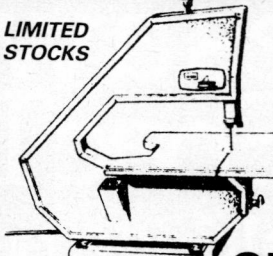

DRYING YOUR TIMBER

8

Here W. H. Brown FIWSc offers some guidelines on constructing a chamber in which to condition smallish sections or piece parts. The article introduces the construction of the chamber. In following issues adaptations of the basic theme and other matters will be discussed.

Previous articles in this series have appeared in March, April, July, August, September and October 1981 and in January 1982

Bearing in mind the time of year and the difficulty of conditioning small quantities of wood during winter months under domestic or semi-domestic situations, we think it expedient to offer some guidelines on the construction of an inexpensive chamber in which to condition smallish sections or piece parts to a reasonable m.c.

While the construction of a suitable shell does not present serious problems, the feasibility and availability of a suitable heat source and the means to prevent stratification of the air can prove difficult.

Since it is probable that in most individual cases some adaptation of the basic theme would be necessary; and since, too, the project will run beyond one article, we think it essential here to introduce the basic construction.

A few years ago Forest Products Laboratory at Madison, Wisconsin, developed three variations on a basic theme of conditioning chambers for wood piece parts and sheet materials intended for furniture and cabinetmaking. This came about because of difficulties regularly experienced when furniture and similar was shipped to different parts of the country. For example, in northern parts of the US exceedingly low relative humidities in heated buildings during the winter are responsible for severely reducing the m.c. in wooden items. This often results in checking, splitting, warping, shrinking and loosening of joints. On the other hand, in seaboard areas, particularly the gulf coast, continuous high humidities frequently cause drawers and doors to swell and stick, as well as warping and telegraphing (or show-through) in some veneered items.

Because of customer complaints FPL developed these low-cost conditioning rooms or chambers and the reason for three types was that each was intended to have an atmosphere suitable for wood that was to be sent to separate areas. In other words, one was designed to produce conditions equal to 12% relative humidity (RH) one at 42% RH and one at 72% RH.

These values need some qualification. It will be understood that here in UK our average m.c. values for wood are a little higher than the average value in the US. For example, we think in terms of 10% m.c. as a national average with only slight geographical variations, whereas in the US the value is 8% m.c. with wide fluctuations.

In this US project, 42% RH in the temperature range of 65° to 90°F corresponded to an equilibrium m.c. (EMC) for wood of 8%, 4 to 5% m.c. for hardboard, 3 to 4% for decorative laminates and typical backing sheets, about 7% in flat-press particleboards and 6 to 9% m.c. for paper. We look for a relative humidity of 50% or slightly more to give an EMC for wood of 10%.

The conditioning room designed for a RH of 12% would have an EMC for wood of about 4%. To us this sounds exceptional but during the coldest weather, wood test pieces in the lobby of FPL reached EMC of 3% over a period of at least a month. We are mentioning this because in the conditioning room concerned, to achieve an EMC of 4% an old domestic refrigerator with the door permanently removed was used to obtain the correct air conditions.*

We have shown this in Fig. 1 but will return to its possible use later. It will no doubt be understood that in the quite common use today of dehumidifying equipment, this extracts moisture from the wood and passes the moisture-laden air into the dehumidifier where the air makes contact with cold evaporator coils, the moisture is condensed and runs out to drain; in other words, refrigeration techniques are employed basically.

We will deal initially with a basic shell as shown in Fig. 1 using FPL method and dimensions of 7 × 7 × 7ft (2.1 × 2.1 × 2.1m). Adaptations would probably be needed dimensionally and particularly in regard to ventilation in the case of fairly wet wood being dried rather than conditioned by a few points of m.c.

Constructional details are as follows:

1 The frame may be built from norminal 2 × 2in. (50 × 50mm) surfaced all-round softwood, preferably liberally brush-treated with an organic solvent preservative. Fabricate the four walls and top separately using suitable corner joints.

No bottom frame is necessary. To provide extra rigidity nail bracing diagonally between the vertical members in the lower half of the wall frames, leaving a door opening of convenient size in one wall. 2 Fasten the four wall frames together on-site with ¼in. (6mm) carriage bolts. Next position the top frame on the walls and bolt down. A door to fit the door opening should be fabricated and hung in place. A vapour-tight gasket or weather-stripping should be fitted completely around the door.

Here we must digress again: the question of whether or not to make the chamber air-tight is dependent on the type of drying and the amount of moisture to be removed. This is something which needs further discussion but at this point a word of caution is absolutely essential.

In any envisaged chamber large enough for a person to enter, the door must open outwards, have no lock and be capable of being opened from the inside. Any stay by a person inside the chamber should be restricted to, say, no more than 1hr. In a chamber likely to need natural air draught, then the base of the door could be modified, in conjunction with a couple of vents in the roof of the chamber, to encourage air flow upwards, in which case close fitting of the door is not essential.

We will continue with the constructional details in a future issue.

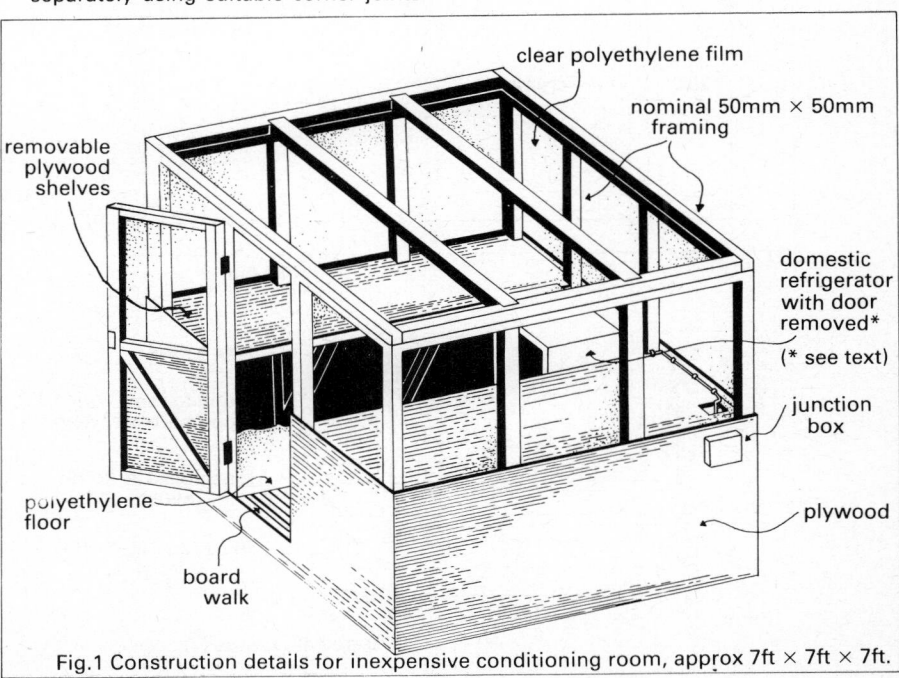

Fig.1 Construction details for inexpensive conditioning room, approx 7ft × 7ft × 7ft.

- clear polyethylene film
- nominal 50mm × 50mm framing
- removable plywood shelves
- domestic refrigerator with door removed* (* see text)
- junction box
- polyethylene floor
- plywood
- board walk

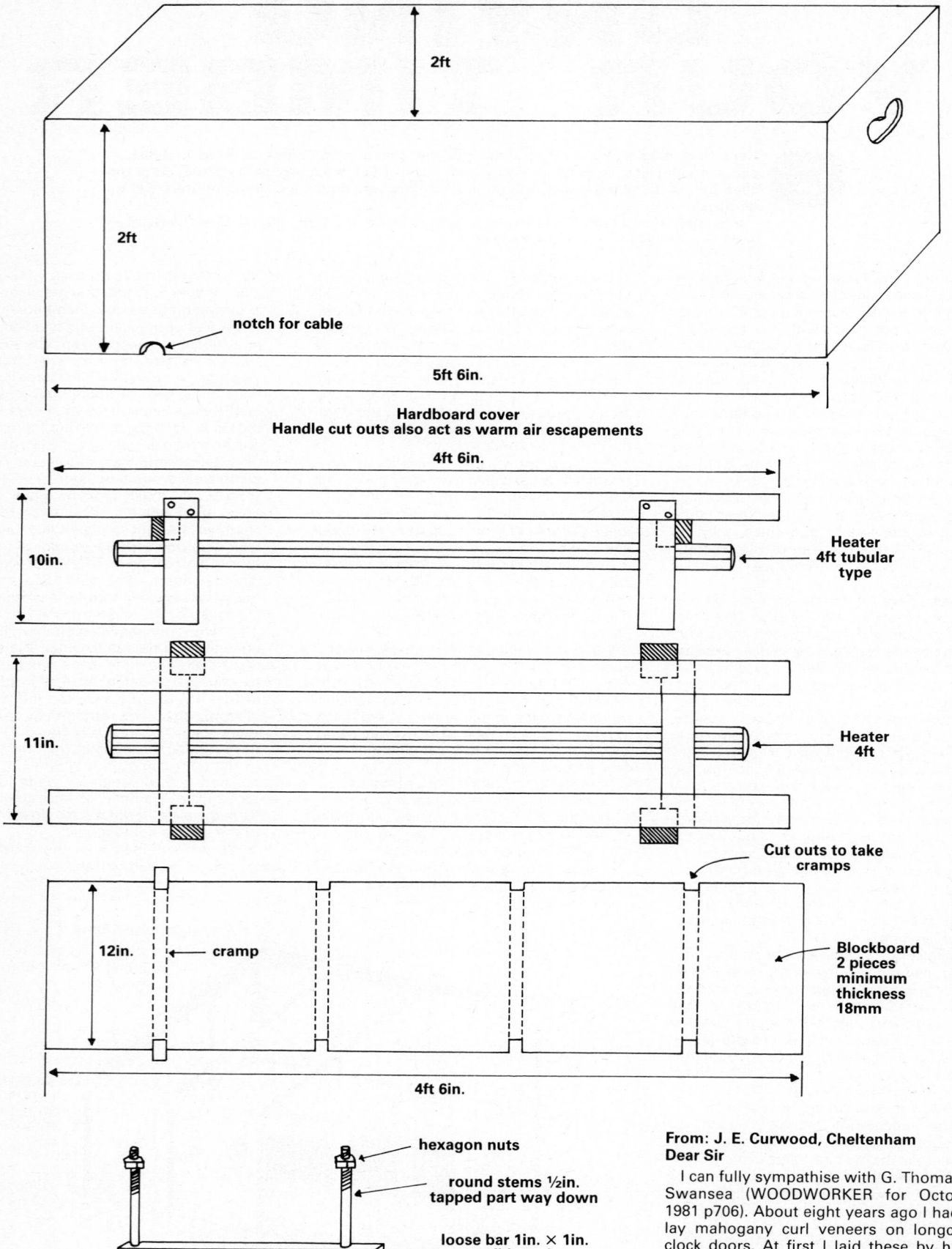

2ft

2ft

notch for cable

5ft 6in.

Hardboard cover
Handle cut outs also act as warm air escapements

4ft 6in.

10in.

Heater
4ft tubular
type

11in.

Heater
4ft

Cut outs to take
cramps

12in. ← **cramp**

Blockboard
2 pieces
minimum
thickness
18mm

4ft 6in.

hexagon nuts

round stems ½in.
tapped part way down

loose bar 1in. × 1in.
mild steel

fixed bar 1in. × 1in.
mild steel

14in.

Detail of cramps (4)

From: J. E. Curwood, Cheltenham
Dear Sir

I can fully sympathise with G. Thomas of Swansea (WOODWORKER for October 1981 p706). About eight years ago I had to lay mahogany curl veneers on longcase clock doors. At first I laid these by hand using scotch glue but the results were disastrous.

Curl is difficult as Mr Thomas suggests. It is difficult because present-day curl is knife-cut and very buckled. Eventually my problem was solved and I pass on the solution in the hope that it will help him and other readers.

The curl is *not* wetted. If this is done it stretches and then shrinks after laying and the darker short grain areas become full of cracks. It should be flattened in a heated press, perfectly dry, for 24hr prior to laying.

Then stick pieces of 1in. wide gummed brown paper tape across the short grain areas and along the sides and top and bottom of the piece of veneer to be laid. If for example the section required is, say, 40 × 9in., this area is marked-out with the tape making the centre of each tape the finished line.

When the tape is dry, with a steel straight-edge and sharp knife the piece is cut from the sheet. As many pieces as required are prepared in this way. The pieces are carefully laid in the press which is gradually tightened, the heat switched on and the press left for 24hr.

At the end of this period the pieces are taken from the press and if the taping has been carried out correctly the veneer will be perfectly flat and ready to lay with Cascamite one-shot adhesive. Burr walnut veneers can be treated in the same manner.

I give sketches of the heated press I made and find very successful. The dimensions given are those that suit my work. Incidentally, the heated chamber can be used for drying-off other work, particularly in winter. I find it useful for quickly drying out work which has been fastened with PVA adhesive.

One improvement to the press is to have a supply of mild steel sheets about ⅛in. thick to place over each piece of veneer (and later each veneered piece). For example, six pieces of veneer or work require the equivalent number of steel sheets. I put a piece of polythene directly on each piece of work before placing the steel sheets in position.

Yours faithfully, **J. E. Curwood**

From: **W. H. Brown FIWSc, Amersham**
Dear Sir

I would like to comment on part of the letter from E. R. Kingdon of Western Australia (WOODWORKER for September 1981, p609); I refer to his method of drying his turnery wood.

This is an interesting point but I do not know how far Mr Kingdon has been guided by what he has read of centrifugal drying, or whether he has developed his technique purely by trial and error. Since the matter could be of general interest, I would make the following remarks:

In 1952 in Salzburg, Eisenmann KG of Stuttgart demonstrated what was called an 'air-conditioning spiral centrifuge' for the drying of timber. Without going into a lot of detail, it consisted of three steel cages arranged around a central, vertical spindle.

The timber to be dried was placed in the steel cages, the bases of which engaged in a steel track in the floor. When the motor was switched on the cages revolved at an ever-increasing speed and water was flung from the wood. The whole machine was housed in a chamber in which heat and humidity could be introduced as required, and the process was claimed to dry wood of all descriptions in a shorter space of time, and at a more attractive cost, than by conventional kilning methods.

The method did not become commercial although the running costs were apparently very economical: the main reason for rejection was the fairly short life of the bearings,

the centrifuge in question being designed to dry 500ft^3 of timber at a time so that centrifugal force would be considerable.

In subsequent experiments carried out in Prague using a small laboratory centrifuge to dry beech and oak parquet blocks, it was reported that drying times were 30-50% shorter than with conventional-type kilns and there did not appear any more danger of seasoning degrade than with normal kiln-drying.

In Mr Kingdon's system what is happening is that much, perhaps most, of the free water in the pore cavities is being removed when the wood is left spinning on the lathe. In other words the fibre saturation point (FSP) is not reached but a lot of unwanted water is removed. The actual seasoning, ie from the FSP of about 30% m.c., commences when the wood is buried in the dry shavings. Here actual drying is brought about by the favourable air conditions.

She-oak is not a true oak (*Quercus*) but is a species of *Casuarina* although the wood does bear a resemblance to our evergreen oak (*Q. ilex*) in that it lacks the rings of large pores typical in the sessile and pedunculate oaks.

She-oak does produce large rays like oak and therefore any attempt to hasten the drying from the FSP tends to cause cracking and splitting. However, unlike the majority of Australian hardwood, ie eucalypts and acacias, which are usually so refractory that the only sensible way of seasoning is to kiln-dry them and then recondition them in order to iron out the stresses, she-oak is a much kinder wood. It requires care but would lend itself quite readily to the drying technique Mr Kingdon employs. It is used extensively for decorative cabinetwork, veneer, shingles, cooperage, and for the manufacture of wooden hand-screws as well as turnery.

Yours faithfully, **W. H. Brown**

Letters

From: **Charles Cliffe, Bexleyheath, Kent**
Dear Sir

It frequently happens that a door is required to close automatically. One popular and neat method of achieving this is to use sprung hinges which contain powerful springs. These cause the hinges to close and although effective in closing doors they are equally so at nipping the fingers of the person fitting them.

The tricky part is to keep the hinge open while running the screws into the door and the frame. I find a simple way of doing this is to use two specially shaped blocks of wood and a nut and bolt which will pass through the screw holes in the hinge leaves.

One leaf of the hinge is gripped in the vice while the other is held open at 90° with a pair of pliers. The bolt is pushed through a screw hole in the leaf which is to be screwed to the door and the nut tightened. A small hardwood block (A) is inserted between the bolt and the other leaf and this keeps the two leaves apart while the hinge is screwed to the door frame (Fig. 1). Three of the screws are driven in, the fourth is prevented from being inserted because of the bolt and wooden block.

A differently shaped block (B) is prepared and wedged between the door stop and the free leaf. This enables the first block and the nut and bolt to be removed while still keeping the hinge open (Fig. 2). The free leaf is then screwed to the door, the fourth screw is driven into the frame and after removing block (B) the hanging is complete.

Yours faithfully, **Charles D. Cliffe**

Closing doors automatically

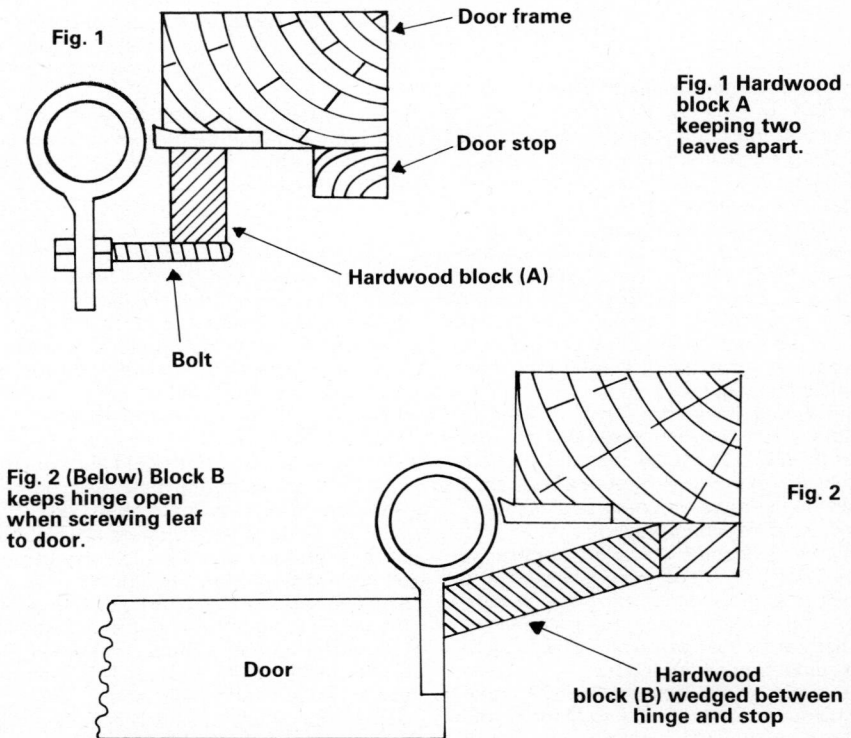

Fig. 1

Door frame

Door stop

Hardwood block (A)

Bolt

Fig. 1 Hardwood block A keeping two leaves apart.

Fig. 2 (Below) Block B keeps hinge open when screwing leaf to door.

Door

Fig. 2

Hardwood block (B) wedged between hinge and stop

Letters

From: James Doak, Louth, Lincs
Dear Sir

The editorial note under the heading Smaller than Small (WOODWORKER for September 1981) underlines the total lack of appreciation of the current difficulties of cottage industry.

While a small industry employing, say, a hundred or so people can qualify for state help in lean times, the one-man-band has no such recourse to government funds. All around him the cottage worker sees public money being poured into a variety of loss-making enterprises while he struggles on to meet the ever-increasing cost of utilities and rates and taxes.

He finds it very difficult in the current economic climate to charge a realistic rate for his work, often accepting jobs at a rate well below his true worth.

It might be of benefit to others contemplating setting-up a new business to warn them to investigate very carefully the tax situation before actually starting. Under the present legislation anyone not fully aware of the rather odd way that inland revenue works could find themselves with a tax bill larger than they had bargained for. In other words you can find you are working for the inland revenue department. Even if forewarned the situation is one of disincentive rather than one where a new venture is helped and encouraged to become successful.

The power to create the right financial and moral climate has been assumed by the government in recent years. It is time government started to exercise that power for the benefit of the small man from whom the future great industries will grow.

Yours faithfully, **James Doak**

From: D. S. Cotter, Denham, Bucks
Dear Sir

Your editorial comment in the September 1981 issue made fascinating reading. Fascinating because you kindly published a letter which I wrote on exactly this subject (WOODWORKER for February 1980 p92).

Since then, in utter frustration, I decided to start my business from 'unapproved' premises. Business has steadily grown thus justifying my faith. However, some weeks ago for reasons beyond my control and unnecessary to explain, I now need new premises fairly quickly.

One would have thought that after 18 months since my first letter to you the situation would be totally changed, particularly in view of this government's frequently stated policy towards small business and with around 3m unemployed.

However, despite so-called 'enterprise zones' (which few people seem to want) and 'strong recommendations to local authorities to relax planning controls,' the situation has hardly changed at all – a fact which I predicted in my earlier letter.

The copy of my November 1979 letter, which you forwarded to David Mitchell MP, elicited a reply which stated 'we recognise this problem as a major one afflicting the small firms sector and we are currently looking into it in order to determine what should be done to provide a remedy'. As it is only too easy to be negatively critical, I again wrote to Mr Mitchell with a series of positive suggestions which I thought, and still think, merit serious consideration – he did not reply.

My suggestions were, briefly, that many existing buildings would be suitable such as redundant farm buildings, chapels/churches; waste land could be used to create workshops/craft centres (and there must be many old buildings in the grounds of stately homes which could be used for such centres); old redundant ministry of defence buildings are another possibility.

If the present government is serious in its intention to help small businesses then it must tackle this problem and I suggest that of all the organisations CoSIRA is ideally placed to carry out some of these suggestions, provided the necessary funds are made available.

Mr Mitchell obviously did not find a 'remedy' and in the unlikely event of him still looking for one, I suggest he contacts CoSIRA to ask about the current property situation. I did and, as always, the waiting list far exceeds the property available list. Lastly he cannot rely on local authorities to do this job for him. They will take as much notice of recommendations to relax planning restrictions as they appear to do with most other directives – little or none.

The penultimate paragraph of your editorial is also interesting as in my letter to Mr Mitchell I stated 'I fully appreciate the authorities have an obligation to exclude unwanted industry from residential/shopping areas but surely it would be simple enough to impose restrictions which if and when exceeded would lead to automatic re-classification as light industry proper. Size of premises, number of people, annual turnover are three possible restrictions'.

Frustration is not a strong enough word to describe my own feelings as my business has gone from considering taking on my first employee to facing closing-down completely – not because of financial problems, or through lack of orders but simply because I cannot find premises in the area I want.

So, what is the answer? Just how can one get something done – or even get someone to listen – I have no idea but, I have again written to Mr Mitchell.

Yours faithfully, **D. S. Cotter**

Editor comments: As James Doak says the tax situation is complex and it is essential to get the right advice before starting-up. It was for this reason that Guild of Woodworkers in co-operation with CoSIRA arranged the seminar at Salisbury in June. Here taxation and finance were explained and discussed in practical terms. We plan to hold seminars in the west midlands and eastern counties during 1982. See report in WOODWORKER for September 1981.

D. S. Cotter's letter refers to CoSIRA. Some time ago we wrote to the department of employment drawing attention to the excellent work being done by this organisation and calling for its remit to be widened to cover urban as well as rural areas. But getting Whitehall to listen, as Mr Cotter has found, is a frustrating task. And as we said in September small business is a favourite waffle of politicians of all parties. Unfortunately the practicalities tend to be ignored.

From: C. W. Bell, North Shields
Dear Sir

Regular readers will know that dotted around the country are various places where one can obtain instruction in the art of woodturning. Many of these are advertised in the classified pages of WOODWORKER and I chose to take the one-day course offered by Alan McNair of Northumberland.

Alan believes that turning is a cutting process not one of scraping. In order to cut, a tool needs the right edge and I spent quite a part of the course leaning to sharpen the tools correctly. Beside learning to turn, I also learnt about timber selection, machinery, techniques and methods, discussed woodturners and the books they have written, the manufacture of turning tools and what to look out for and avoid, plus finishing ancient and modern.

In a way the course was like being a part of a living WOODWORKER magazine.

Yours faithfully, **C. W. Bell**

From: L. S. Paul, Keltek Products, St Giles Mews, Wadebridge PL27 6OR
Dear Sir

The US manufacturer of the Scru-Drill feels that the report on p757 of WOODWORKER for November 1981 is a very fair assessment of the product and adds the following comments:

'The life of the cutting edges of the Scru-Drill is very much dependant on the type of usage but would compare favourably with any quality woodworking tool. The edges are easily maintained with the use of an oil stone.

'On finished surfaces the stop collar should be regarded as a guide only and pressure removed as soon as the collar comes near to contact with the surface being drilled. Should a stop collar setscrew be lost a replacement can be made available on request.'

Yours faithfully, **L. S. Paul**

From: S. G. Oxland, Nottingham
Dear Sir

To my mind none of the explanations put forward on p526 of the August 1981 issue quite 'hit the nail on the head'. While accepting that the cone theory could have some marginal effect, I think it likely that the long screwdriver would still prove more effective if it was prevented from following the conal orbit.

I am convinced the real answer lies in the relative postures adopted by the operator.

With a short screwdriver the hands are close to the work with the forearms fairly near each other and the elbows never far apart. In these circumstances power comes almost entirely from hands and wrists.

Now introduce a long screwdriver which enables the operator to move away from the work where a different posture can be adopted. The forearms open outwards and the elbows are wide apart. Each arm now acts on a brace and bit principle with the biceps supplying additional twisting force.

The fact that a much better grip can be obtained on the handle of a long screwdriver, when the arms come into play is, of course, an important contributory factor.

Yours faithfully, **S. G. Oxland**

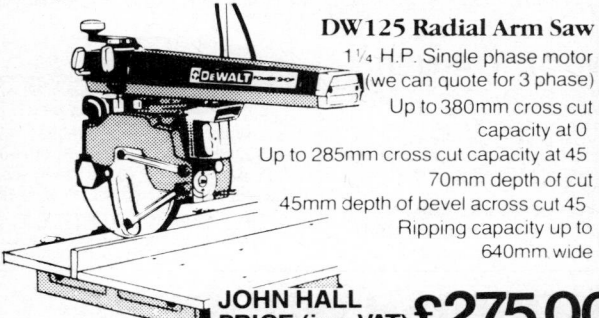

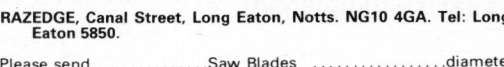

Wood Suppliers

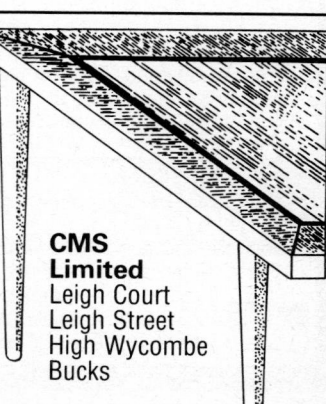

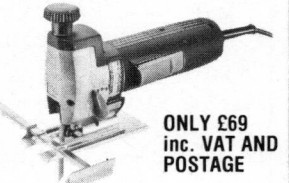

Type M230 — designed and made in England — one of the range of wood turning lathes that we manufacture for amateur hobbyists to professional users. Available as cabinet stand mounted units, motorised and all ready-to-run, or for those preferring to make their own work bench, the lathes and accessories together with the appropriate electrical items (motors and switchgear) can be purchased separately from us or from a limited number of stockists.

For details of the M230 and the other lathes available, also prices and information on motors, grinders, tools, books and other items usually in stock, please send 30p in stamps to:

Arundel
WOOD TURNING LATHES AND ACCESSORIES

D. ARUNDEL & COMPANY LIMITED,
Mills Drive Farndon Road
Newark,
Nottinghamshire.
NG24 4SN

Tel. Newark (0636) 702382

---

17 x 37 WOODWORKING LATHE AND ACCESSORIES

TYME MACHINES (BRISTOL) LTD.

A COMPLETE PACKAGE

The standard equipment supplied with the Tyme 17 x 37 enables the Woodworker to carry out most operations without costly accessories. Bowl turning up to 17″ diameter and an overall length of 37″ between centres give large capacity at low cost.

Standard equipment:
½ H.P. motor • no volt overload switch • 150mm face plate • driving centre • solid centre

For further details write to:
Tyme Machines (Bristol) Ltd.,
Unit 3, Halls Road, Kingswood, Bristol.
Telephone (0272) 603726.

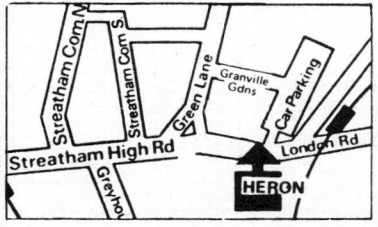

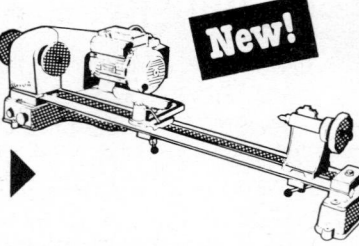

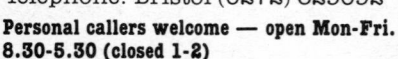
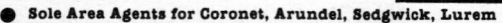

Prices quoted are those prevailing at press date and are subject to alteration due to economic conditions.

QUESTION BOX

Wooden goblets
From: J. R. Allanagh, Ponsarooth, Cornwall

Can you please suggest a suitable finish that will be impervious to alcohol? I am making wooden goblets and would like to apply a finish that will resist alcohol and stand up to washing in warm water.

Modern finishes of the polyurethane type will resist alcohol and dilute acids. But a distinction must be drawn between their normal use which is generally on the side grain of flat surfaces of, say, table tops and their use on turned shapes which contain a variety of grain including end grain surfaces.

These finishes need to adhere firmly to the wood surface and there, by chemical reaction, to form a hard film. This is achieved very easily on side grain but not on end grain where adhesion differs from other parts of the same wood. The result is that although a polyurethane finish applied to the interior of a goblet bowl may appear reasonable, the film probably has weak areas.

If the goblet is used for liquids and is then washed, the progressive slight movement of the wood by swelling and shrinking will break down the polyurethane.

This is only one aspect mentioned to indicate that it is not possible to expect even the best wood finish to stand up very long to the acidic affect of, say, wine and the alkalinity of detergents and soaps used in washing-up.

We must say we are basically reticent to suggest that a wooden goblet is an ideal vehicle from which to drink alcoholic beverages since long-term detrimental characteristics could develop in the wood. Some woods are irritant to some people and particularly to the lips and mucous membranes of the throat; but it is not possible, or desirable, to mention any particular species.

On the other hand the phrase 'matured in the wood' in respect of certain alcoholic drinks is a truism but only under controlled circumstances; old sherry casks made from oak are essential to the ultimate flavour of scotch whisky though the same cannot be said of new oak. There are highly complicated reasons for this connected with the chemistry of the wood and the effect on this of alcohol.

Our advice accordingly must be that while we think decorative wooden goblets are fine as *objets d'art* we cannot recommend their use to hold drinks.

Cabinet doors
From: Robert Stirling, Ballymena

I'm interested in building cabinet doors using astragal moulding. I would have the moulding professionally cut. Could you please tell me: (1) Do I build the glazing bars or the moulding first. (2) Do I mitre or scribe where the moulding joins that of the door? (3) In the case of scribing what hand tools should I use and how do I mark-out in the first instance?

Your questions are too wide-ranging to be answered in detail here and space only permits a review of basic principles. However, the subject is covered in detail in J. Hooper's *Modern Cabinetwork* (New Era Publishing Co). Although this title is out-of-print you should be able to get a copy through your local library.

The wooden glazing bars employed on cabinet doors are usually in two parts: First, there are the bars or slats made from rectangular section pieces of wood which make up the lattice of the door. Second, lengths of astragal moulding are 'saddled' onto the slats by means of a groove worked on the underside of the moulding. The rebate thus formed holds the glass which is secured by beading strips tacked in and mitred at the corners.

A good method of procedure is as follows: Make a backboard of plywood and position the door frame on it. The outline of the slats is drawn on to the backboard and the positions of the stub tenons to the frame and the various intersections marked. The slats may now be cut and fitted by stub tenoning them to the door frame and halving them where they cross.

Pieces of tape or linen about 2in. long are glued into all angles to reinforce the joints. Plywood blocks nailed to the backboard will accurately locate the slats during assembly and gluing.

When dry the slats can be carefully levelled off ready to take the astragal moulding pieces which, in turn, are glued to the slats. Where the mouldings intersect they are mitred, either shot on a mitre board or chiselled using a mitre template.

It is as well to put a piece of slat in the groove underneath the moulding while doing this to prevent the wood breaking-out. For the stiles and rails of the door frame, half the mould is planted on and mitred in the corners.

In cheaper practice it was once common to apply the moulded ornamentation to the face of the glass. All very well until the glass got broken when the whole work would have to be renewd.

Leather cutting board
From: D. R. Shattower, River, Kent

I intend making a cutting board for a leather worker. Would you please advise on the details of construction, suitable woods and possible dimensions of such a block?

Your inquiry is not entirely clear since you refer to both a board and a block. Obviously you will clear this point with your customer together with the maximum sizes of skins he wants to process, but in order to assist you we will give approximate details of both types.

We understand that the leather trade today is going over more and more to nylon-coated boards which are less trouble to resurface, though there are still plenty of wooden types used. In the first place three basic requirements exist: 1 the material used must not blunt the edges of cutting tools too rapidly; 2 the cutting surface must not encourage the tools to wander or be biased in any one direction; and 3 the cutting surface must not tend to snag the leather.

For the construction of cutting boards, the best wood that meets the requirements of 1 and 2 is lime. So far as construction is concerned boards of appropriate length, edge jointed with a loose tongue and well glued to make up a suitable width, with the finished panel 2 or 3in. thick, is all that is usually required.

The points to note however, are that both sides of the board can be used; and the width should be satisfactory not only to the work but to the general run of planing facilities conveniently available locally, bearing in mind that sooner or later the board will need resurfacing by planing and sanding.

Lime is a reasonable wood but it does have a slight tendency to distort; once suitably dry, however, it is a small mover. Whether or not the board is framed-up is a matter of choice but it must be remembered that the top and bottom frame rails would present cross grain to a planer and, since lime is soft, could tear-out.

A frame could be applied and fixed without glue, to be dismantled when the board had to be resurfaced, but see the following details of a cutting block.

We discussed this with a leather manufacturer who uses blocks which, like the boards, simply lie on a bench when in use. These are made up in pine with an overall dimension of 40×24in. and at the moment are 2in. thick, though they probably started off originally at around a nominal 3in.

The body of the block consists of pine blocks, say, 3in. long (to make the thickness) $\times$ about $3\frac{1}{2} \times 3\frac{1}{2}$in. these set upright so as to present an end grain cutting surface in the style of a butcher's block. The blocks are not glued together but rely on being held tightly together by the use of a wood frame which is screwed together and also screwed to the outer blocks.

When the time comes for resurfacing either the whole panel can be planed and sanded on both sides or it can be dismantled and any badly-worn blocks replaced. This type of cutting block is probably the most economic. Comparatively low-cost softwoods such as spruce and fir could be substituted for pine; but none of these woods would be satisfactory for a cutting board where, as we have said, the prime wood is lime.

However, alder, aspen and horse chestnut could also be used. Precise machining is essential and especially in respect of the blocks which, when assembled, must present a more or less homogeneous mass.

Veneering chipboard
From: J Heron, Gedling, Notts

I wish to veneer chipboard with oak to make a carcase assembly. What adhesive should I use? I am told that scotch glue is suitable but my old glue pot has long since gone. Is Resin W suitable for veneer work? And is it necessary to veneer both sides of the chipboard?

I presume that the reference to veneering means the laying of veneers by hand using the hammer method. This can only be done satisfactorily with animal (or scotch) glue. It has been in use for centuries and has stood the test of time. And in my view, in spite of the advances made in adhesives during the past 30-40 years, for hand-veneering there is not one that can better or even equal it.

The reason is that this glue, by virtue of the fact that it needs to be kept hot so as to remain liquid, has almost immediate gel outside the pot, and veneers being laid will

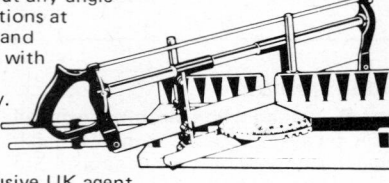
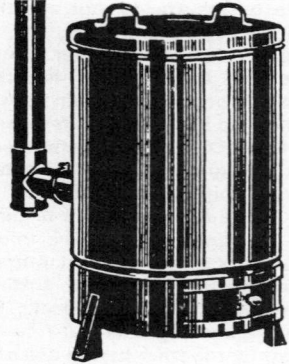

stay in position with veneer hammer pressure only.

This explanation is over-simplified, and there are indeed many occasions when difficulties and problems arise. But these are beyond the scope of this reply.

The glue pot whether heated by gas or electricity is ideal for making and keeping the glue hot. If a glue pot is not available, or the need for one only very occasional, two old saucepans can be used. The outer one containing the water must be quite a bit larger than the inner one containing the glue; this inner one must be raised so that there is direct contact with the flame. This is very important.

Chipboard is not an ideal material, because of its absorbency, for hand-veneering with animal glue, but it can be done. The panel must first be sized with a slightly thinned-down version of the glue, spread generously and as evenly as possible, allowed to dry thoroughly (at least overnight), and lightly glasspapered to remove any nibs or foreign bodies. The main veneer can then be applied in the usual way.

Because of the absorbency of chipboard and the fact that hand-veneering entails the use of quite a lot of water, unless the edges are lipped care must be taken to ensure that they are not soaked or kept wet for any length of time.

Chipboard is an unstable material and unless the panel is fixed to a substantial frame all round its perimeter (and on anything much bigger than about 2 × 1½ft across the centre too), it is advisable to counter-balance the back. Balancing veneers which can be up to 2ft wide, and much cheaper than face veneers, are available for this purpose.

With an assembled carcase there is no easy alternative to the hand method of veneering using the traditional glue. But J. Heron's letter implies that the panels he wishes to veneer are separate. This is rather fortunate for with any other type of glue the pressure method must be used.

Evostik Resin W is a very good adhesive and ideal for use on chipboard, as are all the PVA formulations. But as I have said, the glue line must be kept under pressure. I appreciate that there are not many of us who possess a press capable of doing a fair-size panel, or have a sufficient quantity of large heavy-duty G-cramps to enable the pressure to be applied as described in some technical books. I must say, however, that anyone possessing either of the above should achieve a very good result.

However there is an equally good method of doing this job which does not involve the use of machines or cramps. It is slower than the machine (what handwork is not?) but in my opinion faster than cramps. The method is too detailed to be covered in this reply.

There is another point I must make: when laying oak veneers by hand, due to several factors, it will almost invariably dry with patchy dark-blue staining, very difficult (I think impossible) to clean-off by normal scraping and papering method.

This applies to most light-coloured veneers but oak is particularly vulnerable. The complete cure which is cheap and simple is beyond the scope of this reply.

The impact adhesives are formulated to use mainly with the relatively new Melamine plastics. Here they do a splendid job because the sheets are flat and rigid. They will not distort after being coated and left to gel.

Veneers, on the other hand, are thin and seldom flat in the dry state. Since the veneer as well as the groundwork has to be coated with the adhesive (otherwise it will not work), the veneer will distort. This makes it extremely difficult — if not impossible — to smooth out without getting undesirable air bubbles and glue build-up.

It must also be borne in mind that with this method you do not get a second chance. Of course you could use the pressure method while the glue is still liquid, but then the whole object of using a relatively expensive glue is defeated. I do not recommend the use of impact adhesive for laying wood veneer, by any method.

In conclusion: (1) The only glue suitable for hand-veneering by the hammer method is animal or scotch glue. This can also be (and was in the past frequently) used for pressing too, with hot cauls. (2) PVA and most of the non-staining one-pack synthetic adhesives, designed for woodworking, among other applications, are to be used for the pressure method. (3) The impact adhesives are reserved for the Melamine plastics and mending punctures on bicycle inner tubes.

Hardwood flooring

From: Howard Birkby, Otley, Yorks
Before I lay a wooden floor in a house could you please advise if African mahogany is a suitable timber? What should be its m.c.? What is a suitable adhesive? Can you recommend spacing centres for the battens? What are the best type of fixing pins or nails? Is polyurethane varnish the best finish for the floor?

African mahogany in boards of 72 × 6 × 1in. for conversion to strips 72 × 3 × ½in. is available and the intention is for the strips to be t & g and laid with random end-to-end joints.

When the wood is converted and is machined to t & g the resultant flooring would be about ⅜in. thick with an ⅛in. tongue. As such it would be classed in the trade as overlay strip and not flooring proper. There is nothing wrong in using overlay of course; it does make an excellent floor surface but the general recommendations are that it should be pinned and glued (usually spot glued) to a subfloor of ⅛in. (3mm) plywood or, in the case of upper floors where the strips are laid over an existing suspended floor, on hardboard if preferred.

There are available special hot or cold bitumen/latex-type liquid agents that will bond wood flooring to a sand and cement screed and you may be confusing the use of these with other types of wood flooring that are bonded direct to the screed.

These fall into two types: parquet blocks of normal thickness ex 1in. and mosaic square panels built up from wood fingers often no thicker (ie ⅜in.) than your strips.

There is however a difference: in the case of these thin mosaic panels they are backed with cotton mesh or special paper which not only holds the pieces together but serves to prevent the thin wood either absorbing some of the cold adhesive (which is generally used) or oozing up to the top and thus staining the wood and spoiling the ultimate finish. The thicker blocks do, of course, have a better chance of resisting this tendency.

It is possible to lay your overlay strips this way but we would hesitate to recommend it, not only because of difficulty in keeping the surface clean but in obtaining a truly level surface to the floor. The use of a subfloor would make for a better job but obviously the final levels of that room with the next, taking into account door openings and the position of skirting boards — which, ideally, should sit over and cover the expansion gap left at the perimeter of the floor, must be taken into account.

With regard to the battened floor the same remarks apply: if battens or fillets only were to support the thin flooring they would need to be so close together as to be uneconomic, but if fillets were used to support a subfloor of plywood then this is another matter.

We would strongly advise you to take a second opinion when you have digested our comments. There are in your area two of the leading flooring people, ie Hewetsons Ltd and Hollis Bros Ltd, both of Hull. Their technical departments not only could give confirmation to what we say, or offer an alternative, but they could supply all the required materials. You will appreciate that there are many different materials which can be used to make for better results. But since in most cases they become an integral part of the building it is essential to obtain expert advice before using them, for while they might improve some aspects they might contravene others.

We suggest you discuss with one or other of these companies the improvement of resilience by the use of underlayment to the floor; the probable degree of insulation if the strips are bonded direct to the screed; and, if this has not already been arranged, the provision of a damp-proof membrane in the floor structure.

Other essential information is that where a plywood subfloor is used the strips are set either diagonally or at right-angles to the grain of the plywood. Pinning is by secret nailing, ie lost-head nails are driven through the base of the tongue and punched home; when the next strip is offered up its groove covers the nail hole. Care is needed with thin stock so as not to damage the tongues nor bruise the upper surface of the wood.

With regard to the other points you raise. African mahogany is ideal for light domestic traffic; iroko is considered a little more decorative and being a little harder is also recommended for slightly heavier traffic, say, in offices. The choice is not too important, all other things considered, since it ought to be the finish that takes the wear not the wood.

This is why good, regular maintenance of floors is important. Modern finishes aim at sealing the wood and leaving a good final finish after a few applications. This is then maintained by lightly mopping over or with the occasional use of wax. Suitable m.c. of wood strip flooring is generally reckoned as 10 to 12% at the time of laying on a dry base.

QUESTION BOX COUPON FEBRUARY 1982

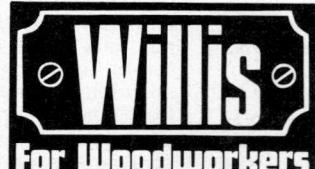
Prices quoted are those prevailing at press date and are subject to alteration due to economic conditions.

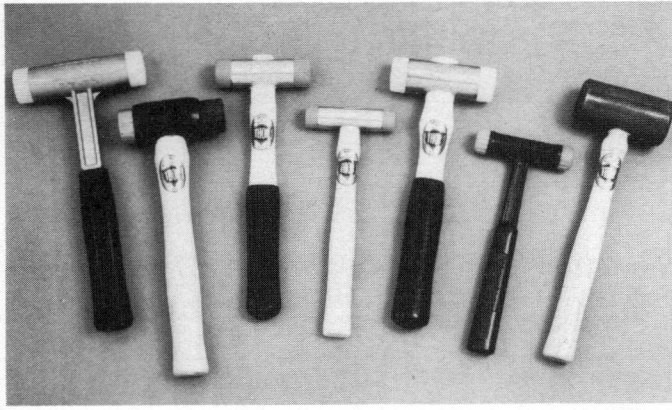

Plunging router

In modified form the Haffner BF304 plunging router has a more powerful motor (720W single phase 220V) operating at 25 000rpm, states C. D. Monninger Ltd, Overbury Road, London N15 6RJ (01-800 5435). In addition the facility to remove the baseplate and replace it with the RF374 head attachment means that the tool can be quickly converted to a trimmer for laminate edges. A dual edge guide on the trimmer head is to prevent overcutting and gouging. Frames with clamping devices and templates for recessing fittings can be supplied.

The BF304 has positive depth location and it is possible to pre-set three cutting depths. It is claimed that the large diameter armature minimises deflection and improves cutting quality in both routing and edge trimming operations.

The baseplate contacting surface is Teflon-coated to prevent marking of the workpiece.

Further details can be had from C. D. Monninger.

TCT blades

TCT blades are now fitted as standard to the Elu MH85 and MH25 portable ripsaws. There is no increase in the price of these models as a result of the modification, states Elu Machinery Ltd, Dallow Road, Luton LU1 1SS, (0582) 425001, which markets these German-made saws in UK.

Model MH85 has a 240mm (9½in.) diameter blade while MH25 has a 100mm (4in.) diameter blade. Both have a.c./d.c. 220V motors, the former operating at 4000rpm and the latter at 8000rpm.

Elu MH85 ripsaw now fitted with TCT blade as standard.

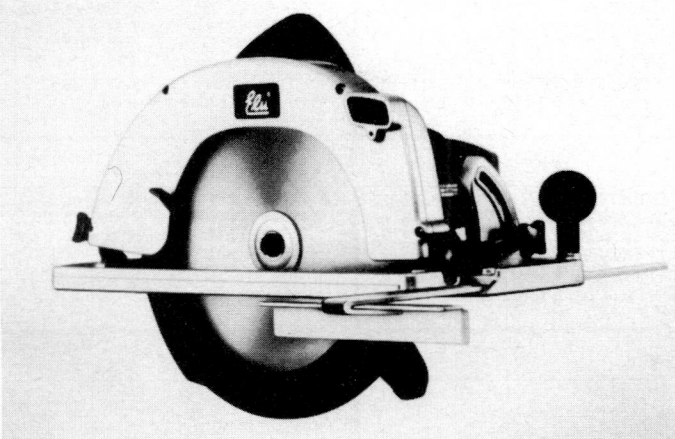

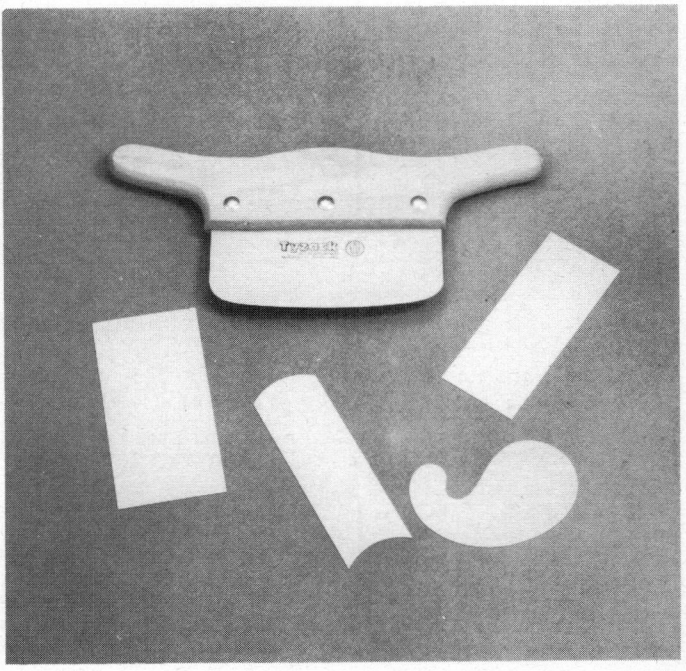

Tools and accessories

Additions to the tools from Toolmail Ltd, Parkwood Industrial Estate, Sutton Road, Maidstone ME15 9LZ (0622 672736), include Schmitt Two Cherries brand chip carving tools in numerous shapes and sizes, hand-forged and with polished hardwood handles. There are also three sizes of rectangular scrapers and curved scrapers in two types; the French block scraper for heavy-duty work has a curved blade of Sheffield steel and hardwood handle.

Thor brand soft-face hammers are available in many types, weights and sizes. A further addition is the Salmen tool cabinet no. 475 for wall-mounting; it is 29 × 21¼ × 8in. No. 473 is the Salmen tool chest measuring 26¾ × 10¾ × 6½in. overall.

Above left: (from the top) Soft face hammers, Salmen's tool cabinet and range of chip carving tools; right: range of cabinet scrapers, all from Toolmail Ltd.

SHOP GUIDE SHOP GUIDE

The quickest and easiest method of reaching all Woodworkers is to advertise in SHOP GUIDE. Telephone **Valerie Tester (0442) 41221 Ext. 266. Rate: £8.00 per unit.** Minimum of 6 months.

Key: H — Hand tools, **P** — Power tools, **W** — Woodworking machinery up to £1000, **WM** — Woodworking machinery over £1000, **D** — Demonstration available on selected machines, **T** — Timber, **CS** — Cutting or sharpening services, **A** — Attachments, **BC** — Books/catalogues, * — Mail order.

AVON

BATH   Tel. Bath 64513
JOHN HALL TOOLS   ★
RAILWAY STREET

Open: Monday-Saturday
9.00 a.m.-5.30 p.m.
H.P.W.WM.D.A.BC.

BRISTOL   Tel. (0272) 311510
JOHN HALL TOOLS LIMITED   ★
CLIFTON DOWN SHOPPING
CENTRE, WHITELADIES ROAD
Open: Monday-Saturday
9.00 a.m.-5.30 p.m.
H.P.W.WM.D.A.BC.

BRISTOL   Tel. 0272-633844
ROBBINS LIMITED   ★
THE WOODWORKER SHOP
MERRYWOOD MILLS, BEDMINSTER
Open: Mon-Fri 8.00 a.m.-5.00 p.m.
Saturday 8.30 a.m.-12.30 p.m.
H.P.T.CS.A.BC.

BRISTOL   Tel. 0272-629092
TRYMWOOD SERVICES
2a DOWNS PARK EAST, (off
North View) WESTBURY PARK
Open: 8.30 a.m.-5.30 p.m. Mon. to
Fri. Closed for lunch 1-2 p.m.
P.W.WM.D.T.A.BC.

BRISTOL   Tel. 0272-667013
V. H. WILLIS & CO. LTD   ★
190-192 WEST STREET,
BEDMINSTER
Open: Mon-Fri 8.30 a.m.-5 p.m.
Saturday 9 a.m.-1 p.m.
H.P.W.WM.D.CS.A.BC.

BERKSHIRE

READING   Tel. Littlewick Green
DAVID HUNT (TOOL   2743
MERCHANTS) LTD   ★
KNOWL HILL, NR. READING
Open: Monday-Saturday
9 a.m.-5.30 p.m.
H.P.W.D.A.BC.

READING   Tel. (0734) 586522
SARJENT'S TOOL STORES   ★
LTD.
44-52 OXFORD ROAD
Open: 8.30 a.m.-5.30 p.m.
Monday-Saturday
H.P.W.WM.D.A.BC.

BUCKINGHAMSHIRE

HIGH WYCOMBE   (0494) 22221
ISAAC LORD LTD
185 DESBOROUGH ROAD

Open: Mon-Fri 8.00 a.m.-5.00 p.m.
Saturday 8.00 a.m.-12.00 noon
H.P.W.D.A.

BUCKINGHAMSHIRE

MILTON KEYNES   Tel. 0908
A. POLLARD & SON   75221
LTD.   ★
51 QUEENSWAY, BLETCHLEY
Open: 8.30 a.m.-5.30 p.m.
Monday-Saturday
H.P.W.WM.D.A.BC.

CAMBRIDGESHIRE

CAMBRIDGE   Tel. 0223-353091
H. B. WOODWORKING
69 LENSFIELD ROAD
Open: 8.30 a.m.-5.30 p.m.
Monday-Friday
8.30 a.m.-1.00 p.m. Sat
P.W.WM.D.CS.BC.

CHESHIRE

NANTWICH   Tel. Crewe 67010
ALAN HOLTHAM   ★
THE OLD STORES TURNERY
WISTASON ROAD, WILLASTON
Open: Tues-Sat 9a.m.-5.30p.m.
Closed Monday
P.W.WM.D.T.C.CS.A.BC.

CLEVELAND

MIDDLESBROUGH   Tel. 0642-
WINTZ   460035/813650
INDUSTRIAL SUPPLIES
2 BESSEMER COURT
GRANGETOWN
Open: Mon-Fri 8.30 a.m.-5 p.m.
H.P.W.D.A.

CORNWALL

HELSTON
SOUTH WEST
POWER TOOLS
Helston (03265) 4961
Truro (0872) 71671
Launceston (0566) 3555
H.P.W.WM.D.CS.A.

NEWQUAY   Tel. 063 73 2516
CONWAY SUPPLIES   ★
(NEWQUAY)
70 FORE STREET
Open: Mon-Fri 9 a.m.-5.30 p.m.
Sat 9 a.m.-12.30 p.m.
H.P.W.WM.D.A.BC.

ST. AUSTELL   Tel. (0726) 65922
TOOLSERV   ★
TRURO ROAD

Open: 8 a.m.-5.30 p.m.
6 days
H.P.W.WM.D.CS.A.BC.

DERBYSHIRE

BUXTON   Tel. 0298-871636
CRAFT SUPPLIES   ★
THE MILL
MILLERSDALE
Open: Mon-Fri 9 a.m.-5 p.m.
Saturday 9 a.m.-1 p.m.
H.P.W.D.T.CS.A.BC.

DEVON

AXMINSTER   Tel. 0297 33656
POWER TOOL CENTRE   ★
STYLES & BROWN
CHARD STREET
Open: 9.00 a.m.-5.30 p.m.
Monday-Saturday
H.P.W.WM.D.CS.A.BC.

EXETER   Tel. 0392 73936
WRIDES TOOL CENTRE
147 FORE STREET

Open: 9.00 a.m.-5.30 p.m.
Wednesday 9.00 a.m.-1.00 p.m.
H.P.W.WM.A.

PLYMOUTH   Tel. 0752 786633
STEENWISE S.W. LTD   ★
BURRINGTON WAY
HONICKNOWLE
Open: Monday-Friday
8.30 a.m.-5.00 p.m.
P.W.WM.D.

PLYMOUTH   Tel. 0752 330303
WESTWARD BUILDING SERVICES
LTD., LISTER CLOSE, NEWNHAM
INDUSTRIAL ESTATE, PLYMPTON
Open: Mon-Fri 8 a.m.-5.30 p.m.
Sat 8.30 a.m.-12.30 p.m.
H.P.W.WM.D.A.BC.

PLYMOUTH   Tel. 0752-266179
JOHN WRIDE & CO (PLYMOUTH) LTD
146 CORNWALL STREET
Open: Monday to Saturday
9.00a.m.-5.30p.m.
Wed 9.00a.m.-1.00p.m.
H.P.W.WM.A.

DORSET

BOURNEMOUTH   Tel: 0202
MACHINE SALES & SERVICES   527780
(BOURNEMOUTH) LTD   527781
56 STROUDEN ROAD   ★

Open: Mon-Fri 8.15 a.m.-5 p.m.
H.P.W.WM.D.A.

WEYMOUTH   Tel: (0305) 787396
WEYMOUTH TOOL CENTRE   ★
30A ABBOTSBURY ROAD

Open: Monday to Saturday
8 a.m.-5.30 p.m.
H.P.W.WM.D.A.BC

CO. DURHAM

BARNARD CASTLE   Tel: (0833)
WOODMEN   38442/31609
27 NEWGATE   ★

Open Monday-Saturday
9 a.m.-5.30 p.m.
P.W.WM.D.A.BC.

GLOUCESTERSHIRE

TEWKESBURY   Tel. 0684
TEWKESBURY SAW CO.   293092
LIMITED
TRADING ESTATE, NEWTOWN
Open: Mon-Fri 8.00 a.m.-5.00 p.m.
Saturday 9.30 a.m.-12.00 p.m.
P.W.WM.D.CS.

HAMPSHIRE

ALDERSHOT   Tel. 0252 28088
BURCH & HILLS LTD
BLACKWATER WAY TRADING
ESTATE
Open: Mon-Fri 8.30 a.m.-5.30 p.m.
Saturday 8.30 a.m.-12.00 p.m.
H.P.W.WM.D.A.BC.

PORTSMOUTH   Tel. 0705
EURO PRECISION TOOLS   67332
LTD   ★
259/263 London Road, North End
Open: Mon-Fri 9 a.m.- 5.30 p.m.
Sat 9.00 a.m.-5.00 p.m.
H.P.W.WM.D.A.BC.

SOUTHAMPTON   Tel. 0703
H.W.M.   776222
THE WOODWORKERS   ★
303 SHIRLEY ROAD, SHIRLEY
Open: Tues-Fri 9.30 a.m.- 6 p.m.
Sat 9.30 a.m.-4.00 p.m.
H.P.W.WM.D.CS.A.BC.T.

HEREFORDSHIRE

HEREFORD   Tel. 0432 3018
PEN TOOLS (HEREFORD) LTD
24 EDGAR STREET

Open Mon.-Fri. 8 a.m.-5.30 p.m.
Sat. 8 a.m.-1 p.m.
H.P.W.D.C.A.

HERTFORDSHIRE

WATFORD   Tel. 0923 48434
HOME CARE CENTRE   ★
20 MARKET STREET
WATFORD, HERTS
Open 9.00 a.m.-5.30 p.m.
Mon.-Sat.
H.P.W.A.WM.BC.D.

WATFORD   Tel. 0923 26052
J. SIMBLE & SONS LTD   ★
76 QUEENS ROAD

Open 8.30 a.m.-5.30 p.m.
Mon.-Sat. Closed Wednesday
H.P.W.WM.D.A.BC.

WATFORD   Tel. (0923) 49911
TREND MACHINERY & CUTTING
TOOLS LTD
UNIT N, PENFOLD WORKS
IMPERIAL WAY
Open: Mon-Fri 9 a.m.-5 p.m.
P.W.WM.D.CS.BC.

Prices quoted are those prevailing at press date and are subject to alteration due to economic conditions.

KENT

MATFIELD   Tel. Brenchley
LEISURECRAFT IN WOOD   (089272)
'ORMONDE', MAIDSTONE RD.   2465
TN12 7JG
Open: Mon-Sun
9 a.m.- 5.30 p.m.
W.WM.D.T.A.

LANCASHIRE

LANCASTER   Tel. 0524 2886
LILE TOOL SHOP
43/45 NORTH ROAD
Open: Monday to Saturday
9.00 a.m.-5.30 p.m.
Wed 9.00 a.m.-12.30 p.m.
H.P.W.D.A.

LEICESTERSHIRE

COALVILLE   Tel. (0533) 415556
POOLE WOOD MACHINERY   (06077)
SERVICES LIMITED   5777
4 SWALLOW DALE
THRINGSTONE
Open: Mon-Fri 9 a.m.-5 p.m.
H.P.W.WM.D.A.BC.

LEICESTER   Tel. 0455 43254
ROY STARTIN LTD
134 WOOD STREET
EARL SHILTON
Open: Mon-Fri 8 a.m.-5.30 p.m.
Saturday 8.00 a.m.-1.30 p.m.
H.P.W.WM.D.T.A.

LINCOLNSHIRE

LINCOLN   Tel. 0522 36168/9
R & S TOOLS (LINCOLN)
LIMITED
BEEVER STREET LN6 7AD
Open: Mon-Fri 8.30 a.m.-5 p.m.
Sat 9.00 p.m.-12.00 p.m.
H.P.W.WM.D.CS.A.BC.

LINCOLN   Tel. 0522 30199/
WOODWISE LIMITED   39871 or
121 HIGH STREET   0522 68428
    & 06077 5777/5288
   (after hours) ★
Open: Mon-Sat 9 a.m.-5.30 p.m.
P.W.WM.D.A.BC.

LONDON

ACTON   Tel. 01-992 4835
A MILLS (ACTON) LTD   ★
32/36 CHURCHFIELD ROAD
W3 6ED
Open: Mon-Fri 9.00 a.m.-5.00 p.m.
Closed Saturday
H.P.W.WM.

HANWELL   Tel. 01-567 2922
G. D. CLEGG & SONS
83 Uxbridge Road, W7 3ST
Open: Monday to Friday
9.00 a.m.-6.00 p.m.
Saturday 9.00 a.m.-5.30 p.m.
H.P.W.WM.D.

LONDON   Tel. 01-636 7475
BUCK & RYAN LIMITED   ★
101 TOTTENHAM COURT ROAD
W1P 0DY
Open: Mon-Fri 8.30 a.m.-5.30 p.m.
Saturday 8.30 a.m.-1.00 p.m.
H.P.W.WM.D.A.

LONDON

LONDON   Tel. 01-739 7126
CECIL W. TYZACK   ★
79-81 KINGSLAND ROAD
SHOREDITCH
Open: Mon-Fri 8.45 a.m.-5.15 p.m.
Saturday 9 a.m.-12 noon
H.P.W.WM.D.A.BC.

NORBURY   Tel: 01-679 6193
HERON TOOLS & HARDWARE LTD
437 STREATHAM HIGH ROAD
S.W.16
Open: Mon-Sat 8.30 a.m. - 6 p.m.
Wednesday 8.30 a.m. - 1 p.m.
H.P.W.A.

WOOLWICH Tel.01-854 7767/8
A. D. SKILLMAN & SONS LTD
108-109 WOOLWICH HIGH ST
SE18 6DW
Open: Mon-Sat 8.30 a.m.-to 5.30 p.m.
Half Day Thursday
H.P.W.CS.A.

MERSEYSIDE

LIVERPOOL   Tel. 051-263 1359
TAYLOR BROS (LIVERPOOL) LTD
5/9 PRESCOTT STREET
Open: Monday to Friday
8.30 a.m.-5.30 p.m.
H.P.W.WM.D.A.BC.

MIDDLESEX

HARROW   Tel. 01-863 9462
ALLIED HARDWARE   ★
219 STATION ROAD
Open: Monday-Saturday
9.00 a.m.-6.00 p.m.
H.P.A.

NORTH HARROW Tel. 01-863 2492
WILLIAMS TECHNICAL SERVICES ★
36 STATION ROAD
Open: Mon-Fri 8 a.m.-5.30 p.m.
Wed 8 a.m.-1 p.m.,
Sat 9 a.m.-5.30 p.m.
H.P.W.WM.D.A.

NORFOLK

NORWICH   Tel. 0603 898695
NORFOLK SAW SERVICES
DOG LAND, HORSFORD
Open: Monday to Friday
8.00 a.m.-5.00 p.m.
Saturday 8.00 a.m.-12.00 p.m.
H.P.W.WM.D.CS.A.

NORWICH   Tel. 0603 400933
WESTGATES WOODWORKING Tx.
MACHINERY, JUPITER ROAD 975412
OFF MILE CROSS LANE
Open: 9 a.m.-5 p.m. weekdays
9 a.m.-12 a.m. Sat.
P.W.WM.D.

NORTHAMPTONSHIRE

RUSHDEN   Tel. 093-34 56424
PETER CRISP LIMITED   ★
7 HIGH STREET
Open: Monday to Saturday
8.30 a.m.-5.30 p.m.
Thursday 8.30 a.m.-1.00 p.m.
H.P.W.D.BC.

NORTHUMBERLAND

BLYTH   Tel. (06706) 69279
ALLAN McNAIR WOODCRAFT ★
69-71 PLESSEY ROAD
Open: Monday to Saturday
9 a.m.-5 p.m.
H.W.WM.D.T.CS.A.BC.

NOTTINGHAMSHIRE

NOTTINGHAM Tel. (0602) 225979
POOLEWOOD   (06077) 5777
EQUIPMENT LTD
5a HOLLY LANE, CHILLWELL
Open: Mon-Fri 9 a.m.-5.30 p.m.
Sat. 9 a.m. to 12.30 p.m.
P.W.WM.D.CS.A.BC.

NOTTINGHAM Tel. 0602 811889
THE WOODCUTTER
5 TUDOR SQUARE
WEST BRIDGFORD
Open: Tues-Sat 9 a.m.-5.30 p.m.
Fri 9 a.m.-7.30 p.m. Closed Mon.
H.P.W.WM.D.T.CS.A.

OXFORDSHIRE

BICESTER   Tel. (08692) 4156/
WOODMEN   3218/3219
104 CHURCHILL ROAD
Open: Monday-Saturday
9 a.m.-5.30 p.m.
P.W.WM.D.A.BC.

OXFORD   Tel. (0865) 45118/9
SARJENT'S TOOL   ★
STORES LTD
150 COWLEY ROAD
Open: Monday to Saturday
8.30 a.m.-5.30 p.m.
H.P.W.WM.D.A.BC.

STAFFORDSHIRE

TAMWORTH Tel. 0827-56188
MATTHEWS BROTHERS LTD
KETTLEBROOK ROAD
Open: Mon.-Sat. 8.30am-6.00pm
Demonstrations Sunday mornings
by appointment only
H.P.WM.D.T.CS.A.BC.

SUFFOLK

BURY ST. EDMUNDS   Tel.
TOOLS & THINGS   0284 62022
21 CHURCHGATE   ★
Open: Monday to Saturday
9.00 a.m.-5.30 p.m.
H.P.W.WM.D.A.BC.

IPSWICH   Tel. 0473 86216
FOX WOODWORKING   ★
'STEBBINGS' BACK LANE
WASHBROOK
Open: Tues. Fri. 9.00am-5.30pm
Sat. 9.00am-12 noon
H.P.W.WM.D.A.B.C.

SURREY

CARSHALTON BEECHES Tel.
SURREY WOOD   01-642 6636
MACHINE SALES LTD   ★
56A BANSTEAD ROAD
Open: Tues-Fri 9.30 am-6.00 pm
Saturday 9.30 am-2.00 pm
P.W.WM.D.BC.CS.

SURREY

CROYDON   Tel. 01-688 5513
L. H. TURTLE LTD   ★
6-12 PARK STREET
Open: Monday to Saturday
8.30 a.m.-5.30 p.m.
H.P.W.WM.D.A.

GUILDFORD   Tel. 0483 61125
MESSINGERS FOR TOOLS
14-18 CHERTSEY STREET
Open: Tuesday to Saturday
8.30 a.m.-5.30 p.m.
Closed all day Monday
H.P.W.D.BC.

SUSSEX

BOGNOR REGIS Tel: (0243) 863100
A. OLBY & SON (BOGNOR REGIS LTD)
"TOOLSHOP", BUILDER'S MERCHANT
HAWTHORN ROAD
Open: Mon-Thurs 8 a.m.-5.15 p.m.
Fri 8 a.m.-8 p.m. Sat 8 a.m.-12.45 p.m.
H.P.W.WM.D.T.C.A.BC.

WORTHING   Tel. 0903 38739
W. HOSKING (TOOLS &
MACHINERY)
96a MONTAGUE STREET
Open: Mon-Sat 8.30am-5.30pm
Wednesday 8.30am-1.00pm
H.P.W.WM.D.CS.A.BC.

WEST MIDLANDS

WEST BROMWICH   Tel: 021-
CONWAY SAW &   533 5461/2
SUPPLY LTD   ★
SWAN LANE
Open: 8 a.m.-6 p.m. Mon-Fri
9 a.m.-1 p.m. Saturday
P.W.WM.D.CS.BC.

WILTSHIRE

SWINDON   Tel. (0793) 31361
SARJENT'S TOOL STORES LTD ★
64 FLEET STREET
Open: Monday to Saturday
8.30 a.m.-5.30 p.m.
H.P.W.WM.D.A.BC

YORKSHIRE

BRADFORD   Tel. 0274 560699
STEENWISE LIMITED   ★
LIMEFIELD MILL,
WOOD STREET, CROSSFLATS
BINGLEY
Open: Mon to Fri 9 a.m.-5 p.m.
H.P.W.WM.D.T.CS.A.BC.

HALIFAX   Tel. 0422 884075/
TIMBERLITE LTD   884788/33575
VICTORIA BUILDINGS
LUDDENDEN FOOT
Open: Monday to Friday
Saturday 9.00 a.m.-5.00 p.m.
H.P.W.WM.D.CS.A.BC.

HARROGATE   Tel. 0423 66245/
MULTI-TOOLS   55328 ★
158 KINGS ROAD
Open: Monday to Saturday
8.30 a.m.-6.00 p.m.
H.P.W.WM.D.A.BC.

SHOP GUIDE SHOP GUIDE

YORKSHIRE

HUDDERSFIELD Tel. (0484)
NEVILLE M. OLDHAM 641219/(0484)
UNIT 1 DAYLE ST. WORKS 42777
DAYLE STREET, LONGWOOD ★
Open: Mon-Fri 9.00am- 5.30pm
Saturday 9.30am-12.00pm
P.W.WM.D.A.BC.

LEEDS Tel. 0532 790507
GEORGE SPENCE & SONS LTD
WELLINGTON ROAD ★
Open: Monday to Friday
8.30 a.m.-5.30 p.m.
Saturday 9.00 a.m.-5.00 p.m.
H.P.W.WM.D.T.A.

SHEFFIELD Tel. 0742-441012
GREGORY & TAYLOR LTD
WORKSOP ROAD
Open: 8.30 a.m.-5.30 p.m.
Monday-Friday
8.30 a.m.-12.30 p.m. Sat.
H.P.W.WM.D.

SHEFFIELD Tel. 0742-24659
GRAHAM OXLEY'S SHOWROOM
BRIDGE STREET ★
Open: Monday to Friday
9.00 a.m.-5.30 p.m.
Saturday 8.30 a.m.-12.30 p.m.
H.W.D.A.BC.

YORKSHIRE

SOWERBY BRIDGE Tel. (0422)
CALDER 31861
WOODWORKING Telex: 517400
MACHINERY LTD.
STATION ROAD
Open: Mon - Fri 9 a.m.-5 p.m.
P.W.WM.D.CS.A.

SCOTLAND

EDINBURGH Tel. 031-337
SCOTSPAN 7788/665 3121
195 BALGREEN ROAD
Open: Monday to Friday
9.00 a.m.-3.00 p.m.
P.W.WM.D.A.

GLASGOW Tel. 041 429 4374/4444
THE SAW CENTRE Telex: 777886
596-602 EGLINTON STREET ★
G5 9RR
Open: Mon.-Fri. 8 a.m.-5.30 p.m.
Saturday 9 a.m.-1 p.m.
H.P.W.WM.D.CS.A.

N. IRELAND

Co. ANTRIM Tel. 0266 6384
GEORGE GARDINER
49 BALLYMONEY STREET
BALLYMENA
Open: Open: Mon-Fri 8.30am-5.30pm
Wednesday 8.30am-1.00pm
H.P.W.D.A.BC.

N. IRELAND

Co. DOWN Tel. (0247) 819800 (day)
NEWTOWNARDS 812506 (night)
NORLYN MACHINERY, UNIT 10
Malcolmson Ind. Est., 80 Bangor Road
Open: Mon-Fri 9.30am-5.30pm
or any other time by request
H.P.W.WM.D.A.BC.

S. IRELAND

COUNTY KILKENNY Tel.
WOODMEN (0409) 5460
CASHEL HOUSE ★
KELLS ROAD, KILKENNY

Open: Monday to Saturday

WALES

BRITON FERRY Tel. (0639)
WOODMEN 820803/4
49 NEATH ROAD ★
Open: Monday to Saturday
9.00 a.m.-5.30 p.m.
P.W.WM.D.A.BC.

CARDIFF Tel. (0222) 373007
JOHN HALL TOOLS LIMITED ★
22 CHURCHILL WAY
Open: Monday to Saturday
9.00 a.m.-5.30 p.m.
H.P.W.WM.D.A.BC.

WALES

CARDIFF Tel. (0222) 30831
F. W. MORGAN & 25562
(CANTON) LTD., 129-133
COWBRIDGE RD EAST,
CANTON, CARDIFF
Mon-Sat 8-5 Sun. 9.30-12.30
H.P.T.CS.A.BC.

CARDIFF Tel. (0222) 36519/
WOODMEN 373793/35221
43 CRWYS ROAD ★
Open: Monday to Saturday
9.00 a.m.-5.30 p.m.

CARMARTHEN Tel. 0267 7219
DO-IT-YOURSELF SUPPLY
BLUE STREET, DYFED
Open: Monday to Saturday
9.00 a.m.-5.30 p.m.
Thursday 9.00 a.m.-1.00 p.m.
H.P.W.WM.D.T.CS.A.BC.

**YOU CAN BUY WITH
CONFIDENCE FROM THE
SHOPS IN THIS
SHOP GUIDE**
★Shops offering a mail
order service are denoted by
an asterisk

SHOP GUIDE SHOP GUIDE

SHOP GUIDE SHOP GUIDE SHOP GUIDE
SHOP GUIDE SHOP GUIDE

The quickest and easiest method of reaching all Woodworkers is to advertise in SHOP GUIDE. Telephone **Valerie Tester (0442) 41221 Ext. 266. Rate: £8.00 per unit.** Minimum of 6 months.

Key: H — Hand tools, **P** — Power tools, **W** — Woodworking machinery up to £1000, **WM** — Woodworking machinery over £1000, **D** — Demonstration available on selected machines, **T** — Timber, **CS** — Cutting or sharpening services, **A** — Attachments, **BC** — Books/catalogues, * — Mail order.

£8.00 per Unit
Minimum of SIX insertions.
I enclose remittance of £48.00 ☐
I wish to be invoiced. ☐
Please tick as appropriate.

To: **Valerie Tester**
WOODWORKER MAGAZINE
P.O. Box 35,
13 Bridge Street, Hemel Hempstead,
HP1 1EE.

COUNTY ....

TOWN ....

NAME OF COMPANY/SHOP ....

....

ADDRESS ....

....

TELEPHONE No ....

DAYS AND HOURS OF BUSINESS

....

....

*TO DENOTE MAIL ORDER SERVICE
AVAILABLE ☐

ADVERTISEMENTS WILL BE INSERTED IN THE FIRST AVAILABLE ISSUE

Prices quoted are those prevailing at press date and are
subject to alteration due to economic conditions. Woodworker, February 1982

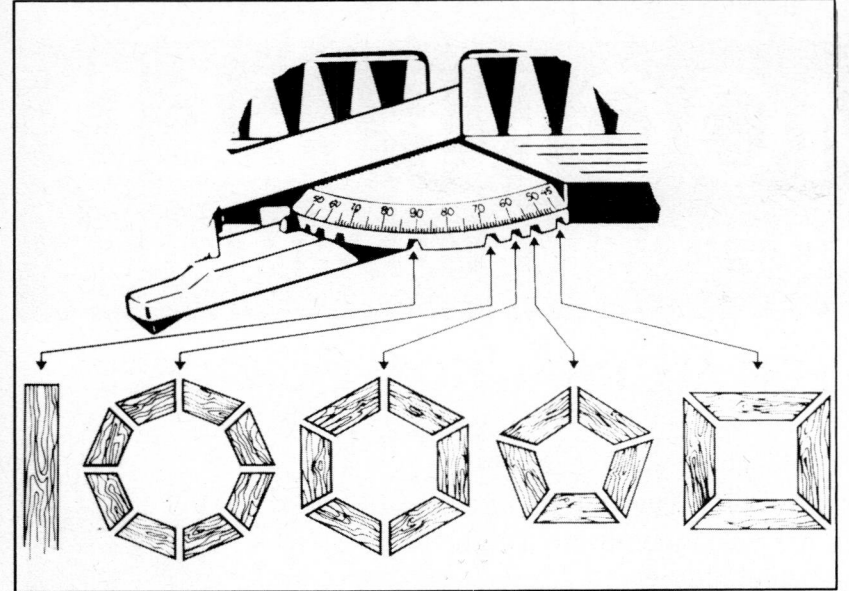

WHAT'S NEW

Nobex is modified

Modified version (model 202) of the Nobex mitre saw incorporates six fixed 'quick-lock' positions and a graduated locking scale for non-standard angles.

The additional fixed positions are said to mean that calculation of angles for the less usual frame shapes, ie pentagonal, hexagonal and octagonal, is unnecessary. Thus there are no errors in calculation or in manually setting the saw.

For further details get in touch with C. D. Monninger Ltd, Overbury Road, London N15 6RJ (01-800 5435). Illustrated leaflet is available.

Melting

Seba medium-temperature melting equipment comprises an outer container with internal insulation and a melting pot mounted on legs and provided with a handle and double-skin lid. The electric heating element is fitted to the exterior of the inner vessel and the standard Seba has integral controls incorporating two adjustable controllers for temperatures over the range 40-180°C.

There are four types of pot with capacities from 2.5 to 20litre (4.4 to 35pt); the equipment can be provided with bottom pour or constructed to individual requirements.

Seba is marketed by Woodcote Developments, Doric House, The Poplars, Brayton, Selby YO8 9HH (0757 708247). Price of a 6litre capacity model is given as £135 plus VAT.

Edgebanding

The T55 edgebander and F10 edgetrimmer, both made by Heinrich Brandt in W Germany, are available here through Jaydee (Machine Sales) Ltd, Copyground Lane, High Wycombe HP12 3HE (High Wycombe 3409). The former machine deals with application of hot-melt adhesive pre-coated material in coils and fixed lengths to straight or shaped workpieces of all forms and sizes at feed speed up to 10m/min.

The latter machine provides synchronous top and bottom flush trimming and chamfering on panels of all shapes and sizes; inside and outside radii can be processed. An optional extra which may be fitted to the F10 is the EK11 endtrimmer. This can be set to deal with front and rear edge material projection.

Log cutting

Use of the Chainhorse log cutter from Hugh Simpson Designs, Banwen Farm, Glanamman, Ammanford SA18 2AA, is said to speed cutting and give the operative a greater measure of safety. It comprises a metal frame with pivoting sawtable to accept most makes and models of chainsaw. There is a solid metal self-retracting hand guard to protect the operative's left hand.

It is claimed that logs from 7in. down to 1in. diameter can be sawn with the attachment; logs up to 12in. diameter are held in a quick-release clamp and sawn freehand with a rocking motion.

Guillotine blades 4in. and spring-loaded can be provided to cut branches etc up to 1¼in. diameter.

Keyless chuck and countersink

The Nylex is a keyless chuck for Black & Decker drills. It is currently available in ⅜in. (nominal), though maker of the chuck (The Jacobs Manufacturing Co Ltd, Archer Road, Millhouses, Sheffield (0742 57481)) states that it plans to introduce other sizes.

The chuck is said to be produced from a nylon derivative which makes it light and easy to operate. The price is given as about £7.27.

Jacobs has also introduced a countersink in HSS as used for industrial tooling. It costs around £2.70 and the company claims that it has a much longer life than countersinks made of low carbon steel.

Right: The keyless Nylex chuck from Jacobs is light, easy to operate and costs approx. £7.27.

Prices quoted are those prevailing at press date and are
subject to alteration due to economic conditions.

The Child Coil Grip Chuck

A COMBINATION CHUCK FOR HAND WOODTURNERS   (copied but not improved on)   Patented

COIL GRIP ASSEMBLY

This unique chuck is the outcome of many years experience by a professional woodturner and teacher, and the patented coil grip method together with the many extra modes of operation safely and neatly overcome the chucking problems encountered by amateur and professional turners. The coil grip, supplied ONLY WITH THIS CHUCK, together with the large (4½") diameter heavy duty body offers unbeatable strength and rigidity for gripping end grain work of ANY size. It grips by compression on the outside of the work so there is no danger of splitting the wood by excessive outward pressure. It holds staved work safely. An almost limitless variety of home-made wooden adaptors can be made which will grip any shape or size of work, internally, externally, dovetail grip, plain grip, or as required. The coil grip feature makes this chuck by far the most versatile of its kind. Made for most lathes (state model) £36.50 inc. VAT & carriage.

WOODTURNERS' SPECIALIST SUPPLIER

The most comprehensive range of tools available. The new ROY CHILD parting tool. Chucks, centres, fittings, drills. Flexicramps. Many types and sizes glass inserts, barometers, hygrometers, thermometers, eggtimers, hourglasses, condiment liners, 160 circular tile patterns, lighters, pens, flower vase tubes, peppermills, STAINLESS saltmills, knives, clocks, pencil sharpeners, ashtrays, clock dials. Abrasives, waxes, finishes. Speed-n-Eze, Rustins. WOOD for turning. MYFORD agents. ROY CHILD pyrography machines. Post Office Parcel Contract for most quick and direct delivery service. Send S.A.E. for catalogue, or $1.00 from overseas enquiries. We EXPORT worldwide.

WOODTURNING AND FINISHING

Two-day intensive course and personal tuition at 17th century Essex-Suffolk farmhouse. Fully equipped workshops. Maximum of two guests for any one course.

PETER CHILD

THE WOODTURNER CRAFTSMAN
The Old Hyde, Little Yeldham, Halstead, Essex. Tel. Gt. Yeldham (0787) 237291

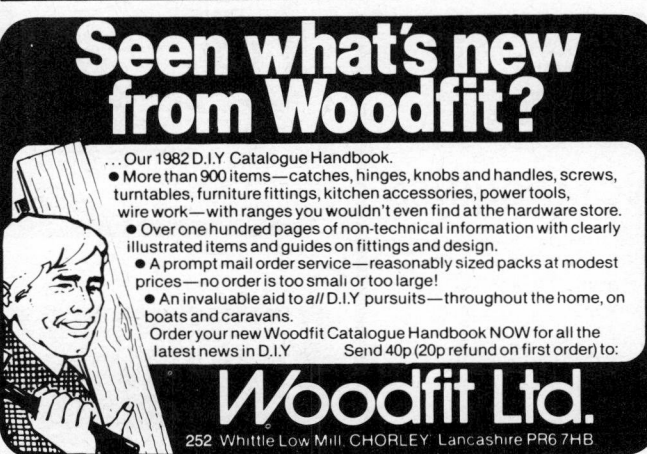
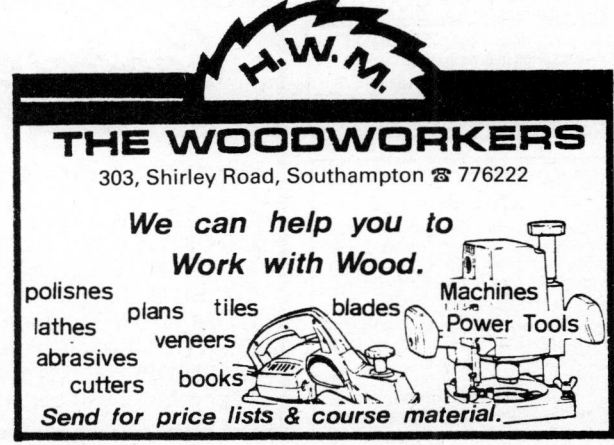

Classified Advertisements

WORKSHOP EQUIPMENT

COPING SAW BLADES and junior hacksaw blades. Details from Lea Blades, 16 Barclay, Hertford Heath, Hertford, Herts.　K-L

GENERATOR 1.5 KVA industrial R/Field S/P A/C 110/240v. Tooley Powered Villiers 4/S petrol engine £365 as new. Maidstone 43872. Today's price £484.　K

CIRCULAR AND BAND saw blades for all applications from: A. A. SMITH of Lancing Ltd., 63 Brighton Road, Shoreham, Sussex. Tel: 07917 61707 (24 hrs).　K-O

BANDSAW ATTACHMENT for Myford ML8 Lathe. Good working order. 40 blades. Offers Halcrow, Homebank, Coldstream TD12 4ND. Tel: 089 083 285.　K

ANTIQUE BRITANNIA 3-speed lathe, 3" c.h., with accessories. Good order £100 o.n.o. Tel: (Tewin) 043871 7323.　K

FRETSAW BLADES, Marquetry saw blades, whetstones. Details and prices Lea Blade Sales, 16 Barclay, Hertford Heath, Herts.　JK

MACHINERY. A comprehensive range of new/used machinery. Check our prices, e.g. HMO 10"×5½" planer/thicknesser £325. HF30 spindle moulder £328. 12" tilt arbor sawbench 2hp motor £121. Shopsmith MK5 home workshop £782. Morso mitring machine £437, (including V.A.T.). See these machines and Ryobi industrial small tools demonstrated at Woodman Woodworking Machinery Co. (Sign of the Axe), Little Malgraves Hall, Lower Dunton Road, Bulphan, Nr. Upminster, Essex. Tel: (0268) 415511 or (0702) 331729.　I-U

MAKE A WOODTURNING LATHE easily, construction details and parts list, send S.A.E. to: Ortan Lathes, P.O. Box 46, Norwich NR7 8PB.　I-K

EBAC TIMBER SEASONERS, Protimeter moisture meters, always good prices and advice from the man who pioneered small scale seasoning. John Arrowsmith, Roadham Cottage, Barton, Richmond, North Yorks. Telephone: (0325) 77362.　T/C

PLANERS 6", 9" planers/thicknessers, 12" × 7", 9" × 6", 12" × 7", sawbenches, 10", 12", combination woodworkers. British made. Particulars, send stamp. Dodd Machine Tools Ltd., South Woodham, Chelmsford. Tel: 320 691.　C-N

WASHITA & ARKANSAS whetstones now readily available from importer. Large selection, SAE for list. C. Rufino, Manor House, South Clifton, Newark, Notts.　T/C

The **'SCRU-DRILL'** Adjustable Woodscrew Bit Specialist tool for Woodworker and DIY enthusiast.

Adjust to size of screw and in one single operation —
● Drill pilot hole for screw thread
● Drill pilot hole for screw body
● Countersink — counterbore
● Drill to accurate preset depth

Screw home with ease in hard or softwoods — no excess strain on screw, timber or yourself — set of four 'SCRU-DRILLS' replaces dozens of other fixed size pilot drills and countersinks — accommodates numbers 5 to 14 woodscrews.

Set of Four £11.50
inc. VAT and carriage

Send cheque or P.O. to:
KELTEK PRODUCTS
PO Box 5, Wadebridge PL27 7YZ

or SAE for further information
— Trade enquiries —

MULTICUT -2 SAW

The world's first universal precision saw, cuts 50mm wood, 10mm metals, plastics, rubber, etc. High performance, safe in use. Do not compare with standard fretsaws. Details 11½p stamp.

Hegner Universal Saws (U.K.) Ltd.
36 Gt. Eastern Road, Hockley, Essex.
Tel: Southend (0702) 205669.

Demonstrations at most of the major exhibitions throughout the year.

WOODCARVING tools

LARGEST STOCK IN EUROPE

Ashley Iles & Henry Taylor
Arkansas Bench & Slip Stones
Strops & Strop Paste
Bench Screws, Carvers' Vices

WOODTURNING tools

Complete range of
Henry Taylor & Ashley Iles
handled or unhandled

send 30p in stamps for illustrated catalogue

ALEC TIRANTI LTD
70 High St. Theale, Reading, Berks
21 Goodge Place, London W.1.

A·Pollard+Son LTD.

Come and browse through our huge stocks of machinery and tools. If you live too far away, privately owned Mini Clipper service will deliver within days to your door.

KITY UNITED KINGDOM **K5**
International Woodworker with Sawbench, Spindle Moulder, Planer/Thicknesser & Slot Mortiser.
Full range in stock.

scheppach **HMO ▶**
2HP 10" × 6" Planer/Thicknesser. HM2 Planer/Thicknesser also in stock.

Elu **MFF 80 Planer**
The ideal machine for use by craftsmen on the building site and in the joinery shop.
£52·99 CARR. £2 EXTRA

DeWALT DW125
Powershop, for Sawing, Grooving, Sanding, Moulding etc.
Dust Extractors, Planer/Thicknessers & Industrial R.A.S. also in stock.

◀ H.F.30
Spindle Moulder 2HP Motor.
Shown with: Overhead Roller, Guard & Sliding Carriage. (Optional Extras)

mafell **BIBEREX**
12", 2.3HP Sawbench with Rise & Fall, Mitre Guide, Fence and Tilting Arbor.
Other Sawbenches in stock.

Dust Extractors, Lathes, Industrial R/A. Saws. Large stocks of Ironmongery & Handtools — Most accessories stocked.
Open 6 days a week 8.30-5.30　Barclaycard, Access　Business Established over 50 years.

A. POLLARD & SON LTD. 51 Queensway, Bletchley, Milton Keynes ☎ (0908) 75221

WOODTURNERS SUPPLIES

Woodturning tools, Peppermills, Salt mills, Barometers, Thermometers, Lighters, Hourglasses, Eggtimers, Ceramic tiles and clock faces, Clock movements, Spinning wheel plans, Sealers & Polishes, etc. Fast and efficient mail order service + competitive prices. S.A.E. for lists.

ERIC TOMKINSON
86 Stockport Road, Cheadle, Cheshire, SK8 2AJ. Tel. 061-491-1726
Shop open Weds., Thurs., Fri. & Sat.

SUMACO **DIRECT LINE**

2 YEAR GUARANTEE

EUMENIA RADIAL SAW

Total accuracy with a feature not available on any other radial saw — extension arm giving 600mm cross-cutting. Optional extra.

£179.50 incl. VAT carr. extra

EXCLUSIVE IN THE UK TO SUMACO

Sumaco Machinery and Tools Ltd.,
Suma House, Huddersfield Road, Elland, West Yorkshire. Tel: Elland (0422) 75491.

ACCESS/BARCLAYCARD WELCOME

Braywood Estates

Comprehensive range of **DeWALT** Accessories plus a super service for spare parts & on site servicing.

BRAYWOOD ESTATES LTD. FREEPOST, SLOUGH SL2 4BL
TELEPHONE : SLOUGH 0753 22567/70792

SHERWOOD WOOD TURNING LATHES

All cast iron constructed. 3¾" CH 24" or 36" B.C. 3 or 4 speed, bowl turning up to 14" dia. ball-bearing spindle c/w face plate, centres etc. Prices from **£75.29** inc. VAT.

Send stamp for leaflets and details of above and other low-priced machines and motors.

JAMES INNS (Engs),
Main St., Bulwell, Nottingham

Cooksley

A. COOKSLEY LIMITED
Riverside Works,
The Causeway, Staines,
Middx. TW18 3AG.
Tel: Staines 57244/5/6.

NEW WOODWORKING MACHINES

SEDGWICK Saws, Planers, Mortisers.
COOKSLEY Universals, Spindles, Planers.
STARTRITE Bandsaws, Dim. Saws, Drills.
WILSON Combined Planer, Spindle.
DOMINION Tenoner, Sander, Moulder.
DEWALT Bench & free standing Crosscut Saws.
MODERN Hand & Foot mitre trimmers.
Wood cutting tools and engineering repairs

Rates
20p per word, minimum £3.00
Box nos. £1.25 extra.
Semi display s.c.c. £4.00
(min £10.00)

140

Prices quoted are those prevailing at press date and are subject to alteration due to economic conditions.

Woodworker, February 1982

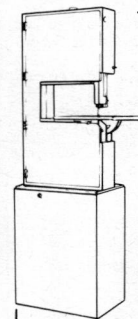

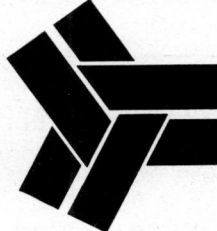

Prices quoted are those prevailing at press date and are subject to alteration due to economic conditions.

THE MAGAZINE FOR THE CRAFTSMAN

MARCH 1982 Vol. 86 No. 1060 ISSN 0043-776X

Front cover: Many of the big cypress *Taxodium distichum* are over 100 years old. They are the same species as the dwarf cypress of the Everglades. *(Photo. P. Curds)* See also p167.

	Editorial	
Advertisement Manager	Polly Curds	
	Glyn Crole-Rees	
Advertisement Director ⎫	MAP Leisure	Michael Merrifield
Managing Director ⎭	Division	Gavin Doyle

MEMBER OF THE AUDIT BUREAU OF CIRCULATIONS

SUBSCRIPTION DEPARTMENT: Remittances to MODEL AND ALLIED PUBLICATIONS, PO Box 35, Hemel Hempstead, Herts HP1 1EE. Price per copy 95p includes p&p. Subscription queries: Tel: Hemel Hempstead 51740. Subscription rate, including index, £11.90 per annum; overseas sterling £12.90; $29.00 US for overseas dollar subscribers. Second class postage paid in US at New York, New York. *Distribution* to North American hobby and craft stores, museums and bookshops by Bill Dean Books Ltd, 166-41 Powells Cove Boulevard, Post Office Box 69, Whitestone, New York 11357, USA. Tel: 1-212-767-6632. *Distribution* to news stand sales by Eastern News Distribution Inc, 111 Eight Avenue, New York, NY10011, USA. Tel: 1-212-255-5620.

WOODWORKER is printed in Great Britain by H. E. Warne Ltd, East Hill, St Austell, Cornwall PL25 4TN for the proprietor and publisher Model & Allied Publications Ltd (a member of the Argus Press Group). Trade sales by Argus Press Sales & Distribution Ltd, 12-18 Paul Street, London EC2A 4JS. WOODWORKER (ISSN 0043-776X) is published on the 3rd Friday of the month.

Model & Allied Publications Ltd

PO Box 35, Bridge Street, Hemel Hempstead, Herts HP1 1EE. Telephone: Hemel Hempstead (0442) 41221.

Mathematical modelling

According to the multinational forest model study that has been initiated by the International Institute for Applied Systems Analysis (IIASA) a new technical tool is joining chainsaws, log runs and the other traditional tools of forestry. The purpose is to enable managers to see not only the forest and its trees, but also their environmental niche, the challenges they face from rising demand for land and fuel, and the industry and international trade they support.

The 'tool' is a computer model...a set of mathematical equations capable of simulating processes in nature. A researcher at IIASA, Dr Risto Seppälä, states that 'While some countries have used models of timber growth, harvesting and land use, not much has been done to provide models covering the entire forest sector.'

The term 'forest sector' refers to the composite of all aspects of forestry and the forest industry, from timber growth to end products, along with associated environmental and socioeconomic factors. This effort to see the whole has been stimulated by the decline in size of the world's forests.

At a recent N American conference on forest sector models an ambitious modelling programme was proposed by IIASA to be carried out in close co-operation with industry, government and researchers in 16 participating nations with the aid of some 40 research organisations.

A central source is to be set up so that forest managers may well avail themselves of data and a set of prototype models will be developed as a nucleus for subsequent national efforts to build mathematical models tailored to the specific characteristics and requirements of each nation. Elements such as: timber production, harvest and labour force, land conversion, erosion, firewood use, wood processing, wood product consumption, and such government policy as relates to subsidies, and national economy, would all be included.

Long term resource potential must also be studied plus restructuring of existing industries, production costs and new technologies. Dr Seppälä points out that the present trend of decline in the accessible forests in SE Asia will ultimately shift trade to another exporter. The effect of this on the present world trade is an unknown quantity. A global framework will therefore need to be developed, linked to national and regional models, focusing on the countries that amount for some 75% of world production, consumption and trade.

Time horizon of the study is of the order of 20-50 years. Forests must be protected as a renewable resource. The effect of atmospheric pollutants on health and species distribution of forests is critical.

The new editor of Woodworker, Christopher Dunn, has joined us, and will be taking over the reins for the May issue. Chris has worked for magazines and newspapers both in this country and overseas. As an amateur woodworker he has specialised in furniture, though his current project is building a cello, under the guidance of Juliet Barker, the Cambridge violin maker. Chris says he looks forward to getting to know readers and immersing himself in the subject closest to his heart, wood.

Simple Reliable-

There's a lot of talk these days about revolutionary, highly sophisticated woodworking machinery – the new, low cost, over complicated little wonders that do almost everything – providing of course you're a keen engineering student with more than a lot of time on your hands.

Well – no one ever said Kity machines were sophisticated or revolutionary – and we're proud of it – in fact we designed and built them to be simple, reliable and easy to use. You don't have to change your woodworking methods or be an engineer, Kity simply adds power and precision to develop your own skills – and sometimes even your bank balance.

Recently Barrie and Lynne Goddard of Bottesford, near Scunthorpe, decided to improve their kitchen. The going rate for the job, from a professional contractor, was around £5,000; however with Kity machinery to help him, Barrie built their dream kitchen for just £2,000.

Ideas can now become reality

All of us at some time have had to scrap excellent creative ideas because we couldn't afford to bring in the professionals and didn't have sufficient expertise to carry them out ourselves. The simplicity of Kity machinery has gone a long way towards removing this frustration and our illustrated instruction sheets will explain step by step the machine techniques needed to transform your ideas into superb reality.

Common base for all functions.

The K5 has units for separate machine functions mounted on a common base and driven by a centrally mounted power unit – the K5 motor. You have all the versatility of separately mounted machines, any change of operation becomes simplicity itself. Just connect the belt to the machine you want to use, adjusting the tension easily by means of a simple, quick release lever. Without losing your pre-set adjustments, you can change from one function to another in a matter of seconds. Continuity of work is thus assured.

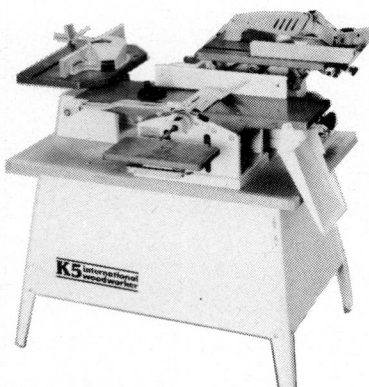

K5 international woodworker

– *complete power workshop for only* **£559**

(plus VAT. £83.85)

Engineering specification

Circular saw.
180mm (7") blade normally fitted but will accept a 200mm (8") blade giving a 57mm (2¼") depth of cut. 2 speeds, 3750 for normal wood and 6200 r.p.m. for laminated boards. Complete with rip fence, mitre guide, repeat cut length stop, wobble washers for grooving, tilting table 0.45°.

Surface planer.
700mm (27½") long × 200mm (8") wide cast bed. Maximum planing width 150mm (6"). Adjustable 90° – 45° fence for bevel planing. Dynamically balanced cutter block rotating at 11,400 cuts per minute.

Thickness planer.
Fully automatic feed, 7.5m (24') per minute. Maximum capacity 100mm (4") deep, 150mm (6") wide. Anti kick-back fingers, calibrated scale.

Spindle moulder
6400 rpm shaft speed. 45mm (1¾") vertical adjustment. Capable of taking 25mm (1") × 25mm (1") rebate in one pass. Accepts both French moulding profiles and white hill type blocks.

Slot mortiser
Rise/fall table with 100mm (4") of adjustment.

---

2 New Books

2 great books from Kity to help improve your craft.

"How to work with Wood"
One of the few books available about **woodworking machine techniques** including setting up and the use of circular saws, spindle moulder planer thicknesser slot mortisers etc. An invaluable manual for anyone using or buying woodworking machinery.

Full colour 260 pages, hard bound 195mm × 275mm, price **£15.00.**

"How to choose your Wood"
A definitive work covering timber types, cutting, storage and use. Including man made boards of all types.

Full colour 141 pages hard bound, 195mm × 275mm, price **£10.00.**

Available from all Kity stockists or direct from **Kity UK.** only **£20 for both books – save 20%.**

Maximum bit diameter 12mm (½"). Produces accurate mortises, also horizontal boring for perfect dowel joints.

2 year guarantee
When you buy a K5, you will be protected against all manufacturing defects (parts and labour) for the first two years after purchase, no matter how hard you work your machine.

The Kity Heavy Duty Range

Arthur is a highly skilled, traditional craftsman who uses the Kity Heavy Duty Range, ideal machinery for the busy modern craftsmen. By purchasing a mixture of independent and combination machines he built a superb workshop that exactly suited his requirements and his pocket. Arthur says... "It's amazing how some woodworkers still use old fashioned methods that belong in the Dark Ages. Mind you – I ought not to criticize them I used to be the same, I was proud to work like my Grandfather did and I believed the results would be better if everything was done by hand. It never occurred to me he had no alternative – and in any case, I always thought machines were complicated and some how difficult to use. Anyhow, I soon found out how wrong I was when I started using Kity machinery. I got better results in a fraction of the time and with very little physical effort. There's no doubt in my mind that Kity machinery is simple and very easy to use – and sure, it makes makes me money."

Kity offers you Heavy Duty Circular Saws, Bandsaws, Planer Thicknessers, Spindle Moulders and Slot Mortisers, along with a complete range of accessories, motors and floor stands. Each machine can be independent or part of a combination for example: you can start your workshop with a circular saw. With Kity you don't have a lot of complicated attachments, nor do you have to swing the machine into different positions or use a special tool. Simply slip the belt from one machine to the next.

The Circular Saw 617

This is the heart of most workshops. The Kity machine has a cast and machined, tilting work table; a rise/fall arbor with hand wheel control; it accepts blades up to 9" in diameter giving a 3⅛"

Prices quoted are those prevailing at press date and are subject to alteration due to economic conditions.

and *very* easy to use

depth of cut; and is capable of running at two speeds; 3400 rpm and 7000 rpm. It is powered by a ½ H.P. motor with No Volt Thermal Overload starter. You will have no difficulty in cutting any wood based material, from melamine faced chipboard to African hardwoods.

Accessories included in the price are the mitre-guide with repeat cut stop, and wobble washers for grooving. The machine is guarded to comply with international standards.

The Planer Thicknessers 535, 635, 636

Kity manufacture three 'under and over' planer/thicknessers, a 10″ × 6″, 8″ × 6″ and a 7″ × 4″.

Each machine is available with stand and motor and can be used as an independent unit or will fit as part of the combination.

Each machine has cast tables and a twin knife cutter block and is of the 'under and over' type. The thicknesser is power fed with an adjustable thicknessing table giving true results along the whole length of the timber; this is usually difficult to achieve with the 'over fed' clamp type thicknesser. The 636 and 635 both have unusually long (40″) surfacing tables ideal for straightening a twist in a plank of timber.

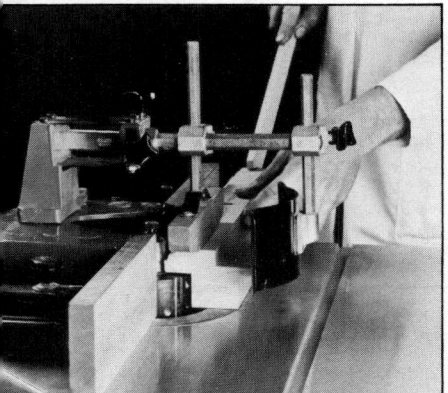

Spindle Moulders 626/627

The Spindle Moulder is a versatile and powerful tool. It does a totally different job to a router, although the system is similar. For example: – The 626 and 627 are capable of making large rebates 1¼″ × 1¼″ in hundreds of feet of timber. They will also produce moulding, deep grooves, tongue and groove joints, V-joints, tenons, profiles and counter profiles.

The 626 has a standard adjustable fence with the capability of positioning the cutting tools over a 4″ vertical range. The 627 has the same specifications but with individual micro adjustable fences. Both machines have cutting speeds of 7000 rpm, and are guarded to full international standards.

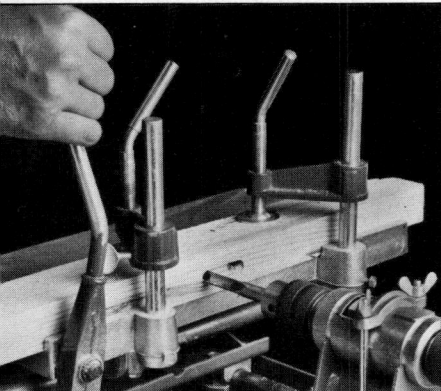

The 625 Slot Mortiser

The only machine in the whole range that is *not* available as an independent machine.
Working from the 700 table it will provide a ½″ slot, up to 5″ long and 4″ deep. An excellent machine for mortise joint production.

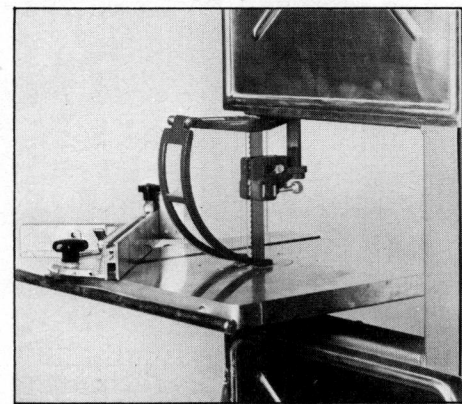

The 612 Bandsaw

Kity make an all steel, two wheel, Bandsaw with a 5½″ depth of cut and an 11½″ throat. It will accept blades from ¼″ for tight turns to ⅞″ for deep cutting and planking of timber. Unlike 'Plastic' Bandsaws the steel construction of the Kity machine allows you to set a high blade tension. This enables you to cut fast and in a straight line through hardwood and knots with a maximum depth of 5½″.

Kity Plan Sheets

These are issued for a nominal charge exclusively to Kity users and titles include, fitted kitchens and furniture. These practical plan sheets include cutting lists and complete manufacturing instructions on the relevant subject.

Nation-wide Service

Kity have 150 fully trained stockists throughout the U.K. and they provide a service second to none – there'll be one near you, ask for a demonstration, before you buy.

If you have a dream project you want to build or if you're a busy craftsman then you need Kity – simple, reliable and easy to use machinery.

Instructions on machines

Each Kity machine has comprehensive instructions to ensure you have the knowledge to use the machine correctly.

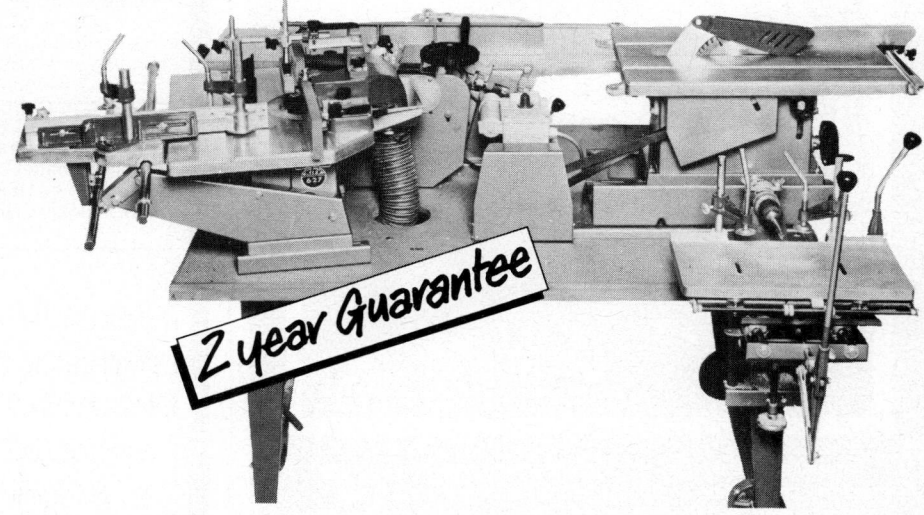

2 year Guarantee

KITY UNITED KINGDOM

Kity U.K., Sizer's Court, Henshaw Lane, Yeadon, Leeds LS19 7DP.
Tel: (0532) 509110. Telex: 557920

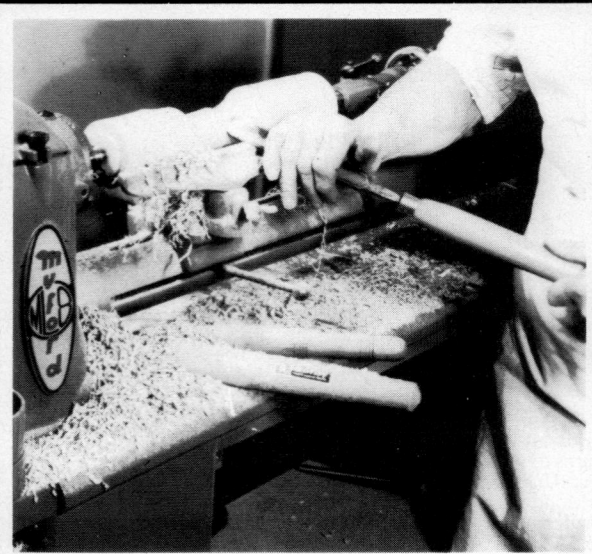

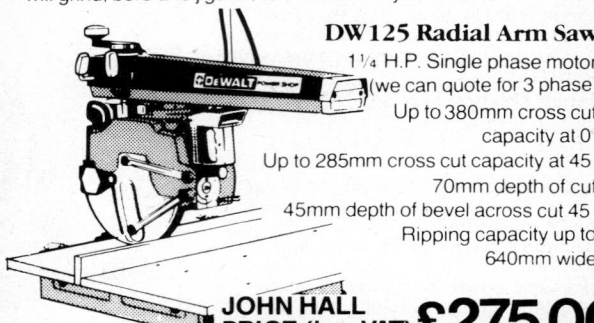

Prices quoted are those prevailing at press date and are subject to alteration due to economic conditions.

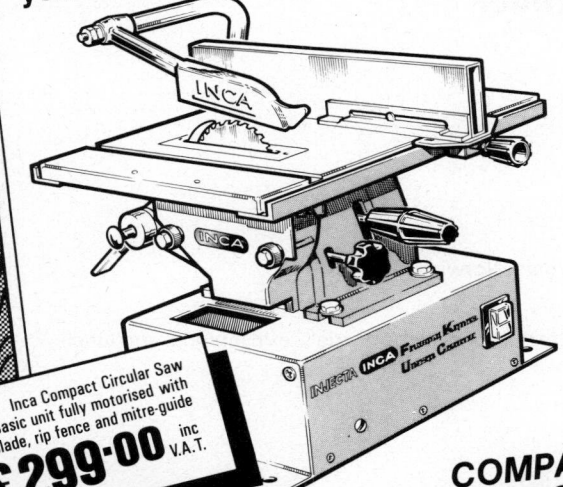

Guild of Woodworkers

Courses on design appreciation and fine craftsmanship

Three separate courses on design and fine craftsmanship have been arranged at Rycotewood College, Priest End, Thame OX9 2AF.

2 day course 6-7 April....a two-day course to introduce the basic principles of design and to apply them to the development of interesting and original small scale woodwork problems. Cost £40.00.

3 day course 14-16 April....a three-day course to introduce the basic principles of design, to show how the 20th century designer/craftsman has developed both the art and craft aspects in modern commis-sioned design, and how they may be applied to a small piece of work. Cost £69.00.

5 day course (date to be advised) in August/September 1982....a five-day course to bring to the woodworker the basic principles of design and to apply these principles to the making of a piece of furniture. Cost £115.00.

Respective charges for the three courses are all inclusive of VAT and all cover accommodation at the college, plus morning coffee and meals. A cancellation charge of half the fee will be made unless the cancellation is received in writing 14 days prior to the date of the course.

Applications should be made as soon as possible, together with remittance to: Administrator, Guild of Woodworkers, PO Box 35, Bridge Street, Hemel Hempstead HP1 1EE.

Machine tools course

Special introductory practical two-day course for members with limited experience of woodworking machinery to be held at various times (bookings accepted any time to suit) in Milton Keynes, Bucks. This is a non-residential course. Price on application to the administrator.

SEMINARS: SKILLS AND PROFIT-MAKING

Guild of Woodworkers – Council for Small Industries in Rural Areas

To: Administrator
Guild of Woodworkers
PO Box 35
Bridge Street
Hemel Hempstead HP1 1EE

Date ....

Please reserve a place for me on the seminar to be held
on 24-25 February 1982 at Lord Hill Hotel, Abbey Foregate, Shrewsbury,
on 28-29 April 1982 at the Pottergate Course & Conference Centre, 83-5 Pottergate, Norwich.
(Tick which seminar you wish to attend).

I enclose cheque/postal order for £57.50 in payment of seminar tuition fee, papers and lecture material, refreshments and lunch.

I contemplate starting my own business
I am already trading on my own account
(Tick whichever applies).

Please reserve accommodation for me at a guest house,
hotel,
bed & breakfast
(Tick whichever applies)

I understand that accommodation is not included in the seminar fee and I will pay for my accommodation direct.

Name .... BLOCK CAPITALS

Address in full ....

....

Telephone number ....

Signed ....

Membership number ....

Attention is drawn to the cancellation charge of half the fee unless the cancellation is received in writing 14 days prior to the date of each seminar.

TEAR OFF AND POST IMMEDIATELY TOGETHER WITH REMITTANCE

Garry Olson (right) and Chris Hall (left) discuss a technical point with guild administrator Albert Beezem at one of last year's polishing courses.

Protecting the ears

Draft proposals for a uniform statutory system of noise control which could extend hearing protection to everyone at work are contained in consultative document ISBN 0 11 883431 2 *Protection of Hearing at Work*. This is available from HMSO at £3 and comments on it should be sent to HSE, Hazardous Substances Division, Branch HSDD3, 25 Chapel Street, London NW1 5DT, not later than 30 April 1982.

As background to the consultative document HSE has issued *Some Aspects of Noise and Hearing Loss* ISBN 0 11 883432 0 through HMSO at £3.50.

Present legislation containing explicit noise requirements applies only to a limited number of industries of which woodworking is one.

Both of the two-day non-residential courses on finishing to be held during the early weeks of March are now FULL.

Further courses are being arranged on this subject at a date to be announced in future issues of WOODWORKER. If you are interested and would like your name added to a provisional waiting list, please let the administrator know, quoting your guild number if possible on all correspondence. Details can then be circulated on a personal basis as soon as they are finalised.

RESIDENTIAL COURSES
DESIGN APPRECIATION AND FINE CRAFTSMANSHIP

To: Administrator
Guild of Woodworkers
PO Box 35, Bridge Street
Hemel Hempstead HP1 1EE

Please reserve a place for me on the course to be held at Rycotewood College, Thame, OX9 2AF

on 6–7 April 1982 ☐ .... £40.00 ☐

on 14–16 April 1982 ☐ ....(Tick which course you wish to attend) .... £69.00 ☐

on Aug/Sept 1982 – date to be advised ☐ .... £115.00 ☐

I enclose cheque/postal order for   £40.00 ☐   inc VAT in payment of course fee, meals,

(Tick whichever applies)   £69.00 ☐   morning coffee and

     £115.00 ☐   accommodation

Name   .... BLOCK CAPITALS

Address in full   ....

....

....

Telephone number   ....

Signed ....

A cancellation charge of half the fee will be made unless the cancellation is received in writing 14 days prior to the date of the course.

Membership number ....

These hard to find tools are readily available at Sarjents

A few basic tools are fairly widely available; the more specialised items however are not so easy to find – up till now. We present here a few items from our enormous stocks, readily available through the post. Remember **all** our tools are fully guaranteed, and the price mentioned is the price you pay – there is no extra for carriage or VAT.

110–108 Lion Mitre Trimmer.

The world famous Lion trimmer has long been renowned for fast and accurate mitring capabilities. The side fences have pre-set (but adjustable) stops for 45° and 90°, and can quickly be set at any other angle. Fitted with high grade tool steel blades, the Lion mitre trimmer will finish joints with a high degree of accuracy.
£143.75 (inc. VAT and carriage).

121–115 Book: Routing Techniques by Jim Phillips.

This comprehensive guide to working with the versatile portable router includes many hints and tips and illustrations of bits, jigs and fixtures to aid novices and craftsmen alike. **£4.50**

123–104 Stanley 265 1¼″ HP Router.

This super heavy duty router is slashed in price! Over 56% off list price (no it's not a mistake!). All ball bearing construction micro-depth adjustment, shaft lock, 27,000 r.p.m. with ¼″ and ⅜″ collets, will take a huge range of cutters. Remember our special price includes postage and packing. Usual catalogue price: £132.25, now down to **£57.85**.

109–146 Picture Frame Cramp.

This simple set consists of a cramping tool, 3 corner angles (with removable base-plates), and a 6ft length of bonding cable. As the tension is set on the cramped object, perfect 90° angles are formed.
£3.95.

SARJENTS TOOLS

Personal shoppers welcome at our branches:

62–64 Fleet Street, Swindon. (0793) 31361

150 Cowley Road, Oxford. (0865) 45118

106–130 Veneer Saw.

Our veneer saw has 2″-3″ curved cutting edges and a polished beech handle. One edge has tapered teeth and one straight-edge teeth.
£1.95.

All these and nearly 2,000 other quality, hard-to-find tools are listed in the Sarjents Tools Woodworking Catalogue. For your copy send £1.00 to include p. & p., or ask for your **free** catalogue when ordering any of the tools above.

Send today to:-
Sarjents Tools,
Dept. PW382,
Oxford Road,
Reading.
(0734) 586522

All prices include post, packing and VAT. No extra to pay.

To pay by Access or Barclaycard, simply write or phone with your number.

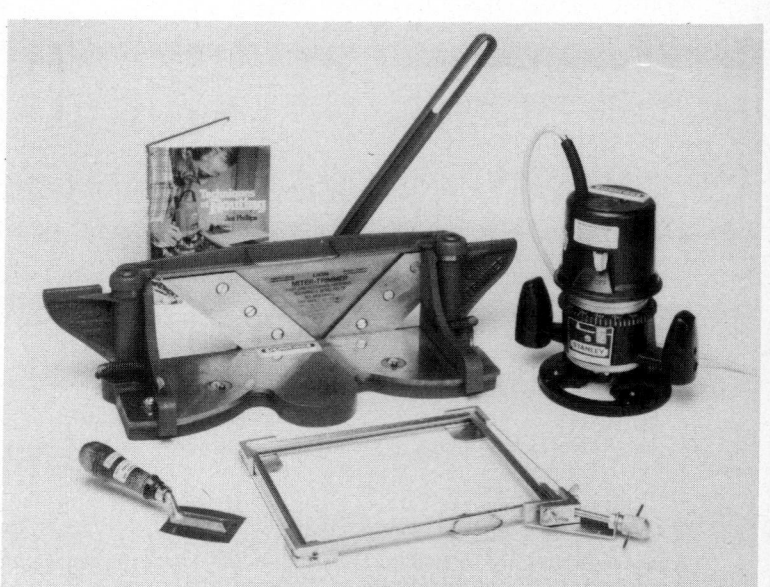

Prices quoted are those prevailing at press date and are subject to alteration due to economic conditions.

DAVID MAKES A POLE LATHE

R. W. Grant tells how David Thrower, a 16-year-old student at an Oxford school made a one-third model pole lathe as one of his projects in last year's O-level GCE examination in design. This type of lathe – and its manually-operated rotative offspring – could enjoy a revival in these energy-conscious days.

The pole lathe is a treadle-operated machine in which the workpiece is alternately rotated towards and away from the operator while the pole (originally a sapling) stores the energy for the return stroke. Its appearance in medieval times heralded a new element in machine construction and such devices continued to be used well into the present century on a commercial basis by the chair-bodgers of the High Wycombe (Bucks) area. These craftsmen in the sylvan setting of the Chilterns turned out innumerable chair legs which were used in the construction of the renowned Windsor chair.

In these energy-conscious days the pole lathe might enjoy a revival of interest, not only because of its cheapness of construction and operating cost but because of its portability. The old chair-bodgers could make the shavings fly at a rate that some of us with electrically-powered lathes would find hard to equal.

The pole lathe shown here is a one-third scale working model taken originally from instructions and sizes given in Aubrey Burstall's book *Simple Working Models of Historic Machines* published by Arnold at around £1.10. It was produced by David Thrower a 16-year-old student at Cowley St John Church of England upper comprehensive school, Oxford, as one of his projects entered for the Associated Examining Board's O-level GCE examination in design.

The book, by the way, is a treasury of ideas for the handy person who likes to make things that work. Although I am not an aficionado of this type of modelling, I certainly had fun making the blacksmith's 'Oliver' (a foot-operated tilt hammer) also shown in the book.

David's model incorporated many refinements over the basic type given in Burstall's book, such as using beech for the construction; steel mandrels; adjustable and locking tailstock; laminated ash pole; and even a supplementary 'dolly' to wind the cord around when turning narrow stock.

Right: Model pole lathe in beech, part of 'O' level design course work by David Thrower. (Photo. John Peacock)

SIMPLICITY OF LINE

Back from America H. C. King tells of his visit to designer and craftsman Sam Maloof who works in California. Pictures by Jonathan Pollack

Sam Maloof and his wife Freda live in a lovely part of California, about 50 miles east of Los Angeles. Sam built their beautiful timber house on a seven-acre site which used to be a lemon grove. In addition to the house, he provided himself with three workshops, a design studio and office, timber stores and a guest house for visitors.

This achievement would have been sufficient for most men, but Sam did not stop there. Without formal training in woodwork, he left a safe job as a graphic designer and set up in business as a designer and cabinetmaker. And he has made a great success of it.

I knew of him and his work so when in California I got in touch with him. There was an immediate invitation from Sam and Freda for my wife and I to go to lunch with them and to see his designs, his methods and to be shown their home. What an experience it was! The house is a masterpiece of design and has grown over the years to the extent that Sam had to count up to admit to 14 rooms. His art training is evident in the interior too. In all the rooms there is something beautiful to see.

Straight from school he worked as a graphic artist until he was 32 with a gap of four years' military service. He made furniture for the home and for his parents, being lucky to have evening-class workshop facilities. By this time he and Freda were married and had a baby. Then came his first commission to furnish a dining room with table, chairs and a buffet, the latter with 16 drawers.

The order came from an interior decorator for one of his clients. The timber was to be birch and the decorator insisted on it being stained to what Sam thought was a horrible colour. The client liked everything except the colour so he had to strip it and finish it natural. Sam has two dislikes: stain and interior decorators, neither of which he uses any more.

Above
Sam in his workshop

On the strength of this job, he forsook graphic art and said that he was going to earn a living by designing and making furniture. His employers told him he was mad, that he had no training and he would never do it. But he had already bought his lemon grove site on which there was a shack and a large chickenhouse. Sam and Freda lived in the former and made do with the latter as a temporary workshop. Then he set about building enough of the house to ensure some comfort and added a timber-frame workshop. He is still working on the house, adding extra accommodation, his design studio doubling as an architect's office.

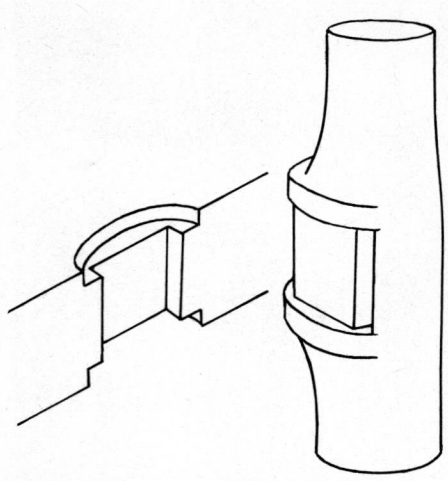

Above: Sam's unusual joint between chair leg and seat. The leg is faired off to seat level after assembly. See photo of finished joint right. *(Sketch by H.C. King.)*

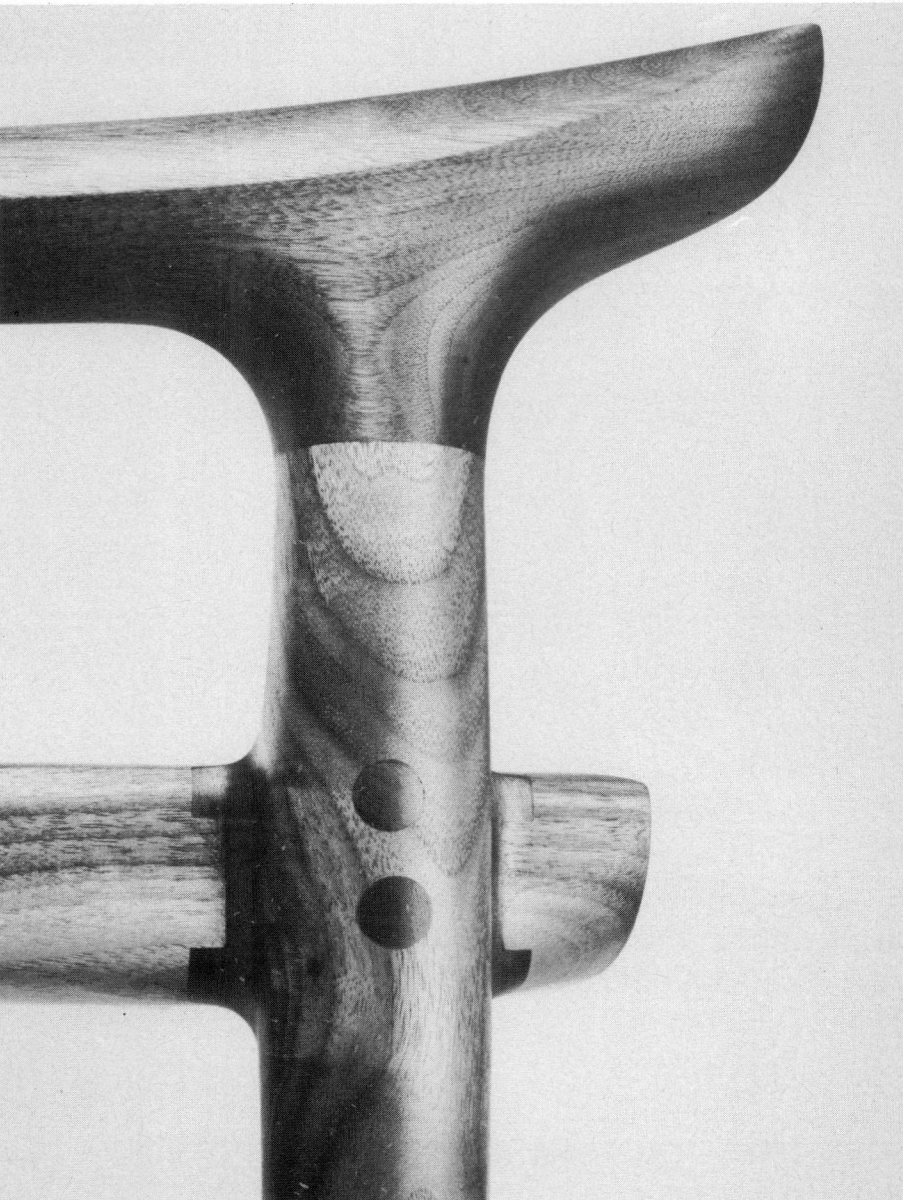

Sam is not quite sure why he specialises in tables and chairs, though is not averse to making whatever the customer wants so long as Sam likes the idea. By far the greater output is in American walnut finished to a lovely lustre by his own process. Incidentally, he leaves any lighter parts of the wood as they are rather than disguising them with stain. All his work is to his own designs. As the photographs show the results involve flowing curves enhanced by impeccable workmanship.

When he first started in business he vowed that nothing would leave his workshops which he was not proud to have designed and made. He aims to make furniture that people will be comfortable to live with. 'I rely on simplicity of line that follows the structure of the piece with an eye to the nature of the wood.' And 'Why make a beautiful joint and then hide it?' These are two of his axioms.

In following the latter he exposes his structural details. He feels that mortise and tenon joints remove too much wood and weaken the piece. He has now changed from dowels on chairs to the use of screws, counter-bored with the plugs making a design feature. These remove even less wood and are stronger. To fix legs to the centre columns of pedestal tables he uses ¾in. dowels and locks them with ¼in. pins.

As Sam Maloof has years of work on order, he can afford to choose to make only the items he enjoys himself. To certify his work, everything goes out signed and dated which I am sure, will result in his products being very much sought-after in the years ahead.

He has the distinction of being the first woodworker to be elected a fellow of the American Craft Council. His work has been shown at the Vatican museum, the Smithsonian, the Renwick gallery in Washington DC and the American Crafts museum in New York. Twelve of his chairs are in the permanent collection of the Museum of Fine Arts in Boston.

Sam never sells at craft fairs or exhibitions except one-man shows, at one of which he sold out on the opening evening. He usually works five or six days a week and is always willing to give lectures and practical workshop sessions. He usually has one student working with him. Freda is busy too, doing the clerical work, entertaining visitors, growing lemons and taking a good many of the photographs.

We had a delightful few hours with them. We had a splendid lunch, too, and sat on Maloof dining chairs at a circular dining table of his make.

TIMBER MARKET

Timber market consultant Arthur Jones says 'Wood is better than money in the bank.'

Timber importers and stockists make their best profits when world prices are rising and demand is high. Every week that passes then sees the value of their stocks increasing without any effort on their part; wood is better than money in the bank.

Recession brings about the reverse process. They have been through a traumatic experience of losing money on stocks for the past year or so; and this at a time of high interest rates and depressed sales. They meet these conditions by reducing stocks and thereby their indebtedness to the banks; and by buying only as the need arises to meet vital gaps in stocks to satisfy customer requirements. No money is spent on wood which cannot be moved fairly quickly into consumption.

The time must surely be coming when we shall see an upturn in the economy worldwide. Then prices will rise and the opportunities for profits return. Few importers will be tempted to speculate upon the timing of this upturn, though the general impression is that it will begin during the second half of the year.

But without this prior heavy investment in new stocks there must inevitably be a period when supplies in this country could be short and prices rise sharply. In the hardwood trade this period could be lengthy due to the long time-lag between placing orders with producers in the far corners of the globe and arrival of the wood in UK yards.

This poses a problem for the woodworker in business. He is heavily dependent upon steady supplies of hardwood – and sometimes softwood and sheet materials – to maintain steady output. At the very least he wants to be assured that the timber will be available when he calls on his merchant.

From what has already been written it will be evident that there is coming a time when he could encounter great problems of supply and will have to pay much higher prices.

Whether this occurs in the second half of 1982 or later is purely a matter of timing. But there are many who believe that it cannot be delayed much into 1983 without irreparable harm being done to the economic structure and industry of Britain.

At the moment most hardwood stockists have run down their holdings to a level which they consider commensurate with sales, though there are still some with too much money tied up in stocks. For all of them there is keen competition for business, resulting in cut prices in many areas.

Woodworkers should seriously consider buying for stock themselves. Such an investment could have at least two major benefits. First, and most important, it could mean stocks in hand to keep them going through any lean stock period. And this period could easily last for six months or even longer by virtue of the nature of imported hardwood trading. Woodworkers could even be forced into using woods they would not normally consider.

Second is a saving on the price of fresh stocks. Assuredly the prices of tropical hardwood will rise once demand increases. The cost of holding a small hardwood stock at today's prices could prove a worthwhile investment in under a year.

We have seen imports of hardwood falling by some 20% and the stockist selling at below replacement cost because of the need to cut down interest charges at a time of inflated overhead costs over which he has no control.

A major ingredient in the final cost of tropical hardwood is freight. Such long

journeys are involved to get most of the hardwood to our yards. Once the world economy improves there will be a heavier demand for shipping space, with higher freight charges and possibly transport delays.

Once the upturn begins we might see a renewed interest in some of the lesser-known hardwood which has disappeared from the scene in recent years while there has been a plentiful supply of the favoured species such as mahogany, lauan, meranti, ramin, afrormosia, keruing, utile and so on.

We have recently seen a ban on the exports of iroko in log form from the Ivory Coast. This follows the trend among many producers of tropical hardwood to ban log shipments and encourage local processing of wood. While this iroko log ban has not damaged the supply of sawn iroko, it has certainly helped to strengthen the price. Some have looked at merbau from Malaysia as an alternative.

Several hardwood species are cheaper today than they were six months ago. How long this will remain true is open to question. Brazilian mahogany and oak are two favourites which have fallen below their 1981 peaks.

What has been suggested on possible stocking by buying hardwood now does not apply to softwood. Here also imports and stocks have been slashed and prices are as low as they have been at any time during the past 12 months. But here there is no danger of any lengthy period of shortage. Indeed, it is doubtful whether any shortages of note will arise because it is possible to get fresh stocks into this country from Europe in a matter of days through the roll-on roll-off ferry services.

Softwood prices are likely to show only small changes in the first half of 1982. Most producers will be content if they can hold their present levels, though they will naturally try their best to push up rates a little.

Certainly there will be sharp price increases when demand for wood eventually rises again, but there should not be any of the supply dangers which are possible in hardwood. For woodworkers this is a sector of the market which they can leave to the timber trade with some assurance that they will get the service they require.

There are some woodworkers who are dependent upon top-quality joinery softwood, and here there could be stock problems. Devaluation of the Swedish krona has helped in both the supply and price of softwood from that country, and Finnish and Canadian woods have had to move a little to stay competitive.

The plywood market has been something of a disaster in 1981, with weak demand and weaker prices. Even the attempts of the Far Eastern producers to impose their minimum selling prices – themselves pitched low – have been a failure.

The Komasi price list of the Far Eastern plywood shippers could not be held last autumn and sales continued at 5% less than the list price. Another attempt is being made this year to put that extra 5% on the selling prices.

Plywood price increases over the past 12 months have been marginal, well below the rate of inflation.

Coniferous plywood supplies have been plentiful from the US and Canada, with the American mills often under-cutting the larger Canadian producers.

Generally, woodworkers are still enjoying the fruits of stiff competition among their wood suppliers to get the grades and species they want at attractive rates. The coming months could see rather more specification problems as stocks continue to fall. But prices should show little variation.

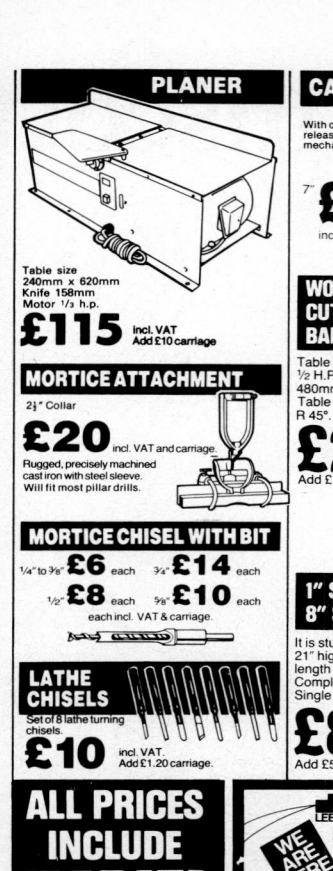

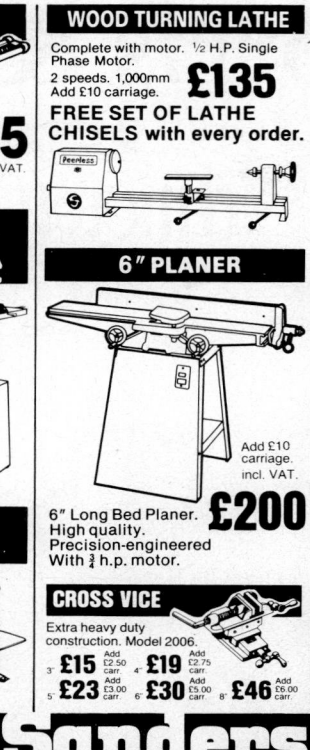

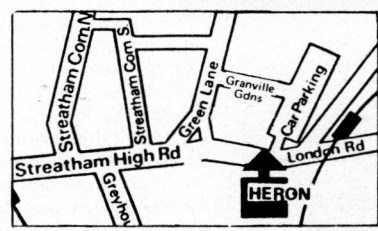

William Morris & Kelmscott

'A full sympathy between the works of man and the land they were made for'.

At the end of 1981 West Surrey College of Art and Design, Farnham, Surrey, held a major exhibition entitled William Morris and Kelmscott, to show for the first time the Society of Antiquaries collection of paintings, prints, textiles, ceramics, fine books, furniture and personal belongings of William Morris, Dante Gabriel Rossetti, Edward Burne-Jones, Philip Webb and William de Morgan from Kelmscott Manor.

The exhibition included much supplementary material from the major national collections and spanned the whole of Morris's life and achievements. Sponsors of the exhibition included Johnson Wax, Sotheby's Crafts Council, South East Arts Association, Marc Fitch Fund and Pasold Fund.

William Morris and Kelmscott is an im-

portant new book from the Design Council in association with West Surrey College of Art and Design, which was published to coincide with the exhibition. (Available from the Design Centre bookshop, Haymarket, London SW1Y 4SU at £7.00 plus p/p. ISBN 0850721210.) The central theme of the book is the 17th century farmhouse which Morris and Dante Gabriel Rossetti held on a joint tenancy in 1871. In 1874 Rossetti left and Morris continued as sole tenant until his death in 1896. During the 25 years Morris was at Kelmscott the house provided a focus for much of his work and that of his friends. It remained a symbol in the moral, social and political thinking of this remarkable man.

Morris loved Kelmscott Manor and it was the 'old house by the Thames' which he depicted so well in his book *News from Nowhere*. After Morris's death, his widow Janey sold their London house, also called Kelmscott House, in Hammersmith and went to live in the Manor House. It was May Morris their daughter who bequeathed the manor and its contents to Oxford University on her death in 1938. Today it is in the care of the Society of Antiquaries who have done much to improve the building and had many of the contents cleaned, repaired and returned to the manor in 1966.

In addition they have greatly added to the collection of books, fine art, furniture and furnishings associated with Morris.

The vargueno in rosewood with ivory, ebony and tortoiseshell inlays — a Spanish type drop-front desk — resting in this instance on a matching cupboard of late 16th century or early 17th century date.

Rectangular rush seat, back rails connected by turned spindle.

on the Arts and Crafts movement of which Morris was a leading figure; John Brandon-Jones, the architect, is also an authority on the Arts and Crafts movement and has written on Philip Webb, a lifelong friend of Morris, who had a great influence on him (see WOODWORKER April 1981 p224) and Ray Watkinson who has written widely on Morris as a designer.

All 14 essays deal with different aspects of Morris's work and they provide a useful and scholarly introduction to the many activities of Morris in his successful revival of the arts and crafts which were in danger of being lost forever and his brave but not

Rossetti armchair, rounded rush seat, more elaborate than rest of the range, with its scroll over-arms and wheatsheaf back of nine sticks slotted through a wooden 'tie', similar to the comb piece of a Windsor chair. Unlike the rest of the range this chair exhibits a curved back rail.

The book includes a comprehensive catalogue to the books, furnishings, ceramics, textiles, prints and drawings of the exhibition and in addition 14 authoritative contributions by eminent writers and artists covering many aspects of Morris's life and achievements. Many of these contributors have already written extensively about Morris and his work. Notable among them is Asa Briggs, Provost of Worcester College, Oxford, whose book *Selected works of William Morris* was universally acclaimed; Gillian Naylor has written a standard work

Armchair, curved and shaped arm terminates in a shaped finial, arm support is inserted into the seat from a special stretcher under the seat to avoid a weak joint if insertion occurred directly over the front leg.

Cruciform back and oval rush seat, design attributed to Ford Madox Brown.

so successful attempt to reform society through socialism.

Anyone not already acquainted with the life and work of Morris and whose appetite was whetted by the exhibition or is whetted by reading the book is guided towards further research and detailed study of the achievements of this extraordinary man by referring to the excellent references at the end of each essay.

The book is in soft covers, beautifully produced and illustrated, and is excellent value.   I. G. C.

This cassone (Italian marriage chest) is in Italian cypress wood with a poker work decoration and was originally placed in the drawing room of Kelmscott House. It was transferred to Kelmscott Manor after Morris's death.

'If a chap can't compose an epic poem while he's weaving tapestry he had better shut up'

The massive centre piece of the exhibition was the beautiful 'Bullerswood' type carpet, almost 25ft long and 13ft wide. The design of the carpet which features birds among intertwined stems and foliage owes much to Morris's study of Persian rugs and is similar to the 'Bullerswood' Morris carpet in the Victoria and Albert museum.

One of the most impressive books in the exhibition was the Kelmscott edition of the works of Geoffrey Chaucer, which represents the height of Morris's achievement as printer, typographer and book designer. It took him nearly 4 years to produce and was completed only 3 months before his death in October 1896.

The smallest item on show was a pen and ink drawing by Rossetti of Janey Morris with whom he was in love. It measures only 2½in. square and was drawn on the flyleaf of Burton's *Anatomy of melancholy*. The relationship between Rossetti and Janey — both artistic and emotional is explored in the Design Council book. She was a favourite model and many of his portraits of her were shown in the exhibition, including *Blue silk dress* painted when she was 26 years old.

The exhibition divided naturally by both time scale and subject. *Early years* covered 1834-53; *young manhood* 1853-59; *Red House and the firm* 1859-71; (see also WOODWORKER April 1981 p224); *Kelmscott Manor* 1871-75; *textiles* 1859-1940; *poet and publisher* 1856-73; *social commitment* 1875-90; *Kelmscott press* 1890-98 and *coda* 1896-.

Among the pictures illustrating this article we have included some of the furniture made by the 'Firm' and also personal items brought to Kelmscott Manor by Morris.

The chairs from the Sussex range were probably the most commercially successful product of the 'Firm'. The different designs were developed and refined by Ford Madox Brown and Dante Gabriel Rossetti from a prototype found by Warrington Taylor (their young business manager) while he was with a carpenter in Sussex. This prototype may well have been a 'Sheraton fancy chair' a country version of a sophisticated Regency design. The exhibition showed 4 distinct designs of 'Sussex' chair — all showing the common characteristics of ebonised wood structure with rush seats; all made from a combination of simple turned parts (front legs, rails, spindles and stretchers) with more complicated carved and shaped pieces (arms and back uprights). Their lightness and delicacy of construction owe a great deal to the knowledge and skill of the 18th century cabinetmakers. This can be seen in the shaping of the back uprights that curve at the 'waist' and alter in section from rounded back to tapering rectangular leg. The use of a mortise and tenon joint at the back to seat frame union gives strength and allows tapering away of superfluous wood to further lighten the chair.   P. CURDS

Top: The main staircase at Kelmscott Among the personal items are Morris's oak 4-poster bed with turned balusters. Clive Wainwright of the department of Furniture and Woodwork, Victoria and Albert museum, has suggested that the bed may be a later remake from earlier pieces. The base shows evidence of restoration between 1964 and 1967 by Archer Cowley & Co Ltd of Oxford.

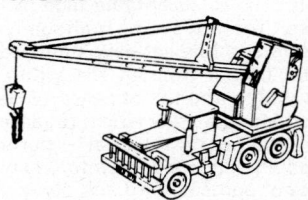
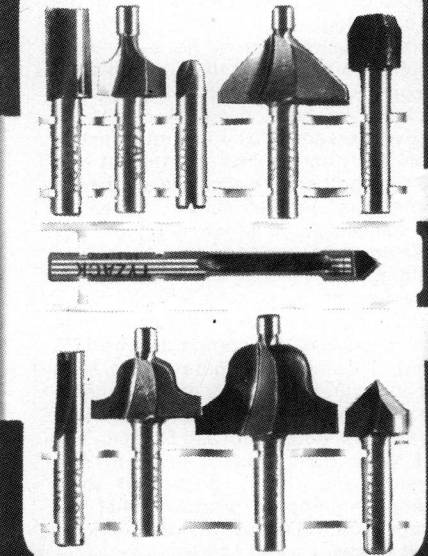

THE TIMBER MERCHANT AND THE CRAFTSMAN

Tony Reardon, editor of *Forestry & British Timber,* advises that craftsmen and merchants should 'forge and maintain close links'

The craftsman woodworker should forge and maintain close links with his timber suppliers. This was the message of the 1981 foresters and craftsmen seminar at Parnham house, Beaminster, Dorset.

Bill Garvey, a furniture maker and timber merchant from Honiton, Devon, called his talk 'The unacceptable face of British timber.' The advent of mahogany some 300 years ago had set new standards for furniture timber in both the width of boards available and the absence of defects. This had led to a view which regarded wood as an engineer's material – perfectly stable and unblemished – reinforced by the wider use of particleboard and plywood.

It had resulted in foresters' and the trade's acceptance of large, long-boled straight oak as the standard of excellence. Mr Garvey made a good case for a return to older standards in which the variation in colour, knots, burrs and shakes in oak timber could all be made into virtues; and blemishes (far from detracting from the quality of the finished item) adding charm and character.

Provocatively, Roger Venables, the Stafford specialist in fine British hardwood, said that to the timber merchant the craftsman was an economic disaster! 'He has exacting requirements with, all too often, not enough money to pay for the quality he demands and the service he receives. His delivery address is some old stable in a remote village which is inaccessible to an articulated lorry. He takes the maximum credit and expects the merchant to interpret his artistic vision through a few words scribbled on a piece of paper or a lengthy, verbal description on the telephone'.

However, Mr Venables emphasised that the craftsman as represented by the Parnham trust had an essential part to play in the overall marketing of British timber. 'It is not the small amount you actually sell that matters but the number of people who see the sheer magnificence of your art and craftsmanship.

'The publicity you get is essential to the promotion of solid hardwood and, although not many people will actually be able to purchase one of your individual pieces of furniture, it will encourage them to look for solid timber in their furniture and joinery. This sort of promotion has a knock-on effect which is to the advantage of the joinery and furniture factory, the timber merchant, forester and woodland owner.'

During the last 20 years, he continued, there had been a tremendous rationalisation and specialisation programme in the British timber industry. The emergence of key round timber merchants – of which his company was one – handling over 1 million cu ft of round hardwood a year had played a large part in that development.

'An essential part of obtaining the best prices for our round timber must be the handling of volume in order to obtain the continuity of supply to the specialist sawmill. That is why the round timber merchant will never disappear and why the forester who tries to grade and market his own round timber will never get as much money as the round timber merchant.

'So, then, the first essential part of any timber merchant's operation is the correct selection and grading of logs in sufficient quantities in order to get efficient sawmill production', Mr Venables continued.

Having obtained a batch of a particular grade and specification, logs were presented to the sawmill for cutting as quickly and accurately as possible, making sure that the heart of the log was lined up with the saw. The log was turned before cutting in order to get the maximum yield from the shape of the log.

The top-quality boards, he said, were then built into kiln sets – that is, well-piled loads some 8 × 8 × 25ft with ½in. strips 9in. apart between each layer. Accuracy of loading was essential to avoid undue distortion of the boards. The control of the humidity, together with accurate air speeds from the fans, enabled careful controlled drying to take place which, Mr Venables maintained, was superior to natural air-seasoning.

The length of drying was reduced some 50 times compared with air-drying and the final moisture was 10% compared with 17% air-dried. The length of time in the kilns varied according to species and thickness: 26mm oak took 23 days; 26mm ash and beech 10 days; and 75mm ash 52 days. The boards were then graded, sawn to size dimension and finally presented to a moulding machine to produce what the customer required in the way of planing or finished shape.

Although, Mr Venables concluded, there were big advantages in the craftsman going direct to the forester for unusual and difficult requirements, he must bear in mind the cost of time in selecting the log, seeing to its transport and supervising the cutting at a local sawmill. But there was no way in which he could escape the interest charge in having a log air-seasoning for two years.

Forestry Commission director of research and amateur furniture maker and author David Johnstone said that as well as the obvious choice of species and provenance, silvicultural practices could influence such factors as ring width, knottiness and the presence of reaction wood.

The effects of misuse, fungal attack, burns, lightning strikes, wire, stones and even shrapnel were vividly displayed as an awful warning to the timber user to choose the right tree.

Peter Marlow, a director of Forestry Investment Management Ltd, explained the mechanics of private investment in woodlands and suggested that the small craftsman-user would probably find a highly sympathetic ear in the private woodland owner and his forester, many of whom would take a good deal of interest in the supply of small quantities of timber – usual or unusual.

Just such a man was John McHardy, head forester to the Marquis of Bath at Longleat. In a lively and amusing talk, he demonstrated the difference between theory and practice and showed how an active and progressive forestry enterprise was run, with emphasis on the silviculture of natural regeneration in his commercial softwood operations but not forgetting the more unusual species for which room was easily found.

David Taylor, a partner in a forestry consultancy (John Clegg & Co) said that the link between grower and user had traditionally been provided by the timber merchant but all too often the small local sawmiller had gone out of business. Because of the cost of holding hardwood stocks, emphasis had changed to softwood.

More direct contact between forester and craftsman would be necessary, Mr Taylor said.

Chairman at the seminar was Donn Small (Forestry Commission deputy surveyor, New Forest) who is a keen woodturner.

Guild of Woodworkers is actively promoting the forging of closer links between craftsman and timber merchant. One-day visits have been arranged with specialist timber merchants in several areas. For details see guild study programme in WOODWORKER.

What Machine?

If you are considering equipment for your workshop, you will probably be looking at a combination machine offering the basic features of SAWBENCH — PLANER/THICKNESSER — SPINDLE MOULDER and MORTISER as the essential requirements with the possibility of adding other items such as BANDSAW — LATHE — SANDER and SHARPENING EQUIPMENT as required.

When choosing a machine it is important to bear in mind that, as you become more ambitious in your projects, your machine must have adequate capacities and the capability of developing with you.

This "What Machine?" report has been prepared by Scheppach Maschinenfabrik in the interests of woodworkers in the United Kingdom.

For further information please contact our sole concessionaire:

Sumaco Machinery & Tools Ltd., Suma House, Huddersfield Road, Elland, West Yorkshire HX5 9AA. Telephone (0422) 75491.

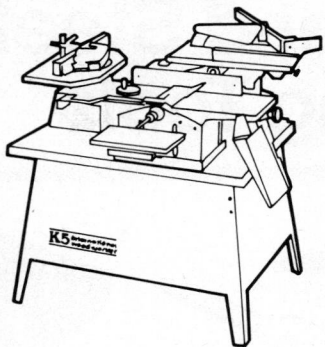

K5 International Woodworker
From Kity UK
Rec. Price £642.85

Mia 6
From Woodmen
Rec. Price £580

Scheppach HM2 KOMBI
From Sumaco
Rec. Price From £627.90

HIGHLY RECOMMENDED

	K5 International Woodworker	Mia 6	Scheppach HM2 KOMBI
Verdict:	Could be attractive to the novice but rather limited. No capability of adding attachments. Offered as a single unit.	Compact machine but again, specification far too limited for anyone with ambition. Purchased only as a single unit.	The exceptional specification should meet requirements of the most demanding woodworkers and more than compensates for any additional initial expense. Attachments can be purchased as required.
HP of motor	1hp	1hp	2hp
Circular Saw:			
Blade diameter	180mm	160mm	300mm
Depth of cut	47mm *	55mm	87mm
Surface Planer:			
Maximum planing width	150mm	155mm	260mm
Maximum stock removal	0-3mm	0-2.5mm	0-3mm
Thicknesser:			
Maximum thicknessing capacity	150 × 100mm	153 × 73mm	250 × 140mm
Automatic feed rate	7.5m/min	7m/min	6m/min
Maximum stock removal	0-3mm	0-2mm	0-5mm
Spindle Moulder:			
Spindle diameter	15mm	25mm	30mm
Rise and fall adjustment	45mm	63mm	55mm
Maximum tooling diameter	100mm	55mm	200mm
Number of spindle speeds	1	1	2
Slot Mortiser:			
Maximum bit diameter	12mm	12mm	16mm
Will Accept:			
Bandsaw	No	No	Yes
Lathe	No	No	Yes
300mm Disc Sander	No	No	Yes

*Will accept 200mm diameter blade.

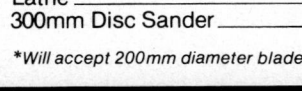
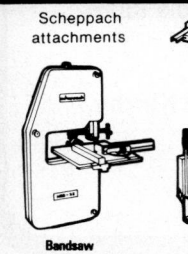
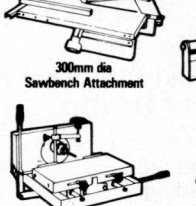

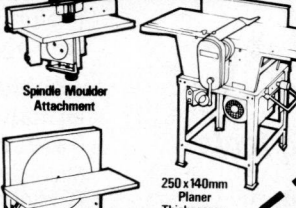
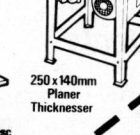

Prices quoted are those prevailing at press date and are subject to alteration due to economic conditions.

workpieces

Tale of a table

During World War II, C. McLaren Reid was adjutant and interpreter at a Royal Air Force PoW camp in Batavia. To while away the time in captivity he carved the 34 × 20in. teak top of the orderly room table with the names of officers and warrant officers in the camp. His tools were a blunt and jagged-edged gouge, pen knife, a nailfile and some sharpened nails. The work took nearly four months. This was in 1942.

The table vanished but four years afterwards Mr McLaren Reid found the top in Malaya and finished off the carving. He also had a silver plate made and autographed by the late Lord Mountbatten of Burma. This plate he set into the top.

Now 35 years later, reader R. M. H. Knotts of Oakham, Rutland, sends these details, adding that the top was at one time in the military museum of Edinburgh castle. 'I have tried to trace C. McLaren Reid without success', writes Mr Knotts. 'I contacted the museum authorities at Edinburgh only to be informed that while the table had been held there for some 10 years, it had been returned to the owner some time ago'.

Advice

Wilcot (Decorative Products) Ltd, Alexandra Park, Fishponds, Bristol BS16 2BQ (0272 543256), has started an advisory service. Mrs Shirley Ayres is available to answer written and telephone inquiries on the use of Nitromors brand paint removers as well as other products such as white spirit, putties and wood preservatives.

Taxation

In January 1981 the Council for Small Industries in Rural Areas (CoSIRA) issued a booklet titled *Taxation and the Smaller Business*. It was an immediate success and is now available as a second edition at £1. This has been prepared (as before) by Arthur Young McClelland Moores & Co, the chartered accountants. Copies can be had from CoSIRA at 141 Castle Street, Salisbury SP1 3TP.

The authors point out that the booklet is for guidance only.

Kity Distributors

Kity UK, Yeadon, Leeds, has appointed as distributors: W. T. Baker & Sons (Aberkenfig) Ltd, Central Buildings, Aberkenfig; J. Ardron & Son (Ironmongers) Ltd, Mowbray Drive, Blackpool; County Tools, 50 Gardner Street, Brighton; D. & S. Enterprises, Old House, Oates Street, Dewsbury; Pen Tools, 24 Edgar Street, Hereford; Hegner Universal Saws (UK) Ltd, 36 Great Eastern Road, Hockley; Williams Technical Services, 36 Station Road, North Harrow; G. W. Farmer, 28 Market Place, Stevenage, Herts; Stourport Timber Supplies, Sandy Lane, Stourport; Tool Centre, 30a Abbotsbury Road, Weymouth.

FLORIDA SYLVA

(Florida: population around 9 million; area 58 560 sq miles (land 54 136, water 4424; over 14 000 acres of environmentally endangered land; altitude 0-345ft; nickname sunshine state; state tree Sabal palm)

The phenomenal success that Florida has had for the past century in attracting visitors is basically rooted in the largess of nature in this subtropical corner of the US. The citrus crop is worth nearly half a billion dollars a year and forestry products 169 million. (1979 figures) Christopher Columbus was not far from Florida when he bumped into the island of Hispaniola (Haiti and Dominican republic) on his way to 'the Indies' in 1492, but credit for the discovery of Florida must go to Juan Ponce de Léon who sailed from Puerto Rico in 1513. He gave the long marshy land its name, inspired by the season Pascua Florida (the Easter feast of flowers) rather than its floral beauty.

The north and panhandle area of Florida is a harmony of moss-draped live oaks. Just west of Tallahassee are the Apalachicola National forests of 557 446 acres. Northern Florida is typified by the Suwannee River, central Florida is a vast citrus belt; south of this citrus area are the Big Cypress swamp and the Corkscrew swamp, but the unique treasure of Florida is the Everglades — a sawgrass prairie rooted in a giant river.

Many of the native trees within this area are found in no other part of the US. The region is sub-tropical, cold snaps accompanied by frosts occur each winter but the growing season is a full 12 months. Rainfall is scanty in autumn and winter, often heavy in spring and summer. Prevailing winds are from the east and south and tropical storms and hurricanes carve paths of destruction through the forests. The soils are mixtures in varying proportions of sand, mud, rock and decomposed vegetable matter. In the Everglades the mud is made up almost entirely of rotted sawgrass; in the redlands the scanty soil is humus from pine forests; the rich, heavy, black soil several feet deep in the hardwood forests is made up from leafmould and broken rock.

The species of trees that grow in any portion are determined by elevation, the amount of standing water, richness and depth of soil and salt content. An Anglicised Indian term, hammock, is in general use to identify a plot of hardwood trees growing at an elevation of a few inches or feet above the water.

All of the trees now native to Florida are thought to have entered the peninsula from other regions. The swampland trees have spread south from the coastal plains of the southern states, they are deciduous and also include a few woodland species. Most of the species of the shoreline and hammocks are of Caribbean Basin origin brought to the area as seeds on the tropical storms. The watery expanse of the Everglades (pa-hay-okee, river of grass to the Indian) acts as a barrier to the southern spread of many species common in the centre of Florida; the heavy mangrove screen has prevented spread from the direction of the bay.

Man's imprint on the flora has been considerable, the Indians burned the pines to prevent the hardwood supplanting the pines, so that they could ensure their crops of coontie (a cycad whose tubers were used for flour and arrowroot). The Spanish logged most of the giant mahogany (*Swietenia mahogani*) and prized the lignum vitae (*Guaiacum sanctum*) for medicines. The first settlers cut the black ironwood (*Krugiodendron ferreum*) for use as foundation posts, felled the pines and cypress for timber. Their primary source of charcoal was buttonwood (*Conocarpus erecta*). Introduced species include coconut palm (*Cocos nucifera*), tamarind (*Tamarindus indica*), Australian pine (*Casuarina glauca*), guava (*Psidium guajava*), seaside-mahoe (*Thespesia populnea*), and Brazilian pepper (*Schinus terebinthefolius*).

The hammocks of the Everglades are scattered islands of hardwood and dense undergrowth on elevated sections within the sawgrass. In size these range from tiny tree clumps to larger forests of Royal palm (*Roystonea elata*) and mahogany (*Swietenia mahogani*). Massive live oaks (*Quercus virginiana*) rise to great heights. Scattered tree islands (known as heads) dot the sawgrass and are named for their dominant species eg cypress dome, bayhead, or willow head. The cypress is a deciduous cone bearing tree which thrives in acid conditions. The dwarf cypress forests of the Everglades are the same species as the big cypress (*Taxodium distichum*) and many are over 100 years old though only a few feet in height. The largest mahogany tree on record in the US grows in mahogany hammock; its circumference is 10ft. 8in. at 4½ft. above ground level and it is thought to be over 100 years old. Mahoganies do not grow in pure stands but are scattered and their shallow root system makes them vulnerable to strong winds and in particular to hurricanes.

Stout trunks of the gumbo limbo (*Bursera simaruba*) may reach heights of 60ft. Their reddish brown bark that peels off in paper-like flakes gives the tree its nickname of tourist tree.

Live oaks are common and their rough barked branches provide a hold for orchids and bromeliads. Strangler figs (*Ficus aurea*) with their smooth grey bark and dark green leathery leaves are to be found standing on their own prop roots or slowly choking their many host trees.

In the US the Royal palm is only native to southern Florida where it may grow to over 100ft; also native in this area is the poisonwood (*Metopium toxiferum*) which belongs to the same family as poison ivy (Anacardiaceae) and whose sap alkaloids also cause severe skin irritation.

The Everglades are a river of grass with scattered hardwood in a delicate ecological balance. Here you sense life's great fragility and its immense determination to endure.

P. CURDS

SOLAR KILN RESEARCH

by R.W. Grant DLC FRSA MSIAD and Robert Wakefield
Photos John Peacock

R. W. Grant is head of the design faculty at one of Oxfordshire's comprehensive schools and Robert Wakefield was, until leaving last year, a VIth form student at the school. Under Mr Grant's aegis Robert sat and passed the Associated Examining Board's new advanced-level GCE in design.

Part of Robert Wakefield's course requirements were that he researched, designed and made three projects which would demonstrate his ability to manipulate design skills. One of his projects was to investigate the field of timber drying using low-energy methods. His conclusions may well appeal to the craftsman wishing to season his own material.

At the start of the project an evaluation was made of the known low-cost methods of drying timber including material or air seasoning, deliquescent salts, polyethylene glycol (PEG), disc and bag method (see WOODWORKER for June and July 1980 (Timber Topics series)) and solar-heating.

Comparisons of all these methods led Robert to conclude that some form of solar-heated kiln offered the most economical method of drying timber within a reasonable period. The photographs show a 1:10 scale model of a prototype kiln initially made to support the theory of solar-kilning.

Satisfactory results were obtained from this model although time prevented the construction of a full-size kiln. However, contact was made with the Oxford University department of forestry which has a battery of similar kilns successfully operating. Robert was able to talk to R. A. Plumptre of the department, Mr Plumptre has done much pioneering work in this field (here and in the tropics) producing kilns that are now operating on a commercial basis.

Main advantage of the solar-operated kiln over conventionally heated kilns is that it uses a free source of energy to provide the heating necessary to dry timber at a faster rate than is possible with natural seasoning. In the UK it is possible to dry timber down to 17-18% m.c. using the natural method, while with the solar kiln it is possible to get it down to 10-12% m.c. — which is ideal for most furniture and and interior work.

An added advantage of the solar kiln is that the timber is subjected to less drying stresses due to the diurnal temperature changes, and checking and end splits are less likely to occur.

Best drying time in UK is between the months of April to October and at other times the drying rate is slightly better than with air seasoning. The length of drying time depends, of course, on the initial m.c. of the timber and the prevailing weather conditions. You cannot expect much drying to take place on overcast and wet days but, even so, the timber remains adequately sheltered.

The performance of one of the Oxford University kilns is worth quoting: during a summer period 2in. thick oak dried from over 40% m.c. to 11% in four months. This should be compared with the normal drying period of six months by natural seasoning and one-and-a-half months conventional kiln-drying for the same section of material.

The accompanying 1:10 scale drawing shows the details of a home-built kiln about 18ft square. The kiln should be placed so that its 32° sloping collector panel is facing south (to maximise on the angle of the sun's rays and length of exposure). The panel itself can be made from corrugated-iron sheeting painted matt black to give a heat-absorbent surface. The false flat roof is made from the same material.

The rest of the structure could be made from reclaimed wood clad with hardboard and again painted matt black. Apart from the collector panel it is important to adequately insulate all interior surfaces including the floor, by using strawboard or similar material, to retain the collected heat. The whole roof should be covered with a clear polythene sheet (preferably ultra-violet inhibited grade) to keep off the rain; it also has a secondary purpose of intensifying the sun's rays.

Air flow in the kiln is indicated by the arrows on the drawing. This is assisted by a four-bladed fan driven by a fhp motor operated during daylight hours only. Fresh air is drawn in through the two flap ports low down on the sides of the kiln and exhausted through the flap vents in the rear and gable ends of the structure. Ports and vents should be opened in the morning and closed at night. Apart from this the kiln is self-operating. The timber to be dried should be stacked with the aid of softwood stickers to allow adequate air movement between the boards.

There would appear to be no restriction on the size of the kiln; the only design factor needing to be taken into account is that the volume of the proposed timber stack must equal the square of the area of the collector panel. Thus, to dry 10cu m of wood the collector panel surface area would need to be 100sq m; this could include the area of the flat false roof as it does serve as a secondary collector.

During his investigations Robert corresponded with the Timber Research & Development Association (TRADA), Hughenden Valley, High Wycombe, and with the National Centre for Alternative Technology in Wales. He would like to thank the officers of those organisations for their advice. Particular thanks are due to Mr Plumptre, (Oxford University forestry department) who kindly allowed Robert to draw freely on his own research material.

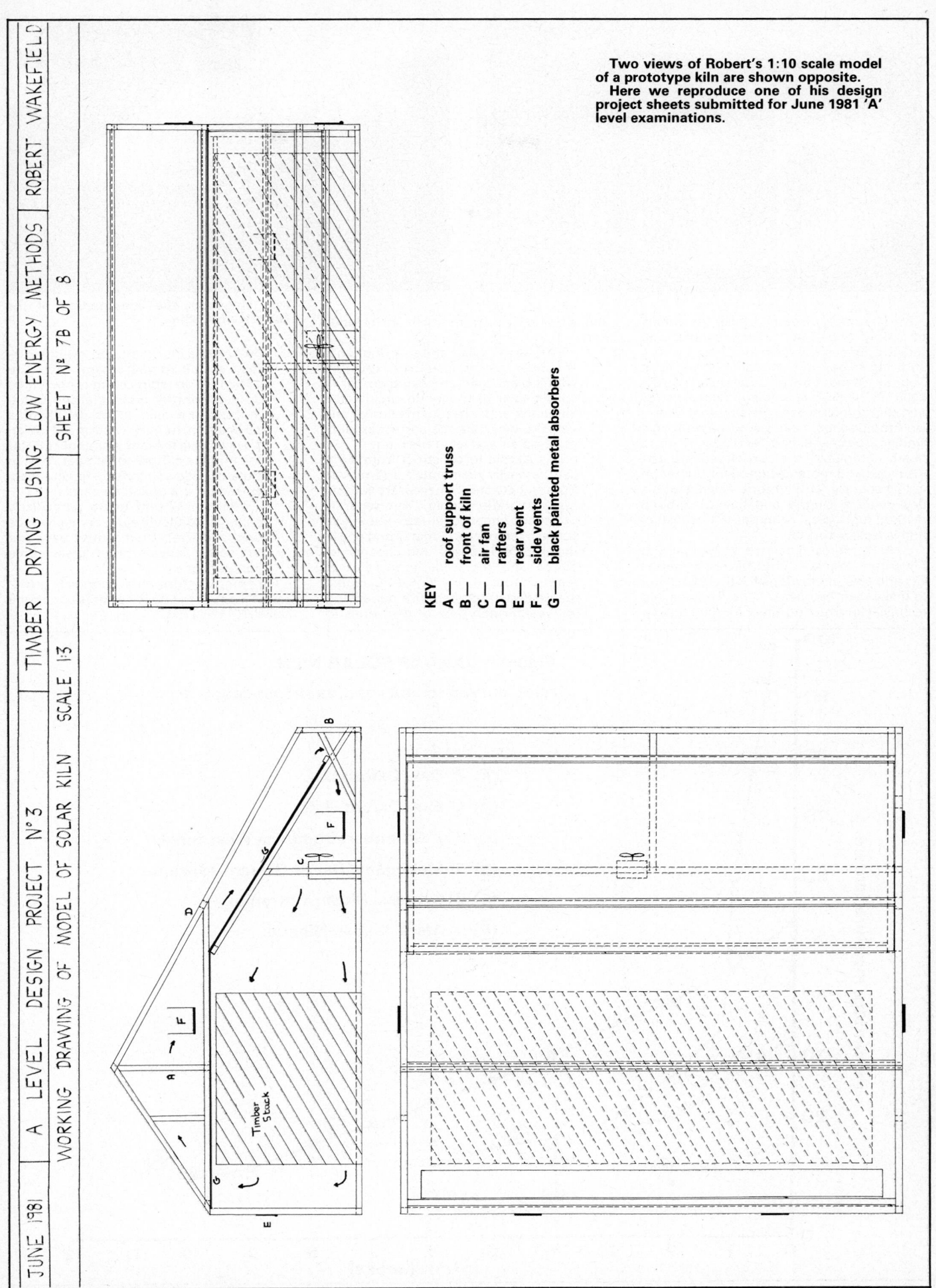

Two views of Robert's 1:10 scale model of a prototype kiln are shown opposite. Here we reproduce one of his design project sheets submitted for June 1981 'A' level examinations.

KEY
A — roof support truss
B — front of kiln
C — air fan
D — rafters
E — rear vent
F — side vents
G — black painted metal absorbers

JUNE 1981 | A LEVEL DESIGN PROJECT N°3 | TIMBER DRYING USING LOW ENERGY METHODS | ROBERT WAKEFIELD

WORKING DRAWING OF MODEL OF SOLAR KILN   SCALE 1:3   SHEET N° 7B OF 8

Timber Stack

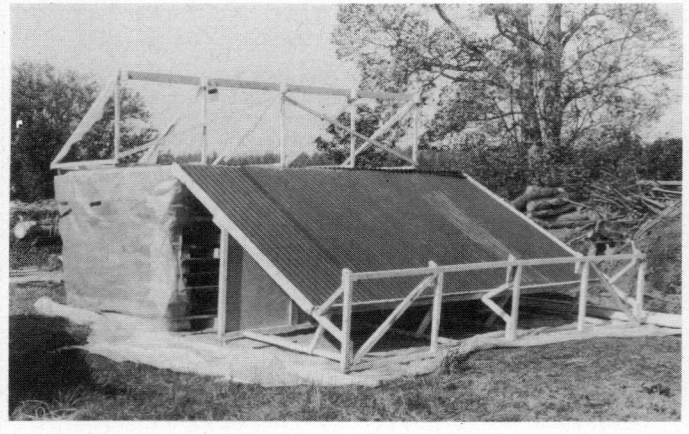

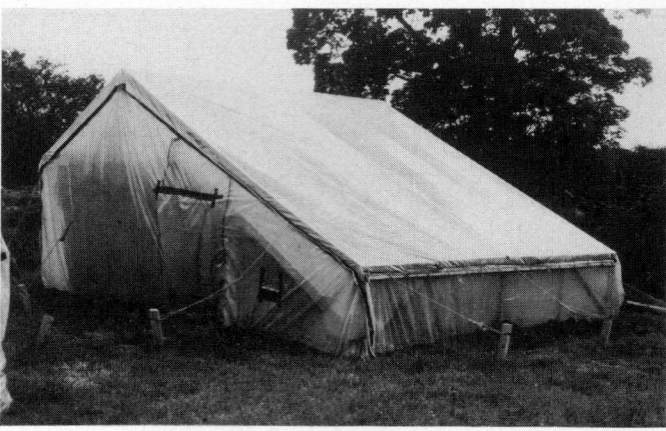

Two stages in the construction of the Tubney wood kiln.

Mr Plumptre, research officer, university of Oxford department of agricultural and forest sciences has sent pictures 3 and 4 showing stages in the building of the kiln at Tubney Wood Sawmill. Capacity is 200-300ft^3 (5.7-8.6m^3) according to timber sizes and sticker thicknesses. He says that Matthew Arnold school have also been running a similar project and their 1m^3 capacity kiln is nearly completed. It is part glazed and part insulated and more designed for operation in this country. Mr Plumptre developed his design as a simple and cheap to build method for tropical countries where insulation is less important.

J. A. K. Forest Fuels of 21 Biggar Rd, Silverburn, Penicuik, EH26 9LQ now market kits and sets of drawings for those wishing to make their own solar kilns. They have a technical information sheet for their Jakrap kiln: a few extracts from which are included here.

The Jakrap solar timber drying kiln is a simple greenhouse type structure with a black painted heat absorber to collect solar heat, fans to circulate air and transfer the heat to the timber and vents to evacuate the correct amount of damp air and let in fresh air.

It is simple to construct from a kit; can be easily dismantled and moved from stack to stack if necessary without restacking the timber. The separate polythene sheet cover lasts about two years in temperate climates and one in the tropics, is easily and cheaply repaired and replaced. It operates at temperatures of up to 0-20°C higher than external temperature depending on weather and time of day; dries to 10-12%m.c.; is said to be 2-3 times as fast as air drying from green to 18%m.c. Too rapid drying is prevented so less distortion is experienced. Capital costs are said to be 1/10th of a normal kiln, running costs much lower, power to run the fans was about £30 for the months of April to October, 1981 in Britain. Little supervision is necessary since fans are on a time clock.

The kiln is said to be particularly suited to difficult slow-drying woods (oak and elm). Drying rates vary and the accompanying graph gives some comparisons.

For more information contact J.A.K. Forest Fuels at the above address or phone (0968) 75112/77790.

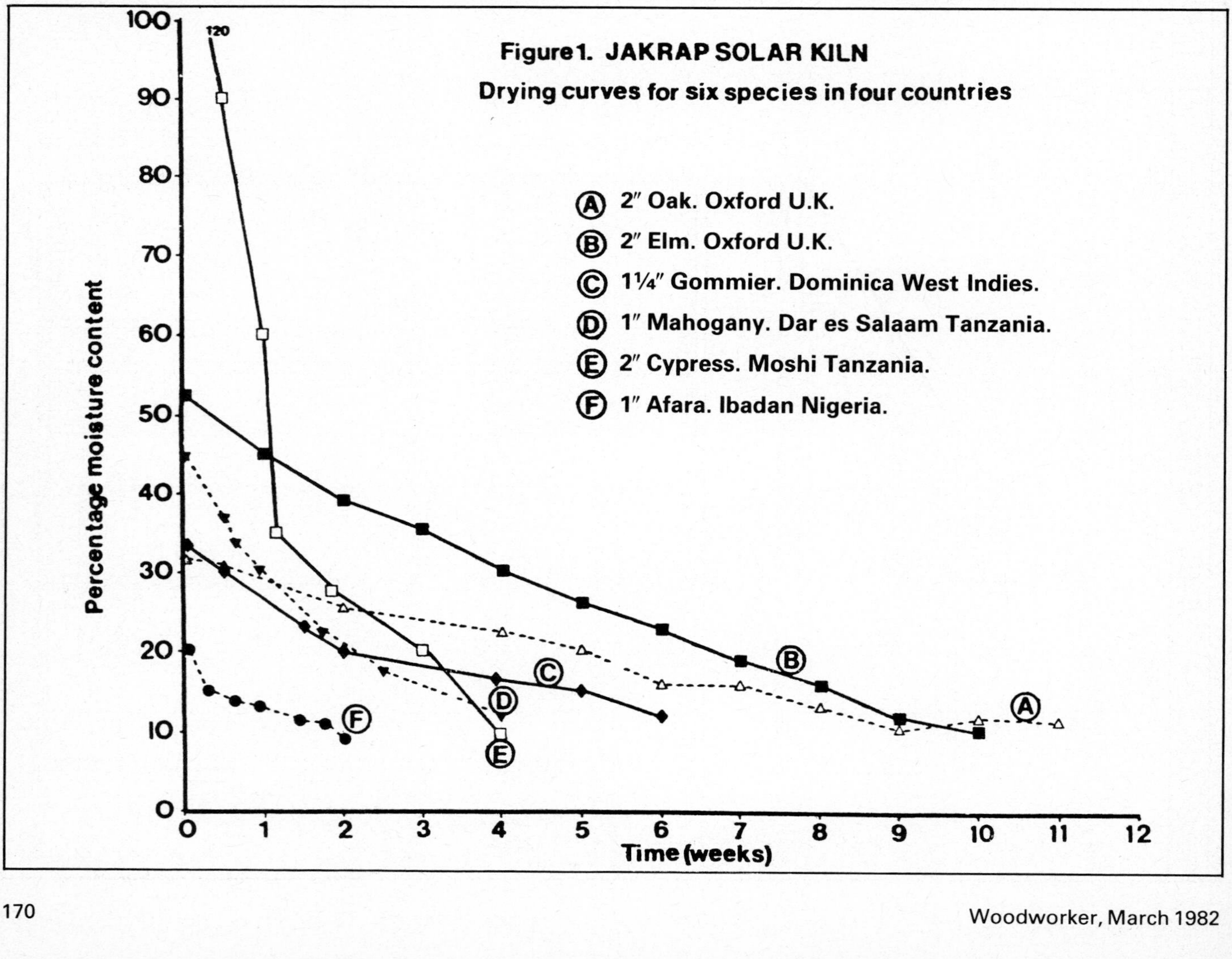

Percentage moisture content
Time (weeks)
0
10
20
30
40
50
60
70
80
90
100
1
2
3
4
5
6
7
8
9
11
12
120
Ⓐ 2″ Oak. Oxford U.K.
Ⓑ 2″ Elm. Oxford U.K.
Ⓒ 1¼″ Gommier. Dominica West Indies.
Ⓓ 1″ Mahogany. Dar es Salaam Tanzania.
Ⓔ 2″ Cypress. Moshi Tanzania.
Ⓕ 1″ Afara. Ibadan Nigeria.

Figure 1. JAKRAP SOLAR KILN
Drying curves for six species in four countries

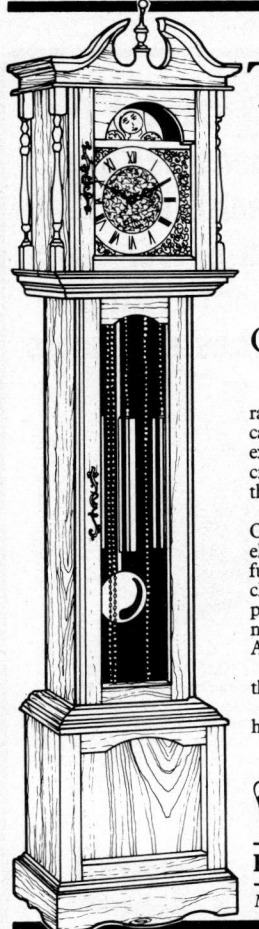

This Grandfather clock solid hardwood case is yours to assemble for as little as £156.34

(Inc VAT).

Complete movement for case from £114.43
(Inc VAT)

Just to feel and handle the solid, beautifully-worked hardwood is a rare pleasure. Yet to assemble your Emperor grandfather clock, rightly called 'the antiques of the future', requires no special woodworking experience. The case you put together with your own hands – our craftsmen have already pre-cut all the mitres and have pre-assembled all the difficult parts and joints.

The cases range in height from 5′ 10″ to 6′ 10″ in a choice of Cherry, Oak, Black Walnut or Mahogany . . . finest hardwoods, ¾″ thick to eliminate warpage and provide greater resonance. The movements come fully assembled, crafted in solid brass by one of West Germany's foremost clockmaking family firms. Included are brass weight shells, brass bob pendulum and embossed solid brass dial with either Roman or Arabic numerals. Either Westminster or triple chimes – the choice is yours. A full five year guarantee backs each movement.

You have the option of buying the case only, the movement only or the whole clock fully assembled.

For our free six page colour brochure with order form use our 24 hour 7 day week telephone brochure answering service, or write to:

EMPEROR CLOCK COMPANY

Emperor Clock Co. Ltd., (Dept W W)
3 The Parade, Trumps Green Road,
Virginia Water, Surrey GU25 4EH.
Tel: Wentworth (09904) 4925.

For details of our special offer send for Free brochure now!

MODEL 120 74″ × 16¾″ × 10″

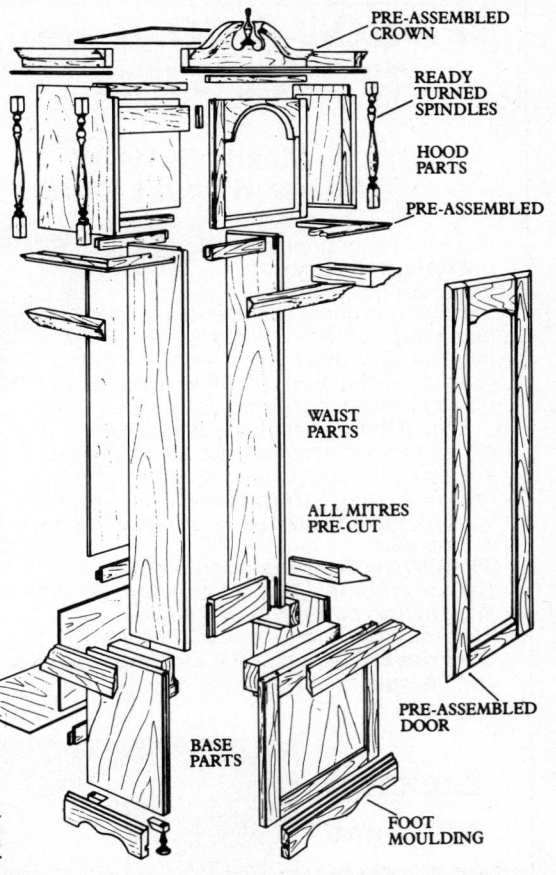

PRE-ASSEMBLED CROWN

READY TURNED SPINDLES

HOOD PARTS

PRE-ASSEMBLED

WAIST PARTS

ALL MITRES PRE-CUT

PRE-ASSEMBLED DOOR

BASE PARTS

FOOT MOULDING

"Here at The Woodsmith our products are made to the highest standards of craftsmanship so our timbers have to be dried perfectly and economically.

Up until 3 years ago I'd been buying ready dried timber and had all the usual problems of ordering, availability, cost, late deliveries quality etc. that you'll know only too well.

Now I've taken care of these with my Ebac Mini Timber Drier. It gives me independence and total control and the few doubts I had about installation, operation and cash outlay were groundless.

I get the exact moisture content I need; I just set it and forget it and week by week I can see the saving.

Even when a few boards of a different timber are required I simply load it in the chamber with the other timber; and I've no trouble with minimum orders.

But the biggest advantage I've found is being able to dry timber to suit the job in hand.

The Woodsmith's products, from wooden spoons to fitted kitchens

Let David Weston tell you himself why he spent £390 on an Ebac Mini Timber Drier.

Like a kitchen I recently fitted. I found that the temperature was always higher than usual so I needed a lower moisture content.

The result was no complaints due to degrade and no hassle sending dried timber back and re-ordering to the correct moisture content.

All I did was re-set the control box.

David Weston, Proprietor, The Woodsmith

If you want to save money, improve quality and limit problems, do what David Weston did and get an Ebac Mini - you'll never regret it.

LET EBAC HELP YOU MAKE THE MOST OF YOUR TIMBER

N.B. David Weston actually paid less than the above, we have used today's prices to avoid misleading.

If you would like to know what an Ebac Mini can do for you, fill in the coupon or 'phone Nick Greenwood on (0388) 661991, direct line.

☐ Please give me details of your interest free credit plan.

NAME _____

ADDRESS _____

BLM AD & DES (91)

Ebac

Greenfields Ind. Est. Bishop Auckland, Co. Durham DL14 9TF, England. Tel. (0388) 605061
Also available from: John Arrowsmith, Barton, N. Yorks. Ebac of America, 1715 Nth. Sherman Drive, Indianapolis, Indiana 46218 Tel. (317) 359 9607.

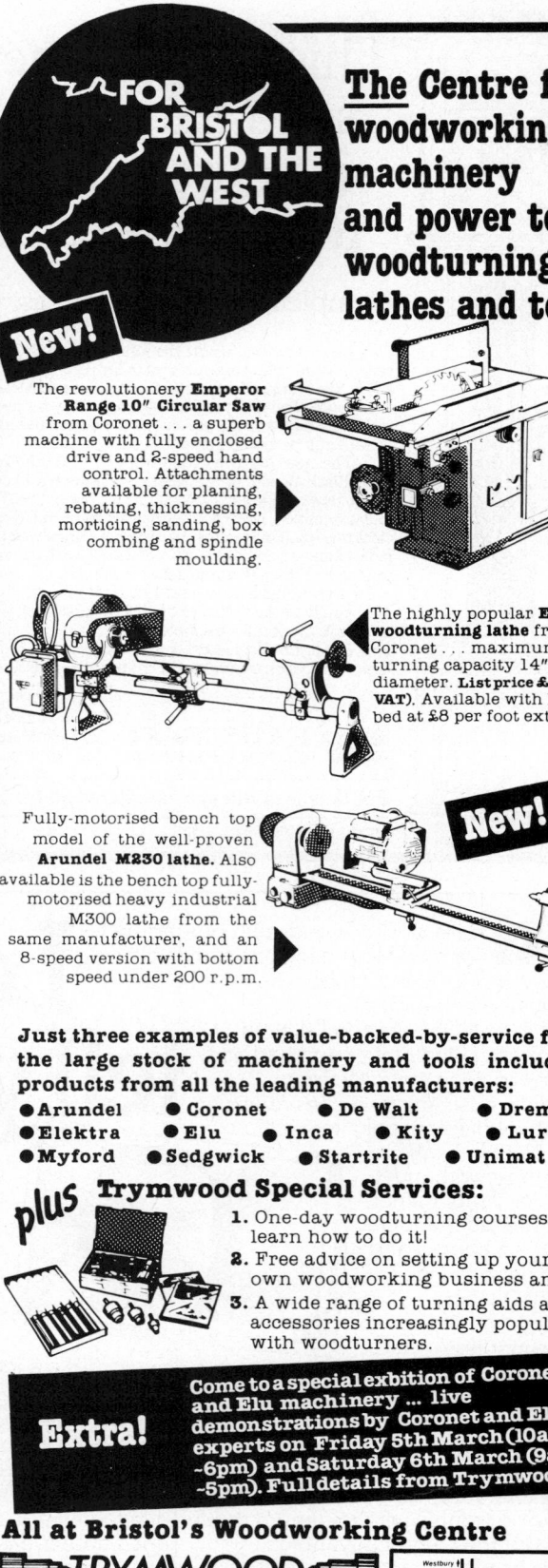

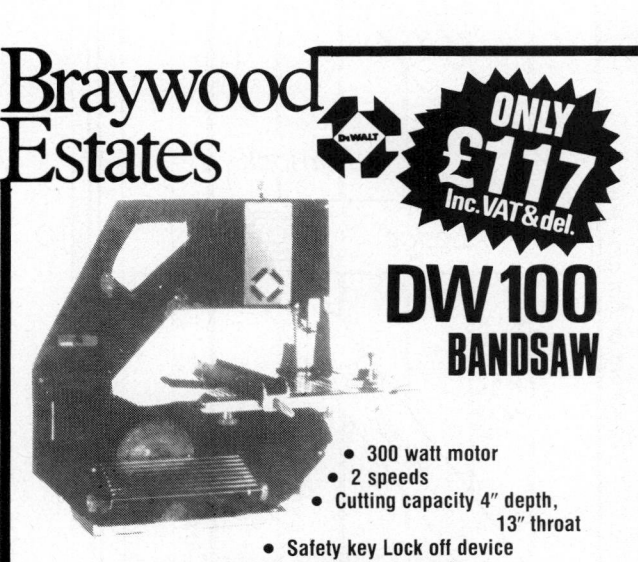

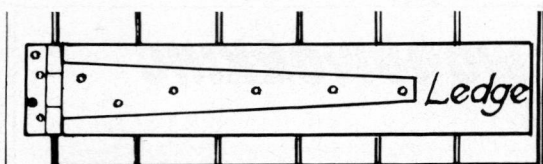

MAKING LEDGED DOORS

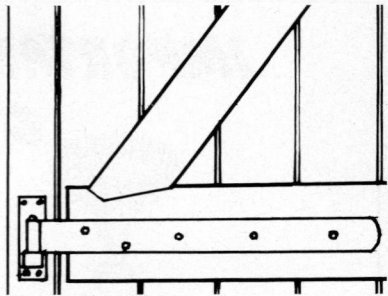

V. J. Taylor who is a former editor of WOODWORKER, explains that there are two designs of ledged door: the ledged and battened (or barred), and the ledged and braced. Here he gives constructional details and drawings for both designs

There can hardly be one house in the country which does not have at least one ledged door, whether it is the back door, or an outhouse or a garden shed door. Almost always they are outside doors which are exposed to the elements and this ought to mean that they are robustly built of seasoned timber and kept well-painted.

Unhappily many of them are, so to speak, on their last legs and since they are straightforward pieces of joinery and made up from readily available softwood, it is worthwhile looking at their proper construction.

Regrettably, many ready-made doors of this type are too flimsy, so let us deal first of all with basics. Obviously, if you are replacing an existing door, the height and width are predetermined for you.

If you are starting from scratch the width can vary from 1ft 10in. (560mm) to 3ft 3in. (990mm), and if you can do so make the height about 3ft 11in. (1,193mm) greater than the width. If the opening is greater than 3ft 6in. you will have to think in terms of double doors. A door width of less than 2ft 5½in. (750mm) is too narrow for conveni-

ence and safety, particularly if fire should break out and several people try to get out at once.

There are two designs of ledged door; the ledged and battened (or barred) (Fig. 1A); and the ledged and braced (Fig. 1B). In both designs matchboarding is used for the main cladding. This should be at least ¾in. (19mm), or preferably ⅞in. (22mm) thick.

There are several kinds of matchboarding

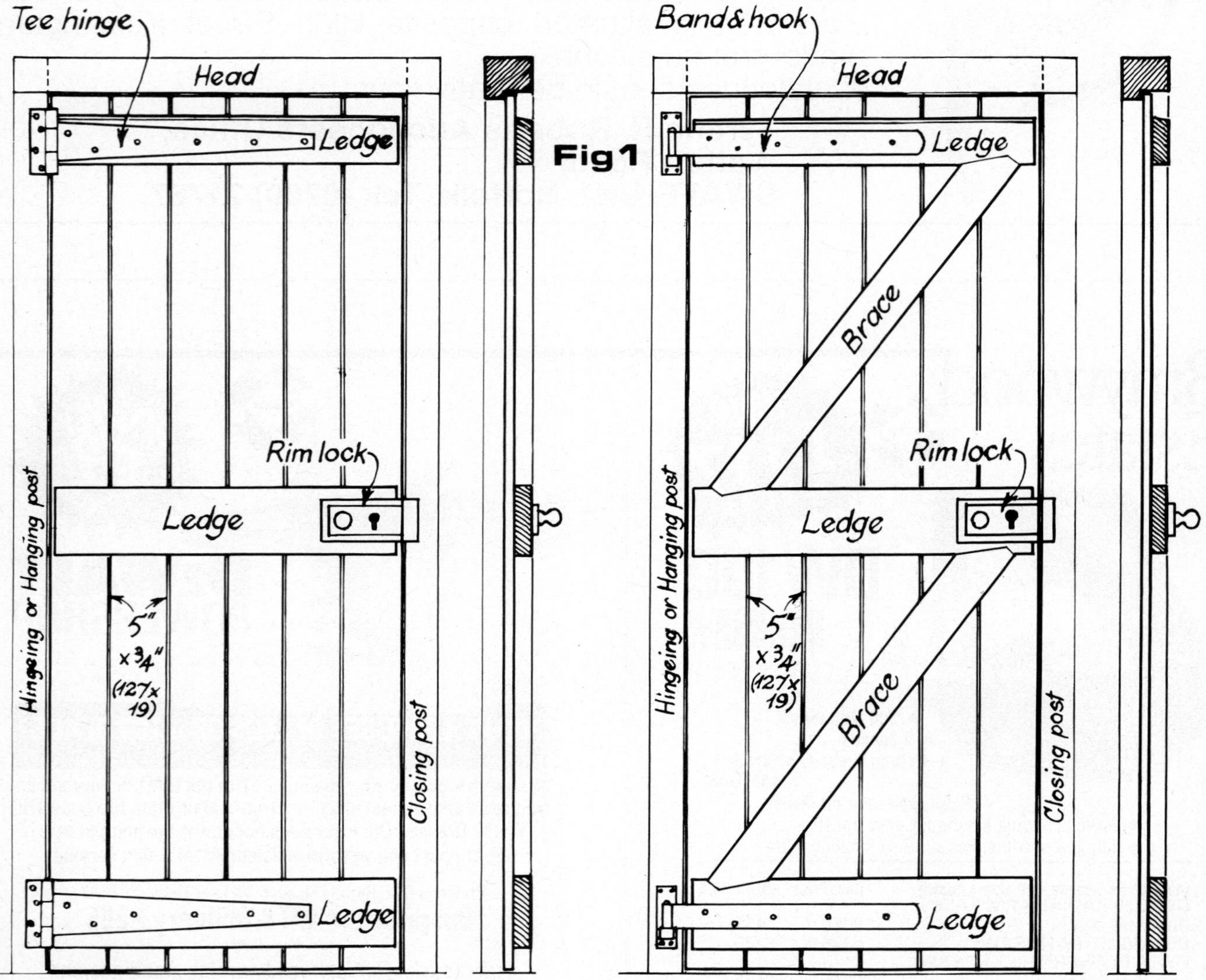

Fig 1

A   Ledged

B   Ledged & braced

REAR ELEVATIONS & SECTIONS

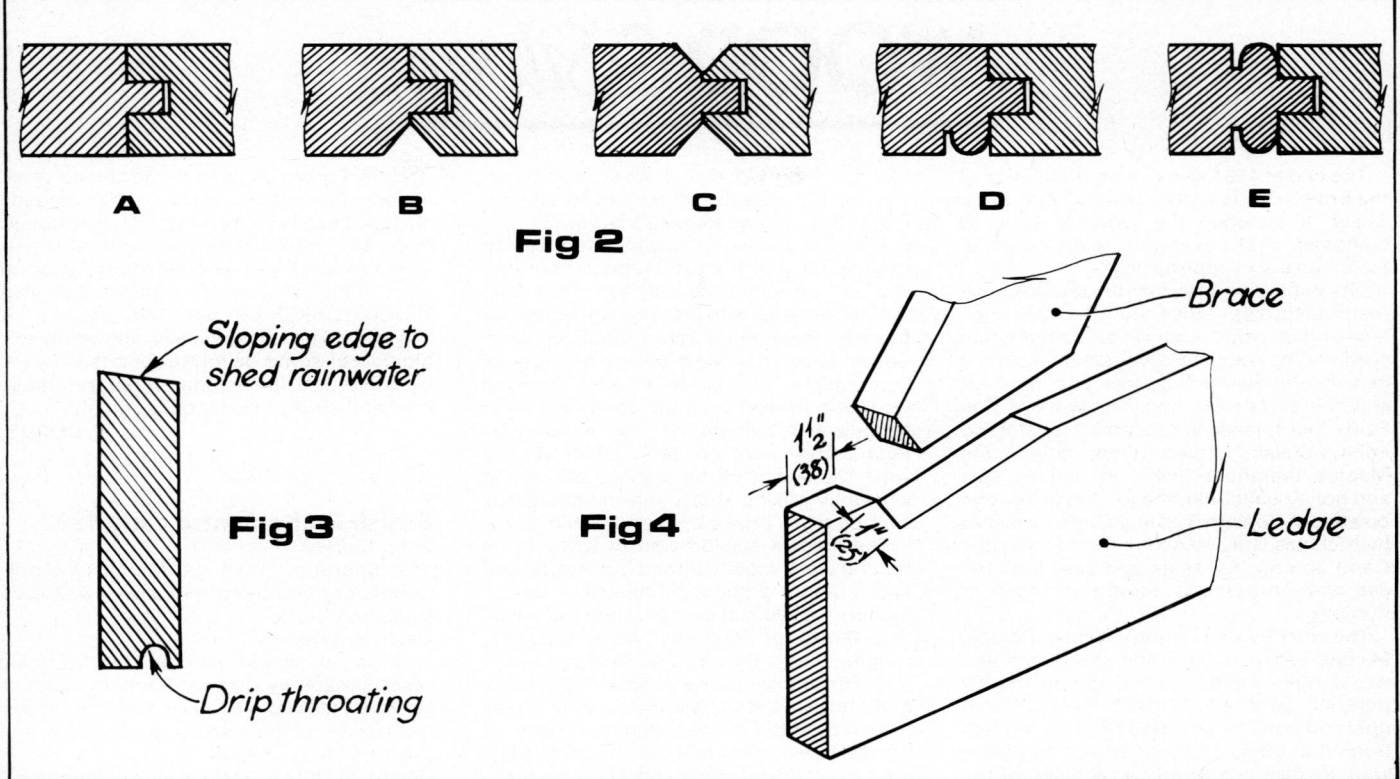

Fig 2

Fig 3

Sloping edge to shed rainwater

Drip throating

Fig 4

Brace

Ledge

1½" (38)

¾ (3)

as shown in Fig. 2. Example A is a plain butted-and-tongued matchboarding more suitable to a floor than an external door, one of the prime considerations being that if the joints open as a result of dry weather shrinking the boards across their widths, the resulting open crack should be as unnoticeable as possible.

Example B shows a typical tongue-and-groove matchboard which is V-jointed on side. This is the common or garden variety that you are likely to meet and it is quite suitable for our own job. There is the disadvantage that although the V-joint helps to mask any shrinkage on one side it does nothing for the other side.

At C we have a similar matchboard but this is V-jointed on both sides which will make the shrinkage less obvious inside and out. At D we see a matchboard not only tongued-and-grooved but incorporating a beading which is worked on one side only. This looks attractive and hides shrinkage even more, but only on one side.

At E the tongue-and-groove joint has a bead worked on both sides. This is the most elegant of them all, presenting the same appearance on both sides.

Note that in all cases the tongue does not reach the bottom of the groove, the 1/16in. (2mm) gap allowing room for the board to swell. You must not attempt to alter this feature. Now for dimensions of the other parts. Of the three ledges, two (the middle and the lower) are the same dimensions, namely 5⅞ × 1¼in. (150mm × 32mm). The top one is the same thickness but narrower

at 3⅞in. (99mm). The two braces are 1¼in. thick (32mm) and 3⅞in. (99mm) wide.

The methods used in constructing both doors are uncomplicated and reasonably easy to follow from the drawings. However, as with most things in woodwork, there are small features which not only contribute to the finished appearance of the job but make it stronger.

So we find that if a small drip-throating is worked on the underside of each of the ledges, rain will drop off instead of running down the matchboarding. Similarly the upper edge of the ledge is angled off slightly so that rainwater will run away and not be blown down behind it. These features are shown in Fig. 3.

Both the top and bottom ledges are set back from their respective edges by 2in. (50mm) or so. This lessens the risk of splits developing when the matchboards are fixed. It also eases the job of trimming the top and bottom edges to size, as you will only have the thickness of the matchboards to contend with. Similarly, the ends of the ledges stand in by ½in. (25mm) to allow for trimming the long edges.

When fixing the matchboards you can use nails for the middle boards but it will make a stronger job if the two outer boards are screwed in place. Not only will it make the whole job more rigid but it will help to keep it square and prevent the outer boards from moving outwards.

One of the strongest ways to nail the matchboards on is to use nails long enough so that at least ½in. (12mm) protrudes; this

protrusion is bent over and hammered down flat (known as clenching). Incidentally, the clenching should be done so that the piece bent over and flattened lies along the grain direction and not across it.

The braces need careful treatment. First of all they must always incline upwards from the hanging side. Otherwise they will be unable to fulfil their function of preventing the door from drooping and sagging (A) The ledges should be positioned so that the angle of the two braces is the same. Otherwise the door will have a decidedly odd appearance.

Next, the braces are housed into the ledges as shown in Fig. 4. They are not tenoned but housed complete. And note that the housings are kept back by 1½in. (38mm) from the ends of the ledges to avoid splitting them.

No adhesive need be used on the joints for the reason that the inevitable movement of the various parts must be allowed for. However, most doors are painted and all joints should be primed before assembly. You could use pink primer though I prefer the aluminium-based wood primer. It is much easier to apply and also seals the knots and prevents resin bleeding through. Alternatively, if you finish the door with a wood preservative all parts should be well-treated before assembly.

The door furniture traditionally comprises: T-hinges one on the top and one on the bottom ledge (Fig. 1A); or bands and hooks (Fig. 1B). A rim lock and (optionally) door bolts complete the furniture.

WOOD & Silver

The end of 1981 saw a major exhibition at the British Crafts Centre entitled *Wood and Silver*. It included the work of over 30 craftsmen and covered a wide range of techniques and approaches.

The exhibition logically divided into five main categories — toys, wood, silver, jewellery and a wood and silver combination section. The colourful toys section included carved and painted figures and toys for children and grown-ups. The work of Ron Fuller (aeroplanes and boats), Mabel Packenham-Walsh (carved totem poles) and Maggie Wareham (fish, caterpillars, cats and hot air balloons); the jointed fishes and bowties of Howard Raybould and the pieces by Nicholas Gray (like Blue Cloud and Little Gem) among his trains and cars took the eye and included a strong element of humour.

The work by silversmiths William Phipps, Michael Lloyd, Julia Drane and Paul Mann was exquisite and included spoons, highly polished hand-raised bowls inlaid with red gold and bowls with a matt finish. Jewellery formed another group of work and pieces were in silver, or wood and a blend of the two elements. Howard Raybould showed some carved and gilded wooden jewellery, Harriet St Leger's pieces combined silver smithing and carving in exotic woods to produce pendants, brooches and earrings of flower heads and flowing lines, webs of silver glistened on the woods. Peter Niczewski showed highly original jewellery pieces of marquetry with a geometric theme. Lesley Miller's work included a necklet of silver in which a blue-dyed ball of wood seemed to hang unsuspended, and bracelets inlaid with various colours. The fan shaped jewellery of Trevor Cowland

incorporating wood and silver was attractive, so too was the chunky bead style of Peter Chatwin and Pamela Martin.

Wood and silver in combination was an exciting facet of the exhibition. Peter Chatwin had exploited his technique of dyeing sycamore veneers to produce some angular boxes incorporating layers of silver. Cecil Colyer showed a silver-rimmed mazer of burr maple and some smaller drinking vessels in the same combination. The silver spoons with slender wooden handles by Poul Larsen were delightful. Also of note were the sword sticks, walking sticks and knives by Miklos Menis and the geometric *trompe d'oeil* boxes by Darrell Whittaker.

The biggest section was of wood in its natural state, mostly turned but also carved and much of a domestic nature — boxes, platters, bowls and scoops. Here the bowls and boxes of Ray Key were exquisite, ranging in size from tiny acorn-sized boxes with lids to thick burr-elm bowls and heavy platters. Paul Caton had large free-form yew bowls as did Christian Nimmo many of whose free forms retained the bark. Cecil Jordan produced some enormous bowls in burr elm and some wee pepper-pot-like boxes with lids. David Pye's boxes showed exquisite swirl patterned mouldings and subtle polish. John Creed had a series of tiny boxes, Richard Raffan showed turned bowls some down to almost paper thin. For almost the utmost in transparency of turning one appreciated the bowls of Scotsman Michael O'Donnell and Jim Partridge whose bowls of unseasoned wood could almost be seen through. Jim also showed his stepped spiral bowls and some laminated bracelets. Don White had tiny scoops in various woods and burr elm bowls;

Andrew Forbes showed some carved work including an otter and fish and an elegant slender boat with bird figure head. Boxes and hand mirrors were the work of David Gregson and ladles and fat chunky spoons the product of John Thompson (see also WOODWORKER February 1982 p102).

A satisfying, aesthetically appealing exhibition of some delightful pieces of work by some of Britain's contemporary craftsmen at their best and most original.

P. CURDS

British Crafts Centre early 1982

Main Gallery
The Sporting Crafts 12 March-17 April. Continues the series of exhibitions of British traditional crafts.
Basement Gallery
A show of carved and painted wooden objects made by Howard Raybould, plus a selection of engraved glass to illustrate the techniques employed by the modern engraver 5 March-3 April.

Details of British Crafts Centre exhibitions can be obtained from Joan Taylor, Exhibitions Organiser on 01-836 6993. The centre is at 43 Earlham Street, Covent Garden, London WC2H 9LD, open Tuesday-Friday 10-5.30, Saturdays 10-4.00.

Below: Group of E. Indian ebony boxes by Cecil Jordan; silver coil bangle, coil earrings and oblong bangle by Alison Baxter; inlaid wood and silver 'trompe d'oeil' boxes by Darrell Whittaker.

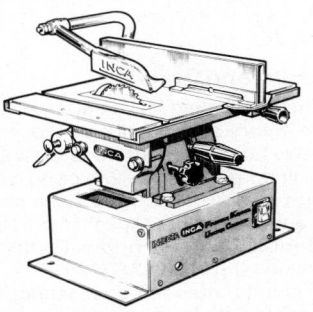

BOOK REVIEWS

Most important place

In his introduction to *Shelves, Closets and Cabinets* author Peter Jones writes: '. . . ask any woman what she considers most important when she is considering a new place to live, and she will probably tell you "the kitchen, the bathroom and the storage place".'

This sums up the whole book; for it is a volume which should prove valuable for any handy husband anxious to please his lady. We men may be adept in the making of shelves, closets and cabinets. But it is the practical women, after all, who make the homes.

There are two aspects in working with wood: the practical and the romantic — I mean romantic in the wider sense, as typified by the annual Woodworker Show. There is not much poetry in the above title and the first thought which came to my mind was of the essential difference between these two views of life, for the processes described in this book are far removed from those displayed in the Woodworker Show. Give me the latter!

However, be that as it may, this is indeed a comprehensive volume of 300 pages, profusely illustrated with clear line drawings which are almost too numerous to assess. Chapter 1 Planning and Utilising Space is an amplification of the title. Chapter 2 is on Tools and 3 is about Wood the Basic Material.

This last is sound so far as it goes, but not so the illustrations. The drawings of 'six major types of wood grain' are poor; and the photographs of softwoods, as a matter of course, all look alike. Those of common American hardwoods are not much better, but it is difficult enough to illustrate wood effectively in colour, let alone in monochrome.

Chapter 4 is Cuts, Bends and Joints, 5 is on Fasteners, leading to Drawers, Doors and Frames, Veneering, Molding and Trim and Finishing Touches, all adding up to a well-worn sequence which, I suppose, is hackneyed but necessary in any book on woodworking.

Then follows a host of fitments of all sorts, each of which 'has a specific purpose'. But I feel that the subject has been somewhat overdone, as there is a certain sameness about the illustrations, this being unavoidable in so narrow a concept.

I found myself slightly at variance with the author, also in the introduction, when he describes the work: 'This is a book for the dedicated craftsman. . . ' My idea of a dedicated craftsman is a man who looks beyond the necessities of life and gropes, however humbly, into the realms of imagination and romanticism, not because his project is of practical worth but because he seeks to emulate in his own way the illimitable handiwork of Nature.

Still, the author must have worked extremely hard and with noble intentions; and the same may be said of the three names responsible for the illustrations. I compliment them all.

The publisher is Van Nostrand Reinhold Co Ltd, Molly Millars Lane, Wokingham RG11 2PY. Price £11.35 cloth; £10.15 paper (reference ISBN 0-442-26424-0).　　**C.B.**

Hardly a handbook

Cabinet Making, Pattern Making and Millwork by Gaspar J. Lewis (ISBN 0-442-24785-0) is a large book of over 400 pages referred to by the publisher as a handbook. A handbook, according to the *Concise Oxford Dictionary*, is a (usually short) treatise, manual or guidebook; hardly a fair reference!

It is not easy to understand why the world of cabinet-making and the world of pattern-making are grouped between the same covers. Granted, the skills of both worlds are much the same, but as soon as the cabinetmaker attains that skill he becomes more and ever more free to express himself as an individual.

This is something, surely, the pattern-maker can never do. He may have great pleasure in his skill and great satisfaction from his contribution to some mighty work of art and engineering; but for all that he is more of a slave. The demands made on his ability are dictated from without, while each example of the cabinetmaker may well be an expression from within.

Try as I might, I cannot agree with these two aspects of woodworking skill being placed together in the same volume.

The title is all-embracing, and while it is self-explanatory, the book consists of six sections. Common to both worlds are the first three: Wood and Woodworking; Woodworking Tools; Joinery. The rest are in the title, and there is a summary of the title in Unit 1. There are 40 of these units, all of which are copiously illustrated. But the photographs are rather small and details of the operations described are not easily appreciated.

The contents of the book are scholastic in general layout and numerous safety hints are conspicuous, being printed in panels; but photographs of mill workers with long hair are questionable.

Units 4 to 14 deal with woodworking tools and they are comprehensive, including hand tools, portable power tools and standard woodworking machines. Unit 15 covers the making of joints and is less comprehensive, most of the joints, well-described and well-illustrated, being comparatively elementary. This is followed by Glues and Clamping. Unit 17 is headed Fasteners and includes nails, screws and various metal appliances. Reference is made to steam bending and the cutting of curved members.

Next, in Cabinetmaking, there are chapters or units on design, layout and planning, casework construction, kitchen cabinets, drawer construction, cabinet doors and plastics laminating. Unit 26 covers tables of usual, if limited constructions. Unit 27 describes various finishes.

Section 5 on Pattern-Making covers sand moulds, pattern details, one-piece patterns, parted patterns, cores, core prints and core boxes, stave construction, match plates.

Section 6 is devoted to Millwork and describes wood mills and machines, mouldings, screens, doors and door frames, sash and window frames, stairways and stair parts.

At the end there is a useful glossary and the inevitable in./m list.

Each unit follows the same pattern: objectives; activities; unit review; and questions, thus giving an educational sequence which the reader would do well to follow.

John Orozco (the jacket designer) might have depicted dovetails with the proper slope. But that is only the jacket. The book itself is a handsome production full of sound advice which is illustrated with over 700 photographs and drawings.

Publisher is Van Nostrand Reinhold Co Ltd, Molly Millars Lane, Wokingham RG11 2PY.　　**C.B.**

Theory and Practice

First published in 1958, George Love's *The Theory and Practice of Woodwork* can receive no greater accolade than that it has remained popular for 23 years. Now, in its fourth edition, it has again been updated by the author (a retired teacher of woodwork) and reissued by its original publisher and classified (ISBN 0 582 23125 0).

Primarily intended as a school textbook — and as such it is undoubtably a classic — the work contains a wealth of easily-understood information and advice. All this is of value not only to the young in school struggling, perhaps, to master the manual dexterity and intellectual skills required of them but also to those of us whose school-days are long, or recently, past but who still need, or want, to learn.

For the prime purpose of George Love's book is to teach. It takes its reader up to and beyond the standard required to take (and hopefully pass) the traditional woodwork examinations at GCE O Level. To this end it contains specimen examination questions and a number of practical exercises.

It should be pointed out that with the current trend in some schools towards craft, design and technology courses rather than traditional woodwork etc, with work emphasising design and problem-solving as opposed to manual skills, some will consider the book rather old-fashioned.

However, in spite of a recently acquired university certificate in design technology, I still believe that craft skills matter and that this book and others like it have their place in the school workshop. And it is for these same reasons that I suggest it for those no longer at school.

The fundamentals of good woodworking practice are amply covered, from basic working out and cutting, through a range of common joints and construction methods to gluing-up and cramping. Further chapters give instruction on veneering, wood-turning and finishing. Tools, their use, care and maintenance and the raw materials for woodworking are also described.

To satisfy examination requirements there is a chapter on technical drawing and another on the history of furniture development; both are interesting and rarely covered in the more popular books (as distinct from textbooks) on woodworking.

Lavishly illustrated throughout with drawings and some photographs it is published by Longman Group Ltd, 5 Bentinck Street, London W1M 5RN, at £2.75 in soft covers. It is excellent value for money and is strongly recommended.　　**J. H.**

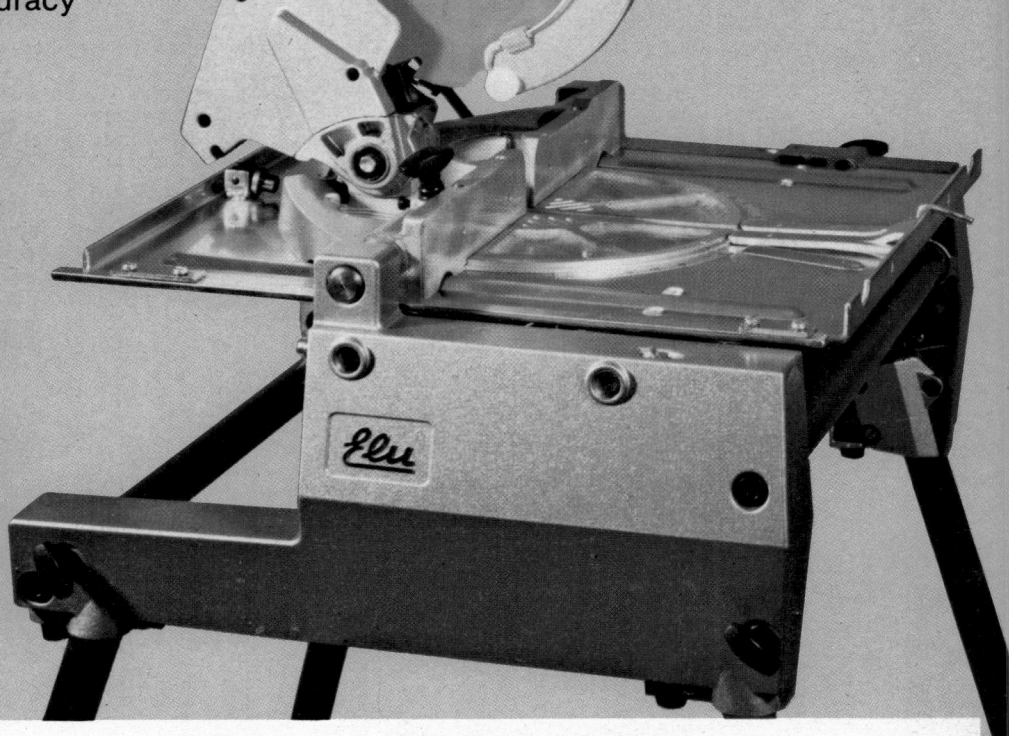

and see all that's new in Europe's most
Continuous machinery demonstrations
furniture construction - Hundreds of ge:

All at the 1982 WOODME

NEW MACHINES

You can, for example, see and try-out an entirely new bandsaw (the MINI-MAX PROFESSIONAL). This machine is without question the most superbly engineered and accurate unit we have ever seen in this price range.

All tables, wheels, guide assemblies and adjusting mechanisms are in precision ground, fine-grain cast iron. Paint work is mirror finished and the total cost will be less than £250 (inc. VAT)!

A low-cost table sander for perfect finishing of wide panels etc. will also be shown for the first time. This machine is literally half the price of any previously available and if you are in full-time woodworking is a unit which simply must be seen.

Other new developments include a 6 operation universal with a uniquely efficient function changing system - a new copying lathe - MULTICO's latest long-bed planers - an 18 inch floor-standing, cast-iron bandsaw at under £500 - an 8 inch wet-stone grinder for just £59 and the new WOODMASTER universal system amongst many others.

Apart from new machines, you can of course, see the full range of universal and independent machines currently produced by Britain's and Europe's leading manufacturers including CORONET, ARUNDEL, DeWALT, ELEKTRA, HARRISON, LUNA, MULTICO, MYFORD, MODERN, SEDGWICK, STARTRITE, ZINKEN and so on.

FRENCH POLISHING & RESTORATION

Furniture restoration has become a lucrative and rewarding part of the woodworking scene, but matching and finishing components to traditional standards presents problems for most woodworkers.

At this year's show you can see a professional french polisher at work and learn a great deal from the demonstrations, advice and tips on the basic requirements for success in this most fascinating craft.

A full range of professional quality stains, fillers, french polishes, wadding, etc. will be available from his stand.

A1 HARDWOODS AT 50% SAVINGS

Top quality hardwoods are not only difficult to obtain but can be prohibitively expensive. English Oak for example, costs on average about £23 per cubic foot.

David Gratch of the "Timber Purchasing Pool" will have stocks of this timber at prices from just £14 per cube; Olive Ash at £7 per cube, Lebanon Cedar at £6, English Walnut at £11 and so on. In fact more than 70 species of common, rare and exotic timbers will be on sale at similar substantial savings.

Don't miss this opportunity to see before you buy and of course save on carriage costs.

1400 SPECIALIST HANDTOOLS

Rogers of Hitchin offer a unique range of woodworking handtools from their catalogue. Virtually all of these will be on display for the first time at the show.

Top quality tools for cabinet making, carpentry, musical instrument making, veneering, carving, turning and every conceivable woodworking need will be directly available from Rogers' stand at special show prices.

Of particular interest to all woodworkers will be the new range of Japanese laminated steel tools. The repeated forging and doubling of a single piece of high quality tool steel produces blades of peerless strength, resilience and edge-holding capability. (Samurai swords were made by this process.) As a real incentive to try the difference for yourself, these tools will be offered at a full 20% under the normal price for the duration of the show.

THE BEST IN FURNITURE DESIGN & CONSTRUCTION

Rycotewood College was established for training qualified students in the highest traditional standards of woodworking. Work from the College ranks with the best produced anywhere in the world and many outstanding examples of their originality and craft will be on display.

Live demonstrations will also be a feature of their stand and you can see much of the work of final year students in progress during the course of the exhibition.

13	
22	
23	

1 Woodworking
2 Coronet Macl
3 DeWalt Mach
4 Startrite, Rob
5 Timber purch
6 Luna Internat
7 Multico demo
8 Lazzari "Profe
9 Mini-Max Wo
10 Copying Lath
11 Zinken Unive
12 Elm Machine
13 Bargain Corn
14 Ashley Iles w
15 Gordon Stoke
16 Meber Bands:
17 French Polish
18 Rogers Tool S
19 Sales Office/M
20 Council for Ri
21 Rycotewood (
22 Toilets
23 Reception & R

ehensive range of light woodworking machinery.
tuition in woodturning, french polishing, carving and traditional
show offers on machines, tools and finishing materials.

EXHIBITION

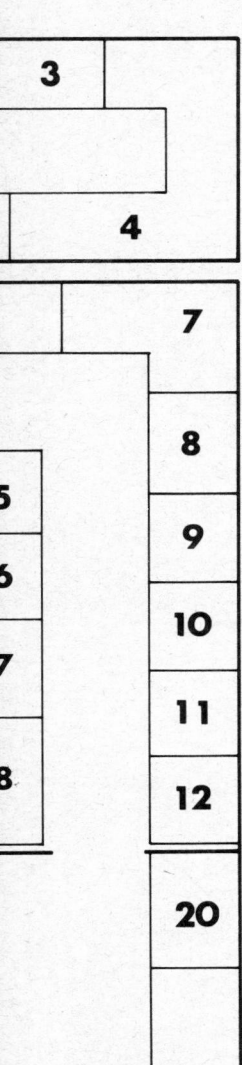

WOODTURNING TEACH-IN

Gordon Stokes is world-famous as the author of many woodturning and woodworking books. His expertise in the practical application of the principals he writes about (and the ability to impart that knowledge) is evident from the fact that many successful businesses have been established as a direct result of his 2 day basic and advanced woodturning courses. In fact WOODMEN, now the largest light woodworking machinery distributors in Europe, was originally inspired in just this way.

If you would like to start woodturning or have a particular problem in this field, you are certain to benefit from the free advice and personal tuition that Mr. Stokes will be on hand to give for the duration of the show.

STARTING YOUR OWN BUSINESS

An idea and the enthusiasm to carry it through will take you more than half way to starting a business of your own. Unfortunately, many people with both these requisites have nevertheless failed to take account of the particular problems associated with trading in today's climate.

Finance, marketing, accounting, insurance, cash control, production planning, legislative restrictions and Government subsidies; even in a one-man business; will all play an important part in the establishment and continuing success of your venture.

COSIRA (Council for Small Industries in Rural Areas) give expert advice on every aspect of running a small business and can employ experienced consultants at every level to analyse plans and prospects in the light of their experience. Grants, subsidies, finance, forecasting, raw material and market location, etc., etc., are all a part of the FREE SERVICE they can offer you or arrange on your behalf.

In addition, many of the demonstrators and people you will meet at the exhibition have a wealth of practical experience in setting-up and running a business of their own. Talk to them and benefit from their advice and experience.

Immediate finance arrangements can be further discussed with a senior representative of MERCANTILE CREDIT (a subsidiary of BARCLAYS BANK). Personal loans and hire purchase facilities are offered on purchases of £200 or more and attractive leasing arrangements on larger plant and equipment, if required.

BARGAIN CORNER

Shop-soiled, ex-demonstration and part-exchanged machines, accessories and attachments will be on sale here at stock clearance prices. Planer/thicknessers, spindle moulders, grinders, saws, bandsaws, etc. together with a huge selection of tooling at savings of up to 50%.

& books service

Machinery display
tration
onstration
nstration
tion
ration
ols demonstration

carving tools
g teach-in
ration
ation demonstration

edit Consultant
s Service
nstration

The 1982
WOODMEN EXHIBITION
brings you the complete spectrum of woodworking

 **A real chance to win £1,000 to spend on equipment of your choice in our limited entry competition!**

Entry forms and rules for the BEST HOME WORKSHOP DESIGN competition will be available at the show. Submissions will be judged by Geoff Peters and Alan Mitchell of "PRACTICAL WOODWORKING" magazine.

plus **A holiday for two in Sweden at a time of your choice! (Includes air fares & hotel accomodation.)**

Every customer spending £10 or more at the exhibition on equipment of any description will automatically qualify for this prize draw.

plus **Premium Vouchers, hundreds of special show offers & FREE refreshments every day!**

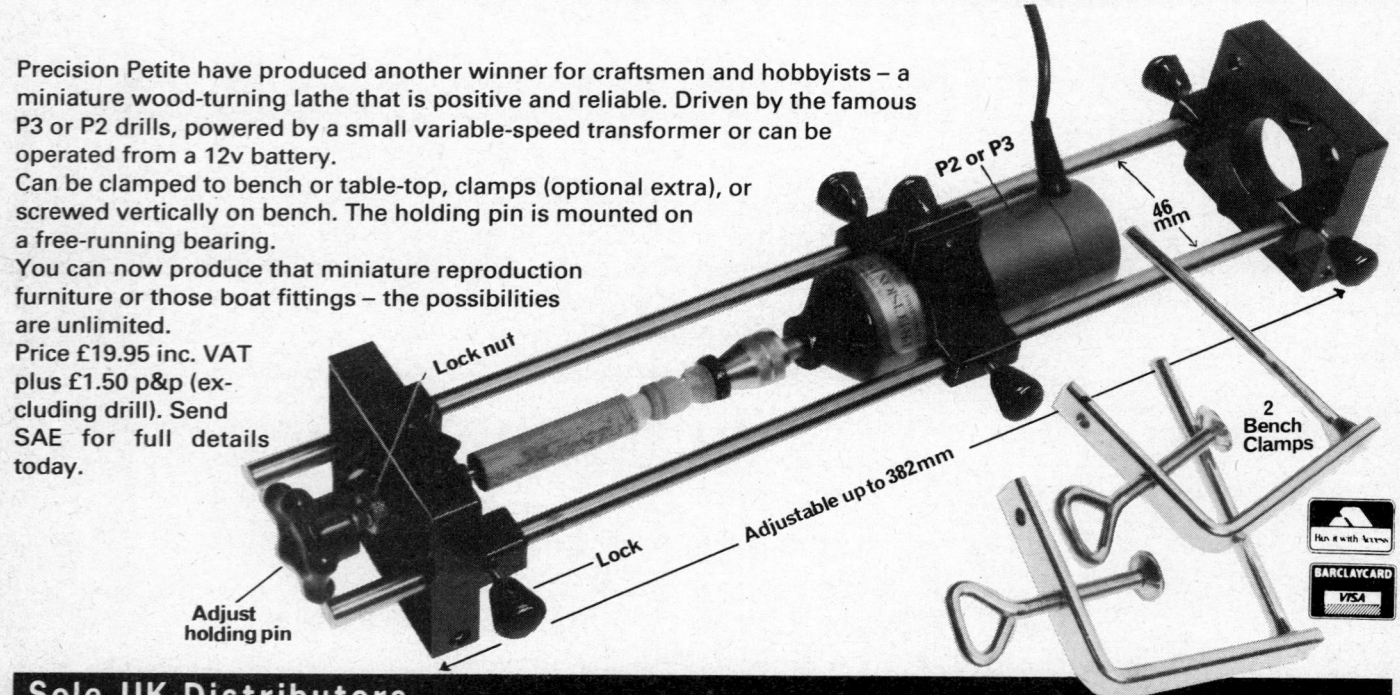
182

Prices quoted are those prevailing at press date and are subject to alteration due to economic conditions.

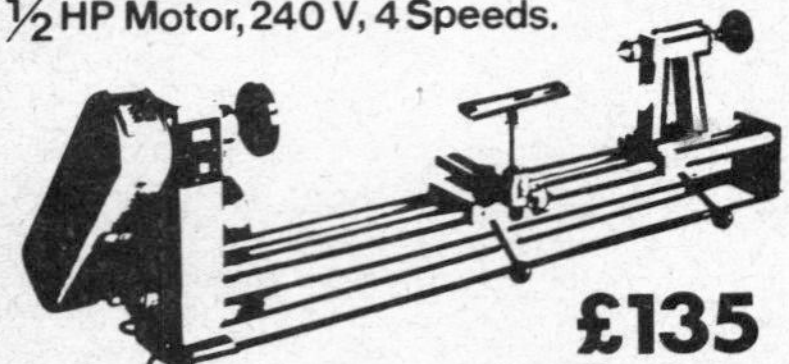

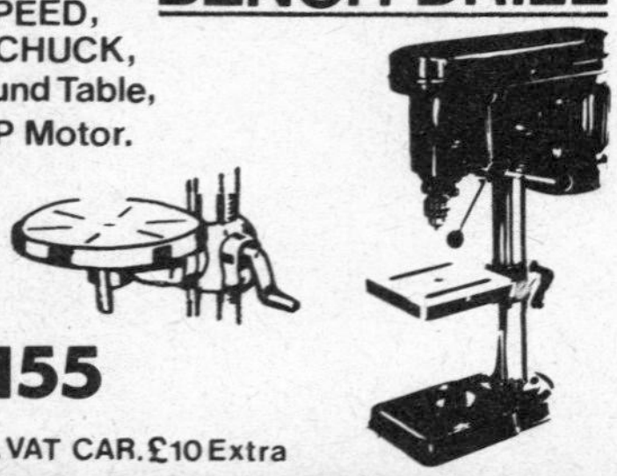

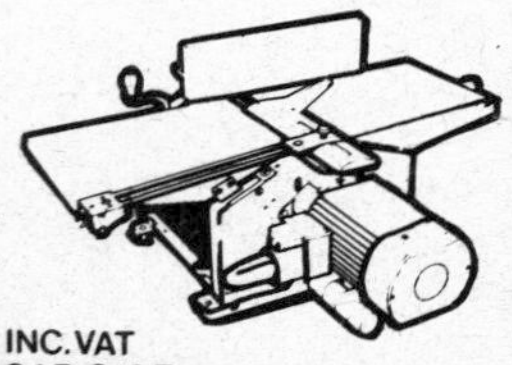

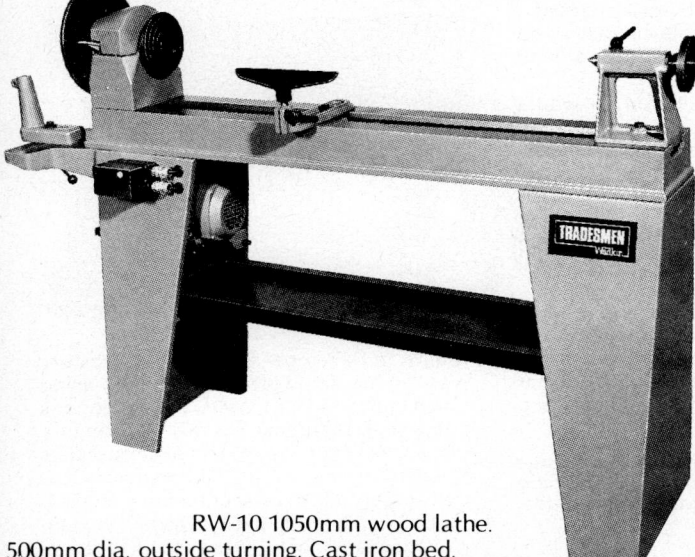

AUCTION

Tyrone R. Roberts' annual auction of woodworking and allied trade tools is once again being held at Kensington new town hall in London, on March 30th. (See WOODWORKER March 1981 p152 for last year's report.)

Readers will have the opportunity to evaluate over 2000 tools that were once the pride and joy of the wheelwright, cooper, joiner, shipwright and pattern maker.

Any one who missed last year's block-busting performance by Tyrone R. Roberts, when he sold 600 lots at an average of 132 lots an hour, can look forward to an encore with this year's huge collection of fine tools.

Of particular note this year is the wide selection of braces representing those of the chair-maker, cooper and coach-builder, showing the individuality of design for the various trades.

There are 7 metallic framed braces, more commonly known as the *Ultamatum* so called by William Marples, the first and largest manufacturer who introduced this type of brace in the early 1850's. All the examples are in good condition with some in ebony, beech, rosewood and the very rare horn-filled Ultamatum.

The mid 19th century saw a plethora of patented and registered designs emerge from the Sheffield tool makers; several rare types are on offer including those by Schofield, Joseph Cooper, Bloomer & Phillips, Pilkington & Marsden Bros, also others of the 18th century from England, Scotland and the continent.

While mentioning Scotland, Stewart Spiers of Ayr immediately springs to mind as the most prolific of all the metal plane-makers north of the border. Almost every model of his extensive stock lines are represented, from a gunmetal bullnose plane to the long dovetailed jointer. Two very rare items are worthy of special mention, a smoothing plane with a Norris type vertical adjustment and an improved mitre plane, one of Spiers' specially made tools with an iron 2½in. wide. (The auctioneer's estimate for this is £400-£500.) Two other, as yet unrecorded makers from Ayr, are also noted, both mitre planes, one bearing the name Rutherford Ayr, and the other Spier Ayr, whether the latter's name and provenance was actually an attempt to confuse craftsmen with the proprietary maker is a matter for conjecture but seems quite likely.

While Spiers concentrated wholly on metal planes, Mathieson of Glasgow (and later Edinburgh, Dundee and Liverpool) sold the complete range of woodworking tools, as shown by the ivory rules, screwboxes, a wide variety of wooden moulding and other specialised planes, to braces and ebony spirit levels, most of which were his

Right: a very rare adjustable smoothing plane stamped J. Fenn Reg 12th Nov. 1844.

own manufacture especially in the early years of the business. Later when the range of items became too great he had to buy a large percentage of them as can be seen clearly by the Norris A7 rebate plane just as clearly stamped Mathieson, also a Spiers' panel plane with the Mathieson stamp.

Scottish wooden planes are of special interest to the collector as the variety of unusual types far surpassed English planes, although two irons are not particularly scarce, when it comes to three or even four irons these are rare and were only produced in Scotland. A four-ironed sash plane in last year's auction made £200. One with more intricate moulding and in better condition is in this year's sale.

Stanley tools are well to the fore as usual being mostly sought after by American dealers and collectors, but will meet with stiff opposition from some of our own knowledgeable enthusiasts in particular numbers 9¾in. (early) block plane, Nos 10¼ & 10½ carriage-makers' rabbet planes, No. 39 dado plane, Nos 45 & 55 combination planes, No. 72 chamfer plane, No. 98/99 rabbet planes, No. 444 dovetail plane and four variations of adjustable circular soled planes, plus a whole range of good early usable Stanley tools.

The craftsman is well catered for with a dozen American Disston saws, literally hundreds of carving gouges and chisels, moulding planes of every imaginable pro-

Right: a Kimberly patent plough plane.

file, as well as sets of hollows and rounds, beads etc. Anyone wishing to take up the trades of shipwright, wallpaper block maker or pattern maker will have to look no further for there are complete chests of these and other trades.

Left: a four-ironed quirk ogee with double fillet moulding plane by A. Mathieson, Dundee.

What is probably one of the finest collections of planes by the celebrated maker Thomas Norris, offered at auction, will be on view, notably two smoothing planes, a shoulder and a bullnose plane, all in gunmetal and pristine condition, a rare adjustable A7 shoulder plane, as well as a large assortment of rebate, jointing, smoothing and the sought after Nos 71 and 72 wooden planes (in all over 25 items). Other contemporaries of Norris have also contributed to the sale; names like Holland, Buck, Slater, Holtzapffel and Preston which are names to conjure with in the rhykenological (plane collecting) world, are represented.

Prices over the last year have not seen any real escalation except for the exceptional piece, for like every other aspect of the antique trade the recession has taken its toll, in fact some items, notably metal planes in anything other than very good condition have fallen in value at the sale-

rooms. In December for example, ordinary wooden moulding planes were not making much more than £1 each, the exceptions being special purpose or early 18th century planes. While on the subject of early planes Robert Wooding (1710-39), S. Holbeck, Cogdell, Rogers and several unrecorded makers (Lots 350-370) will always have their aficionados amongst serious collectors and should hold their price.

Illustrated catalogues (this year with four extra pages of photographs) and estimated prices, £2 (sae if prices-realised list required) from Tyrone R. Roberts, Auctioneers Office, Watton Road, Swaffham, Norfolk (0760-21767) which also provides full postal bidding and shipping facilities. Viewing is from 12.00 noon-9.00 p.m. on 29 March and 8 a.m.-12 noon on sale day 30 March.

R. EATON

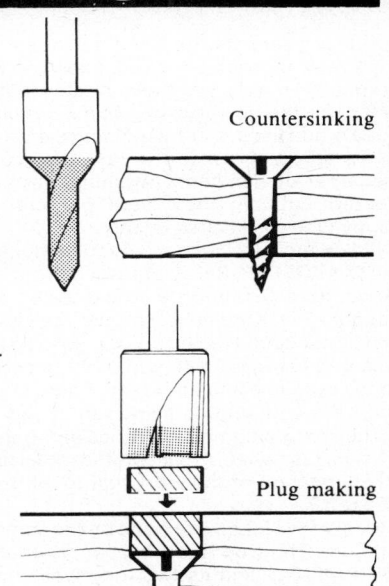
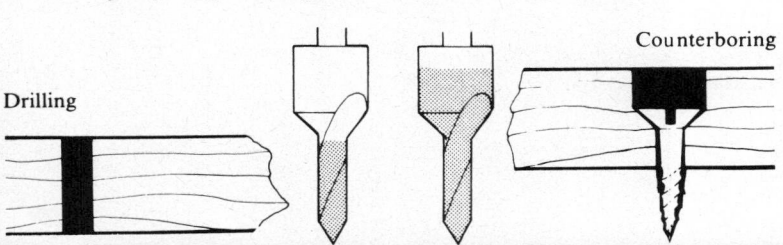

Laurence Archer from Yorkshire Press and Publicity follows the story of a competition winner and finds a
DREAM KITCHEN

Fifteen years ago Barrie and Lynne Goddard were married and like all newly-weds gradually improved their home, Barrie being in the joinery and cabinetmaking trade made life easier by building a 4ft × 6ft single storey extension to house some of the larger kitchen items (washing machine, freezer) but still they were not entirely happy with the kitchen layout.

Following reading an advertisement in WOODWORKER Barrie travelled from his home near Scunthorpe to Leicester and bought a Kity K5 which he transported in his estate car and erected in his garage. He enlarged its range with some of the accessories available and at the same time heard about the competition being run by Kity.

The competition meant redesigning their kitchen, just what Lynne wanted, rules said ninety percent of the work had to be done on the K5.

Most of the jobs were done on the spindle moulder. The Goddards' kitchen measures 15ft × 8ft 6in. and its two long walls both contain new units which incorporate oven and hob, the fridge is now hidden behind an oak door. All the ⅝in. unit carcases were made of white Melamine, laminated to both sides of chipboard. Barrie further stiffened the structure by using the same material for the solid backs as for the sides. At any point where there was an end seam he put ⅛in. oak-faced plywood so that no white ends would be showing. Glue and KD fittings finished the whole job which was carefully squared up.

Shopping list
8 cubes well seasoned oak
8 sheets 8ft × 4ft white laminated chipboard
29 solid brass handles
20 pairs flush hinges
24 sq ft laminated leather finish worktop
19 sq yds ceramic wall and floor tiles stainless steel sink, taps and fittings, oven and hob units, light fittings and fan, stain, polish, paint, screws and glues.

Method
Read and carefully study Kity plan sheets on kitchen layout and construction details eg joints, rebates and mouldings. Plan carefully and make the fullest use of Kity machinery.

The units now have solid oak doors on one side and leaded glass doors on the other. The solid oak doors were all made using the spindle moulder and framed with separate fielded panels. The fielding is a 1½in. × ¼in. rebate with a mould. Top door rails were serpentined. The framing is 2½in. × 1in. with a roman ogee mould (one of the extras bought for the K5). To gain the required effect it was necessary to groove out ¾in. × ⅜in. around the frame to take the fielded panels before gluing up.

Barrie used the Kity *Cottage kitchen* plans to design his solid oak drawers. All worktop edgings and corners were laminated.

To complete his oak kitchen Barrie gave an aged effect to his ⅜in. softwood beamed ceiling, using various techniques including

a water stain, rubbing down and shellac sanding sealer. Lacquer and brown wax completed the job. All the tiling in the kitchens is in an oak framework for which the spindle moulder was an ideal machine. Barrie appears 'hooked' on that accessory, he has made new architraves, skirting boards and cornices plus mouldings and pelmets.

The kitchen, completed on the closing day of the competition, cost in all about £2 000 to construct, it is estimated to be worth over £5 000. The overall effect is now warm and welcoming as the photograph shows.

Lynne is still waiting for the coffee table she had asked for when Barrie started on the kitchen.

Above: a view of the Goddards' kitchen. Below: Barrie using the K5 in his garage.

THE MOST EXCITING NEW HOBBY EVENT THE MIDLANDS HAS YET SEEN

Whatever your hobby interest, make a note in your diary now to visit the Midlands' own new modelling and craft exhibition.

Jointly staged by the Royal Agricultural Society of England and Model & Allied Publications Ltd, this great weekend show will demonstrate the best of what Midland hobby and crafts people can achieve. Each of the seven exhibition halls will concentrate on different aspects of skilled hobbies. In one hall woodworking and model engineering, in the next model railways, boats and aeroplanes and in three other halls, gem crafts

and crafts. A packed programme of lectures and films throughout the weekend will stimulate and inform.

Our of doors there will be live steam tracks, model cars and boats in action and all types of model flying.

Crafts clubs will be exhibiting and there will be many woodworking demonstrations and lectures.

Whatever your hobby interest you are going to enjoy your day out with your family and friends. Car parking is free, there are full catering and snack facilities.

Adults £2.00
Children and OAP's £1.00
Car Parking Free

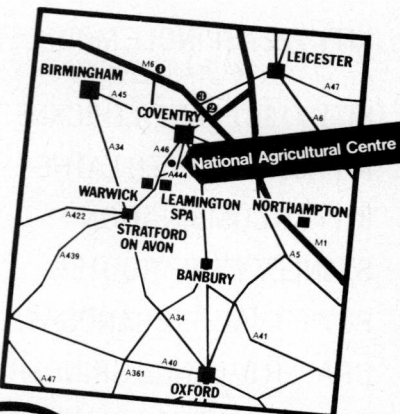

Gemcraft

Woodworking

Modelling

Flying Helicopters

Woodworking Displays

1982

MODEL CRAFT & COUNTRY SHOW

Model Boats outdoors

General Crafts & Equipment

Flying Models outdoors

Home Craft & Country pursuits

Model Engineering

SAT·SUN MAY 22/23
STONELEIGH, KENILWORTH

10 am - 6 pm
Each day

JOINT ORGANISERS

ROYAL AGRICULTURAL SOCIETY OF ENGLAND
NAC Stoneleigh, Nr. Kenilworth, Warwickshire CV8 2LZ Tel: Royal Show (0203) 565100

Model & Allied Publications
P.O. Box 35 Hemel Hempstead, Herts HP1 1EE Tel: Hemel Hempstead (0442) 41221

Prices quoted are those prevailing at press date and are
subject to alteration due to economic conditions.

BEFORE

by Richard J. Webber

Scarcity of good-quality furniture is helping to make people realise that restoration is a viable proposition when the cost is equated with current prices.

This is the view of John Harrap from Ludgershall, Wilts, who specialises in restoration and repair of period and fine pieces. A recent commission is shown in the before-and-after pictures here of an 18th century chair. Extensive work had to be done to the crest and back and to interpret the missing pieces was a fair test of Mr Harrap's skills.

Work comes to him by personal recommendation and though his speciality is furniture he undertakes other jobs; for example billiard tables and, on the 'small side', he once turned a set of chessmen for a dolls house. If a piece is considered too far gone for restoration he is perfectly honest with the customer and refuses the commission. Generally speaking, though, he finds he has the capability and the capacity to undertake most jobs.

It was during the 1950s while working in local woodland that he gained appreciation of what was to become his primary raw material. To complement this he attended Southampton and Newbury art colleges classes on art appreciation. He has built-up an extensive library of reference titles on design, art and antiques. This is necessary because there are problems when trying to interpret a missing part.

Matching and authenticity are very important and on occasions it has been necessary to 'home-make' nails to match the originals.

What started as Mr Harrap's hobby has now developed into a full-time business.

The work of John Harrap photographed by Peter R. Beadle

AND AFTER THE RESTORATION

WORKSHEET 10 NEW SERIES

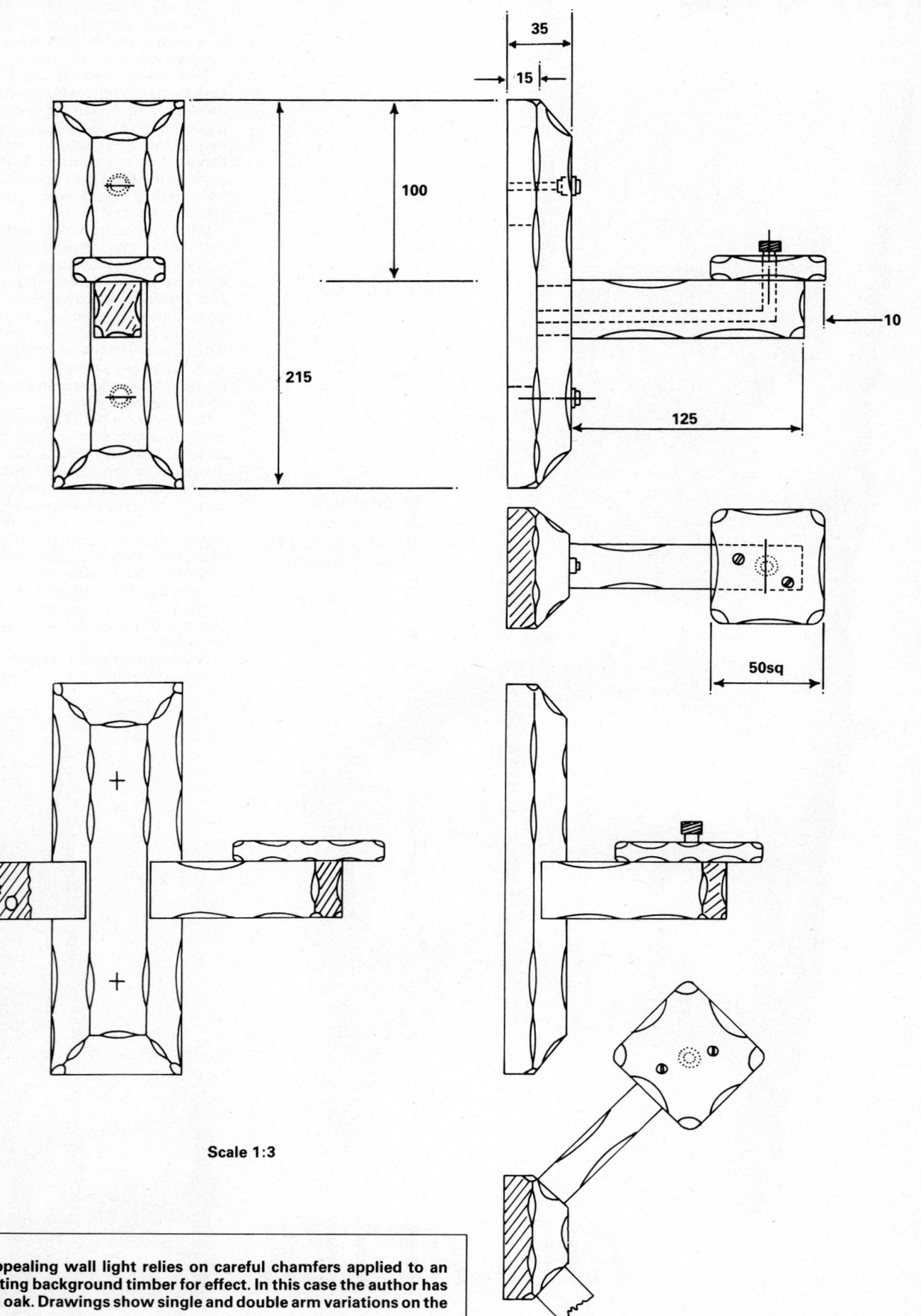

Scale 1:3

This appealing wall light relies on careful chamfers applied to an interesting background timber for effect. In this case the author has chosen oak. Drawings show single and double arm variations on the theme.

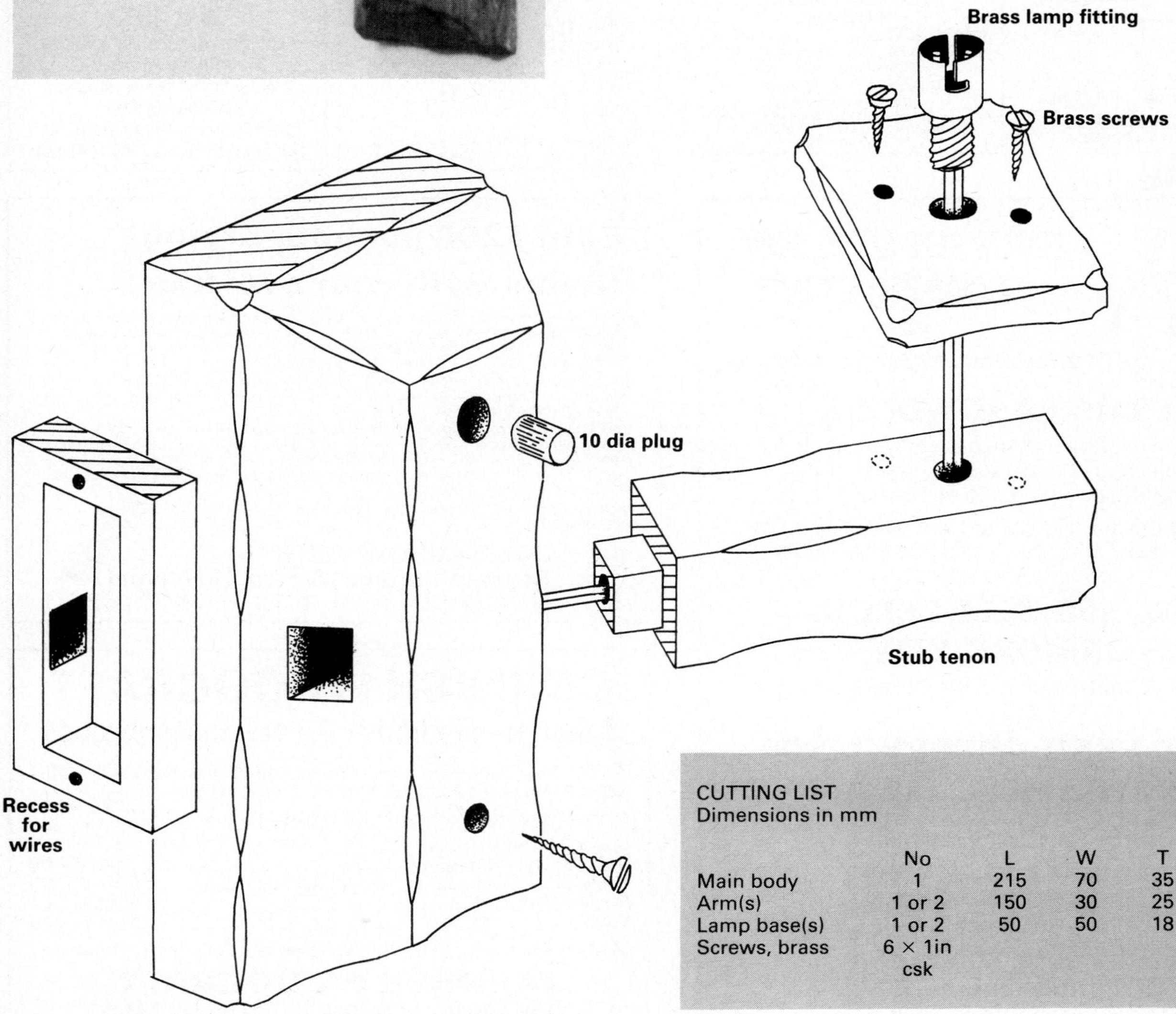

Brass lamp fitting

Brass screws

10 dia plug

Stub tenon

Recess for wires

CUTTING LIST Dimensions in mm					
	No	L	W	T	Material
Main body	1	215	70	35	Oak
Arm(s)	1 or 2	150	30	25	Oak
Lamp base(s)	1 or 2	50	50	18	Oak
Screws, brass	6 × 1in csk				

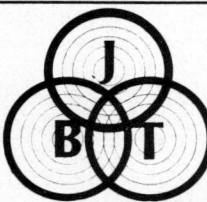
Prices quoted are those prevailing at press date and are subject to alteration due to economic conditions.

Wood Suppliers

Especially aimed at the readers who require to buy and sell timber and allied materials. Make sure you reach the market.

Let Woodworker Wood Suppliers section work for you. Sizes available — Full Page £300. Half Page £160. Quarter Page £88. Eighth Page £50. Classified — Semi Display £4.00 per single column cm (Minimum £10.00). Lineage rate 20p per word (Minimum £3.00). Box Number £1.25 extra

For further details give Valerie Tester a ring on (0442) 41221 Ext. 266.

British Hardwoods

Kiln Dried—Air Dried—Fresh Sawn

Specialising in Kiln Dried Oak

Sawn to size and delivery arranged

For details and quotations apply to:

R.E. & R. Duffield & Sons Ltd.,

**The Boathouse, River View Road,
Ripon, N. YORKS.
Tel: (0765) 3667**

or our Sales Depot at:

**The Old Creamery, Currock Road,
CARLISLE. Tel: (0228) 46478**

YORKSHIRE HARDWOODS

KILN DRIED HARDWOOD FOR CRAFTSMEN

We specialize in English Oak and can supply anything from long waney edged boards up to 36" wide to small turning blanks. We will cut and machine to your exact requirements

**Yorkshire Hardwoods Limited
Pocklington Grange,
Bielby Lane, Pocklington, York YO4 2NT**

Pocklington
075 92-2870

GREEN TIMBER CONVERTED ON SITE

Timber felled, kilning facilities available, green timber for sale. Countrywide service.

Telephone: Shrewsbury (0743) 66702

ENGLISH HARDWOODS

Oak, Ash, Sycamore, Beech etc. Air & Kiln dried
All sizes in stock
**HOGHTON TIMBER
HIGHER WALTON TRADING ESTATE
PRESTON, LANCS.
Tel: Preston 36193**

THE COMPLETE VENEER SERVICE

Offers 60 fine veneers for D.I.Y. restoration, marquetry to customer requirements; advisory, quotation, matching facilities; chess boards, project ideas. **Catalogue** 3 × 14p stamps to:
**I. & R. E. HENDERSON, Seahouses, Northumberland. Tel: 0665 720324.
SUPPLIERS OVERSEAS.
CATALOGUE: £1 International Money Order.**

VENEERS, inlay bandings, stringing and marquetry panels. Large selection. *Mail order and callers welcome. S.A.E. for list.*
**R. AARONSON (VENEERS) LTD
45 Redchurch St., London E2.
Tel: 01-739 3107**

TIMBER

cut to your requirements

We cut and prepare to your cutting list

TEAK, OAK, ROSEWOOD, MAHOGANY, BEECH, BOXWOOD, etc. —VENEERS and PLYWOODS

We carry large stocks of dry hardwoods for cabinet and joinery trade. Turning done to your drawing. Brassware and cabinet fittings available.

**Open all day Saturday — early closing Thursday.
Send S.A.E. with your cutting list for quote.**

GENERAL WOODWORK SUPPLIES

Dept. W.W., 76-80 STOKE NEWINGTON HIGH STREET, LONDON N16_____ Phone: 01-254 6052

ENGLISH TIMBERS
SEASONED HOMEGROWN AND IMPORTED HARDWOODS FOR THE CRAFTSMAN.
Please Contact:
P. Smith, Furniture Maker,
The Old Chapel,
Kirkburn,
Driffield.
E. Yorks.

Tel: 0377 89301

**To:
Valerie Tester, Woodworker,
PO Box 35, Bridge Street,
Hemel Hempstead,
HP1 1EE**

*PLEASE NOTE
On lineage advertisements, copy to be submitted (pre-paid) with this form.*

Full page £300 ☐ Half page £160 ☐ Quarter page £88 ☐ Eighth page £50 ☐
Semi-display £4.00 per single column cm (minimum £10.00)   Lineage rate 20p per word (minimum £3.00)   Series discounts available on request.
No. of insertions_____ Name_____
Address_____
Semi-display size_____cms_____   Tel. No._____

Woodworker, March 1982   KINDLY MENTION 'WOODWORKER' WHEN REPLYING TO ADVERTISEMENTS   193

THE WORLD'S TIMBER TREES

In no. 24 of this series (January 1982) C.W. Bond FIWSc, described the original Cuban or 'Spanish' mahogany which brought a new era to furniture making. This month he completes the study of the Meliaceae by describing one of the lesser known members of the mahogany family, avodiré, which is white and more familiar in veneer form, frequently sold as 'avodiré curls'.

AVODIRÉ: 25

Turraeanthus spp. Meliaceae *Turraeanthus* — having a flower like *Turraea,* of the same family. *Turraea* being named in honour of Giorgio della Turra 1607-1688, professor of botany at Padua university.

This timber is from a tree which is considerably smaller than the mahoganies and sometimes of rather poor shape, so that large size straight-grained boards are not generally available. It is very similar in texture and hardness to mahogany but is very white indeed when freshly cut. This whiteness, however, quickly becomes off-white on exposure and eventually turns to a pale but quite definite yellow.

The grain is often wavy and good quality veneers which are easy to handle are produced, the most striking type of figure from this wood being that of 'curls' which are effective in panelling, either singly or as quartered designs. These curls have a somewhat translucent quality. In this form it may be most frequently met commercially. The wood, should it be encountered, can be recommended for artistic work both in the solid and as veneer it being exceptionally clean and pleasant to work.

The photomicrograph shows a very regular structure. The tree is very beautiful with its compound leaves of fifteen to twenty pairs of leaflets and panicles of flowers up to three feet long.

Among the many timbers of the Meliaceae are Australian mahogany *Dysoxylum fraserianum*, toon *Cedrela toona* and tiama or gedu nohor *Entandrophragma angolense*. These apart from tiama are unlikely to be met commercially but are important locally in the countries of

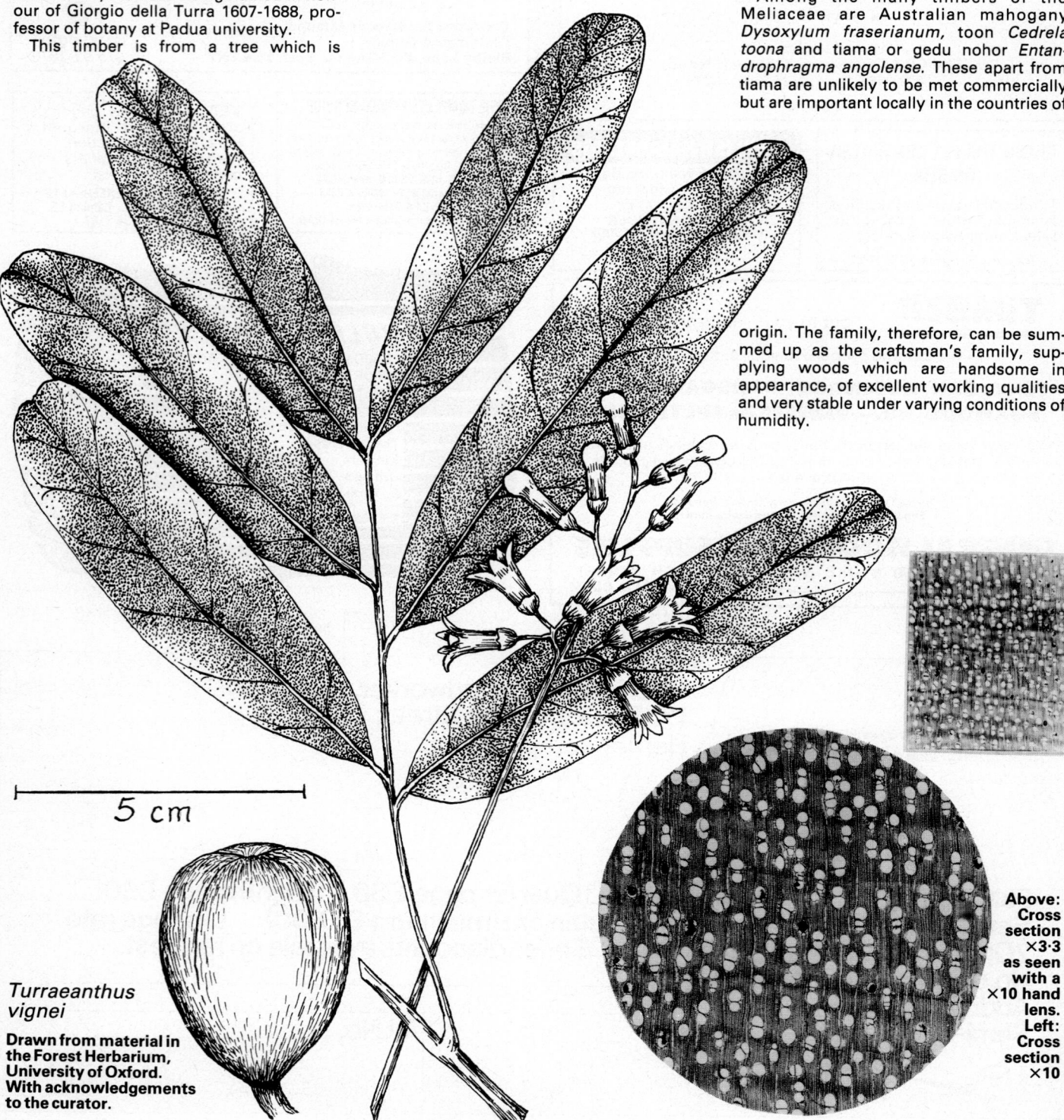

origin. The family, therefore, can be summed up as the craftsman's family, supplying woods which are handsome in appearance, of excellent working qualities and very stable under varying conditions of humidity.

5 cm

Turraeanthus vignei

Drawn from material in the Forest Herbarium, University of Oxford. With acknowledgements to the curator.

Above: Cross section ×3·3 as seen with a ×10 hand lens. Left: Cross section ×10

194

SURFACES

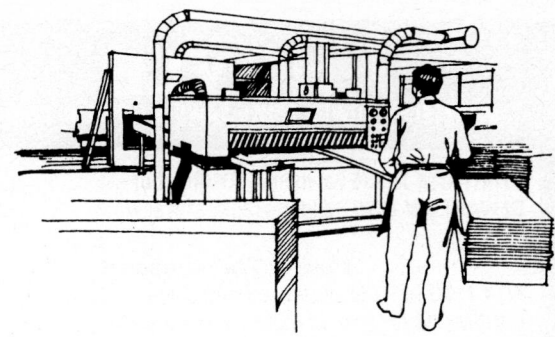

Use of pigments, colour staining and treatments to enhance the decorative value of woods and composition boards.

A small exhibition was recently held at the Royal College of Art showing the results of three years' work recently completed by two of the college's research fellows Sarah Bungey and Steve Mantej.

Their research was sponsored by the Worshipful Company of Furniture Makers and the Worshipful Company of Painter-Stainers. It produced a number of important aspects for the furniture industry to consider. The project commenced on 21 March 1978 and had the following aims: to instigate a research programme in the use of pigments, colour staining and treatments to enhance the decorative value of woods and composition boards. 'The project arose because of the conviction of Professors Heritage and Nicholson that the decorative surface value of woods, composition boards and surfaces are of high importance in product value, are underdeveloped industrially and that some dedicated work should be carried out into some of their possibilities.

Being a part-time research project and of short duration the main object was not to carry out an information research into say the Building and Decorating Industries and the Furniture Industries but to act practically and creatively to see what could be achieved. The subject extends into wide areas of application and could be conceived as including all surfaces natural or manmade which are used by man in his environment and his products.

It is thought that the use of composition board will be with us for ever as a substitute for wood. While there is considerable research in progress into the physical properties and application of boards, there is relatively no enquiry being undertaken into the visual and tactile appearance of the surface. Yet the aesthetic value of a surface is of major importance, affecting its acceptance by the consumer. Normal thinking so far has followed the obvious idea of covering the board with laminated skins. Other alternatives are relatively unexplored.

Sarah Bungey MA (RCA) is a member of the textile school at the RCA and she concentrated her studies on 1 the use of lasers for the decoration of wood in conjunction with Pyroform Ltd 2 the use of colour and staining in conjunction with tooling effects and 3 the use of upholstery as both a functional and decorative part of furniture.

Steve Mantej MDes RCA, is in the furniture school and his brief covered 1 instant inlay techniques 2 cutting-back technique using water-based vinyl paints and 3 sand blasting. In the examples of sand blasting on show the various wood grains were picked out and the various laminations of the timber exposed to differing degrees giving some very pleasing and unique effects. Various lacquers were applied to boards, oak and teak veneered plywoods were coloured with pva and then hand sanded to give differing effects.

Approximately 100 sample finishes were shown produced by Sarah and Steve (with the help of Aideen Sturgeon, Nancy Nicholson and Jane Kelvey) in two sizes . . . small

Badge of the Worshipful Company of Furniture Makers.

5 × 5in. panels to illustrate techniques and larger 12 × 18in. panels developing the designs and indicating their use in furniture and panelling. Many of Steve's designs were also on show to illustrate the various techniques and these included a wooden frame screen in coloured lacquer, a gate leg dining table in pine with sandblasted decoration, various decorated wall shelves and stools (designed by Steve, made by Ercol Furniture). A display of wallhide designed by Adrian Emck and work produced by Pyroform showing laser cutting of decoration was also on show.

The Worshipful Company of Furniture Makers offers a selection of scholarships, prizes and awards each year, for the advancement of the British Furniture Industry. In 1981 the Master's prize was won by Nigel Piercy, graduate in business and management studies of Heriot-Watt university and Durham university business school, now a lecturer in business policy and marketing at UWIST, Cardiff. The thesis for the Master's prize was a study of export market strategy and pricing policies in medium-sized and smaller furniture producers, drawing on a recent survey carried out by the author.

WOODWORKER January 1982 p16 gave details of the manufacturing awards for 1981 — the Bowen award to I. M. Barker of Buckinghamshire College of Higher Education *to visit colleges training designers and craftsmen in Scandinavia.* Other awards in 1981 included the Wrighton scholarship to E. J. Kennedy of Younger Furniture Ltd *to examine veneering methods and machinery in Germany;* the Schreiber award to K. P. Leonard of London College of Furniture *to study the use of fibre re-inforced board materials in the USA* (see WOODWORKER October 1981 p659); and the Wood Brothers scholarship to R. J. Saunders of Restall, Brown & Clennel *to discuss recruitment and the training of apprentices at factories and colleges in the UK.*

P. CURDS

WHAT'S ON

Tecnoforest '82
The Pacific International Trade Fair in Lima will be organising a second Tecnoforest from 19-28 November.

Maker's eye
Fourteen leading craftsmen and women have selected a range of contemporary work to demonstrate the richness and diversity of British craft. The exhibition at the Crafts Council gallery, 12 Waterloo Place, London SW1Y 4AU has over 500 objects of contemporary design to give an insight into the quality and sheer fun of British craft. Admission charge 50p, new gallery opening hours Tuesday-Saturday

10.00-17.00, Thursday 10.00-19.00, Sunday 14.00-17.00 closed Mondays. *Maker's eye* is open until 28 March. A fully illustrated catalogue is available price £5.95 from the exhibition or £6.95 by post.

Model exhibition
Reading Society of Model Engineers will be staging another exhibition of models on Saturday/Sunday 3/4 April at the Hexagon, Civic Centre, Reading. The whole area is devoted to displays of working models and layouts, stationary engines, traction engines, aircraft, boats and cars with live steam. Entries from individuals and other societies are welcome. Contact the exhibition manager, A. B. Milne, 39 Springhill Rd, Goring on Thames, Reading RG8 0BY (phone: Goring 2949).

French trade exhibition for 1982
The two major trade fair centres in Paris are the Parc des Expositions, Porte de Versailles and the CNIT Palace, Rond-Point de la Defense, both served by the metro. This year's shows include International Games and Toys exhibition 13-19 February; International Woodworking Machinery and Wood Industry exhibition (EXPOBOIS) 18-23 March; International Exhibition of wallpapers, wallcoverings, furnishing textiles, nets and household linen (PARITEX) 22-26 April. Further details of these and all other French exhibitions can be obtained from French Trade Exhibitions, French Chamber of Commerce House, 54 Conduit St, London.

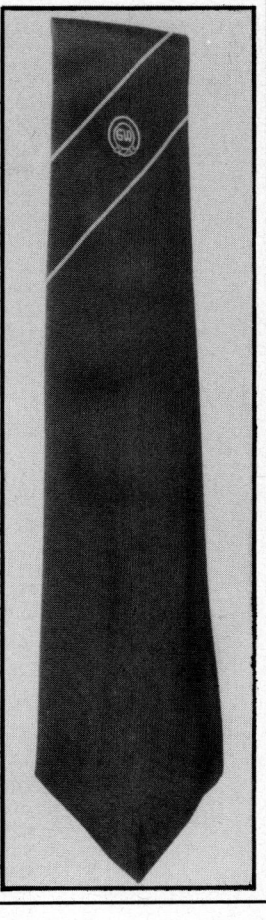

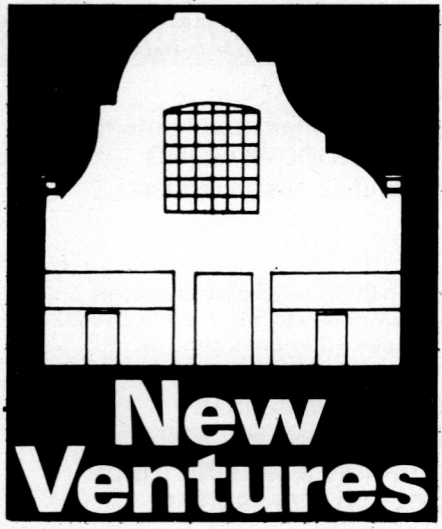

New Ventures

New to you

There is no doubting that throughout the country there is the need to consider very seriously the problems of the present recession and the consequences of unemployment and redundancy. There is whole hearted support for the concept that the future economic success of this country lies in the promotion and encouragement of small business ventures which by their future growth and employment requirements will help to reduce the numbers of unemployed.

In April 1981 Letchworth Garden City Corporation gave serious thought to just this situation and on 4 December 1981, the chairman of the corporation, Sidney Melman, officially opened *New Ventures*. This new workspace centre is based in previously unoccupied corporation property, once used as a body building plant and now designed as a series of small 'starter units'. Six new local businesses are in residence, all first-time users chosen from the 54 replies the corporation received in response to their initiative.

In most cases the applicants needed advice relating to the mechanics of starting in business, keeping records, sources of finance and provision of premises. 'In all appropriate cases,' said the chairman, 'the corporation acted as a confidence booster.' In all 20 people have been helped so far, 7 are still talking to the bank and 19 have been told 'don't do it'. Several old traditional crafts are in residence in the Glebe Rd premises. They include a book binder, potter, sign writer, joiner, picture framer, cabinet maker and small engineering firm.

Morgan Prints is the name given to a collection of limited edition pictures produced by the Letchworth artist, Brian Morgan. These are line and tone pictures of life in Victorian Britain inspired by photographs taken between 1870 and 1910 and as such are also historically accurate. All are elegantly framed. Morgan Prints also offer a general picture framing service and can cope with one off or quantity picture framing.

The beauty of the scheme devised by the corporation is that all the businesses pay a single weekly rent which covers the cost of all the facilities used so that all outgoings are consolidated into this single payment. The individual craftsmen and women are thus free from all the separate budgetting problems that normally beset a small business trying to get off the ground.

John Sandwell of Capability Kitchens has recently completed a local Skillcentre course in joinery and he is specialising in producing high-quality fitted kitchen units to individual requirements using a variety of hardwoods and composition boards.

On this page and opposite we show some of Graham Peterkin's exquisite cabinet-making. Left and below: details of his cabinet in English cherry with walnut handles. The fitted interior of the cabinet section is also in walnut. Opposite top and centre: details of his dining table. Top and underframe in sweet chestnut, legs in ash.

MORGAN PRINTS

Hitchin cabinet maker Graham Peterkin is another member of the group. He trained for two years at Parnham House, Dorset, under John Makepeace where he perfected his skills and learnt about setting up in business. He previously made wooden toys and billiard tables and now designs and makes to individual commissions of either domestic and/or office furniture. He aims to make a to a high standard in a variety of indigenous hardwoods especially for local clients thereby offering a much needed personal service. He had on display several of his excellent pieces including; a dining chair (seat and back rails in sweet chestnut, legs and underframe in ash), cabinet (English cherry with walnut handles and walnut inside top cabinet), miniature chest of drawers (in a variety of timbers including South American mahogany, teak, sycamore, rosewood and cedar), shove ha'penny board (in mahogany and sycamore) and a carved mirror in sweet chestnut plus a low brown oak table that split into three sections. Details of his cabinet and dining table are shown here.

The corporation had also gathered to the opening ceremony representatives of other craft businesses based elsewhere in Letchworth starter units or small premises. These included Uncle Ned's beds in oak, mahogany or pine (specialist in water beds) of Unit 10 Norton Hall Yard, Norton Road, Letchworth SG6 1AG; and Martin Groves (Spirella Building, Bridge Rd, Letchworth SG6 4EJ) who specialises in hand engraving and repair of glass.

The other businesses at New Ventures are Osprey Print Finishing, RAB Engineering and Letchworth Iceni Pottery. The workspace is at Glebe Rd, Letchworth SG6 1DS (phone Letchworth 2888).

Exhibition

Masterclass '82 sponsored by Roger's of Hitchin, organised by The White Knight Gallery of Cheltenham, brings together a series of lectures, demonstrations and exhibitions. Speakers include John Makepeace, Alan Peters, Mary Comino, Cecil Jordan, Brian Cohen, Robert Brett and Richard Maude. Demonstrations will be of carving, turning and musical instrument making. At the Sun Hotel, Hitchin, 14-17 April, 10am-6pm, details from Betty Norbury (0242) 38582.

Letters

From: R. R. Gillies, Weybridge, Surrey
Dear Sir

Readers may be interested in a solution to a problem I have always found somewhat vexing, ie the grinding of plane and chisel blades.

Over the years I have tried an electric grinder bench-mounted but find it is difficult to maintain a constant grinding angle; not to mention the associated heat and temper problems. The wet grinder is messy and arduous unless motorised. I now rely on a flat-bed sander fitted with an aluminium oxide belt.

I apply only gentle pressure when grinding the blades and easily obtain a flat, accurate bevel without the heat and temper problems arising. The required grinding angle is fairly easily judged by eye though if necessary a honing guide can be used.

Recently I tried making my own sanding belts. I bought a 5yd roll of 4in. wide belting — grit size of 120 seems about right. Split down the middle this provided enough 2in. wide belting to make 16 belts at a cost of just under 8p apiece.

Making the belts is straightforward. I find the length by measuring an old one. Alternatively you can run a tapemeasure round the driving wheels of the machine making due allowance for the spring-loaded tensioning adjustment.

I then mark-off the length required and cut the ends at an angle of 45° (Fig.1). To butt joint the ends together I use a 1in. wide strip of cotton fabric — curtain lining material is ideal; I avoid using man-made fabrics which might fail if heat is generated by friction.

I coat the back of the belt ends with Evostik woodworking adhesive and bring the angled ends closely together. I press the cotton fabric over the ends and cramp the joint between two blocks of wood, having first interleaved two scraps of polythene to prevent belt and fabric sticking to the wooden blocks. When the adhesive has set I fasten another strip of fabric over the first one but this time use a 1½in. wide strip so that there is a small overlap (Fig.2).

The result is a sound belt which stands up well in use. I have had no failures to date.

Yours faithfully, **R. R. Gillies**

From: Rev Fr D. K. Bonisch SM, 88 Hobson St, Wellington, New Zealand
Dear Sir,

I was a regular subscriber to WOODWORKER over a number of years. Ever since I was a youngster I have loved working in wood. I once dreamed of being a cabinetmaker but, instead, here I am a middle-aged Catholic priest who has managed to fit a certain amount of woodworking into a very busy life.

After a gap of some years I have come back to it again. For the most part I make children's toys and the pleasure that youngsters obviously get from them is wonderful to see.

I found much fascinating reading in WOODWORKER and have made many of the projects over the years. Some that come to mind are the jardiniere in the January 1964 issue; the needlework box of September 1962; and the occasional table of February 1961 which I did in Queensland maple with a mahogany veneered top.

I still see these and other pieces in the houses of the people I gave them to so they still give me pleasure. I especially enjoyed making the Elizabethan doll's house of December 1962 for a niece then 11 years old.

She has recently called for me to stay with her and her husband and put all things in order with it for her daughter! Indeed woodworking can be a joy for ever.

I have WOODWORKER almost complete and mostly in bound volumes from 1958 to 1969. Would any New Zealand reader like to make me an offer for these volumes? They are occupying rather too much space on my shelves now.

Yours faithfully, **D. K. Bonisch**

From: Richard Stanford, Brixham, Devon
Dear Sir

I was interested in B. P. Moor's 'Tips for timber buyers' on p464 of the July 1981 issue but would like to ask why timber cannot be sold to the nearest 100mm or even 10mm, instead of the present 300mm, with a view to reducing waste?

I can see only one advantage in having the metric system: the ease with which prices can be worked out on a calculator to any number of mm.

Time after time I have to buy 200mm plus more than I need, which has to be cut to waste; only a few of these small ends can be put to use. If all the short ends wasted in this country each day could be calculated I imagine the total would appal those who are concerned about our balance of imports and exports.

Next time you pass a new building nearing completion, cast your eye over the piles of ends of treated joists, rafters and other sections. Then ponder anew on the folly of mankind.

Yours faithfully, **Richard Stanford**

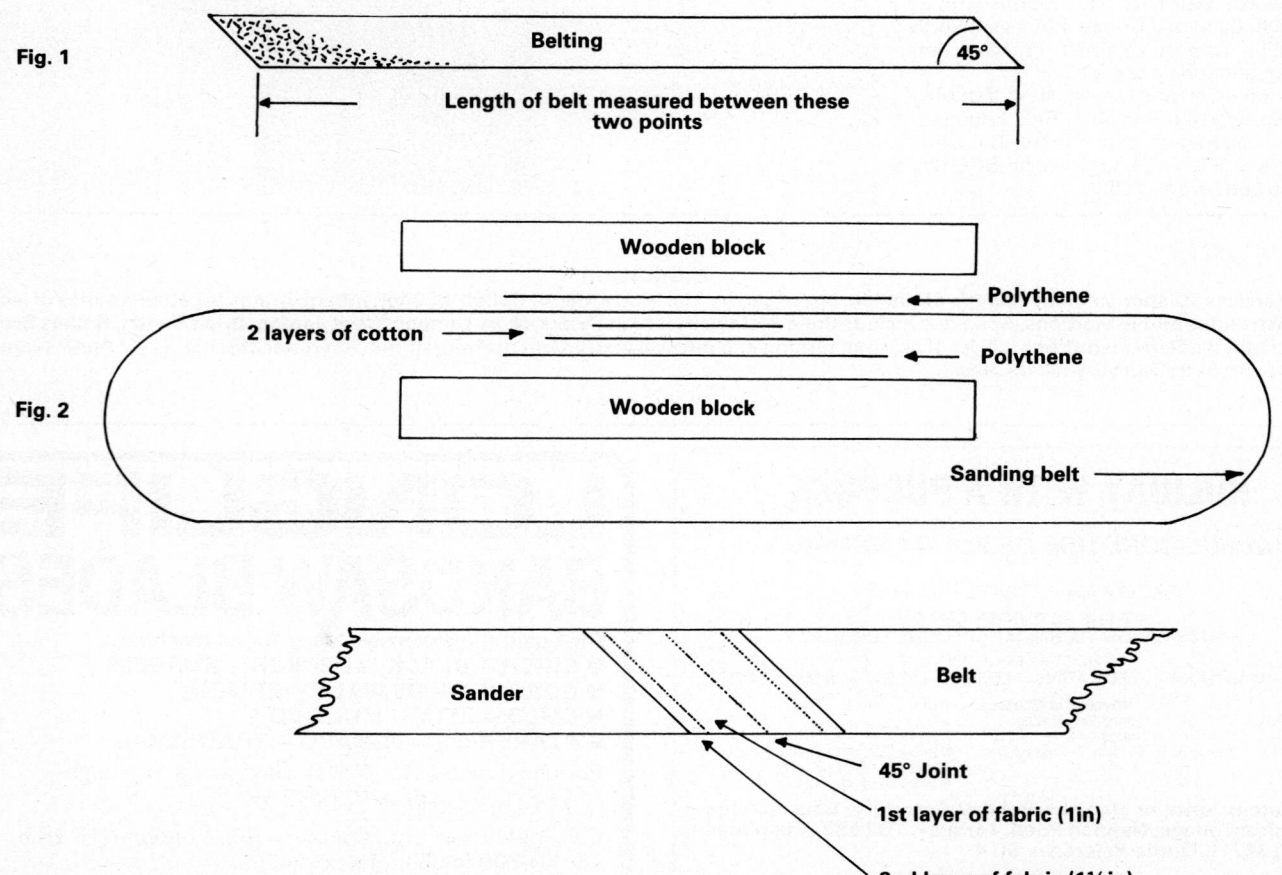

Fig. 1

Belting 45°

Length of belt measured between these two points

Fig. 2

Wooden block

Polythene

2 layers of cotton

Polythene

Wooden block

Sanding belt

Sander Belt

45° Joint

1st layer of fabric (1in)

2nd layer of fabric (1½in)

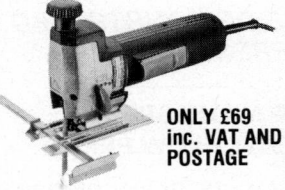
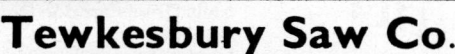

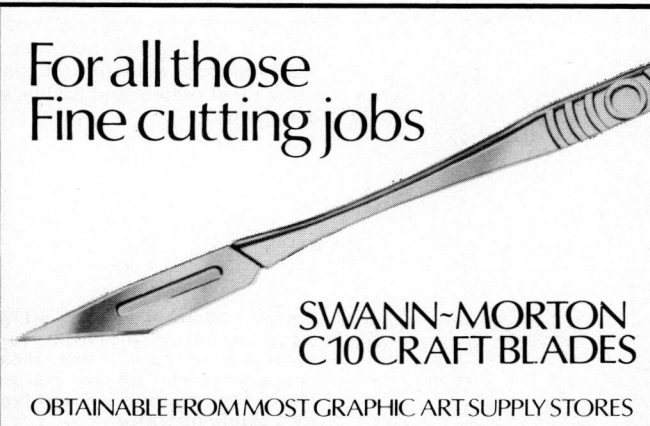

Edge banding machines

Stefani Spa of Italy is manufacturing a range of edge banding machines to the specification of Wadkin Ltd, Green Lane Works, Leicester LE5 4PF (0533 769111). The first two models — HFM and MTS — have been introduced to the UK market by Wadkin Agencies. Illustrated leaflets and specifications are available on application to Wadkin Agencies at the above address.

Briefly, model HFM is a single-sided universal edge bander for straight, circular and free-shaped panels up to 60mm thick. The machine is hand-fed by a single operative who uses the machine to completely band and edge-trim each workpiece in turn. PVC rollform strip, veneers or solid edging up to 5mm thick can be applied to a board edge, including a capability of bevelled edging up to 45° by use of the tiltable worktable.

Hot-melt is heated in a low-level table beneath the worktable and is delivered at the correct temperature to the edge of the workpiece through a spiral roller working within a confined tube arrangement. The correct amount of adhesive is metered automatically.

Model MTS is a larger and more sophisticated machine taking straight panels up to 50mm thick and handling edging materials up to 8mm thick. It is provided with an infeed guide with adjustable roller bar. This permits any sized panels to be worked from a minimum of 240 × 110mm, positive feeding being controlled by a wide rubber-coated bottom feed chain and adjustable top pressure rollers. End trimming is undertaken by an electrically-pneumatically controlled trimmer having twin-bladed saw and angled feed for final pass bevelling.

Wadkin states that it has found a need for single and double-sided machines using both standard hot-melts and PVAC cold adhesives, including post-forming and soft-forming techniques, and special machines such as a double-sider for lipping rebated doors.

Jigsaw

To its portable power tool range Wadkin has now added model JSE60 electronically-controlled orbital jigsaw. It weighs 2kg, is rated at 400W and

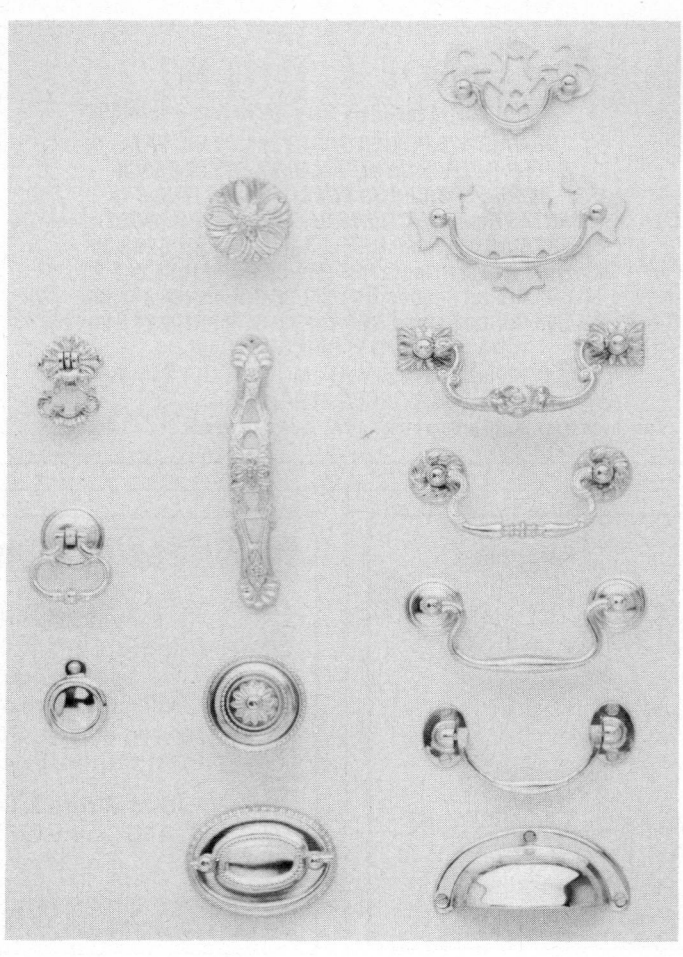

available for 240V or 110V operation. The speed control provides full torque and constant speed at any setting from 1000-2700 strokes/min. The orbiting mechanism has a four-position setting. A tilting base can be used for cutting bevels up to 45°. List price is given as £99 plus VAT.

Further details can be had from the portable power tool division of Wadkin which is at Trent Lane, Castle Donington, Derby DE7 2PU.

Cabinet furniture

Craftsmen in Brass is the range of solid brass cabinet handles and fittings from B. Lilly & Sons Ltd, Baltimore Road, Birmingham B42 1DJ (021-357 1761). Many of the designs are said to be reproduced from patterns used by the company when it was established in the jewellery quarter of Birmingham in 1861.

Details of the items are given in a colour leaflet which also lists dimensions (imperial and metric) and the finishes available. The furniture is sold through the usual retail outlets and builders merchants.

Below: Wadkin model HFM edge banding machine for straight, circular and free shaped panels up to 60mm thick. The machine is hand fed by a single operator.

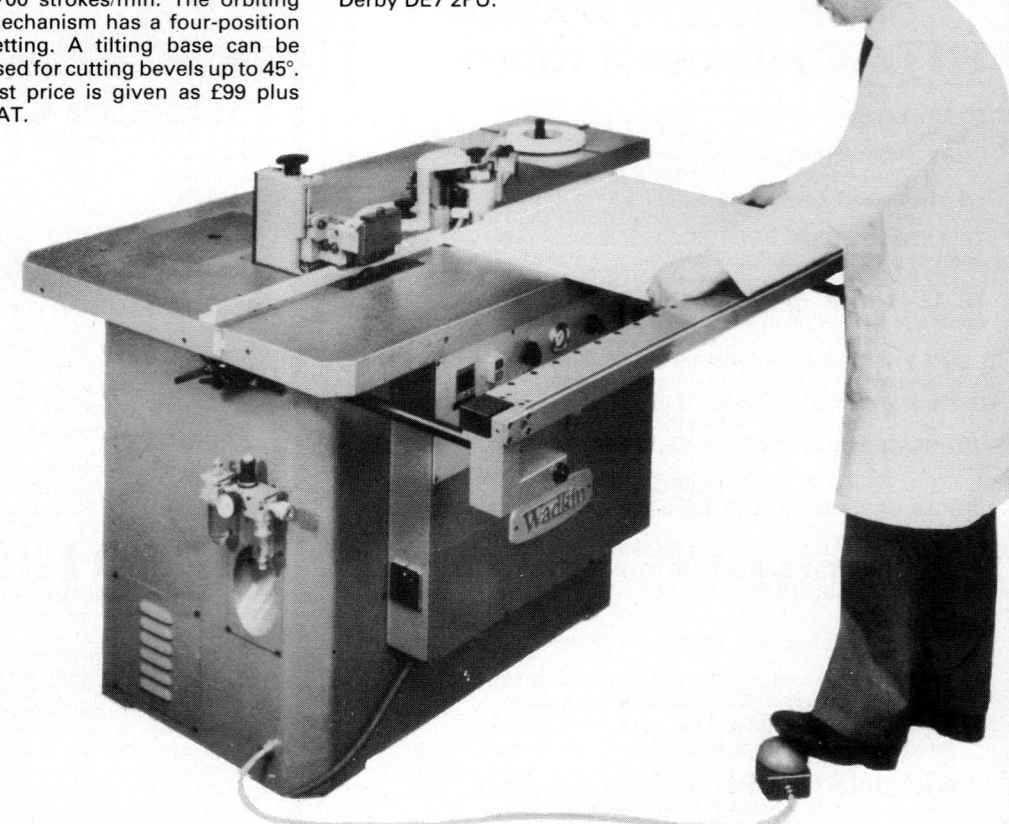

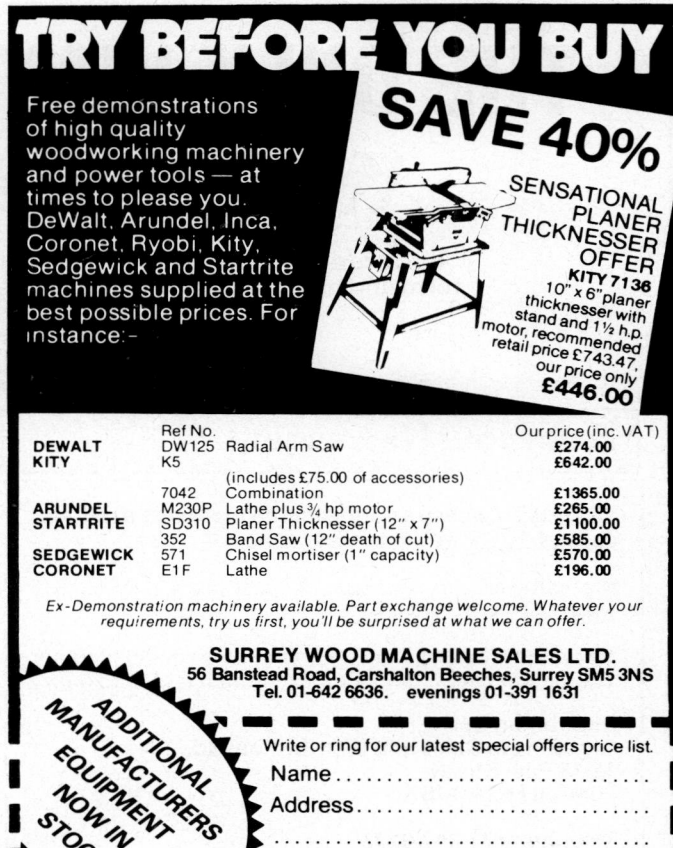
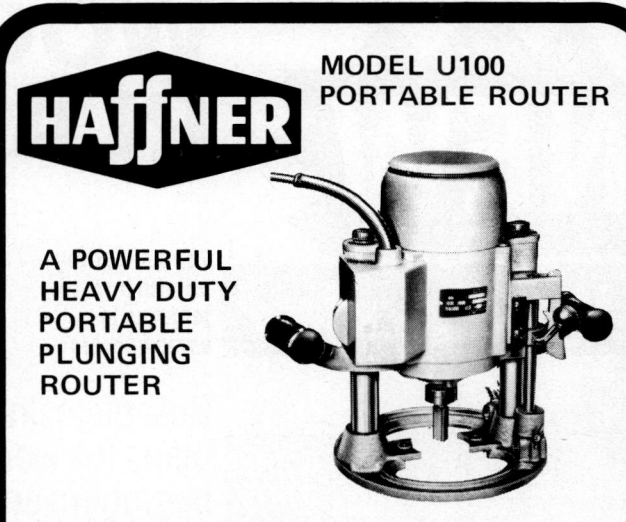

 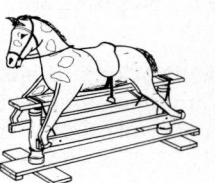  

AVON

BATH   Tel. Bath 64513
JOHN HALL TOOLS   ★
RAILWAY STREET

Open: Monday-Saturday
9.00 a.m.-5.30 p.m.
H.P.W.WM.D.A.BC.

BRISTOL   Tel. (0272) 311510
JOHN HALL TOOLS LIMITED   ★
CLIFTON DOWN SHOPPING
CENTRE, WHITELADIES ROAD
Open: Monday-Saturday
9.00 a.m.-5.30 p.m.
H.P.W.WM.D.A.BC.

BRISTOL   Tel. 0272-633844
ROBBINS LIMITED   ★
THE WOODWORKER SHOP
MERRYWOOD MILLS, BEDMINSTER
Open: Mon-Fri 8.00 a.m.-5.00 p.m.
Saturday 8.30 a.m.-12.30 p.m.
H.P.T.CS.A.BC.

BRISTOL   Tel. 0272-629092
TRYMWOOD SERVICES   ★
2a DOWNS PARK EAST, (off
North View) WESTBURY PARK
Open: 8.30 a.m.-5.30 p.m. Mon. to
Fri. Closed for lunch 1-2 p.m.
P.W.WM.D.T.A.BC.

BRISTOL   Tel. 0272-667013
V. H. WILLIS & CO. LTD   ★
190-192 WEST STREET,
BEDMINSTER
Open: Mon-Fri 8.30 a.m.-5 p.m.
Saturday 9 a.m.-1 p.m.
H.P.W.WM.D.CS.A.BC.

BERKSHIRE

READING   Tel. Littlewick Green
DAVID HUNT (TOOL   2743
MERCHANTS) LTD   ★
KNOWL HILL, NR. READING
Open: Monday-Saturday
9 a.m.-5.30 p.m.
H.P.W.D.A.BC.

READING   Tel. (0734) 586522
SARJENT'S TOOL STORES   ★
LTD.
44-52 OXFORD ROAD
Open: 8.30 a.m.-5.30 p.m.
Monday-Saturday
H.P.W.WM.D.A.BC.

BUCKINGHAMSHIRE

HIGH WYCOMBE   (0494) 22221
ISAAC LORD LTD
185 DESBOROUGH ROAD

Open: Mon-Fri 8.00 a.m.-5.00 p.m.
Saturday 8.00 a.m.-12.00 noon
H.P.W.D.A.

BUCKINGHAMSHIRE

MILTON KEYNES   Tel. 0908
A. POLLARD & SON   75221
LTD.
51 QUEENSWAY, BLETCHLEY
Open: 8.30 a.m.-5.30 p.m.
Monday-Saturday
H.P.W.WM.D.A.BC.

CAMBRIDGESHIRE

CAMBRIDGE   Tel. 0223-353091
H. B. WOODWORKING
69 LENSFIELD ROAD
Open: 8.30 a.m.-5.30 p.m.
Monday-Friday
8.30 a.m.-1.00 p.m. Sat
P.W.WM.D.CS.BC.

CHESHIRE

NANTWICH   Tel. Crewe 67010
ALAN HOLTHAM
THE OLD STORES TURNERY
WISTASON ROAD, WILLASTON
Open: Tues-Sat 9a.m.-5.30p.m.
Closed Monday
P.W.WM.D.T.C.CS.A.BC.

CLEVELAND

MIDDLESBROUGH   Tel. 0642-
WINTZ   460035/813650
INDUSTRIAL SUPPLIES   ★
2 BESSEMER COURT
GRANGETOWN
Open: Mon-Fri 8.30 a.m.-5 p.m.
H.P.W.D.A.

CORNWALL

HELSTON
SOUTH WEST
POWER TOOLS
Helston (03265) 4961
Truro (0872) 71671
Launceston (0566) 3555
H.P.W.WM.D.CS.A.

NEWQUAY   Tel. 063 73 2516
CONWAY SUPPLIES   ★
(NEWQUAY)
70 FORE STREET
Open: Mon-Fri 9 a.m.-5.30 p.m.
Sat 9 a.m.-12.30 p.m.
H.P.W.WM.D.A.BC.

ST. AUSTELL   Tel. (0726) 65922
TOOLSERV   ★
TRURO ROAD

Open: 8 a.m.-5.30 p.m.
6 days
H.P.W.WM.D.CS.A.BC.

DERBYSHIRE

BUXTON   Tel. 0298-871636
CRAFT SUPPLIES   ★
THE MILL
MILLERSDALE
Open: Mon-Fri 9 a.m.-5 p.m.
Saturday 9 a.m.-1 p.m.
H.P.W.D.T.CS.A.BC.

DEVON

AXMINSTER   Tel. 0297 33656
POWER TOOL CENTRE   ★
STYLES & BROWN
CHARD STREET
Open: 9.00 a.m.-5.30 p.m.
Monday-Saturday
H.P.W.WM.D.CS.A.BC.

EXETER   Tel. 0392 73936
WRIDES TOOL CENTRE
147 FORE STREET

Open: 9.00 a.m.-5.30 p.m.
Wednesday 9.00 a.m.-1.00 p.m.
H.P.W.WM.A.

PLYMOUTH   Tel. 0752 786633
STEENWISE S.W. LTD   ★
BURRINGTON WAY
HONICKNOWLE
Open: Monday-Friday
8.30 a.m.-5.00 p.m.
P.W.WM.D.

PLYMOUTH   Tel. 0752 330303
WESTWARD BUILDING SERVICES   ★
LTD., LISTER CLOSE, NEWNHAM
INDUSTRIAL ESTATE, PLYMPTON
Open: Mon-Fri 8 a.m.-5.30 p.m.
Sat 8.30 a.m.-12.30 p.m.
H.P.W.WM.D.A.BC.

PLYMOUTH   Tel. 0752-266179
JOHN WRIDE & CO (PLYMOUTH) LTD   ★
146 CORNWALL STREET
Open: Monday to Saturday
9.00a.m.-5.30p.m.
Wed 9.00a.m.-1.00p.m.
H.P.W.WM.A.

DORSET

BOURNEMOUTH   Tel: 0202
MACHINE SALES & SERVICES   527780
(BOURNEMOUTH) LTD   527781
56 STROUDEN ROAD   ★

Open: Mon-Fri 8.15 a.m.-5 p.m.
H.P.W.WM.D.A.

WEYMOUTH   Tel: (0305) 787396
WEYMOUTH TOOL CENTRE   ★
30A ABBOTSBURY ROAD

Open: Monday to Saturday
8 a.m.-5.30 p.m.
H.P.W.WM.D.A.BC

CO. DURHAM

BARNARD CASTLE   Tel: (0833)
WOODMEN   38442/31609
27 NEWGATE   ★

Open Monday-Saturday
9 a.m.-5.30 p.m.
P.W.WM.D.A.BC.

ESSEX

LEIGH ON SEA   Tel. (0702)
MARSHALL &   710404
PARSONS LTD
1111 LONDON ROAD
Open: 8.30 am-5.30 pm Mon-Fri.
9.00 am-5.00 om Sat.
H.P.W.WM.D.CS.A.

GLOUCESTERSHIRE

TEWKESBURY   Tel. 0684
TEWKESBURY SAW CO.   293092
LIMITED
TRADING ESTATE, NEWTOWN
Open: Mon-Fri 8.00 a.m.-5.00 p.m.
Saturday 9.30 a.m.-12.00 p.m.
P.W.WM.D.CS.

HAMPSHIRE

ALDERSHOT   Tel. 0252 28088
BURCH & HILLS LTD
BLACKWATER WAY TRADING
ESTATE
Open: Mon-Fri 8.30 a.m.-5.30 p.m.
Saturday 8.30 a.m.-12.00 p.m.
H.P.W.WM.D.A.BC.

PORTSMOUTH   Tel. 0705
EURO PRECISION TOOLS   67332
LTD   ★
259/263 London Road, North End
Open: Mon-Fri 9 a.m.-5.30 p.m.
Sat 9.00 a.m.-5.00 p.m.
H.P.W.WM.D.A.BC.

SOUTHAMPTON   Tel. 0703
H.W.M.   776222
THE WOODWORKERS   ★
303 SHIRLEY ROAD, SHIRLEY
Open: Tues-Fri 9.30 a.m.- 6 p.m.
Sat 9.30 a.m.-4.00 p.m.
H.P.W.WM.D.CS.A.BC.T.

HEREFORDSHIRE

HEREFORD   Tel. 0432 3018
PEN TOOLS (HEREFORD) LTD
24 EDGAR STREET

Open Mon.-Fri. 8 a.m.-5.30 p.m.
Sat. 8 a.m.-1 p.m.
H.P.W.D.C.A.

HERTFORDSHIRE

WATFORD   Tel. 0923 48434
HOME CARE CENTRE   ★
20 MARKET STREET
WATFORD, HERTS
Open 9.00 a.m.-5.30 p.m.
Mon.-Sat.
H.P.W.A.WM.BC.D.

WATFORD   Tel. 0923 26052
J. SIMBLE & SONS LTD   ★
76 QUEENS ROAD

Open 8.30 a.m.-5.30 p.m.
Mon.-Sat. Closed Wednesday
H.P.W.WM.D.A.BC.

Prices quoted are those prevailing at press date and are
subject to alteration due to economic conditions.

SHOP GUIDE SHOP GUIDE

HERTFORDSHIRE
WATFORD   Tel. (0923) 49911
TREND MACHINERY & CUTTING
TOOLS LTD
UNIT N, PENFOLD WORKS
IMPERIAL WAY
    Open: Mon-Fri 9 a.m.-5 p.m.
P.W.WM.D.CS.BC.

KENT
MATFIELD   Tel. Brenchley
LEISURECRAFT IN WOOD   (089272)
'ORMONDE', MAIDSTONE RD.   2465
TN12 7JG
    Open: Mon-Sun
     9 a.m.- 5.30 p.m.
W.WM.D.T.A.

LANCASHIRE
LANCASTER   Tel. 0524 2886
LILE TOOL SHOP
43/45 NORTH ROAD
   Open: Monday to Saturday
     9.00 a.m.-5.30 p.m.
    Wed 9.00 a.m.-12.30 p.m.
H.P.W.D.A.

LEICESTERSHIRE
COALVILLE   Tel. (0533) 415556
POOLE WOOD MACHINERY   (06077)
SERVICES LIMITED,   5777
4 SWALLOW DALE
THRINGSTONE
    Open: Mon-Fri 9 a.m.-5 p.m.
H.P.W.WM.D.A.BC.

LEICESTER   Tel. 0455 43254
ROY STARTIN LTD
134 WOOD STREET
EARL SHILTON
    Open: Mon-Fri 8 a.m.-5.30 p.m.
     Saturday 8.00 a.m.-1.30 p.m.
H.P.W.WM.D.T.A.

LINCOLNSHIRE
LINCOLN   Tel. 0522 36168/9
R & S TOOLS (LINCOLN)
LIMITED
BEEVER STREET LN6 7AD
    Open: Mon-Fri 8.30 a.m.-5 p.m.
     Sat 9.00 p.m.-12.00 p.m.
H.P.W.WM.D.CS.A.BC.

LINCOLN   Tel. 0522 30199/
WOODWISE LIMITED   39871 or
121 HIGH STREET   0522 68428
    & 06077 5777/5288
    (after hours) ★
    Open: Mon-Sat 9 a.m.-5.30 p.m.
P.W.WM.D.A.BC.

LONDON
ACTON   Tel. 01-992 4835
A MILLS (ACTON) LTD   ★
32/36 CHURCHFIELD ROAD
W3 6ED
    Open: Mon-Fri 9.00 a.m.-5.00 p.m.
     Closed Saturday
H.P.W.WM.

HANWELL   Tel. 01-567 2922
G. D. CLEGG & SONS
83 Uxbridge Road, W7 3ST
    Open: Monday to Friday
     9.00 a.m.-6.00 p.m.
    Saturday 9.00 a.m.-5.30 p.m.
H.P.W.WM.D.

LONDON
LONDON   Tel. 01-636 7475
BUCK & RYAN LIMITED   ★
101 TOTTENHAM COURT ROAD
W1P 0DY
    Open: Mon-Fri 8.30 a.m.-5.30 p.m.
    Saturday 8.30 a.m.-1.00 p.m.
H.P.W.WM.D.A.

LONDON   Tel. 01-739 7126
CECIL W. TYZACK   ★
79-81 KINGSLAND ROAD
SHOREDITCH
    Open: Mon-Fri 8.45 a.m.-5.15 p.m.
     Saturday 9 a.m.-12 noon
H.P.W.WM.D.A.BC.

NORBURY   Tel: 01-679 6193
HERON TOOLS & HARDWARE LTD
437 STREATHAM HIGH ROAD
S.W.16
    Open: Mon-Sat 8.30 a.m. - 6 p.m.
     Wednesday 8.30 a.m. - 1 p.m.
H.P.W.A.

WOOLWICH   Tel. 01-854 7767/8
A. D. SKILLMAN & SONS LTD
108-109 WOOLWICH HIGH ST
SE18 6DW
    Open: Mon-Sat 8.30 a.m.-to 5.30 p.m.
     Half Day Thursday
H.P.W.CS.A.

MERSEYSIDE
LIVERPOOL   Tel. 051-263 1359
TAYLOR BROS (LIVERPOOL) LTD
5/9 PRESCOTT STREET
    Open: Monday to Friday
     8.30 a.m.-5.30 p.m.
H.P.W.WM.D.A.BC.

MIDDLESEX
HARROW   Tel. 01-863 9462
ALLIED HARDWARE   ★
219 STATION ROAD
    Open: Monday-Saturday
     9.00 a.m.-6.00 p.m.
H.P.A.

NORTH HARROW   Tel. 01-863 2492
WILLIAMS TECHNICAL SERVICES   ★
36 STATION ROAD
    Open: Mon-Fri 8 a.m.-5.30 p.m.
     Wed 8 a.m.-1 p.m.,
     Sat 9 a.m.-5.30 p.m.
H.P.W.WM.D.A.

NORFOLK
NORWICH   Tel. 0603 898695
NORFOLK SAW SERVICES
DOG LAND, HORSFORD
    Open: Monday to Friday
     8.00 a.m.-5.00 p.m.
    Saturday 8.00 a.m.-12.00 p.m.
H.P.W.WM.D.CS.A.

NORWICH   Tel. 0603 400933
WESTGATES WOODWORKING   Tx.
MACHINERY, JUPITER ROAD   975412
OFF MILE CROSS LANE
    Open: 9 a.m.-5 p.m. weekdays
     9 a.m.-12 a.m. Sat.
P.W.WM.D.

NORTHAMPTONSHIRE
RUSHDEN   Tel. 093-34 56424
PETER CRISP LIMITED   ★
7 HIGH STREET
    Open: Monday to Saturday
     8.30 a.m.-5.30 p.m.
    Thursday 8.30 a.m.-1.00 p.m.
H.P.W.D.BC.

NORTHUMBERLAND
BLYTH   Tel. (06706) 69279
ALLAN McNAIR WOODCRAFT   ★
69-71 PLESSEY ROAD
    Open: Monday to Saturday
     9 a.m.-5 p.m.
H.W.WM.D.T.CS.A.BC.

NOTTINGHAMSHIRE
NOTTINGHAM   Tel. (0602) 225979
POOLEWOOD   (06077) 5777
EQUIPMENT LTD
5a HOLLY LANE, CHILLWELL
    Open: Mon-Fri 9 a.m.-5.30 p.m.
     Sat. 9 a.m. to 12.30 p.m.
P.W.WM.D.CS.A.BC.

NOTTINGHAM   Tel. 0602 811889
THE WOODCUTTER
5 TUDOR SQUARE
WEST BRIDGFORD
    Open: Tues-Sat 9 a.m.-5.30 p.m.
    Fri 9 a.m.-7.30 p.m. Closed Mon.
H.P.W.WM.D.T.CS.A.

OXFORDSHIRE
BICESTER   Tel. (08692) 4156/
WOODMEN   3218/3219
104 CHURCHILL ROAD
    Open: Monday-Saturday
     9 a.m.-5.30 p.m.
P.W.WM.D.A.BC.

OXFORD   Tel. (0865) 45118/9
SARJENT'S TOOL   ★
STORES LTD
150 COWLEY ROAD
    Open: Monday to Saturday
     8.30 a.m.-5.30 p.m.
H.P.W.WM.D.A.BC.

STAFFORDSHIRE
TAMWORTH   Tel. 0827-56188
MATTHEWS BROTHERS LTD
KETTLEBROOK ROAD
    Open: Mon.-Sat. 8.30am-6.00pm
    Demonstrations Sunday mornings
     by appointment only
H.P.WM.D.T.CS.A.BC.

SUFFOLK
BURY ST. EDMUNDS   Tel.
TOOLS & THINGS   0284 62022
21 CHURCHGATE   ★
    Open: Monday to Saturday
     9.00 a.m.-5.30 p.m.
H.P.W.WM.D.A.BC.

IPSWICH   Tel. 0473 86216
FOX WOODWORKING   ★
'STEBBINGS' BACK LANE
WASHBROOK
    Open: Tues. Fri. 9.00am-5.30pm
     Sat. 9.00am-12 noon
H.P.W.WM.D.A.B.C.

SURREY
CARSHALTON BEECHES   Tel.
SURREY WOOD   01-642 6636
MACHINE SALES LTD   ★
56A BANSTEAD ROAD
    Open: Tues-Fri 9.30 am-6.00 pm
     Saturday 9.30 am-2.00 pm
P.W.WM.D.BC.CS.

CROYDON   Tel. 01-688 5513
L. H. TURTLE LTD   ★
6-12 PARK STREET
    Open: Monday to Saturday
     8.30 a.m.-5.30 p.m.
H.P.W.WM.D.A.

GUILDFORD   Tel. 0483 61125
MESSINGERS FOR TOOLS
14-18 CHERTSEY STREET
    Open: Tuesday to Saturday
     8.30 a.m.-5.30 p.m.
     Closed all day Monday
H.P.W.D.BC.

SUSSEX
BOGNOR REGIS   Tel: (0243) 863100
A. OLBY & SON (BOGNOR REGIS LTD)
"TOOLSHOP", BUILDER'S MERCHANT
HAWTHORN ROAD
    Open: Mon-Thurs 8 a.m.-5.15 p.m.
    Fri 8 a.m.-8 p.m. Sat 8 a.m.-12.45 p.m.
H.P.W.WM.D.T.C.A.BC.

WORTHING   Tel. 0903 38739
W. HOSKING (TOOLS &
MACHINERY)
96a MONTAGUE STREET
    Open: Mon-Sat 8.30am-5.30pm
     Wednesday 8.30am-1.00pm
H.P.W.WM.D.CS.A.BC.

WEST MIDLANDS
WEST BROMWICH   Tel: 021-
CONWAY SAW &   533 5461/2
SUPPLY LTD   ★
SWAN LANE
    Open: 8 a.m.-6 p.m. Mon-Fri
     9 a.m.-1 p.m. Saturday
P.W.WM.D.CS.BC.

WILTSHIRE
SWINDON   Tel. (0793) 31361
SARJENT'S TOOL STORES LTD   ★
64 FLEET STREET
    Open: Monday to Saturday
     8.30 a.m.-5.30 p.m.
H.P.W.WM.D.A.BC

YORKSHIRE
BRADFORD   Tel. 0274 560699
STEENWISE LIMITED   ★
LIMEFIELD MILL,
WOOD STREET, CROSSFLATS
BINGLEY
    Open: Mon to Fri 9 a.m.-5 p.m.
H.P.W.WM.D.T.CS.A.BC.

HALIFAX   Tel. 0422 884075/
TIMBERLITE LTD   884788/33575
VICTORIA BUILDINGS   ★
LUDDENDEN FOOT
    Open: Monday to Friday
    Saturday 9.00 a.m.-5.00 p.m.
H.P.W.WM.D.CS.A.BC.

SHOP GUIDE SHOP GUIDE

YORKSHIRE

HARROGATE   Tel. 0423 66245/
MULTI-TOOLS   55328 ★
158 KINGS ROAD

Open: Monday to Saturday
8.30 a.m.-6.00 p.m.
H.P.W.WM.D.A.BC.

HUDDERSFIELD   Tel. (0484)
NEVILLE M. OLDHAM   641219/(0484)
UNIT 1 DAYLE ST. WORKS   42777
DAYLE STREET, LONGWOOD   ★
Open: Mon-Fri 9.00am- 5.30pm
Saturday 9.30am-12.00pm
P.W.WM.D.A.BC.

LEEDS   Tel. 0532 790507
GEORGE SPENCE & SONS LTD
WELLINGTON ROAD   ★
Open: Monday to Friday
8.30 a.m.-5.30 p.m.
Saturday 9.00 a.m.-5.00 p.m.
H.P.W.WM.D.T.A.

SHEFFIELD   Tel. 0742-441012
GREGORY & TAYLOR LTD
WORKSOP ROAD
Open: 8.30 a.m.-5.30 p.m.
Monday-Friday
8.30 a.m.-12.30 p.m. Sat.
H.P.W.WM.D.

YORKSHIRE

SHEFFIELD   Tel. 0742-24659
GRAHAM OXLEY'S SHOWROOM
BRIDGE STREET   ★
Open: Monday to Friday
9.00 a.m.-5.30 p.m.
Saturday 8.30 a.m.-12.30 p.m.
H.W.D.A.BC.

SOWERBY BRIDGE   Tel. (0422)
CALDER   31861
WOODWORKING   Telex: 517400
MACHINERY LTD.
STATION ROAD
Open: Mon - Fri 9 a.m.-5 p.m.
P.W.WM.D.CS.A.

SCOTLAND

EDINBURGH   Tel. 031-337
SCOTSPAN   7788/665 3121
195 BALGREEN ROAD

Open: Monday to Friday
9.00 a.m.-3.00 p.m.
P.W.WM.D.A.

GLASGOW Tel. 041 429 4374/4444
THE SAW CENTRE   Telex: 777886
596-602 EGLINGTON STREET ★
G5 9RR
Open: Mon.-Fri. 8 a.m.-5.30 p.m.
Saturday 9 a.m.-1 p.m.
H.P.W.WM.D.CS.A.

N. IRELAND

Co. ANTRIM   Tel. 0266 6384
GEORGE GARDINER
49 BALLYMONEY STREET
BALLYMENA
Open: Open: Mon-Fri 8.30am-5.30pm
Wednesday 8.30am-1.00pm
H.P.W.D.A.BC.

Co. DOWN   Tel. (0247) 819800 (day)
NEWTOWNARDS   812506 (night)
NORLYN MACHINERY, UNIT 10
Malcolmson Ind. Est., 80 Bangor Road
Open: Mon-Fri 9.30am-5.30pm
or any other time by request
H.P.W.WM.D.BC.

S. IRELAND

COUNTY KILKENNY   Tel.
WOODMEN   (0409) 5460
CASHEL HOUSE   ★
KELLS ROAD, KILKENNY

Open: Monday to Saturday

WALES

BRITON FERRY   Tel. (0639)
WOODMEN   820803/4
49 NEATH ROAD   ★
Open: Monday to Saturday
9.00 a.m.-5.30 p.m.
P.W.WM.D.A.BC.

WALES

CARDIFF   Tel. (0222) 373007
JOHN HALL TOOLS LIMITED   ★
22 CHURCHILL WAY

Open: Monday to Saturday
9.00 a.m.-5.30 p.m.
H.P.W.WM.D.A.BC.

CARDIFF   Tel. (0222) 30831
F. W. MORGAN   & 25562
(CANTON) LTD., 129-133
COWBRIDGE RD EAST,
CANTON, CARDIFF
Mon-Sat 8-5 Sun. 9.30-12.30
H.P.T.CS.A.BC.

CARDIFF   Tel. (0222) 36519/
WOODMEN   373793/35221
43 CRWYS ROAD   ★

Open: Monday to Saturday
9.00 a.m.-5.30 p.m.

CARMARTHEN   Tel. 0267 7219
DO-IT-YOURSELF SUPPLY
BLUE STREET, DYFED
Open: Monday to Saturday
9.00 a.m.-5.30 p.m.
Thursday 9.00 a.m.-1.00 p.m.
H.P.W.WM.D.T.CS.A.BC.

SWANSEA   Tel. (0792) 55680
SWANSEA TIMBER &   ★
PLYWOOD CO LTD
57-59 OXFORD STREET
Open: Mon. to Fri. 9 am-5.30 pm
Sat. 9 am-1 pm
H.P.W.D.T.CS.A.BC.

YOU CAN BUY WITH CONFIDENCE FROM THE
SHOPS IN THIS SHOP GUIDE

★Shops offering a mail order service are denoted by an asterisk

---

SHOP GUIDE SHOP GUIDE

The quickest and easiest method of reaching all Woodworkers is to advertise in SHOP GUIDE. Telephone **Valerie Tester (0442) 41221 Ext. 266. Rate: £8.00 per unit.** Minimum of 6 months.

Key: H — Hand tools, **P** — Power tools, **W** — Woodworking machinery up to £1000, **WM** — Woodworking machinery over £1000, **D** — Demonstration available on selected machines, **T** — Timber, **CS** — Cutting or sharpening services, **A** — Attachments, **BC** — Books/catalogues, ＊ — Mail order.

£8.00 per Unit
Minimum of SIX insertions.
I enclose remittance of £48.00 ☐
I wish to be invoiced.   ☐
Please tick as appropriate.

COUNTY ....

TOWN ....

NAME OF COMPANY/SHOP ....

....

ADDRESS ....

To: **Valerie Tester**
WOODWORKER MAGAZINE
P.O. Box 35,
13 Bridge Street, Hemel Hempstead,
HP1 1EE.

TELEPHONE No ....

DAYS AND HOURS OF BUSINESS

....

....

*TO DENOTE MAIL ORDER SERVICE
AVAILABLE ☐

Prices quoted are those prevailing at press date and are subject to alteration due to economic conditions.

Classified Advertisements

Telephone Valerie Tester
(0442) 41221 Ex.266

All classified Advertisements must be pre-paid.
Private and trade rate 20p per word (minimum £3.00). Box Numbers £1.25 extra. Display box rates s.c.c. £4.00 (min £10.00). All advertisements are inserted in the first available issue.
Box replies to be sent care of Advertisement Department, PO Box 35, Bridge Street, Hemel Hempstead, Herts, England HP1 1EE. There are no reimbursements for cancellations.

FOR SALE

ADVERTISERS please note
FINAL COPY DATE for
APRIL ISSUE
(Published 19th March)
is **5th February**
MAY ISSUE
(Published 16th April)
is **3rd March**

KITY COMBINATION TABLE C/W with machinery inc accessories and extractor system. Excellent condition. £1,500. Can be seen by appointment. Tel: after 5pm, Petersfield 0730-66155 (home). L

CANOES, KAYAKS, punts, dinghies in Kayel D.I.Y. Kit form and ready built. Brochures available. Granta Boats (WW) Ramsey, Cambs. Tel: (0487) 813777. K-L

TIMBER SEASONERS, moisture meters, polymeters. Everything you require for seasoning your own timber. For free advice and lowest prices, consult the experts, 15 years in the trade. Some reconditioned seasoners available. Wyco Moisture control. Tel: Weybridge 40864. K-P

WOODWORKER MAGAZINE 1939-1981 not quite complete, offers. Buyer collects. Telephone Kenilworth, Warwicks 57963. L

INCA BANDSAW, Brook Gryphon motor. Little used — £170. Telephone: Ashford (Middx.) 57304. L

WELSH SLATE oil stones for sale at very competitive prices. Send S.A.E. for details:- INIGO JONES & Co. Ltd., Groeslon, Caernarfon, Gwynedd. Tel: 0286-830242. F-R

HEAVY DUTY GERMAN 'LORCH' WOODTURNING LATHE ONLY. 10½" swing diameter cast iron bed collet chuck and 6-1 chuck face plate No 2 morse tail stock £185. Also 'S and G' DIY 2w bandsaw £25. Tel: Welwyn Garden 26117. L

DENFORD VICEROY LATHE with metal turning facility 10" × 36 B.C. 20" rear handrest, 8 speeds, compound slide, centres, F. plate, D. plate, chuck, fixed steady, v.g.c. £420.00 o.n.o. Windsor: 65819 eve. L

SHERWOOD 36" WOOD LATHE ½hp motor, 8 Sorby tools, handy collett chuck, Auger sizing tool etc. Stock of seasoned timber £120. Phone Shirebrook 2486. L

PILLAR DRILLING MACHINE half an inch to one thirty-second of an inch chuck. Foot or belt driven. Excellent working order and condition. Collectors item suitable for craft workshop or museum. £100. Telephone Beckley 275. L

CORONET INTERNATIONAL WOODWORKER Universal Woodworking Machine, infinite variations of speed from 800rpm to 4,000rpm with tilting arbor saw. Many attachments which include sawing, planing, rebating, thicknessing, moulding, mortising, sanding, turning. £1,000 ono. Tel: 0734 732091 evenings/weekends.

FOR ALL SUPPLIES
FOR THE

Craft of Enamelling

ON METAL

Including
LEAD-FREE ENAMELS

PLEASE SEND 2 × 10p STAMPS
FOR FREE CATALOGUE, PRICE
LIST AND WORKING
INSTRUCTIONS

W. G. BALL LTD.

ENAMEL MANUFACTURERS

Dept. W. LONGTON
STOKE-ON-TRENT
ST3 1JW

R & S TOOLS (LINCOLN) LTD.

BEEVOR STREET, LINCOLN. Tel: Lincoln 0522 36168/9

Why pay more when you can get up to 25% discount off most leading makes of power tools and hand tools?

Stockists of:

ELECTRIC POWER TOOLS:
AEG—ELU—BOSCH—MAKITA—SUPER STORK—SKIL WOLF—METABO—WADKIN—KANGO

WOODWORKING MACHINES
DEWALT—MULTICO—SEDGWICK—WADKIN—STARTRITE

SAWBLADES
SANDVIK—TEX—MICOR—FIRTH—BROWN

HAND TOOLS
ALL LEADING MAKES OF BUILDING AND ENGINEERING TOOLS

ABRASIVES
ENGLISH—TEX—KLINGSPOR—UNIVERSAL GRINDING WHEELS

Up to 30% off most leading brands of coated abrasive

TCT CIRCULAR SAW BLADES
Contact us for the best price.

For the first time ever we can now offer an A.E.G. Drill of industrial quality at D.I.Y. price – £44.85 (inc. V.A.T.) Carriage extra.
Access & Barclaycard welcome.

SOLE AGENTS FOR SWIFTSURE CUTTING & CUTTING DISCS
FOR YOUR QUOTATION—PLEASE PHONE BETWEEN 8.30 am and 5 pm

BARRIE IRONS MACHINERY LTD

A leading distributor of POWER TOOLS
offer
Cash and carry or cash and carrier prices
JUST TO LIST A FEW

	RRP	OUR PRICE
MOF 31 15⁄8hp Plunging Router	£132.25	£79.50
MOF 98 2¼hp Plunging Router	£161.00	£99.50
MVS 47 H/O Orbital Sander	£102.35	£74.50
MH 151 2in. depth Circular Saw	£56.35	£43.50
MHB 90/10 4in. Belt Sander c/w sanding frame	£186.30	£135.00

Our prices include VAT; carriage £3.50 per machine
Having worked for Elu for over 20 years we consider ourselves second to none in expertise and service
Also distributors of DeWalt, Multico, Startrite, Kango, Bosch, all at discount prices
Why not drop us a line or visit our new showroom
81 UXBRIDGE ROAD, STANMORE
MIDDLESEX HA7 3NH
Telephone 01-954 0181

TOOLS TO TREASURE

Adzes, Drawknives, and other high quality tools for the Woodcraftsman, including a fine selection of "Pax" Hand and Panel Saws.
**CATALOGUE 45p.
EXPORT ENQUIRIES
WELCOME**
CORBETT TOOLS, Dept WW/3, 224 Puxton Drive, Kidderminster, Worc's

---

CLASSIFIED
Telephone Valerie Tester
(0442) 41221 Ext. 266

FINAL PRICE SLASH
ELU-DE WALT
Before buying phone
Machine Sales & Services (Bournemouth) Ltd.,
0202 527781 or 527780
WE CAN PROVE WE ARE CHEAPER!
E. G. DW 30 – £140

HAND CARVED
'Adam Style' motifs in Mahogany — Example 10" × 5" centre lamp and two side pieces — £25.00
Send S.A.E. for details and quotation. Your own design quoted for if required.
SAM NICHOLSON
22 Lisnagarvey Drive,
Lisburn, Co. Antrim,
N. Ireland. Phone Lisburn 3510

WORKSHOP EQUIPMENT

PROFESSIONAL QUALITY HAND TOOLS and power tool accessories at discount prices, by leading manufacturers:- Barrus, Record, Stanley, Leytool, Footprint, Ridgeway, Guys, Marples, Tyzack, Rabone Chesterman, Skarsten, Eclipse, Paramo, Raaco, Sandvik, Spear and Jackson, Bahco etc. Wood and metal working. Send 22p stamp for lists (refundable with first order). Trade enquiries welcome. Dalewood Tools, 31 Dalewood Avenue, Sheffield S8 0EG. Phone Sheffield (0742) 350665. XY

COPING SAW BLADES and junior hacksaw blades. Details from Lea Blades, 16 Barclay, Hertford Heath, Hertford, Herts. K-L

PLANERS 6", 9" planers/thicknessers, 12" × 7", 9" × 6", 12" × 7", sawbenches, 10", 12", combination woodworkers. British made. Particulars, send stamp. Dodd Machine Tools Ltd., South Woodham, Chelmsford. Tel: 320 691. C-N

MACHINERY. A comprehensive range of new/used machinery. Check our prices, e.g. HMO 10"×5½" planer/thicknesser £325. HF30 spindle moulder £328. 12" tilt arbour sawbench 2hp motor £121. Shopsmith MK5 home workshop £782. Morso mitring machine £437, (including V.A.T.). See these machines and Ryobi industrial small tools demonstrated at Woodman Woodworking Machinery Co. (Sign of the Axe), Little Malgraves Hall, Lower Dunton Road, Bulphan, Nr. Upminster, Essex. Tel: (0268) 415511 or (0702) 331729. I-U

WASHITA & ARKANSAS whetstones now readily available from importer. Large selection, SAE for list. C. Rufino, Manor House, South Clifton, Newark, Notts. T/C

EBAC TIMBER SEASONERS, Protimeter moisture meters, always good prices and advice from the man who pioneered small scale seasoning. John Arrowsmith, Roadham Cottage, Barton, Richmond, North Yorks. Telephone: (0325) 77362. T/C

Prices quoted are those prevailing at press date and are subject to alteration due to economic conditions.

How to get the most from your advertisement in

Give a full description of the product or service which you want to sell. Book a series of advertisements to ensure that you reach the whole potential market. Remember your customer could quite easily miss the issue which contains your advertisement.

If you want to cancel your advertisement then simply pick up the 'phone and tell us. You will only be charged for the ones which have appeared.

Lastly, get the most from your advertisement consult us first. We are here to help you.

Telephone Valerie Tester (0442) 41221 Ext. 266

Prices quoted are those prevailing at press date and are subject to alteration due to economic conditions.

Woodworker
THE MAGAZINE FOR THE CRAFTSMAN

APRIL 1982 Vol. 86 No. 1061 ISSN 0043-776X

Front cover: Entrance doors at the headquarters of the Cornhill Insurance Group in London (*Photo. courtesy Cornhill Group*). See story History on the doors pp234, 235.

Editor	Chris Dunn	
Deputy Editor	Polly Curds	
Advertisement Manager	Glyn Crole-Rees	
Advertisement Director ⎫	MAP Leisure	Michael Merrifield
Managing Director ⎭	Division	Gavin Doyle

MEMBER OF THE AUDIT
BUREAU OF CIRCULATIONS

SUBSCRIPTION DEPARTMENT: Remittances to MODEL AND ALLIED PUBLICATIONS, PO Box 35, Hemel Hempstead, Herts HP1 1EE. Price per copy 95p includes p&p. Subscription queries: Tel: Hemel Hempstead 51740. Subscription rate, including index, £11.90 per annum; overseas sterling £12.90; $29.00 US for overseas dollar subscribers. Second class postage paid in US at New York, New York. *Distribution* to North American hobby and craft stores, museums and bookshops by Bill Dean Books Ltd, 166-41 Powells Cove Boulevard, Post Office Box 69, Whitestone, New York 11357, USA. Tel: 1-212-767-6632. *Distribution* to news stand sales by Eastern News Distribution Inc, 111 Eight Avenue, New York, NY10011, USA. Tel: 1-212-255-5620.

WOODWORKER is printed in Great Britain by H. E. Warne Ltd, East Hill, St Austell, Cornwall PL25 4TN for the proprietor and publisher Model & Allied Publications Ltd (a member of the Argus Press Group). Trade sales by Argus Press Sales & Distribution Ltd, 12-18 Paul Street, London EC2A 4JS. WOODWORKER (ISSN 0043-776X) is published on the 3rd Friday of the month.

Model & Allied Publications Ltd

PO Box 35, Bridge Street, Hemel Hempstead, Herts HP1 1EE. Telephone: Hemel Hempstead (0442) 41221.

Timber framing

As this magazine reaches the bookstall this year's Ideal Home exhibition is in its second week. Last year all the show houses were of timber frame construction, at least 20% of new homes built in 1980 were timber frame and the proportion was expected to rise sharply. In response to this trend the British Woodworking Federation and the House Builders Federation have been running special half-day courses on timber frame housing organised regionally for site managers and supervisors.

James Riley, chairman of the BWF timber frame construction section comments 'It is gratifying that so many firms are taking a responsible attitude towards maintaining high standards of efficiency on site by sending staff to the courses. The dramatic swing to timber frame as a leading method of house building is clearly going to continue. The latest figures show nearly a quarter of all private houses started in GB during December were timber frame (compared with 13% in June 1981) and the swing is continuing.'

Maker's eye

HRH Prince Charles opened the new Crafts Council Gallery and Information Centre at 12 Waterloo Place, London SW1, on 2 February. The interior of the building (designed by Terry Farrell Partnership) has been designed as a contemporary paraphrase of the neo-classical exterior; many specially commissioned pieces have been incorporated into the scheme, along with a special provision for disabled people.

The inaugural exhibition is The Maker's Eye (open until 27 March) and is made up of groups of objects chosen by 14 craftsmen and women as examples of their own appreciation and enjoyment of craftsmanship. The selections are therefore diverse but include all the traditional crafts.

On 2 February the Prince of Wales unveiled a commemorative inscription commissioned from Tom Perkins (one of the youngest letterers on the Crafts Council Index) and was presented with a child's high chair made in cleft oak by Richard La Trobe Bateman. The chair has been made from an oak tree felled on the estate of the Marquis of Bath at Longleat. Oak being considered a most appropriate wood for a chair which may be used by a future heir to the British throne. The chair has been made from green timber employing the techniques discussed in *Making a chair from a tree* by John D. Alexander published by Taunton Press 1979 (reviewed Woodworker January 1979). A similar chair in cleft ash is a part of the current exhibition.

Boom over

A piece of advice in the letters column of the quarterly newsletter on crafts produced by the Welsh Arts Council and Crafts Council stated. 'The craft boom is over. . . buyers are no longer conned by the magic word *crafts*. If there is genuine sincerity in the work, however, confidence is established. Do not attempt to compete with the machine, make it by hand and made this obvious. Make it well to good design and with first class materials, charge realistic prices in line with your own needs—do not be over influenced by what others earn. Remember a good craftsman will always be busy. . .'

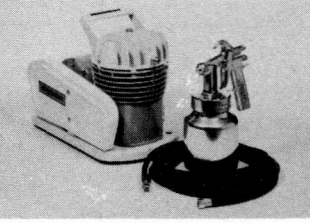

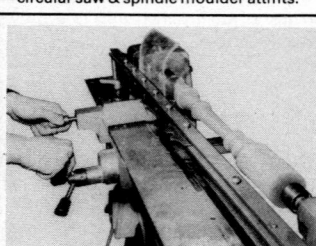

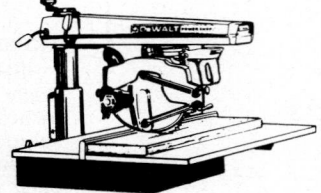
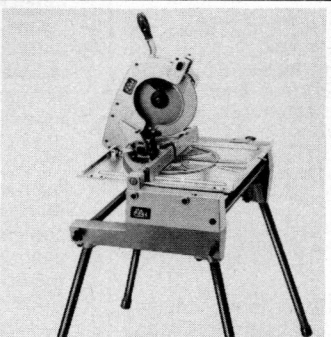
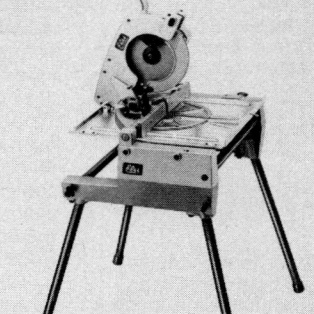

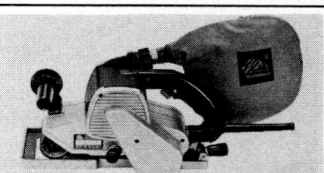

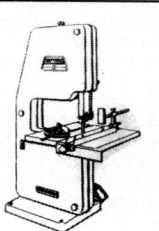

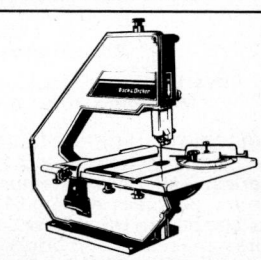

Prices quoted are those prevailing at press date and are subject to alteration due to economic conditions.

New! High Speed Steel Turning Tools

High Speed Steel 1" Roughing-out Gouge
Unhandled **£18.80**
Handled **£20.13**
(Including VAT)

High Speed Steel Skew Chisel
Unhandled **£8.45**
Handled **£9.78**
(Including VAT)

High Speed Steel Scraper
Designed by Gordon Stokes
Hand ground — Black finish **£5.46**
(Including VAT)

The above and many more new exciting tools are in the Ashley Iles catalogue supplement sent free on request.

Balinese Style Carving Tools

Some of the finest wood carving in the world is produced on the Indonesian Island of Bali. The tools they use are here replicated by Ashley Iles with the addition of a reinforced sleeve.

The set comprises 6 solid steel fishtail pattern tools, length 9" from the finest carbon steel. Black backed, straw-tempered used with a mallet or hardwood shaft.

£23.00 including VAT for the set of six.

Cranked Parting Tools

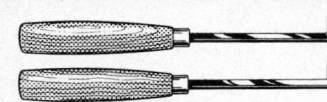

Save valuable timber, making rings from bowl waste (Useful for picture frames, radius corners etc.)
£12.50 a pair including VAT
Hand ground, black backed with wooden handles.

In conjunction with Ashley Iles Gordon Stokes offers a free phone or mail advisory service. Full details in the catalogue supplement.

Courses of Tuition by Gordon Stokes
A step by step introduction to woodcarving from sharpening to finishing **£7.50** post free.

Woodturning Course — a solid introduction to woodturning based on 20 years experience. Vol. 1 **£7.50**, Vol. 2 **£7.50** both post free.

All Gordon Stokes books are listed in the catalogue supplement.

Ashley Iles
woodcarving & turning tools
made in the old tradition
Ashley Iles (Edge Tools) Ltd., East Kirkby, Spilsby, Lincolnshire PE23 4DD. Telephone (07903) 372

Send for our 12 page full colour catalogue showing the full range of carving and turning tools (50p). There is also a free supplement showing recent additions

Main Distributors
Alec Tiranti Ltd., 70 High St., Theale, Reading.

Heron Tools Ltd., 437 Streatham High Rd., Norbury SW16.

Scotland
Allan McNair Woodcraft 69 Plessey Rd., Blythe, Northumberland.

THE MOST EXCITING NEW HOBBY EVENT
THE MIDLANDS HAS YET SEEN

Whatever your hobby interest, make a note in your diary now to visit the Midlands' own new modelling and craft exhibition.

Jointly staged by the Royal Agricultural Society of England and Model & Allied Publications Ltd, this great weekend show will demonstrate the best of what Midland hobby and crafts people can achieve. Each of the seven exhibition halls will concentrate on different aspects of skilled hobbies. In one hall woodworking and model engineering, in the next model railways, boats and aeroplanes and in three other halls, gem crafts and crafts. A packed programme of lectures and films throughout the weekend will stimulate and inform.

Our of doors there will be live steam tracks, model cars and boats in action and all types of model flying.

Crafts clubs will be exhibiting and there will be many woodworking demonstrations and lectures.

Whatever your hobby interest you are going to enjoy your day out with your family and friends.

Car parking is free, there are full catering and snack facilities.

Adults £2.00
Children and OAP's £1.00
Car Parking Free

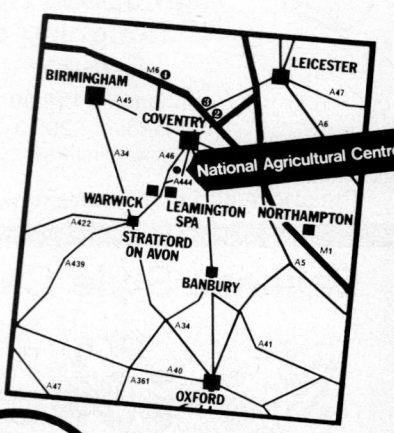

Gemcraft

Woodworking

Modelling

Flying Helicopters

Woodworking Displays

Model Boats outdoors

General Crafts & Equipment

Flying Models outdoors

Home Craft & Country pursuits

Model Engineering

1982 MODEL CRAFT & COUNTRY SHOW

SAT·SUN MAY 22/23
STONELEIGH, KENILWORTH
10 am - 6 pm
Each day

JOINT ORGANISERS

ROYAL AGRICULTURAL SOCIETY OF ENGLAND
NAC Stoneleigh, Nr. Kenilworth, Warwickshire CV8 2LZ Tel: Royal Show (0203) 555100

Model & Allied Publications
P.O. Box 35 Hemel Hempstead, Herts HP1 1EE Tel: Hemel Hempstead (0442) 41221

Prices quoted are those prevailing at press date and are subject to alteration due to economic conditions.

Quality or price?

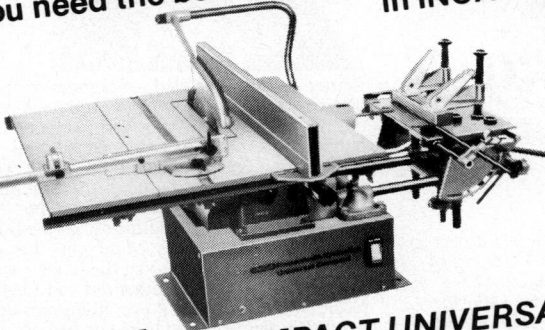

Simple Reliable

There's a lot of talk these days about revolutionary, highly sophisticated woodworking machinery – the new, low cost, over complicated little wonders that do almost everything – providing of course you're a keen engineering student with more than a lot of time on your hands.

Well – no one ever said Kity machines were sophisticated or revolutionary – and we're proud of it – in fact we designed and built them to be simple, reliable and easy to use. You don't have to change your woodworking methods or be an engineer, Kity simply adds power and precision to develop your own skills – and sometimes even your bank balance.

Recently Barrie and Lynne Goddard of Bottesford, near Scunthorpe, decided to improve their kitchen. The going rate for the job, from a professional contractor, was around £5,000; however with Kity machinery to help him, Barrie built their dream kitchen for just £2,000.

Ideas can now become reality

All of us at some time have had to scrap excellent creative ideas because we couldn't afford to bring in the professionals and didn't have sufficient expertise to carry them out ourselves. The simplicity of Kity machinery has gone a long way towards removing this frustration and our illustrated instruction sheets will explain step by step the machine techniques needed to transform your ideas into superb reality.

Common base for all functions.

The K5 has units for separate machine functions mounted on a common base and driven by a centrally mounted power unit – the K5 motor. You have all the versatility of separately mounted machines, any change of operation becomes simplicity itself. Just connect the belt to the machine you want to use, adjusting the tension easily by means of a simple, quick release lever. Without losing your pre-set adjustments, you can change from one function to another in a matter of seconds. Continuity of work is thus assured.

K5 international woodworker

– *complete power workshop for only* **£559**

(plus VAT. £83.85)

Engineering specification

Circular saw.
180mm (7″) blade normally fitted but will accept a 200mm (8″) blade giving a 57mm (2¼″) depth of cut. 2 speeds, 3750 for normal wood and 6200 r.p.m. for laminated boards. Complete with rip fence, mitre guide, repeat cut length stop, wobble washers for grooving, tilting table 0.45°.

Surface planer.
700mm (27½″) long × 200mm (8″) wide cast bed. Maximum planing width 150mm (6″). Adjustable 90° – 45° fence for bevel planing. Dynamically balanced cutter block rotating at 11,400 cuts per minute.

Thickness planer.
Fully automatic feed, 7.5m (24′) per minute. Maximum capacity 100mm (4″) deep, 150mm (6″) wide. Anti kick-back fingers, calibrated scale.

Spindle moulder
6400 rpm shaft speed. 45mm (1¾″) vertical adjustment. Capable of taking 25mm (1″) × 25mm (1″) rebate in one pass. Accepts both French moulding profiles and white hill type blocks.

Slot mortiser
Rise/fall table with 100mm (4″) of adjustment.

2 New Books

2 great books from Kity to help improve your craft.

"How to work with Wood"
One of the few books available about **woodworking machine techniques** including setting up and the use of circular saws, spindle moulder planer thicknesser slot mortisers etc. An invaluable manual for anyone using or buying woodworking machinery.

Full colour 260 pages, hard bound 195mm × 275mm, price **£15.00**.

"How to choose your Wood"
A definitive work covering timber types, cutting, storage and use. Including man made boards of all types.

Full colour 141 pages hard bound, 195mm × 275mm, price **£10.00**.

Available from all Kity stockists or direct from **Kity UK**. only **£20 for both books** – save 20%.

Maximum bit diameter 12mm (½″). Produces accurate mortises, also horizontal boring for perfect dowel joints.

2 year guarantee

When you buy a K5, you will be protected against all manufacturing defects (parts and labour) for the first two years after purchase, no matter how hard you work your machine.

The Kity Heavy Duty Range

Arthur is a highly skilled, traditional craftsman who uses the Kity Heavy Duty Range, ideal machinery for the busy modern craftsmen. By purchasing a mixture of independent and combination machines he built a superb workshop that exactly suited his requirements and his pocket. Arthur says… "It's amazing how some woodworkers still use old fashioned methods that belong in the Dark Ages. Mind you – I ought not to criticize them I used to be the same, I was proud to work like my Grandfather did and I believed the results would be better if everything was done by hand. It never occurred to me he had no alternative – and in any case, I always thought machines were complicated and some how difficult to use. Anyhow, I soon found out how wrong I was when I started using Kity machinery. I got better results in a fraction of the time and with very little physical effort. There's no doubt in my mind that Kity machinery is simple and very easy to use – and sure, it makes makes me money."

Kity offers you Heavy Duty Circular Saws, Bandsaws, Planer Thicknessers, Spindle Moulders and Slot Mortisers, along with a complete range of accessories, motors and floor stands. Each machine can be independent or part of a combination for example: you can start your workshop with a circular saw. With Kity you don't have a lot of complicated attachments, nor do you have to swing the machine into different positions or use a special tool. Simply slip the belt from one machine to the next.

The Circular Saw 617

This is the heart of most workshops. The Kity machine has a cast and machined, tilting work table; a rise/fall arbor with hand wheel control; it accepts blades up to 9″ in diameter giving a 3⅛″

Prices quoted are those prevailing at press date and are subject to alteration due to economic conditions.

and ᵛᵉʳʸ easy to use

depth of cut; and is capable of running at two speeds; 3400 rpm and 7000 rpm. It is powered by a 1½ H.P. motor with No Volt Thermal Overload Starter. You will have no difficulty in cutting any wood based material, from melamine faced chipboard to African hardwoods.

Accessories included in the price are the mitre-guide with repeat cut stop, and wobble washers for grooving. The machine is guarded to comply with international standards.

The Planer Thicknessers 535, 635, 636

Kity manufacture three 'under and over' planer/thicknessers, a 10″ × 6″, 8″ × 6″ and a 6″ × 4″.

Each machine is available with stand and motor and can be used as an independent unit or will fit as part of the combination.

Each machine has cast tables and a twin knife cutter block and is of the 'under and over' type. The thicknesser is power fed with an adjustable thicknessing table giving true results along the whole length of the timber; this is usually difficult to achieve with the 'over fed' clamp type thicknesser. The 636 and 635 both have unusually long (40″) surfacing tables ideal for straightening a twist in a plank of timber.

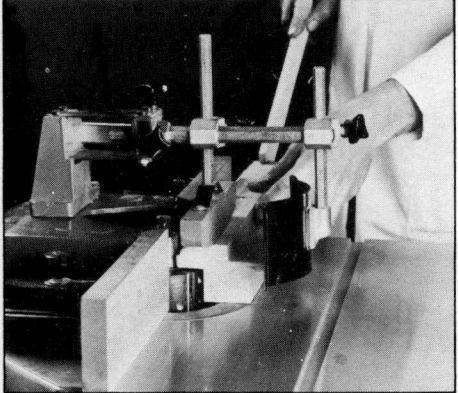

Spindle Moulders 626/627

The Spindle Moulder is a versatile and powerful tool. It does a totally different job to a router, although the system is similar. For example: — The 626 and 627 are capable of making large rebates 1¼″ × 1¼″ in hundreds of feet of timber. They will also produce moulding, deep grooves, tongue and groove joints, V-joints, tenons, profiles and counter profiles.

The 626 has a standard adjustable fence with the capability of positioning the cutting tools over a 4″ vertical range. The 627 has the same specifications but with individual micro adjustable fences. Both machines have cutting speeds of 7000 rpm, and are guarded to full international standards.

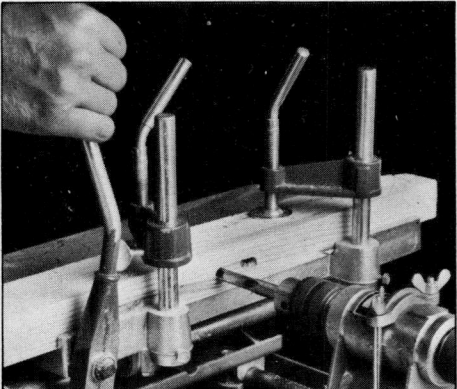

The 625 Slot Mortiser

The only machine in the whole range that is *not* available as an independent machine.
Working from the 700 table it will provide a ½″ slot, up to 5″ long and 4″ deep. An excellent machine for mortise joint production.

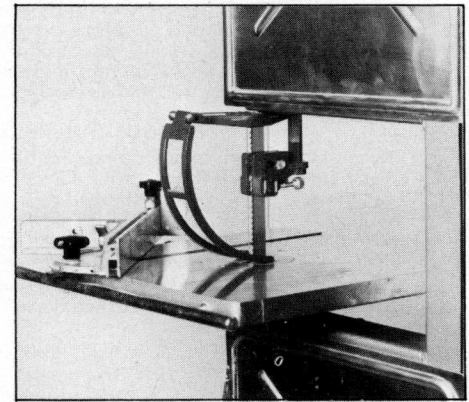

The 612 Bandsaw

Kity make an all steel, two wheel, Bandsaw with a 5½″ depth of cut and an 11½″ throat. It will accept blades from ¼″ for tight turns to ⅞″ for deep cutting and planking of timber. Unlike 'Plastic' Bandsaws the steel construction of the Kity machine allows you to set a high blade tension. This enables you to cut fast and in a straight line through hardwood and knots with a maximum depth of 5½″.

Kity Plan Sheets

These are issued for a nominal charge exclusively to Kity users and titles include, fitted kitchens and furniture. These practical plan sheets include cutting lists and complete manufacturing instructions on the relevant subject.

Nation-wide Service

Kity have 150 fully trained stockists throughout the U.K. and they provide a service second to none – there'll be one near you, ask for a demonstration, before you buy.

If you have a dream project you want to build or if you're a busy craftsman then you need Kity – simple, reliable and easy to use machinery.

Instructions on machines

Each Kity machine has comprehensive instructions to ensure you have the knowledge to use the machine correctly.

2 year Guarantee

The Child Coil Grip Chuck

A COMBINATION CHUCK FOR HAND WOODTURNERS   (copied but not improved on)   Patented

COIL GRIP ASSEMBLY

This unique chuck is the outcome of many years experience by a professional woodturner and teacher, and the patented coil grip method together with the many extra modes of operation safely and neatly overcome the chucking problems encountered by amateur and professional turners. The coil grip, supplied ONLY WITH THIS CHUCK, together with the large (4½") diameter heavy duty body offers unbeatable strength and rigidity for gripping end grain work of ANY size. It grips by compression on the outside of the work so there is no danger of splitting the wood by excessive outward pressure. It holds staved work safely. An almost limitless variety of home-made wooden adaptors can be made which will grip any shape or size of work, internally, externally, dovetail grip, plain grip, or as required. The coil grip feature makes this chuck by far the most versatile of its kind. Made for most lathes (state model) £36.50 inc. VAT & carriage.

WOODTURNERS' SPECIALIST SUPPLIER

The most comprehensive range of tools available. The new ROY CHILD parting tool. Chucks, centres, fittings, drills. Flexicramps. Many types and sizes glass inserts, barometers, hygrometers, thermometers, eggtimers, hourglasses, condiment liners, 160 circular tile patterns, lighters, pens, flower vase tubes, peppermills, STAINLESS saltmills, knives, clocks, pencil sharpeners, ashtrays, clock dials. Abrasives, waxes, finishes. Speed-n-Eze, Rustins. WOOD for turning. MYFORD agents. ROY CHILD pyrography machines. Post Office Parcel Contract for most quick and direct delivery service. Send S.A.E. for catalogue, or $1.00 from overseas enquiries. We EXPORT worldwide.

WOODTURNING AND FINISHING

Two-day intensive course and personal tuition at 17th century Essex-Suffolk farmhouse. Fully equipped workshops. Maximum of two guests for any one course.

PETER CHILD

THE WOODTURNER CRAFTSMAN
The Old Hyde, Little Yeldham, Halstead, Essex. Tel. Gt. Yeldham (0787) 237291

Prices quoted are those prevailing at press date and are subject to alteration due to economic conditions.

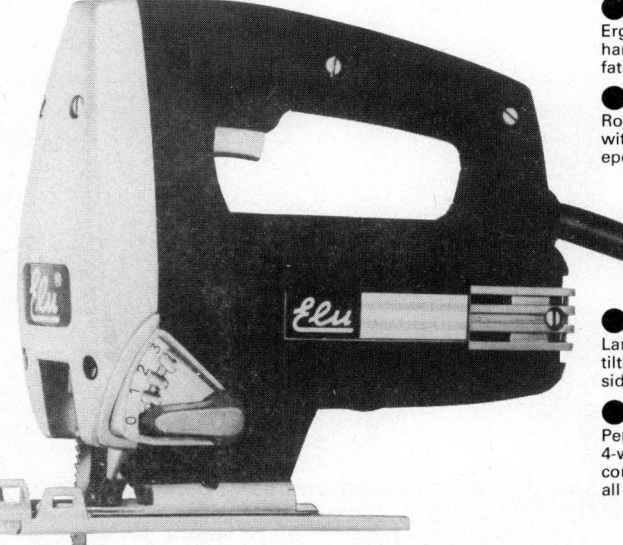

Roger's Mail Order Catalogue

Still the best way to buy all your specialist tools through the post.

-: SPRING OFFERS :-

SOCKET PARING CHISELS

Roger's have commissioned these fine reproductions of a traditional style of chisel - long absent from the market - from an old established Sheffield forging company. Hand crafted and finished to a high polish, they represent the finest examples of the forger's art. Because of small production runs and the amount of handwork carried out in the completion of each tool they are by no means cheap, but they represent excellent value for money to those who appreciate a fine quality tool, each lovingly completed by the best forgers, grinders, polishers and craftsmen.

Cat. No.	Size	Price	Cat. No.	Size	Price
500200	1/4	£10.89	500204	3/4	£11.50
500201	3/8	£10.89	500205	1	£12.36
500202	1/2	£10.89	500206	1 1/4	£13.60
500203	5/8	£11.50			

COMPLETE SET ONLY £69.95

STOCK CLEARANCE OF HANDLED TURNING TOOLS

Description :	M.R.P.	Clearance Price
Standard Strength Skew 1/2in	£ 4.09	£3.27
Standard Strength Skew 1 in	£ 4.76	£3.80
Standard Strength Diamond Pt. 1/2	£ 4.44	£3.55
Standard Strength Round Nose 1/2	£ 4.44	£3.55
Standard Strength Gouge 3/8in	£ 5.56	£4.44
Roughing Gouge 3/4in	£ 8.97	£7.17
L & S Deep Fluting Gouge 1/4in	£11.70	£9.36
L & S Deep Fluting Gouge 3/8in	£11.70	£9.36
L & S Deep Fluting Gouge 1/2in	£11.70	£9.36
Standard Strength Parting Tool	£ 4.41	£3.52
L&S Beading & Parting Tool 3/8in	£ 5.91	£4.70

MEMBER OF WOODWORKING MACHINERY DEALERS ASSOCIATION

MACHINERY

We can supply and demonstrate tools and machinery by the following manufacturers ; ARUNDEL, BOSCH, BURGESS, De WALT, ELECTRA BECKUM, ELU, KITY, INCA, SHOPSMITH, STARTRITE & TYNE LATHES All on display at our Hitchin shop.

ROGER'S CATALOGUE

With 160 pages showing over 1400 Specialist Woodcraft Tools at realistic prices, gives you the widest range of Quality Specialist Woodcraft tools available through the post.
So why pay more when Roger's Mail Order Catalogue can save you money.
Send for your Catalogue today and see what we offer. U.K. and Eire send £1.50 inc. p&p, Overseas £3.00 in sterling.
Cost of Catalogue refunded on your first order over £30.00.
Allow 14 days for delivery of your order

SEND ALL ORDERS TO :-

ROGER'S Dept. W.
47 Walsworth Road
Hitchin
Herts. SG4 9SU
Telephone: Hitchin 4177

Closed all day Wednesday

masterclass '82

AN EXHIBITION of handmade furniture and artistry in wood, over 100 selected pieces by leading contemporary craftsmen.

CONTINUOUS DEMONSTRATIONS by 7 professional craftsmen, eg WOODCARVING by IAN NORBURY, MUSICAL INSTRUMENT MAKING by JOHN UNDERHILL.

LECTURES by 16 leading national and international craftsmen, designers and experts in associated fields, eg JOHN MAKEPEACE, ALAN PETERS, CHARLES HAYWARD, STOBARTS BOOKS, MARY COMINO.

to be held at
THE SUN HOTEL,
SUN STREET,
HITCHIN, HERTFORDSHIRE.
Sponsored by **roger's**
from 14th-17th APRIL inclusive — 10 a.m. to 6 p.m.

Entrance to the exhibition and demonstrations by illustrated brochure £2.00 available at the door, or in advance, further information and reservation details for lectures from:
BETTY NORBURY, THE WHITE KNIGHT GALLERY,
28 PAINSWICK RD., CHELTENHAM, GLOS.
Tel (0242) 38582.

Special rates for families and parties. Please enclose S.A.E. for information.

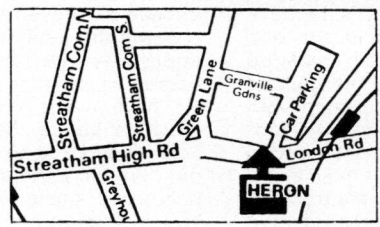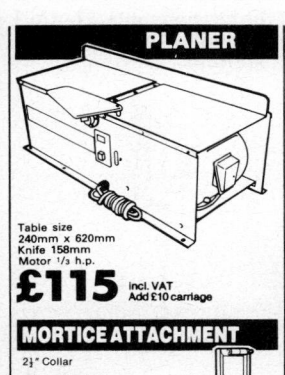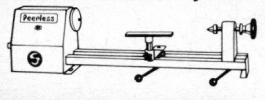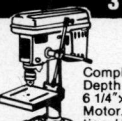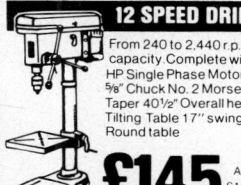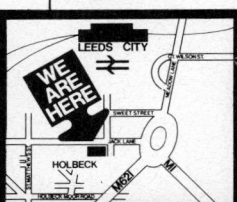

Woodworker, April 1982   KINDLY MENTION 'WOODWORKER' WHEN REPLYING TO ADVERTISEMENTS   229

R. W. Grant researches a kitchen table to find more than meets the eye. Pictures by John Peacock.

At first sight photo 1 hardly justifies my cryptic title, says Robert Grant. True it is a kitchen table, an old and sturdy one at that. The top is some 7ft long and 1½in. thick. All joints are pegged with dowels and the absent spreader bar once dovetailed in is evidence of the ravages that time has wrought upon this piece during long service. It has also suffered from the attentions of the furniture beetle; the wood is sycamore and many a grub has dined well on this venerable piece.

That the table is Welsh in origin is borne out by the fact that the present owner, T. Charles-Edwards esq. recalls it has been in his family at least since his grandfather's day (he was born in Bala around the time of the battle of Trafalgar), the family later moving to Aberystwyth. Mr Edward's uncle rose in church circles to positions of eminence, becoming the Queen's chaplain and eventually retired as Bishop of Worcester – as a boy he would have known this table at his father's house.

The puzzle of the table is shown in close-up in photo 2. It appears to be a unique method used to secure the butt joints between the planks which made up the top. Three 7ft boards are butt-jointed along their lengths and are cleated with 1½in. wide pieces at the ends. At four equidistant points the boards are secured with ¼in. dowels laid out in equilateral fashion. These pierce through the top and, one suspects also through a hardwood tongue which is let into the thickness of each board.

A nail file run along the now opened joints stops abruptly near to the line of the outer dowels.

I am convinced that this curious feature is part of the original construction and was intended, along with the end cleats to impede the movement of the timber and so prevent the boards from opening. It is impossible with the passage of time to determine whether any glue was used.

I have never seen this form of construction before. Reference to the Welsh Folk museum at St Fagans, Cardiff, bears out that while the table is similar to some half-dozen kitchen tables still existing in Wales which are known to date from the early 19th century none of these show this form of locking the top boards together. Perhaps readers may know of other instances and WOODWORKER would like to hear if this is the case.

Interestingly enough, Ernest Gimson (1864-1919) the great furniture designer who along with Ernest and Sidney Barnsley was to bring the vernacular arts and crafts style of furniture to such high peaks of perfection, often employed a 'butterfly' or dovetailed-shaped piece of wood inlaid across table top butt-joints in a similar manner to hold the boards together. Perhaps this was Gimson's refinement of a once widespread and well known method, after all he first picked up his notions of woodworking as a craft in Herefordshire – not all that far away from the home of our puzzling table.

Photo. 1 (Above) the kitchen table. Photo. 2 (Below) close-up showing the method of securing the butt jointing.

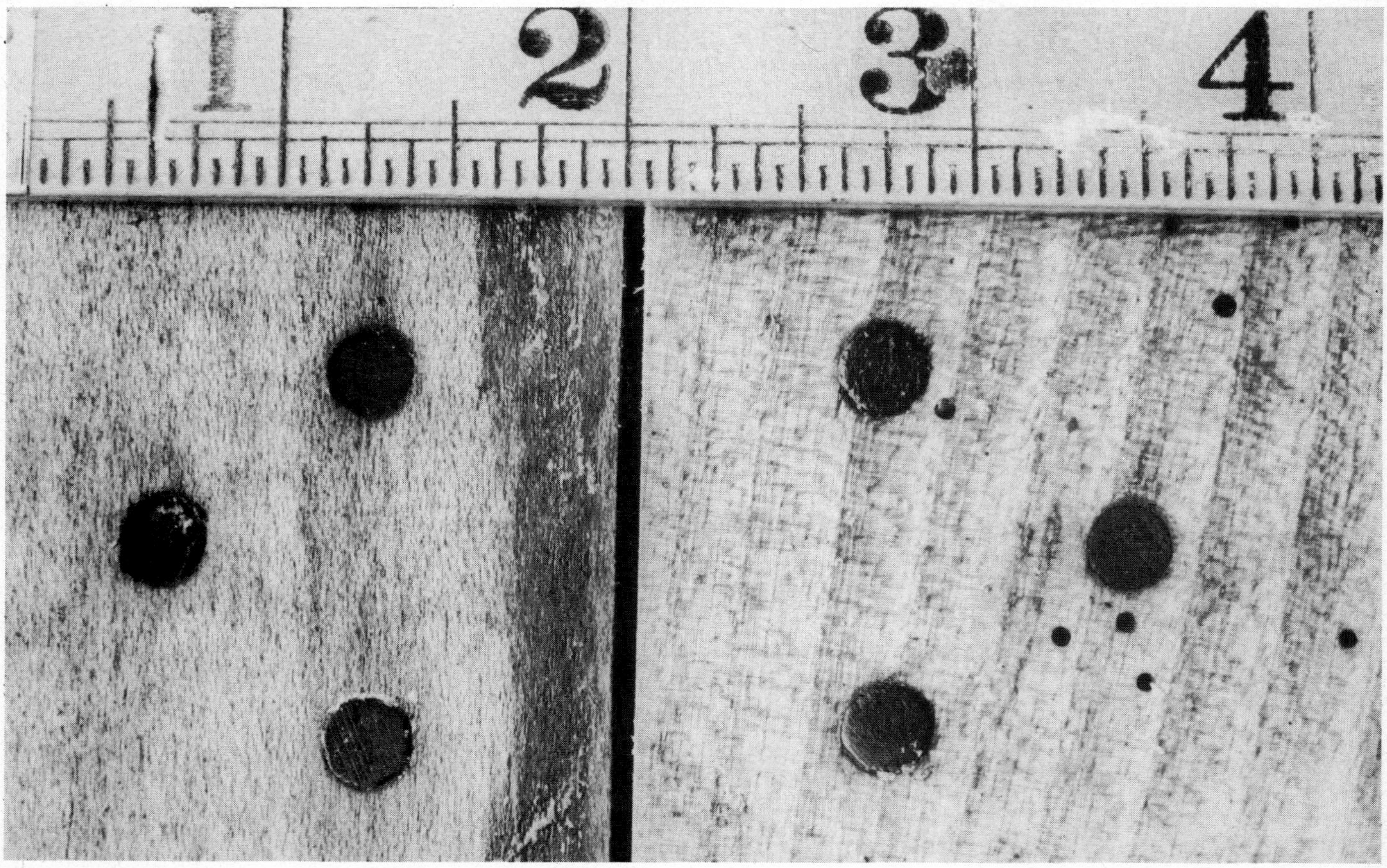

As invaluable as a dictionary, as informative as an encyclopaedia, as revered as the Bible... Now as near as your local stockist!

It's no exaggeration that our readers regard Fine Woodworking more as an indispensable reference source than a magazine. And it's not difficult to see why.

Each richly detailed bi-monthly issue is filled with articles that go well beyond the usual 'how to' pieces in other craft magazines. Written by professionals, Fine Woodworking uncovers a wealth of information about materials, design, tools, techniques, cabinet making, carving, turning, veneering – in the sort of detail that's practically impossible to find elsewhere. Which makes the news that Fine Woodworking is now as near as your local stockist all the more astonishing.

Stockists

AVON
V H Willis Ltd., 190-192 West Street, Bedminster, Bristol ● Trymwood Services, 2A Downs Park East, Off North View, Westbury Park, Bristol.

BERKSHIRE
David Hunt, Bath Road, Littlewick Green, Knowle Hill, Nr Reading

BUCKINGHAMSHIRE
A Pollard & Son, 51 Queens Way, Bletchley, Milton Keynes

CAMBRIDGESHIRE
Cyril Ridgeon & Sons Ltd., Tenison Road, Cambridge

CHESHIRE
Robert Kelly & Sons Ltd., 19 Newgate Row, Chester ● Linacre Plant & Power Tools Ltd., 11 Bewsey Road, Warrington

CLEVELAND
Kayes Middlesbrough Ltd., 63 Newport Road, Middlesbrough

CORNWALL
South West Power Tools, Monument Rd., Helston ● Tool Serve, 27 Truro Road, St Austell

DERBYSHIRE
Bradley Fernie & Co Ltd., 413 Sheffield Road, Whittington Moor, Chesterfield ● Derbyshire Hire Services, 115 Nottingham Road, Alfreton, Derbyshire

DEVON
Axminster Power Tool Centre, Chard Street, Axminster ● Totem Timber Ltd., St John's Road, Cattedown, Plymouth

DORSET
Power Tool Services, 851 Christ Church Rd., Boscombe, Bournemouth

DURHAM
George Mitchie, Northgate, Darlington

ESSEX
Marshall & Parsons, 1111 London Road, Leigh-on-Sea, Essex

GLOUCESTERSHIRE
Tewkesbury Saw Co Ltd., Trading Estate, Newton, Tewkesbury

HAMPSHIRE
Burch & Hills Ltd., Blackwater Way Industrial Estate, Aldershot

HEREFORD
Hereford Industrial Supplies, Unit 18/19 Block D, Three Elms Trading Estate

HERTFORDSHIRE
J Simble & Sons Ltd., 76 Queens Road, Watford ● Rogers Walkareach Ltd., 47 Walsworth Road, Hitchin

HUMBERSIDE
Humberside Factoring Co., Main Street, Hull ● J E Siddle Ltd., 83 Victoria Road, Grimsby

ISLE OF WIGHT
ITS Tools Ltd., Plot 3A, Dodnor Lane Industrial Estate, Newport

KENT
Leisurecraft In Wood, 124 Camden Road, Tunbridge Wells ● Ashford Tool Centre, 14 Elwick Road, Ashford

LANCASHIRE
Lancashire Saw Co., Wharf Street, Eanham, Blackburn ● J Ardron & Son Ltd., Mowbray Drive, Blackpool

LEICESTERSHIRE
Middleton Mail Order, 33-37 St Mary's Road, Market Harborough

LINCOLNSHIRE
Woodwise, 121 High Street, Lincoln

GREATER LONDON
G H Chappell (MT) Ltd. 586 Lea Bridge Road, Leyton, London, E10 7DN

MERSEYSIDE
Linacre Plant & Power Tools Ltd., Glover Street, St Helens

WEST MIDLANDS
Atkin & Sons Ltd., 110 Bradford Street, Birmingham 12 ● Webbs Power Tools, 1752 Pershore Road, Birmingham

NORFOLK
Windmill Enterprises, The Old Mill, Gayton, Kings Lynn

NOTTINGHAMSHIRE
Poole Wood Equipment Ltd., 5 Holly Lane, Chilwell

OXFORDSHIRE
Hopkins of Cowley, 117/125 Hollow Way, Cowley

SHROPSHIRE
J A Morgan Ltd., Pre Cast Concrete Works, Nantmawr, Nr. Oswestry

SOMERSET
Mitchell Tools, 61 Priory Bridge Road, Taunton

STAFFORDSHIRE
Matthews Bros., Kettlebrook Road, Tamworth

SUFFOLK
Suffolk Saw Services, Bridge Road Works, Felixstowe

SURREY
L H Turtle Ltd., Tait Road, off Gloucester Road, Croydon

SUSSEX
Thorcraft, Queens Road, Hastings ● B J Tools Ltd., 41 Broadwater St West, Broadwater, Worthing ● W Hosking, 96a Montague Street, Worthing

NORTH YORKSHIRE
Elcock Power Tools Ltd., Hospital Fields Road, Fulford Road, York ● Multi-Tools (Harrogate) Ltd., 158 Kings Road, Harrogate

SOUTH YORKSHIRE
Middleton Mail Order, Middlewood Road, Sheffield

WEST YORKSHIRE
Neville Oldham, 16 Thornhill Road, Lindley, Huddersfield ● Neil Rushworth, (M&T), Greencroft, Kirk Lane, Yeadon, Leeds

SCOTLAND
Lanark Saw Services, Cleghorn, Lanark ● Powercraft, 15 Peebles Street, Ayr ● Scotspan, 195 Ballgreen Road, Edinburgh

SOUTH WALES
Scimitar Eng Power House, 81 Mansell Road, Swansea ● The Tool Centre, 36 Frogmore Street, Abergavenny, Gwent ● The Tool Centre, 5 The Strand, Cwmbran, Gwent ● The Tool Centre, 138A High Street, Myrther Tydfyl, Mid Glamorgan

CHANNEL ISLANDS
Norman Ltd., Commercial Buildings, St Helier, Jersey

SUMACO
Woodworking Library

Sumaco Woodworking Library, Suma House, Huddersfield Road, Elland, West Yorkshire HX5 9AA. Telephone Elland (0422) 79811.

These hard to find tools are readily available at Sarjents

A few basic tools are fairly widely available; the more specialised items however are not so easy to find – up till now. We present here a few items from our enormous stocks readily available through the post. Remember **all** our tools are fully guaranteed, and the price mentioned is the price you pay – there is no extra for carriage or VAT.

110–108 Lion Mitre Trimmer.

The world famous Lion trimmer has long been renowned for fast and accurate mitring capabilities. The side fences have pre-set (but adjustable) stops for 45° and 90°, and can quickly be set at any other angle. Fitted with high grade tool steel blades, the Lion mitre trimmer will finish joints with a high degree of accuracy.
£143.75 (inc. VAT and carriage).

121–115 Book: Routing Techniques by Jim Phillips.

This comprehensive guide to working with the versatile portable router includes many hints and tips and illustrations of bits, jigs and fixtures to aid novices and craftsmen alike.   **£4.50**

123–104 Stanley 265 1¼″ HP Router.

This super heavy duty router is slashed in price! Over 56% off list price (no it's not a mistake!). All ball bearing construction micro-depth adjustment, shaft lock, 27,000 r.p.m. with ¼″ and ⅜″ collets, will take a huge range of cutters. Remember our special price includes postage and packing. Usual catalogue price: £132.25, now down to **£57.85.**

109–146 Picture Frame Cramp.

This simple set consists of a cramping tool, 3 corner angles (with removable base-plates), and a 6ft length of bonding cable. As the tension is set on the cramped object, perfect 90° angles are formed.
£3.95.

SARJENTS TOOLS

Personal shoppers welcome at our branches:

62–64 Fleet Street,
Swindon.
(0793) 31361

150 Cowley Road,
Oxford.
(0865) 45118

106–130 Veneer Saw.

Our veneer saw has 2″-3″ curved cutting edges and a polished beech handle. One edge has tapered teeth and one straight-edge teeth.
£1.95.

All these and nearly 2,000 other quality, hard-to-find tools are listed in the Sarjents Tools Woodworking Catalogue. For your copy send £1.00 to include p. & p., or ask for your **free** catalogue when ordering any of the tools above.

Send today to:-
Sarjents Tools,
Dept. PW382,
Oxford Road,
Reading.
(0734) 586522

All prices include post, packing and VAT. No extra to pay.

 To pay by Access or Barclaycard, simply write or phone with your number.

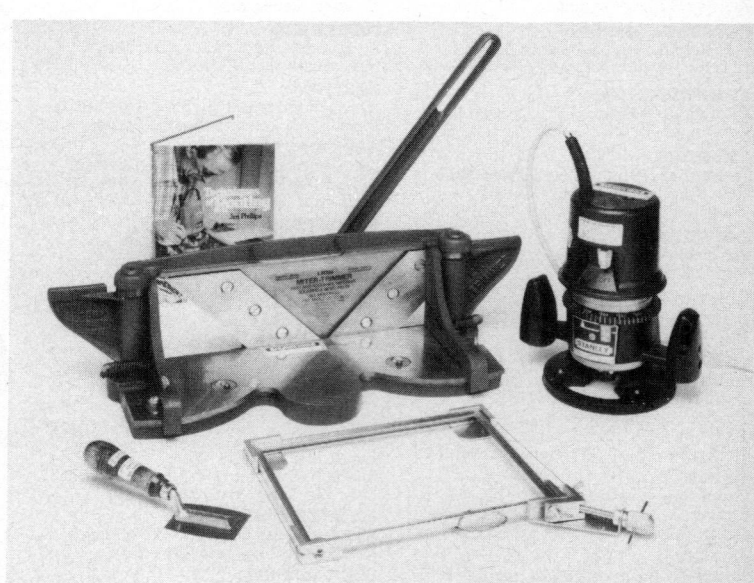

Prices quoted are those prevailing at press date and are subject to alteration due to economic conditions.

CRAFT EDUCATION ADVANCES AT OXFORD

Important advances in craft education have been introduced at Cowley St John C of E upper school, Oxford. This is a mixed comprehensive foundation with a design faculty headed by R. W. Grant DLC FRSA MSIAD. A new course in product design and construction leading to a City & Guilds of London foundation certificate (devised by Mr Grant) was announced by Mrs E. F. Storrar BA, head teacher at Cowley St John, to industrialists and representatives of commercial interests in the Oxford area who attended a meeting at the school on 26 November 1981.

The school is also to have a 'craftsman in residence' (WOODWORKER for August 1980), though the craftsman will, in fact, be a young woman — Miss Lucinda Leech — who studied at Rycotewood College, Thame, and for the past three and a half years has been designing and making furniture in her workshop at Oxford (WOODWORKER for November 1981).

Her initial project will be a table for use at the school. The 'craftsman in residence' idea is essentially two-way: it leads to a better appreciation of what craftsmanship involves in practical terms; and what the students themselves can achieve. Though not formally linked with the product design and construction course, Miss Leech will be closely associated with it and it is visualised that the students will undertake practical work on the project.

The course is of two years' duration and it is probable that the examination will take the place of the CSE in technical studies in the Cowley St John curriculum. Mr Grant has devised the course in co-operation with officials of the C & G to meet the needs of students wishing to gain a valid qualification in practical work.

Some of the audience of teachers and industrialists in the Oxford area who heard the announcement of the C&G foundation certificate course drawn up by R. W. Grant.

Left to right: P. Alexander (City & Guilds of London Institute), Miss Lucinda Leech (craftsman in residence, Cowley St John), Mrs E. F. Storrar (head teacher, Cowley St John); R. W. Grant (head of design, Cowley St John); E. Lord (City & Guilds of London Institute).

Lucinda Leech, who is acquiring a national reputation as a young designer and maker of furniture based in her Oxford workshop, has been commissioned by Cowley St John school to make a table to enhance the school foyer and also to act as the focal point on formal occasions, such as presentations. Miss Leech will produce the table in the school workshops and will actively involve the pupils in its manufacture.

The table will be in two contrasting woods, rose zebrano top and white beech legs and framing, finished with two coats of matt lacquer and wax. It will be used for display in the foyer against a wall and on the stage viewed from front and above to seat 3-4 people behind.

The enterprise is being funded jointly by the Southern Arts Association and the school.

The course is available for boys and girls and aims to help students make an informed choice about a career. It is also intended to introduce them to the discipline of a working environment; safety in the workshop and to a practical experience of making things; plus widening their knowledge of the social and industrial environment. The course is also intended to develop the students' personal qualities and to assist them to reach a level of attainment which will facilitate entry into employment or further education.

At the end of the course students will have to set-up a display of their work which will be looked at by a visiting examiner who will ask questions. The display will contain: projects made; the folio which goes with it, containing all design sheets and a working drawing; project journal; 3rd and 4th year design homework folder; folder or exercise book showing work done respectively in the english, maths and humanities faculties; and an example showing the students' personal qualities and interests.

Throughout the course in the workshops students will have a series of half-termly theory tests and the marks gained for these will go towards the final grading.

The objectives of the course as explained by Mr Grant at the meeting on 26 November last year, are in designing and making useful and decorative objects within a wide range of materials; development of skills with tools and processes; acquisition of theoretical knowledge and incidental technology on tools, materials and processes; and communication, ie writing, drawing and speaking and to achieve basic competence in literacy and numeracy.

Mr Grant told the meeting: 'I would ask you to return to your boardrooms and your chambers of commerce and spread the news of this course which at the moment is unique to Cowley St John, though it may well be emulated by other schools. Indeed, we have already received inquiries.'

Other speakers welcoming the initiative of Mrs Storrar and Mr Grant were P. Alexander who is in charge of C & G foundation courses and E. Lord, the C & G assessor of the Cowley St John course work.

HISTORY ON THE DOORS

The entrance doors to number 32 Cornhill in the city of London are decorated with eight panels, each 18 × 19in. The panels were carved by the well-known sculptor Walter Gilbert whose other work includes the gates at Buckingham palace and many war memorials. The doors which lead into the head office of Cornhill Insurance Group, were designed by B. P. Arnold who took much of the material for the panel designs from city of London records.

Erected in 1939 each door is 6ft 8in. high and 30in. wide in what is believed to be one of the mahoganies. The original working drawings and specifications were destroyed during the wartime blitz on London.

By courtesy of Cornhill Insurance Bill Gates was able to take pictures of some of the panels. Cornhill also kindly provided the descriptive material.

The door panels

1. Depicts the founding of St Peter's-upon-Cornhill as an Archbishop's See by King Lucius in Roman times. Reputed to be the first Christian church in London.

2. A notable medieval incident in Cornhill was the penance imposed upon Eleanor, Duchess of Gloucester in 1441. The charges were sorcery and treason and she was compelled to walk barefoot, carrying a lighted candle, from Queen's hithe to St Michael's church, Cornhill. She was afterwards banished.

Panels 1 and 2 are shown on the front cover of this month's issue.

3

In ancient times Cornhill was a soke (domain) of the Bishop of London. His tenants were not allowed to bake bread in their own ovens and had to use the seigneurial oven – and pay dues accordingly! However, apart from 'raising the wind' for his treasury, the bishop may well have realised that many ovens would constitute a serious fire risk whereas a single one under the control of his officers would be less hazardous.

4

Cornhill market was until 1369 the only one permitted to remain open until a late hour. But some of the traders sold old goods as new to those coming to the market after dark. Consequently the privilege was curtailed and the market ordered to close at sunset.

5

Birchin Lane probably takes its name from the original builder or owner. Until the end of the 16th century it was a street favoured by wealthy drapers and tailors who lived above their warehouses and shops. This panel represents an Elizabethan dandy having a 'fitting' at his tailor in Birchin Lane.

6

Pope's Head tavern in Cornhill in existence in 1756 was granted to the Merchant Taylors' Co of London (the company still owns part of Pope's Head Alley). This panel shows an 18th century scene in the tavern.

7

Garraway's coffee house in Exchange Alley (now Lombard Street) was in the 17th and 18th centuries the resort of men of business, fashion and learning. In those times the coffee houses of London became important as places where business was transacted. Lloyds – the insurance market – started as a coffee house.

▶ 3

◀ 4

◀ 5

6 ▲   7 ▲

◀8

8
The publishers Smith, Elder & Co had their premises in Cornhill which were visited (as shown in the panel) by such well-known authors as Thomas Thackeray and the Brontës. The poets William Cowper and Thomas Gray lived in Cornhill as did Thomas Guy, the wealthy bookseller and financier who founded Guy's hospital in London.

This piece is a continuation of the series on designs for furniture by Edward Barnsley and as originally produced in his Froxfield (Hampshire) workshops. The settee was made in English cherry and the elegance and simplicity of the design belies a robustness yielding comfort and security to the sitter.

A competent furniture maker wishing to attempt this piece would need to secure sound straight-grained stock and make templates of the shaped legs, arms and rails by scaling up the profile drawing shown. Interestingly enough these drawings were prepared from the actual templates used in Mr Barnsley's workshops.

Access to a bandsaw would, of course, facilitate the cutting out of the curved members which then would be cleaned-up with a spokeshave. A certain amount of the blending of the curves could not be completed until the piece was assembled, particularly the fit of the splice pieces at the junction of the arms and back legs.

The cutaway drawing indicates the general construction of the settee which is principally mortise and tenon work. The foam seat is supported on a ½in. ply base (the original specification states that it is to be 'well ventilated'). The back pad is supported on a light weight framework of 2 × ½in. ash, bridled in the corners and skinned with hardboard each side. The intervening hollow carries a cardboard honeycomb which lends a surprising rigidity to the structure. The foam is stuck to the hardboard face and the upholstery fabric applied overall, including the back of the panel.

A $\frac{5}{16}$in. bead mould is worked along the top of the back, front and side rails. Although this is best worked on a spindle moulder it could be worked with a scratch-stock formed from a piece of broken bandsaw blade suitably filed to shape.

Cherry wood is capable of providing a lustrous finish and any of the usual lacquers or wax polish could be used, burnished to a delicate shine.

SETTEE

Design by Edward Barnsley

Described and illustrated by R. W. Grant DLC FRSA MSIAD

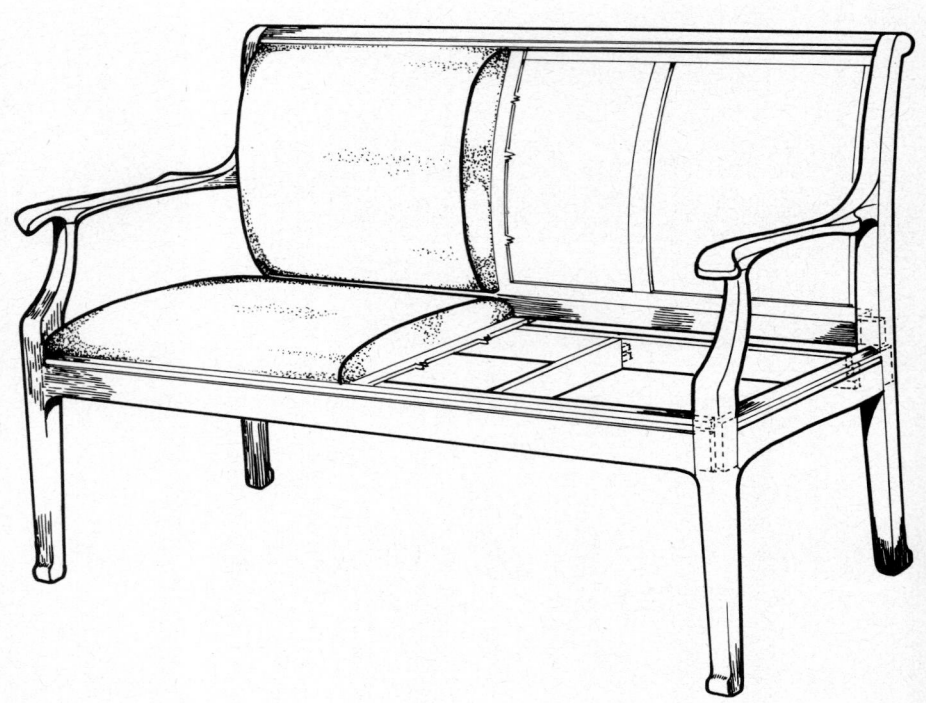

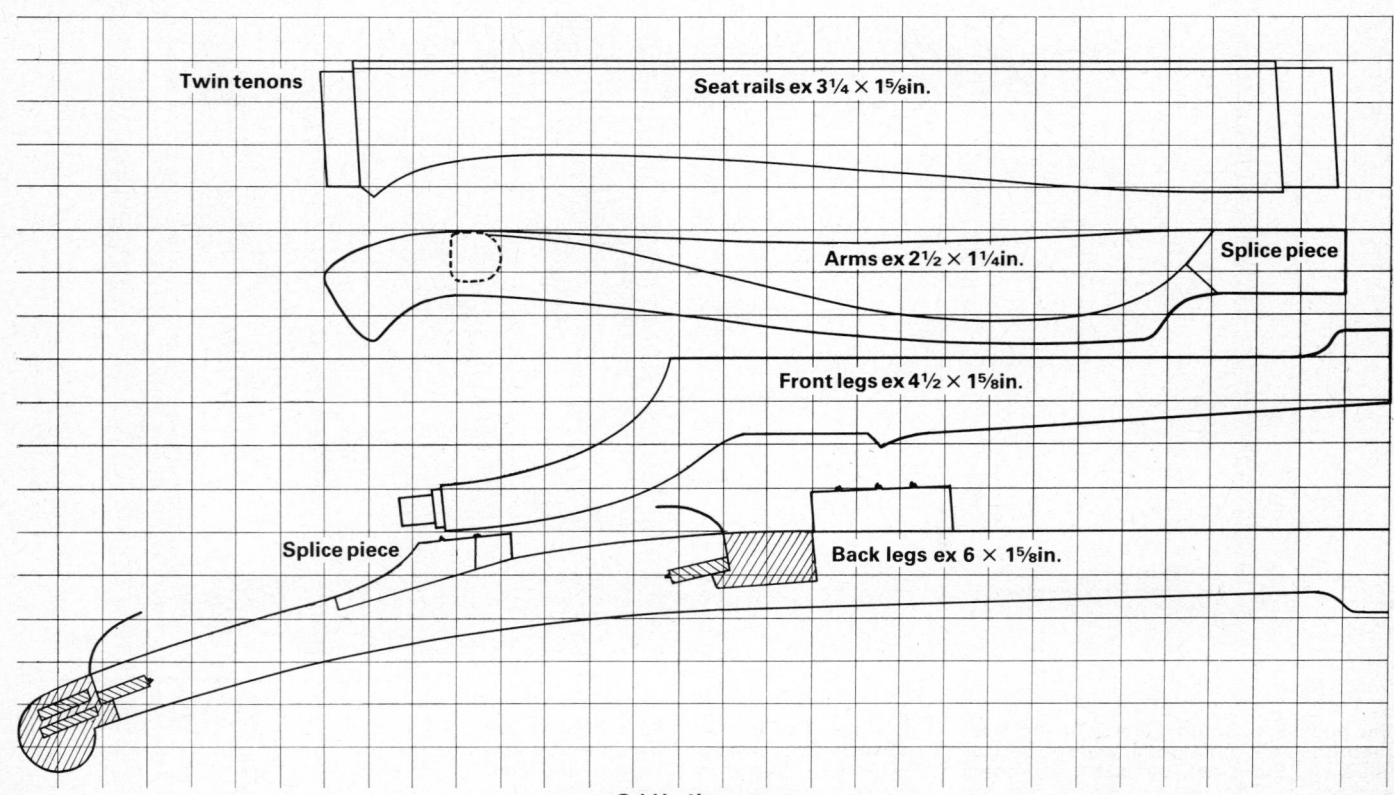

Twin tenons

Seat rails ex 3¼ × 1⅝in.

Arms ex 2½ × 1¼in.

Splice piece

Front legs ex 4½ × 1⅝in.

Splice piece

Back legs ex 6 × 1⅝in.

Grid in 1in. squares

Cutting list

Net sizes given

Note: Cutting curved pieces can be extremely wasteful of stock unless care is given to economical marking-out and 'fitting' pieces closely together. The sizes given in this list are for 'notional' blocks of wood. In practice the careful arrangement of the templates should result in considerably less wood being used than is shown in the list.

No.	Description	L	W	T	Material
2	Back legs	31¼in.	ex 6in.	1⅝in.	Cherry
2	Front legs	22½in.	ex 3¼in.	1⅝in.	Cherry
2	Arms	23½in.	ex 2½in.	1¼in.	Cherry
2	Splice pieces	3¼in.	ex 3¼in.	1⅝in.	Cherry
2	Side rails	22½in.	ex 3¼in.	1⅝in.	Cherry
1	Front rail	4ft.	3¼in.	1in.	Cherry
1	Back rail	4ft.	2⅜in.	1in.	Cherry
1	Top rail (back)	4ft.	2¼in.	1¾in.	Cherry
1	Lower rail (back)	4ft.	2½in.	1¼in.	Cherry
2	Seat support rails	21in.	2½in.	⅞in.	Cherry
2	Back frame rails	4ft.	2in.	½in.	Ash
2	Back frame stiles	14½in.	2in.	ex 1¼in.	Ash
2	Back frame muntins	14in.	2in.	ex 1¼in.	Ash
2	Back frame cover pieces	4ft.	14½in.	⅛in.	Hardboard
1	Seat base	4ft.	22in.	½in.	Plywood
4	Seat blocks for corners	3in.	3in.	1¼in.	Cherry

3in. thick foam and upholstery materials to suit.

WHAT'S ON

Masterclass '82

A series of lectures, demonstrations and exhibitions organised by Roger's of Hitchin and the White Knight Gallery, Cheltenham at the Sun Hotel, Hitchin 14 April-17 April; 10am-6pm, details from Betty Norbury (0242) 38582.

Tecnoforest '82

The Pacific International Trade Fair in Lima will be organising a second Tecnoforest from 19-28 November.

Maker's eye

The exhibition at the Crafts Council gallery, 12 Waterloo Place, has over 500 objects of contemporary design to give an insight into the quality and sheer fun of British craft. Admission charge 50p, new gallery opening hours Tuesday-Saturday 10am-5pm; Thursday 10am-7pm; sunday 2pm-5pm, closed Mondays. Open until 28 March. Fully illustrated catalogue available £5.95 from the exhibition or £6.95 by post.

Model exhibition

Reading Society of Model Engineers will be staging another exhibition of models on Saturday/Sunday 3-4 April at the Hexagon Civic Centre, Reading. Entries from individuals and other societies are welcome. Contact the exhibition manager A. B. Milne, 39 Springhill Road, Goring on Thames, Reading RG8 0BY (phone Goring 2949).

Spring/Summer '82

The current programme of spring and summer courses at the Earnley Concourse, Chichester is now available. Phone Bracklesham Bay 670392 or write to the administrator Owain Roberts at the Concourse, nr Chichester, Sussex PO20 7JL. Courses of interest to *Woodworker* readers include mounting and framing pictures, woodcarving and sculpture, marquetry, practical upholstery, arts and antiques of the 18th and 19th centuries.

Special Concession for advance ticket holders to the 1982 Model Engineer Exhibition

Due to the exceptionally bad weather conditions and the national rail strike, quite a large number of advance ticket holders, particularly from Wales, the West Country, the Midlands and the North, were unable to travel to the recently held Model Engineer Exhibition.

The Organisers, Model & Allied Publications Ltd, are therefore making an exceptional concession which will allow all such ticket holders to use their ticket(s) to visit the 1983 Model Engineer Exhibition. This concession is of course, an exception to the general rule by which advance ticket bookings are non-returnable, and applies only to those who have retained their tickets.

Those who, in the meantime, would like to visit the next major modelling exhibition spanning all the modelling hobbies, are reminded that the Model, Craft & Country Show will be held on 22-23 May at Stoneleigh, the headquarters of the Royal Agricultural Society, near Kenilworth, Warwickshire.

Leisure courses

City and Guilds of London are holding leisure courses during the summer holidays (June-August) in woodcarving, rural crafts, toymaking and soft furnishing. To find out more about the content of the courses, the colleges and how to enrol contact City & Guild of London (Leisure Courses) 76 Portland Place, London W1N 4AA (01-580 3050).

Carved and painted wood

Howard Raybould: Carved and painted wood until 3 April, British Crafts Centre, 43 Earlham St, Covent Garden, London WC2H 9LD, open Tuesday-Friday 10 am-5.30 pm, Saturdays 10 am-4 pm. A one man show of the work of this highly original designer.

French trade exhibitions

The major trade fair centres in Paris are the Parc des Expositions, Porte de Versailles and the CNIT Palace, Rond-Point de la Defense, both served by the metro. Details of French exhibitions can be obtained from French Trade Exhibitions, French Chamber of Commerce House, 54 Conduit St, London.

Interbimall '82

The International Biennial Exhibition of Woodworking Machinery and Tools will be held from 20-25 May at the Milan Fair.

Craft Fair

On the 27 March in the Civic Hall, Wimbledon, sponsored by the Lions Club of Merton in aid of charity. Admission 20p adults, children and OAPs free, open 10 am-5 pm.

John Penney describes his method of making a

DRESSING TABLE STOOL

I needed a stool but wanted something which looked craftsman-made.

I think the neo-classical curves of the finished piece achieve this. The curves also presented quite a challenging little carving exercise. Moreover, I had a stock of short offcuts in 4 × 2in. pine and wanted to put these to some productive use.

Pedestal: I made this first because it provides a template when cutting the mortises in the seat and base. First (using PVA woodworking glue throughout), I glued and cramped together five 305mm pieces along their 93mm wide faces. After planing the faces of the resulting block true I marked the outline of the pedestal on both faces. I drilled three 10mm holes through this block at A, B and C (Fig.1) to simplify cutting-out of the waste. I was able to saw out the two triangular pieces on either side of the block, to produce the waisted shape (Fig.1).

I then removed the waste on both faces of the block by cutting a saw slot down the centre of each face and then chiselling out the rest of the waste (Fig.2). I was careful not to cut deeper than 35mm each side, or the block could have split into two pieces along A—D. I cut out the V-neck at the top of the pedestal down to the hole already drilled at A (Fig.1). I was left with the two 20mm long

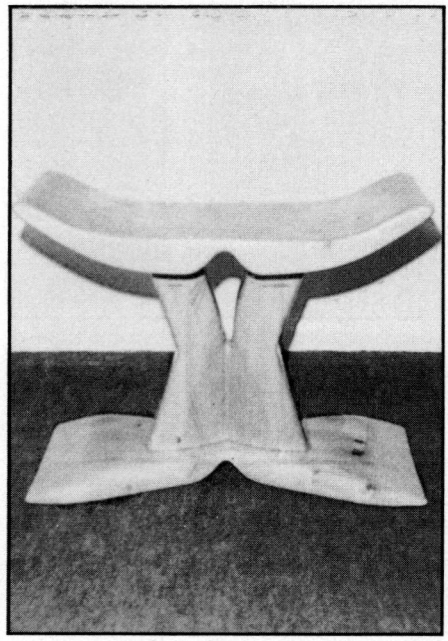

tenon stubs to cut out at both ends of the pedestal. X and Y were easy enough with a tenon saw, plus a small hacksaw for the inside edge of the pedestal top.

On the bottom I found it easiest to make a number of saw cuts 20mm deep across the bottom of the pedestal between the stubs W and Z, down to H—G. I chopped the waste between the kerfs out with a sharp chisel and rounded all the vertical edges and sanded the pedestal smooth.

Seat: I glued and cramped together six of the 510mm pieces along their 93mm faces and planed the resulting block true. I made an accurate template of the curved side of the seat out of card and traced this outline on to both sides of the block.

I used a circular saw attachment to my drill to cut a series of kerfs across the top of the block down to the seat outline (Fig.3). I then chiselled the waste out — a long job and one for which I wore goggles as the chips can achieve some velocity.

Before removing the waste on the underside of the seat in the way just described, I used the pedestal piece to mark-out the two mortises needed to accommodate tenons X and Y. I cut these out using a plunge router freehand. This is easy providing the outline is cut first using a series of straight-down

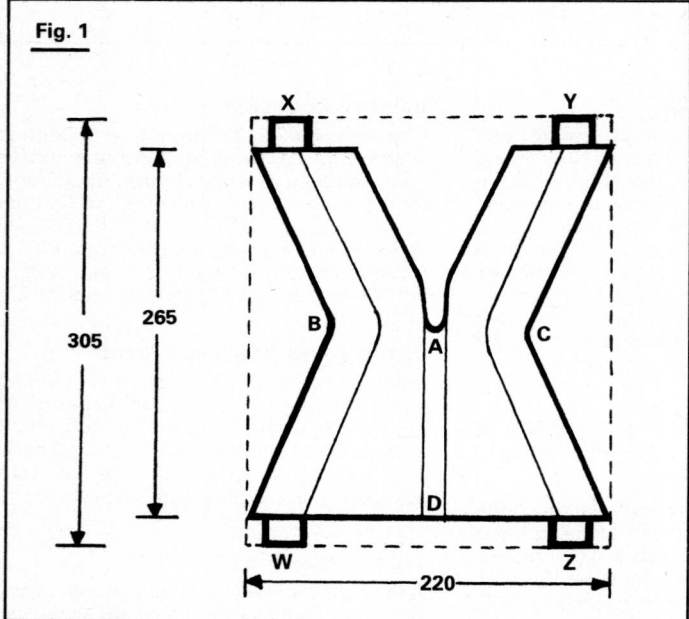

Fig. 1

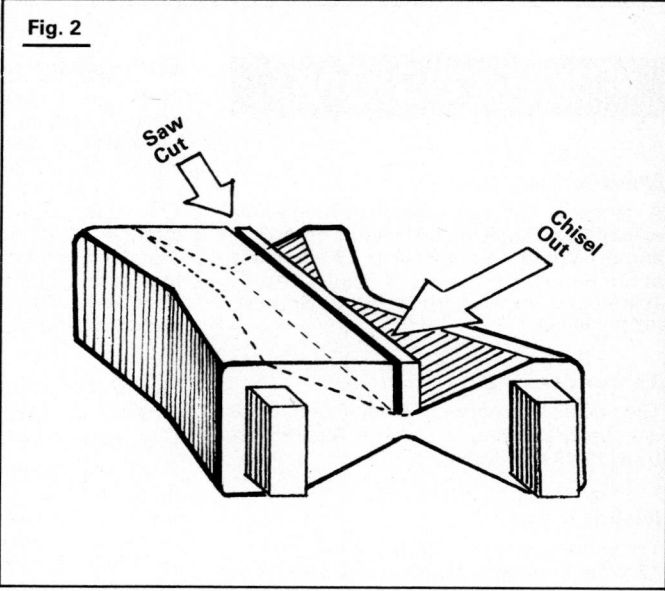

Fig. 2

CUTTING LIST

(These are finished dimensions — based on 4" × 2" P.A.R. Pine)

		mm	in
SEAT:	6 pieces	510 × 93 × 44	20 1/16 × 3 5/8 × 1 3/4
PEDESTAL:	5 pieces	305 × 93 × 44	12 × 3 5/8 × 1 3/4
BASE:	3 pieces	510 × 93 × 44	20 1/16 × 3 5/8 × 1 3/4

DRESSING TABLE STOOL

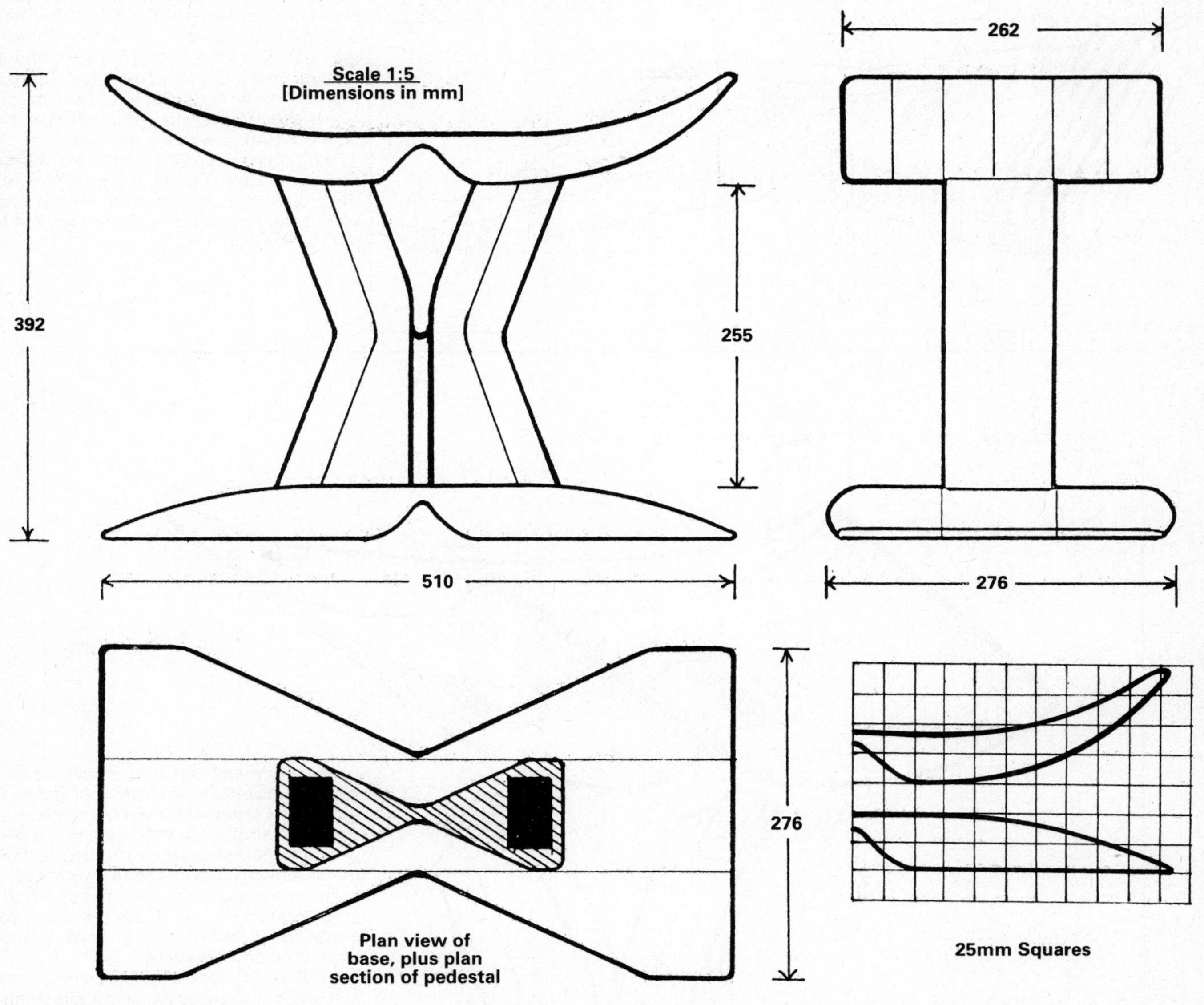

Scale 1:5
[Dimensions in mm]

392

255

510

262

276

276

Plan view of
base, plus plan
section of pedestal

25mm Squares

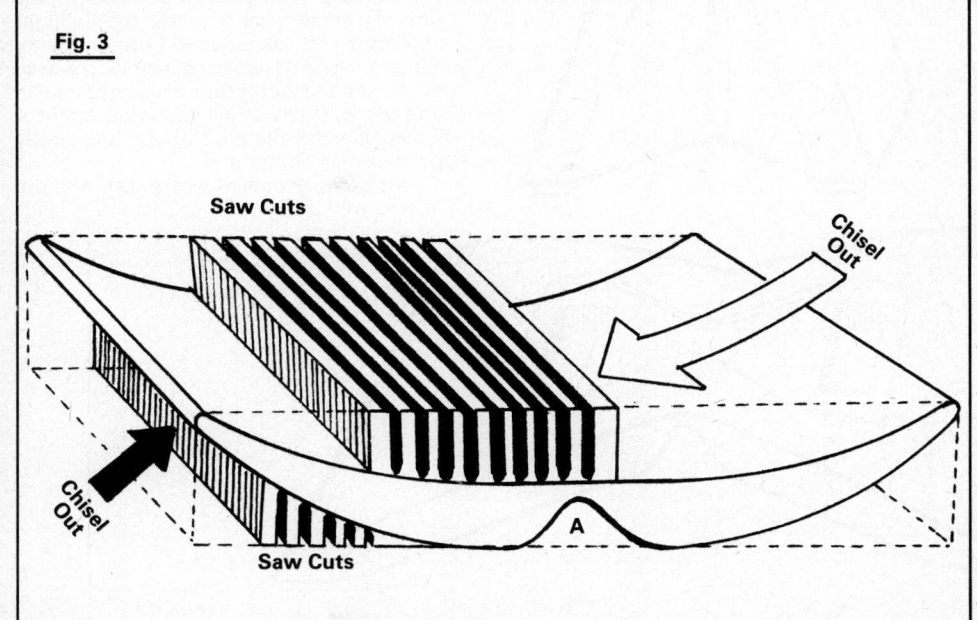

Fig. 3

Saw Cuts

Chisel
Out

Chisel
Out

Saw Cuts

A

plunges round the inside of the required outline.

The mortises were cut 25mm deep because the pedestal top was next recessed 5mm into the seat by pushing the tenons into their mortises and marking round the outline of the pedestal top on the seat bottom. This was then cut out using the router freehand, though a template could have been used. This recess avoids the problem of matching the top of the pedestal with the curved bottom of the seat. I cut the 30mm deep groove (A in Fig.3) across the bottom of the seat, using circular saw and chisel and a round Surform tool to shape the bottom of the groove.

Lastly I removed the rest of the waste on the seat bottom as with the seat top (Fig.3). I rounded all the edges and sanded the part smooth.

Base: I glued and cramped the remaining pieces together along their 44mm deep sides and planed true the resulting block. I made out of card a template of the base side shape and marked the outline of this on both edges of the block. Before going further I cut out the mortises in the top of the base for the pedestal tenon stubs W and Z.

Dressing table stool continued

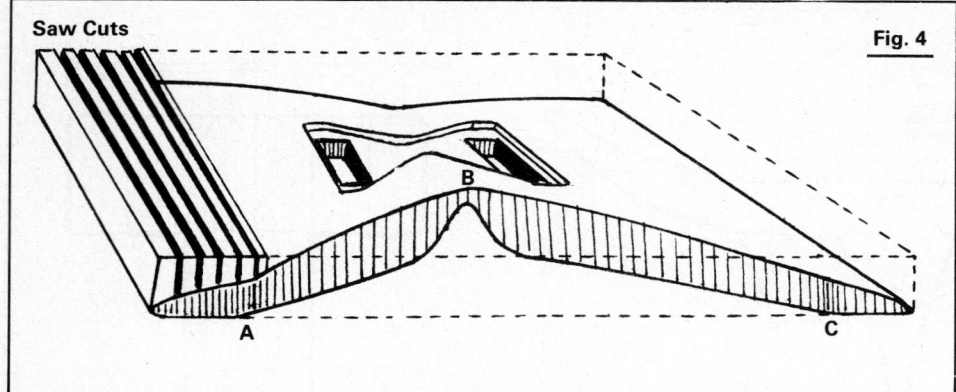

Saw Cuts   **Fig. 4**

As with the seat I cut a 5mm recess for the bottom of the pedestal around the mortises (Fig.4).

I removed the waste above the template outline using the circular saw to produce a series of kerfs across the top of the base, down to the template outline, and chiselled this out (Fig.4). I marked the triangular cutouts on either side of the base. (A, B, C in Fig.4). A hole drilled at the apex of each triangle (B in Fig.4) made this cutting easier. I did the cutting with a hand saw.

The 30mm deep groove across the bottom of the base was cut in the same way as the groove in the seat bottom. All the edges were rounded with a Surform tool and the part sanded smooth.

Fig. 5 Exploded drawing of the three completed components

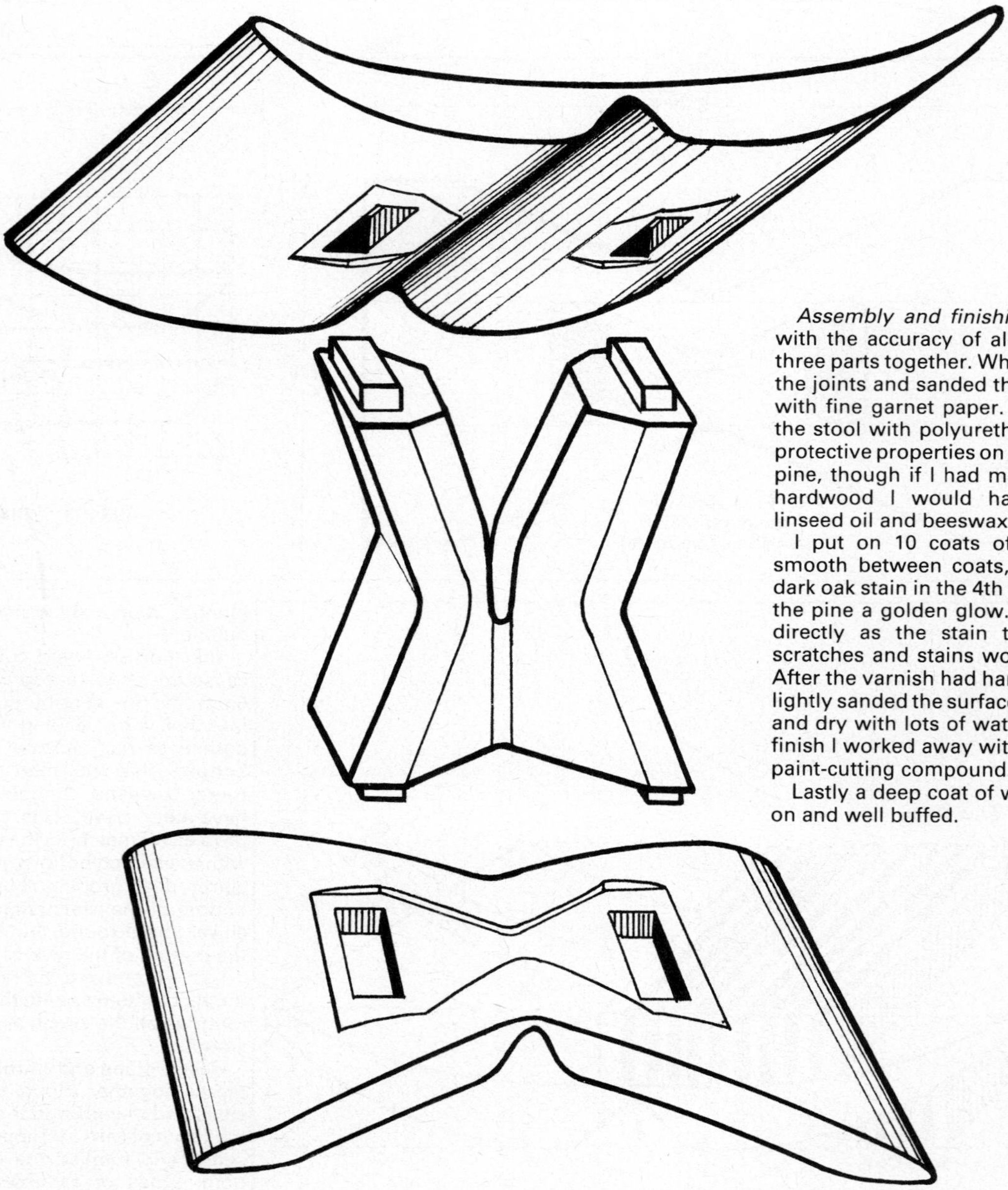

Assembly and finishing: Once satisfied with the accuracy of all joints I glued the three parts together. When dry I cleaned-up the joints and sanded the assembled piece with fine garnet paper. I decided to finish the stool with polyurethane varnish for its protective properties on such a soft wood as pine, though if I had made the stool from hardwood I would have used perhaps linseed oil and beeswax.

I put on 10 coats of varnish, sanding smooth between coats, with very diluted dark oak stain in the 4th to 8th coats to give the pine a golden glow. (I don't stain pine directly as the stain tends to highlight scratches and stains wood filler too dark). After the varnish had hardened for a week I lightly sanded the surface with very fine wet and dry with lots of water. To get a mirror finish I worked away with T-cut, a car body paint-cutting compound.

Lastly a deep coat of wax polish was put on and well buffed.

Boring HOLES

with Ralph Fellows

Turners at some time or another need to bore holes symmetrically around a circular block, pillar or such like. I devised an apparatus which seems to eliminate the guesswork and also provide the accuracy needed.

It takes the form of a previously made dividing plate (Photos 1, 2) with the addition of a locator and drilling jig. The dividing plate stays on my lathe all the time and is useful for turning the mandrel by hand.

As it is perfectly smooth I also use it as a handbrake. It is divided into 24 divisions which is probably more than most wood-workers need.

Photo 2 shows the locator about to be positioned; Photo 1 shows the locator in position. For ease of identification I have numbered the holes in the plate: 2 for half; 3 for thirds; 4 for quarters and so on. I used Letraset transfers and fixed them by spraying with a clear lacquer such as is used for protecting chrome plate on cars.

Components for making the drilling jig are few and simple (see Photos 3, 4). A small length of 2in. diameter steel tube is fitted to a standard which then fits into the toolrest holder in the normal way.

Into the tube a hardwood insert is fitted and secured in place by a small locking screw. This insert is the guide and the drill or bit used needs to have a straight shank with the insert drilled to suit, ie with no side play. A number of inserts are quickly turned and drilled to requirements) or they can be stored for future needs.

If, for example, Photos 5, 6 are taken to represent a three-legged stool being drilled for the legs, you can see how quickly and accurately you are able to set-up and drill the holes symmetrically and at the desired angle by using no. 3 on the dividing plate. Photo 7 shows the same set-up, though with a greater angle, eg to produce a splay to the leg fixing. The drive can be an ordinary portable drill or flexible shaft. I have omitted to show this for clarity.

You may need to drill a number of equally-spaced holes around the edge of a circular piece (Photo 8). The same principle applies whether you need to drill faceplate or spindle work. With this jig the operation is quite simple and accurate. Photo 9 shows the complete set-up on the lathe.

1 ◄

2 ◄

▼ 3

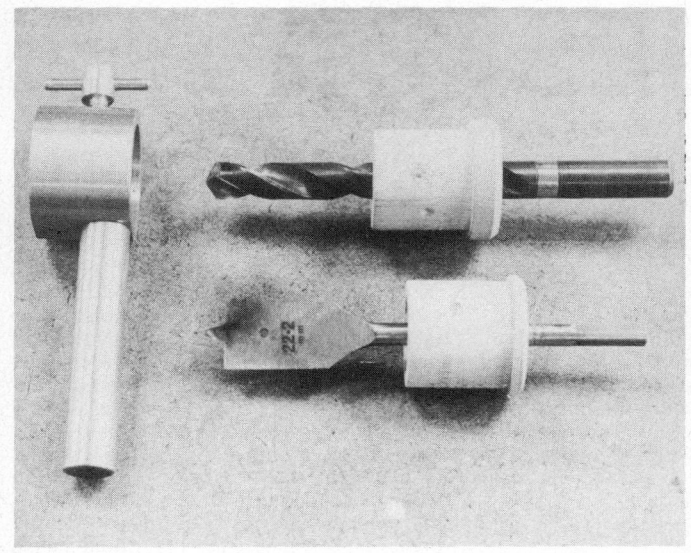

4 ▲

5 ▲

6 ▲

7 ▲

8▲

9▲

GATES

by V. J. Taylor

These gate designs are intended to cope with two sets of circumstances which occur very frequently and call for really robust woodwork.

Design A (Fig. 1) is a farm or estate gate, and although the opening width shown is only 8ft 6in. (2m 590mm) the dimensions of timber could certainly be employed for a gate of 10ft (3m 46mm) width. Over this width it would, of course, be advisable to use a pair of gates.

Design B (Fig. 1) is designed as a house entrance gate and incorporates a wicket gate which allows casual visitors to call without using the main gate and thoughtlessly leaving it open. It would not be difficult to fix a spring-closing device to the wicket in conjunction with a trip-catch and this would prevent the dog getting out.

The first requirement is to settle on the timber to be utilised and there are three conditions to bear in mind, namely cost, type of finish required and ease of working. If expense is not a prime factor hardwoods like English oak, rock elm or iroko would be ideal, although cheaper ones like ash or sweet chestnut (NOT horse chestnut) are not to be sneezed at. The first three are liable to be pretty hard to work while the last two are comparatively easy. It would be a pity to paint any of them, and an attractive and serviceable finish could be obtained with several coats of good quality marine varnish. However, it is more likely that most people will prefer to use softwood, with a paint finish. In this case, try to choose the timber yourself and look for sound, knot-free stuff. If you can it's a good idea to buy the stuff some months in advance so that you can season it before using it.

Design A

The two stiles plus the top and bottom rails are all from 4 by 2½in. (100 × 65mm), while the brace, strut, and intermediate rails are from 3½ by 2in. (90 × 50mm) stuff. The two posts really need to be oak and are 8 inches (200mm) square. As they need to be sunk into the ground to a depth of 1ft 6in.-2ft (460 - 610mm), there will not be much waste from pieces 6 feet (1m 830mm) long.

You will see that there is a 45° by ½in. deep chamfer worked on both designs on some of the rails. The parts, in general, are both long and heavy and it would be as well to work the chamfers by hand, the running-out of the ends being finished by means of a rasp or shaper tool.

Now we come to the jointing which, if we tackle it methodically, can be enjoyable and rewarding. One type of joint, the wedged tenon, is used to join the top and bottom rails to the stiles in both designs, and the principle of how it works is shown in Fig. 2. Note that the mouth of the mortise is sloped to allow for the expansion of the tenon when the wedges are driven in. The slots for the wedges are not taken down the full depth of the tenon as this would cause undue strain, and the mortise sides are sloped correspondingly. Always use hardwood wedges, even with softwood joints, and make sure they are bone dry.

The draw-bored mortise and tenon, is used for joining the intermediate rails to the stiles (Fig. 3). The tenon here is a 'stub tenon' — in other words, it does not pass right through. Cut it in the usual way, making sure the shoulders are a good square fit, and then (with the tenon removed from the mortise and replaced by a suitably-sized piece of scrap wood) bore two holes right through both walls of the mortise. The diameter of these holes depends on the size of the dowels you are employing, and ⅜in. (10mm) would be about right.

Position the centre of each hole as shown in Fig. 3, about ½in. (12mm) in from the edge. Next, fit the tenon into the mortise and cramp the joint up. Use the point of a twist-bit inserted in the hole to make a mark on the tenon and then take the joint apart

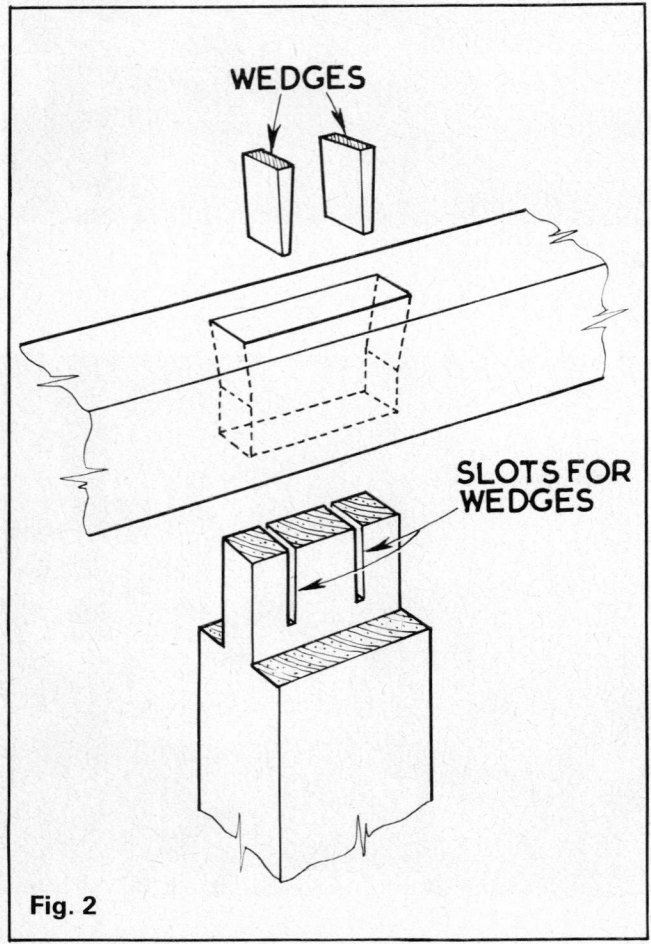

WEDGES

SLOTS FOR WEDGES

Fig. 2

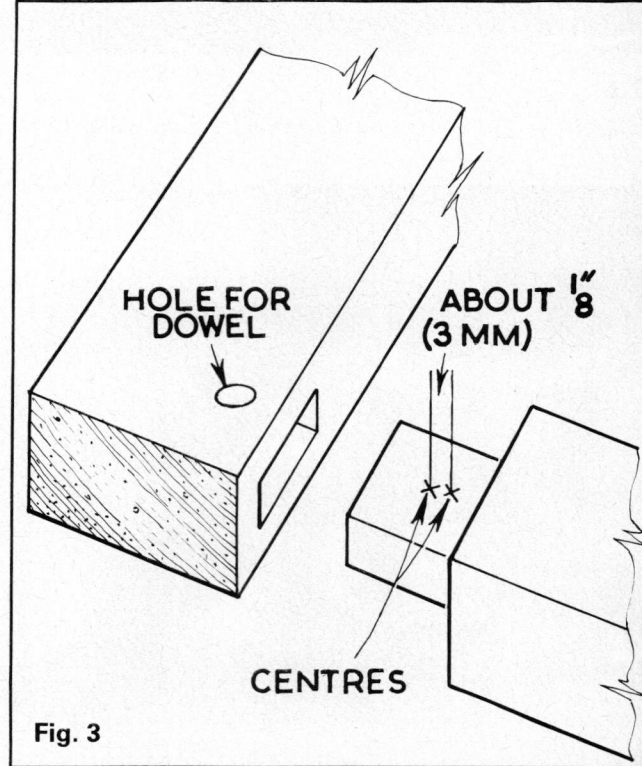

HOLE FOR DOWEL

ABOUT 1"/8 (3 MM)

CENTRES

Fig. 3

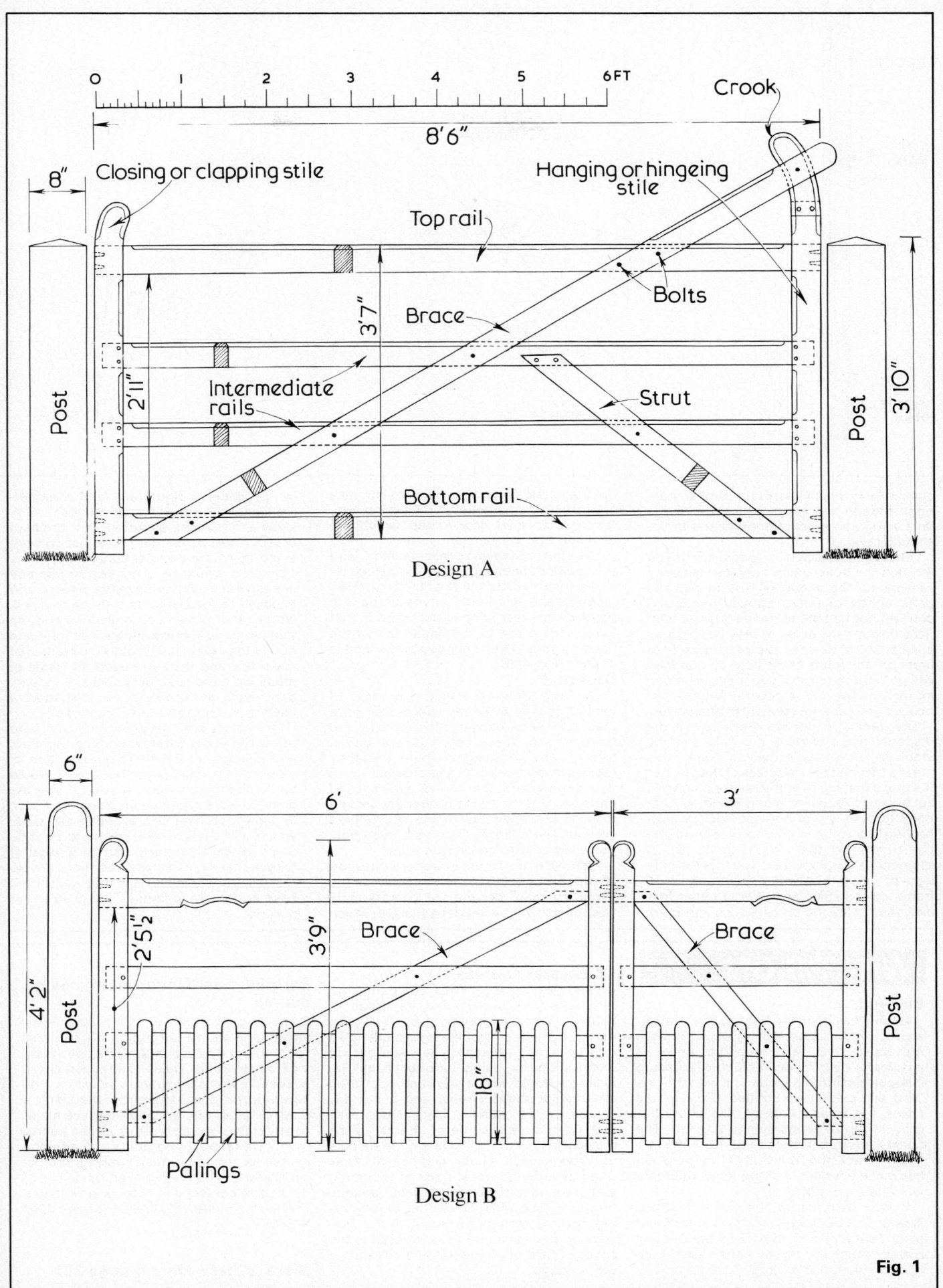

Design A

Design B

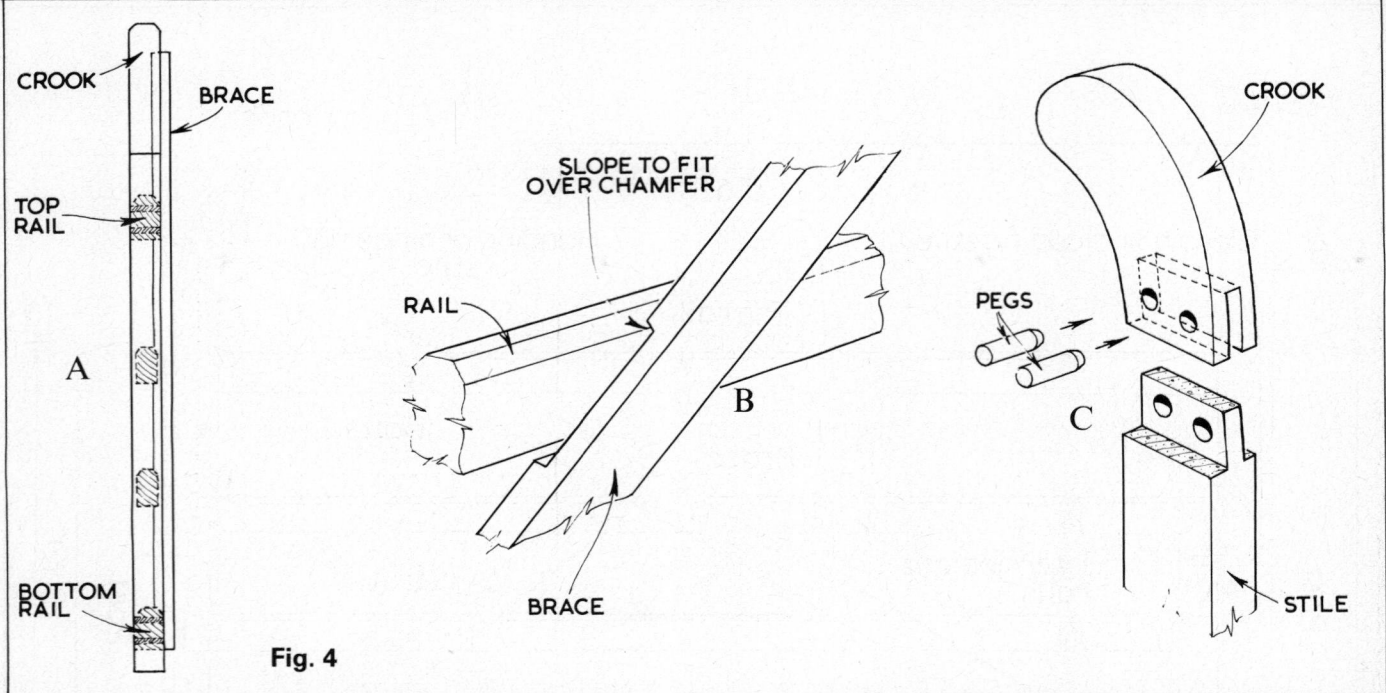

Fig. 4

again. Carry on by boring a similar hole right through the tenon, the centre of this hole being about ⅛in. (3mm) nearer to the shoulder (Fig. 3).

Obviously, if dowels or 'pegs' are driven through the holes when the joint has been assembled, the action will be to pull the parts tightly together. Equally obviously, you will not be able to drive square-ended pegs through the holes as they will stop up against the tenons, so the procedure is to taper off the points of the pegs so that they will go right through. If you make each peg an inch or two (25 to 50mm) longer than needed you can trim them flush afterwards.

The joint used at the areas where the diagonal brace crosses the rails and the crook is known as a 'halved' joint. This means that half the thickness of the parts of the brace that lap over the rails and crook is cut away as shown at A and B (Fig. 4). One point to note is that one shoulder of each halving has to be sloped to accommodate the bevels on the rails (Fig. 4) (B). A moment's thought will tell you that the only way to cut the halvings accurately is to frame up the stiles and rails together first and then to lay the brace across and mark out the joints. When the joints are cut, they are further strengthened by inserting ¼in. (6mm) dia. steel coach-bolts which are fastened with washers and nuts.

The strut is fixed in a similar fashion, with the addition that its upper end is halved on to the intermediate rail to a depth of 1½in. (38mm), and this joint is draw-bored and pegged. The last joint to deal with is that joining the crook to the upper end of the hanging stile. Here, a pegged bridle joint is utilised (Fig. 4) (C).

Design B

The only difference in the method of jointing is that while the two braces have their two ends halved over the top and bottom rails, these halvings are bolted through and not pegged. There is slightly more ornamentation in the chamfering of this design, and the curved and shaped parts can best be accomplished by using a rasp or a shaper tool of the appropriate section. The palings, of course, need only be nailed on with galvanised nails.

Now we come to the important question of whether or not to use any adhesive in the joints. If you do, then the one to use is an RF (resorcinol formaldehyde) adhesive, which is completely waterproof and weather-resistant; UF (urea formaldehyde) adhesives are almost as good but ordinary casein, PVA, or animal glues just will not stand up to the weather conditions. In my opinion it would be a mistake to use any adhesive at all. Anything made of wood and exposed to the elements is going to swell, shrink, and move in all directions and the thing to do is to make allowances for it and not try to prevent it. The old-time craftsmen knew this and therefore used the kinds of joints we have been describing — indeed, they had to, as the only glues they had were useless in damp and wet conditions.

One thing is worth doing and that is to prime the joints before cramping them up, and this applies whether you use paint or varnish as a finish. In either case I would apply aluminium wood primer. If you are going to have a varnish finish you will have to paint it on carefully, avoiding any parts which will show. There seems to be little point in specifying any particular type of hinges, hasps, or catches as there are so many kinds to choose from that you should have no trouble in finding one to suit your purpose.

WHAT'S ON

Bird Art

Quality has been the bottom line in every aspect of the Leigh Yawley Woodson Art museum's Bird Art Exhibition since its inception in 1976. In 1976 the museum inaugurated its public opening with the first 'bird art' exhibition entitled *Birds of the Lakes, Fields and Forests.* The show has grown from 23 artists then to 100 now. The quality of work is becoming more diversified. A grant from the Gulf Oil Corporation has made a 'selections from the exhibition' world tour possible.

It was featured at the Royal Scottish Academy, Edinburgh, in late January and early February and moves to the Natural History museum, South Kensington, London for the period 4 March-1 May.

Chichester courses

West Dean college, West Dean, Chichester, Sussex, has extended its range of courses. Wood engraving proved popular during the winter months and is extended into the summer season; a new approach to woodcarving is being introduced by Howard Raybould with a weekend course on ornamental shallow relief and a five-day course on the same subject. Oboe reed making in June may be of interest to the musical instrument makers among readers of *Woodworker*. Other courses at West Dean include the usual ones of mounting and framing pictures, caring for antique furniture, cane and rush seating, woodcarving, making cottage furniture, and upholstery. Inquiries should be addressed to the college office of phone 0243-63 301 during office hours.

Early keyboard instrument making course

Coinciding with this year's Chichester Festivities John Storrs is running his summer course in early keyboard instrument making from 9-19 July. These 10 day courses are residential and participants can with a little hard work produce at the end of the course a playing spinet or clavichord, or have made considerable progress on a larger instrument. There are opportunities during the course for informal music making, discussions and theatre outings. For full details of the course contact John Storrs at Hunston, Chichester Sussex PO20 6NR (phone 0243 789605).

More 'What's On' on page 237

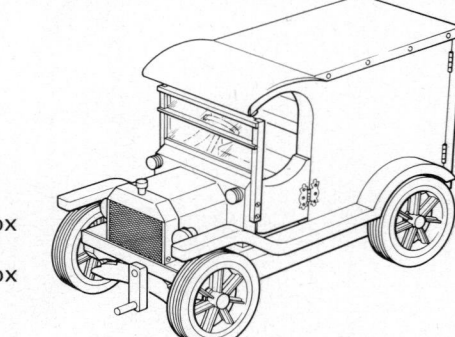

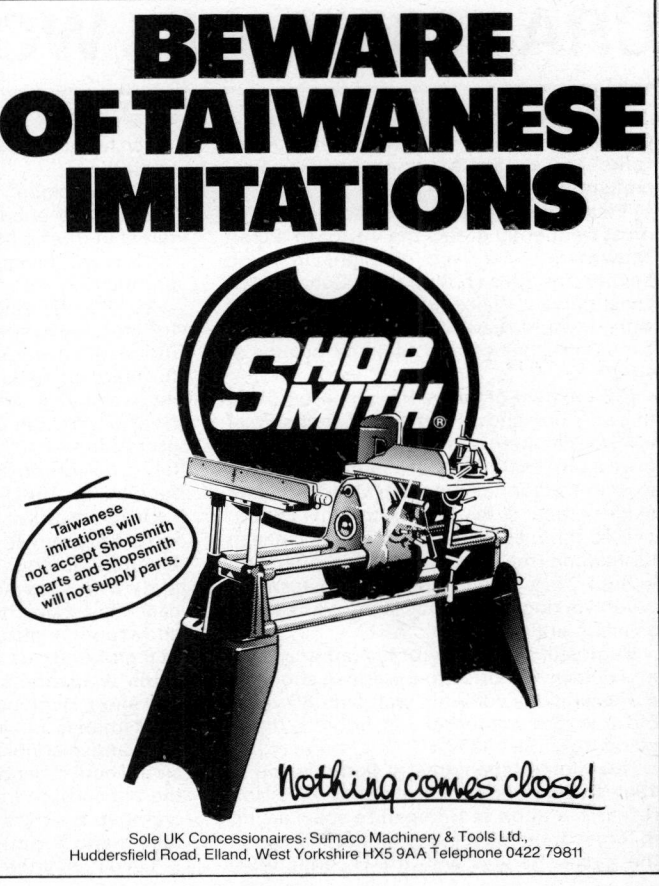

CRAFTSMAN IN WOOD

Above: Hugh Loughborough in his show-room with some of his pieces. Below: At work on the Evenwood bandsaw.

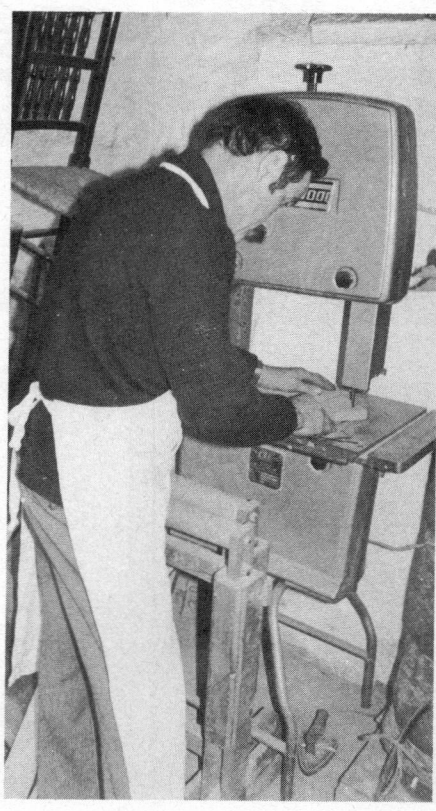

On the west coast of Wales Arthur Jones talks to a 'Satisfaction millionaire' craftsman.

'Please do not handle' is the sign which most frequently greets the visitor to a craft showroom. There are no signs in Hugh Loughborough's showroom at Solva on the coast of west Wales. But if he did put up a sign it would read: 'Please run your hand over these pieces and feel the beauty of wood.'

He is a lover of native British timbers and this affection shows in the craftsmanship of the wooden items he displays. These range from a modest little stool in elm priced at £7 to a 4ft traditional-style elm Welsh dresser at £990. Most of his work is commissioned.

Throughout his life he has stayed close to timber and trees. Even as a boy growing up in Surrey he saw his father's enthusiasm for woodworking, though his living was earned as an engineer.

Hugh still uses some of his father's tools and points with pride to a wooden shooting plane which is certainly well over 80 years old and perfect; or to his father's metal plane from the 1920s.

Hugh joined the Forestry Commission in 1941 and worked as a forester at Alice Holt research station in Hampshire specialising in forest pathology. Except for four years in the forces, he was with the FC until 1955,

when he went into farm management for 12 years.

As he explains, this close contact with the countryside enabled him to retain his interest in trees while his skills in woodworking proved invaluable for odd job repairs around the farm.

In 1969 he decided to set-up his own furniture workshop as a small rural craft industry, producing traditional country furniture in native timbers. He had been inspired by the fine chair-making of Neville Neal of Stockton, Warwickshire, and he is a great admirer of the furniture designs by the late Sir Gordon Russell, (WOODWORKER for October 1981).

He chose Solva for his workshop, acquiring small premises in the High Street of this beautiful harbour, a delight with fishermen and owners of small craft. Appropriately he called his shop The Craftsman, with a small showroom to attract the visitors who come in their hundreds every summer to Solva.

His workshop is behind the showroom and shop. Hugh needs more space, but The Craftsman is in the Pembrokeshire national park and planners will not permit expansion. There is barely room to move between the benches and machines, but from such cramped quarters comes a flow of beautifully-made furniture.

'Obviously I feel strongly that traditional

furniture and woodware is superior if made from solid wood, and even better when native timbers are used,' says Hugh. 'I aim to produce pieces to a high standard, but I'm anxious to show visitors that you don't have to pay the earth for craftsman-made furniture, whether to traditional or original designs. What I make is practical and pleasing to the eye — something people will want to use and keep for a lifetime.

'Even so, my prices bear comparison with the best of mass-produced furniture. But my customers know they are not buying fashion pieces which will break or show their age and be discarded in a few years. I work in the knowledge that much of my output will be in use and giving pleasure long after I've departed this world!'

He admits readily to a prejudice for native hardwood and does not stock either soft-wood or imported hardwood. Nor does he favour ornamentation, but sticks to designs possessing their own simple charm.

Perhaps use of the word 'design' is a little misleading because Hugh never works to detailed drawings so no two pieces are identical. From his books of traditional furniture styles, customers can select a piece which approximates to their needs and then discuss the variations they would like, including the actual size of the piece. And from these instructions he will produce the finished article.

'I do the smaller pieces so that I have something to sell immediately to visitors, but I cannot make the bigger pieces for stock — I simply haven't the spare room for them,' he explain.

He produces tables of various kinds up to 10ft; a 5ft 6in. refectory table in elm costs £650. A popular line is the rush-seat ladder-back chair.

Above: His father's shooting and metal planes — still in fine working condition.

Great care is taken with the selection of the right wood for the job. He works in oak, elm, ash, chestnut, sycamore and some-times in cherry. From experience he has proved it is worthwhile to stick with a single supplier, and he trades with a Leicestershire merchant who knows his requirements.

'I visit his yard to select the logs which are cut through-and-through into planks of thicknesses from ¾ to 6in. but mainly I need the smaller sizes,' says Hugh. Cheapest hardwood at the moment is elm and the dearest is oak, which can cost up to £20 a cu ft. 'I find it difficult to get all the wood I want of the required high quality,' he comments.

Below: An interior shot of the workshop at The Craftsman.

CRAFTSMAN IN WOOD

All wood has to be thoroughly seasoned and he keeps his stock of hardwood planks in-stick under cover so that the drying process is continuous. 'Modern houses are so often heated to a high level, and this is the bane of the furniture maker,' he says despairingly. 'Central heating can mean a m.c. requirement of 12% or less. This has a diabolical effect upon furniture if the wood has not been properly dried beforehand.

'I need my wood down to at least 16% when it comes into the workshop. I sometimes bring it down much farther, especially where I want a tight fit with chair rungs,' he comments 'As drier rungs take up moisture and swell so the tight fit becomes even tighter. Old woodworkers used this method so they needed hardly any glue in the joint.' Care has to be taken not to dry wood too quickly or splits develop.

Elm he uses in considerable quantities though he finds it somewhat of a woolly character. But it has the advantage of being among the least expensive hardwood. It is a tough wood, ideal for Windsor chairs and stools.

Dutch elm disease has taken its toll and supplies could become short in the future, but the disease does not affect the timber if the tree is felled, cut and seasoned within 18 months of the attack. If logs are left lying around too long the wood begins to yellow and rot appears.

Ash he finds excellent for chairs, tables and tool handles. 'It is a really strong wood, but it must be fast-grown,' says Hugh. 'The colour is attractive for furniture.' He finds that people tend to select wood for colour rather than other characteristics.

Oak is the prestige wood at The Craftsman. 'It has a beautiful figure and doesn't break away from the chisel — you can get a lot more detail when working in oak,' is Hugh's opinion. He uses it mainly for tables and dressers.

Sycamore is wood which he uses mainly for kitchen items like chopping boards — 'But it has little character.' Yew he sometimes uses for decorative items. 'It's a hard wood with a beauty all its own,' he claims.

The subtle colour of cherry he likes for dressing tables, but it is a brittle wood demanding care in the workshop.

His workshop equipment includes a Coronet lathe to turn chair and table legs and rungs, for example, with an extra long bed for chair backs having the back and leg pieces in one. 'It's been in constant use for 10 years without giving any trouble,' he says which is tribute indeed. Hugh is also full of praise for his Evenwood bandsaw, the Multico sawbench and planer, and a DeWalt overhead saw and sander. He has a German drilling machine and a wide range of hand tools.

Sawdust is used in the workshop to provide all the heat required, burning in an efficient stove-heater.

The ash goes into his greenhouse to help feed the plants.

Most of his furniture is given a final wax finish, but where resistance to heat and stain is needed he applies a polyurethane finish.

His shop is rightly named. Hugh Loughborough is indeed a craftsman — a man who works with loving care and skill in wood. His output is limited so he will never make a fortune. But if satisfaction were to figure in his profit-and-loss account, then Hugh is a millionaire.

Shavings fly as Hugh turns a stool leg on his lathe.

BOOK REVIEWS

Before the roof sagged

Ever-increasing charges for maintenance work around the home coupled with the seeming unwillingness of some 'trades' to call when wanted (ever tried to get a plumber to attend to a burst pipe after 5.00 pm?) encourages homeowners to attempt their own repairs and renovations. There are even redecorating schemes operated by some local authorities whereby tenants carry out the work themselves.

Thus the diy army advances and as with all operations there are casualties. Surely you have heard the one about the chap who attempted to put an extra room in his loft and sawed through the purlin to make more headroom, heedless of the creaking sag of the rafters and rattle of slates as they cascaded to the ground? This story may be apochryphal but there are others founded on truth. Their unwitting and hapless authors would do well to get a copy of the *Which? Book of Do-it-Yourself*, along with those others who want a reliable and authoritative manual which deals with every aspect of home maintenance — including legal aspects of building regulations and planning permission.

Wood has always been a major building material and brick-and-tile constructions employ large amounts of it. There are indications that the domestic dwellings of the near future will contain even more timber — the November 1981 issue of WOODWORKER had something to say about this.

It is no surprise therefore that of the 12 chapters which comprise the book, six cover topics that come directly within the woodworker's sphere: floors, stairs, roofs, doors, windows etc, and one is devoted exclusively to woodworking itself. Tools, materials, processes and techniques are covered in detail although I would not heed the advice to hang up planes to store them, nor would I sharpen a saw then set it — rather the other way round.

Like its stablemate *Which? Way to Repair and Restore Furniture* reviewed in WOODWORKER for September 1981, this is a thoroughly useful book, clearly written, accompanied by excellent diagrams. It is a veritable compendium of knowledge and instruction on the repair and maintenance of the structure, services and decoration of the home.

Published by Consumer's Association, 14 Buckingham Street, London WC2N 6DS (ISBN 0-340-26237-0); it is priced at £11.95.

R.W.G.

Get carving!

Apart from a chapter on carving for casting (which may seem inappropriate for such a title), *Woodcarving: An Introduction* by Maurice Woods follows the general style and content of several books on the subject which have appeared before. Nevertheless it is well written and illustrated; it could be recommended to the prospective carver.

The basic tool requirements are described and procedures for handling and sharpening chisels are dealt with in detail. The explanations are helped by many good illustrations. The section on relief carving is particularly clear. Choosing a single example of a carved wooden plaque, the author sets out the step-by-step procedure from start to finish in a way that should encourage the reader to have a go.

Carving in the round is dealt with along the same lines. Other chapters cover carving heads (understandably not so easy to follow); letter carving; chip carving and finishing. This is dealt with rather sketchily and omits any direct reference to the polyurethane finishes which can be so satisfactory and easy to apply.

The list of timbers for carving omits several of the best domestic woods which are available in some districts, and several of which are advertised by suppliers in WOODWORKER. These include holly, boxwood, hornbeam and fruit woods, especially pear.

The author may have deliberately avoided any more than a brief reference to the use of machine tools in carving. However machine tools are owned by so many woodworkers that they might have deserved a special chapter. I refer particularly to the valuable part that can be played by the bandsaw, router and small high-speed rotary carving tools.

Similarly, in the important aspect of securing the carving, alternative methods are available today which allow greater speed and flexibility in changing the position of the carving while working on it.

The question frequently asked by prospective carvers is: 'Where do I get the materials and special tools required to make a start?' In a book introducing the subject it would have been helpful to have had a list of suppliers or, at least, reference to specialist publications such as WOODWORKER which carry many advertisements by timber and tool suppliers.

Publisher is Adam & Charles Black Ltd, 35 Bedford Row, London WC1R 4JH (reference ISBN 0-7136-2148-6) and the price is £6.95

A. A.

Who's for a taco tweezer?

Yet another book by an American author has come my way for review. There seems to be a plethora of such publications, either direct from American pubishers or through English publishing houses, an arrangement which may be financially advantageous to the publishers concerned. But it seems to me to be a sad comment in the long term on British publishers and British authors.

Our once thriving film industry disappeared under the weight of American and then other foreign films and our cinemas almost all became bingo halls. What will be made of obsolete British publishing houses I wonder?

But to return to the *Woodworker's Book of Wooden Kitchen Utensils* by Vance Studley, a large-format hardback of only 128 pages at £13.55. It contains instructions for making over 40 wooden utensils suitable for use in the preparation and serving of food; from stirrers and scoops to storage and display accessories. These range from the simple, well-known implements to more exotic gadgets such as a kibbi hammer (no kitchen should be without one) and a Mexican taco tweezer (yes I, too, asked 'what's that?').

Each piece of work is discussed as a separate project under sub-headings: wood, equipment, procedure. Each project includes a sketch of the finished object and dimensioned line drawings showing stages of work, some of which can be used as patterns for enlarging and transferring to the workpiece. There are no photographs in the book.

With text, each project occupies two or three pages and all instructions are for making the items using hand tools only. No lathe work is involved, even for things such as egg cups, spice 'jars' etc, which would normally be turned. Although the author makes it all sound very simple some of the projects will require a great deal of skill and a lot of time spent on finishing.

A number of items are made from bamboo, others from a wide range of woods both hard and soft, several of which I would not consider suitable for utensils in touch with food. My own preference is always sycamore, then beech; neither taint food and both can be kept properly clean by scrubbing with old-fashioned water.

With several introductory pages on wood and tools etc and a short glossary and selected bibliography — mainly of American publications — the book is a useful but very expensive source of ideas. My own experience of making kitchen utensils is that it is almost always cheaper to buy them at specialist stores.

But hand-made and well-made in the right material utensils are nice to use and are appreciated by some. And anyway it is always satisfying to be able to say 'I made that'.

The *Woodworker's Book of Wooden Kitchen Utensils* is published by Van Nostrand Reinhold Co Ltd, Molly Millers Lane, Wokingham RG11 2PY. Reference is ISBN 0-442-24726-5.

J.H.

Right way crooked

The crooked man (physically not mentally) and the crooked cat and mouse 'all live together in a little crooked house', so the nursery rhyme tells us.

The toymaker of Pebble Mill fame, Richard Blizzard, has created the crooked house by crooked building (not to be confused with jerry-building so he assures us in *Top Toys from Pebble Mill* (ISBN 0-950-7781-17) published by Chestnut Tree, Five Leaves, Bussage, Stroud GL6 8AT, at £2. It can be had from this address or through selected booksellers.

The book runs to 32 pages of dimensioned drawings and cutting lists for the crooked house, a baby-walker, Model T Ford van, fisherman, wheelbarrow, castle, rocking cradle, waddling duck, timber waggon and a fire appliance. In addition there are a number of excellent colour pictures of some of the items and the delightful Blizzard children who, as Marian Foster writes in her foreword, had much pleasure in 'consumer-testing their father's work'.

In addition to the drawings and cutting lists the author gives good instructions for making the items. He also includes useful addresses for such things as wheels, axles and spring caps, non-toxic paints and varnish and tools.

The book is well-produced and the colour pictures both inside and on the soft covers are of excellent quality. They really make you want to start work on a crooked house, the model T Ford van or any of the other toys.

By the way dimensions are given in mm and in. which is particularly useful for grandfathers or others who have still to catch up with the EEC!

Richard Blizzard must be one of the best-known toymakers with a huge following on his Pebble Mill programmes. The popularity of his latest book seems assured; 7000 copies were sold within three and a half weeks.

G.P.

Quality joinery

In his introduction to *Contract Joinery* the author Ken Austin says it is his considered opinion that the standards of workmanship have dropped considerably since pre-war times. Economic requirements of industry demand that any improvement in quality must be made without additional labour costs. The solution can only lie in better training. The City & Guilds of London Institute, the Institute of Carpenters and other examining bodies are making worthwhile efforts in this direction by conducting yearly examinations in the woodworking crafts.

Ken Austin has been an examiner for the City & Guilds of London Institute over the last 18 years, the last 10 of these in 'purpose made joinery'. He proposes that his book covers the subject of purpose made joinery; not specifically working from the City & Guilds syllabus but taking the term to express one-off or low multiples of work to an architect's specification using machines where economically viable.

He introduces connected ancillaries (geometry, calculations, scientific principles and special tools) where convenient and at the end of each chapter gives 3 or 4 questions about the subject covered; usually drawn from a past public examination paper.

The book ends with a chapter of answers to these questions. A discussion and model answer is provided to illustrate each point.

Basically the book is a manual of good craftsmanship, lucidly expressed and illustrated with simple well proportioned sketches and the general principles of technical drawing.

Tools and materials does not duplicate the information easily obtained from popular textbooks or trade catalogues. It concentrates on the principles behind tool design and tool classification, details the differences to be found between modern adhesives, explains the various categories of sheet materials and timbers and their uses.

The safety aspects of powered hand tools and woodworking machinery are emphasised and much of the layman's confusion over electrical terms and ratings is explained. Several pages are taken to explain the principles of machine woodworking, calculating pitch and angles of planing cutters are detailed also.

Complete chapters are deovted to single subjects – doors, windows, partitions and panelling, staircases, handrails, glulam timbers and plywood constructions. All these chapters contain calculations, projections, assembly, design and building. A chapter on veneers is particularly useful, it gives a wealth of advice on pattern hammer veneering, adhesives, preparation of the ground, pattern veneering under pressure, cutting and fitting complicated veneers eg curved rails and panels. Chapter 10 deals with ecclesiastical joinery and fitments. It includes linen-fold panels, church benches and pews, litany desks, altar rails, pulpits, doors, fonts and galleries.

This beautifully produced book is excellent and exceptionally good value at £9.25 (hardback) from Northwood Publications Ltd (Book Dept), Northwood House, 93-99 Goswell Road, London EC1V 7QA (ISBN 7198 2950X). Detailed as a building trades journal book it is invaluable for anyone wishing to produce good quality joinery, a standard 'classic' of the future for joinery apprentices. The examination techniques proposed by the author, if followed by the reader, should produce excellent results and lift the standards of craftsmanship among the young and old alike. **P.C.**

Stobart and Son Ltd, long associated with books for the craftsman, have recently brought out their revised catalogue, which boasts a bibliography of available woodwork, metalwork and craft books comprising more than 900 titles.

The catalogue, called *Books for Craftsmen*, contains sections on carving and sculpture, turning, treen and woodware, crafts in wood, toys and dolls' houses, furniture history, furniture making, restoration and repair, finishing, tools, carpentry and joinery, boat building, school woodwork, musical instruments, as well as many other craft subjects.

Certainly there can be no more comprehensive range of books for the woodworker than Stobarts carry, so anyone who likes to read about the subject as well as getting on with the practical side will find the catalogue a valuable reference source.

It is available from the publisher at 67-73 Worship Street, London EC2A 2EL, price £1. **C.D.**

Advice for the non-expert

Whether you want to repair bubbled veneer, a broken picture frame of gesso and gilt, torn antique leather or replace a missing leg this handy compact A-Z guide contains much of the information you require.

Advice on cleaning and renovation of more than 250 types of collectable antiques is given in *A-Z guide to cleaning and renovating antiques* by Tom Rowland, price £5.95, published by Constable & Co Ltd, 10 Orange Street, London WC2H 7EG (ISBN 0-09-463630-3). Many useful tips known to the antique trade are included by the author who has been an antique renovator for many years.

A book that claims to be an A-Z guide needs to be systematically arranged to be of any practical value. This one divides naturally into 3 alphabetical sections. Section 1 gives directions on the care of the most common categories of antiques, deals with simple care and cleaning and simple specialist renovation and repair. Section 2 lists the materials recommended for cleaning and repairing, details their specialised uses, availability and sources of supply. Section 3 is a list of useful addresses of specialist suppliers cross-referenced to sections 1 and 2. (Capitals or bold type are used to denote the relevant section.)

The author states that great pleasure can be obtained in cleaning, polishing and repairing one's own antiques, however, only minor repairs should be attempted by the layman and the advice, if not the actual help of experts should always be sought. Never jump in with both feet since valuable antiques require care and expertise.

Use the specialists at your local museum but do not abuse their services and time by overloading them with trivial enquiries. Gain confidence and expertise yourself as you progress from the easy to the more complicated repairs.

About 120 materials recommended for cleaning and repairing are listed in part 2 and about 64 specialist suppliers in part 3. Many of these latter will supply by mail order so do not be deterred if you live in a remote area.

A useful pocket-sized guide for the beginner in restoration, with a readable and knowledgeable text that gives historical anecdotes as well as sound practical advice. **P.C.**

Joys of rebirth

L. Donald Meyers author of *The Furniture Lover's Book, finding, fixing, finishing,* says basically furniture repair and refinishing are not difficult jobs. If you have the interest, the right tools and the right materials; you can do it. In the States, at least, there has been a renewal of interest in the renovation of furniture. Timber prices and labour costs are rising and good furniture is expensive. However, a trained eye is needed to spot the 'jewel' from the 'junk', to determine 'built to last' from 'built for quick sale'.

The first four chapters of *The Furniture Lover's Book* deal with exploring and explaining the furniture-making-process, what is good and what is not-so-good construction. Woods and jointing techniques are emphasised. Later chapters cover construction and finishing techniques (both home and factory), basic repair, upholstery and plans for building one's own furniture.

From personal experience the author states 'start on something portable, don't tackle a big long-term job until you have had some experience'. Since this is another American book the four appendices are not very useful to the UK reader dealing as they do with popular US woods, their price and availability, adhesives, abrasive papers and mail order supply houses in the US.

The plans too have more appeal on the other side of the Atlantic. But having said that much of the practical side of the book is valid and sound information. The text is eminently readable, obviously drawn from personal experience as the many anecdotes suggest. The Boston *Globe* said: 'Meyers has a passion for furniture and it shows in his writing,' this is true.

The book is for those who want to salvage old furniture and it covers all the faults one is likely to find from simple dents, scratches and burns to replacing seats, table tops, wobbly legs and refinishing, reupholstery and complete rebuilding.

Available in UK from Van Nostrand Reinhold Co Ltd, Molly Millars Lane, Wokingham RG11 2PY (ISBN 0-442-26314-7) at £7.60 (paperback). **P.C.**

THE WORLD'S TIMBER TREES

In no25 of his series (March 1982) C. W. Bond FIWSc completed his survey of a group of woods from the mahogany family by commenting on avodiré. This month he continues with an outstanding timber, ekki, a wood of great weight, strength and durability, too hard for general handworking but which should prove of value for ornamental turnery.

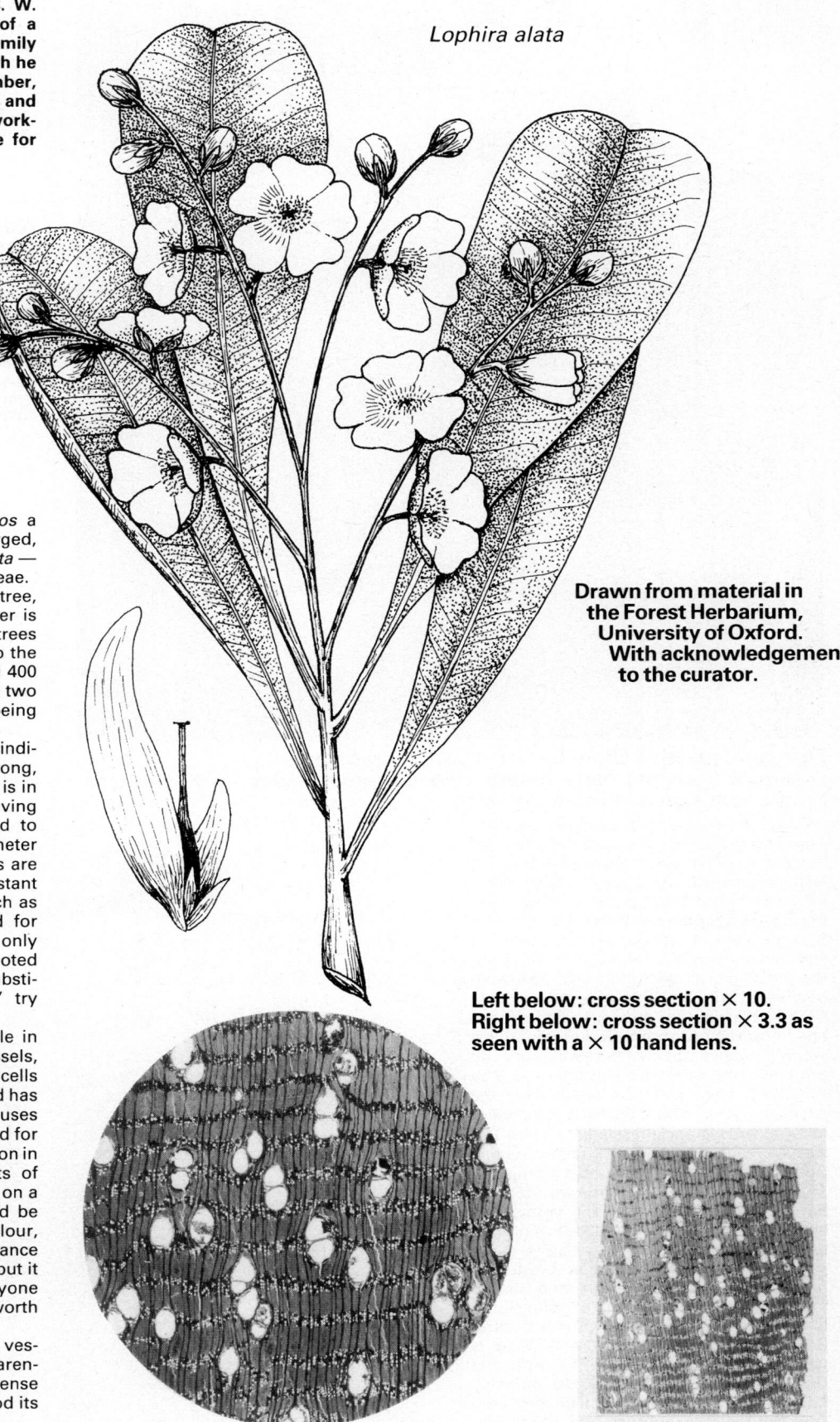

Lophira alata

EKKI (HENDUI or RED IRONWOOD):26

Lophira alata, Lophira — from *lophos* a crest. Two of the sepals become enlarged, one to form a crest over the seed, *alata* — winged; referring to the seed. Ochnaceae.

This wood is from a large rain-forest tree, up to 100ft tall and when in full flower is regarded as one of the most beautiful trees in the world. The family is confined to the tropics and consists of 20 genera and 400 species of trees and shrubs. There are two species of *Lophira, L. lanceolata* being similar but with longer leaves.

The wood, as the alternative name indicates, is extremely heavy, hard and strong, density up to 1.3 (80 lbs per cu ft) and is in the same category as greenheart, having great resistance to fungal decay and to marine borers and termites. The diameter of the bole being up to 5ft, large sizes are available and the wood is in constant demand for heavy structural work such as piers, jetties, bridges and piles, and for railway wagons and sleepers. The only instance of smaller use which I have noted was immediately after the war as a substitute for rosewood in woodworkers' try squares.

It is a uniform dark brownish-purple in colour with a white deposit in the vessels, and the regular bands of parenchyma cells form a characteristic feature. The wood has been exported for many years for the uses mentioned above, but is much too hard for handworking. The reason for its inclusion in the present series is in the interests of turnery. Although I have never used it on a lathe, I have always thought it would be worthwhile to do so. Its handsome colour, coarse texture and general appearance suggest high decorative values, and I put it forward for ornamental turnery to anyone willing to give it a trial. It might be worth searching for.

The photomicrograph shows large vessels and the apotracheal bands of parenchyma show sharp contrast to the dense thick-walled fibres which give the wood its great weight.

Drawn from material in the Forest Herbarium, University of Oxford. With acknowledgements to the curator.

Left below: cross section × 10. Right below: cross section × 3.3 as seen with a × 10 hand lens.

EDWARD BARNSLEY

Exhibition reviewed by Polly Curds

First retrospective show for British artist-craftsman. Furniture from the early twenties to the present day — 60 years of furniture design and cabinetmaking.

Left: Edward Barnsley sitting in a black-bean chair made by Herbert Upton. Below: Dining chair and carver in walnut with green leather seats, designed for Mrs John Lucas, made by Malcolm Clubley in 1970 and bow-fronted chest in yew with ebony inlay, made by Oskar Dawson in 1976. Right: Oskar Dawson and Edward Barnsley discuss the pieces. Far right: Hanging curved corner cupboard in padauk with sycamore inlay and glass front made by George Taylor in 1973.

Forty works by the designer Edward Barnsley were on show at the Fine Art Society, 148 New Bond Street, London W1 from 25 January - 19 February. The furniture included major and minor pieces made during the period from 1919 right up to the present day. A catalogue illustrating a selection of over 80 of his works taken from the 7 000 pieces designed and produced between 1919 and 1981 of which at least 1 500 were unique, and including essays and information about Barnsley and his workshop, accompanied the exhibition. The printing of the catalogue was sponsored by Christie's. The exhibition was under the auspices of the Edward Barnsley Educational Trust with financial assistance from The Art Worker's Guild, The Crafts Council, Sotheby's and The Carpenter's Company. The research for the catalogue was done by Edward Barnsley himself, his wife Tania and their daughter Contessa Karin Antonini with assistance from Dr Mary Capes.

Edward Barnsley has been producing furniture of superb design and craftsmanship for 60 years, he is the son of the late Sidney Barnsley, who, with his brother Ernest and the architect Ernest Gimson, is well known for his part in The Arts and Crafts Movement. The Edward Barnsley Educational Trust was established in 1980 (see *Woodworker* August 1980 p509) and

has charitable status. Since its foundation it has received approx. £43 000 (against a target of £200 000) and already has three young apprentices receiving training in the workshop. The training scheme offers a three year apprenticeship followed by at least two further years of workshop experience with day release to Guildford Polytechnic for timber technology and machine courses. Design is studied with Edward Barnsley and then discussed with Edward Barnsley, David Butcher and Mark

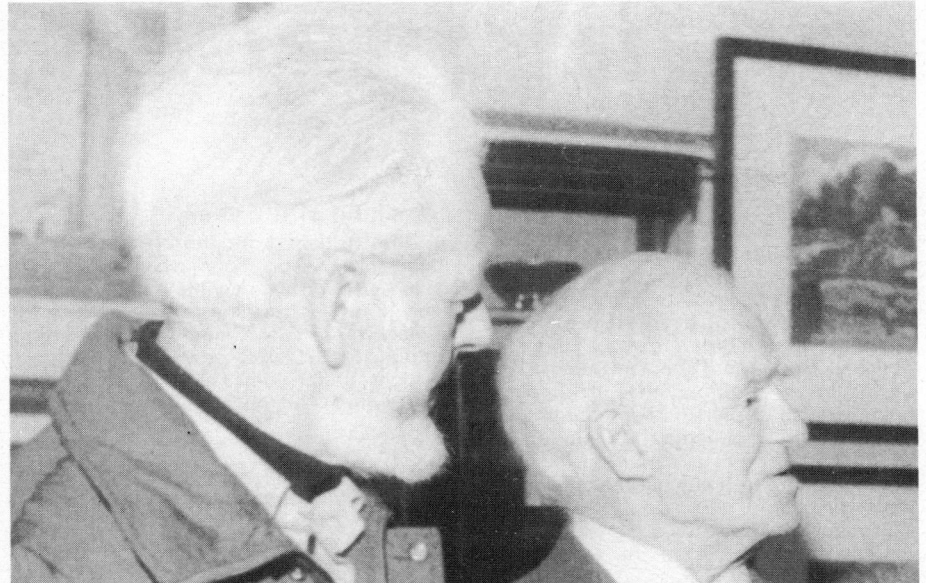

Nicholas. As the course proceeds they are able to call upon the unique skills and experience of Oskar Dawson (who joined the firm in 1947) and George Taylor (joined as an apprentice in 1937 and still a part time member of staff).

Bald words indeed to describe the impact of a man like Edward Barnsley who is visited by school children, students, clients and connoisseurs from all over the world and who has had a decisive influence on design and cabinetmaking during the last 60 years. The Trust was established in 1980 to save the artist craftsmanship of the Barnsley workshop's apprenticeship tradition; to carry on the traditions of design and craftsmanship started by his father Sidney, inspired by William Morris when Sidney, Ernest Gimson and Edward Barnsley left London almost 100 years ago to live and work in the Cotswolds.

Scant words too, to convey the sense of perfection, design, admiration, love, warmth and affection that radiated from this exhibition, both from the master himself, his wife and family and craftsmen and also from the pieces of furniture obviously chosen with love for the exhibition.

The director of The Fine Art Society, Peyton Skipwith, is to be congratulated on his generosity in making the premises available for this exhibition, the owners of the items lent for the exhibition are to be thanked for making it possible to see 'so much' in such a small space.

Edward Barnsley says that he has built on the foundations of his father and Gimson who 'were men of greatness in a small orbit'. This exhibition was one of 'greatness in a small orbit'. It followed a chronological order and showed the progression of his designs from heavy oak pieces (no 1 1919, cupboard in English oak with fielded panel doors, made at Sapperton) to the present light elegant furniture of considerable sophistication (no 90 1980, refectory table in rosewood with sycamore inlay and raised ebony hexagons round the edge of the table top, laminated wish-bone stretcher between two pedestal legs).

One delightful touch to the catalogue is the thoroughness of the catalogue entry; each item is listed chronologically, the assistant craftsman who made the piece is named, cost and the number of hours spent on the project are given along with the

dimensions and often a short history of the piece including for whom it was designed and many of Edward Barnsley's personal comments.

I was fortunate to have Edward Barnsley beside me when I visited the exhibition and to be privileged to hear his thoughts on many of the pieces. Edward last made a piece with his own hands in 1976. . . an oak blanket chest for Dr Mary Capes ; now he says he can stand back and admire perfection. . . his craftsmen produce beauty in wood, many would say unequalled in the world today. A stream of beautiful pieces has flowed from the Froxfield workshops, a lasting tribute to the quality of the men who work there. Edward Barnsley has a special regard for all of these men; one of these Oskar Dawson was also present to talk about his work. Listening to these two gifted men talking was an experience, their love of wood and their faith in their own strength and ability was evident. I think for me, in spite of being 'spoilt for choice' my favourite piece of the exhibition was a bow fronted yew chest with ebony inlay, designed by Edward Barnsley for Mr and Mrs John Wedgbury and made in 1976 by Oskar Dawson.

Early pieces included in the exhibition were a small walnut cabinet (1924) an occasional table in walnut with a crisp holly and ebony inlay (1924); a large oak sideboard with circular metal handles (1931) and a doctor's writing desk (1932). Both of these latter Edward Barnsley is now critical about, he feels he has now progressed from these solid early pieces. The conductor's stand in walnut Herbert Upton made in 1934 for Sir Adrian Boult in 73hrs at a cost of £7.15s stood next to the much photographed and noted Jubilee cabinet of 1977, made by Herbert Upton, George Taylor, Oskar Dawson and Mark Nicholas in over 900hrs for £3769.99p. Edward Barnsley says of the cabinet 'the work of my craftsmen cannot be faulted; it is perfection'. The walnut for that cabinet had matured in his sheds for 30 years waiting for the right occasion. (See *Woodworker* August 1980 p509).

Furniture from the 60s was included, no 51 lady's bedside table in walnut with sycamore inlay; no 68 small kneehole desk in blackbean and desk-chair no 69 to match; no 66 a beautiful serpentine fronted display

cabinet in yew with sycamore and ebony inlay.

Tania Barnsley expressed regret that a side table (made by George Taylor in 1967) with drawer fronts and top in padauk, legs and stretcher in rosewood and sycamore inlay had faded across the front 'I remember it brighter and richer than that' she said wistfully. Contessa Karin Antonini was happy to include her 'slipped disc' armchair, she says 'it has given me considerable relief and comfort since it was made'.

Pride of place was given to the Archbishop's chair, prie Dieu and stool in walnut inlaid with sycamore, upholstered in duck-egg green leather. It was first used in 1971 by Archbishop Michael Ramsey. 'I'm making another like that at the moment' said Oskar Dawson, of a circular dining table in padauk with sycamore and inlaid laminate pedestal. Again it was with a warm feeling I heard him take the trouble to explain how he inlaid the top, how he laminated and jointed the pedestal.

Cigarette boxes and a coffee table in walnut with ebony and sycamore inlay by apprentice Colin Eden-Eadon; an uphol-

stered walnut stool with a soft yellow top by Robert Lawrence plus a trinket box by Giles Garnham were on display. A promise here of things to come. 'If it's not correct they must do it again, it must always achieve accuracy' said Karin Antonini. 'At present they work to high standards', she told *Woodworker*, 'and so time is not important; they are not viable craftsmen, they are learning, they must learn thoroughly and well before they can hope to achieve'.

If you missed this exhibition try to visit the follow up one at The Crafts Study Centre, Holburne Museum, Great Pulteney St, Bath from 3 April - 13 June when a further selection of 14 pieces of furniture, working drawings and photographs will be on show. B. G. Burrough echoes my sentiments, in his short appreciation of Edward Barnsley included in the catalogue 'Edward Barnsley's life's work has, I am quite sure, been so successful, influential and important because it has been based on sound foundations; humility, honesty, sincerity, fitness for purpose, harmony and repose'.

workpieces

Beware — Beetles

A recent letter to the trade press mentioned an incidence of woodworm discovered when some dead elm posts were felled. The grubs were identified as those of the furniture beetle, *Anobium punctatum*, and a warning was given regarding the potential danger, to wood and furniture in the home, if such timber found its way indoors as firewood. This reference should serve as a timely reminder to all woodworkers that any dead wood, tree stumps, rotting fencing posts and other wood debris offers ideal breeding grounds for a variety of beetle pests and should be removed and immediately burned. There is one point to make however; the causes of Dutch elm disease are in no way connected with the furniture beetle. In the context of this comment there are two beetle pests of economic significance to look for; *Lyctus* or powder post beetle, and *Anobium* or furniture beetle.

The natural habitat of the furniture beetle in this country is outdoors in dead parts of trees and hedges and infestation is mainly confined to the sapwood of softwood and hardwood, especially severe in the area closest to the bark, due to higher protein content. The heartwood is not immune however, particularly when decay is also a factor. Many wood species are liable to attack, including alder, beech, birch, elm and spruce. Oak and pine are to some extent resistant to outdoor attack unless and until decay of the white-rot type also occurs.

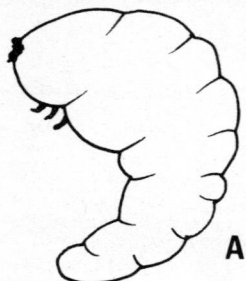
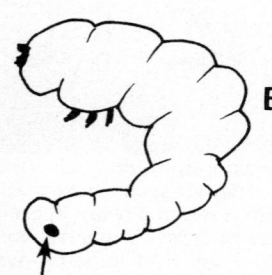

Breathing pore

Larvae of (a) *Anobium* (b) *Lyctus* beetles. Note profile of *Anobium* more swollen than in *Lyctus* while black breathing pore present in *Lyctus*, absent in *Anobium*.

Anobium larvae are white and curved, about 5mm long with three pairs of legs and two dark-coloured jaws. *Lyctus* beetle also breeds outdoors but there are limiting factors; firstly, the pores of the wood must be large enough to accept the female beetle's ovipositor for egg laying, (something like 0.05mm) and secondly, there must be adequate starch available as food. This is principally found in sapwood. Suit-

Bostik M890 two part acrylic adhesive being applied to a teak door locker frame at Sadler Yachts Ltd, Dorset.

able host trees and stumps in this country are ash, elm, oak, and walnut. Beech and birch are generally not attacked because their starch content is low, while lime and cherry escape because their pores are too small. Other woods that are susceptible are agba, antiaris, limba, iroko, mahogany, obeche, ramin and seraya. Superficially *Lyctus* larvae resemble those of *Anobium*, being whitish, curved, and up to 5mm long when fully grown, but may be distinguished by the presence of a dark spot, called a breathing pore located near the tail end, on either side.

Probably the easiest way for the layman to distinguish one from the other is by examination of the frass, or bore dust. Under hand-lens examination, this will be seen to contain ellipsoidal or lemon-shaped pellets in the case of *Anobium* and if rubbed between thumb and forefinger will feel slightly gritty, like fine sand. On the other hand, *Lyctus* bore dust is a very fine powder (hence the common name, powder post) with a smooth feel, like rubbing talcum powder. Where either of these beetle pests are suspected in outdoor wood it is important to make a correct diagnosis because this will determine the possible degree of infestation, and what steps to take. *Lyctus* attack for example will not spread to softwood timbers, but pieces of wood infested with *Anobium* are a different matter. The danger period (ie for the beetles to emerge from infested wood and commence egg laying) is from May until September, with the greatest activity during June, July and August. Both beetles can fly, but only sluggishly.

Bond boats with Bostik

Bostik M890 has been used by Sadler Yachts Ltd of Poole, Dorset since its introduction in 1977. This two-part adhesive speeds up production and achieves cost savings as no pre-mixing is required and there is no waste. The Bostik is conveniently supplied in cartridges which fit standard guns. The company bond large quantities of teak and plywood panelling, teak door locker frames and decorative trims to the moulded glass fibre interiors of their boats.

Machine of the year

The British Agricultural and Garden Machinery Association have voted the Stihl 010 AV chainsaw machine of the year from the 12 power machines nominated for the award. It has a 37cc single cylinder engine producing 1.1kw of power at 7000rpm. It weighs under 10lbs. and costs £119 exc. VAT with a 12in. guidebar and chain.

Firm success

It is always heartening to hear about a company establishing itself in a highly competitive market. This is the position of Woodworking Machines of Switzerland after only 5 months trading in Milton Keynes.

Right from the start md Bruce Pollard believed that with the right products and a carefully chosen distribution network, success would be assured. 'We were convinced with the quality and range of Inca, response to our advertising has been tremendous and our stand at the Woodworker show was yet another justification of the faith we put into this venture.'

Woodworking Machines of Swtizerland are the sole UK importers of Inca and they are fully backed by the Swiss company.

Courses in basic woodworking skills are being run twice a week in purpose/built workshops at Milton Keynes and the company hope to offer more advanced courses in the near future.

Design prize

Sixteen year old Diane George's design for an electronic spirit level helped her father regain his interest in carpentry after more than 10 years of blindness. The judges of this year's schools design prize (organised by the Design Council and sponsored by Rolls-Royce Ltd) agreed that Diane's design was an inventive solution to a specific problem, tackled with limited resources.

It relies on a circuit using photocells and if the level is on an uneven surface the mercury moves between the light source and transistor thus triggering one of two differing tone buzzers showing whether the tilt is to the left or right.

Apprentice wins competition

Paul Butcher was the winner of the carpentry/joinery craft trainees' competition at this year's Interbuild exhibition. Paul is an apprentice joiner at J. R. & E. Russell of Wednesbury. The senior partner of the firm is Gordon G. Bates, president of the British Woodworking Federation, and he was naturally delighted with Paul's performance which he saw as an opportunity to show the general public just what is being done to train the craftsmen of the future. In this current period of recession the encouragement of training in every possible way must remain top priority, he said. The wood used in the competition was sponsored by the federation's Architectural and General Joinery section. 23 teams took part in the four day competition.

DRYING YOUR TIMBER

9

In the February 1982 issue of WOODWORKER W. H. Brown FIWSc began a discussion centred round inexpensive conditioning rooms for wood designed by the Forest Products Laboratory at Madison, Wisconsin, a few years ago and which he felt could provide a basis for home or small business adaptation, either to condition relatively small sections or piece parts from a doubtful moisture content to a lower, uniform and more satisfactory one, or to achieve similar results from rather wetter wood, but in either case by relative humidity control. Previous articles in this series have appeared in March, April, July, August, September and October 1981 and in January and February 1982.

So far (February 1982 p119) we have given details of the suggested frame construction, as items 1 and 2; we propose to continue the sequence.

3 After assembling the walls and top, cover the entire frame structure including the bottom and door, with a clear polyethylene film. Wherever possible and feasible use continuous film, otherwise allow about a 6in (150mm) overlap. Attach the film to the framing members with staples or tacks. Later cover all frame members with battens or moulding and carefully cut the film round the door frame. 4 To help prevent damage to the polyethylene film, cover the lower section of the walls and doors with ¼in (6mm) plywood. A removable board-walk made from 1in × 6in (25mm × 150mm) boards on 2in × 2in (50mm × 50mm) framing, (with felt on the bottom side) and carefully installed inside is sufficient to protect the polyethylene floor from damage. 5 Two removable ¾in (18mm) plywood shelves, approximately 7ft × 2ft (2.1m × 0.6m) may be installed inside the cabinet on which to place small sections and test pieces.

6 Consider the feasibility of installing a junction box and properly grounded electrical outlets in the chamber. This would be a necessity where a discarded domestic refrigerator was available for use or if a heat source was to be electric but, in consideration of these points, a humidistat and appropriate relay, or similar controls, should be added to the electrical outlet to cycle the equipment that maintains the required humidity conditions in the chamber. 7 A sling psychrometer, an accurate direct reading humidity indicator, or a calibrated wood sample or similar device should be available to check periodically the relative humidity within the room or chamber.

With the construction so far described (see also February 1982 WOODWORKER), the basic shell of the room would be more or less air-tight, necessary if a used household refrigerator with its door permanently removed is going to be used, sited on the floor at the far end of the room and connected to the electrical service. Used in conjunction with a humidistat installed at the outlet to control the cycling of the unit, the conditions within a room of the dimensions given, ie 7ft × 7ft × 7ft can be maintained at a relative humidity of 12%.

Before proceeding further, there are several points needing clarification. Very few woodworkers would have access to a used refrigerator, nevertheless it is not an impossible acquisition, therefore we feel we should explain a little more of its possibili-

ties. The Forest Products Laboratory at Madison, evolved this 12% RH chamber because it gave an equilibrium condition for wood of 4% m.c. which was needed in the US. We in this country do not need our wood as dry as this, unless of course we intended to export the finished article to a similarly dry area. Accordingly, if such a room was available, with the same control system, then any wood placed in it could be withdrawn either before it had reached equilibrium or the humidistat could be adjusted to give an RH of a higher value, say 50%.

At this point it is as well to understand the basic techniques employed generally in the commercial drying of timber. With timber drying kilns there are controlled facilities including a heat source, variable fans to circulate the air for periods in one direction then in reverse, baffles to direct the air, means with which to introduce wet steam for humidification and vents to discharge moisture-laden air, together with other refinements, the whole under automatic or semi-automatic control, working to a 'safe' drying schedule.

In any attempt to make up a room or chamber to achieve a reasonable form of timber drying, obviously one must improvise on the above system, and if an inexpensive shell, such as the FPL one is to be adapted, then the essentials like heat, humidity and air circulation cannot be ignored, unless of course, one can turn to a refrigeration method.

Apart from the commercial steam-heated kiln, the other general method of drying timber is by means of a refrigeration type dehumidifier placed in an air-tight chamber and by adapting a used household refrigerator in the FPL system the same method of moisture extraction is being followed. Since in any consideration of a unit that will dry wood we must talk of heat, it is necessary to qualify heat, which has no precise meaning purely as a word. Actually, there are two types of heat, latent and sensible. Latent heat is energy required to change ice to water, or water to steam, while sensible heat is energy required to cause a temperature change, in other words, in kiln drying we use sensible heat to raise the temperature of 1lb of pure air 1°F, but to change 1lb of water to 1lb of steam, we use latent heat.

In the commercial drying of timber the use of refrigeration type dehumidifiers effects a definite economy in the heat used since the latent heat given up to the refrigerant in the cold coils by the vapour consensing on them is returned to the circulating air via the warm coils. (Fig 1) By contrast, in a conventional steam-heated kiln, the latent heat is lost in the vapour going out through the vents, while the cool air drawn in has to be warmed up to the working temperature of the kiln. It would therefore be to great advantage if a used refrigerator could be employed in a home-produced drying or conditioning room.

We will continue this discussion in a future issue of WOODWORKER.

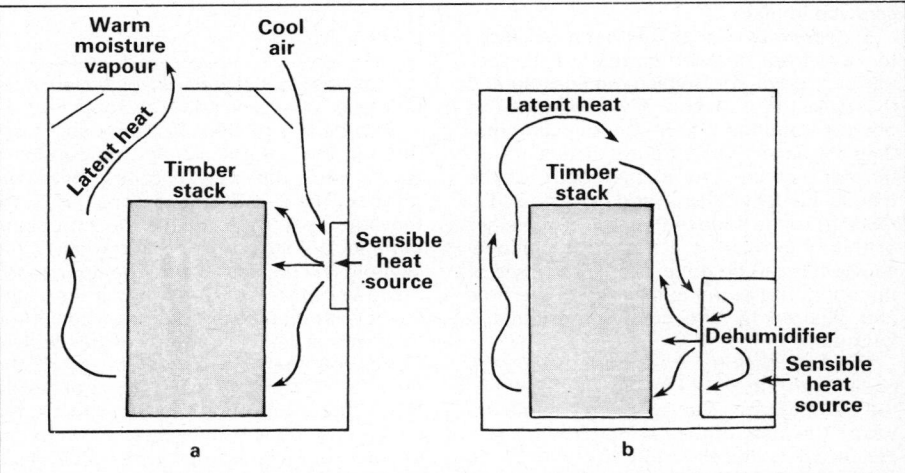

Fig. 1. In a steam heated kiln (a) much latent heat is lost in moisture vapour discharged through vents, while incoming cool air must be warmed to working temperature by sensible heat.

In an air tight chamber housing a dehumidifier this not only supplies sensible heat but also recovers latent heat for recirculating.

THE KEY TO FITTING LOCKS

According to the old saw, 'love laughs at locksmiths.' Be that as it may, fitting locks can be a job that brings not the glimmer of a smile. Here Charles Cliffe and Bill Gates discuss some of the locks used by woodworkers and the method of marking, cutting and fitting.

Hasp and staple (Fig. 1) In its simplest form the staple is secured to the frame by two countersunk screws and three screws fix the hasp to the door. A more robust form has four stout screws holding the staple which is covered by a hinged hasp fixed by six screws and a coach bolt going right through the door. In both cases locking is by padlock.

Rim lock (Fig. 2) These inexpensive locks require the minimum of fitting being screwed to the inner face of the door while the metal box into which the bolt shoots is screwed to the frame. They are often fitted to doors of greenhouses and garden sheds and are sometimes found on the back doors of older properties.

Mortise lock (Fig. 3) As the name implies, these locks are housed in a mortise cut in the door stile. The catch and bolt shoot through the striker plate into mortises cut in the door frame. Various qualities are available ranging from the straightforward to the multi-lever lock which encourages burglars to try elsewhere.

To fit, place the lock in position on the side of the door stile and mark the top and bottom of the body of the lock. Square these lines on to the door edge and gauge a line down the centre of the edge. Mark the depth of lock on a twist bit of appropriate diameter (usually ¾in.). Bore out, placing the point of the bit on the centre line. Clean out waste with a chisel.

If many locks are to be fitted it is worth buying a mortise lock chisel to make a clean job of cutting the bottom of the mortise.

The lock is pushed into the mortise and a pencil line drawn round the front plate. After withdrawing the lock sufficient wood is removed from the pencilled area to sink the front plate sightly below the level of the door edge. In the event of the door swelling a shaving can be removed without endangering the plane iron. Holes for the door handle and the key are bored, the lock screwed home and the door furniture screwed in place.

Cylinder lock (Fig. 4) This is the lock fitted to most front doors. It comprises the lock barrel, the bolt mechanism and casing and the striker box. A hole 1¼in. diameter is bored through the door stile to accommodate the barrel. Measure the distance from the edge of the lock to the centre of the handle (usually 2⅜in.) and bore this distance from the edge of the door. The height of this hole may be a matter of personal choice but can be governed by the style of the door. The barrel is inserted in the hole and secured by two screws through the back plate.

The bolt casing is positioned with the connecting bar entering the centre slot in the rotating disc. The door edge is marked where the plate of the casing overlaps and the recess is chiselled out after which the casing is screwed to the back of the door. The striker plate box is placed on the door frame with the bolt in the centre of the opening and the frame is marked. The frame is recessed and the box screwed in place.

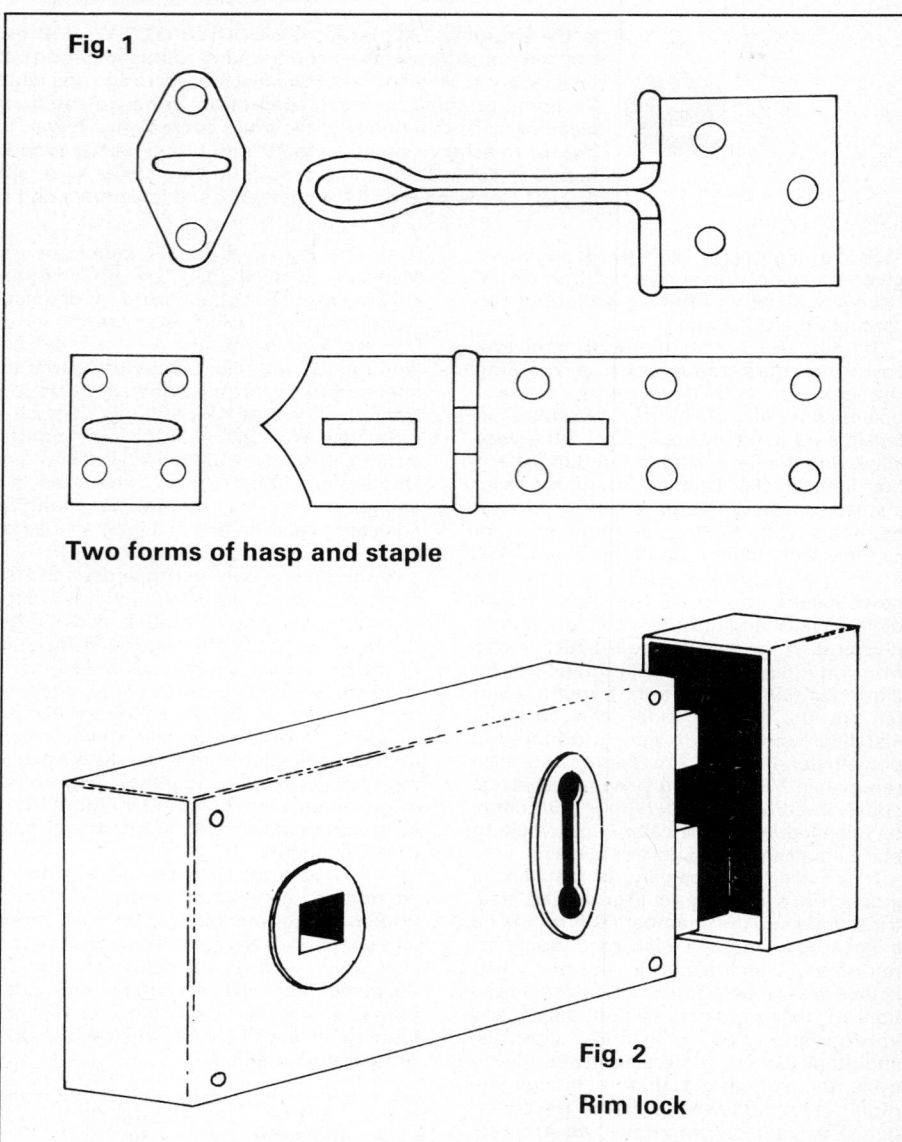

Fig. 1

Two forms of hasp and staple

Fig. 2

Rim lock

If the door opens inwards the bevel on the bolt faces outwards and *vice versa*.

Cupboard lock (Fig. 5) These locks are fitted in the upright position on cupboard doors with the bolt shooting into the pilaster. The first factor to consider is the measurement 'to pin'. This means obtaining a lock of such a size that the pin in the keyhole will be central with the door stile.

Drawer lock (Fig. 6) The position of the keyhole is obtained by squaring a pencil line vertically at half the length of the drawer front. The marking gauge is set to the distance from plate A to the centre of the pin B and the gauge point is pressed on the pencil line. Bore a hole right through the drawer front with a small centre bit and cut the lower part C to allow the key to pass through.

If a brass escutcheon is to be fitted due allowance to the size of the hole has to be made. Insert the key through the hole and into the lock and mark on the back of the drawer front the outline of the part of the lock containing the mechanism. Cut out the sinking for the lock followed by the sinkings for plates A and D.

Screw the lock in position and having checked that the mechanism works smoothly shoot the bolt and smear it with black oil from the oilstone. Turn down the bolt, push in the drawer and turn up the bolt so that a black impression is left on the lower side of the drawer rail. A special drawer lock chisel is used to cut away the marked area to a depth sufficient to accommodate the bolt.

Hook lock (Fig. 7) These locks are similar in appearance to drawer locks except that the bolt is curved like a hook and engages in a brass plate. They are to be found on pianos, the lock being fitted to the piano case and the brass plate let into the fall. Fitting follows along the lines of the drawer lock.

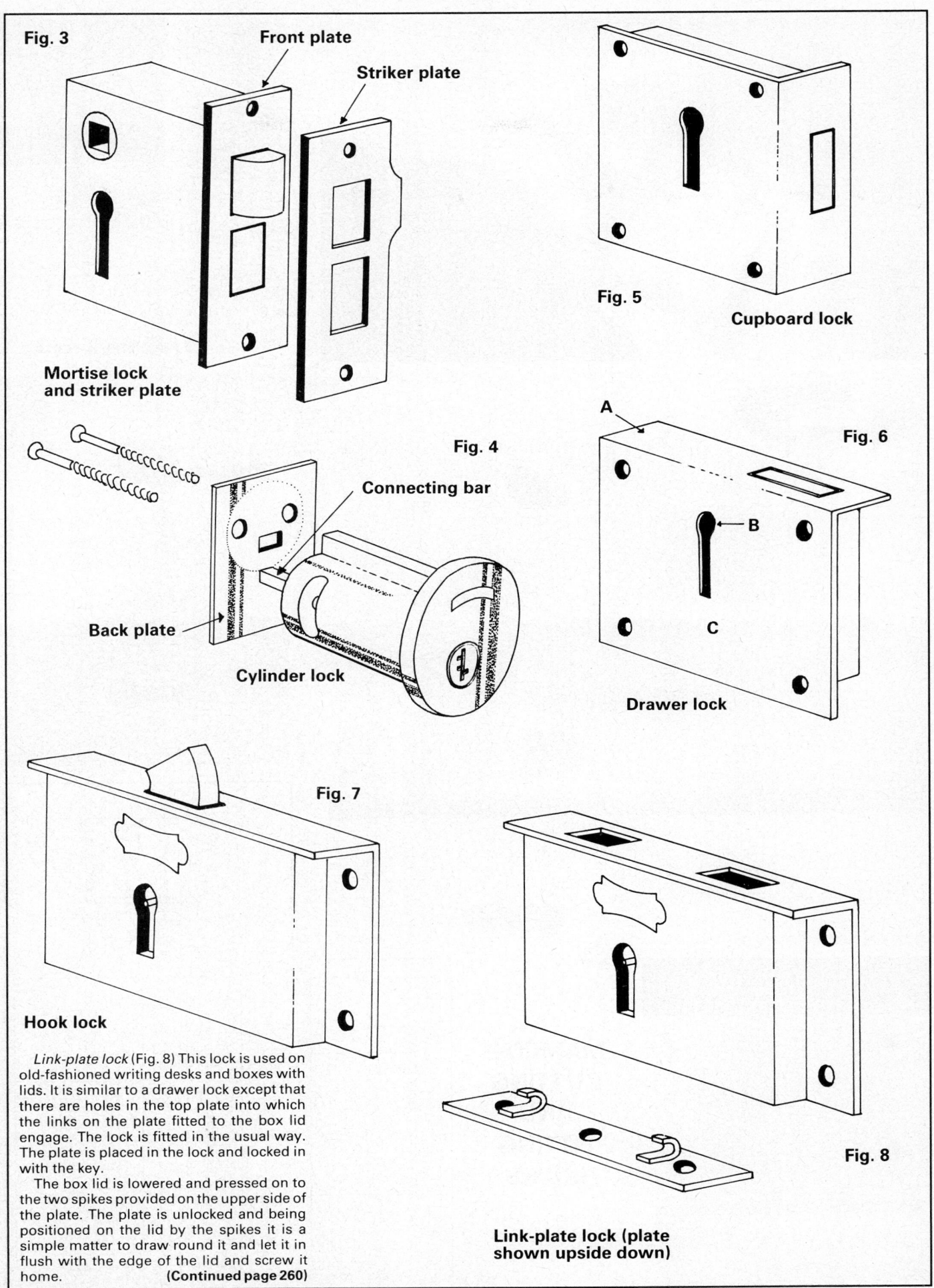

Fig. 3

Front plate

Striker plate

Mortise lock and striker plate

Fig. 5

Cupboard lock

Fig. 4

Connecting bar

Back plate

Cylinder lock

A

B

C

Fig. 6

Drawer lock

Fig. 7

Hook lock

Fig. 8

Link-plate lock (Fig. 8) This lock is used on old-fashioned writing desks and boxes with lids. It is similar to a drawer lock except that there are holes in the top plate into which the links on the plate fitted to the box lid engage. The lock is fitted in the usual way. The plate is placed in the lock and locked in with the key.

The box lid is lowered and pressed on to the two spikes provided on the upper side of the plate. The plate is unlocked and being positioned on the lid by the spikes it is a simple matter to draw round it and let it in flush with the edge of the lid and screw it home. (Continued page 260)

Link-plate lock (plate shown upside down)

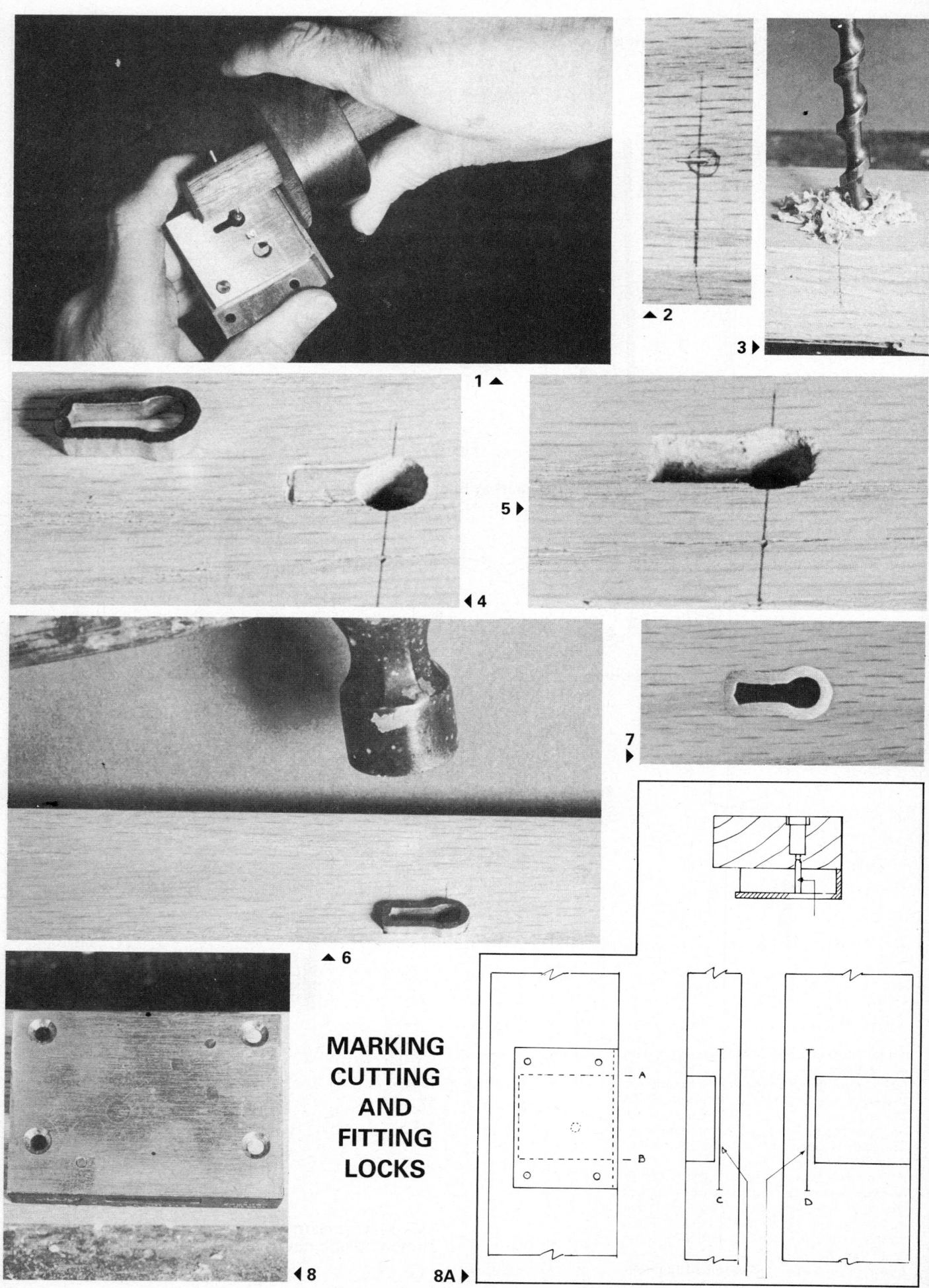

MARKING CUTTING AND FITTING LOCKS

1 ▲

▲ 2

3 ▶

5 ▶

◀ 4

7 ▶

▲ 6

◀ 8

8A ▶

A

B

C

D

9

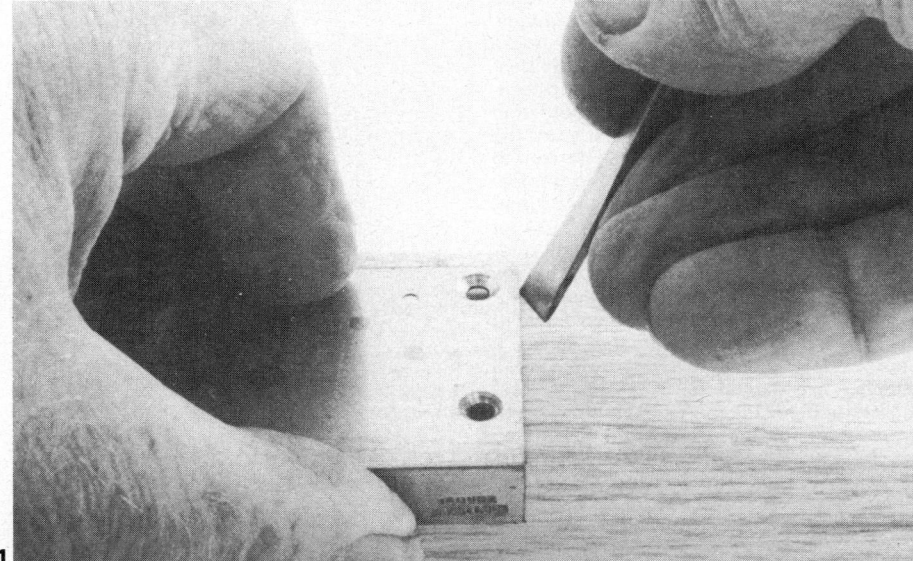
10

11

12

Photo 1 Hold the lock in one hand and set a marking gauge to the centre of the lock pin.

Photo 2 When the position of the lock has been decided mark in pencil a line of the face side square to the edge. Use the marking gauge previously set to mark the centre of the keyhole.

Photo 3 Drill a hole to suit the size of the flush escutcheon. As this must be a tight-drive fit check the drill size by first drilling a piece of waste wood. Do not turn the work over to complete the drilling because the small hole made by the screw point of the bit is used to locate the lock by pressing the lock pin into this hole.

Photo 4 Place the flush escutcheon over the hole and strike this lightly with a hammer. Cut away the waste to the impression marks. The depth of the keyhole must be cut halfway through the thickness.

Photo 5 Completed hole.

Photo 6 Drive in the escutcheon.

Photo 7 Escutcheon driven in flush and finished with glasspaper.

Photo 8 Work is turned over and lock placed in position by pressing the pin into drilling. Mark against the body of the lock at points A and B (Fig. 8A). Lines C and D are gauged before removing the waste. The lock measures $1\frac{3}{4} \times 2\frac{1}{2}$in. (46 × 63mm).

Photo 9 Remove the waste and sawcuts by drilling with Forstner-type bit; finish with chisel.

Photo 10 Cut out the recess to expose the keyhole.

Photo 11 Place lock in the recess, check that the keyhole is in alignment and mark with cut lines against the edges of the lock.

Photo 12 This is the completed recess.

Photo 13 Place lock in the recess and check with the key before final fixing.
13

BRYNMAWR

I. G. Cleaver looks back at an earlier 'recession' in this review of the work of Paul Matt and his social experiment in making BRYNMAWR FURNITURE 1931-40

In 1931 International Voluntary Service (IVS), the UK branch of Service Civil International, went to Brynmawr, S Wales, to set up the first international voluntary workcamp ever to be held in Britain. One hundred and sixteen volunteers, many of them students from a dozen different countries arrived on this venture. They lived with local families. After some initial prejudice they were accepted and joined in the town's activities.

Brynmawr is situated on the northernmost edge of the S Wales coalfield and 1200ft above sea level. Formerly in the county of Brecon, it was transferred to Gwent when local government reorganisation took place in 1973. At that time, Brynmawr had a population of 7694 of which 74% was unemployed. Well over 1000 of its youth had left the town to seek employment in other parts of the country.

The Society of Friends had been active in Brynmawr for some years and had started a boot factory for the local unemployed miners. The arrival of IVS was a great morale booster for the Quakers who organised meetings throughout the country to see how they could further alleviate the sufferings of the community which had lost all hope.

To one of these meetings held in London went a young furniture maker Paul Matt. At the end of the meeting he volunteered to help and when asked what he could do replied: 'I can make furniture'. He was encouraged to go to Brynmawr and after a short time there working on other projects, he set up a furniture workshop in part of the boot factory, and for the next nine years or so of its existence produced the Brynmawr furniture which is now eagerly collected all over Britain.

Above: Brecon bureau bookcase (2ft 9in wide, 1ft 7in deep at base, 9½in deep at top, 6ft 5in high, leather-lined fall and automatic slides). Left: Mount armchair (loose seat upholstered in hide or old Glamis fabric, also supplied with loose seagrass seat). Below: Dining room group.

Paul Matt was the son of a German cabinetmaker, then living in London and specialising in high-class reproduction furniture. Paul had been apprenticed to his father for three years.

Soon after setting up the workshop at Brynmawr, Paul Matt and a few trained men began making prototype pieces in readiness for the arrival of the first group of young men. Some had been to a government training centre, others were unemployed miners whom Matt undertook to train to assemble the furniture designed by him.

From the start each worker had two unemployed boys working with him and in time these also had helpers, so the workshop was able to keep pace with growth.

Early in 1931, several large orders were forthcoming including one for 400 oak chairs for a Quakers girls' school assembly hall at York. When these were completed, orders from other schools and institutions started to flow in. So busy was the factory that it was reluctant to show some furniture at a rural industries exhibition. This, however, proved most successful. In the first year £400 worth of orders were taken which doubled in succeeding years and this kept the factory going while Matt was developing new items to widen the scope of the work.

The furniture was not sold through retailers, but direct to customers and institutions through the medium of exhibitions held at large department stores throughout the country. One such store was David Morgan of Cardiff which gave its showroom free of charge for eight years.

An exhibition held at Manchester in October 1937 was opened by the late Duke of Kent. A year later the permanent London showroom in Cavendish Square was opened by Mrs Neville Chamberlain, wife of the then Prime Minister. Exhibitions had a number of advantages: they reduced the necessity of holding large stocks; orders

Right: Gilwern corner cupboard (wall measurements 21in × 21in. 22½in across doors, height 6ft 2½in).

were placed and furniture made to the customers' requirements. The uniqueness and high-quality of Brynmawr furniture attracted to the exhibitions all classes of people who, for various reasons, wished to associate themselves with the sufferings of the unemployed.

Early in 1937, when extensions to meet these increasing sales had been started, the factory was completely destroyed by fire. But this disaster neither destroyed the skill gained by the men in a new craft, nor dampened their enthusiasm. Work was recommenced under temporary conditions within a few weeks.

For the first three years oak was the only wood used and since mass-produced furniture was not selling, so severe was the slump, Paul Matt had to design pieces that were attractive in appearance, soundly constructed and of the best material. The conventional method of construction with solid ends and tops for cabinets, wardrobes and sideboards was beyond the ability of his unskilled workers, so he devised a form of construction to overcome this.

Laminated board at that time was a comparatively recent invention; it had been badly misused and had earned an undeservedly bad name. It does not shrink yet it was being used in the same way as solid wood panels which were grooved into the framework. Matt approached this problem in a new way by inserting the veneered laminated panels into a rebated picture frame, bevelling the edges and fixing this into the framework of a piece of furniture. This, Matt claimed, gave the pieces a rounded appearance that was bold and outstanding. An example of this construction may be seen in the Merthyr desk.

Other characteristic features of Brynmawr furniture were the use of bold chamfers on legs and handles; the square fielded panels for the rails of stools and tables, and single and doubly fielded drawer fronts. All Brynmawr furniture was treated with a hard

All pictures illustrating this article have been taken from the original catalogue and are reproduced here courtesy of the curator, Welsh Folk museum, St Fagans, Cardiff.

wax polish that could easily be kept in good condition.

Later furniture was also made of mahogany, American black walnut and Australian (Queensland) walnut. Experience showed that mahogany, to be at its best, needed a highly-polished surface. The most effective method then was by french polishing, but the damp climate of Brynmawr was quite unsuited to this method of finishing, Matt therefore utilised more of the two walnuts which were readily available at that time. English walnut was then, as now, not easily obtainable in the solid which is the reason why it was not used. The walnuts were much more expensive than oak so nothing like as much furniture was made of these woods up to the closure of the factory.

With the approach of war, profitability decreased greatly. Peter Scott, a Quaker closely associated with the marketing of the furniture, said that 'Londoners were more interested in gas masks than sideboards'. Sales for 1938-39 totalled just over £10 000 whereas over £19 000 was needed to break even. In late 1939 the London showroom was closed and the factory wound-up in March 1940.

An interesting feature of the catalogue issued was that each item of furniture was named after a Welsh town or district, for example Merthyr desk, Brecon bureau-bookcase and so on.

This year an exhibition of Brynmawr furniture is to be held at Newport museum and art gallery. This will be an opportunity to see at first-hand the results of an extraordinarily successful experiment which did so much to provide employment and at the same time restore a large measure of dignity as well as to release the creative spirit of those who otherwise would have been doomed to enforced idleness.

Welsh dresser (length 4ft 6in depth 1ft 8in height 6ft 6in).

Below: Talgarth sideboard (5ft 0in. Also made 4ft 6in sliding trays in centre cupboard, top tray fitted for cutlery and baize lined).

FIGURE & DECORATIVE CARVING 2

by Harry Turner

The first article in this series appeared in the January issue and considered the beginner's approach. Here the author leads the beginner on to three dimensional work.

The Dolphin

There are two approaches to three-dimensional work: one is 'free expression', the other is 'controlled'. In the former the carving is done straight on to the wood, occasional pencil marks being made to give direction. Alternatively, the pencil marks can be omitted and the carving progressed by vision alone and alterations made during the work.

This is appropriate for those with experience.

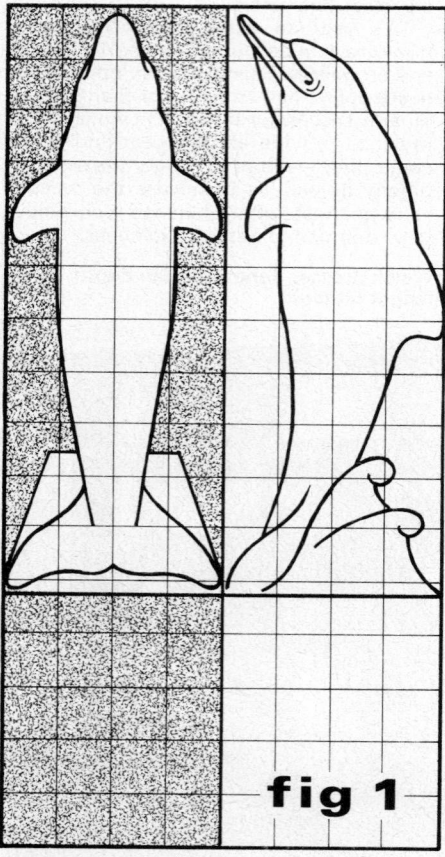

fig 1

Fig. 1 (Above)

This shows the drawings on two faces only. The outlines are on squared paper so as to be enlarged to suit the dimensions of the block.

Fig. 2 (Right)

The drawings can be laid over carbon paper, folded round the block and taped in position.

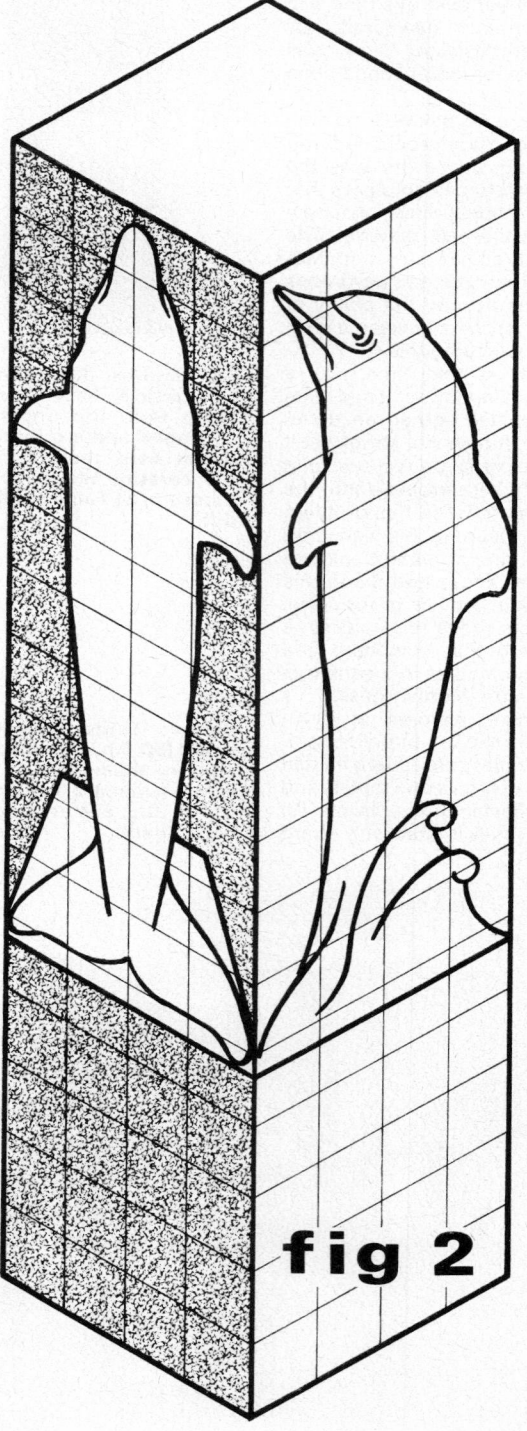

fig 2

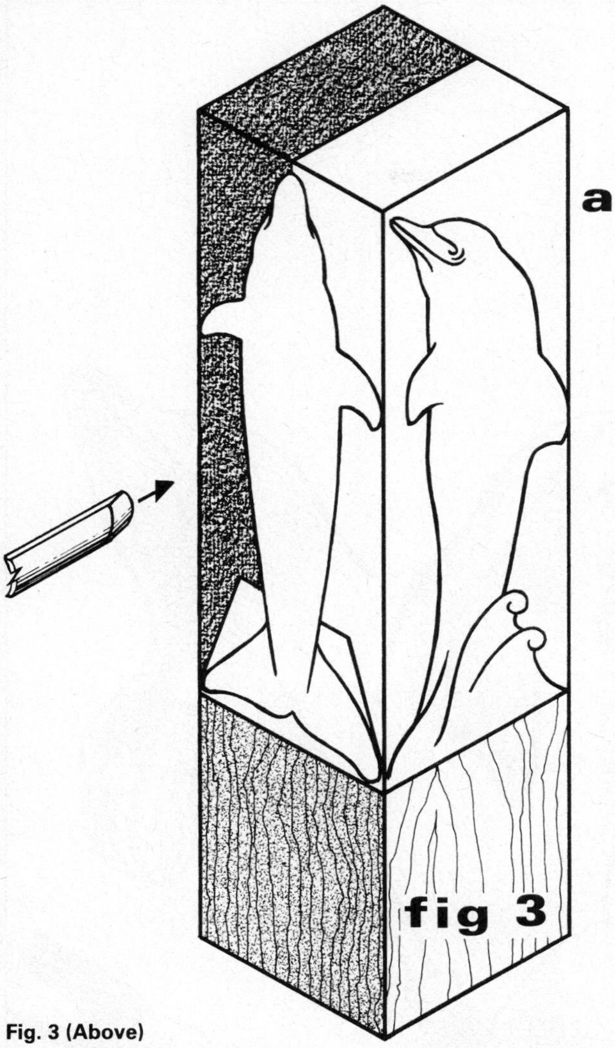

a

fig 3

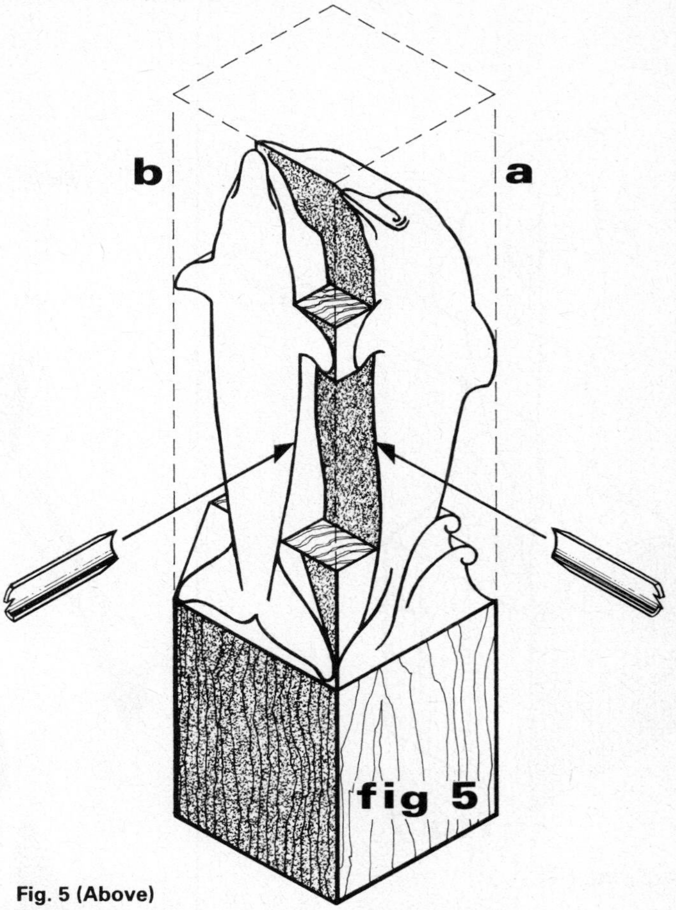

b   **a**

fig 5

Fig. 3 (Above)

The block is laid on side (a), clamped to bench and then cut across the grain with gouge and mallet to just clear of the dolphin body outline. This is followed by careful paring of the wood across the grain with a flat chisel or medium rasp to touch the body line.

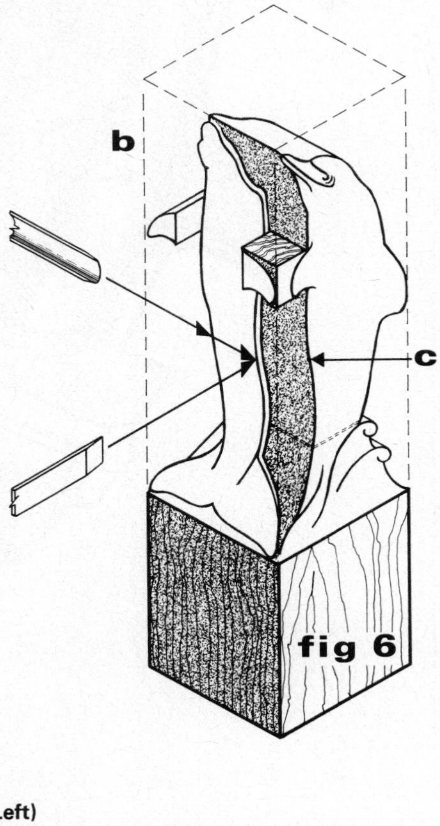

Fig. 5 (Above)

This shows cutting into sides (a) and (b) just clear of the body line using gouge and mallet; paring to body contour follows.

Fig. 6 (Left)

On side (b) use small chisel and mallet to provide a cut drawing line, then with gouge cut across the grain down to line (c). Also cut at double dotted line with chisel to maintain top of the wave line.

b   **c**

fig 6

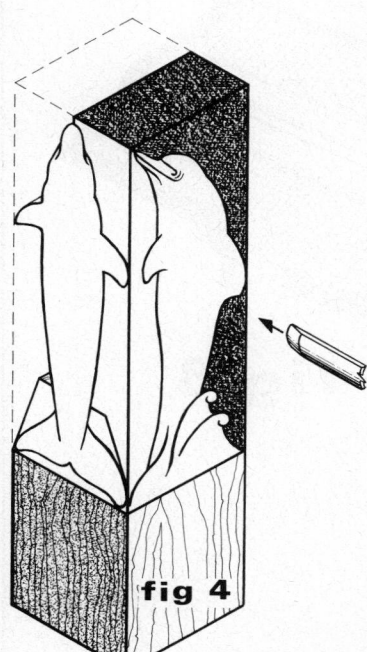

fig 4

Fig. 4 (Left)

Applying the same approach as illustrated in Fig. 3.

In the latter or 'controlled' method (outlined in the first article), the carver is master of the wood. This method is more appropriate for the beginner because for him (or her) 'free expression' can often result in loss of form and proportions and to too much wood being taken away too soon.

For the carving shown in the accompanying drawings a piece of seasoned oak fencing post has been selected 3¾ × 3¾in. actual section (95 × 95mm). This wood has excellent carving properties and permits crisp cuts and fine detail.

The drawing faces should be prepared and painted and the drawings transferred to the surfaces and sealed with two coats of polyurethane varnish. (Details were given in the first article). It is particularly important for the drawings to be properly sealed to avoid erasure due to handling.

It will be noted that a section of the block is left below the drawing for clamping while the carving is done.

For mounting the finished work turned plinths of various designs could be adopted; or a stylised wave effect given to the clamping portion. Alternatively, the

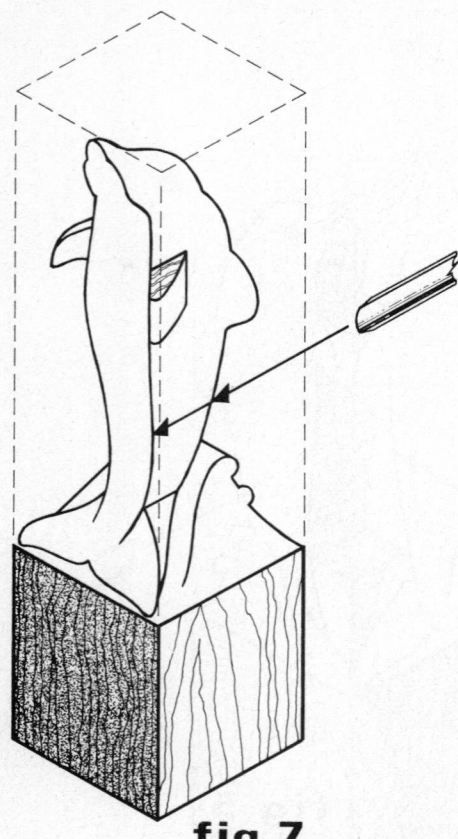

fig 7

Fig. 7 (Above)

With gouge and mallet hew down to the cut drawing line. (See also Fig. 6).

dolphin could be mounted on a brass rod or dowel set in a base of stone.

The surface texture can be left with fine gouge marks showing, or sanded smooth. Texture is a matter of personal taste as is the final finish treatment. Some would prefer to have the wood in its natural state while others would apply, say, one coat of polyurethane varnish, allow this to dry before cutting back with fine wirewool and then applying a wax polish to achieve a slight sheen. Too much burnishing can result in a plastics appearance.

But it is all a matter of personal taste.

The beginner should bear in mind that in three-dimensional carving a Plasticine model of the work is a valuable aid. Model and work can be compared as the carving continues. Trying to convert from a 'flat' guide, such as a photograph, to three-dimensional work is to court disaster.

The beginner will generally find it better to use small gouges or chisels rather than large ones which require more force. Light hand pressure or light tapping with the mallet permit more control over the cutting. It is, of course, essential that gouges and chisels should be kept sharp.

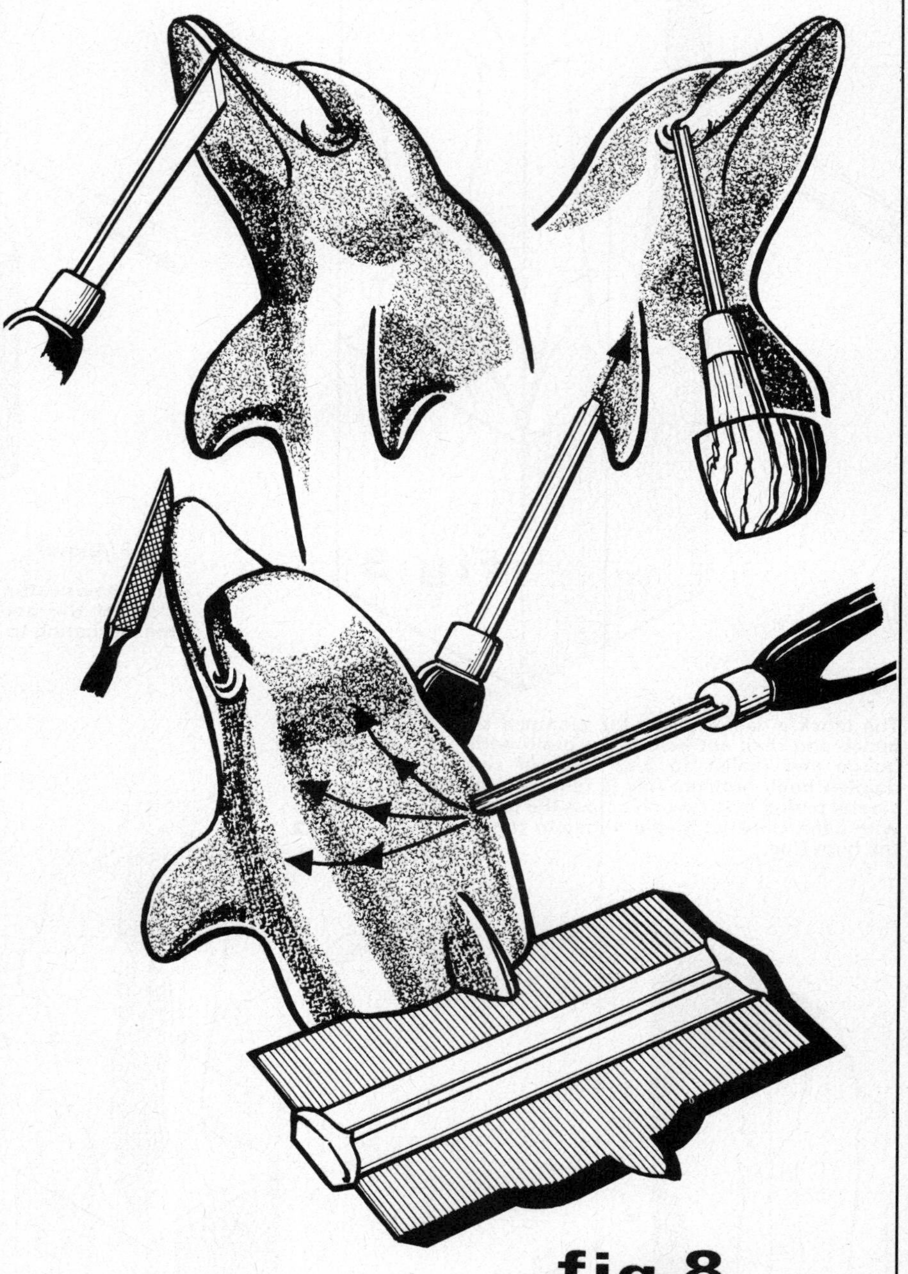

Fig. 8 (Right)

Stages in the final carving to shape. The contour gauge shown is a useful piece of equipment as is a pair of callipers.

fig 8

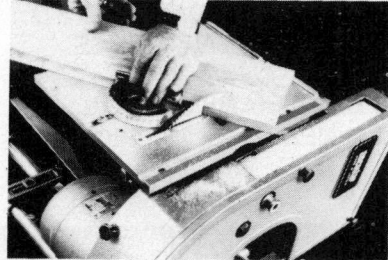
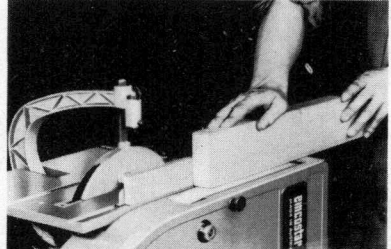

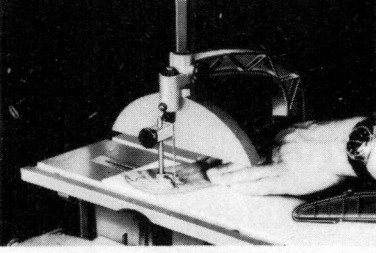

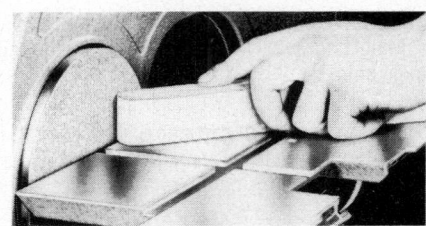

FOR PRECISION WORK.. THIS IS THE DRILL

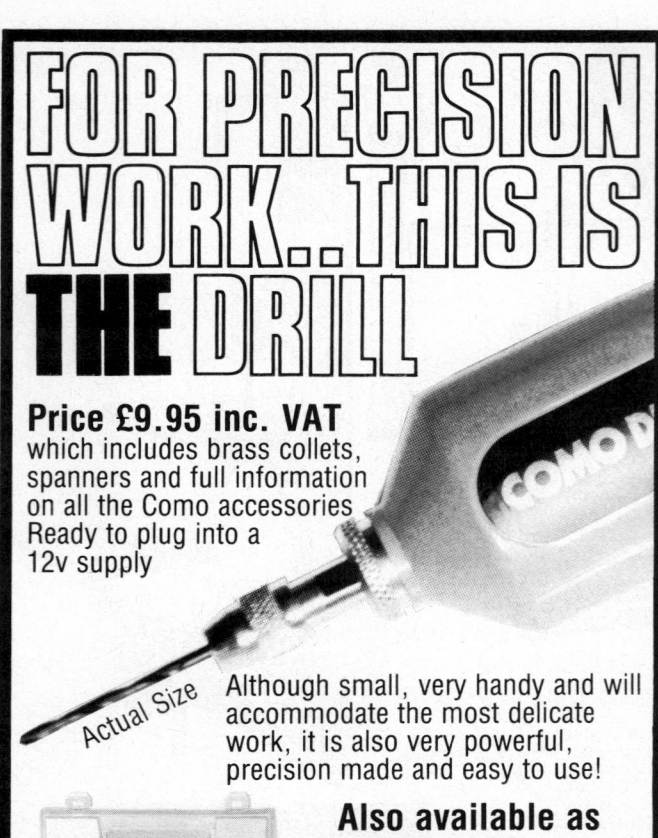

Actual Size

Price £9.95 inc. VAT
which includes brass collets, spanners and full information on all the Como accessories. Ready to plug into a 12v supply

Although small, very handy and will accommodate the most delicate work, it is also very powerful, precision made and easy to use!

Also available as complete kits

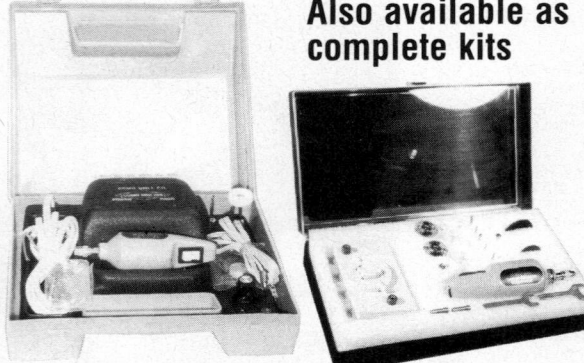

COMPLETE SUITCASE OUTFIT
Includes Como drill, built in variable speed transformer, selection of tools, full information and instructions. Just plug into mains and you're away **Price £39.95 inc. VAT**

BATTERY POWERED SET
includes Como drill, battery adaptor (for 4 *Ever Ready 1289* batteries), selection of tools, full information and instructions. Can be used anywhere! **Price £19.95 inc VAT**

Ideal for * Marquetry * Wood Carving * Miniature Furniture * Metal Engraving and all precision drilling, cutting, grinding and polishing

No extra charges for carriage or credit cards. Remember also that all Como products carry our 'NO QUIBBLE' guarantee! S.A.E. for full illustrated information on all the accessories

COMO DRILLS

Access

The Mill, Mill Lane, Worth, Deal, Kent
Tel: (Sandwich) 0304 612734

BARCLAYCARD
welcome here

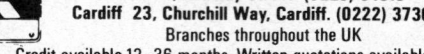

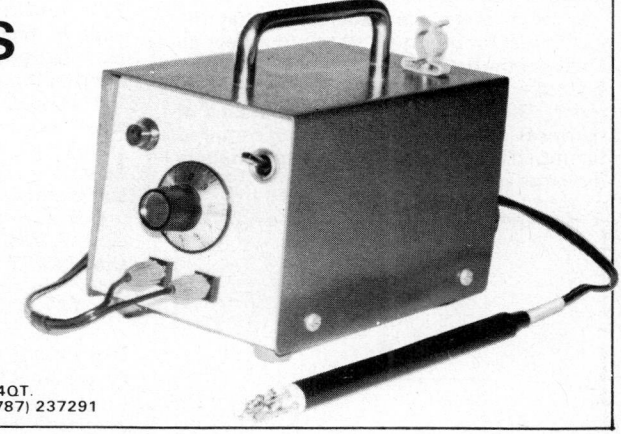
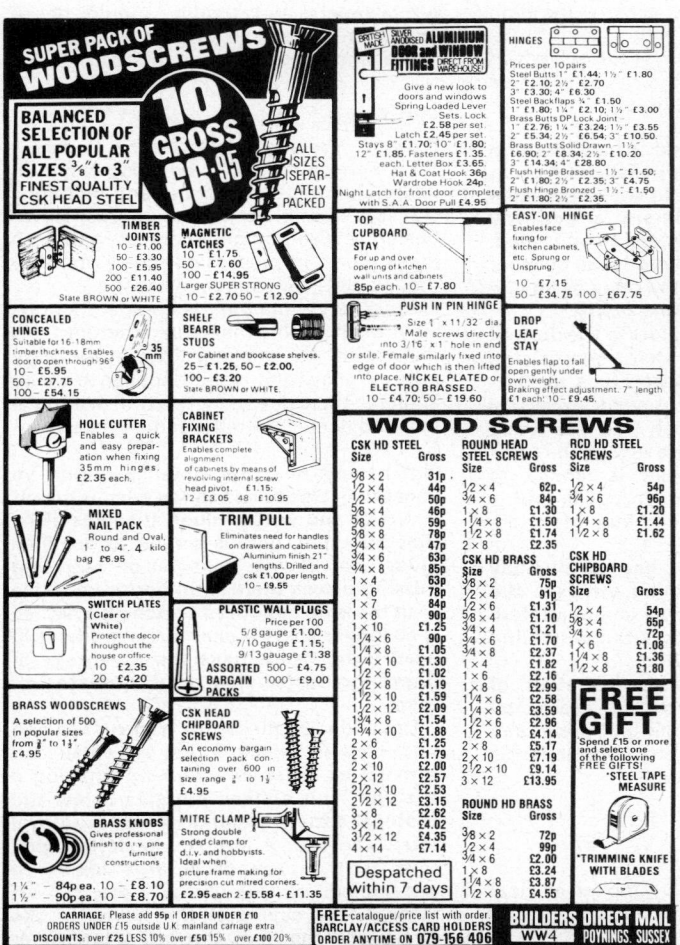
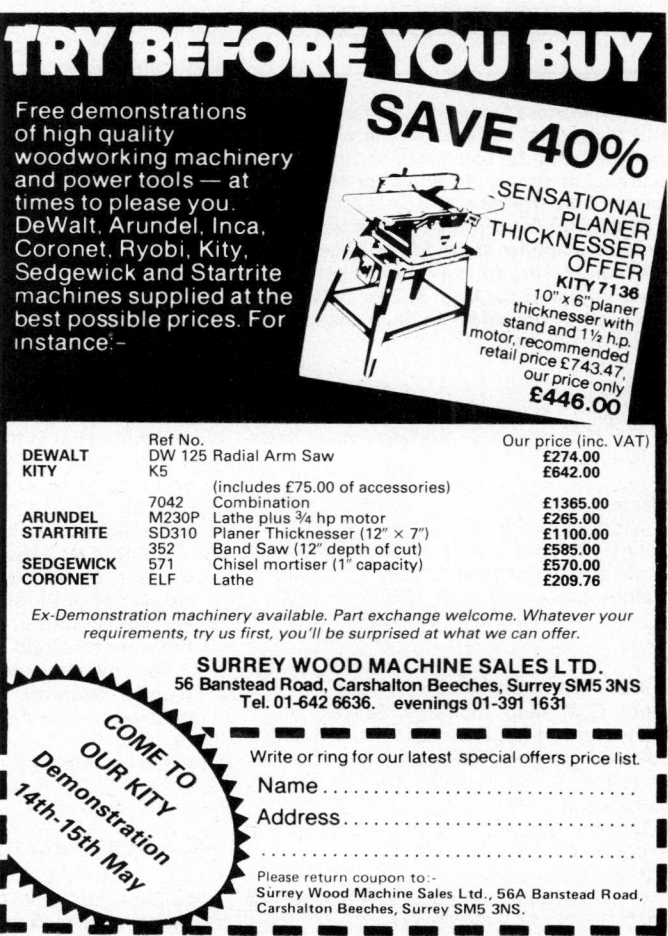

Hardness test

From: Hugh Blogg, Broadstairs

I am acquainted with the various hardness tests for metals; but can you please inform me of the Janka hardness test for timbers and how it is conducted?

Hardness in wood is primarily its resistance to indentation although the relative resistance to cutting tools is also a reference to hardness. However, there is a difference: in the latter context it depends not only on the nature of the cell walls but also on their possible contents, irregularities of grain and so on. In the former, hardness depends upon the thickness and composition of the cell walls.

An example could be serayah or lauan, woods which are relatively easy to indent by stiletto heels when used as flooring, but which offer some resistance to planing because of silica deposits.

It must further be understood that the Janka test for hardness does not reflect an ability of the wood to resist abrasion; other tests are used for this purpose of assessment. The Janka test is the measure of hardness determined by the load required to embed a 0.444in. steel ball to one half its diameter in the wood.

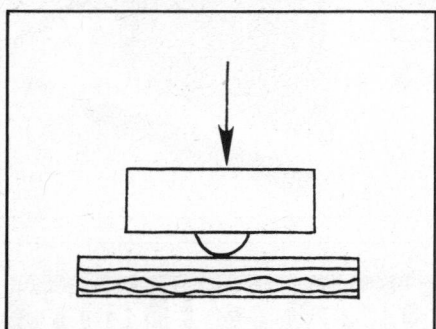

The hardness test is applied to end, radial and tangential surfaces of the wood sample. The result for side grain hardness is the average of those obtained for radial and tangential surfaces.

Dimension of the test pieces is 2 × 2in. and assessments are made on green specimens and on dry specimens whose m.c. has been adjusted to 12%. A few results are given for information, in each case for dry wood at 12% m.c.:

Wood species	Hardness On end grain	On side grain
	lb	lb
Western red cedar	660	350
Western hemlock	940	580
Douglas fir (coastal)	760	670
White oak (American)	1420	1330
Walnut, black	1050	1010

Motor conversion

From: C. J. Allen, Hastings, Sussex

I have an industrial electric motor used to power a general purpose vacuum cleaner. Its rating is 750 watts, 3.2 amps at 240V continuous.

1. Given the rating could I use this motor to power an electric saw?
2. What size of saw blade can I use?
3. Is a formula available for me to work it out?

Varying degrees of success are met with in using motors of this kind, but if the motor has been in service on a cleaner it may well be in a poor condition. If this is the case the results could be disappointing. The rating seems to be in order and assuming the motor to be in *first class* condition it should do the job. . . but circular saws, when used on hardwood of any significant thickness, draw a lot of power. IT IS NOT ADVISABLE TO EXCEED 10 IN. in blade diameter, and eight would be far better, aiming to provide maximum depth of cut of a little over two ins.

Formulae for working out 'required' tip speed on small circular saws are frequently published, but the speed of the tooth tip is far from critical in small diameter blades and it must be borne in mind that they make little sense in any case unless applied to a specific rate of feed.

Assuming the motor to have a speed of 2850 rpm (not quoted in your query) an eight in. blade can be tried at motor speed and its rpm varied to suit the user by altering the pulley sizes.

It should be pointed out that circular saws need to be constructed to high standards of engineering, both from a safety viewpoint and in order for them to be sufficiently accurate.

Our advice, with any proposed conversion, is WHEN IN DOUBT (on any aspect) then DON'T.

Polishing goblets

From: John Ball, Great Yarmouth

I am turning a number of goblets in utile and need to finish them with a high gloss. I have tried polyurethane but find it necessary to apply up to six coats to achieve the high gloss I want.

Is there any preparation (sealer etc) which I can apply so that the gloss can be produced after a shorter time?

Utile is open-grained and is considered a 'hungry' wood by french polishers. A great deal of polish is needed to choke the open pores of the grain before a perfectly smooth, brilliant surface can be achieved. When working on such woods the polisher uses a grain filler to fill the open grain and thereby save both time and polish.

Having stained the goblets to the desired colour, it is suggested that you seal the grain with Jackson's Sealer-D, a shellac-based filler. This will prevent excessive absorption of the varnish into the wood and will assist in the more rapid build up of a high gloss. The sealer is similar in appearance to white french polish and is suitable for use on any colour of wood, either light or dark.

Guild of Woodworkers has run two-day courses on wood finishing whereat the subject of grain filling was demonstrated. Further courses are being arranged during this year for Guild members.

The syllabus includes preparation of wood, staining, filling the grain, oil polishing, waxing, french polishing and repolishing. Overnight accommodation is available nearby if required.

Can you help us?

We would like to find a supplier of clear cellulose in aerosol cans for one of our readers in the West Midlands.

Trenails

From: W. H. Brown, Amersham, Bucks

I would refer to the reply to E. Minost, Lymington (Question Box, December 1981 WOODWORKER, page 868). This dealt admirably with the question that was asked but it occurred to me that on inquiring about the trenails Mr Minost might have overlooked two further and important points.

Oak heartwood has a good natural resistance to decay, but the sapwood is by definition, non-durable. Accordingly for all exposed wooden members, ie, windows and external doors, sills, thresholds etc, all sapwood ought to be removed. There are two reasons, wet rot can quite quickly develop in any sapwood that can get wet and be unable to dry out again very quickly, and secondly, particularly early on, there is the chance for the sapwood to be attacked by *Lyctus* beetle. This latter contingency would tend to die out after a few years but if it did occur it would cause severe structural damage. If it is too late to take action to remove the sapwood, or if it is not considered a practical measure then our further advice would be to well brush-treat the sapwood portions with a clear organic solvent wood preservative. It should contain an insecticide and a fungicide. Allow at least 48 hrs for the spirit base to evaporate before applying your final decorative finish. All fasteners and fittings should be of non-ferrous metal in order to avoid 'ink-stains' and early corrosion of metal.

White and yellow glues

From: G. Vergine, Priest Weston, Powys

An American book on veneering refers to white glue and yellow glue and mentions that it is possible to heat and press down blisters, caused by poor contact, with both these glues, in presumably the same way that we deal with animal glues.

American white glue is apparently polyvinyl resin. Is this markedly different from the commonly available PVA in its properties? Yellow glue would appear to be an aliphatic-type glue. Is there a British equivalent and does it have the same properties?

Not having read the American book on veneering it is difficult to say what is meant by white and yellow glues. It seems likely that the white glue is similar to our PVA glues. For laying veneers or replacing missing pieces there is no better adhesive than the time honoured scotch glue, which is no longer sold in cakes but is available in pearl form. Pearls have the advantage of dissolving faster than broken pieces of cake.

Occasionally pieces of veneer lift and form blisters, which, if they are small, can sometimes be stuck down by applying a hot iron. This softens the glue below the blister and the application of a hot caul will retain the veneer in place while the glue sets. In the case of a large blister, a slim-bladed craft knife is used to cut through the centre of the blister in the direction of the grain. One half of the blister is lifted at a time and hot glue is worked underneath the raised veneer. The newly glued pieces are pressed into position and held down by weights until the glue sets. If a single slit is insufficient to allow glue to be worked far enough in, a second cut is made at right angles to the first. All four pieces are gently lifted in turn as the glue is introduced, after which the weights are applied. The use of PVA glues for this purpose is not recommended.

A useful directory which classifies glues by type of basic material and end use, gives an adhesives check list, trade names, associations, names and addresses plus selection chart is published annually by A. S. O'Connor & Co Ltd, 26 Sheen Park, Richmond, Surrey.

Saw problems
From: R. Hassell, Brighton
I have recently acquired a Nobex mitre saw (featured in November WOODWORKER 1981 p762) and am now able to cut with accuracy 8-sided and 5-sided frames. I am, however, experiencing difficulty in clamping, gluing and pinning and would be grateful for any advice and help.

The problem of positioning your pieces while gluing and pinning polygonal frames could be solved by making up a locating jig. In its simplest form this is a plywood baseboard some inches larger than the finished frame and onto which is glued a further piece of plywood which is the exact shape and size of the rebate size of the framework to be glued.

The jig should be sealed and then waxed to prevent excess glue sticking the frame to the jig. Given the accuracy with which your Nobex saw will cut frame members to precision length and angle it is worthwhile making sure that the jig is accurate. With the glue applied to all the mitres, position the pieces on the jig and hold all in place with a stout rubber band. Larger frames are better held with a string cramp tensioned with a tourniquet in exactly the same manner that a bow saw is tightened. The use of string and tourniquet cramps is adequately described in the opening chapter of *Woodwork aids and devices* by Robert Wearing, published by Evans Bros. Commercially made cramps which employ adaptations of the same principle are available eg Flexicramps. An elaboration of the jig for heavier frameworks would be to fix stop bars to the base board, of the same length and parallel to, the jig sides at some distance away and drive a pair of folding wedges against each frame side to 'pull' the pieces up. This arrangement would have the added advantage of allowing you to pin and glue at the same time, whereas with the string cramp you would have to wait until the glue had set and the cramp was dismantled before you could pin the joint.

Finish for oak
From: C. M. Harthan, Bristol
Some years ago I made an oak dining table which was finished with cellulose and is now regularly wax polished. It has proved very susceptible to marking, particularly with red wine. I would be grateful for your advice on:
1. How should I remove the existing stains?

2. What finish would you recommend? (I do not like a plastic finish)
3. I am in the process of making an oak hi-fi cabinet, would you recommend a similar finish?

It is generally agreed that wax polish is the best finish for oak. The deep mellow shine which repeated applications of beeswax imparts, reveals the beauty of oak better than any other finish. The brilliance of a plastic finish would give a gaudy appearance although it would withstand alcohol.

It is suggested that the stained wax polish is cleaned off with white spirit and then the cellulose carefully examined. If it is badly damaged it should be removed with a stripper but if it is in good order it will only need smoothing with a fine abrasive paper. This is to provide a good key for the subsequent finish.

A shellac finish *Imperva* is obtainable from James Jackson & Co (London) Ltd, Major Works, 76/89 Alscot Road, London SE1 5SX. It is applied either by pad or brush and withstands alcohol better than ordinary french polish. If, however, wine glasses are frequently placed on the table is would be more satisfactory to brush on Jackson's bar-top polish. This is a one part polish which can be thinned with cellulose thinners. It stands up well to both alcohol and water.

With regard to the oak hi-fi cabinet we would advise a wax polish. Having stained the work to the desired colour, brush on several applications of white french polish until the grain is fairly full. When the polish is hard it is smoothed with a fine garnet paper and then thoroughly dusted. Light and dark antique wax finishes are available.

Apply the polish evenly with a clean rag and allow it to stand for about ten minutes, then polish briskly along the grain with a soft duster. Repeat several times until the required depth of finish is obtained.

Storing teak
From: J. George, High Wycombe
I have for some time been using teak for faceplate turning. The pieces I use are 1in. thick with 9 and 11in. diameters. Occasionally a finished piece will shrink slightly (approx. 1/16/1/8in. across the grain) although thought to be dry before turning.

I purchase the teak from a local timber yard (covered) and immediately cut the wood into 9 and 11in. diameter discs and stack them indoors (approx. 65°F) for about a month before turning. I treat the finished piece with bourne seal and beeswax. Please could you tell me if this method of storing the teak is satisfactory for my intended use and whether I am allowing enough drying time. (The wood is not 'wet' when I purchase it from the timber merchants) Any other information you might have on teak would be most welcome.

I use teak for its pleasant appearance and apart from this shrinkage it is the most stable wood I have used and found suitable to my needs. Do you know of any other wood more stable for consideration?

Taking all things into consideration, you will not find another wood behaving any better than teak, since in terms of movement its classification is 'small'. What is wrong is that your working environment is such that all your wood is not coming to

equilibrium in the same exposure time, in other words, 'about a month' is not long enough. What you should do is to cut your blanks, 1/8in. (3mm) larger than your present off-saw diameter and then draw a pencil line across the centre of the blank, marking the exact diameter on this line. If you check the dimensions periodically, the wood will be at equilibrium when any shrinkage has stopped. Since presumably you have no trouble after turning and sealing the wood, it is the preliminary preparation that is at fault.

It will no doubt help you to understand the position more clearly if we explain that the temperature you mention is only subsidiary to air conditions, for example, if in your timber suppliers's store the temperature is 65°F with a relative humidity of 75% then timber stored there would, if left long enough come to an equilibrium moisture content of about 12%. In your home, at the same temperature, the atmosphere would no doubt be drier, the average for well-heated rooms being about 50% RH providing an equilibrium for wood of about 10%, so that wood moved from one environment to the other would readjust its moisture content accordingly. When laboratory tests are made to assess a timber's movement value (by shrinking or swelling), samples are first conditioned in wet air and then in dry air and the differences in dimensions noted. The tests for teak were as follows, Equilibrium m.c. in 90% RH = 15%: Equilibrium m.c. in 60% RH = 10%

Corresponding tangential (plain sawn) movement = 5/32in. per ft (4mm in 300mm) You will note that movement by shrinking (5/32in.) is for a m.c. change of 5% (15% to 10%). Taking your worst case, ie 1/8in. across a 9in. face; this equals 5/32in. roughly across a 12in. face which in theory at least suggests your wood when bought was 5% higher in moisture content than was desired. We do not think this was so however, for several reasons but mainly because we have taken your worst case and, in practice, the RH of covered, dry timber storage would doubtless be lower than the wettest condition used in the test, 90% RH being almost saturated air. We suspect that when bought your teak is around 12 to 13% m.c. and is drying down in your home to 9 or 10%, and needs just that little longer drying. Of course, if your teak was radially cut (quarter sawn), then the movement value would be reduced from 5/32in. to 3/32in. per foot of width.

QUESTION
BOX
COUPON
APRIL 1982

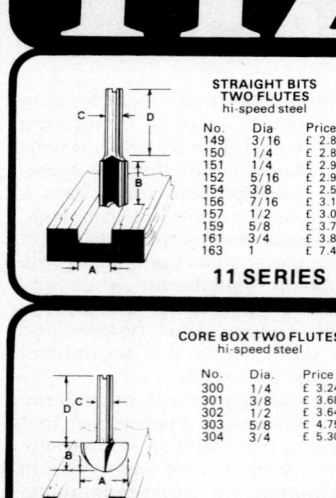
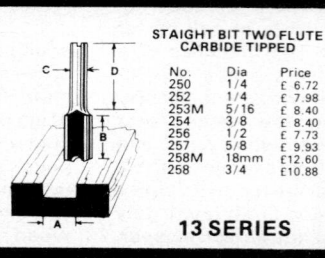
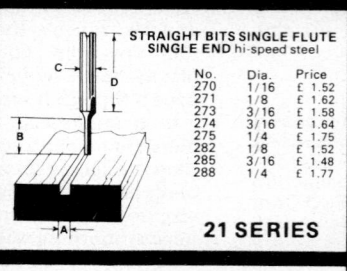
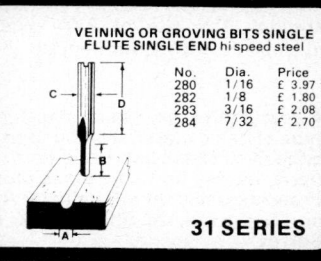
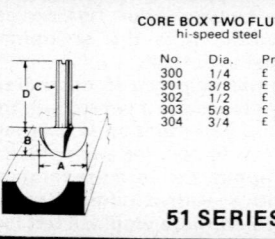
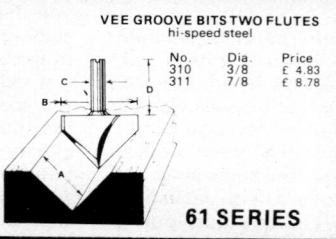
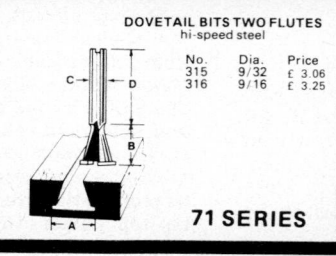
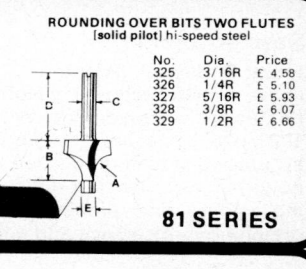
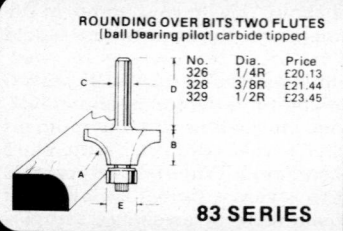
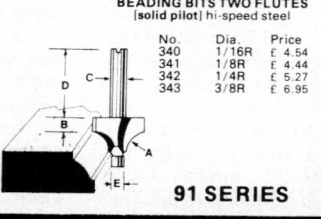
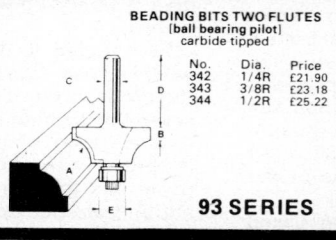
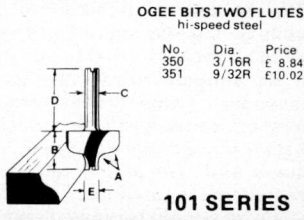
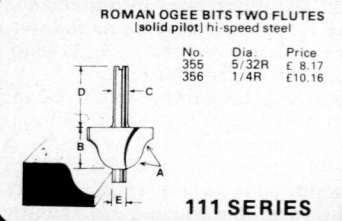
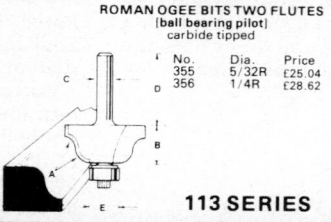
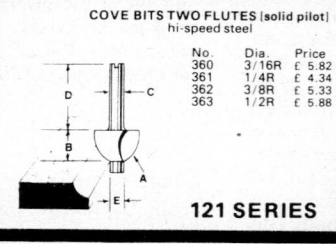
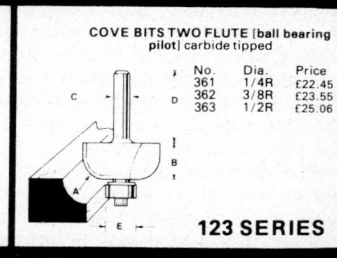
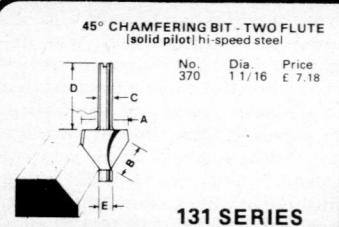
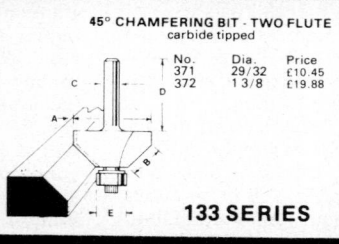
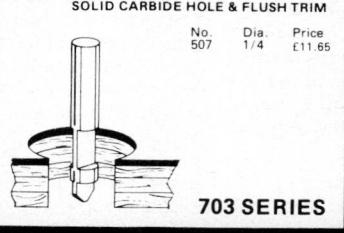
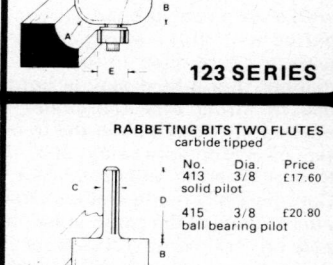
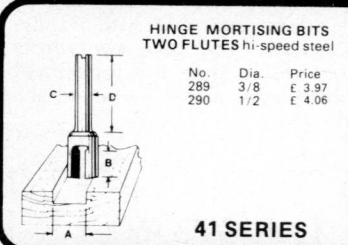
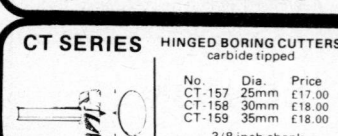
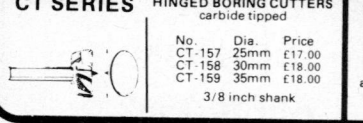
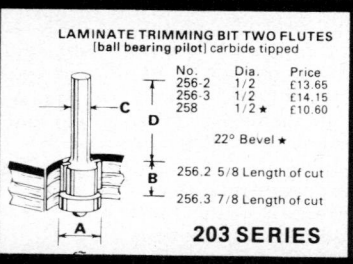

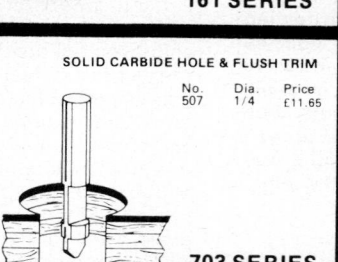
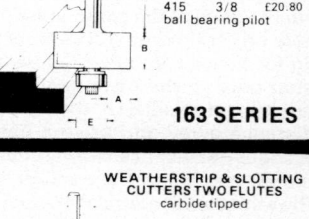
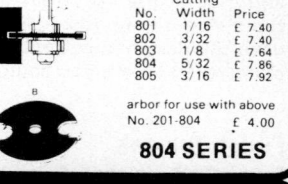

Guild of Woodworkers

DESIGN

Courses on design appreciation and fine craftsmanship

Three separate courses on design and fine craftsmanship have been arranged at Rycotewood College, Priest End, Thame OX9 2AF.

2 day course 6-7 April....a two-day course to introduce the basic principles of design and to apply them to the development of interesting and original small scale woodwork problems. Cost £40.00.

3 day course 14-16 April....a three-day course to introduce the basic principles of design, to show how the 20th century designer/craftsman has developed both the art and craft aspects in modern commissioned design, and how they may be applied to a small piece of work. Cost £69.00.

5 day course (date to be advised) in August/September 1982....a five-day course to bring to the woodworker the basic principles of design and to apply these principles to the making of a piece of furniture. Cost £115.00.

Respective charges for the three courses are all inclusive of VAT and all cover accommodation at the college, plus morning coffee and meals. A cancellation charge of half the fee will be made unless the cancellation is received in writing 14 days prior to the date of the course.

Applications should be made as soon as possible, together with remittance to: Administrator, Guild of Woodworkers, PO Box 35, Bridge Street, Hemel Hempstead HP1 1EE.

Application forms for all Guild of Woodworkers courses have been published in previous issues of Woodworker. They may be obtained direct from the Administrator, please enclose a SAE. Applications for all courses should be made as early as possible so as to avoid disappointment. Some courses fill almost immediately they are published.

SKILLS AND PROFIT-MAKING

Following the success of the two-day seminar on skills and profit-making held at Salisbury last June in co-operation with the Council for Small Industries in Rural Areas (CoSIRA), the guild has arranged a further series of two-day seminars on the same subject.

The first was held at the Lord Hill Hotel, Abbey Foregate, Shrewsbury, on Wednesday and Thursday 24 and 25 February. The second will be at the Pottergate Course & Conference Centre, 83-5 Pottergate, Norwich, on Wednesday and Thursday 28 and 29 April. The fee for the seminar is £50 plus £7.50 VAT (total £57.50) which includes tuition, papers and lecture material, morning coffee, lunch and tea in the afternoon. Accommodation is not included but arrangements can be made on request.

Subjects will include business principles, business skills; marketing; production utilisation; financial control; budgets; tax; planning for growth and much more. The programme is carefully tailored to meet the requirements of those who contemplate starting their own businesses or who have recently set up in the woodworking sector.

The instructors are CoSIRA officers all of whom have much practical experience in small business operation and each seminar allows time for discussion and exchange of views. As reported in WOODWORKER for September last year: 'It (the seminar at Salisbury) was all done in a practical way and with good humour, informality and quick-fire question-and-answer technique.' One member said afterwards: 'It's all a matter of commonsense really but I did not realise it until now. The seminar has certainly opened my eyes.'

The whole purpose of being in business is to make a profit. At the Salisbury seminar, John Matthews (CoSIRA senior production management officer) said: 'If you want to make £10,000 a year you've got to make £1 every 10 minutes, so when you are on your own you can't afford to just stand around.'

Machine tools course

Special introductory practical two-day course for members with limited experience of woodworking machinery to be held at various times (bookings accepted any time to suit) in Milton Keynes, Bucks. This is a non-residential course. Price on application to the administrator.

Tool Insurance

In April 1980 WOODWORKER p219, we announced an insurance scheme to cover members' woodworking tools and machinery had been arranged at an average cost of 2½% of total value. (Subject to variation in certain high-risk areas.) In May 1981 WOODWORKER p302 we announced that several members had asked if the total amount of £500 could be increased to a figure more closely related to current values.

We are now able to announce that improved facilities are available. Members may now insure their tools and machinery for £500 (premium £5.00 per annum) or £1000 (£12.50 per annum). The underwriters still require an excess of £10 to obviate a large number of small claims. Other exceptions are wear and tear, electrical and mechanical breakdown, gradual deterioration and losses due to climatic conditions. The success of an 'all risks' policy depends on maximum support. Forms and details from: The Administrator, Guild of Woodworkers, PO Box 35, Bridge Street, Hemel Hempstead HP1 1EE.

Enforcement notices

In 1979 HM Factory Inspectorate issued 284 enforcement notices under the Woodworking Machines Regulations 1974. There were 347 contraventions mentioned in the notices: 299 relating to improvements; seven deferred prohibitions; and 41 immediate prohibitions. A total of 295 notices were complied with in full, 46 notices received an extension granted by factory inspectors and one was extended by a tribunal. Three notices were withdrawn by the inspector while on two no further action was taken.

Prosecutions by the inspectorate under WMR in 1979 totalled 102 (103 in 1978) and in 97 convictions were obtained. The average fine was £154. There were three dismissals and two withdrawals.

Details are given in *Health & Safety Statistics 1978-9* (ISBN 0-11-883438-X) published by HMSO at £4.50.

GUILD OF WOODWORKERS

Guild necktie in green with two narrow gold-coloured 'bandings' between which is the guild badge also gold-coloured, is now available at £3.50 inclusive of VAT, postage and packing. Members requiring a tie should send cheque or crossed postal order together with their guild number and address to:

Administrator, Guild of Woodworkers, PO Box 35, Bridge Street, Hemel Hempstead HP1 1EE.

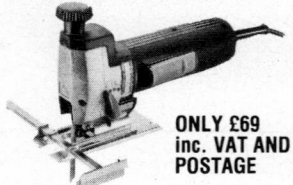

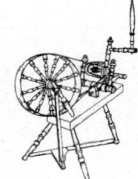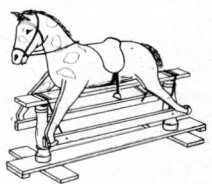

masterclass '82

Masterclass '82 is being held at the Sun Hotel, Sun St, Hitchin, Herts, a beautiful old coaching house dating back to the 14 century.

Sponsored by Roger Buse of Roger's Tool Store, and organised by Betty Norbury of The White Knight Gallery, Masterclass '82 takes place from 14-17 April inclusive, in Hitchin, Herts. The original concept was a display of woodworking products but in response to increasing demand from professionals and amateurs for quality information it has become a series of lectures, demonstrations and exhibitions.

Questions or problems can be discussed over continuous demonstrations of marquetry, cabinetmaking, carving, turning, chairmaking, musical instrument and model making, by experts in their individual fields.

16 lectures will be given by some of the top personalities in today's woodworking

Chair in ash with rush seat by Paul Spriggs.

fraternity. These include John Makepeace, Alan Peters, Charles Hayward, Cecil Jordan, Mary Comino, Richard Maude and advisors on sales promotion, marketing and design. The reference works on the subject will be discussed by Brian Davies of Stobarts and Bob Brett will discuss the raw material – wood and its availability.

Information, reservation forms for lectures, prices etc from: Betty Norbury, The White Knight Gallery, 28 Painswick Rd, Cheltenham, Glos. (0242) 38582. Please include sae with enquiries.

Over 150 carefully selected exhibits from some 50 leading craftsmen in wood, furniture makers, wood turners, wood carvers, musical instrument makers, covering most aspects of the contemporary scene. Plus a range of modern hand tools and books, backed by expert advice on qualities and uses.

Programme of lectures

Wednesday 14 April at 2.00pm, under the heading *Availability* Brian Davies, Robert Brett, Roger Buse, Richard Maude and Ian Fiddes-Gooding will speak on woodworking books, timber, new tools, old tools and stains and finishes respectively.

Thursday 15 April at 2.00pm under the heading *Makers* four craftsmen give an insight into their skills: John Makepeace (eminent designer) Alan Peters (craftsman designer) Cecil Jordan (craftsman woodturner) and Brian Cohen (musical instrument maker).

Friday 16 April at 2.00pm *A step into the past* brings together 3 speakers Mary Comino (Gimson and the Barnsleys) Charles Hayward (craftsman and writer) and John Beer (Arts and Crafts Movement).

Saturday 17 April at 2.00pm. How do you market a product? Will the public want it? Helpful, positive advice in *Craftsman and consumer* by Chris Simpson (head of the department of Fine Craftsmanship and Design, Rycotewood College), Richard Collins (PR consultant), Alan Mitchell (Editor, *Practical Woodworking)* and Lucinda Leach (cabinetmaker).

Eric Gill: Man of Flesh and Spirit, by Malcolm Yorke (Constable £12.50) ISBN 0 09 463740 7

Eric Gill was an extraordinary man, both in personality and in the diversity of his work. So it is surprising that he is really only remembered today as a designer of print typefaces, while his reckonable achievements spanned a so much greater range.

Perhaps it is this very artistic diversity that is responsible for his comparative obscurity now, though to suggest that he was a 'jack of all trades and master of none' would be a grave misjudgement of his prodigious talent.

For Eric Gill (1882-1940) was, during the course of his varied life, a book designer and illustrator, a stone-cutter, a sculptor in wood and stone and a wood-engraver, in addition to his prolific writing of radical words on subjects ranging from politics to clothing.

The various aspects of Gill's work have been assessed individually by several previous authors, but Malcolm Yorke has taken the broadest possible brief in this new work. The result is that Gill emerges for the first time in print as the whole man; the man driven equally by an extraordinary sexual appetite and a profound sense of religious significance.

This apparent conflict of nature was evidently less opposed in Gill's own mind than might be expected, but his acceptance of the duality of flesh and spirit is quite clear in his work. The key is, perhaps, that even religious figures which appear in his va-

rious mediums have about them an undisguised and unashamed sexuality. Indeed, Gill's approach to figure drawing is often salacious, if not downright pornographic.

For the wood-engraver, the illustrations in this book give away much useful technical detail, particularly interesting in that

Gill was a leading light in the revival of the art, along with Noel Rooke, Gwen Raverat and John Nash, during the 1920s.

At its lightest this volume is recommended as an enjoyably readable book for the bed-side, but it is a credit to Dr Yorke that its contents will sustain the serious student of Gill as well.   **C.D.**

Wryly entitled 'The Sofa', this wood engraving by Eric Gill, printed in *intaglio*, was produced in 1925. Note the end-grain shadows in the print.

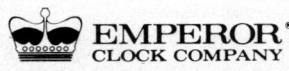
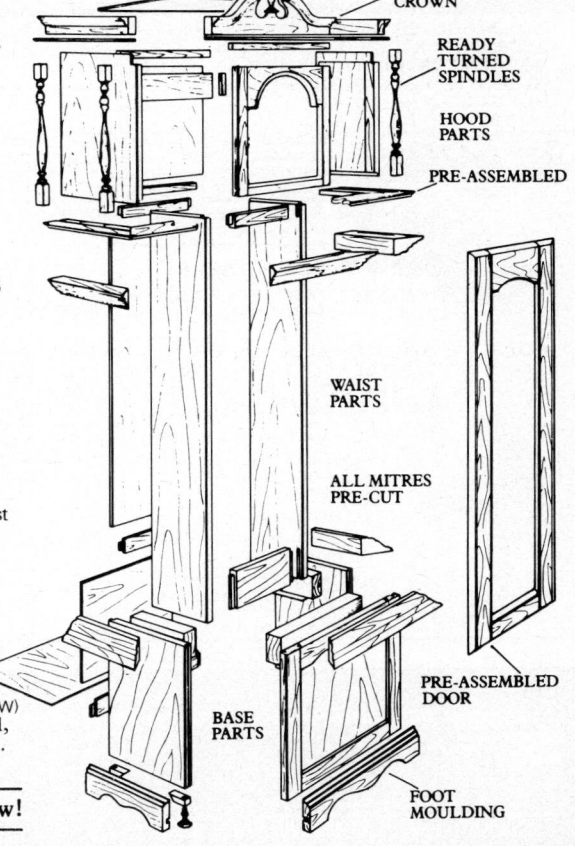

G. K. HADFIELD

SCARCE OR OUT OF PRINT BOOKS

TREDGOLD: **Elementary Principles of Carpentry.** Revised from original and partly re-written by Hurst. 5th ed. 1886 527pp. plus plates. Together with carpentry and joinery and atlas of engravings. 1873 – The two ... **£48.00**

STURT: **The Wheelwright's Shop.** 1st ed. 1923 v.g.c.
.... **£30.00**

paperback edition **£5.25**

FASTNEDGE: **Sheraton Furniture.** 1962. Well ill. **£18.75**

BARTER: **Woodwork.** 1905 305 ills. **£16.00**

PARRY: **Woodworking Machinery and Electric Tools, and Accessories.** 2nd ed. 1,500 ills. 500 pp. **£9.50**

Send today for your list of over 500 scarce or out of print titles on clocks, watches, lathes, turning, woodwork, sundials, automata etc. 30p stamps please.

Barclaycard/Visa/Access/Mastercard welcomed – it's quick, efficient and easy. **Phone 050 95 3014 Now!**

Blackbrook Hill House, Tickow Lane, Shepshed, Leics LE12 9EY.

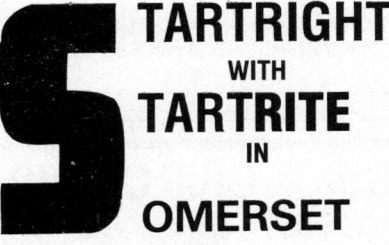

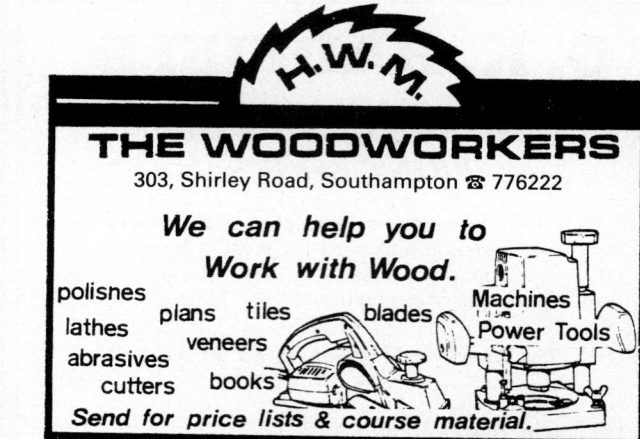
PHOTOCOPY SERVICE

We are able to supply photocopies of articles from many past issues of WOODWORKER at a nominal cost of 15p a page (minimum 75p) plus 25p postage. Readers are asked to give month and year of the issue required to Mrs Anne Duncan at WOODWORKER office which is PO Box 35, Bridge Street, Hemel Hempstead HP1 1EE (0442 41221).

We cannot guarantee to supply photocopies from all past issues as unfortunately the office files of back-numbers are not complete.

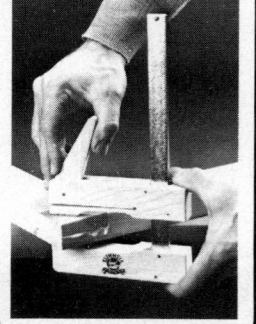
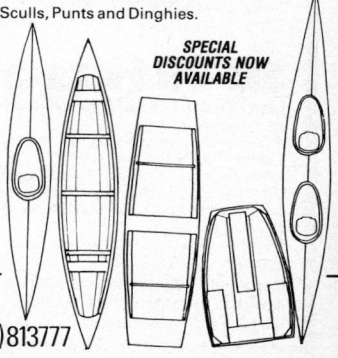

Whittling knives

Whittling (chip carving) knives from Warren Tool Co Inc of the US are available in UK through Ashley Iles (Edge Tools) Ltd, East Kirkby, Spilsby, Lincs (07903 372). Two of the smaller kits (packed in clear plastics boxes are KB3 comprising 4⅛in. long handle with six (one each style) ⁵⁄₁₆in. tang blades; and KBL3 which includes a 3⅜in. handle and three (one each style) ½in. tang blades.

Ashley Iles tells WOODWORKER: In June last year I visited a number of cities in the US. The products of Warren Tools were of particular interest as a solution to our long-standing problem of chip carving knives and we negotiated a substantial delivery. The presentation and quality of these items are excellent.

Preservatives

Xylamon preservatives in various formulations for specific applications are marketed by Kay-Metzeler Ltd, Waterhouse Mill, Bollington, Macclesfield, Cheshire, in 2½, 5 and 25 litre containers and household spray cans. There are formulations to combat blue stain, fungi and borers as well as Xylamon LX Hardening which is resin-based and said to preserve timber that has been heavily attacked by borers.

Advice on application etc of these preservatives can be had from the company's wood preservative division at the Bollington address.

Xylamon preservatives available from Kay-Metzeler Ltd to combat blue stain, fungi and borers.

Through-feed moulder

Addition to the moulders by Wadkin Ltd, Green Lane Works, Leicester LE5 4PF (0533 769111), is the FDR170, a belt-driven through-feed machine of modular construction with integral sound enclosure and outfeed and built-in extraction.

Below: Whittling knives from Warren Tool Co Inc of the US now available from Ashley Iles (Edge Tools) Ltd packed in clear plastics boxes.

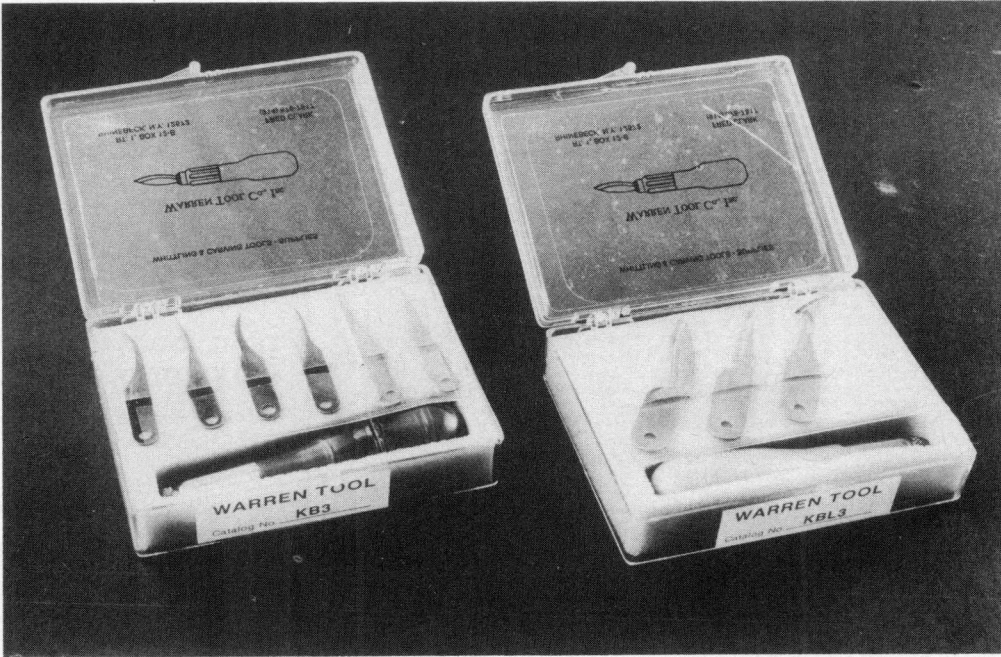

Straight and profile jointing is provided via cutter spindles operating at 6000rpm. Where a single-knife finish is required spindle speeds of 7500 and 9000rpm can be provided.

Close centre pneumatically-loaded feed rolls provide first-class traction for all types of timber whatever its condition, states the company. The machine has a grooved bed and is equipped with Hydrogrip tooling for greater accuracy and finer finish.

Right: range of adhesives and waterproofing products introduced by Bostik Ltd to complement their House Holders range of repair adhesives.

Cutting tools

Cutting tools made by the Vermont American Corp are being handled in UK by E. P. Barrus Ltd, Launton Road, Bicester OX6 0UR (08692 3355). Products include Krome-King chrome-nickel alloy, Fire Tooth (R) and TCT circular saw blades, all in various diameters and tooth patterns, as well as industrial TCT up to 20in. diameter and a variety of tooth patterns. There are jigsaw blades and bi-metal jigsaw blades, the latter having HSS teeth welded to the carbon steel back. Four tang designs are available to cover all jigsaws made by the major power tool companies.

Another item is no. 398 portable saw table to fit portable circular saws with blades up to 7½in. diameter. The table height

Bigger sizes

No. 8 woodworking adhesive manufactured by Bostik Ltd, Ulverscroft Road, Leicester, is now available in 500ml and 1 litre polybottles at £1.95 and

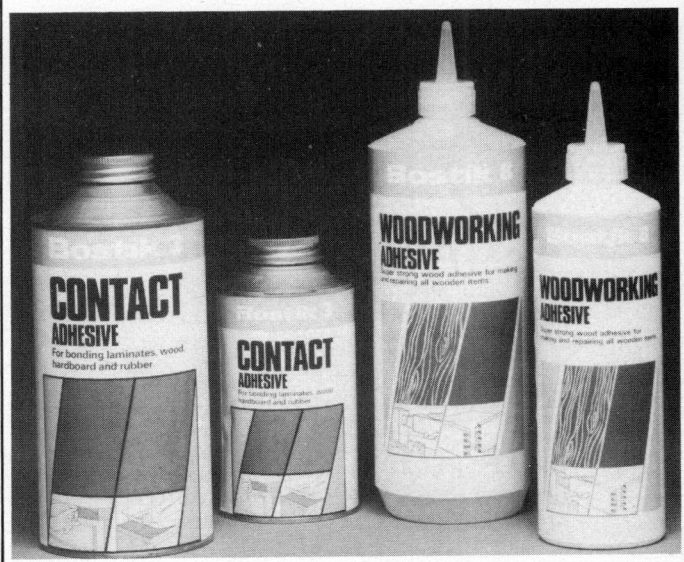

£3.45 (incl VAT) respectively. The smaller packs of 70 and 120cc capacity are continued. The company's Weatherproof, Contact and other adhesives are also offered in larger capacities.

is 11in.

The range of routing equipment includes router bits in TC and HSS (individually and four sets); no. 852 router lathe; no. 396 router table; no. 850 router pantograph; no. 855 sign template set of letters and numbers; no. 859 template guide and edge kit; no. 857 door hinge template set; no. 860 dovetail fixture template.

An attachment to convert ¼ and ⅜in. chuck power drills into an impact wrench is offered in two models branded U-Impact-

It. There is also a range of holesaws in bi-metal, TCT and carbon steel.

Barrus has also made an addition to its Shapercraft tools in the form of the MitreMate (no. 6050) clamping jig for sawing etc. operations where a 90° or 45° angle cutting left or right is required.

The range of drill stands has been revised and comprises the DrillMate (no. 1129); DrillMate Plus (no. 1130); Drillmate Combi-Workshop (no. 1131); and shaping table (no. 1121).

Wood Suppliers

Especially aimed at the readers who require to buy and sell timber and allied materials. Make sure you reach the market.
Let Woodworker Wood Suppliers section work for you. Sizes available — Full Page £300. Half Page £160. Quarter Page £88. Eighth Page £50. Classified — Semi Display £4.00 per single column cm (Minimum £10.00). Lineage rate 20p per word (Minimum £3.00). Box Number £1.25 extra
For further details give Valerie Tester a ring on (0442) 41221 Ext. 266.

KILN DRIED, Acacia, Ash, Cherry, Elm, Lime, Yew etc. Rustic wood slices. Telephone (0222) 861584. L-N

VENEERS AND MARQUETRY equipment, materials and books now in stock. Phone or send for details to: H.W.M., The Woodworkers, 303 Shirley Road, Shirley, Southampton. Tel: 0703 776222. T/C

VENEERS, all types. SAE List—S. Gould (Veneers), 342 Uxbridge Road, W12. Tel: 01-743 8561. T/C

CONVERT TIMBER YOURSELF, with a portable chain saw mill. Cuts a 36" width 200 sq. ft. per hour. Keenest prices. Brochure, demonstration. Philip Cole, 16 Kings Lane, Flore, Northampton. Tel: Weedon 0327 40337 (evenings) T/C

SEASONED English Hardwoods. Air and kiln dried timbers for the discerning craftsman. P. Smith, Furniture Makers, Chapel Workshops, Kirkburn, Driffield, E. Yorkshire. Tel: Driffield 89301. Alt. T/C

VENEERS from 20p per square foot. Send SAE for list to Veneers, Bridgemount, Headlands Road, Liversedge, West Yorkshire WF15 6PR. M

ROSEWOOD MAXIMUM 16' × 1' 6" Burr Walnut, mahogany curls and crotches. Half price. Telephone: 0203 410045. I-N

AIR DRY BEECH, forest grown 1⅛", 2", 2¼", 2½", 3¼", 4¼", 6" from around £8.00 per cu. ft. Ring Will Tyers, Hornby (0468) 21292 (Nr. Lancaster). J-O

Earn £200 per hour drying timber with your own kiln . . .

My seasoners need so little attention that your time could hardly be better spent than by drying your own timber. Can you afford to invest a few hundred pounds in order to guarantee your work is stable in central heating and ensure that your English hardwoods will cost half as much for many years to come.

No need to keep large untidy stacks of timber slowly drying and spoiling for years and years — these machines work from green in a few weeks and cost only a few pence per cubic foot to run.

The smallest seasoner costs less than £340 and will dry enough timber to keep several people busy or make you some money selling surplus timber. It can live outside and does not usually need a box much larger than 8' × 4' × 4'. As I am the man who developed these machines, I hope that my information, prices, references etc., are second to none.

Write for details or ring me any time for answers to your questions completely without obligation.

JOHN ARROWSMITH
Roadam Cottage, Barton, Richmond,
N. Yorks. DL10 6HR. Tel. 0325 77 362

TIMBER
cut to your requirements

We cut and prepare to your cutting list

TEAK, OAK, ROSEWOOD, MAHOGANY, BEECH, BOXWOOD, etc. —VENEERS and PLYWOODS

We carry large stocks of dry hardwoods for cabinet and joinery trade. Turning done to your drawing. Brassware and cabinet fittings available.

Open all day Saturday — early closing Thursday.
Send S.A.E. with your cutting list for quote.

GENERAL WOODWORK SUPPLIES
Dept. W.W., 76-80 STOKE NEWINGTON HIGH STREET, LONDON N16 ———————— Phone: 01-254 6052

VENEERS
SHORT AND FULL LEAVES
In all popular timbers. Send S.A.E. for FREE price list or 55p for samples of 12 pieces 4" × 3" to:
ELLIOTT BROS
Four Winds, Moorwoods Lane, Dore
All letters to PO Box No. 6, Glossop, Derby. Reg. No. 2064782

Telephone Valerie Tester
(0442) 41221
Ex. 266

CRAFTWOODS
Good stocks of many hardwoods — Mahogany, Ash, Lime, Bubinga, Cherry, Lignum Vitae, Ebony, Meranti, Maple, Padauk, Pear, Oaks, Rosewood, Teak, Wenge, Sapele, Afrormosia.
Also Fingerboards, squares, veneers, panelling, carving kits, doors, plywood, tools, books.
Logs and Billets for carving.
Send SAE for price list to
CRAFTWOODS,
Smiths Yard, Water Lane, Sherington, Bucks.
Tel: Newport Pagnell (0908) 615050.
Callers Welcome.

Portable Tree Milling Service

WE SUPPLY ENGLISH HARDWOODS. In the round, fresh sawn, or dried. Species in stock include: Oak, Burr Oak, Walnut, Ash, Elm, Yew, Sycamore, Tree of Heaven, Acacia, Beech, Lacewood.
SOON TO BE MILLED. Acacia, Apple, Ash, Beech, Cedar, Cherry, Chestnut, Elm, Holly, Holm Oak, Lacewood, Lime, Maple, Oak, Pear, Sycamore, Tree of Heaven, Tulip Tree, Walnut, Yew.
QUARTER SAWN AND STRAIGHT EDGED OAK SUPPLIED.
YOUR OWN TREES MILLED on site, to your specifications.
JOHN EMERY
THE OLD RECTORY, PILGRIMS WAY, CHEW STOKE, NR. BRISTOL.
TEL: CHEW MAGNA 3222

JOHN BODDY & SON (TIMBER) LTD.

offer

Direct from our Sawmill and Kilns

BRITISH HARDWOODS

As one of the few British Timber Merchants specialising in the production of kiln dried hardwoods in planking and dimension stock.

We invite craftsmen to inspect and select from our stock of over 20,000 cubic feet of kiln dried timber. Stored under cover.

OAK, ASH, ELM, BEECH, SYCAMORE, YEW.

available from stock in most thicknesses.
Also

APPLE, PEAR, CHERRY, LIME, RIPPLE SYCAMORE & WALNUT

Round logs are available in all species for selection and conversion to customers' individual requirements.

---

*Please send for our Stock List or call and inspect
Open Monday to Friday 8 a.m. - 5 p.m.
Saturday 8 a.m. - 12 noon*

Riverside Sawmills,
Boroughbridge, YO5 9LJ, North Yorkshire.
Telephone (09012) 2370 Telex 57526

NORTH HEIGHAM SAWMILLS
Good, Kiln-Dried stocks of most Home-Grown timbers, and exotic, Imported Hardwoods.
Stocks include: Apple, ash, beech, blackwood, box, cedar, cherry, cocobolo, ebony, elm, holly, lemonwood, lignum, lime, mahogany, maple, oak, padauk, pear, plane, rosewood, satinwood, sycamore, walnut, yew, zelkova.
Please send S.A.E. for priced stock list to:
North Heigham Sawmills, Paddock St. (off Barker St.), NORWICH NR2 4TW. Tel: Norwich 22978.

WOOD TURNERS SUPPLIES
Hardwood Blocks for bowls, lamps etc. cut from seasoned timbers— assortment of sizes and woods for £7.00 + £4.50 p&c to any UK mainland address.

TRADITIONAL DOORS, BIDDENDEN, ASHFORD, KENT

VENEERS, inlay bandings, stringing and marquetry panels. Large selection.
Mail order and callers welcome. S.A.E. for list.
R. AARONSON (VENEERS) LTD
45 Redchurch St., London E2.
Tel: 01-739 3107

ACACIA, ASH, CHESTNUT, MAPLE, OAK, YEW, SYCAMORE, WALNUT.
Fresh Sawn, Air Dry or Kilned. Machining Available.
William and Penny Garvey, Furniture Makers,
Leyhill, Payhembury, Honiton.
Tel: Broadhembury (040 484) 430.

Prices quoted are those prevailing at press date and are subject to alteration due to economic conditions.

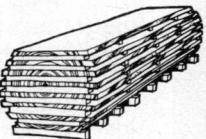

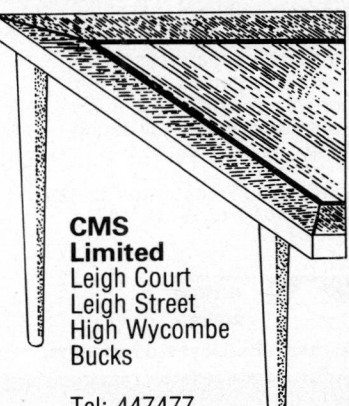

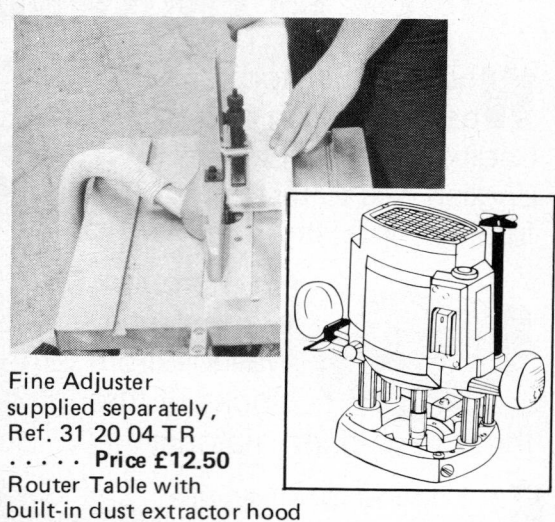

Prices quoted are those prevailing at press date and are subject to alteration due to economic conditions.

SHOP GUIDE SHOP GUIDE

The quickest and easiest method of reaching all Woodworkers is to advertise in SHOP GUIDE. Telephone **Valerie Tester (0442) 41221 Ext. 266. Rate: £8.00 per unit.** Minimum of 6 months.

Key: H — Hand tools, **P** — Power tools, **W** — Woodworking machinery up to £1000, **WM** — Woodworking machinery over £1000, **D** — Demonstration available on selected machines, **T** — Timber, **CS** — Cutting or sharpening services, **A** — Attachments, **BC** — Books/catalogues, * — Mail order.

AVON

BATH   Tel. Bath 64513
JOHN HALL TOOLS   ★
RAILWAY STREET

Open: Monday-Saturday
9.00 a.m.-5.30 p.m.
H.P.W.WM.D.A.BC.

BRISTOL   Tel. (0272) 311510
JOHN HALL TOOLS LIMITED   ★
CLIFTON DOWN SHOPPING
CENTRE, WHITELADIES ROAD

Open: Monday-Saturday
9.00 a.m.-5.30 p.m.
H.P.W.WM.D.A.BC.

BRISTOL   Tel. 0272-633844
ROBBINS LIMITED
THE WOODWORKER SHOP
MERRYWOOD MILLS, BEDMINSTER

Open: Mon-Fri 8.00 a.m.-5.00 p.m.
Saturday 8.30 a.m.-12.30 p.m.
H.P.T.CS.A.BC.

BRISTOL   Tel. 0272-629092
TRYMWOOD SERVICES   ★
2a DOWNS PARK EAST, (off
North View) WESTBURY PARK

Open: 8.30 a.m.-5.30 p.m. Mon. to
Fri. Closed for lunch 1-2 p.m.
P.W.WM.D.T.A.BC.

BRISTOL   Tel. 0272-667013
V. H. WILLIS & CO. LTD   ★
190-192 WEST STREET,
BEDMINSTER

Open: Mon-Fri 8.30 a.m.-5 p.m.
Saturday 9 a.m.-1 p.m.
H.P.W.WM.D.CS.A.BC.

BERKSHIRE

READING   Tel. Littlewick Green
DAVID HUNT (TOOL   2743
MERCHANTS) LTD   ★
KNOWL HILL, NR. READING

Open: Monday-Saturday
9 a.m.-5.30 p.m.
H.P.W.D.A.BC.

READING   Tel. (0734) 586522
SARJENT'S TOOL STORES   ★
LTD.
44-52 OXFORD ROAD

Open: 8.30 a.m.-5.30 p.m.
Monday-Saturday
H.P.W.WM.D.A.BC.

BUCKINGHAMSHIRE

HIGH WYCOMBE   (0494) 22221
ISAAC LORD LTD
185 DESBOROUGH ROAD

Open: Mon-Fri 8.00 a.m.-5.00 p.m.
Saturday 8.00 a.m.-12.00 noon
H.P.W.D.A.

BUCKINGHAMSHIRE

MILTON KEYNES   Tel. 0908
A. POLLARD & SON   75221
LTD.   ★
51 QUEENSWAY, BLETCHLEY

Open: 8.30 a.m.-5.30 p.m.
Monday-Saturday
H.P.W.WM.D.A.BC.

CAMBRIDGESHIRE

CAMBRIDGE   Tel. 0223-353091
H. B. WOODWORKING
69 LENSFIELD ROAD

Open: 8.30 a.m.-5.30 p.m.
Monday-Friday
8.30 a.m.-1.00 p.m. Sat
P.W.WM.D.CS.BC.

CHESHIRE

NANTWICH   Tel. Crewe 67010
ALAN HOLTHAM   ★
THE OLD STORES TURNERY
WISTASON ROAD, WILLASTON

Open: Tues-Sat 9a.m.-5.30p.m.
Closed Monday
P.W.WM.D.T.C.CS.A.BC.

CLEVELAND

MIDDLESBROUGH   Tel. 0642-
WINTZ   460035/813650
INDUSTRIAL SUPPLIES   ★
2 BESSEMER COURT
GRANGETOWN

Open: Mon-Fri 8.30 a.m.-5 p.m.
H.P.W.D.A.

CORNWALL

FALMOUTH   Tel. 0326-312915
WOODSTOCK
(HARDWOODS) S.W.,
ASHFIELD, PONSHARDEN,

Open: Mon-Fri 8.30 a.m.-5.30 p.m.
Sat 9 a.m.-1.00 p.m.
T.

HELSTON
SOUTH WEST
POWER TOOLS

Helston (03265) 4961
Truro (0872) 71671
Launceston (0566) 3555
H.P.W.WM.D.CS.A.

NEWQUAY   Tel. 063 73 2516
CONWAY SUPPLIES   ★
(NEWQUAY)
70 FORE STREET

Open: Mon-Fri 9 a.m.-5.30 p.m.
Sat 9 a.m.-12.30 p.m.
H.P.W.WM.D.A.BC.

ST. AUSTELL   Tel. (0726) 65922
TOOLSERV   ★
TRURO ROAD

Open: 8 a.m.-5.30 p.m.
6 days
H.P.W.WM.D.CS.A.BC.

DERBYSHIRE

BUXTON   Tel. 0298-871636
CRAFT SUPPLIES   ★
THE MILL
MILLERSDALE

Open: Mon-Fri 9 a.m.-5 p.m.
Saturday 9 a.m.-1 p.m.
H.P.W.D.T.CS.A.BC.

DEVON

AXMINSTER   Tel. 0297 33656
POWER TOOL CENTRE   ★
STYLES & BROWN
CHARD STREET

Open: 9.00 a.m.-5.30 p.m.
Monday-Saturday
H.P.W.WM.D.CS.A.BC.

EXETER   Tel. 0392 73936
WRIDES TOOL CENTRE
147 FORE STREET

Open: 9.00 a.m.-5.30 p.m.
Wednesday 9.00 a.m.-1.00 p.m.
H.P.W.WM.A.

PLYMOUTH   Tel. 0752 330303
WESTWARD BUILDING SERVICES   ★
LTD., LISTER CLOSE, NEWNHAM
INDUSTRIAL ESTATE, PLYMPTON

Open: Mon-Fri 8 a.m.-5.30 p.m.
Sat 8.30 a.m.-12.30 p.m.
H.P.W.WM.D.A.BC.

PLYMOUTH   Tel. 0752-266179
JOHN WRIDE & CO (PLYMOUTH) LTD
146 CORNWALL STREET

Open: Monday to Saturday
9.00.a.m.-5.30.p.m.
Wed 9.00a.m.-1.00p.m.
H.P.W.WM.A.

DORSET

BOURNEMOUTH   Tel: 0202
MACHINE SALES & SERVICES   527780
(BOURNEMOUTH) LTD   527781
56 STROUDEN ROAD   ★

Open: Mon-Fri 8.15 a.m.-5 p.m.
H.P.W.WM.D.A.

WEYMOUTH   Tel: (0305) 787396
WEYMOUTH TOOL CENTRE   ★
30A ABBOTSBURY ROAD

Open: Monday to Saturday
8 a.m.-5.30 p.m.
H.P.W.WM.D.A.BC

CO. DURHAM

BARNARD CASTLE   Tel: (0833)
WOODMEN   38442/31609
27 NEWGATE

Open Monday-Saturday
9 a.m.-5.30 p.m.
P.W.WM.D.A.BC.

ESSEX

LEIGH ON SEA   Tel. (0702)
MARSHALL &   710404
PARSONS LTD   ★
1111 LONDON ROAD

Open: 8.30 am-5.30 pm Mon-Fri.
9.00 am-5.00 om Sat.
H.P.W.WM.D.CS.A.

GLOUCESTERSHIRE

TEWKESBURY   Tel. 0684
TEWKESBURY SAW CO.   293092
LIMITED
TRADING ESTATE, NEWTOWN

Open: Mon-Fri 8.00 a.m.-5.00 p.m.
Saturday 9.30 a.m.-12.00 p.m.
P.W.WM.D.CS.

HAMPSHIRE

ALDERSHOT   Tel. 0252 28088
BURCH & HILLS LTD
BLACKWATER WAY TRADING
ESTATE

Open: Mon-Fri 8.30 a.m.-5.30 p.m.
Saturday 8.30 a.m.-12.00 p.m.
H.P.W.WM.D.A.BC.

PORTSMOUTH   Tel. 0705
EURO PRECISION TOOLS   67332
LTD   ★
259/263 London Road, North End

Open: Mon-Fri 9 a.m.-5.30 p.m.
Sat 9.00 a.m.-5.00 p.m.
H.P.W.WM.D.A.BC.

SOUTHAMPTON   Tel. 0703
H.W.M.   776222
THE WOODWORKERS   ★
303 SHIRLEY ROAD, SHIRLEY

Open: Tues-Fri 9.30 a.m.- 6 p.m.
Sat 9.30 a.m.-4.00 p.m.
H.P.W.WM.D.CS.A.BC.T.

HEREFORDSHIRE

HEREFORD   Tel. 0432 3018
PEN TOOLS (HEREFORD) LTD
24 EDGAR STREET

Open Mon.-Fri. 8 a.m.-5.30 p.m.
Sat. 8 a.m.-1 p.m.
H.P.W.D.C.A.

HERTFORDSHIRE

WATFORD   Tel. 0923 48434
HOME CARE CENTRE   ★
20 MARKET STREET
WATFORD, HERTS

Open 9.00 a.m.-5.30 p.m.
Mon.-Sat.
H.P.W.A.WM.BC.D.

WATFORD   Tel. 0923 26052
J. SIMBLE & SONS LTD   ★
76 QUEENS ROAD

Open 8.30 a.m.-5.30 p.m.
Mon.-Sat. Closed Wednesday
H.P.W.WM.D.A.BC.

SHOP GUIDE SHOP GUIDE

HERTFORDSHIRE

WATFORD   Tel. (0923) 49911
TREND MACHINERY & CUTTING
TOOLS LTD
UNIT N, PENFOLD WORKS
IMPERIAL WAY
 Open: Mon-Fri 9 a.m.-5 p.m.
P.W.WM.D.CS.BC.

KENT

MATFIELD   Tel. Brenchley
LEISURECRAFT IN WOOD   (089272)
'ORMONDE', MAIDSTONE RD.   2465
TN12 7JG
 Open: Mon-Sun
 9 a.m.- 5.30 p.m.
W.WM.D.T.A.

LANCASHIRE

LANCASTER   Tel. 0524 2886
LILE TOOL SHOP
43/45 NORTH ROAD
 Open: Monday to Saturday
 9.00 a.m.-5.30 p.m.
 Wed 9.00 a.m.-12.30 p.m.
H.P.W.D.A.

LEICESTERSHIRE

COALVILLE   Tel. (0533) 415556
POOLE WOOD MACHINERY   (06077)
SERVICES LIMITED,   5777
4 SWALLOW DALE
THRINGSTONE
 Open: Mon-Fri 9 a.m.-5 p.m.
H.P.W.WM.D.A.BC.

LEICESTER   Tel. 0455 43254
ROY STARTIN LTD
134 WOOD STREET
EARL SHILTON
 Open: Mon-Fri 8 a.m.-5.30 p.m.
 Saturday 8.00 a.m.-1.30 p.m.
H.P.W.WM.D.T.A.

LINCOLNSHIRE

LINCOLN   Tel. 0522 36168/9
R & S TOOLS (LINCOLN)
LIMITED
BEEVER STREET LN6 7AD
 Open: Mon-Fri 8.30 a.m.-5 p.m.
 Sat 9.00 p.m.-12.00 p.m.
H.P.W.WM.D.CS.A.BC.

LINCOLN   Tel. 0522 30199/
WOODWISE LIMITED   39871 or
121 HIGH STREET   0522 68428
 & 06077 5777/5288
 (after hours) ★
 Open: Mon-Sat 9 a.m.-5.30 p.m.
P.W.WM.D.A.BC.

LONDON

ACTON   Tel. 01-992 4835
A MILLS (ACTON) LTD   ★
32/36 CHURCHFIELD ROAD
W3 6ED
 Open: Mon-Fri 9.00 a.m.-5.00 p.m.
 Closed Saturday
H.P.W.WM.

HANWELL   Tel. 01-567 2922
G. D. CLEGG & SONS
83 Uxbridge Road, W7 3ST
 Open: Monday to Friday
 9.00 a.m.-6.00 p.m.
 Saturday 9.00 a.m.-5.30 p.m.
H.P.W.WM.D.

LONDON

LONDON   Tel. 01-636 7475
BUCK & RYAN LIMITED   ★
101 TOTTENHAM COURT ROAD
W1P 0DY
 Open: Mon-Fri 8.30 a.m.-5.30 p.m.
 Saturday 8.30 a.m.-1.00 p.m.
H.P.W.WM.D.A.

LONDON   Tel. 01-739 7126
CECIL W. TYZACK   ★
79-81 KINGSLAND ROAD
SHOREDITCH
 Open: Mon-Fri 8.45 a.m.-5.15 p.m.
 Saturday 9 a.m.-12 noon
H.P.W.WM.D.A.BC.

NORBURY   Tel: 01-679 6193
HERON TOOLS & HARDWARE LTD
437 STREATHAM HIGH ROAD
S.W.16
 Open: Mon-Sat 8.30 a.m. - 6 p.m.
 Wednesday 8.30 a.m. - 1 p.m.
H.P.W.A.

WOOLWICH   Tel. 01-854 7767/8
A. D. SKILLMAN & SONS LTD
108-109 WOOLWICH HIGH ST
SE18 6DW
 Open: Mon-Sat 8.30 a.m.-to 5.30 p.m.
 Half Day Thursday
H.P.W.CS.A.

MERSEYSIDE

LIVERPOOL   Tel. 051-263 1359
TAYLOR BROS (LIVERPOOL) LTD
5/9 PRESCOTT STREET
 Open: Monday to Friday
 8.30 a.m.-5.30 p.m.
H.P.W.WM.D.A.BC.

MIDDLESEX

NORTH HARROW   Tel. 01-863 2492
WILLIAMS TECHNICAL SERVICES   ★
36 STATION ROAD
 Open: Mon-Fri 8 a.m.-5.30 p.m.
 Wed 8 a.m.-1 p.m.,
 Sat 9 a.m.-5.30 p.m.
H.P.W.WM.D.A.

NORFOLK

KINGS LYNN   Tel. (0553) 2443
WALKER & ANDERSON (Kings Lynn) LTD
WINDSOR ROAD, KINGS LYNN
 Open: Monday to Saturday
 7.45 a.m.-5.30 p.m.
 Wednesday 1 p.m. Saturday 5.00 p.m.
H.P.W.WM.D.CS.A.

NORWICH   Tel. 0603 898695
NORFOLK SAW SERVICES
DOG LAND, HORSFORD
 Open: Monday to Friday
 8.00 a.m.-5.00 p.m.
 Saturday 8.00 a.m.-12.00 p.m.
H.P.W.WM.D.CS.A.

NORWICH   Tel. 0603 400933
WESTGATES WOODWORKING   Tx.
MACHINERY, JUPITER ROAD   975412
OFF MILE CROSS LANE
 Open: 9 a.m.-5 p.m. weekdays
 9 a.m.-12 a.m. Sat.
P.W.WM.D.

NORTHAMPTONSHIRE

RUSHDEN   Tel. 093-34 56424
PETER CRISP LIMITED   ★
7 HIGH STREET
 Open: Monday to Saturday
 8.30 a.m.-5.30 p.m.
 Thursday 8.30 a.m.-1.00 p.m.
H.P.W.D.BC.

NORTHUMBERLAND

BLYTH   Tel. (06706) 69279
ALLAN McNAIR WOODCRAFT   ★
69-71 PLESSEY ROAD
 Open: Monday to Saturday
 9 a.m.-5 p.m.
H.W.WM.D.T.CS.A.BC.

NOTTINGHAMSHIRE

NOTTINGHAM   Tel. (0602) 225979
POOLEWOOD   (06077) 5777
EQUIPMENT LTD
5a HOLLY LANE, CHILLWELL
 Open: Mon-Fri 9 a.m.-5.30 p.m.
 Sat. 9 a.m. to 12.30 p.m.
P.W.WM.D.CS.A.BC.

NOTTINGHAM   Tel. 0602 811889
THE WOODCUTTER
5 TUDOR SQUARE
WEST BRIDGFORD
 Open: Tues-Sat 9 a.m.-5.30 p.m.
 Fri 9 a.m.-7.30 p.m. Closed Mon.
H.P.W.WM.D.T.CS.A.

OXFORDSHIRE

BICESTER   Tel. (08692) 4156/
WOODMEN   3218/3219
104 CHURCHILL ROAD
 Open: Monday-Saturday
 9 a.m.-5.30 p.m.
P.W.WM.D.A.BC.

OXFORD   Tel. (0865) 45118/9
SARJENT'S TOOL   ★
STORES LTD
150 COWLEY ROAD
 Open: Monday to Saturday
 8.30 a.m.-5.30 p.m.
H.P.W.WM.D.A.BC.

STAFFORDSHIRE

TAMWORTH   Tel. 0827-56188
MATTHEWS BROTHERS LTD
KETTLEBROOK ROAD
 Open: Mon.-Sat. 8.30am-6.00pm
 Demonstrations Sunday mornings
 by appointment only
H.P.W.WM.D.T.CS.A.BC.

SUFFOLK

BURY ST. EDMUNDS   Tel.
TOOLS & THINGS   0284 62022
21 CHURCHGATE   ★
 Open: Monday to Saturday
 9.00 a.m.-5.30 p.m.
H.P.W.WM.D.A.BC.

IPSWICH   Tel. 0473 86216
FOX WOODWORKING   ★
'STEBBINGS' BACK LANE
WASHBROOK
 Open: Tues. Fri. 9.00am-5.30pm
 Sat. 9.00am-5pm
H.P.W.WM.D.A.B.C.

SURREY

CARSHALTON BEECHES   Tel.
SURREY WOOD   01-642 6636
MACHINE SALES LTD   ★
56A BANSTEAD ROAD
 Open: Tues-Fri 9.30 am-6.00 pm
 Saturday 9.30 am-2.00 pm
P.W.WM.D.BC.CS.

CROYDON   Tel. 01-688 5513
L. H. TURTLE LTD   ★
6-12 PARK STREET
 Open: Monday to Saturday
 8.30 a.m.-5.30 p.m.
H.P.W.WM.D.A.

GUILDFORD   Tel. 0483 61125
MESSINGERS FOR TOOLS
14-18 CHERTSEY STREET
 Open: Tuesday to Saturday
 8.30 a.m.-5.30 p.m.
 Closed all day Monday
H.P.W.D.BC.

SUSSEX

BOGNOR REGIS Tel: (0243) 863100
A. OLBY & SON (BOGNOR REGIS LTD)
"TOOLSHOP", BUILDER'S MERCHANT
HAWTHORN ROAD
 Open: Mon-Thurs 8 a.m.-5.15 p.m.
 Fri 8 a.m.-8 p.m. Sat 8 a.m.-12.45 p.m.
H.P.W.WM.D.T.C.A.BC.

WORTHING   Tel. 0903 38739
W. HOSKING (TOOLS &
MACHINERY)
96a MONTAGUE STREET
 Open: Mon-Sat 8.30am-5.30pm
 Wednesday 8.30am-1.00pm
H.P.W.WM.D.CS.A.BC.

WEST MIDLANDS

WEST BROMWICH   Tel: 021-
CONWAY SAW &   533 5461/2
SUPPLY LTD   ★
SWAN LANE
 Open: 8 a.m.-6 p.m. Mon-Fri
 9 a.m.-1 p.m. Saturday
P.W.WM.D.CS.BC.

WILTSHIRE

SWINDON   Tel. (0793) 31361
SARJENT'S TOOL STORES LTD ★
64 FLEET STREET
 Open: Monday to Saturday
 8.30 a.m.-5.30 p.m.
H.P.W.WM.D.A.BC

YORKSHIRE

HALIFAX   Tel. 0422 884075/
TIMBERLITE LTD   884788/33575
VICTORIA BUILDINGS   ★
LUDDENDEN FOOT
 Open: Monday to Friday
 Saturday 9.00 a.m.-5.00 p.m.
H.P.W.WM.D.CS.A.BC.

HARROGATE   Tel. 0423 66245/
MULTI-TOOLS   55328 ★
158 KINGS ROAD
 Open: Monday to Saturday
 8.30 a.m.-6.00 p.m.
H.P.W.WM.D.A.BC.

YORKSHIRE	YORKSHIRE	N. IRELAND	WALES

YORKSHIRE

HUDDERSFIELD   Tel. (0484)
NEVILLE M. OLDHAM   641219/(0484)
UNIT 1 DAYLE ST. WORKS   42777
DAYLE STREET, LONGWOOD   ★
Open: Mon-Fri 9.00am- 5.30pm
Saturday 9.30am-12.00pm
P.W.WM.D.A.BC.

LEEDS   Tel. 0532 790507
GEORGE SPENCE & SONS LTD   ★
WELLINGTON ROAD
Open: Monday to Friday
8.30 a.m.-5.30 p.m.
Saturday 9.00 a.m.-5.00 p.m.
H.P.W.WM.D.T.A.

SHEFFIELD   Tel. 0742-441012
GREGORY & TAYLOR LTD
WORKSOP ROAD
Open: 8.30 a.m.-5.30 p.m.
Monday-Friday
8.30 a.m.-12.30 p.m. Sat.
H.P.W.WM.D.

SHEFFIELD   Tel. 0742-24659
GRAHAM OXLEY'S SHOWROOM
BRIDGE STREET   ★
Open: Monday to Friday
9.00 a.m.-5.30 p.m.
Saturday 8.30 a.m.-12.30 p.m.
H.W.D.A.BC.

YORKSHIRE

SOWERBY BRIDGE   Tel. (0422)
CALDER   31861
WOODWORKING   Telex: 517400
MACHINERY LTD.
STATION ROAD
Open: Mon - Fri 9 a.m.-5 p.m.
P.W.WM.D.CS.A.

SCOTLAND

EDINBURGH   Tel. 031-337
SCOTSPAN   7788/665 3121
195 BALGREEN ROAD
Open: Monday to Friday
9.00 a.m.-3.00 p.m.
P.W.WM.D.A.

GLASGOW   Tel. 041 429 4374/4444
THE SAW CENTRE   Telex: 777886
596-602 EGLINGTON STREET
G5 9RR
Open: Mon.-Fri. 8 a.m.-5.30 p.m.
Saturday 9 a.m.-1 p.m.
H.P.W.WM.D.CS.A.

N. IRELAND

Co. ANTRIM   Tel. 0266 6384
GEORGE GARDINER
49 BALLYMONEY STREET
BALLYMENA
Also: Open: Mon-Fri 8.30am-5.30pm
Wednesday 8.30am-1.00pm
H.P.W.D.A.BC.

N. IRELAND

Co. DOWN   Tel. (0247) 819800 (day)
NEWTOWNARDS   812506 (night)
NORLYN MACHINERY, UNIT 10
Malcolmson Ind. Est., 80 Bangor Road
Open: Mon-Fri 9.30am-5.30pm
or any other time by request
H.P.W.WM.D.A.BC.

S. IRELAND

COUNTY KILKENNY   Tel.
WOODMEN   (0409) 5460
CASHEL HOUSE   ★
KELLS ROAD, KILKENNY
Open: Monday to Saturday

WALES

BRITON FERRY   Tel. (0639)
WOODMEN   820803/4
49 NEATH ROAD   ★
Open: Monday to Saturday
9.00 a.m.-5.30 p.m.
P.W.WM.D.A.BC.

CARDIFF   Tel. (0222) 373007
JOHN HALL TOOLS LIMITED
22 CHURCHILL WAY   ★
Open: Monday to Saturday
9.00 a.m.-5.30 p.m.
H.P.W.WM.D.A.BC.

WALES

CARDIFF   Tel. (0222) 30831
F. W. MORGAN   & 25562
(CANTON) LTD., 129-133
COWBRIDGE RD EAST,
CANTON, CARDIFF
Mon-Sat 8-5 Sun. 9.30-12.30
H.P.T.CS.A.BC.

CARDIFF   Tel. (0222) 36519/
WOODMEN   373793/35221
43 CRWYS ROAD   ★
Open: Monday to Saturday
9.00 a.m.-5.30 p.m.

CARMARTHEN   Tel. 0267 7219
DO-IT-YOURSELF SUPPLY
BLUE STREET, DYFED
Open: Monday to Saturday
9.00 a.m.-5.30 p.m.
Thursday 9.00 a.m.-1.00 p.m.
H.P.W.WM.D.T.CS.A.BC.

SWANSEA   Tel. (0792) 55680
SWANSEA TIMBER &   ★
PLYWOOD CO LTD
57-59 OXFORD STREET
Open: Mon. to Fri. 9 am-5.30 pm
Sat. 9 am-1 pm
H.P.W.D.T.CS.A.BC.

Classified Advertisements

FOR SALE

EMCOSTAR SUPER Universal Woodworking Machine comprising bench saw and band saw. 2½ years old. Excellent condition. £370. Write to B. Luck, St. Michaels College, Llandaff, Cardiff.   M

WOODWORKERS. 15 copies 1903-4 £40. Bland, 23 Kenley Avenue, Bradford BD6 3JB. Telephone (0274) 573150.   M

MYFORD MLS 42" Bed, Cabinet and Stand. Planer/thicknesser. Saw Table, Bandsaw. Mortiser. As new used privately. Sell complete or separate. Offers invited. Write to: Box No. 502 (Tenbury Wells), c/o Woodworker Magazine, 35 Bridge Street, Hemel Hempstead, Herts.   M

DEWALT RADIAL arm saw, model 1420. 5hp single-phase motor. Little used, £500. Peter Marshall, Porthwidden, St Ives, Cornwall. Tel: Penzance 794497.   M

LARGE WORKSHOP, peaceful old Devon cottage, 4/6 berth caravan, large greenhouse, ⅓ acre £30,000. Details Bratton Clovelly. (Code 083787) 224.   M-N

MULTICUT 2 SAW as new; cost over £200, offers. Fretsaw motorised, £50 o.n.o. 01-800 4019.   M

TIMBER SEASONERS, moisture meters, polymeters. Everything you require for seasoning your own timber. For free advice and lowest prices, consult the experts, 15 years in the trade. Some reconditioned seasoners available. Wyco Moisture control. Tel: Weybridge 40864.   K-P

LATHE ATTACHMENT for Consort, £85 End turning rest, £25 as new. Tel: Newcastle-upon-Tyne 860634.   M

WOODWORKER MAGAZINES FOR SALE: June 1928 - February 1942 complete. January 1946 - December 1955 missing. November and December 1949, October 1950, September 1954. Offers to: Jarvis, 19 Ladbrooke Drive, Potters Bar, Herts.   M

SMALL TIMBER MILLING & DRYING CONCERN. Comprising Sawmill, Kiln with 12' cabinet, and timber stocks. Profitable sideline to be disposed of owing to other commitments. £2,000 plus VAT. Telephone 021-706 2497. Evenings.   M

HARRISON GRADUATE LATHE, tools, chucks, £250.00 worth of timber. Good condition — little used and many extras. £550.00. Tel: 05827-4574 (Hertfordshire) after 7pm.   M

DEWALT BAND SAW as new, model BS/1310 £200. Wolf electric portable saw 9¼" with two saw blades as new £100. Electric motor ½H.P. £15. Black and Decker drill ½" as new £15. Cash only. Telephone Portsmouth 839050. M

KITY 7136 10" surface and thicknesser planer, with dust extractor, as new £520 o.n.o. Tel: 021-707 8090.   M-N

BRASS FRAMED and ebony ultimatum type brace by Alfred Ridge, Ecclesfield. Enquiries: King, 0253 68888.   M

WOOD LATHE: Myford ML8. Little used. Good set Sorby tools. Face plates. Woodscrew chuck. £250. Langtree (N. Devon) 430.   M

SURPLUS KITY machinery at bargain prices. Trymwood, Bristol (0272) 629092.   M

The Complete Works
IN ONE COMPREHENSIVE CATALOGUE

NEW UPDATED 32 PAGE COLOUR CATALOGUE AND FULL DESCRIPTIVE PRICE AND SPECIFICATION LIST NOW AVAILABLE.

Join the fastest-growing hobby of clock building. Build your own clock — Grandfather or Mother, Traditional or Modern, Bracket or Battery, Carriage or Cuckoo.

We can offer you from stock the most comprehensive range of Europe's finest movements and dials, as well as full kits with easy-to-follow simple instructions. Trust in the experts and let this established Family business help you start a fascinating and satisfying hobby. Build a clock, or even a musical box. Restore an antique clock.

Send today for the NEW updated, fully comprehensive 32 page colour catalogue, and descriptive price list.

To help cover costs, please send 50p which will be refunded with your first order.

Charles Greville & Co. Ltd.
Dept (W4) Unit 5, Rear Airport House, Purley Way, Croydon, Surrey. Tel: 01-686 2972. Ample car park. Personal callers most welcome. Open: Mon—Fri: 9.30—5.30. Sat: 9.00—12.30.

FOR ALL SUPPLIES
FOR THE

Craft of Enamelling
ON METAL

Including
LEAD-FREE ENAMELS

PLEASE SEND 2 × 10p STAMPS FOR FREE CATALOGUE, PRICE LIST AND WORKING INSTRUCTIONS

W. G. BALL LTD.
ENAMEL MANUFACTURERS

Dept. W. LONGTON
STOKE-ON-TRENT
ST3 1JW

SEDGWICK 12" × 8" Planer/thicknesser, single phase. P. Smith, Furniture Maker, The Old Chapel, Kirkburn, Driffield, E. Yorks. Telephone: 0377 89301.   M

CORONET MAJOR WOOD LATHE — blue with saw planer and extension table, hardly used. £500. Uphill Farm, Uphill, Weston-super-Mare. Telephone 20031.   M

RECORD MULTI-PLANE 405 boxed, immaculate £65. Set of additional cutters £30. Oakwood Hill (0306 79) 545.   M-N

MYFORD ML8A LATHE plus cabinet stand £395. 3-jaw & 4-jaw chucks for the above, £85 the two. All immaculate and almost unused. Oakwood Hill (0306 79) 545.   M-N

MAKE A WOODTURNING LATHE easily, construction details and parts list, send SAE to: ORTAN LATHES, P.O. Box 46, Norwich NR7 8PB.   M-R

TREADLE LATHE. Excellent condition, 9" throw. Wood turning rests plus carriage and apron for metal turning. Offers. Redditch 23768.   M

PROFESSIONAL QUALITY HAND TOOLS and power tool accessories at discount prices, by leading manufacturers:- Barrus, Record, Stanley, Leytool, Footprint, Ridgeway, Guys, Marples, Tyzack, Rabone Chesterman, Skarsten, Eclipse, Paramo, Raaco, Sandvik, Spear and Jackson, Bahco etc. Wood and metal working. Send 22p stamp for lists (refundable with first order). Trade enquiries welcome. Dalewood Tools, 31 Dalewood Avenue, Sheffield S8 0EG. Phone Sheffield (0742) 350665.   L-M

WASHITA & ARKANSAS whetstones now readily available from importer. Large selection, SAE for list. C. Rufino, Manor House, South Clifton, Newark, Notts.   T/C

CIRCULAR AND BAND saw blades for all applications from: A. A. SMITH of Lancing Ltd., 63 Brighton Road, Shoreham, Sussex. Tel: 07917 61707 (24 hrs).   K-O

MACHINERY. A comprehensive range of new/used machinery. Check our prices, e.g. HMO 10"×5½" planer/thicknesser £374. HF30 spindle moulder £365. 12" tilt arbour sawbench 2hp motor £140. Shopsmith MK5 home workshop £897. Morso mitring machine £437, (including V.A.T.). Kity K-5. See these machines and Ryobi industrial small tools demonstrated at Woodman Woodworking Machinery Co. (Sign of the Axe), Little Malgraves Hall, Lower Dunton Road, Bulphan, Nr. Upminster, Essex. Tel: (0268) 415511 or (0702) 331729.   I-U

EBAC TIMBER SEASONERS, Protimeter moisture meters, always good prices and advice from the man who pioneered small scale seasoning. John Arrowsmith, Roadham Cottage, Barton, Richmond, North Yorks. Telephone: (0325) 77362.   T/C

PLANERS 6", 9" planers/thicknessers, 12" × 7", 9" × 6", 12" × 7", sawbenches, 10", 12", combination woodworkers. British made. Particulars, send stamp. Dodd Machine Tools Ltd., South Woodham, Chelmsford. Tel: 320 691.   C-N

Braywood Estates
Comprehensive range of **DeWALT** Accessories plus a super service for spare parts & on site servicing.

BRAYWOOD ESTATES LTD. FREEPOST, SLOUGH SL2 4BL
TELEPHONE : SLOUGH 0753 22567/ 70792

The **'SCRU-DRILL' Adjustable Woodscrew Bit** Specialist tool for Woodworker and DIY enthusiast.

Adjust to size of screw and in one single operation —
● Drill pilot hole for screw thread
● Drill pilot hole for screw body
● Countersink — counterbore
● Drill to accurate preset depth
Screw home with ease in hard or softwoods — no excess strain on screw, timber or yourself — set of four 'SCRU-DRILLS' replaces dozens of other fixed size pilot drills and countersinks — accommodates numbers 5 to 14 woodscrews.

Set of Four £13.80 inc. VAT and carriage

Send cheque or P.O. to:
KELTEK PRODUCTS
PO Box 5, Wadebridge PL27 7YZ

or SAE for further information
— Trade enquiries —

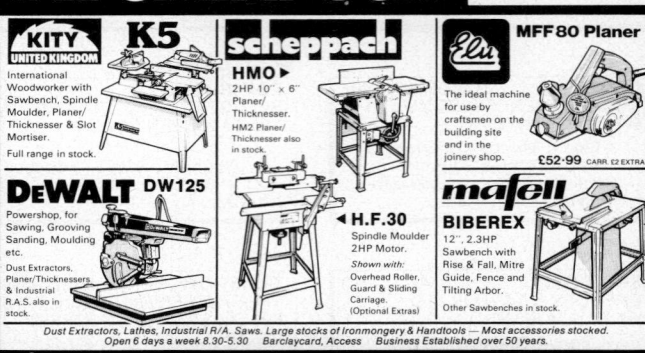

A·Pollard+Son LTD.

Come and browse through our huge stocks of machinery and tools. If you live too far away, privately owned Mini Clipper service will deliver within days to your door.

KITY UNITED KINGDOM — **K5** International Woodworker with Sawbench, Spindle Moulder, Planer/Thicknesser & Slot Mortiser. Full range in stock.

scheppach — HMO ▶ 2HP 10" × 6" Planer/Thicknesser. HM2 Planer/Thicknesser also in stock.

Elu **MFF 80 Planer** The ideal machine for use by craftsmen on the building site and in the joinery shop. £52·99 CARR. £2 EXTRA

DeWALT DW125 Powershop, for Sawing, Grooving Sanding, Moulding etc. Dust Extractors, Planer/Thicknessers & Industrial R.A.S. also in stock.

◀ **H.F.30** Spindle Moulder 2HP Motor. *Shown with:* Overhead Roller, Guard & Sliding Carriage. (Optional Extras)

mafell **BIBEREX** 12", 2.3HP Sawbench with Rise & Fall, Mitre Guide, Fence and Tilting Arbor. Other Sawbenches in stock.

Dust Extractors, Lathes, Industrial R/A. Saws. Large stocks of Ironmongery & Handtools — Most accessories stocked. Open 6 days a week 8.30-5.30   Barclaycard, Access   Business Established over 50 years.

A. POLLARD & SON LTD. 51 Queensway, Bletchley, Milton Keynes ☎ (0908) 75221

The **L/1 T.C.T. Router cutter** with ball bearing guide. Will trim laminates at 90° to a professional finish. Many other uses. ¼" shank. Fits any router.
Only £9.98
Send cheque or P.O. to:-
WOODCUTTER SERVICES,
88 Thornhill Road, Heaton, Mersey,
Stockport SK4 3DH, Cheshire.
Telephone: 061-432 4294

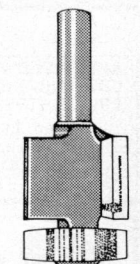

WOOD TURNING LATHES

550mm between centres. 65mm centre height. Lever action tailstock. No.2 Morse tapers. Rear turning attachment takes 220mm dia. Various bed lengths available.
Prices from £80 + VAT
Send SAE for details

GREENFIELDS ENGINEERING

Building 3A, Site 1, Newport Road, High Ercall, Telford, TF6 6JA. Telephone High Ercall (0952) 770672

TOP QUALITY SHEFFIELD WOODTURNING TOOLS

A complete range of top quality Chisels and Gouges. Full size and long and strong.
EXAMPLES: FULL SIZE

1" gouge £4.25	½" skew £3.25
½" gouge £3.95	½" diamond £3.25
1" skew £3.95	½" round £3.25

S.A.E. for full price list

TOOLSHOP, 29 Walcot Street, Bath. Avon. Tel: Bath (0225) 61838

Chisel Sharpening-
How EdgeRider Makes it Easier:

Easy, natural action — just slip chisel (1" max) into guide, steady with fingertips, then back and forwards against spring-mounted stone above edge.

Sharpening angle (range 23°-37°) quickly set by scale on stone holder; locked by wingnut. You can sharpen to chosen angle again and again, so —

Ideal for keeping a working edge 'touched-up' — just a quick few strokes whenever the edge starts to get dull for peak performance right through the job.

'an excellent device' — DL, Middlesex.

Selected for Design Centre. Works bench or vice mounted or hand-held. Sharpener with long-life stone plus spare, fixing screws and detailed instructions; £6.45 post free, UK or Overseas (extra stones 70p each) from manufacturers, W G & O I Parr, Dept WW8, 16 Greenway, Harrogate, North Yorkshire HG2 9LR

POWER TOOL HOTLINE!
(0533) 761676.

Phone Peter Exton at Wadkin for all the powerful facts on portable power tools. **Wadkin**

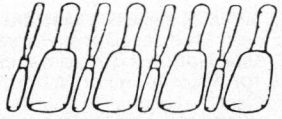
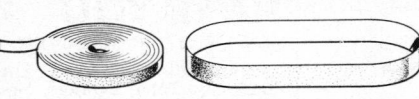
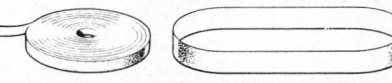

ROBBINS LIMITED — the complete timber merchants. Hardwoods, including exotic Softwoods, Plywoods, Mouldings, Veneers, Lines, Bandings, Nails, Screws, Fittings, Clear Finishes, Adhesives, Tools, Books. Complete list (35p stamp) Merrywood Mills, Bedminster, Bristol. Phone 633022.　　　　T/C

QUARTZ CLOCK MOVEMENTS and barometer inserts. Competitive prices. Efficient mail order service. SAE for illustrated brochure. Tudorcraft, 57 Honeyborne Road, Sutton Coldfield, West Midlands B75 6BN. Tel: 021-378 2685.　　　　L-M

UPHOLSTERY MATERIALS, cabinet brassware, wheels and DIY supplies by post. SAE for catalogue to Dept Z, J. W. & A. J. Turner, Handymans Store, High St., Cranleigh, Surrey GU6 8AE.　　　　G-M

FIRST QUALITY Black Forest longcase movements, all dials, Battery Movements, Quartz movements, all accessories, Clock Kits in Solid Oak or Mahogany from £63.80. Send large stamped addressed envelope: TIMECRAFT, 10 Edinburgh Road, Formby, Liverpool.　　　　T/C

D.I.Y. PICTURE FRAMING. Suppliers of mitred mouldings. 79 patterns to choose from. Also ready-mades, ovals, tools, mounts, accessories, illustrated catalogue 45p. Westward, 16 Minton Close, St. Austell, Cornwall.　　　　I-T

CLOCKMAKING MATERIALS

German quartz clock movements by Kienzle and Junghans, prices from only £2.95 inclusive! Also excellent range of quartz pendulum and insertion movements, hands, dials and numerals.

S.A.E. for free illustrated brochure.

BATH CLOCK COMPANY (Dept W),
13 Welton Road, Radstock, Bath,
Avon BA3 3UA.

MAKE HANDSOME CLOCKS
for Pleasure or Profit . . . with

. . . our superb electronic and quartz battery movements from the world famous **KIENZLE** Works. Other high quality movements and accessories available, plus a special dials offer to help everyone enjoy clockmaking at reasonable cost. SAE details now: **SMS/Kingswoode (W1), 24 Holwood Road, Bromley, Kent, BR1 3EB**

HAVE YOU

COMPARED OUR PRICES FOR:-

Turning tools, Ceramic Tiles, Eggtimers, Table Lighters, Hourglasses, Barometers, Cheese Blades, Peppermills, Polishes, Waxes, etc. PRICE LIST S.A.E.

COUNTRY CRAFT STUDIO
LAWSHALL,
BURY ST. EDMUNDS,
SUFFOLK.

Tel: (STD 0284) 828661

MANCHESTER　　061-236 2477

FRED ALDOUS LTD
37 LEVER STREET

Supply materials for Basketry, Stool Seating, Lampshade making, Marquetry, Modelling, Pewter, Copper, Enamelling, Leather Work.

CHAIR CANE SUPPLIES

Chair cane, Seagrass, Pre-woven cane etc. Tools, Books & advice. SAE for list
BERRY'S CRAFT SUPPLIES
10 Hill Rd., Theydon Bois, Epping, Essex. CM16 7LX. Tel: 037 881 3532 (anytime)

CRAFTSMAN'S FRENCH POLISHING KIT

No skill is required whatsoever, it can be used to patch up without the need for stripping all the surface. The kit comes complete with full instructions.

200 mls £3.10
1 Litre £8.75
Price inc. VAT p/p

Send to **MAIL ORDER DEPARTMENT**
J. L. PRODUCTS, 6 NEWINGTON DRIVE, BURY, LANCS BL8 2NE.
Telephone: 061 764 6769

MARQUETRY VENEERS
Mixture Packs — our speciality
Send S.A.E. for details of our basic Mixture Packs. Prompt attention; noted for value. "Marquetry Magic," a Beginner's Guide, 50p plus stamp.
TERRY MILLS (W),
23 Maplestead Avenue, Wilford, Nottingham NG11 7AS

FRENCH POLISHES WAXES

and full range of sundries French polishes, Varnish and knotting, Wax polish, Cellulose lacquer, Pigments, Dyes & Stains, Wood fillers & stoppers, Wire wool

Send for Catalogue:
JOHN MYLAND LTD.
80 Norwood High St., London
SE27 9NW Tel: 01 670 9161

Rates
20p per word, minimum £3.00
Box nos. £1.25 extra.
Semi display s.c.c. £4.00
(min £10.00)

SOUVENIR MAKERS' TRANSFERS
Floral, Mottoes, Dogs, Horses, Crests, National Emblems, etc., for decorations on Wood, Plastics, Leather, Fabric, etc.
PLASTIC-STICKER INQUIRIES
Trade Catalogue and samples 50p
A. P. AXON & HARRISON LTD.
JERSEY, Channel Islands

ART VENEERS
Suppliers to the Marquetarian Cabinetmaker and Home Woodcraftsman

• Large range of rare and exotic veneers for Marquetry and Cabinet Making.
• Complete range of marquetry Art Sets — beginner to expert – including the NEW '300 Range' of modern Action Pictures for quicker results.
• Expanding range of Craft Kits.
• 4 New Clock Kits incl. marquetry wall clocks, pine kitchen clock and fully machined mahogany mantlepiece clock.
• All necessary back-up materials, polishes, adhesives, motifs and banding, tools, longcase movements, books, etc.

WORLD OF WOOD　The Art Veneers Co. Ltd., Industrial Estate, Mildenhall, Suffolk 1P28 7AY

CRAFTEX RUBBERISED ABRASIVES

Impregnate high grade neoprene rubber with Silicon Carbide grit and you have a material which will give you a super sharp cutting edge and produce a highly polished bevel on cutting tools. CRAFTEX available in Wheels, Blocks, Sticks and Slips – invaluable to every Woodcraftsman.

To learn more of this remarkable material, send a stamp for our illustrated catalogue.

WOODCRAFT SUPPLY (U.K.) LTD.
2 Drew Street, Brixham, Devon TO5 9JU.
Sole distributors for CRAFTEX in the U.K.

HARNESS KITS

for heavy and light horses should suit all model wagon and carriage builders in ⅛, ¹⁄₁₀th and ¹⁄₁₂th scales. Send 3 × 1st class stamps for price lists and illustrated brochure of horses to:

LENHAM POTTERY
215 Wroxham Road, Norwich,
Norfolk NR7 8AQ

ONE DAY WOODTURNING COURSE: Trymwood Services, 2a Downs Park East, (Off North View), Westbury Park, Bristol. Phone Bristol 629092.　　　　T/C

COURSES IN WOOD MACHINING AND WOODTURNING. Bookable by the hour—the most convenient and flexible way! all for £6.00 an hour (inc. VAT). H.W.M., The Woodworkers, 303 Shirley Rd., Shirley, Southampton. Tel: (0703) 776222.　　　　T/C

TWO-DAY Woodturning Course for beginners in mid-Norfolk village. Two students only. Accomodation available. SAE for details please. Doug Keeling, Church Lane, Beetley, Norfolk NR20 4AB.　　　　T/C

POWERED WOODCARVING — 2 or 3 day courses in the use of Dupli-Carver woodcarving machines. Expert personal tuition covering all aspects of this absorbing craft. For full details write the comprehensive Woodcraft Projects Ltd., Unit 10, Kernick Road Industrial Estate, Penryn, Cornwall. 0326 73846.　　　　L-W

VIOLIN MAKING AND RESTORING. Full time courses in professional workshop. For details write or telephone Paul Bickle, 42 Langton Road, Bishops Waltham, Hants. SO3 1GF (04893) 5292.　　　　K-M

RESIDENTIAL/NON-RESIDENTIAL Woodcarving courses, July, September. Somerset Studio. S.A.E. Gertner, Deans Cottage, Bagley, Wedmore. Telephone: (0934) 712679.　　M

WOODTURNING COURSES

Maximum 2 students
Write or telephone for details:
Allan McNair Woodcraft,
69/71 Plessey Road,
Blyth, Northumberland.
Tel: Blyth (067 06) 69279

WOODTURNING COURSES

2 or 3 Day
Courses in the creative art of
WOODTURNING. Professional tuition in the heart of the **GARDEN OF ENGLAND.** lathes & accessories by **CORONET.**

SAE please for brochure:
RHYS M. LEWIS,
50 Gladstone Rd.,
Sth. Willesborough,
Ashford, Kent TN24 0BY.
Ashford (0233) 28556

Australian Readers WOODTURNING

40 Years of woodturning experience available to you in a 2 day course. Basic or advanced. Personal tuition to your needs in a fully equipped workshop. Write for details:
PHILIP ELFORD 407 Peel St. N., Ballarat, Vic. 3350.

GORDON STOKES
Author of Modern Woodturning Beginner's Guide to Woodturning Woodturning for Pleasure, etc. etc Will be pleased to send you full details of his intensive two day Woodturning and Woodcarving courses. Personal instruction based on thirty years experience. Don't struggle along the hard way. Foolscap S.A.E. to: 202 The Hollow, Bath, Avon BA2 1NG Tel: Bath 22617

Woodturning Courses

four days with
MIKE LAW
(Thos Harrison & Sons)

Relax into a four-day long woodturning course in the informal atmosphere of our farmhouse home. We offer comfortable accommodation, good food, and professional tuition in the heart of this beautiful countryside.

Please write or telephone for details: Mike Law, The Longhouse, Maxworthy Cross, North Petherwin, Launceston, North Cornwall. Tel: STD (056685) 322.

LEARN THE ART AND CRAFT OF RESTORING ANTIQUES AND DESIGNING AND MAKING YOUR OWN FURNITURE

Situated in a charming Norfolk village we offer professional tuition in courses of antique restoration, wood turning, machining, woodworking and finishing. Come to The Old Mill at Gayton for good food and comfortable accommodation in very pleasant surroundings.

WINDMILL ENTERPRISES

For full details send SAE to MR R Hirons, The Old Mill, Gayton, Norfolk.

Prices quoted are those prevailing at press date and are subject to alteration due to economic conditions.

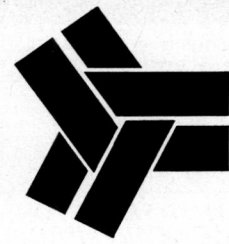

B.A. Hons. ART AND DESIGN COURSES
B.Sc. TIMBER TECHNOLOGY COURSE
FURNITURE PRODUCTION DIPLOMA COURSE

We offer three year full-time courses for all these subjects. Send for a copy of our prospectus from The Head of School, School of Art and Design, Furniture and Timber, Buckinghamshire College of Higher Education, Queen Alexandra Road, High Wycombe, Bucks HP11 2JZ. Tel: 0494 22141.

Rawdon Woodturners

Comprehensive courses geared to suit individual requirements offered in
Woodmachining
Woodturning
Take advantage of my 20 years of industrial and educational experience and realize the full potential of your machinery. Write or phone for details

Rawdon Woodturners
Peter Clark Woodcraft Ltd.,
Old Friends School, Low Green
Rawdon, Nr Leeds, West Yorkshire
Tel: Leeds (0532) 676068 (evenings preferred)

WOODTURNING COURSES

2 Day courses, mid-week or weekend. Expert personal tuition in modern well equipped workshop. Comfortable accommodation available in pleasant surroundings. SAE for details to
Cliff Willetts, Gables, Frisby On The Wreake, Melton Mowbray, Leics.

Wood machining Course

A craftsman of forty years experience offers a unique two-day course to learn the basics of machine woodworking including spindle moulding and routing in his fully equipped modern workshop.
S.A.E. for details please to:
ROY SUTTON
14 St. Georges Avenue,
Herne Bay, Kent CT6 8JU
Telephone: Herne Bay 3297 or Whitstable 272136 (evenings).

COURSES IN BASIC ANTIQUE RESTORATION

Weekend Courses carried out monthly in our workshops on the basic skills of restoring furniture. Course includes laying and repairing veneers, staining distressing and french polishing.
Full details from:
EDWIN TURNER, Home Farm, Gislingham, Eye, Suffolk. Tel: Mellis 280.

Woodworking Machines of Switzerland LIMITED

SCHOOL OF WOODWORKING

NEW ONE-DAY INTRODUCTORY COURSES

The Official INCA School of Woodworking is pleased to announce vacancies for Introductory One-Day Courses using the famous 'COMPACT UNIVERSAL SAW'.
These intensive courses are limited to 2 or 3 students each using a 'COMPACT' under the tuition of experienced instructors.
The cost of a one-day introductory course including lunch, refreshments and VAT is **£35**.
For full details of this and other woodworking courses using the finest INCA equipment and held in our purpose-built workshops, write now to:
**Woodworking Machines of Switzerland Ltd.,
Inca House, Peverel Drive, Granby, Milton Keynes MK1 1NL.
Telephone: Milton Keynes (0908) 641492.**

MUSICAL INSTRUMENTS

MAKE YOUR OWN CLAVICHORD full size plans and instruction manual. SAE for details to: Early Keyboard Instruments, Morley Farm, Brancepeth, Durham DH7 8DS.   T/C

HARPSICHORD MAKER supplies keyboards, registers jacks. SAE for details. William Groom, 7 Basildene Close, Gilwern, Abergavenny, Gwent.   L-M

Harpsichord, spinet, clavichord kits for home or educational projects. Traditional materials are used, and no special skills are needed for kit assembly. Stool kits and instrument covers are also available. Visitors are welcome.

John Storrs Maker of Early Keyboard Instruments
Hunston Chichester West Sussex PO20 6NR England

HARPS

Celtic Harp, Clarsach, Knee harp, Gothic Harp, Miniature Harp. Full size detailed plans and instruction sheets for the above Harps as well as the complete range of hardware, gut and brass strings and tonewood for their construction. They are also available as complete kits. Also available: complete kits for Bowed Psalteries, Appalachian and Hammered Dulcimers.
For full, illustrated details and price list please send a stamped addressed envelope to:
Michael Saunders (Luthier)
1 Waterloo Cottages, Letton,
Hereford HR3 6DN
Tel: Eardisley 352

TONEWOOD CATALOGUE

If you make, repair or restore any stringed instrument you will find our new free catalogue invaluable. We hold large stocks of selected materials for:
VIOLIN, VIOLA, 'CELLO, BASS, LUTE, GUITAR, BAROQUE VIOLS, ETC.
Callers welcome or return of post mail order service available. Open 10am - 4pm Tues/Sat.
A. HIGHFIELD & €O, Rosewood House, Bridge Road, Downham Market, Norfolk PE38 0AE.
Tel: Downham Mkt. 2614.

MUSICAL INSTRUMENT
Makers and Repairer's supplies

Largest selection of tonewoods, parts and tools in the country. Callers or mail order welcome. Also Ebony offcuts, assorted sizes.

TOUCHSTONE TONEWOODS LTD.,
27 Lesbourne Rd., Reigate, Surrey RH2 7JS

Materials for the
Amateur and Professional
VIOLIN & GUITAR MAKER

Send S.A.E. 16p
plus 50p for either cat.
50p deductible
from purchase £5.00 or over

SYDNEY EVANS LTD.
45 Regent Place,
Birmingham, B1 3BN
Tel: (021) 233-1741

BUILD YOUR OWN HARPSICHORD
from a kit by Frank Hubbard.

All materials provided including comprehensive instruction manual and full scale drawing. Choose from spinets, virginals, harpsichords and forte-pianos. Free colour catalogue and price list on request. Donald Mackinnon and Mimi Waitzman, 11 Sprowston Road, Forest Gate, London E7 9AD. Tel: 01-519 1170.

CLASSIFIED
Telephone Valerie Tester
(0442) 41221 Ext. 266

GENERAL

TEACH WOODWORK IN AMERICA for summer '82. Hundreds of Woodwork enthusiasts needed by BUNACAMP as counsellors in U.S. children's summer camps. Over 12,000 BUNACAMPers have enjoyed the most unforgettable rewarding summer of their lives. 8 sunny weeks, hard, fun work, then up to 6 weeks holiday. Flight, work visa papers, job, board, lodging all provided. $200-$230 salary. Contact Tim Wilkins, BUNACAMP, 58 Berners Street, London W1P 3AE. Telephone: 01-580 9458.   J-M

SOLID BRASS DOOR, cabinet and window fittings, in period and modern designs. Full colour catalogue illustrates over 300 different items. Send 50p (refundable with first order) to: Classic Brass (Dept. WW2), West Road, Westcliff on Sea, Essex.   I-N

¹/₁₂th SCALE BRASS HARDWARE

Period handles, hinges, grille
S.A.E. for list
MARGARET VARNEY (MINIATURES)
10 Hardays Lane,
West Haddon, Northampton

WOODTURNERS & WOODWORKERS

Visit our showroom in Blyth where we welcome visitors and are open Monday to Saturday from 9.30 a.m. to 5.30 p.m.
Drop in for a chat
with practical craftsmen and see a demonstration of
● CORONET WOODWORKING MACHINES
● ASHLEY ILES TURNING TOOLS
● ROBERT SORBY CHISELS AND OTHER FINE QUALITY TOOLS AND ACCESSORIES
Allan McNair Woodcraft
69-71 Plessey Rd., Blyth, Northumberland.
Telephone: Blyth (06706) 69279

Prices quoted are those prevailing at press date and are subject to alteration due to economic conditions.

THE MAGAZINE FOR THE CRAFTSMAN

MAY 1982 Vol. 86 No. 1062 ISSN 0043-776X

Front cover: Dan Morris of Dolgellau who plays fiddle with the Welsh folk group Cilmeri, playing his crwth.
(Photo. Peter Murphy) See also pages 298, 299.

Editor	Chris Dunn
Deputy Editor	Polly Curds
Advertisement Manager	Glyn Crole-Rees
Advertisement Director } MAP Leisure	Michael Merrifield
Managing Director } Division	Gavin Doyle

MEMBER OF THE AUDIT
BUREAU OF CIRCULATIONS

SUBSCRIPTION DEPARTMENT: Remittances to MODEL AND ALLIED PUBLICATIONS, PO Box 35, Hemel Hempstead, Herts HP1 1EE. Price per copy 95p includes p&p. Subscription queries: Tel: Hemel Hempstead 51740. Subscription rate, including index, £11.90 per annum; overseas sterling £12.90; $29.00 US for overseas dollar subscribers. Second class postage paid in US at New York, New York. *Distribution* to North American hobby and craft stores, museums and bookshops by Bill Dean Books Ltd, 166-41 Powells Cove Boulevard, Post Office Box 69, Whitestone, New York 11357, USA. Tel: 1-212-767-6632. *Distribution* to news stand sales by Eastern News Distribution Inc, 111 Eight Avenue, New York, NY10011, USA. Tel: 1-212-255-5620.

WOODWORKER is printed in Great Britain by H. E. Warne Ltd, East Hill, St Austell, Cornwall PL25 4TN for the proprietor and publisher Model & Allied Publications Ltd (a member of the Argus Press Group). Trade sales by Argus Press Sales & Distribution Ltd, 12-18 Paul Street, London EC2A 4JS. WOODWORKER (ISSN 0043-776X) is published on the 3rd Friday of the month.

Model & Allied Publications Ltd

PO Box 35, Bridge Street, Hemel Hempstead, Herts HP1 1EE. Telephone: Hemel Hempstead (0442) 41221.

Of wood and words

As this is my first issue as editor of *Woodworker,* perhaps I should introduce myself to you by way of saying hello. And having said that, the next move is to sit and look blankly at the typewriter for half an hour thinking only how difficult it is to 'introduce' oneself in print without seeming immodest, insincere or just plain daft.

However, in the hope that I can steer a course between these hazards, here goes:

My working background has been in magazines and newspapers, a career that has taken me to places as far apart as Cape Town and Cambridge, but while the process of earning a living has gone on, there has always been wood and woodworking to help sustain the spirit.

My first contact with beautiful wooden things was the cot in which I was parked a few hours after getting born. This remarkable piece of furniture, which is still in service now with my own small children, was made from rosewood grown on the coffee estate in south India where I was born. As the marks still to be seen on the cot rails record, I cut my teeth on rosewood. I think that's why I have been hooked on timber ever since!

Many pieces of rosewood furniture made by the same Indian estate carpenter are still in the possession of my family, now back at home in England, and as time goes on I hope to publish photographs and details of some of the pieces. Made with great skill by a workaday chippy using only the simplest of woodworking tools and a treadle lathe, they are wonderful examples of what can be done without all the sophistication of the modern workshop.

My own efforts at making furniture have been less distinguished, but the pieces have come in handy, and at least I am proud of that. I have also taken a special interest in musical instrument making, and my current project is building a cello under the joint guidance of Juliet Barker, the Cambridge violin-maker, and Roland Gentle, whose reputation as a violin-maker is fast being outstripped by his growing renown as a maker of fine bows.

It is rather awesome for me to be taking over editorship of *Woodworker,* with its long and proud tradition stretching back to the very beginning of this century. But the magazine can only have survived these 81 years by adapting and changing with the times, so I commit myself to continuing that process of evolution.

But while I intend that *Woodworker* will continue to reflect, report and comment upon the craft of woodwork in its most contemporary context, I hope the magazine will also uphold the elevated standards of aesthetic excellence and masterly skill as handed down to us by previous generations of wood craftsmen.

For me it is a joyful challenge to combining the two things I enjoy most, words and wood. I hope I shall serve you well.

Chris Dunn

Simple Reliable

There's a lot of talk these days about revolutionary, highly sophisticated woodworking machinery – the new, low cost, over complicated little wonders that do almost everything – providing of course you're a keen engineering student with more than a lot of time on your hands.

Well – no one ever said Kity machines were sophisticated or revolutionary – and we're proud of it – in fact we designed and built them to be simple, reliable and easy to use. You don't have to change your woodworking methods or be an engineer, Kity simply adds power and precision to develop your own skills – and sometimes even your bank balance.

Recently Barrie and Lynne Goddard of Bottesford, near Scunthorpe, decided to improve their kitchen. The going rate for the job, from a professional contractor, was around £5,000; however with Kity machinery to help him, Barrie built their dream kitchen for just £2,000.

Ideas can now become reality

All of us at some time have had to scrap excellent creative ideas because we couldn't afford to bring in the professionals and didn't have sufficient expertise to carry them out ourselves. The simplicity of Kity machinery has gone a long way towards removing this frustration and our illustrated instruction sheets will explain step by step the machine techniques needed to transform your ideas into superb reality.

Common base for all functions.

The K5 has units for separate machine functions mounted on a common base and driven by a centrally mounted power unit – the K5 motor. You have all the versatility of separately mounted machines, any change of operation becomes simplicity itself. Just connect the belt to the machine you want to use, adjusting the tension easily by means of a simple, quick release lever. Without losing your pre-set adjustments, you can change from one function to another in a matter of seconds. Continuity of work is thus assured.

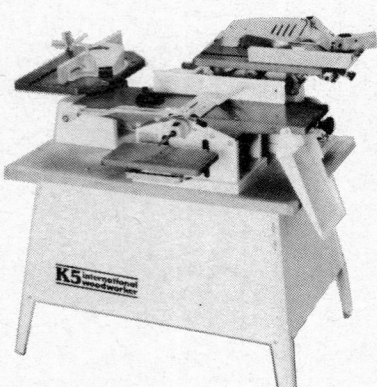

K5 international woodworker

– complete power workshop for only **£559**
(plus VAT. £83.85)

Engineering specification

Circular saw.
180mm (7″) blade normally fitted but will accept a 200mm (8″) blade giving a 57mm (2¼″) depth of cut. 2 speeds, 3750 for normal wood and 6200 r.p.m. for laminated boards. Complete with rip fence, mitre guide, repeat cut length stop, wobble washers for grooving, tilting table 0.45°.

Surface planer.
700mm (27½″) long × 200mm (8″) wide cast bed. Maximum planing width 150mm (6″). Adjustable 90° – 45° fence for bevel planing. Dynamically balanced cutter block rotating at 11,400 cuts per minute.

Thickness planer.
Fully automatic feed, 7.5m (24′) per minute. Maximum capacity 100mm (4″) deep, 150mm (6″) wide. Anti kick-back fingers, calibrated scale.

Spindle moulder
6400 rpm shaft speed. 45mm (1¾″) vertical adjustment. Capable of taking 25mm (1″) × 25mm (1″) rebate in one pass. Accepts both French moulding profiles and white hill type blocks.

Slot mortiser
Rise/fall table with 100mm (4″) of adjustment.

2 New Books

2 great books from Kity to help improve your craft.

"How to work with Wood"
One of the few books available about **woodworking machine techniques** including setting up and the use of circular saws, spindle moulder planer thicknesser slot mortisers etc. An invaluable manual for anyone using or buying woodworking machinery.

Full colour 260 pages, hard bound 195mm × 275mm, price **£15.00**.

"How to choose your Wood"
A definitive work covering timber types, cutting, storage and use. Including man made boards of all types.

Full colour 141 pages hard bound, 195mm × 275mm, price **£10.00**.

Available from all Kity stockists or direct from **Kity UK.** only **£20** for both books – save 20%.

Maximum bit diameter 12mm (½″). Produces accurate mortises, also horizontal boring for perfect dowel joints.

2 year guarantee
When you buy a K5, you will be protected against all manufacturing defects (parts and labour) for the first two years after purchase, no matter how hard you work your machine.

The Kity Heavy Duty Range

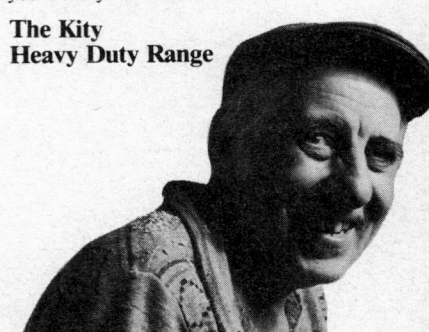

Arthur is a highly skilled, traditional craftsman who uses the Kity Heavy Duty Range, ideal machinery for the busy modern craftsmen. By purchasing a mixture of independent and combination machines he built a superb workshop that exactly suited his requirements and his pocket. Arthur says… "It's amazing how some woodworkers still use old fashioned methods that belong in the Dark Ages. Mind you – I ought not to criticize them I used to be the same, I was proud to work like my Grandfather did and I believed the results would be better if everything was done by hand. It never occurred to me he had no alternative – and in any case, I always thought machines were complicated and some how difficult to use. Anyhow, I soon found out how wrong I was when I started using Kity machinery. I got better results in a fraction of the time and with very little physical effort. There's no doubt in my mind that Kity machinery is simple and very easy to use – and sure, it makes makes me money."

Kity offers you Heavy Duty Circular Saws, Bandsaws, Planer Thicknessers, Spindle Moulders and Slot Mortisers, along with a complete range of accessories, motors and floor stands. Each machine can be independent or part of a combination for example: you can start your workshop with a circular saw. With Kity you don't have a lot of complicated attachments, nor do you have to swing the machine into different positions or use a special tool. Simply slip the belt from one machine to the next.

The Circular Saw 617
This is the heart of most workshops. The Kity machine has a cast and machined, tilting work table; a rise/fall arbor with hand wheel control; it accepts blades up to 9″ in diameter giving a 3⅛″

and ꞈVery easy to use

...th of cut; and is capable of running at two ...eds; 3400 rpm and 7000 rpm. It is powered by a ...H.P. motor with No Volt Thermal Overload ...rter. You will have no difficulty in cutting any ...od based material, from melamine faced chip-...rd to African hardwoods. ...cessories included in the price are the mitre-...de with repeat cut stop, and wobble washers for ...oving. The machine is guarded to comply with ...rnational standards.

...e Planer Thicknessers 535, 635, 636
...y manufacture three 'under and over' ...ner/thicknessers, a 10″ × 6″, 8″ × 6″ and a ...× 4″.
...h machine is available with stand and motor ...l can be used as an independent unit or will fit ...art of the combination.
...h machine has cast tables and a twin knife ...er block and is of the 'under and over' type.
...e thicknesser is power fed with an adjustable ...knessing table giving true results along the ...ole length of the timber; this is usually difficult ...chieve with the 'over fed' clamp type ...knesser. The 636 and 635 both have unusually ...g (40″) surfacing tables ideal for straightening a ...st in a plank of timber.

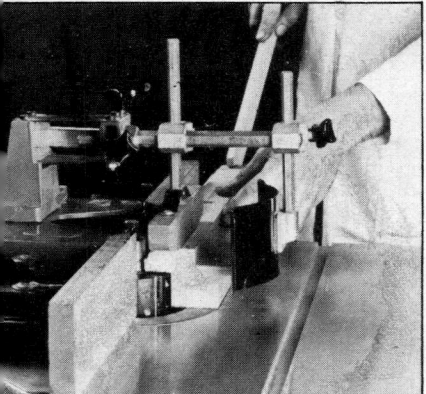

...indle Moulders 626/627
...e Spindle Moulder is a versatile and powerful ...l. It does a totally different job to a router, ...ough the system is similar. For example: –
...626 and 627 are capable of making large ...ates 1¼″ × 1¼″ in hundreds of feet of timber.
...y will also produce moulding, deep grooves, ...gue and groove joints, V-joints, tenons, profiles ... counter profiles.
...626 has a standard adjustable fence with the ...ability of positioning the cutting tools over a 4″ ...ical range. The 627 has the same specifications ...with individual micro adjustable fences. Both ...chines have cutting speeds of 7000 rpm, and are ...rded to full international standards.

...e 625 Slot Mortiser

The only machine in the whole range that is *not* available as an independent machine.
Working from the 700 table it will provide a ½″ slot, up to 5″ long and 4″ deep. An excellent machine for mortise joint production.

The 612 Bandsaw
Kity make an all steel, two wheel, Bandsaw with a 5½″ depth of cut and an 11½″ throat. It will accept blades from ¼″ for tight turns to ⅞″ for deep cutting and planking of timber. Unlike 'Plastic' Bandsaws the steel construction of the Kity machine allows you to set a high blade tension. This enables you to cut fast and in a straight line through hardwood and knots with a maximum depth of 5½″.

Kity Plan Sheets
These are issued for a nominal charge exclusively to Kity users and titles include, fitted kitchens and furniture. These practical plan sheets include cutting lists and complete manufacturing instructions on the relevant subject.

Nation-wide Service
Kity have 150 fully trained stockists throughout the U.K. and they provide a service second to none – there'll be one near you, ask for a demonstration, before you buy.

If you have a dream project you want to build or if you're a busy craftsman then you need Kity – simple, reliable and easy to use machinery.

Instructions on machines
Each Kity machine has comprehensive instructions to ensure you have the knowledge to use the machine correctly.

2 year Guarantee

IMPROVE YOUR SKILLS

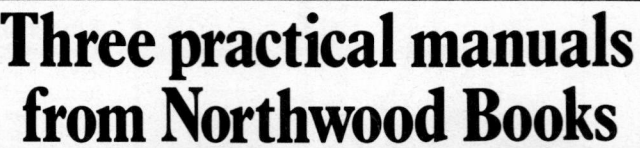

Three practical manuals from Northwood Books

Contract Joinery

Ken Austin

Companion volume to the highly acclaimed *Site Carpentry* and written by the same author, *Contract Joinery* is a comprehensive guide to the construction of individual, purpose-made items in wood.

The ten chapters cover the use and care of tools, both hand and powered; the selection and treatment of materials; the manufacture of doors, windows, partitions, panelling, staircases and handrails; glulam timbers and plywood construction; veneers; and ecclestiastical joinery and fitments.

The book contains over 580 illustrations which are used in every chapter to explain each form of construction in the clearest possible terms. Written with students and teachers in mind, it will be equally valuable to all involved in the design, manufacture or installation of purpose-made joinery.

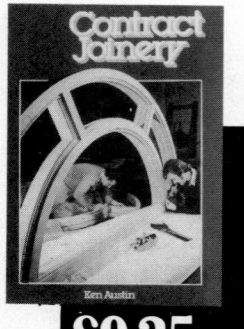

£9.25
168 pages A4 size

Site Carpentry

Ken Austin

Based on a series of articles which originally appeared in *Building Trades Journal*, this book imparts a thorough knowledge of all building site carpentry and joinery.

The eleven chapters, copiously illustrated, encompass such subjects as the basic tool kit, formwork, timber floor construction, centres and arches, shoring, roofing, stair construction, partitions, windows and doors, internal fitments and temporary timber buildings. For ease of reference, much of the information is presented in graphic and tabular form; there are over 600 illustrations. A welcome, practical guide for students and professional carpenter alike.

£5.95
144 pages A4 size
£4.50 Spiro binding

Techniques of Routing

Jim Phillips

The first book to be devoted exclusively to the craft of routing, this is an operating manual on all aspects of handling portable routers.

Written by an acknowledged expert on the subject, the book deals with the many and manifold uses of the machine, stressing its versatility to both amateur and professional craftsman. It can be used for jobs as simple as bevelling the edge of a shelf or as complex as making an accurate reproduction of a Chippendale chair!

The concise text is fully illustrated with photographs and line drawings and has a comprehensive appendix covering the numerous cutters available and their specific uses.

£4.50
144 pages A5 size

To: Northwood Books, 93-99 Goswell Road, London EC1V 7QA.

Please send me:

_____ copy/ies of Contract Joinery at £10.25 (includes p&p)

_____ copy/ies of Techniques of Routing at £5 (includes p&p)

_____ copy/ies of Site Carpentry (Hardback) at £6.95 (includes p&p)

_____ copy/ies of Site Carpentry (Spiro binding) at £5 (includes p&p)

I enclose a cheque/PO for £_____
made payable to Northwood Publications Ltd.

Name _____

Address _____

_____

_____

WW

Prices quoted are those prevailing at press date and are subject to alteration due to economic conditions.

Quality or price?

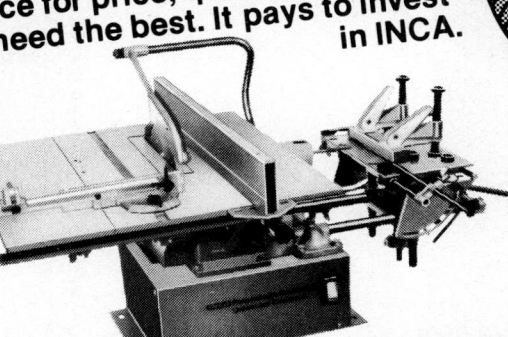

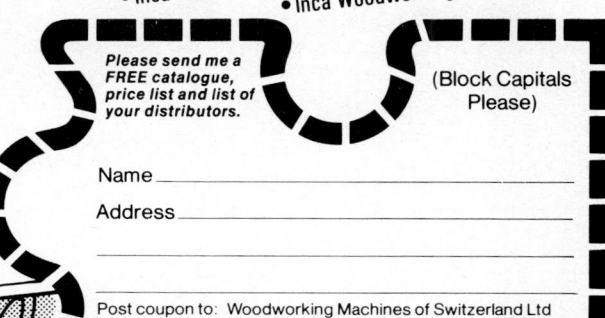

Comeback for the Crwth

Dan Morris who plays fiddle with the Welsh folk group Cilmeri, believes the time has come for a revival of the crwth (pronounced crooth). The crwth — crowd in England, crot or cruit in Ireland — was played from the 6th century to the early part of the last century. Its decline has been attributed to the rise in popularity of the violin, though in Wales the religous revivalists frowned on the crwth and folk songs and dances too.

Dan Morris' wish to transfer the crwth from museum to stage could not be satisfied until he met Bernard Ellis, a former steelworker, who makes early stringed instruments at Dilwyn in Herefordshire. Bernard's catalogue lists a crwth based on the Foelas crwth which is in the collection of the Welsh Folk museum at St Fagans castle near Cardiff.

Until now Bernard has made the crwth for Scandinavian players so he was pleased to have a request from the principality for this traditional Welsh instrument. He and Dan Morris discussed ideas and decided that the Cilmeri crwth would differ in design and weight from the Foelas and be more like the Hayward crwth now in the Welsh national library at Aberystwyth.

The Cilmeri instrument is made from one solid piece of plane with the arms and soundbox as one, the latter being worked with mallet and chisel to a depth of 5cm before the Sitka spruce front is put on. White of egg is the sealant and the polish is beeswax.

The crwth is rectangular in shape with six strings passing over an oblique bridge. One foot of the bridge passes through a hole in the belly of the instrument and rests on the back to act as a sound-post. The sound is closer to the viola than the violin and has a

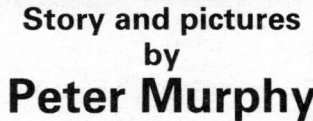

Story and pictures
by
Peter Murphy

● *Above: Dan Morris playing his Cilmeri crwth. Left and opposite: views of Bernard Ellis of Dilwyn carving, cutting and shaping the crwth.*

folksy flavour more Irish than Welsh.

Will the crwth enjoy lasting revival? Attempts have been made before — towards the end of last century when Owen Tudor, a carpenter of Dolgellau in N Wales made one which is now believed to be an exhibit in the Boston (US) museum of fine arts.

Dan Morris who lives at Dolgellau believes the 1890s revival failed because the motive was academic rather than musical. However, he is optimistic that nearly a hundred years later the crwth, perhaps altered in tuning and in the number of strings, will be varied enough to meet the needs of contemporary folk music.

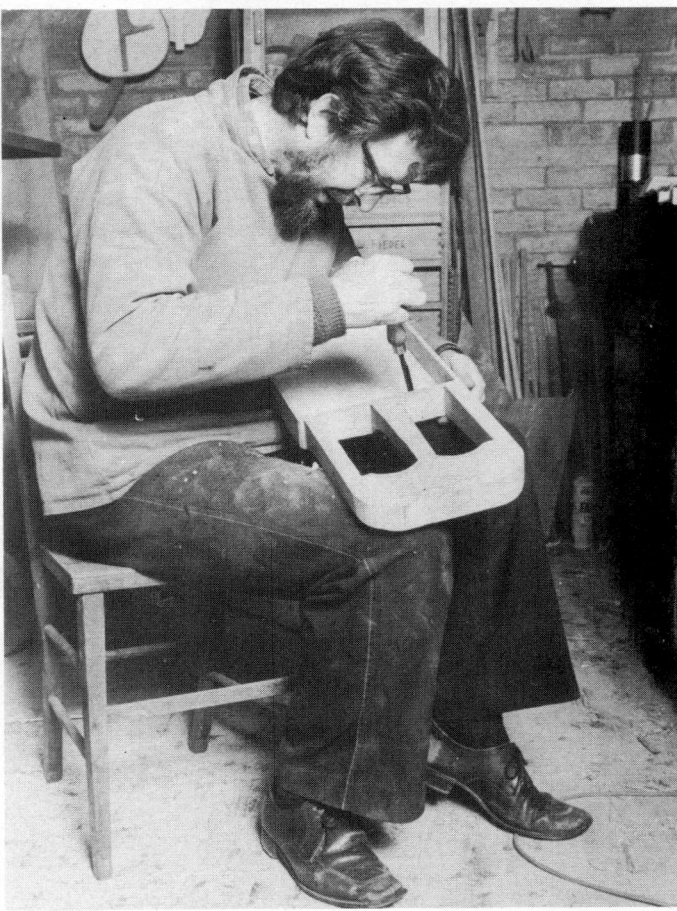

Three-tier dumbwaiter

Readers will recall that we showed an illustration of a three-tier dumbwaiter, belonging to Peter Francis of London, in the November issue. This was such a graceful piece that we asked Vic Taylor to draw up a similar design for publication. And here it is

In the Georgian House at Bristol, a real treasure trove of elegant Georgian period furniture, I was very attracted to a magnificent specimen of a dumbwaiter. It has three revolving trays, each of which carries flaps, but they are rather larger than Peter Francis' piece at 17in (431mm), 21in (533mm), and 24½in (622mm) diameters. Heights of the two pieces are comparable, so I have compromised by making the diameters 14in (356mm), 17in (431mm), and 20in (508mm); I have also made the legs a little heavier, and there are one or two other small differences.

The design is suitable for making up in mahogany or walnut, but be warned – it will be expensive, as you will need some pretty large pieces. Obviously, the three trays call for comparatively wide planks and you may well have to think about jointing two pieces together to arrive at the requisite width. If so, you could use a rubbed glue joint or a tongued and grooved joint; for the former it is best to use animal (scotch) glue, while for the latter one of the modern synthetic resin adhesives will make a reliable joint.

Turning the trays on the face-plate of the lathe, and the columns between centres, is straightforward enough. You will find patterns for the columns in Fig 1, where they are superimposed on a grid representing one inch (25.4mm) squares. If you draw out a corresponding grid full size on a piece of paper you will be able to plot the curves. Also shown is a section of the top showing the dishing.

This is probably a good place to explain the method of jointing the columns and the trays together so that they can revolve freely. Starting with the top tray, you have to bore a ¾in (19mm) diameter hole to a depth of ⅜in (10mm) into the underside. This may sound simple and indeed it is, provided you bear in mind that you should not use any bit that has a screw point which leads the point in. If you do, the screw point is liable to break through the face side and spoil it. The ideal bit for this kind of work is a Forstner (Fig 2A) which has only a tiny screw point to start it and then relies on its circular shape to do the rest.

However, it's quite likely you do not have one as they are quite rare these days – both in woodworkers' tool kits and on sale at tool stores. If so, do not despair as it is only a shallow hole and can be formed by drilling three or four holes with an ordinary HS drill and joining them up with a small gouge or chisel. Of course, if you intend to veneer the

Fig 1. Elevation is shown at (A); plan at (B). Drawing (C) is on a grid representing one-inch (25·4mm) squares. Dovetail joint is shown at (D).

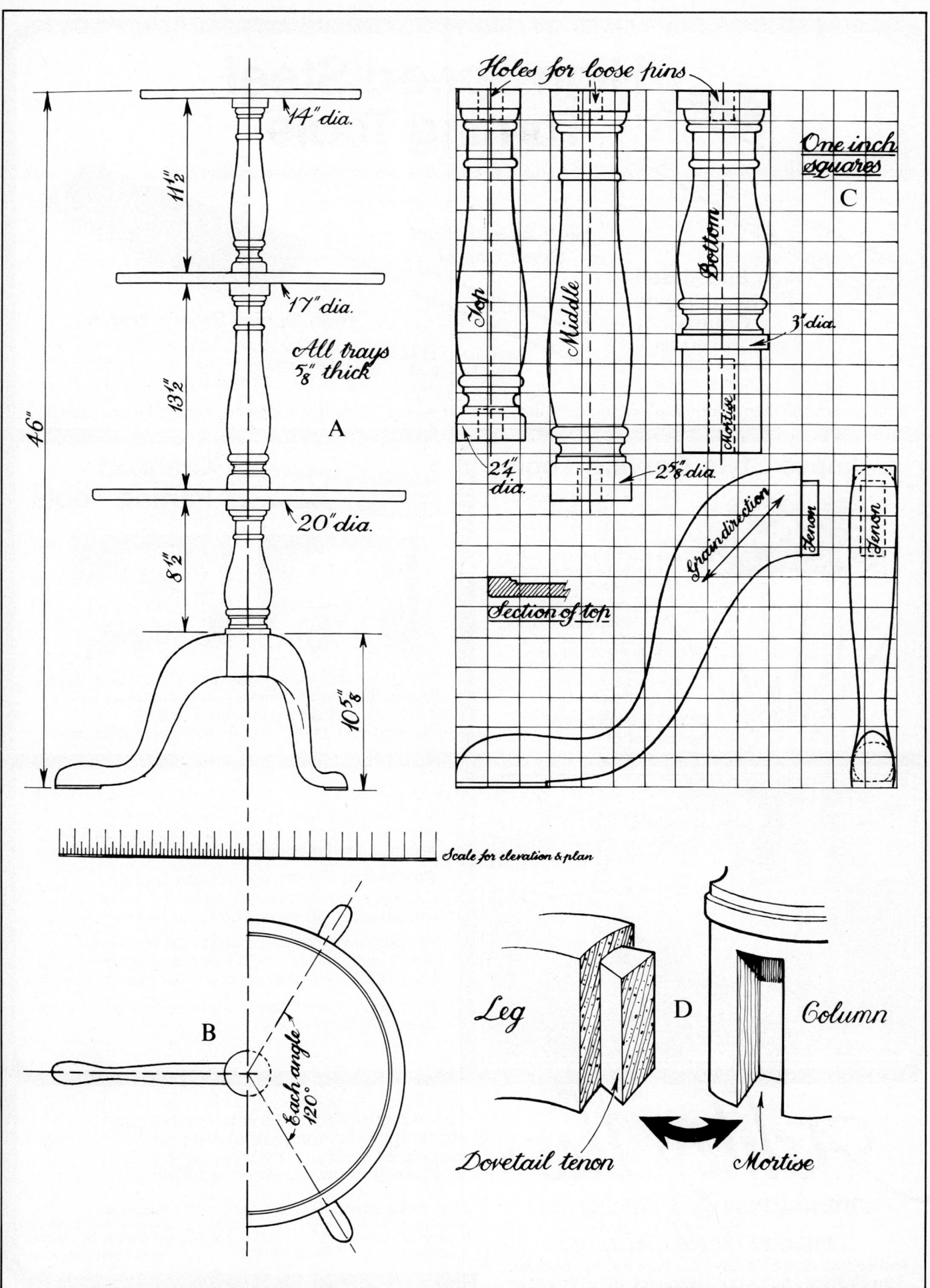

Holes for loose pins

One inch squares

C

14" dia.

11½"

17" dia.

All trays ⅝" thick

A

13½"

20"dia.

46"

8½"

10⅝"

Top

Middle

Bottom

2¼" dia.

2⅝" dia.

3"dia.

Mortise

Section of top

Grain direction

Tenon

Tenon

Scale for elevation & plan

B

Each angle 120°

Leg

D

Column

Dovetail tenon

Mortise

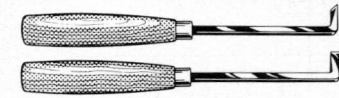

Prices quoted are those prevailing at press date and are subject to alteration due to economic conditions.

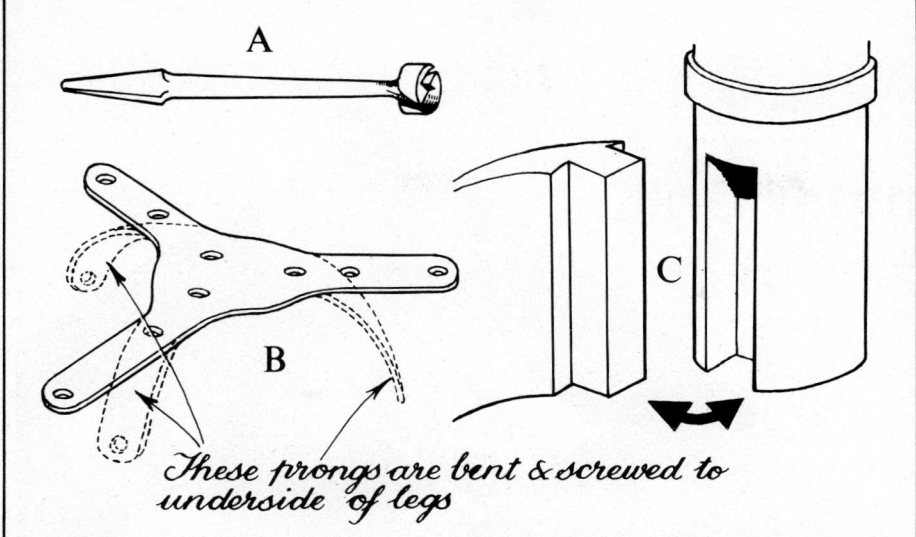

Fig 2. Forstner bit is shown at (A), metal strapping at (B), and square mortise and tenon joint at (C).

Three-tier dumbwaiter

trays, all this is unnecessary as any small holes on the face side can be filled and veneered over.

Once you have made the hole it needs a ¾in (19mm) pin gluing into it so that the pin protrudes by an inch – this means that the pin itself needs to be 1⅜in (35mm) long. A corresponding socket 1in (25mm) deep by ¾in (19mm) diameter has to be bored out of the upper end of the top column to accept the pin. You will probably have to ease the pin with glasspaper so that it rotates smoothly.

Moving down to the middle and lower trays, each of these has a ¾in (19mm) diameter hole bored right through the centre, and a 2⅝in (67mm) long pin is fitted into each end so that 1in (25mm) protrudes each side. These protrusions are then glued into sockets bored in the ends of the columns. Obviously the holes in the trays may need easing a trifle so that they can rotate easily.

This brings us to the stool part, where strength and rigidity are the keywords. The first prerequisite is that the legs are cut from as small a piece of solid timber as possible, and the second is that the joint between the legs and the column is the strongest you can achieve.

Dealing with the legs, you will naturally try to nest them one into another to save as much wood as possible. This is all right, but you must ensure that the grain of each leg runs diagonally in the direction shown by the arrow in Fig 1C. This is not just desirable but essential, as otherwise the grain in the narrow neck just behind the foot will be liable to shear.

Save the offcuts, by the way, as they are invaluable as cramping blocks when you come to cramp up the legs. Cutting out the outline shapes of the legs can really only be done on a bandsaw, and rounding off the edges (called 'benching' in the trade) is accomplished by hand with spokeshave and scrapers – probably the most enjoyable part of the job. It's most difficult to show the subtle curves and sculptured shapes of the legs in a drawing and if you could visit a museum or 'stately home' to look at a genuine example it would help you a lot.

But make sure you are looking at an authentic piece, as the shapes of the legs on some modern reproductions are really appalling.

Fig 1A shows the best way of joining the leg to the base of the column, and it calls for careful cutting and fitting. It is essentially a dovetailed tenon and mortise joint, with the mortise left open at the bottom so that the tenon can be inserted into it easily. The dovetailing feature gives a positive fit and good rigidity.

An alternative method is shown at Fig 2C. Here the joint is a simple mortise and tenon which should not trouble anyone in the making – again, the mortise is open-ended but it could equally well be closed, although this would entail shouldering the tenon at the bottom. It's evident that such a joint is not as strong as the dovetailed one already described and, if you do use it, I would strongly recommend a metal 'strapping' as shown in Fig 2B. This is screwed to the underside of the upper parts of the legs and to the bottom end of the column.

Unfortunately this is definitely not a fitting that can be shop-bought and it will have to be hand-made by a metalworker to your pattern. It should be of malleable mild steel about 2mm thick – malleable because you will have to bend the prongs yourself.

There are one or two other points to note which may save you time and trouble. For instance, it would be advisable to make the tenons on the legs before you do the final shaping, as you will be able to hold them in the vice more easily and any scratches or marks can be removed when you are benching the legs.

Cutting the plain mortises in the column base is straightforward enough, but the dovetail-shaped ones will be trickier. Probably the best way to clear away the waste would be to drill a series of holes and clean out the socket with a sharp chisel. Also, I would be inclined to make the mortises first and fit the dovetail tenons to them – trimming a tenon is a lot easier than digging about with a mortise chisel.

I advised you to keep the offcuts when sawing out the leg shapes and their usefulness will become apparent when you have to cramp up the legs to the column, as they can be re-positioned to form cramping blocks. They have another function too, as if you are going to use a metal strapping you can employ them as shaping blocks when bending the curves on the prongs.

Events

College exhibition

The dates of the college exhibition of fine furniture produced by students training as designer/craftsmen at Shrewsbury College of Arts and Technology, are 24 June-30 June from 9.00-5.00 (not Sunday). The college can be found in London Road, Shrewsbury.

Shoreditch Campus exhibition

Each year the specialist Design Technology training establishment, Shoreditch college (now a part of Brunel University) holds an exhibition of student work. This year the exhibition will be opened by the Hon William Waldegrave MP parliamentary under-secretary for education. As in previous years there will also be a selection of trade stands run by commercial organisations associated with the needs of design, craft and technology teachers. This year's exhibition is from 14-16 May inclusive, opening times 10am-6pm.

Turned wood

Ray Key's 5th one-man show will be at Key Crafts, 20 Vine St, Evesham, Worcs from 3-22 May. Bowls, boxes and platters in over 30 woods will be featured. Ray will be on hand to discuss his work on 3 May, 10 May and 17 May.

Miniature venue

First Leeds doll and miniature fair at Pudsey Civic Hall, Dawsons Corner, Pudsey, Leeds on Saturday 22 May 10.30-5.00, admission 30p. Further details from Doreen Jeffries on 0274 616539.

Coronet Open Week

At Alfreton Road, Derby 27 April to 3 May, Monday to Saturday 10-7, Sunday 10-2, refreshments available.

Tour arrangements to trade fairs

Pressplan Travel, 17 Verulam Rd, St Albans AL3 4DA offer various inclusive tour arrangements to trade fairs being held later this year in Europe and N America. The company say that they represent a saving on independent reservations and their tour selections are also capable of a maximum flexibility of movement for participants.

Exhibitions covered include Paritex (Paris 22-26 April); Star/Sasmil and Interbimall (Milan, 20-25 May), and Neocon (Chicago, 16-18 June). Full details from Pressplan at the above address or phone St Albans 33291.

Cost of conservation

A symposium organised by the United Kingdom Institute for Conservation is to be held on Thursday 29 April at the Victoria and Albert museum, South Kensington, London with the aim to get freelance and institutional conservators and their clients to discuss the financial side of their business. Price per attendance including lunch and refreshments UKIC members £10, Friends of the V&A £10, others £14. Applications to Jane Reynolds, Conservation Dept, Victoria and Albert museum, London SW7 2RL.

Prices quoted are those prevailing at press date and are subject to alteration due to economic conditions.

FRETSAW MARQUETRY

In WOODWORKER for November and December 1980 and March, June and November 1981, Ernie Ives has discussed basic marquetry and given step-by-step instructions to produce a simple picture. Here he considers fretsaw marquetry which involves learning a different skill and using a few extra tools.

Some woods are harder than others. Some shapes are difficult to cut. Readers who have tried making the picture given in the basic marquetry series will appreciate the truth of these statements. And I did not recommend any woods that are particularly hard; neither did I recommend shapes that are abnormally intricate.

However, the design in this present series involves some tortuous cutting and I am suggesting that it is done either in Macassar ebony or Indian rosewood (both nearly black in colour) to contrast with the whiteness of sycamore. Nasty? No not when a fretsaw is used.

But fretsaw marquetry does involve learning a different skill — and most pictures really need a combination of knife and saw techniques: the knife for the straighter cuts and the saw to deal quickly with the very curly shapes and very hard woods.

Only a few extra tools will have to be bought and the outlay need not be great. For the time being I will not deal with fretsaw machines (hand, treadle or power) and confine my remarks to handframes.

These are still available although you are unlikely to be able to get my favourite which has a toggle-tensioning device (Fig. 1A) except second-hand. The frame shown in Fig. 1B relies on the springiness of the metal to hold the blade taut; it is quite satisfactory. If you have a choice get the frame having greatest depth of throat. Some practitioners, particularly Americans, make their own wooden frames, occasionally so large that they have to be suspended by a cord from the ceiling in order to maintain control. For most purposes, however, a throat of 12-14in. is adequate.

2▼

1▼

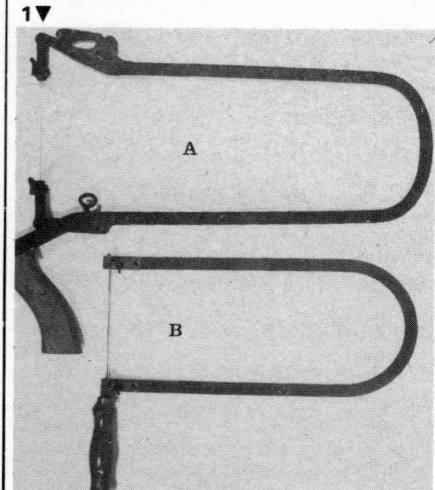

3▶

Piercing saw blades. Even the finest fretsaw blades are too coarse for marquetry so we have to go to the jeweller for the piercing saw blades he uses to cut tiny shapes from precious metals. These are the same length as fretsaw blades and the table below gives the sizes suitable for marquetry.

Size	Width in in.	Thickness in in.
2/0	0.024	0.010
4/0	0.0165	0.0095
6/0	0.015	0.007
8/0	0.012	0.006

Sizes vary with different makes but the dimensions given are measured from my own stock. These blades are available from some tool shops and veneer suppliers or from silversmiths' supply houses but although those from the last named seem to be the best the supply is in packets of 1 gross. Usually I recommend beginners to start with the 4/0 size. They are not much thinner than the 2/0 but are narrower and easier to get round sharply-pointed corners; and the teeth are finer and less likely to shatter the veneer. On the other hand the 2/0 blades are more robust and less likely to break. After some practice you can graduate to the 6/0 grade. This I use for all but the most intricate detail.

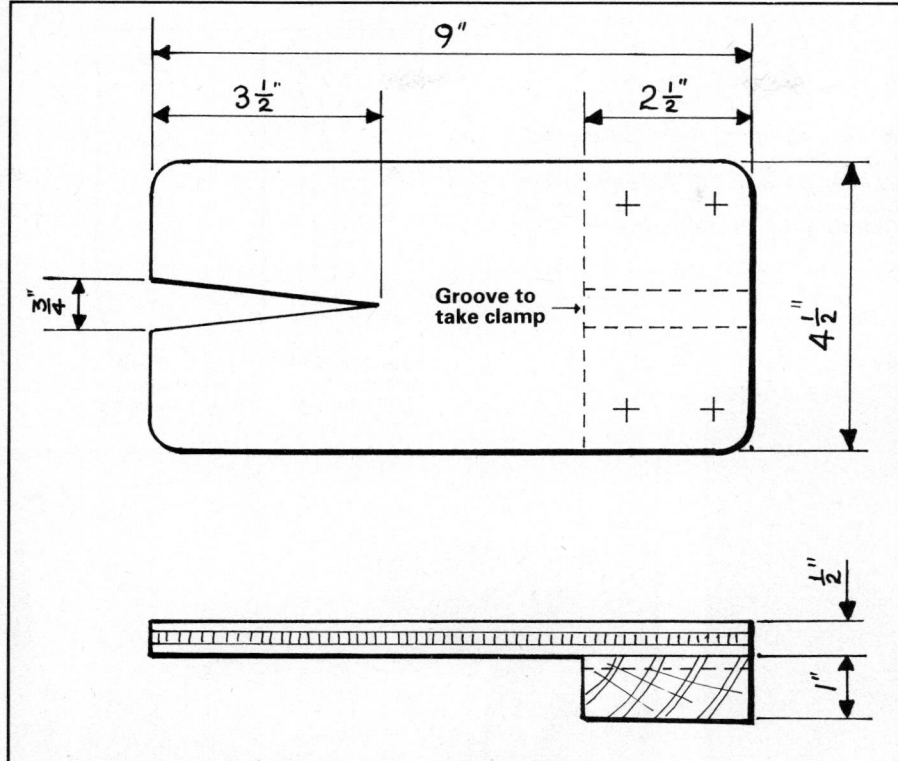

9"

3½"

2½"

¼"

Groove to take clamp

4½"

½"

1"

▲4

6▼

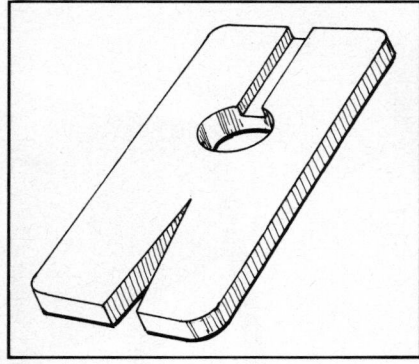

5▲

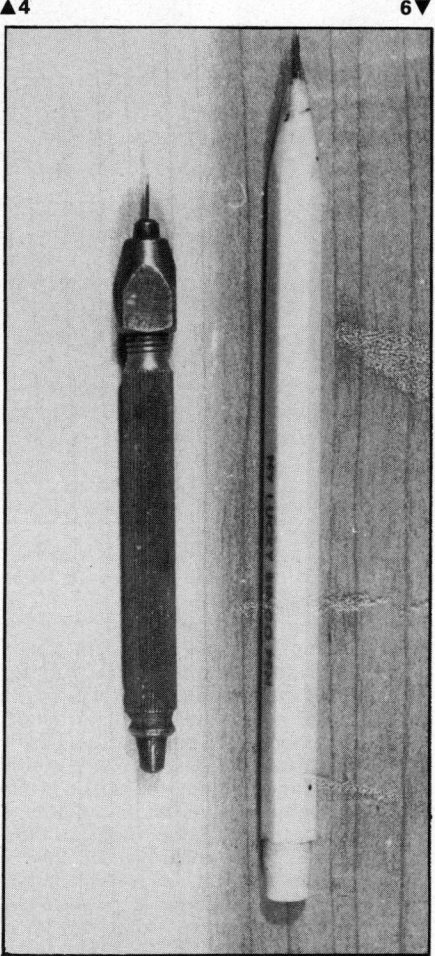

Piercing saw blades are meant for cutting metal and therefore they should be more than hard enough to cut wood. But some are too hard and brittle and with such a batch the only way I have found to draw the temper satisfactorily is to melt some lead in a shallow rectangular tin and dip each blade into it. Keeping it under the surface for a few seconds allows the blade to get up to the temperature of the lead (Fig. 2) and when removed it cools almost instantly. I then scrape off any lead adhering to the blade with thumbnail or forceps. Tests with one particularly brittle batch that I treated like this indicated the blade life was increased by over eight times.

Once the wire from each pack of blades is removed it is all to easy to mislay and mix up the various sizes. A convenient way to store them is in 6in. lengths of ⅜in. rigid plastics tube obtainable from aquarium shops. Tightly plug one end with a cork and cut off flush and fit a loose cork into the

● *Fig 1 Two types of fretsaw. Fig 2 Using a bath of molten lead to soften piercing saw blades. Fig 3 Containers for blades made from plastics tubes. Fig 4 Sawing table. Fig 5 Alternative sawing table (sizes as Fig 4). Fig 6 Needle holders.*

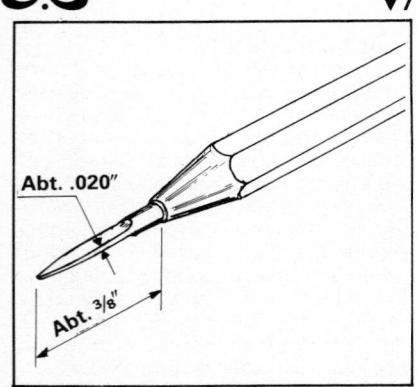

Abt. .020"

Abt. ³/₈"

▼7

● Fig 7 Shaping the needle point. Fig 8 Making a hole through the veneer pack. Fig 9 Threading the blade through the work. Fig 10 Pointing the blade ends.

▶ 10

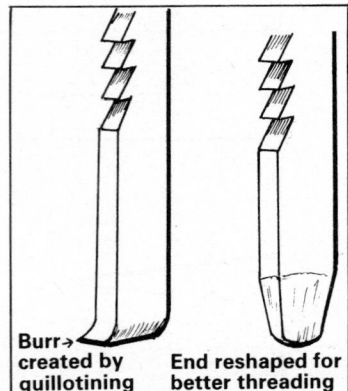

Burr→ created by guillotining

End reshaped for better threading

8▼

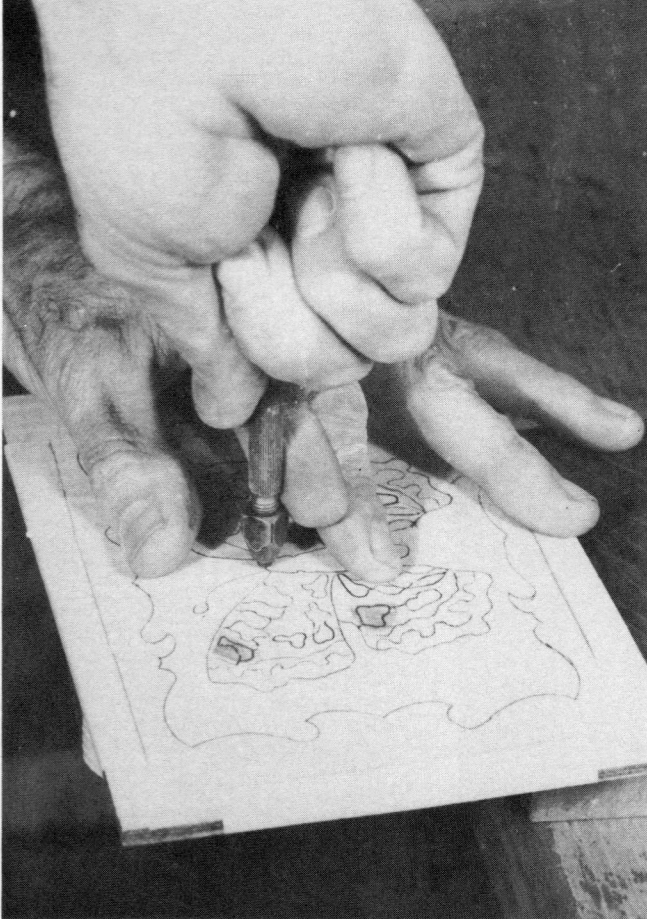

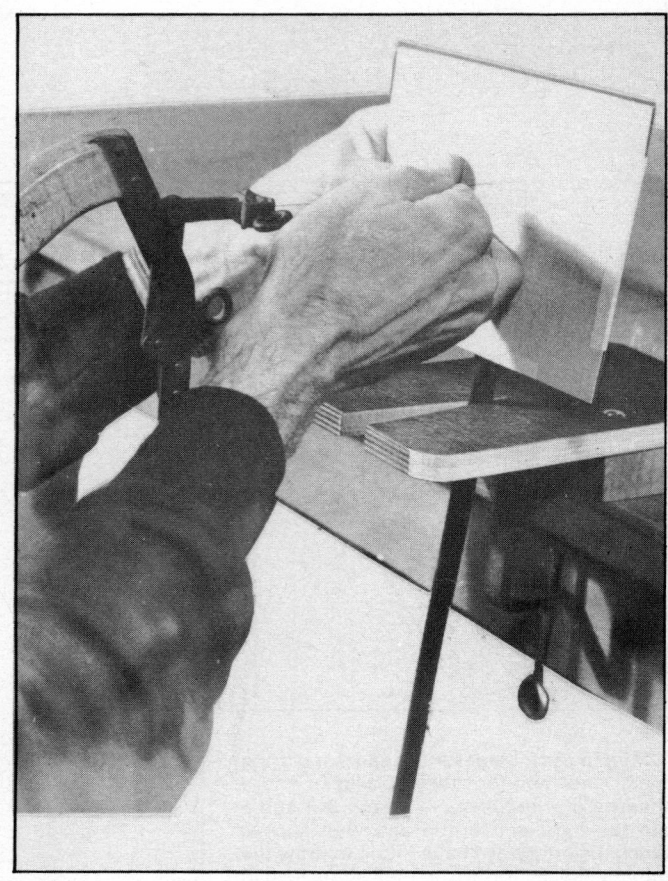

▲9

other end (Fig. 3).

Sawing table. For the first fretsawing project you will need a simple, level sawing table, sometimes called a 'birds mouth' (Fig. 4). Keep the vee quite narrow so as to adequately support the veneer; the vee in most commercial tables is too wide for marquetry. The block on the underside has a slot cut across it to take a small G-cramp and is fixed with four 1in. × 8g screws. Alternatively, the top piece can have a 1in. hole bored through and the slot to take the cramp cut into the top surface (Fig. 5). This gives a lower working position.

Needle holder. Holes will have to be made in the pack of veneers to thread the blade through at the start of the cut. Fine drills are

available but are not as suitable as a needle. Drills remove the wood and leave a hole; the needle pushes the fibres apart and these close up again when dampness from the glue soaks in. Choose a needle about 0.020in. thick (a medium-fine one from an assorted packet). The needle has to be put in some kind of holder but the often recommended method of driving it into a piece of dowel is not successful and can be dangerous as the dowel handle easily pulls off when the needle get stuck in the work.

Two better ways are shown in Fig. 6. One is a bought pin vice which has the advantage that the needles can easily be changed. The other way (and cheaper) is to use an old ball-point or felt-tip pen — one having a

small opening when the pen itself is removed. Make a small wooden plug that fits the bore of the plastics case (I found the end ½in. off an artist's brush to be just right), make up a small quantity of epoxy resin glue and poke this into the top end of the pen. Insert the wooden plug and force it down inside the handle with a stout piece of wire. This will push all the glue before it until it comes out of the other end.

Put in the eye end of the needle and tap into the wooden plug for a very short distance to keep the needle centralised. I find it best to hold the needle in a vice and tap the wooden plug on to it by hitting the

13►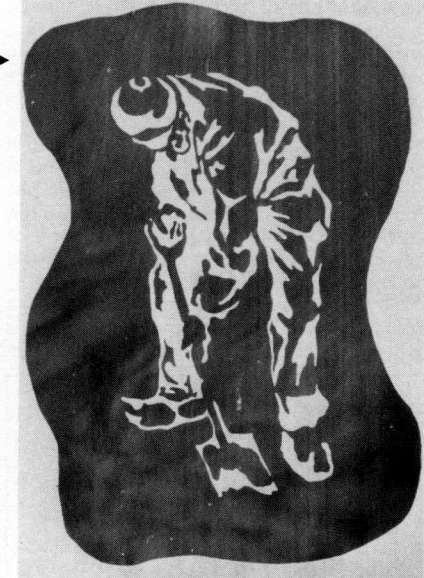

● *Fig 11 Holding the fretsaw. Fig 12 Using the fingers to hold down the work. Fig 13 The Peasant. Fig 14 (overleaf) The Bait Digger.*

end of the rod used to push the plug down the tube. Leave abut ⅜in. of the needle projecting, set the holder upright and allow the glue to dry.

The needle in its holder can be used as it is but it is better if the needle is sharpened to a bradawl-like point (Fig. 7). This can be done on a fine oilstone or with the fine side of the sandpaper file.

Fig. 8 shows the tool in use. Wherever possible make the hole where the line runs with the grain of the wood so that it has a better chance of closing again afterwards.

Inserting the blade. Beginners often break more blades at this stage than when cutting. It takes time to judge just how much of the blade to insert into the clamps to give the right amount of tension. The job seems to require at least two pairs of hands to hold the frame, the work, the blade and to tighten the clamp. Overcome this difficulty by using the sawing table and your chest!

The teeth of the blade should point towards the handle so that they cut when the saw is pulled downwards through the work. The teeth are so fine that it is difficult

to see which way they point — but they can be felt.

Fasten the blade into the lower (handle end) clamp. Catch the top of the frame an inch or two below the clamps, into the vee of the sawing table. Rest the end of the handle on to your chest and insert the blade through the hole in the underside of the work (Fig. 9). Some cheaper blades have burrs on the ends and these may make it difficult to thread a blade through the hole. If you find this, taper the ends to a blunt point with the fine side of the sandpaper file or a slipstone (Fig. 10).

Slide the work right along the blade as far as the lower clamp. Now if the free end of the blade is held with one hand you can let go of the work and the other hand is then ready to tighten the top clamp. With the chest, press on the frame to close it slightly, insert the blade into the top clamp and tighten. When the pressure is removed the frame will spring out and, if your judgement has been correct, tension the blade to give a high vibrant tone when plucked. Too much tension and the blade will break, too little

and it will be too slack and soggy for use. The technique for inserting the blade in a frame with the toggle tensioning device is similar, except that the frame is not sprung together when inserting the blade. The correct tension is put on afterwards by the lever cam and the fine adjusting screw.

Using the saw. Keep the blade upright and keep the place being cut near to the apex of the vee in the sawing table to support the work as much as possible. Keep the round end of the frame alongside your arm (Fig. 11) and hold the work firmly down with your fingers close to the blade. Sometimes I use finger and thumb as shown in Fig. 12 and at other times I use the first and second fingers.

With this hand steer the work to the saw rather than the other way round. Try and imitate the action of a machine with the saw moving up and down more or less in the same place in the table. Do not force the saw

GUILD OF WOODWORKERS

into the work. Let it cut at its own pace. At the sharp corners keep the saw marking-time (moving up and down in the same place) while the work is steered round to the new direction. It may save hunting for a small piece in the pile of the carpet if a sheet of white paper is put on the floor; or if you wear an apron and pin or Blutak the ends to the underside of the worktable to catch any pieces that fall.

Supporting veneer. For nearly all hand fretsawn marquetry a waste or supporting veneer, preferably slightly thicker than normal, is taped under the other veneers being cut. As the name suggests it supports them and helps to prevent them being torn away by the saw. Supporting veneer is not absolutely necessary when the finest blades (6/0 or 8/0) are used.

Techniques for fretsawing. While there are a number of techniques that can be employed in pictorial marquetry to get a perfect fit with any thickness of blade, I will suggest a simpler method in order to make a silhouette type of picture. The one I have chosen for this series started out as a drawing by Van Gogh. I did a version of it that I called *The Peasant* (Fig. 13). A friend of mine, a keen fisherman, suggested that I put a pair of Wellington boots and a bobble hat on the figure and make a picture of one of the men who go out on the mud flats around the coasts to dig lug and ragworm for bait. *The Bait Digger* is thus the subject for this project but you can look for designs of your own and follow the methods I use. Adver-

Fig 14

tisements in newspapers and magazines are a good source and it is worthwhile keeping a folder of pictures which could make likely designs.

When you study *The Bait Digger* (Fig. 14) I am sure you will see how difficult the shapes would be to prick round with a knife, even in mild veneers. You will also note all the fragile areas of short grain. I do not say it would be impossible to cut with a knife, even using ebony (someone with masochistic tendencies would be bound to prove me wrong); but it would be much more difficult.

Post bag

The first few weeks of 1982 have brought an interesting selection of letters to the guild desk. Guild members are not restricted to the UK and now include woodworkers in the US, Australia, Canada, New Zealand, many of the countries in Africa, Holland, Hong Kong, Greece, Malaysia and a high percentage of the Arab states. We are pleased that *Woodworker* is reaching these countries and still meeting the needs of people who are there for a short time on business or are natives of the various countries.

Guild members are experienced in a wide range of skills relating to woodworking. Our post bag includes letters from '40 years experience as a joiner, now considering self-employment', 'a trading craftsman specialising in house signs and number boards' and 'a teacher of design and craft in schools who has retired early with the intention of designing, making and selling his own pieces.'

We have a plea from a member who is moving from Herts to Godmanchester, Huntingdon, and would like to contact other guild members in his new area. Any letters to us in the Guild office will be forwarded to Mr O'Carroll.

Members include students eg a 20 year old student teacher studying education in Glasgow and hoping to qualify as a technical teacher in two years time. Good luck for the future John. Another plea, this time from Ghana. Students taking cabinet-making courses at City & Guilds level find the acquisition of suitable text books, catalogues and magazines very difficult. Any assistance would be appreciated, the colleges are both in Accra but we do not have complete addresses. Perhaps local members of the guild would consider helping.

A member from Lillingstone Lovell specialises in traditional window replacements and cabinetmaking; another in Needingworth is a maker of classical guitars. He writes to say that he is finding it increasingly difficult to find woods in top quality that his work demands. Mr Young is mainly in need of good quality pine, rosewood, mahogany and ebony. Frank Insall from Pershore has told us he has had some of his marquetry pictures and boxes exhibited at the Jennie Hill Gallery in Pershore. How about entering the marquetry section of the Woodworker Show this year Frank and letting more of us see your work? Frank is a member of the Marquetry Society and we hope that they will be joining us at the show in October with a display stand of members work to complement our competition classes.

We are a little late to help a member from Blackrock, Co Dublin who is searching for assistance in 'furniture wood carving'. He has been practising ball and claw, rope edge and acanthus leaf carving but though there are many books on the subject he feels that to really improve his skills he would like some personal tuition. Dr Spain was looking for help in March when he visited the Kent area but perhaps he will be

visiting some other time and members can suggest some future aid.

Many of our members have specialised in the restoration side of woodwork and we regularly note the full or part-time occupation of antique furniture restorer and cabinetmaker in the letters we receive.

In early January we heard from Mr Davies of Barnsley who enclosed a photograph of a regulator style clock which he had made from a walnut shop-counter that had seen some hard wear in its time. The clock sides are dovetail housed into top and bottom, back deep sawn and joined, rebated to fit in a groove in the sides and with finials which are three pieces thick in order to get the required diameter. The split turnings on the door are in one length each with a waisted centre to give a better effect. The whole case is solid timber. The photograph shows a clock with a battery movement but other clocks in walnut and mahogany that Mr Davies has made have 'wind up, strike on coil' movements. Mr Davies says he has exhibited at several craft shows and can now sell all he makes. Unfortunately his photograph is in colour and so we cannot show his work on this page. If readers are interested in sharing their work and details of their craft with other guild members, would they please send black and white prints that are as sharp as possible so that they can be faithfully reproduced to do justice to quality.

FINISHING COURSE

Another two-day finishing course has been arranged for guild members on 10-11 May 1982 at the Hudson Hall, rear of 40 Bean Road, Bexleyheath, Kent. The course starts at 10.00am and will end about 4.30pm each day with an hour (12.30-1.30pm) for lunch. Refreshments can be obtained at a nearby pub.

The course will be restricted to six to permit individual instruction to be given.

Cost of the two-day course is £31.60 for each member inc. VAT. This does not inlude cost of lunch.

SKILLS AND PROFIT-MAKING

There are still a limited number of vacancies to be filled on a further two-day seminar arranged in co-operation with the Council for Small Industries in Rural Areas (CoSIRA). To be held at the Pottergate Course & Conference Centre, 83-5 Pottergate, Norwich on Wednesday and Thursday 28 and 29 April.

The fee for the seminar is £50 plus £7.50 VAT (total £57.50) which includes tuition, papers and lecture material, morning coffee, lunch and tea in the afternoon. Accommodation is not included but arrangements can be made on request.

Application forms for all Guild of Woodworkers courses have been published in previous issues of Woodworker. They may be obtained direct from the Administrator, please enclose a SAE.

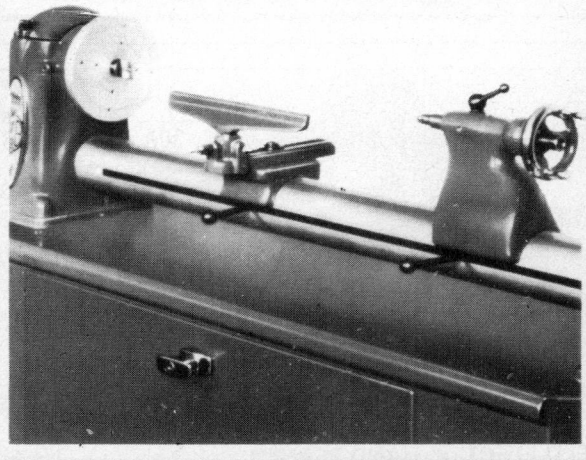

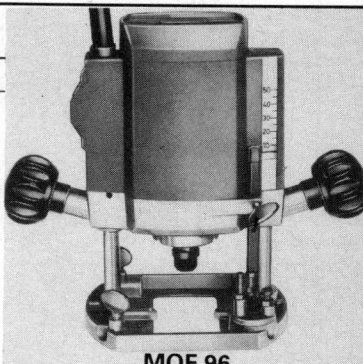
Prices quoted are those prevailing at press date and are subject to alteration due to economic conditions.

Where there's a wheel there's a way

Bert Bailey of Kingsnorth in Kent is a wheelwright, as his father, grandfather and great grandfather were before him. Here his wife, Jocelyn Bailey, records some of the demands made upon a wheelwright by modern-day customers

It is interesting to see old agricultural items of the kind that were originally made in village workshops like ours, now being brought in for restoration as collectors' items.

Old Kent shims, Kent ploughs and seed drills hold pride of place in the heart of any collector of bygone agricultural things, and whenever my husband does restorations to such implements, he is reminded of how his father, grandfather or great grandfather would have made similar things of more practical use for the local farmers of yesterday.

Recently a collector brought an old Kent plough to the shop for restoration. Off went my husband to a fellow rural craftsman, a hurdlemaker, and returned with some chestnut butts. I was mystified, until he explained that they are traditionally correct in making up implement handles such as those on horsedrawn ploughs and shims. The photograph shows the ideal shape of the butts, with the grain running naturally to the shape of a curved handle.

The wooden billets, which are connected to the horse's harness with chains and hooked on to the implement behind, are also of interest. They were made from chestnut or ash poles at the carpenter's shop and then sent to the blacksmith's, where the iron fittings were applied hot and then cooled with water, which shrunk them to a very tight fit on the wood. Incidentally, these wooden billets have different names in other areas and I note in the *Heavy Horse Handbook*, published by Southern Counties Heavy Horse Association, such names as whippletrees and badikins, used in this context.

Then there are the hames, which fit over the collar of a horse's harness, which are traditionally made of chestnut or ash. Like the billets, the hames were also made from suitably curved butts and the iron fittings were made by the blacksmith, bent round to fit on the wood whilst hot. Nowadays a pair of old hames are often used as a wall decoration in a room.

Some of my husband's customers go so far as to have a new wooden waggon wheel made especially for use as a decorative feature in the home. Such a wheel need not be painted, of course, and looks very attractive in the wood, showing the elm of the nave, the oak of the spokes and the ash, beech or elm of the felloes. How grandfather would have scoffed at the idea of anyone standing a waggon wheel in the

lounge or hallway!

Although the bulk of my husband's work naturally consists of ordinary things, the occasional demand for repairs to old things or for new articles made in traditional way does give him the interest of utilising a range of those older skills his father taught him.

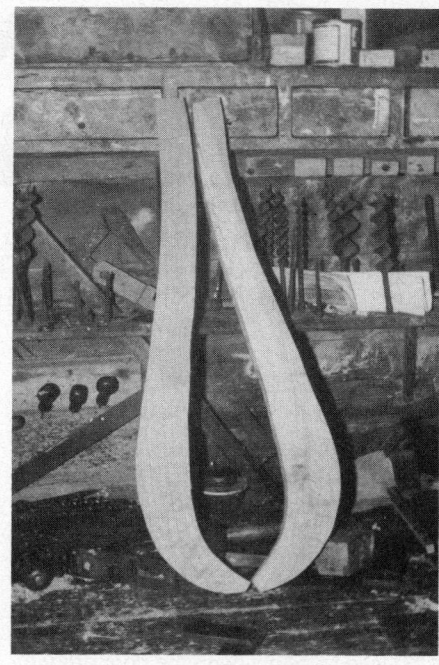

● Hames cut out in ash before trimming.

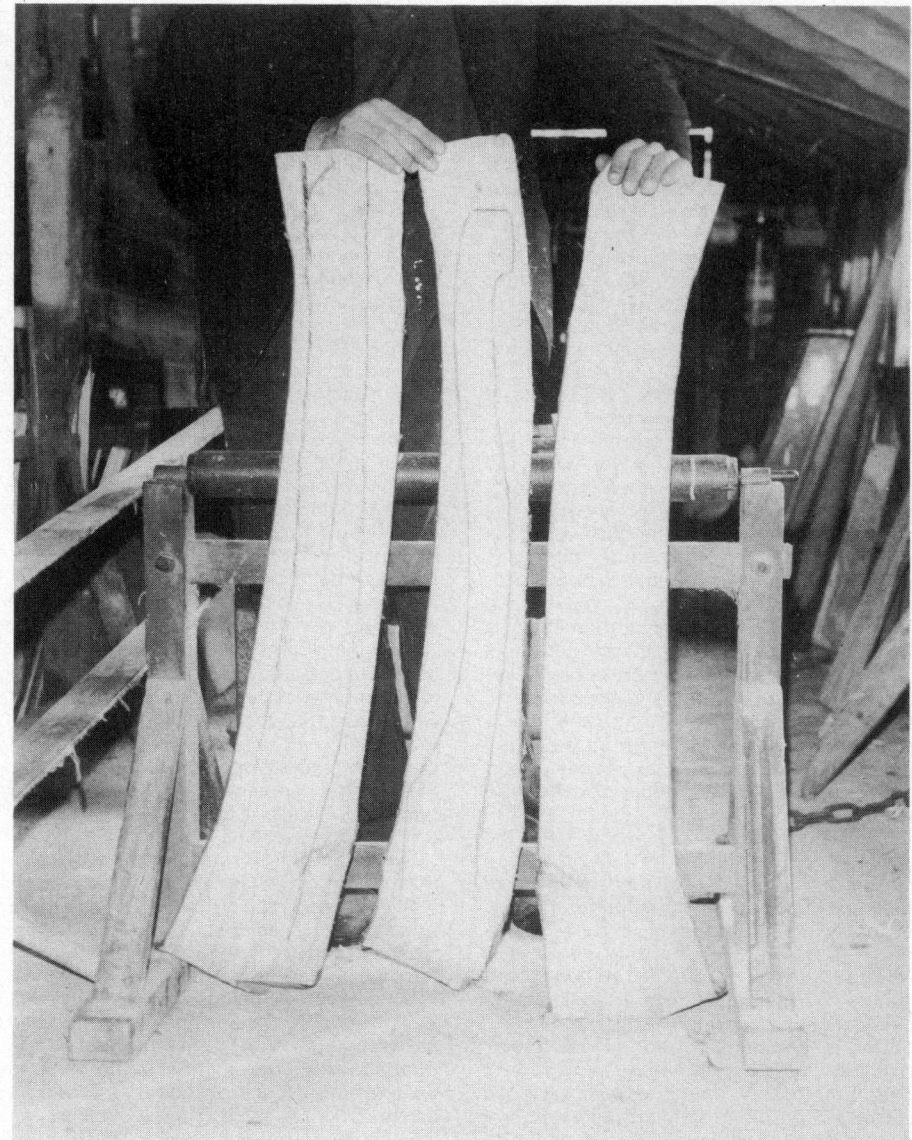

● Butts of poles cut down in halves with two marked out as for handles.

DRYING YOUR TIMBER 10

Our timber expert, Bill Brown, continues his series on the art and science of drying timber. This month he looks at further adaptations of the basic conditioning chamber described in previous articles

In recent issues of *Woodworker* we have been discussing the feasibility of making up a small chamber for the drying or conditioning of wood, and we mentioned in the original American design, an old domestic refrigerator with the door removed, was installed.

We included this in the constructional sketch (February p119) and again referred to its use in the April issue.

It is essential to the sense of the discussion to understand that if the structure is produced faithfully (with the door draught-proofed, the refrigerator connected to the power supply, with a humidistat fitted to control the cycling of the unit, and with the size of the chamber no more or less than the dimensions given) then the relative humidity of the air in the chamber should easily be maintained at 12%, equal to an equilibrium moisture content for wood of 4%.

This atmosphere is much drier than we would generally require for conditioning. 50% RH would suit just as well, but since drying, as opposed to conditioning, could be the requirement, it is as well to examine all the possibilities.

While the chances of obtaining an old refrigerator may be small, this is important only in terms of cost, because there are on the market small, portable dehumidifiers and moisture extraction units ideally suited to timber drying, as they require a more or less air-tight chamber. These are regularly being advertised in *Woodworker*.

With this mode of drying, the air within the chamber is not exchanged with the outside air and therefore does not require periodic reheating. It is recirculated and the moisture extracted from the wood is allowed to drain away as condensate.

Such a chamber as we have been describing could accordingly be sited anywhere in a workshop. Whether or not the cost of a dehumidifier in lieu of an old refrigerator is justified would depend upon personal requirements of dry timber or piece parts, and in some circumstances it might be necessary for additional equipment to be installed. It would be best to discuss your requirements with a supplier of dehumidifiers.

In many instances of wood use, the principal requirement is for the material to be brought to a fairly uniform level of moisture content, which in general terms probably means reducing it from 15-18% down to about 10%. In other words, it is reduced from an air-dried condition to one suiting wood that will be used in warm living-room conditions.

The reason why wood usually needs conditioning is because there is no control over ambient air conditions. If air-dried wood is brought into a warm workshop or similar area it will gradually dry down to equilibrium with that air, but the time in

● *Fig 1 Top of chamber modified to take two adjustable vents. Domestic fan heater to provide heat and encourage upward diagonal movement of air. See also detailed sketch February Woodworker p 119.*

which it takes to do this and the resulting quality of the wood is often conjectural.

Accordingly, if an enclosed chamber is available in which the air conditions can be regulated, even if not completely controlled, then any wood placed therein stands a better chance of being uniformly conditioned, and in quicker time.

Proper control of the air within a chamber implies that temperatures can be improved beyond ambient in order to hasten the drying, that a suitable relative humidity of the air can be maintained, and that the air can be moved, encouraging the removal of excess moisture by ventilation. This means the provision of a thermometer, a direct reading relative humidity meter, or a wet and dry bulb hygrometer, and possibly a fan to move the air.

A chamber such as we have been describing could be placed within an enclosed working area for the purpose of quickly conditioning wood. Ventilation of the chamber could be achieved by modifying the top to incorporate a couple of hinged flaps fitted with adjustable stays to facilitate partial or full opening as required. Bearing in mind that the bigger the openings are, the greater the ventilation potential, but remember too that this will also mean a greater influx of cold air to be warmed up.

Unless air movement is adequate throughout the chamber, the sluggish air will tend to become stratified and therefore non-uniform in its affect at different levels. However, since the temperature within the chamber must be warmer than without, it might be feasible to employ a small domestic fan heater to provide both heat and good air circulation, siting it on the floor at the opposite end of the chamber to the vents, so as to promote a diagonal air flow upwards, as shown in Fig 1.

Some experimentation is inevitable; for example, initially, the pick up of moisture

from the wood by virtue of the warm air could raise the relative humidity a lot higher than that aimed for. This would mean the vents needed to be opened more, or the heat shut off for a time with only the fan working.

The quality of the wood would need watching and the relative humidity adjusted to suit. In one of the American chambers, designed to develop 42% RH equal to a moisture content of 8%, a room type dehumidifier was installed together with a vaporizer and controlled by the slight movement across the grain of a 12in wide maple wood element which actuated two snap-type electrical contacts (one normally on, the other normally off). The wood sliver was set so that a movement of a few thousandths of an inch actuated one or the other.

A relative humidity of 50% at temperatures of 40°F (5°C) to 80°F (27°C) provides equilibrium moisture contents for wood of 9.4% at the lowest temperature and 9% at the highest. Corresponding values for 60% RH are 11.3% and 10.7% EMC and for 70% RH, 13.4% and 12.8% EMC.

It will be noted that, in effect, it is the relative humidity of the air that is important in bringing wood to suitable condition. Increases in temperature bring this about more quickly, but there is a limit to how much dry heat wood can tolerate without splitting and checking.

A chamber with vents, if used only for conditioning should operate comfortably in an enclosed area (say a workshop), the moisture vented from the chamber being dispersed under the normal ventilation of the workshop. Any variation from this, where wetter wood was being dried, would call for extended vents leading directly to the open air. These could be made from plywood or other material, but the inside surfaces would need protecting with bituminous paint.

NEW

BURGESS POWERLINE

2 SPEED BANDSAW MODEL BK2/FJA

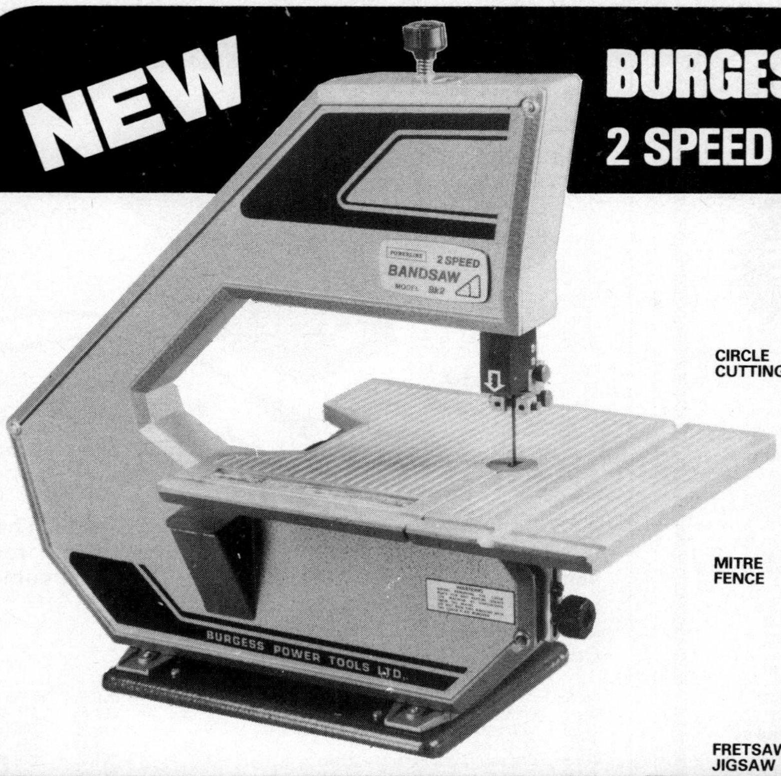

CIRCLE CUTTING

MITRE FENCE

FRETSAW JIGSAW

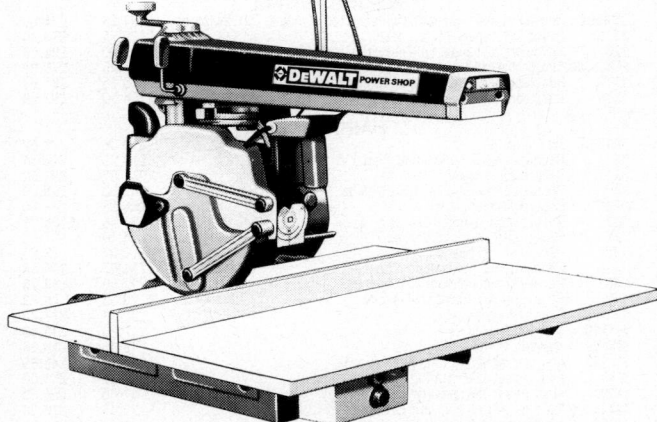

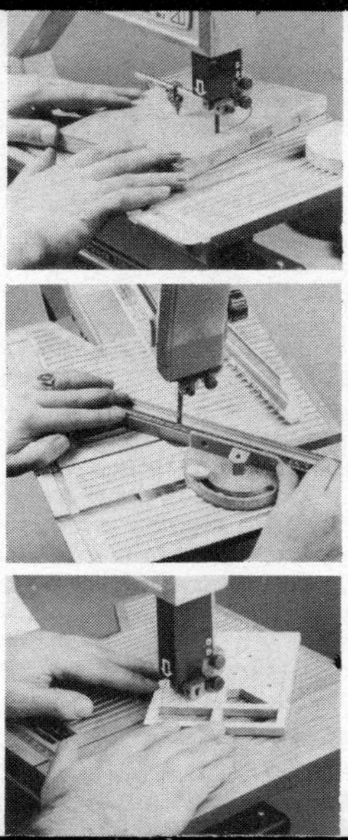

COMPLETE WITH:-

- ★ FRETSAW/JIGSAW ATTACHMENT
- ★ GENERAL PURPOSE BANDSAW BLADE
- ★ JIG SAW BLADE
- ★ PLUS 3" FRETSAW BLADES

Price

£109.55

(inc. VAT)

Carriage £5.00

Access

Cecil W. Tyzack LTD. TOOLS AND MACHINERY

VISA

79/81 Kingsland Rd., Shoreditch, E2 8AG Tel: 01-739 7126 & 2630

Turn yourself into a craftsman with the DeWalt Powershop.

How would you like to bring the stamp of a craftsman to your home woodworking? Well, with the DeWalt DW125 Powershop you can.

Basically the Powershop is a sophisticated saw that can be set to cross cut, rip cut, bevel and mitre to a wide range of lengths, depths and angles. By itself it can satisfy the needs of the most demanding home woodworker with speed and ease.

But when fitted with its various attachments it gives you the opportunity to add real craftsman's touches to your work, and opens up new horizons in home woodworking.

Grooves, rebates, decorative edges, intricate shapes, housings and mouldings appear as if by magic. Perfect joints become commonplace. And the sanding attachments add the final finishing touches that really make all the difference.

The DeWalt Powershop is one of the most versatile woodworking machines available today. Not only can it help you realise the most from your own skills, but its ease of operation makes it a pleasure to work with as your ideas take shape.

It's a must for every serious woodworker who wants to be admired as a craftsman. You'll soon wonder how you ever managed without one.

The DeWalt DW125 Powershop is available from all good tool and machinery shops and you can call Teledata on 01-200 0200 for further details.

DEWALT®

A Division of Black and Decker, Canon Lane, Maidenhead, Berks.

Prices quoted are those prevailing at press date and are subject to alteration due to economic conditions.

Woodturning from A to Z

Gordon Stokes of Bath is a well known and respected craftsman in the woodturning field. As a teacher and author of many books on woodturning, he has encountered pretty well every problem that faces a novice at the lathe, so when we decided to run a linked and progressive series of articles on woodturning, we turned, if you will pardon the pun, to Gordon Stokes. In this the first of the series, he goes back to basics with the lathe itself.

● *Typical view of professional lathe. Plenty of shavings, no dust, and rarely tidy!*

LOOKING AT LATHES

Gordon Stokes writes: My aim over the coming months will be to give a general introduction to the craft, with appropriate information regarding selection and purchase of machinery and ancillary equipment, tools, timber, and the setting up of a workshop. I hope also to deal with the commercial or semi-commercial aspects, since many are now seeking profitable sidelines, or opportunities for starting in a small way of business.

The series will progress logically through tool sharpening, basic cutting techniques, and simple projects, then move on to intermediate and advanced work, so there should be something for everyone.

The articles will be as clear as I can make them, but I will be pleased to answer any queries, which should be sent initially to the Editor, with a stamped envelope.

□   □   □

Before discussing the selection of a lathe and the essential equipment in detail, we should perhaps dispose of the perennial question – should a 'universal' machine by purchased?

From a woodturning viewpoint, where turning is the main interest, the answer is no. A separate lathe is without doubt the best choice. In an ideal situation, where neither space nor capital is limited, all machines should be individual. Most of us do not enjoy freedom from restrictions of cash or space, however, and a composite machine may well be the only possibility. If this is so, then – again from the turner's viewpoint – the Coronet Major leads the field, in my opinion. Whatever the final choice, however, do make sure that the lathe part of the machine is satisfactory, which is frequently not the case.

At a later stage we can consider machinery and equipment which is desirable, as distinct from necessary. But the immediate question at this point is the lathe itself. What points should the intending purchaser look out for, and what is the likely cost?

On the latter point it is essential to note that the woodworking machinery scene has now regrettably become discount orientated. However, there remains the fact that the best machines have little or no discount potential, since they sell well on merit and recommendation, while in general those which carry high discounts do so because they must if they are to sell.

'Caveat emptor' – let the buyer beware!

In the selection of a lathe, which hopefully will be the main item of woodturning equipment for many years to come, serious consideration is required on certain points.

Don't buy too small a machine. It is advisable to consider the possible requirements which may arise once the craft has been mastered. A small lathe will do well if woodturning is to be no more than a pleasant hobby, but if there is any idea of augmenting income, or using the machine on a commercial basis, the small machine will soon prove to be inadequate.

A lathe which will accept about 2ft 6in between centres, and is capable of swinging a disc around 18in diameter, will do virtually all the work likely to be attempted by any normal woodturner. Avoid the flimsy lightweight machines, which are most frustrating to operate, since they suffer badly from vibration problems, and which can in some cases be downright dangerous. The main points of a good lathe are as follows.

1. As heavy as possible commensurate with cash available.
2. Well made and finished, with all castings properly machined.
3. A good headstock bearing, preferably of the phosphor bronze variety, or a high quality bearing which can be adjusted or replaced by the user.
4. Rigidity in the headstock itself.
5. A bed which can be kept clean and free from build-up of shavings, so that tailstock and saddles (or banjos if no saddles are used) can be moved easily.
6. Sufficient clearance between bed and

● *Sturdy tailstock which does its job well. Centre fitted here is Coronet heavy duty type.*

● *Good quality revolving centre from Arrand Engineering (left). Drive centre (right) fits through centre ejector which is then screwed onto lathe mandrel.*

● *Drive system on older Coronet Majors gave three speeds. The current system gives five, using Poly-Vee drive. The machine shown here is the one I use, which has a gearbox, giving total of six speeds over two drive ratios.*

Woodturning

(Continued from page 317)

bench top to permit tools to be laid on the bench without difficulty.

7. ALL clamps on the machine must be solid, efficient in operation, easily operated, and out of the way of the hands and tools when in use.

8. Sensibly shaped and well made tool rests (I doubt if you'll find these!) A badly shaped tool rest makes the work awkward, and can often be a source of danger. It may be necessary to have some made up locally.

9. Speed in woodturning will be dealt with later in the series, but choose a machine which offers at least four speeds in its range, covering 5-600rpm up to about 3,000.

10. Drive and tailstock centres should be no1 Morse taper, except on the larger machines, where no2 is often used. Such machines are designed for constant use in the turning of very large and often heavy items, and so do not concern us here.

11. The best lathes are provided with *two* toolrest holders (banjos) so that a twin pinned toolrest which runs the full length of the lathe can be employed. This is essential on long workpieces.

12. The tailstock must be heavily constructed so that no significant movement is possible in use, and well engineered so that head and tailstock centres will line up accurately. Before buying, slide the tailstock up as close as possible to the headstock, with centres in both, and check the alignment when the tailstock clamp is tightened.

13. Avoid gimmicks or fiddly attachments such as lathe 'steadies' – at least for the time being.

14. Try to select a machine which will accept as wide a range of chucks and other equipment as possible.

15. A good electric motor is important, and there are some strange ones about. Look for a Brook, or perhaps a Newman, continuously rated, which should be ¾ or 1hp for the larger home user machines, and ½ or ¾hp for the smaller ones.

16. There is nothing wrong with a grinding wheel mounted on the outboard side if the lathe permits – though I prefer a separate grinder.

That covers all the important features, but remember that the headstock is there to support the lathe spindle and permit it to rotate about its longitudinal axis *without any other significant movement.*

Newcomers to the craft should also bear in mind that although a woodturning lathe is mechanical, in the sense that it is normally driven by a motor, it does nothing whatsoever for the woodturner other than to rotate the material. Metal turning lathes, if correctly set and sufficiently sophisticated, will perform a variety of tasks with little or no help from the operator. Woodturning lathes merely rotate the material and the turning itself depends for its quality and accuracy upon the manipulative skill of the turner.

It is this manipulative skill, together with a satisfactory comprehension of the fundamentals of woodturning which will make up this series.

Woodworker's bookshelf

Painted chairs

The reader who last year asked Question Box for guidance on restoring painted furniture may find additional information in *How to Restore and Decorate Chairs in Early American Styles*. This is a long title for a book of 127 pages in soft covers; it is written by Roberta R. Blanchard and comes from Dover Publications Inc of New York. Sales in UK are handled by Constable & Co Ltd, 10 Orange Street, London WC2H 7EG. The price is £3 and the ISBN 0-486-24177-7.

It should be added that this 1981 edition is an unabridged reproduction of a work originally issued in 1952 by another American publisher. Obviously, therefore, the edition does not take account of more up-to-date information on the subject.

Why paint furniture? It seems that American cabinetmakers who admired the brass inlays and costly filigree of the imported French furniture in the early days of the 19th century, substituted for the expensive metal inlays clever brushwork in bronze powders and gold leaf. As business expanded more and more short cuts were taken by means of stencils. Painting could also have been adopted as a means of camouflaging pieces in which differing species of timber were used.

Styles covered include early and late Sheraton fancy; ladder, arrow and fiddle-backs; early and late Boston rockers; Hitch-cocks; country-type Windsors; landscape medallion Pennsylvania style; and thumb-backs. The author discusses the types of decoration; terms, materials, surface preparation; background finishes; brush-stroke painting; stencilling techniques; and gold leaf and other techniques. This comprises part 1.

In part 2 she deals with the history of the various styles and working designs. Throughout she gives step-by-step directions and a great many recipes which make interesting reading and have possible application in other sectors of woodworking.

The many illustrations – photographs, line drawings, diagrams – are adequate, though the reproduction of the photographs, in particular, lacks some of the fine detail on the original pieces. The stencils seem rather clumsy as shown in the book but they serve as guides. **G.P.**

□   □   □

Woodwork one and two

Woodwork 1 (third edition) and *Woodwork 2* (second edition) by David Willacy, published by Thomas Nelson & Sons Ltd, Nelson House, Mayfield Road, Walton, Surrey at £3.35 each, are companion volume text books written with woodwork examinations in secondary schools firmly in mind and as such are excellent examples of their type. Their popularity is proved; they are now in their second and third editions, the format is clear and excellent line drawings complement the text. However, the contents represent a corpus of knowledge that school's examination boards (CSE and GCE) deem to be relevant and examinable but which in my experience stirs agony in the breasts of the intended readers.

Pupils coming eagerly into school workshops do not want to be told 'theory lesson today, get out your books'; they want to make something. Time was when workshop theory was taught as some incidental to a practical demonstration by a master and the knowledge came from the practice. Yet, in some of our modern woodworking examinations theoretical expertise is approaching 50% of the total and much valuable workshop time has to be devoted to the study of the theoretical aspects of the craft.

Perhaps schools and examinations boards are in danger of debasing what C. R. Ashbee called the education of the 'head, hands and heart'.

Even the word workshop is becoming suspect. Its use has spread to other spheres of life and we now hear of 'music workshops' instead of rehearsals and 'oral workshops' instead of discussions, we cannot be far from 'theory workshops'!

None of this is Mr Willacy's fault (although he is a chief woodwork examiner) but his books are a response to the academic demands of what is surely a practical craft.

Volume 1 is a virtual catalogue of woodworking tools, equipment and materials with specific chapters devoted to workshop drawing and that most complicated of subjects, design. Volume 2 deals with designing for both traditional and modern constructions concluding with a miscellany of chapters devoted to turning, carving, laminating etc. All of these are necessarily simplified and would need supplementing by reference to specialist books in carrying out a practical task.

Despite my reservations about existing examinations requirements these books are admirable and might also serve anyone starting out on the fascinating activity of making things from wood. They are thorough and excellent background primers.

R.W.G.

□   □   □

Tricks of the trade

There cannot be a craftsman in the country who has not, at one time or another, had to invent a device or system to solve a technical problem. It should be no surprise to discover that such problems are rarely unique. What Robert Wearing has done in *Woodwork aids and devices* is to collect 200 solutions to as many problems and presented them in this fascinating compendium of tried and tested 'tricks of the trade'.

The aids and devices are described with clear line drawings and a concise text in seven sections which cover not only solutions to the common problems of holding materials, but aids to marking out and cutting. The latter either speed-up work or eliminate error. Sections on lathework, drilling and disc-sanding acknowledge the expanding use of machines by the home craftsman.

A well produced bound book printed on an attractive cream paper, it will be a useful source of reference for many home craftsmen. Others may simply use it to refine their existing aids and devices. Published by Evans Bros Ltd, Montague House, Russell Square, London WC1B 5BX at £6.95 (ISBN 0-237-44995-1).

D.M.W.

Beginners start here

The latest Newnes Technical Book, *Beginners Guide to Woodturning,* is a good introductory book to this most ancient of woodcrafts. A small paperback of just over 180pp, it is packed with essential basic know-how for those who have just started turning and for those who are still thinking about getting started.

Woodturning seems to hold a special fascination, unique among the woodcrafts. As the long shavings curl away from the chisel or gouge, the cutting edge of the tool seeming only to gently kiss the wood as it revolves, the workpiece takes shape, its contoured outline revealing rich grain patterns previously hidden within the wood. There is an ease about the turner's work which is deceptive, however, for good turning comes only with knowledge, with experience and with practice. This book, based on the author's experience, provides a good start to acquiring that knowledge. For practice, a lathe is required.

As is pointed out in the preface the book is not large enough to cover the subject fully. But I think the authors, Frank Underwood and Gordon Warr, who also wrote *Beginners Guide to Woodworking* in the same series, have got the essentials together in one place and this is what really matters.

Published by The Butterworth Group, Borough Green, Sevenoaks TN15 8PH in the Newnes Technical Book series at £3.60 (soft cover) ISBN 0-408-00507-6.

J.H.

□ □ □

This one's a classic

Stanley Doubtfire, an engraver by training and a guitar maker by persuasion and inspiration, has produced an extraordinary book. *Make your own classical guitar* published by Victor Gollancz Ltd, 14 Henrietta St, London WC2E 8QJ at £15.00 (ISBN 0-575-02980 3) It combines a grasp of his craft with a keen appreciation of the musical implications for that craft. His exposition shows clearly that he is an experienced player. He communicates his method at just the right level, and has also persuaded four famous makers to discuss their craft in a chapter at the end of the book.

It is a most attractive book, well illustrated with the author's own drawings and photographs, and is a pleasure to handle. Perhaps at this price we could have offered a few colour plates, in particular where subtleties of the grain matching are being discussed. This would have made his point more clearly. However, he is usually well served by the illustrations.

The book is in three parts. In the first part there is a brief discussion of how what Berlioz called 'the orchestra in miniature' works; what materials are traditionally used; sizes required and a useful list of suppliers; what tools are required and some tools that the maker can and should make himself.

Part two is concerned with the making of the instrument and part three describes the work of five famous makers.

My one concern for such a finely produced book is that if it is to adorn one's bookshelf and be of use in the workshop,

one needs to buy two copies or devise some way of transcribing the information for workshop use.

Instruction books are not usually such a good read as this.

We learn that Mr Doubtfire is teaching himself to play the lute. Can we look forward to a similar volume on lute making?

E.J.C.

□ □ □

● *Master housewright Roy Underhill, author of* The Woodwright's Shop *with some of the old tools of his trade.*

Technology of the past

The Woodwright's Shop by Roy Underhill is, as its subtitle clearly states, a practical guide to traditional woodcraft. It is an American book and describes the American scene, but for all this it is an excellent guide to old ways of working wood using old tools and the simple technology of a bygone age.

As a traditional woodcraftsman the book has a great deal of appeal for me. And I am sure it will interest all who like to experience the intimate relationship with real wood that the old craftsmen enjoyed before machinery took away some of that joy in the imposed needs of speed. There is pleasure in the book, too, for those who share the idea that wood is one of our most valuable resources and that treated with understanding, it can, as it did so adequately in the past, provide so many of man's needs.

The book is packed with good, general information and illustrated with over 340 photographs, including four pages in colour. There is sufficient detail to enable the practical-minded to try out much, if not all, of the work described. But those who just like to learn about craftsmanship in a historical context will find the work very readable and equally interesting.

It is published in US by University of North Carolina Press, PO Box 2288, Chapel Hill, North Carolina 27514, at $11.95 paper $19.95 cloth.

J.H.

□ □ □

Sitting duck

The prospective buyer of *Carving duck decoys* by Harry Shourds and Anthony Hillman who might look forward to some hours of interesting and informative reading, is in for some disappointment. It takes

less than quarter of an hour to read from cover to cover. On the positive side almost the whole of the book is taken up with full-scale working drawings for the construction of sixteen varieties of duck decoys. These are intended to be removed, cut out and mounted on plywood for use as templates.

It seems unlikely that this book will be of wide interest in this country. If decoy ducks are used here to any extent, manufacture from moulded plastics would be cheaper and more practical. There may be some demand as collectors' items, but from a carver's point of view, one duck decoy is very much like another, and producing these in quantity would become monotonous and give little scope for self-expression.

Available in this country from Constable and Co, 10 Orange St, London WC2, price £3.20, ISBN 0-486-24083-5.

A.A.

□ □ □

Flashy but comprehensive

Apart from its title — *General Woodworking* — Chris H. Groneman's book on first sight looks more like a treatise on confectionery, for the cover unfortunately resembles a half-opened box of candy. There is far too much lurid colour throughout its pages, which is a pity in view of the fact that nature's most subtle and beautiful shades of colour are to be found in wood.

The book is essentially scholastic in character and while it is 'widely used for the first-year course in woodworking' the contents are far too comprehensive to be so described. In fact it is one of the fullest descriptions of elementary woodworking that I have ever seen.

Most profusely illustrated, the book is in its 6th edition. Apart from its flashy appearance, it is an excellent work for schools; but it is written for American pupils and as such has a somewhat limited appeal in this country.

It is published by McGraw-Hill Book Co (UK) Ltd, Shoppenhangers Road, Maidenhead SL6 2QL, at £12.50 (ISBN 0-07-025003-0)

C.B.

□ □ □

Anatomy of a housebuilder

The author of *The housebuilding experience* Jack McLaughlin teaches humanities at Clemson University, South Carolina, and has previously written on various popular culture subjects, particularly concentrating on the way we respond subjectively to creative experiences. After building his own house, in spite of a total lack of construction experience and skills, he began to investigate how other owner builders felt about constructing their own dwellings.

An entertaining book in the American style. Designing for identity and some of the sections such as time, skills and building materials and tools cross the Atlantic; but chapters on zoning regulations, building codes, costs, finance, etc do not. Published by Van Nostrand Reinhold Co Ltd, Molly Millars Lane, Wokingham RG11 2PY at £12.70 hardback (ISBN 0-442-25398-2). **P.C.**

Carving a cormorant

Harry Turner has been guiding the novice woodcarver through the basic stages of the craft in recent issues of Woodworker. In this his third article, Harry takes the subject a step further by inviting readers to try their hand at carving a cormorant

Fig 1

In the first two articles in the series you have seen the controlled approach to wood carving, which achieves mass form in the simplest possible way. Now we can apply this method to a further subject.

Any tendency to rush at the work to achieve detail as soon as possible must be curbed; patience is needed. It is preferable to slowly carve a detail several times to obtain the desired result, bearing in mind that having detailed one portion the remainder goes out of proportion. Therefore a continued balancing and carving to detail must proceed together.

In Fig 1 a front and side view of a cormorant is illustrated with proportional squaring.

With Fig 2 a variation to approach is introduced, basically on account of a thinner piece of wood. The method of priming the surfaces white and 'fixing' the drawings is as previously described, but in this instance the original full-size drawing (side view only) should be on stout tracing paper. The drawing is then accurately located and superimposed over carbon paper on to the wood.

This applies to both sides of the wood, by reversing tracing paper to apply second drawing. Although we have produced a front view drawing (Fig 1) this is ignored for the time being.

All preparation having been made, initial hewing can take place as shown in Fig 3, but to reduce gouge and mallet work, saw off surplus wood behind the cormorant. In front of the bird it is easier to make a series of cuts with a tenon saw, spaced at approximately ½in (12mm) centres to required depth, but keeping outside the drawn line. It is then simple to remove surplus wood with gouge and mallet with minimum of effort.

With Fig 4 reference is made to the front view drawing. Draw a centre line down the wood, with the drawing pencilled in about this line, if required with the aid of a rule or calipers. At this stage it is of personal choice if one thin coat of varnish is applied over this secondary drawn detail.

The toned portions containing the head detail, on both sides, are removed with a tenon saw and carefully retained.

Fig 5 illustrates cutting away surplus wood down to drawn lines, this results in the somewhat strange appearance shown in Fig 6, where the form of the bird comprises four flat sides.

The really satisfying part of the work can now proceed as shown in Fig 7, by searching for and realising the true form. As an extra aid to the normal human eye balancing, a contour gauge is very helpful. This can be depressed on to one side, held in position, and a pencil line drawn.

It is then reversed and placed against the ends of the previous pencil line and marked with a further pencil line. By this method we achieve a series of contour lines which can easily be reinstated with pencil after careful paring and balancing with a gouge.

At this point the two off-cuts (Fig 4) will be found to be very useful, by placing alongside the work for systematically drawing in detail with a pencil as the carved detail proceeds, it is infinitely easier than trying to hold the original drawing against the work.

Finally with Fig 8 directional cutting is illustrated on the finished work.

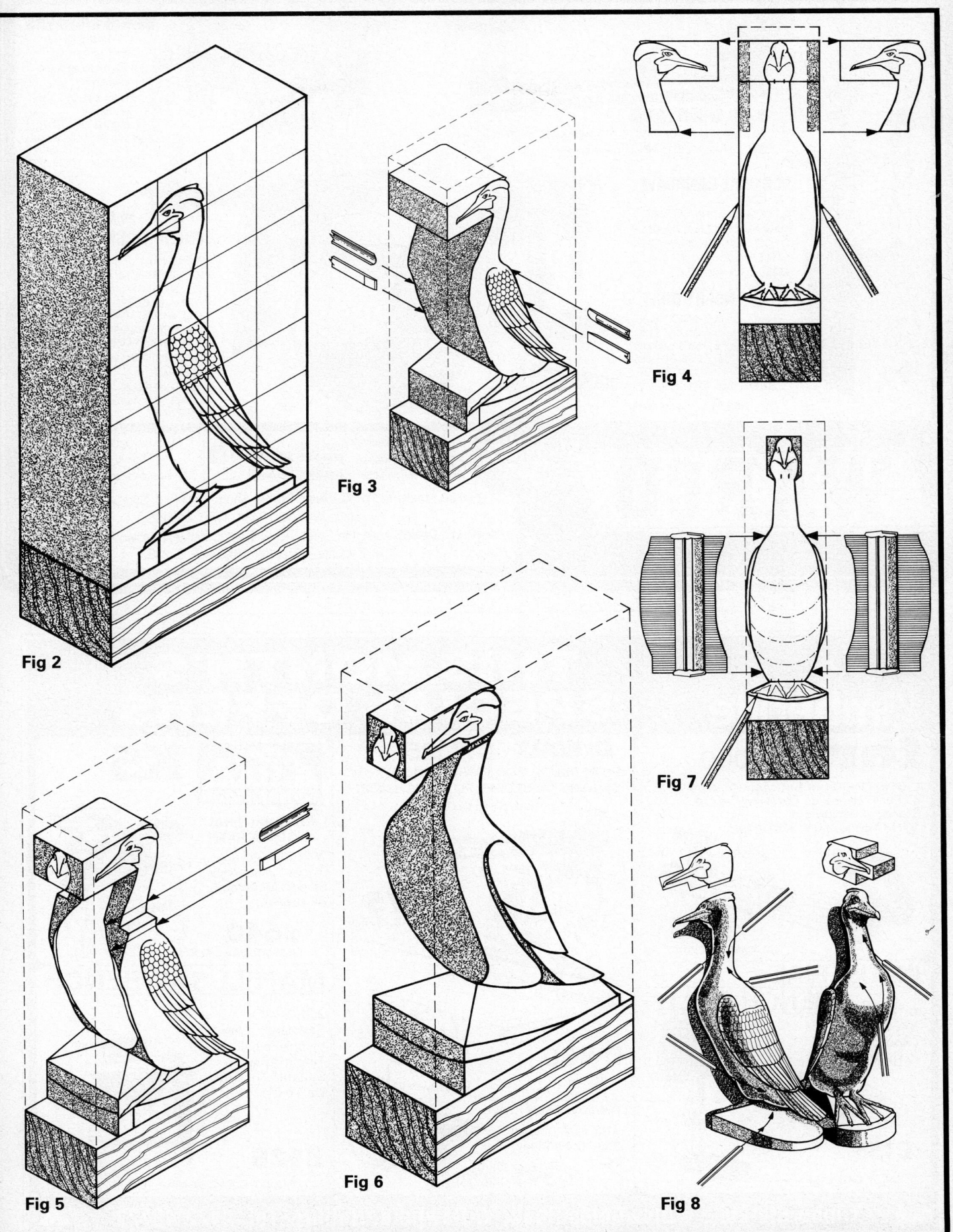

Fig 2

Fig 3

Fig 4

Fig 5

Fig 6

Fig 7

Fig 8

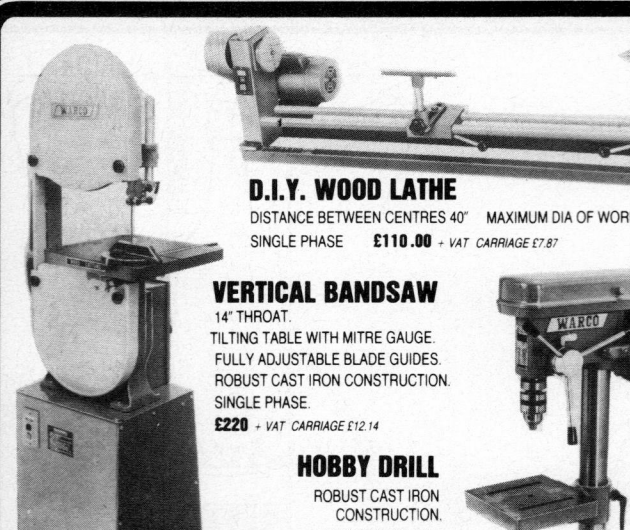
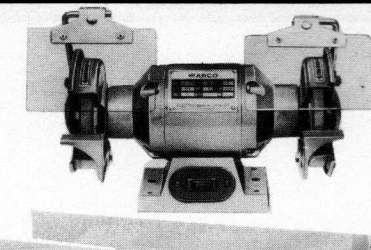

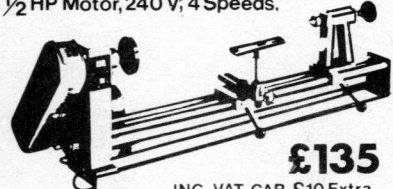

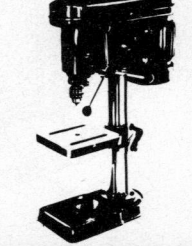
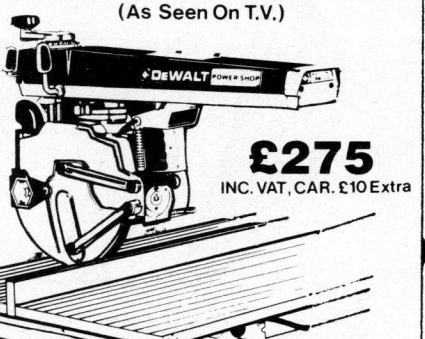

Almost instant patina

J. H. McCormick explains his methods for obtaining an almost instant patina and details his hot wax method which he says produces a lovely honey smell as an added bonus

The essence of hot-waxing is to seal the grain of new surfaces, or surfaces that have been cleaned-off by, for example, a chemical agent which leaves the grain open and absorbent. The method is to melt pure beeswax on the surface and then by friction (vigorous rubbing with a cloth) to impregnate the surface as deeply as possible with the molten wax.

To seal the grain I apply a mixture of turps and beeswax on the wood surface (white spirit will not do). I add 1pt of turps to 10oz of flaked wax then melt in a water-bath or double saucepan. The mixture must not be placed over direct heat as it is flammable. This mixture is then painted on everywhere by brush.

On an absorbent surface there will be an immediate darkening after waxing but this will disappear within about 24hr. That period of time must elapse before any subsequent application of wax.

There are several ways of applying the wax. You can borrow the cheesegrater from the kitchen and by means of the coarsest section liberally sprinkle the scrapings of wax all over the surface (Fig. 1). Obviously this way is suitable only for horizontal or near-horizontal surfaces. Or you can hold the mass of wax in your hand and soften its surface with a flame from a gas blowtorch and immediately rub the softened area on to the wood until no more comes away.

But the way I find most satisfactory is to melt the wax in the water-bath and when molten paint it into the grain with a brush (Fig. 2). Not only is this a quick way but it is suitable for use on angled, upright or upside down surfaces. I take care not to put too much on and find a dab here and there is sufficient, covering about 75% of the total area. Cover thinly is a good motto as the wax is expensive. Moreover, a thick coating leaves a lot of waste to deal with when applying the heat source (the gas blowtorch).

To melt the wax thoroughly on the surface of the workpiece I use the gas blowtorch with fish-tail burner. I keep a lighted candle handy during this operation in case the nozzle gets blocked and the flame goes out. It is essential to keep the flame moving as otherwise charring can occur or the wax catch alight. If you are unfortunate enough to get charring, such as on the raised sections of a moulding, fine glasspaper will remove it.

Having made what is in effect a flowing wax puddle, I rub vigorously with an absorbent cloth in the form of a large pad which fills my hand. I find that towelling or cheesecloth are suitable; even an old woollen garment can be used. If I have applied too much wax at once the pad becomes saturated. I keep turning the pad so as to offer a fresh clean surface to the hot wax. When the pad has become completely saturated I discard it. I have tried boiling the wax out of cloths for re-use, but without success.

Subsequently, the surface will need an occasional rub with a soft cloth to bring-up the patina.

For readers who are interested in all aspects of finishing and polishing furniture, Guild of Woodworkers regularly run courses on the subject. For details of these contact the Administrator, Guild of Woodworkers, PO Box 35, Bridge Street, Hemel Hempstead HP1 1EE. Please enclose a sae.

● Left: softening the wax using a gentle blow torch flame

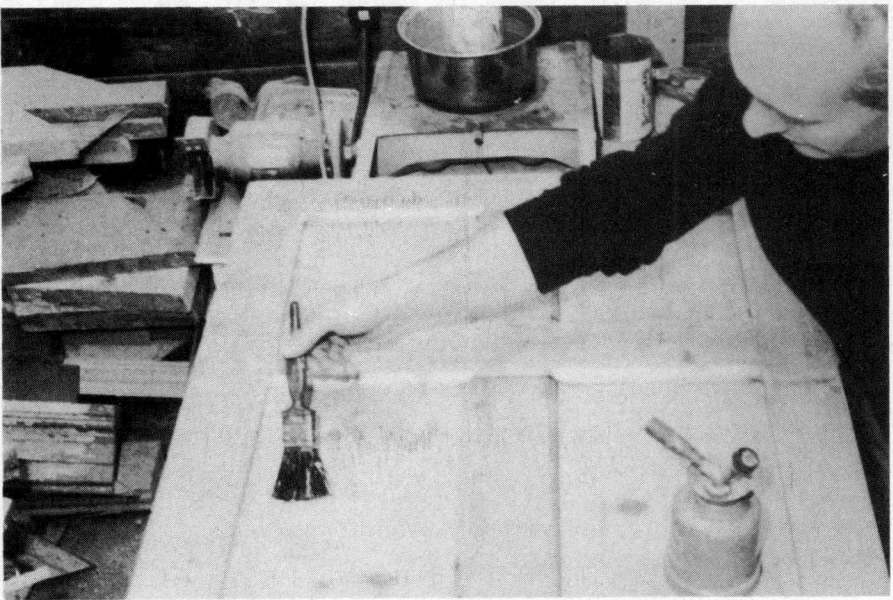

● Painting the wax into the grain with a brush

When renovating old furniture I apply the hot wax sparingly after first making sure that the original finish was wax. I keep the flame of the blowtorch on the move and vigorously rub the surface with a dry cloth. This brings off a great amount of dirt but leaves a patina you did not imagine could exist.

To me the great satisfaction of the hot-wax method is the instant patina; and of course there is a lovely smell of honey everywhere!

Another 'STAR-TURN' from PRECISION PETITE

A fully adjustable MINI WOOD-TURNING LATHE

Precision Petite have produced another winner for craftsmen and hobbyists – a miniature wood-turning lathe that is positive and reliable. Driven by the famous P3 or P2 drills, powered by a small variable-speed transformer or can be operated from a 12v battery.

Can be clamped to bench or table-top, clamps (optional extra), or screwed vertically on bench. The holding pin is mounted on a free-running bearing.

You can now produce that miniature reproduction furniture or those boat fittings – the possibilities are unlimited.

Price £19.95 inc. VAT plus £1.50 p&p (excluding drill). Send SAE for full details today.

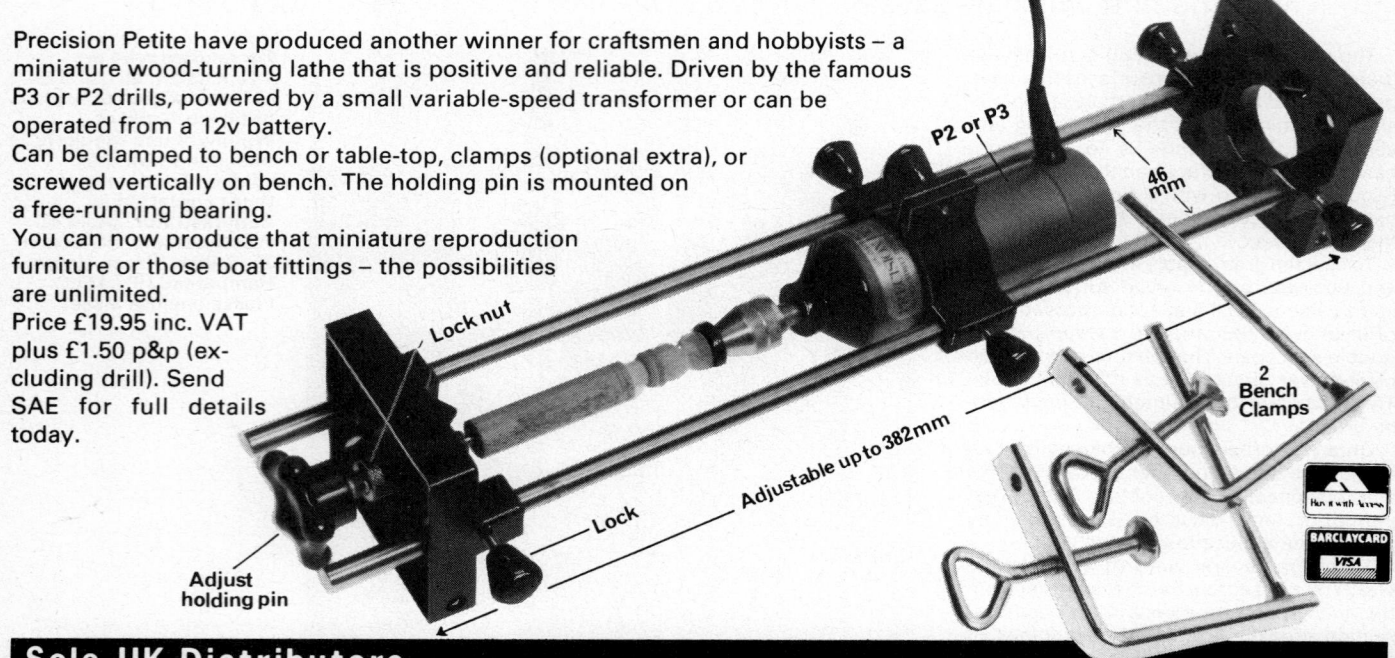

Lock nut

P2 or P3

46 mm

2 Bench Clamps

Adjust holding pin

Lock

Adjustable up to 382mm

Prices quoted are those prevailing at press date and are subject to alteration due to economic conditions.

Our panel of experts
answer queries about
your workshop problems

Woodworker's Question Box

Write to: Question Box
Woodworker
PO Box 35
Bridge Street
Hemel Hempstead HP1 1EE

Inlaying a chess board
From: T. G. Prior, Market Drayton

I have been commissioned to make a coffee table in oak. My client is supplying the wood, which was originally the head and foot boards of a solid oak bedstead, the wood is old and should be well seasoned, it is about ¾in. thick.

Making the table does not present any particular problems, but my client has asked me to inlay a chess board, which will not be covered and will therefore be permanently visible in the finished table top.

I am writing to you for advice regarding the best materials to use for the chess board and the best method of inlaying these in the oak top. If there is any risk of the top warping how best can this be avoided?

We note that your client has stipulated an inlaid top which precludes the use of interesting techniques such as dyeing or texturing the wood and you will have to employ veneers for the job. To gain the necessary effect you will have to select contrasting woods such as a light coloured beech, holly or sycamore placed against a darker wood. (You could of course dye/stain the light wood selected for the dark pieces. In view of the fact that the whole job is to be made from oak, why not try fuming oak veneers for the dark squares? This would ensure that the whole job would have some harmony and continuity.

The inlaying of the chequered square into a solid top will present problems and even access to a portable machine router will necessitate guide pieces and a false bed to carry out the job. We would therefore advise you to adopt the more usual method adopted in these circumstances and veneer the whole top. This is carried out on a suitable ground such as chipboard which is then lipped on its edges with a solid wood moulding. In your case this would entail laying the games board in the centre portion of the top and surrounding it with strips of oak veneer which could be mitred at the corners to give the whole top a framed effect. At the junction of the games board edge and the surrounding frame it would be as well to put in a piece of contrasting stringing to define the limits of the board. It should be noted that the reverse of the top will also have to be veneered to counterbalance the pull of the face veneer.

A simple way to make the chequered board itself is to prepare alternate strips of the contrasting veneers (of sufficient length to span the playing surface plus a bit for trimming) and glue them edge to edge down onto a sheet of newspaper. When dry strips can be cut off across the width staggering each piece so obtained by one square. The whole can be reglued onto another sheet of newspaper and when dry turned over and stuck to its ground. Scraping and glasspapering will remove the newspaper to reveal the chequerboard.

Finally any of the conventional methods of fixing a top to an underframe should prevent warping and these are given in the article by C. D. Cliffe in *Woodworker* February 1982 p103.

Skew chisels
From: B. E. Nicholson, Harrogate

I am relatively new to woodturning and would like some advice regarding skew chisels. I understand from reading that the bevels on a chisel should be flat, underlined that the bevels should at all times be kept rubbing on the wood to avoid digging-in. I have lately been given a skew chisel which looks fairly unused and the cutting edge appears to have been professionally ground. In a copy of *Woodworker* I have seen a picture of a similar chisel but do not understand how it is possible to keep the bevel 'rubbing' as the slight radius prevents this. I would be grateful for any help.

Confusion on the correct shape for the bevel of a gouge or chisel is quite common, and is due at least in part to the fact that at one time these tools were manufactured with bevels which were convex in shape. It is possible for an expert to use a tool which is shaped so, but it is highly unlikely that an expert would bother to do so.

A bevel with a flat surface is better, but ideally the tool should be ground on the convex curve of a grindstone, so that it is hollow ground. The only exception is the bevel of a gouge which is to be used on the inside of bowls, which is sometimes ground with a slight convex shape.

A skew chisel should *never* have a convex curve to its bevel, though constant use of an oilstone – rarely used by experts on turning tools – can bring about this undesirable condition quite quickly.

THE ATTRACTIVE FACE OF DISEASE

Mr James Crutchlow of Welwyn Garden City didn't just stand by and watch when some trees were being felled on the green. He made sure that some of the timber, at least, was put to good use.

'I collared two trunks, stood them for a year, then proceeded to saw them into manageable sizes,' he told us, enclosing in his letter some small samples of the wood for our comments.

'They come from a small (8ft high) ornamental tree with a reasonable sized girth and a very straight trunk, and my naturalist GP informs me they are called "whippy elm". Stricken by the elm disease, they were felled a year after dying back.'

Mr Crutchlow reckoned they would only be good for inlay or veneer facings.

'I was very surprised at the configurations and colours,' he reports. 'Some of the work I have done is very attractive.'

We sent the samples to our timber consultant, who responds thus:

These are typical of what the trade would call doaty, dopey, or dozy wood and what the Americans call spalted wood. Actually, the figuration is due to the initiation of fungal decay, technically known as incipient decay.

The regard with which Mr Crutchlow has paid his wood is interesting because we tend, as individuals, to see wood in different lights according to what we hope to use it for.

Many years ago, there was much adverse publicity given in the press to a suite of furniture whose drawer sides carried the stencilled trade mark of a well-known food company. 'Furniture made from sugar boxes?' was the cry; had the stencil been sanded off, no one would have complained, because technically, there was nothing wrong with the soundness, appearance, and functional ability of the wood in question.

Just so with incipient decay. In the trade, it is considered extremely bad practice to stack timber in such a way that it becomes doaty, while in good class furniture production, and this includes school furniture in beech, doaty wood is rejected, quite often even from unseen underframes. At the other end of the wood-using scale, people with an eye to the aesthetic appeal of wood can turn doaty wood to good account. The Japanese have been doing this for many years, and more recently wood turners here and in America have begun to recognise how attractive this type of wood can be.

The reference above to bad stacking of timber needs explanation. All wood species have a degree of natural resistance to decay, some like beech are classified as perishable, while elm is non-durable. If woods like these in board or plank form are stacked wet but in such a way that air cannot flow easily over the wood, and this often happens if the ends of boards in one layer rest on those in the layer below, the one or other of dozens of fungal types could start to develop.

Initially, the attacked wood loses its colour in patches, generally becoming cream-coloured or yellowish; later the zones are often enclosed by a blackish line of corky material and is so contained. This is decay in incipient form; if the wood is allowed to remain wet, the yellow zones gradually soften and decay.

In the case of Mr Crutchlow's logs (tree killed by Dutch elm disease) the wood would already have some fungal spores and evidence of attack present in the tree at the time of felling.

Death of the tree would be due to combined beetle and fungal attack which is responsible for tyloses to become over-developed, so blocking the large pores in the wood. Other fungal forms could also attack the dead tree or the logs left standing on end.

Accordingly, the wood could have already been marked with incipient decay at the time of felling or it could have developed in the log since the blocked pores would slow down or defeat drying, or it could be a combination of both. The wood needs proper drying now, otherwise it could become porous enough as to interfere with good finishing treatment. There is already evidence in one sample piece of the cross fracturing typical of actual decay.

May notes

Ply that fails to comply

Growing concern about the quality and reliability of certain brands of marine plywood has led the British Standards Institution to test some suspect products.

Eleven boards, all generally available in the market place and all purporting to comply with BS1088 (plywood for marine craft), though not stamped with the official Kitemark, were rigorously tested according to BSI specifications.

And the results were alarming.

Not one complied fully with the requirements of BS1088. Although some of the points of failure could be considered minor, others were decidedly major. Four boards failed because of manufacturing defects and three failed the bonding test, one seriously.

Other failures concerned aspects such as veneer quality, which the purchaser could perhaps identify by visual examination. Three boards failed to identify either manufacturer or country of origin, with a further four not identifying country of origin – both requirements of the standard and important for traceability in the event of subsequent failure in use.

Although any manufacturer can claim compliance with this standard – and use words to that effect on his product – only plywood bearing the Kitemark has BSI's independent assurance that this is indeed the case.

From the results of the tests, the message is clear – to be confident of conformity with BS1088, look for the Kitemark on marine plywood.

Recent purchase

In 1981, Cheltenham Art Gallery and Museum organised the first major exhibition on the work of the architect/designer, Charles Robert Ashbee and the Guild of Handicraft. The museum is especially pleased to be able to add one of the most striking exhibits from that show, a cabinet designed by Ashbee and made by the Guild of Handicraft, to its permanent collection of Arts and Crafts furniture.

This cabinet is a particularly ingenious and colourful reworking of the traditional Spanish vargueno: a basic box structure

● Goshawk with grouse by William Vernon Hazzard, one of the sculptures in the exhibition organised by the Leigh Yawkey Woodson Art Museum of Wisconsin and sponsored by Gulf Oil. 50 paintings and 10 sculptures are at the Natural History Museum, South Kensington, London until 1 May.

equipped with drawers, cupboards and pigeonholes and supported on a stand which inspired many Arts and Crafts designers. Veneered in willow and ebony, its surfaces are additionally inlaid, painted or lined with morocco leather. The original silver-plated and wrought-iron fittings have survived intact.

Bon mould

Bonhams, the Knightsbridge auctioneers and valuers, held a sale of unusual interest recently, for the lots up for auction all came from a long-established but unnamed framing business.

Among the 200 lots there were 100 reverse moulds, some dating back as far as Robert Adam and several known to have been made by Thomas Wall, an 18th century reverse carver of great renown.

The technique of using reverse moulds in framing began around 1780, when it was realised that demand was far outstripping the possible supply of elaborately carved picture frames of the period.

A cheaper and quicker method of producing carved frames was required, to allow greater flexibility, so framers turned to moulded decoration rather than individually carved figuring.

There was a profession of reverse carvers who did nothing but carve these moulds for fine composition frames. Framemakers would buy their designs and then mass-produce mouldings in their own workshops. A composition of resin, glue and plaster, with the consistency of putty, was pressed into the oiled mould, and when it had hardened it was stuck to the wooden frame with a mixture called whiting.

The moulds in Bonhams' sale were principally of boxwood and mahogany, among other hardwoods, dating from 1780 to 1850.

Sack cloth and ashes

In April 1981 *Woodworker* p228 we published an article on Cheltenham museum and the collections of furniture of the Cotswold group. We are indebted to Ms Carruthers, assistant keeper of decorative arts at Leicestershire museums group for pointing out that we had omitted to include an acknowledgement to the catalogue from which we obtained a large proportion of our information. We rectify that omission here, with apologies to all concerned. The catalogue of works by *Ernest Gimson and the Cotswold Group* can be obtained from the Publications Assistant, Leicestershire Museums, Art Galleries and Records Service, 96 New Walk, Leicester at £2.50 plus 50p p/p.

Correction

We would like to point out that the wrong caption was appended to the picture at the foot of page 186 in our March issue. The caption should read Below: Barrie using the K627 spindle moulder.

● The Ashbee cabinet – see 'recent purchase'.

WATER, WIND AND WOOD

Pictures by Nigel Barklie (Venn Mill) and Bill Wilkinson (Marsh Mill)

The restoration in recent years of wind and water mills, which has done so much to enhance the rural skyline, has also vividly recalled the millwright's skilful use of timber. Though the milling process itself was effected by grinding stones, a mill relied upon the strength and durability of timber for much of its structure and mechanism. Here we celebrate in pictures the age-old partnership between wood and milling, taking in three famous mills: Venn watermill at Garford in Oxfordshire, Marsh Mill at Thornton, near Blackpool, and Brill Mill in Buckinghamshire.

■   ■   ■

Wednesday for Walter Heapy never varies. Because for the past 15 years, Walter, of School Road, Thornton Cleveleys, has reserved that day for the love of his life — Marsh Mill, Thornton.

There Walter has put his efforts and dedication into restoring the former flour mill and Fylde landmark to its former glory.

Walter, a retired engineer who will be 70 in April, had always admired the mill, which was built in 1794, but after seeing the interior he was so impressed with the craftsmanship that he decided to attempt to restore it.

With finance from the council, contributions from the public and an occasional government grant, Walter and his volunteer working party got to work, systematically making their way from the top down the five floors, repairing rotting timber, strengthening supports and floors and painting and generally renovating the workings of the mill to its original state.

Thornton Mill has a tapering circular brick tower about 50ft

● *Brill Mill, a 17th century post mill, stands sentinel over the Buckinghamshire landscape. (Picture: David Askham)*

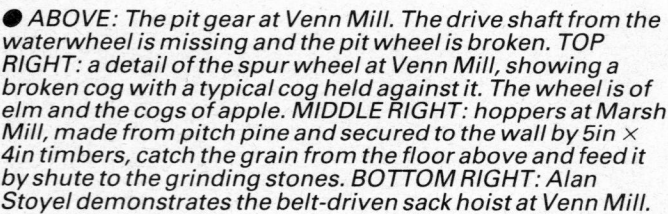

● ABOVE: The pit gear at Venn Mill. The drive shaft from the waterwheel is missing and the pit wheel is broken. TOP RIGHT: a detail of the spur wheel at Venn Mill, showing a broken cog with a typical cog held against it. The wheel is of elm and the cogs of apple. MIDDLE RIGHT: hoppers at Marsh Mill, made from pitch pine and secured to the wall by 5in × 4in timbers, catch the grain from the floor above and feed it by shute to the grinding stones. BOTTOM RIGHT: Alan Stoyel demonstrates the belt-driven sack hoist at Venn Mill.

high with five storeys. The wooden caps are of ther typical north-western style shaped like inverted boats and turning on blocks or rollers resting on a curb at the top of the tower.

The earlier common sails were later replaced by patent sails with shutters. Two were blown off in a gale in 1962, but were replaced later during restoration.

The caps were turned by a fantail mounted on a wooden staging at the opposite end to the sails and connected by gearing to a rack and curb at the top of the tower.

There is a wooden staging or gallery round the tower at second floor level to give access to the sail, enabling the miller to adjust the sailcloth according to the wind. The staging is supported by timber props resting on projecting stone corbels.

A cast-iron windshaft replaced a wooden one in 1895. Inside the cap the brake wheel was mounted vertically on the windshaft and the drive taken to the horizontal wheel at the top of the vertical main shaft, which runs down to the floor below.

The sacks of grain were lifted to the top storey by a sack hoist and emptied through shutes into wooden hoppers which fed the grain, so that the grain gradually worked its way down through the different processes, until it was finally bagged and stored at the bottom.

Bill Wilkinson

VENN MILL
Built on a site recorded in the Doomsday Book, the present structure of Venn Mill was completed about 1806 and advertised in the local paper for rent. However its rural craftsmen used technology of an earlier age and the style of the gearing construction is mid-18th century.

The milling of flour stopped in 1913 and animal feed could only keep the mill in partial operation. Consequently hard

● ABOVE: Walter Heapy poses proudly with Marsh Mill, which he has done so much to restore. TOP LEFT: Marsh Mill's 10ft diameter brake wheel is built of oak and beech. The 80 or so cast iron cogs were originally of hornbeam or apple, and elm has been used with iron links on the brake-hand strap which surrounds the wheel. MIDDLE LEFT: Oak is chosen for the cogs at Venn Mill, to minimise the warping problems in the damp conditions of the pit. BOTTOM LEFT: Walter Heapy attends to a detail of repair to the Marsh Mill sack hoist.

● *PICTURED RIGHT: one of the wooden wheels at Marsh Mill which drive the belt in the mealhouse. FACING PAGE: top left shows how Marsh Mill's brake wheel drives the crown wheel, or 'wallower'. The job of the wallower is to convert the horizontal rotary motion of the sails to a vertical drive. The picture below it shows the auxiliary pinion shaft, meshed on to the teeth of the great spur wheel, and far right: all the timber here on the stone floor, where the grinding is done, is elm.*

times set in, the mill becoming run down with botched-up repairs, such as a gate post being used to support the drive shaft when the original bearings wore out.

1940 saw the last miller hang his hat on the door. The building then saw service as a chicken coop, at great expense to the milling machinery which has been lost.

Restoration work is being carried out by Mr Alan Stoyel. Work is restricted to spare time, but he hopes the water wheel will be turning by the summer, when visitors will be welcome on Sundays.

Nigel Barklie

Now, simply by looking for the right new Humbrol packs on your uppliers shelves, you know that

you're buying the best ... to bring out the best in your woodworking from start to finish. **HUMBROL** (Borden)

Humbrol Consumer Products Division of Borden (UK) Ltd., Marfleet, Hull, England.

TART...TO FINISH

Prices quoted are those prevailing at press date and are
subject to alteration due to economic conditions.

-STAR TEAM ATES.

All the way from America we're proud to present, the ...sh all-star team, a new range of DIY products.

Just take a close look at the host of useful and unique ...ms featured here.

And when you see the shop prices you'll understand ...y Hirsh has been a best seller with the Yanks for years.

What's more, because the complete Hirsh range is flat ...cked, it's easy to transport, yet simple to assemble once ...u're home.

They'll be in your stores soon.

...ST A FEW OF HIRSH'S LOW COST PRODUCTS.

1. WORK CENTRE Rugged, modular system with sliding door cabinets and adjustable shelving. Available in two sizes.

2. SAW GUIDE Gives a circular saw the combined versatility of a radial arm saw and panel cutting sawbench. Portable, folds flat for easy storage.

3. THE CUTTER'S EDGE A precision, all ...rpose, cutting guide with clamps. Ensures accuracy on all ...ose long lengths. Extends to 8 ft.

...SAW TABLE Gives a circular saw the accuracy of a ...wbench – can also be used with most routers and jig saws. ...lds flat for easy storage.

...ROUTER AND JIG SAW TABLE Converts portable router ...d jig saw into stationary power tool. Offers untold ...ssibilities to owners of these popular workshop power tools.

...MITRE MAKER Makes perfect mitre cuts with most types of ...rtable circular saw. Fast, accurate cross-cutting and mitre cuts ...ery time.

...WORKBENCH LEGS Steel, enamelled legs. Perfect for ...aking workbench, potting, picnic or garden table, desk etc. ...awer unit also available.

...FRAME CLAMP Self-squaring. Clamps four corners at one ...ne. Any size up to 26 ins x 30 ins.

...WORK GRABBER Heavy duty portable vice/saw horse. ...aves your hands free to use tools properly and safely. ...amps on both top and sides.

...IRON HORSE A sturdy, yet lightweight saw horse that folds flat for easy ...prage. Will hold over 2,000 lbs distributed load.

...ULTRA CLAMPS A range of adjustable bar clamps, will clamp or spread ...d can be used as a vice – up to 1000 lbs pressure.

...ADJUST-A-TABLE Portable, folding, all purpose table. Adjusts from ...orizontal to vertical. Suitable as artist's, games, homework or general ...obby table.

...MEDITERRANEAN SHELVING Self-assembly, distressed, ...alnut woodgrain-look steel shelving. One of many styles of ...omestic and workshop shelving.

...DE LUXE WORKBENCH All steel frame with drawer, ...elves, tool rack and hardware bins.

...WORK'N HOBBY BENCH A complete workshop centre ...the home. Includes tool rack and hardware bins.

If you would like more details and free colour leaflets, ...nd s.a.e. stating which product(s) interest you, to the ...umaco Merchandising address opposite, or ask your local ...rdware shop to get you details.

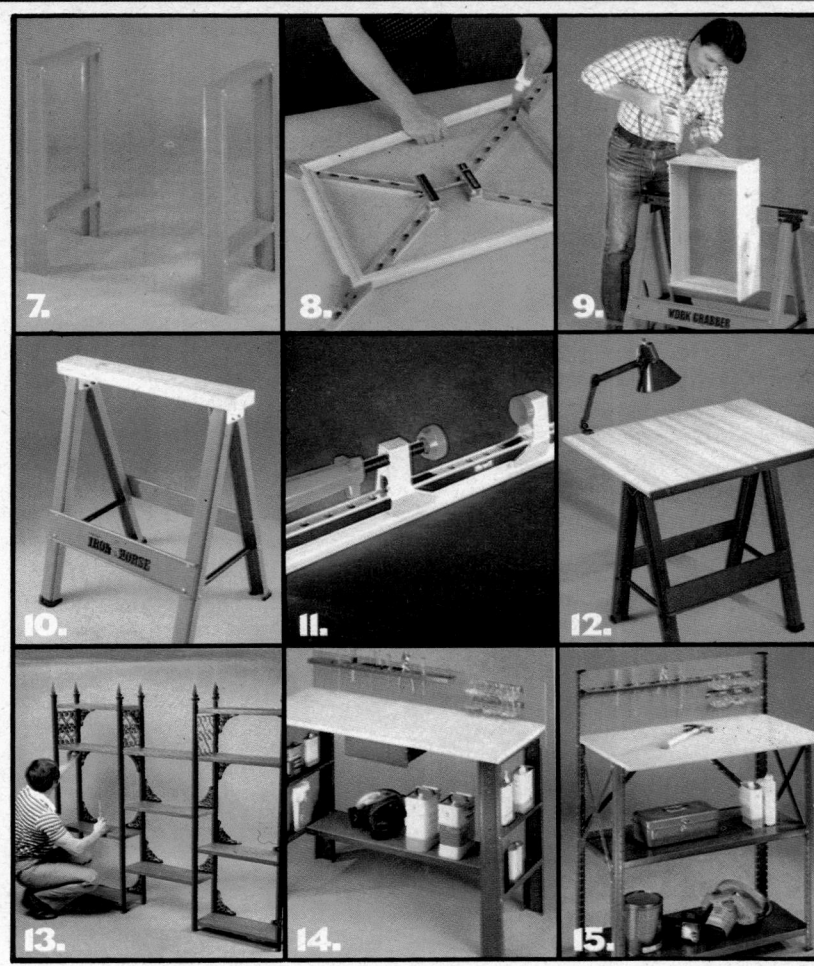

7. 8. 9.

10. 11. 12.

13. 14. 15.

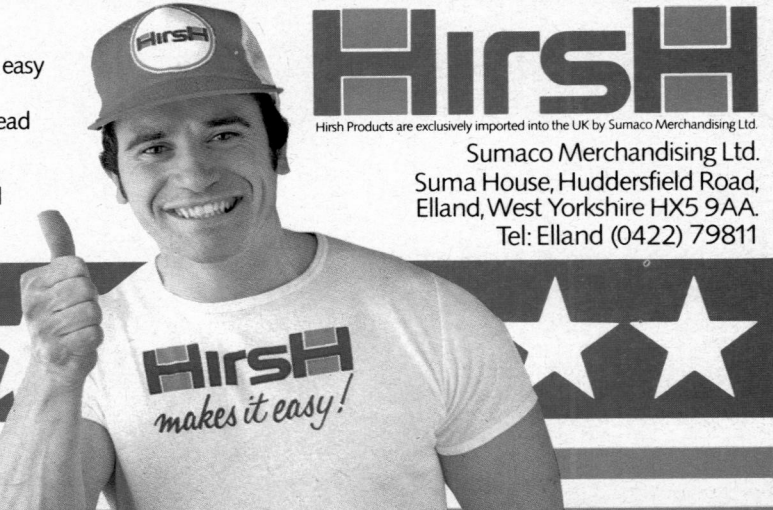

HirsH

Hirsh Products are exclusively imported into the UK by Sumaco Merchandising Ltd.

Sumaco Merchandising Ltd.
Suma House, Huddersfield Road,
Elland, West Yorkshire HX5 9AA.
Tel: Elland (0422) 79811

HirsH
makes it easy!

In praise of the carpenter as builder

For the serious woodworker who likes sometimes to stand back and look at the way things used to be done, timber framed buildings, so many of which survive as proof of their builders' great skill, provide a rich area of study. The Arts Council's touring exhibition on timber framed buildings draws attention to the remarkable development in building between the 12th and 18th centuries, and is particularly relevant in light of the current revival in timber frame building. We asked Geoff Pratt, former editor of *Woodworker*, to review the exhibition for us by way of its accompanying illustrated catalogue.

Readers who are following the timber-frame house plans advertised in the March 1982 issue of *Woodworker*, could gain useful background information from the catalogue which accompanies the Arts Council's touring exhibition on timber-frame buildings.

Titled *Timber Framed Buildings* the catalogue has been written by Richard Harris who has made a study of the buildings and has reconstructed several in his capacity as advisor to the open-air museums at Singleton, near Chichester, and Bromsgrove, Worcestershire. He is also author of the Shire Publications Ltd *Discovering Timber-Framed Buildings*.

The exhibition guide costs 60p (ISBN 0 7287 0256 8). It includes a useful list of publications and an introductory reading list. The author suggests that the best textbooks on timber-frame buildings are the buildings themselves and a great deal can be learned by 'reading' the design of the building from its facade.

He says: 'The elements to look for are the bay divisions and the positions of doors, windows and chimneys. In many cases the former existence of windows, particularly projecting bays or oriels, can be inferred from the pattern of framing and of empty mortises, grooves and pegholes.'

In the guide are numerous photographs of timber-frame buildings in different parts of the country. In addition there are line drawings showing constructional details, which would be of particular value to model makers.

Richard Harris explains that everyone who looks at timber-frame buildings must

● *The skill of the timber frame builders is displayed at its zenith in the beauty of Grange Court at Leominster, Herefordshire. (Picture: David Askham)*

sooner or later become aware that, no matter what place or period particular examples may occupy, they have certain technical features of importance which never vary. They are technical features of importance only to the carpenter, not at all to his client.

Perhaps the most important of them is the bay system of the structure and its relationship with the plan. A related feature concerns the placing of the upper face of frames, which are always placed facing outwards. The third feature, universal in British box-frame and aisled buildings though it does not occur in cruck frames, is the tying joint between cross frames and wall frames which is in the form of a lap dovetail. This first appears in 13th century buildings, although it may have been used before, and was still in use in many rural areas in the late 19th century.

According to the author, other features could be found, but the bay system, the direction of the upper face and the tie beam lap dovetail assembly, belong together and form a system which is internally consistent.

The exhibition guide has an interesting section on regional characteristics, making the point that virtually every feature of a building is subject to regional variations which themselves alter with time. The features which most clearly define regional variations fall into four groups: roof construction, the patterns of wall framing, decorative treatment and house plan.

Richard Harris emphasises the importance of the carpenter as a *builder* of

timber-frame. Traditionally he was responsible for the whole process of transforming logs into beams and fitting beams into a frame. This, says Mr Harris, 'enabled him to keep the beams in a proper relationship to one another, the logic of their positions in the tree being transformed into the logic of their positions in the frame.'

'A timber-frame building is two-dimensional until the day when, after weeks of cutting and fitting the joints of each component frame, the whole structure is erected ("raised" is the word used in old documents). The bay system, its relationship with the plan; the tying joint; and the geometry of the roof structure, ensure between them the coherence of the frame in three dimensions. They enabled the carpenter to approach any project in the knowledge that whatever the size, shape and purpose of the building, if he followed the rules the result would come out right every time!

'If a lesson for the present can be drawn from the study of timber-frame buildings, this is where it may lie. No one would advocate a return to past methods but a similar set of rules for modern architects and builders, not to restrict their freedom but to ensure their success, would be much to be desired.'

The Arts Council touring exhibition on timber-frame buildings was displayed at Chichester (Sussex) district museum from 23 January to 13 February and augmented by the museum's collection of carpenters' tools.

● This exhibition is currently at Hitchin Museum, Hertfordshire, where it remains until 1 May. From 19 June to 11 July you can catch up with it again at the Weald and Downland Open Air Museum, Singleton.

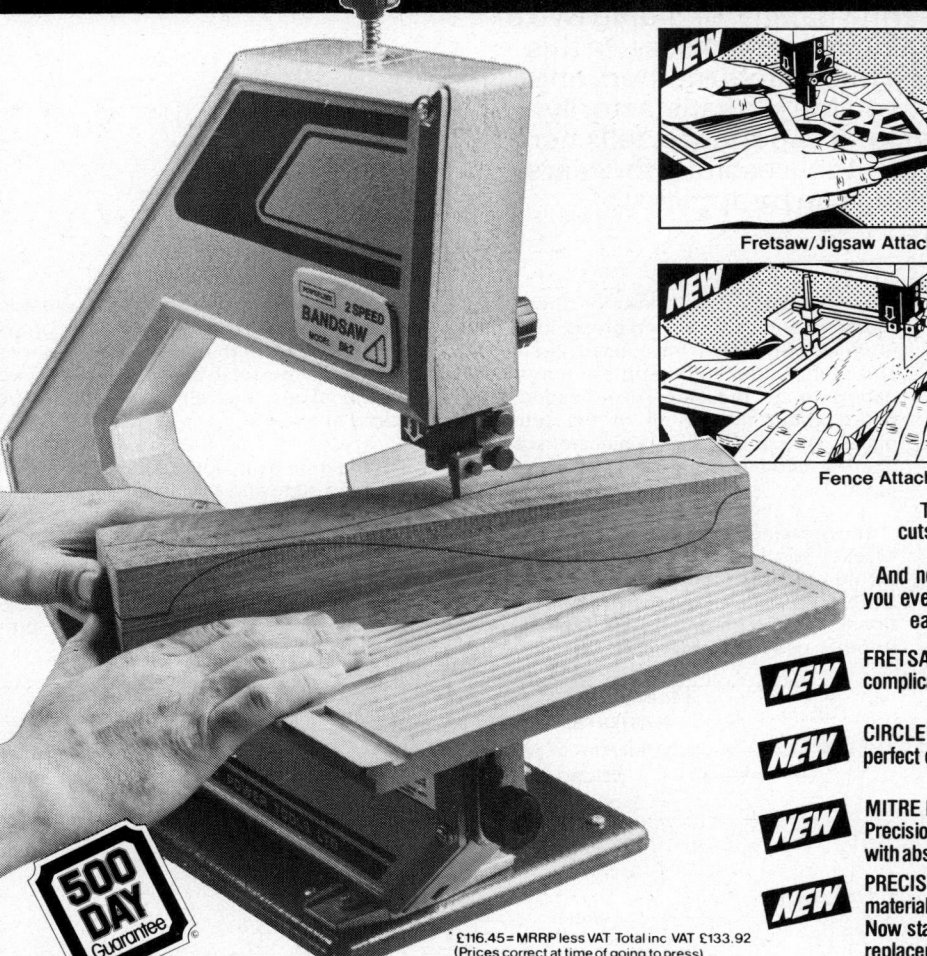

BURGESS POWERLINE
BK2 BANDSAW HUNDREDS OF UNEXPECTED USES AT AN UNEXPECTED PRICE OF £116.45* or less

Fretsaw/Jigsaw Attachment.

Circle Cutting Attachment.

Fence Attachment.

Mitre Fence Attachment.

The famous Burgess 2-speed Bandsaw cuts an enormous range of materials — faster and cleaner than you'd ever thought possible. And now there's a new range of attachments to give you even greater versatility and precision. Simple and easy to fit — and just look what they'll do!

NEW FRETSAW/JIGSAW ATTACHMENT enables you to cut complicated shapes exactly — inside or outside perimeters.
£14.95 inc VAT (MRRP)

NEW CIRCLE CUTTING & FENCE ATTACHMENTS give you perfect circles or controlled dead-straight lines.
£5.95 inc VAT (MRRP)

NEW MITRE FENCE ATTACHMENT in conjunction with the Precision Table, ensures that pre-set angles can be cut with absolute precision.
£5.69 inc VAT (MRRP)

NEW PRECISION TABLE is grooved for easy mobility of materials, making accuracy and control easier. Now standard fitting on all BK2 Bandsaws. Available as replacements for older models.
£10.35 inc VAT (MRRP)

£116.45 = MRRP less VAT Total inc VAT £133.92
(Prices correct at time of going to press)

500 DAY Guarantee®

SPARE BLADES
Choice of 5.
ASK FOR DETAILS.

BURGESS
POWERLINE
Power to your elbow

BURGESS POWER TOOLS LTD.
FREEPOST, SAPCOTE, LEICESTER LE9 6JZ

THERE'S A WIDE RANGE OF OTHER BURGESS POWERLINE POWER TOOLS — SEND FOR FREE LITERATURE. NO STAMP REQUIRED.

Now there's no end to the variety of complex shapes you can make with a Burgess Powerline BK2.

CLOCK PLANS ONLY £3.85 inc. VAT

You too can make this ingenious wall clock in wood with a set of Burgess Powerline clock plans — 6 sheets and full instructions.

See the BK2 and accessories at your local DIY/Hardware Counter or send for list of stockists and FREE literature on this and other Burgess Powerline power tools.

Name: _____
Address: _____
_____
_____
_____

W/5/82

A simple press for veneering your own panels

Anyone working with wood will inevitably, at some time, encounter the problem of veneering panels, or gluing two or more panels together in order to build up thickness. In this instance, veneering by hand is an unsuitable method, and some form of press is required to do the job satisfactorily. Mark Kenning, a woodworker of long experience, tells here of a method of pressing he has used successfully for years, proving how a bit of lateral thinking can be applied to overcome a workshop problem

The text books give a method of veneer pressing which requires quite a number of large heavy duty G cramps and/or hand-screws.

But the other method, simpler in my opinion, requires no special tools or equipment, although there are certain conditions. The first is that there must be an un-obstructed corner of the room or workshop where one does not need to worry about spoiling floor coverings or decorations. The second is that the ceiling above this area should be spanned by joists, whether visible or not, the reason for which will become clear later.

The materials needed are: two stout pressing plates (I will describe them in a moment) and some strong props, 2in × 2in is ideal, although I have used 2in × 1in successfully, depending on the number of panels to be pressed. Also needed is a board about the length of the pressing plates, around 9in wide (a piece of scaffold board would be ideal). This I call the 'ceiling plate'.

The pressing plates consist of two boards at least ¾in thick. Blockboard or plywood would be perfect, but chipboard would do almost as well, although it requires additional reinforcement, as we shall see. Another possible material is 1in t&g board or similar, provided they are cleated together with the faces level. The props should be of a length to reach from floor to ceiling, less the total thickness of the two pressing plates plus all the panels to be pressed at one go.

For the time being ignore the thickness of the ceiling plate and any packing or wedges that may be needed. There should be two props for every 12-18in of panel lengths plus two extra, so a panel size of 36in × 18in would require a minimum of eight props. The beauty of this method is that all of the materials can be re-used for other purposes.

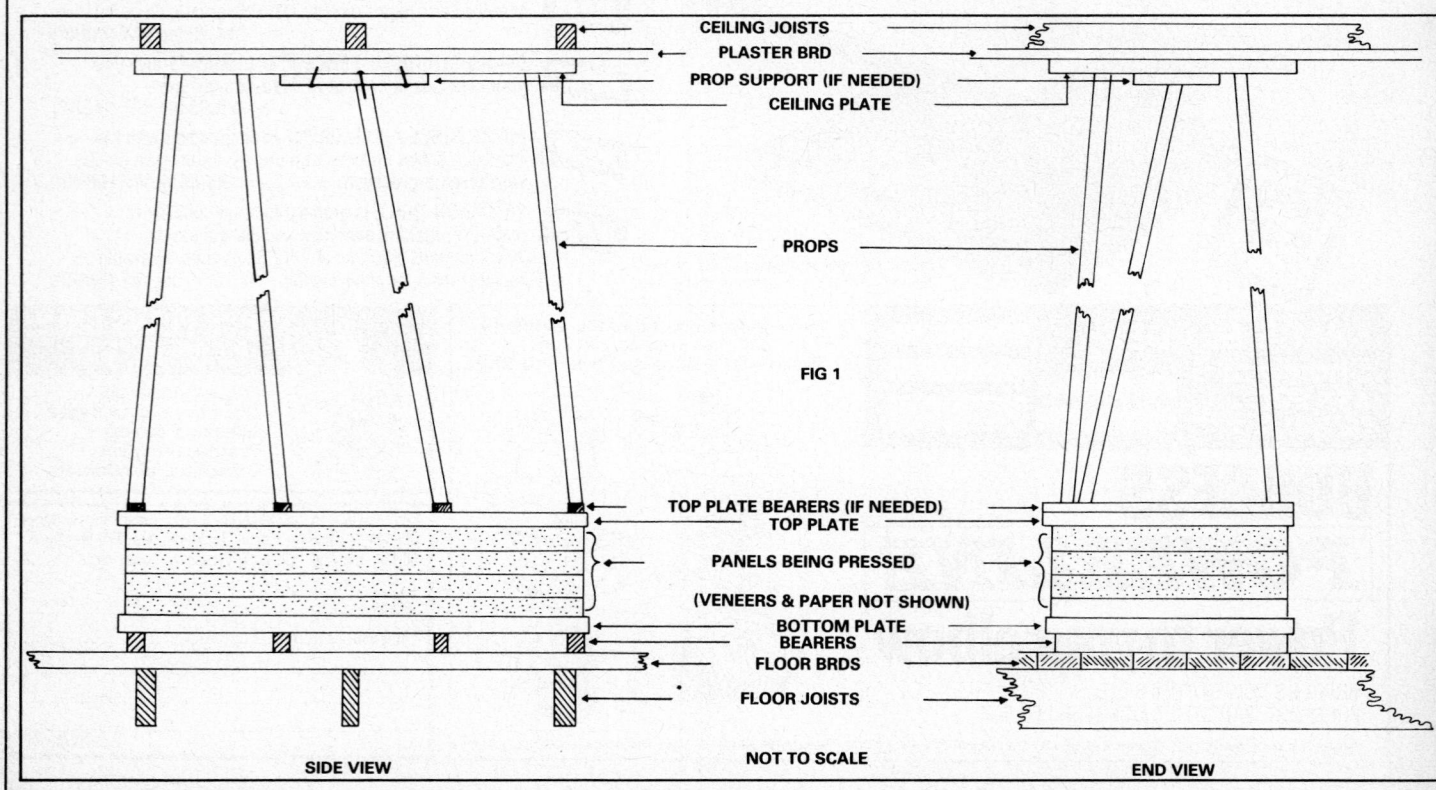

CEILING JOISTS
PLASTER BRD
PROP SUPPORT (IF NEEDED)
CEILING PLATE

PROPS

FIG 1

TOP PLATE BEARERS (IF NEEDED)
TOP PLATE
PANELS BEING PRESSED
(VENEERS & PAPER NOT SHOWN)
BOTTOM PLATE BEARERS
FLOOR BRDS
FLOOR JOISTS

SIDE VIEW
NOT TO SCALE
END VIEW

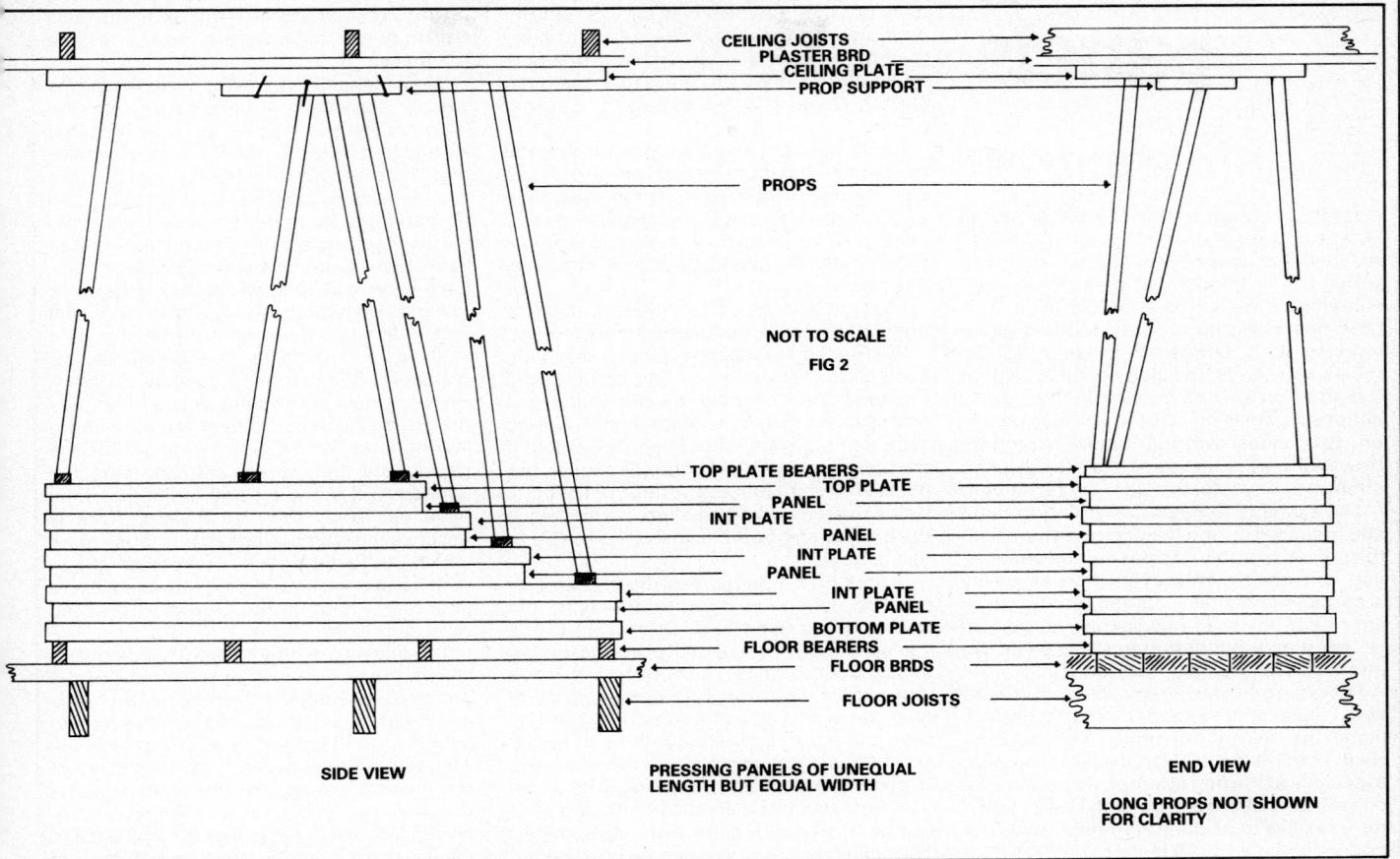

CEILING JOISTS
PLASTER BRD
CEILING PLATE
PROP SUPPORT

PROPS

NOT TO SCALE

FIG 2

TOP PLATE BEARERS
TOP PLATE
PANEL
INT PLATE
PANEL
INT PLATE
PANEL
INT PLATE
PANEL
BOTTOM PLATE
FLOOR BEARERS
FLOOR BRDS
FLOOR JOISTS

SIDE VIEW

PRESSING PANELS OF UNEQUAL
LENGTH BUT EQUAL WIDTH

END VIEW

LONG PROPS NOT SHOWN
FOR CLARITY

The press is prepared in the following manner:

If the floor is level then one of the pressing plates (I call this the bottom plate) can lay directly on it. It is worthwhile spreading some old newspaper on the floor first, well beyond the edges of the plate to prevent any excess glue getting on it. If the floor is uneven it will be necessary to support the bottom plate on 2in × 1in battens, set at 16in centres to coincide with the floor joists. For the sake of stability it is advisable to have the length of the supports at least as long, and preferably longer than the width of the bottom plate.

On a wood floor lay the bottom plate so that its length spans the joists, and try to place supporting battens to coincide as near as possible with the joists. The nails running across the floorboards indicate the joist positions. If the floor is of concrete then the bottom plate should be laid on it so that it spans across the ceiling joists above. These can be ascertained by the run of the floorboards in the room above or, if on one level, from the loft space. Having done this, place a sighting stick at each end of the floor plate and wedge or pack as needed between the supports and floor (never between the supports and plate) to true it up. Now it is ready for the pressing to start.

Obviously this method would be unsuitable where the workroom is in a barn with no ceiling joists or where the ceiling is of unsupported asbestos. In cases where the ceiling is unusually high, say over 9ft, the press can be raised on to a stout table, which will reduce the height by around 2ft 6in.

The panels and veneers will have been prepared in the usual way, the veneers being oversize to allow for trimming. This is normal practice, but the allowance may be omitted under certain circumstances, such as when the edge will eventually have a moulding worked into it. It is helpful if the panels to be pressed at any one time are all of the same size, as will be obvious from Fig 1.

Where the panels are of varying sizes, the job can still be done, but it would require intermediate plates and possibly extra props (see Fig 2). The only other requirement is that the largest panel is at the bottom and that every successive panel is either the same size or smaller than the preceding one. Under no circumstances should a higher panel overlap unsupported the one below. Occasions do arise however when it is not possible to place an upper panel without overlap. Here one would need to insert dummy filler pieces, but I would advise that under these circumstances, and until experience and confidence has been gained, the panels should be veneered one at a time.

We will assume that the panels are of chipboard and that PVA glue will be used. The veneers must, of course, be flat and if this has been done by damping them and keeping them under pressure overnight they will, and should, be damp when ready for use. PVA is water based and will tolerate a little dampness. With any other synthetic glue it must first be ascertained whether it is compatible with water. With scotch glue, hot cauls would have to be used but otherwise the method is the same. Incidentally, anyone contemplating pressing any

but the plainest of veneers in their dry state should bear in mind that dry veneers are brittle. Some, like the burrs, are very brittle and liable to split and crack when pressure is applied.

It is good practice to do a trial dry run before commencing the work proper. The veneers would not normally be used at this stage since, being fragile, the less they are handled the better.

When all the panels and the plates are in position the props should be cut to length, about ¾-1in longer than the distance between the top plate of the press and the ceiling plate. If there are insufficient long lengths, then two pieces nailed together with long nails clenched at the back will do just as well.

A difficulty, if doing the job single-handed, is to hold the ceiling plate up while trying to insert the first prop. There are several ways, and readers may find methods more suitable to their needs, but the following is a solution which has worked for me for many years. Cut one of the props shorter than the others by a little less than the thickness of the ceiling plate. Nail a 2in × 1in batten about 2-3ft long centrally into the end grain of the prop, with at least two 2in or longer nails slightly skewed to prevent the batten from rotating. Then nail the batten, as centrally as possible to the face of the ceiling plate. There is now a prop and plate as one piece in the form of a large T which is easy to handle and to place in position.

The number of panels that can be pressed at any one time is generally limited by the gelling time of the glue. With most adhe-

Veneering panels

(from page 337)

sives this depends on the local temperature. PVA is no exception. It is generally recommended that assembly or pressure be done within 10-15 minutes of application, presumably at a temperature of 65-70F. But this time factor can be at least doubled when working with dampened veneers, as the moisture retards the gelling time. Within this time factor I have been able to press either six panels on one side or four panels on two sides without undue hurrying. However I would suggest that, for the first attempt at any rate, this quantity be halved.

The secret is to have everything to hand and prepared during the dry run. Apart from the press assembly, the panels and veneers, you will need plenty of glue in an easily accessible container, a large glue brush or 4in roller, plenty of newspaper, some ¾in veneer pins, a pin hammer, some clean rag and water for washing the hands.

The gluing can now begin, but first spread two layers of newspaper on the bottom plate, the reason for which will become clear later. It could also be very helpful, especially at the first attempt, if another pair of hands are available, but don't be put off if the work has to be done single-handed. The dry run will give sufficient confidence.

Spread the glue generously and as evenly as possible over the whole panel; this is where a roller comes into its own. Make certain that there are no dry spots. Lay the first sheet of prepared veneer on the panel. It is unnecessary, undesirable in fact, to spread glue on the veneers as well. The veneers must be held in position, otherwise when the pressure is applied they could slide out of place. This is done by tapping a veneer pin in at each of the four corners of the veneer, an inch or so from the long edge of the panel, into the sharp edge of the panel, and bending down into the waste.

Of course, if an allowance has been left on the panel for trimming, the pins can be tapped into this and bent. Do not hammer the pins right home as the heads have very little holding power, very difficult to remove without damage to the veneers and if left in could result in notched cutting edges. For the same reason, when prising up the pins for removal, be gentle as they can easily break. In instances where the veneers are shorter than the panels and pin holes are not permissible, a short length of Sellotape at each of the four corners will hold them firm.

If the reverse face is to be done at the same time then carefully turn the panel over on to two clean sticks, so that a minimum of veneer is in contact with the bench and repeat the previous operation.

You will find that the long edges of the veneer, while unsupported, will curl upward slightly within a few minutes of making contact with the glued panel. This should be ignored. The veneers will flatten out as soon as any weight is put on them.

When satisfied that the veneer is firmly in position on the panel, place it carefully and centrally on the papered bottom plate. It does not matter which way up it is, but my own practice is to stack them face-to-face, the bottom one face up, the next one face down and so on. After the panel has been placed, cover it with two layers of newspaper.

Continue in the same way with the rest of the panels, making sure that they are placed directly over and level with the preceding one, with two layers of paper between every veneered surface. If you use polythene sheet instead of newspaper only one layer need be used.

The method of dealing with panels of unequal size will be explained in a moment.

When all the panels have been placed in position the top pressing plate is put on and the pressure can now be applied. Fig 1 shows battens across the top plate beneath each pair of props. These can be omitted if the top plate is of blockboard or similar, but if it is important that the surface of the plate is not bruised or marked, then use battens. If the plate is chipboard it is also advisable to use battens.

If working single-handed the first prop to position is obviously the one with the ceiling board fixed to it. Offer it up to the ceiling directly above the press assembly and across the joists. The bottom end of this first prop should reach the pressing plate near the centre of its length and about 1in from the edge. Tighten it with hand pressure by pushing the bottom of the prop towards the centre. The ceiling board will now hold up of its own accord and the prop can be further tightened with the hammer. The ceiling board too may now be adjusted if necessary by tapping it with the hammer. Subsequent props should be inserted by placing them on the pressing plate about 1½-2in from the long edge, then on to the ceiling board and tightened from the top. The props must be worked in pairs and from the middle out towards the ends.

You may find that as sbsequent props are tightened, previous ones loosen, so as each one is tightened up, lightly tap the others to make sure they are tight. The props should not stand perpendicular, at which point the maximum point of efficiency would have been reached and any further action would tend to make them loose. Should this happen they should be withdrawn and wedges or packing inserted. The final assembly will look like a crazy petrified forest. When they are all in position go around tapping each one with the hammer in rotation from the middle outward to make sure they are all tight. This final tightening may be done from either end.

A lot of force is not necessary. Obviously this method is not a scientific one and there is no gauge to measure the psi, but a 'feel' is soon developed. Do not be afraid that the floor above will lift. This would require much more pressure than one can generate with an ordinary woodworking hammer.

From time to time during the tightening-up stages take a look at the edges of the panels. Tear away any paper that is obscuring the view and you will get the satisfying sight of the excess glue running down the edges. Leave at least overnight in warm weather or in a heated workshop. In cold or in unheated conditions I would advise 24-48 hours of curing time. I have not known PVA glue fail to cure in 48 hours, even under extreme cold conditions. A good indication is the excess glue on the edges. If this feels soft to finger nail pressure, do not release the press.

When satisfied that all is well, the props can be removed. A light blow with the hammer at the bottom of each one is all that should be needed to free them, making sure that the one with the ceiling board is not accidentally freed till last, as it could fall and do damage. Separate the panels and now you will appreciate why it was essential to have two layers of paper between them. Each layer will be stuck, at least in part, to the panel it was touching. With only one layer of paper there is a possibility of it sticking to both faces of adjacent panels making it difficult to separate them. Trim off excess veneer in the usual way and remove the stuck-on paper by wetting, allowing a few minutes for the water to penetrate the paper, and then scrape off. Damping the veneers will show up any faults that may have occurred, such as blisters. This is because the water will swell any loose parts which can then be seen in reflected light, in which case you would deal with them there and then, before the glue has reached maximum cure.

The panels can now be stood aside to dry. Where the veneers reach to the end of the panels, especially on both faces, the edge on which it is to stand must be raised slightly off the floor to prevent possible damage to the veneers. If the long edge of the panel is unimportant or is going to be veneered, two 1½in wire nails partly hammered into it will act as legs on which it can safely stand. Where the edge must not show any holes, a couple of small blocks thinner than the thickness of the panel, can be glued on temporarily. Do not stand or lay the panels close together while they are wet as this could encourage mould growth.

When one needs to press panels of varying sizes, so that each successive one is contained within the area of the preceding one, it can be done, as I said earlier, but a few extra provisions must be made. It is essential that this be done during the dry trial run when no harm will be done if the set-up needs to be altered or adjusted in any way.

The pressing plates, bottom, top and intermediates, must be at least an inch longer and wider than the longest and widest panels. If the largest (in area) panel is 36in × 18in and the next largest 30in × 20in then the bottom and intermediate plate must be at least 37in × 21in and so on. Filler pieces, from waste material of the same thickness as the panel, plus the same number of veneers (again from waste) must be provided to fill the spaces below the upper overhanging boards but there is no need to glue them on. Where more than one or two filler pieces have to be provided it might be a good idea to number or identify them in some way so that they will go into their exact position when actually setting up for pressing.

While I have tried to cover many eventualities in this article, it is not possible to cover them all. Nevertheless the basic principles remain the same. Any minor problems that may arise, not covered in the article, will be quite easily dealt with by the operator because the whole of the operation is visual. But the key to success is to solve any problems at the trial dry run.

When paint seals it in,

Bosch breaks it out.

Screws that have been painted over or become rusty are no joke. Try and get them out with a screwdriver and the chances are you won't.

Take a new Bosch 650-2 R LE Drill to them and they'll come out without a fight.

Because it's everything a reversible action hammer drill should be.

A powerful 650W motor drives three fully synchronised, mechanical gears (two forward and one reverse rotation).

The constant Electronic Control gets you through the hardest of materials with the minimum of effort.

The variable speed control, which takes you from 0-3400 rev/min, gives you precise, on-the-dot pilot drilling (useful for drilling through ceramic tiles).

And the robust lightweight body is ergonomically designed, fully insulated and suppressed.

So next time you've a job to do and you want to make it easy, you'll know the drill.

It's called the new Bosch 650-2 R LE.

BOSCH

The more professional D.I.Y. power tools.

WORKSHEET 11

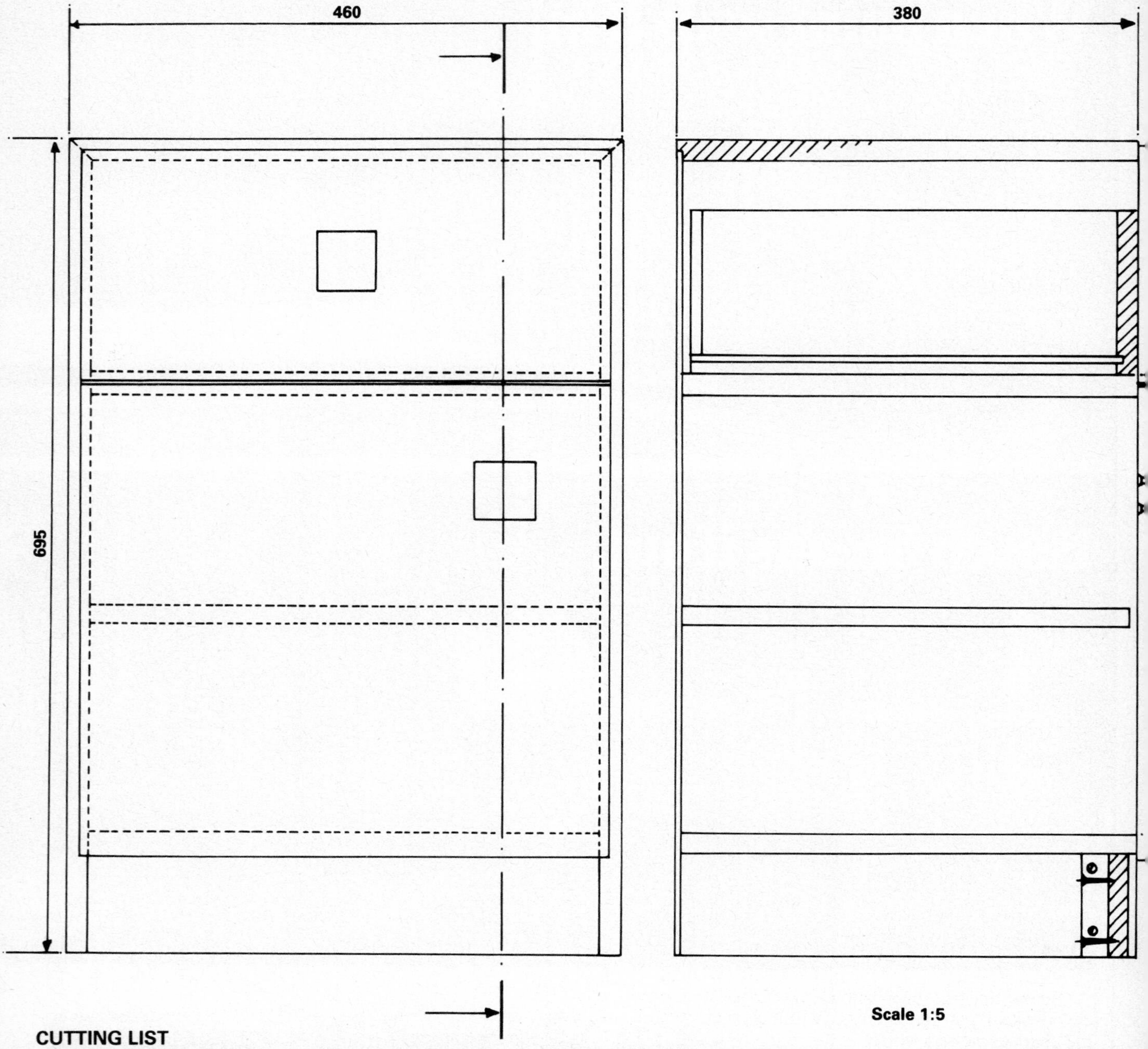

460

380

695

Scale 1:5

CUTTING LIST

	No	L	W	T	MATERIAL
Cabinet sides	2	695	380	16	Veneered or laminated chipboard
Cabinet top, base + shelves	4	460	380	16	" "
Cabinet door	1	400	435	16	Veneered or laminated chipboard
Cabinet kicking board	1	425	90	16	" "
Cabinet back	1	600	460	4	Ply
Drawer sides	2	365	140	16	Pine
Drawer back	1	430	125	12	Pine
Drawer front	1	430	140	16	Pine
Drawer false front	1	435	200	16	Veneered or laminated chipboard
Drawer bottom	1	430	360	6	Ply

Handles — bought or made from hardwood
Magnetic catch, self adhesive edging strip
Hinges (two pair) screw-in lift-off for chipboard use

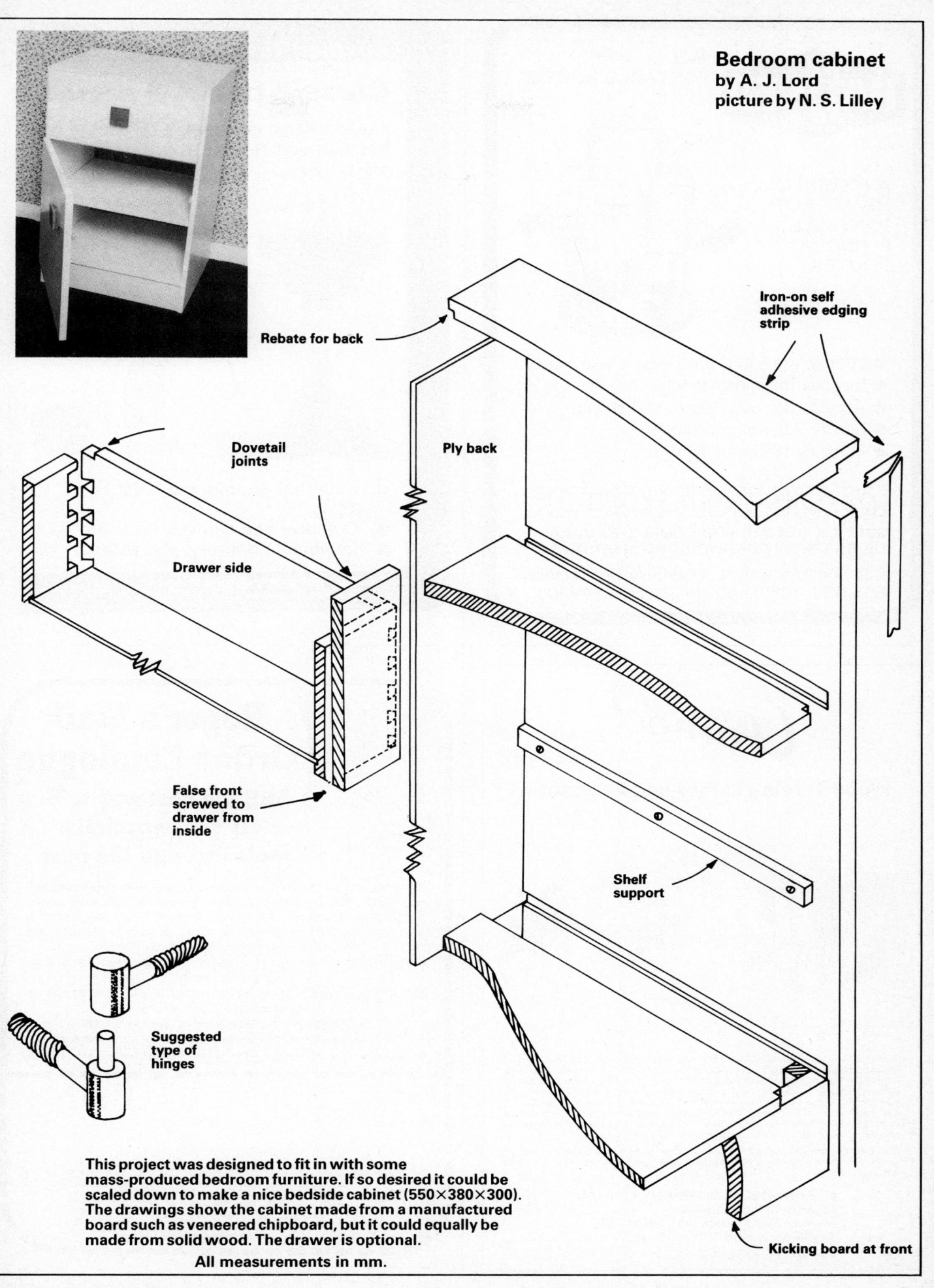

Bedroom cabinet
by A. J. Lord
picture by N. S. Lilley

Iron-on self adhesive edging strip

Rebate for back

Dovetail joints

Ply back

Drawer side

False front screwed to drawer from inside

Shelf support

Suggested type of hinges

Kicking board at front

This project was designed to fit in with some mass-produced bedroom furniture. If so desired it could be scaled down to make a nice bedside cabinet (550×380×300). The drawings show the cabinet made from a manufactured board such as veneered chipboard, but it could equally be made from solid wood. The drawer is optional.

All measurements in mm.

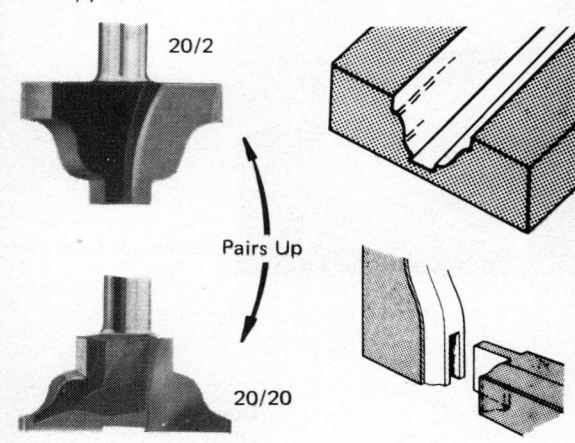

The saw designed to give you perfect results in modern materials

NOT JUST FOR PROFESSIONALS

Advanced production systems bring this precision tool within your reach. For little more than the cost of a light pressed steel sawbench, you can enjoy the accuracy and precision of the TGS171.

Add the sliding table and you can cut boards and panels up to 36" at a perfect 90°

FREE with your TGS171, a super hard TCT Sawblade, adjustable cutting guides, and quickly detachable legs for storage and transport.

Versatility

Simply pull the plunge table locking lever, and the overhead mitre cutting saw swivels through 180° to become a conventional bench saw.

A sawbench . . . . A simple flip over . . A perfect Mitre saw.

Superb Accuracy

Positive locking at any precise angle between square and 45°.

Stability

Wide bearing point of pivot precision, ground for stability.

Whether you need to cut delicate veneered boards for cabinet building or even alloy extrusions for mitred frames, the new TGS171 has been developed to give the performance and consistent accuracy you want.

Further Information

Elu have a nationwide network of over 200 authorised distributors. Contact us today for your FREE fully illustrated colour brochure and full list of stockists.

Elu Machinery Ltd.
310 Dallow Road,
Luton LU1 1SS
Tel: (0582) 425001 Telex: 825540

Elu

KITS from The Early Music Shop

Crumhorn Kits

The skill needed to build this instrument is minimal. You will find the instruction book thorough and the kit very complete – even to the various polishes. The bent section is supplied pre-formed.
Available: soprano in C, alto in F, tenor in C, bass in F.

Glastonbury Pipe Kit

An alto windcap with chromatic compass f-b' based in part on medieval iconography. Suitable for folk music or more serious early music.
Simple to construct from the pre-formed parts supplied.

The Early Music Shop
Main showroom, sales and postal service
28 Sunbridge Road, Bradford, Yorkshire
telephone (Bradford) 0274-20014

London sales
47 Chiltern Street, London W1M 1HN
telephone (London) 01-935 1242

Scotland
Sanderson and Taylor
23 Bruntsfield Place, Edinburgh
telephone (Edinburgh) 031-229-2051

Samurai

TRADITIONAL TOOLS FROM THE EAST
2,000 YEARS OF CRAFTSMANSHIP GIVES YOU THE ULTIMATE IN CHISELS

USU NOMI - TEMPLE CARPENTERS CHISELS

Japanese USU NOMI - Temple Carpenters Chisels are used for heavy joinery work as their name implies. Hand forged from EXTRA high carbon steel laminated to a low carbon front, these chisels offer the Western woodworker a tool with exceptional edge holding properties combined with strength. The backs of the chisel blades are hollow ground to facilitate fine paring cuts of a standard difficult to obtain with Western chisels. Fitted with high quality Japanese Red Oak handles and hooped to avoid splitting.

Cat. No.	Size	Price	Cat. No.	Size	Price
150120	3mm	£ 10.25	150125	18mm	£ 12.89
150121	6mm	£ 10.25	150127	24mm	£ 13.28
150122	9mm	£ 10.25	150128	30mm	£14.35
150123	12mm	£ 10.45	150129	36mm	£ 16.00
150124	15mm	£ 11.33			
150139	Complete set of 9 Chisels £ 98.15				

Send Stirling Cheques and Postal Orders made payable to ROGER'S to the address below ;-

Roger's Department W
47. Walsworth Road. Hitchin.
Hertfordshire SG4 9SU
Telephone: Hitchin (0462) 4177

Prices quoted are those prevailing at press date and are subject to alteration due to economic conditions.

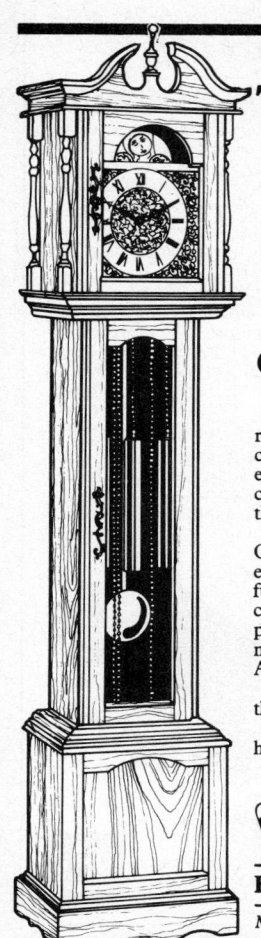
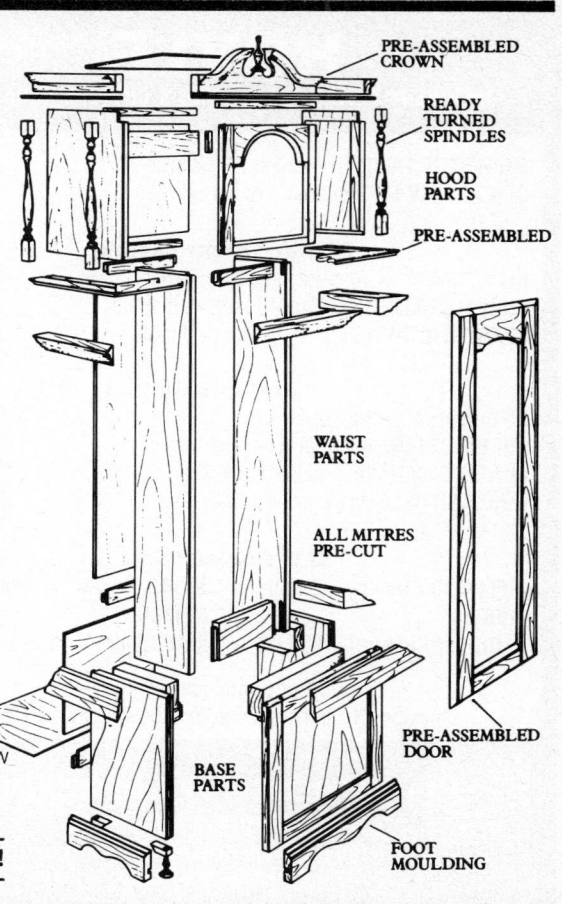

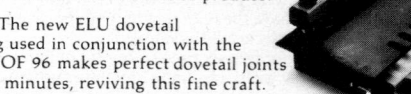

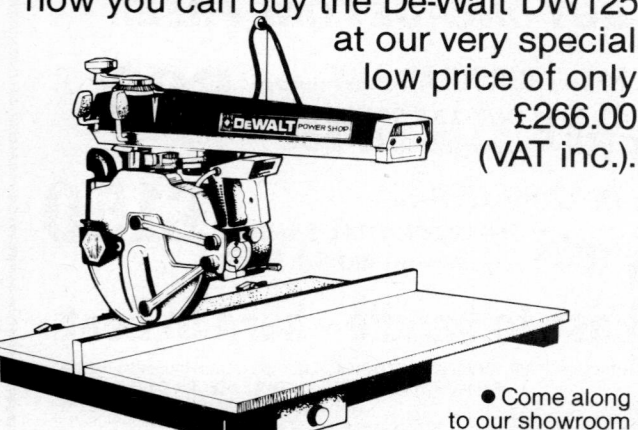

Prices quoted are those prevailing at press date and are subject to alteration due to economic conditions.

THE MOST EXCITING NEW HOBBY EVENT THE MIDLANDS HAS YET SEEN

Whatever your hobby interest bring all your family to the MODEL, CRAFT & COUNTRY SHOW at the NATIONAL AGRICULTURAL CENTRE at Stoneleigh nr Kenilworth, Warwickshire, on the weekend of May 22nd and 23rd.

This big and stimulating event will be action packed for modelling, woodworking and craft enthusiasts and for those who want to learn new skills, hobbies and pastimes.
Just study this list of the Show's content:-
★ 7 specialist exhibition halls filled with exhibits, trade stands, demonstrations, and hobbies in action
★ 4 big working model railway layouts
★ 3 live steam tracks
★ 7¼" gauge Echills Wood Railway in steam
★ The models from the TV series 'Flambards' and 'Wings' flying
★ Non-stop model flying demonstrations by top clubs and teams, R/C, control line, helicopters, gliders and ducted fan jet fighter models

★ Model boating championships
★ Famous model boats on the lake
★ Top woodworkers demonstrating and explaining a wide range of skills
★ Model horse-drawn vehicles
★ Model & Craft clubs helping and advising
★ Model engineering and wood working machinery and tool suppliers
★ Lectures and films across a wide range of hobbies
★ 3 craft halls demonstrating and selling a huge range of rewarding craft skills for the home, including home economy ideas
★ Learn how to make your craft pay at the Small Business Forum
★ Spaceship models, wargames, military models
Whether you are an expert or a beginner, the MODEL, CRAFT & COUNTRY SHOW is the hobby get-together you, your wife, your family and friends must visit.

The Midlands has never seen anything like it — don't miss it!

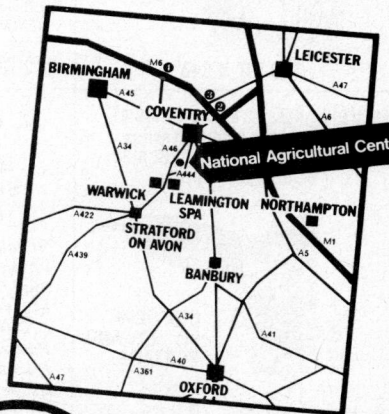

★ SPECIAL BUS SERVICE FROM COVENTRY AND LEAMINGTON B.R. STATIONS

Gemcraft

Woodworking

Modelling

Flying Helicopters

Woodworking Displays

Model Boats outdoors

General Crafts & Equipment

1982 MODEL CRAFT & COUNTRY SHOW

Flying Models outdoors

Home Craft & Country pursuits

Model Engineering

SAT·SUN MAY 22/23

Adults £2.00
Children and OAPs £1

STONELEIGH, KENILWORTH

10 am - 6 pm
Car Parking Free

—JOINT ORGANISERS—

ROYAL AGRICULTURAL SOCIETY OF ENGLAND
NAC Stoneleigh, Nr. Kenilworth, Warwickshire CV8 2LZ Tel: Royal Show (0203) 555100

Model & Allied Publications
P.O. Box 35 Hemel Hempstead, Herts HP1 1EE Tel: Hemel Hempstead (0442) 41221

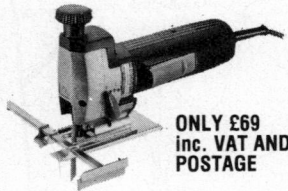

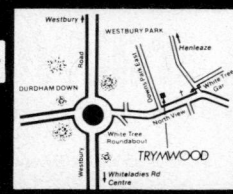
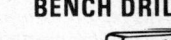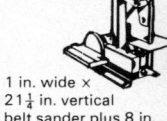
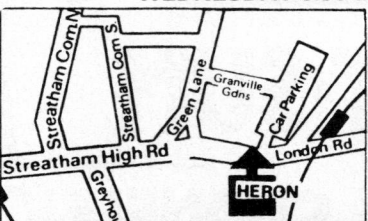
Prices quoted are those prevailing at press date and are subject to alteration due to economic conditions.

THE SHREWD CHOICE

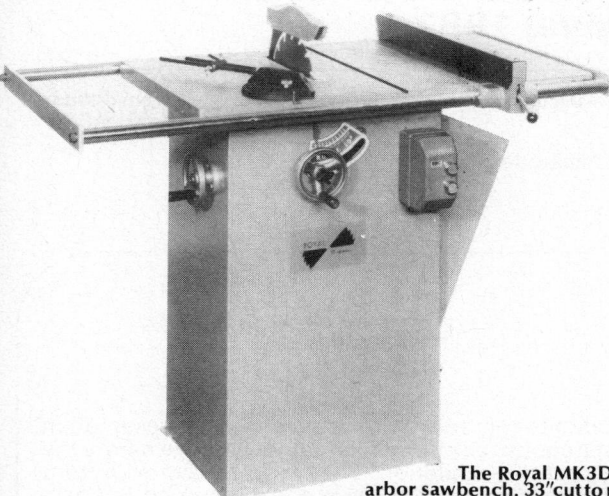

The Royal MK3DL 10" tilt arbor sawbench. 33" cut to right of saw up to rip fence • Large supported area for the easy handling of big sheets • Finely ground cast iron table • Sliding subtable moves within rip fence traverse • Single action, front and rear locking rip fence with twin fixture position for hold–down unit • Wide range of accessories •

Royal MK3DL R.L.P. £556.00
exc. v.a.t.

ROYAL
Always the right machine at the right price

Manufactured in England by Merrifield Engineers Ltd London 01-874 3042

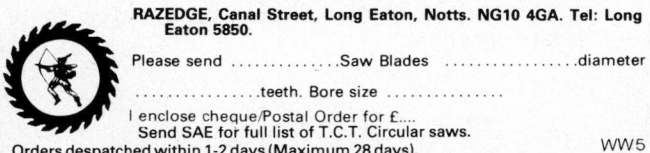

Woodworker Show

Royal Horticultural Society's New and Old Halls
19-24 October (inclusive) 1982

Royal Horticultural Society's New and Old Halls, London SW1 (10.00am to 6.00pm Tuesday-Saturday inclusive; 10.00am to 5.00pm Sunday)

COMPETITION RULES:
All correspondence and entry forms to: Exhibitions Manager, Model and Allied Publications Ltd,
PO Box 35, Bridge Street, Hemel Hempstead HP1 1EE.

GENERAL CONDITIONS OF ENTRY

1. Each entry shall be made separately on the official form and every question must be answered. Be sure to include the estimated value of your model. LAST DAY OF ENTRY WILL BE FRIDAY, 3 SEPTEMBER 1982.
2. All entry forms must be accompanied by a remittance for the appropriate entry fee(s).
3. The competition entry fee will be £2.00 for seniors, £1.50 for juniors. Subsequent entries will carry an entry fee of £1.50 for seniors and £1.00 for juniors.
4. A junior shall mean a person under 18 years of age on 1 October 1982.
5. No exhibit which has previously won a bronze medal, rosette or higher award at any of the exhibitions promoted by this company shall be accepted for these competitions. The organisers reserve the right to transfer an entry to a more appropriate class.
6. Entries may be submitted by amateur or professional workers.
7. The decision of the judges shall be final.
8. Competitors shall state on the entry form:
   (a) that the exhibit is their own work and property;
   (b) any parts or kits which were purchased or were not the outcome of their own work;
   (c) the origin of the design.
9. Exhibits will be insured for the period during which they will be at the exhibition. Insurance of exhibits in transit to and from the exhibition is the responsibility of the competitor.
10. Model and Allied Publications Ltd reserves the right to refuse any entry or exhibit on arrival at the exhibition and shall not be required to furnish any reason for doing so.
11. Model and Allied Publications Ltd reserves the exclusive rights to describe and photograph any exhibits entered for competition or display and to make use of any such photograph or descriptions in any way the company may think fit.
12. Competitors will be issued with a free non-transferable competitor's pass to the exhibition on presentation of their exhibit to the organisers.

RECEPTION

13. All exhibits must be delivered to Royal Horticultural Society's New Hall, Greycoat Street, Westminster, London SW1 (near Victoria station) on Sunday, 17 October between 10.30am and 4.00pm. Exhibitors must take away all empty cases, packing materials etc.

COLLECTION

14. Exhibits can only be reclaimed on the presentation of a control card, and this cannot be done before the end of the exhibition. They may be removed from the Halls between 5.30pm and 7.00pm on Sunday, 24 October or between 10.00am and 12.00 noon on Monday, 25 October. Any remaining uncollected exhibits will be removed to the offices of Model and Allied Publications Ltd and the organisers reserve the right to dispose of any for which collection arrangements have not been made by 30 November 1982.

AWARDS

15. All awards are made entirely at the discretion of the judges who may deem a particular class or section to be not worthy of any particular award.

16. A challenge cup will be awarded for the best entry in each of the following classes:
    WA — Cabinetmaking
    WB — Woodcarving
    WC — Woodturning
    WD — Musical instruments
    WE — Marquetry and inlay
    WF — Toys and Miniatures
    WG — Model horse-drawn vehicles
    WH — Junior (under 18) section
    WJ — Clocks
    WK — Carpentry and Joinery

17. Awards of 1st, 2nd and 3rd will be made in each section. 'Gold' medals will be awarded to all 1st prize winners in each of the individual sections. The awards for 2nd and 3rd will take the form of Certificates of Merit.

18. Any additional prizes may be made by personal donation of individuals or companies but are, as such, not part of the official *Woodworker Show* award schedule.

COMPETITION CLASSES

CABINETMAKING

WA1 Furniture: Any piece of work of any size and style. Finish to competitors' choice.

These may be individual pieces such as dining or card table, display cabinet, armchair etc each of which would represent one entry.

If, however, the exhibit were to be a dining suite, a maximum of three entries may be made: entry would be accepted on the following basis: dining chair – one entry; dining table – one entry; carver chair – one entry.

WOODCARVING

Exhibits in this class may be coloured using conventional water- or spirit-based woodstains and may be finished using a clear transparent sealer if desired, but no opaque paints or finishes may be applied.

WB1 Architectural: Any piece of architectural carving such as fireplace surround panel, church carving. A complete fireplace surround (three panels) would represent three entries.

WB2 Figure carving: Any sculpture not more than 36in high. Abstract forms will not be acceptable neither will, for example, polished branch or driftwood. The forms must be fully representational.

WB3 Relief carving: Any subject, overall size not to exceed 18 × 12in.

WOODTURNING

WC1 Any piece of spindle turning, or set of pieces.

WC2 Any example of faceplate turning including laminated work.

WC3 Any segmental turned item.

MUSICAL INSTRUMENTS

WD1 Any wind instrument.
WD2 Any string instrument.
WD3 Accessories

MARQUETRY AND INLAY

WE1 Any marquetry picture of any subject with overall face area greater than 12sq in.

WE2 Any miniature marquetry picture of any subject with overall face area, including frame, not exceeding 12sq in.

WE3 Any marquetry picture of any subject made from a kit.

WE4 Any work of pictorial or geometric decorative veneering, or parquetry, applied to a suitable article, eg tray, box, gameboard etc.

TOYS AND MINIATURES

WF1 Toys made in solid timber or wood-based sheet material.

WF2 Miniature buildings, furniture, or other items to ¹⁄₁₂ scale.

To qualify as a toy the entry should have play-value, it should be capable of being played with. Miniatures should all conform to the correct ¹⁄₁₂ scale and not be just smaller versions of standard pieces.

MODEL HORSE-DRAWN VEHICLES

WG1 Any farm cart or waggon or agricultural implement, drawn by horses, or horse-drawn vehicles for industrial purposes such as brewers' dray, coal cart, delivery vehicle etc.

WG2 Any caravan, coach, carriage or horse-drawn vehicle used for passenger transport (public and private).

WG3 Any horse-drawn vehicle made up from a kit. Horses that are carved or modelled or made in ceramics may be included with the exhibit but they will be disregarded in judging.

JUNIOR SECTION

WH1 Any item of woodwork made by a junior under the age of 18 on 1 October 1982.

CLOCKS

WJ1 Longcase clocks.
WJ2 Bracket clocks.
WJ3 Workshop regulators

CARPENTRY AND JOINERY

WK1 Carpentry } Any items
WK2 Joinery

Which would you rather work with?

More than 200 joinery workshops last year chose to work in a healthier, safer, cleaner environment. They bought one of our range of mobile dust extraction units. We're sure you and your staff would make the same decision if you saw one working. They are in use with almost all types of woodworking machinery and in all situations from large joinery plants to school craft rooms. So we're confident we have the unit to suit your needs at prices starting from £235 + VAT. And our extractors are tough. They're built from 16 gauge steel plate. The impeller fan is dynamically balanced in two planes to virtually eliminate vibration and keep noise to a minimum.

We understand the conditions under which our units must work, if we didn't build them like battleships we wouldn't be able to unconditionally guarantee them for a year!

Fill in the coupon now and we'll show you, on your machinery, how to clean up.

Specification

Capacity	950 Cu. mtrs per hr.
Fan Motor	0.75 h.p.
Motor Speed	2,800 rpm
Collection Capacity	0.1 Cu. mtr.
Inlet Diameter	125mm
O/A Length	740mm
O/A Width	390mm
Weight	49 Kg

Air-Ventilation & Fan Systems Ltd.
Priestly Way, Crawley, Sussex RH10 2NT
Telephone: Crawley 24266

Show me how to clean up!

Company ....

Address ....

Name .... Position .... Tel ....

AVFS **Air-Ventilation & Fan Systems Ltd.**
Priestly Way, Crawley, Sussex RH10 2NT
Telephone: Crawley 24266

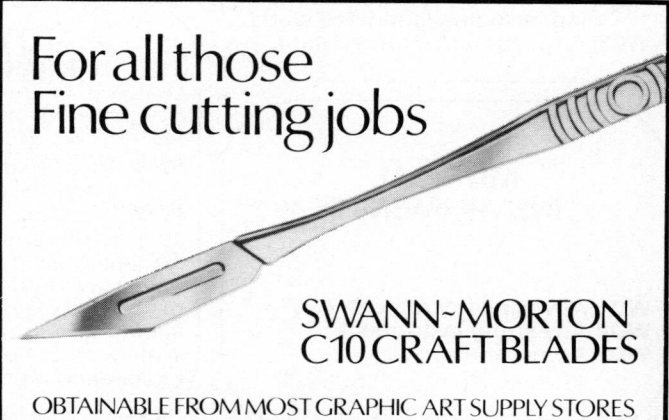
Prices quoted are those prevailing at press date and are subject to alteration due to economic conditions.

Woodworker Show
Competition Extra

PIRATES AND SEA-DOGS

The 1982 competition is again figure carving only. This follows the indications of previous years that figure carving is more popular than relief. The organiser has therefore, agreed that this year's competition shall be for one section only, namely figure carving.

Subject is **Sea Dogs and Pirates** which will allow entrants the widest choice of design, expression and finish for their work. The subject also allows for a great deal of artistic and original experiment.

Ashley Iles (Edge Tools) Ltd, East Kirkby, Spilsby, Lincs, is co-sponsor of the competition and has generously agreed to award substantial voucher prizes to be redeemed against his current catalogue. The attention of entrants is drawn to the importance of correctly packaging their work. The GPO has issued a leaflet *Wrap up well* (copies can be obtained from head post masters) which tells how parcels should be packed to minimise damage during transit. Adequate packaging is essential to avoid disappointment.

Closing date is Friday 1 October 1982. This will enable entries to be sent to *Woodworker*, PO Box 35, Bridge Street, Hemel Hempstead HP1 1EE, in time for judging to take place at the Woodworker Show which is being held at both the RHS Halls (New and Old), Greycoat Street, Westminster, London SW1 from 19-24 October (inclusive).

General conditions of entry

1 Entry is open to professional and amateur craftsmen. There is no entry fee.
2 The decision of the judges shall be final.
3 Entries must be received by Friday 1 October at the latest.
4 Entries must not be submitted before Friday 3 September.
5 Maximum dimensions of figure carvings: 18 × 9 × 9in.
6 Entrant's full name, address and telephone number must be securely attached to each piece submitted together with a statement that: a) the exhibit is their own work and property and b) the origin of the design.
7 Each entry must include the appropriate return postage, and packing should be of adequate quality to allow for safe return of the piece.
8 Each entry must be accompanied by a statement of its approximate value. (This is required for insurance purposes).
9 Each entry will be acknowledged on receipt.
10 Pieces entered in the Ashley Iles competition are not eligible for entry in the woodcarving classes of the Woodworker Show.
11 Pieces may be coloured using conventional water or spirit-based woodstains and may be finished using a clear transparent sealer if desired, but no opaque paints or finishes of any description may be applied.
12 Model and Allied Publications Ltd reserves the exclusive rights to describe and photograph any piece entered for this competition and to make use of any such photographs or descriptions in any way the company may think fit.

ROUTING

With the considerable interest in routing techniques, we felt this year the subject of routing should receive special consideration. The power router with purpose-made accessories, offers huge possibilities for development.

At the exhibition this year a cup, and three sets of Trend router cutters will be presented as 1st, 2nd and 3rd prizes in this special class. Here are some suggestions for those who might be tempted to enter:
a) Special attachments for the router, which enable it to perform either standard applications in a much improved fashion, or non-standard applications.
b) A special device or machine, powered by a router, ie a static machine and not used portably.
c) Special templates or copy-routing processes to assist those wishing to reproduce their products for sale.

Special consideration will be given to those showing originality, and giving clear and concise instructions, accompanied by a well-finished end product (if applicable).

All explanations or sketches, also parts (those which are not designed to be free-standing) should be mounted on plywood panels 10mm or 12mm thick in multiple sizes of 2ft.

A top hung leg (or legs) to allow the exhibit to free-stand on a table will be required.

Entry forms are available from the Exhibitions Manager, Model and Allied Publications Ltd, PO Box 35, Bridge Street, Hemel Hempstead HP1 1EE

POWERED WOODCARVING

Microflame UK Ltd of Diss in Norfolk have put up a trophy for a power-tool carving competition, in reaction to an apparent growing interest in this new dimension to the age-old art of carving.

So a competition has been devised for power-tool carvers in conjunction with this year's Woodworker Show, to be held at the Royal Horticultural Halls in London from 19-24 October. Entries are invited under the following guidelines:

The subject will simply be 'The Fox', which entrants may interpret entirely as they wish. The longest overall dimension should be no larger than 9in, but any wood may be used for the piece.

Malcolm Woodward of Microflame will award the Moto-Tool Challenge Trophy to the entry judged to be the most outstanding by a panel of three judges, to be announced later. The winner will also receive a replica trophy to keep, while the challenge cup will pass from winner to winner on an annual basis.

Entries should be delivered to the show, according to the specifications stated on page 350 while the general conditions of entry and arrangements for reception and collection of entries will also apply.

Entry forms are available now from the Exhibitions Manager, address above.

Offcuts

by Chris Dunn

This is the spot where we relax a little and take
time to examine the off-beat, the humorous,
the curious, and even the scandalous, or
anything else that attracts attention as being
entertaining or informative

'Enery weighs in

Our 'Enery – otherwise known as Henry
Cooper OBE KSG, former heavyweight
boxing champ – is apparently diversifying
from his TV advertising image as the sweet
smelling brute.

His latest promotional adventure is on
behalf of a tool company, and the name of
that company is (you guessed) Cooper
Tools Ltd.

The company, however, makes surprisingly little capital out of the namesake
aspect of the new alliance. Rather they have
signed up the popular pugilist-turned-
showbiz star because, say Cooper Tools,
Henry's image is 'entirely consistent with
that which the company wishes to portray
for its products: quality, ruggedness, reliability and suitability for the job'.

So we can no doubt look forward to some
punny advertising lines from Cooper Tools
in the future, such as promises of 'knock-out
prices' and an entirely new meaning for the
term 'Enery's 'Ammer, which used to refer
to the boxer's block-busting left hook in the
old days.

Cooper Tools' branded items include
wrenches, screwdrivers, tapes, files, hammers, soldering irons and guns, snips and
pliers. Surely they won't pass up this
opportunity of adding a range of punches to
their product list.

Out of stock

'This,' says an impassioned letter to Woodworker from Peter Sanford of Walsall, 'is a
sincere cry for help'.

Peter is a maker of hand-crafted black
powder guns and is finding it difficult to get
his hands on the right woods for the stocks
of his guns.

'Due to the recession and the general high
cost of the woods used in making full-
stocked guns,' says Peter, 'my supplier has
had to give up his business in hard woods
and is concentrating on soft woods, which
he states is more profitable.'

The search for a supplier has led him to
many stockists, but none has so far been

able to meet his requirements. 'In fact,' says
Peter rather despairingly, 'many just found
my requests over the telephone highly
hilarious.'

But it's no joke.

'Please,' he asks, 'can you or the readers
of your excellent magazine help me in
trying to find a source of the appropriate
woods?'

Peter's requirements are English or European walnut, American black walnut and
curly or tiger-stripe maple. The dimensions
he needs are 60in × 8in × 2in, with a five per
cent moisture content.

Can you help? Let me know and I will pass
on to him any good news.

Spinning a yarn

'The only thing I know about wood is that
you can set fire to it,' says Jack Donaldson,
describing himself rather as 'a metalworker
that makes clocks'. But he must be spinning
an over-modest yarn, wouldn't you say
when you look at this photograph of the
magnificent spinning wheel he has recently
built?

'The spinning wheel was made because I
am not very good at woodwork,' he told me
when he brought it to the office from his
Watford home for us to have a look at. 'But I
keep trying and one of the tries was the
spinning wheel.'

Jack worked from a plan by David Bryant,
bought from MAP's Plans Service, but he
found the instructions ambiguous in several respects. His further research took him to
any place where he might find an upright

● Jack
Donaldson's
spinning wheel.

spinning wheel to inspect, including the
Science Museum in London.

His search proved fruitless, so he was
obliged to 'make his own salvation' as he
says. If any reader is similarly having
trouble with this plan, they can write to me
(Woodworker, PO Box 35, Bridge Street,
Hemel Hempstead) and I will put them in
touch with Jack Donaldson.

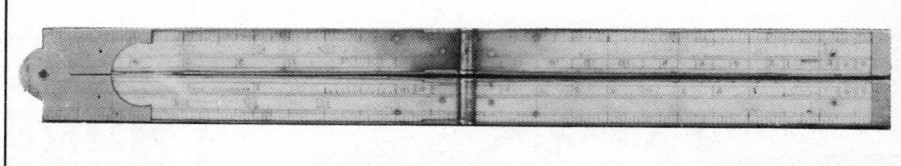

Exception to the rule

● Woodworker reader Mr J. Broadbent
of Wallasey was puzzled when he acquired
this 2ft rule. For the first thing he noticed
was that the markings were calibrated from
right to left, instead of the more customary
left to right.

We were as puzzled as Mr Broadbent by
the photographs which he sent us of the
rule. But I think there must be a more
sensible explanation than that it was made
for a left-handed Chinese chippy.

Mr Broadbent tells me: 'The rule is faced

with what appears to be ivory or bone. The
edges are faced with nickel plated brass,
and the two ends and hinge are of the same
material. The rule weighs 5oz, and is
stamped Stanley Rule and Level Co, New
Britain, Conn.'

There are three things Mr Broadbent is
keen to know: for which trade this rule was
made, its approximate date of manufacture,
and its possible value as an antique.

Does anyone know the answers? Drop me
a line at Woodworker, PO Box 35, Bridge
Street, Hemel Hempstead.

Mr Castle's lumber jacket

● *A variation on the lumber-jacket? This delightful and brilliantly executed piece of woodwork is by American furnituremaker Wendell Castle, giving full range to great skill and an engaging sense of humour, I think. Mr Castle will be among the list of eminent speakers at the International Seminar on Woodcarving, to be held at Parnham House, Beaminster, Dorset, on the weekend of 12 and 13 June. The seminar, together with an accompanying exhibition, takes the theme 'drawing in wood', and is intended to convey the essential ability of the imaginative carver to perceive in three dimensions. Also billed to speak at the seminar, held under the auspices of John Makepeace's School for Craftsmen in Wood, are American sculptor Michael Cooper, architect and designer Theo Crosby, Frederick Oughton, who is an authority on Grinling Gibbons, British woodcarver Howard Raybould, wood-engraver Leonard Baskin, and Dick Reid, president of the Master-Carvers Association. Further details Beaminster (0308) 862204.*

The return of Stan

Veteran cabinetmaker Stan Thomas of Treorchy was recalling the days of 1964/65 in a recent letter, telling of the time when he was a regular consultant to Woodworker, answering readers' questions in Question Box.

'Some of these queries came from women,' Stan recalled. 'They usually took the theme: My husband doesn't know how to set about this or that job; could you tell him?

'One day I had a note from one of these husbands. It said: Dear S. R. Thomas, why don't you get stuffed?'

Well, there's gratitude for you!

Readers who remember Stan's contributions to Woodworker will be happy to know that he has agreed to get writing for us again, always ready to bring his subject alive with wit and a good anecdote.

● The knight in search of a name.

● A jacket hanging carelessly on the back of a chair – all in wood carved by American furniture-maker Wendell Castle.

The knight with no name—yet

● *Exhibition goers have already had the chance to wonder at this outstanding example of work by Cheltenham wood craftsman Ian Norbury. But the beautiful equestrian figure, in full battle armour with visor raised to show only a glaring skull within and firmly in the saddle of a great rearing charger, has no name.*

And that's where you come in, as we ask you to name the knight.

This magnificent piece of carving, standing three feet and some in height, was made by Ian between Christmas and the end of January. The wood is lime, acquired from stocks laid down ten years ago by monks of a Benedictine monastery in the Cotswolds, and the finish is three coats of wax.

The main body of the horse is one block of wood, while the knight himself is separate, with detachable cape and fittings.

But what is the significance of the skull? Ian Norbury offers no explanation. Perhaps you have an idea of its possible symbolism... so we decided to invite readers to suggest names for the figure. The name chosen as best or most apt by a panel of judges will receive as a prize a 12-piece set of carving tools, donated with generosity by Roger Buse, always a loyal friend to Woodworker, of Roger's Tools in Hitchin, Herts.

Send your suggestions on a postcard please to the Editor, Woodworker, PO Box 35, Bridge Street, Hemel Hempstead, Herts, giving your name and address. And let us have your suggestions (as many as you like) by 30 June.

A free timber-identification service

Woodworker is now able to offer a free service to readers who want timber samples identified. In the past we have had to refer readers to Princes Risborough Laboratories or TRADA, both of which make a charge. So if you have a mystery timber, let us have a sample and we will get the necessary tests done.

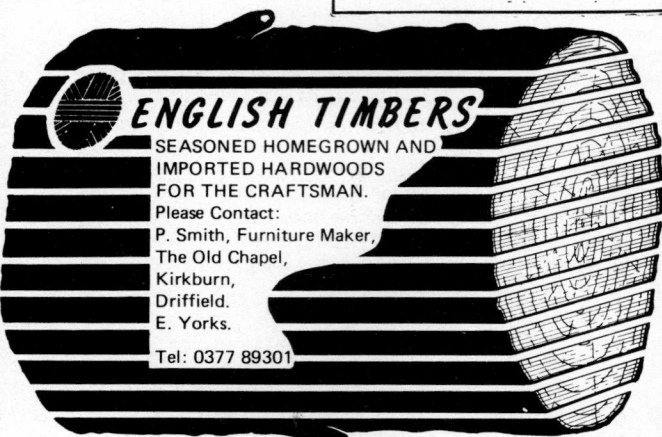

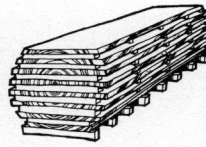

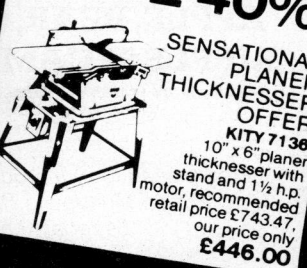

AVON

BATH Tel. Bath 64513
JOHN HALL TOOLS
RAILWAY STREET ★

Open: Monday-Saturday
9.00 a.m.-5.30 p.m.
H.P.W.WM.D.A.BC.

BRISTOL Tel. (0272) 311510
JOHN HALL TOOLS LIMITED ★
CLIFTON DOWN SHOPPING
CENTRE, WHITELADIES ROAD
Open: Monday-Saturday
9.00 a.m.-5.30 p.m.
H.P.W.WM.D.A.BC.

BRISTOL Tel. 0272-633844
ROBBINS LIMITED ★
THE WOODWORKER SHOP
MERRYWOOD MILLS, BEDMINSTER
Open: Mon-Fri 8.00 a.m.-5.00 p.m.
Saturday 8.30 a.m.-12.30 p.m.
H.P.T.CS.A.BC.

BRISTOL Tel. 0272-629092
TRYMWOOD SERVICES
2a DOWNS PARK EAST, (off
North View) WESTBURY PARK
Open: 8.30 a.m.-5.30 p.m. Mon. to
Fri. Closed for lunch 1-2 p.m.
P.W.WM.D.T.A.BC.

BRISTOL Tel. 0272-667013
V. H. WILLIS & CO. LTD ★
190-192 WEST STREET,
BEDMINSTER
Open: Mon-Fri 8.30 a.m.-5 p.m.
Saturday 9 a.m.-1 p.m.
H.P.W.WM.D.CS.A.BC.

BERKSHIRE

READING Tel. Littlewick Green
DAVID HUNT (TOOL 2743
MERCHANTS) LTD ★
KNOWL HILL, NR. READING
Open: Monday-Saturday
9 a.m.-5.30 p.m.
H.P.W.D.A.BC.

READING Tel. (0734) 586522
SARJENT'S TOOL STORES ★
LTD.
44-52 OXFORD ROAD
Open: 8.30 a.m.-5.30 p.m.
Monday-Saturday
H.P.W.WM.D.A.BC.

READING Tel. Reading 661511
WOKINGHAM TOOL CO. LTD
99 WOKINGHAM ROAD

Open: Mon-Fri 9am-5.30pm
Closed 1-2pm for lunch
H.P.W.WM.D.CS.A.BC.

BUCKINGHAMSHIRE

HIGH WYCOMBE (0494) 22221
ISAAC LORD LTD
185 DESBOROUGH ROAD

Open: Mon-Fri 8.00 a.m.-5.00 p.m.
Saturday 8.00 a.m.-12.00 noon
H.P.W.D.A.

MILTON KEYNES Tel. 0908
A. POLLARD & SON 75221
LTD ★
51 QUEENSWAY, BLETCHLEY
Open: 8.30 a.m.-5.30 p.m.
Monday-Saturday
H.P.W.WM.D.A.BC.

CAMBRIDGESHIRE

CAMBRIDGE Tel. 0223-353091
H. B. WOODWORKING
69 LENSFIELD ROAD
Open: 8.30 a.m.-5.30 p.m.
Monday-Friday
8.30 a.m.-1.00 p.m. Sat
P.W.WM.D.CS.BC.

CHESHIRE

NANTWICH Tel. Crewe 67010
ALAN HOLTHAM ★
THE OLD STORES TURNERY
WISTASON ROAD, WILLASTON
Open: Tues-Sat 9a.m.-5.30p.m.
Closed Monday
P.W.WM.D.T.C.CS.A.BC.

CLEVELAND

MIDDLESBROUGH Tel. 0642-
WINTZ 460035/813650
INDUSTRIAL SUPPLIES ★
2 BESSEMER COURT
GRANGETOWN
Open: Mon-Fri 8.30 a.m.-5 p.m.
H.P.W.D.A.

CORNWALL

FALMOUTH Tel. 0326-312915
WOODSTOCK
(HARDWOODS) S.W.,
ASHFIELD, PONSHARDEN,
Open: Mon-Fri 8.30 a.m.-5.30 p.m.
Sat 9 a.m.-1.00 p.m.
T.

HELSTON
SOUTH WEST
POWER TOOLS
Helston (03265) 4961
Truro (0872) 71671
Launceston (0566) 3555
H.P.W.WM.D.CS.A.

NEWQUAY Tel. 063 73 2516
CONWAY SUPPLIES ★
(NEWQUAY)
70 FORE STREET
Open: Mon-Fri 9 a.m.-5.30 p.m.
Sat 9 a.m.-12.30 p.m.
H.P.W.WM.D.A.BC.

CORNWALL

ST. AUSTELL Tel. (0726) 65922
TOOLSERV ★
TRURO ROAD

Open: 8 a.m.-5.30 p.m.
6 days
H.P.W.WM.D.CS.A.BC.

DERBYSHIRE

BUXTON Tel. 0298-871636
CRAFT SUPPLIES ★
THE MILL
MILLERSDALE
Open: Mon-Fri 9 a.m.-5 p.m.
Saturday 9 a.m.-1 p.m.
H.P.W.D.T.CS.A.BC.

DEVON

EXETER Tel. 0392 73936
WRIDES TOOL CENTRE
147 FORE STREET

Open: 9.00 a.m.-5.30 p.m.
Wednesday 9.00 a.m.-1.00 p.m.
H.P.W.WM.A.

PLYMOUTH Tel. 0752 330303
WESTWARD BUILDING SERVICES ★
LTD., LISTER CLOSE, NEWNHAM
INDUSTRIAL ESTATE, PLYMPTON
Open: Mon-Fri 8 a.m.-5.30 p.m.
Sat 8.30 a.m.-12.30 p.m.
H.P.W.WM.D.A.BC.

PLYMOUTH Tel. 0752-266179
JOHN WRIDE & CO (PLYMOUTH) LTD
146 CORNWALL STREET
Open: Monday to Saturday
9.00a.m.-5.30p.m.
Wed 9.00a.m.-1.00p.m.
H.P.W.WM.A.

DORSET

BOURNEMOUTH Tel: 0202
MACHINE SALES & SERVICES 527780
(BOURNEMOUTH) LTD 527781
56 STROUDEN ROAD ★

Open: Mon-Fri 8.15 a.m.-5 p.m.
H.P.W.WM.D.A.

WEYMOUTH Tel: (0305) 787396
WEYMOUTH TOOL CENTRE ★
30A ABBOTSBURY ROAD

Open: Monday to Saturday
8 a.m.-5.30 p.m.
H.P.W.WM.D.A.BC

CO. DURHAM

BARNARD CASTLE Tel: (0833)
WOODMEN 38442/31609
27 NEWGATE ★

Open Monday-Saturday
9 a.m.-5.30 p.m.
P.W.WM.D.A.BC.

ESSEX

LEIGH ON SEA Tel. (0702)
MARSHALL & 710404
PARSONS LTD ★
1111 LONDON ROAD
Open: 8.30 am-5.30 pm Mon-Fri.
9.00 am-5.00 om Sat.
H.P.W.WM.D.CS.A.

GLOUCESTERSHIRE

TEWKESBURY Tel. 0684
TEWKESBURY SAW CO. 293092
LIMITED
TRADING ESTATE, NEWTOWN
Open: Mon-Fri 8.00 a.m.-5.00 p.m.
Saturday 9.30 a.m.-12.00 p.m.
P.W.WM.D.CS.

HAMPSHIRE

ALDERSHOT Tel. 0252 28088
BURCH & HILLS LTD
BLACKWATER WAY TRADING
ESTATE
Open: Mon-Fri 8.30 a.m.-5.30 p.m.
Saturday 8.30 a.m.-12.00 noon.
H.P.W.WM.D.A.BC.

PORTSMOUTH Tel. 0705
EURO PRECISION TOOLS 67332
LTD ★
259/263 London Road, North End
Open: Mon-Fri 9 a.m.- 5.30 p.m.
Sat 9.00 a.m.-5.00 p.m.
H.P.W.WM.D.A.BC.

SOUTHAMPTON Tel. 0703
H.W.M. 776222
THE WOODWORKERS ★
303 SHIRLEY ROAD, SHIRLEY
Open: Tues-Fri 9.30 a.m.- 6 p.m.
Sat 9.30 a.m.-4.00 p.m.
H.P.W.WM.D.CS.A.BC.T.

HEREFORDSHIRE

HEREFORD Tel. 0432 3018
PEN TOOLS (HEREFORD) LTD
24 EDGAR STREET

Open Mon.-Fri. 8 a.m.-5.30 p.m.
Sat. 8 a.m.-1 p.m.
H.P.W.D.C.A.

HERTFORDSHIRE

WATFORD Tel. 0923 48434
HOME CARE CENTRE ★
20 MARKET STREET
WATFORD, HERTS
Open 9.00 a.m.-5.30 p.m.
Mon.-Sat.
H.P.W.A.WM.BC.D.

WATFORD Tel. 0923 26052
J. SIMBLE & SONS LTD
76 QUEENS ROAD

Open 8.30 a.m.-5.30 p.m.
Mon.-Sat. Closed Wednesday
H.P.W.WM.D.A.BC.

SHOP GUIDE SHOP GUIDE

HERTFORDSHIRE

WATFORD Tel. (0923) 49911
TREND MACHINERY & CUTTING
TOOLS LTD
UNIT N, PENFOLD WORKS
IMPERIAL WAY
Open: Mon-Fri 9 a.m.-5 p.m.
P.W.WM.D.CS.BC.

KENT

MATFIELD Tel. Brenchley
LEISURECRAFT IN WOOD (089272)
'ORMONDE', MAIDSTONE RD. 2465
TN12 7JG
Open: Mon-Sun
9 a.m. - 5.30 p.m.
W.WM.D.T.A.

SITTINGBOURNE Tel.
B.T.S. (TOOLS), Sittingbourne
Unit 25, SITTINGBOURNE 79551
INDUSTRIAL PARK ★
Open: Monday - Friday
8.00 a.m. - 5.00 p.m.
H.P.W.BC.CS.

LANCASHIRE

LANCASTER Tel. 0524 2886
LILE TOOL SHOP
43/45 NORTH ROAD
Open: Monday to Saturday
9.00 a.m.-5.30 p.m.
Wed 9.00 a.m.-12.30 p.m.
H.P.W.D.A.

LEICESTERSHIRE

COALVILLE Tel. (0533) 415556
POOLE WOOD MACHINERY (06077)
SERVICES LIMITED, 5777
4 SWALLOW DALE
THRINGSTONE
Open: Mon-Fri 9 a.m.-5 p.m.
H.P.W.WM.D.A.BC.

LEICESTER Tel. 0455 43254
ROY STARTIN LTD
134 WOOD STREET
EARL SHILTON
Open: Mon-Fri 8 a.m.-5.30 p.m.
Saturday 8.00 a.m.-1.30 p.m.
H.P.W.WM.D.T.A.

LINCOLNSHIRE

LINCOLN Tel. 0522 36168/9
R & S TOOLS (LINCOLN)
LIMITED
BEEVER STREET LN6 7AD
Open: Mon-Fri 8.30 a.m.-5 p.m.
Sat 9.00 p.m.-12.00 a.m.
H.P.W.WM.D.CS.A.BC.

LINCOLN Tel. 0522 30199/
WOODWISE LIMITED 39871 or
121 HIGH STREET 0522 68428
& 06077 5777/5288
(after hours) ★
Open: Mon-Sat 9 a.m.-5.30 p.m.
P.W.WM.D.A.BC.

LONDON

ACTON Tel. 01-992 4835
A MILLS (ACTON) LTD ★
32/36 CHURCHFIELD ROAD
W3 6ED
Open: Mon-Fri 9.00 a.m.-5.00 p.m.
Closed Saturday
H.P.W.WM.

LONDON

HANWELL Tel. 01-567 2922
G. D. CLEGG & SONS
83 Uxbridge Road, W7 3ST
Open: Monday to Friday
9.00 a.m.-6.00 p.m.
Saturday 9.00 a.m.-5.30 p.m.
H.P.W.WM.D.

LONDON Tel. 01-636 7475
BUCK & RYAN LIMITED ★
101 TOTTENHAM COURT ROAD
W1P 0DY
Open: Mon-Fri 8.30 a.m.-5.30 p.m.
Saturday 8.30 a.m.-1.00 p.m.
H.P.W.WM.D.A.

LONDON Tel. 01-739 7126
CECIL W. TYZACK ★
79-81 KINGSLAND ROAD
SHOREDITCH
Open: Mon-Fri 8.45 a.m.-5.15 p.m.
Saturday 9 a.m.-12 noon
H.P.W.WM.D.A.BC.

NORBURY Tel: 01-679 6193
HERON TOOLS & HARDWARE LTD
437 STREATHAM HIGH ROAD
S.W.16
Open: Mon-Sat 8.30 a.m. - 6 p.m.
Wednesday 8.30 a.m. - 1 p.m.
H.P.W.A.

MERSEYSIDE

LIVERPOOL Tel. 051-263 1359
TAYLOR BROS (LIVERPOOL) LTD
5/9 PRESCOTT STREET
Open: Monday to Friday
8.30 a.m.-5.30 p.m.
H.P.W.WM.D.A.BC.

MIDDLESEX

NORTH HARROW Tel. 01-863 2492
WILLIAMS TECHNICAL SERVICES ★
36 STATION ROAD
Open: Mon-Fri 8 a.m.-5.30 p.m.
Wed 8 a.m.-1 p.m.,
Sat 9 a.m.-5.30 p.m.
H.P.W.WM.D.A.

NORFOLK

KINGS LYNN Tel. (0553) 2443
WALKER & ANDERSON (Kings Lynn) LTD
WINDSOR ROAD, KINGS LYNN
Open: Monday to Saturday
7.45 a.m.-5.30 p.m.
Wednesday 1 p.m. Saturday 5.00 p.m.
H.P.W.WM.D.CS.A.

NORWICH Tel. 0603 898695
NORFOLK SAW SERVICES
DOG LAND, HORSFORD
Open: Monday to Friday
8.00 a.m.-5.00 p.m.
Saturday 8.00 a.m.-12.00 p.m.
H.P.W.WM.D.CS.A.

NORWICH Tel. 0603 400933
WESTGATES WOODWORKING Tx.
MACHINERY, JUPITER ROAD 975412
OFF MILE CROSS LANE
Open: 9 a.m.-5 p.m. weekdays
9 a.m.-12 a.m. Sat.
P.W.WM.D.

NORTHAMPTONSHIRE

RUSHDEN Tel. 093-34 56424
PETER CRISP LIMITED ★
7 HIGH STREET
Open: Monday to Saturday
8.30 a.m.-5.30 p.m.
Thursday 8.30 a.m.-1.00 p.m.
H.P.W.D.BC.

NORTHUMBERLAND

BLYTH Tel. (06706) 69279
ALLAN McNAIR WOODCRAFT ★
69-71 PLESSEY ROAD
Open: Monday to Saturday
9 a.m.-5 p.m.
H.W.WM.D.T.CS.A.BC.

NOTTINGHAMSHIRE

NOTTINGHAM Tel. (0602) 225979
POOLEWOOD (06077) 5777
EQUIPMENT LTD
5a HOLLY LANE, CHILLWELL
Open: Mon-Fri 9 a.m.-5.30 p.m.
Sat. 9 a.m. to 12.30 p.m.
P.W.WM.D.CS.A.BC.

NOTTINGHAM Tel. 0602 811889
THE WOODCUTTER
5 TUDOR SQUARE
WEST BRIDGFORD
Open: Tues-Sat 9 a.m.-5.30 p.m.
Fri 9 a.m.-7.30 p.m. Closed Mon.
H.P.W.WM.D.T.CS.A.

OXFORDSHIRE

BICESTER Tel. (08692) 4156/
WOODMEN 3218/3219
104 CHURCHILL ROAD
Open: Monday-Saturday
9 a.m.-5.30 p.m.
P.W.WM.D.A.BC.

OXFORD Tel. (0865) 45118/9
SARJENT'S TOOL ★
STORES LTD
150 COWLEY ROAD
Open: Monday to Saturday
8.30 a.m.-5.30 p.m.
H.P.W.WM.D.A.BC.

STAFFORDSHIRE

TAMWORTH Tel. 0827-56188
MATTHEWS BROTHERS LTD
KETTLEBROOK ROAD
Open: Mon.-Sat. 8.30am-6.00pm
Demonstrations Sunday mornings
by appointment only
H.P.W.WM.D.T.CS.A.BC.

SUFFOLK

BURY ST. EDMUNDS Tel.
TOOLS & THINGS 0284 62022
21 CHURCHGATE ★
Open: Monday to Saturday
9.00 a.m.-5.30 p.m.
H.P.W.WM.D.A.BC.

IPSWICH Tel. 0473 86216
FOX WOODWORKING ★
'STEBBINGS' BACK LANE
WASHBROOK
Open: Tues. Fri. 9.00am-5.30pm
Sat. 9.00am-5pm
H.P.W.WM.D.A.B.C.

SURREY

CARSHALTON BEECHES Tel.
SURREY WOOD 01-642 6636
MACHINE SALES LTD ★
56A BANSTEAD ROAD
Open: Tues-Fri 9.30 am-6.00 pm
Saturday 9.30 am-2.00 pm
P.W.WM.D.BC.CS.

CROYDON Tel. 01-688 5513
L. H. TURTLE LTD ★
6-12 PARK STREET
Open: Monday to Saturday
8.30 a.m.-5.30 p.m.
H.P.W.WM.D.A.

GUILDFORD Tel. 0483 61125
MESSINGERS FOR TOOLS
14-18 CHERTSEY STREET
Open: Tuesday to Saturday
8.30 a.m.-5.30 p.m.
Closed all day Monday
H.P.W.D.BC.

SUSSEX

BOGNOR REGIS Tel: (0243) 863100
A. OLBY & SON (BOGNOR REGIS LTD)
"TOOLSHOP", BUILDER'S MERCHANT
HAWTHORN ROAD
Open: Mon-Thurs 8 a.m.-5.15 p.m.
Fri 8 a.m.-8 p.m. Sat 8 a.m.-12.45 p.m.
H.P.W.WM.D.T.C.A.BC.

WORTHING Tel. 0903 38739
W. HOSKING (TOOLS &
MACHINERY)
28 PORTLAND RD BN11 1QN
Open: Mon-Sat 8.30am-5.30pm
Wednesday 8.30am-1.00pm
H.P.W.WM.D.CS.A.BC.

WEST MIDLANDS

WEST BROMWICH Tel: 021-
CONWAY SAW & 533 5461/2
SUPPLY LTD ★
SWAN LANE
Open: 8 a.m.-6 p.m. Mon-Fri
9 a.m.-1 p.m. Saturday
P.W.WM.D.CS.BC.

WILTSHIRE

SWINDON Tel. (0793) 31361
SARJENT'S TOOL STORES LTD ★
64 FLEET STREET
Open: Monday to Saturday
8.30 a.m.-5.30 p.m.
H.P.W.WM.D.A.BC

YORKSHIRE

HALIFAX Tel. 0422 884075/
TIMBERLITE LTD 884788/33575
VICTORIA BUILDINGS ★
LUDDENDEN FOOT
Open: Monday to Friday
Saturday 9.00 a.m.-5.00 p.m.
H.P.W.WM.D.CS.A.BC.

HARROGATE Tel. 0423 66245/
MULTI-TOOLS 55328 ★
158 KINGS ROAD
Open: Monday to Saturday
8.30 a.m.-6.00 p.m.
H.P.W.WM.D.A.BC.

Prices quoted are those prevailing at press date and are
subject to alteration due to economic conditions.

Classified Advertisements

WORKSHOP EQUIPMENT

MACHINERY. A comprehensive range of new/used machinery. Check our prices, e.g. HMO 10"×5½" planer/thicknesser £374. HF30; spindle moulder £365. 12" tilt arbour sawbench 2hp motor £140. Shopsmith MK5 home workshop £897. Morso mitring machine £437, (including V.A.T.). Kity K-5. See these machines and Ryobi industrial small tools demonstrated at Woodman Woodworking Machinery Co. (Sign of the Axe), Little Malgraves Hall, Lower Dunton Road, Bulphan, Nr. Upminster, Essex. Tel: (0268) 415511 or (0702) 331729. I-U

EBAC TIMBER SEASONERS. Protimeter moisture meters, always good prices and advice from the man who pioneered small scale seasoning. John Arrowsmith, Roadham Cottage, Barton, Richmond, North Yorks. Telephone: (0325) 77362. T/C

BANDSAWS 16" throat, 7" depth, 2 speed, complete £198.00 inc. H.A. Birch, 32 Pickwick Grove, Moseley, Birmingham 13. Tel: 021-777 6577. N

PLANERS 6", 9" planers/thicknessers, 12" × 7", 9" × 6", 12" × 7", sawbenches, 10", 12", combination woodworkers. British made. Particulars, send stamp. Dodd Machine Tools Ltd., South Woodham, Chelmsford. Tel: 320 691. C-N

CORONET MAJOR UNIVERSAL MK I sawbench, wobble-saw, box comb jig, grindstone, planer/thicknesser, tool rests, b/c and face plate, basic turning tools, mounted on 2 vice heavy duty workbench £650.00 complete. Telephone: Astall Leigh (099 387) 8024. N

WASHITA & ARKANSAS whetstones now readily available from importer. Large selection, SAE for list. C. Rufino, Manor House, South Clifton, Newark, Notts. T/C

MAKE A WOODTURNING LATHE easily, construction details and parts list, send SAE to: ORTAN LATHES, P.O. Box 46, Norwich NR7 8PB. M-R

CIRCULAR AND BAND saw blades for all applications from: A.A. SMITH of Lancing Ltd., 63 Brighton Road, Shoreham, Sussex. Tel: 07917 61707 (24 hrs). K-O

5000 ELECTRIC MOTORS, FANS & BLOWERS

New & Used. Single & 3 Phase

ALWAYS IN STOCK

RING

(0742) 78088

FOR FREE STOCKLIST

**Beatson & Co (Elec.) Ltd.,
17-21 Mowbray St.,
Sheffield S3 8EN**

Viking Machinery Ltd.

Quality Machines from Viking Can Actually 'SAVE' You Money

SPRING SPECIAL
DW125 complete with standard blade PLUS disc or drum sander
R.A.S. £275.00 inc. v.a.t.
DW1370 R.A.S. £465.00 inc. v.a.t.

L-1323 Planer
£89.00 inc. v.a.t.

SU-6200 Orbital Sander
£95.00 inc. v.a.t.

Woodworking Machines
DeWalt Range
DeWalt DW1420/S
& DW1600/S (industrial)
DeWalt MC20 Mitre Saw
DeWalt DW50 Planer Thicknesser
Wadkin Tradesman Range
Wadkin EDA-2 Chisel Mortiser
Wadkin RF-15 Belt & Disc Sander
Wadkin RS-10 Spindle Moulder
Wadkin RW-10 Lathe
DeWalt Carr. £10 — Wadkin £28.00
T.C.T. Blades Bandsaw Blades
Router Cutters Plus Tooling &
Accs for all machines.

Builders/Plumbers Equipment
Circular Saws
Cement Mixers
Site Saws
Stone Cutters
Rotary Hammer Drills
Two Speed Impact Drills
Metal Cutting Saws
Angle Grinders
Carr. £5.00
14" Site Saw with T.C.T. Blade
£239 inc. v.a.t Carr £6.00
G-1800 Angle Grinder
£105.00 inc. v.a.t.

**Portable Hand Tools
WADKIN RANGE**
Wadkin Orbital Sander
Wadkin Belt Sander
Wadkin Super Sander
Wadkin Handy Trimmer
Wadkin Orbital Jig Saw
Wadkin
Hand Planer 3 Models
Wadkin Router
Power Tool Carr. £3.50

Speedy Delivery UK Mainland 48Hr.

REMEMBER! Quality Always Lasts

Phone your order direct to Val Criddle on Halifax (0422) 64178 (Works & Showroom). Halifax (0422) 34422 (Home) with 7 day, 24 hour personal Contact & Service plus late night opening until 8pm Thurs (or anytime by prior arrangement).
VIKING MACHINERY LTD.
Henry Street, Kings Cross Lane, Halifax, West Yorks HX1 2SY
(Rear of Beehive & Crosskeys)
3 ample car parks

20% OFF TREND ROUTER CUTTERS

Same day despatch, post free, write or phone for **free wall chart**, **Axminster Power Tool Centre**, Chard St, Axminster, Devon
Tel: (0297) 33656 (after 6pm 33535)

WOODTURNERS SUPPLIES

Woodturning tools, Peppermills, Salt mills, Barometers, Thermometers, Lighters, Hourglasses, Eggtimers, Ceramic tiles and clock faces, Clock movements, Spinning wheel plans, Sealers & Polishes, etc. Fast and efficient mail order service + competitive prices. S.A.E. for lists.

ERIC TOMKINSON
86 Stockport Road, Cheadle, Cheshire, SK8 2AJ. Tel: 061-491 1726

Shop open Mon-Fri from 9am to 4pm, Sat 9am to 1pm.

WOODWORKING MACHINES

STOCKISTS OF
Wadkin, Multico, Kity, Coronet, Myford, Elu, Shopsmith, Mafel, Scheppach, Bosch, DeWalt, Myblo, Trend Cutters, Monninger, Toolkraft, Elektra Beckum, Taylors Wood Turning Tools, Bennets TCT Saw Blades, Wadkin Portable Powered Tools etc

RING FOR BEST PRICES

ELU MOF 969 — £66.90 incl.
Trend cutters — can we quote you?

MATTHEWS
Matthews Brothers (Woodworkers) Ltd.,
Kettlebrook Road, Kettlebrook, Tamworth, Staffs.
Telephone: Tamworth 56188

PETER CRISP OF RUSHDEN
THE CARPENTER'S SHOP

Hand Tools by leading makers. Stockists of:
- **Craftsmen, Coronet, Elu, Kity Woodworking Machinery**
- **Sorby Turning Chisels**
- **Taylor Carving Chisels**
- **Gomex T/Carbide Circular Saws**

High Street, Rushden, Northants.
Telephone:
093 34 56424-7

TOP QUALITY SHEFFIELD WOODTURNING TOOLS

A complete range of top quality Chisels and Gouges. Full size and long and strong.
EXAMPLES: FULL SIZE

	FULL SIZE	
1" gouge £4.25	½" skew £3.25	
½" gouge £3.95	½" diamond £3.25	
1" skew £3.95	½" round £3.25	

S.A.E. for full price list

TOOLSHOP, 29 Walcot Street, Bath. Avon. Tel. Bath (0225) 61838

Braywood Estates

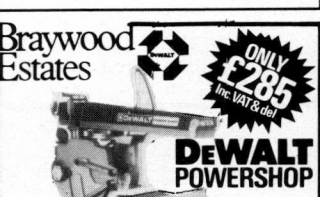

ONLY £285 inc VAT & del

DeWALT POWERSHOP

PLUS A FREE SET OF LEGS OR A T.C.T. BLADE

A superb woodworking machine. With the DW125 Powershop you can make almost anything from a piano stool to a beautiful Welsh Dresser. Our offer does not end at the point of sale! We support you with an efficient After Sales Service.

Previous Rec. Retail Price inc. VAT and Delivery £547
Our price inc. VAT & Delivery £285
(UK Mainland)

Full range of DeWalt woodworking machines and accessories in stock at discount prices.
All machines are new & current models with a 12 month guarantee

For further details contact
Braywood Estates Ltd.
(Dept. WW), Stoke Green House, Stoke Poges, Slough SL2 4HN.
Tel Slough 0753 22567/70792

SHERWOOD WOOD TURNING LATHES

All cast iron constructed. 3¾" CH 24" or 36" B.C. 3 or 4 speed, bowl turning up to 14" dia. ball-bearing spindle c/w face plate, centres etc. Prices from £75.29 inc. VAT.

Send stamp for leaflets and details of above and other low-priced machines and motors.

**JAMES INNS (Engs),
Main St., Bulwell, Nottingham**

Braywood Estates

Comprehensive range of **DeWALT** Accessories plus a super service for spare parts & on site servicing.

BRAYWOOD ESTATES LTD. FREEPOST, SLOUGH SL2 4BL
TELEPHONE : SLOUGH 0753 22567/70792

The 'SCRU-DRILL' Adjustable Woodscrew Bit
Specialist tool for Woodworker and DIY enthusiast.

Adjust to size of screw and in one single operation —
- Drill pilot hole for screw thread
- Drill pilot hole for screw body
- Countersink — counterbore
- Drill to accurate preset depth

Screw home with ease in hard or softwoods — no excess strain on screw, timber or yourself — set of four 'SCRU-DRILLS' replaces dozens of other fixed size pilot drills and countersinks — accommodates numbers 5 to 14 woodscrews.

Set of Four £13.80
inc. VAT and carriage

Send cheque or P.O. to:
KELTEK PRODUCTS
PO Box 5, Wadebridge PL27 7YZ

or SAE for further information
— Trade enquiries —

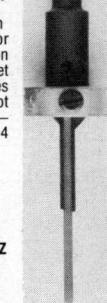

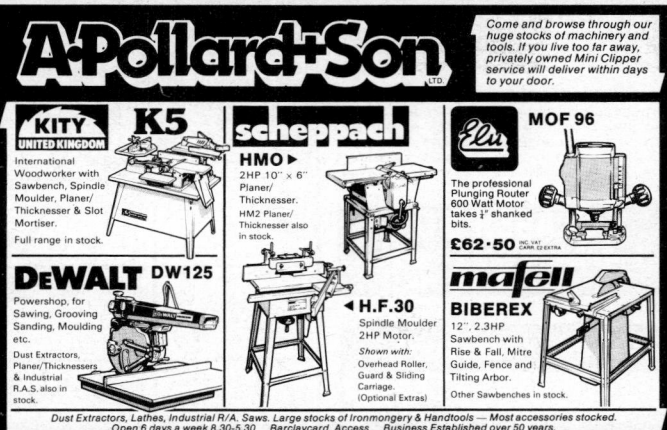

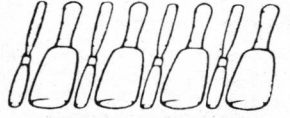

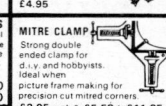

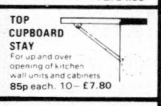
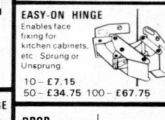

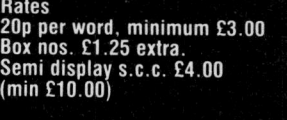
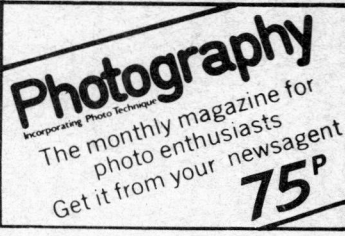

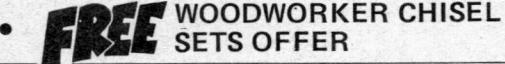

THE MAGAZINE FOR THE CRAFTSMAN

JUNE 1982 Vol. 86 No. 1063 ISSN 0043-776X

Front cover: Stanley Yates, creator of 'pictures in wood' at work at his Mawdesley, Lancashire workbench.
(Photo. Michael Edwards) Story: pages 409, 410.

Editor	Chris Dunn	
Deputy Editor	Polly Curds	
Advertisement Manager	Glyn Crole-Rees	
Advertisement Director ⎫	MAP Leisure	Michael Merrifield
Managing Director ⎭	Division	Gavin Doyle

MEMBER OF THE AUDIT
BUREAU OF CIRCULATIONS

SUBSCRIPTION DEPARTMENT: Remittances to MODEL AND ALLIED PUBLICATIONS, PO Box 35, Hemel Hempstead, Herts HP1 1EE. Price per copy 95p includes p&p. Subscription queries: Tel: Hemel Hempstead 51740. Subscription rate, including index, £11.90 per annum; overseas sterling £12.90; $29.00 US for overseas dollar subscribers. Second class postage paid in US at New York, New York. *Distribution* to North American hobby and craft stores, museums and bookshops by Bill Dean Books Ltd, 166-41 Powells Cove Boulevard, Post Office Box 69, Whitestone, New York 11357, USA. Tel: 1-212-767-6632. *Distribution* to news stand sales by Eastern News Distribution Inc, 111 Eight Avenue, New York, NY10011, USA Tel: 1-212-255-5620. (POSTMASTER: Send address changes to England).

WOODWORKER is printed in Great Britain by H. E. Warne Ltd, East Hill, St Austell, Cornwall PL25 4TN for the proprietor and publisher Model & Allied Publications Ltd (a member of the Argus Press Group). Trade sales by Argus Press Sales & Distribution Ltd, 12-18 Paul Street, London EC2A 4JS. WOODWORKER (ISSN 0043-776X) is published on the 3rd Friday of the month.

Model & Allied Publications Ltd

PO Box 35, Bridge Street, Hemel Hempstead, Herts HP1 1EE. Telephone: Hemel Hempstead (0442) 41221.

Art or craft?

Woodworker reader N. O. Potter, who lives in Lindfield, Sussex, did a double take when he saw our pictorial round-up of last year's Woodworker Show. For the photograph of the winning entry in the 'Four Legs' carving competition gave him a distinct feeling of déja vu.

'That winning entry,' he told us in a rather indignant letter, 'is an exact copy, right down to the spikes on the collar, of a well-known and widely-sold casting.' And Mr Potter was able to make direct comparisons because, as he told us, he has this particular casting on his bedside cabinet.

'As an artist myself,' Mr Potter went on, 'I have always understood that you do not copy another artist's work, except when copying the Old Masters, which is a recognised aid for students. Surely it is ethical to submit only work you have originated, or which is based on recognised sources of reference, such as the plaster statues and casts in art school, classical leaf patterns and decorations for woodcarving and modelling, etc. This surely must be so, particularly if prizes are being given'.

A good point, to be sure.

So I put the point to Ashley Iles, who sponsors this particular carving competition at the Woodworker Show. Mr Iles was unaware of the casting which had obviously been the source of inspiration for the winning work, but even when informed of the fact, he remained unrepentent.

'I do not know the opinions of my fellow judges,' wrote Ashley Iles in reply to Mr Potter's comments, 'but had I known of the existence of this model, in an amateur competition I would still have awarded first prize in this instance. We are, in my opinion, judging woodcarving, which is craftsmanship with a very small amount of art content, and all skill and craftsmanship is based on the works of previous masters.

'In the cabinetmaking section the entries are judged on the models and craftsmanship of existing pieces by Chippendale and other original craftsmen.'

And that is a good point too.

But it does seem that this question of ethics creeps into woodwork at some point, and perhaps it is not a bad idea to try and determine just at what point it happens. Certainly it is an accepted, and highly desirable, practice to copy the works of the great furniture designers, but do the same rules apply to the carver who decides to knock out a copy of Michelangelo's David?

Possibly one could try to draw a line at the point where craft and art meet, though such a line would simply disappear into what is called "a grey area". There is, however, a fairly well-defined line between artefacts that have a functional base in their design, and those which are intended purely as ornament. Can we take this line as the division at which copying makes that subtle change from being acceptable to unacceptable?

Our letters columns await your comment.

Chris Dunn

a WIDE CHOICE helps you make a WISE CHOICE

Here are some Machines and Tools we normally have available from stock.

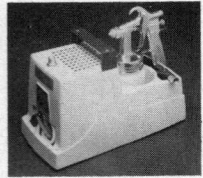

BURGESS S.R.122 Diaphragm Compressor Sprayer. 14 psi. with pressure feed gun.

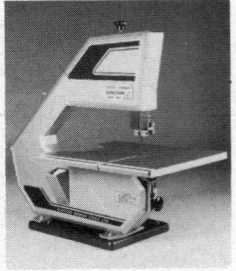

BURGESS B.K.2 Band Saw 2 speed. Max: cut 1" thick × 12" wide or 3' × 10".

MYFORD ML8A Woodturning Lathe. 30" between centres with rear turning attachment.

ELU MWA61W Grinder/Honer. 125mm dia: wheel, leather honing belt & grinding clamp guide. 0.35 hp.

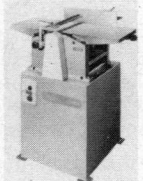

STARTRITE 352 Band Saw. 2 speed. Max: cut 11.8" thick × 13.7" wide. 1 hp.

ELU 055 Combi Bench. Can be fitted with portable circular saw or router. Snip-Off attachment available.

EMCO TS-5 Circular Saw. Max: cut 55mm thick, tilting table. Sanding & Combing accs: available. 1.20 hp.

MULTICO Type M Chisel Mortiser. Takes ¼"-1" Chisels. Can be used as drilling machine. ¾ hp.

STARTRITE-INCA AF.190M Planer-Thicknesser. Planes up to 10¼" wide. Thicknessing up to 6¼". 1¼ hp.

Please name the items that interest you when asking for details and our Price Lists.

EMCO-STAR Multi-Purpose Machine. Combines Circular, Band, Jig & Fret Saws. Belt & Disc Sanders. 2 speed. 0.5/0.7 hp. Planer-Thicknesser & Lathe attachments can be fitted.

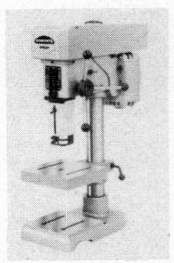

STARTRITE S.P.50 Bench Drill. ½" Chuck. 5 speeds. ½ hp. 5 Ball Bearings. Floor type available.

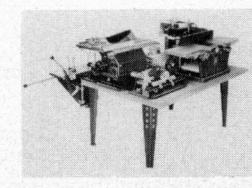

KITY Combination Set. Circular saw, spindle moulder, planer-thicknesser, mortiser & grinders on table with 1½ hp. motor.

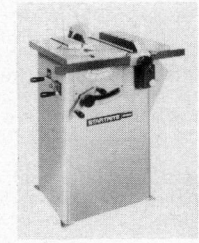

STARTRITE TA/SP.145 Saw Bench. Max: cut 3⅛" deep. Tilt arbor. 1 hp.

STANLEY 268 Heavy Duty Router. Takes ¼" & ⅜" shank cutters. All ball bearings. 1½ hp.

ELU MFF 80/00 Planer/Rabbetter. 80mm wide TCT. blades. 650 watts. Inversion stand available.

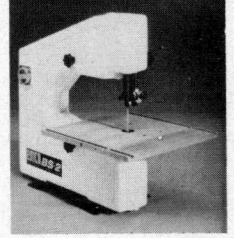

EMCO BS.2. Band Saw for wood, metal or plastic. 3 speed. Max: cut 145mm thick × 360mm wide. 370 watts.

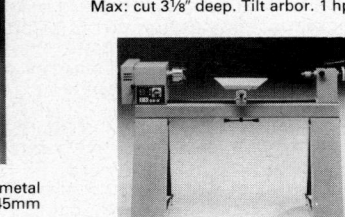

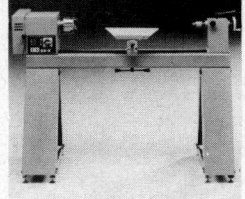

EMCO DB.5. Wood Turning Lathe. 1000mm between centres, 200mm centre height. 4 speeds. ¾ hp. Copying attachment available.

KITY 7227 Spindle Moulder. 20mm dia: spindle. Takes cutters in slot or block. 6200 rpm. 1½ hp. on stand.

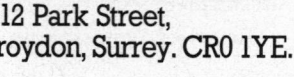

Open 6 days per week 8.30-5.30

L.H. Turtle Ltd.
6-12 Park Street,
Croydon, Surrey. CR0 1YE.

Established 1894

01-688-5513

Quality or price?

Swiss precision engineering and highly efficient production techniques together give INCA the edge for quality and value for money.

You won't find a more versatile and reliable range of woodworking equipment.

Price for price, quality for quality, you need the best. It pays to invest in INCA.

INCA solves the problem!

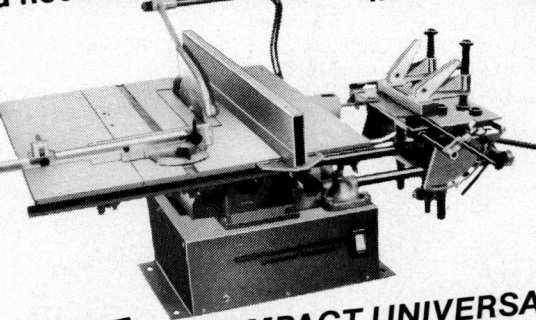

COMPACT UNIVERSAL CIRCULAR SAW

Inca Compact Circular Saw Basic unit fully motorised with blade, rip fence and mitre-guide

£299·00 inc V.A.T.

Table Extension, Mortising Table, Chuck and Miller Bit not included.

The 'Compact' is easy and safe to use, has a wide range of functions, yet weighs only 25kg.

This incredibly accurate machine is precision built to give years of pleasure to the amateur cabinet maker.

Full range of accessories include:

- **Micro Adjuster** for rip fence making cutting adjustment of 0.1mm possible.
- **Tenoning Jig**–indispensable for making a series of tenons and grooves.
- **Comb Jointing Device**–produce the perfect comb joint quickly and easily.
- **Dado Blades** (Grooving Cutters). 6 widths available. Wobble washers standard with saw.
- **Moulding Head and Cutters**–for safe spindle moulding cutters have soft metal core and hard steel cutting edge. Suva protecting device holds workpiece down and at the same time presses it against rip fence.
- **Mortising Table** for precision drilling, boring and slot mortising.
- **3 Jaw Chuck**–special taper fit design for drills and slot mortice bits.
- **Sanding Disc and Drum**–for use in chuck or on flexible driving shaft.
- **Saw Blades**–many different types available.

INCA BANDSAW

- Precision built 10" throat bandsaw with all essential parts in pressure cast alloy. Ideal for wood, non-ferrous metals and plastics.
- Professional blade tracking control capable of cutting 6" of hardwood and accurate tilt table (45° one way) **dove tailed** for optional mitre guide.
- Separate saw blade micro adjusting screw guides and thrust rollers fitted above and below table.
- **Blade tension indicator** and moveable brush on lower wheel to remove sawdust.
- Standard equipment includes rip fence and depth stop.
- Optional extras include 8 different blades, **sanding attachment, fret saw** with special guides to allow 3mm minimum radius. **Micro-adjuster** for rip fence giving accuracy of 0.1mm.
- **Unmotorised** version available for belt or electric drill power.

Basic unit, fully motorised **£279·00** inc V.A.T.

Basic unit, unmotorised **£169·00** inc V.A.T.

Prices correct at January 1982

Woodworking Machines of Switzerland LIMITED

Sole U.K. Agents for INCA Woodworking Machinery.

INCA distributors in the following locations:
Aberdeen, Ashford (Kent), Ayr, Biggen Hill, Blackpool, Blythe (Newcastle), Bristol, Bury St. Edmunds, Cambridge, Cardigan (Dyfed), Carlisle, Carshalton Beeches, Croydon, Dinas (Gwynedd), Doncaster, Edinburgh, Enfield, Exeter, Glasgow, Hastings, Hay-on-Wye, Helston, Hitchen, Hull, Ilford, Ipswich, King's Lynn, Launceston, Leeds, Leigh-on-Sea, Leominster, Lincoln, Liverpool, London West End, Manchester, Matfield (Kent), Middlesbrough, Milton Keynes, Nantwich, Newquay, Northern Ireland, Norwich, Nottingham, Oxford, Peterborough, Ramsgate, Reading, Southampton, Swindon, Taunton, Truro, Watford, Worthing.

THE COMPLETE INCA RANGE INCLUDES:
- Inca Major Circular Saw
- Inca Multi-Purpose Circular Saw
- Inca Jointer-Planer
- Inca Combined Jointer-Planer/Automatic Feed Thicknesser
- Inca Rabbeting Planer
- Inca Bandsaw
- Inca Spindle Moulder
- Inca Blades / Cutters
- Inca Benches and Work Stands
- Inca Woodworking Project Plans

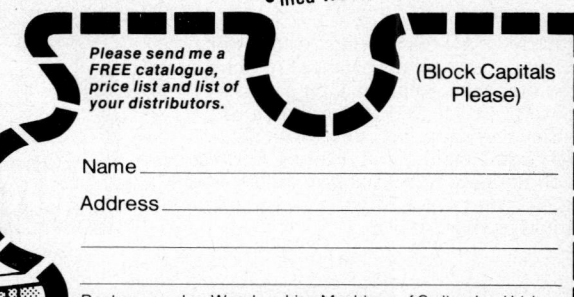

Please send me a FREE catalogue, price list and list of your distributors.

(Block Capitals Please)

Name _____

Address _____

Post coupon to: Woodworking Machines of Switzerland Ltd Inca House, 7 Peverel Drive, Granby Milton Keynes, MK1 1NL Telephone: Milton Keynes (0908) 641492   WW5

5 YEAR WARRANTY

`Kity' Quality Machines For Craftsmen

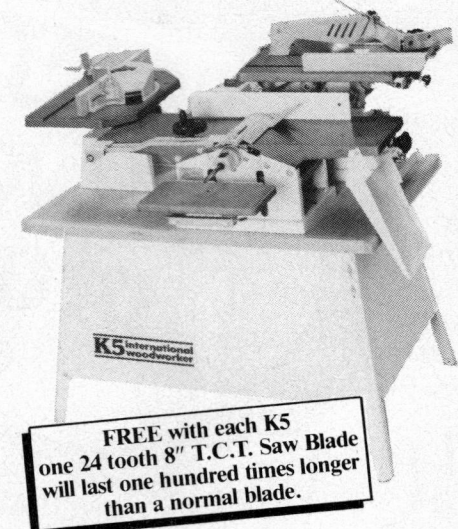

K5 international woodworker

FREE with each K5 one 24 tooth 8″ T.C.T. Saw Blade will last one hundred times longer than a normal blade.

Your craft depends on the skill of your hands, together with the quality of your tools.

The results you achieve reflect the care you have taken to choose the raw materials, the thought you have put into your design. As a true craftsman, every purchase for your workshop will have been chosen with consideration and care, attention paid to the quality of construction and value for money. When you purchase machinery these standards are important and must not be compromised.

Value for Money
At Kity we understand the needs of the craftsman, in consequence, we produce a range of machines unique in their versatility, adequate in capacity and manufactured to a very high standard. Machines which are unconditionally guaranteed and are excellent value for money.

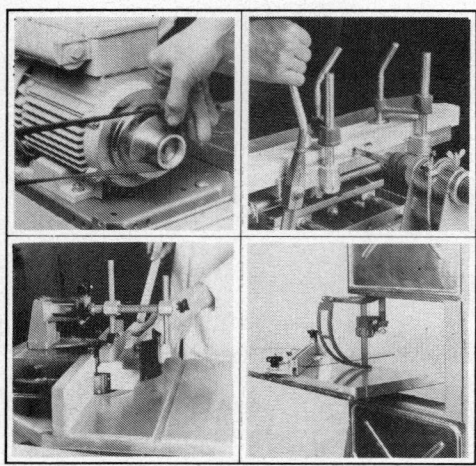

Simple and Easy to use
All Kity machines are of cast construction with sealed bearings, dynamically balanced rotating blocks and precision machined components. You will expect to achieve a high standard of workmanship with Kity. Moreover, with the unique Kity combinations your existing working methods do not need to be changed, unlike other combinations you can use Kity machinery exactly as you would use hand tools.

The K5 Combination
Specifically designed for the craftsman who requires the quality of the 700 series without the capacity, ideal for most household projects including fitted kitchens and wardrobes, boat building, replacement windows and doors, architrave and skirting boards. A versatile unit at a very attractive price: **£559.00** + V.A.T.

Buy direct from Kity U.K. and use a K5 for 30 days, if you are not entirely satisfied for whatever reason, we will refund your total costs.

The K5 Consists Of:

512 Saw	2″ depth of cut, rise and fall, two speeds, mitre guide and rip fence.
535 Planer	6″ wide, 30″ bed, 6″ × 4″ thicknesser, single speed.
511 Spindle Moulder	¾″ × ¾″ rebate, 2″ rise and fall.
550 Slot Mortiser	3″ depth, 5″ wide, 4″ rise and fall.
500 Work Bench	with 1hp motor and drive.

The 700 Series
Each machine is available independently, just add a stand and motor, or you can make up your own combination by fitting the machines of your choice around a motor on a 700 stand.

617 Saw	3″ depth of cut, rise and fall, two speeds, mitre guide, rip fence.
612 Bandsaw	5¾″ depth, 11½″ throat, steel construction.
636 Planer	10″ wide, 40″ bed, 10″ × 6″ two speed thicknesser.
635 Planer	8″ wide, 40″ bed, 8″ × 6″ two speed thicknesser.
535 Planer	6″ wide, 30″ bed, 6″ × 4″ one speed thicknesser.
627 Spindle Moulder	1¼″ × 1¼″ rebate, 2½″ rise and fall.
652 Slot Mortiser	4″ depth, 6″ wide, 6″ rise and fall.

Plus a wide range of accessories, including 6″ Belt Sander, 4″ Disc Sander, 3″ Drum Sander, Planer Knife Sharpener.

KITY
UNITED KINGDOM

Now in Australia and South Africa.
Please write for details.

Kity U.K., Sizer's Court, Henshaw Lane, Yeadon, Leeds LS19 7DP. Tel: (0532) 509110. Telex: 55792

Prices quoted are those prevailing at press date and are subject to alteration due to economic conditions.

HERON TOOLS - THE WOODWORKERS SHOP

OVER 11,000 ITEMS OF TOOLS ★ MACHINERY ★ ACCESSORIES

RECORD ★ STANLEY ★ MARPLES ★ RABONE CHESTERMAN ★ SPEAR & JACKSON ★ WOLF ★ BLACK & DECKER ★ BOSCH ★ RIDGEWAY ★ ECLIPSE ★ STABILA ★ DISSTON ★ MAKITA ★ SKIL ★ BURGESS ★ PICADOR ★ RYOBI ★ CRAFTSMAN (USA) ★ DEWALT ★ SHOPMATE (USA) ★ ASHLEY ILES ★ ELU ★ TOOL CRAFT (USA) ★ R.SORBY

HARDWARE & IRONMONGERY ITEMS BY THE THOUSAND!

BOLTS, SCREWS, WASHERS & NUTS OVER 6000 ITEMS & SIZES STOCKED

MOST ITEMS DISCOUNTED ALSO SPECIAL OFFERS

  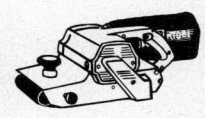

'PERFECTION' IN PORTABLE POWER TOOLS!

Superbly made, and with ample power the Ryobi range of power tools offers the complete answer to your needs. What's more despite their precision engineering they don't cost the earth either. In fact we recommend that you

DO NOT BUY A POWER TOOL UNTIL YOU HAVE EXAMINED A RYOBI!

WE WILL GLADLY SEND YOU A CATALOGUE AND WE GUARANTEE YOU WILL BE GLAD WE DID!

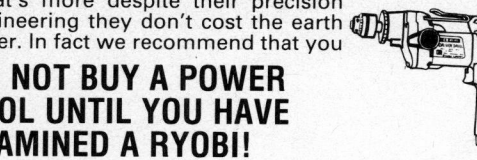

OVER 3500 DIFFERENT STYLES & TYPES & FINISHES ESPECIALLY FOR CABINETMAKERS

CABINET HANDLES, FURNITURE & CLOCK CASE FITTINGS, KNOBS & KNOCKERS FROM THE EARLIEST PERIOD TO ULTRA MODERN – POSSIBLY THE UK's LARGEST SELECTION

HIGH QUALITY MACHINES – VAT INCLUSIVE PRICES – ALL CAST IRON AND STEEL CONSTRUCTION (EXCEPT WHERE STATED OTHERWISE)

10 INCH SAW BENCH
Precision cast iron table 40 × 27 in. incorporating rise and fall and tilt mechanisms **£250**

8 INCH SAW BENCH
Rise and fall tilt table size 11 × 13 in. Less motor and floor stand **£77.98**

BENCH GRINDERS
5 in. wheel, $\frac{1}{8}$ h.p. motor **£22**
6 in. wheel, $\frac{1}{4}$ h.p. motor **£35**
8 in. wheel, $\frac{1}{2}$ h.p. motor **£52**
All models incorporate single-phase motors, safety eye shields, etc.

6 INCH PLANER

Bed 6 × 45 in., overall height 32 in., $\frac{3}{4}$ h.p. motor
£200

WOOD TURNING LATHE

£135
$\frac{1}{2}$ h.p. motor, 2 speeds. 40 in. between centres, 18 in. swing.

10 INCH DISC SANDER
Large precision tilting table. $\frac{1}{2}$ h.p. motor. No volt release starter. Cast aluminium construction. **£178.55**

7" SAW BENCH
7 in. saw blade, rise and fall tilt table 14 × 13 in. Heavy duty ball bearings, cast aluminium construction. With $\frac{1}{2}$ h.p. motor, bench stand, switch, etc.
£163.95 less motor, etc. **£87.15**

COMBINED SAW BENCH-PLANER
7 in. saw blade, rise and fall tilt table. 4 in. wide planer blades. Cast aluminium construction, heavy duty ball bearings. $\frac{1}{2}$ h.p. motor **£245.18**

WOOD BANDSAW
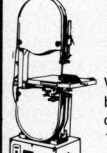
Wood cutting bandsaw, $5\frac{1}{2}$ in. depth of cut and 14 in. throat, $\frac{1}{2}$ h.p. motor, tilting table 14 × 14 in. Overall height 65 in. **£225**

3-SPEED MODEL
$\frac{1}{6}$ h.p. motor, $\frac{1}{2}$ in. chuck. Depth gauge and tilting table **£65**

5-SPEED MODEL
As above but with $\frac{1}{4}$ h.p. motor **£94**

12-SPEED MODEL
$\frac{1}{3}$ h.p. motor, $\frac{5}{8}$ in. chuck, No. 2 Morse Taper. Rack operated rise and fall tilting table (round or square) **£145**

BENCH DRILLS

BELT SANDERS/GRINDERS
4 in. wide × $39\frac{1}{2}$ in. belt. 8 in. dia. grinding wheel. $\frac{1}{2}$ h.p. motor **£135**
With $1\frac{3}{4}$ in. wide × $32\frac{1}{2}$ in. belt. 6in. dia. grinding wheel. $\frac{1}{3}$ h.p. motor **£80**
(Belt sander on both machines adjustable to horizontal or vertical positions

4 INCH PLANER

Table size $15\frac{1}{2}$ in. × 5 in. 4 in. blades. Both tables fully adjustable. Cast aluminium construction with heavy duty ball bearings. With $\frac{1}{2}$ h.p. motor, bench stand, switch etc. **£152.00**
Without motor, etc **£87.99**
4 INCH PLANER similar to above but ground cast iron bed and plain bearings. Less motor **£69.95**

BELT/DISC SANDER
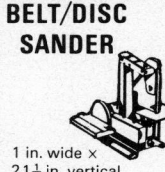
1 in. wide × $21\frac{1}{4}$ in. vertical belt sander plus 8 in. dia. disc, tilt table **£82**

MORTICE ATTACHMENT

$2\frac{1}{4}$" Collar
£20 incl. VAT
Rugged, precisely machined cast iron with steel sleeve. Will fit most pillar drills.

MORTICE CHISEL WITH BIT
$\frac{1}{4}$" to $\frac{3}{8}$" **£6** each $\frac{3}{4}$" **£14** each
$\frac{1}{2}$" **£8** each $\frac{5}{8}$" **£10** each
each incl. VAT

CARPENTER'S VICE

With quick release mechanism.
7" **£18** incl. VAT   9" **£25** incl. VAT

CROSS VICE
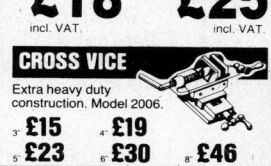
Extra heavy duty construction. Model 2006.
3" **£15**   4" **£19**
5" **£23**   6" **£30**   8" **£46**

OPEN
MONDAY TO SATURDAY
8.30 a.m.—6 p.m.
WEDNESDAY 8.30 a.m.—1 p.m.

Free Parking for 200 cars at rear
Entrance in Granville Gdns.

HERON TOOLS & HARDWARE LTD
Tel: 01-679 6193
437–439 STREATHAM HIGH ROAD, NORBURY, LONDON SW16

WHEN THE NURSERY COT GETS TOO SMALL...

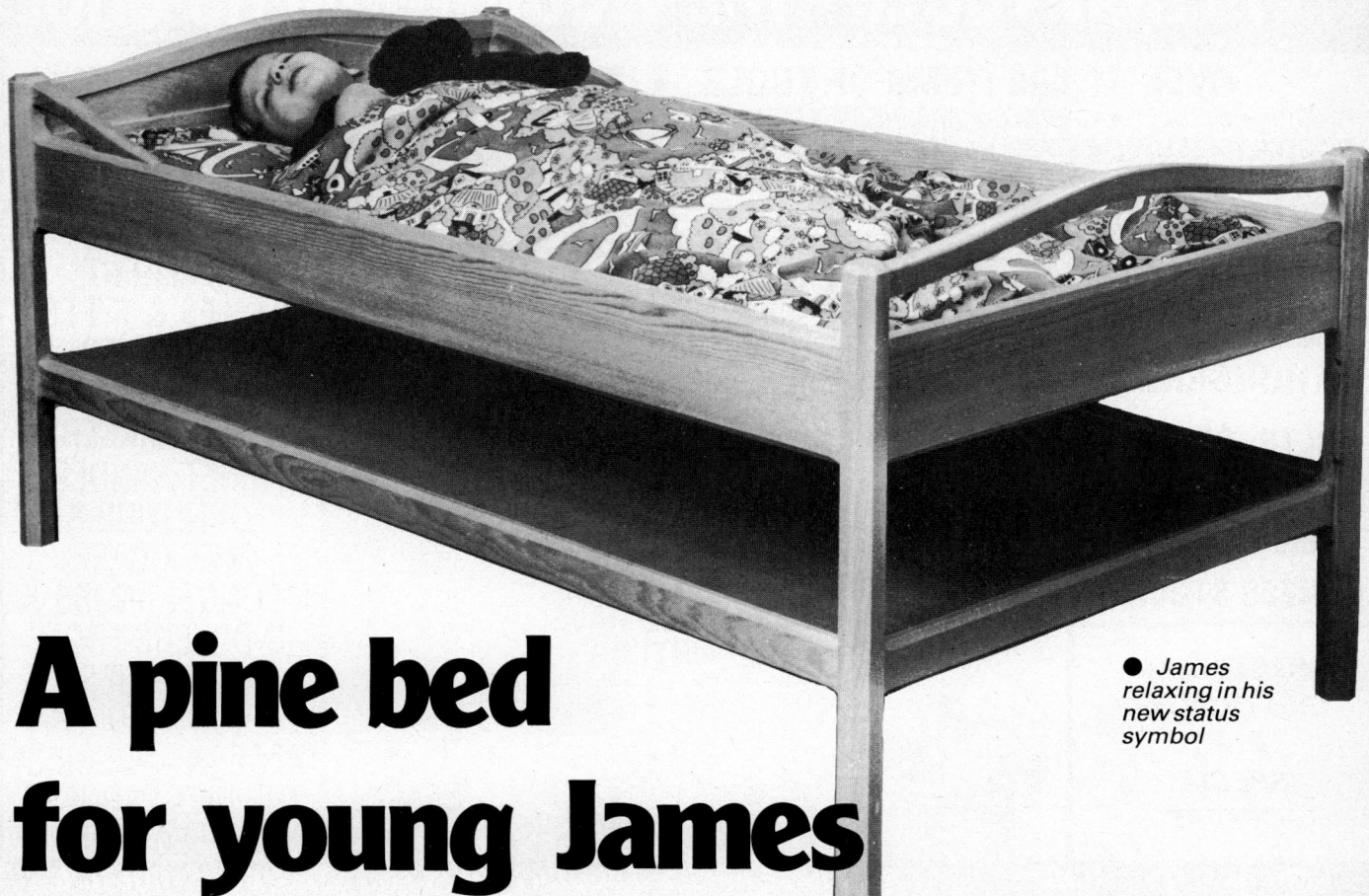

● *James relaxing in his new status symbol*

A pine bed for young James

When young James Grant demanded an upgrade in status from infancy to childhood by moving from his cot into a proper bed, his Dad had to admit this was a perfectly reasonable request. In fact Dad, better known to *Woodworker* readers as Bob Grant, did more than just comply. He designed and built a bed guaranteed to be the envy of James' friends, and here he explains his design criteria, along with details of construction. The pictures were taken by John Peacock

CUTTING LIST

Nett sizes given in inches

No.	Description	L	W	T	Material
4	legs	24	1¾	1¾	Pine or hardwood
2	top side-rails	56	4¾	1⅛	Pine or hardwood
2	top end-rails	29	4¾	1⅛	Pine or hardwood
2	ox-bow rails	29	ex4	1⅛	Pine or hardwood
2	pillow-retaining rails	11	ex3	1⅛	Pine or hardwood
1	headboard panel	29	ex4	¼	Plywood
1	mattress base-board	55	29	½	Plywood
2	bottom side-rails	56	2	1⅛	Pine or hardwood
2	bottom end-rails	29	2	1⅛	Pine or hardwood
1	tie bar	28½	1¾	1⅛	Pine or hardwood
1	shelf base	55	28	¼	Plywood
1	mattress (snugfit)			2 or 3	Foam
1	fabric top to shelf				Vinyl simulated leather

Somewhere between the first two of Shakespeare's famous 'seven ages of man', lies that period when every utterance of the offspring begins with 'I want'. In my experience few such demands are really justified, although perhaps in the case of wanting a bed rather than a cot some heed should be paid to the request, heralding as it does a change from infant status to proper childhood.

Among the considerations that I took into account when designing this bed were the needs to provide a convenient height from the floor for the child to scramble in and out of bed; a well for the mattress which would also provide sufficient side depth to prevent toppling out; no sharp arrises to injure little bodies (hence the chamfering and octagonal legs); storage space for the inevitable clutter of toys and perhaps a suitcase. Lastly, thought was given to the production of a piece of furniture that was recognisably 'up-market' of the nursery type that the child could importantly call its own – even to the extent of initials and date burnt into the headboard.

The dimensions fit the standard size bed linen for children, whilst the foam mattress was obtained from Direct Foam of Lane End Road, High Wycombe, Bucks, who advertise nationally and market foams with a specification suitable for mattresses.

The construction is straightforward mortise and tenon work and the accompanying scale drawings show the details of the piece whilst the half sectional front elevation shows how the mattress base and shelf

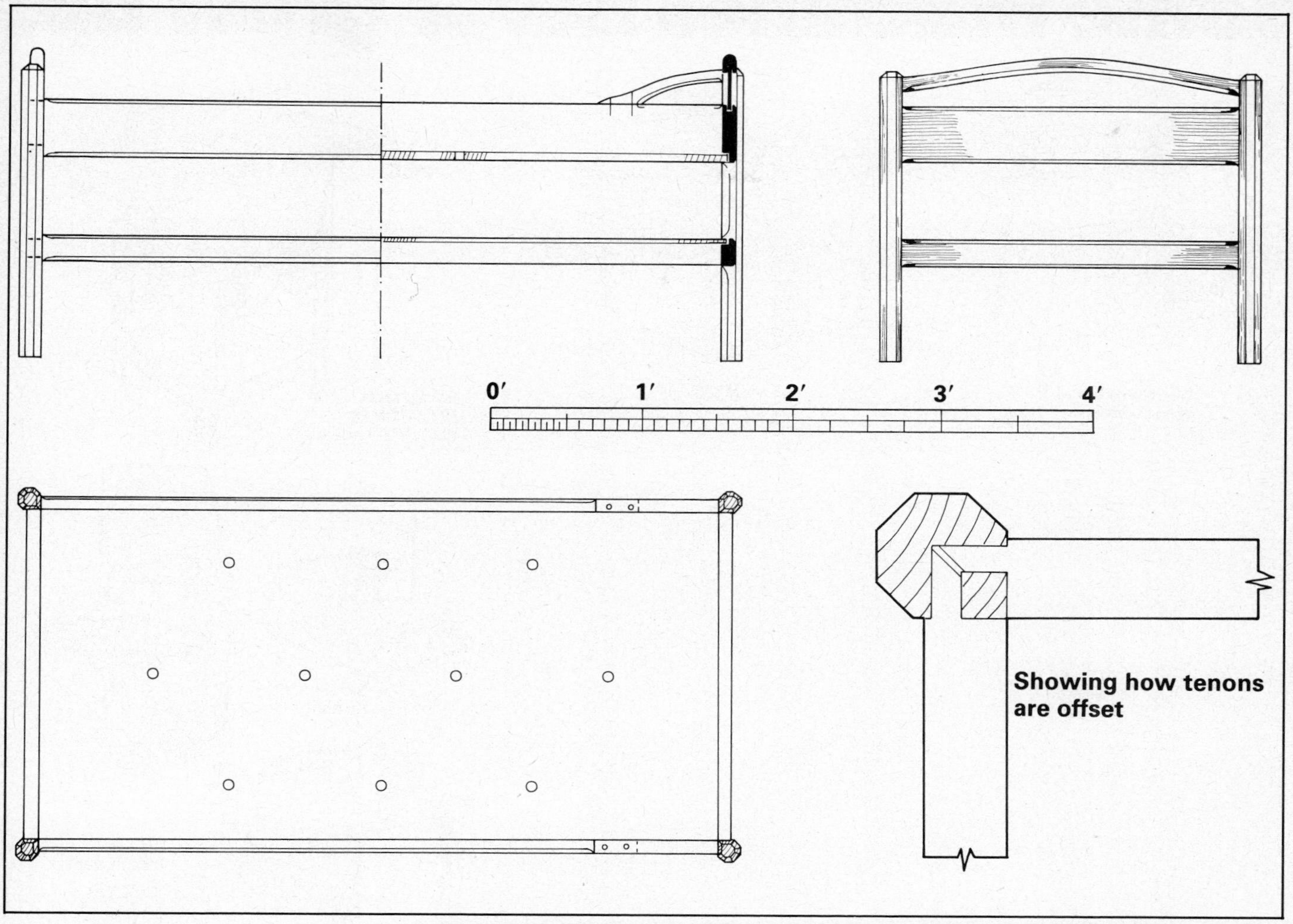

Showing how tenons
are offset

boards are rebated in. The sketch shows
how the tenons are offset on the rails to give
an improved penetration into the legs – the
octagons at these points being left square
on the inside faces.

The end frames should be made up as
sub-assemblies and before gluing the side
rails on. It is important to place the mattress
and shelf boards loosely in place as they
cannot be manipulated into position once
the bed is together. The mattress board
should be drilled with sufficient holes to
provide ventilation to the mattress itself and
the board is well screwed and glued up into
its rebate. The ¼in ply shelf has a simulated
leather covering, although a slatted shelf
would serve just as well. There is a mid-way
tie bar set across the shelf which is dovetail
housed into the two bottom side rails.

Photograph no 1 shows the junction of the
pillow retaining rails at the headboard
end. These are tenoned into the legs and
screwed and pelleted into the rails. If two
pillows are likely to be used then it would be
as well to heighten the headboard end
dimensions by a further 6in or so.

All edges are well dubbed over except
where chamfered (photo no 2) and a
'grubby hand proof' finish could be cellulose lacquer, matted with 00 steel wool and
buffed to a dull gloss. The stearates in this
type of finish make it slightly waxy and
marks are easily removed with a damp
cloth.

The original bed was made in pine but
any straight grained hardwood (particularly
oak) would suit.

● *Above photo
1 shows the
junction of the
pillow
retaining rails
at the
headboard
end. Right
photo 2
details the
chamfering
which neatly
finishes the
pine bed*

Some machines never grow up.

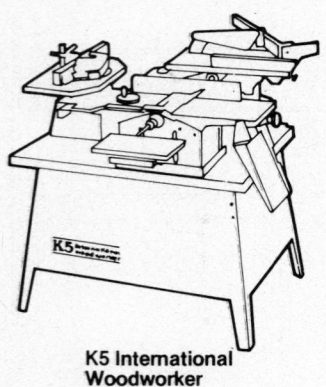

K5 International Woodworker

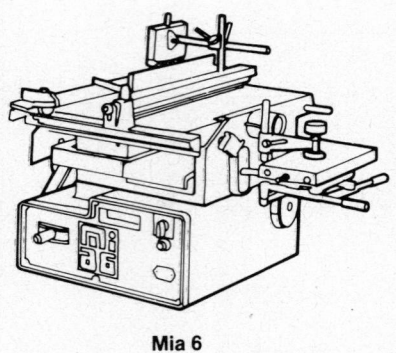

Mia 6

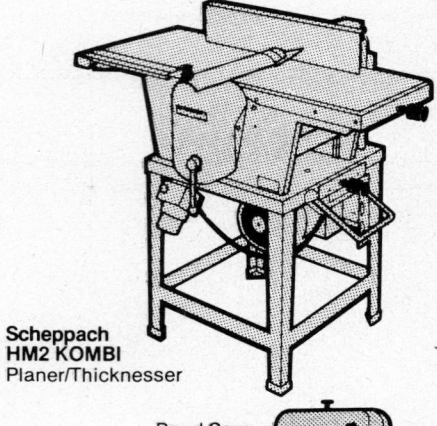

Scheppach HM2 KOMBI Planer/Thicknesser

Band Saw Attachment

Slot Mortiser Attachment

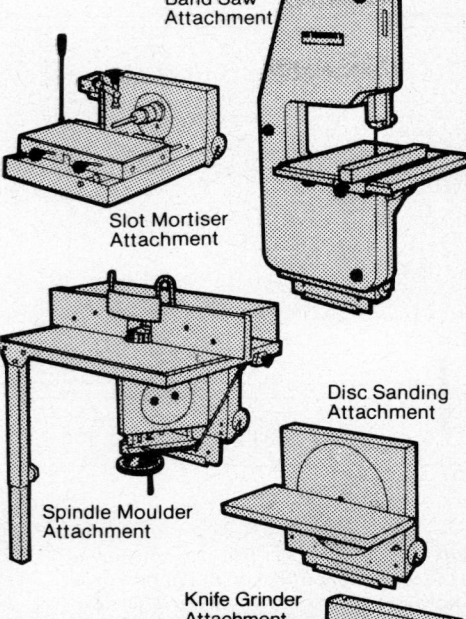

Spindle Moulder Attachment

Disc Sanding Attachment

Knife Grinder Attachment

Saw Table Attachment

scheppach

The more you think ahead

Lathe Attachment

Look at any popular multi-purpose woodworking machine and you will find that they do not only offer an extremely limited working capacity, but also provide no more than a sawbench, planer, thicknesser, mortiser and spindle moulder which, of course, is very acceptable to start with. But what happens "tomorrow" when you also need a bandsaw, or sander etc? New, separate machines? More expense?

Not with Scheppach. This is a machine with more than adequate working capacity, plus the capability to develop and grow with you. Add a lathe, disc or belt sander, bandsaw or knife grinder. Scheppach is the only machine to offer all these features.

Sumaco Machinery & Tools,
Suma House, Huddersfield Road,
Elland, West Yorkshire HX5 9AA.
Tel. (0422) 79811   WW/6

Prices quoted are those prevailing at press date and are subject to alteration due to economic conditions.

 # High Speed Steel Turning Tools

High Speed Steel 1″ Roughing-out Gouge
Unhandled **£18.80**
Handled **£20.13**
(Including VAT)

High Speed Steel Skew Chisel
Unhandled **£8.45**
Handled **£9.78**
(Including VAT)

High Speed Steel Scraper
Designed by Gordon Stokes
Hand ground – Black finish **£5.46**
(Including VAT)

The above and many more new exciting tools are in the Ashley Iles catalogue supplement sent free on request.

Balinese Style Carving Tools

Some of the finest wood carving in the world is produced on the Indonesian Island of Bali. The tools they use are here replicated by Ashley Iles with the addition of a reinforced sleeve.

The set comprises 6 solid steel fishtail pattern tools, length 9″ from the finest carbon steel. Black backed, straw-tempered used with a mallet or hardwood shaft.

£23.00 including VAT for the set of six.

 ## Cranked Parting Tools

Save valuable timber, making rings from bowl waste (Useful for picture frames, radius corners etc.)
£12.50 a pair including VAT
Hand ground, black backed with wooden handles.

In conjunction with Ashley Iles Gordon Stokes offers a free phone or mail advisory service. Full details in the catalogue supplement.

Courses of Tuition by Gordon Stokes
A step by step introduction to woodcarving from sharpening to finishing **£7.50** post free.

Woodturning Course – a solid introduction to woodturning based on 20 years experience. Vol. 1 **£7.50**, Vol. 2 **£7.50** both post free.

All Gordon Stokes books are listed in the catalogue supplement.

Ashley Iles
woodcarving & turning tools
made in the old tradition

Ashley Iles (Edge Tools) Ltd., East Kirkby, Spilsby, Lincolnshire PE23 4DD. Telephone (07903) 372

Send for our 12 page full colour catalogue showing the full range of carving and turning tools (50p). There is also a free supplement showing recent additions

Main Distributors
Alec Tiranti Ltd., 70 High St., Theale, Reading.

Heron Tools Ltd., 437 Streatham High Rd., Norbury SW16.

Scotland
Allan McNair Woodcraft 69 Plessey Rd., Blythe, Northumberland.

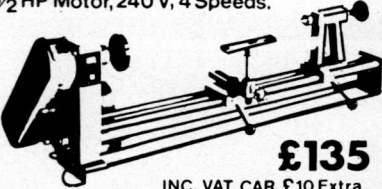

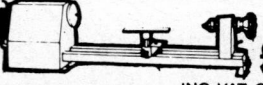
Prices quoted are those prevailing at press date and are subject to alteration due to economic conditions.

RAY KEY
Woodturner

Ray Key is one of the judging panel at the annual Woodworker Show and a well respected craftsman in the woodturning scene both here and abroad. His work, characterised by its modern philosophy and innovative approach, is to be found in most of the important galleries and crafts centres. Polly Curds visited him in his Evesham workshop recently, and this is her report

Profile of a craftsman

● Ray and the raw material

Evesham is set in a loop of the River Avon, dating from the foundation of the abbey in AD 708. Abbot Reginald's Gateway, a 12th century timber-framed building at the end of a passage from the market place, leads to the abbey remains and the two churchyards of the 12th century All Saints Church and the 16th century Church of St Lawrence. At the centre of Evesham stands the 110ft Bell Tower built in 1539, part of the ruined Benedictine abbey, where a plaque marks the burial place of Simon de Montfort, father of the English parliament, who was killed fighting at the Battle of Evesham on 4 August 1265. In Vine Street the 14th century Abbey Almonry has a museum of local history and the old town stocks are preserved on the green outside the museum.

Also in Vine Street, but not needing stocks to hold him still, *Woodworker* found woodturner Ray Key and his wife Liz, who runs Key Crafts. Ray was born in Kenilworth

in 1942 and as a young lad served a five-year apprenticeship as a pattern maker. He followed this with seven years as a clay modeller with Chrysler Styling Studios, where he translated the designs and sketches of the design team into 3D models. It was here among artists that his eye was trained to appreciate the complicated geometry of forms, the circles, spheres, cylinders and spirals. One of the most difficult forms to translate from two to three dimensions, he says, was the ogee curve necessitated by many of the surface changes that are seen in the motor industry.

Ray bought himself a simple lathe and practised woodturning for nearly eight years as a hobby before he made it a full-time living in 1973. He says during these eight years he read and reread Fred Pain's book, *The Practical Woodturner,* and taught himself all the techniques and skills contained in it. Woodturning books now are mostly pictorial in content, so learning from text was more of a struggle. When one looks at his work today it is obvious Ray made the effort and succeeded. He was forcefully nudged in the right direction – 'not pushed but rather guided' – by Liz. She bought him a stock of timber with her end-of-year bonus and gradually his hobby became a way of life.

Ray says in these early days he was influenced by the standard of craftsmen around at that time, not necessarily by their style but by their quality and craftsmanship. The three men to whom he feels he owes most are George Sneed (a turner in the late 1950s and early 1960s who sold work at Heals), Dennis French (whom Ray regards as one of the best production turners in this country) and John Trippas of Devon, who now makes mostly furniture rather than concentrating on turning.

Liz gave up her job and opened a small gallery in Coventry to sell Ray's work. This lasted for 18 months and the couple then moved to Evesham, where they have been for the last nine years.

In tiny premises behind their Vine Street shop Ray started by producing domestic table woodware. Ninety per cent of his production was in teak with elm and a little yew making up the other 10 per cent. He cringes a little now at his early attempts, he knows now that he was lucky to make a living at first with a product that was not widely accepted as anything other than a

functional piece and therefore not commanding a high price. Domestic woodware such as platters, goblets, bowls and boards are the ordinary kitchen utensils that for more than 3,000 years have graced man's table, but they now have to be something more, to have a special something, while the useful bowl in wood has been supplanted by the mass-produced plastic or ceramic bowl.

Sculpture and wood carvings have always been acceptable as collectors' items and have found their way readily into museums. Now a new age of woodturning is emerging. Bowls are finding a place on the shelves of art galleries, museums and private collections, and photographs appear in magazines, as an aesthetically pleasing and decorative art form emerges. Faster in the States, but gathering momentum here, is a new feeling about wood, and the beauty of objects made from wood for sheer pleasure of form, not fundamental necessity.

Since 1977 Ray has been interested in producing items of a more aesthetic nature, in a wide range of exotic and unusual timbers. He tries to show the full beauty of the material by way of simple design form, and always has a high quality of workmanship behind each piece.

He says in the last two to three years turning in this country has taken gigantic strides forward; the aesthetically pleasing is coming into its own. He finds he is being

● Tall knobbed box in Indian rosewood

(continued on page 380)

RAY KEY
Woodturner

(continued from page 379)

● *Shaped bowl in Indian ebony*

● *A selection of woods, and turned shapes from the lathe of Ray Key demonstrate his versatility*

asked increasingly often to produce a special piece – a one off – a higher priced quality product. Because of the quality of his work he is becoming known in this country and abroad and so is finding he is being constantly challenged to make pieces that are adventures in themselves. But he still needs the bread and butter side, the mini-production line, and his various gallery and craft shop outlets. The emphasis is changing here too; galleries ask for more work, but are choosey about what they take, while the craft shops are dwindling in number.

Ray now has a 'proper' workshop some two miles from his home, he is a disciplined man (it was being in industry that fostered the nine to five habit) often working 60-65 hours a week, now mainly in exotics. He usually has 50 or so different timbers in stock, half of which are from South America and India. Bob Brett of North Heigham Sawmills is a good friend and, as many other turners and cabinetmakers have found, Bob stocks a good range of excellent timber.

Ray doesn't work from sketches or drawings. 'The grain dictates the bowl', he says. 'The eye and hand have learnt cunning over the years. But I'm not quite like Bob Stocksdale of the US, who looks at a log and normally works out the number of bowls it will make.'

In 1977 Ray's work was accepted by the Crafts Council and placed on their Index. He put five pieces into their New Faces exhibition at the British Crafts Centre, and five galleries approached him and asked to show his work. Ray admits he was lucky. For five years he didn't have to worry too much, and he didn't have to search for orders. He had five years when work came in steadily and he could consolidate and plough money into timber stocks. Not many can claim to have started that way.

In fact Ray Key has gone from strength to strength. He is hon secretary of the Worcestershire Guild of Designer-Craftsmen, of which he has been a member since 1973. His work was purchased by West Midland Arts for their collection in 1978, and he has had five one-man exhibitions – at Harvest and Charles-De-Temple, in London, at Centre Craft Coventry, at Key Crafts, Evesham and at Blackhorse Craft Centre, Norwich. His work has been exhibited widely, including Gallerie Kraus in Paris, the Westminster Gallery in Boston, USA, at the Edinburgh Festival, the British Craft Centre and the Crafts Council Gallery.

In 1980 he chaired the hand woodturning section of the International Woodturning Seminar at Parnham House, in Dorset, and in 1981 lectured and demonstrated at the 10th Woodturning Symposium in Philadelphia, USA.

Ray aims to bring out the natural beauty of wood in his turnery. Using chisels and gouges from Craft Supplies, he turns on a Union Graduate lathe and finds his three-jaw chucks and spigot chucks excellent aids to quality work that shows no sanding scratches, no torn end-grain and no screw holes. He says he owes a lot to Peter Dingley of Meer Street, Stratford upon Avon, not only for early encouragement but also for continued and valued comment and criticism of his work.

He talks with real affection about his colleagues in the States, Bob Stocksdale, David Ellsworth, Bruce Mitchell, Ed Moulthrop and Dale Nish, and he obviously derived a great deal of pleasure from the woodturning symposium in Philadelphia last year, organised by Albert Le Coff.

Ray is not a shy man. He will argue over his work and he welcomes every chance to share his art with others. 'I want to put something back into the craft,' he says. 'I want to impart information to those who will listen.' He is now experimenting with thinness, with wormy, spalted timber, and burrs feature largely in his woodpile. Once turners searched for a perfect piece of timber, now they see beauty in many different faces.

The most stunning piece at Philadelphia, Ray thinks, was a buckeye wafer-thin bowl by Hap Sakwa. In his opinion England is now the poorer since Richard Raffan has left for Australia, 'a great technician and a tremendous extrovert with his work'; the boxes of David Pye are among the best anywhere, he says, and probably the most original young turner in the country at the moment is Jim Patridge. That is Ray's personal opinion, but in my opinion some of the most aesthetically pleasing pieces are coming out of Evesham.

Ray has several favourite woods but admits that he gets special pleasure from paraki (kingwood) and thuya root burrs from the Atlas mountains of Morocco. He mostly produces bowls, boxes and platters and spends almost an equal time on the finish and the turning of each piece.

Wood is a growing material and Ray Key is a growing force in the world of turning. While there is beauty in wood there will always be turners of his calibre ready and able to show it to the world. ■

● *A variation in boxes making use of the impact of the grain to add to the design qualities*

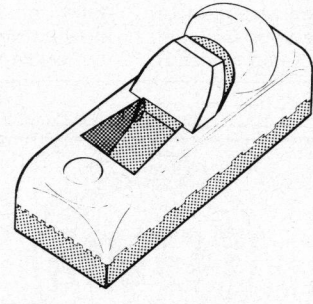

GUILD OF WOODWORKERS

Morgan plus four

Looking through old files is often a pleasure and often something comes to light of interest. The photograph shown here is one of those instances. Ray Jones of Gidea Park, sent us photographs of a 1961 Morgan plus four carved from a piece of walnut by guild member B. D. Swain. The car is 15in long, 6in wide and 3½in high. Headlights and side lights were carved separately, the wheels were first turned and then the spokes were scribed on. The picture was taken by Graham Murrell.

Wood Finishing Courses

Guild members attended courses on wood finishing at Bexleyheath, Kent, on 15/16 March and 22/23 March. Their interests ranged from furniture making, antique restoration and dealing, remedial hospital work and musical instrument making to general repair work. Members came from as far afield as Ayrshire, Durham, Lancashire, the Midlands, mid-Wales, Dorset and Wiltshire.

A wide variety of stains, fillers and polishes were available and their uses were fully described and demonstrated. The merits and drawbacks of oil, water and spirit stains were discussed, examined and smel-

led, particularly the one made from burnt sienna and stale beer!

The last hour or so of the second day was devoted to question time when the guild administrator, Albert Beezem and the course instructor, Charles Cliffe answered members' polishing problems. Mr. Ken Coney of James Jackson & Co advised on the different finishes available and how best to apply them. He also gave each member a tin of their special wax polish.

Finally certificates of attendance and a folder containing articles on wood finishing were handed out amidst farewells and promises of 'See you at the Show in October'.

Furniture design

If we can obtain sufficient support from members we will be able to take advantage of a first class opportunity of receiving quality, professional tuition in the basic principles of design and furniture making.

A five day course is to be arranged in August/September at Rycotewood College, Thame OX9 2AF (exact date to be advised)

● *Mr Swain's walnut Morgan*

to bring to the woodworker the basic principles of design and to apply these to the *making of a piece of furniture*.

Cost, which is inclusive of VAT and all accommodation at the college, plus morning coffee and all meals is £115.00.

The usual cancellation charge of half the fee will be made unless the cancellation is received in writing 14 days prior to the date of the course.

We would like provisional bookings as soon as possible with any comments as to course content or members' wishes so that we may accurately assess response.

Re-stocking pistols

We have had a request from a gentleman in Sussex which may be of interest to guild members. He has a number of antique pistols which need to be re-stocked and is looking for assistance in this matter. If any guild members in East Sussex are interested we would like to hear from them so that we can put both parties in touch.

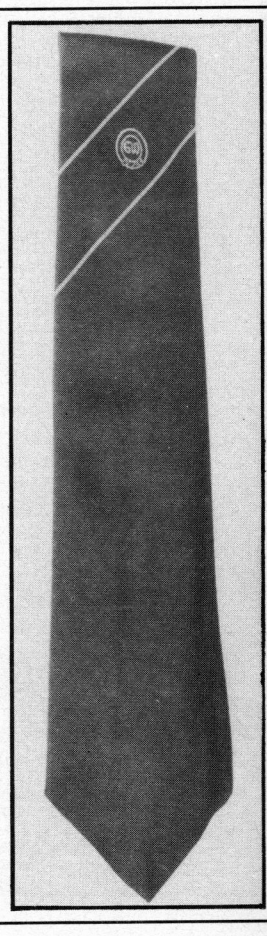

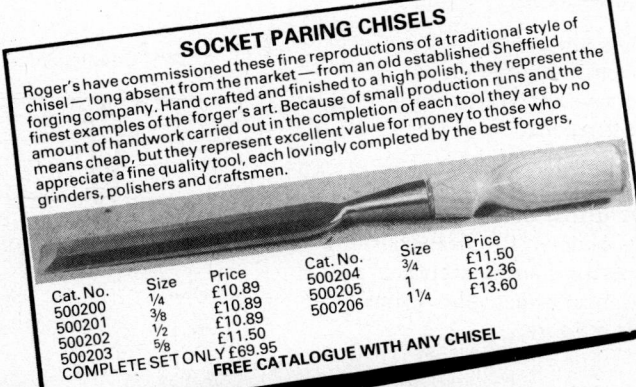

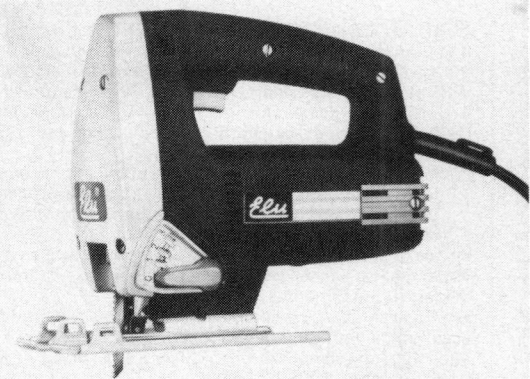

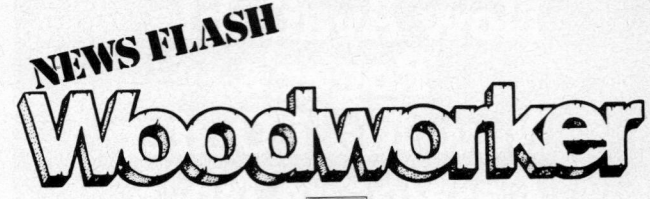

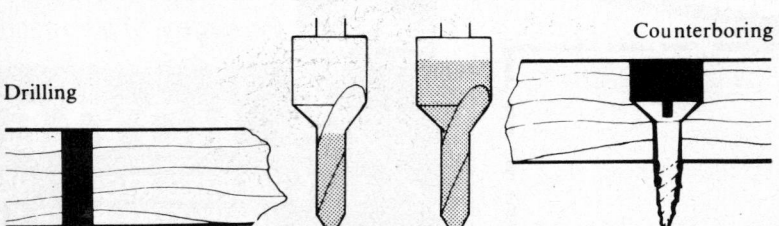
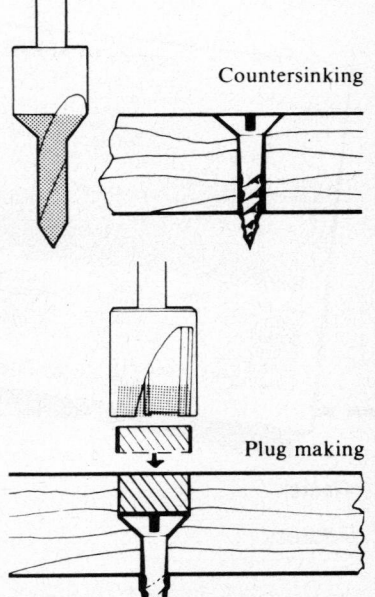

TIMBER TOPICS · 17

Over the past months Bill Brown has guided us through various technical and practical aspects of timber. In this article, taking heed of the widespread sales of woodburning stoves these days, he takes a slightly different approach to the use of timber by discussing its properties as burnable fuel

The thermal properties of wood are important, particularly when used for building. Thermal conductivity (K-value) for example, is the ability of wood, regardless of thickness, to transmit heat, and is defined as the quantity of heat which will pass through unit area of unit thickness in unit time when there is one degree F difference from the warmer to the cooler side.

Three factors determine heat conductivity: specific gravity of the wood at a given moisture content; percentage of moisture content, and a constant which depends upon actual moisture content and is 0.028 below 40% m.c. and 0.038 for values at or above 40% m.c.

The thermal resistance of wood, or its insulating value, is the reciprocal of conductivity (1/K = R-value). Therefore, the insulating value of wood is inversely proportional to its specific gravity and moisture content. This relationship explains the use of low density, dry, balsa wood for the highest insulating requirements. In terms of insulation, the higher the R-value, the better the insulator.

Wood is more of an insulator than a conductor of heat; the conductivity K-value of glass is approximately 5 and brick is around 4.5, while western red cedar at 12% m.c. has a value of 0.735 which is not bad when considered against building insulation material like rock wool, foam and fibreglass with values of about 0.2 to 0.3. Using the same comparisons, the relative insulation or R-values are as follows, glass 0.2; brick 0.22; western red cedar at 12% m.c. 1.36; building insulating material 3.3 to 5.0.

In the English Imperial system, thermal properties were measured in British thermal units (Btu) and to some extent they still apply, although since metrication was introduced into Britain, the construction industry has applied the measure, Watt per metre degree Celsius (W/M°C). For convenience the K and R-values given above are in Btu. The conversion factor is 1Btu (IN/FT^2/HR/°F) = 0.1442 W/M°C.

The calorific value of wood is a measure of its heat value when burnt as fuel, which can be defined as any combustible substance burnt for the sake of the heat evolved in the process. Most people are aware that different woods burn at different rates. Spruce tends to explode and send out live sparks, fruit tree wood like apple burns with a pleasant aroma and some woods appear dull-burning. But few realise the actual heat value of different woods. This aspect is especially relevant today, bearing in mind the need for heat conservation generally and the increasing use of woodburning stoves in the home.

Calorie is a metric unit of heat and the calorific value of a fuel is represented by the number of units of heat which the complete combustion of unit weight of fuel will evolve. Where the calorific value is measured in Btu it is based on the number of Btu generated by the combustion of one lb of the fuel, the Btu being the amount of heat which raises one lb of water through 1°F.

Fuels vary considerably in heating power; crude petroleum may have a calorific value of 20,000 Btu; best coal 17,000 to 18,000; poor coal 10,000; dry wood 9,000 to 10,000; and dry straw 8,000 Btu. Since metrication these values may be expressed in Kcal/kg or kJ/kg, 1 Btu = 0.45359 Kcal/kg or 2.326 kJ/kg.

The reference to 'dry' wood is pertinent to the discussion since much heat is lost in heating and evaporating off excess moisture when wet wood is burned. Gross calorific value is based on oven dry wood, of 0% m.c., but practical values are lower, based on actual moisture content of the wood and the efficiency of the fireplace or stove. In one test, an average value of 4,500 kCal/kg at 0% m.c. fell to 3,800 Kcal/kg at a m.c. of 15% and only 3,300 when the wood was at 30% m.c.

The differences between calorific values of timber species is basically small, but in terms of heat value it will be noted from the table shown here that dry beech, for example, is better than wet oak, but dry birch is better than beech, while hornbeam, even at high moisture content, has very good heating potential.

Everything is relative however, and so much depends upon the efficiency of the heating appliance. One thing is certain though; if wood is being regularly used as fuel, the wetter it is, the greater the heat loss and the higher the rate of inflammable substances deposited in flues and chimneys capable of initiating a chimney fire.

GROSS CALORIFIC VALUES OF BRITISH TIMBERS

Wood		Calorific Value Kcal/kg	
		Wet	Dry
Alder	trunk	4404	4715
	branches	4240	4500
Ash	trunk	4406	4662
	branches	4350	4550
Aspen	trunk	3810	4061
	branches	4348	4655
Beech	trunk	4350	4579
	branches	4296	4546
Birch	trunk	4514	4802
	branches	4402	4648
Chestnut, Sweet	trunk	4388	4734
	branches	4404	4680
Elm	trunk	—	4728
Hornbeam	trunk	4676	4927
	branches	4568	4885
Larch	trunk	4286	4586
	branches	4498	4821
Lime	trunk	4350	4579
	branches	4404	4694
Maple	trunk	4557	4848
	branches	4458	4673
Pine, Scots	trunk	4242	4556
	branches	4458	4809
Poplar	trunk	4080	4375
Oak	trunk	4296	4551
	branches	4294	4568
Spruce	trunk	4350	4589
	branches	4350	4613
Sycamore	trunk	4295	4658

First of all, let's eliminate those things you cannot, or should not, do. If your circular saws are the TCT (tungsten-carbide-tipped) kind, don't attempt to sharpen them as it needs special equipment – mind you, as they last three or four times as long as the ordinary steel ones, it's not uneconomic to replace worn-out saws with new ones. The non-stick Teflon-S coated blades can, however, be sharpened in the normal way.

Never try to correct a buckled blade; either get it done professionally or buy a new one. When hand saws are made they are specially tensioned, so that they are 'springy', and a buckled one will just sag lifelessly if you hold it out in front of you by the handle. Incidentally, the main cause of buckling is hitting the tip of the saw on the floor while sawing because the support for the work is too low.

Don't let the saw teeth get too blunt before re-sharpening as little and often is the rule; otherwise you may have to file the teeth so much that the saw will be ruined. But this prohibition does not apply to setting the teeth, as too much bending will weaken them and eventually cause them to snap off.

One more thing before we get down to work. It is vital to understand just how saw teeth work, and the two types (cross-cut or panel saws, and rip saws) are shown at A to F, Fig 1.

The action of a cross-cut or panel saw is similar to two knife cuts being made ACROSS the grain, about 1/16th of an inch apart, and the wood fibres between the two cuts are so short that they crumble away (Fig 1, A and E).

On the other hand, the action of the rip saw teeth simulates that of a series of moving chisels (Fig 1, B and F) and this is what is required for sawing along the grain.

Now to get down to work. Before sharpening or setting, the teeth must be 'topped'. At H, Fig 1, you can see the two most typical faults – on the left, blunt or chipped teeth; and on the right, a hollow edge. The first fault can be caused by striking metal while sawing (nails in the timber, or holding the work in a vice and accidentally running the teeth across the vice jaws), and by constantly sawing through tough knots or hard glue lines. The hollow edge is almost always the result of not using the full length of the saw and confining the use to the centre only – the remedy is obvious.

In any event, the tips of the teeth must be levelled off and this is done with a flat file – preferably a well-worn one as you do not want to take off too much at a stroke. If you don't have a flat file at all, the best one to buy is a 10inch second-cut file, which must be used lightly.

Obviously, the saw will have to be supported in a vice while this operation is being done. At J, Fig 1, you will see a gadget which is easily made and which ensures that the file is held exactly at right angles to the saw.

I have emphasised that the flatting must only be done lightly. But what do you do when the teeth are grossly mis-shapen? The answer still is, to flat lightly, and then use a triangular file to re-shape the shallowest teeth; if necessary, you may have to repeat the procedure several times before the shape is satisfactory.

Next we come to the shaping of the teeth,

THE CRAFTSMAN IN HIS WORKSHOP: No1

Getting saws sharpened is one of the major headaches for the serious woodworker, whether professional or amateur. Most of us have to do the job ourselves, and here Vic Taylor points the right way to making a success of it.

This is part one of a series on tool sharpening we have asked Vic to write for us under the title of *The Craftsman in His Workshop,* and in later issues he will be covering machine saws, electric planer knives, chisels, plane irons and gouges, plus anything else that needs a keen cutting edge

Keep handsaws sharp and sure

and to do this accurately the saw needs to be supported correctly. Professionals use a special saw vice but we can make do with an ordinary bench vice, plus a pair of wooden strips about 9 or 10 inches long by 1 inch wide and ½ inch thick; put the saw in the vice with a strip on each side of it and with the teeth protruding about ¼ inch or so.

Shape the teeth with a triangular file, but make sure the face of the file is at least twice the depth of the saw teeth, as too small a file could distort the shape; recommended sizes by Spear and Jackson are:

Saw points per inch
5(Rip saw) 6   7 to 8   10 to 12

Length of taper-saw file
8inch 7inch   6inch   6inch(Slim taper)

Holding the file properly is important and is best achieved by placing it firmly in the gullet between two teeth and pressing it down firmly with the left hand, the right hand holding the file handle with the thumb on top and a finger alongside. File across the saw exactly at right angles and with the file held horizontally, maintaining the same grip throughout. In Fig 1 you will see the angle of pitch at (C) is 14 degrees for cross-cut and panel saws, and at (D) is 3 degrees for rip saws; you need not worry too much about this as the file will automatically follow the existing angle of pitch, and this very rarely changes provided the saw is used normally.

At this juncture, all the flats on the saw teeth should have been removed and they should all have been brought to a point with the fronts and backs sloping at the correct angle; disregard bevelling the teeth at this stage as this is dealt with after the teeth

have been set.

Setting the teeth is the next step. In effect, this involves bending alternate teeth, but there are several points to watch for, and all of them are important.

First, just how much 'set' should we apply? The answer is – not too much and, in fact, rarely does it mean making a kerf more than one and a half times the thickness of the blade. A 'kerf' is a saw cut and is illustrated at Fig 1 E; in general, most woodworkers tend to over-set the teeth and this in no way helps the saw to cut; all that happens is that you expend unnecessary effort in cutting an over-size kerf, and that you waste wood as sawdust.

Secondly, do we bend over the complete depth of each tooth, or only part of it? In Fig 2A you can see that the correct procedure is to bend over only the upper half – actually, slightly less than half is best of all. If you do bend the whole of each tooth, the results could be distortion of the gullet at the root of each tooth, possibly accompanied by cracks and teeth breaking out.

Moving on to the actual methods of setting the teeth, there are two methods, the first one being that used by manufacturers and professionals. The set-up is shown in Fig 2F, and consists of a wooden baseboard with a steel plate screwed or cramped to it. This steel plate does not have to be any exact thickness, and 3/16 inch (4mm) would be quite suitable; a bevel is filed off the front edge at an angle corresponding to the amount of 'set' required; in fact, you could file all the four edges at different angles to suit the various sizes of saws you are sharpening. You could then choose the appropriate bevel, and screw or cramp the

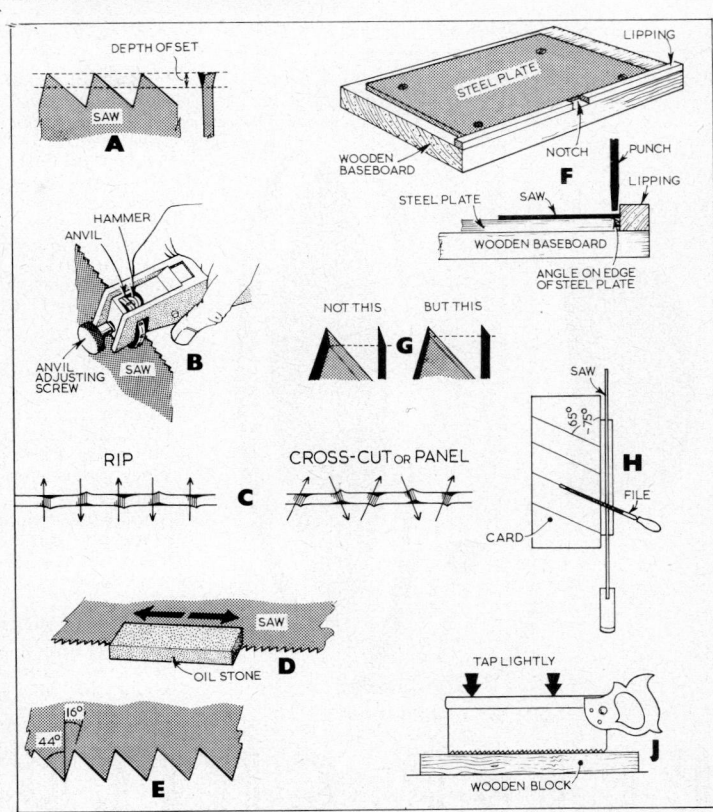

plate to the baseboard. You will note that there is a lipping attached to the front edge, and this fulfils the important function of determining the depth of the 'set'.

The procedure is to lay the saw on the steel plate with the teeth butting against the lipping, and then to use a punch to bend the teeth to the required angle, working at the point where the notch has been cut out. A three or four inch nail with the point filed off to a flat makes a good punch; and needless to say, you should only tap the punch two or three times with a hammer. Obviously, you start at one end of the saw, setting every other tooth, and then turn the saw over and repeat the process on the teeth you omitted the first time. Equally obviously, the teeth must be set to conform with their original setting, as forcing them to the opposite sides will almost certainly break them off.

The other way to set the teeth is by using a pliers-type saw-set, which is shown in Fig 2B. This is called the Eclipse Saw Set and is made by Neill Tools Ltd, who seem to be the only firm offering accessories for tool sharpening. To use the tool, place the jaws over a tooth and squeeze the handles, which causes a plunger to push the tooth over against an anvil. This anvil is adjustable to take account of the number of teeth points per inch – from 4 to 12 points actually; both the amount and depth of 'set' are automatically controlled by turning the anvil adjusting screw. Their latest model incorporates a magnifying eye-piece set just above the hammer, which is an enormous help to those whose eyesight is not as good as it was.

Whichever method you choose, once the teeth have been set you should lay the saw

blade flat on the bench and run an oilstone backwards and forwards as at D, Fig 2. Just a light pressure is needed, as the aim is to reduce any teeth that are too prominent, and when you have dealt with one side, turn the saw over and do the other.

We have almost finished, as we have come to the last stage – the final sharpening. This is where the remarks about the two different ways in which rip saws and cross-cut saws actually have to be borne in mind, and they are shown at A to F, Fig 1. In other words, when we sharpen rip saws, we hold the file horizontally and at right angles to the saw throughout the work; while in the case of crosscut and panel saws, we still hold the file horizontally but at an angle of 65 to 75 degrees to the saw. To ensure a consistent angle throughout, it is a good idea to mark ink or pencil lines at the required angle on a piece of card which can be placed at the side of the vice, as shown in Fig 2H where it will serve as a handy guide. At G, Fig 2, you can see the result of filing at too shallow an angle, which produces a fragile tooth.

Naturally, in all cases the file is used on alternate teeth in the first pass and then you have to reverse the saw in the vice and deal with the others. To help you to see how far you have got, give all the teeth a light 'topping' before you start so that they shine, and you will find that as the teeth are filed, the shine will be removed.

So far we have treated rip, cross-cut, and panel saws, but there is still another class to consider, namely Back Saws, including tenon and dovetail saws.

The procedure is just the same for tenon saws as it is for cross-cut saws but as the

teeth are smaller, you should use a 5 inch slim taper file for those with 13 teeth points per inch, and for 15 points per inch, a 4 or 4½ inch slim taper file. Note, too, that the teeth have a 16 degree angle of pitch (Fig 2E), but the final sharpening angle is, like the cross-cut saw, 65 to 75 degrees.

Dovetail saws only need topping, shaping and sharpening like a rip saw; you should not put any 'set' on the teeth. The sharpening angle of pitch is the same as for the tenon saw – 16 degrees.

Fig 2J illustrates a useful tip. After a period of use the blades of both tenon and dovetail saws may work slightly loose in the back. By standing the saw upright on a wooden block and tapping the back gently with a hammer as indicated, the blade will re-set itself in the back and the sawing action will be greatly improved.

In conclusion, may I mention one or two points that I have found useful? It's most important to do the job in a good light, and a desk-lamp strategically placed, plus your strongest spectacles (if you wear them) will make the work much easier.

It's worthwhile keeping an old paint brush and some white spirit handy; give the teeth a thorough cleaning before you start to remove any gummy deposits which may have built up as they may cause the file to be tilted at the wrong angle. White spirit is ideal for this job as it evaporates quickly and does not cause rust. When not in use, hang your saws up by their handles and give them an occasional rub over with Vaseline or a light machine oil (not a vegetable oil such as linseed, which tends to become gummy) to keep them bright, shining, and in good working order. ■

The Child Coil Grip Chuck

A COMBINATION CHUCK FOR HAND WOODTURNERS   *(copied but not improved on)*   *Patented*

COIL GRIP ASSEMBLY

This unique chuck is the outcome of many years experience by a professional woodturner and teacher, and the patented coil grip method together with the many extra modes of operation safely and neatly overcome the chucking problems encountered by amateur and professional turners. The coil grip, supplied ONLY WITH THIS CHUCK, together with the large (4½") diameter heavy duty body offers unbeatable strength and rigidity for gripping end grain work of ANY size. It grips by compression on the outside of the work so there is no danger of splitting the wood by excessive outward pressure. It holds staved work safely. An almost limitless variety of home-made wooden adaptors can be made which will grip any shape or size of work, internally, externally, dovetail grip, plain grip, or as required. The coil grip feature makes this chuck by far the most versatile of its kind. Made for most lathes (state model) £36.50 inc. VAT & carriage.

WOODTURNERS' SPECIALIST SUPPLIER

The most comprehensive range of tools available. The new ROY CHILD parting tool. Chucks, centres, fittings, drills. Flexicramps. Many types and sizes glass inserts, barometers, hygrometers, thermometers, eggtimers, hourglasses, condiment liners, 160 circular tile patterns, lighters, pens, flower vase tubes, peppermills, STAINLESS saltmills, knives, clocks, pencil sharpeners, ashtrays, clock dials. Abrasives, waxes, finishes. Speed-n-Eze, Rustins. WOOD for turning. MYFORD agents. ROY CHILD pyrography machines. Post Office Parcel Contract for most quick and direct delivery service. Send S.A.E. for catalogue, or $1.00 from overseas enquiries. We EXPORT worldwide.

WOODTURNING AND FINISHING

Two-day intensive course and personal tuition at 17th century Essex-Suffolk farmhouse. Fully equipped workshops. Maximum of two guests for any one course.

PETER CHILD

THE WOODTURNER CRAFTSMAN
The Old Hyde, Little Yeldham, Halstead, Essex. Tel. Gt. Yeldham (0787) 237291

Prices quoted are those prevailing at press date and are subject to alteration due to economic conditions.

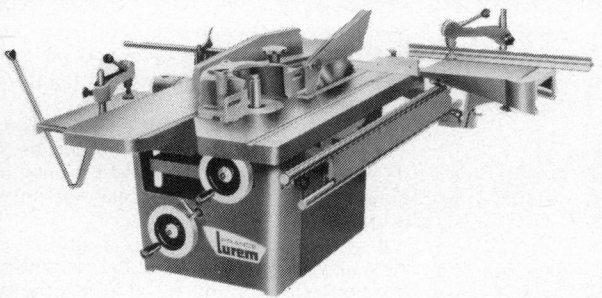
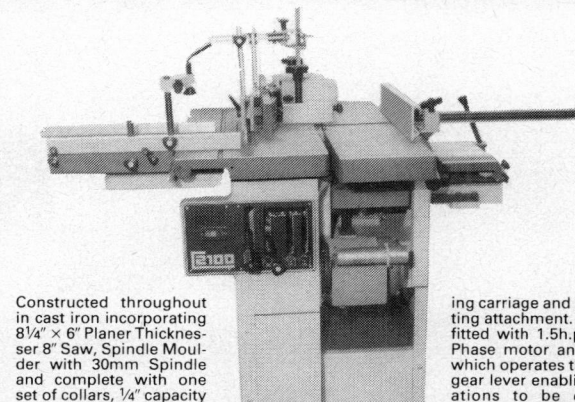

Woodturning from A to Z

In the second of his series of instructional articles on woodturning, Gordon Stokes discusses some general points about siting a lathe in the workshop and then details the best tools to get the learner turner started

INTO THE WORKSHOP

● 1½in woodscrew chuck. Work-pieces on these chucks should not be more than 3in in length.

● Expanding collett type chuck for Coronet, here fitted with 'mini' unit for small jobs. A larger diameter insert is available for bowls, plates etc.

● Jacobs pattern chuck with tapered shank will be found useful.

Last month we considered the features which should be inherent in a good wood-turning lathe, and can now move on to look at some other matters which will be of importance to the beginner.

There is the initial layout of the workshop, or work area, and this we can return to from time to time to review it in the light of additional equipment which may need to be placed. The other really vital thing of course is the wise and careful selection of wood-turning tools with which to learn the craft.

Once a good quality lathe has been purchased, it will need to be installed in a sensible manner which will enable it to be used with maximum comfort and safety. As a first step, stand in a normal erect posture and ask someone to measure the distance between your elbow and the floor. The resulting figure is the ideal height for the lathe centres, enabling the machine to be used for long periods without the need to stand like a half shut knife and so develop back problems.

This naturally brings us to the question of how the lathe is to be supported. If you have laid out a lot of money on a 'cabinet stand' for the machine — which in fact I would not advise — then unless you are very short, the cabinet will need to be mounted on some-thing in order to bring the centres to elbow height. If this is the case, make sure that the supporting timber or platform is steady and well secured to the workshop floor. The cabinet must also be secured to the plat-form.

Light is obviously important, and begin-ners are often advised to position the machine under a window. It would be far better under a skylight really, since a lathe which is in front of a window receives the best illumination on the side away from the turner. There are also legends in plenty referring to tools being torn from perspiring hands and hurled up the garden — but those who follow my instructions carefully will have no need to fear this.

I like to use an electric light source, and whilst strip lighting is fine for general illumination, it is not so good for working on a lathe, since it provides a flat and relatively shadow free light, which hides imperfec-tions in the work.

I keep my tools in heaps on the lathe bench all the time, and do not use a rack, but those who decide to have one should position it where they will not need to reach over the lathe to get at it.

The positioning of the on-off switch for the machine also needs thought, unless it is already built into the cabinet. This switch MUST be placed where it can be reached and operated quickly in an emergency, possibly even by means of the knee. Try also to avoid creating an area at the back of the machine which is difficult to reach once the bolting down has been done. Shavings will accumulate there, and small tools will fall among them.

In my own view, after 35 years of setting lathes up in all sorts of odd places, there is nothing to beat a really solid wooden bench for mounting a lathe — and it can hardly be too heavily built. This may have cupboards built in for chucks and other odds and ends, and its height can be arranged so as to position the lathe at the correct height for the operator.

Don't economise on leg thickness, 3in × 3in will be fine, and the top should be 2in minimum thickness. Hardwood is best, but pine will do at a pinch, and reclaimed timber is ideal.

If the lathe comes with a grindstone which is designed to be left permanently in position, all well and good. The operator will soon be accustomed to it, and all should be well. My own preference is for a separate free-standing double-ended grinder, but this is by no means obligatory.

The grinding wheel is of great signifi-cance for those who wish to follow my methods, as will quickly become apparent, and if free-standing it should be placed in a position which suits the user, and left there. It should not have a wheel diameter of less than 6in, and there is no need to go for anything larger than eight, which would be very expensive. Most such machines are double-ended, having a wheel on each end of the spindle, which should be coarse and medium grades respectively. Fine wheels will be likely to overheat the tools.

● Main bearing on the Coronet Major is one of the phosphor bronze type, fully adjustable in a few moments by means of the castellated rings. These bearings are capable of long and hard service.

The coarser wheel will be useful for the rapid removal of metal when reshaping tools, and the medium — 60 to 80 grit — will be used for the sharpening process as such. The care of these wheels, and the grinding procedures, will be dealt with in detail in due course.

A 'devil stone' (dressing stone for a carborundum wheel) will also be required, and can be obtained from the manufacturer. This stone is very important. Do *not* use a 'dressing tool' which is unsuitable for our particular purpose.

THE TOOLS

The tools used in woodturning may seem to be expensive, or at least initially so, but their cost has to be considered against their relatively long expectation of life. Most gouges and chisels will last for several years, even in the constant and heavy use which I give them — certainly there is something badly wrong if they do not. My scrapers last indefinitely, since I rarely use them.

Woodturners are also better placed when starting out in the craft than are woodcarvers, who are faced with the ridiculous situation of having more than a thousand patterns to choose from. There are very few patterns of tool in turning, so the confusion is greatly reduced.

For instructional purposes I use a carefully selected set of nine tools. This is the 'Gordon Stokes' set, and can be obtained from Ashley Iles Ltd. The set is the result of a great deal of thought, and provides all that is needed in learning the craft. I could easily earn my living with this particular set, and the beginner using them will not be confused by unnecessary chisels and gouges.

If you are offered 'sets' of tools in boxes, ask the supplier to explain *exactly* what each tool is meant to be used for, and if he is unable to do this — don't buy them. Weird assortments of tools are gathered together quite arbitrarily in boxes and sold to the unwary as 'sets', and in many cases without any apparent logic. Woodturners are rarely expert toolmakers, and toolmakers are rarely expert woodturners, so between the two there is a great gulf fixed. Sad, but true,

The set to which I refer — and I should add that I have no financial interest in the matter — is listed here, with brief comments on size and purpose. These tools will be examined in greater detail later in the series when we begin to look at cutting techniques. Those who already possess some of these can purchase the others individually to complete the set. If you have any tools which are not listed, then for your own sake I suggest that you put them away in a drawer until you can use all nine of the set really well.

Roughing Gouge ¾in
Designed for the safe, rapid, and efficient reduction of a 'stick' to a cylindrical blank. Not for use on discs except in skilled hands.

Spindle Gouge ½in
Spindle gouges are used in the cutting of curves of all kinds in jobs which are secured between centres (spindles) and in chuck work where the grain is running in the same direction as the lathe bed. Not for use on discs except in skilled hands.

Spindle Gouge ¼in
As above, but also very useful in the rapid removal of waste when hollowing small end grain items, such as vases, pots, or egg cups.

Skew Chisels ¾in and 1¼in
The evil reputation which these tools enjoy rightly belongs to those who attempt to use them without proper instruction, not to the chisels! They are not difficult to use when they are fully understood, and any man or woman who has not mastered the skews is not really a woodturner. Basic understanding and practice will bring competence in time. Functions are the smoothing cut, in which the tool is used like a plane, and decorative detail cutting, which is done with the point, or 'long corner'. The best example of this is the bead.

Parting Tool
More about this later, but for now suffice it to say that it is a square ended chisel, usually of ¼in width, which has a number of purposes. It is easy to use, but produces poor surface finishes.

Deep Fluted Gouge ⅜in
This is the 'bowl turning gouge' so frequently referred to in books and articles. It is more accurately described as a disc turning tool, and its use will be the subject of detailed examination at a later stage.

Scrapers 1in round nose and 1¼in square ended
The round nose is used in hollowing pots, vases, boxes, tankards, etc, and the square ended one is for levelling recessed surfaces which are required to be completely flat.

I hope that by the end of this series, many readers who are now complete beginners will be using all these tools with a fair degree of skill. ∎

NEXT MONTH: THE RIGHT CHUCKS

● *Coronet taper chuck system is based on headstock unit with internal thread (right) and tailstock unit with tapered shank (left).*

● *Business ends of saw tooth pattern bits. These can be used — at low speed — in a Jacobs chuck and will cut large holes cleanly and efficiently. They will be overheated and spoiled if run too fast.*

● *2½in woodscrew chuck. Note extra screw holes in rim.*

● *Range of inserts of various sizes greatly increases the versatility of the chucks shown at the top of the page.*

What some sanders leave behind,

Bosch takes away.

Sanding down a surface can get up your nose. Quite literally.

Unless, of course, you use the Bosch PSS 280-A which comes fitted with a dust collection bag.

Thanks to the suction fan, which is integrated into the motor housing, dust is removed as you work. With the result that the sanding sheet lasts a lot longer.

It has a powerful 250 watt motor, delivering 10,000 rev/min.

A sheet holder designed for quick changes. And a large (114 mm x 227 mm) sanding pad.

Together, they enable you to complete the job quicker. And achieve a smoother, more even result.

While the sponge rubber pad provides just the right amount of elasticity for every kind of sanding job. Whether it's flat, or curved like the wing of a car, for instance.

What's more, it weighs in at only 2.9 kg with a well-designed, doubly-insulated body, a comfortable grip and a low-noise, low-vibration, suppressed motor.

So where some sanders can only leave dust behind, it's easy to see why the only thing the Bosch PSS 280-A leaves behind is the competition.

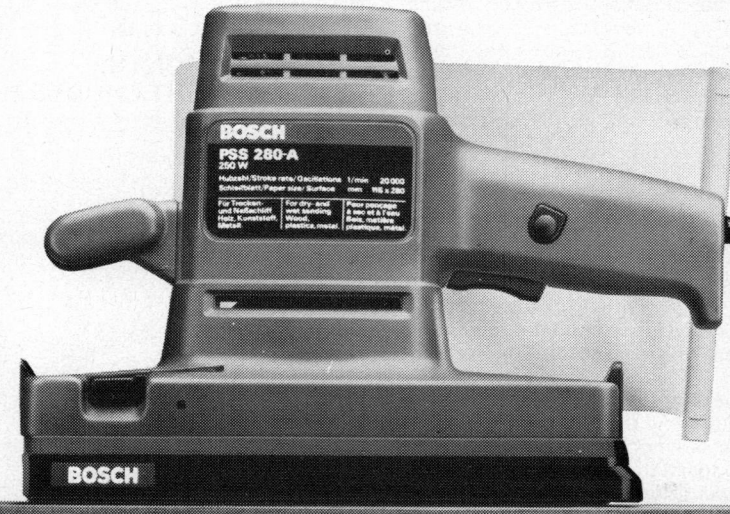

BOSCH ⊕
The more professional D.I.Y. power tools.

The world's timber trees

In no 26 of this series (April 1982) C. W. Bond FIWSc described ekki from a tropical family, the Ochnaceae. This month he begins a survey of comparatively well-known tropical timbers from the family Combretaceae. These woods are good for handworking, and in their best quality can be classed as highly decorative.

NARGUSTA or WHITE OLIVIER: 27

Terminalia amazonia, *Terminalia* from terminus — end or limit, *amazonia* — from the Amazon region; family Combretaceae.

The family Combretaceae occurs throughout the tropics and is named from the type genus *Combretum* which contains 350 species, many of them climbers. It supplies the woodworker with a number of woods which are distinctive and which are regarded as high-class furniture woods with good working qualities. The name *Combretum* was used by Pliny with reference to a climbing plant, but which plant is uncertain.

Five timbers from the family are selected for this series, all of them being species of *Terminalia*. This genus contains over one hundred species. The flowers, in elongated spikes, have ten stamens, no petals, and are sessile (without stalks). These woods are nargusta (*T. amazonia*) from Central America, Indian silver greywood (*T. bialata*), idigbo (*T. ivorensis*), afara (*T. superba*) both from Africa and Indian laurel (*T. alata* and *tomentosa*).

The 'regalia' of these trees, if the word can be used to refer to the leaves and flowers are clustered together at the ends of the branches. The seeds are winged and the whole arrangement, conspicuous enough for the generic name to be suggested and authorised by Linnaeus, must be very beautiful. Small wonder that one of the species from Africa, in its specific name, is referred to as superb or splendid.

The colour of the woods of *T. bialata* and *superba* varies considerably, some specimens being greenish grey and showing handsome dark markings, others being without this coloration. Names for the

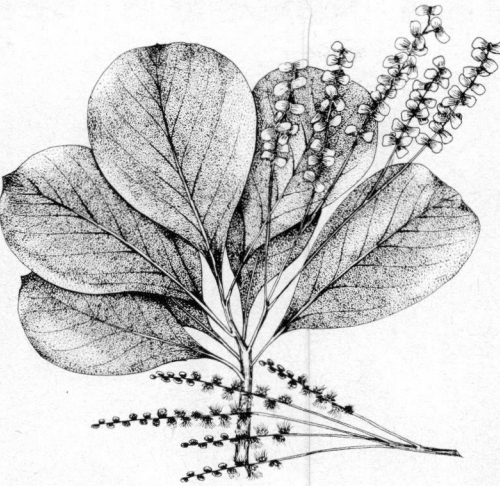

Terminalia amazonia
Drawn from material in The Forest Herbarium, University of Oxford, acknowledgement to the curator.

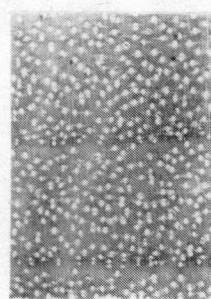

Right: Cross section × 3.3 as seen with a × 10 hand lens. Below: Cross section × 10

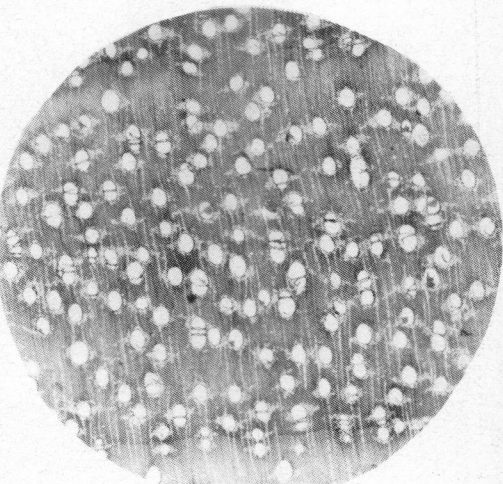

plainer examples which might be encountered are from India — white bombway or bombwe and white chuglam which includes *T. procera* — possibly mixed and difficult to segregate. Names for the darker examples of afara are *Limba* and *Limba noire*.

Nargusta (also called aromilla, guayabo and nacastillo) is a large tree, widely distributed from Mexico to Brazil. The winged seeds are small and numerous and are shed in clusters after ripening in a few weeks.

The wood is mainly yellowish, variously striped with red. This mixture of colours, comparatively rare in wood, makes this an unusual timber and as it has been reported

to be the principal species of *Terminalia* in Central and South America, having a pleasing appearance and good working qualities, one feels that it should be better known in the export market. The wood is very attractive when showing a fiddle-back figure.

The photomicrograph shows an even fine-to-medium texture with very small rays. There is slight evidence of growth rings, and parenchyma cells can be seen, being vasicentric with a tendency to a confluent arrangement.

Chicago here we come!

Woodworker is planning to visit the Excellence in Woodworking exhibition, to be held in Chicago, USA, 12-14 November, and offers readers the chance to come along too.

We are able to take advantage of cheap group rates and offer an attractive package of seven nights in Chicago, with the exhibition as the centrepiece, for only £575 a head. And if money exchange rates and air fares change between now and November, it could be even cheaper than that.

The price, which works out cheaper than a four-day package, includes return flight from Heathrow to O'Hare Airport, Chicago, by jumbo jet, with seven nights' accommodation at a central hotel, plus entrance to the exhibition. The plan is that our *Woodworker* party will take a lunchtime flight on Wednesday 10 November and arrive at the

hotel in Chicago around 8pm. The following day will be set aside for relaxing and recovering from jet lag, in preparation for taking in the woodworking exhibition on Friday, Saturday and Sunday.

Monday 15 November will be sightseeing day, or shopping day, or whatever sort of a day you want to make of it, and on Tuesday the party will regroup for the return flight to London.

Sounds like a wonderful winter break, doesn't it? The arrangements are still in the planning stage, but if you would like to take this opportunity of spending an exciting week in Chicago, including the chance to take in all that's best in the American woodworking scene, then fill in the coupon and let us have it back as soon as possible. Places on the trip will be limited, so act now if you mean to be there.

To the Editor, *Woodworker*, PO Box 35, Bridge Street, Hemel Hempstead HP1 1EE.

Please send me further details of the *Woodworker* trip to Chicago's Excellence in Woodworking exhibition, as soon as they are available.

Name ....

Address ....

....

....

....

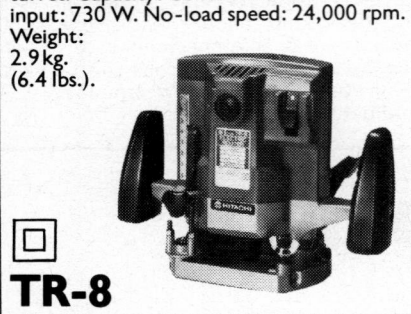

Prices quoted are those prevailing at press date and are subject to alteration due to economic conditions.

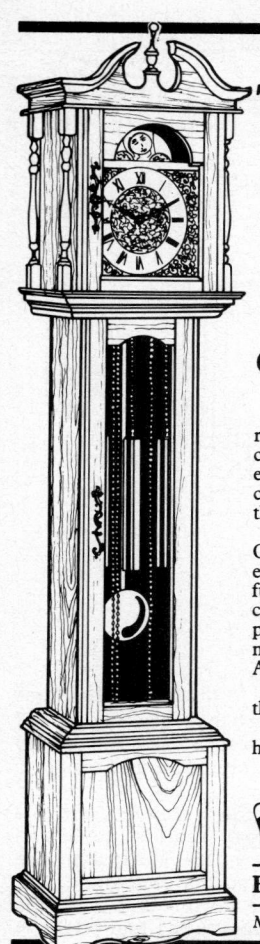
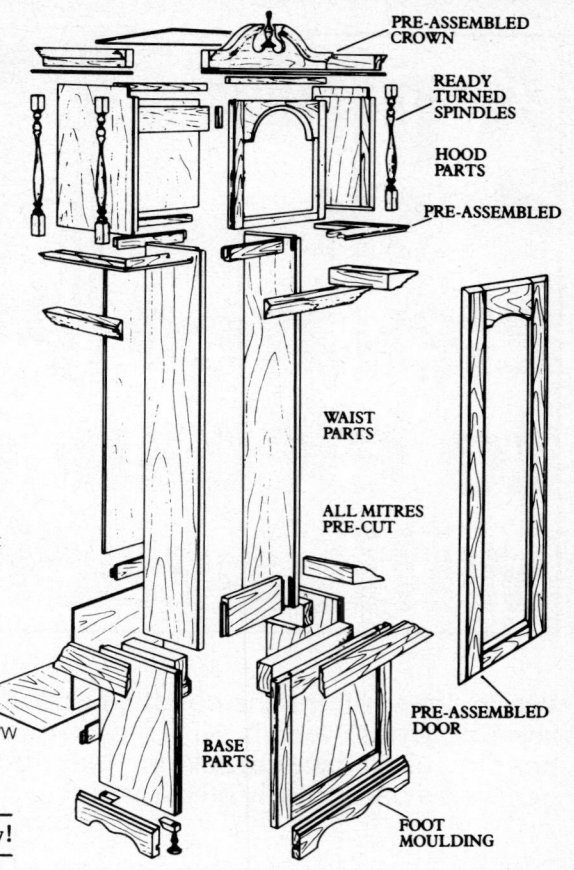

A plain desk elevated to elegance with beading

Fig 1

Vic Taylor explains the construction of a straightforward knee-hole desk which, with the simple addition of cocked beading and corner brackets, rises above the ordinary to become a particularly elegant piece

Although many people would describe this design as a 'pedestal' desk, it would not be strictly true as the pedestals are not separate but part of the whole structure, which cannot be dismantled.

At the moment I am drawing up some period furniture from various stately homes over a considerable area, and I have been struck by the fact that judiciously placed cocked beading can very quickly bestow an air of elegance on an otherwise undistinguished piece. Although this desk is a straightforward design, I hope you will agree that the cocked beading and the corner brackets lift it out of the ordinary run.

Construction is shown in exploded form in Fig 2 and follows orthodox framing methods. There are four pilasters (or posts), nos1 and 2, at the front and they are connected by an extra-wide front rail (no5). The outside corner posts, no1, have a dovetail socket in the upper end which accepts a dovetail formed on the end of the front rail, no5; the posts also have two mortises cut in their rear faces which accept the tenons on the top (no8) and bottom (no9) end rails, and a groove is worked on each post to join the mortises and to house the plywood panel. Lastly, three mortises are cut in each post to take the tenons of the drawer rails (no7).

Turning now to the two intermediate posts (no2), these are each twin-tenoned right through the front rail (no5) and then wedged. At the bottom end, on the rear face, you will need to cut mortises to take the tenons on the intermediate division rails (no13), plus three mortises on the inner faces to match the tenons on the drawer rails (no7), just as you did on the two corner posts. There are two more jobs on these posts – one is to cut mortises for the tenons on the centre drawer rail (no6 – remembering that this stands back by 1in or 25mm);

and the other is to form a rebate on the back edge of each for the plywood panels, noting that the rebate stops at the level of the centre drawer rail.

The back framing is built up from a long top back rail (no11), which is dowelled into a back corner post (no3) at each end: if you can, it would be a decided advantage if these dowels could pin the tenon on the end of the top end rail, no8. Other work on the top back rail (no11) consists of working a rebate throughout its length to accept the back panel. The last job is to cut a mortise to match the tenon on the intermediate top rail, no12.

Now for the two bottom back rails, (no10) which are, of course, shorter. They both have a rebate on their top edges to take the back panel, and they are both dowelled into the back corner posts, (no3), in a way similar to the top back rail, no11.

The back corner posts (no3) are grooved as shown in Fig 2A for the end panel, and also have mortises cut at top and bottom for the tenons on the top (no8) and bottom (no9) end rails. These end rails are also grooved for the end panel.

Two more constructional members remain to be dealt with, and they are the intermediate back posts, no4. At Fig 3A you will see the treatment each one receives at its upper end, where it is stop-rebated on one side to accept the ply panel at the back of the centre drawer, and rebated on the other side for the plywood back panel. There is another stopped rebate on the third edge for the panel enclosing the inner side of the pedestal. Other jobs are to make a mortise at the foot for the tenon on the lower intermediate rail (no13), and to bore holes for the dowels on the lower back rail, no10.

The centre drawer rail (no6) needs a special mention as it is tenoned into the

posts (no2) with its front edge set back one inch (25mm) to match the recessed shape of the top. There is also a back rail (no12) which is dowelled into no14, and supports the centre drawer at the back.

This leaves the drawer framing, and this comprises the drawer bearers (no15) and the drawer guides, (no16). The bearers are notched to fit around the posts (nos1,2,3, and 4) and can be dowelled to both the posts themselves and to the rear edges in the drawer rails, no7, while the guides need only be pinned and glued in place as they are not structural members.

The drawers are made up in the conventional way and details are given in Fig 3B. The sides are lap-dovetailed into the fronts, and each drawer bottom is grooved into the back of the drawer front and also into the drawer sides at a height which does not cut into the lowest dovetail. Note that the drawer back rests its lower edge on the drawer bottom and is pinned and glued to it from beneath; it can be dovetailed to the drawer side if you are determined to follow the best practice, but alternatively it can be pinned and glued to a shallow rebate in the drawer side.

Unless you have a slab of solid mahogany (!) you will have to use a man-made board for the top. A piece of multi-plywood is by far the best as it makes a stable groundwork for veneering and it also has good screw-holding properties. Fig 3C is a suggestion for lipping a suitably-sized piece of plywood, bearing in mind that the shaped recess on the front edge must be contained within the width of the lipping. The thumb moulding worked on the edge of the top is optional and if you haven't a spindle moulder or a moulding plane I would be inclined to leave it plain with just the arrises taken off.

Fixing the top can be accomplished by either pocket screwing, or buttoning. If you have a plywood top, pocket screwing will suffice, as buttoning is meant for fixing down solid tops that are liable to move. Anyway, both methods are shown in Fig 4.

Now we come to the question of whether or not to line the top. If it is finished with a modern synthetic resin lacquer, it could be well left unlined, as the lacquer is resistant

(continued on page 398)

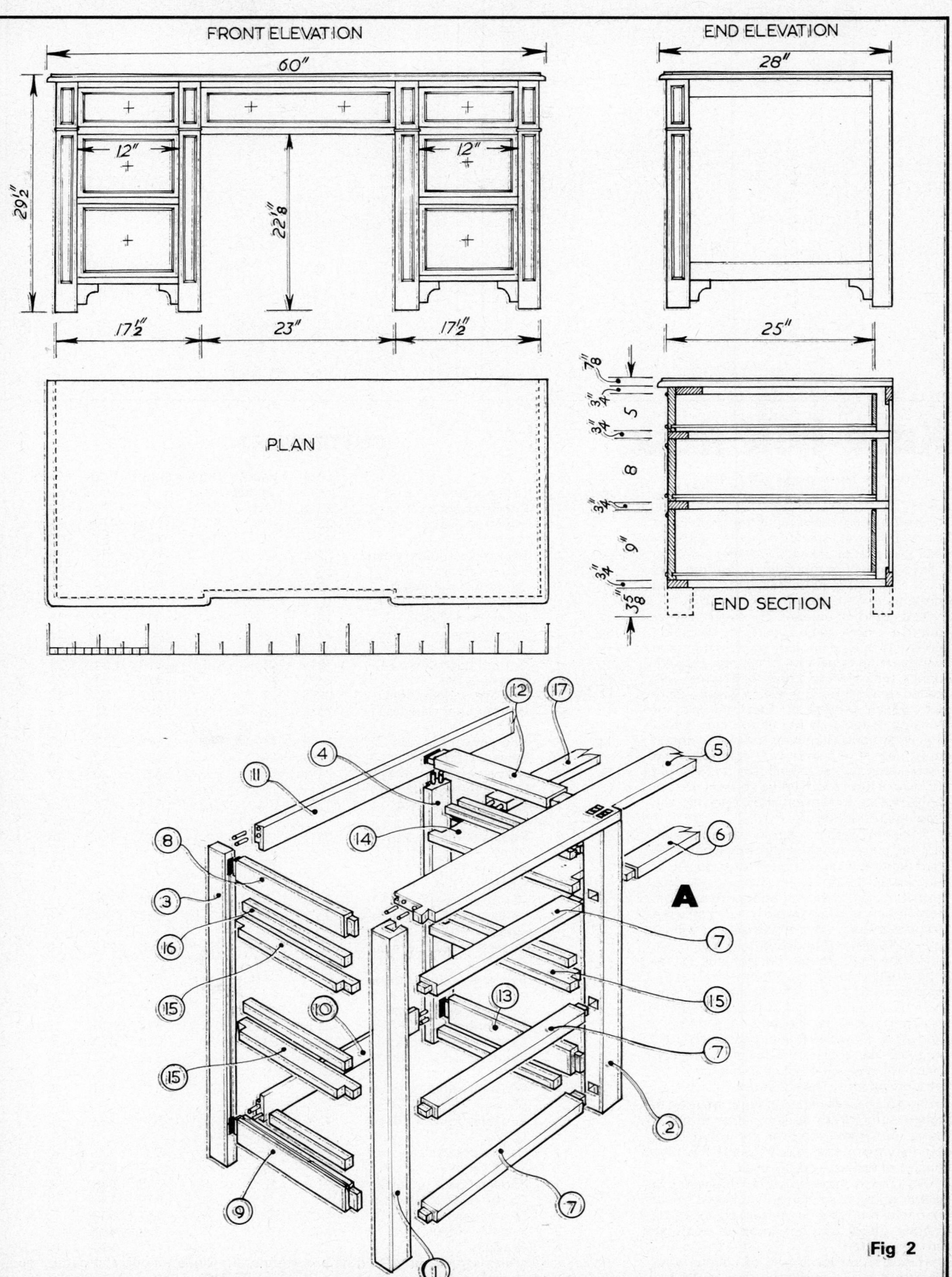

FRONT ELEVATION

60"

29½"

12"

22⅞"

12"

17½"   23"   17½"

END ELEVATION

28"

25"

PLAN

7⅛"
3" 3" ¾"   5
¾"
8
3" ¾"
9"
3" ¾"
3⅝"

END SECTION

A

Fig 2

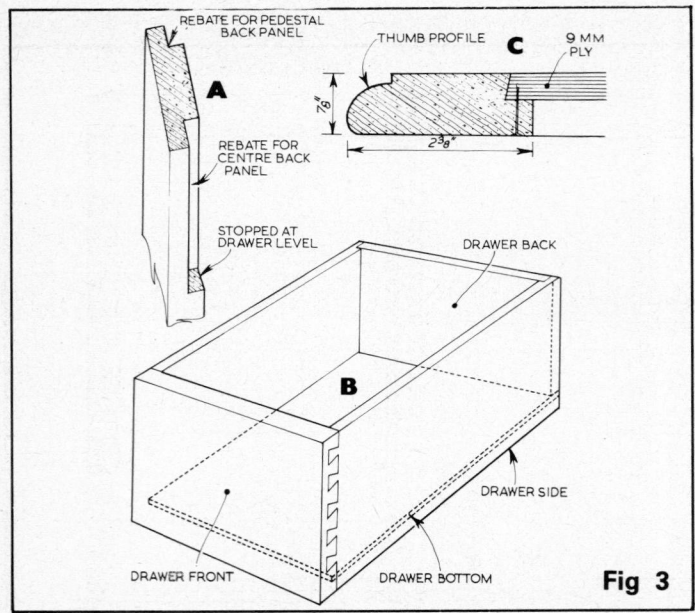

Fig 3

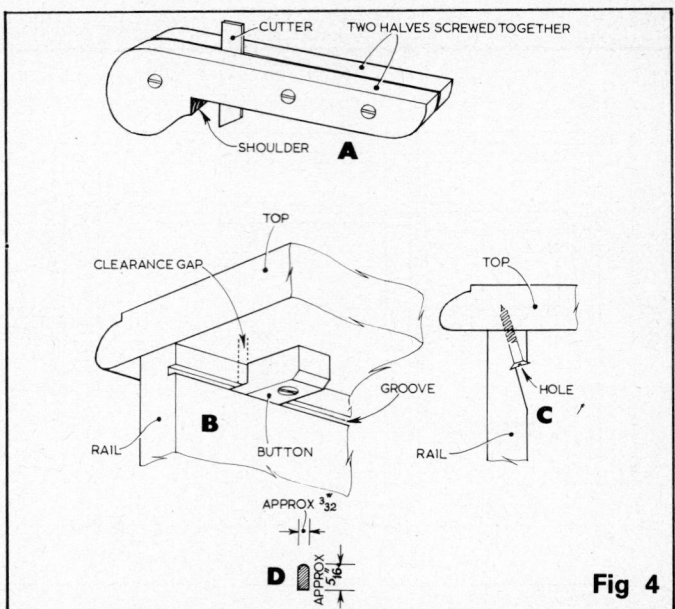

Fig 4

Knee-hole desk

(continued from page 396)

to scuffing and marking but french polishes and wax finishes are not. However, you may feel (like me) that a hard wooden top is an unsympathetic surface when writing and that something more resilient would be preferable.

You could, of course, line it with leather but this is likely to be expensive, so could I enter a plea for a linoleum top? In the trade we made up quite a lot of counter-tops for banks which were lined with what was called 'bank lino'. This was a good quality lino which offered an ideal surface for moving ledgers, books, and coins about easily; although it may be difficult to obtain now, I am sure a plain vinyl floor covering would answer just as well. The point is that if you use this type of lining you will have to allow for its thickness when applying the lipping around the top.

The small corner brackets can be dowelled into place, and the only other woodwork that remains is the cutting of the grooves for the cocked beads. If you have a powered router, this will be straightforward enough, remembering that it would be advisable not to go right into the corners as you will be bound to get a rounded corner which will spoil the appearance. So stop the router about half an inch or so (12mm) short of the corners and finish off by hand. If you haven't a router, why not make yourself a 'scratch stock' as shown in Fig 4A? It's known as a 'revolver' stock because it looks vaguely like one (rather an old-fashioned one, I must say), but you'll find it useful for all kinds of jobs. The construction is shown in Fig 4A and is obvious enough: we used to make cutters from broken pieces of bandsaws and shape them on the grindstone, but very good ones can be made from the blades of ordinary craft knives.

Fig 4D also shows you the dimensions of a typical cross-section of a cocked bead; normally this is made up from scrap, and is simply glued into the grooves with all corners mitred.

Handles and locks are, of course, your choice. ■

CUTTING LIST

Part No.	No. req'd.	Description	Long	Wide (inches)	Thick	Long	Wide (millimetres)	Thick
1	2	Corner posts	29½	2¾	2½	750	70	64
2	2	Intermediate posts	29½	2¾	2½	750	70	64
3	2	Corner back posts	29½	2	⅞	750	51	23
4	2	Back intermediate posts	27¾	2	⅞	705	51	23
5	1	Top front rail	56	4¼	⅞	1422	108	23
6	1	Centre front drawer rail	25¼	1¾	¾	641	45	19
7	6	Front drawer rails	13	1¾	¾	330	45	19
8	2	Top end rails	23⅞	2	⅞	607	51	23
9	2	Bottom end rails	23⅞	2	⅞	607	51	23
10	2	Bottom back rails	12½	2	⅞	318	51	23
11	1	Top back rail	56¼	2	⅞	1429	51	23
12	2	Top intermediate rails	23⅞	2	⅞	607	51	23
13	2	Bottom intermediate rails	23⅞	2	⅞	607	51	23
14	2	Top drawer bearers	26⅝	4½	¾	677	115	19
15	6	Drawer bearers	26⅝	1⅞	¾	677	48	19
16	14	Drawer guides	24⅞	1	¾	632	25	19
17	1	Back intermediate rail	23½	1¾	¾	597	45	19
	2	Pedestal top drawer fronts	12½	5¼	⅝	318	134	16
	2	Pedestal middle drawer fronts	12½	8¼	⅝	318	210	16
	2	Pedestal bottom drawer fronts	12½	9¼	⅝	318	235	16
	1	Centre drawer front	23	5¼	⅝	584	134	16
	4	Pedestal top drawer sides	25	5¼	⅜	635	134	10
	4	Pedestal middle drawer sides	25	8¼	⅜	635	210	10
	4	Pedestal bottom drawer sides	25	9¼	⅜	635	235	10
	2	Centre drawer sides	24	5¼	⅜	610	134	10
	6	Drawer bottoms	25	12½	¼	635	318	6
	1	Centre drawer bottom	24	24	¼	610	610	6
	2	Pedestal top drawer backs	12½	5	⅜	318	127	10
	2	Pedestal middle drawer backs	12½	8	⅜	318	203	10
	2	Pedestal bottom drawer backs	12½	9	⅜	318	229	10
	1	Centre drawer back	23	5	⅜	584	127	10
	1	Top (if solid)	61	29	⅞	1549	737	23
	2	Pedestal back panels	21	17½	¼	533	445	6
	1	Centre back panel	24	7	¼	610	178	6
	2	End panels	23½	21	¼	597	533	6
	2	Knee-hole panels	23½	19	¼	597	482	6
	8	Brackets	3	2¾	⅜	77	70	10

Allowances have been made to lengths and widths to include tenons and cutting etc; thicknesses are net.

Kenton & Co

A company of architects

In April 1981 we drew the attention of craft, woodwork and design teachers to the current series of features in *Woodworker* which should be of help and interest to boys and girls taking the A level paper in Craft and Design... Wood. The course covers the historical development of furniture design from 1850 to the present day. Kenton & Co continues this series which has so far covered the work of Gimson and the Barnsleys, Philip Webb, Peter van der Waals, William Morris and the arts and crafts movement, Gordon Russell and machine made furniture, Brynmawr furniture, the collections of the Cheltenham museum and the recent Edward Barnsley exhibition plus several of Edward Barnsley's designs

A review by Idris Cleaver

Shortly after the formation of the Arts and Crafts Exhibition Society in 1888, a number of its members were deputed to visit the principal London furniture stores to ascertain if they were producing furniture suitable for inclusion in the 1889 exhibition. The results were disappointing. What they saw was quite unsatisfactory and, moreover, they found the furniture trade most uncooperative. Among those members were two young architects, Reginald Blomfield (later Sir Reginald) and Mervyn Macartney.

As a result of their experience, and inspired by another architect W. R. Lethaby, they joined forces with another two young architects in Ernest Gimson and Sidney Barnsley to form themselves into a firm of architects to produce furniture of a high standard of design and workmanship. They were further joined by Stephen Webb, an able young draughtsman and Colonel Mallet, a friend of Macartney's, who had no real interest in furniture, but who had the right connections. All the members contributed £100 each; Col. Mallet £200, and Stephen Webb nothing at all and left shortly afterwards.

They occupied a workshop over some stables at the back of Bedford Row and called the firm *Kenton and Co* after the name of a street which they had to pass on their way to the workshops.

At least five cabinetmakers were employed to execute their designs, with A. H. Mason as their foreman. They bought their own materials and the designs were carried out by the skilled cabinetmakers under the personal supervision of the architect members.

The craftsmen were responsible for executing each piece of furniture from start to

● Cabinet on stand made in 1891 by Ernest Gimson, in palm, ebony and orangewood marquetry geometric design. Inside fitted with 12 drawers and two doors in holly. The stand is finished in ebony. (Photo: courtesy of the Fine Art Society Ltd, New Bond Street)

● Above: The famous ship chest and Right: a workbox in walnut with ebony insets, both by W. R. Lethaby and now in the possession of Major and Mrs Biddulph, Rodmarton Manor. (Photos: courtesy Cheltenham Art Gallery and Museum)

finish which was an essential part of the arts and crafts movement. Perhaps more important was the fact that each piece was stamped with the initials of the maker and the designer. This recognition of the workman was at that time a great step forward in line with the teaching of Ruskin and Morris.

All the members, except Mallet, had already shown an interest in furniture and some had previously exhibited at the 1888 exhibition. They had been greatly influenced by the furniture produced by the firm of Morris & Co of which Philip Webb and his assistant George Jack were the principal designers. Indeed, according to Lethaby, Philip Webb was 'their particular prophet'. Although they all admired Webb's furniture they were at this time also showing an interest in the Queen Anne furniture in the Victoria and Albert museum and what could be seen in the London antique shops, there was no common style in Kenton & Co. Each designer went his own way according to his interests and predilections, with the result that most of the furniture produced was different, and quite a lot of it original.

Reginald Blomfield (1856-1942) distinguished himself as a sportsman in Exeter College, Oxford by winning Blues at both cricket and rugby football. On leaving Oxford he entered the Royal Academy School and the architectural practice of his uncle A. W. Blomfield. Both he and Mervyn Macartney (1853-1932) who also went straight from university into the office of Norman Shaw, produced the eclectic walnut, mahogany and rosewood pieces in adaptations of 18th century pieces.

Ernest Gimson (1864-1919) had already shown a great interest in furniture making and had previously apprenticed himself to Philip Clissett of Bosbury in 1888 to learn the art of making turned ash chairs (*Woodworker* July 1979 p 376). His work was almost entirely original. One of the cabinetmakers employed by the firm — W. Hall — specialised in chamfered work and it is probable that this sparked off Gimson's prolific use of the chamfer, especially in his earlier work. He would certainly have been familiar with the chamfer as a decorative feature because his grandfather was a wheelwright in Leicester. Gimson had for some time before Kenton & Co been interested in starting up a furniture workshop in the country and had been looking for a place in Yorkshire or the Cotswolds.

Sidney Barnsley (1865-1926). His work was mostly in solid unstained oak heavily influenced by that of Philip Webb. He did, however, design a mirror frame which was Persian in design, inlaid with mother-of-pearl, probably reflecting the influence of a visit to Greece where he made a study of Byzantine churches. In conjunction with his friend and fellow architect Robert Weir Schultz he published a book on the Monastery of St. Luke of Stiris in Phocis. He also designed a wardrobe veneered in Indian walnut. In 1893 he moved with Gimson first to Ewen near Cirencester and later to Pinbury, where for the remainder of his life he designed and made his own furniture, mostly in English oak.

W. R. Lethaby (1857-1930) worked with Sidney Barnsley and Macartney in Norman Shaw's office until 1890 and then left to work on his own. He started designing furniture at about this time and worked mostly in oak, mahogany and rosewood. He was fond of a coarse type of floral marquetry using unstained woods. His chair in oak inlaid with ships was later used by Gimson as a model for one of his chairs. Lethaby's Kenton & Co chest with inlaid ships had the ends dovetailed and cogged, a construction which was very popular at the time.

The firm exhibited at the Arts and Crafts Exhibition in 1890 and held its own exhibition at Barnard's Inn in 1891. At this latter exhibition, more than £700 worth of furniture was sold, but that was not enough to prevent the firm from folding up. Apart from the fact that the furniture was sold at only a little over cost price, with nothing charged for the design or the time expended by the architects in supervision, it was obvious that the firm was underfinanced, but none of the members was inclined to put up more capital to keep it going. It probably did not occur to them that they could have obtained financial support from outside the firm. So after less than two years duration, the firm packed up and the unsold pieces were divided among the members according to the amount due to them. In general each member chose his own designs with the remainder being distributed by drawing lots.

Each member architect then went his own way. Blomfield and Macartney returned to

● *Sideboard in oak, carved and inlaid with ebony, sycamore and bleached mahogany, designed by W. R. Lethaby for Melsetter House, Hoy, Orkneys in 1900. This sideboard is visible in a photograph of the dining room at Melsetter House, illustrated in Sir Reginald Blomfield's obituary tribute of 1932. (Photo: courtesy Victoria and Albert Museum)*

architecture. Lethaby also returned to architecture and later became the joint Principal of the LCC Central School of Art & Crafts before becoming the first Professor of Architecture at the Royal College of Art.

Ernest Gimson and Sidney Barnsley moved to the Cotswolds and opened their own furniture workshops where they were joined by Sidney's brother Ernest. Most of the skilled craftsmen moved with Gimson and settled down to produce the superb furniture which has since had such a great influence on the course of modern furniture both in this country and on the continent.

All the members concerned enjoyed and learnt much from the experience of being in direct touch with materials which Lethaby had always insisted was the only road to architectural salvation.

The influence of Kenton & Co is in no way reflected by its short existence. This is evidenced in a letter which Gimson wrote to Lethaby some time later. Writing of their experience of Kenton & Co, he said, 'After all it seems to have been our craft Eden that made possible the German Werkbund.'

(A number of pieces produced by 'Kenton & Co' may be seen at the Victoria & Albert museum, South Kensington.) ■

June notes

New angle on hardwoods

As a longstanding supplier of hardwoods, Anthony Broughton-Head says he has become increasingly aware of the problems of obtaining quality timber in small quantities at reasonable prices.

This has led him to set up a new company with the intention of putting things right for the small-scale user of hardwoods who, he says, is only too often subjected to buying low quality timber at high prices.

His stated objectives in this new enterprise are: to stock selected first quality kiln-dried and air-dried timber; to sell in small quantities; to encourage selection; to sell at reasonable prices; and to establish large stocks of all species and thicknesses.

His current stocks offer English oak, cherry, ash, walnut, American red oak and ash, cedar of Lebanon, Brazilian mahogany, chestnut, yew, elm and sycamore.

Mr Broughton-Head will be glad to supply price lists and further details. You can get him on 02357-67811, or drop him a line at 2 Elizabeth Drive, Wantage, Oxon.

The French connection

Reports from the 23rd French Furniture Exhibition in January provide some pointers about the general state of demand for furniture on the continent, which probably translates into our own market in much the same way.

Response to exhibits seems to suggest a continuing demand for country style and 19th century romantic type pieces, though there is still an increasing market for contemporary designs.

Of the 46,000 visitors to the exhibition, 5,500 were from outside France, and 57 per cent of exhibitors declared that they had achieved positive results (only 52 per cent said this at the '81 show).

The organisers also report a trend towards lighter wood colouring, and brightly painted furniture is increasingly popular. Although a newcomer on the scene, furniture sold in kit form made a substantial impact. Kits both worry and intrigue manufacturers and dealers, but all foresee that they probably represent a large part of tomorrow's market.

Buyer's guide

The ninth edition of the *Educational Institute of Design, Craft and Technology Craft Buyer's Guide 1982* runs to 80 pages and is published by Kogan Page Ltd, 120 Pentonville Road, London N1 9JN at £5.95 (paperback, large format). Emphasis in the editorial section of this edition is on 'technology' aspects of CDT. This the editor claims follows the bias and thematic approach of recent editions of *Practical Education* the journal of EIDCT. The second part of the book consists of a directory listing manufacturers and suppliers of tools, machines and materials for some 37 different crafts including woodworking, canoe and boat building, treen and woodturning, musical instruments, sculpture, upholstery and picture framing. This year's guide has a more open aspect than previous editions. The index to suppliers is separated from the classified list giving a less cluttered look to the pages and also accounting for the drop in their numbers.

● *Detail taken from a 16th century oak panel (see 'Early carving')*

And then there were two

Two full-time advanced courses on timber technology as well as many part-time block release specialist training courses are now offered by Buckinghamshire College of Higher Education. The BSc Timber Technology course has been running for eight years and alongside this is the one-year Diploma in Timber Studies course. Both courses also cover law, economics, accounts, management and marketing. Also available are courses in saw doctoring, wood machining, timber infestation surveying and various wood science courses. Full details from D. G. Patterson at the college in Queen Alexandra Road, High Wycombe HP11 2JZ.

A lock on prison doors

Who could stifle an ironical (and perhaps slightly unkind) smile on discovering inmates of prisons in this country are making doors?

In fact the volume of doors manufactured in HM Prison establishments now numbers around 1,650 each week, and the British Woodworking Federation is getting worried about the effect this output is having upon the door-making industry.

So concerned is the BWF that it has written to Patrick Mayhew, Minister of State at the Home Office, asking for a temporary suspension of the manufacture of hardwood exterior doors and the assembly of Canadian door stock, while also requesting a freeze on the release of several thousand doors which are believed to be in stock.

Originally the BWF agreed to the limited manufacture of doors in HM Prisons, but at that time demand was outstripping output. Redundancies in the industry brought on by the recession and by the enormous increase in imports from the Far East have changed all that, and now the federation contends that it is insupportable to keep prisoners employed at the expense of jobs in the industry.

The BWF suggests switching to the manufacture of small kitchen doors, since most of this market is currently supplied by imports.

Early carving

Celia Jennings has produced a small booklet (12pp) designed and printed by Surrey Graphics Ltd, Dorking, Surrey, on *An introduction to early woodcarving*.

The five pages of photographs concentrate on 15th, 16th and 17th century ecclesiastical carvings. The text leads the reader through the medieval background, woodcarving, themes and symbolism, to the Renaissance and its religious, pagan and animal symbolism.

A useful little booklet to read before visiting churches so that a fuller appreciation can be gained of the woodcarvings.

Jarrah on the tracks

The sleepers supplied to keep the British trains running are of jarrah, a reddish-brown timber found only in a small area of SW Australia and renowned for its durability and attractive appearance. Brunning Bros who hold the contract also supply to Belgium Railways, they supply mine shaft timber to Germany, flooring to Greece and timber for other structural projects eg bridges and sea-defence work. The company also supply panelling and glue laminated kauri useful for church communion rails, tavern bar counters and kitchen tops. Available in easy to work solid sections, pre-packed in set lengths. Fuller details from Peter Mott at the Australian department of trade on 01-438 8000.

High standard of vehicles

In newsletter no 55 John Pearce secretary of the Model Horse Drawn Vehicles Club says that the standard of models entered in the 51st Model Engineer exhibition was extremely high. In reply to numerous letters asking how the winners are chosen he has this to say: 'The answer is simple, judging is split into several headings with a set maximum mark for each of the following, scale, authenticity, suitability of materials, complexity, painting/finish with a grand maximum total of 600 marks. Each vehicle is thus individually judged and the total marks totted up.'

John Pearce expresses disappointment at the low number of models entered by club members. He says a Mr Binns virtually ran away with the honours receiving gold, silver and bronze medals plus 2 highly commended. The rest of the newsletter contains, as usual, tips and hints, replies to queries and trade news plus wanted and for sale columns. John Pearce can be reached at 4 Brentlea Crescent, Higher Heysham, Lancs LA3 2BT.

Ornamental bulletin

Another interesting bulletin from the Society of Ornamental Turners has arrived. The new secretary is P. J. (Phil) Holden, 17 Chichester Drive, East Saltdean, Brighton BN2 8LD, to whom any correspondence concerning the society should be addressed. The latest bulletin reports on the 33rd AGM of the society held at Caxton Hall last November, William Hartley's four part geometric chuck, shops log, rose-engine turning, spherical turning, re-cycled wine glass and a remarkable turning, plus an appreciation of the president of the society and news from last year's auction.

CUBE CRAZY!

Erno Rubik has already made a pretty comprehensive job of driving the whole world crazy with his maddening Cube. Now *Woodworker* exclusively unveils a puzzle cube made of wood, designed and built by Jon Millington of Bristol, who is a published authority on unravelling Mr Rubik's ingenious brain-teaser

Now make one in wood

As author of a book on Rubik's Cube, I am sometimes asked to talk about my method for solving it. So since the normal plastic cubes are not big enough to be seen by more than a few dozen people, I decided to make a wooden demonstration model.

After some experiments, I chose an over-all edge length of 12cm which in practice has proved to be about the right size to be held and moved by one person. Anything larger would have been too heavy and cumbersome for this, but the measurements given here can be scaled up or down to produce a model of whatever size is wanted.

Wood is the ideal material for this model which was enjoyable and straightforward to make, while it can easily be taken apart.

The eight corner pieces and 12 edge pieces are made from 4cm cubes, and the six centre pieces are 4 × 4 × 2.5cm blocks. Opposite centre pieces are joined by a strong coil spring linked to a swivel.

Elm was the wood used, although the choice is not critical and others would be equally suitable. What is critical is the accuracy with which the 20 cubes and six blocks are cut, and a tolerance of ±½mm should be aimed for to ensure the smooth working of the model.

Three templates made from zinc or other thin and rigid material help to obtain the correct profile of the inner surfaces. They are much easier to use on cubes and blocks whose edges have not yet been rounded.

CONSTRUCTION

Corner pieces (8 off). Cut away a 1.5cm cube from one corner of a 4cm cube and glue a 2.5cm cube in this cavity. Then use template A to obtain the correct radius on three corners of the 2.5cm cube.

Edge pieces (12 off). Glue a 2 × 1.8 × 1cm block to one face of a 4cm cube and glue a 3 × 1.8 × 1cm block overlapping the first to the adjoining face, retaining each of them with a 25mm panel pin. Use template B to ensure that these blocks are in their right places. Then cut away the two corners of the cube next to the glued blocks to the curvature of template A. I used a 6 to 7cm diameter grinding wheel to finish these off.

Centre pieces (6 off). Select one of the two 4 × 4cm surfaces of a 4 × 4 × 2.5cm block and cut it to the profile of template C. This should reduce the thickness at the centre of all four 4 × 2.5cm faces to 2cm. Again, a grinding wheel came in useful. Alternatively, use 4 × 4 × 2cm half cubes which do not need any further shaping at this stage, although the model will not operate as smoothly with these.

Springing (3 off). Brass swivels are secured by dome-headed screws to three centre pieces while the other three have a strong spring screwed to them. The loop is cut off one end of each spring and a thin 5 × 14mm brass strip pushed between the last turn and the one before. A screw inserted into the other end of the spring is located in the strip's hole and is then screwed into the centre piece.

The looped end of each spring is linked to its swivel on the opposite centre piece by a stout wire about 5cm long bent round at both ends. Its exact length will depend on that of the spring, and should be adjusted so

(Continued on page 406)

TEMPLATES

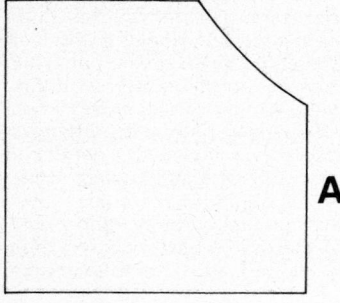

A

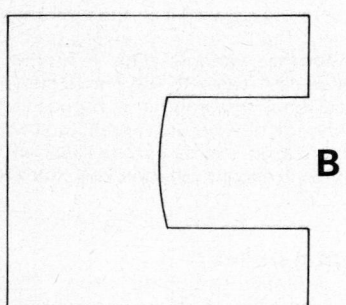

B

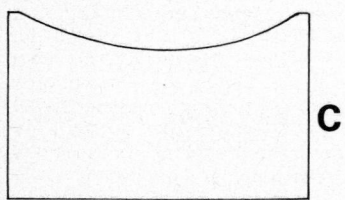

C

● The wooden cube as designed and built by Jon Millington

CORNER PIEC

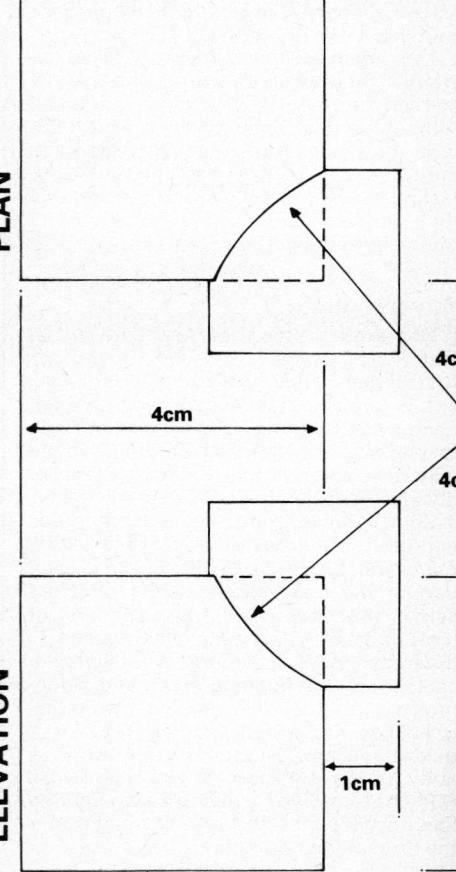

PLAN

ELEVATION

4cm

4cm

4cm

1cm

PLAN VIEW OF MIDDLE LAYER

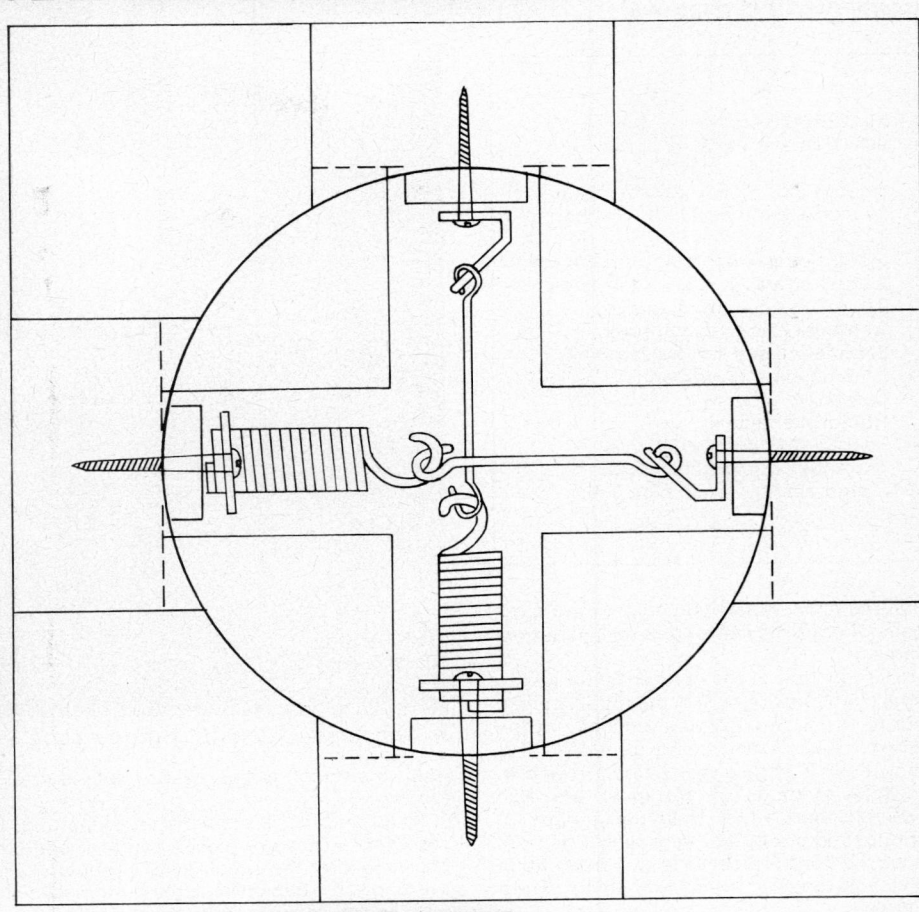

EDGE PIECE

4cmR

1.8 cm

4cm

4cmR

1cm

2cm

CENTRE PIECE

1.6 cm

4cm

2.5 cm

4cmR

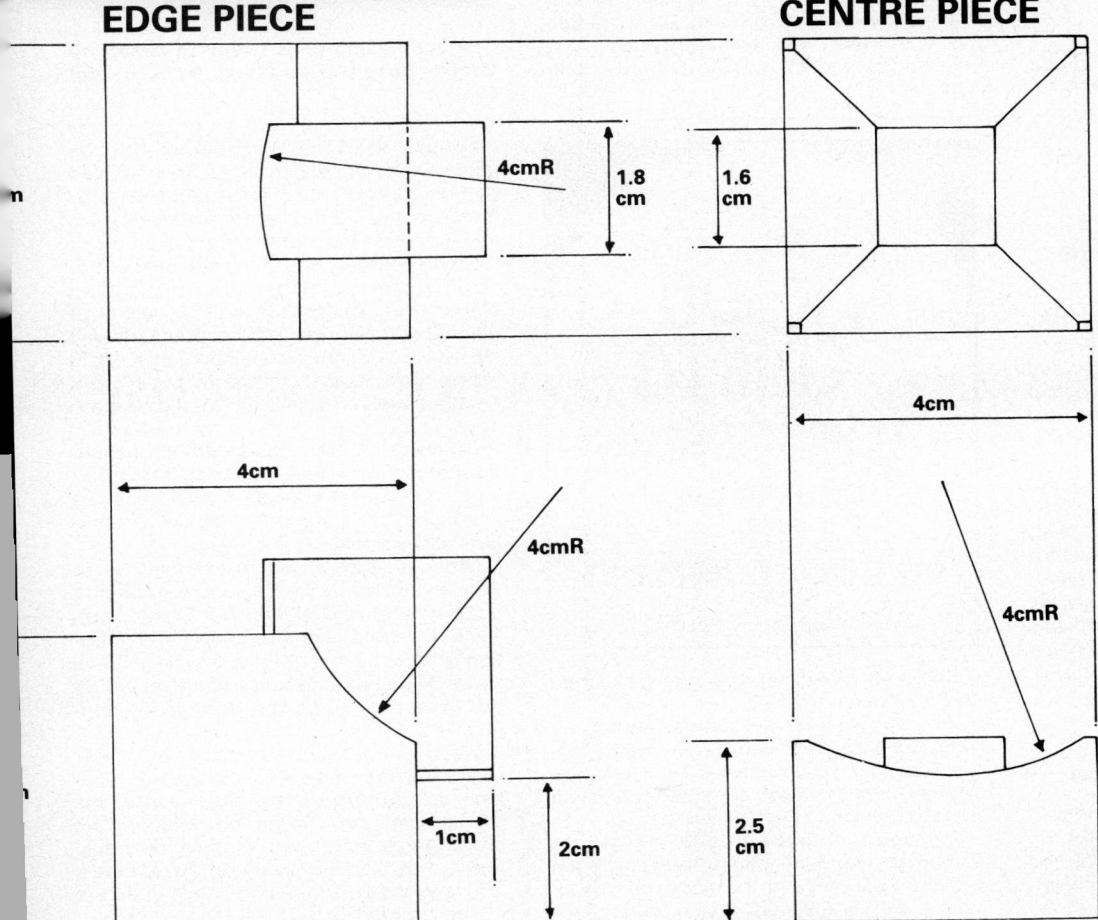

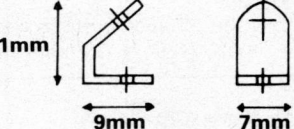

11mm

9mm

7mm

- *Swivel holes to suit screw and wire developed length 22mm*

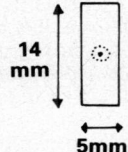

14 mm

5mm

- *Spring insert hole to suit screw*

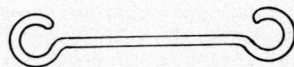

- *Linking wire developed length about 5cm*

● Rubik's Cube is a trademark of the Ideal Toy Corporation, New York.

Wooden cube

(continued from page 404)

MATERIALS
20 cubes 4 × 4 × 4cm
6 blocks 4 × 4 × 2.5cm
8 cubes 2.5 × 2.5 × 2.5cm
12 blocks 2 × 1.8 × 1cm
12 blocks 3 × 1.8 × 1cm
3 brass strips 14 × 5 × 1mm approx.
3 brass strips 22 × 7 × 1mm approx.
3 wire links 5cm long approx.
3 springs 2.5cm long approx.
6 dome-headed screws 2cm no4
24 panel pins 25mm long
Cascamite glue
Humbrol Enamels:
   white (22), yellow (69)
   orange (18), bright red (19)
   emerald (2), french blue (14).

● *The heart of Jon Millington's cube, showing its workings*

that the tension between each of the three pairs of opposite centre pieces is about the same.

The function of the springs is not just to apply light tension within the model at rest, but to resist strongly any tendency of the layers to part when being turned, as this may result in edge pieces being forced out.

Other methods of springing are also possible, and I first tried using pairs of springs (without the wire links) to join opposite centre pieces. This worked quite well and required swivels on all six centre pieces.

FINISHING

When the 26 pieces have been made, every single edge is rounded except the four innermost edges of the six centre pieces.

To assemble the model, start by putting together four centre pieces and four edge pieces to form the middle layer as shown in the diagram. Then build up the bottom layer with its centre piece, four edge pieces and four corner pieces. Fit these to the middle layer and then add the top layer by first linking the top centre piece to the one opposite.

Now the external squares have to be primed and then painted with about three coats of enamel paint. It does not really matter which colour goes on which face, but I put a light colour opposite a dark one with white/blue, yellow/green and orange/red.■

● **Jon Millington is author of** *Resolving Rubik's Cube* **(Abson Books, Wick, Bristol 95p).**

Events

Craftsman's directory of events

Compiled and published by Stephen and Jean Lance the *Craftsman's directory 1982* gives a comprehensive list of craft events, guilds etc to be held during 1982. Times and venues should be verified before setting out as dates are often changed at the last minute or information received for catalogues can often be inaccurate.

The directory gives the names and addresses of the organisers of the various events to aid readers in advance. Also included are details of venues available for hire, craft books, centres, shops and galleries, craft demonstrators, suppliers, schools and courses and magazines and periodicals of interest to the craft world. Obtainable direct from the publishers at Brook House, Mint Street, Godalming GU7 1HE.

Model, Craft and Country Show

As publicised in earlier issues of *Woodworker* May 22 and 23 are the dates for the Model, Craft and Country Show at the National Agricultural Centre at Stoneleigh in Warwickshire. Entry £2 for adults, £1 for

children and OAPs, car parking free, open 10-6 each day.

Woodworking is well represented in the Tate and Lyle Hall with trade stands, displays and a special Woodworker Workshop where round the clock demonstrations will be taking place.

On hand both days will be Jack Hill whose series on windsor chairs was a much acclaimed success in the pages of *Woodworker*. Jack's speciality is traditional chair-

making by hand and he will be demonstrating this and the use of rotary planes devised by Fred Lambert. Jack is also an expert on most country crafts, having written on them and practised most of them in his time.

Stan Thomas of Treorchy will be demonstrating the use of traditional moulding planes, the correct use of tools, principles of planing and setting out procedures. He will also have a display consisting of a scale model geometrical staircase, raised and fielded panelling with ogee-moulded spandrils.

Gordon Hall, from the school of art and design, furniture and timber at Bucks College of Higher Education will also be sharing his skills and knowledge with members of the public.

Other displays include model horse drawn vehicles by B. P. Young of Chipping Sodbury and R. D. Paxford of Stratford on Avon, a turned, laminated vase and selection of work by Arthur F. Allen. These items by Mr Allen were discussed and shown on BBC *Midlands Today* programme in January 1980.

Trade stands will cover hand and power tools. A programme of lectures and films back up all these events and of course the model side is not forgotten. Military and scale models, gems and needlework, model horse drawn vehicles, model cars, boats, railways, model engineering and planes are all represented.

THE EMCOSTAR

More Craft . . . Less Space!!

This truly universal Woodworking Machine gives you results everytime! This incredible machine requires a space of only 40″ × 28″; and will provide apart from the six functions as illustrated, the following:
Moulding ● Planing ● Thicknessing
● Mortising ● Combing ● Grooving
● Coving ● Wood-turning
● Tool-sharpening ● Working
with Flexible Shaft

£558 (incl. VAT) and free delivery from your nearest EMCO Leisure Centre

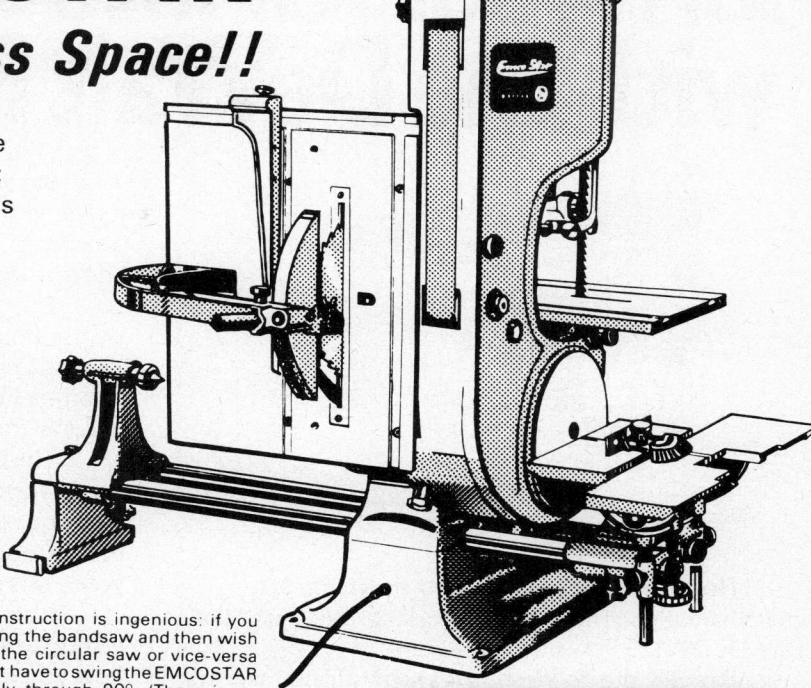

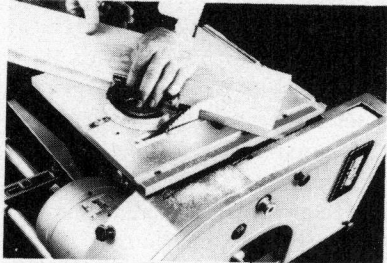

Circular Sawing, Ripping.

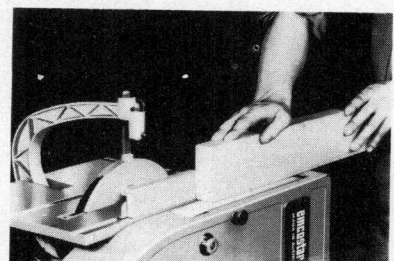

Using the belt sander for finishing ledges.

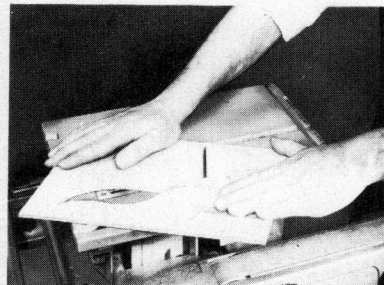

Sawing a curved design from a piece of wood with the jig saw (blade guard and support arm removed to provide a clear work table).

The construction is ingenious: if you are using the bandsaw and then wish to use the circular saw or vice-versa you just have to swing the EMCOSTAR vertically through 90°. (There is no other machine with such an ingenious feature.)

All 6 operations are possible without any conversion. It's a compact unit working with a precision that surprises the home-worker and attracts the professional carpenter.

The possibilities of making things are endless, such as: built-in cupboards, antique replicas, wooden models, play-room furniture, garden furniture, cellar-bars, etc., there are no limits.

With the EMCOSTAR also the unskilled can extend his handicraft-abilities and work as a carpenter. The fascinating versatility of the EMCOSTAR is the secret of its success. Every user is enthusiastic about it. Your tool dealer will demonstrate the machine to you and you will be amazed.

That's what you can do already with the basic EMCOSTAR unit: 6 operations namely: Circular Sawing ● Band Sawing Jig Sawing ● Fret Sawing ● Belt Sanding ● Disc Sanding

Cutting an intricate shape with the fret saw using wood support and blade guide.

Cutting decorative shapes with the band saw.

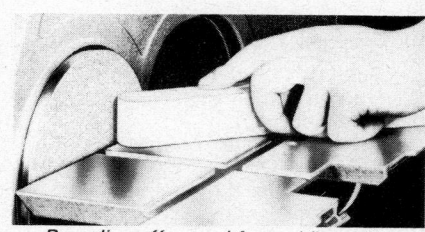

Rounding off an end face with sanding tables as a work support.

Turn yourself into a craftsman with the DeWalt Powershop.

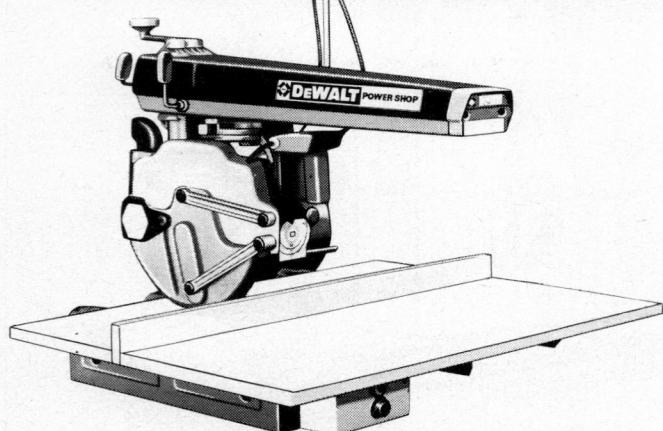

How would you like to bring the stamp of a craftsman to your home woodworking? Well, with the DeWalt DW125 Powershop you can.

Basically the Powershop is a sophisticated saw that can be set to cross cut, rip cut, bevel and mitre to a wide range of lengths, depths and angles. By itself it can satisfy the needs of the most demanding home woodworker with speed and ease.

But when fitted with its various attachments it gives you the opportunity to add real craftsman's touches to your work, and opens up new horizons in home woodworking.

Grooves, rebates, decorative edges, intricate shapes, housings and mouldings appear as if by magic. Perfect joints become commonplace. And the sanding attachments add the final finishing touches that really make all the difference.

The DeWalt Powershop is one of the most versatile woodworking machines available today. Not only can it help you realise the most from your own skills, but its ease of operation makes it a pleasure to work with as your ideas take shape.

It's a must for every serious woodworker who wants to be admired as a craftsman. You'll soon wonder how you ever managed without one.

The DeWalt DW125 Powershop is available from all good tool and machinery shops and you can call Teledata on 01-200 0200 for further details.

DeWALT®

A Division of Black and Decker, Canon Lane, Maidenhead, Berks.

Prices quoted are those prevailing at press date and are subject to alteration due to economic conditions.

● The tiny interior of the carpenter's workshop as seen by miniaturist Stanley Yates

Mastery in miniature

In a small workshop in Mawdesley, Lancs, an even smaller workshop takes shape, a part of the tiny world created by miniaturist Stanley Yates. Michael Edwards went to see Mr Yates and discovered how he sets about constructing his beguiling 'living pictures'

● ● ●

Stanley Yates' miniature works have an unsettling effect on the viewer. Look at them long enough and you seem to shrink to his 1/32 scale yourself.

Stanley is an internationally known miniaturist who creates his miniscule masterpieces in a dusty shed next to a piggery in Mawdesley, Lancashire. He is self-taught and proud of it, but few people realise that behind the practical skill of his craft are the long hours of pre-production research he must spend, working at old books, photographs and documents in his efforts to perfect his work.

He has been making his 'living pictures' for seven years full-time, after working for 22 years in the licensing trade. After quitting the pub life at the age of 50, he built a cottage at Coniston in the Lake District, drawing on his 14 years' experience in the building trade after leaving school. Stanley and his wife stayed in the Lake District for four years, selling his 'pictures in wood' from premises in Ambleside, but due to poor out-of-season business they decided to move back to Lancashire where they could live and sell his work from one building.

Most of his miniatures are designed as though they are going to be lived in, and

(continued overleaf)

● Stanley at his workbench, surrounded by the tools of his craft

Miniaturist

(from previous page)

many are based on characters in real life. For instance, the character that inhabits his miniature 19th century country carpenter's shop is, in Stanley's eyes, a traditional village carpenter. He makes coffins on the side, but he also knows how to bend and heat iron, so if he makes a gate he need not call on a blacksmith to fashion bands and gudgeons. Hence the forge.

Stanley Yates' most popular commissions depict scenes from Victorian times up to the late 30s. Unlike an artist who works in two dimensions conveying three dimensions with perspective, he does not like flat surfaces. Length, height and depth are important. He always wants to know what lies beyond a door. One of these days, he says, he'll pass through and into...

On the day I called a customer asked for a farm kitchen complete with a dog lying in front of the fire, a slop-stone and a ladling-can, used to fill the tub with hot water from the boiler. Also to be included was a black leaded grate with an oven, a maiden and a tin bath on the wall. Another person wanted baking day depicted, with dough on the table, bread tins, and loaves and yeast rising in a big bread mug by the fire.

The worn appearance of the range is achieved with judicious applications of black and silver paint. Detail takes account of the fact that the area around the fire would be dull, while the top would be a little brighter, since it was always being wiped. The oven door knob would always sparkle due to it being opened with a cloth because of the heat.

A farm kitchen, on the other hand, would include a big open stone fireplace with a skillet hung over it on a chain and where bannocks were cooked. There would be a cauldron with logs piled up at the side; fishing tackle, hams and a shotgun would hang about the room, with skins and antlers on the walls. The windows would be shuttered.

How many hours does it take him to make something like this? Stanley could not answer that one. Rather than working by the hour, he starts at 8 o'clock every morning and often goes through until 11pm, or until his eyes give way. He charges not by the hour but on the subject and the number of days it takes.

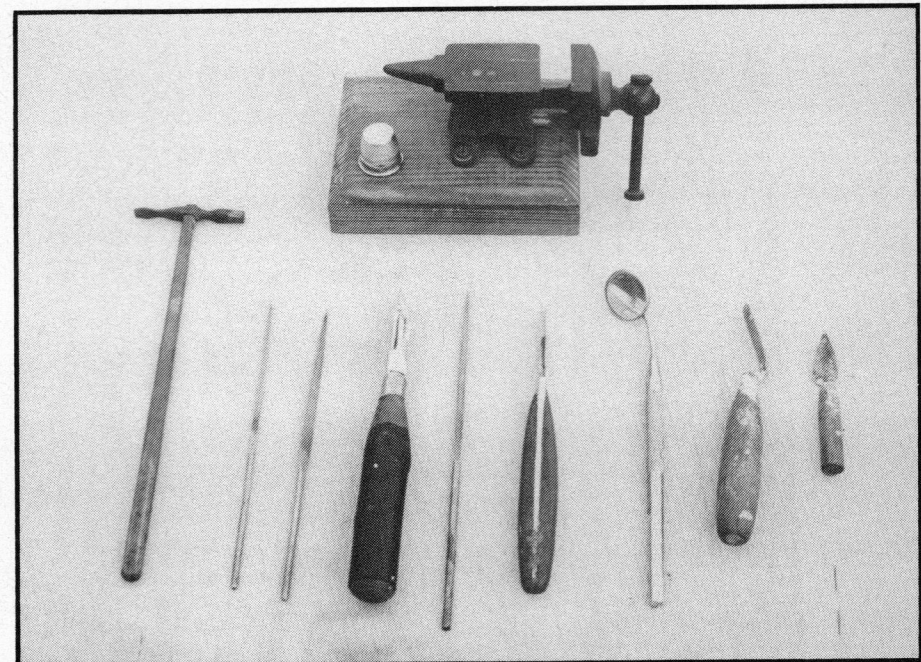

● *Part of the miniaturist's armoury — scalpels, dental tools and a mini-vice*

His thirst for detail is never quenched. Carving a historical piece can involve considerable research, for he would not like it said by an expert in any particular period that such and such an item was incorrect. As an instance, he cited a mediaeval hall which hasn't a flue or fireplace, the smoke escaping through a hole in the roof. A weaver's cottage would have mullioned windows, long and low facing a certain direction. There would be a hole in the kitchen floor which was filled with water to keep the thread damp. A building's king post roof truss must have the correct wooden mitre; the rafters and purlins must be spot on. Even the door must hang on the correct side.

On the day of my visit Stanley was just completing the country carpenter's shop. The door is ajar as though the man has just nipped out for a minute, and the workshop is complete with firpole scaffolding under the beams, dolls, trestles, saw blocks, paint pots and brushes, chisels, hammers, rules and even a joiner's bass. Being part blacksmith, he has a forge in the left of the room. The fire has gone out, but it is still warm because his chair is pulled up against the forge with his brew-can on it.

Everything must be identifiably correct in every way, which may explain Stanley's success in selling his pieces. Yates originals are now to be found in America, Canada, Germany, Japan, Australia, France, New Zealand and Spain, and he also supplies a London gift shop.

The cases are made in a variety of woods – oak veneer, Canadian redwood, mahogany and pitch pine, while the carved interiors are all from yellow pine, a light, easily worked wood with a long, straight and knotless grain that will not warp or move. This timber from the Baltic is no longer imported into this country, so Stanley's supplies have to come from demolished buildings such as churches, barns and mills.

The complete items are assembled with pearl glue heated in an electric waterbath, stained and french polished, using a mixture of shellac and meths. Commercial stain, says Stanley, looks artificial and too glossy.

As a maker in miniature, Stanley gets some unusual requests, including the Victorian dental surgery that is now a fixture on the QE2. This piece incorporates such horrors as a foot-driven treadle drill, a tiny chair for the patient, a spittoon and even a blood-spattered bib. ■

Events

Courses in Wiltshire

Details of courses being held during spring and summer 1982 at Urchfont Manor College, Urchfont, Devizes, Wilts, are now available from the secretary of the college Miss Audrey Brent. They include french polishing and wood colouring, English period furniture, restoring furniture, woodcarving, wood engraving and rush and cane seating.

Craft courses

Micklethwaite Studio workshops enter their eighth season of craft courses at their restored early 19th century textile mill in West Yorkshire. Courses are of varying lengths (full week, mid week and weekend) and in addition to the usual courses previously offered in woodturning, wood carving, furniture making, clock making, this year they are introducing a series of building courses. Due to start in the autumn the three new courses include property renovation, brick laying, stonework and plastering and build your own house. Full details of all the courses and fees from Robert Ellwood, Micklethwaite Studio Workshops, Holroyd Mill, Beck Road, Micklethwaite, nr Bingley, W. Yorks.

Crafts show

British Craft Show 1982 will be held at Syon Park from 16-19 September. Full details from David Bennett/Maurice Brown, 3 Rothesay Drive, Highcliffe, Christchurch, Dorset.

Toys

Until 30 May an exhibition of toys by Sam Smith from the Crafts Council collection, at Carlisle Museum and Art Gallery, Castle St, Carlisle.

Exhibition mix

British designer-makers and artists 5th year of exhibitions at Prescote Gallery, Cropredy, Oxon. This year's mix includes: Carved and painted toys and mobiles by Jim Edmiston 20 June-18 July, Bowls by Paul Caton 25 July-12 September, Decorated wooden objects by Eleanor Glover 19 September-17 October. All these exhibitions start at noon on the first date given. The gallery is normally open from 10-5 Wednesday to Sunday and Bank Holidays inclusive.

The Inca bandsaw

ON TEST

The small bandsaw, now very much more versatile than purely a profile cutting device, is fast establishing itself in the amateur workshop as a useful general purpose woodworking machine. One of this new breed of small bandsaws is the Inca model, imported by Woodworking Machines of Switzerland, who are based at Milton Keynes. We asked Alan Holtham, a woodturner and supplier of light woodworking machinery, to put the Inca through its paces for us. Here is his verdict

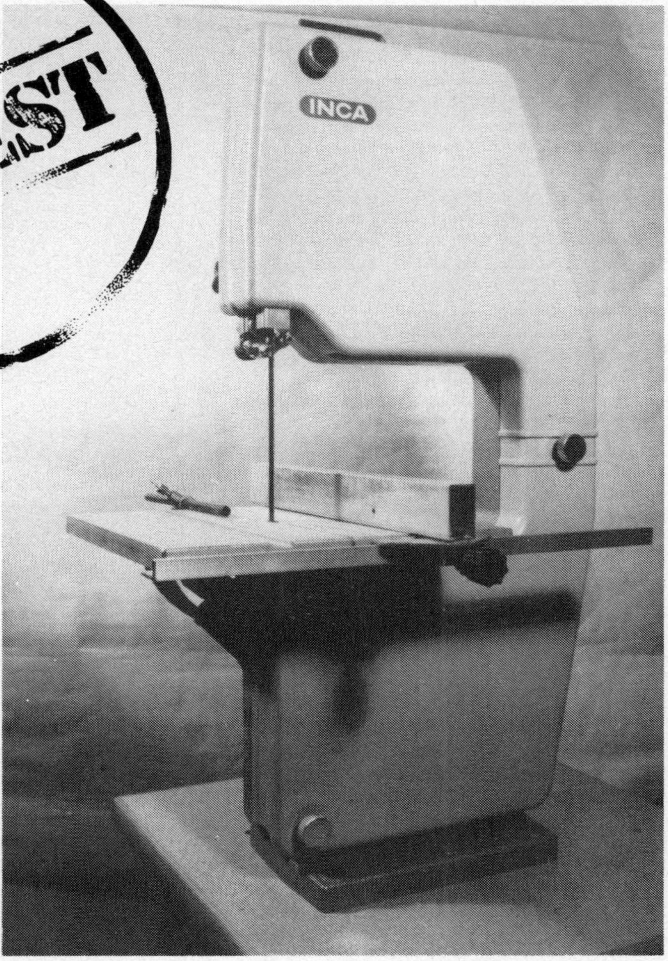

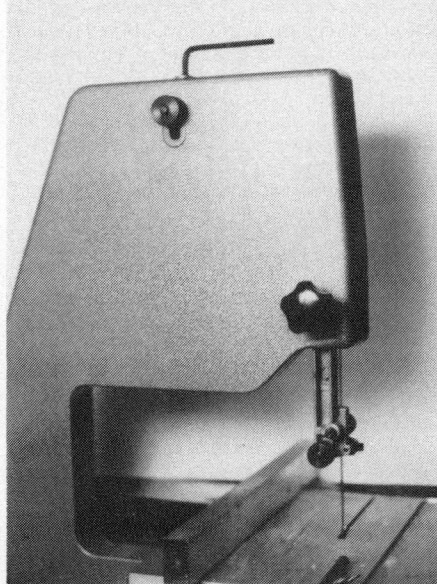

Fig 1 (above).

Fig 2 (right) the main controls.

Fig 3 (left) tilting mechanism.

One always associates Swiss engineering with quality, and this is exemplified on the Inca. In fact, so confident are the manufacturers in their product that the non-electrical parts are guaranteed for five years.

Although at first glance the Inca appears to be conventional in format, the serious bandsaw user will quickly notice that it is left handed, which is apparently no problem to the new user, but having only ever used right handed machines myself, I found it took some getting used to. This does cause a rather amusing difficulty with some people though, since a folded blade welded up for a right hand machine will usually unfold the wrong way round for the Inca. We regularly have customers complaining that blades have been welded with the teeth pointing the wrong way round! Just turn the blade inside out and all is returned to normal.

Viewed from the rear (Fig 2) there are three main controls visible, the allen type handle in the top of the frame is the adjustment for the blade tension. The lock nut and adjuster below are used to alter the tracking of the blade, and this works by simply tilting the top wheel backwards and forwards to take account of the different widths of blades that can be fitted. The large

black knob is the lock for the height adjustment of the top blade guide system, and it is interesting to note that on virtually all the Incas I have used, the up and down movement of this guide has been extremely stiff, and requires a little attention before it all operates smoothly.

Underneath the table is a first class tilting mechanism which alters easily, and unlike many more expensive machines has a graduated scale that actually works, and is not just a token gesture. The standard motor is a 0.6 HP single phase flange mounted unit which provides a blade speed of about 3,000ft per minute, which although satisfactory for wood cutting is a little too fast for metal cutting. However, one of the nice features of this machine is that it is available unmotorised, so one can quite easily rig up a three or four step pulley drive system if you want to cut materials other than wood.

The heart of any bandsaw is the blade, and correct maintenance of the guides is essential to maximise the performance of that blade, so it is a credit to the Inca that changing the sawblade and making subsequent guide adjustments, is not at all difficult. A screw adjustment makes positioning of the guides very simple, so there should be no excuses for poorly running

blades and the provision of a tension indicator is a particularly useful feature, as many amateur users of bandsaws find that blade tensioning is the most off-putting aspect. Here it is foolproof.

It is always interesting to start up a bandsaw for the first time with a new blade in, though if the basic setting up procedure has been followed there will be no problem. I always smile when I think of a wood-

(continued on page 412)

(continued on page 412)

Inca on test

(continued from page 411)

turning friend of mine who could not understand the need for correct blade tracking, which always resulted in the blades on his machine coming flying forward off the wheels unless you quickly jammed in a piece of wood. This was more difficult since his nerves were by now so tattered that he would crouch behind a large pile of wood and start the machine with a long stick! Such extremes are quite unnecessary with the Inca.

Another useful feature on this machine is the small nylon brush to keep the bottom wheel clean. Normally this sort of thing is only found on the much larger machines. Though it is not very much, it is a nice little touch.

I started the test by cutting some patterns I wanted in some 3in mahogany. As the curves were relatively gentle I used the standard ⅜in × 6 tooth per inch blade. This cut very cleanly and easily, and in fact with a good blade one becomes quite carried away cutting up all sorts of bits of timber just for the fun of it.

As these patterns seemed to be no problem to the Inca I thought I would really give it something to think about, and since the literature said it would cut 6¼in deep hardwood, I cut the end off a large iroko beam and ran it through the planer to 6¼in. To be fair to the machine I replaced the blade with a ½in × 4 tpi section and prepared to do battle with this monster piece, but the subsequent results took me completely by surprise. The Inca whizzed through this as if it had been cheese and I was so impressed that I tried a square on it to see just how straight the cut was. Quite amazing! Even on a larger machine I would have expected some degree of bowing on the cut, but there wasn't a trace here, just a perfect 90° cut.

As ripping ability is another test of a bandsaw, I thought it would be interesting to give this the full treatment as well. The manufacturers were kind enough to lend me the fine fence adjuster which screws on to the standard rip fence to allow micro adjustments to be made. With this in place I managed to run off veneers 3in deep by less than ¹⁄₁₆in thick in Honduras mahogany without any problem at all. Once again I was truly impressed. I think the success of the Inca lies in the direct drive of the motor straight on to the bandwheel, with no intermediate belt drive, so the power transmission is consequently more positive and more even. This straight ripping ability is also ideal for any tennoning work, and a simple back stop is provided as standard on the machine for just this type of work.

There is quite a range of accessories available for the Inca, the mitre fence probably being one of the most useful. This is quite substantial, and very accurate, due mainly to the long dovetailed slide which provides a really positive location in the table. This also means that you can pull the slide out beyond the edge of the table without it falling off, if wider panels have to be cut. The mitre fence also incorporates a handy cut-off device for sawing a series of pieces to length, though my criticism here is that it is the wrong way round if you want to cut a long length down.

Another interesting feature is the fret cutting set, which is basically a set of roller guides which allow the use of a fine ⅛in blade for very tight cutting. These guides replace the side blade guides and give a very positive support to the tiny fret blade. You start using this blade with some trepidation, but it is surprisingly strong, and I managed to cut 3mm radius circles in 2in material quite easily. This starts off all sorts of ideas for puzzles and toys and with the table tilted at various angles the possibilities are endless.

The other main accessory is the sanding attachment, and I must admit that I was a little sceptical about this when I first saw it. You just replace the blade with a sanding belt, which runs against a support piece held between the top and bottom guides, and with an enlarged table insert. This

Fig 4 Cutting gentle curves in 3in mahogany.

Fig 5 Iroko behaves like Swiss cheese.

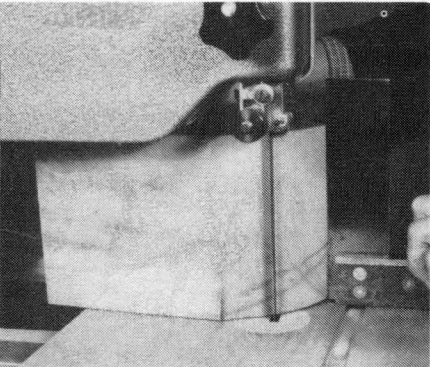

Fig 6 Taking a 90° cut through 6¼in deep iroko.

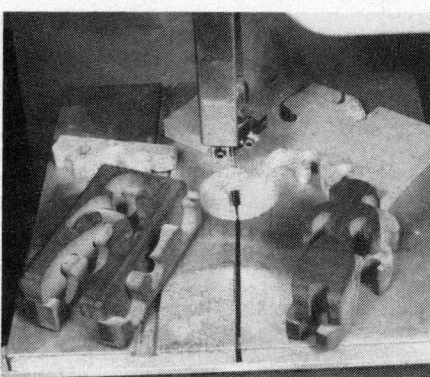

Fig 7 Ideas for puzzles and toys.

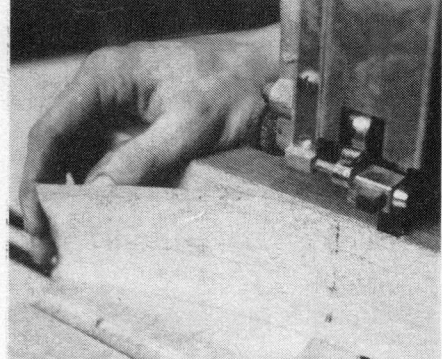

Fig 8 Producing Honduras mahogany veneers.

upright support is flat on one side and half round on the other, so that most profiles can be sanded. In practice, it was extraordinarily effective, reaching those parts other sanders certainly wouldn't reach! A variety of different grit belts are available, so again most materials can be handled.

After many happy hours working on this bandsaw, I can only say that it certainly lives up to its claims, and the range of extras available increases its potential use beyond that of many other bandsaws. There were a few minor niggles; for instance, why not put a decent handle for tension adjustment rather than the very crude allen key? But otherwise I have no major complaints, and I would recommend the Inca as worth a serious look if you are in the market for a medium range bandsaw. ■

Woodworker's bookshelf

What the French say

Some 20 years ago I regularly travelled to France to buy timber, plywood and veneer, and I absorbed something of the atmosphere of the trade there. Accordingly it was with pleasure I picked up *How to Choose Your Wood?* and noted this was a translation from the French of a publication titled *Comment Choisir Son Bois*.

I must record my disappointment. Here was a book full of good intentions but, surprisingly, unable to augment them.

Aim of the book is admirable; firstly to familiarise the reader with wood as a material; secondly to prepare the reader for a second book, on the principles of working in wood.

This is obviously a suitable approach and the table of contents does cover a wide field (too wide in my opinion) but the text is inadequate and often misleading, showing a confused knowledge on the part of the authors and indicating insufficient research on certain of the subjects.

There is a set of tables suggesting suitable end uses for different woods (most of them traditional) but there are some I find impossible to reconcile. Afrormosia is an expensive furniture wood. It is not listed under that heading but, rather strangely, under the headings for scaffolding and shuttering. It could, I suppose, be used for either purpose, except no one would dream of doing so.

A section in the book is devoted to biological agencies, but the whole text is confused and incomplete. Beetles, for example may damage wood, and frequently do, but if in a book they are to be mentioned in connection with choosing wood, then the text should reflect the degree of association.

The book is divided into four chapters: Progressing through wood and its structure; Commercial timbers: sawing, grading, buying etc; Species of wood and the derivatives; Products derived from wood, plywood, chipboard etc.

There are some excellent photographs and line drawings. The text offers advice on drilling, jointing, gluing and so on, much of it elementary. The book is nicely set out but in its present form no doubt offers more attraction to the French market than here. The authors are Yves Touchard and Alphonse Meyer. The publisher is Kity, 14 Rue des Casernes, F-67240 Bischwiller, France. It is available in UK from Kity stockists at £8.50. **W.H.B.**

Woodwork for you and you

For some time the way woodwork is taught in many schools has been undergoing a change in emphasis. The idea that 'skills exercises' should predominate — with every pupil making the same ubiquitous teapot stand from the teacher's dimensioned drawing on the blackboard — has (or has not in some cases) given way to courses intended to provide a more individual involvement in designing and making 'real' things.

A broader understanding of materials and the ways in which these are used to good purpose both by industry and in the home is the underlying theme of these courses. Arguably, it must be said that some such courses have gone overboard on the design aspect, relegating skills and craftsmanship to second place — here the pendulum has swung too far in my opinion. Design and technology are the 'in' words.

Indeed, craft, design and technology (CDT) is fast becoming the accepted synonym for those subjects hitherto timetabled as woodwork, metalwork etc, and a number of examining boards now set CSE and GCE examinations in line with this trend.

Woodwork For You is written by David M. Willacy, a chief examiner and moderator to one of these examining boards. The book therefore reflects some of the current thinking in woodwork education and provides a good deal of information relevant to the work now being done in school workshops.

It does more than this, however, for it is packed with information relevant to the needs of many whose schooldays are over with but who still want to learn about working with wood.

While the book includes a section on designing and two further short sections on school project work and examinations, the bulk of the work is given over to more practical matters of wider interest: Which wood or man-made board to use? Which tool for which job? How to use that particular tool and how to keep it sharp? Which joint and how to make it? Plus ways of joining wood without making joints; nails, screws, adhesives, construction, assembly; suitable hardware (hinges etc) and how to fix them. There are also sections on simple veneering; wood carving, turning, laminating and finishing; and also on upholstery and portable electric tools.

Predominantly visual, the book has illustrations on each of its 192 pages: clear photographs and diagrams, each keyed into the page's concise text which is given in the form of short, easy-to-read notes.

A criticism might be that the written information is too concise until you remember that the book is intended first as a school textbook and second to be of interest to adult beginners. For the first of these purposes it says quite enough and for the second it provides a sound introduction to the subject.

Some of the material was first published as *Crafts and Design in Wood* (Books 1, 2 & 3) by the same author. This single volume, which contains additional material and updated examination questions, is a good buy at £2.95. It is published by Hutchinson & Co, 3 Fitzroy Sq, London W1 (ISBN 0-09-145521-9) **J.H.**

Woodcarving: a three-way look

Few readers need an introduction to the name of Gordon Stokes. Many will have had the good fortune to receive tuition from him in woodturning and woodcarving. His explicit books on aspects of woodturning have enjoyed a wide circulation and the latest volume in his tuition series *Basic Woodcarving* is to be welcomed.

It is good that the author recommends the use of bandsaw and router, though stressing that these tools are not essential for success in the first stages.

He emphasises the importance of purchasing the best carving tools and keeping them in good condition, properly ground and sharpened. He explains how to prepare the tools for use and suggests the minimum number the beginner should acquire. However it is a pity that illustrations of honing and stropping chisels and gouges are not included.

The book is essentially a textbook for taking a course of woodcarving under the personal tuition of the author. It is published by the author from 202 The Hollow, Bath, Avon, at £7.50 in flexible heavy paperback.

It is well worth buying but its value would be enhanced if more step-by-step illustrations were included. In this reviewer's opinion the book would benefit considerably from being printed on better quality paper, stitched and cased in boards and cloth in a conventional manner.

Another book on woodcarving which has much to recommend it comes from the American collection of Dover books published by Constable at £3.40. It is, in fact, the transcription of 30hr of tape recordings made in 1967 by William S. Brown in conversation with Cecil C. Carstenson whose wood sculptures are widely distributed in the US. Titled *The Craft and Creation of Wood Sculpture* the book is well produced and although in a flexible binding is good to handle and lavishly illustrated with 84 photographs.

The reader is taken through easy stages from the type of tools and workshop facilities required to start woodcarving, to the importance of grinding, honing and stropping all cutting edges.

Another Dover book published in UK by Constable at £1.90 describes how to make amusing caricatures of country folks. . . . all, of course, in the numerous illustrations of US origin; there are 105 black and white illustrations and four in full colour on the flexible covers.

It is called *Carving Country Characters* and the author is Bill Higginbotham. Like the previous books this one describes the tools required. Since the 18 projects dealt with are examples of what can be done with whittling knives the author, after his introduction and chapter on carving woods (not all readily available this side of the Atlantic) explains how to make your own whittling knives. There is a short chapter on the production of patterns which can be used for creating the model caricatures and the carving of faces is shown step-by-step photographically. This is followed by a few notes and drawings on the subject of whittling hands suitable for the 18 projects.

As this type of carved object needs colouring in the final stages more should have been devoted to the finishing, colouring and staining process.

The 18 caricatures are all shown as line drawings which are very clear. The whittling techniques are illustrated very well and the text is quite adequate.

This is a jolly book revealing the lighter side of woodcarving but the creation of the odd little figures does suggest that the craftsman must have artistic ability if he, or she, wishes to be a creative artist rather than just a copyist. **F.D.A.**

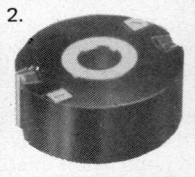
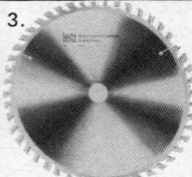
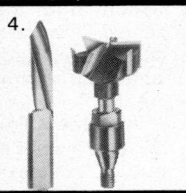

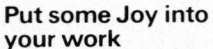

PHOTOCOPY SERVICE

We are able to supply photocopies of articles from many past issues of WOODWORKER at a nominal cost of 15p a page (minimum 75p) plus 25p postage. Readers are asked to give month and year of the issue required to Mrs Anne Duncan at WOODWORKER office which is PO Box 35, Bridge Street, Hemel Hempstead HP1 1EE (0442 41221).

We cannot guarantee to supply photocopies from all past issues as unfortunately the office files of back-numbers are not complete.

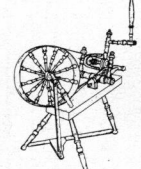 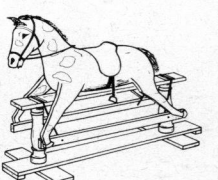 

Prices quoted are those prevailing at press date and are
subject to alteration due to economic conditions.

Letters to the editor

WOODWORKER
PO Box 35
Bridge Street
Hemel Hempstead

From: M. J. Perryman, Redhill, Surrey
Dear Sir,

Recently when making a comb-back Windsor chair I needed for the first time to do some steam bending. As I am not likely to do this very often, the equipment needed to be cheap, easily stored and reasonably small.

I eventually decided to make the steam chamber from a large polythene bag and to use an electric kettle for the source of steam. The kettle was connected to the bag by a piece of cycle inner tube and a short length of garden hosepipe secured to the bag with plastic insulation tape. The inner tube was taped to the kettle spout and the other end formed a steam-tight joint with the hose.

The wood to be bent was placed in the bag and the neck tied with string, then hung over the kettle so that the condensed steam could run back into the kettle. Some steam was naturally lost through the top of the bag and so 1pt of water was added to the kettle every ½hr. To regulate the amount of steam produced, the electricity supply was fed through a simmerstat (hot plate controller salvaged from an old electric cooker).

A 'V' cut into the bag-end of the hose enabled the water to flow without affecting the upward flow of steam. Polythene sheet is an alternative if a large enough polythene bag for your wood is not available.

The wood to be bent was a 2ft length of 6×1in. oak, the middle needed to be bent 2in. to give the required curve. To give it the required shape a former was made in two parts.

a) a piece of 1in. blockboard to which were screwed two pieces of wood, moulded to the required shape for the ends of the work piece.

b) another piece of wood shaped to the required inside curve.

When ready for bending, the workpiece is placed on the first former with the second on top, all clamped together and bent with a 'G' cramp.

The first time I used too short a piece for the inside curve former (following diagrams I had seen previously) so the ends not in contact with this piece remained straight and had to be rebent

Yours faithfully, **Michael Perryman**

editor: We were delighted to hear from Michael Perryman, he entered our wood-turning classes at last year's Woodworker Show with a set of egg cups on a stand and a spinning wheel. Due to disabilities Michael is unable to use a die and so had the metal threads for his wheel cut for him. It was good to have his entry during the year of the disabled, Michael himself does

not let his disability stand in the way of his woodwork. From an early age he became used to people saying 'you can't do that' so he proved to them that 'yes he could'.

Articles on steam bending have been published in *Woodworker*... July 1980 in the series *Country chairs and chairmaking* by Jack Hill pp458-461 and in December 1981 in *Windsor chairs made at home* by Harold Collinson p852.

From: D. R. Maddock, Fleet, Hants
Dear Sir,

A few months ago my faithful Arcoy Buccaneer power drill finally gave up the ghost and I had trouble in finding another drill of similar specification to use with the Arcoy drill stand. The particular point was that the drill stand required a drill with 38mm collar and nearly all the bigger more powerful drills seem to have gone over to 43mm collar.

However, I was able to have the drill stand clamp hole enlarged to take a 43mm collar drill and I then bought a B & D GD3099E electronic drill. An additional advantage (and a considerable one) is that the stand now takes the body of my Bosch router which, together with a table to use CK cutters, makes a very useful overhead moulder.

Of course, the Stanley Bridges jigsaw and orbital sander attachments that I previously used with the Arcoy drill are no longer any use but I managed to persuade my wife that I needed to buy better machines — and I'm now working away again!

Yours faithfully, **D. R. Maddock**

From: A. E. Tyler, Wembley, Middx.
Dear Sir,

Much has been said of a warning nature recently regarding cross slides relating mainly to rear tool posts. However, any set-up on the cross slide requiring firm

clamping tends to strain the tee slots and tighten the action of the cross screw. I have overcome this risk by mounting a ⅝in false plate on top of the slide secured in the corners by 4 Allen screws in counterbored holes. The rest of the plate is laid out with ⁵⁄₁₆in Whit tapped holes which are used for clamping any tool posts or components.

Yours faithfully, **A. E. Tyler**

From: I. Lauder, Brisbane, Australia
Dear Sir,

In the January 1982 WOODWORKER journal p34, my letter concerning the attempted determination of the moisture content of wood by a method described by Mr Wheatley is published. You also publish a letter from Mr Harper on the same topic.

The equation derived by Mr Harper, lines 9 and 10 from the bottom of the left-hand column, is mathematically confused. The correct formula is given at the top of the middle column p34. It should be noted, however, that this formula is derived on the assumption that the beam is uniform and that the weight and the wood sample are suspended at the ends of the beam.

I agree with the other formula given by Mr Harper, $\%\text{m.c.} = \dfrac{(L2 - L1)}{L1} \times 100$

Yours faithfully, **I. Lauder**

From: E. Langsdon, Chichester, W. Sussex
Dear Sir,

I have made a tea trolley, which while being quite nice to look at is not completely successful. The polished mahogany top makes moving the trolley when loaded with the usual tea things (tea pot, cups etc) quite a problem. A surrounding galley of decorative pierced brass would help if I only knew where one of light gauge and pleasing design could be obtained.

Yours faithfully, **E. Langsdon**

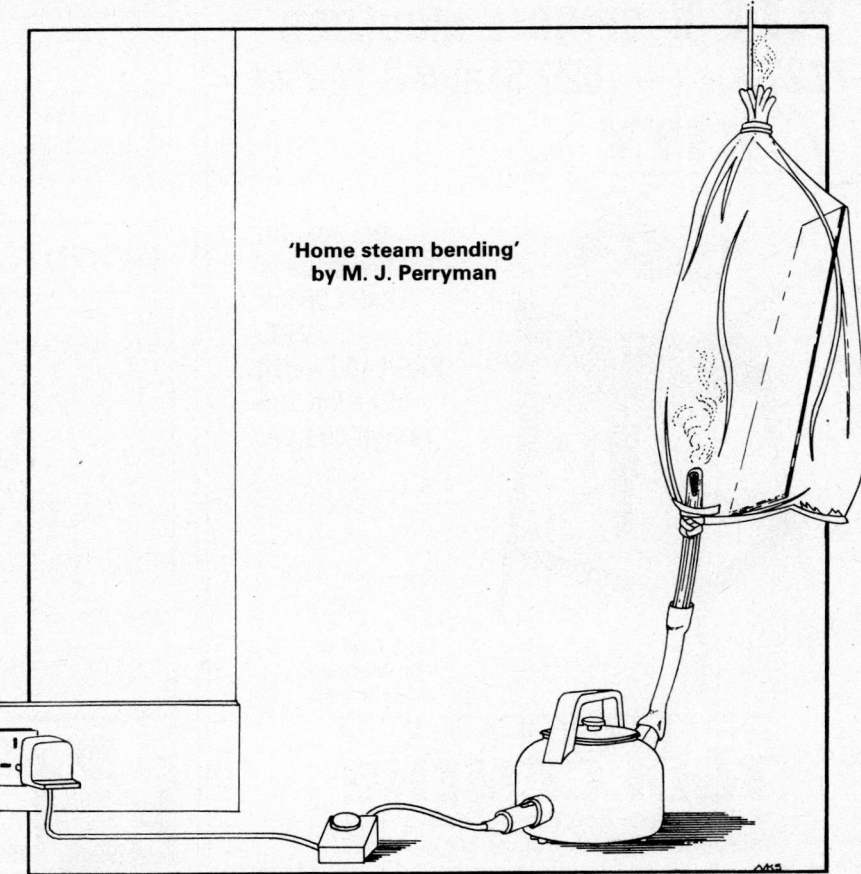

'Home steam bending'
by M. J. Perryman

Woodworker, June 1982

417

Prices quoted are those prevailing at press date and are subject to alteration due to economic conditions.

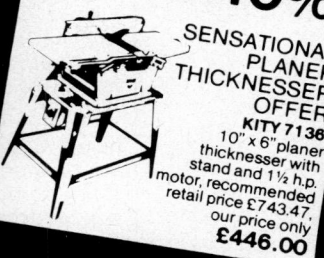

Offcuts

by Chris Dunn

Heart of Oak...

English oak has for centuries symbolised the steadfastness and durability of the English people, and it occurred to me in a cynical moment that there may be some dark significance in the currently widespread belief that English oak is in rather short supply.

But if stock levels of oak have any real connection with the condition of our national characteristics, I have some extremely good news both for the battered English ego and for craftsmen in search of that most durable of timbers.

For the fact is that English oak is in plentiful supply. And you may henceforth regard anything you hear to the contrary as a subversive plot to undermine the reputation of English excellence.

This encouraging news comes from Stephen Goody, who is managing director of Wheelers Ltd in Sudbury, Suffolk, and who knows a thing or two about English oak, since his company specialises in the production of high grade oak for joinery, construction and furniture.

But if I make light of English oak's reputation as being rather hard to find, Mr Goody sees this sort of widespread misconception as a serious handicap to the timber trade in general.

'Timber merchants seem to be very good at telling each other what they have in stock,' he told me, 'but when it comes to informing the public about the availability of various species, communications seem to break down.'

This suggests that Stephen Goody will be making vigorous attempts to rectify the situation among members of the English Timber Merchants' Association now that he has become their new chairman.

And if you are still doubtful about the availability of English oak, let me tell you that Wheelers alone currently hold stocks in excess of 70,000 cu ft.

... and start of oak

While on the subject of English oak, it is nice to record that 130 oak saplings have recently been planted on Cannock Chase, near Stafford. The area of the Chase known as Brocton Coppice is the only remaining part of Cannock Wood, which in the 16th century covered 38,000 acres with English oaks.

Alas, since the time of Elizabeth I the oaks have been steadily depleted by the requirements of the industrial West Midlands, but now Furniglas Ltd, whose headquarters are nearby Cannock Chase, decided to plant 130 new oaks to mark the 25th anniversary of the company's founding.

So Laurie Powell and Eric Jones of Furniglas and Vee Vohralik, who is managing director of Evode Ltd, the parent company, got their wellies on and started digging. They were assisted by two students working on their Duke of Edinburgh's Gold Award, Adele Greenfield and Wendy Meacham.

Hot-foot from the Sun

By the time you read this a month will already have passed since the Masterclass 82 extravaganza of woodworking excellence took place. But at this time of writing I come hot-foot from the old Sun Hotel in Hitchin, Herts, where the four-day exhibition, with craft demonstrations and lectures, was staged.

There is neither space nor time to produce a full account of the event in this issue, but I couldn't let pass the opportunity of a spare corner without at least recording what a success Masterclass 82 turned out to be.

Organised by that tireless champion of good craftsmanship, Betty Norbury of the White Knight Gallery in Cheltenham, and sponsored by Roger Buse of Roger's Tools in Hitchin, Masterclass was designed to promote the work of outstanding wood craftsmen. But it did more than that. The four days of the exhibition generated a special air of magic that seemed to fire the imaginations of professionals and amateurs alike.

The magnetic quality of Masterclass is perhaps best illustrated by the reaction of Alan Peters, surely one of the most significant names in the world of contemporary woodworking. Alan arrived at the Sun Hotel at lunchtime on the Wednesday to deliver a lecture on his work, but it was Thursday lunchtime before he could tear himself away. On his own admission, he was quite captivated by the occasion.

● A full review of Masterclass 82 will appear in your July WOODWORKER.

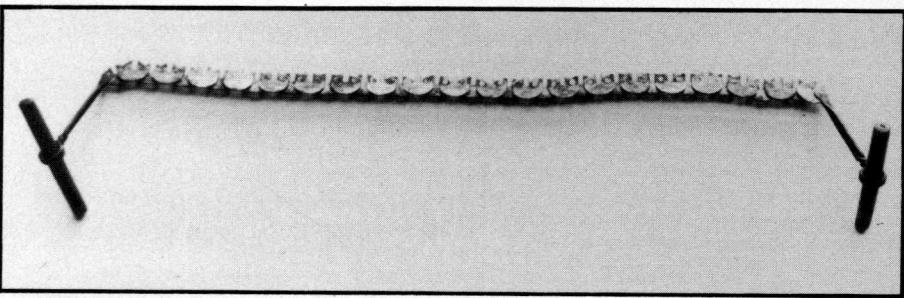

● The chain saw ready for action (above) and folded away (left).

Man-powered chainsaw

● On taking over the editor's chair at Woodworker, I was having a sort-out of articles, photographs and other such material that I inherited from Geoff Pratt's term of office. Among the files we came across these pictures of an interesting and elderly sawing device that was obviously made for work in the field.

A rather natty fold-away tool, wouldn't you say? A sort of cross between the traditional two-handed cross-cut saw used by foresters and the modern chainsaw. If anyone can tell anything more about this tool and its application, I would be interested to hear.

And there's one other thing... to whom do these pictures belong? When they came out of the file there was no indication of their source, so if they are yours and you would like them back, drop me a line.

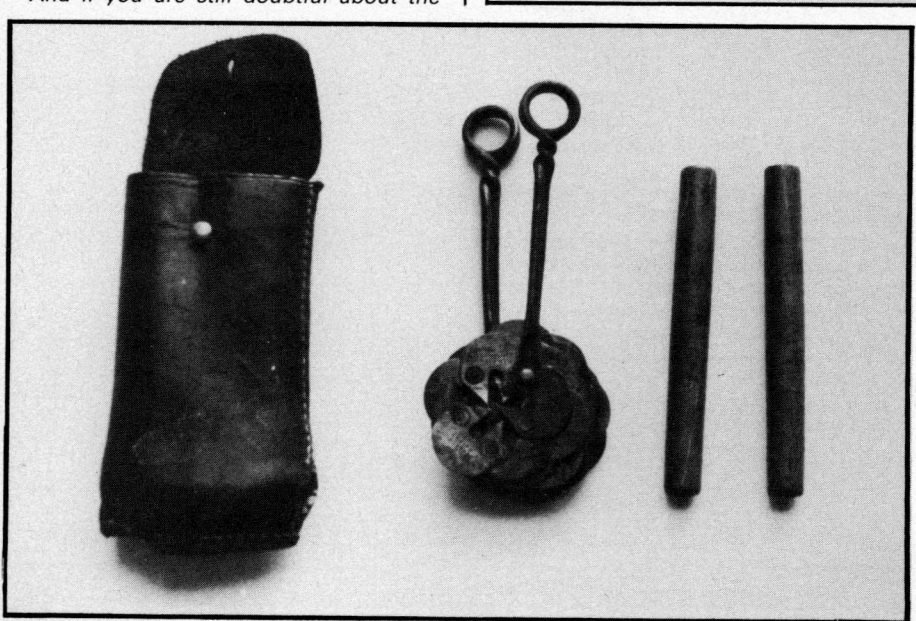

Happy customer

When amateur woodworker John Johnson's new Zincen M16 universal woodworking machine developed a fault, he braced himself for a battle with the suppliers over getting it put right.

'My work involves quite a bit of buying,' Mr Johnson, who lives in Coventry, told me. 'So I know how difficult after-sales service can often prove to be.'

He telephoned Woodmen at Bicester in Oxfordshire, from whom he had bought the machine. Mr Johnson takes up the tale:

'Woodmen made an investigation on their own demonstration model and decided that my problem was due to adverse tolerancing in manufacture. They immediately contacted me by phone to let me know that an exchange of machines would be necessary.'

Mr Johnson's replacement M16 arrived promptly, much to his delight. But what impressed him most was that all this happened – from complaint to satisfaction – in less than one week.

It is perhaps a shaming reflection on the general standards of service in modern commerce that this example set by Woodmen should be so notable, but it is certainly heartening to hear about it.

Turn of speed

In all his years in the woodworking trade, you would think that Ashley Iles had seen it all. But he confessed to me the other day that woodturner Alan McNair of Blyth, Northumberland, had recently changed all his ideas of what constitutes a speedy service.

Ashley was visiting Alan McNair, who is agent for Ashley's tools north of the border, and while they were talking in the shop a customer came in.

'Alan told me to hang on a minute while he dealt with the customer,' Ashley said. 'Having spoken briefly to the chap, he then went off upstairs to his workshop. And in the time that it took me to drink a cup of coffee, Alan returned with four tiny turned knobs, which he had just run off on the lathe for his customer.'

That's what you call an impressive turn of speed.

Cuban crisis

When John Baggs of Craftwoods in Sherrington, Bucks, read our profile of Cuban mahogany in the series 'The World's Timber Trees', he felt he couldn't let it pass without comment.

'It seems a little unfair,' he says, 'to have woodworkers the length and breadth of the country trembling with excitement having read this article on a magnificent species – particularly when the writer, C. W. Bond is most assuredly aware of the fact that Cuban mahogany is virtually unobtainable.'

So if the prospect of getting a chisel into some Cuban mahogany got you all a'tremble, you will be gratified by Mr Baggs' final paragraph:

'Your readers may be interested to know that supplies are available from Craftwoods!'

Crafty, Mr Baggs!

Woodpecker woes

Not long from now there will be much buzzing going on in the orchards of north Kent, when bee-farmer Ken Beevor lets

● What a nice plug for UniBond! Ken Beevor plugs a hole hacked in one of his hives by a woodpecker while UniBond, who supplied the picture, take the opportunity of getting a tin of their PVA adhesive up-front. But eagle-eyed readers will spot that it's not just UniBond who get the free plug. The picture shows Ken holding another tin, in which he has evidently mixed up his anti-woodpecker paste, and that tin bears the legend 'Sainsbury's Seville Orange Marmalade'. Marmalade on a honey farm? Outrageous!

loose his eight million busy little workers to gather pollen.

Ken has 400 hives on his bee farm near Sittingbourne, each hive housing around 20,000 bees, and when the orchards come into blossom his bees will be out there helping the fruit growers towards bumper crops by cross-pollinating the trees.

So everything in the Garden of England sounds rosy enough, you may think. But now we introduce the villain of the piece (booo!): the woodpecker. These accomplished feathered woodworkers, though not generally held to be pests, are playing havoc with Ken's bees by pecking holes in his wooden hives. In little more than an hour a woodpecker can gouge a four-inch diameter hole in the toughest beehive and, having gained access, then starts devouring the bees. And the bees don't help matters any, because while the woodpecker rat-a-tats outside the hive, the workers crawl towards the source of the noise, so provid-

ing a woodpecker with the quickest fast-food service in town.

And now we introduce the hero (hooray!): UniBond Ltd. Ken Beevor has discovered that UniBond's PVA adhesive does a tough job when it comes to repairing woodpecker holes. On one side of the hole he pins a piece of perforated metal sheet, lined with polythene, then he fills the hole with a pasty mix of sawdust and PVA glue. This hardens after a couple of days, whereupon Ken removes the backing piece, rubs down the filler and then finishes with creosote.

The chaps at UniBond were most chuffed to hear about this, and so they told us about it. They were even more pleased to hear that in Ken's experience a woodpecker which returns for a further feast from a repaired hive leaves the filled area well alone.

The message is clear: all bee-keepers should build their hives out of glue and sawdust.

Events

English furniture holiday course

English furniture is the title of a summer holiday course to be held at Ammerdown nr Bath from Friday 25 June to Friday 2 July. The course will study the history and development of English furniture and furnishings in their architectural settings from the age of oak in the 16th century to Victorian times. Materials, constructions and decorative processes will also be examined. Morning lectures and discussions will be followed by afternoon visits to various country houses including Dyrham Park, Corsham Court, Laycock Abbey and Bath. Whole day excursions include visits to Wilton House, Stourhead, Montague House and Parnham House. This latter includes a lecture by John Makepeace. Cost of the course is £150 which covers accommodation in single rooms at Ammerdown (modern conference centre in the grounds of Ammerdown House) full board (except for three lunches) all admissions, lectures and coach travel from and to London. Course director H. Jan Scott Hutchinson (lecturer in fine and decorative arts at Keele University). Full details from The Association for Cultural Exchange, Babraham, Cambridge CB2 4AP, phone Cambridge 835977.

One-off

First international crafts fair of one-off pieces, Nimes Palais des Expositions 3-6 June. Further information from Maison des Metiers d'Art Français, 27 rue de l'Université 75007, Paris.

Pots and Wood

Work by Jim Partridge and Robin Welch from 28 June to 17 July at Collection Craft Gallery and Studio, 13 The Southend, Ledbury, Herefordshire.

Timber frame

For details of half-day timber frame seminars organised by BWF and BAS on 3 June and 6 July in Edinburgh and Cambridge resp. or in the autumn in South Wales and Yorkshire contact BWF, 82 New Cavendish St, London (01-580 5588).

Business Boost

Business to Business exhibition, Earls Court, London 6-9 June incl. organised by Silver Collins & Co Ltd, 10-11 Holywell Lane, London (01-729 0677).

Miniature weekend

Miniatures '82 will be held at Dorking Halls, Dorking on 12 June from 10.30-5.00. This will be an extended version of last year's exhibition to include both old and new dolls houses, rooms etc and many new exhibitors in the world of dolls houses, shops and furniture. A special miniatures weekend has been arranged at the White Horse hotel, Dorking, from the evening of 11 June to mid-day on 13 June. Price of this weekend is £21.75 per night inc. VAT and service and applies for a two night stay. Full details of stay and programme of events from Johan L. Bolling, manager White Horse hotel, High St, Dorking RH4 1BE phone Dorking 881138.

Edward Barnsley

Until 13 June at the Crafts Study Centre, Holburne museum, Great Pulteney St, Bath.

24-hour call

The Victoria and Albert museum has launched a 24-hour recorded information telephone service. By dialling 01-581 4894 potential visitors can get details such as opening hours, current exhibitions and their admission prices, other special openings and events at the V&A. The two minute recording is to be changed each week to ensure that the information is never out of date.

Information not on the recording can still be obtained by phoning the V&A Press Office on 01-589 6371 ext 411.

Music in Morden

If you wish to learn the craft of Musical Instrument Repair/Making Merton Technical College will be continuing to run its popular courses commencing September 1982. Full-time and part-time courses are available concerned with the repair of brass, woodwind, bowed and fretted stringed instruments and the making of bowed and fretted stringed instruments.

Applications are invited from those wishing to be considered for entry in September 1982. Further details from D. S.

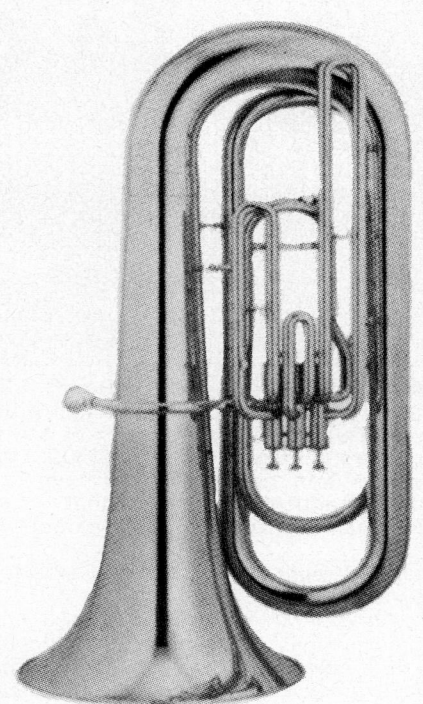

Tulloch, Head of Dept of Gen. Education & Science, Merton Technical College, Morden Park, London Road, Morden, Surrey (01-640 3001 ext 37).

Wood exhibition

Spock Woodcarvings of Birmingham are holding a three day Birmingham and area wood show on 17, 18 and 19 June (Thursday and Friday 12-6, Saturday 10-6) which will include turning, tools, wood for sale and general advice plus an exhibition. Further details from Spock Woodcarvings, 810 Bristol Rd, Selly Oak, Birmingham B29 6NA (sae please) or phone 021-472 4969 Tuesdays to Saturdays 10-6.

Make a trophy

The TCB Maritime England Race Trophy award is a competition organised by Brighton Museum and sponsored by TCB to celebrate Maritime England Year. The award complements a major summer exhibition at Brighton Museum *Simply mes-*

sing about in boats (1 May-30 August) which traces the history of boating for pleasure from Charles II up to the present day. Entries are invited from amateur, professional and student craftsmen over the age of 18 years to make a suitable trophy to be presented to the winners of the Maritime England Race. The trophy must be a unique piece of work, a sculpture, a boat model, a cup or an engraved glass. It may be made in any durable material. Registration forms and full competition details from Lianne Jarrett, Exhibitions Assistant, Brighton Museum, Church Street, Brighton (phone 0273 603005 extn. 48). Entries will need to be delivered on 17, 20 or 21 July.

Woodcarving Seminar

Drawing in wood, an international seminar on woodcarving to be held at Parnham House, Beaminster, Dorset on 11-13 June. Principal contributors include Wendell Castle, Michael Cooper, Theo Crosby, Howard Raybould, Frederick Oughton, Leonard Baskin, Dick Reid and Kevin Perkins. Plus exhibition of work by contemporary woodcarvers and a selection of historic pieces. Full details from Brian James, Beaminster 862204.

Art in action

Waterperry House near Wheatley, Oxon, is the venue again this year for Art in Action to be held from 14-18 July inclusive (10.30-5.30). Admission £3, children under 6 free, 6-16 years, OAP's and students with a valid card £1.50. Over 100 professional artists and craftsmen demonstrating and answering questions on techniques, plus concert, dance and theatre, craft market and homemade food.

Craft Fairs

The Derbyshire Country Craft Co (phone Glossop 63022) are organising a series of craft and country fairs in the midlands and the north during 1982 in conjunction with local authorities, stately homes and the National Trust. If you are interested in exhibiting your craft at any of these events the organisers would like to hear from you. They can be contacted at the above phone number or write with sae to 9 Peaknaze Close, Simmondley, Glossop SK13 9UN.

Our panel of experts answer queries about your workshop problems

Woodworker's Question Box

Write to: Question Box
Woodworker
PO Box 35
Bridge Street
Hemel Hempstead HP1 1EE

Cellulose thinners
From: D. H. Poole, Hythe, Kent

Further to an enquiry of mine in December 1981 *Woodworker* p864 I have been experimenting with the removal of the old finish on woodwork. I have found that cellulose thinners do the job best and most easily and a new finish can then be applied without the need to neutralise.

Can you advise whether the use of cellulose thinners is detrimental to the wood or to the subsequent finish. Is cellulose thinner the same as denatured alcohol? (Mentioned in *The Complete Book of Furniture Repair and Refinishing* by R. P. Kinney).

The use of cellulose thinners to clean down the woodwork should not harm the wood, or any subsequent finish that might be applied provided the fluid has been allowed to evaporate properly.

We understand cellulose thinners is based principally on amyl acetate which you no doubt recognise from its pear-drop aroma. This material is not the same as denatured alcohol, which, in effect, is methylated spirit; in other words it has been made undrinkable by the addition of a dye.

Chair match
From: M. S. McQuire, London N14

I was fortunate recently to be able to obtain five rosewood chairs at auction. I enclose a sketch of one with the upholstery removed. I would like to make a sixth chair to match, a major snag would appear to be the wood which seems to be difficult or impossible to obtain and would presumably be outrageously expensive if available. Can you recommend an alternative wood which has the correct characteristics to enable the design to be reproduced exactly and which could be stained to match the original chairs? Should the curved sections be cut from solid or bent to shape?

No wood has the exact characteristics of rosewood, therefore, both rarity and individuality are reflected in its price. If you have to be cost conscious in tackling your problem, and you are unable to obtain by any other means, then regrettably you must opt for substitution rather than an exact match.

For this, I would suggest cocobolo. Because of its similar grain characteristics and density the slightly more orangy red could be matched by experimentation. The wood is not too difficult to work, and finishes well. Drawbacks are that there is an inherent natural oil problem, unhelpful when gluing, and the dust has been known to have irritant properties. An excursion to a timber merchant may prove lucky and yield other alternatives by way of a bastard piece of African padauk, or bubinga.

Regarding the curved sections, I would advise cutting from the solid. You may be lucky in that the grain will follow on for the rear legs. The curve in the horizontal back bars are no problem from the solid, because

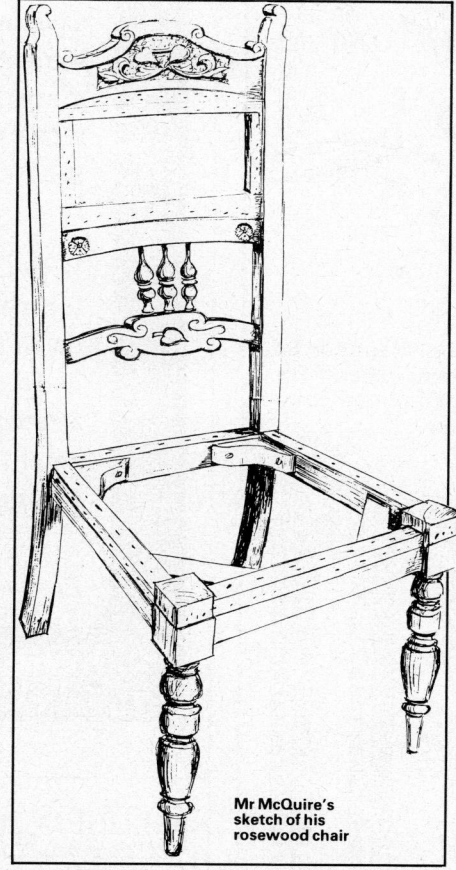

Mr McQuire's sketch of his rosewood chair

of the short length involved. In my work, I encounter many problems such as the one expressed by Mr McQuire, and I always take a long hard look at the fine old originals to see how our earlier craftsmen coped.

Renovating problems
From: R. F. Dowling, Shetland

I have been asked the best way to approach two problems in renovating. I can make guesses but would appreciate some advice.
1 An intricately carved oak altar which under strong lighting appears dry and lifeless. What kind of oil/wax finish would be appropriate and how best should it be applied? It is a large altar and lack of time for its upkeep is an important consideration.
2 A nest of tables with a quartered walnut burr veneer varnish finish which is in a bad state. How can this be removed without affecting the veneer glues? Would a polyurethane varnish be best from the point of view of wear and tear?

1 We are not sure of the age of the altar. If it is an old one in need of restoration it will be necessary to remove all the dust and dirt before applying any finish. Vacuum cleaning and careful washing with warm water and toilet soap should leave the surfaces clean. Let the wood dry thoroughly.

Oak looks very well when finished with linseed oil but this laborious process is suited to plain surfaces rather than intricate

carvings. We would therefore advise a waxed finish. Using a bear hair mop, brush on two or three applications of white french polish. This will seal the grain. After the polish has hardened it is smoothed with worn, fine garnet paper. Wax polish can then be applied by rag or by brush and should be allowed to stand for about ten minutes before polishing briskly with a soft duster. A special emulsion wax is obtainable which is very suitable for applying on carvings and it can be polished using a clean shoe brush. Several applications of wax will give a deep lasting shine.

2 The finish on the veneered walnut tables could be removed with a steel cabinet scraper or if there are difficult mouldings, a proprietary stripper would be more effective. Smoothing with wire wool followed by a fine garnet paper will prepare the wood for staining should that be necessary. It is difficult to advise a finish when the subsequent use of the tables is not known. French polishing with white polish brings out the beauty of veneers but if there is a danger of liquids being spilled then a less vulnerable finish for the top is advised. Both oil varnish and polyurethane are resistant to alcohol and also stand up to hard wear. Flow on the varnish with a bear hair mop taking care not to over brush. The brush marks will even themselves out as the varnish dries.

Teak finish
From: P. Tulloch, Shetland

I am at present making a sideboard in teak and would like to finish it in a spirit resistant varnish, such as polyurethane. I would appreciate it if you could give me any information on how to achieve the rich golden colour seen on some of the modern teak furniture.

Advising on what colour stain to apply is difficult without seeing the wood which is to be stained or knowing precisely what the desired finishing colour is to be. For these reasons we would always recommend carrying out experiments on waste pieces of wood so that the resultant colour can be checked.

Careful blending of spirit-soluble stains may yield the required colour but these stains dry very rapidly which makes an even colour difficult to achieve. Far easier to apply are oil stains which have the added advantage of not raising the grain. A suitable teak oil can be obtained from James Jackson, 76/89 Alscot Rd, London SE1 5SX (01-237 2862/3).

The stain can be applied with a rag and if it can be left for a couple of days before varnishing, so much the better. An oil varnish should be used rather than a polyurethane as the latter may adversely affect the stain.

Apply the varnish liberally with a bear hair mop and flow it on rather than brush it on, taking care not to dwell in one particular place. Over brushing should be avoided, any brush marks will even themselves out before drying.

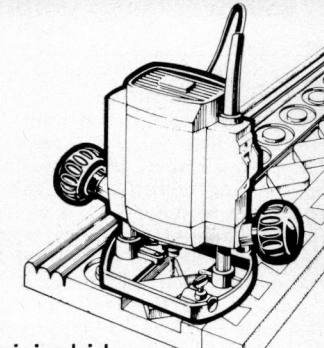
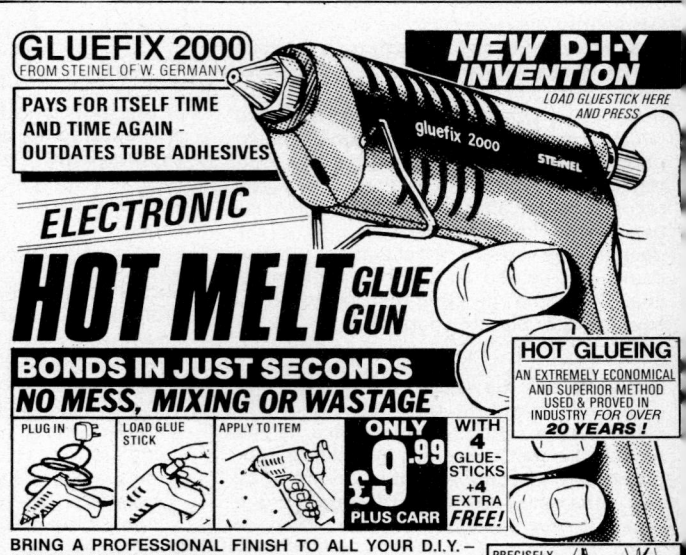

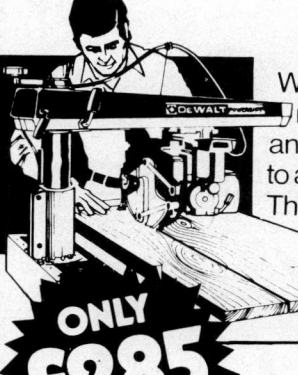

Our panel of experts answer queries about your workshop problems

Woodworker's Question Box

Write to: Question Box
Woodworker
PO Box 35
Bridge Street
Hemel Hempstead HP1 1EE

Record cabinet

From: G. Roche, Mulhuddart, Co Dublin

I wish to seek advice on two points:

1. I wish to make a record cabinet which would have a top 20in deep and ¾in thick. I have bought some kiln dried sweet chestnut and I have some wide pieces (over 20in). Could I plane this down or would I be better off, from the point of view of stability, in ripping these wide pieces and then rejoining them by dowelling?

2. Could you tell me how best to finish the sweet chestnut and also some ramin that I wish to use as bookshelves?

We note that the record cabinet will be 20in deep and that some of your pieces of sweet chestnut exceed this width. It is therefore possible to make the carcase of the cabinet out of one piece rather than the usual method of jointing several pieces together. Using very wide pieces can be disadvantageous. As the wood dries out it will shrink across the grain and also it may distort. If several narrower pieces are dowelled together it is advisable to arrange the pieces so that the heartsides face alternate directions as in Fig. 1. Any bowing caused by changes in moisture content will thus be less apparent.

If the cabinet top is dovetailed or otherwise jointed to the sides then it will stay flat because the joints will hold it securely. If however, the top is to be in the form of a hinged lid then plain clamps fitted across the ends as in Fig. 2 will keep the top flat. End grain will be visible on the front edge of the lid and if this is considered undesirable mitred clamps (Fig. 3) should be used. These can be dowelled to the ends (Fig. 4) or a better arrangement would be to mortise and stub tenon (Fig. 5). The clamp is grooved with a plough plane and the ends are mitred. The haunched tenons and mitres are set out on the top where the clamps will be fitted and the waste is cut away with a tenon saw and chisel. If required a bullnose plane may be used to level the haunches. The clamp is laid in position over the tenons and marked where the mortises are to be cut.

The type of finish used may depend on what other furniture is in the same room as the record cabinet and how best to harmonise with it. The grain of sweet chestnut bears a close resemblence to oak and it is accordingly suggested that a wax finish would be most suitable. To assist in a more rapid build up of a wax film the open pores are sealed by brushing on two coats of white french polish. When hard this is smoothed with worn fine garnet paper, dusted off and wax polished. The wax polish is applied evenly to the work with a clean rag and allowed to stand for about ten minutes before being briskly polished with a soft duster. Several applications will be needed to produce a durable shine.

Ramin will take the usual wood finishes quite well. If the bookcase is to stand near the record cabinet then this too could be wax polished using the same procedure.

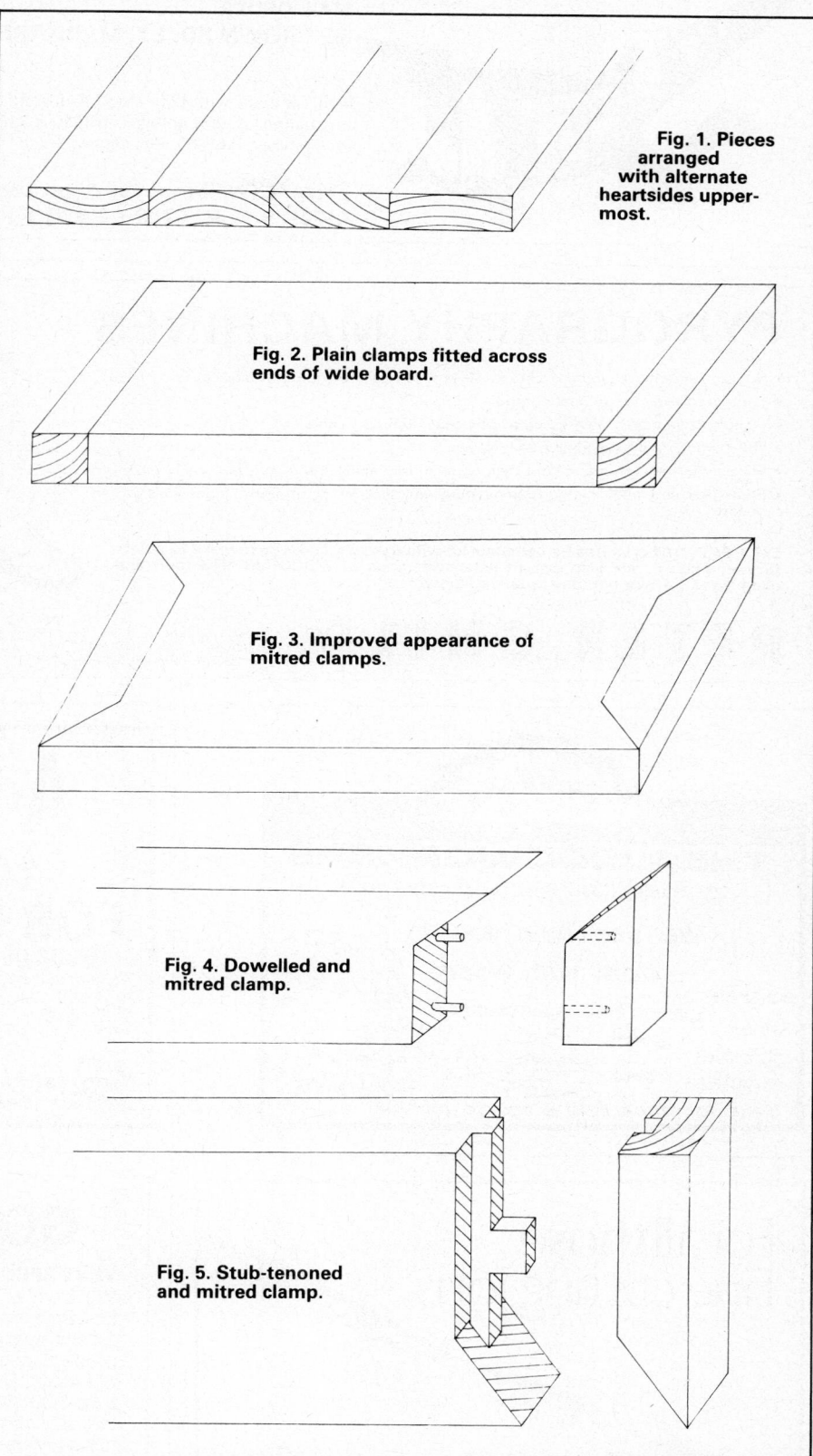

Fig. 1. Pieces arranged with alternate heartsides uppermost.

Fig. 2. Plain clamps fitted across ends of wide board.

Fig. 3. Improved appearance of mitred clamps.

Fig. 4. Dowelled and mitred clamp.

Fig. 5. Stub-tenoned and mitred clamp.

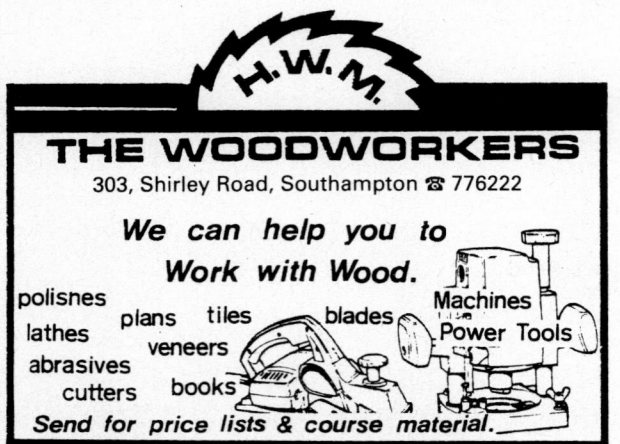
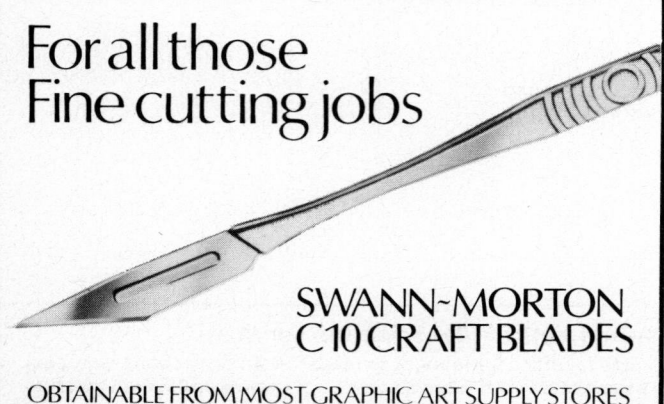

SHOP GUIDE SHOP GUIDE

AVON

BATH Tel. Bath 64513
JOHN HALL TOOLS ★
RAILWAY STREET

Open: Monday-Saturday
9.00 a.m.-5.30 p.m.
H.P.W.WM.D.A.BC.

BRISTOL Tel. (0272) 311510
JOHN HALL TOOLS LIMITED ★
CLIFTON DOWN SHOPPING
CENTRE, WHITELADIES ROAD
Open: Monday-Saturday
9.00 a.m.-5.30 p.m.
H.P.W.WM.D.A.BC.

BRISTOL Tel. 0272-633844
ROBBINS LIMITED ★
THE WOODWORKER SHOP
MERRYWOOD MILLS, BEDMINSTER
Open: Mon-Fri 8.00 a.m.-5.00 p.m.
Saturday 8.30 a.m.-12.30 p.m.
H.P.T.CS.A.BC.

BRISTOL Tel. 0272-629092
TRYMWOOD SERVICES ★
2a DOWNS PARK EAST, (off
North View) WESTBURY PARK
Open: 8.30 a.m.-5.30 p.m. Mon. to
Fri. Closed for lunch 1-2 p.m.
P.W.WM.D.T.A.BC.

BRISTOL Tel. 0272-667013
V. H. WILLIS & CO. LTD ★
190-192 WEST STREET,
BEDMINSTER
Open: Mon-Fri 8.30 a.m.-5 p.m.
Saturday 9 a.m.-1 p.m.
H.P.W.WM.D.CS.A.BC.

BERKSHIRE

READING Tel. Littlewick Green
DAVID HUNT (TOOL 2743
MERCHANTS) LTD ★
KNOWL HILL, NR. READING
Open: Monday-Saturday
9 a.m.-5.30 p.m.
H.P.W.D.A.BC.

READING Tel. (0734) 586522
SARJENT'S TOOL STORES ★
LTD.
44-52 OXFORD ROAD
Open: 8.30 a.m.-5.30 p.m.
Monday-Saturday
H.P.W.WM.D.A.BC.

READING Tel. Reading 661511
WOKINGHAM TOOL CO. LTD
99 WOKINGHAM ROAD

Open: Mon-Sat 9am-5.30pm
Closed 1-2pm for lunch
H.P.W.WM.D.CS.A.BC.

BUCKINGHAMSHIRE

HIGH WYCOMBE (0494) 22221
ISAAC LORD LTD
185 DESBOROUGH ROAD

Open: Mon-Fri 8.00 a.m.-5.00 p.m.
Saturday 8.00 a.m.-12.00 noon
H.P.W.D.A.

MILTON KEYNES Tel. 0908
A. POLLARD & SON 75221
LTD.
51 QUEENSWAY, BLETCHLEY
Open: 8.30 a.m.-5.30 p.m.
Monday-Saturday
H.P.W.WM.D.A.BC.

CAMBRIDGESHIRE

CAMBRIDGE Tel. 0223-353091
H. B. WOODWORKING
69 LENSFIELD ROAD

Open: 8.30 a.m.-5.30 p.m.
Monday-Friday
8.30 a.m.-1.00 p.m. Sat
P.W.WM.D.CS.BC.

CHESHIRE

NANTWICH Tel. Crewe 67010
ALAN HOLTHAM ★
THE OLD STORES TURNERY
WISTASON ROAD, WILLASTON
Open: Tues-Sat 9a.m.-5.30p.m.
Closed Monday
P.W.WM.D.T.CS.A.BC.

CLEVELAND

MIDDLESBROUGH Tel. 0642-
WINTZ 460035/813650
INDUSTRIAL SUPPLIES ★
2 BESSEMER COURT
GRANGETOWN
Open: Mon-Fri 8.30 a.m.-5 p.m.
H.P.W.D.A.

CORNWALL

FALMOUTH Tel. 0326-312915
WOODSTOCK
(HARDWOODS) S.W.,
ASHFIELD, PONSHARDEN,
Open: Mon-Fri 8.30 a.m.-5.30 p.m.
Sat 9 a.m.-1.00 p.m.
T.

HELSTON
SOUTH WEST
POWER TOOLS
Helston (03265) 4961
Truro (0872) 71671
Launceston (0566) 3555
H.P.W.WM.D.CS.A.

NEWQUAY Tel. 063 73 2516
CONWAY SUPPLIES ★
(NEWQUAY)
70 FORE STREET
Open: Mon-Fri 9 a.m.-5.30 p.m.
Sat 9 a.m.-12.30 p.m.
H.P.W.WM.D.A.BC.

CORNWALL

ST. AUSTELL Tel. (0726) 65922
TOOLSERV ★
TRURO ROAD

Open: 8 a.m.-5.30 p.m.
6 days
H.P.W.WM.D.CS.A.BC.

DERBYSHIRE

BUXTON Tel. 0298-871636
CRAFT SUPPLIES ★
THE MILL
MILLERSDALE
Open: Mon-Fri 9 a.m.-5 p.m.
Saturday 9 a.m.-1 p.m.
H.P.W.D.T.CS.A.BC.

DEVON

EXETER Tel. 0392 73936
WRIDES TOOL CENTRE
147 FORE STREET

Open: 9.00 a.m.-5.30 p.m.
Wednesday 9.00 a.m.-1.00 p.m.
H.P.W.WM.A.

PLYMOUTH Tel. 0752 330303
WESTWARD BUILDING SERVICES ★
LTD., LISTER CLOSE, NEWNHAM
INDUSTRIAL ESTATE, PLYMPTON
Open: Mon-Fri 8 a.m.-5.30 p.m.
Sat 8.30 a.m.-12.30 p.m.
H.P.W.WM.D.A.BC.

PLYMOUTH Tel. 0752-266179
JOHN WRIDE & CO (PLYMOUTH) LTD
146 CORNWALL STREET

Open: Monday to Saturday
9.00a.m.-5.30p.m.
Wed 9.00a.m.-1.00p.m.
H.P.W.WM.A.

DORSET

BOURNEMOUTH Tel: 0202
MACHINE SALES & SERVICES 527780
(BOURNEMOUTH) LTD 527781
56 STROUDEN ROAD ★

Open: Mon-Fri 8.15 a.m.-5 p.m.
H.P.W.WM.D.A.

WEYMOUTH Tel: (0305) 787396
WEYMOUTH TOOL CENTRE ★
30A ABBOTSBURY ROAD

Open: Monday to Saturday
8 a.m.-5.30 p.m.
H.P.W.WM.D.A.BC

CO. DURHAM

BARNARD CASTLE Tel: (0833)
WOODMEN 38442/31609
27 NEWGATE ★

Open Monday-Saturday
9 a.m.-5.30 p.m.
P.W.WM.D.A.BC.

ESSEX

LEIGH ON SEA Tel. (0702)
MARSHALL & 710404
PARSONS LTD ★
1111 LONDON ROAD
Open: 8.30 am-5.30 pm Mon-Fri.
9.00 am-5.00 om Sat.
H.P.W.WM.D.CS.A.

GLOUCESTERSHIRE

TEWKESBURY Tel. 0684
TEWKESBURY SAW CO. 293092
LIMITED
TRADING ESTATE, NEWTOWN
Open: Mon-Fri 8.00 a.m.-5.00 p.m.
Saturday 9.30 a.m.-12.00 p.m.
P.W.WM.D.CS.

HAMPSHIRE

ALDERSHOT Tel. 0252 28088
BURCH & HILLS LTD
BLACKWATER WAY TRADING
ESTATE
Open: Mon-Fri 8.30 a.m.-5.30 p.m.
Saturday 8.30 a.m.-12.00 p.m.
H.P.W.WM.D.A.BC.

PORTSMOUTH Tel. 0705
EURO PRECISION TOOLS 67332
LTD ★
259/263 London Road, North End
Open: Mon-Fri 9 a.m.- 5.30 p.m.
Sat 9.00 a.m.-5.00 p.m.
H.P.W.WM.D.A.BC.

SOUTHAMPTON Tel. 0703
H.W.M. 776222
THE WOODWORKERS ★
303 SHIRLEY ROAD, SHIRLEY
Open: Tues-Fri 9.30 a.m.- 6 p.m.
Sat 9.30 a.m.-4.00 p.m.
H.P.W.WM.D.CS.A.BC.T.

HEREFORDSHIRE

HEREFORD Tel. 0432 3018
PEN TOOLS (HEREFORD) LTD
24 EDGAR STREET

Open Mon.-Fri. 8 a.m.-5.30 p.m.
Sat. 8 a.m.-1 p.m.
H.P.W.D.C.A.

HERTFORDSHIRE

WATFORD Tel. 0923 48434
HOME CARE CENTRE ★
20 MARKET STREET
WATFORD, HERTS
Open 9.00 a.m.-5.30 p.m.
Mon.-Sat.
H.P.W.A.WM.BC.D.

WATFORD Tel. 0923 26052
J. SIMBLE & SONS LTD ★
76 QUEENS ROAD

Open 8.30 a.m.-5.30 p.m.
Mon.-Sat. Closed Wednesday
H.P.W.WM.D.A.BC.

SHOP GUIDE SHOP GUIDE

HERTFORDSHIRE

WATFORD   Tel. (0923) 49911
TREND MACHINERY & CUTTING
TOOLS LTD
UNIT N, PENFOLD WORKS
IMPERIAL WAY
   Open: Mon-Fri 9 a.m.-5 p.m.
P.W.WM.D.CS.BC.

KENT

MATFIELD   Tel. Brenchley
LEISURECRAFT IN WOOD   (089272)
'ORMONDE', MAIDSTONE RD.   2465
TN12 7JG
   Open: Mon-Sun
   9 a.m. - 5.30 p.m.
W.WM.D.T.A.

SITTINGBOURNE   Tel.
B.T.S. (TOOLS),   Sittingbourne
Unit 25, SITTINGBOURNE   79551
INDUSTRIAL PARK   ★
   Open: Monday - Friday
   8.00 a.m. - 5.00 p.m.
H.P.W.BC.CS.

LANCASHIRE

LANCASTER   Tel. 0524 2886
LILE TOOL SHOP
43/45 NORTH ROAD
   Open: Monday to Saturday
   9.00 a.m.-5.30 p.m.
   Wed 9.00 a.m.-12.30 p.m.
H.P.W.D.A.

LEICESTERSHIRE

COALVILLE   Tel. (0533) 415556
POOLE WOOD MACHINERY   (06077)
SERVICES LIMITED,   5777
4 SWALLOW DALE
THRINGSTONE
   Open: Mon-Fri 9 a.m.-5 p.m.
H.P.W.WM.D.A.BC.

LEICESTER   Tel. 0455 43254
ROY STARTIN LTD
134 WOOD STREET
EARL SHILTON
   Open: Mon-Fri 8 a.m.-5.30 p.m.
   Saturday 8.00 a.m.-1.30 p.m.
H.P.W.WM.D.T.A.

LINCOLNSHIRE

LINCOLN   Tel. 0522 30199/
WOODWISE LIMITED   39871 or
121 HIGH STREET   0522 68428
   & 06077 5777/5288
   (after hours)   ★
   Open: Mon-Sat 9 a.m.-5.30 p.m.
P.W.WM.D.A.BC.

LONDON

ACTON   Tel. 01-992 4835
A MILLS (ACTON) LTD   ★
32/36 CHURCHFIELD ROAD
W3 6ED
   Open: Mon-Fri 9.00 a.m.-5.00 p.m.
   Closed Saturday
H.P.W.WM.

HANWELL   Tel. 01-567 2922
G. D. CLEGG & SONS
83 Uxbridge Road, W7 3ST
   Open: Monday to Friday
   9.00 a.m.-6.00 p.m.
   Saturday 9.00 a.m.-5.30 p.m.
H.P.W.WM.D.

LONDON

KILBURN   Tel. 01-624 5146
W. THATCHER & SON LTD   ★
POWER TOOL CENTRE
AT THE TECHNICAL LEISURE CENTRE
1 THE GRANGEWAY, N.W.6.
   Open: Mon-Sat 9 a.m.-5.30 p.m.
P.H.W.D.CS.A.BC.

LONDON   Tel. 01-636 7475
BUCK & RYAN LIMITED   ★
101 TOTTENHAM COURT ROAD
W1P 0DY
   Open: Mon-Fri 8.30 a.m.-5.30 p.m.
   Saturday 8.30 a.m.-1.00 p.m.
H.P.W.WM.D.A.

LONDON   Tel. 01-739 7126
CECIL W. TYZACK   ★
79-81 KINGSLAND ROAD
SHOREDITCH
   Open: Mon-Fri 8.45 a.m.-5.15 p.m.
   Saturday 9 a.m.-12 noon
H.P.W.WM.D.A.BC.

NORBURY   Tel: 01-679 6193
HERON TOOLS & HARDWARE LTD
437 STREATHAM HIGH ROAD
S.W.16
   Open: Mon-Sat 8.30 a.m. - 6 p.m.
   Wednesday 8.30 a.m. - 1 p.m.
H.P.W.A.

MERSEYSIDE

LIVERPOOL   Tel. 051-263 1359
TAYLOR BROS (LIVERPOOL) LTD
5/9 PRESCOTT STREET
   Open: Monday to Friday
   8.30 a.m.-5.30 p.m.
H.P.W.WM.D.A.BC.

MIDDLESEX

NORTH HARROW   Tel. 01-863 2492
WILLIAMS TECHNICAL SERVICES   ★
36 STATION ROAD
   Open: Mon-Fri 8 a.m.-5.30 p.m.
   Wed 8 a.m.-1 p.m.,
   Sat 9 a.m.-5.30 p.m.
H.P.W.WM.D.A.

HOUNSLOW   Tel. 01-570 2103/5135
Q. R. TOOLS LTD
251-253 HANWORTH ROAD
   Open: Mon-Fri 8.30 a.m.-5.30 p.m.
   Sat 9 a.m.-1 p.m.
P.W.WM.D.CS.A.

NORFOLK

KINGS LYNN   Tel. (0553) 2443
WALKER & ANDERSON (Kings Lynn) LTD
WINDSOR ROAD, KINGS LYNN
   Open: Monday to Saturday
   7.45 a.m.-5.30 p.m.
   Wednesday 1 p.m. Saturday 5.00 p.m.
H.P.W.WM.D.CS.A.

NORWICH   Tel. 0603 898695
NORFOLK SAW SERVICES
DOG LAND, HORSFORD
   Open: Monday to Friday
   8.00 a.m.-5.00 p.m.
   Saturday 8.00 a.m.-12.00 p.m.
H.P.W.WM.D.CS.A.

NORFOLK

NORWICH   Tel. 0603 400933
WESTGATES WOODWORKING   Tx.
MACHINERY, JUPITER ROAD   975412
OFF MILE CROSS LANE
   Open: 9 a.m.-5 p.m. weekdays
   9 a.m.-12 a.m. Sat.
P.W.WM.D.

NORTHAMPTONSHIRE

RUSHDEN   Tel. 093-34 56424
PETER CRISP LIMITED   ★
7 HIGH STREET
   Open: Monday to Saturday
   8.30 a.m.-5.30 p.m.
   Thursday 8.30 a.m.-1.00 p.m.
H.P.W.D.BC.

NORTHUMBERLAND

BLYTH   Tel. (06706) 69279
ALLAN McNAIR WOODCRAFT   ★
69-71 PLESSEY ROAD
   Open: Monday to Saturday
   9 a.m.-5 p.m.
H.W.WM.D.T.CS.A.BC.

NOTTINGHAMSHIRE

NOTTINGHAM   Tel. (0602) 225979
POOLEWOOD   (06077) 5777
EQUIPMENT LTD
5a HOLLY LANE, CHILLWELL
   Open: Mon-Fri 9 a.m.-5.30 p.m.
   Sat. 9 a.m. to 12.30 p.m.
P.W.WM.D.CS.A.BC.

NOTTINGHAM   Tel. 0602 811889
THE WOODCUTTER
5 TUDOR SQUARE
WEST BRIDGFORD
   Open: Tues-Sat 9 a.m.-5.30 p.m.
   Fri 9 a.m.-7.30 p.m. Closed Mon.
H.P.W.WM.D.T.CS.A.

OXFORDSHIRE

BICESTER   Tel. (08692) 4156/
WOODMEN   3218/3219
104 CHURCHILL ROAD
   Open: Monday-Saturday
   9 a.m.-5.30 p.m.
P.W.WM.D.A.BC.

OXFORD   Tel. (0865) 45118/9
SARJENT'S TOOL   ★
STORES LTD
150 COWLEY ROAD
   Open: Monday to Saturday
   8.30 a.m.-5.30 p.m.
H.P.W.WM.D.A.BC.

STAFFORDSHIRE

TAMWORTH   Tel. 0827-56188
MATTHEWS BROTHERS LTD
KETTLEBROOK ROAD
   Open: Mon.-Sat. 8.30am-6.00pm
   Demonstrations Sunday mornings
   by appointment only
H.P.WM.D.T.CS.A.BC.

SUFFOLK

BURY ST. EDMUNDS   Tel.
TOOLS & THINGS   0284 62022
21 CHURCHGATE
   ★
   Open: Monday to Saturday
   9.00 a.m.-5.30 p.m.
H.P.W.WM.D.A.BC.

SUFFOLK

IPSWICH   Tel. 0473 86216
FOX WOODWORKING   ★
'STEBBINGS' BACK LANE
WASHBROOK
   Open: Tues. Fri. 9.00am-5.30pm
   Sat. 9.00am-5pm
H.P.W.WM.D.A.B.C.

SURREY

CARSHALTON BEECHES   Tel.
SURREY WOOD   01-642 6636
MACHINE SALES LTD   ★
56A BANSTEAD ROAD
   Open: Tues-Fri 9.30 am-6.00 pm
   Saturday 9.30 am-2.00 pm
P.W.WM.D.BC.CS.

CROYDON   Tel. 01-688 5513
L. H. TURTLE LTD   ★
6-12 PARK STREET
   Open: Monday to Saturday
   8.30 a.m.-5.30 p.m.
H.P.W.WM.D.A.

GUILDFORD   Tel. 0483 61125
MESSINGERS FOR TOOLS
14-18 CHERTSEY STREET
   Open: Tuesday to Saturday
   8.30 a.m.-5.30 p.m.
   Closed all day Monday
H.P.W.D.BC.

SUSSEX

BOGNOR REGIS   Tel: (0243) 863100
A. OLBY & SON (BOGNOR REGIS LTD)
"TOOLSHOP", BUILDER'S MERCHANT
HAWTHORN ROAD
   Open: Mon-Thurs 8 a.m.-5.15 p.m.
   Fri 8 a.m.-8 p.m. Sat 8 a.m.-12.45 p.m.
H.P.W.WM.D.T.C.A.BC.

WORTHING   Tel. 0903 38739
W. HOSKING LTD (TOOLS &   ★
MACHINERY)
28 PORTLAND RD, BN11 1QN
   Open: Mon-Sat 8.30am-5.30pm
   Wednesday 8.30am-1.00pm
H.P.W.WM.D.CS.A.BC.

WEST MIDLANDS

WEST BROMWICH   Tel: 021-
CONWAY SAW &   533 5461/2
SUPPLY LTD   ★
SWAN LANE
   Open: 8 a.m.-6 p.m. Mon-Fri
   9 a.m.-1 p.m. Saturday
P.W.WM.D.CS.BC.

WILTSHIRE

SWINDON   Tel. (0793) 31361
SARJENT'S TOOL STORES LTD ★
64 FLEET STREET
   Open: Monday to Saturday
   8.30 a.m.-5.30 p.m.
H.P.W.WM.D.A.BC

YORKSHIRE

HALIFAX   Tel. 0422 43722/
TIMBERLITE LTD   884788/33575
WILLOWFIELDS ROAD   ★
WILLOWFIELD
   Open: Monday to Friday
   Saturday 9.00 a.m.-5.00 p.m.
H.P.W.WM.D.CS.A.BC.

Prices quoted are those prevailing at press date and are
subject to alteration due to economic conditions.

Woodworker, June 1982

SHOP GUIDE SHOP GUIDE

YORKSHIRE

HARROGATE   Tel. 0423 66245/
MULTI-TOOLS   55328 ★
158 KINGS ROAD

Open: Monday to Saturday
8.30 a.m.-6.00 p.m.
H.P.W.WM.D.A.BC.

HUDDERSFIELD   Tel. (0484)
NEVILLE M. OLDHAM   641219//(0484)
UNIT 1 DAYLE ST. WORKS   42777
DAYLE STREET, LONGWOOD   ★
Open: Mon-Fri 9.00am- 5.30pm
Saturday 9.30am-12.00pm
P.W.WM.D.A.BC.

LEEDS   Tel. 0532 790507
GEORGE SPENCE & SONS LTD
WELLINGTON ROAD   ★
Open: Monday to Friday
8.30 a.m.-5.30 p.m.
Saturday 9.00 a.m.-5.00 p.m.
H.P.W.WM.D.T.A.

SHEFFIELD   Tel. 0742-441012
GREGORY & TAYLOR LTD
WORKSOP ROAD
Open: 8.30 a.m.-5.30 p.m.
Monday-Friday
8.30 a.m.-12.30 p.m. Sat.
H.P.W.WM.D.

YORKSHIRE

SHEFFIELD   Tel. 0742-24659
GRAHAM OXLEY'S SHOWROOM
BRIDGE STREET   ★
Open: Monday to Friday
9.00 a.m.-5.30 p.m.
Saturday 8.30 a.m.-12.30 p.m.
H.W.D.A.BC.

SOWERBY BRIDGE   Tel. (0422)
CALDER   31861
WOODWORKING   Telex: 517400
MACHINERY LTD.
STATION ROAD
Open: Mon - Fri 9 a.m.-5 p.m.
P.W.WM.D.CS.A.

SCOTLAND

EDINBURGH   Tel. 031-337
SCOTSPAN   7788/665 3121
195 BALGREEN ROAD

Open: Monday to Friday
9.00 a.m.-3.00 p.m.
P.W.WM.D.A.

GLASGOW   Tel. 041 429 4374/4444
THE SAW CENTRE   Telex: 777886
596-602 EGLINGTON STREET   ★
G5 9RR
Open: Mon.-Fri. 8 a.m.-5.30 p.m.
Saturday 9 a.m.-1 p.m.
H.P.W.WM.D.CS.A.

N. IRELAND

Co. ANTRIM   Tel. 0266 6384
GEORGE GARDINER
49 BALLYMONEY STREET
BALLYMENA
Open: Open: Mon-Fri 8.30am-5.30pm
Wednesday 8.30am-1.00pm
H.P.W.D.A.BC.

Co. DOWN   Tel. (0247) 819800 (day)
NEWTOWNARDS   812506 (night)
NORLYN MACHINERY, UNIT 10
Malcolmson Ind. Est., 80 Bangor Road
Open: Mon-Fri 9.30am-5.30pm
or any other time by request
H.P.W.WM.D.A.BC.

S. IRELAND

COUNTY KILKENNY   Tel.
WOODMEN   (0409) 5460
CASHEL HOUSE   ★
KELLS ROAD, KILKENNY

Open: Monday to Saturday

WALES

BRITON FERRY   Tel. (0639)
WOODMEN   820803/4
49 NEATH ROAD

Open: Monday to Saturday
9.00 a.m.-5.30 p.m.
P.W.WM.D.A.BC.

WALES

CARDIFF   Tel. (0222) 373007
JOHN HALL TOOLS LIMITED   ★
22 CHURCHILL WAY

Open: Monday to Saturday
9.00 a.m.-5.30 p.m.
H.P.W.WM.D.A.BC.

CARDIFF   Tel. (0222) 30831
F. W. MORGAN   & 25562
(CANTON) LTD., 129-133
COWBRIDGE RD EAST,
CANTON, CARDIFF
Mon-Sat 8-5 Sun. 9.30-12.30
H.P.T.CS.A.BC.

CARDIFF   Tel. (0222) 36519/
WOODMEN   373793/35221
74-76 PARK ROAD
WHITCHURCH, CARDIFF   ★

Open: Monday to Saturday
9.00 a.m.-5.30 p.m.

CARMARTHEN   Tel. 0267 7219
DO-IT-YOURSELF SUPPLY
BLUE STREET, DYFED
Open: Monday to Saturday
9.00 a.m.-5.30 p.m.
Thursday 9.00 a.m.-1.00 p.m.
H.P.W.WM.D.T.CS.A.BC.

YOU CAN BUY WITH CONFIDENCE FROM THE SHOPS IN THIS SHOP GUIDE

★ *Shops offering a mail order service are denoted by an asterisk*

SWANSEA   Tel. (0792) 55680
SWANSEA TIMBER &   ★
PLYWOOD CO LTD
57-59 OXFORD STREET
Open: Mon. to Fri. 9 am-5.30 pm
Sat. 9 am-1 pm
H.P.W.D.T.CS.A.BC.

Wood Suppliers Wood Suppliers

Especially aimed at the readers who require to buy and sell timber and allied materials. Make sure you reach the market.
Let *Woodworker Wood Suppliers* section work for you. Sizes available —
*Full Page £300. Half Page £160. Quarter Page £88. Eighth Page £50.
Classified — Semi Display £4.00 per single column cm (Minimum £10.00).
Lineage rate 20p per word (Minimum £3.00). Box Number £1.25 extra*

For further details give Valerie Tester a ring on (0442) 41221 Ext. 262.

Earn £200 per hour drying timber with your own kiln...

My seasoners need so little attention that your time could hardly be better spent than by drying your own timber. Can you afford to invest a few hundred pounds in order to guarantee your work is stable in central heating and ensure that your English hardwoods will cost half as much for many years to come.

No need to keep large untidy stacks of timber slowly drying and spoiling for years and years — these machines work from green in a few weeks and cost only a few pence per cubic foot to run.

The smallest seasoner costs less than £340 and will dry enough timber to keep several people busy or make you some money selling surplus timber. It can live outside and does not usually need a box much larger than 8' × 4' × 4'. As I am the man who developed these machines, I hope that my information, prices, references etc., are second to none.

Write for details or ring me any time for answers to your questions completely without obligation.

JOHN ARROWSMITH
74 Wilson Street, Darlington,
Co. Durham DL3 6QZ. Tel: 0325 481970

ENGLISH HARDWOODS. Oak Specialists, also Elm, Ash, Beech, Sycamore. Over 4,000 cu ft. Send for stock list to W. H. Mason & Son Ltd, The Sawmills, Wetmore Road, Burton-on-Trent, Staffs. Telephone 64651/2. Also imported hardwoods, softwoods and full machining facilities.   N-S

KILNED — ALL ENGLISH HARDWOODS, also Teak £10 per cubic foot, Mahogany £5. Great Stour 470 (Kent) evenings.   N-O

ROSEWOOD. One ton. Up to ⅞" thick in boards and shorts. J. D'Agapeyeff, Talbot House, Crickhowell, Powys. Tel: 0873-810 620.   N-O

SEASONED English Hardwoods. Air and kiln dried timbers for the discerning craftsman. P. Smith, Furniture Makers, Chapel Workshops, Kirkburn, Driffield, E. Yorkshire. Tel: Driffield 89301.   Alt. T/C

AIR DRIED ELM. 12ft, 10ft, 8ft and 7ft. 2", 1½" and 1". £8.00 per cubic foot. Tel. Brixham 51155 evenings.   N-O

EXOTICWOODS. Boxwood, Cocobolo, Ebony, Kingwood, Olivewood, Partridge-wood, Purpleheart, Grande Pallisander, Rosewoods, Tulipwood. Many others. CHART, Reading (0734) 695336. Evenings/Saturdays.   O

AIR DRY BEECH, forest grown 1⅛", 2", 2¼", 2½", 3¼", 4¼", 6" from around £8.00 per cu ft. Ring Will Tyers, Hornby (0468) 21292 (Nr. Lancaster).   J-O

VENEERS AND MARQUETRY equipment, materials and books now in stock. Phone or send for details to: H.W.M., The Woodworkers, 303 Shirley Road, Shirley, Southampton. Tel: 0703 776222.   T/C

CONVERT TIMBER YOURSELF, with a portable chain saw mill. Cuts a 36" width 200 sq. ft. per hour. Keenest prices. Brochure, demonstration. Philip Cole, 16 Kings Lane, Flore, Northampton. Tel: Weedon 0327 40337 (evenings)   T/C

STOCK CLEARANCE. Oak, Yew, Elm, Ash, Sycamore, air day. Quantity discounts. Telephone: Mr. Rees, (0782) 643023.   O-P

VENEERS, all types. SAE List—S. Gould (Veneers), 342 Uxbridge Road, W12. Tel: 01-743 8561.   T/C

Continued
Overleaf

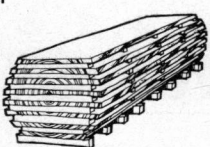

Classified Advertisements

Telephone Valerie Tester
(0442) 41221 Ex. 262

All classified Advertisements must be pre-paid.
Private and trade rate 20p per word (minimum £3.00). Box Numbers £1.25 extra. Display box rates s.c.c. £4.00 (min £10.00). All advertisements are inserted in the first available issue.
Box replies to be sent care of Advertisement Department, PO Box 35, Bridge Street, Hemel Hempstead, Herts, England HP1 1EE. There are no reimbursements for cancellations.

FOR SALE

TIMBER SEASONERS, moisture meters, polymeters. Everything you require for seasoning your own timber. For free advice and lowest prices, consult the experts, 15 years in the trade. Some reconditioned seasoners available, Wyco Moisture control. Tel: Weybridge 40864. K-P

SURPLUS KITY and Lurem machinery at bargain prices. Trymwood. Bristol 629092. O

YEW THREE DRAWER CABRIOLE leg dresser base kit. All stock joined, planed and thicknessed. Legs shaped and morticed sides tennoned. Ideal project for the discerning woodworker, £148. Northampton 412268. O

CORONET MINOR Universal Woodworking machine with too many accessories to list. £350. Please telephone Luton (0582) 27864 for details. O

MYFORD ML8 attachments. Bandsaw. Sanding Table. R.H. 8" Plate. Saw Table. Wobble Arbor. £250.00. Lincoln 751288 (evenings). O

WOODWORKER ANNUALS 1943 to 1979. Also Woodcarving tools by Sargents. All unused due to bereavement. Telephone: Bolton (Lancashire) 656601. O

CORONET MINOR Woodturning lathe with saw attachment and planer with thicknesser. Some turning attachments. £450. Excellent condition. East Horsley (04865) 2099. O

MULTICO 10" PLANER, 2 h.p., single phase motor. Very good condition. £350. Telephone Kings Lynn 672673 after 6 p.m. O

NEW MYFORD ML8B 36" B.C. on steel stand 1 h.p. motor and starter £450. Used Myford ML8B 36" B.C. on steel stand ¾ h.p. and starter £350. Part exchange welcome. Also used ML8 attachments, bandsaw and circular saw. Telephone: Heathfield (043 52) 2593. Sussex. Anytime. O

LACE BOBBIN turning blanks in exotic hardwoods. S.A.E. for list. J. Ford, 5 Squirrels Hollow, Walsall WS7 8YS.

EBAC TIMBER SEASONERS. Two Minor models £550 each, two Proportional Timers £70 each. Absolutely unused in original packing. Bargain, chance of a lifetime. Tel: Great Shefford 558. O

FOR ALL SUPPLIES
FOR THE

Craft of Enamelling

ON METAL

Including
LEAD-FREE ENAMELS

PLEASE SEND 2 × 10p STAMPS
FOR FREE CATALOGUE, PRICE
LIST AND WORKING
INSTRUCTIONS

W. G. BALL LTD.

ENAMEL MANUFACTURERS

Dept. W. LONGTON
STOKE-ON-TRENT
ST3 1JW

ADVERTISERS please note
FINAL COPY DATE for
AUGUST ISSUE
(Published 16th July)
is **4th June**

SEPTEMBER ISSUE
(Published 20th August)
is **9th July**

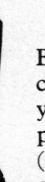

PENS AND HOLDERS

Beautiful modern desk pens and holders in 5 exciting colours — brown, ivory, black, gold and red. Turn your craft objects into useful pen sets. **£2.40 for 6** (3 pens and 3 holders) including postage and VAT (minimum order). Pens are 6" long with gold finish on barrel. Holders nearly 3" high with swivel base.
HIRSH JACOBSON, 91 Marylebone High Street, London W1.

HAND CARVED
'Adam Style' motifs in Mahogany — Example 10" × 5" centre lamp and two side pieces — £25.00
Send S.A.E. for details and quotation. Your own design quoted for if required.
SAM NICHOLSON
22 Lisnagarvey Drive,
Lisburn, Co. Antrim,
N. Ireland. Phone Lisburn 3510

For best results when buying or selling use the CLASSIFIED COLUMNS — Telephone: Valerie Tester, (0442) 41221. Ext. 262

BARRIE IRONS MACHINERY LTD

We are pleased to announce that in 1981 we were the largest distributor for ELU machinery. We may not be the cheapest but we are competitive with excellent service and technical back-up facilities.
Also distributors of DeWalt, Multico, Startrite, Kango, Bosch, all at discount prices.
Why not drop us a line, telephone for further information or even pay us a visit to our new showroom.
81 UXBRIDGE ROAD, STANMORE, MIDDLESEX HA7 3NH
Telephone: 01-954-0181

R & S TOOLS (LINCOLN) LTD.

BEEVOR STREET, LINCOLN. Tel: Lincoln 0522 36168/9

Why pay more when you can get up to 25% discount off most leading makes of power tools and hand tools?

Stockists of:
ELECTRIC POWER TOOLS:
AEG—ELU—BOSCH—MAKITA—SUPER STORK—SKIL WOLF—METABO—WADKIN—KANGO

WOODWORKING MACHINES
DEWALT—MULTICO—SEDGWICK—WADKIN—STARTRITE

SAWBLADES
SANDVIK—TEX—MICOR—FIRTH—BROWN

HAND TOOLS
ALL LEADING MAKES OF BUILDING AND ENGINEERING TOOLS

ELU MVS 93 less list 30%
ABRASIVES
ENGLISH—TEX—KLINGSPOR—UNIVERSAL GRINDING WHEELS

Up to 30% off most leading brands of coated abrasive

TCT CIRCULAR SAW BLADES
Contact us for the best price.

ACCESS & BARCLAYCARD WELCOME

SOLE AGENTS FOR SWIFTSURE CUTTING & CUTTING DISCS
FOR YOUR QUOTATION—PLEASE PHONE BETWEEN 8.30 am and 5 pm

The Complete Works
IN ONE COMPREHENSIVE CATALOGUE

NEW UPDATED 32 PAGE COLOUR CATALOGUE AND FULL DESCRIPTIVE PRICE AND SPECIFICATION LIST NOW AVAILABLE.
Join the fastest-growing hobby of clock building. Build your own clock — Grandfather or Mother, Traditional or Modern, Bracket or Battery, Carriage or Cuckoo.
We can offer you from stock the most comprehensive range of Europe's finest movements and dials, as well as full kits with easy-to-follow simple instructions. Trust in the experts and let this established Family business help you start a fascinating and satisfying hobby. Build a clock, or even a musical box. Restore an antique clock.
Send today for the NEW updated, fully comprehensive 32 page colour catalogue, and descriptive price list.
To help cover costs, please send 50p which will be refunded with your first order.

Charles Greville & Co. Ltd.
Dept (W.6) Unit 5, Rear Airport House, Purley Way, Croydon, Surrey. Tel: 01-686 2972. Ample car park. Personal callers most welcome. Open: Mon–Fri: 9.30–5.30. Sat: 9.00–12.30.

434

Prices quoted are those prevailing at press date and are subject to alteration due to economic conditions.

Woodworker, June 1982

SUPER PACK OF WOODSCREWS

10 GROSS £6.95

BALANCED SELECTION OF ALL POPULAR SIZES ⅜" to 3" FINEST QUALITY CSK HEAD STEEL

ALL SIZES SEPARATELY PACKED

TIMBER JOINTS
10 – £1.00
50 – £3.30
100 – £6.95
200 – £11.40
500 – £26.40
State BROWN or WHITE

MAGNETIC CATCHES
10 – £1.75
50 – £7.60
100 – £14.95
Larger SUPER STRONG
10 – £2.70 50 – £12.90

CONCEALED HINGES
Suitable for 16-18mm timber thickness. Enables door to open through 96°
10 – £5.95
50 – £27.75
100 – £54.15
State BROWN or WHITE

SHELF BEARER STUDS
For Cabinet and bookcase shelves.
25 – £1.25, 50 – £2.00,
100 – £3.20
State BROWN or WHITE

HOLE CUTTER
Enables a quick and easy preparation when fixing 35mm hinges. £2.35 each.

CABINET FIXING BRACKETS
Enables complete alignment of cabinets by means of revolving internal screw and moved either. £1.15; 12 – £3.05 48 – £10.95

MIXED NAIL PACK
Round and Oval. 1" to 4'. 4 kilo bag £6.95

TRIM PULL
Eliminates need for handles on drawers and cabinets. Aluminium finish 21" lengths. Drilled and csk £1.00 per length.

SWITCH PLATES
(Clear or White) Protect the decor throughout the house or office.
10 £2.35
20 £4.20

PLASTIC WALL PLUGS
Price per 100
5/8 gauge £1.00:
7/.0 gauge £1.15;
9/13 gauge £1.38
ASSORTED 500 – £4.75
BARGAIN 1000 – £9.00 PACKS

BRASS WOODSCREWS
A selection of 500 in popular sizes from ⅜" to 1⅛"
£4.95

CSK HEAD CHIPBOARD SCREWS
An economy bargain selection pack containing over 600 in size range ⅜" to 1½"
£4.95

BRASS KNOBS
Gives professional finish to d.i.y. pine furniture constructions
1¼" – 84p ea. 10 – £8.10
1½" – 90p ea. 10 – £8.70

MITRE CLAMP
Strong double ended clamp for d.i.y. and hobbyists. Ideal when picture frame making for precision cut mitred corners.
£2.95 each 2 £5.58 4 £11.35

BRITISH MADE ANODISED ALUMINIUM DOOR AND WINDOW FITTINGS DIRECT FROM WAREHOUSE
Give a new look to doors and windows
Spring Loaded Lever Sets. Lock £2.58 per set.
Latch £2.45 per set.
Stays 8" £1.70; 10" £1.80;
12" £1.85. Fasteners £1.35 each. Letter Box £3.65.
Hat & Coat Hook £2.00
Wardrobe Hook 24p
Night Latch for front door – complete with S.A.A. Door Pull £4.95

HINGES
Prices per 10 pairs
Steel Butts 1" £1.44; 1½" £1.80
2" £2.10; 2½" £2.70
3" £3.30; 4" £6.30
Steel Backflaps ¾" £1.50
1" £1.80; 1½" £2.10; 1½" £3.00
Brass Butts DP Lock Joint –
2" £6.76; 1¼" £3.24; 1½" £3.55
2" £5.34; 2½" £6.34; 3" £10.50
Brass Butts Solid Drawn – 1½"
£6.90; 2" £8.34; 2½" £10.20
3" £14.34; 4" £28.80
Flush Hinge Brassed – 1½" £1.50;
2" £1.80; 2½" £2.35; 3" £4.75
Flush Hinge Bronzed – 1½" £1.50
2" £1.80; 2½" £2.35.

TOP CUPBOARD STAY
Up and over opening of kitchen wall units and cabinets
85p each. 10 – £7.80

EASY-ON HINGE
Enables face fixing for kitchen cabinets, etc. Sprung or Unsprung.
10 – £7.15
50 – £34.75 100 – £67.75

PUSH IN PIN HINGE
Size 1" x 11/32" dia.
Male screws directly into 3/16" x 1" hole in end or stile. Female similarly fixed into edge of door which is then lifted into place. NICKEL PLATED or ELECTRO BRASSED.
10 – £4.70; 50 – £19.60

DROP LEAF STAY
Enables flap to fall open gently under own weight.
Braking effect adjustment. 7" length
Each. 10 – £9.45

WOOD SCREWS

CSK HD STEEL Size	Gross	ROUND HEAD STEEL SCREWS Size	Gross	RCD HD STEEL SCREWS Size	Gross
⅜ × 2	31p	½ × 4	62p	½ × 4	54p
½ × 4	44p	⅝ × 6	99p	¾ × 6	96p
½ × 6	50p	1 × 8	£1.30	1 × 8	£1.20
⅝ × 6	46p	1¼ × 8	£1.50	1¼ × 8	£1.44
⅝ × 6	59p	1½ × 8	£1.74	1½ × 8	£1.62
⅝ × 8	78p	2 × 8	£2.35		
¾ × 4	47p				
¾ × 6	63p	CSK HD BRASS Size	Gross	CSK HD CHIPBOARD SCREWS Size	Gross
¾ × 8	85p	⅜ × 2	75p		
1 × 4	63p	½ × 4	91p	½ × 4	54p
1 × 6	78p	⅝ × 6	£1.31	⅝ × 6	65p
1 × 7	84p	¾ × 4	£1.10	¾ × 4	72p
1 × 8	90p	¾ × 6	£1.21	1 × 8	£1.08
1 × 10	£1.25	¾ × 8	£1.70	1¼ × 8	£1.36
1¼ × 6	90p	1 × 4	£2.37	1½ × 8	£1.80
1¼ × 8	£1.05	1 × 6	£1.82		
1¼ × 10	£1.30	1 × 8	£2.16		
1½ × 6	£1.02	1¼ × 4	£2.99		
1½ × 8	£1.19	1¼ × 6	£2.58		
1½ × 10	£1.59	1¼ × 8	£3.59		
1½ × 12	£2.09	1½ × 6	£2.96		
1¾ × 12	£1.54	1½ × 8	£3.39		
1¾ × 10	£1.88	1½ × 10	£4.59		
2 × 6	£1.25	2 × 8	£5.17		
2 × 8	£1.79	2 × 10	£7.19		
2 × 10	£2.20	2½ × 10	£9.14		
2 × 12	£2.57	3 × 12	£13.95		
2½ × 12	£3.15				
3 × 8	£2.52	ROUND HD BRASS Size	Gross		
3 × 12	£4.02				
3½ × 12	£4.35	⅜ × 2	72p		
4 × 14	£7.14	½ × 4	99p		
		¾ × 6	£2.00		
		1 × 8	£3.24		
		1¼ × 8	£3.87		
		1½ × 8	£4.55		

FREE GIFT
Spend £15 or more and select one of the following FREE GIFTS!
"STEEL TAPE MEASURE"
"TRIMMING KNIFE WITH BLADES"

Despatched within 7 days

CARRIAGE Please add 95p if ORDER UNDER £10 over £10 and UNDER £15 outside U.K. mainland add 95p. DISCOUNTS over £25 LESS 10% over £50 15% over £100 20%

FREE catalogue/price list with order. BARCLAY/ACCESS CARD HOLDERS ORDER ANYTIME on 079-156 406

BUILDERS DIRECT MAIL
WW 6 POYNINGS, SUSSEX.

FOR SALE

CORBETT TOOLS HAVE THE EDGE

Adzes, Drawknives, Inshaves, Bowsaws, Carving Sets, and other unusual and high quality tools for the Craftsman in Wood.

EXPORT ENQUIRIES WELCOME
CATALOGUE AVAILABLE
Send 45p to:-
CORBETT TOOLS (Dept, WW/6), 224 Puxton Drive, Kidderminster, Worc's.

EXCLUSIVE To KENYONS
this specially designed **D.I.Y. Apron**

Made in 100% Heavy Duty Cotton, with 9 Pockets and a Hammer Holder, an ideal gift for any do-it-yourselfer at only:

£4.90 + 65p P&P

Price per 100
- Chuck Key
- Drills
- Screwdrivers
- Hammer Holder
- Sandpaper Pencils
- Tape Measure
- Screws & Nails

KENYONS (mail order) Co. Ltd., (W)
Oxen Road, CREWKERNE, Somerset.
Please allow 21-28 days for delivery.

TOOLS MENTIONED ABOVE ARE NOT SUPPLIED

MATERIALS

ROBBINS LIMITED — the complete timber merchants. Hardwoods, including exotic Softwoods, Plywoods, Mouldings, Veneers, Lines, Bandings, Nails, Screws, Fittings, Clear Finishes, Adhesives, Tools, Books, Complete list (35p stamp) Merrywood Mills, Bedminster, Bristol. Phone 633022. T/C

D.I.Y. PICTURE FRAMING. Suppliers of mitred mouldings. 79 patterns to choose from. Also ready-mades, ovals, tools, mounts, accessories, illustrated catalogue 45p. Westward, 16 Minton Close, St. Austell, Cornwall. I-T

FIRST QUALITY Black Forest longcase movements, all dials, Battery Movements, Quartz movements, all accessories, Clock Kits in Solid Oak or Mahogany from £63.80. Send large stamped addressed envelope: TIMECRAFT, 10 Edinburgh Road, Formby, Liverpool. T/C

We manufacture and sell a complete range of wood care products such as wood dyes, wax and French polishes. Wax filler sticks, seal etc.
To receive our catalogue please send two first class stamps to:

LIBERON WAXES

6-7 Park Street, Lydd, Kent.

Our shop is also open by appointment or on a Saturday from 10-1pm/2-5pm. For more information call Lydd 20107.

Rates
20p per word, minimum £3.00
Box nos. £1.25 extra.
Semi display s.c.c. £4.00
(min £10.00)

MATERIALS

The Perfect Adhesive for all kinds of jobs!

4 MINUTE EPOXY GLUE
in economy non-breakable squeeze bottles.

Ideal for bonding: wood, glass, metal, costume jewellery, tool handles, china, most plastics and fibreglass.

WATERPROOF – PERMANENT HEATPROOF – CLEAR
10 oz. size **£4.62** +35p p&p
4 oz. size **£3.09** +32p p&p

Send cheque/P.O. to:
DE LUXE MATERIALS 4a Waterloo Place, Crowthorne, Berks
TRADE ENQUIRIES VERY WELCOME SAE for details of other products

---

MAKE HANDSOME CLOCKS for Pleasure or Profit . . . with
. . . our superb electronic and quartz battery movements from the world famous KIENZLE Works. Other high quality movements and accessories available, plus a special dials offer to help everyone enjoy clockmaking at reasonable cost. SAE details now: SMS/Kingswoode (W1), 24 Holwood Road, Bromley, Kent, BR1 3EB

CRAFTSMAN'S FRENCH POLISHING KIT

No skill is required whatsoever, it can be used to patch up without the need for stripping all the surface. The kit comes complete with full instructions.

200 mls £3.10
1 Litre £8.75
Price inc. VAT p/p

Send to MAIL ORDER DEPARTMENT
J. L. PRODUCTS, 6 NEWINGTON DRIVE, BURY, LANCS BL8 2NE.
Telephone: 061 764 6769

CHAIR CANE SUPPLIES

Chair cane, Seagrass, Pre-woven cane etc. Tools, Books & advice. SAE for list
BERRY'S CRAFT SUPPLIES
10 Hill Rd., Theydon Bois, Epping, Essex. CM16 7LX. Tel: 037 881 3532 (anytime)

CLASSIFIED
Telephone Valerie Tester
(0442) 41221 Ext. 262

CREATE A BEAUTIFUL PICTURE IN WOOD VENEERS

We have the world's largest range of rare and exotic veneers for Marquetry and a New '300 Range' of modern Action Pictures for quicker results. We use the WINDOW METHOD of construction in all our kits. Decorative veneers, brasswares, tools, adhesives, books, plans and much more... even 8-day clock movements.
Send for combined Instruction Manual and Illustrated Catalogue, 70p inc post. Special offer: Catalogue with MINI WOOD COLLECTION (3 cards containing 45 sample veneers) £2.50p.

THE ART VENEERS CO. LTD.,
WORLD OF WOOD
Industrial Estate
Mildenhall Suffolk
IP28 7AY

RUSH

Good quality flat rush, suitable for chair seating 0-20 lbs £1.65 per lb. 200 lbs plus 95p per lb. Intermediate weight by quotation. Ex Hereford + V.A.T. (Quantity guide: 2/3 lbs. for single chair).
Chair re-rushing service
I. & J. L. BROWN, 58 Commercial Road, Hereford, HR1 2BP
Telephone: (0432) 58895

MARQUETRY VENEERS

Mixture Packs — our speciality
Send S.A.E. for details of our basic Mixture Packs. Prompt attention; noted for value. "Marquetry Magic," a Beginner's Guide, 50p plus stamp.
TERRY MILLS (W),
23 Maplestead Avenue, Wilford, Nottingham NG11 7AS

CLOCKMAKING MATERIALS

German quartz clock movements by Kienzle and Junghans, prices from only £2.95 inclusive! Also excellent range of quartz pendulum and insertion movements, hands, dials and numerals.
S.A.E. for free illustrated brochure.
BATH CLOCK COMPANY (Dept W),
13 Welton Road, Radstock, Bath, Avon BA3 3UA.

HAVE YOU

COMPARED OUR PRICES FOR:-

Turning tools, Ceramic Tiles, Eggtimers, Table Lighters, Hourglasses, Barometers, Cheese Blades, Peppermills, Polishes, Waxes, etc. PRICE LIST S.A.E.
COUNTRY CRAFT STUDIO LAWSHALL, BURY ST. EDMUNDS, SUFFOLK.
Tel: (STD 0284) 828661

SOUVENIR MAKERS' TRANSFERS

Floral, Mottoes, Dogs, Horses, Crests, National Emblems, etc., for decorations on Wood, Plastics, Leather, Fabric, etc.
PLASTIC-STICKER INQUIRIES
Trade Catalogue and samples 50p
A. P. AXON & HARRISON LTD.
JERSEY, Channel Islands

MODEL COACH BOLTS, DOME AND SQUARE HEAD WITH SQUARE NUTS

Now available in all steel and all brass. Increased range of steel and brass rod, bar and strip. Send 3 × 1st class stamps for detailed price lists and coloured brochure of horses for model wagons to:
LENHAM POTTERY, 215 Wroxham Road, Norwich, Norfolk NR7 8AQ.

MANCHESTER 061-236 2477
FRED ALDOUS LTD
37 LEVER STREET

Supply materials for Basketry, Stool Seating, Lampshade making, Marquetry, Modelling, Pewter, Copper, Enamelling, Leather Work.

CRAFTEX RUBBERISED ABRASIVES

Impregnate high grade neoprene rubber with Silicon Carbide grit and you have a material which will give you a super sharp cutting edge and produce a highly polished bevel on cutting tools. CRAFTEX available in Wheels, Blocks, Sticks and Slips – invaluable to every Woodcraftsman.

To learn more of this remarkable material, send a stamp for our illustrated catalogue.

WOODCRAFT SUPPLY (U.K.) LTD.
2 Drew Street, Brixham, Devon TQ5 9JU.
Sole distributors for CRAFTEX in the U.K.

MACHINERY. A comprehensive range of new/used machinery. Check our prices, e.g. HMO 10"×5½" planer/thicknesser £374. HF30; spindle moulder £365. 12" tilt arbour sawbench 2hp motor £140. Shopsmith MK5 home workshop £897. Morso mitring machine £437, (including V.A.T.). Kity K-5. See these machines and Ryobi industrial small tools demonstrated at Woodman Woodworking Machinery Co. (Sign of the Axe), Little Malgraves Hall, Lower Dunton Road, Bulphan, Nr. Upminster, Essex. Tel: (0268) 415511 or (0702) 331729. I-U

MAKE A WOODTURNING LATHE easily, construction details and parts list, send SAE to: ORTAN LATHES, P.O. Box 46, Norwich NR7 8PB. M-R

CIRCULAR AND BAND saw blades for all applications from: A.A. SMITH of Lancing Ltd., 63 Brighton Road, Shoreham, Sussex. Tel: 07917 61707 (24 hrs). K-O

PLANERS 6" × 9", planers/thicknessers, 12" × 7", 9" × 6", 12" × 7", sawbenches, 10" × 2" combination woodworkers. British made. Particulars, send stamp. Dodd Machine Tools Ltd., South Woodham, Chelmsford. Telephone: (0245) 320 691 O-Z

WASHITA & ARKANSAS whetstones now readily available from importer. Large selection, SAE for list. C. Rufino, Manor House, South Clifton, Newark, Notts. T/C

T.C.T. ROUTER CUTTERS with ball bearing guide will trim laminates at 90° to a professional finish, ¼ inch shank, fits any router, only £10.99. Send cheque:- Woodcutter Services, 88 Thornhill Road, Heaton Mersey, Stockport SK4 3DH. Telephone 061-432 4294. O

RECORD COMBINATION PLANE 050C with 18 Blades £35. Record Bench Holdfast 145 £10. Record Dowelling jig complete with extension rods £20. Everything still boxed and as new. Craftsman Model 748-2 1 H.P. Router complete with the following craftsman accessories: 2544 H.D. Table, Trim-A-Form 25174 Trammel point, micro adjustment edge and contour guide, guide bushings (Templet Guides), router bit sharpening kit. All in excellent condition £175 complete. Startrite 12 S 1 Bandit Bandsaw with good supply spare blades. Protractor. Rip fence. Circle cutting attachment. Cutting height 7¼" throat 11⅜". Good condition. £200. G. M. Grimwade, 14 Thorpe Avenue, Peterborough. Telephone 0733 66487. O

EBAC TIMBER SEASONERS, Protimeter moisture meters, always good prices and advice from the man who pioneer small scale seasoning. John Arrowsmith, 74, Wilson Street, Darlington, Co. Durham BL3 6QZ. Tel: 0325 481970. T/C

MORTISING ATTACHMENT, chuck, five mortise chisels and holder for Myford ML8. Good condition, £195. Telephone Glemsford 280520 (Suffolk). O

SAW BLADES. Fretsaw. Marquetry. Coping. Price list from Lea Blades, 16 Barclay, Hertford Heath, Hertford. O

Braywood Estates
Comprehensive range of **DeWALT** Accessories plus a super service for spare parts & on site servicing.
BRAYWOOD ESTATES LTD. FREEPOST, SLOUGH SL2 4BL
TELEPHONE : SLOUGH 0753 22567/70792

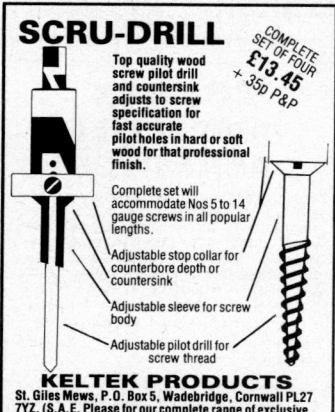

SCRU-DRILL
COMPLETE SET OF FOUR £13.45 + 35p P&P

Top quality wood screw pilot drill and countersink adjusts to screw specification for fast accurate pilot holes in hard or soft wood for that professional finish.

Complete set will accommodate Nos 5 to 14 gauge screws in all popular lengths.

Adjustable stop collar for counterbore depth or countersink

Adjustable sleeve for screw body

Adjustable pilot drill for screw thread

KELTEK PRODUCTS
St. Giles Mews, P.O. Box 5, Wadebridge, Cornwall PL27 7YZ. (S.A.E. Please for our complete range of exclusive products).

A·Pollard·Son LTD.
Come and browse through our huge stocks of machinery and tools. If you live too far away, privately owned Mini Clipper service will deliver within days to your door.

KITY UNITED KINGDOM **K5**
International Woodworker with Sawbench, Spindle Moulder, Planer/Thicknesser & Slot Mortiser.
Full range in stock.

scheppach HMO ▶
2HP 10" × 6" Planer/Thicknesser. HM2 Planer/Thicknesser also in stock.

Elu MOF 96
The professional Plunging Router 600 Watt Motor takes ¼" shanked bits.
£62·50 INC VAT CARR. £2 EXTRA

DeWALT DW125
Powershop, for Sawing, Grooving, Sanding, Moulding. Dust Extractors, Planer/Thicknessers & Industrial R.A.S. also in stock.

◀ H.F.30
Spindle Moulder 2HP Motor. Shown with: Overhead Roller, Guard & Sliding Carriage. (Optional Extras)

mafell BIBEREX
12", 2.3HP Sawbench with Rise & Fall, Mitre Guide. Fence and Tilting Arbor. Other Sawbenches in stock.

Dust Extractors, Lathes, Industrial R/A. Saws. Large stocks of Ironmongery & Handtools — Most accessories stocked.
Open 6 days a week 8.30-5.30   Barclaycard, Access   Business Established over 50 years.

A. POLLARD & SON LTD. 51 Queensway, Bletchley, Milton Keynes ☎ (0908) 75221

JOHN HALL WOODWORKING CENTRE

	JOHN HALL (inc. VAT)
DeWalt Dw125 Radial Saw	£275.00
Elektra TF100 Spindle Moulder with 6 Free Cutters & Block	£349.95
Elektra HC260 K Planer/Thicknesser with stand	£449.95
DeWalt DW50 Planer/Thicknesser	£430.00
DeWalt DW100 Mini Bandsaw	£115.00
DeWalt BS1310 12" Bandsaw	£237.00
Elekra Combi 2200 2.9 H.P. Saw Bench	£139.50
Elekra Spa 1000 Dust Extractor	£155.00
Kity 7227 Spindle Moulder with Free Cutters	£419.95
Kity 7136 Planer/Thicknesser with stand	£449.95
Kity K5 Combination Machine	£642.85

Carriage £9.50 per unit (UK mainland only)
Bristol Clifton Down Shopping Centre, Whiteladies Road, Bristol. (0272) 741510
Bath 2, Railway Street. (0225) 64513
Cardiff 23, Churchill Way, Cardiff. (0222) 373007
Branches throughout the UK
BARCLAYCARD   VISA

BURGESS BANDSAWS

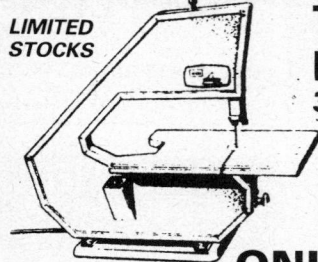

LIMITED STOCKS

TWO SPEED MODEL BK2
3" CUTTING DEPTH
12" THROAT

FULLY GUARANTEED NEW MACHINES with full after sales service from our own workshop.
Price still held at
(LIST PRICE £125.35) **ONLY £79.95**
SPARE BLADES — **£2.58**; ADJUSTABLE FENCE — **£3.62**
when ordered with machine
Prices include V.A.T. Carriage and Insurance. Send cheque or P.O. to:

PEN TOOLS
EDGAR STREET HEREFORD 3018

TYME WOOD LATHE
SINGLE PHASE, 5 SPEED, 37" B.C. 17" BOWL TURNING. SELF LOCKING SYSTEM, COMPLETE WITH WOOD SCREW SET, FACE PLATE LIVE CENTRE, 2 PRONG CENTRE, SOLID CENTRE.
Price £285.00 complete — inc. V.A.T.
DEWALT HEAD AND KNIVES
Set comprising cutter head, nut and spacer plus **12 pairs of knives** Complete in carrying case **£86.50** (inclusive V.A.T.)
Literature available
CONWAY SAW & SUPPLY CO LTD.
Swan Lane, West Bromwich,
W. Midlands B70 0NU.
Tel: 021-553 5461/021-525 6400

CLASSIFIED
Telephone Valerie Tester
(0442) 41221 Ext. 262

B/DECKER, SKIL, BOSCH, MAKITA TOOLS ALL IN STOCK
NEW LUTZ SAWBENCH NOW IN STOCK ONLY £165.00

BEST QUALITY TCT SAWS, 5" DIAMETER UP TO 36" GUARANTEED PERFORMANCE
24 HOUR RETURN POST SHARPENING SERVICE.
PHONE OR WRITE TO MAYS HIGH SPEED SAWS LTD. NEW ROAD (Nr. CHANDLER CORNER), RAINHAM, ESSEX.
Tel: (04027) 55371/21331
(7 DAYS A WEEK)
TCT   ALLOY

5000 ELECTRIC MOTORS, FANS & BLOWERS
New & Used. Single & 3 Phase
ALWAYS IN STOCK
RING
(0742) 78088
FOR FREE STOCKLIST
Beatson & Co (Elec.) Ltd,
17-21 Mowbray St.,
Sheffield S3 8EN

MULTICUT -2 SAW
The world's first universal precision saw, cuts 50mm wood, 10mm metals, plastics, rubber, etc. High performance, safe in use. Do not compare with standard fretsaws. Details 11½ stamp.
Hegner Universal Saws (U.K.) Ltd.
36 Gt. Eastern Road, Hockley, Essex.
Tel: Southend (0702) 205669

Demonstrations:
Wessex Craft Show,
Breamore House, Fordingbridge, Dorset.
30th May to 1st June 1982
and
Model Craft & Country Show,
Stoneleigh, Kenilworth, Warwicks.
22nd/23rd May 1982

WOOD TURNING LATHES
550mm between centres. 65mm centre height. Lever action tailstock. No.2 Morse tapers. Rear turning attachment takes 220mm dia. Various bed lengths available.
Prices from £80 + VAT
Send SAE for details

GREENFIELDS ENGINEERING
Building 3A, Site 1, Newport Road, High Ercall, Telford, TF6 6JA. Telephone High Ercall (0952) 770672

WOODTURNERS SUPPLIES
Woodturning tools, Peppermills, Salt mills, Barometers, Thermometers, Lighters, Hourglasses, Eggtimers, Ceramic tiles and clock faces, Clock movements, Spinning wheel plans, Sealers & Polishes, etc. Fast and efficient mail order service + competitive prices. S.A.E. for lists.

ERIC TOMKINSON
86 Stockport Road, Cheadle, Cheshire, SK8 2AJ. Tel. 061-491 1726
Shop open Mon-Fri from 9am to 4pm,
Sat 9am to 1pm.

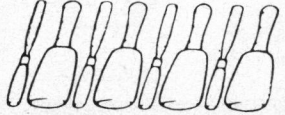

Harpsichord, spinet, clavichord kits for home or educational projects. Traditional materials are used, and no special skills are needed for kit assembly. Stool kits and instrument covers are also available. Visitors are welcome.

John Storrs Maker of Early Keyboard Instruments
Hunston Chichester West Sussex PO20 6NR England

PROFESSIONALLY MADE keyboards for Harpsichord etc. from £29/Octave Jacks from 60p. each. William Groom. Telephone (0873) 831117.　　　　　　　　　　　　　　O

MAKE YOUR OWN CLAVICHORD full size plans and instruction manual. SAE for details to: Early Keyboard Instruments, Morley Farm, Brancepeth, Durham DH7 8DS.　　T/C

BUILD YOUR OWN HARPSICHORD
from a kit by Frank Hubbard.
All materials provided including comprehensive instruction manual and full scale drawing. Choose from spinets, virginals, harpsichords and forte-pianos. Free colour catalogue and price list on request.
Donald Mackinnon and Mimi Waitzman, 11 Sprowston Road, Forest Gate, London E7 9AD. Tel: 01-519 1170.

TONEWOOD CATALOGUE
If you make, repair or restore any stringed instrument you will find our new free catalogue invaluable. We hold large stocks of selected materials for:

VIOLIN, VIOLA, 'CELLO, BASS, LUTE, GUITAR, BAROQUE VIOLS, ETC.
Callers welcome or return of post mail order service available. Open 10am - 4pm Tues/Sat.

A. HIGHFIELD & CO, Rosewood House, Bridge Road, Downham Market, Norfolk PE38 0AE.
Tel: Downham Mkt. 2614.

WOODWORKER SHOW
Royal Horticultural Society's New Hall, London SW1.
19-24 October '82 inclusive

MUSICAL INSTRUMENT
Makers and Repairer's supplies
Largest selection of tonewoods, parts and tools in the country. Callers or mail order welcome. Also Ebony offcuts, assorted sizes.
TOUCHSTONE TONEWOODS LTD.,
27 Lesbourne Rd., Reigate, Surrey RH2 7JS

HARPSICHORD KITS
Unique new basic kit enables you to build a good harpsichord first time at half the price of a full kit.
SAE for details: D. H. Bolton, Harpsichord Maker, 17 The Crescent, Linthorpe, Middlesbrough, Cleveland TS5 6SG.

HARPS
Celtic Harp, Clarsach, Knee harp, Gothic Harp, Miniature Harp. Full size detailed plans and instruction sheets for the above Harps as well as the complete range of hardware, gut and brass strings and tonewood for their construction. They are also available as complete kits. Also available: complete kits for Bowed Psalteries, Appalachian and Hammered Dulcimers.
For full, illustrated details and price list please send a stamped addressed envelope to:
Michael Saunders (Luthier)
1 Waterloo Cottages, Letton, Hereford HR3 6DN
Tel: Eardisley 352

Materials for the
Amateur and Professional
VIOLIN & GUITAR MAKER

Send S.A.E. 16p
plus 50p for either cat.
50p deductible
from purchase £5.00 or over

SYDNEY EVANS LTD.
45 Regent Place,
Birmingham, B1 3BN
Tel: (021) 233-1741

Telephone Valerie Tester (0442) 41221 Ext 262 for further information regarding advertising in these columns.

Classified Advertisements

From:

....

....

....

I enclose remittance value......................to cover ....

Insertions under the heading:

WORKSHOP EQUIPMENT	☐	BOOKS & PUBLICATIONS	☐
COURSES	☐	PLANS	☐
CRAFT/ANTIQUE/SECOND-		MATERIALS	☐
HAND TOOLS	☐	FOR SALE	☐
WANTED	☐	SERVICES	☐
MUSICAL INSTRUMENTS	☐	WOOD SUPPLIERS	☐

To: Valerie Tester
WOODWORKER

CLASSIFIED ADVERTISEMENT DEPT.
PO BOX 35, BRIDGE STREET,
HEMEL HEMPSTEAD, HERTS HP1 1EE

★ Lineage rate 20p per word. Minimum charge £3.00
★ Semi display single column cm = £4.00 (Minimum £10.00)
★ Box numbers £1.25 extra

Name and address if to appear must be paid for

◖BLOCK CAPITALS PLEASE◗

Prices quoted are those prevailing at press date and are subject to alteration due to economic conditions.

Woodworker

THE MAGAZINE FOR THE CRAFTSMAN

JULY 1982 Vol. 86 No. 1064 ISSN 0043 776X

Front cover: Ralph Fellows, subject of this month's profile of a craftsman pp 457, 458 at his workbench.

Editor	Chris Dunn
Deputy Editor	Polly Curds
Advertisement Manager	Glyn Crole-Rees
Advertisement Director ⎱ MAP Leisure	Michael Merrifield
Managing Director ⎰ Division	Gavin Doyle

MEMBER OF THE AUDIT
BUREAU OF CIRCULATIONS

SUBSCRIPTION DEPARTMENT: Remittances to MODEL AND ALLIED PUBLICATIONS, PO Box 35, Hemel Hempstead, Herts HP1 1EE. Price per copy 95p includes p&p. Subscription queries: Tel: Hemel Hempstead 51740. Subscription rate, including index, £11.90 per annum; overseas sterling £12.90; $29.00 US for overseas dollar subscribers. Second class postage paid in US at New York, New York. *Distribution* to North American hobby and craft stores, museums and bookshops by Bill Dean Books Ltd, 166-41 Powells Cove Boulevard, Post Office Box 69, Whitestone, New York 11357, USA. Tel: 1-212-767-6632. *Distribution* to news stand sales by Eastern News Distribution Inc, 111 Eight Avenue, New York, NY10011, USA Tel: 1-212-255-5620. (POSTMASTER: Send address changes to England).

WOODWORKER is printed in Great Britain by H. E. Warne Ltd, East Hill, St Austell, Cornwall PL25 4TN for the proprietor and publisher Model & Allied Publications Ltd (a member of the Argus Press Group). Trade sales by Argus Press Sales & Distribution Ltd, 12-18 Paul Street, London EC2A 4JS. WOODWORKER (ISSN 0043-776X) is published on the 3rd Friday of the month.

Model & Allied Publications Ltd

PO Box 35, Bridge Street, Hemel Hempstead, Herts HP1 1EE. Telephone: Hemel Hempstead (0442) 41221.

What...no woodworkers?

I was disappointed – and most surprised – to learn from the organisers of the Festival of India, which is currently raging all about us, that among the 12 demonstrating Indian craftsmen of various disciplines now working their way round Britain as part of the festival, there is not a single woodworker.

Readers who managed to stay the course with the editorial I wrote in the May issue will recall perhaps that I alluded to a personal affection for Indian furniture, having been swaddled as a babe in a magnificent rosewood cot and having lived thereafter in the company of Indian-made furniture and artefacts gathered by my colonial forebears. So the omission of woodwork in its own right from the Festival of India seems to me a particularly glaring one.

However, where the festival organisers have left a gap, *Woodworker* is going to oblige with its own contribution to this celebration of all things Indian. At this very moment my correspondent in India, Mr K. P. Uthappa, is scouring that continent on *Woodworker's* behalf in search of the finest craftsmen, while I have been gathering examples of Indian furniture and cabinet work on the home front. Also, a nice bloke called Bob Martin, who has a keen interest in contemporary Indian artefacts (and who will have become my brother-in-law by the time you read this) has promised *Woodworker* free access to the collection he gathered during his days as a bus-driver on the now legendary overland trail to India.

If any readers have outstanding examples of Indian woodcraft that they would like to share, please do let us know about it, preferably with a photograph alongside.

If the Festival of India won't do it for us, let us do it ourselves.

□   □   □

In this issue you will read about Ralph Fellows, who has scored such notable successes at recent Woodworker Shows. Ralph is aiming to take the overall woodturning award at this year's show, having already taken top honours in recent years in the cabinetmaking, carving and clock sections.

I hope that news of a threat of conquest by this aimiable Midlander at Show 82 will help to elevate yet further the standards in the turning section, and I hope also that it will serve to remind intending competitors in all classes that it is already time to start thinking about entries. You know how each summer passes more swiftly than the one before? Don't be caught out by tempus fugiting, will you.

Chris Dunn

July notes

Prizewinners

Sutton Coldfield town hall was the venue for the recent presentation of medals to the winners in the national craft competition 'Skill-Build' organised by the National Joint Council for the Building Industry. First prize in the carpentry section was awarded to 20 year old Timothy Sansome of Hinckley, who is employed by F. E. Downes Ltd and attends Hinckley College of Further Education. Second place went to Timothy Hancock (Slough Borough Council and Langley College of Further Education) and third prize to Ramon Dias (Taylor Woodrow Construction and Willesden College of Technology).

Joinery section winners were: first Quintin Pearmine who is 17 years old and employed by J.C.M. Shopfitters Ltd and attends the Isle of Wight College of Arts and Technology, second place went to Ian Gardner (Lancaster & Morecambe College of Further Education) and third to Neil Lewis of Barnwood Joinery Ltd and Gloucestershire College of Arts and Technology.

All the winners received vouchers from Magnet & Southerns who are one of the major sponsors of the competition. Congratulations all round.

Pips and Cops

New methods mean greater efficiency, more cost effectiveness and better quality control

say Jaydee of High Wycombe, who are now marketing the Plan-It system which operates with a micro-computer to (they say) provide an inexpensive approach to production planning for the furniture industry. Time savings are reported on batch determination and best possible material utilisation can be achieved in cutting boards and rails to required sizes. Hard or/and software can be supplied from Jaydee at Copyground Lane, High Wycombe. Contact Heinz Baron on (0494) 28697.

The go-anywhere bench

Hyett Adams have recently announced a potentially useful tool for use in the field or workshop. Called the Convertabench, it is a sturdy but lightweight bench which converts to a saw bench with the addition of a chainsaw.

It has a metal framework, with collapsible legs for transportation and is independent of any power source. When folded it measures 35in × 21in × 9in and it takes most chainsaws over 60cc with automatic oiling.

The Convertabench takes logs up to a 12in. diameter and enables timber to be converted into planks, fencing boards, posts and slabs on site anywhere. It is available from Hyett Adams at £169.00 plus VAT. The company's address is Oldends Lane, Stonehouse, Glos GL10 3SY.

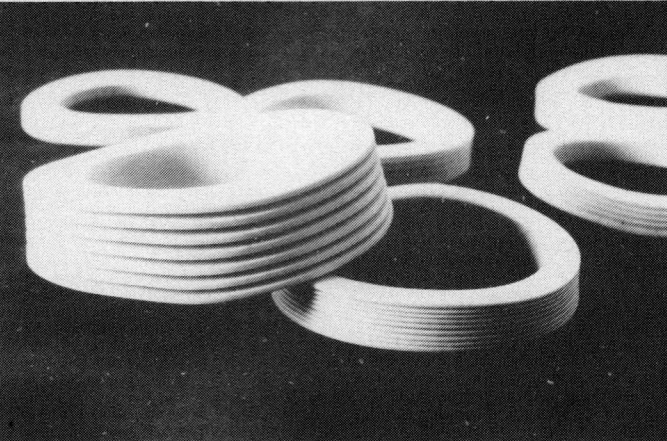

● *Bracelets turned from solid, unseasoned holly. The grooves are cut in with a thin parting-off tool; they add visual detail and allow the wood to dry out quickly and evenly without splitting. Maker Jim Partridge of Sutton Mandeville says they 'warp to a wrist shaped oval'.*

Still in the doldrums

According to the BWF the woodworking manufacturing industry is still in the doldrums but should improve during the year. Only one in seven firms were operating at full capacity at the start of the year, blamed on the weather (!), the economy and competition. One favourable sign is the report of increased export enquiries and a continued rise in demand is being shown for timber frame housing. So someone is happy.

Prison Industries have reported a reduction in levels of door production: down to 900 per week for hardwood external doors, and a cessation of production of softwood doors in

response to a request from BWF. The Home Office stress the revised plan represents a reduction in door manufacturing larger than the one-third drop in the market over the last decade.

Mail order catalogue

Catalogues arrive with clockwork regularity on the editorial desk but occasionally one can offer something just that little bit extra or unusual which catches the eye. The 1982 mail order catalogue from Leonard Ball of Lutterworth, Leics, caught my eye for just that reason. Here is a catalogue that spells out to potential customers a few facts about mail order... did you know that the GPO parcel length limit is 36in? Parcels of mouldings are therefore too long and must travel by Roadline (a minimum of £7.50) or they can be cut to stated lengths under the 36in limit (reasonable charge for this service 50p).

Leonard Ball offer a special service... they will attempt to make, repair, or supply any part, decoration or fitting. A real help to those antique dealers or clock makers restoring or refitting clocks without the facilities or know how to attempt perhaps one part of the restoration.

Some of the services and supplies which they offer include: frets for any type of clock, wood turning to order, dial painting and resilvering, lacquered case restoration, inlays from stock, a wide range of brass screws, panel pins, polishes and stains, veneers and adhesives.

Catalogue costs 50p (refunded with first order) from the company at 44 Market Street, Lutterworth.

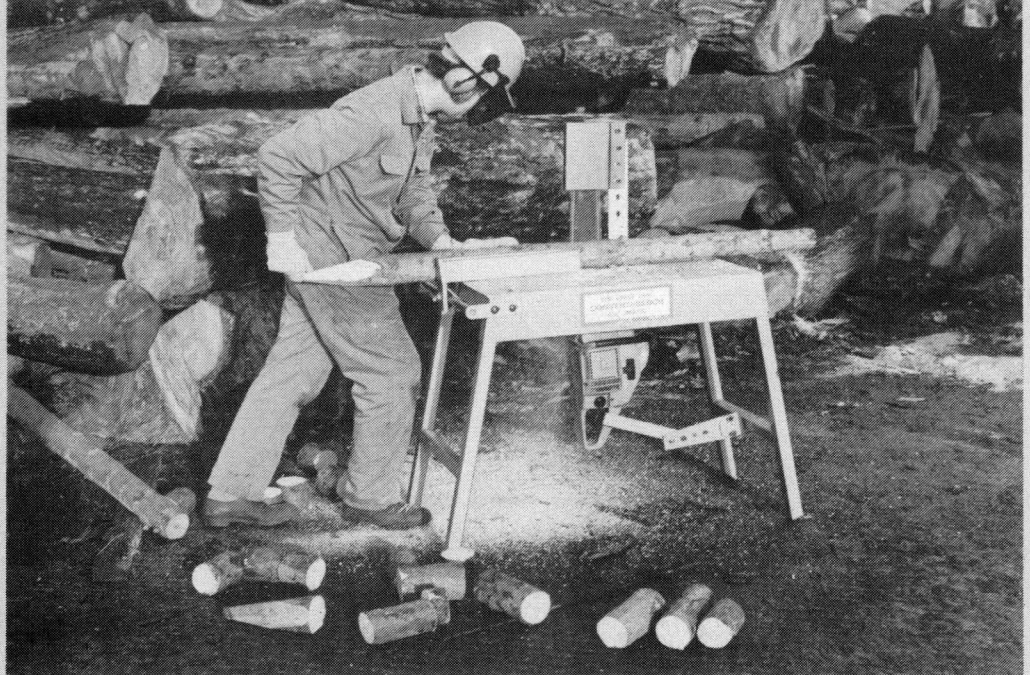

● *Using the universal Convertabench. See 'the go-anywhere bench'*

Around the world

Byrom International Corp of Chardon, Ohio 44024, have introduced a line of small hand tools from Holland. These include the Combi 4 razor blade plane capable of planing both concave and convex surfaces and trimming into tight butt corners with three individual blade locations.

To complement the plane there is also available a David Fixer... a low profile fast wedge action vice to accommodate any length of board.

Also from Byrom come Tiny-tools, precision engineered, light weight power tools in the German tradition. These miniature size power tools include a variety of variable speed electric drills, router, sander, lathe and assemblies. Table saw and variety of attachments give each tool maximum versatility. Suitable for miniature dolls house and furniture builders, model makers and power wood-carvers.

Fifty years in April

The Ashford (Kent) based firm of Emmerich (Berlon) Ltd, celebrated its 50th anniversary in April. During this half century most school boys will not have appreciated that they were working on Emmerich benches but the UK education market has been one of the firm's biggest customers over this period. The company also supply the famous range of Harris looms, and under the Emir brand name market mitre boxes, mallets, marking gauges and builders' floats.

Macpherson's combination

Designed for use in limited space or as a stand-by machine Macpherson Components Ltd, of Barking, Essex, have produced the Sicar model 250 combination machine. It serves as a planer, thicknesser, mortiser, spindle moulder and circular saw and is also provided with a tenoning table.

Socket paring chisels

Ash handles and Sheffield steel combine in the bevel edged socket paring chisels that Roger's of Hitchin have added to their comprehensive range of hand tools. Available in seven sizes between ¼in and 1½in and priced from £10.89 inc VAT from Roger's, 47 Walsworth Road, Hitchin.

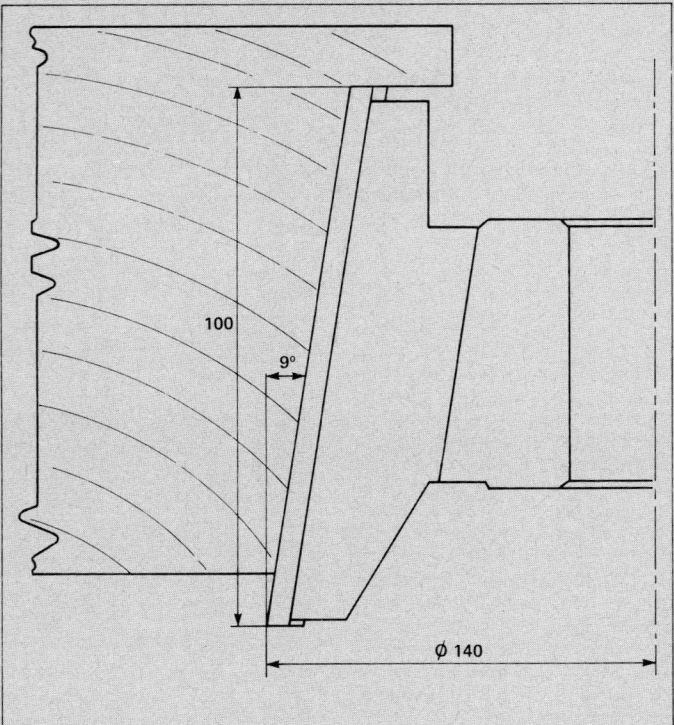

● *Line drawing showing the profile and principal dimensions of the Leitz bevel cutter for external sill sections. See 'bevel'*

Boom in the gloom

It is not all gloom and bad news on the industrial front. Boulton and Paul of Norwich, who claim to be Europe's largest manufacturers of standard joinery products, are busy enough to have felt the need to appoint a joinery export manager for the first time. This move is in response to considerable overseas interest in the company's Flowline kitchen units, currently being produced by their £3.5m factory at Maldon in Essex.

The man in the hot seat is to be Jim Wakefield, whose brief will also cover exports of B and P's other products, including flush doors, windows and stairs.

New drill from AEG

AEG have just launched the latest in their range of New Generation percussion drills.

Called the SBE-401 RL, it is a reversible hammer drill which they have packaged up as an introductory offer with three drill bits, a universal screwdriver bit, a box of fixings and screws, plus a dust collector.

It features right and left revolutions, smooth electronic speed control and a fast change-over from normal drilling to hammer drilling. The price of the introductory package is £54.75 including VAT.

Bevel

Monninger of London announce that they can now supply a special purpose bevel cutter made by Leitz of W Germany.

It is designed for cutting external window sill sections in hard or softwoods, intended for use in conjunction with standard spindle moulding machines. The three-blade cutter (ref MON267) has a bevel profile of diameter 140mm, height 100mm and a 9° angle of taper.

Full details from C. D. Monninger Ltd, Overbury Road, London N15 6RJ.

Saw point

Stanley have a new 22in fleam tooth saw on the market. With 8 points to the inch and precision ground teeth on a Swedish steel blade, it is suitable for use on plastics as well as all types of wood and composite boards. The retail price, including VAT, is £7.40.

More July notes over

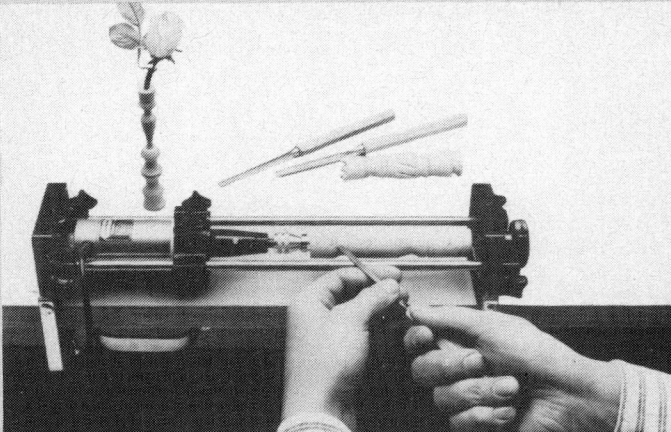

● *Miniature power tools from Byrom. See 'around the world'*

● *Combi 4-razor blade plane. See 'around the world'*

July notes

Keep young and beautiful...

One of the latest in a range of timber care products from Rentokil their Clear Water Repellent contains a transparent pigment that they claim prevents timber fading in sunlight. Unlike polyurethanes and yacht varnishes it does not form a surface film and therefore should not crack or flake. Two coats are claimed to be sufficient for new timbers. Care is limited to the occasional wash down in soapy water and the application of a new coat. A 500ml can is sufficient for a new hardwood door; five litre cans are also available.

Colour leaflets

One of the constant battles when buying machinery is the seeming lack of literature telling the intending buyer exactly what the machine is capable of and giving dimensions that will ensure that when he gets it home, it will fit the available space. Multico of Redhill, Surrey, have recently introduced three woodworking machines: surface planer, circular saw and thicknesser all backed with full colour leaflets.

The front of each leaflet sets out the principal features of the machine while the reverse is used to illustrate operating procedures. Technical specifications are also given, front and side elevation line drawings provide all necessary dimensions and show the location of fixing holes.

Where are they?

The latest newsletter from the Model Horse Drawn Vehicles Club has an interesting section on 'Where to see vehicles'. We are often asked to supply details of the correct livery of vehicles (eg the Lord Mayor's coach) and it is always good to know where to find the original. As John Pearce says the Museum of London is well worth a visit, as are the Country Life Museum, Sandy Bay, Exmouth, Devon (open 1 May-27 September daily at 10.30am) and the Museum of Lincolnshire Life, Burton Road, Lincoln.

'Wet ice on wet ice'

Polytetrafluoroethylene. Try saying that with a mouthful of mashed potato! No wonder it is more usually referred to as PTFE. Plumbers know this material well as a clean modern alternative to the old hemp and paste compound for sealing pipe joints, but it has recently found a new role as a clean modern alternative to candle wax in the furniture trade.

For PTFE is the only known material whose co-efficient of friction actually decreases with increasing pressure between two surfaces. In fact its frictional properties are such that when PTFE slides on PTFE the movement has been likened to 'wet ice on wet ice'.

Apply these properties to the action of drawers, or any other working parts used in furniture, and you will begin to see the possibilities. Fluorocarbon Ltd of Manchester have developed the possibilities of PTFE tape, by nature a glue resisting material, by etching one side of the tape to take a pressure-sensitive silicone adhesive, and it is now being taken up by furniture manufacturers.

The company's self-adhesive PTFE tape is available in widths up to a metre, and if you want to know more the address is Fluorocarbon Sheet and Tape Division, Unit 5, Lyons Motorway Estate, Stretford, Manchester.

Frame jointing

The Fairmitre system of jointing timber window frames is described as 'a new and simpler way... heart of the system is a patented plug which secures a mitre joint with powerful adhesive.'

The system comprises power saws for cutting the mitres, a computer-controlled router which cuts the profile apertures to receive the plugs and a power cramp to insert the adhesive-covered plugs.

It is available in one complete package deal. All the necessary equipment, an initial stock of pre-moulded, treated timber, a training programme plus a licence to produce the frames. Fairmitre will service the equipment and supply the materials.

The machines used are all single-phase and can be connected to 13A socket outlets. The pre-moulded material is given as U/S quality Scandinavian redwood, kiln-dried, preservative treated and finished with one coat of base coat primer. Also available are the same mouldings in a dark red mahogany-type timber, kiln-dried to 12% m.c. Mouldings are delivered in foil-wrapped bundles either 3.6, 3.9 or 4.2m lengths.

Details of the system are available from Fairmitre Joinery Systems, Howley, Warrington, Cheshire (0925 32214). The equipment has been developed from the T120 clamping unit by Charnwood division of Cooks Export Services Ltd, Unit 3A, Mill Lane Industrial Estate, Glenfield, Leicester (0533 878534) (WOODWORKER for April 1981 p258).

● *Some of the wide range of hardwood beads, mouldings and strip wood available from H. Burbridge of Oswestry. See 'more mouldings'*

● *PTFE tape applied to swivel-top table. See 'wet ice on dry ice'*

More mouldings

Anyone who has searched high and low for sources of good hardwood mouldings will find it surprising that we British woodworkers apparently buy around £40 million-worth of the stuff each year.

Where we manage to get it from is a bit of a mystery, since anyone will tell you that shops who provide a comprehensive range of hardwood mouldings are few and far between.

But this impressive sales figure has prompted H. Burbridge and Son Ltd of Oswestry to get into this market in a big way. Now, in conjunction with the Dutch firm Jéwé, they are offering what they describe as 'the most comprehensive and decorative range of mouldings yet seen in the UK'.

Their stock of 107 different items comes from Europe, and includes mahogany, red cedar, American oak and ramin.

Details from the company at Whittington Road, Oswestry, Salop SY11 1HZ.

Moisture meter

From the US come details of the Triton 1000 digital moisture meter referred to as model P5. It is said to be suitable for testing samples up to 3in. thick and has hardened steel probes giving a penetration up to 1½in. Other probes are available for use on thinner stock.

● *Minor plus. See 'timber wet…'*

Valley Products & Design Inc, RT418, PO Box 396, Milford Pa 18337, USA, states that a single adjustment allows the user full control over instrument calibration and the digital display registers m.c. readings over a range of less than 5% to over 80%. An integral light will illuminate the meter when it is used in dark areas. Jumpy readings in the low m.c. range are virtually eliminated, adds Valley Products.

Timber dry… timber wet

Timber moisture meters designed to measure up to the higher moisture content values have been released by Cubbage-Bollmann. Two models are available, a pocket-sized unit (moisture content range 4-60%m.c.) and a larger model (moisture content range 4-120%m.c.) Both have liquid crystal digital display and in-built temperature compensation. They come complete with Ramin electrodes for taking surface or deep probe readings.

Kiln Remote Read-out Packs are also available which use up to five electrode probes inserted directly into the timber stack during the drying cycle and save the time and effort of removing and weighing samples. For leaflets detailing these products phone High Wycombe 41368.

From Ebac, the company who manufacture a range of timber dryers, comes news of a series of small scale timber drying machines designed for the cabinet maker and joiner. To supplement their range the LD82 has been developed, amongst other improvements this machine incorporates a small heater to assist the drying process during the colder months and to increase efficiency. A new control system which features a chamber temperature display is supplied with the LD82 giving the operator complete control of the drying process, and yet remains simple to operate. Other new features include a powerful fan to promote even drying, and a slim shape which takes up little room inside the drying chamber.

The LD82 is intended for the user requiring between 10 and 200 cubic feet of timber, dried sufficiently to be used for furniture in centrally heated homes.

The same control system is now supplied with the Minor timber dryer which also features a heating facility, this machine is suitable for drying between 120 and 600 cubic feet of wood per load. It has been designed for the medium sized furniture making company, or the timber yard that needs a facility to dry wood to the exacting standards demanded by their customers.

Further details on the Ebac products phone (0388) 605061.

Flatpack furniture

Furniture for self-assembly is offered by Artisan Solid Wood Products, 321 Fulham Road, London SW10 9QL (01-351 5441). Pieces are a desk; TV cabinet; refectory tables in 4ft and 5ft 6in. lengths; lamp table; coffee table. The refectory tables are in oak but the other pieces come in either mahogany or cherry, though the TV cabinet is available in oak as well.

All pieces can be had in kit form or assembled ready for finishing. The desk is described as Regency style and the TV cabinet period style; the refectory table is traditional and the coffee and lamp tables contemporary.

Timber is American white and red oak and cherry. A finishing kit is available as an optional extra. All pieces can be supplied assembled and completely finished as well as in kit form or assembled ready for finishing.

Artisan also offers solid wood kitchen cabinet doors and drawer fronts in white and red oak and cherry. Styles are in a choice of period or contemporary.

● *Triton 1000 moisture meter model P5 eliminates jumpy readings. See 'moisture meter'*

Wood machining

EMCO Rex 2000 comprises a 10in. and 6in. planer/thicknesser operated by 2.5hp motor single-phase, though three-phase is available, to take accessories that include 3.5in. depth of cut circular saw, spindle moulder and slot mortiser. It can be supplied as a complete machine centre though the accessories can be purchased as and when required.

This, states distributor EME Ltd, makes it a useful equipment for industry or the home workshop. It is a totally new concept: space-saving, easy to operate, versatile. The machine has a large work capacity. With it the operative can surface plane, thickness, saw, flute, dovetail, mould, sand, drill, mortise and comb.

Illustrated leaflet giving full information is available from EME at B.E.C. House, Victoria Road, London NW10 6NY (01-965 4050).

● *Range of meters and electrodes available from Cubbage-Bollmann. See 'timber dry…'*

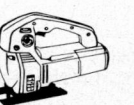
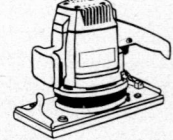

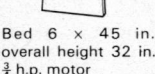

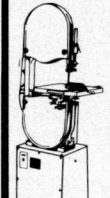

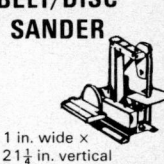
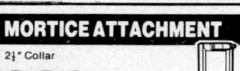

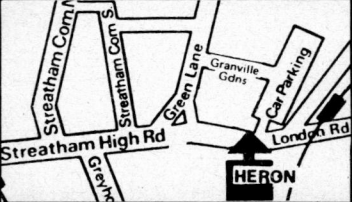
446

Prices quoted are those prevailing at press date and are subject to alteration due to economic conditions.

'Kity' Quality Machines For Craftsmen

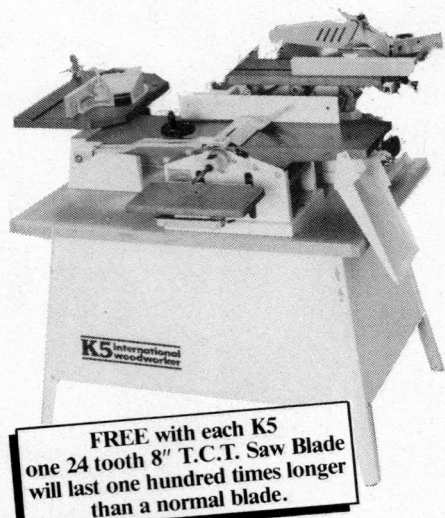

K5 international woodworker

FREE with each K5 one 24 tooth 8″ T.C.T. Saw Blade will last one hundred times longer than a normal blade.

Your craft depends on the skill of your hands, together with the quality of your tools.

The results you achieve reflect the care you have taken to choose the raw materials, the thought you have put into your design. As a true craftsman, every purchase for your workshop will have been chosen with consideration and care, attention paid to the quality of construction and value for money. When you purchase machinery these standards are important and must not be compromised.

Value for Money
At Kity we understand the needs of the craftsman, in consequence, we produce a range of machines unique in their versatility, adequate in capacity and manufactured to a very high standard. Machines which are unconditionally guaranteed and are excellent value for money.

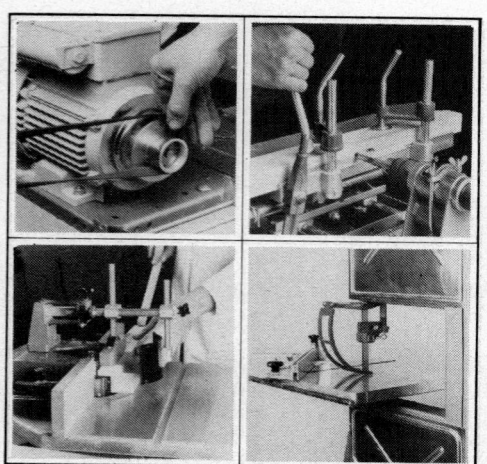

Simple and Easy to use
All Kity machines are of cast construction with sealed bearings, dynamically balanced rotating blocks and precision machined components. You will expect to achieve a high standard of workmanship with Kity. Moreover, with the unique Kity combinations your existing working methods do not need to be changed, unlike other combinations you can use Kity machinery exactly as you would use hand tools.

The K5 Combination
Specifically designed for the craftsman who requires the quality of the 700 series without the capacity, ideal for most household projects including fitted kitchens and wardrobes, boat building, replacement windows and doors, architrave and skirting boards. A versatile unit at a very attractive price: **£559.00 + V.A.T.**

Buy direct from Kity U.K. and use a K5 for 30 days, if you are not entirely satisfied for whatever reason, we will refund your total costs.

The K5 Consists Of:
512 Saw	2″ depth of cut, rise and fall, two speeds, mitre guide and rip fence.
535 Planer	6″ wide, 30″ bed, 6″ × 4″ thicknesser, single speed.
511 Spindle Moulder	¾″ × ¾″ rebate, 2″ rise and fall.
550 Slot Mortiser	3″ depth, 5″ wide, 4″ rise and fall.
500 Work Bench with 1hp motor and drive.	

The 700 Series
Each machine is available independently, just add a stand and motor, or you can make up your own combination by fitting the machines of your choice around a motor on a 700 stand.

617 Saw	3″ depth of cut, rise and fall, two speeds, mitre guide, rip fence.
612 Bandsaw	5¾″ depth, 11½″ throat, steel construction.
636 Planer	10″ wide, 40″ bed, 10″ × 6″ two speed thicknesser.

635 Planer	8″ wide, 40″ bed, 8″ × 6″ two speed thicknesser.
535 Planer	6″ wide, 30″ bed, 6″ × 4″ one speed thicknesser.
627 Spindle Moulder	1¼″ × 1¼″ rebate, 2½″ rise and fall.
652 Slot Mortiser	4″ depth, 6″ wide, 6″ rise and fall.

Plus a wide range of accessories, including 6″ Belt Sander, 4″ Disc Sander, 3″ Drum Sander, Planer Knife Sharpener.

KITY
UNITED KINGDOM

Now in Australia and South Africa. Please write for details.

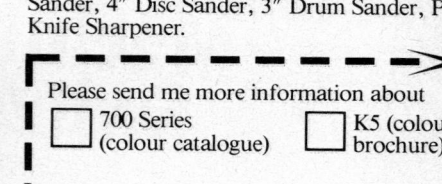

Please send me more information about
☐ 700 Series (colour catalogue)   ☐ K5 (colour brochure)

NAME _____

ADDRESS _____

_____

W

Kity U.K., Sizer's Court, Henshaw Lane, Yeadon, Leeds LS19 7DP. Tel: (0532) 509110. Telex: 55792

Prices quoted are those prevailing at press date and are subject to alteration due to economic conditions.

We have still more problems.

TECNOFOREST '82

2nd International Fair
and Technical Consultation for the forestry and woodworking industry

BACKGROUND:

TECNOFOREST '79, the first event of its kind, was held in Lima in November 1979. The ten day exhibition, combined with the Technical Consultation, permitted a concentrated Latin American market to choose the most effective technological alternatives for present and/or future needs.

At the Technical Consultation, the Latin American industry presented 764 technical problems. 726 solutions (now published in the "Book of Solutions") were given by international experts, who demonstrated the advantages of their technology both theoretically (at the Round Tables) and practically (at the Fair).

A request to repeat the success was immediately presented by the participants, which is the reason why TECNOFOREST '82 is now announced.

TECNOFOREST '82:

Both the Fair and the Technical Consultation will be held within the precincts of the PACIFIC INTERNATIONAL TRADE FAIR, organising entity of these two events.

The Fair will be held from 19 to 28 November 1982. The Technical Consultation from 20 to 23 November 1982.

The Technical Consultation is based on a five-month pre-survey. Fifteen hundred forestry and woodworking industries in Argentina, Brazil, Central America, Colombia, Chile, Ecuador, Mexico, Paraguay, Peru and Venezuela have been visited by a group of experts, identifying and compiling a list of present technical problems faced by each industry.

The result of the pre-survey has been screened and arranged under the corresponding "Round Table Discussion Topics" and published in book form ("Book of Problems"), which is distributed in two phases:

1) Worldwide to "solution givers" such as machinery manufacturers, consultants, technological institutions, associations, etc. with an invitation to give their possible solutions to the Latin American Industry that will be present at the Technical Consultation.

2) In Latin America to all industrialists that might feel themselves identified with the problems, with an invitation to meet with the world's experts who have or belive they have the best solutions.

The "Book of Problems" for TECNOFOREST '82 is being prepared in English and Spanish and is available at no cost from the PACIFIC INTERNATIONAL TRADE FAIR in Lima.

Sponsored by the Peruvian Government, international organisations, and the governments of the Federal Republic of Germany and the Netherlands, the high-level performance of TECNOFOREST '82 is assured. International experts will act as moderators for each Round Table, keeping the sessions strictly technical. Those who have or believe they have some solutions will be allowed a five-minute speech for each problem. Competition will be strong.

An extract of all presented solutions will later be published in the "Book of Solutions", representing the final document of the event.

THE ORGANISER:

The PACIFIC INTERNATIONAL TRADE FAIR is the organiser of the dual event TECNOFOREST '82 as it was in 1979. During its 22 years of activity, it has held a large number of general and specialised trade fairs, shows, exhibitions, congresses and technical consultations.

It has at its disposal 35 permanent pavillons in 240,000 sq.mts. precincts. Situated in Lima, Peru, the geographical and logical center of the Andean Group countries, it is also considered the most important fair organisation in Latin America.

The PACIFIC INTERNATIONAL TRADE FAIR invites interested solution givers, as well as those who are interested in finding solutions to their problems, to TECNOFOREST '82.

Welcome to Lima! Welcome to TECNOFOREST '82!

Pacific International Trade Fair
P.O. Box 4900
Lima 100, Perú
Phone: 52-8140
Telex: 25504PE FERIA

TECNOFOREST '82
Pacific International Trade Fair
P.O. Box 4900, Lima 100, Peru
Please send me the "Book of Problems"

TECHNICAL CONSULTATION (Nov. 20-23)
I am interested in attending ☐
the following Round Table (s):

A   Reforestation and Forest Management ☐
B   Harvesting and Transport ☐
C   Saw Milling and related activities ☐
D   Veneer and Wood Panels ☐
E   Wooden Houses ☐
F   Furniture ☐
G   Marketing of Forest Products ☐

SPECIALISED FAIR (Nov. 19-28)
I am interested in exhibiting ☐

Name: _____

Title: _____

Organization: _____

_____

Address: _____

_____

City: _____   Country: _____

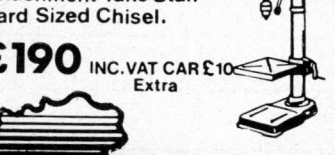

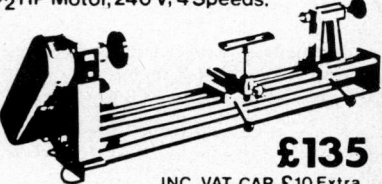

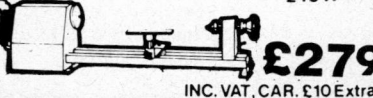
Prices quoted are those prevailing at press date and are subject to alteration due to economic conditions.

452

Prices quoted are those prevailing at press date and are subject to alteration due to economic conditions.

Woodworker, July 1982

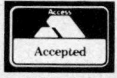

Prices quoted are those prevailing at press date and are subject to alteration due to economic conditions.

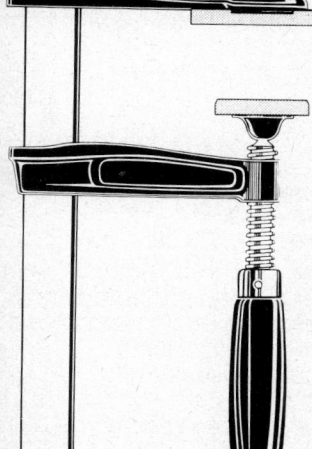

Build your own kitchen

 Polished Brass or Wood Knobs

 Concealed Hinges

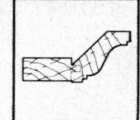 Cornice Mouldings

 Convertible Worktops

 Pull-out Ironing Tables

 Adjustable Legs

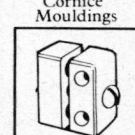 4 hole K/D Blocks

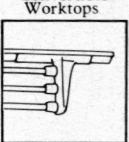 Pull-out Towel Rails

 Shelf Baskets

 Waste Bins

 Unit Carcase

 Solid Oak Doors

We supply all the components you need including doors and drawers.

Send for list of accessories and photo.

Name ....

Address ....

.... Tel: ....

Post to: P.W.S. Fittings Department, Garden Street, Darlington, Co. Durham. Tel: 0325 53511.

WOODTURNERS & WOODCARVERS

Visit our showroom in Blyth, where we welcome visitors and are open Monday to Saturday from 9.30 a.m. to 5.30 p.m. and see a demonstration of woodturning.
(or send for details)

- ARUNDEL WOODTURNING LATHES
- INCA WOODWORKING MACHINERY
- CORONET WOODWORKING MACHINES
- ASHLEY ILES TURNING & CARVING TOOLS
- NEW CHUCKS AND ACCESSORIES
- and other fine quality Tools and Accessories

The full range of these universal and independent machines on show

- WOODTURNING COURSES in fully equipped workshop with personal tuition (Details on request). Permanent Demonstration facilities

Allan McNair Woodcraft

69/71, Plessey Rd., Blyth, Northumberland.
Telephone Blyth (06706) 69279

ACCESS — BARCLAYCARD

EXAMPLES OF OUR GREAT PRICES

AEG

AEG SBE401
Hammer drill and screwdriver. The new Electronic Drill is a heavy duty reversible Hammer Drill that doubles as a screwdriver.
Free with each drill:
3 Drill bits, Universal S/D Bit
Box of fixings. Only **£49.95**

STANLEY

263 Laminate Trimmer — £75.00
The powerful Stanley 425 watt motor is specially designed for smoother running. Standard equipment includes 85288 Combination Straight and Bevel Trim Bit. Swivel Base, swivels 45° either way for trimming acute, obtuse or right angles. Bevel or flush finish.
Trims and scribes the back edge of a counter top in one operation to give a perfect fit against an irregular wall. Roller guide and fine depth adjustment assures accurate smooth following and trimming.

BOSCH

Bosch PST 55PE Orbital Action/Variable Speed Jigsaw — £66.95
Three stage orbital action blade movement, reduces blade wear, gives greater cutting performance, and superb manoeuvrability particularly on curved cuts.
Variable speed control, ideal for cutting many types of material as hard as ceramic tiles or soft as plasterboard.
Mitre cuts up to 45°, by tilting footplate, footplate can also be retracted to allow cutting right into corners.
Balanced plunger for vibration free effortless cutting, all you do is guide the jigsaw.
Complete with parallel and circle guide to assist cutting straight lines and making perfect circle cuts.
Power input: 380 watts; Maximum cutting capacities wood: 2¼″ (55mm), steel: ³⁄₁₆″ (5mm), no load stroke rate: 55-3000 per min variable.

Black & Decker Power Tools

Black & Decker DN750 – Electric Plane
A DN750 Plane, giving the combination of 75mm cutting width, 1.5mm cutting depth, and high blade speed, makes smooth work of preparing the roughest old timber or finish planing new timber. Rebates up to 20mm deep can be machined with ease and the baseplate incorporates two grooves enabling chamfers up to 4.5mm deep to be cut at a single pass. Two handles and an extra long baseplate enable a high degree of control to be achieved. **Only £36.95.**
7470 – Master Sander
A complete sanding system in itself, the 7470 can sand flat, contoured and intricate shapes such as chair legs. Can also be used with a polishing bonnet (£2.15), wire wheel brush (£5.99) or clean and strip wheel (£4.99). Features include: Two speed switch. Flapwheel (shown fitted) for intricate shapes. Cushion pad and adhesive discs for flat and gently curved surfaces. Bench mounting bracket. Only **£28.95.**

Elu Power Tools

Elu MH182 Circular Saw
Depth of cut up to 78mm (3⅛″), 1400 watt motor, fitted with TCT Blade.

Only **£69.95.**

MVS 94 ½ Sheet Sander
Powerful 350 watt motor, 24,000 orbits per minute. Complete with dust collections.

Only **£69.95.**

All prices inc. VAT, p&p £2.50 per tool. Stockists of AEG, Black & Decker, Bosch, Burgess, ELU, Kity, Makita, Metabo, Skil, Startrite, Stanley and Wolf Power Tools. Please ring for prices of tools not listed.

Home Care Centre
20 Market Street
Watford, Herts.
0923 48434

We welcome Access and Visa card, simply quote card No. by telephone or letter.

Prices quoted are those prevailing at press date and are subject to alteration due to economic conditions.

RALPH FELLOWS

● Ralph Fellows inspects an example of his turning work, a segmented wooden vase with lid

Profile of a craftsman

Though Ralph Fellows is well placed in Division One of amateur wood craftsmen, he shows little interest in turning his skills to financial gain, preferring to maintain the standards of high quality work that he believes are no longer possible in the professional sphere of woodcraft. Chris Dunn went to see him at his home in Dudley, Worcestershire, where he lives with his wife Doreen and Mick the Mongrel

■ ■ ■

If you want to see *real* craftsmanship these days, says Ralph Fellows, you have to look in the amateur home workshops. A highly contentious statement, to be sure, and there's many a professional who would argue with it, but it is indisputably true that *real* craftsmanship flourishes unbounded in Ralph's own amateur workshop.

Recognition of Ralph Fellows' extensive woodworking skills has become a regular feature of the annual Woodworker Show in London. For over the last three years he has walked away with three major titles: in 1979 his superb oak chest took first prize overall in the cabinet-making section, in 1980 he won the clocks section with his long-case clock built from reclaimed mahogany, and at last year's show he took the top award overall in the carving section with his scroll, hewn from a joined block of ash and incised with the motto 'Home Sweet Home'.

He was, he admits, surprised to have won the carving award, and even went as far as to ask the judges whether there hadn't been a mistake. The irony was that Ralph had

been making an all-out effort to take the woodturning title, but he could only manage a couple of third places in that section.

Nevertheless, the carving prize established him as the only competitor in the history of the Woodworker Show to have won the top award in three separate sections. But not content to rest on any laurels with his 'triple crown' feat, this year Ralph means to complete the 'grand slam' by taking overall first in the turning section.

At 55, Ralph Fellows has also made it to the top of the tree in his job. Starting his working life as a bricklayer, he has risen to become Chief Clerk of Works for Dudley Metropolitan Borough's Architectural Services Department. He has never had the inclination to turn to woodwork professionally, and shows a marked indifference to making money from his remarkable skills, though when he retires in about five years' time, he might take a more active interest in income.

'I do take on some commissioned work,' he told me, 'but only if I am sufficiently interested in the project.'

He accepted, for instance, a small but enormously prestigious commission which came about as a result of his success in the 1979 Woodworker Show. He was asked to carve two panels, mainly involving the incised lettering which he does so well, for the bishop's chair in Liverpool's Anglican Cathedral.

However, while Ralph Fellows doesn't look to his woodwork for any financial reward, when it comes to trophies, awards and accolades he is very much more enthusiastic. What is most important to him, it seems, is the approval and respect of his peers. He has unequivocally achieved that, for the bungalow, which he built himself in the pretty valley just outside Dudley where he has lived all his life, is chock-full of every manner of trophy, certificate, award and prize for woodwork. Even

Continued on page 458

● Ralph at work on the panel he was commissioned to carve for the bishop's chair in Liverpool's Anglican Cathedral

Profile of a craftsman –from page 457

the aquarium in the hall has been emptied of water and filled with trophies.

Ralph likes to work with reclaimed timber most of all, both because this eliminates drying problems and because old wood has that colour of history that allows good workmanship to pay homage to the continuity in the nature of things. His long-case clock was made from reclaimed mahogany that came from an old pub, and the oak for that magnificent chest was also chosen from various sources of old timber.

It's small wonder, when you look at the exquisite examples of his work to be seen around Ralph's home, that he considers pure craftsmanship to be only within the practical capacity of the amateur these days. The pressure of time on economics makes it almost impossible for a professional to apply standards of real craft to his work in the modern world, says Ralph, and he believes that the most elevated quality of workmanship now survives only in the world's garden workshops. Readers will probably have something to say about that view, and, of course, *Woodworker's* letters page is always open for your comments.

Meanwhile, Ralph is turning his thoughts and his hand to turning, in preparation for this autumn's Woodworker Show and that coveted first prize. Be warned, all you woodturners… Ralph Fellows intends to be extremely hard to beat! ■

● Lettering carved on oak proclaims the name of a house. A small commission

Secrets of an old lacebox

Sydney Reynolds finds himself beguiled by the magic of an old box he spotted in an antique shop recently

● A flurry of oyster veneering decorates the lid of the lacebox

People in Berkhamsted High Street, Herts, have been wondering how a beautifully veneered lacebox dating from the late 17th century has come to end up in an antique shop sandwiched between the local labour party office and an undertaker's.

The walnut lacebox, 21in × 15in × 5in deep, is designed in oyster-veneer — a technique using cross-sections of wood to display the grain, resembling an oyster shell, graded in increasing sizes.

Much has happened to English society since 1700 and the pages of history are torn with world wars, but the lacebox appears to have been unscathed by unsettling events. Only a rich inimitable patina bears witness to years of devotion and the effect of 'light years' on wood.

The appearance of the lacebox in the shop raises several questions. Who would conceivably part with it in the late 20th century? And for what reason? History of this type is almost irreplaceable today and surely money can never be a truly satisfactory substitute for a thing of lasting beauty. What is its provenance? What kind of person is likely to buy it at £295 and what purpose would he have in mind for it?

Mr Mike Armson, owner of the antique shop at 370 High Street, Berkhamsted, told me that the lacebox was purchased from a dealer in Northampton. He said that the sort of person interested in buying it would be a collector.

It is a curious phenomenon that in times of high inflation and unemployment the antique busines has enjoyed something of a boom. There is a philosophy attached to the love of antiques. In unsettled times, economically and socially, antiques represent lasting values in workmanship and style and, not least, in the very fact that they have clearly been cherished above all things to be passed on to succeeding generations.

Could *this* be the secret magic of the lacebox? ■

Work from the schools

It is always encouraging to see both boys and girls producing grade one work in school examinations. Here Bob Grant introduces readers to the work of some of his 16 year old pupils at Cowley St John school. Photos by John Peacock

● Above: CSE woodwork course 1981. Back left: mahogany bedside unit by Peter Shefford. Centre: bookcase by Christopher Coles. Right: bedside cabinet in pine by Simon Hornblow. Front left: table with leathercloth top by Terrence Chandler. Centre: table with smoked-glass top by Raj Garewal. Right: pine table by Clive Morgan; this piece has mahogany 'socks.'

● Examples of work by Samantha Jones who was awarded CSE grade 1, July 1981.

Cowley St John C of E upper school is a mixed comprehensive foundation within the boundaries of the city of Oxford. Its design faculty is headed by R. W. Grant DLC FRSA MSIAD who, although a busy head of department, finds time to prepare 16-year-old pupils for the southern region examinations board's certificate of secondary education (CSE) in woodworking.

Photo 1 shows a selection of pupils' project work (all were awarded a grade 1 certificate) from among some 30 pupils who were also successful in the examination for 1981. Each piece is supported by a design folio which shows the development of the project culminating in a working drawing. Candidates also have to sit a 2½hr theory paper which tests their knowledge of the technical details of the craft in order to gain a final award.

Successful candidates are encouraged to stay on and enter the VIth form of the school studying for the associated examining board's new advanced level general certificate of education (GCE) in design. They also undertake research projects.

Girls as well as boys are able to undertake workshop studies in the school. Photo 2 shows the coursework of Samantha Jones which was submitted for the CSE examination. She, too, was awarded a grade 1 certificate for her endeavours. These centred around wooden items of kitchenware incorporating techniques of lathe work (platters and rolling pin); carving (salad servers); laminating (chopping board); and pyrography (bread board). ■

FRETSAW MARQUETRY: Part 2

In positive and negative

In the first part of this article (*Woodworker* for May) Ernie Ives explained that most marquetry pictures really need a combination of knife and saw techniques. Here he considers the silhouette technique and related matters. The author's series on basic marquetry appeared in the November and December issues of 1980 and the March, June and November issues of 1981

With the silhouette technique the two veneers making up the design are cut through simultaneously and the two pieces interchanged. Often they can be made up into two separate pictures, one positive, one negative. Both are often equally attractive. Two pictures from two pieces of veneer should appeal to cost-conscious readers.

Theoretically you leave the thickness of the saw kerf around each piece. In practice this is almost invisible if a PVA glue and a press are used to lay the picture, provided care is taken to keep each piece central in its opening: pushed hard up to one end will give a double width gap at the other. Areas of small pieces are more likely to show gaps, the ratio of saw kerfs to the size of pieces being higher; and the wood may be unable to swell sufficiently to close the joins.

Preparation of the veneer pack First you must decide how large you wish the background of the design to be. The minimum

size of the veneer required is that size, plus the width of two borders, plus the width of two edges (Fig 15). Thus if the background is, say, 12 × 9in with ¾in borders and mounted on ½in chipboard, the minimum size (allowing a little for trimming) will be 13½ × 10½in.

Three pieces of this size will be needed, one of a light veneer (sycamore, aspen, birch etc); one dark (Macassar ebony, Indian rosewood or Indian laurel); and one piece of any common veneer that is not too fragile (mahogany, beech etc). They must all be exactly the same size but they can be larger than the minimum size. Macassar ebony is expensive (about £1.30/sq ft) and is usually only available as a narrow sliced veneer. However at the time of writing 13½in wide rotary-cut ebony is available from I. & R. E. Henderson of Seahouses, Northumberland.

If you decide, as I did, to have the grain of the veneers running horizontally across the

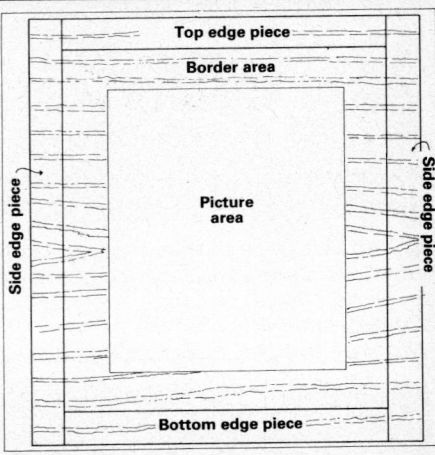

● Fig 15 Borders and edges cut from one piece

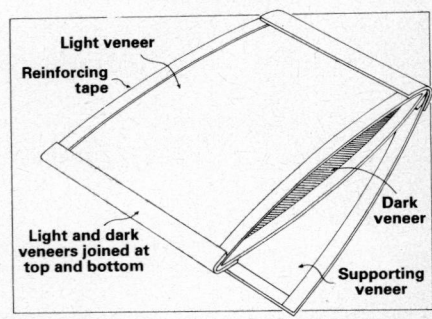

● Fig 16 Assembly of veneers before cutting

picture, reinforce the end grain with masking tape to prevent it splitting. Tape together the top and bottom edges of the two picture veneers and hinge the supporting veneer to the underside of the dark veneer with masking tape along the top edge only (Fig 16). Reinforce also the edges of the supporting veneer. The light veneer is kept on the top so that the marking out will show clearly. All marking out is done at one go and the drawing is removed.

Cutting the picture As a general rule, cut all the 'island' pieces (pieces that are surrounded by others) before the pieces that enclose them. Thus all the white pieces surrounded by black on the drawing must be cut before the black. If you do not do this the white pieces will have to be re-marked. This means that the drawing will have to be registered again to the markings and white or yellow carbon paper used to get the lines to show on the dark veneer. A lot of unnecessary work.

The cutting is normally done from the face side as the saw makes the underside slightly rougher and furry. But if all the pieces are glued in without taping you can usually choose which side to make the face side after all the cutting is completed. It is quite feasible to make a pair which are a mirror image of each other. Indeed that is what I did.

I suggest you start on the mud patches that surround the bucket. These are fairly simple and it matters little if the shape is not exactly as drawn.

Fasten the free end of the supporting veneer to the rest of the pack with a couple of paper clips or a small piece of masking tape to prevent it flapping about. Place this pack on an expanded polystyrene or cork block to give a firm, resilient pad for the needle to penetrate and pierce a hole at any point on the line where the grain of the wood runs parallel to the line.

Insert the blade (see the first article in this current series) and carefully saw round the piece. If the saw wanders from the line do not go back and try and correct it — this will leave an unsightly cut. Just carry on and work your way back to the line but it is essential that you end up in the same place as you began. Nobody will know that the shape you end up with was not the proper shape. Remember to keep the saw upright. Any sloping of the blade will mean that one piece will be larger than the other and therefore will not be interchangeable. Cut with long easy strokes. Do not try to force the pace.

When the piece has been cut release the tension on the blade and remove it from the work. Free the end of the supporting veneer again and glue the piece cut from it back in place again. It can be held with tape if necessary. This keeps a flat surface under the veneers, one which will not catch or snag on the saw table.

Slide a piece of Formica or metal sheet between the two layers of the picture and glue the white piece into the black and *vice versa*. I find it is better to apply the glue after the piece has been fitted in place, a little being put round the joint and rubbed in with the end of the knife handle. This makes the surface messy, especially on the front where the carbon from the marking-out tends to mix with the glue but this is easily removed with a round blade in the knife or a hacksaw blade ground to a similar shape.

If the glue is put round the hole first more of it gets between the two layers and can cause them to stick although the plastics sheet should prevent this. Remove the plastics sheet, tape the supporting veneer back again and cut the next piece.

Several pieces, if not too large, can be cut out at a time provided they are spaced well apart and then all glued at one go. If the wood is buckled put a weight on the piece for a few minutes until the glue has started to set and to hold. But do not leave it too long otherwise it will stick to the Formica with potentially disastrous results.

You may find it necessary to use Sellotape on some of the narrow short-grain pieces before cutting them although sawing is far less likely to break the veneers than knife cutting is. It is easy enough to position the Sellotape on the white side where the marking out is but positioning on the other side will largely be a matter of guesswork. If however other pieces have been put in around it this should not be too difficult.

The white 'island' pieces will in the first instance be glued into the lower dark layer

● *Fig 17 The cutting completed*

and then when their surrounding piece is cut, will surface again into the white top layer.

Continue cutting in this way until the picture is complete. (Fig 17).

Borders and edges You can saw an irregular shape around the picture as I did with the *Peasant* or an oval can be drawn and cut as with *Happiness in Ebony* (Fig 18). I was not pleased with the effect of the former method and there was not enough veneer for the latter. This is why I decided to have the rectangular frame but not one made by *adding* borders and edges in the usual way. In this method (Fig 15) the borders are cut from the backgrounds and interchanged. The edges are then cut from the outside of the borders which can give the appearance at first glance at least, of the picture having been inlayed into a solid block. Some may like to interchange the edges as well so that the white borders have a dark edge and *vice versa*. You can now see the reason for the earlier calculation for the size of the backgrounds.

To do this mark out both the inside and outside edges of the borders on to the light background veneer (Fig 19). Check that the marking is square and then with a knife cut along the inside line (Fig 20) being careful not to overrun the corners. Cutting Macassar ebony with a knife is hard work but ensures a straighter result than if the saw is used.

Put identification marks on the outer lines of the borders so that the edge pieces can be returned to their matching pieces later. Cut off the edge pieces and keep them safely. I

● *Fig 18 Happiness in ebony*

● *Fig 19 Mark the inside and outside edges of the borders*

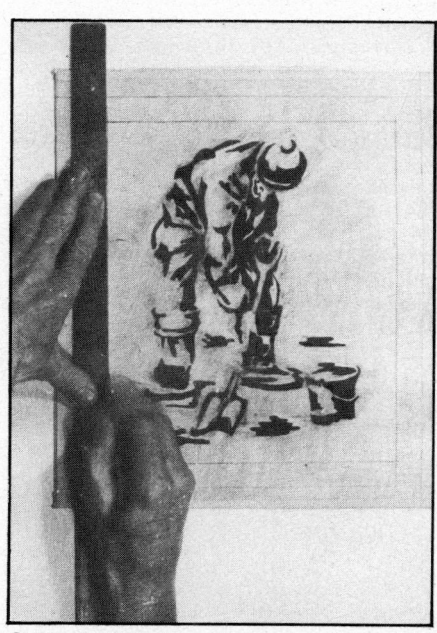

● *Fig 20 Cut along the inside line of the border*

Continued on p 462

FRETSAW MARQUETRY: Part 2

Continued from p 461

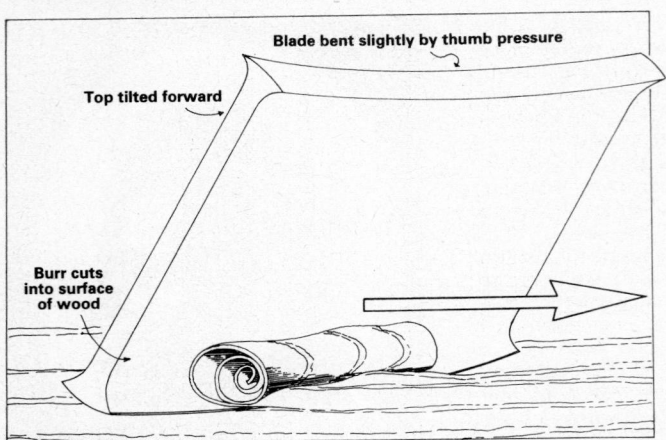

● Fig 21 Sketch of the cutting action of a cabinet scraper

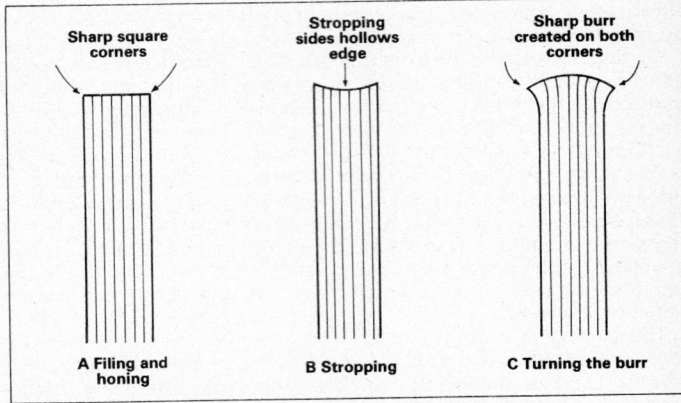

● Fig 22 Stages in sharpening a cabinet scraper

like to cut the lines that go across the grain first. Then if the veneer does split at the end nearest to you, the split is in the waste area. This splitting can be prevented by cutting through the last ½in first.

Interchange the borders with the pictures, choose which side of each you prefer and tape the borders on. Cut and prepare a baseboard and backing veneer, both slightly oversize and lay the picture. The PVA glue and press method is much the best as the moisture of the glue and the pressure will cause the veneer to swell and close the saw kerfs. When the glue has dried saw the baseboard to the size of the picture/border assembly. Plane or sand the edges and glue on the edge veneers.

If you have followed my advice about cutting across the grain first when severing the edges from the borders, the two long-grain ones will be just the length of the baseboard so put them on first. (They would be a fraction too short if they had to cover the ends of the short-grained ones as well). Keep the cut edge of the edge veneer flush with the face of the picture and line-up the grain markings so that they follow round the wood. The identification marks indicate which edge goes where.

Cleaning up the picture Some problems can arise when cleaning-up this type of picture. If it is hand sanded dust from the darker veneer can get into the pores of the lighter one and make it look muddy. Sometimes this can be overcome by using an orbital sander which to some extent blows the dust away before it gets lodged in the grain. The best way is to use a cabinet scraper. But it must be sharp. A sharp scraper should take off shavings and not produce dust. Not only will the two veneers that have been used contrast in colour, they

● Fig 23 (Right) File the edge straight

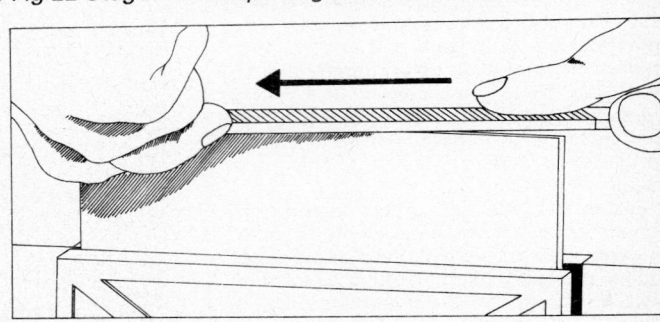

will contrast in hardness. A dull scraper will slide over one and bite into the other.

Sharpening a cabinet scraper Although the cabinet scraper is simply a rectangular piece of tool steel care should be exercised choosing a good one. Many are too thick for our purpose but I bought a good one recently from Roger's of Hitchin. This one is 0.027in thick. As a tool it is extremely simple but the sharpening is not so I have tried to illustrate each step. I have tried various textbook ways of doing this but I always fall back on the way I was taught as an apprentice. But whatever the method the scraper must be sharp enough to take off clean, fine shavings.

The scraper cuts because a sharp burr is created on the cutting edge and this acts like a plane (Fig 21). In my technique sharpening is carried out in three stages: A squaring-up the edge; B stropping to remove any remaining burrs and to burnish and stretch the edge; and C putting on the new burr (Fig 22). The sharpness is dependent on how well each stage is done.

Start by setting the scraper up in a vice and with a smooth hand or flat file, file the two long edges straight and square. Keep the file lengthways with the edge, hold it by the blade with your hands close together

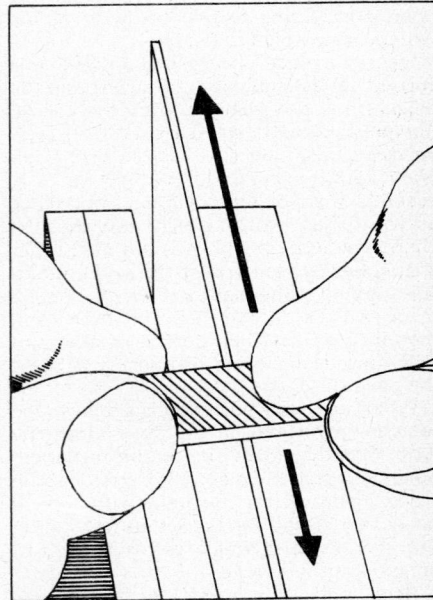

● Fig 24 Draw file edge smooth. (Keep file square to sides)

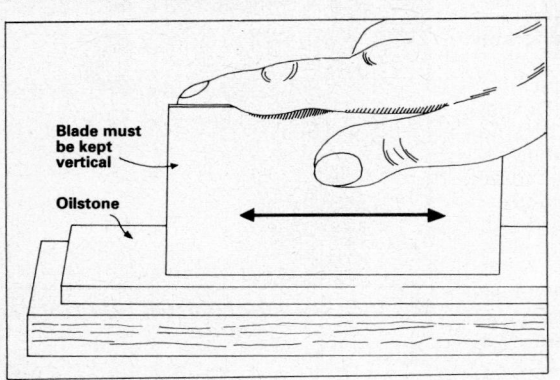

● Fig 25 (Left) Honing the edge

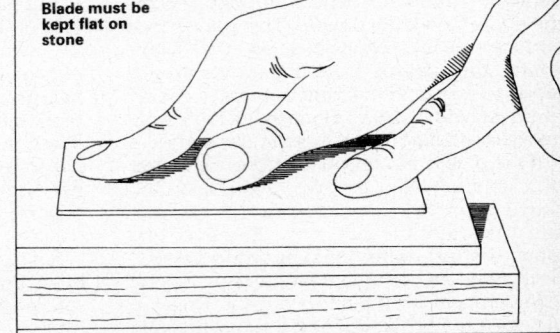

● Fig 26 (Right) Removing the burrs

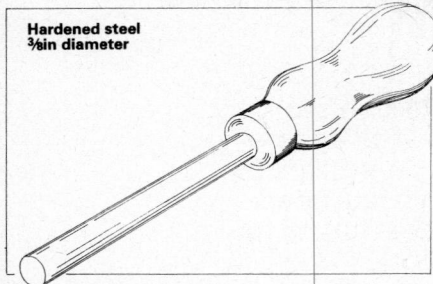

Hardened steel
⅜in diameter

● Fig 27 Ticketer

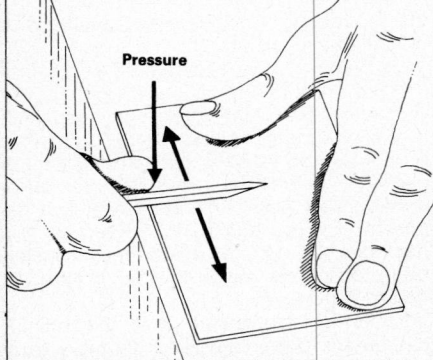

Pressure

● Fig 28 Stropping the edge

and push it to and fro sideways along the edge to draw-file the edge smooth (Fig 24). This should remove most of the file marks from the previous stage. As the keenness of the cutting edge is governed by the sharpness of the square corners at this stage, the edges should be honed on a fine oilstone, first with the scraper on edge as in Fig 25 and then on the flats (Fig 26). The four sharp corners should produce four sharp cutting edges.

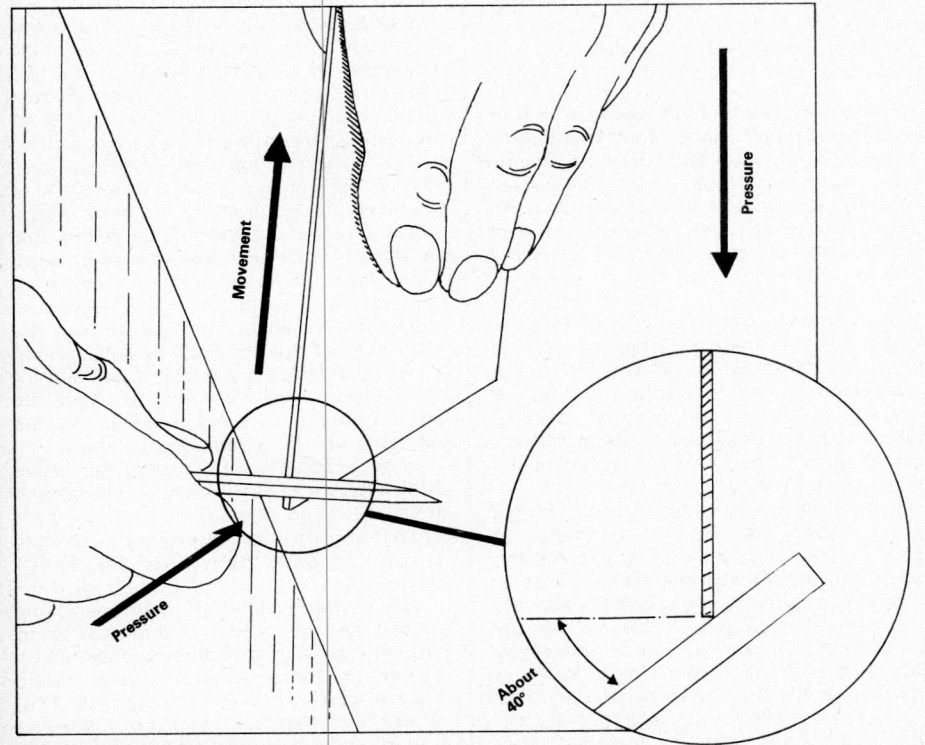

Movement

Pressure

Pressure

About 40°

● Fig 29 Turning the burr

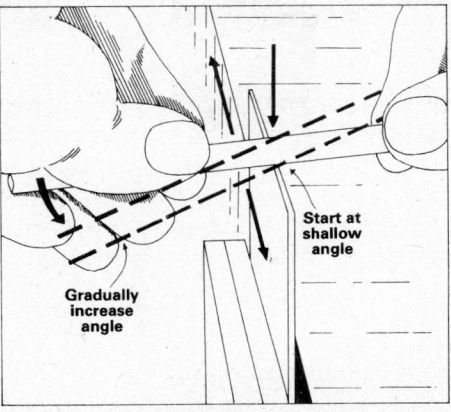

Start at shallow angle

Gradually increase angle

● Fig 30 Using ticketer to form burr

Most craftsmen have their favourite tools for stages B and C. Mine is a worn-down 1in bevel edged chisel but of course the correct tool is a ticketer — a hardened steel rod set into a handle (Fig 27). Lubricate the chisel or ticketer with a little spittle before stropping the sides of the scraper. Use plenty of pressure and keep the ticketer flat with the surface of the scraper to burnish and slightly stretch the corners and, in theory at least, give a hollowground effect to the edge (Fig 28).

Now to the part that needs the knack: the edge has to be turned and a burr set up. I hold the scraper vertically with the chisel at 30 to 40° to the edge (Fig 29) and apply considerable pressure as I draw the chisel along the corner once only. Each of the four corners is treated in the same way.

An alternative method (regarded where I worked as more for amateurs possibly because it was a little slower) is shown in Fig 30. After stropping, the scraper is placed in a vice and the ticketer worked backwards and forwards along the corner starting with

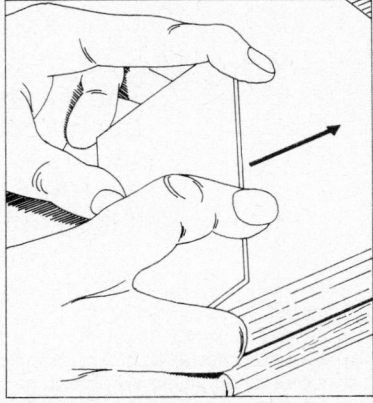

● Fig 31 Holding the scraper

a slight angle and gradually increasing the angle until a good burr is formed. You may not be able to see the burr as clearly as I have drawn it but you should be able to feel it.

There is a knack in using the scraper, especially on marquetry pictures built up from many types of veneer, some hard, some soft and with the grain running in all directions. The scraper is more likely to dig into the softer and fibrous veneers if you go across them. Whenever possible, therefore, push the scraper with the grain of the softer woods and leave the harder ones to take care of themselves — these will cut almost equally well in any direction. Be careful not to chip the edge veneer by running the scraper across the borders and over the side.

Two methods of holding the tool are normally used: In one place the thumbs in the centre of the bottom edge and curl the fingers round the ends (Fig 31). In the other the bend can be put in over the palm of the hand as shown at Fig 32. The more the scraper is bent the quicker the wood is removed but the surface will be less flat. For marquetry the bend is kept to minimum consistent with good cutting. Small areas near the edge can be done with the last inch or so of the scraper.

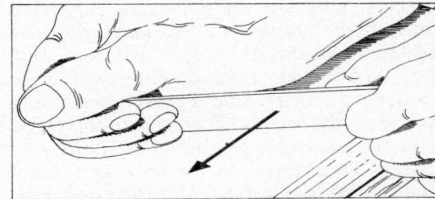

● Fig 32 Alternative way of holding the scraper

When the surface has been made level it can be sealed. This, too, can bring problems if certain of the rosewoods (particularly coral and San Domingo) have been used for the dark veneer as the colour may bleed from them into the sycamore and give a muddy effect. The easiest way to overcome this is to spray the sealer on fairly dry. If you do not have spraying equipment you have to paint the sealer on to the individual dark areas with an artist's brush. When all is dry the surface can be sealed in the usual way. Great care must be taken when sanding the sealer — if you go through to the basewood the colour will bleed-out again. The final finish can be matt or gloss as desired. ■

The calling of the carpenter

The carpenter has had a various career throughout history, but his consistent importance to communities of all ages is well illustrated by the frequency with which his doings are to be found recorded in old documents. Bill Brown has been seeking out the carpenter in history, and concludes that he has always been much more than just a 'chippy'

In shop floor parlance a cabinet maker is a maker, a wood machinist is a wood butcher, and a carpenter is a chippy. The latter cognomen suggests an individual happy only when chopping away with mallet and chisel, which may be partially true but it is an injustice nevertheless, since historically, a carpenter was, as he still is, an important person in the community.

The word carpenter is derived from the Latin *carpentum,* a carriage or wagon, but in monastery records and Pipe Rolls the word *carpentarius* is used for the craftsman who had to turn his hand to an amazing variety of jobs. He had, for example, not only to assist in many ways in the building of a cathedral or monastery, by making the *cintra* (centres) for the vaulted ribs and arches of the roof, he also had to make a *wyndas* (hoist) with which to lift the heavy timber members into position. Even before this could be done he had to provide and make the *carrectar* (type of cart) for hauling the materials to site.

In 1236 Simon, one of the king's carpenters at Windsor was told, according to the Pipe Rolls of the time, to repair the kitchen with two twisted posts (to support the spit) and also to mend the gutter, while another entry shows one of his next jobs was to make tables for the use of the cooks, from a beech tree supplied from the royal forest. It was the general practice in medieval times for the employer to provide the timber, the carpenter being paid piece-work, sometimes in kind. Towards the end of the 14th century, some carpenters were supplying their own timber and other materials; William Wright of Ripon, we are told, worked on repairs to Ripon Minster and was paid 18s 7d for making a door in the Choir, including the supply of 'bords' for the work.

In the building of the great halls and cathedrals of the past it would seem most responsibility rested with the master mason and master carpenter. They were expected not only to interpret the master plan, but to devise means of carrying out the work, and finally to make, fabricate and install, everything from below ground to the apex of the building. The general supervision was usually in the hands of a Clerk in Holy Orders, who not only was 'Clerk of Works', but was charged 'to sell branches, bark, and other remnants of trees, accounting for the monies received and receiving', the reference here being to the discarded parts of trees delivered to site by the customer, often the king.

The famous hammer beam roof of Westminster Hall is a good example of the medieval craftsman's skill. It was planned and executed by Master Hugh Herland, the king's carpenter, with much of the oak

● 'The Carpenter' as seen by The Book of English Trades and Library of the Useful Arts in 1824 (Picture courtesy of Verulamium Museum, St Albans)

coming from woods near Farnham in Surrey. As a student a good many years ago, I was shown some portions of timber beams removed from Westminster Hall which needed replacing; they had always been considered to be made from oak, but were in fact sweet chestnut, a wood resembling oak in appearance but being inferior in strength by about 20 %. Since structural timbers in those days were invariably overdesigned, the load bearing capacity of chestnut mixed with oak was no doubt adequate but, as a young man full of scepticism, I wondered whether the incidence had been inspired by ulterior motives rather than by human error in felling the wrong tree. Perhaps it was economics.

In 1247 the maintenance of the structures of Windsor Castle was in the hands of Master John Silvester, the king's mason, and the previously mentioned Master Simon, the carpenter, but in 1255 Alexander succeeded Simon and in 1257, on January 14 precisely, Alexander was appointed by patent master of all the king's works of carpentry. Master Alexander was the first holder of this office and, as a recognition of his status, he received fur-trimmed robes twice a year in addition to his fees which

were doubled when he was travelling on official business.

He held the post for about 12 years until he died around 1269, and during that time carried out a lot of important work, especially at Westminster Abbey, where some of his original scissor trusses still stand, although partially covered by more recent strengthening members. The importance of his position can be judged from the fact that between 1256 and his death, he was called upon to witness many charters granted at Westminster.

While it is probable that the master carpenters formed a guild in the very early days, it was in 1477 that Edward IV granted a charter to the Carpenters' Company which was to become one of the leading livery companies of London. The Carpenters' Hall was actually started in 1429, but its completion took many years and it was eventually destroyed in the Blitz of 1941.

By the time the charter was granted, the Carpenters' Livery in the City of London had more or less assumed complete control of the building industry and it was necessary to obtain their licence before even contemplating to build a pig pen, let alone a house. On the other hand, they made it their duty to see that anything they licensed was properly built, somewhat as our present day National House-Builders' Council operate. A case in 1543 concerned a house which collapsed soon after completion. The two carpenters responsible has to share the cost of its rebuilding, 'as well for ther own honystie as the honystie of the crafte'.

The Livery Companies were also concerned with ensuring the pay and conditions were appropriate to the work undertaken. After the Great Fire of London in 1666 an Act of Parliament was altered so as to allow tradesmen, including carpenters, to become freemen of the city. This was to attract craftsmen to the rebuilding of the city. The act operated for an initial seven years, but artificers working in the city for this entire period were able to 'enjoy the same liberty to work as freemen of the said city for and during their natural lives'.

In more recent years, a carpenter in the British navy was a warrant officer promoted from the rating of shipwright and eligible after 15 years for further promotion to chief carpenter and thence to carpenter-lieutenant.

The modern carpenter may spend the greater part of his life on some particular type of work, while another spends his on something totally different. Each would have a lot to learn if they changed jobs, which is perhaps the best side of work; a day in which one learns nothing is a day wasted. ∎

Woodturning from A to Z

What is the best wood for turning? Tree wood, says Gordon Stokes. And he is not joking. In this the third article in his A to Z of woodturning, Gordon advises on the basic ancillary equipment necessary, before directing some thought to the subject of the wood itself

YOU'LL ALSO NEED...

● Lamp blanks should be drilled for the flex before turning

One might perhaps think that with a good lathe and a set of tools, only the timber is missing. Up to a point this is true, but a certain amount of ancillary equipment is necessary if the versatility of the lathe is to be exploited. The items described here will all be useful in the early stages, and I will bring in others as the series proceeds.

Lathes are normally supplied complete with drive centre, tailstock centre (in some cases this will be of the 'live' or rotating variety) and a faceplate. This enables the purchaser to make a start, but the need for further equipment will soon arise.

The purchase of two woodscrew chucks will be a wise move, since these have a wide variety of uses. They are normally available in two sizes, these being 1½in and 2½in — the figures indicating the diameter of the chuck face. The smaller version is a single screw chuck, which has a woodscrew projecting from its centre. The best size of screw for the job is a number fourteen, and I use them about one inch in length. In the better makes of chuck provision is made for the user to replace the screw when it is worn or damaged, or when a longer or shorter screw is needed for a particular project.

The smaller of the screw chucks is used for items such as furniture knobs, small finials, chessmen, egg cups, and other projects where a larger chuck would make the work awkward. The larger version has extra holes in its rim which permit the use of more screws, additional to the central one. Usually there are only two of these extra holes, but I feel that three or even four would be better. This size of chuck is suitable for pots, vases, tankards, and so on, and I use them for bowls up to eight or nine inches in diameter, where a seven or eight inch faceplate would be awkward.

Faceplates tend to obstruct the movement of the tools in some jobs, and I have always felt that a four or five inch diameter version should be available. Most makers do not provide this however, so you will have to do as I do — have one made locally. On large discs, such as big bowls, plates, or trays, a large faceplate is required to provide the necessary support. The two screw chucks and the Jacobs pattern chuck, illustrated in my previous article, can be regarded as essential.

There are now numerous other chucks and holding devices, most of which are worth buying, provided that their purpose is understood, and that the particular purchaser is likely to use them often enough to justify the expenditure. All woodturning equipment is now relatively expensive, so full investigation should be made into the purpose and efficiency of any items before spending good money. This series will examine the uses of many such chucks, and

in the later stages they will be shown in use on various projects.

Many beginners seem to number among their early requirements some equipment for the drilling of long holes. Kits can be obtained for this purpose for almost every make of lathe, but the cost is high, and until the basics of the craft have been thoroughly covered and practised, it is as well to leave them off the shopping list. The idea behind these kits is really to enable the turner to drill through blanks which are intended for tall table lamps, to provide a passage for the cable. Such lamps should really be left until later, and shorter ones can be drilled from each end. using a Jacobs chuck and a Jennings pattern bit — as used in a hand brace — with the square sectioned piece cut off, and the thread of the lead screw removed. Note that such drilling is done in the square blank, before it is turned. There are several good reasons for this, which we can examine when the series has progressed to actual projects.

Insofar as the holding of workpieces is concerned it is best to avoid the use of Jacobs chucks or engineers' chucks. These have jaws which are designed to grip metal, but when used on wood they compress it, so that the workpiece can rapidly become loose. The engineers' chuck is large and very heavy — not to mention its incredible price — and it has projecting jaws which can be extremely dangerous when rotating at woodturning speeds, unles they are properly guarded. Beware also of the oddments which appear on the market from time to time with extravagant claims as to their value in facilitating certain turning operations. Many such items are more trouble than they are worth, and will be found in few, if any, professional workshops. The best guide here is to select only those which are endorsed by at least one reputable woodturner, who has actually tried the product in question.

Before we can begin to cut wood in the lathe, we should consider one or two points which are highly relevant, and which seem to cause a great deal of unnecessary confusion among beginners. The three which instantly come to my mind, because they are constantly the subject of queries, are speed in turning, tool grinding and sharpening, and timber varieties.

The importance of speed lies mainly in the fact that beginners need to appreciate its relative unimportance. My usual advice to students is that a lathe should be run at a speed which is comfortable for the operator, and which will allow the tools to produce clean cuts.

Do not waste too much of your time in studying the quaint little charts which are so often published to indicate 'correct' speeds

● Square blank for vase once hollowed out, can be supported by tapered plug at tailstock end with slight tailstock pressure

for given diameters. These are of no real value, since most workpieces have widely varying diameters within their own ranges, and the speed of the machine cannot be varied to suit these while cutting.

Most lathes are strictly limited in their speed ranges, having perhaps three or four speeds. One of these will be too low for general spindle work because it is intended for large discs, and the other end of the range will give a speed which is too fast since it is intended for use on very small diameters. This leaves little choice, but in practice a speed between 1,500 and 2,000 rpm will serve well for spindles which vary between, say, six inches and one inch. Keep the speed on the low side until the basic cutting has been mastered. In suggesting that beginners should use a speed which feels comfortable, I am allowing for the increasing confidence — and competence — which will come with practice.

Any man or woman taking up woodturning, and hoping to achieve a high degree of skill, should put aside any knowledge of tool sharpening which may have been acquired. I spend hours on my carving tools, and guard the resulting fine edges with great care, but sharpening of this kind is not required for turning tools. They will be used

(continued on p 466)

Woodturning

(continued from page 465)

in situations where considerable frictional heat is produced as their bevels rub on the wood, and where the relative speed between timber and cutting edge is very high indeed. As a result, a fine edge which has been produced with great care will be destroyed in seconds. I do not use oilstones of any kind on my turning tools — ever — yet they peel off shavings, and in most cases leave a finish which requires no sanding. Some may find this hard to accept, but all the students who have passed through my workshops have seen this for themselves — as indeed have the thousands who have watched me at exhibitions. Since all this is a matter of fact, rather than of opinion, the importance of the grinding equipment will be appreciated. Any old grindstone just will not do. A good quality grinder is essential, and the stone used for sharpening should be medium grade, about 60 or 80 grit.

So far, so good, but that is not the end of it. The stone should be kept for the sharpening of woodturning tools, and never abused by use in rough grinding of a general nature. Something has to be done about keeping its surface flat, because the gouges will quickly produce hollows, and like any other cutting tool it must be sharpened. If it is allowed to become blunt and glazed, the degree of frictional heat imparted to the tools will be unacceptable, and even an experienced turner would be unable to use it without overheating the blades, and so destroying the temper of the steel.

The 'devil stone' is the device which takes care of both these points. Used correctly, it will remove just enough grains from the surface of the wheel to expose fresh cutting points. These will be sharp, and will cut cleanly with the minimum of heat.

Grinding and sharpening woodturning tools is *not* a difficult matter, provided of course that it is fully understood. Detailed coverage of this essential part of the craft will be the subject of my next article.

What is the best wood for turning? I wonder how many times I have been asked that question — it must run into thousands. I am tempted to say 'tree wood' which is a serious and sensible answer, in no way meant to be facetious. Almost all timbers can be turned — certainly all European woods can — and it is important for beginners to try out every piece they can get hold of, rather than stick to one variety. Professionals of course have to use timber varieties as required by their customers, and would not be in business for long if they could not cope with this.

Many people who seek the 'best' wood for turning, are in fact looking for the timber which will respond in the most satisfactory manner to unskilled tool application. One might as well be content with the 'easiest' or 'best' tune to play on a certain musical instrument! All timber is worth a try, if it is completely free from cracks, loose knots, nails and other hazards. A few varieties are very abrasive, and blunt the tools more quickly than others. Some get up your nose — literally — and aggravate the sinuses. Some workers find that they are allergic to the odd type, but the vast majority of species can be turned with relative ease — once the necessary skill has been acquired.■

Windsor chair

This is a straightforward design for a windsor chair which involves some interesting turning and practice in the accurate boring of angled holes. It is made mainly from beech though other homegrown hardwoods such as oak, ash or fruitwoods would be suitable. The seat, however, should be made from elm and is sculpted using gouges and an abrasive disc

Cutting List

PART	No	L	W	T	MATERIAL
seat	1	370	350	32	elm
back	1	460	120	60	beech
front legs	2	460	38	38	beech
back legs	2	460	38	38	beech
stretchers	2	320	32	32	beech
cross rail	1	300	30	30	beech
back rail	2	370	38	38	beech
sticks	4	370	18	18	beech

by Tony Lord

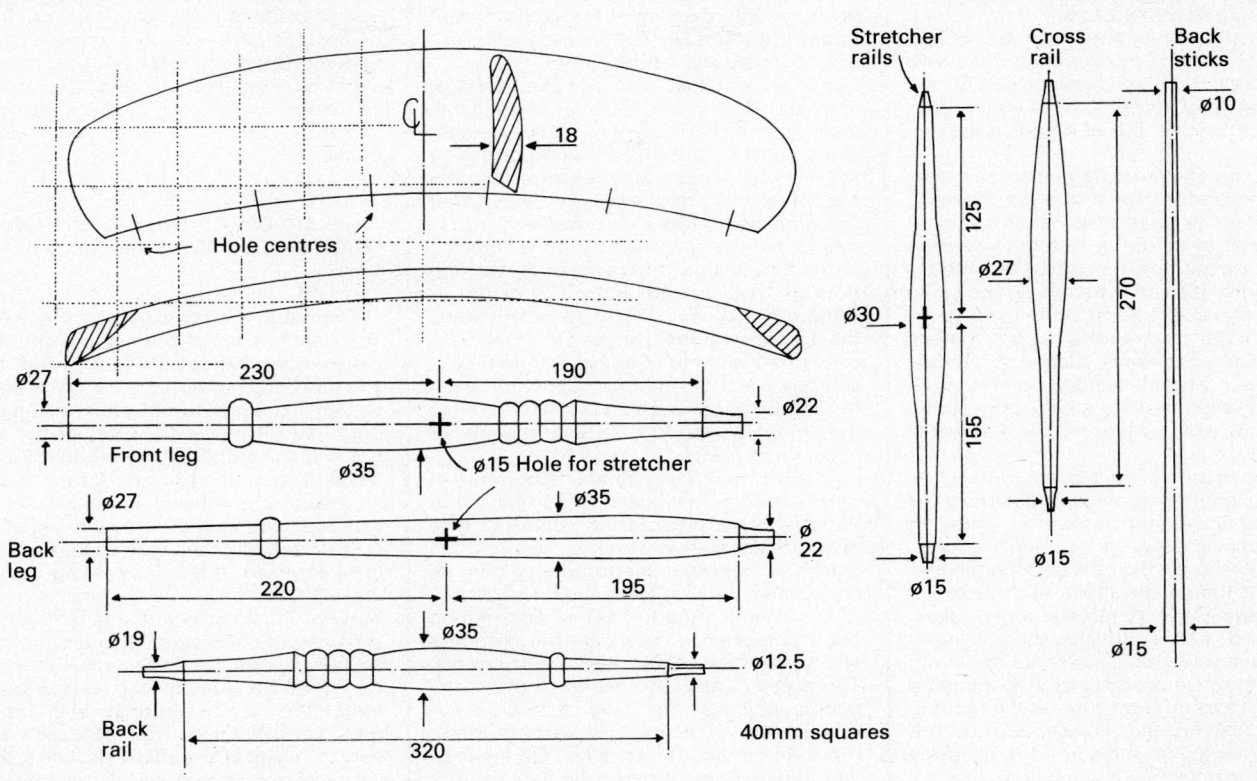

18

Hole centres

Stretcher rails

Cross rail

Back sticks

ø10

125

ø27

270

ø30

155

ø15

ø15

ø15

ø27   230   190   ø22

Front leg

ø35   ø15 Hole for stretcher

ø27   ø35

Back leg   ø 22

220   195

ø19   ø35

Back rail   ø12.5

320   40mm squares

Fox-wedged joint

850

290

415

380

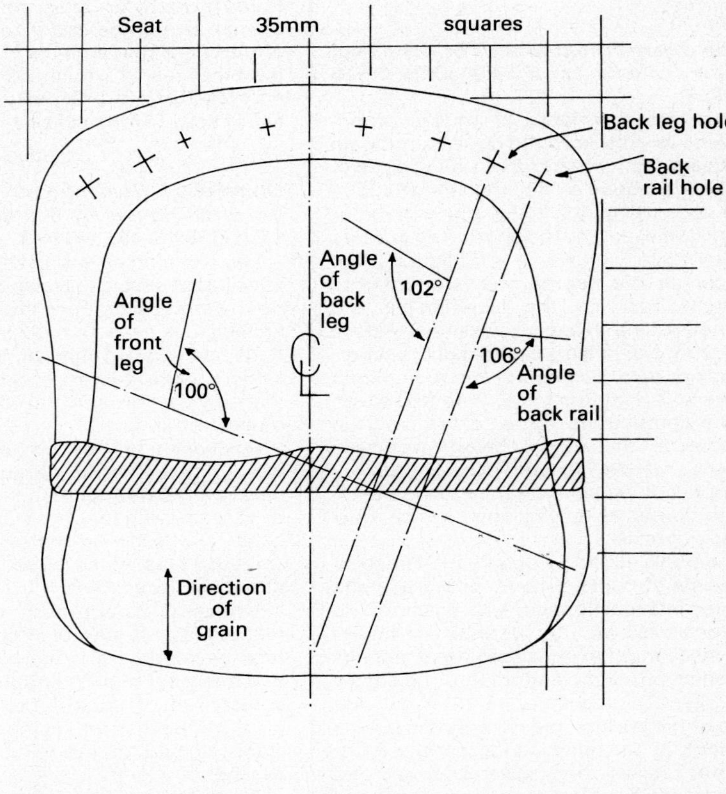

Seat   35mm   squares

Back leg hole

Back rail hole

Angle of back leg   102°

Angle of front leg   100°

106°

Angle of back rail

Direction of grain

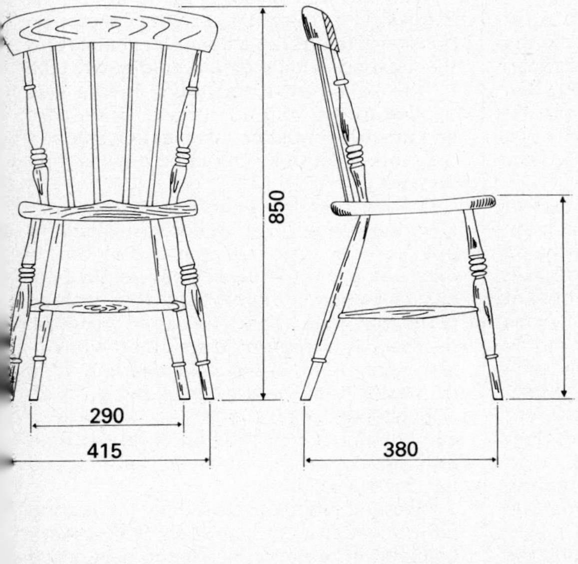

Woodworker's bookshelf

The Complete Home Carpenter, edited by Stuart Laing (Hamlyn £4.95)

There are many books aimed at the person who wants to take care of his own home, rather than pay someone else to do it for him. Most of them claim to be thoroughly comprehensive, but of course none can be so.

The Complete Home Carpenter, now in its umpteenth reprint since first appearing in 1972, comes as close as any such book can to its claim of being 'complete', however, cleverly introducing the actual techniques of carpentry as and when they appear in projects that are detailed along the way.

What better place to discuss the making of drawers, for instance, than in the middle of a project centred round building kitchen units? Or when making a box, to expound the theme and variations on a dovetail joint?

The production of the book is immaculate and the illustrations are stimulating to the reader while lacking nothing in clarity of explanation. It takes as its brief the maintenance and care of all things wooden that appear in the construction and interior of the average house. Windows, doors, floors, roofs and stairs all get pretty comprehensive coverage, interspersed with more decorative projects such as building various items of furniture and repairing veneers. Also included is a useful section on power tools, along with some sound advice on how best to equip a workshop.

As for the book being the 'complete' volume on its subject, that is another matter. Let us just say that this is an extremely competent addition to a home reference library on carpentry. It will certainly find a well-thumbed place on my own reference shelves.   **C.D.**

☐   ☐   ☐

Modern harpsichord makers by John Paul (Victor Gollancz Ltd £15.50) ISBN 0 575 02985 4

Have you experience of intricate woodworking or a background of performing on keyboard instruments? Even if the answer to either question is 'No', then this magnificent book will give you the urge to try your hand at making a harpsichord. The success of the first venture is problematic but almost all the contributors started from scratch. Studying the experiences and methods of the sixteen professional makers and groups of makers cannot fail to encourage and help beginners and competent workers. It is interesting to note that seven of the contributors came to the craft via woodwork, the others being musicians already. Of the sixteen, two started by chance and two because they saw building harpsichords as a challenge which they could not resist.

The book, edited by John Paul, himself a harpsichord builder, starts with a 66 page learned introduction to the harpsichord. He relates its revival after a century in limbo, the mechanics of the instrument and its various types and elaborations. The author then gives the results of an interview with each of the makers, followed by the latter's account of the way he became a harpsichord maker, his researches and his methods. Difficulties in the early stages and how they were overcome are recounted,

these give a great deal of help and encouragement to beginners. All the contributors give freely of their expertise in a most friendly and helpful way.

It is evident that although the essential features of the instruments are explainable and relatively easily copied, there are other characteristics that are only incorporated by the knowledge and experience of the physics of sound. This leads to each maker having his own ideas on producing instruments with a satisfactory tone quality. Some can design a harpsichord, knowing how it will sound before making it. Although they are willing to help others, they cannot put their finger on what might be termed 'secrets'. Choice of materials is discussed by contributors. The wood used for soundboards is given consideration so too are bristle, leather, delrin and quills for making the plectra.

One contribution is by two decorators of harpsichords. The husband specialises in marquetry and restoration while his wife does the decorative painting, having done extensive research on original pigments and media. Illustrations shown the beauty of their work. Another gives information about published plans of early harpsichords and other famous keyboard instruments. These are particularly useful to the many people who do not have access to the originals to measure and inspect them. However, another writer says that the man who only copies, learns a limited amount about harpsichord making. A few of the contributors have designed and made instruments which produced a tone they liked after ignoring standard practice.

This excellently produced volume is a wealth of information and opinion. It is printed on good quality paper and is illustrated by many first class photographs. It is unique as a guide and inspiration to both professional and amateur. The insight into the other fellow's methods, expertise and successes are of great value to the established harpsichord maker.   **H.C.K.**

☐   ☐   ☐

Ornamental Carpentry on 19th Century American Houses by Ben Karp (Constable £5.25) ISBN 0-486-24144-0

This is almost exclusively a book of photographs which take as their theme the sawn-wood decorations found in American architecture from the 1820s to 1910. Ben Karp has allowed himself full rein on the subject, with the sort of celebratory style that suggests ornamental carpentry is very much his thing.

What distinguishes this particular type of work is that it is the product of the sawblade alone, without refinements added by chisel or carving tool. It is stark and rough in detail, a reflection of the same flamboyant spirit that created the legendary folk heroes of the age, says Karp. It is certainly highly individual in its approach, but really only relevant in its context of gratuitous architectural decoration. It is therefore a criticism that many of the photographs present their subject out of context by homing in on detail, rather than letting the ornamentation stand as part of the whole architectural concept.

To the average reader this side of the Atlantic, the pictures will be of little more

than passing interest, a brief education in a certain colonial mode of woodwork that is of no real relevance to our own cultural heritage. But at its most useful, the book will serve as a source of good ideas for the craftsman looking for unusual decorative designs and devices to adapt or develop for himself.   **C.D.**

☐   ☐   ☐

Restoring Old Furniture Better than New (BBC £4.75) by Albert Jackson and David Day.

This is a new book to accompany the BBC Television series of the same name. If the reader does not get the feeling that he or she must start furniture restoration classes at the first opportunity after reading this book then it is not the fault of the book, because the authors have produced a book which is easy to read and follow, and the illustrations have been drawn to a very high standard, showing the smallest detail.

The book has been written for those who are interested in this fascinating craft and are willing to 'have a go'. It must be realised however that complete restoration from stripping (if necessary), staining, polishing by the various methods available, and all the structural repairs and veneering and upholstery by traditional and modern methods call for considerable skill and a very wide knowledge. To do justice to all the various facets of this work is not possible in 142 pages.

As stated under the chapter on upholstery, the reader must consult specialised books to carry out more advanced work. The book would have been improved by the addition of a reading list, so that if the reader wished to study any part or all the subjects concerned in this book in greater depth he would have been made aware of the available material.

The technical content is strongest under the chapter covering structural repairs, at the expense, one feels, of the subject of polishing and finishing. For instance most traditional polishers understand the meaning of 'spiriting off' but very few would actually pour a few drops of meths on to the rubber that was virtually free of polish. As suggested by the authors in the chapter on polishing, meths is a solvent for shellac and the inexperienced worker could easily take all the polish off if too much meths was applied to the built up surface. Great care and attention must be taken at this stage of the work. The rubber must be only slightly damp.

The chapter on upholstery deals with covering stuffed-over and drop-in seats. At one point in this chapter a diagram is misleading as it shows heavyweight hessian tacked on to the bevelled edge instead of the top of the frame; the use of ½in tacks necessary for this would splinter the bevelled edge. Also under this heading it is suggested that the second stuffing on an upholstered seat should be fibre. If a combination of hair and fibre is chosen then fibre should be used for the first stuffing and hair for the second.

Overall the book is extremely interesting and informative and one cannot fail to learn the basic information needed to get started in the field of furniture restoration.   **G.H.**

Making Wooden Toys (John Murray £5.95) by Richard Blizzard

Richard Blizzard has wasted no time in capitalising most sensibly on the stardom thrust upon him by appearances on Pebble Mill at One. His toy-making exploits on television have created an interest far in excess of anything the pundits at the BBC predicted, and Mr Blizzard's own plans service has been cheerfully working overtime to keep up with demand for his designs.

His previous books have been published to go hand-in-hand with the television series (he is currently planning a new project for BBC2) but on this occasion Mr Blizzard has produced a volume of toy designs on his own account, and it is a pretty safe bet commercially, I would say.

As a former teacher Richard Blizzard has had plenty of opportunity to observe children (including his own) at play, and clearly he has a skilful eye for spotting what attracts a child to one toy rather than another. The secret, one deduces from the projects in *Making Wooden Toys*, seems to be in providing plenty of moving parts — toys that actually do something in their own right as opposed to those which can only be played *with*. This enterprising new book gives working drawings for 12 different projects, ranging from a mechanical shark for terrorising bath-time (or the gold-fish in the garden pond) to a go-cart with trailer.

Although I haven't made up any of the designs myself, I can say that the clear drawings seem to be both comprehensive and comprehensible, but I would like to have seen photographs, rather than just line drawings, of the finished items. It occurred to me that if the book had been produced in paperback, instead of its glossy hard-bound cover, the costing might have allowed for more stimulating illustration of each project within.

However, this is a quibble, and Mr Blizzard's proven fame as a designer and maker of good solid wooden toys is going to be recommendation enough to ensure huge sales. I am sure that *Making Wooden Toys* will swell even further Richard Blizzard's legion of happy customers. **C.D.**

□ □ □

Sainsbury's woodturning projects for dining by John Sainsbury, published by Sterling Publishing Co Inc, distributed in UK by Oak Tree Press Ltd at £7.95.

Those who are not woodturners always complain and say 'oh anyone can turn' then in the same breath they follow with 'but they never get further than the egg cup or goblet of the two day class and once they get home they forget it all anyway'. Here is a practical book to alter all that which the publishers punningly quote as 'an appetising book for hungry woodworkers to take them from soup to nuts on the lathe'.

No one can over-emphasise the warmth and beauty of natural wood. What better then, than to sit down to a complete meal (eight courses in this book!) and have settings, service, implements all made by you to complement the food and wine.

John Sainsbury has come up with 42 projects shown in over 300 step-by-step

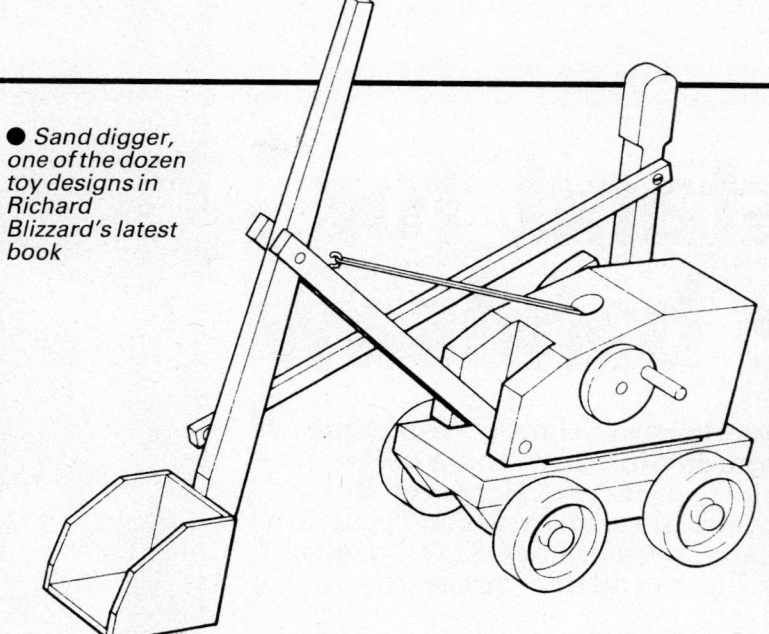

● *Sand digger, one of the dozen toy designs in Richard Blizzard's latest book*

photographs; precisely detailing mounting, shaping and finishing. Procedures and techniques, wood selection, lathe speed, tools and pointers are clearly and concisely explained. Appendices inform on holding wood for turning, sharpening, using and grinding tools.

The author has been a teacher, lecturer and technical advisor for some time (he has just retired), he is widely travelled and sought after as a lecturer on TV both at home and abroad. All this experience comes over in his admirable book. Other turners aspiring to publish their art, watch out, your book will have to be very good to rival this one. A real bargain at the price, full of simple to follow and dateless information. **P.C.**

□ □ □

Carving flora and fables in wood by E. J. Tangerman published by Sterling Publishing Co Inc (distributed by Oak Tree Press Co Ltd) one of their Home Craftsman series in paperback at £3.50.

Fifty years of experience in the woodcarving field back up E. J. Tangerman's fourth title in the Sterling Home Craftsman series. Both informative and fun to read whether you are a simple whittler or a carver of 50ft heroic statues, a beginner or a professional, this is a book covering a wide variety of subjects. Among the projects which range from flower panels to Atlas 'a nude in stress' are 91 flowers, four birds, four insects a gnome and a worm plus 'in the round' information for Hercules and Ulysses and others. The Little Mermaid is covered by step-by-step photographs. For the beginner the author has included chapters on choosing wood, using, sharpening and caring for tools, how to choose the size of your piece and suitable finishes.

His chapter on floral polyglot panels is a small treasure within a greater work, demonstrating what I consider to be E. J. Tangerman's forte. The other three books in the series are *Carving wooden animals*, *Carving faces and figures in wood* and *Carving religious motifs in wood*. They can all be obtained from Blandford Press, Poole, Dorset. **P.C.**

Woodturning by W. J. Wooldridge published by B. T. Batsford at £8.95.

This generous book of 150 large and closely printed pages, profusely illustrated with many photographs and numerous line drawings and diagrams joins the growing collection of books on this universally fascinating subject. To begin with, it follows the general pattern and content of a number of other books on the same topic. There are chapters on the selection of tools and some type of available lathes, tool sharpening and lathe accessories, marking out and setting up. Instructions for spindle turning are followed by instructions for faceplate work.

By far the largest proportion of the book is, however, given over to a number of chapters in which are described many of those specialist techniques about which both the beginner and the more advanced woodturner often asks, 'How do you do that?' I don't say that Mr. Wooldridge has all the answers but many will find this part of his book most helpful.

A variety of chucking methods are discussed as is offset turning, boring and long hole boring and some decorative work. Individual projects put each technique into practice. In addition the author, who has an engineering background, describes a number of tools and devices, jigs etc., which can be 'home-made' and suggests several novel turning techniques.

The book has a number of points, mainly on aspects of method, with which some experienced turners would perhaps not entirely agree. But, in fairness I think it is true to say that craftsmen are, and rightly too, highly individualistic. Woodturners especially so! Whilst it is easy to say that certain ways are wrong — usually because they are either counter productive or positively dangerous — it is much more difficult to say with certainty that there is any one *right* way to do a job. There may in fact be several 'right ways' and in the final analysis I believe it becomes a matter of common sense and personal preference. My advice is to read more than just this or any other one book, to watch and listen to a working woodturner if possible and then try for yourself the different methods advocated. **J. H.**

A stand for the bandsaw

For woodworkers with limited workshop area the introduction of machine tools presents space problems. However, Bill Gates has come up with a neat and practical design for a mobile bandsaw stand, which saves both bench and floor space in the workshop.

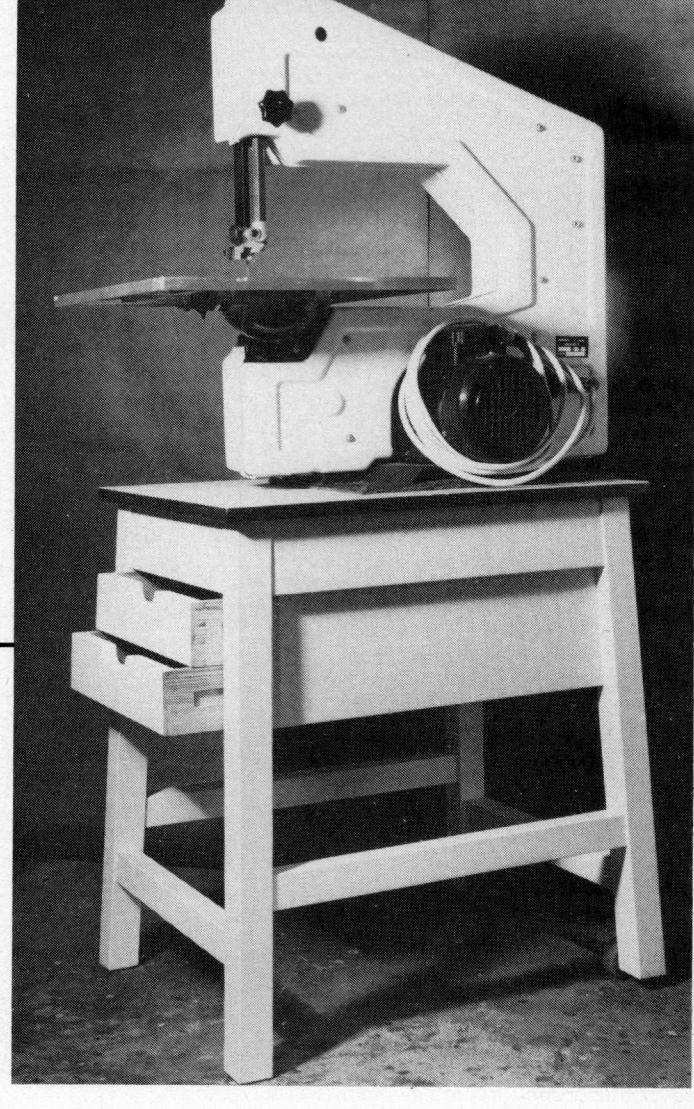

● Bill Gates' bandsaw stand, with wheels between the rear legs to give the unit mobility

Fig 1 shows the main dimensions. The height to the top of the stand should be between 700 and 800mm. This is suitable for a person of average height. The legs are splayed outwards to give additional stability. This requires extra care in setting out but it does add to the interest of the job. Mortise and tenon joints were used for the construction.

Fig 3 shows the top of a leg with a parallel haunch. The bandsaw was used to cut the tenons and haunch and mitre the ends to provide the maximum length of tenon on the top rails. Fgs 2 and 2a show two methods of making and fitting the rollers. The bottom of the legs must be well chamfered to prevent damage when moving the stand.

Assembly The two sides were glued and cramped. After the glue had set the drawer supports were fitted and finally the end rails were glued and cramped. (A rod to check the diagonals is essential for frames that are not parallel). The drawers are supported on hardwood runners (Fig 4). The drawer fronts and sides were fitted individually in their relative positions. I consider this is the only satisfactory way of making a drawer to fit perfectly, and is particularly necessary with inclined sides and fronts. The arrangement of the dovetails is given in Fig 5.

To conceal the drawers and to keep them reasonably dust-free, pieces of hardboard are fitted. These are fixed to the inside of the top rails with screws and to the drawer runners with glued blocks.

Blockboard of 19mm was used for the top and edged with mahogany. The method I used to fix these pieces was to glue and fix with veneer pins driven in sufficiently to hold the edging sections in place until the glue had set. The pins were than removed and the edges lightly damped which almost closes the pin holes.

The top was secured by screws into the top rails, a bed of felt being first fixed to the edges of the rails with rubber-based adhesive to reduce transmission of noise. The machine baseplate rests on a thick layer of felt and is secured with bolts to the stand.■

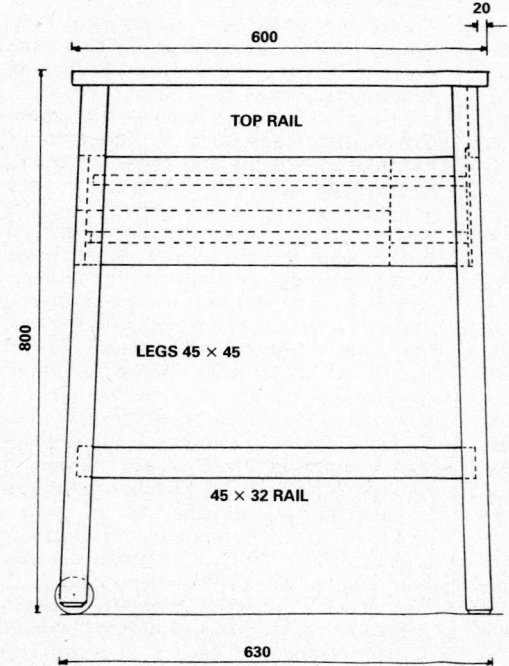
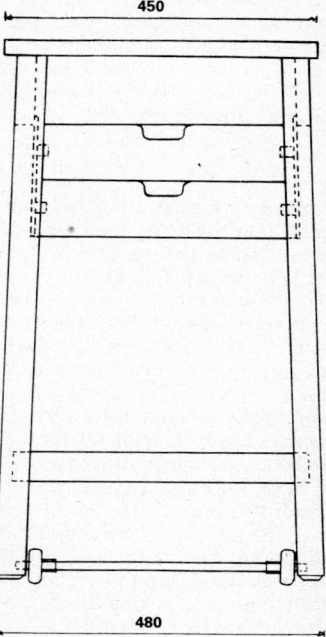

600   20   450

TOP RAIL

800

LEGS 45 × 45

45 × 32 RAIL

630   480

FIG 1

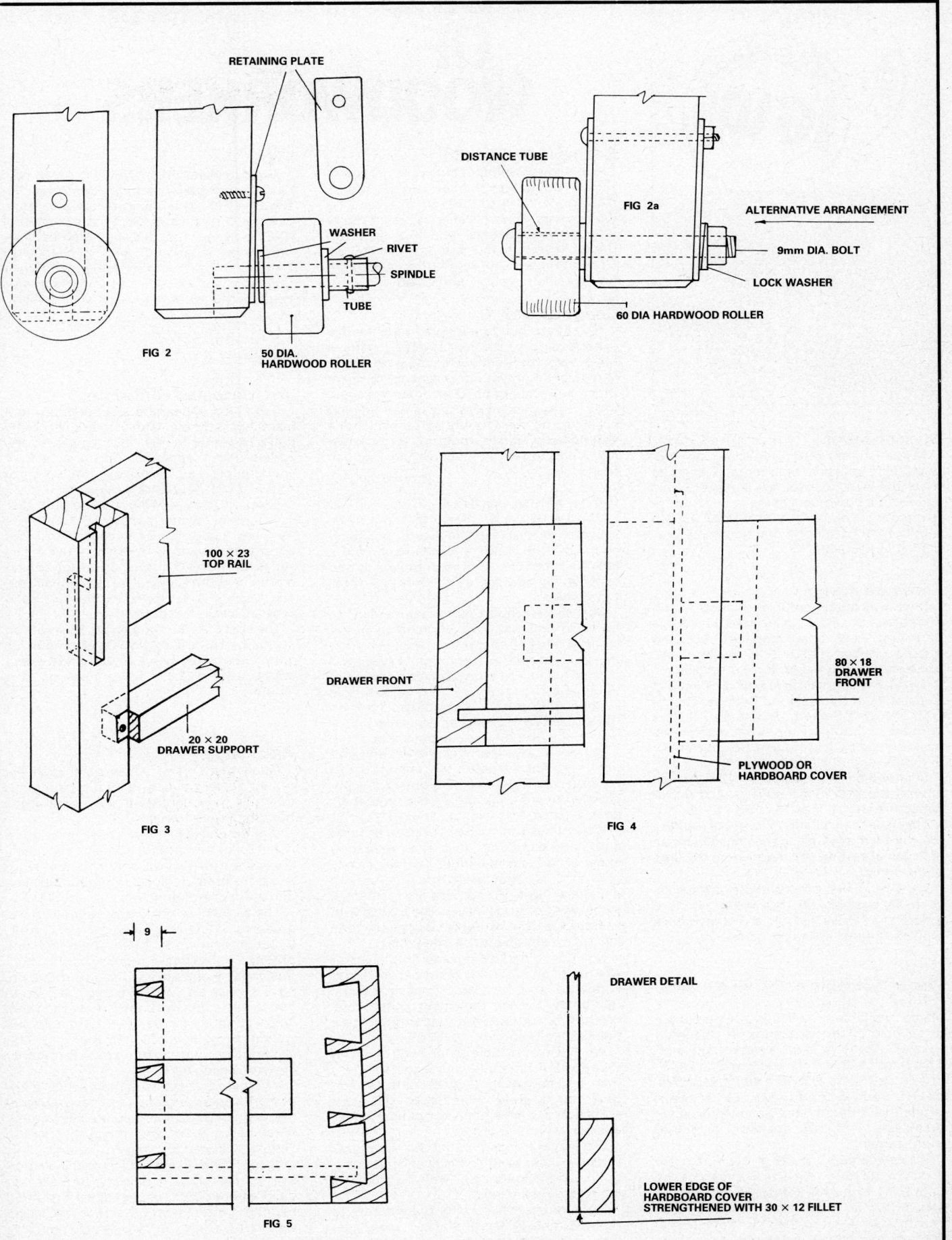

RETAINING PLATE

FIG 2

WASHER

RIVET

SPINDLE

TUBE

50 DIA.
HARDWOOD ROLLER

DISTANCE TUBE

FIG 2a

ALTERNATIVE ARRANGEMENT

9mm DIA. BOLT

LOCK WASHER

60 DIA HARDWOOD ROLLER

100 × 23
TOP RAIL

20 × 20
DRAWER SUPPORT

FIG 3

DRAWER FRONT

80 × 18
DRAWER
FRONT

PLYWOOD OR
HARDBOARD COVER

FIG 4

9

FIG 5

DRAWER DETAIL

LOWER EDGE OF
HARDBOARD COVER
STRENGTHENED WITH 30 × 12 FILLET

GUILD OF WOODWORKERS

Stick on motif

Manufacturers often publicise new products 'In response to popular request' or 'to meet the ever increasing demand'... well Guild of Woodworkers present 'in response to members' requests'... at last that **stick on motif** of the Guild logo that has up till now eluded all requests.

Furniture design

If we can obtain sufficient support from members we will be able to take advantage of a first class opportunity of receiving quality professional tuition in the basic principles of design and furniture making.

Two 3-day courses have been arranged in September at Rycotewood College, Thame OX9 2AF (1-3 September and/or 7-9 September) to bring to the woodworker the basic principles of design and to apply these to the *making of a piece of furniture*.

Cost, which is inclusive of VAT and all accommodation in the college plus morning coffee and all meals is *£69*.

The usual cancellation charge of half the fee will be made unless the cancellation is received in writing 14 days prior to the date of the course.

We would like provisional bookings as soon as possible so that we may more accurately assess response. Fuller details on Guild pages of August issue.

Places available on carving course

There are still a very limited number of places available on a **Woodcarving course** to be held 20-26 September at Dillington House College & Arts Centre, Ilminster, Somerset TA19 9DT (phone Ilminster 2427). The course is either residential (tuition, full board and accommodation) or non-residential (tuition and all meals except breakfast) at £112.50 (resident) or £66.50 (non-resident).

All newcomers including beginners are welcome to this practical course run by Capt G. M. Hines RN (Retd.). For full details and notice of which tools to bring, plus booking forms etc contact Mrs Pat Elliott at the address above. Bookings cannot be accepted by phone.

Calling New Zealand

Guild member and enthusiastic woodturner, Doug Keeling, is visiting Nelson, New Zealand, in October of this year. He would very much like to contact other woodturners/teachers while he is 'down under'. If you are interested please contact Doug at Hintern House, Church Lane, Beetley, Dereham, Norfolk NR20 4AB.

Can you help?

One of our guild members in Scotland is experiencing problems in setting himself up as a woodturner now that he is no longer in regular employment. These mainly relate to the high cost of purchasing new turning tools. If any guild member is contemplating selling some of his tools and is looking for a second hand market would you let me know and I can forward details to our Scottish friend?

Finish at the border

We are delighted, bearing in mind the success of our finishing and polishing courses in the south — Bexleyheath, to be able to announce — **French polishing and re-finishing courses** in the north – Roxburghshire.

This should enable guild members in the north of England and Scotland to heave sighs of relief — no more expensive travelling south to seek expert tuition. We knew it existed in the north it was just a question of finding it!

Colin Campbell was apprenticed on Christmas Day 1939 and says his work is his way of life, like all famous polishers of the past he is always learning and experimenting. He uses traditional and modern methods and materials and finds the combination of old skills and modern materials an interesting and exciting subject.

His courses will not be a series of lectures and demonstrations, but real workshop experience for a maximum of four at any one time so that work may be on an individual basis. His courses are residential in his own home (a 200 year old manse with salmon and trout fishing) and prices include full board, tuition and all materials.

He offers a two day course (mid week or weekend), or a four day course (Tuesday to Friday) to cover preparation of new work, traditional French polishing, alternative finishes, brush finishing, restoring antique finishes, stripping and re-finishing.

We have been able to arrange with Mr Campbell to run guild courses at 10% less than he charges to outside contacts. You must be a guild member to get your reduction and give him your guild number when you write to him.

We have decided to let Mr Campbell organise dates to suit himself and intending guild participants. He will be running courses all year round.

Write direct therefore for fuller details to Colin Campbell, South Manse, Newcastleton, Roxburghshire or phone him on Liddesdale (054-121) 206.

Ties

Guild neckties are available in green with two narrow gold-coloured 'bandings' between which is the guild badge also gold-coloured. Ties are £3.50 each inclusive of VAT, postage and packing. Members requiring a tie should send a cheque or crossed postal order together with their guild number and address to the administrator at the usual *Woodworker* address.

Insurance and confusion

Confusion appears to exist over our tool insurance scheme. The conditions of the policy were not made fully known to me earlier and I apologise for any lack of cooperation that I may have shown since April. To put the matter straight:

The premiums payable relate to a full year of insurance or any part thereof. If therefore, any new member wishes to take out cover with, say, three months of the policy still to run, he will have to pay the full annual premium without any pro-rata adjustment. The premiums run from October 17 of one year to October 16 of the next.

The limit of £500 is still being offered at an unchanged premium of £5.00 per annum or part thereof. Alternative £1,000 cover is also available at £12.50 per annum or part thereof.

All change

Guild members who have been receiving reminders that their annual subscription is due may have spotted a new name at the bottom of their forms.

Though I have been with the magazine on its editorial and production side for nearly six years now; I have only recently (since April) become involved with guild running and administration duties.

The combining of my posts should give a greater guild coverage within the magazine, a better service to guild members and produce a thriving energetic guild both in this country and abroad. You as members have a voice on your own page, it is up to you to use it. Let me know what I can do to help you in your area. If you are able and willing to give instruction in your particular skills perhaps we can bring people together and run a course.

If you are pleased with a particular piece of work you have completed, take a photograph — let us all share your achievement. Most newspapers and magazines run a 'letters to the editor' page or column. This reflects on the lively nature of the readership (or lack of it) — help me to make our guild and our guild pages reflect that guild members are craftsmen and women who want to have a say in today's woodworking scene.

Polly Curds
Guild Administrator

masterclass
'82

Celebration of wood

● Don White demonstrates at the lathe during Masterclass 82

Chris Dunn reviews
Masterclass 82, staged at the
Sun Hotel in Hitchin, Herts,
from 14-17 April

☐   ☐   ☐

Regardless of how good he may be, the craftsman needs a shop window, for if potential customers don't get to see his work he will be out of business before you can say 'Crafts Council'.

With so few sales outlets open to the maker who hasn't yet established a reputation, it is left to a few enterprising gallery owners like Betty Norbury of the White Knight Gallery in Cheltenham to promote outstanding craftsmanship in the way that the Crafts Council ought to, but does not.

Betty's tireless efforts on behalf of the skilled craftsman (and therefore on behalf of her own gallery, of course) are already widely known among woodworking people, and her most recent enterprise, Masterclass 82, was a good example of the entrepreneurial talents that single out Betty Norbury as a significant figure on the contemporary crafts scene.

However, organisation is one thing, and cash is another. Masterclass could not have happened without the sponsorship of Roger Buse, whose vested interest in the well-being of craftsmen is his specialist mail order and retail tool company, Roger's Tools of Hitchin. If he was looking a little apprehensive, it must have been the effects of worrying about the safety of his £7,500 investment in Masterclass. But he need not have worried, for regardless of whether or not it turned out to be an instant financial success, long-term rewards were assured simply by the association of his name with such a prestigious occasion.

So what was Masterclass 82 all about? A standing exhibition of work by 44 craftsmen in the various disciplines of woodworking; a constant demonstration of skills and techniques by seven working craftsmen; and a series of daily lectures, covering many aspects of woodworking. It was an event that celebrated wood.

The standing exhibition was as varied in subject as it was in price, ranging from £2,906.25 for Max Cooper's unfaultable marquetry dressing table and stool in satinwood (plus another £487.50 if you want the matching mirror) to £1.50 for one of Tobias Kaye's wooden eggs. While the asking prices varied, however, for the most part there was a strong common theme of sure quality throughout.

John Makepeace's sewing chair in sycamore, with red leather seat (£2,187.50) drew

Continued on page 474

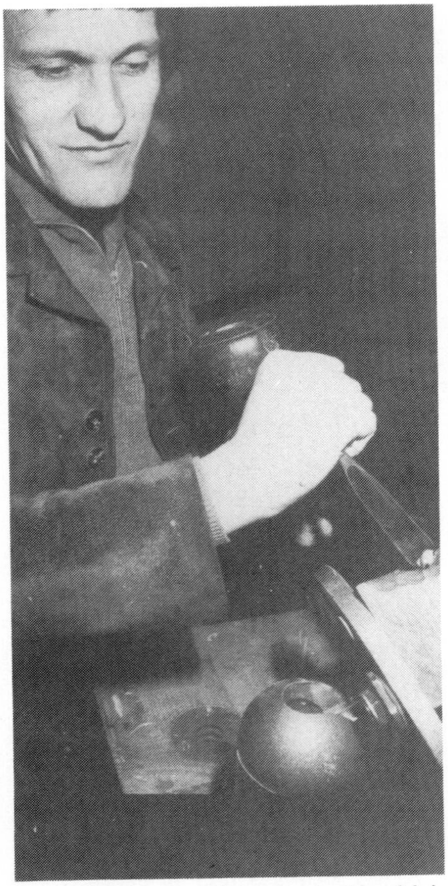

Masterclass

from page 473

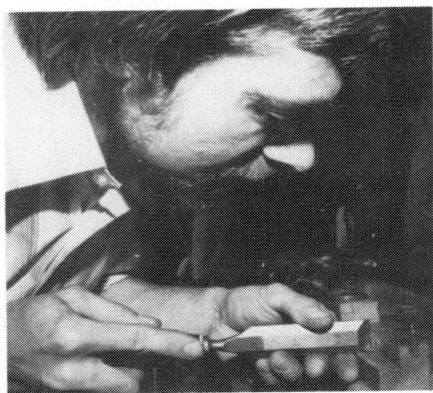

● *Ian Norbury... 'the speed with which he finds the shape in a lump of wood is awesome'*

● *Paul Spriggs works on rushing a ladderback chair*

● *Fraser Budd... 'sure-handed skill with a chisel'*

much attention from visitors, and it was evidently as controversial as it was striking. One comment overheard was: 'He may be a good designer of seats, but he sure as hell doesn't know anything about sewing!' There was interest too in the work of Alan Peters, both because of his well-earned status of superstardom in the woodwork world, and because of the dependable, solid and peaceful nature of his furniture.

Personally I was strongly drawn to the lute and renaissance flutes made by John Underhill of Cheltenham. The flutes, so simple and pure in appearance and so sweet in tone, are immediately identifiable as the work of a talented maker. It was also a pleasure to meet up again with Ian Norbury's almost unbelievably good 'Knight on Horseback' carved in limewood (now priced at £1,120 and still a bargain at that) and to see again Bob Ansell's cradle in yew (£393.75) which attracted so much attention at the Woodworker Show.

Unlisted in the catalogue, but quite an eye-catcher, was a child's high-chair made by Graham Peterkin of Letchworth. When I chanced to meet up with Graham later in Hitchin town centre I took the opportunity of asking whether we could feature the high-chair in *Woodworker*, so keep an eye out for it in a later issue and you will see what I mean about the piece being rather special.

There were turners and carvers and modelmakers and chairmakers and cabinet-

---

makers and boxmakers all represented – and two fine traditional rocking horses by Harold Wakefield, by the way – but there is regrettably not the space here to accord them all the recognition they should rightly have.

Meanwhile the exhibition was being somewhat up-staged by the working demonstrators. Modelmaker Eric Davis from Evesham was being kept busy by visitors' questions as he worked on a model wagon, and John Underhill's lute was the subject of careful scrutiny as it took shape. The catalogue cordially invited visitors to ask questions, and it was no surprise that the nature of the questions suggested that most had come to learn something, rather than to assuage casual curiosity.

Many showed a keen interest in Paul Spriggs' work on rush-seated ladderback chairs, and such was the sure-handed skill of Bristol cabinetmaker Fraser Budd that a good crowd even gathered to watch him perform the comparatively prosaic task of cutting mortices. Woodturning always makes compelling viewing, especially when performed by such a skilled operator as Don White from Bristol, who was turning out articles such as bowls and children's rattles at a prodigious rate.

As one of this country's premier wood-

Continued on page 476

● A lute takes shape under the experienced hands of John Underhill

● Eric Davis, modelmaker, applies a close eye to an intricate job

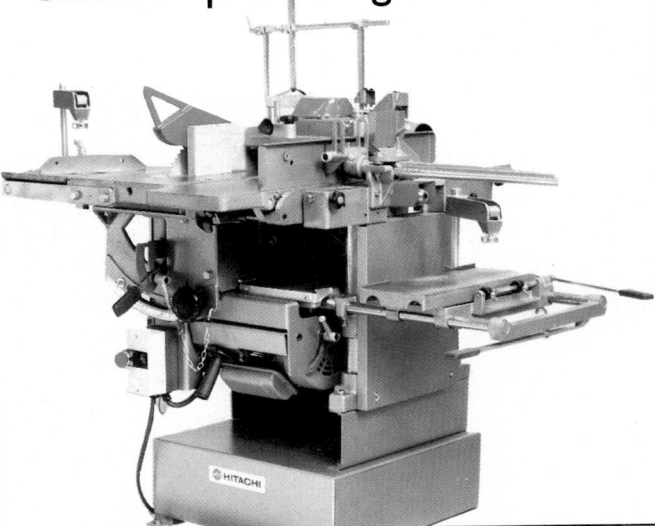
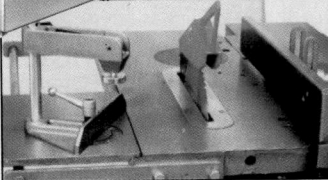
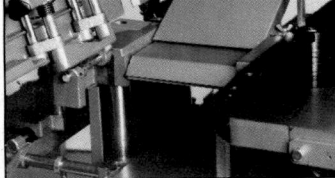
Masterclass Continued from page 475

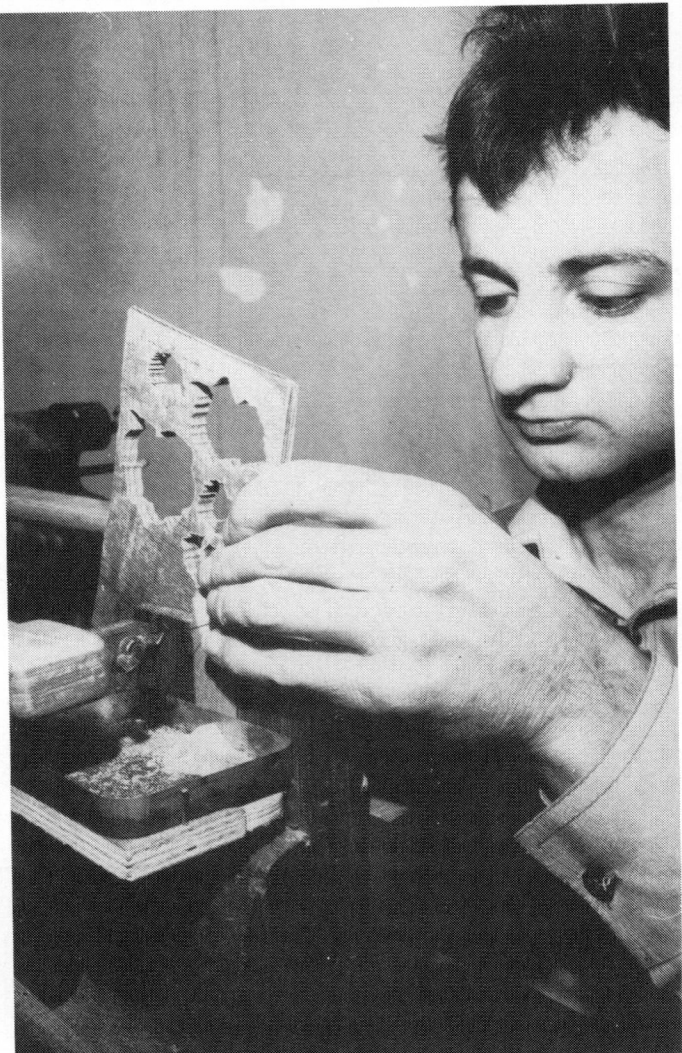

● *Max Cooper at work cutting inlays on his home-built 'donkey'*

● *Opposite; No rush! Paul Spriggs settled comfortably in one of his exquisite ladderback chairs*

carvers there were many who wanted to talk to Ian Norbury of course. The speed with which he finds the shape in a lump of hardwood is quite awesome. At least one customer was able to watch his purchase unfold before his own eyes, and an exquisite horse's head was ready for collection by teatime.

Those who had marvelled at Max Cooper's marquetry dressing table were able to watch the man at work, cutting out intricate designs in multiple on the marquetry 'donkey' he built himself.

The afternoons of the four-day event were set aside for a series of lectures, given by such luminary figures as Alan Peters, Cecil Jordan, Charles Hayward (still going strong, I am happy to report, though now well into his 80s) and John Makepeace. The difficulties of marketing for the craftsman were not unnaturally a consistent theme of questions fired at the speakers during ensuing discussions, and this general preoccupation evoked widely differing responses from different speakers. Cecil Jordan, for instance, had little time for those who complain of a lack of success or recognition. He took the view: if you are good enough you'll make it inevitably, while John Makepeace, who has probably made it bigger in the world of wooden things than anyone, was more inclined to stimulate the craftsman into taking a positive attitude to selling. It is not enough to be

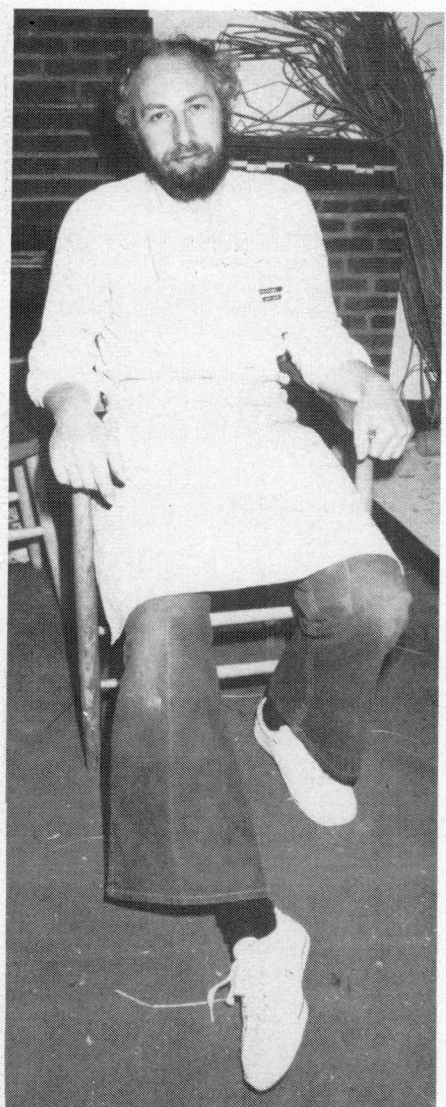

TREE & MAN

Vic Taylor takes a quick look at the recent 'Tree and Man, Hand and Eye' exhibition held in Bath (pictures by Tony Marsh)

This was a small exhibition arranged by an enthusiastic group of folk concerned with conserving small woodlands and making the most of such timber as they can offer. The displays are predictable – small turnery and treen, wood sculpture, and furniture. All are of high quality and do demonstrate, as the hand-out claims, that highly individual and attractive products can result from using this kind of timber.

What did come over was the group's dedication to its purpose, and they will need all of this when they take the exhibition on tour, as all too often such preaching is to the already converted, and the impact on the public-at-large is negligible.

There are already several associations with similar objectives (the Woodland Trust is a notable one) and in my opinion the group would be well advised to ally itself with one of them. Recently I saw the TV programme *Pebble Mill at One* talking of a new project launched recently by David Bellamy called the Conservation Foundation. This has been formed to gather the many small associations into one large body which will have the necessary clout to make its voice heard where it matters.

For those interested, the address is: The Conservation Foundation, Aviation House, 129 Kingsway, London WC2B 6NH. ■

● *Two woodcarvings (above and below) by Chris Pye, both in the exhibition*

good enough, he said. The craftsman must discover that promoting and marketing his wares is actually a most interesting and enjoyable extension of the making process.

Other speakers, spread over the four afternoons were Brian Davies of Stobarts, the publishers, Bob Brett of North Heigham Sawmills, Roger Buse himself, Richard Maude, who spoke about antique tools, and Ian Fiddes-Gooding of the stains and polishes firm, Fiddes and Son. Brian Cohen discussed his techniques as a guitarmaker, and Mary Comino and John Beer gave an in-depth review of the Arts and Crafts Movement, Gimson, Barnsley *et al*. On the final day it was the turn of Chris Simpson from Rycotewood College, and a former Rycotewood student, Lucinda Leech, along with public relations consultant David Hide, and Alan Mitchell, editor of er... what's it called? Oh yes, *Practical Woodworking!*

I noticed in the catalogue that enquiries were already being invited for Masterclass 83, but in the meanwhile let me remind you that Betty's next enterprise, her Woodworkers of Excellence show, takes place at the Queen's Hotel in Cheltenham, on the weekend of July 16/17/18. Fine woodwork needs to put itself prominently before the public in this way, and if woodcraft begins to attract the interest of discerning people the way I think it is going to, it will be the likes of Roger Buse and Betty Norbury who we shall have to thank. ■

● *Don White (see also Masterclass review) showed some fine examples of what Man, Hand and Eye can do for a piece of wood*

Events

Timber frame

The Arts Council touring exhibition on timber frame buildings which was the subject of an article in the May issue of *Woodworker* will be at the Weald and Downland Open Air Museum, Singleton, from 19 June-11 July; from 27 July-15 August it will be at the Cooper Gallery, Barnsley; 6-28 November at the Herbert Art Gallery, Coventry; 11 December-8 January at the Gosport Museum and Art Gallery, Hants. It will continue wandering through 1983 ending in June 1984 though dates and venues are not yet finalised.

Furniture and woodwork

The Victoria and Albert museum announce that the musical instruments gallery is now open but at present can only be reached via the ironwork gallery (rooms 113-114E). The English principal galleries (52-54) are closed and should reopen in mid-October. No opening date is given at this stage but rooms 8 and 9 will be housing the splendid furniture and other items of art at present in the Bethnal Green Museum which form the collections of the continental 19th century principal galleries.

Ham House

Near Richmond (phone 01-940 1950). The gilding of the restored great staircase has just been completed so it now once again looks very much as it must have done when new in 1638.

Osterley Park House

Osterley, Middx (phone 01-560 3918). This spring sees the redecoration of the hall and staircase in their correct colours. The restoration of the state bed is expected to be completed by 1 July.

Wellington Museum

At Apsley House, Hyde Park Corner, London (phone 01-499 5676). The restoration of the dining room will be finished this summer. The so-called slip room has been restored.

Indian Heritage

A major exhibition mounted as part of the Festival of India in room 45 at the Victoria and Albert Museum until 15 August. Admission £1.50p for children, students (with ID) OAP's and UB40 holders. The Indian Heritage covers court life and arts under Mughal rule. 24 June sees an important lecture at 6.30pm to complement this exhibition, entitled Crafts for the court it will be given by Robert Skelton in the lecture theatre on the first floor (off room 66).

Diary date in Peru

Woodworking Machinery Exhibition (TECHNO-FOREST) 20-23 November, at Lima, details from ECL (Exhibition Agencies) Ltd, 11 Manchester Square, London W1M 5AB.

Diary date in Poland

International Trade Fair of Woodworking Machines, 26-30 October, at Poznan, details from Management of the Poznan International Fair, Glogowska Street, 14, 60-734 Poznan.

Lectures
Sunday at the V&A

Under the heading 'A closer look' comes Gillian Darby's lecture at 3.30pm on the Duchess of Manchester's cabinet. This is one of a series of lectures to encourage visitors to the V&A to examine masterpieces from technical, stylistic and historical viewpoints. It is one of a series of slide lectures. This one is on 27 June.

Wednesdays at the V&A

Sarah Bowles has been giving a series of lectures at lunchtime at the V&A (1.15) tracing the development of the skills of the cabinetmaker. On 23 June she covers the late 18th century 'To Mr Adam's taste in the ornament of his buildings and furniture, we stand indebted'. On 30 June she gives the Victorian view 'Tis now the living room, where guests to whim, a taste, or fancy true, Scattered in groups their different plans to pursue.'

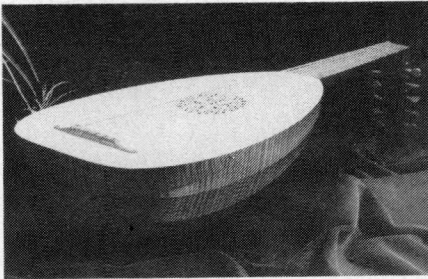

● *Renaissance lute by John Underhill destined for Woodworkers of Excellence*

Diary dates in London

British Craft Show to be held at Syon Park, London, 16-18 September, details from International Craft and Hobby Fair Ltd, 3 Rothesay Drive, Highcliffe, Christchurch, Dorset.

Antiques Fair at the Park Lane Hotel, London, 5-9 October, details from Marlowe Exhibitions Ltd, 57 Mill Lane, London NW6.

London International Building/Home Improvements Exhibition at Earls Court, London, 12-17 October, details from London Building Exhibitions Ltd, 11 Manchester Square, London W1M 5AB.

Woodworker Show at the Royal Horticultural Society Halls, London, 19-24 October, details from Model and Allied Publications Ltd, PO Box 35, Bridge Street, Hemel Hempstead, Herts HP1 1EE.

Kensington Antiques Fair at Kensington New Town Hall, London, 4-9 November, details from Cultural Exhibitions Ltd, 8 Meadrow, Godalming, Surrey GU7 2HN.

Dairy dates in Birmingham

International Woodworking Industries Exhibition (IWIE) 12-16 September at the N.E.C. Details from Andry Montgomery Ltd, 11 Manchester Square, London W1M 5AB.

International Furniture Show, 14-17 November, at the N.E.C. Details from BFM Exhibitions Ltd, 30 Harcourt Street, London W1H 2AA.

Diary date in Denmark

Danish Furniture Trade Fair (MOBELMESSE) 19-22 August at Herning, details from A/S Herning Hallen, DK-7400, Herning.

Diary dates in France

European Furniture and Furnishing Industries Fair, 2-5 October, at Lyon, details from Foire International de Lyon, Palais des Congres, 69459 Lyon, Cedex 3.

Do-it-yourself exhibition, 30 October-11 November, at Paris, details from French Trade Exhibitions, 54 Conduit Street, London W1R 9SD.

Diary dates in USA

World Woodworking Exhibition, 18-22 August at Atlanta, details from Cahners Exposition Group, c/o Show Company International Division, 8687 Melrose Avenue, Los Angeles Ca90069.

International Woodworking Machinery and Furniture Supply Fair 11-14 September at Louisville, details from Show Manager, Suite 907, 8401 Connecticut Avenue, Chevy Chase, Maryland 20015.

Woodworkers of Excellence

Exhibition to be held in the ballroom of the Queens Hotel, Cheltenham on 16, 17, 18 July. (10-7 daily).

Technical Leisure Centre

Bank holiday weekend 29-31 May heralded the opening of the Technical Leisure Centre at 1 Grangeway, Kilburn, London NW6 2BW. The idea behind the centre, set up by Nathan Shestopal Ltd, is to provide a home for advice, knowledge and guidance plus tools and materials in a club environment to serve model engineers, home computer enthusiasts and woodworking craftsmen. Membership of TLC costs £3.00 per annum. Other events planned so far include: 1 June Kity woodworking machinery; 11, 12 June Bosch electric power tools and Trend router cutters; 16, 17, 18 June Elektra Beckum woodworking machinery and woodturning lathes; 25, 26 June Elu machinery and hand power tools.

For violinmakers

The violinmakers' summer schools held annually at Cambridge already have the touch of legend about them, and such is the demand for places that this year there are to be two courses in consecutive weeks.

The dates are 11-17 and 18-24 July, and there are just a few places still available. The two courses, directed by Juliet Barker and Roland Gentle, offer intensive workshop time and instruction, and will be backed up by talks. Lecturers: Wilf Saunders (violinmaker), Philip Walker (authority on woodworking tools) and Harry Danks (retired viola player). A choice of wood will also be on sale, by arrangement with Sydney Evans.

If you would like to join one of the courses (£45 for tuition, with accommodation available at extra cost) get in touch with Juliet Barker, 19 Marshall Road, Cambridge.

After the game . . .

Jack Maynard, a former principal lecturer at Shoreditch College, has made a wall-hanging chess unit. 'Too often,' he says, 'the board and pieces are stowed away when not in use. Yet they have an intrinsic design value of their own and are worthy of a place on the lounge wall.'

His unit consists of the basic frame, the board and two boxes for the pieces

Fig. 1

Basically the movable parts are supported on rods protruding from the frame and are held firmly in position by magnetic catches. They are easy to put up and take down (Fig 2).

The frame This is a simple haunched mortise and tenon frame. The main dimensions are given in Fig 3. Prepare all material to a cross-sectional size and arrange as required. Initially mark-out (Fig 4); mark-out the joints, cut them and test for fit. Take apart and mark the positions for the magnetic catches in the rails (Fig 3) and remove the waste. The catches are those used for cabinet doors but with the plastics covers removed. They can then be held in position with round-headed screws.

Clean-up all the inside edges of the frame; Sellotape to the joint lines where necessary and polish. Glue and cramp-up the frame testing for square and wind. When dry, clean-up the frame to a uniform thickness, mark-out the shape of the top and bottom edges, remove the waste and clean-up. Do not complete the polishing at this stage.

The chessboard This is made basically from 12mm ply veneered on both faces and lipped all round (Fig 5). The veneered ply will finish at just over ½in (13mm) thick and the hardwood lippings should be prepared to ⅝in (15mm) thickness. Start with a piece of ply about 14in (355mm) square. The upper face will be covered with contrasting veneers, eg teak and sycamore.

Produce four strips 13in (330mm) long of light veneer and four of dark, using method shown in Fig 6. The cramping block must be carefully prepared from a solid piece of hardwood; it is vital that it be the same width throughout its length. By this method the strips of veneer will all be the same and the cutting operation (using a new Stanley blade) may be done with confidence. After cutting, the strips are put together with Sellotape (Fig 7).

Initially a pair is pulled together by short pieces of tape and then the joint is covered lengthwise. When the eight strips are joined cut across them at right angles to produce eight alternating strips. These are then Sellotaped together to produce the 64 squares necessary for the board.

If this work has been done accurately it will produce a perfect 12in (305mm) square. The margin round this basic square is made from strips of whichever veneer is prefer-

red, mitred at the corners and taped to the centre piece.

The underneath face of the ply has to be veneered to balance the structure, and a piece of veneer is cut to just under the size of the baseboard.

Garnet paper both faces of the ply to a smooth finish. (Toothing the surface is not required when using adhesives such as

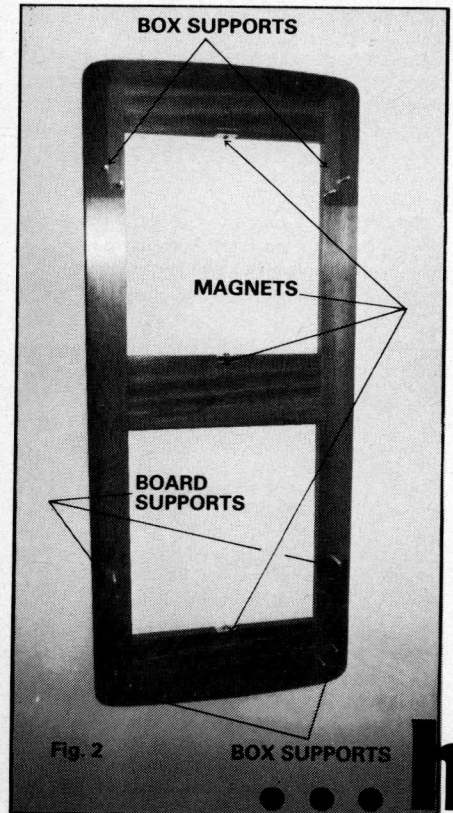

Fig. 2

BOX SUPPORTS

MAGNETS

BOARD SUPPORTS

BOX SUPPORTS

Fig 3 (dimensions: 12¼ (310), 3⅛ (80), 9¾ (245), 3½ (90), (19), ¾, 10⅛ (255), 3½ (90), 30 (760), 1⅝, (40), Magnetic catches)

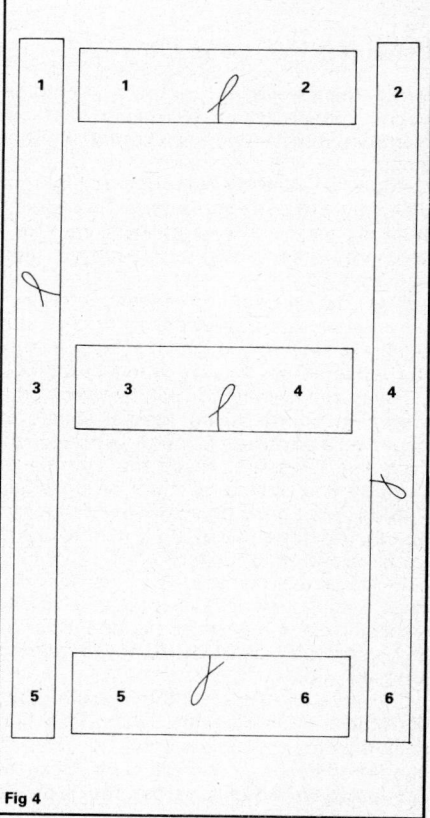

Fig 4 (panels numbered 1 2, 3 4, 5 6)

. . .hang it on the wall

After the game...

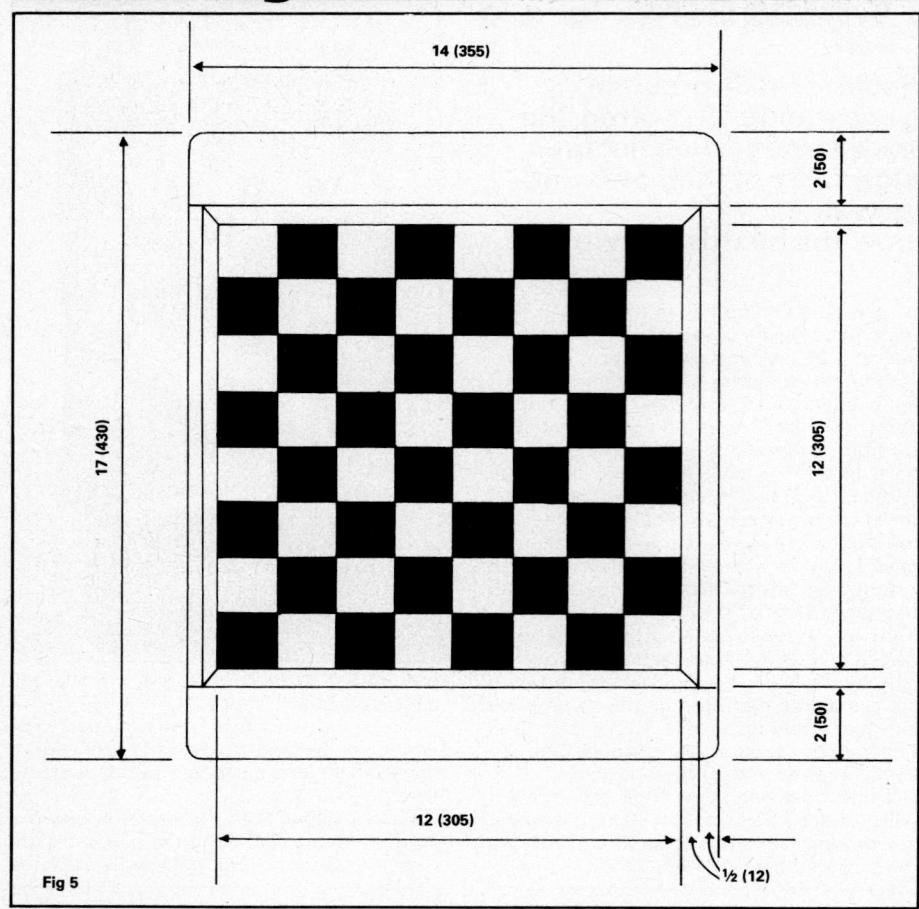

Fig 5

14 (355)
2 (50)
17 (430)
12 (305)
12 (305)
2 (50)
½ (12)

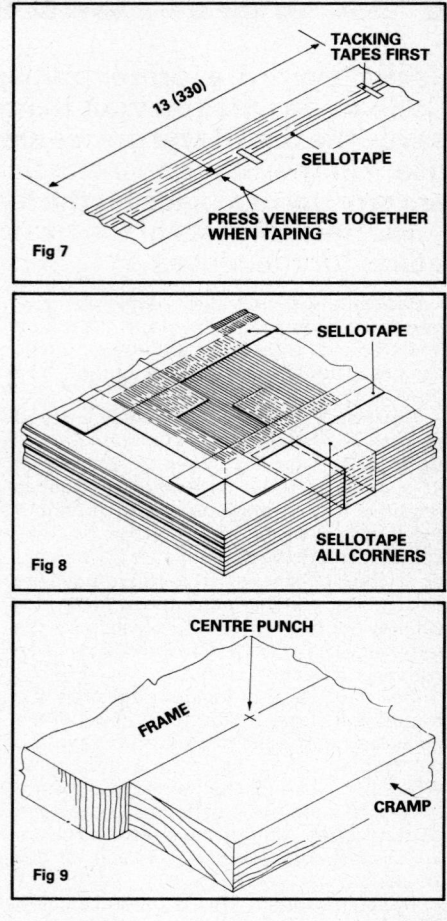

Fig 7

TACKING TAPES FIRST
13 (330)
SELLOTAPE
PRESS VENEERS TOGETHER WHEN TAPING

Fig 8

SELLOTAPE
SELLOTAPE ALL CORNERS

Fig 9

CENTRE PUNCH
FRAME
CRAMP

Continued from page 479

PVA.) Before gluing, prepare cramping boards, paper, and G-cramps so that the operation may be done quickly and without a hitch.

Apply the adhesive uniformly to one side of the ply. Place the underneath side veneer centrally on it and smooth over with firm pressure of the hands. Turn over and glue the upper ply face.

Place the chessboard veneer centrally in place, apply hand pressure as before, and Sellotape each corner (Fig 8). (This prevents the veneers from moving when cramping).

Place the veneered ply between the cramping boards using several sheets of paper on both faces to help distribute the cramping pressure. Place the cramps in position and tighten as much as possible. Putting the cramps on single-handed is not an easy operation and help is useful. Leave under pressure for at least 6hr.

Remove the cramps and clean-off any paper which may have become stuck to the veneer. Next remove the Sellotape. This has to be done very carefully to prevent tearing up the grain.

Cut the ply back to the margin, thus forming a perfect square. Using PVA butt joint the narrow lippings down two sides of the board ensuring that the extra thickness is distributed equally across the T of the veneered ply.

When dry saw off the surplus ends and plane back to the edges of the ply. Remove surplus thickness without damaging the veneers on either side of the ply. Butt joint the wide lippings on to the board and when

dry repeat the process already described. Finally, all surfaces should be carefully scraped and the corners rounded to taste.

The board rests on two aluminium rods in the frame and is held in position by a magnetic catch. The half-holes in the lower edge of the board are produced as shown in Fig 9. The diameter of the hole needs to be slightly larger than that of the supporting rod.

The board may now be positioned on the frame and the exact centres of the rods established. Test drill holes for the rods on a waste piece of wood and choose a drill which will give a drive fit for the diameter rod used. The rods have a domed top end and a slight bevel on the lower to facilitate

entry into the holes (Fig 10). Partially tap the rods in the holes drilled in the frame and support the chessboard on them. From the back mark the position of the magnetic catch on the back of the board. Remove the rods.

Cut out a suitable rectangular-shaped piece of steel plate and inlay it at the marked position flush with the surface, using Araldite adhesive. Drill and countersink two holes in the frame rails to fix to the wall. The board may be cleaned-up with garnet paper and finally polished.

Boxes for the pieces Basically these are simple through dovetail boxes the joints of which are adjusted where necessary to cope with the rebates at the back and

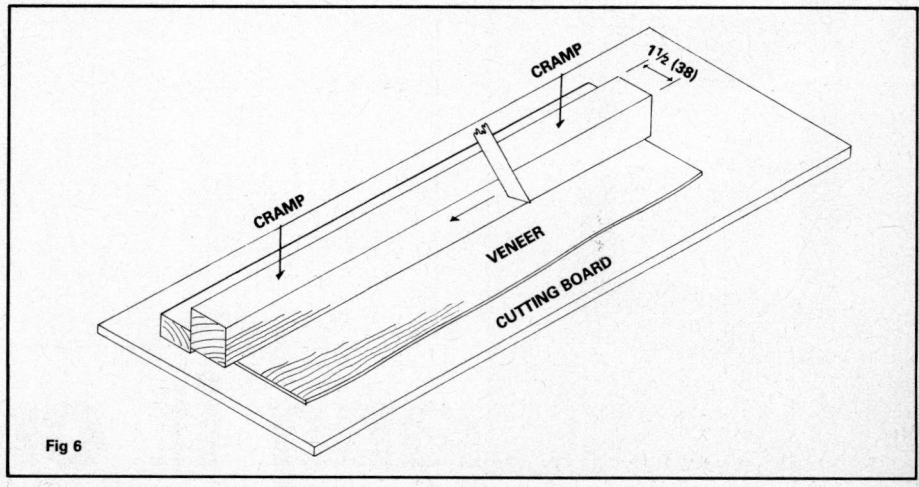

Fig 6

CRAMP
1½ (38)
CRAMP
VENEER
CUTTING BOARD

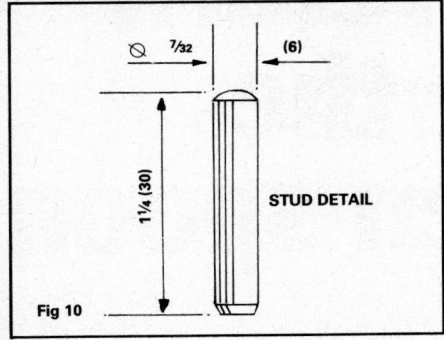

STUD DETAIL

Fig 10

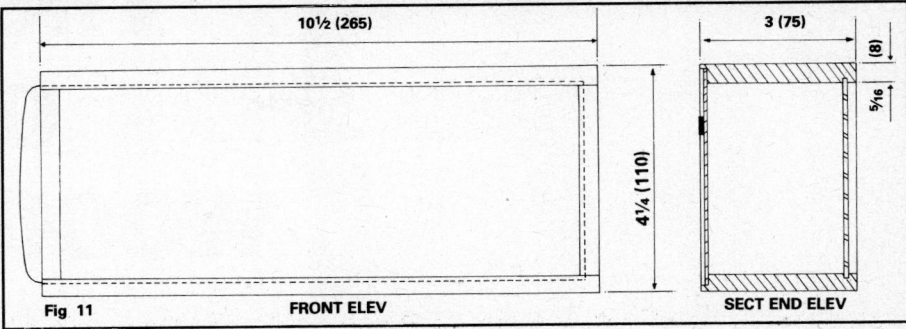

FRONT ELEV

SECT END ELEV

Fig 11

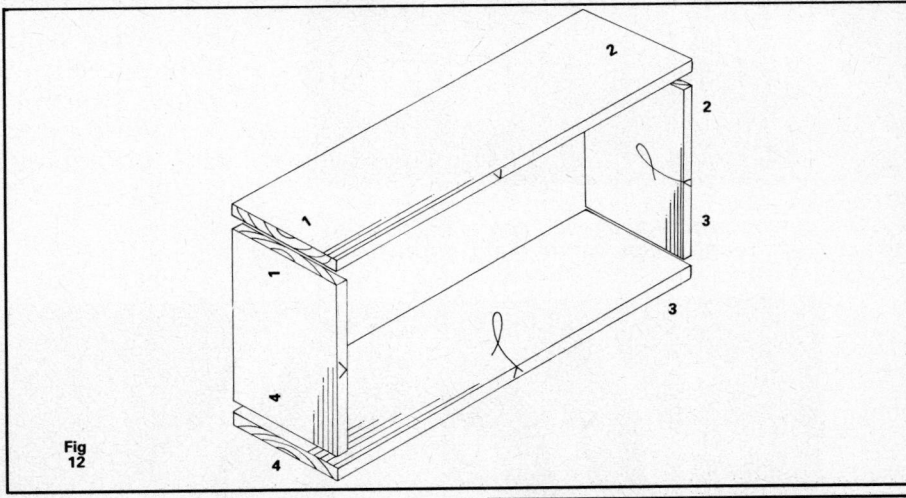

Fig 12

grooves at the front. The overall sizes given in Fig 11.

Prepare all material to a cross-sectional size and shoot all ends square and to length. Arrange the material as required and mark initially (Fig 12). Run out the rebates on all the back edges; and grooves on the fronts of two sides and one end of each box. The size of the grooves will depend on the gauge of glass used.

Mark-out and cut the joints, the detail of which is as Fig 13. One end of the carcase is narrower than the other but do not remove this excess until after the joints have been cut. The new edge can then be accurately lined-up with the inner side of the groove.

Having cut and fitted the joints, clean-up the inner surfaces, mask-off the joint areas with Sellotape and polish. The boxes are glued-up and tested for square and wind. When dry clean-up the outer faces.

The thin ply back may now be glued into the rebate. The inside face of the back is covered with a suitably textured material cut to size and glued into position.

The boxes are carefully positioned on the frame and held there by cramps while the rod positions are marked. This is a tricky operation and may be assisted by using a simple jig (Fig 14). A spare piece of rod with a pointed end is used as a centre punch and a slight tap with a hammer gives the exact drilling position.

The holes in the frame must all be of the same depth and normal to the surface. When the frame has been finally polished the rods are tapped into position to the bottom of each hole using a hammer and small softening block.

The unpolished box should be placed on the rods and the position of the magnet marked on the ply back. A metal plate is

fastened in position on the back (using Araldite) so that the upper face of the metal is in the same plane as the back edge of the box. This ensures good contact with the magnet in the vertical position.

The boxes may now be polished and the glass fronts with ground edges fitted.

Last job is to fix the frame on the wall. Mark, drill and plug the upper hole first. Screw the frame in position and check that it is vertical. Mark the position of the lower hole. Remove the frame. Drill, plug and screw the frame in position.

Fill the boxes with the pieces and place in position, together with the board, on the frame. ∎

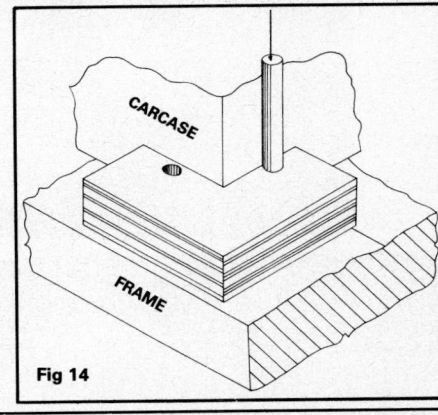

CARCASE

FRAME

Fig 14

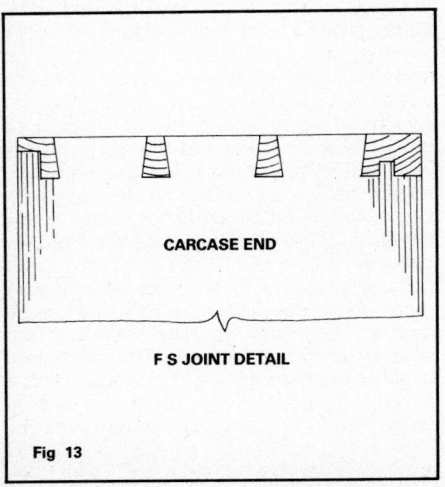

CARCASE END

F S JOINT DETAIL

Fig 13

CUTTING LIST

Working allowance has been made in lengths and widths. Thicknesses are net. Dimensions in inches and mm

	L	W	T
FRAME			
2 Stiles	30½ (770)	1⅞ (45)	¾ (19)
1 Upper rail	12 (305)	3⅜ (85)	¾ (19)
2 Mid/low/rail	12 (305)	3¾ (95)	¾ (19)
2 Br csk 1½ × No. 8 screws			
3 Magnets			
3 Br rd hd ½ × No. 6 screws			
10 Aluminium rods	1¼ (30)	⌀7/32 (6)	
BOARD			
1 Ply	14 (355)	14 (355)	½ (12)
2 Lipping/narrow	14 (355)	¾ (19)	⅝ (15)
2 Lipping/wide	15 (380)	2¼ (55)	⅝ (15)
1 Steel plate	1 (25)	⅜ (10)	16G
Veneers to suit			
BOXES			
4 Tops/bottoms	11 (270)	3¼ (80)	5/16 (8)
4 Ends	4¾ (120)	3¼ (80)	5/16 (8)
2 Backs/ply	10½ (265)	4¼ (110)	⅛ (3)
2 Steel plates (for magnets)			
2 Textured material to suit			
2 Glass fronts to suit			

The return of the wooden spoon

The craft of wooden spoon making had to move over when metal and plastics began to offer a cheaper alternative. However, this ancient craft is now making a revival, not least in the hands of Jack Hill, who gives away some of the secrets here

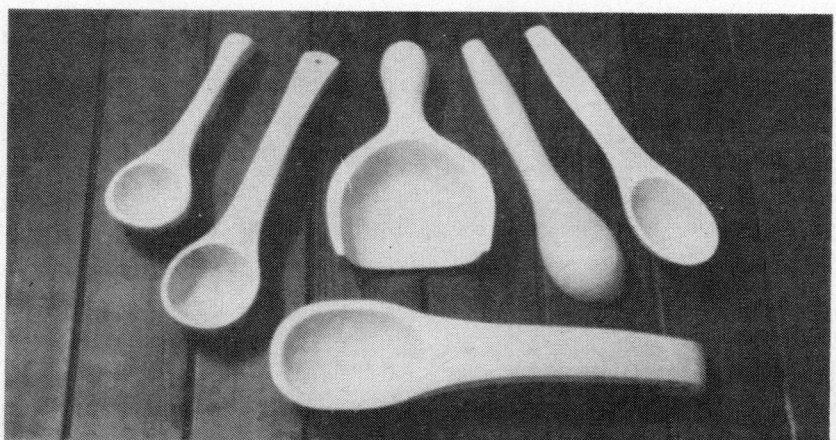

● Early stages in making a spoon, from right to left, sycamore block, roughly shaped spoon made with an axe and a rough shape cut on the bandsaw

● Above: wooden spoons, scoop and a ladle. The lathe turned spoons are at top right. All in sycamore

● Left: hollowing a traditional wooden spoon using the hooking knife (pre 1939) Copyright CoSIRA

The making of spoons, ladles, and scoops in wood was once a thriving village craft. Since metal and plastic products have replaced these wooden utensils in our kitchens and at the table, the craftsmen who made them have almost all disappeared. It is interesting to note, however, that there is still a market for certain of these wooden implements — there are still those who prefer the more pleasing wood to even the brightest coloured plastic variety, but choice is largely limited to cheap foreign imports, often made in the wrong kind of wood.

The right kind of wood for utensils used in the preparation of and in contact with food is sycamore. Its smooth, white surface wears well even after constant use and washing — it can be scrubbed clean when necessary — and, as it has neither taste or smell, it does not taint food in any way. Another suitable wood is beech, which, although a little darker in colour, has properties similar to sycamore. Birch was sometimes used in the past and so was holly. Winter felled sycamore is best, stacked on end in the early stages of seasoning to obtain clean surfaces free from sap stain.

The old spoon makers preferred cleft material for their work to ensure strength along the grain, hewing sections roughly to shape with an axe, the bowl being partly hollowed with a small, one handed adze. Large spoons and ladles, such as those used in jam making and for stirring and serving the porridge, were often made from a suitable size log split down the middle into two half-rounds and then cut roughly to shape. Many carvers did this stage of the work while the wood was still green (unseasoned), taking advantage of the ease with which wood can be worked by hand in this condition. Final shaping came after further seasoning.

Further hollowing of the bowl then took place using the adze or with a half-round gouge. The rough surface was next cut smooth using a special curved knife. Known in some areas as a hooking knife this has a short, bent blade fixed into a remarkably long handle. For this stage of the work the carver sat on a low stool, the roughly shaped spoon held against his left knee by

● *Shaping hollow of bowl with a gouge and mallet. Spoon gouge on bench top*

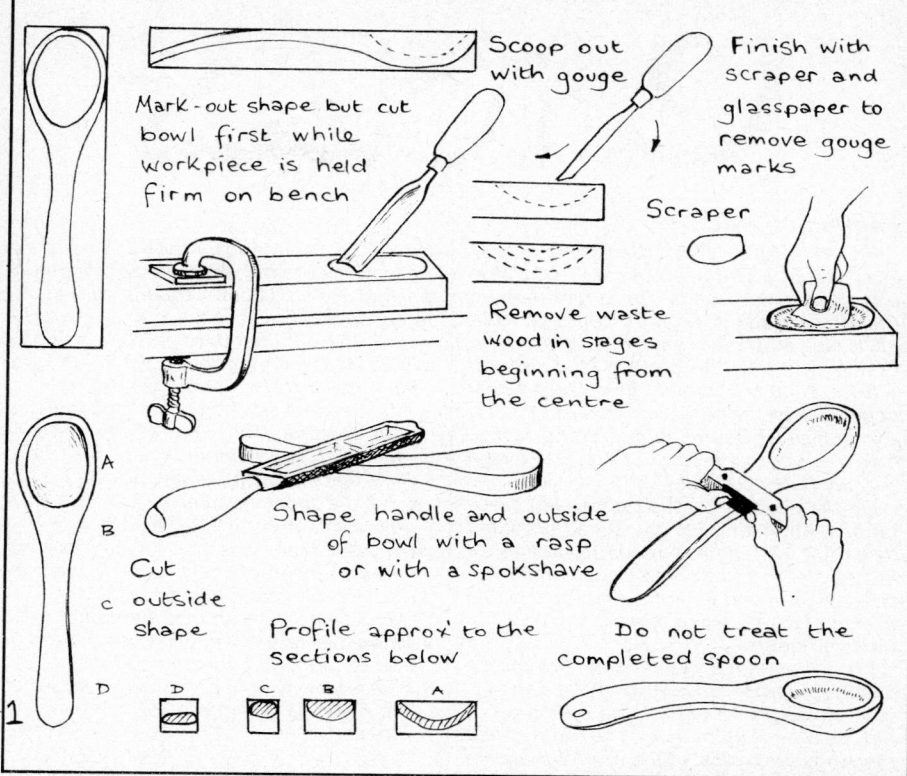

Mark-out shape but cut bowl first while workpiece is held firm on bench

Scoop out with gouge

Finish with scraper and glasspaper to remove gouge marks

Scraper

Remove waste wood in stages beginning from the centre

A

B

Cut

C outside

shape

Shape handle and outside of bowl with a rasp or with a spokshave

Profile approx to the sections below

Do not treat the completed spoon

D   D   C   B   A

1

his left hand. With the long handle of the curved knife held stiffly below his right forearm resting on the right upper leg to give extra leverage, he scooped and smoothed the bowl with a twisting movement of the wrist. Finally, the outside surface would be finished off with a spokeshave.

The beauty of these hand carved spoons is that their handles can be given nicely curved or bent shapes; large spoons and ladles often had hooked handles so that they could hang on a rail when not in use.

Diagram 1 shows how this method of carving could be closely followed using more readily available tools. When a gouge and mallet is used for hollowing the bowl it is best to do this first and avoid problems of holding the workpiece firm to the bench after the outside has been shaped. The gouge should be of the outside bevel or out-cannel type; use with a scooping action to avoid digging in and take small cuts rather than large ones. Work all round the bowl and go progressively deeper — but not too deep! A straight gouge can be used initially — about ¾in is ideal — but a bent or spoon gouge makes finishing by hand easier.

The old craftsmen worked almost entirely by eye, making few measurements as they worked. For symmetry, at least a centre line is recommended or use a paper template to make accurate shapes. Shapes can be cut on a band saw or by hand with a bow saw.

Not all spoons were entirely hand carved; some were part carved and part turned on the lathe. In this method the basic shape

would be roughed out and the bowl hollowed and smoothed as described. The outside of the bowl was finished by hand also but then the whole spoon was set-up in the lathe and a straight, round handle turned on it. A small 'stub' left on the bowl for the lathe centre was cleaned off by hand on completion.

A novel way to make straight handled spoons is to make them in pairs using the split turning technique. Cup chucks are normally used to hold the two halves whilst turning. This gives the shape to the outside of the spoons and, when removed from the lathe, each half is hollowed to form the bowl. Alternatively two halves can be glued and turned as one between centres then parted or a solid piece can be carefully sawn down the middle after being turned and the bowls hollowed as before. These methods have the disadvantage of difficulty in holding the workpiece firm when the bowl is hollowed by gouge and mallet; to overcome this problem in the first two cases bowls can be hollowed before being turned

but beware of breaking through into the hidden hollows.

Wooden scoops are nice to make and have many uses when handling dry goods such as flour or sugar. They can be made in several sizes using methods similar to spoon and ladle making. If anything, scoops are actually easier to make than spoons.

Utensils used in contact with food should *not* be given any surface treatment, no polyurethane, no wax polish; nothing. Some sources suggest using a vegetable oil such as olive oil. This is fine for some items, fruit bowls, for example, but it is not recommended here. The right kind of wood needs no treatment — it can be kept clean and more hygienic simply by being washed in water when necessary.

A small hand adze with either a straight or a curved cutting edge, similar to that described, is available from Roger's of Hitchin. Their catalogue also lists 'carver's hooks' which have blades similar to the spoon carver's hooking knife but fitted into much shorter handles. ■

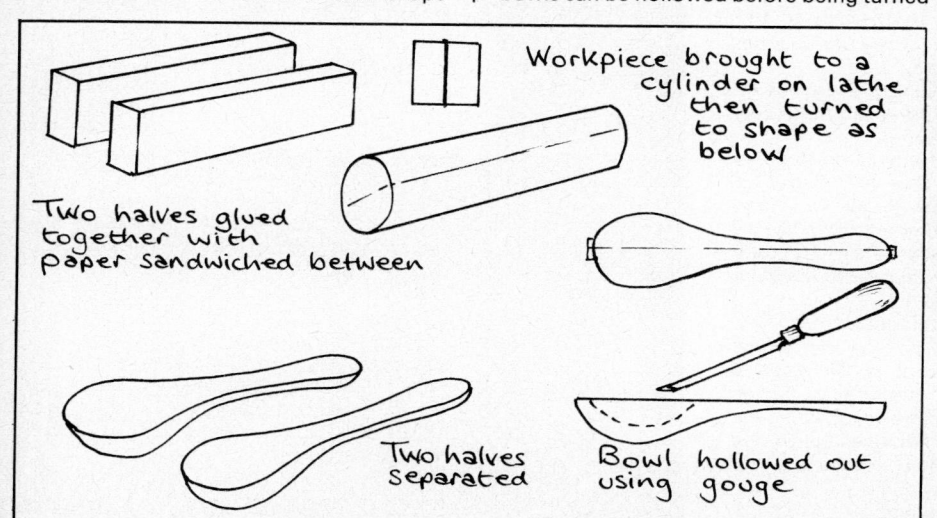

Two halves glued together with paper sandwiched between

Workpiece brought to a cylinder on lathe then turned to shape as below

Two halves separated

Bowl hollowed out using gouge

● *Author shaping a spoon with an axe*

Offcuts

by Chris Dunn

Regulation rule

So I was right. . . Mr Broadbent's elderly Stanley rule, pictured in 'Offcuts' of the May issue, was not made for a left-handed Chinese chippy! A prompt response from no lesser authority than Stanley Tools in Connecticut USA has provided the answer.

Says Stanley's Robert West: 'It certainly appears to be the no 87 ivory rule, arch joint, German silver bound, with drafting scales. This rule was made from 1859 to 1924 by the Stanley Rule and Level Co.'

On the question of the right-to-left calibrations, Mr West goes on: 'When unfolded to its full 2ft length it reads from 1 to 24 inches starting from either end, which is a time saver in that it avoids flipping the rule from end to end when making a number of measurements.'

Mr Broadbent's query also brought a swift reply from F. Seward of London W7, who appears to have a large collection of old Stanley catalogues. 'The right-to-left markings are typical of the fourfold rules of this kind made by SRL for their domestic market,' says Mr Seward. 'For export, at any rate to the UK, they were marked conventionally — hence "American" markings and "English" markings.'

As for the reverse figuring, Mr Seward is in accord with Mr West. 'The explanation for the so-called American marking appears to be this: a carpenter, possibly on piece work, having to cross-cut timbers to varying lengths would (if right-handed) have his saw in the right hand, rule in left, and time would be saved marginally by the markings falling naturally in the reverse order.'

Mr Seward is, however, unconvinced about the practical value of this marking system: 'It seems the Americans themselves were doubtful of any advantage, for by far the most popular rule in the USA, until supplanted by the flexible-rigid coilable steel tape, was the "zigzag" spring-jointed rule. All of these that I have seen listed are marked conventionally.'

Mr Seward gives much additional information besides, which has been passed on to Mr Broadbent, but I think the left-handed Chinese chippy should have the last word.

He say: 'Stanley rules OK.'

Ah-so.

Just for the record

A friend of mine who is currently giving his house a thorough refit came across a piece of skirting board, on the back of which were the names of the two chippies who had put it there in the first place. The signatures have a certain flourish about them, suggesting that the carpenters had taken some pride in their work, and alongside the names of George Blunt and Jesse Young is the date, April 6th, 1912.

This nice little historical record put me in mind of a conversation I had with John Beer, an expert on the Arts and Crafts Movement, at the Masterclass '82 event recently. 'If only', said John, 'if only cabinetmakers would sign their work, it would make life so much easier for historians and furniture specialists.'

It is easy to see how a discreet signature and date on a piece of fine furniture would save people like John Beer, who is a consultant to a London gallery, a great deal of time and detective work.

It strikes me as odd that it is not the natural inclination of a craftsman to sign his work as a matter of course, particularly if he is proud of it. Makers of keyboard instruments, for instance, are always ready to observe the custom of proclaiming 'Fecit Ernie Boggins' or whatever in bold letters just where the world is most likely to see it. Turners seem to stamp their names on their work, and I am sure that woodcarvers like to get their autographs on their work too. Perhaps the cabinetmaker regards the excellence and style of his artefacts to be a sufficient mark of his hand.

Nevertheless, I put it to all you cabinetmakers, on behalf of John Beer and his colleagues: if George Blunt and Jesse Young could sign a piece of skirting board, then a name and a date in some discreet corner of your work would not go amiss.

The good, the bad and the ugly ▶

The unusual frontage pictured right demonstrates intriguingly two extremes of the carpenter's work. As the top half suggests, it must once have been a very pretty feature of its position near the market in Hitchin, Herts. But the need to extend evidently overcame aesthetic considerations at some stage, so somebody nailed that dreadful white box on the front of it.

Fortunately the extension looks to be so badly built that it will just drop off before long, and the people of Hitchin will have the lovely old original to look at again.

Turn of the screw

The Great Screwdriver Controversy which raged in our letters columns recently got many readers going on at some length about the more arcane aspects of driving screws. But all our British talk of torque and leverage has prompted a pithy letter from Mr G. Heighington of the Industrial Arts Department of Cosburn Junior High School in Toronto, Canada.

'Hopefully,' says he, 'in future we may be spared these trivial letters talking of force, slip, drive, angle and all that.'

Mr Heighington's remedy is, on the face of it, quite simple. 'Buy the Canadian designed and patented Robertson Head Screws,' he advises. 'They are ideal for all cabinet work. The drive is by a square recess in the head, quite similar to the allen head bolt.'

He has sent me catalogues from P. L. Robertson Plant in Milton, Ontario, which show this socket-headed screw amid a bewildering range of fastenings for all purposes. 'Given an enterprising importer, or even manufacturer, I'm sure that Britain could also have its share of square screws,' he concludes.

Perhaps we already have?

Home Sweet Hive ▶

Last month I reported on how a Kent bee-farmer was coping with the ravages of woodpeckers which were woodpecking their way into his hives and eating the bees. This month we keep up the theme of apiary (well it's a bee-keeping time of year, isn't it?) with news of how a Lowestoft apiarist has been keeping his little workers happy.

Known to me only as Mr Beckett, this thoughtful bee-man has decided to cheer up his bees by giving their hive windows, eaves, a porch and even a smoking chimney. The workers seem to be most appreciative of their homely hive, since Mr Beckett reports that he has not lost a swarm yet.

By now there will already be plenty of honey in the attic, so if you hear a bee humming 'Home Sweet Home' as it goes about its work, chances are it's one of Mr Beckett's workforce.

For Thumb-Thumpers

The thumped thumb is a rather tedious cliché that clings to the business of hammering nails, but like all tedious clichés it has its own painful truth. Be honest. Have you never thumped your thumb instead of the nail?

John Barratt of Waves, a company based at Corscombe in Dorset which markets Wessex aids and visual systems principally for the disabled, tells me that some market research on one of their products has generated some interesting facts relating to the thumped thumb.

The product under research was a little device which holds steel nails and screws clear of fingers by magnet. 'Before full production commenced we carried out some local market research,' says John Barratt. 'We were astounded at the number of damaged digits shown to us. They could best be described as self-inflicted disablement by professional and amateur experts, whether left-handed, right-handed or otherwise.'

He concluded from the research that the device had possibilities among able-bodied woodworkers as well as the disabled, so he sent us one to have a look at.

It certainly seems a potentially handy thing to have by on the workbench. Its 4kg magnetic pull should prove a useful aid to retrieving stray nails and screws from awkward places, quite aside from its ability to hold vertically nails up to 5in long. (If you want one, by the way, they cost £2.80 including VAT, p & p from Waves, Corscombe, Dorchester DT2 0NU).

On the face of it the nail holder is a neat little device that is rather brilliant in its simplicity. There is however one small catch which will amuse those who are fairly consistent thumb-thumpers. A note in small type at the bottom of the card on which the device is supplied says: Do not hit magnets with hammer.

Are you there, Jack?

Jack Watson, where are you now? A neighbour of mine, Mac Dowdy, was recalling happy days of the early 1960s spent as a teacher at Eastholm Boys School in Peterborough, and the extraordinary teaching talents of a cabinetmaker and woodwork instructor called Jack Watson.

'He arrived as number two in the department,' Mac Dowdy remembers. 'The wood-

● Be it ever so bumble, there's no place like home! More an example of good humour than it is of good woodwork, Mr Beckett's homely bee-hive. (Picture by David Askham)

work department was split into two sections, one of which Jack took over. The first thing he did was to pack up all the nails and screws and send them over to the other section, which was more the sort of woodwork class you expect to find in a school. But while this other section was turning out coat-hangers and toast racks and funny wooden aeroplanes, Jack's boys were making beautiful tables, chairs and chests-of-drawers.

'The boys took a great pride in what they did and the standard was very high – real craftsmanship in fact.'

Jack Watson moved from Peterborough back to his home in Newcastle, but Mac has always remembered his admiration for the skills of this super-teacher of woodwork, and he has also remained grateful to Jack for introducing him to the joys of walking in the Pennines.

'We'll put out a call in Woodworker,' I said, confident that cabinetmakers of Jack Watson's reputed calibre naturally take this magazine.

And that is why I say: Jack Watson, where are you now?

Planting policy

There are different ways of looking at trees. Some people like looking at them purely because they are nice to look at. Others are grateful to the trees for giving off oxygen into the earth's atmosphere. Some enjoy the scientific study of trees, while woodworkers appreciate a good tree not least for the timber it will yield when the chips are down.

But the city fathers of Birmingham have been looking at trees in a more sinister way. Recent discussion at council meetings has concluded that in future the city will only plant thin-trunked trees such as hedge maple, almond and cherry, rather than the old favourites of urban foliation like plane and lime.

The reason for this decision is a dark reflection on the state of our society: it is simply that thin trees are difficult for muggers, bag-snatchers, rapists and other species of urban bandit to hide behind.

Depressing, isn't it?

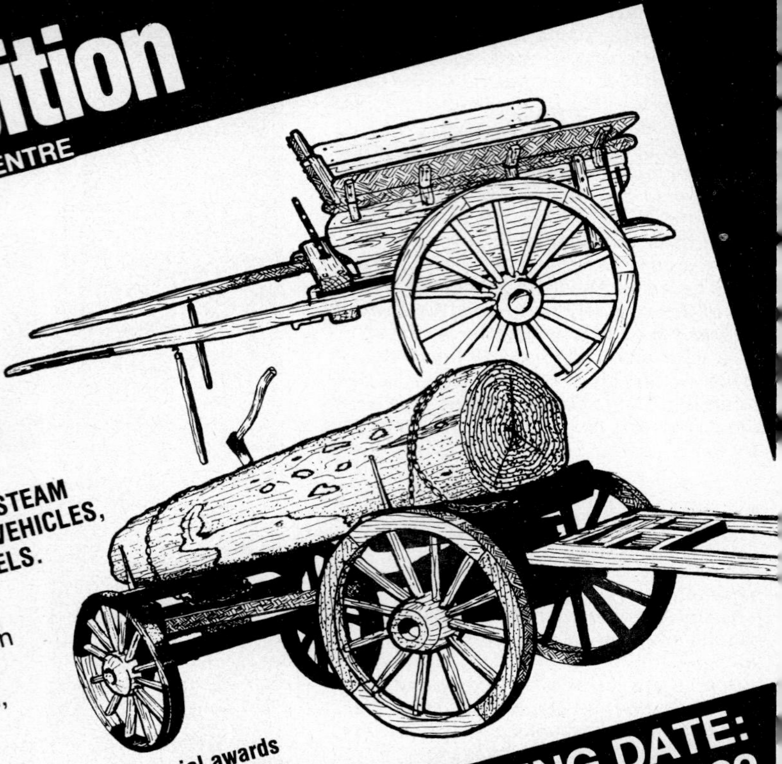

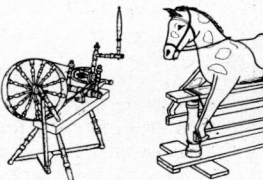  

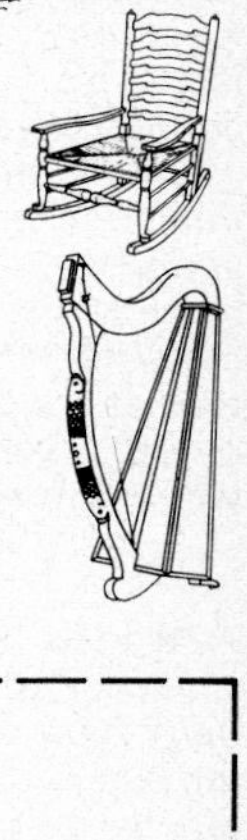

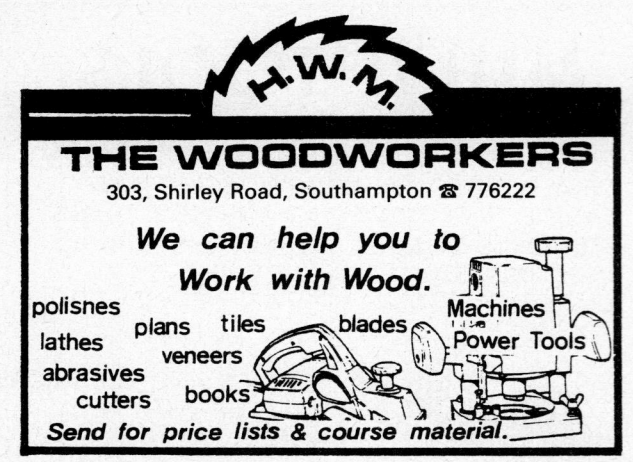
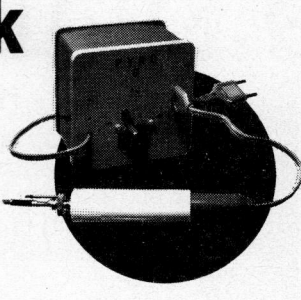

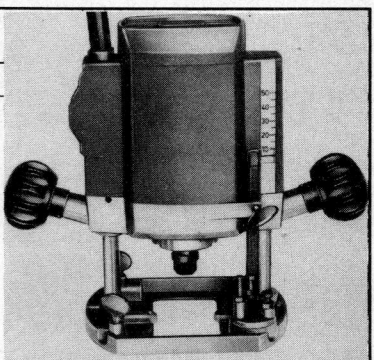

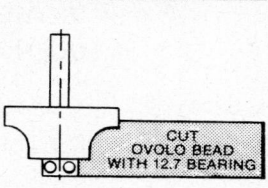

Wood Suppliers

Telephone Valerie Tester
(0442) 41221 Ex. 262

JOHN BODDY & SON (TIMBER) LTD.

offer

Direct from our Sawmill and Kilns

BRITISH HARDWOODS

As one of the few British Timber Merchants specialising in the production of kiln dried hardwoods in planking and dimension stock.

We invite craftsmen to inspect and select from our stock of over 20,000 cubic feet of kiln dried timber. Stored under cover.

OAK, ASH, ELM, BEECH, SYCAMORE, YEW.

available from stock in most thicknesses.

Also

APPLE, PEAR, CHERRY, LIME, RIPPLE SYCAMORE & WALNUT

Round logs are available in all species for selection and conversion to customers' individual requirements.

Please send for our Stock List or call and inspect
Open Monday to Friday 8 a.m. - 5 p.m.
Saturday 8 a.m. - 12 noon

Riverside Sawmills,

Boroughbridge, YO5 9LJ, North Yorkshire.
Telephone (09012) 2370 Telex 57526

YORKSHIRE HARDWOODS

KILN DRIED HARDWOOD FOR CRAFTSMEN

We specialize in English Oak and can supply waney edged boards or dimensioned stock. We welcome enquiries for small quantities cut and machined to your exact requirements. ☎

Yorkshire Hardwoods Limited
Pocklington Grange,
Bielby Lane, Pocklington, York YO4 2NT

Pocklington
075 92-2870

Tree Work Services

WE SUPPLY HOME GROWN HARDWOODS IN THE ROUND, FRESH SAWN, OR DRIED.

SPECIES IN STOCK INCLUDE: Acacia, Apple, Ash, Beech, Cedar, Cherry, Chestnut, Elm, Holly, Holm Oak, Lacewood, Lime, Maple, Oak, Pear, Sycamore, Tree of Heaven, Tulip Tree, Walnut, Yew.

QUARTER SAWN AND STRAIGHT EDGED OAK SUPPLIED.
YOUR OWN TREES MILLED on site, to your specifications.

JOHN EMERY
THE OLD RECTORY, PILGRIMS WAY, CHEW STOKE, NR. BRISTOL.
TEL: CHEW MAGNA 3222

NORTH HEIGHAM SAWMILLS

Good, Kiln-Dried stocks of most Home-Grown timbers, and exotic, Imported Hardwoods.
Stocks include: Apple, ash, beech, blackwood, box, cedar, cherry, cocobolo, ebony, elm, holly, lemonwood, lignum, lime, mahogany, maple, oak, padauk, pear, plane, rosewood, satinwood, sycamore, walnut, yew, zelkova.
Please send S.A.E. for priced stock list to:

North Heigham Sawmills, Paddock St. (off Barker St.), NORWICH NR2 4TW. Tel: Norwich 22978.

ENGLISH HARDWOODS

Air dried T & T Plank Walnut and Oak £12, Yew £8, Ash £6.50, S. Chestnut £7, Sycamore, Elm and Lime £5, Cherry £6, Beech & Hornbeam £5 per cu. ft. approx. prices, plus carriage and V.A.T.

Other timber prices on application

We welcome you to call and inspect our large stocks.

Enquiries: Harry Adcock, Saw Mills, Corby Glen, Grantham, Corby Glen 231.

Fact 1 from Ebac

Ebac help you make the most of your timber. Ebac

Greenfields Ind. Est.
Bishop Auckland, Co. Durham,
England DL14 9TF.
Tel: (0388) 605061

Rustic Woodslices

For House Signs, Wall Plaques, etc., seasoned hardwoods. Sawn obliquely with Bark on, up to 30" long **£2.00** each or three for **£5.00**. Post Free.

A. CRACKNELL
2 ORFORD ROAD, BROMESWELL, WOODBRIDGE, SUFFOLK.

VENEERS, inlay bandings, stringing and marquetry panels. Large selection. *Mail order and callers welcome. S.A.E. for list.*
R. AARONSON (VENEERS) LTD
45 Redchurch St., London E2.
Tel: 01-739 3107

ENGLISH HARDWOODS

Oak, Ash, Sycamore, Beech etc. Air & Kiln dried
All sizes in stock
HOGHTON TIMBER
HIGHER WALTON TRADING ESTATE
PRESTON, LANCS.
Tel: Preston 36193

British Hardwoods

Kiln Dried—Air Dried—Fresh Sawn
Specialising in Kiln Dried Oak
Sawn to size and delivery arranged

For details and quotations apply to:

R.E. & R. Duffield & Sons Ltd.,
The Boathouse, River View Road,
Ripon, N. YORKS.
Tel: (0765) 3667

or our Sales Depot at:
The Old Creamery, Currock Road,
CARLISLE. Tel: (0228) 46478

Phone Valerie Tester (0442) 41221 Ext. 262

Telephone Valerie Tester
(0442) 41221 Ex. 262

ENGLISH TIMBERS
SEASONED HOMEGROWN AND
IMPORTED HARDWOODS
FOR THE CRAFTSMAN.
Please Contact:
P. Smith, Furniture Maker,
The Old Chapel,
Kirkburn,
Driffield,
E. Yorks.

Tel: 0377 89301

TIMBER cut to your requirements

We cut and prepare to your cutting list

TEAK, OAK, ROSEWOOD, MAHOGANY, BEECH, BOXWOOD, etc. —VENEERS and PLYWOODS

We carry large stocks of dry hardwoods for cabinet and joinery trade. Turning done to your drawing. Brassware and cabinet fittings available.

Open all day Saturday — early closing Thursday.
Send S.A.E. with your cutting list for quote.

GENERAL WOODWORK SUPPLIES

Dept. W.W., 76-80 STOKE NEWINGTON HIGH STREET,
LONDON N16 ———————— Phone: 01-254 6052

MIDLAND FORESTRY LIMITED

TIMBER MERCHANTS AND CONTRACTORS

ENGLISH HARDWOOD

Oak plank T & T from £7.80 per cube
Ash plank T & T from £6.00 per cube
Elm plank T & T from £4.30 per cube
Other hardwood and softwood from £4.20. Odd mixed lots of hardwood approximately 10 cube lots at £50.00.

Wood turning blocks
Delivery within 70 miles

**Cleobury Lane, Earlswood,
Solihull, West Midlands.**
Telephone: Earlswood 3195 or 3456

CRAFTWOODS

Good stocks of many hardwoods
— Mahogany, Ash, Lime, Bubinga,
Cherry, Lignum Vitae, Ebony,
Meranti, Maple, Padauk, Pear,
Oaks, Rosewood, Teak, Wenge,
Sapele, Afrormosia.
Also Fingerboards, squares,
veneers, panelling, carving kits,
doors, plywood, tools, books.
Logs and Billets for carving.
Send SAE for price list to
CRAFTWOODS,
**Smiths Yard, Water Lane,
Sherington, Bucks.**
Tel: Newport Pagnell (0908) 615050.
Callers Welcome.

VENEERS
SHORT AND FULL LEAVES
In all popular timbers. Send S.A.E.
for FREE price list or 55p for
samples of 12 pieces 4" × 3" to:
ELLIOTT BROS
Four Winds, Moorwoods Lane, Dore
**All letters to PO Box No. 6, Glossop,
Derby. Reg. No. 2064782**

WOOD VENEERS

Come and select your own from our
extensive range of exotic timbers —
from 0.6mm to 3 mm thick.
C. B. VENEERS LTD., River Pinn
Works, Yiewsley High Street, West
Drayton, Middx UB7 7TA.
Telephone: West Drayton (08954)
41986

Calling all Wood Suppliers —

Let WOODWORKER
supply the buyers.
Ring now to advertise
Valerie Tester

(0442) 41221 Ext. 262

SHOP GUIDE SHOP GUIDE

The quickest and easiest method of reaching all Woodworkers is to advertise in
SHOP GUIDE. Telephone **Valerie Tester** (0442) 41221 Ext. 266. Rate: **£8.00 per unit.**
Minimum of 6 months.

Key: H — Hand tools, **P** — Power tools, **W** — Woodworking machinery up to £1000, **WM** — Woodworking
machinery over £1000, **D** — Demonstration available on selected machines, **T** — Timber, **CS** — Cutting or
sharpening services, **A** — Attachments, **BC** — Books/catalogues, ***** — Mail order.

£8.00 per Unit
Minimum of SIX insertions.
I enclose remittance of £48.00 ☐
I wish to be invoiced. ☐
Please tick as appropriate.

COUNTY ....

TOWN ....

NAME OF COMPANY/SHOP ....

....

ADDRESS ....

To: Valerie Tester
WOODWORKER MAGAZINE
P.O. Box 35,
13 Bridge Street, Hemel Hempstead,
HP1 1EE.

TELEPHONE No ....

DAYS AND HOURS OF BUSINESS

....

....

**TO DENOTE MAIL ORDER SERVICE
AVAILABLE ☐*

Prices quoted are those prevailing at press date and are
subject to alteration due to economic conditions.

SHOP GUIDE SHOP GUIDE

The quickest and easiest method of reaching all Woodworkers is to advertise in SHOP GUIDE. Telephone **Valerie Tester (0442) 41221 Ext. 266. Rate: £8.00 per unit.** Minimum of 6 months.

Key: H — Hand tools, **P** — Power tools, **W** — Woodworking machinery up to £1000, **WM** — Woodworking machinery over £1000, **D** — Demonstration available on selected machines, **T** — Timber, **CS** — Cutting or sharpening services, **A** — Attachments, **BC** — Books/catalogues, * — Mail order.

AVON

BATH Tel. Bath 64513
JOHN HALL TOOLS ★
RAILWAY STREET

Open: Monday-Saturday
9.00 a.m.-5.30 p.m.
H.P.W.WM.D.A.BC.

BRISTOL Tel. (0272) 311510
JOHN HALL TOOLS LIMITED ★
CLIFTON DOWN SHOPPING
CENTRE, WHITELADIES ROAD
Open: Monday-Saturday
9.00 a.m.-5.30 p.m.
H.P.W.WM.D.A.BC.

BRISTOL Tel. 0272-633844
ROBBINS LIMITED ★
THE WOODWORKER SHOP
MERRYWOOD MILLS, BEDMINSTER
Open: Mon-Fri 8.00 a.m.-5.00 p.m.
Saturday 8.30 a.m.-12.30 p.m.
H.P.T.CS.A.BC.

BRISTOL Tel. 0272-629092
TRYMWOOD SERVICES ★
2a DOWNS PARK EAST, (off
North View) WESTBURY PARK
Open: 8.30 a.m.-5.30 p.m. Mon. to
Fri. Closed for lunch 1-2 p.m.
P.W.WM.D.T.A.BC.

BRISTOL Tel. 0272-667013
V. H. WILLIS & CO. LTD ★
190-192 WEST STREET,
BEDMINSTER
Open: Mon-Fri 8.30 a.m.-5 p.m.
Saturday 9 a.m.-1 p.m.
H.P.W.WM.D.CS.A.BC.

BERKSHIRE

READING Tel. Littlewick Green
DAVID HUNT (TOOL 2743
MERCHANTS) LTD ★
KNOWL HILL, NR. READING
Open: Monday-Saturday
9 a.m.-5.30 p.m.
H.P.W.D.A.BC.

READING Tel. (0734) 586522
SARJENT'S TOOL STORES ★
LTD.
44-52 OXFORD ROAD
Open: 8.30 a.m.-5.30 p.m.
Monday-Saturday
H.P.W.WM.D.A.BC.

READING Tel. Reading 661511
WOKINGHAM TOOL CO. LTD
99 WOKINGHAM ROAD

Open: Mon-Sat 9am-5.30pm
Closed 1-2pm for lunch
H.P.W.WM.D.CS.A.BC.

BUCKINGHAMSHIRE

HIGH WYCOMBE (0494) 22221
ISAAC LORD LTD
185 DESBOROUGH ROAD

Open: Mon-Fri 8.00 a.m.-5.00 p.m.
Saturday 8.00 a.m.-12.00 noon
H.P.W.D.A.

MILTON KEYNES Tel. 0908
A. POLLARD & SON 75221
LTD. ★
51 QUEENSWAY, BLETCHLEY
Open: 8.30 a.m.-5.30 p.m.
Monday-Saturday
H.P.W.WM.D.A.BC.

CAMBRIDGESHIRE

CAMBRIDGE Tel. 0223-353091
H. B. WOODWORKING
69 LENSFIELD ROAD

Open: 8.30 a.m.-5.30 p.m.
Monday-Friday
8.30 a.m.-1.00 p.m. Sat
P.W.WM.D.CS.BC.

CHESHIRE

NANTWICH Tel. Crewe 67010
ALAN HOLTHAM ★
THE OLD STORES TURNERY
WISTASON ROAD, WILLASTON
Open: Tues-Sat 9a.m.-5.30p.m.
Closed Monday
P.W.WM.D.T.C.CS.A.BC.

CLEVELAND

MIDDLESBROUGH Tel. 0642-
WINTZ 460035/813650
INDUSTRIAL SUPPLIES ★
2 BESSEMER COURT
GRANGETOWN
Open: Mon-Fri 8.30 a.m.-5 p.m.
H.P.W.D.A.

CORNWALL

FALMOUTH Tel. 0326-312915
WOODSTOCK ★
(HARDWOODS) S.W.,
ASHFIELD, PONSHARDEN,
Open: Mon-Fri 8.30 a.m.-5.30 p.m.
Sat 9 a.m.-1.00 p.m.
T.

HELSTON
SOUTH WEST
POWER TOOLS

Helston (03265) 4961
Truro (0872) 71671
Launceston (0566) 3555
H.P.W.WM.D.CS.A.

NEWQUAY Tel. 063 73 2516
CONWAY SUPPLIES ★
(NEWQUAY)
70 FORE STREET
Open: Mon-Fri 9 a.m.-5.30 p.m.
Sat 9 a.m.-12.30 p.m.
H.P.W.WM.D.A.BC.

CORNWALL

ST. AUSTELL Tel. (0726) 65922
TOOLSERV ★
TRURO ROAD

Open: 8 a.m.-5.30 p.m.
6 days
H.P.W.WM.D.CS.A.BC.

DERBYSHIRE

BUXTON Tel. 0298-871636
CRAFT SUPPLIES ★
THE MILL
MILLERSDALE
Open: Mon-Fri 9 a.m.-5 p.m.
Saturday 9 a.m.-1 p.m.
H.P.W.D.T.CS.A.BC.

DEVON

EXETER Tel. 0392 73936
WRIDES TOOL CENTRE
147 FORE STREET

Open: 9.00 a.m.-5.30 p.m.
Wednesday 9.00 a.m.-1.00 p.m.
H.P.W.WM.A.

PLYMOUTH Tel. 0752 330303
WESTWARD BUILDING SERVICES ★
LTD., LISTER CLOSE, NEWNHAM
INDUSTRIAL ESTATE, PLYMPTON
Open: Mon-Fri 8 a.m.-5.30 p.m.
Sat 8.30 a.m.-12.30 p.m.
H.P.W.WM.D.A.BC.

PLYMOUTH Tel. 0752-266179
JOHN WRIDE & CO (PLYMOUTH) LTD
146 CORNWALL STREET

Open: Monday to Saturday
9.00a.m.-5.30p.m.
Wed 9.00a.m.-1.00p.m.
H.P.W.WM.A.

DORSET

BOURNEMOUTH Tel: 0202
MACHINE SALES & SERVICES 527780
(BOURNEMOUTH) LTD 527781
56 STROUDEN ROAD ★

Open: Mon-Fri 8.15 a.m.-5 p.m.
H.P.W.WM.D.A.

WEYMOUTH Tel: (0305) 787396
WEYMOUTH TOOL CENTRE ★
30A ABBOTSBURY ROAD

Open: Monday to Saturday
8 a.m.-5.30 p.m.
H.P.W.WM.D.A.BC

CO. DURHAM

BARNARD CASTLE Tel: (0833)
WOODMEN 38442/31609
27 NEWGATE ★

Open Monday-Saturday
9 a.m.-5.30 p.m.
P.W.WM.D.A.BC.

ESSEX

LEIGH ON SEA Tel. (0702)
MARSHALL & 710404
PARSONS LTD ★
1111 LONDON ROAD
Open: 8.30 am-5.30 pm Mon-Fri.
9.00 am-5.00 om Sat.
H.P.W.WM.D.CS.A.

LEIGH ON SEA Tel. (0702)
WEBBERS TOOLS 76503
204 ELM ROAD

Open: 9 am-5.30 pm
Monday to Saturday
H.P.W.

GLOUCESTERSHIRE

TEWKESBURY Tel. 0684
TEWKESBURY SAW CO. 293092
LIMITED
TRADING ESTATE, NEWTOWN
Open: Mon-Fri 8.00 a.m.-5.00 p.m.
Saturday 9.30 a.m.-12.00 p.m.
P.W.WM.D.CS.

HAMPSHIRE

ALDERSHOT Tel. 0252 28088
BURCH & HILLS LTD
BLACKWATER WAY TRADING
ESTATE
Open: Mon-Fri 8.30 a.m.-5.30 p.m.
Saturday 8.30 a.m.-12.00 p.m.
H.P.W.WM.D.A.BC.

PORTSMOUTH Tel. 0705
EURO PRECISION TOOLS 67332
LTD ★
259/263 London Road, North End
Open: Mon-Fri 9 a.m.- 5.30 p.m.
Sat 9.00 a.m.-5.00 p.m.
H.P.W.WM.D.A.BC.

SOUTHAMPTON Tel. 0703
H.W.M. 776222
THE WOODWORKERS ★
303 SHIRLEY ROAD, SHIRLEY
Open: Tues-Fri 9.30 a.m.- 6 p.m.
Sat 9.30 a.m.-4.00 p.m.
H.P.W.WM.D.CS.A.BC.T.

HERTFORDSHIRE

WATFORD Tel. 0923 48434
HOME CARE CENTRE ★
20 MARKET STREET
WATFORD, HERTS
Open 9.00 a.m.-5.30 p.m.
Mon.-Sat.
H.P.W.A.WM.BC.D.

WATFORD Tel. 0923 26052
J. SIMBLE & SONS LTD ★
76 QUEENS ROAD

Open 8.30 a.m.-5.30 p.m.
Mon.-Sat. Closed Wednesday
H.P.W.WM.D.A.BC.

SHOP GUIDE SHOP GUIDE

HERTFORDSHIRE

WATFORD   Tel. (0923) 49911
TREND MACHINERY & CUTTING
TOOLS LTD
UNIT N, PENFOLD WORKS
IMPERIAL WAY
Open: Mon-Fri 9 a.m.-5 p.m.
P.W.WM.D.CS.BC.

KENT

MATFIELD   Tel. Brenchley
LEISURECRAFT IN WOOD   (089272)
'ORMONDE', MAIDSTONE RD.   2465
TN12 7JG
Open: Mon-Sun
9 a.m. - 5.30 p.m.
W.WM.D.T.A.

SITTINGBOURNE   Tel.
B.T.S. (TOOLS),   Sittingbourne
Unit 25, SITTINGBOURNE   79551
INDUSTRIAL PARK   ★
Open: Monday - Friday
8.00 a.m. - 5.00 p.m.
H.P.W.BC.CS.

LANCASHIRE

LANCASTER   Tel. 0524 2886
LILE TOOL SHOP
43/45 NORTH ROAD
Open: Monday to Saturday
9.00 a.m.-5.30 p.m.
Wed 9.00 a.m.-12.30 p.m.
H.P.W.D.A.

LEICESTERSHIRE

COALVILLE   Tel. (0533) 415556
POOLE WOOD   (06077) 5777
MACHINERY
SERVICES LIMITED,
30 VALENTINE ROAD
Open: Mon-Fri 9 a.m.-5 p.m.
H.P.W.WM.D.A.BC.

LEICESTER   Tel. 0455 43254
ROY STARTIN LTD
134 WOOD STREET
EARL SHILTON
Open: Mon-Fri 8 a.m.-5.30 p.m.
Saturday 8.00 a.m.-1.30 p.m.
H.P.W.WM.D.T.A.

LINCOLNSHIRE

LINCOLN   Tel. 0522 30199/
WOODWISE LIMITED   39871 or
121 HIGH STREET   0522 68428
& (06077) 2421/5777/5288
(after hours)   ★
Open: Mon-Sat 9 a.m.-5.30 p.m.
P.W.WM.D.A.BC.

LONDON

ACTON   Tel. 01-992 4835
A MILLS (ACTON) LTD   ★
32/36 CHURCHFIELD ROAD
W3 6ED
Open: Mon-Fri 9.00 a.m.-5.00 p.m.
Closed Saturday
H.P.W.WM.

HANWELL   Tel. 01-567 2922
G. D. CLEGG & SONS
83 Uxbridge Road, W7 3ST
Open: Monday to Friday
9.00 a.m.-6.00 p.m.
Saturday 9.00 a.m.-5.30 p.m.
H.P.W.WM.D.

LONDON

KILBURN   Tel. 01-624 5146
W. THATCHER & SON LTD   ★
POWER TOOL CENTRE
AT THE TECHNICAL LEISURE CENTRE
1 THE GRANGEWAY, N.W.6.
Open: Mon-Sat 9 a.m.-5.30 p.m.
P.H.W.D.CS.A.BC.

LONDON   Tel. 01-636 7475
BUCK & RYAN LIMITED   ★
101 TOTTENHAM COURT ROAD
W1P 0DY
Open: Mon-Fri 8.30 a.m.-5.30 p.m.
Saturday 8.30 a.m.-1.00 p.m.
H.P.W.WM.D.A.

LONDON   Tel. 01-739 7126
CECIL W. TYZACK   ★
79-81 KINGSLAND ROAD
SHOREDITCH
Open: Mon-Fri 8.45 a.m.-5.15 p.m.
Saturday 9 a.m.-12 noon
H.P.W.WM.D.A.BC.

NORBURY   Tel: 01-679 6193
HERON TOOLS & HARDWARE LTD
437 STREATHAM HIGH ROAD
S.W.16
Open: Mon-Sat 8.30 a.m. - 6 p.m.
Wednesday 8.30 a.m. - 1 p.m.
H.P.W.A.

MERSEYSIDE

LIVERPOOL   Tel. 051-263 1359
TAYLOR BROS (LIVERPOOL) LTD
5/9 PRESCOTT STREET
Open: Monday to Friday
8.30 a.m.-5.30 p.m.
H.P.W.WM.D.A.BC.

MIDDLESEX

NORTH HARROW   Tel. 01-863 2492
WILLIAMS TECHNICAL SERVICES   ★
36 STATION ROAD
Open: Mon-Fri 8 a.m.-5.30 p.m.
Wed 8 a.m.-1 p.m.,
Sat 9 a.m.-5.30 p.m.
H.P.W.WM.D.A.

HOUNSLOW   Tel. 01-570 2103/5135
Q. R. TOOLS LTD
251-253 HANWORTH ROAD
Open: Mon-Fri 8.30 a.m.-5.30 p.m.
Sat 9 a.m.-1 p.m.
P.W.WM.D.CS.A.

NORFOLK

KINGS LYNN   Tel. (0553) 2443
WALKER & ANDERSON (Kings Lynn) LTD
WINDSOR ROAD, KINGS LYNN
Open: Monday to Saturday
7.45 a.m.-5.30 p.m.
Wednesday 1 p.m. Saturday 5.00 p.m.
H.P.W.WM.D.CS.A.

NORWICH   Tel. 0603 898695
NORFOLK SAW SERVICES
DOG LAND, HORSFORD
Open: Monday to Friday
8.00 a.m.-5.00 p.m.
Saturday 8.00 a.m.-12.00 p.m.
H.P.W.WM.D.CS.A.

NORFOLK

NORWICH   Tel. 0603 400933
WESTGATES WOODWORKING   Tx.
MACHINERY, JUPITER ROAD   975412
OFF MILE CROSS LANE
Open: 9 a.m.-5 p.m. weekdays
9 a.m.-12 a.m. Sat.
P.W.WM.D.

NORTHAMPTONSHIRE

RUSHDEN   Tel. 093-34 56424
PETER CRISP LIMITED   ★
7 HIGH STREET
Open: Monday to Saturday
8.30 a.m.-5.30 p.m.
Thursday 8.30 a.m.-1.00 p.m.
H.P.W.D.BC.

NORTHUMBERLAND

BLYTH   Tel. (06706) 69279
ALLAN McNAIR WOODCRAFT   ★
69-71 PLESSEY ROAD
Open: Monday to Saturday
9 a.m.-5 p.m.
H.W.WM.D.T.CS.A.BC.

NOTTINGHAMSHIRE

NOTTINGHAM   Tel. (0602) 225979
POOLEWOOD   and 227929
EQUIPMENT LTD   (06077) 2421/5777
5a HOLLY LANE, CHILLWELL
Open: Mon-Fri 9 a.m.-5.30 p.m.
Sat. 9 a.m. to 12.30 p.m.
P.W.WM.D.CS.A.BC.

NOTTINGHAM   Tel. 0602 811889
THE WOODCUTTER
5 TUDOR SQUARE
WEST BRIDGFORD
Open: Tues-Sat 9 a.m.-5.30 p.m.
Fri 9 a.m.-7.30 p.m. Closed Mon.
H.P.W.WM.D.T.CS.A.

OXFORDSHIRE

BICESTER   Tel. (08692) 4156/
WOODMEN   3218/3219
104 CHURCHILL ROAD
Open: Monday-Saturday
9 a.m.-5.30 p.m.
P.W.WM.D.A.BC.

OXFORD   Tel. (0865) 45118/9
SARJENT'S TOOL   ★
STORES LTD
150 COWLEY ROAD
Open: Monday to Saturday
8.30 a.m.-5.30 p.m.
H.P.W.WM.D.A.BC.

SHROPSHIRE

TELFORD   Tel. Telford
ASLES LTD   (0952) 48054
VINEYARD ROAD
WELLINGTON
Open: Mon-Fri 8.30am-5.30pm
Saturday 8.30am-4.00pm
H.P.WM.D.A.

SOMERSET

TAUNTON   Tel. Taunton 79078
KEITH MITCHELL   ★
TOOLS AND EQUIPMENT
66 PRIORY BRIDGE ROAD
Open: Mon-Fri 8.30am-5.30pm
Saturday 9am-4pm
H.P.W.WM.D.CS.A.BC.

SOMERSET

WESTON-SUPER-MARE   Tel.
JOHN TERRY   0934 21803
TOOL SALES   ★
36 ALFRED STREET
Open: Monday to Saturday
9am-5.30pm inclusive
H.P.W.WM.D.CS.A.

STAFFORDSHIRE

TAMWORTH   Tel. 0827-56188
MATTHEWS BROTHERS LTD
KETTLEBROOK ROAD
Open: Mon.-Sat. 8.30am-6.00pm
Demonstrations Sunday mornings
by appointment only
H.P.W.WM.D.T.CS.A.BC.

SUFFOLK

BURY ST. EDMUNDS   Tel.
TOOLS & THINGS   0284 62022
21 CHURCHGATE   ★
Open: Monday to Saturday
9.00 a.m.-5.30 p.m.
H.P.W.WM.D.A.BC.

IPSWICH   Tel. 0473 86216
FOX WOODWORKING   ★
'STEBBINGS' BACK LANE
WASHBROOK
Open: Tues. Fri. 9.00am-5.30pm
Sat. 9.00am-5pm
H.P.W.WM.D.A.BC.

SURREY

CARSHALTON BEECHES   Tel.
SURREY WOOD   01-642 6636
MACHINE SALES LTD   ★
56A BANSTEAD ROAD
Open: Tues-Fri 9.30 am-6.00 pm
Saturday 9.30 am-2.00 pm
P.W.WM.D.BC.CS.

CROYDON   Tel. 01-688 5513
L. H. TURTLE LTD   ★
6-12 PARK STREET
Open: Monday to Saturday
8.30 a.m.-5.30 p.m.
H.P.W.WM.D.A.

GUILDFORD   Tel. 0483 61125
MESSINGERS FOR TOOLS
14-18 CHERTSEY STREET
Open: Tuesday to Saturday
8.30 a.m.-5.30 p.m.
Closed all day Monday
H.P.W.D.BC.

SUSSEX

BOGNOR REGIS Tel: (0243) 863100
A. OLBY & SON (BOGNOR REGIS LTD)
"TOOLSHOP", BUILDER'S MERCHANT
HAWTHORN ROAD
Open: Mon-Thurs 8 a.m.-5.15 p.m.
Fri 8 a.m.-8 p.m. Sat 8 a.m.-12.45 p.m.
H.P.W.WM.D.T.C.A.BC.

WORTHING   Tel. 0903 38739
W. HOSKING LTD (TOOLS &   ★
MACHINERY)
28 PORTLAND RD, BN11 1QN
Open: Mon-Sat 8.30am-5.30pm
Wednesday 8.30am-1.00pm
H.P.W.WM.D.CS.A.BC.

Prices quoted are those prevailing at press date and are
subject to alteration due to economic conditions.

SHOP GUIDE SHOP GUIDE

WEST MIDLANDS

WEST BROMWICH   Tel: 021-
CONWAY SAW &   553 5461/2
SUPPLY LTD   ★
SWAN LANE
   Open: 8 a.m.-6 p.m. Mon-Fri
   9 a.m.-1 p.m. Saturday
P.W.WM.D.CS.BC.

WILTSHIRE

SWINDON   Tel. (0793) 31361
SARJENT'S TOOL STORES LTD ★
64 FLEET STREET
   Open: Monday to Saturday
   8.30 a.m.-5.30 p.m.
H.P.W.WM.D.A.BC

YORKSHIRE

HALIFAX   Tel. 0422 43722/
TIMBERLITE LTD   884788/33575
WILLOWFIELDS ROAD   ★
WILLOWFIELD
   Open: Monday to Friday
   Saturday 9.00 a.m.-5.00 p.m.
H.P.W.WM.D.CS.A.BC.

HARROGATE   Tel. 0423 66245/
MULTI-TOOLS   55328   ★
158 KINGS ROAD
   Open: Monday to Saturday
   8.30 a.m.-6.00 p.m.
H.P.W.WM.D.A.BC.

HUDDERSFIELD   Tel. (0484)
NEVILLE M. OLDHAM   641219/(0484)
UNIT 1 DAYLE ST. WORKS   42777
DAYLE STREET, LONGWOOD   ★
   Open: Mon-Fri 9.00am- 5.30pm
   Saturday 9.30am-12.00pm
P.W.WM.D.A.BC.

YORKSHIRE

LEEDS   Tel. 0532 574736
D. B. KEIGHLEY MACHINERY LTD   ★
VICKERS PLACE
STANNINGLEY
   Open: Mon-Fri 9am-5pm
   Saturday 9am-1pm
P.W.WM.D.CS.A.BC.

LEEDS   Tel. 0532 790507
GEORGE SPENCE & SONS LTD
WELLINGTON ROAD   ★
   Open: Monday to Friday
   8.30 a.m.-5.30 p.m.
   Saturday 9.00 a.m.-5.00 p.m.
H.P.W.WM.D.T.A.

SHEFFIELD   Tel. 0742-441012
GREGORY & TAYLOR LTD
WORKSOP ROAD
   Open: 8.30 a.m.-5.30 p.m.
   Monday-Friday
   8.30 a.m.-12.30 p.m. Sat.
H.P.W.WM.D.

SHEFFIELD   Tel. 0742-24659
GRAHAM OXLEY'S SHOWROOM
BRIDGE STREET   ★
   Open: Monday to Friday
   9.00 a.m.-5.30 p.m.
   Saturday 8.30 a.m.-12.30 p.m.
H.W.D.A.BC.

SOWERBY BRIDGE   Tel. (0422)
CALDER   31861
WOODWORKING   Telex: 517400
MACHINERY LTD.
STATION ROAD
   Open: Mon - Fri 9 a.m.-5 p.m.
P.W.WM.D.CS.A.

SCOTLAND

EDINBURGH   Tel. 031-337
SCOTSPAN   7788/665 3121
195 BALGREEN ROAD
   Open: Monday to Friday
   9.00 a.m.-3.00 p.m.
P.W.WM.D.A.

GLASGOW   Tel. 041 429 4374/4444
THE SAW CENTRE   Telex: 777886
596-602 EGLINGTON STREET   ★
G5 9RR
   Open: Mon.-Fri. 8 a.m.-5.30 p.m.
   Saturday 9 a.m.-1 p.m.
H.P.W.WM.D.CS.A.

N. IRELAND

Co. ANTRIM   Tel. 0266 6384
GEORGE GARDINER
49 BALLYMONEY STREET
BALLYMENA
   Open: Open: Mon-Fri 8.30am-5.30pm
   Wednesday 8.30am-1.00pm
H.P.W.D.A.BC.

Co. DOWN   Tel. (0247) 819800 (day)
NEWTOWNARDS   812506 (night)
NORLYN MACHINERY, UNIT 10
Malcolmson Ind. Est., 80 Bangor Road
   Open: Mon-Fri 9.30am-5.30pm
   or any other time by request
H.P.W.WM.D.A.BC.

S. IRELAND

COUNTY KILKENNY   Tel.
WOODMEN   (0409) 5460
CASHEL HOUSE   ★
KELLS ROAD, KILKENNY
   Open: Monday to Saturday

WALES

BRITON FERRY   Tel. (0639)
WOODMEN   820803/4
49 NEATH ROAD   ★
   Open: Monday to Saturday
   9.00 a.m.-5.30 p.m.
P.W.WM.D.A.BC.

CARDIFF   Tel. (0222) 373007
JOHN HALL TOOLS LIMITED   ★
22 CHURCHILL WAY
   Open: Monday to Saturday
   9.00 a.m.-5.30 p.m.
H.P.W.WM.D.A.BC.

CARDIFF   Tel. (0222) 30831
F. W. MORGAN   & 25562
(CANTON) LTD., 129-133
COWBRIDGE RD EAST,
CANTON, CARDIFF
   Mon-Sat 8-5 Sun. 9.30-12.30
H.P.T.CS.A.BC.

CARDIFF   Tel. (0222) 36519/
WOODMEN   373793/35221
74-76 PARK ROAD   ★
WHITCHURCH, CARDIFF
   Open: Monday to Saturday
   9.00 a.m.-5.30 p.m.

CARMARTHEN   Tel. 0267 7219
DO-IT-YOURSELF SUPPLY
BLUE STREET, DYFED
   Open: Monday to Saturday
   9.00 a.m.-5.30 p.m.
   Thursday 9.00 a.m.-1.00 p.m.
H.P.W.WM.D.T.CS.A.BC.

SWANSEA   Tel. (0792) 55680
SWANSEA TIMBER &   ★
PLYWOOD CO LTD
57-59 OXFORD STREET
   Open: Mon. to Fri. 9 am-5.30 pm
   Sat. 9 am-1 pm
H.P.W.D.T.CS.A.BC.

YOU CAN BUY WITH CONFIDENCE FROM THE SHOPS IN THIS SHOP GUIDE

★*Shops offering a mail order service are denoted by an asterisk*

KLEMMSIA QUICK-GRIP CLAMP

From £3.45 m.r.p. inc VAT

- Inexpensive
- Clamping in seconds
- Light and strong
- Nine standard sizes
- Span 8″ to 48″
- Jaw reach 4½″ to 6″

For details and your local stockist,
write or phone:

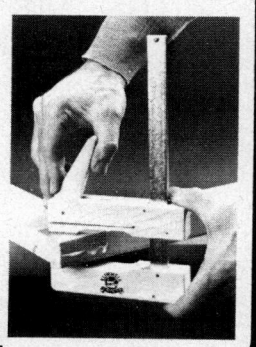

MONNINGER
C.D. Monninger Ltd., Overbury Rd.,
London N15 6RJ. Tel: 01-800 5435.

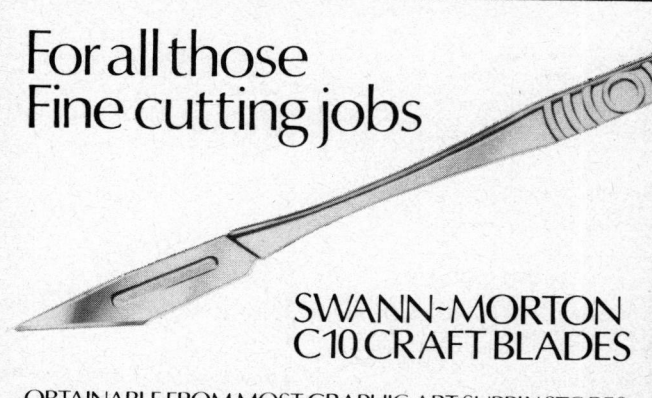

For all those Fine cutting jobs

SWANN-MORTON C10 CRAFT BLADES

OBTAINABLE FROM MOST GRAPHIC ART SUPPLY STORES

Classified Advertisements

FOR SALE

LACE BOBBIN turning blanks in exotic hardwoods. S.A.E. for list. J. Ford, 5 Squirrels Hollow, Walsall WS7 8YS.   O-P

CORONET CONSORT — Saw Bench, Mortiser, Planer, Thicknesser. Little used. £225 o.n.o. Telephone: Nailsea (0272) 854608 Evenings.   P

WOODWORKER MAGAZINES. June 1950 to June 1979. Reasonable offer. Telephone Abingdon (0235) 25706.   P

WELSH SLATE oil stones for sale at very competitive prices. Send S.A.E. for details:- Inigo Jones & Co. Ltd., Groesion, Caernarfon, Gwynedd. Tel: 0286-830242.   F-R

ROBINSON Hand Mortising — Drilling Machine, used until last month. £100. Mathison Mitre machine £35. Telephone Alnwick (Northumberland) 711268.   P

DOUBLE ENDED 4" Grinder at £15.00. 050 Record plane 18 cutters £40.00. Shopmate Router £30.00. Telephone: (0903) 45862.   P

RECORD MODEL 52½ Spring-load, 9" woodwork vice. New £55. Spaven, 117 Birchwood Lane, South Normanton, Derby. Telephone Ripley 811335. Evenings.   P

HOBBIES WEEKLY 1946 to 1960 inclusive. 722 copies including plans. Offers. Telephone 0268 742395 Evenings.   P

COMPOUND SLIDE (1543) for Myford ML8. Good condition £65. Telephone: Glemsford 280520 (Suffolk).   P

CORONET Mk II MAJOR Lathe (Blue), 5'6" bed, saw table, combination table, box jig, bowl rest, various chucks and accessories. Excellent condition £640. Inca Bandsaw ¾ h.p. motor, mitre gauge. Excellent condition £170. Telephone (073087) 313. (Hampshire).   P

ARUNDEL J4 Mk II 3-speed lathe, 32" centres, ½ h.p. motor. Tripod, Sorby tools. Excellent condition, £125. Hertford 54851.   P

HAND CARVED
'Adam Style' motifs in Mahogany — Example 10" × 5" centre lamp and two side pieces — £25.00
Send S.A.E. for details and quotation. Your own design quoted for if required.
SAM NICHOLSON
22 Lisnagarvey Drive,
Lisburn, Co. Antrim,
N. Ireland. Phone Lisburn 3510

TIMBER SEASONERS, moisture meters, polymeters. Everything you require for seasoning your own timber. For free advice and lowest prices, consult the experts, 15 years in the trade. Some reconditioned seasoners available, Wyco Moisture control. Tel: Weybridge 40864.   K-P

FINAL PRICE SLASH
ELU-DE WALT
Before buying phone
Machine Sales & Services (Bournemouth) Ltd.,
0202 527781 or 527780
WE CAN PROVE WE ARE CHEAPER!
E. G. DW 30 – £140

CORBETT TOOLS HAVE THE EDGE
Adzes, Drawknives, Inshaves, Bowsaws, Carving Sets, and other unusual and high quality tools for the Craftsman in Wood.
EXPORT ENQUIRIES WELCOME CATALOGUE AVAILABLE
Send 45p to:-
CORBETT TOOLS (Dept. WW/6), 224 Puxton Drive, Kidderminster, Worc's.

PENS AND HOLDERS
Beautiful modern desk pens and holders in 5 exciting colours — brown, ivory, black, gold and red. Turn your craft objects into useful pen sets. **£2.40 for 6** (3 pens and 3 holders) including postage and VAT (minimum order). Pens are 6" long with gold finish on barrel. Holders nearly 3" high with swivel base.
HIRSH JACOBSON, 91 Marylebone High Street, London W1.

EXCLUSIVE To KENYONS
this specially designed
D.I.Y. Apron
Made in 100% Heavy Duty Cotton, with 9 Pockets and a Hammer Holder, an ideal gift for any do-it-yourselfer at only:
£4·90
+65p P&P

Chuck Key
Drills
Screwdrivers
Hammer Holder
Sandpaper Pencils
Tape Measure
Screws & Nails

KENYONS (mail order) Co. Ltd., *(W)*
Oxen Road, CREWKERNE, Somerset.
Please allow 21-28 days for delivery.

TOOLS MENTIONED ABOVE ARE NOT SUPPLIED

R & S TOOLS (LINCOLN) LTD.
BEEVOR STREET, LINCOLN. Tel: Lincoln 0522 36168/9

Why pay more when you can get up to 25% discount off most leading makes of power tools and hand tools?

Stockists of:
ELECTRIC POWER TOOLS:
AEG—ELU—BOSCH—MAKITA—SUPER STORK—SKIL WOLF—METABO—WADKIN—KANGO

WOODWORKING MACHINES
DEWALT—MULTICO—SEDGWICK—WADKIN—STARTRITE

SAWBLADES
SANDVIK—TEX—MICOR—FIRTH—BROWN

HAND TOOLS
ALL LEADING MAKES OF BUILDING AND ENGINEERING TOOLS

ELU MVS 93 less list 30%
ABRASIVES
ENGLISH—TEX—KLINGSPOR—UNIVERSAL GRINDING WHEELS

Up to 30% off most leading brands of coated abrasive

TCT CIRCULAR SAW BLADES
Contact us for the best price.

ACCESS & BARCLAYCARD WELCOME

SOLE AGENTS FOR SWIFTSURE CUTTING & CUTTING DISCS
FOR YOUR QUOTATION—PLEASE PHONE BETWEEN 8.30 am and 5 pm

BARRIE IRONS MACHINERY LTD
Elu

We are pleased to announce that in 1981 we were the largest distributor of ELU machinery. We may not be the cheapest but we are competitive with excellent service and technical back-up facilities.
Also distributors of DeWalt, Multico, Startrite, Kango, Bosch, all at discount prices.
Why not drop us a line, telephone for further information or even pay us a visit to our new showroom.
81 UXBRIDGE ROAD, STANMORE, MIDDLESEX HA7 3NH
Telephone: 01-954-0181

FOR ALL SUPPLIES FOR THE

Craft of Enamelling
ON METAL

Including LEAD-FREE ENAMELS

PLEASE SEND 2 × 10p STAMPS FOR FREE CATALOGUE, PRICE LIST AND WORKING INSTRUCTIONS

W. G. BALL LTD.
ENAMEL MANUFACTURERS

Dept. W. LONGTON
STOKE-ON-TRENT
ST3 1JW

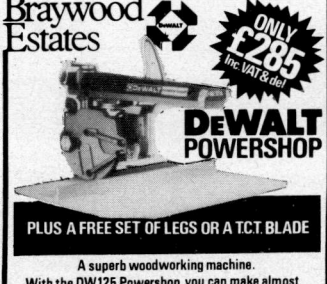
Prices quoted are those prevailing at press date and are subject to alteration due to economic conditions.

COURSES IN WOOD MACHINING AND WOODTURNING. Bookable by the hour—the most convenient and flexible way! all for £6.00 an hour (inc. VAT), H.W.M., The Woodworkers, 303 Shirley Rd., Shirley, Southampton. Tel: (0703) 776222. T/C

POWERED WOODCARVING — 2 or 3 day courses in the use of Dupli-Carver woodcarving machines. Expert personal tuition covering all aspects of this absorbing craft. For full details write or telephone Woodcraft Projects Ltd., Unit 10, Kernick Road Industrial Estate, Penryn, Cornwall. 0326 73846. L-W

Wood machining Course
A craftsman of forty years experience offers a unique two-day course to learn the basics of machine woodworking including spindle moulding and routing in his fully equipped modern workshop.
S.A.E. for details please to:
ROY SUTTON
14 St. Georges Avenue,
Herne Bay, Kent CT6 8JU
Telephone: Herne Bay 3297 or Whitstable 272136 (evenings).

CRAFT HOLIDAYS AND COURSES in the Yorkshire Dales. Woodturning, Carving, Furnituremaking, Spinning, Silversmithing, Copper and Brasswork, Property Renovation. Professional tuition in well equipped workshops with full-board accommodation. SAE Rob and Jan Ellwood, Holroyd Mill, Micklethwaite, Bingley, W. Yorks. N-S

ONE DAY WOODTURNING COURSE: carefully designed, inexpensive. Trymwood, 2a Downs Park East, Westbury Park, Bristol. Telephone Bristol 629092. T/C

Rawdon Woodturners
Comprehensive courses geared to suit individual requirements offered in
Woodmachining
Woodturning
Take advantage of my 20 years of industrial and educational experience and realize the full potential of your machinery. Write or phone for details
Rawdon Woodturners
Peter Clark Woodcraft Ltd.,
Old Friends School, Low Green
Rawdon, Nr Leeds, West Yorkshire
Tel: Leeds (0532) 676068 (evenings preferred)

TWO-DAY Woodturning Course for beginners in mid-Norfolk village. Two students only. Accommodation available. SAE for details please. Doug Keeling, Church Lane, Beetley, Norfolk NR20 4AB. T/C

WOODTURNING COURSE in Scottish borders. Two day professional tuition. For details S.A.E. to: Monteviot Woodcraft, Tower Workshop, Harestanes Mill, Jedburgh, Roxburghshire TD8 6UF. Tel: 0450-87446 (evenings) N-Q

Australian Readers WOODTURNING
40 Years of woodturning experience available to you in a 2 day course. Basic or advanced. Personal tuition to your needs in a fully equipped workshop. Write for details:
PHILIP ELFORD 407 Peel St. N., Ballarat, Vic. 3350.

GORDON STOKES
Author of Modern Woodturning
Beginner's Guide to Woodturning Woodturning for Pleasure, etc. etc
Will be pleased to send you full details of his intensive two day Woodturning and Woodcarving courses. Personal instruction based on thirty years experience. Don't struggle along the hard way. Foolscap S.A.E. to:
202 The Hollow, Bath, Avon BA2 1NG
Tel: Bath 22617

WOODTURNING COURSES
2 Day courses, mid-week or weekend in modern well equipped workshop. Comfortable accommodation available in pleasant surroundings. SAE for details to
Cliff Willetts, Gables, Frisby On The Wreake, Melton Mowbray, Leics.

FREE WOODTURNING LESSONS
Combine your family holiday with instruction. Book for June or September. One week two persons minimum. Rooms, sea view, licensed bar *(to wash down sawdust).* 3 miles of sandy beach, short stroll from hotel. *Send for colour brochure to*
HEADLANDS HOTEL
(AA and RAC One Star)
Beach Road, Woolacombe, Devon.
or telephone (0271) 870320

Woodturning Courses
four days with
MIKE LAW
(Thos Harrison & Sons)

Relax into a four-day long woodturning course in the informal atmosphere of our farmhouse home. We offer comfortable accommodation, good food, and professional tuition in the heart of this beautiful countryside.
Please write or telephone for details: Mike Law, The Longhouse, Maxworthy Cross, North Petherwin, Launceston, North Cornwall. Tel: STD (056685) 322.

LEARN THE ART AND CRAFT OF RESTORING ANTIQUES AND DESIGNING AND MAKING YOUR OWN FURNITURE
Situated in a charming Norfolk village we offer professional tuition in courses of antique restoration, wood turning, machining, woodworking and finishing. Come to The Old Mill at Gayton for good food and comfortable accommodation in very pleasant surroundings.
WINDMILL ENTERPRISES
For full details send SAE to MR R Hirons, The Old Mill, Gayton, Norfolk. Tel: (055386) 613/717

Woodworking Machines of Switzerland **SCHOOL OF WOODWORKING**

NEW ONE-DAY INTRODUCTORY COURSES

The Official **INCA** School of Woodworking is pleased to announce vacancies for Introductory One-Day Courses using the famous 'COMPACT UNIVERSAL SAW'.
These intensive courses are limited to 2 or 3 students each using a 'COMPACT' under the tuition of experienced instructors.
The cost of a one-day introductory course including lunch, refreshments and VAT is **£35**.
For full details of this and other woodworking courses using the finest **INCA** equipment and held in our purpose-built workshops, write now to:
Woodworking Machines of Switzerland Ltd.,
Inca House, Peverel Drive, Granby, Milton Keynes MK1 1NL.
Telephone: Milton Keynes (0908) 641492.

FRENCH POLISHING AND RE-FINISHING COURSES
Intensive, in depth, 2 or 4 day residential courses, geared to suit individual requirements. Small groups. Personal tuition based on my own 40 years experience. Informal atmosphere and **REAL WORK EXPERIENCE**.
Full board and comfortable accommodation in our Riverside home, in beautiful Scottish Border Countryside.
Write or phone for details
COLIN CAMPBELL,
SOUTH MANSE, NEWCASTLETON,
ROXBURGHSHIRE.
TEL. LIDDESDALE (054 121) 206.

CLASSIFIED ADVERTISING IN WOODWORKER BRINGS QUICK RESULTS
This space could cost you as little as £20.00. For further details contact Valerie Tester now on (0442) 41221 Ext. 262

WANTED

BANDSAW and rear sanding attachments for ML8 Lathe. Also separate planer thicknesser. Telephone (0903) 45862. P

WANTED URGENTLY Norris planes, Mitre and low angle planes. Any gun metal planes. Ultamatum braces. Stanley planes up to £200 paid for No 51/52 — 10¼-444. Top cash prices paid for all tools. R. Lowe, 45 Temple Hill, Whitwick, Nr Leicester. Telephone Coalville (0530) 34581 evenings. N-P

WANTED. MORTISING ATTACHMENT and disc sander for Myford ML8. Telephone 02406 5484 Daytime. 049481 2017 Evenings (Bucks.) P

FEELING CRAFTY? Anyone interested in crafts knows how difficult it is to find suppliers of the material. Whether it is tiny hinges for Miniature Furniture or Silvercraft supplies, tracking down stockists can be frustrating. The problem is solved with POPULAR CRAFTS' GUIDE TO GOOD CRAFT SUPPLIERS, listing over 2,000 outlets, plus Courses, Guild and Associations. A mine of useful information at £1.25 inc. P&P, direct from Popular Crafts, P.O. Box 35, Bridge Street, Hemel Hempstead, Herts. T/C

SOLID BRASS DOOR, cabinet and window fittings, in period and modern designs. Full colour catalogue illustrates over 300 different items. Send 50p (refundable with first order) to: Classic Brass (Dept. WW2), West Road, Westcliff on Sea, Essex. T/C

¹⁄₁₂th SCALE BRASS HARDWARE
Period handles, hinges, grille
S.A.E. for list
MARGARET VARNEY (MINIATURES)
10 Hardays Lane,
West Haddon, Northampton

For best results when buying or selling use the CLASSIFIED COLUMNS — Telephone: Valerie Tester, (0442) 41221. Ext. 262

Prices quoted are those prevailing at press date and are subject to alteration due to economic conditions.

Our panel of experts answer queries about your workshop problems

Woodworker's Question Box

Write to: Question Box
Woodworker
PO Box 35
Bridge Street
Hemel Hempstead HP1 1EE

Cleaning teeth
From: P. G. Handley, Truro

Could you please advise me if there is any chemical solution manufactured which facilitates the easy removal of the encrustation of saw dust etc which tends to build up around circular saw teeth and planer knives when machining resinous timber. Failing this is there any method you can recommend? I have tried washing it off with various spirits but to no avail.

There may be chemicals produced for industrial use in the removal of resinous deposits from sawblades and planer knives, but we are not aware of any which are available to the home user.

Various liquids will help, but none will do the whole job, unless the deposits are very light.

The usual approach is to soak the areas in cellulose thinners, methylated spirit, or paraffin, to soften the material, and then to remove it by means of soft wire brushes, such as are sold for cleaning suede shoes, or by scraping with a small knife. If the deposits are not allowed to build up and harden there is really no problem, so perhaps 'little and often' should be the motto.

Porch mahogany
From: P. Conisbee, West Ealing

I wish to build a porch in mahogany. Could you please advise me as to which mahogany or mahogany-type of hardwood is most suitable for exterior joinery.

Where timber is used for this type of construction, its degree of natural resistance to decay must be taken into account, in this context it means 'when in contact with the ground'. You will appreciate that a piece of wood used as a post is at risk whether set in, on the ground, or resting on a brick or concrete plinth; the situation being the same since any wetting, and holding of rain water applies in each case. Similar remarks apply to wood whose side grain is in contact with the ground except here its ability to absorb water is much slower. Practically all commercial woods have been tested for degree of natural durability and have been placed in certain categories, so that at one end of the scale are species like teak and afrormosia which are classified as very durable while at the lower end are those like beech, birch and lime which are deemed perishable. These classifications apply only to heartwood; sapwood of any species should be considered perishable; a few are a little better than this but one ought to play safe.

With regard to hardwoods African mahogany and sapele are considered to be moderately durable; Brazilian mahogany and utile are classified as durable. Many manufacturers of Georgian-type doors, sills and surrounds for double glazing, picture windows and so on, use dark-red meranti/seraya. This is a dullish reddish-brown hardwood, excellent for exterior work and classified as durable as opposed to only moderately durable for ordinary red meran-

ti/seraya. From the above you will note that the highest classifications are for Brazilian mahogany, utile and dark-red meranti/seraya; the last named probably being the cheapest. In practical terms, durable means that a section of 2in × 2in (50mm × 50mm) all heartwood, has a potential resistance to decay of 15 to 25 years when in contact with the ground. A liberal brushing, spraying or steeping of sections like posts in an organic wood preservative could double this life. Clear organic solvent preservatives or those coloured for mahogany or western red cedar are produced by many companies.

Most can be painted or varnished over when dry, but the tinted formulations serve the dual purpose of protection and relatively maintenance free decoration. Doubtless you will obtain a few quotations for suitable dimension stock or sawn to your specification and in this respect there are several advertisers in *Woodworker* who could help if you find difficulty with local suppliers.

Moulding planes
From: B. E. Serth, Lincoln

I have a set of wooden moulding planes comprising various hollows, rounds and ogees, but do not know how to use them correctly. I have tried various books but they only mention that the planes are used by starting on the front of the timber and working backwards (sic) I should appreciate some advice on the subject.

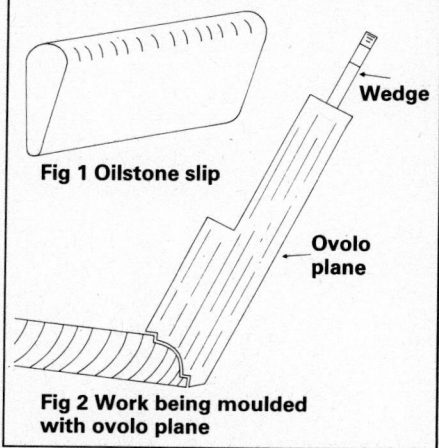

Fig 1 Oilstone slip

Wedge

Ovolo plane

Fig 2 Work being moulded with ovolo plane

The first essential to the successful use of any plane is to be able to sharpen it correctly. The usual flat oilstone is suitable for sharpening the irons of rebate planes, ploughs and rounds. The latter are sharpened by imparting a rotary action to the blade as it is pushed back and forth along the oilstone. The blades of hollows, ogees and ovolos cannot be sharpened in this way. Instead a shaped oilstone slip (Fig. 1) is used by carefully following the contours of the cutting edge. Removal of the ensuing burr is effected in the usual way by placing the blade, bevel side up, flat on the ordinary oilstone and rubbing it a few times to remove the burr.

The blade is placed in the plane and

projects below the sole so that when sighting along the sole the edge is seen as a thin black line. Tapping home the wedge secures the blade in position.

The wood to be moulded is either gripped in the vice or clamped between dogs fitted in the bench top and the tail vice. The planes are grasped by curling the fingers of the left hand around the front end of the plane with the thumb on top. The right hand grips the rear end of the plane.

Planing is commenced at the end of the work farthest away from the worker. Short shavings are removed at first and gradually as more wood is removed the plane is brought towards the near end until finally it is run through from one end to the other.

Ovolo and ogee planes are not held upright but at an angle as shown in Fig. 2. Planing is automatically stopped when the two outer edges of the sole meet the face side and face edge of the work.

Amateur polishing
From: L. Rider, York

Could you advise on any product that could be used to finish off an amateur's attempt at french polishing; such as a mild abrasive combined with a polish to rid the surface of minute specks of dust etc and give it a more uniform finish?

French polishing should be carried on in a dry, draught and dust-free room with a temperature around 65°F. If dust is spoiling the finish, take a critical look at the workshop to locate the source of the dust. Vacuum cleaning may be all that is needed to dispose of sawdust and odd bits.

The polish is applied with a rubber made of wadding wrapped in a clean lint-free rag, preferably a well washed handkerchief. An unsuitable covering can leave undesirable bits in the shellac. Check that the rag covering has not worn into a hole as this too can lead to poor results. The method of application greatly affects the results and if the polish is applied too generously the surface is bound to become sticky and dust will adhere to it.

These few suggestions may prevent difficulties arising in future but to rectify the job in hand we would advise the following: Allow the polished surface to harden for three or four days, then smooth it with fine pumice powder obtainable from a polish supply house. Damp a piece of felt with water, sprinkle some pumice on the felt and gently and evenly rub the work in straight lines in the direction of the grain. This will produce a perfectly smooth matt surface which is wiped clean with a chamois leather.

Apply a good quality wax polish with a clean rag and after about ten minutes rub it vigorously with a soft duster. Three or four applications will give an excellent finish.

We would advise any reader who is experiencing difficulties with french polishing to attend a two-day course on wood finishing organised for members of the Guild of Woodworkers. Full details are available on request from the Administrator, PO Box 35, Bridge Street, Hemel Hempstead, Herts HP1 1EE.

<table>
<tr>
<td>

Our panel of experts
answer queries about
your workshop problems

</td>
<td>

Woodworker's
Question Box

</td>
<td>

Write to: Question Box
Woodworker
PO Box 35
Bridge Street
Hemel Hempstead HP1 1EE

</td>
</tr>
</table>

Blotchy yew
From: D. Gunn, Todmorden

I am having a problem with blotchy yew. The timber was bought from a local sawmill, then dried in my kiln (Ebac mini dehumidifier in a 4 × 4 × 12ft kiln constructed as the manufacturers recommended). When removed it was dry (9-11%m.c.) but appeared to be very red. When cut this was seen to be a surface feature as if all the colour had moved to the outsides of the planks along with the water.

I would be grateful for any information about this. Has anyone else had this problem? Can I avoid it by drying the timber differently? Was the tree cut at the wrong time of the year? Was it grown in a chemically anomalous area? As a one man business producing high quality furniture in mainly English woods my kiln has been a great success in drying elm, ash, oak, walnut, cherry, sweet chestnut and pear.

The discoloration obvious in the samples is of chemical origin and impossible to diagnose specifically. There are many occasions where a particular wood develops a stain for no obvious reason and frequent occasions where the stain disappears after the wood has been exposed to light. This is not likely to happen in your case because a partial clue lies in the fact of the forced drying that was applied. This must not be construed as meaning your drying unit is unsuitable, on the contrary, it is probable you had a 'rogue' parcel of wood on this occasion.

However, to explain: different woods contain a variety of chemicals including colouring pigments and under some circumstances, certain constituents will combine with oxygen during the drying process and so produce oxidation stains. At other times, colour changes are brought about by the action of enzymes in the wood. Probably the most common phenomenon occurring in wood that is dried under certain conditions is that known as hydrolysis, a word meaning decomposition of a chemical compound by the addition of water. You are probably acquainted with 'red' or 'steamed' beech which is uniformly reddish throughout and is brought about by subjecting green beech to a high temperature, high humidity treatment in a drying kiln for three or four days prior to actual drying. If, however, 'white' or 'unsteamed' beech is required, the temperature in the kiln, and we are talking of a conventional kiln, is lowered and the relative humidity reduced by suitable venting. The colour change in the red beech is generally agreed to be due to hydrolysis. There are a number of things you have not told us, for example, the working temperature in your dryer; the initial moisture content of the wood; the average moisture extraction rate of the dehumidifier at the time of drying the yew, and the thickness of the wood, although we assume this to be around 25mm from the samples.

Basically, dehumidifiers operate at relatively low temperatures, but it is now quite common for many to be fitted with a

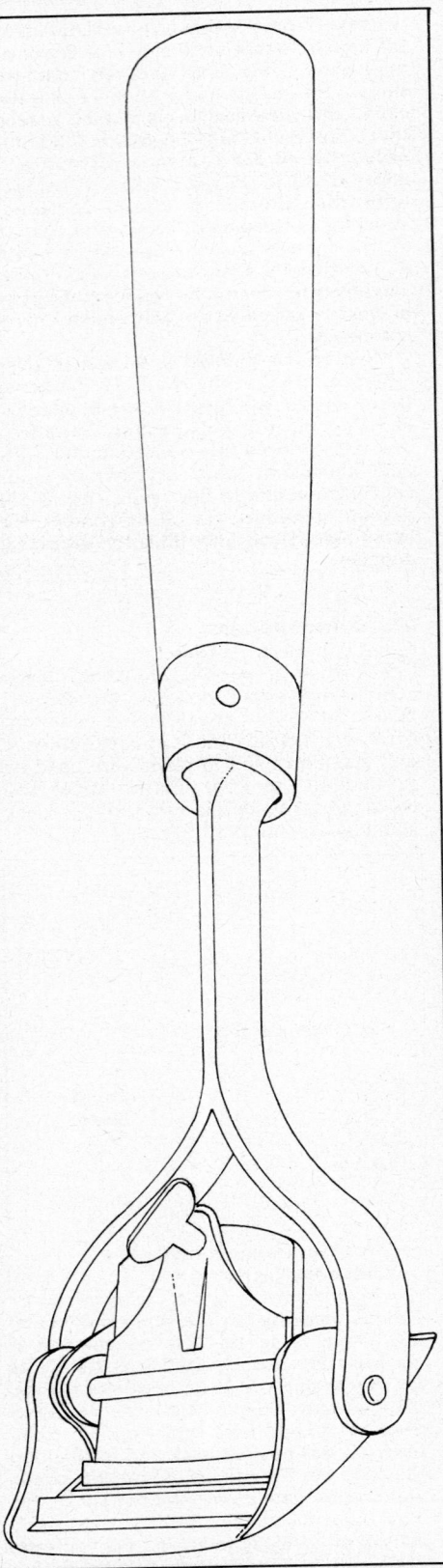

booster so as to promote quicker drying. If your problem is due to hydrolysis, and we are not entirely convinced that it is, allowing your yew to air-dry for a few months prior to final drying, and reducing the

temperature to below 100°F (38°C) ought to supply an answer. We would however, refer to oxidative staining: you may have seen, at some time or other, white-painted interior trim such as skirtings, in wet-constructed houses, showing brownish patchy stains under the paint after only a few months of occupation of the premises. Largely, this is due to the backs of the skirtings being left unprimed, with the result that as the building dries out and becomes warmed, salts in the bricks, plaster, and wood, are drawn, combined with moisture to the front face of the wood where, in the presence of light and oxygen, the unsightly stains appear.

In the case of yew this is a coniferous species and as such, consists anatomically, of a systematic series of pores called tracheids. In other words, unlike the more complex hardwoods, with a high proportion of closed, or very thick fibres, the tracheids, once the free moisture is removed in drying, have a vast number of open orifices that could now retain air. We therefore incline to the view that what has happened with your yew is that by chance, certain water soluble pigments in the wood have been drawn to the surface by the drying process, there to combine with the available oxygen in the tracheids that have dried below the saturation point, and so to oxidise and produce this unnatural red colouration.

As mentioned, we do not think the problem was entirely due to hydrolysis, and we suspect oxidation. Either way, slowing down the drying rate by reducing the temperature, and reducing the initial m.c. prior to placing the wood in the dryer would be helpful in future, but frankly, we would not anticipate similar problems with other parcels.

Box scraper
From: H. R. Driffield, Taunton

In a recent purchase of a job lot of tools I have come across one which I have sketched. It is a small hand plane or shaver, the blade being about two inches wide and similar to that used in a metal spokeshave. It has a small cap iron and is capable of rough adjustment using the thumbscrew on the cap. The wood and iron stirrup handle is pivoted at the base. It is clearly used for shaving wood, but I should be grateful for your advice on the precise use for which it has been designed.

The tool that you have so neatly illustrated is a box scraper of a type still made by Messrs Record Tools catalogue no 070. Its stated purpose is to 'scrape stencils and marks from the surface of boxes, floors etc'. It certainly does this efficiently and although it is rare that I need to remove stencils from boxes I have used it as an alternative to the chair adze for hollowing solid chair seats where its curved sole can be used to advantage.

Incidentally the tool has been on the market for some time. In 1935 it cost 4/- and 30 years later could be bought for 21/6 with spare irons costing 3/6.

Woodworker's Question Box

Write to: Question Box
Woodworker
PO Box 35
Bridge Street
Hemel Hempstead HP1 1EE

Baffling timber

From: G. T. Hall, Gt Abington, Cambs

When I first started turning two years ago I acquired four pieces of yew in the log form. Three of these were obviously still very green the other appeared to be from a dead branch. It was very dry, had splits and little bark. After a week or so I cut a short length to use on the lathe. To my surprise the wood was extremely dry and the splits were not deep. But what really baffled me was the colour. The heartwood was a deep mauve-ed and the sapwood off-white. On turning the wood gives off a very distinct perfume and after a short time white crystals form on the heartwood even after finishing with sanding sealer and polish. These crystals can be wiped off and eventually cease to form.

Over the last two years I have acquired a substantial amount of yew in log form from several trees, mostly green but also some dead branches and have never come across any like the branch in question. Is it yew? It turns beautifully and I would very much like to acquire some more.

The samples you sent in had a few crystals adhering to them and these appear to be of calcium oxalate. This fact, coupled with the aroma you say you notice when working the wood, leads us to the conclusion that the branch was not yew (*Taxus baccata*) but cedar (*Cedrus* spp.). Crystals are not very common in the softwoods and, so far as recorded instances show, they are con-fined to the Abietoideae and yew does not belong to this group. It is not possible to say which species of cedar is involved, but it could be Atlantic, Lebanon, or deodar, all of which are planted for ornamental pur-poses as you probably know. Microscopic investigation would confirm what we say, but unfortunately we do not have suitable equipment.

Steam bending

From: Martin Jeffries, Nottingham

At present I am a student on my second year of a BA (Hons) Furniture Design course at Trent Polytechnic, Nottingham. I have re-cently been researching steam bending as a method of manufacture for a proposed dining chair. What I have tried to create is a mould that will not only bend a section of wood through one plane, but will also induce a twist at both ends of the hoop. The dimensions of the hoop are 370mm high by 430mm wide and the section is 35mm × 20mm beech.

Initially, I started using laminates but had many problems with tension and com-pression on the twists and as a result the fibres split. Later I was introduced to a local steam-bender in Nottingham who steamed some of my solid beech sections of 35mm × 20mm. The wood was steamed for twenty minutes at a constant 5psi. After this period one length was removed from the steamer and we tried to bend it around the mould. The section was too large to bend manually and the twist was impossible. What I would

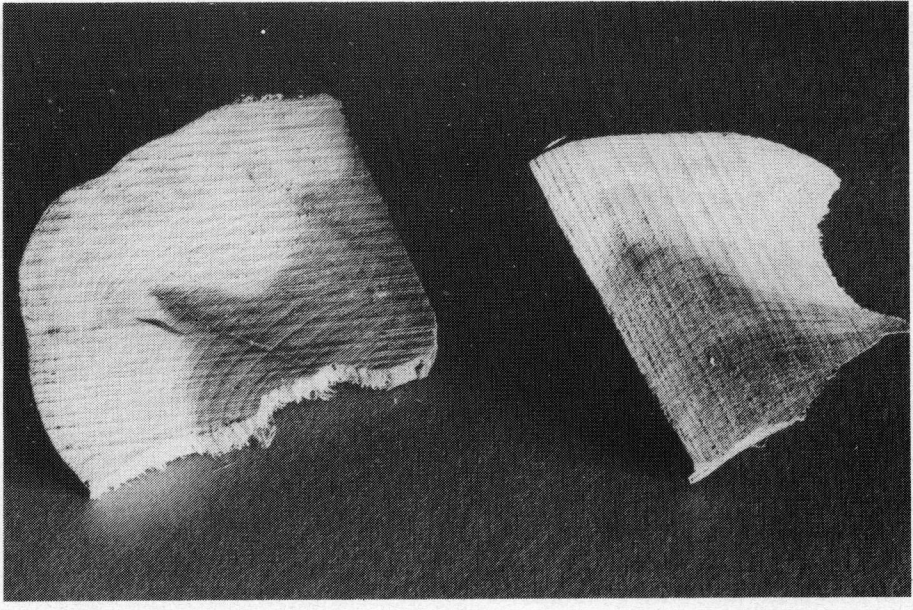

● Above: Photograph of the 'baffling' timber sample sent in by G. T. Hall of Cambridgeshire clearly demonstrating the dark heartwood and the lighter sapwood to which he refers in his query.

like to know is:

1 Is it possible to bend and twist a section of 35mm × 20mm beech, or perhaps a thinner section of 35mm × 10mm into a hoop shape?

2 If it were possible to bend and twist for example the 35mm × 10mm section, would it be strong enough in the pro-posed chair frame.

Any information obtained at this stage relating to steam-bending would be benefi-cial to not only myself but to the whole department as we will shortly be having a steamer installed. I would be very grateful for any advice whatsoever.

Your letter poses quite a problem! Ironical-ly, I believe it to be a basic design problem and I find it rather surprising that you seem to have got to such an advanced stage in your design brief without corrective advice. Personally, I think a serious re-think is called for. However, I will try to be con-structive and limit my reply to a discussion of your bending/twisting difficulty.

I regularly steam bend ash and beech of 1⅛in × 1⅛in (about 28mm²) section into half hoops for chair backs and arm bows. Occasionally one splits on the outside (tension surface) of the bend but most are OK. I use a metal backing strap and end blocks as advocated by Stevens and Turner in their *Wood Bending* handbook. I steam in a simple, home-made steam box at atmos-pheric pressure for about 45 minutes. It takes two fairly strong people to do the actual bending by hand but I shall one day overcome this problem by using a windlass arrangement. So there need be no technical problems in bending your 35mm × 20mm (that's about 1½in × ¾in) sections. (35mm × 10mm sections would not, I think, be strong enough for your chair.)

However, I use straight grained, air dried and often unseasoned wood – I fell and cleave my own ash. I also put the backing

strap either in or on the steamer so that it is at the same temperature as the wood to be bent and I work very quickly when bending. It is *hot* wood fibres which bend most easily – any cooling effect is detrimental. If you have been trying to bend kiln dried stuff, forget it. It is much too dry and brittle to give more than occasional success.

My opinion about the twist at the ex-treme ends of your bend is that you are simply asking too much of your material and that this constitutes a major design weakness. Even with hydraulic bending equipment it would present production difficulties – which explains why it is not done. Chairs which incorporate similar features of what appears to be a bend and two twists use three separate parts joined by clever joints.

Your problems with laminates (pre-sumably you were using constructional veneers) are understandable. You would need a very sophisticated male and female former or mould to achieve any measure of success. Have you tried making the bend with longer ends than required, then cut-ting back to the desired size? This could result in less fibre splitting at the twisted area perhaps? Or you might try laminating with 2mm ply – cut in the right direction this twists quite readily. Again in both cases, the construction of a suitable former would be an important first consideration.

In conclusion, I do recommend you to think again about your design and especial-ly to appreciate the limitations of the material you have chosen to use.

Letters to the editor

WOODWORKER
PO Box 35
Bridge Street
Hemel Hempstead

From: W. McGregor, Aberdeen
Dear Sir

I am very interested in the craft of violin making and would like to have some practical tuition on the subject. Are there any courses available (near at hand) or alternatively would any reader with practical experience be prepared to help?

Yours faithfully, **W. McGregor**
Over to the violin makers of Scotland, can you help Mr McGregor? Letters to the *Woodworker* office with any advice or help will be forwarded. We would like to hear from anyone in Scotland who offers courses or practical instruction in any of the fields of woodworking not just musical instrument making as we are constantly being asked for such details.

From: M. B. Fisher, Whittington, Staffs
Dear Sir

I have been a regular reader of *Woodworker* for a number of years and as a result of reading an advertisement in it have recently attended a course on antique restoration at Edwin Turner's of Gislingham, Eye.

Naturally when one embarks on a venture of this kind there are a lot of questions one asks oneself, such as, will we derive any benefit? Will it be a rip off? Will we understand what is said, meant, or intended? Will it be too basic or too advanced?

However it soon became apparent when the course started that all these doubts and forebodings were unfounded.

The course was most instructive and presented with considerable expertise and in a language that explained technical terms in a manner easily understood by the layman.

The practical applications of the course were presented in a most professional manner when questions on any aspect were encouraged and answered.

Everyone on the course was made very welcome and soon put at ease by our host and hostess Mr and Mrs Turner.

I thought the course was a great success and value for money even though for me it involved a round trip of some 400 miles.

Yours faithfully, **M. B. Fisher**

From: Gordon Stokes, Bath
Dear Sir

I am puzzled by the reply given in the February issue of *Woodworker* p129 to the gentleman who enquired about the finishing of wooden goblets. Perhaps it was meant to be a joke?

If not, I feel I must point out that it goes to great length in explaining what is NOT suitable, without answering the original question. After many years of woodturning — more than thirty five — during which I have made and sold or given away hundreds of goblets, tankards, wine glasses, and so forth, it now appears that I may have left a trail of inflamed mucous membranes and swollen lips, of which I have, until now, been blissfully unaware. Perhaps the fingers are affected also, which might account for the fact that there has been not a single complaint.

Wooden utensils were used for centuries for food and drink — and indeed they still are in some countries. How our ancestors must have suffered! Do the wooden spoons used in our kitchens have a sinsister and hitherto unobserved effect upon our health, I ask myself?

A two part catalyst resin, such as Rustins *Plastic Coating*, does a very good job on items of this kind, two or three coats being desirable — but I make this suggestion with suitable humility, in the light of this new and shattering revelation. Was the question answered by a woodturner, I wonder, or an anonymous 'authority'?

I appeal to you, sirs, do not encourage the abolition of wooden bowls and mugs — it could mean the end for us peasants!

Yours faithfully, **Gordon Stokes**

From: Frank Penty, Masham, Yorks
Dear Sir

Your last two magazines have been full of interest to me.

In one magazine I saw that carbon tetrachloride was a good depressor but was dangerous as being inflammable. CCl_4 is commercially called Pyrene and as such is used in fire extinguishers.

January was interesting because of its wood drying article. Lately I had a job in a grist mill and part of my work was checking grain for moisture content. The usual way of doing this is to use a similar piece of gear as is used on wood, two prongs being inserted into pressed ground of grain to check its resistance.

There was often discrepancy between these moisture measurements and what I got. My readings were obtained by drying ground grains and finding the loss in weight expressed directly as a percentage loss.

This made me wonder if the sort of grain itself had a different resistance from one to another and if this was the same with different sorts of wood. For instance, is the resistance of dry oats any different to, say, ash or elm. This would throw out the moisture content readings as it seems to me that weighing of wet grain and then dry would be a far better and more accurate method if sawdust was used in the same way to get moisture content of timber.

I did try this on sawdust and got a reasonable reading but the original m/c was not known, so I had no proper check.

Yours faithfully, **Frank Penty**

From: B. C. Blyth, Beaconsfield, Bucks
Dear Sir

I wonder if readers can throw any light on W. Mackay. I have a desk of solid yew inlaid with cross-cut yew on the top. It is of the 1900 period, signed W. Mackay.

Yours faithfully, **B. C. Blyth**

Editor: In the absence of a town it is very difficult to trace W. Mackay from trade directories. He is not listed in the Victoria and Albert museum's index. There is at present no ready printed source, that we know of, for identifying Victorian furniture makers, apart from consulting commercial trade directories and these are listed by town or county. Has any reader of *Woodworker* come across W. Mackay in his or her researches. We should be interested to hear and would forward any help to Mr Blyth.

From: P. W. Glenville, Stevenage, Herts
Dear Sir

I am 27 years of age and a fireman by trade. I have just started taking a keen interest in wood and what I can make from it. Instruction in the working of wood is literally nil, apart from what I have learned from books and the 'once a week' (two hours) night class at the local college, started this school year. I am making a roll top desk.

What I am looking for is proper instruction from a course or from a craftsman, local or near local to where I live. Being a fireman I work a shift system. This allows me nearly four days off in eight (ie four days on-four off). It is during these days off that I am willing to work (with the object of learning) with someone.

I understand that this may not be within your field or horizons but all the help I can get in learning about such a fantastic subject is worthwhile. Please can you help?

Yours faithfully, **P. W. Glenville**

Editor: Can anyone help or suggest a course of study in the Hertfordshire area?

From: R. Shann, Caernarfon, Gwynedd
Dear Sir

I am copying some 17th century Flemish furniture, and have a couple of problems. One concerns the small (18mm) tapered iron nails with large heads which one finds. Is it possible to buy these today, either here or abroad (I could imagine nail making by hand might still be going on in the third world...) I have a very interesting article on nail making from the 1950's in the *Woodworker* magazine, but it would be a lot of sweat to set up making them for the few I want.

The other question I have concerns a suitable tool for cutting internal shapes in 1½in oak (that is I'm faced with sawing out internal holes in a solid plank of wood, the tightest curve involved is about 100mm dia.) My bandsaw, of course, can't do internal cuts, and my jigsaw (a cheap one) just burns its blades. (That's a hand held jigsaw). There's a conversion kit for my Burgess bandsaw to make it into a bench jigsaw, would this be likely to be powerful enough (the bandsaw itself cuts quite happily thro' the oak). If not what sort of machine should I be contemplating, in what sort of price range? I suppose I could do the job with my (hand held Mof 96 router) plunging router, or would 1½in be a bit deep? Are the top price hand held jigsaws intended for this sort of work?

Yours faithfully, **R. Shann**

Editor: Readers' replies wanted on this one please. We would also like to hear from firms offering ranges of nail types as we are frequently asked for many different types from upholstery to small brass pins, to large headed tacks, etc. Come on all you experts with jigsaws and routers. We will forward any help you can give to Mr Shann.

Woodworker

THE MAGAZINE FOR THE CRAFTSMAN

AUGUST 1982 Vol. 86 No. 1065 ISSN 0043 776X

Front cover: Work in progress at Kingston Cooperage (Photo Nigel Barklie) Story pp 526-8.

Editor	Chris Dunn	
Deputy Editor	Polly Curds	
Advertisement Manager	Glyn Crole-Rees	
Advertisement Director ⎱	MAP Leisure	Michael Merrifield
Managing Director ⎰	Division	Gavin Doyle

MEMBER OF THE AUDIT BUREAU OF CIRCULATIONS

SUBSCRIPTION DEPARTMENT: Remittances to MODEL AND ALLIED PUBLICATIONS, PO Box 35, Hemel Hempstead, Herts HP1 1EE. Price per copy 95p includes p&p. Subscription queries: Tel: Hemel Hempstead 51740. Subscription rate, including index, £11.90 per annum; overseas sterling £12.90; $29.00 US for overseas dollar subscribers. Second class postage paid in US at New York, New York. *Distribution* to North American hobby and craft stores, museums and bookshops by Bill Dean Books Ltd, 166-41 Powells Cove Boulevard, Post Office Box 69, Whitestone, New York 11357, USA. Tel: 1-212-767-6632. *Distribution* to news stand sales by Eastern News Distribution Inc, 111 Eight Avenue, New York, NY10011, USA Tel: 1-212-255-5620. (POSTMASTER: Send address changes to England).

WOODWORKER is printed in Great Britain by H. E. Warne Ltd, East Hill, St Austell, Cornwall PL25 4TN for the proprietor and publisher Model & Allied Publications Ltd (a member of the Argus Press Group). Trade sales by Argus Press Sales & Distribution Ltd, 12-18 Paul Street, London EC2A 4JS. WOODWORKER (ISSN 0043-776X) is published on the 3rd Friday of the month.

Model & Allied Publications Ltd

PO Box 35, Bridge Street, Hemel Hempstead, Herts HP1 1EE. Telephone: Hemel Hempstead (0442) 41221.

Minding the machine

Woodworkers are constantly assailed with tempting offers of sophisticated weaponry to make the workshop ever more efficient, and the effect of machinery has certainly made an enormous impact on standards of finish and workmanship accordingly.

The versatility that machines offer the woodworker is well illustrated by a recent conversation I had with John Canvey, an outstanding amateur wood craftsman, but what made the subject even more interesting was the note of caution that John expressed in respect of machinery. He told me that his father had been a cabinetmaker all his life — a good one too — but although he had inherited a love of good wood and fine workmanship from his father, John chose to make his living as an engineer, retaining woodwork as a pleasure and a pastime.

John's workshop at home is a monument to modern technology, with every kind of machine and power tool on hand, and the work that emanates from the shop is an enviable example of the standards that a serious woodworker can achieve. But John confessed that the quality of his work, assisted by power, troubled him whenever he thought of his father's fine work, produced by hand.

'The fact is,' he said, 'I am only half the craftsman that my father was, and yet I can employ machinery to produce, quite effortlessly, the sort of finish and accuracy that my old man strove for all his life.'

The modern mind would argue here that this is the beauty of Progress and that everyone should take full advantage of whatever tools and equipment the contemporary world provides him with, otherwise we might as well be chipping away with bits of flint. But John Canvey's experience tells him that there is more to it than that.

He said he now tends to use his machinery more selectively, rather than as a matter of course, both because he doesn't need to rely on speed and efficiency as a professional does and because he fears that machines might eventually undermine the natural skill of his hands, instead of enhancing it. As he pointed out, it is jolly handy to have a pocket calculator to do your sums for you, but you could easily lose the ability to do the sums for yourself. Thus the machine becomes master instead of tool.

John admitted that he wouldn't be without his technological back-up for anything, but he maintains strong reservations about its use and is determined that his tools will remain his tools, and he the master of them.

I thought that was worth passing on.

Chris Dunn

August notes

Latest tools directory

British Machine Tools & Equipment 1982, latest in the long series of directories published by the Machine Tool Trades Association, is now available.

This authoritative 132 page A4 size directory lists the products of 203 British machine tool, component and associated equipment and woodworking machinery manufacturers. The book is intended for both UK and export markets and contains comprehensive cross-referenced indices listing products, manufacturers and trade names, together with a trilingual English, German and Spanish product index.

It costs £10 inclusive of post and packaging and is available direct from MTTA Publications, 62 Bayswater Road, London W2 3PH.

Heavy duty hole saws

A set of heavy duty, steel blade hole saws is now available in the Wolfcraft range of universal power tool accessories.

The blades, seven in total and in diameters of 25mm, 32mm, 38mm, 45mm, 50mm, 56mm and 62mm, are supplied complete with a 6mm centre drill and a robust, blade-holding assembly, in a polystyrene box.

Buy British, says BWF

A buy-British policy has been called for by Gordon Bates, president of the British Woodworking Federation. Speaking at the federation's AGM in London, he said that other industries, public organisations and the public at large would be well advised to support the home woodworking manufacturing industry by buying its products

where they believed this to be justified on cost and performance.

The BWF was not looking for total protection or featherbedding. It was also well understood that the government was precluded from a total buy-British policy because of international trading responsibilities and treaty obligations.

But, said Mr Bates, there are a number of reasons why purchasing home-manufactured wood products makes good sense:

- BWF members provide a wide range of expertise and work which is carried out consistently to high standards.
- They provide an excellent competitive service to clients.
- They provide many jobs – directly or indirectly.
- Encouraging a flood-tide of imports is the surest way to permanent unemployment and recession.
- A sound home manufacturing base provides the springboard for an expanding export trade.

Workshop space

A major factor in setting up a business is finding suitable premises and in this harsh economic climate, costs of rent and rates are all too often prohibitive. New industrial estates, although extremely welcome, pose a greater threat to small rural firms because of the distance and time involved in travel.

With this in mind, Alan Medforth who has successfully run his own woodworking business for the past 13 years, is making 5,500sq ft available to one-man bands who are looking for space

in the Holderness area of North Humberside.

The workshop space includes a full range of modern woodworking machinery, which can be placed at the disposal of small businesses. The firms using these premises would be required to pay a weekly rent which would include use of the machinery, but running costs would have to be shared out. A further 5,500sq ft could be made available if required.

There is sufficient space for at least six new businesses and, if required, Alan Medforth would be willing to give practical advice and help in the use of the machinery, as well as basic business administration backed up by the experience gained by working for 13 years on his own.

If you are thinking of starting your own business or you are already a small business owner in general woodwork or in allied industries, and are looking for premises, contact Alan Medforth on Patrington 70704. His address is: Four Winds, Ellifoot Lane, Burstwick, Nr Hull.

For your toolkit

Paramo Tools Group Ltd, manufacture and distribute a rosewood square and gauges and a wooden handled screwdriver still manufactured in one of their Sheffield works.

Cabinet screwdrivers, London pattern screwdrivers and in particular the perfect pattern screwdrivers were an integral part of the craftsmens tool kit and Warwick Pridham, group m.d. says: 'these products have still a large part to play though demand is now obviously much lower than in the distant past. For sheer satisfaction in use you cannot beat the pleasure of solid rosewood, solid brass and ground steel hand made and finely polished'.

Acclaim for ripsaw

Reg Bater, general manager of Wadkin Cleveland is quoted as saying, 'The power band rip saw is far exceeding all of our original forecasts. After only 2 months we have already needed to increase our production by over 400 per cent.'

In many cases the PBR can not only operate as a rip saw, but also as a narrow blade band saw, so Wadkin say the PBR is installed for less than the cost of a conventional rip saw bench and band saw.

From Germany

The third edition of the reference work 'German Woodworking Machinery' has just been published.

● *Third edition of reference work. See 'from Germany'*

This catalogue of products of the members of the Fachgemeinschaft Holzbearbeitungsmaschinen im VDMA (Trade Association of Woodworking Machinery Manufacturers) is available free of charge from the Fachgemeinschaft Holzbearbeitungsmaschinen im VDMA e.V., Lyoner Strasse 18, PO Box 71 01 09 D-6000 Frankfurt-Niederrad 71, W-Germany.

The 500-page work, presented in German, English, French Spanish and Italian, contains some 550 photographs showing the principal products of the 185 members. Besides these, the firms provide short entries describing their main products.

Back in action

The 'Notes' desk is delighted to hear that Gordon Stokes, our ace woodturning man whose articles on the subject are always so popular, is now on the way to full recovery from his recent heart attack. Gordon tells us he is now back at the lathe, and very much back in action, although he is taking his doctor's advice not to overdo it.

Nice to have you back on board Gordon!

No such book

Thank you Mr Jerrett (or is it Serrett?) for pointing out an error in the book reviews page of October 1981 issue of this magazine.

The ISBN was incorrectly quoted for Jim Phillip's book *Techniques of Routing.* It should have read 7198 2860 0. Now you can all go out and buy it! Remember there is a special cup and prizes being offered at this year's Woodworker Show for innovations connected with the power router.

(See page 555 for details).

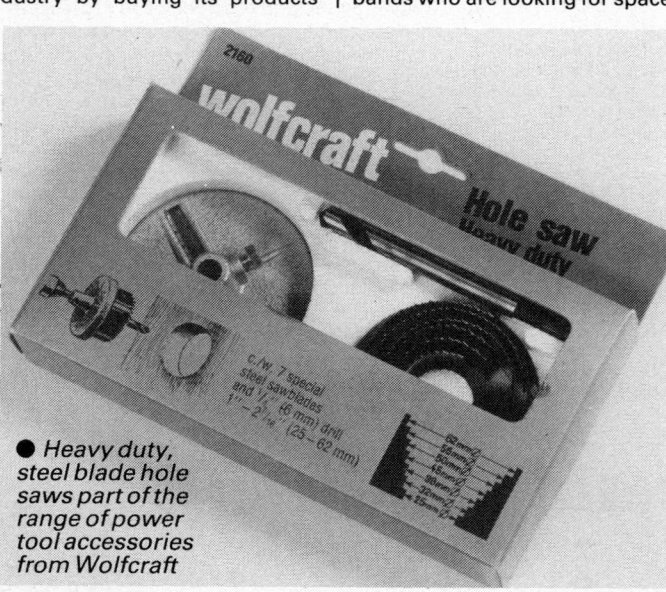

● *Heavy duty, steel blade hole saws part of the range of power tool accessories from Wolfcraft*

Super Stork sander

The BR3 random orbit sander, offered in both standard and dust extraction versions, designed for finishing, flatting and rubbing down, is available from Super Stork (IPT) Ltd, of Edgware. The 150mm diameter sanding pad is mounted on an eccentric spindle to provide a dual action rotary and elliptical movement in a random and non-repetitive pattern. The drive spindle is fitted with a special locking device which facilitates fitting and removal of the pad. The sander body is constructed in Durathane BKV glass-filled resin and incorporates a simple on/off slide switch with special lock-on capability. Single or two-hand operation is provided for. The sander is double-insulated, measures 267mm long and weighs 1.9kg, incorporates a 400w motor operating at 7200rpm. Spares and service facilities are available throughout the UK say Super Stork.

Shaping and carving kit

A powered shaping kit, based on a 350W Bosch high-speed motor with 26,000rpm operating speed, has just been produced by Trend Machinery and Cutting Tools Ltd.

The kit, supplied with carrying case, includes a set of tungsten rasps of various shapes. Trend says the rasps are ideally suited to shaping, cutting and carving wood, plastics and metal. The Trend Shaper Kit costs £86. Further details from Trend, Unit N, Penfold Works, Imperial Way, Watford. (Tel: Watford 49911).

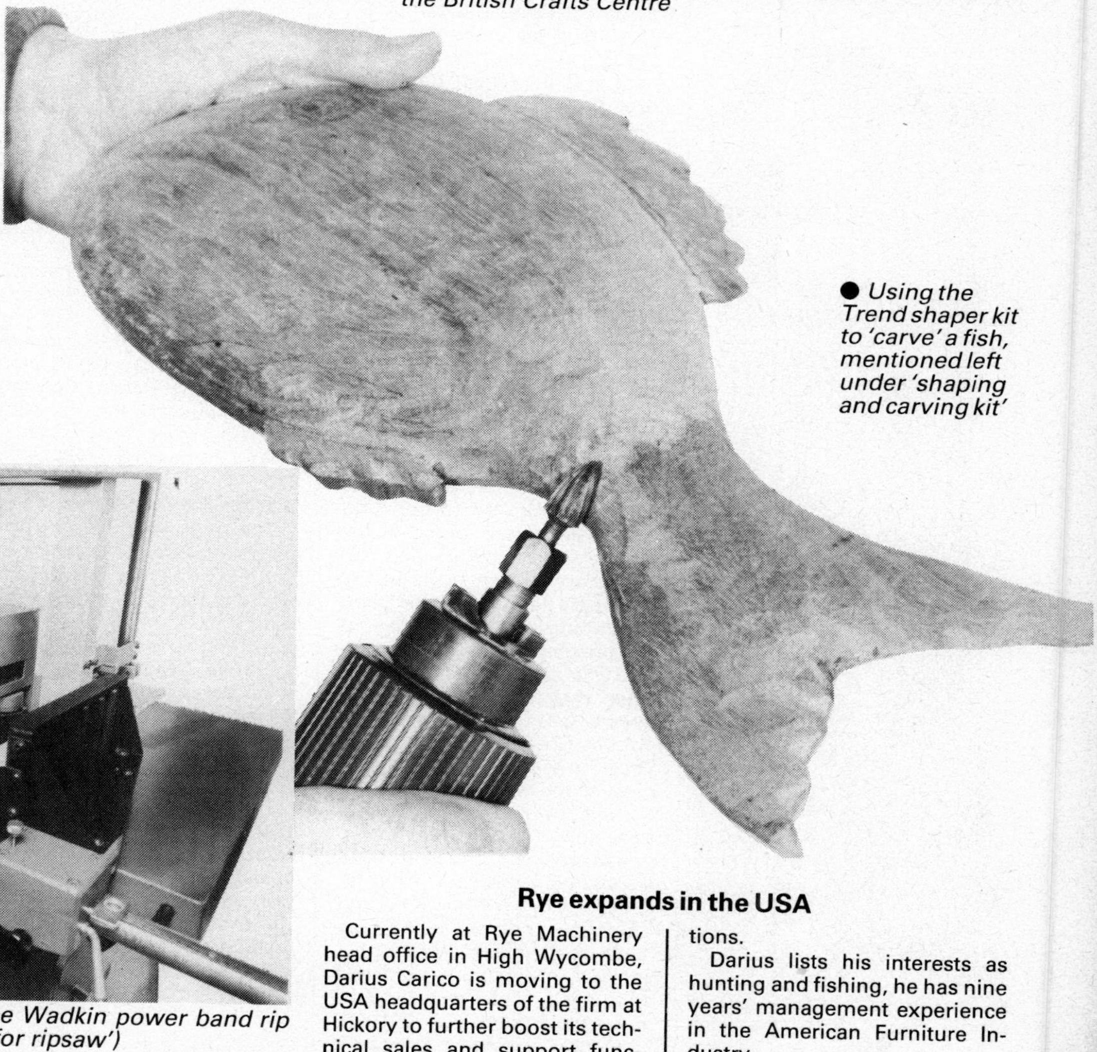

● Monoplane with approx 12in wing span by Nicholas Gray, shown in a recent exhibition at the British Crafts Centre

● Using the Trend shaper kit to 'carve' a fish, mentioned left under 'shaping and carving kit'

● Power feed arrangement of the Wadkin power band rip saw (see 'Acclaim for ripsaw')

Rye expands in the USA

Currently at Rye Machinery head office in High Wycombe, Darius Carico is moving to the USA headquarters of the firm at Hickory to further boost its technical sales and support functions.

Darius lists his interests as hunting and fishing, he has nine years' management experience in the American Furniture Industry.

August notes

Band of eight

Eight models in a new series of woodworker's bandsaws have just been announced by Thomas White and Sons of Cleckheaton. The series is called the White NRA range, and the designers have tried to offer quality features while keeping prices competitive and allowing selection to be made according to each user's particular requirements.

The smallest is the Model 300, with 16 × 18in table, 1in max blade width, 12in dia wheels, and 7in high by 11in wide cutting capacity. Largest is the Model 1050, for which the corresponding figures are 41 × 58in, 2.5in, 42in dia, and 26in high by 41in wide. Motor sizes and wheel speeds for these two models are 0.8hp × 1400rpm and 12.5hp×580rpm, respectively.

Most sizes are available ex-stock, and further details can be obtained from Thomas White and Sons, PO Box 30, Hightown Road, Cleckheaton, Yorks. Telephone (0274) 870311.

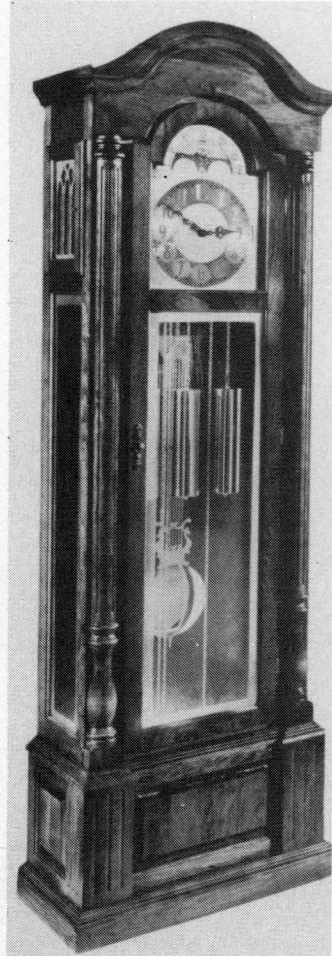

● *Model 450 grandfather clock. See 'kit for grandfather'*

Kit for a grandfather

Emperor Clock Co has announced a new grandfather clock, the model 450. Available as a kit or assembled and finished, it comes in solid ¾in oak or cherry. It features a bonnet top, turned and fluted columns, sculptured base panels, arched dial face door and pierced chime ports. The dial face and movement are constructed of solid brass by West German clocksmiths. Movements feature a self-regulation escapement which makes clock-leveling unnecessary.

In kit form, pieces come completely pre-cut and ready to assemble. Wood is kiln-dried to prevent warping or shrinking. Side frames, front frames and door are pre-assembled. Instructions, screws and all hardware are included. The company say no woodworking experience is necessary. More information from Emperor Clock Co, Emperor Industrial Park, Fairhope.

New woodworm office

To help meet the ever increasing demand for the treatment of timber decay problems throughout Cleveland, County Durham and Teesside, Rentokil's woodworm and dry rot service has opened a new branch office at Rentokil House, Princess Street, Thornaby, Stockton-on-Tees, Cleveland TS17 6AQ. A free timber survey of any building may be obtained by telephoning Stockton (0642) 613911/5.

Catalogue

The latest catalogue to reach the editorial desk is from House of Harbru, a long established family firm in the formulation and manufacture of specialist products. Originally their interests were exclusively in the silver care field, researching and developing methods of delaying and preventing tarnishing of silver. One of their first products when they expanded their interests was a traditional wax polish *Craftsman's original*. They now manufacture many items to the old original recipes.

Their catalogue contains a selection of items including french polishes and spirit varnishes, oil varnishes, wood fillers and dyes, wax polishes and finishes, and miscellaneous items like pumice powder, rosin, shellacs, rottenstone, gold leaf and leather restorers. Special discounts for schools and colleges are available on request.

● *Shepherd carved in acacia wood by Zoë Gertner of Wedmore, Somerset. Zoë's work was exhibited in May and June at Foyles, Charing Cross Road, London. Woodworker readers are reminded that woodcarving courses are run at Zoë's workshop in Somerset, the next one is from 23-29 October (details on p.546)*

Applications must be counter-signed by headmasters/principals.

Further details of the firm and the catalogue can be obtained from House of Harbru, Common Lane, Industrial Estate, Wath-upon-Dearne, Rotherham, S Yorks (phone 0709 874887).

North-West man

Doug Price has been appointed area manager for the North-West by the Nail Division of Gunnebo Ltd, of Ashford, Middlesex. Gunnebo is the UK marketing subsidiary of Gunnebo Bruks AB of Sweden, who have been a leading manufacturer of nails and fixings for more than two hundred years.

Safe conduct

The latest in the Machine Tool Trades Association's series of codes of practice is now available. It is the 13th code, dealing with woodworking machines in general and with sawing machines in particular.

The general part of the code deals with basic design requirements for safeguarding, describes types of guard together with their construction and interlocking, the use of safety colours and signs. Reference is made to controls, woodholding and feeding devices, tool-holding and lubrication systems. Also, to environmental aspects, such as dust and fumes, noise and work space lighting. There is advice on plant layout, installation, operation and maintenance instruction, suppliers' and users' responsibilities and other matters, such as lifting and handling.

That part of the code concerned with sawing machines covers the recommendations for circular saw benches, cross-cutting machines, panel saws, and multiple rip sawing/straight line edging machines. The band sawing section deals with table bandsaws, band resawing and log band sawing machines of the vertical and horizontal types.

Code of Practice – *Safeguarding Woodworking Machines: Part 1 General and Sawing Machines* can be obtained from MTTA, 62 Bayswater Road, London W2 3PH for £7.00 (including post and packing), cash with order.

Corrugated fastener

Atro has brought out a pneumatic tool for driving small corrugated fasteners, 11mm long by 4 or 8mm high, to fasten two timber parts placed on the same level. Known as the Mini CF Roll, it has a magazine capacity of 320 CF fasteners in a roll, manufactured from a continuous metal strip.

Mini CF Roll fasteners employ three reinforcement ribs, diverging downwards so that they draw the edges of the two parts together on penetration. Used in conjunction with glue or cement, they ensure firm, strong butt joints.

Further details from Atro Limited, 62 Norden Road, Maidenhead, Berks SL6 4AY, telephone (0628) 34456.

New abrasives

A three-year product development programme at English Abrasives has resulted in the production of two new woodworking products.

The first of the new abrasive materials, Product 144, is an extra flexible cloth for fine finishing, specifically designed for contour sanding of wood and metal on backstand machines (with soft contact wheels), pad sanders and pneumatic drum sanders.

Also new, Product 150 is an aluminium oxide paper 'E', the open coat structure which reduces clogging when sanding soft and resinous woods.

A full colour wall chart is available as a guide to product selection. Details from English Abrasives Ltd, Marsh Lane, London N17 0XA.

Handbook for the amateur

A 76 page booklet entitled *Plasplugs book of do-it-yourself* is available either from your local diy stockist or direct from Plasplugs Ltd, Sheridan House, Vernon St, Derby DE1 1FR. The booklet is free and is full of practical tips, safety advice, and general rules to use around the home in the form of easy to follow line illustrations and colour photographs with the minimum of text necessary to clarify matters. It is not intended as an encyclopedia of diy but it should give the amateur the confidence to tackle a variety of jobs. I found it particularly useful to learn the range of products available in the shops for diy projects and to learn the correct term for them. Several relatively new products are also detailed within the pages. **P.C.**

● *Dining chair in cherry with tweed seat by Charles Wheeler-Carmichael who graduates from Parnham House in July this year*

Shaper and Sander

Semco, Unit 3, Millbrook Industrial Estate, Southampton, has produced the Tantec, an adaptation of the belt sanding principle designed to fit most conventional 2-speed electric hand drills. It comprises a belt sander fitted with guides and rollers and mounted on a bracket which allows it to be fixed in a number of positions, either hand held or clamped to a bench. With a variety of belts and attachments it can sand and shape wood, plastic and metal, sharpen knives, drills and chisels, make curves and smooth tiles. It retails at £29.95 inc VAT is 280mm long, 200mm wide and weighs 3k.

● *Wooden beer barrels are a fairly rare sight nowadays although CAMRA (the campaign for real ale) may see a resurrection of their manufacture. Pensioned-off barrels were once a common sight as water butts, a utilitarian if unglamorous application. Far more artistic is the conversion shown below taken at the Courage Shire Horse Centre near Maidenhead, Berks. (Photo David Askham). More cooperage on pp 526-8 and the front cover*

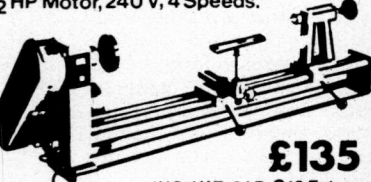
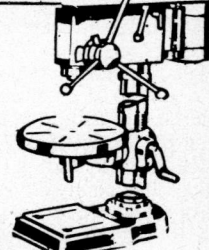
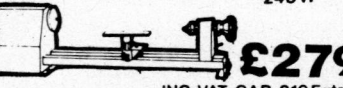

Prices quoted are those prevailing at press date and are subject to alteration due to economic conditions.

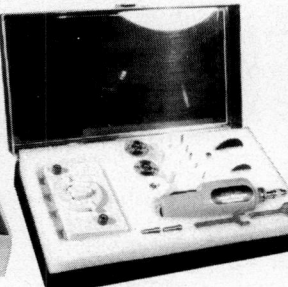

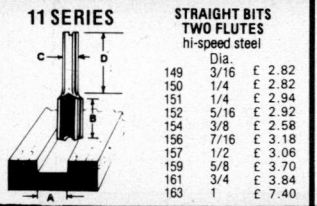
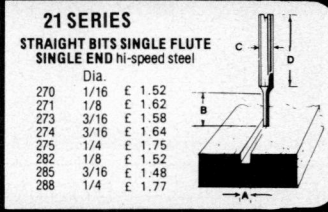
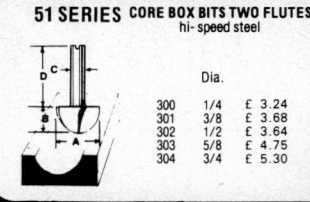
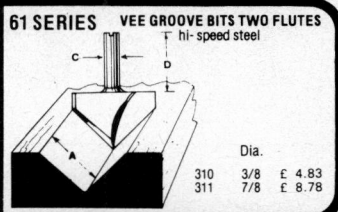
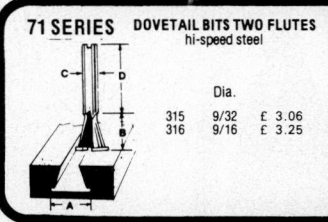
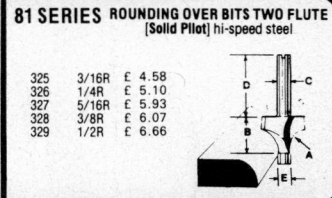
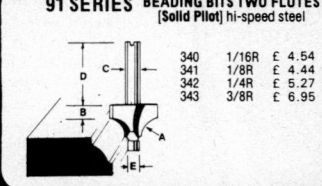
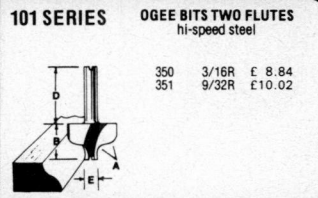
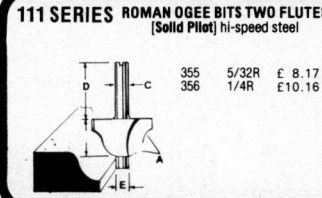
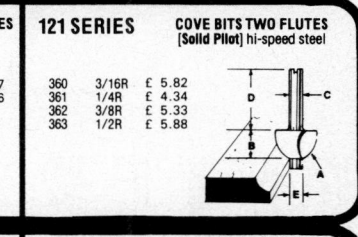
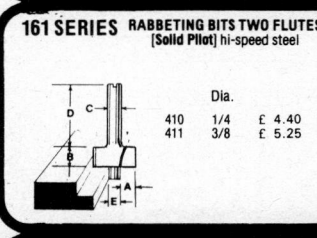
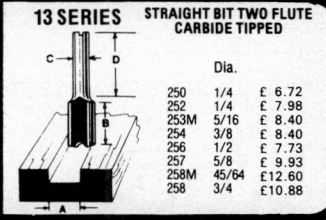

LONDON'S SIXTH

Woodworker Show '82

THE ROYAL HORTICULTURAL SOCIETY'S NEW & OLD HALLS VINCENT SQUARE & GREYCOAT STREET

NEW HALL

OLD HALL

Such is the increasing popularity of the Woodworker Show, now in its 6th year, that this year the Show is to be staged in the attractive Old Hall as well as the New Hall. Tickets will be issued daily enabling visitors to pass from one hall to another and return later on the same day.

Both halls will display the competition exhibits in the many classes. There will be many more trade stands fulfilling every need of the amateur or professional craft woodworker.

The colleges and demonstration areas will be considerably expanded and so will the lecture programme.

Don't miss this year's super Woodworker Show.

For Advance Tickets see advertisement on page 516

Open 10 am – 6 pm each day; 10 am – 5 pm on Sunday 24th October. Restaurant, Bar and Snack Bars.

19th–24th OCTOBER 1982

Admission:
Adults £2.00
Children and OAPs £1.50
Advance booking details from the Organiser, Woodworker Show, 13/35 Bridge Street, Hemel Hempstead, Herts, HP1 1EE

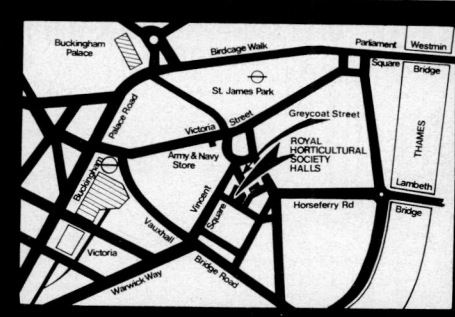

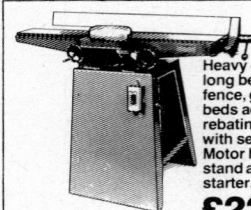

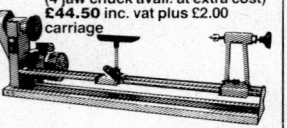

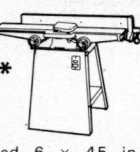

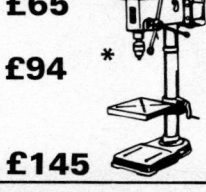

518

Prices quoted are those prevailing at press date and are subject to alteration due to economic conditions.

Woodworker, August 1982

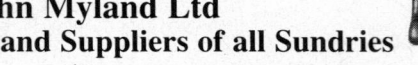

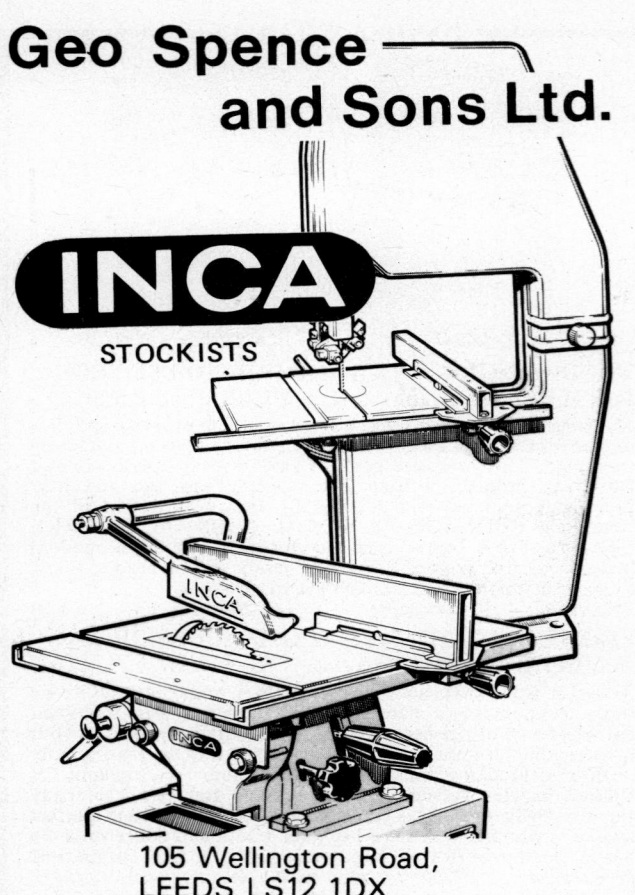

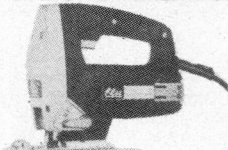
Prices quoted are those prevailing at press date and are subject to alteration due to economic conditions.

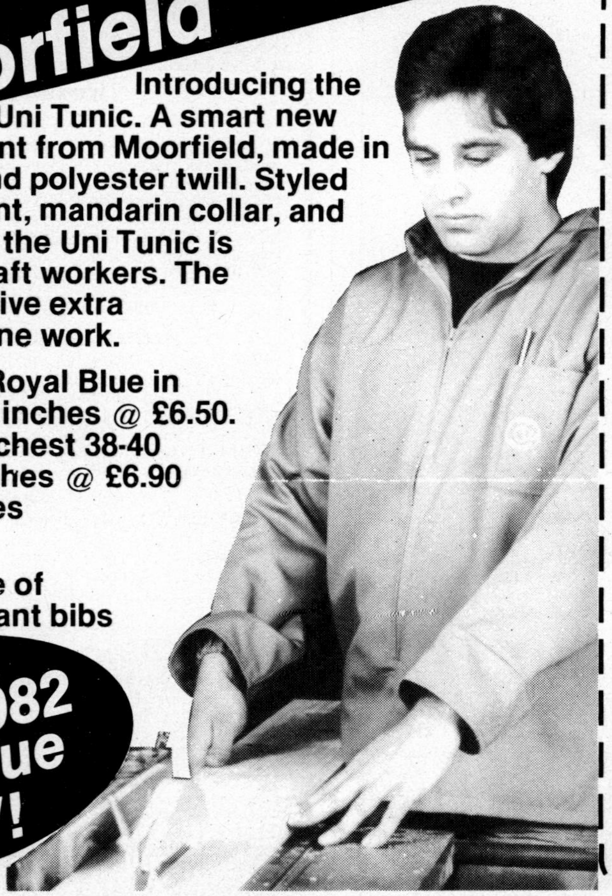

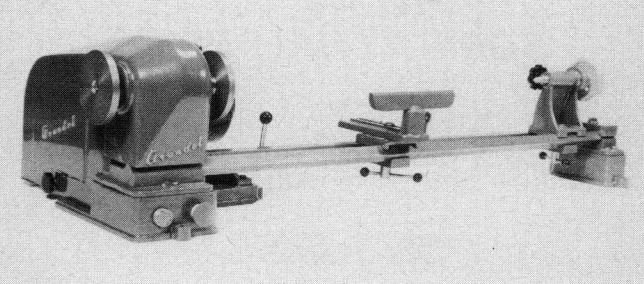
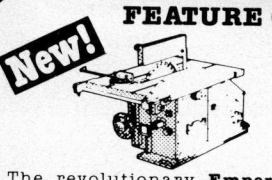

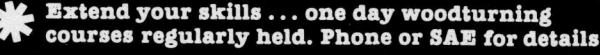
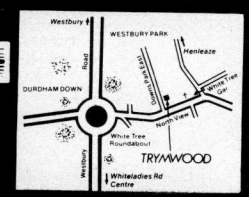

SALE

Our Latest Sale Sheet Is Now Ready

Over 50 offers at **unbeatable sale prices** while stocks last

SOME AT HALF PRICE

Write Or 'Phone For Your **Free Copy**
Today
or will be sent with each order

DON'T MISS IT

POWER TOOLS ETC

Cat No.		M.R.P.	Our Price
2571	Craftsman 12" dovetail kit	£59.50	£44.50
096-2	Craftsman 7½" circular saw, 2⅛hp	£94.45	£70.80
26269	Craftsman Trim-a-Form Router Attachment	£45.95	£33.00
25444	Craftsman Heavy Duty Router/Jigsaw Table	89.05	£74.00
577	Dremel Deluxe Moto Shop	£51.15	£43.00
2509	Dremel Moto-Tool Kit with 35 accessories	£25.50	£21.60
215	Dremel Foot operated speed control	£50.45	£42.50
358	Dremel Variable Speed Moto-Tool	£63.05	£52.50
359	Dremel Variable Speed Moto-Tool Kit with 35 accessories	£65.00	£55.00
284	Dremel Moto Tool Woodcarver's Kit	£76.15	£64.00
384	Dremel Variable Speed Woodcarvers Kit	£13.70	£11.50
292	Dremel engraver	£80.39	£67.00
96H	Skil power plane, 480 watt	£67.74	£55.00
1474H	Skil ½" reversing hammer drill, 500 watt	£62.10	£52.00
574U	Skil 7¼" circular saw, 1000 watt	£52.50	£41.00
400-E	Bosch ½" variable speed hammer drill, 400 watt	£88.80	£60.00
450-2E	Bosch ½" variable speed hammer drill, 450 watt with kit	£75.50	£60.00
500-2E	Bosch ½" variable speed hammer drill, 500 watt	£89.00	£71.00
620-2E	Bosch ½" variable speed hammer drill, 620 watt	£25.15	£20.00
S33	Bosch 6" circular saw attachment	£48.50	£38.50
PST50E	Bosch variable speed jigsaw	£42.50	£34.00
PSS230	Bosch orbital sander	£51.00	£40.00
PSP250	Bosch spray gun set	£59.50	£47.00
PKS46	Bosch 6" circular saw	£43.75	£35.00
S9	Bosch saw table for PKS46 saw	£89.50	£69.00
PKS65	Bosch 7½" circular saw	£59.50	£47.00
POF50	Bosch plunging router with 1 router bit	£49.50	£39.50
S7	Bosch milling stand	£23.00	£18.50
S8	Bosch routing bench for above	£23.00	£18.50
S2	Bosch drill stand	£65.25	£52.00
S18	Bosch lathe kit		

BOSCH INDUSTRIAL

SB4502	Bosch 2 speed impact drill with free tool handy & 750 rawlplugs	£94.88	£74.00
1179	Bosch ½" 2 speed impact drill	£120.75	£94.00
1287-1	Bosch orbital sander with induction motor	£121.90	£95.00
PWS6000	Bosch 7" angle sander/grinder	£97.75	£76.00
1577	Bosch orbital action jigsaw in metal case	£116.15	£91.00

HAND TOOLS

781000	Jet Clamp	£10.35	£9.00
04	Record 2" blade smoothing plane	£19.90	£15.50
311	Record 3 in 1 plane	£37.52	£31.50
778	Record rebate plane	£28.34	£24.00
050C	Record combination plane, 18 blade	£65.50	£55.00
020C	Record circular plane	£56.93	£48.00
405	Record multi plane, 24 blade	£161.46	£136.00
52E	Record Q.R. woodwork vice, 7"	£44.19	£37.50
413	Record 3" drill press vice	£20.53	£17.40
130	Record cramp heads	£10.27	£8.60
145	Record bench holdfast 6⅞" opening	£18.07	£15.30
146	Record bench holdfast 7⅝" opening	£22.60	£19.20
140	Record corner cramp 2" capacity	£8.05	£6.80
148	Record dowelling jig	£32.11	£27.00
M1160	Record dowelling jig	£17.83	£15.00
M2400	Marples draw knife	£19.25	£16.25
M1002	Marples 12" bow saw	£51.41	£43.50
M60	Marples set of 8 turning tools	£73.37	£62.00
M60A	Marples set of 12 carving tools	£41.40	£35.00
M444/S5	Marples set of 6 carving tools	£21.47	£18.20
M260	Marples set of 5 blue chip chisels	£37.49	£31.75
M277	Marples set of 5 wood sculpture tools	£9.60	£7.60
13-052	Marples wood carver's screw	£41.35	£34.50
13-050	Stanley plough plane, 10 blade	£63.00	£52.95
5½	Stanley combination plane, 18 blade	£28.99	£24.00
7	Stanley 15" jack plane	£36.55	£30.95
71	Stanley 22" jointer/try plane	£24.70	£20.50
TS	Stanley hand router, 3 blade	£22.35	£19.00
	Henry Taylor superflute turning gouge	£12.65	£10.75
	Henry Taylor 6 supersharp carving tools	£14.95	£12.70
	Henry Taylor Wood Carver's Adze, Chisel	£19.55	£16.55
	Henry Taylor Wood Carver's Adze, Gouge		

All prices include VAT. Carriage free on orders over £20 (UK Mainland)
Henry Taylor and Marples Woodcarving and Turning Tools in stock

BENMAIL, 48 Station Road, St. Georges, Weston-s-Mare, Avon BS22 0XL
Tel: 0934 24385 *We close Thursdays*

From tuns to garden tubs

Nigel Barklie visited one of Britain's last remaining cooperages, at Kingston-upon-Thames in Surrey, and records here how the cooper, whose skill was once so vital to commerce and conquest, now survives by making umbrella stands and garden tubs

THE COOPERS CARRY ON

● David finishes a 'gun-barrel' umbrella stand, tapping the hoop home with hammer and driver after fitting the head

The cooper's trade is an ancient one. Murals in Egyptian tombs dated around 1900BC show that the art of making casks was already well established 4,000 years ago, and references in the *Book of Kings* prove that the cooper was certainly in business during Biblical times.

It is easy to imagine how essential the cask, or barrel, was to the early traders on the river of Babylon, as a container that could hold every type of commodity, including liquids, securely and conveniently. Empires were built around this simple container. Julius Caesar's armies were kept supplied by the barrel and he used the spent casks filled with tar to burn enemy towns and villages.

Trade in Britain was founded upon the importing of wine after the Norman Conquest, the port of Bristol handling up to 20,000 tuns of wine annually. The navy had a particular reliance on coopers. It was no good sending out a fleet of ships on a long voyage only to be scuppered by rotting food and sour water resulting from poorly made casks. Sir Francis Drake knew this fact well and during his famous raid on Cadiz he is known to have destroyed thousands of Spanish barrels. The Armada of 1588 must, therefore, have been severely affected by deteriorating supplies kept in unseasoned casks.

So at one time the cooper was a prestigious worker, in constant demand, and even at the time of the Industrial Revolution it was a craft which machines failed to supplant. The Bass cooper's yard at Burton-on-Trent stretched to 25 acres of stored timber for the 127,592 barrels that were produced by their 400 coopers in 1889.

Now, however, the cooper's trade is all but dead. At Kingston-upon-Thames Cooperage in Surrey only a single cooper and perhaps the last apprentice cooper work on garden containers, umbrella stands and the occasional made-to-order homebrew beer cask.

They still work with pride. David Carpenter, used to the exacting demands of the beer trade, ensures that measurements are right and that each stave is sound and perfectly fitted, while his apprentice, 18-year-old Paul Black, does all those things apprentice coopers have done for centuries.

By way of describing the cooper's work, let us picture a busy cooper's shop producing beer barrels at the turn of the century. Imagine yourself reporting for your first day's work amidst the smoke and noise of hammer and driver ringing against the iron raising-hoops.

This is the first day of your seven-year apprenticeship, so we'll briefly run through the work and show why you've got so long before we'll let you put your name on a

barrel. What we are doing here is making good casks that will serve the brewery for up to 50 years, given a good dray-man. So let us start with the first essential – wood.

Ideally we would use Memel oak, free from knots and strong. It is straight grained and easy to work, so your tools keep sharp, but we use Scots oak now, which is nearly as good. We buy it already cut into rough staves and shape these on the jointer plane so that they will make a water-tight seal when we raise the casks. We make five sizes of cask here, the pin (4½ gallons), firkin (9 gallons), kilderkin (18 gallons), barrel (36 gallons) and hogshead (54 gallons). Each size needs a different angle of joint, so you have got to learn to judge these by eye. You should also look for any cracks in the wood because they will open out and spoil the work.

When we have done that you can give me a hand to put the truss-hoop on. We place the staves into the hoop and then hammer the raising hoops on to hold the barrel together. The next job will be yours. The barrels have to be fired for 20 minutes over a cresset of oak chippings. We do this in 'Chimney-Corner'. The heating takes the spring out of the wood and sets it to the barrel shape, but if you have used a cracked stave it will break with a bang, and we shall have to start again.

After that we hammer the raising hoops fully home, you working on one side, hitting them in time with me. It has got to be done evenly or else we'll have a 'lord' – the barrel leaning drunkenly to one side. The next stage will be your main job and so I'll show you that now on this barrel which was

● *Above: David marks the diameter of the head. The compasses are passed six times around the barrel before the measurement is accepted as true*

● *Right: Chimney Corner. Paul places a gun-barrel over a cresset of oak chippings*

started yesterday. This is the chiming-hoop which fits lower than the raising hoop, allowing you to work on the tops of the staves. Now we shape the staves with an adze so that they are clean and even. Next use the topping plane, which runs around the top of the barrel, cutting the ends of the staves to an even length. Now you can shave the inside clean so that no bacteria will sour the beer, and then smarten up the outside edges, moving the hoops so the whole barrel is clean. The last tool you need to know is the jigger, a hollow bladed knife used to cut a groove on the inside of the barrel neck, to take the heads (the flat pieces at top and bottom).

While you are doing that I'll be making the heads by dowelling four pieces of wood together. Then we cut a channel in the middle of the groove made by the jigger, put some flag (or river rushes) in the channel like a gasket, and fit the head. That is easy for the first one as you can loosen the hoops and work the head into place from underneath. With the other head you have first got to measure where to cut the grooves so that the barrel holds exactly the right amount of beer. Then when you come to lever the head into place you have to push an iron through the loosened staves and push the head up from underneath. Then we hammer the hoops on tight, paint the bottom to stop it rotting from the outside and brand the top with my initials, so when the barrel needs repairing we'll get the work. But before you do any of that, here's a broom to sweep up the yard!

● Recommended further reading: *The Cooper and His Trade* by Kenneth Kilby, published by John Baker Ltd. ISBN 0 212 983997. ■

● *Above: raising a barrel. David places the final 'raising-hoop' to a 'gun-barrel' which will be used as an umbrella stand*

● *Right: Paul uses hammer and driver to tap home a booge-hoop on a garden tub*

Anatomy of a sturdy workhorse

The length and height of this useful cutting-stool can be varied to suit the user, as can the thickness of the timber used. The cutting-list given is that for a stool measuring 2ft 6in long × 2ft high and of 6in × 1in material. Cost about £6. The timber can be dressed or off-saw, but in the case of the latter should be regularised in width.

Having cut the various parts to length, the feet should be shaped as shown on the drawing. 1ft 2in is long enough for them if the stool is to be used in the workshop, but they should be lengthened to 1ft 8in if intended for use on site in order to span joists set at 18in centres.

Take the two ends, draw a square line across them 5in from one end of each and nail the feet to the ends, with the top edge in line with the square marks, making sure they are positioned centrally. Fix with 2½in wire nails, driven in on the skew and clenched over. Five nails should be used and it is worth remembering that, when face-nailing, if the nails are positioned in the same way as the equivalent number on a domino you won't be far wrong.

Enter three 2½in wire nails ½in from each end of the bottom piece and nail to the top edge of the feet with the edges of the bottom piece in line with those of the ends.

On one edge of the top, put a mark 2in from each end. Enter three 2½in nails 1½in from each end of the top and, with the marks on the top in line with the inside edges of the ends, nail the top to the ends. Punch the nails. Having got this far in a matter of a few minutes, you can fix the rails in position using once again 2½in wire nails. Enter three nails 1⅛in from each end of the rails and another three, evenly spaced, ½in in from one edge of the rails. Lay the stool on its side and check it for square by measuring it diagonally, and nail the rail to the ends and to the edge of the bottom piece. Turn the stool over and repeat the process.

Nail the two 2in × ¾in pieces to the ends of the rails and you now have a stool you can stand on or cut on, a rack at each end to hold screwdrivers and chisels and a well to hold other tools, nails and other small items.

When you have a bit of time and material to spare make another one, for two are much better than one. ∎

William Sinnott is a joiner of many years' experience whose work currently includes, among other things, restoring a 150-year-old cottage in South Lanarkshire for rock star John Martyn. The value of the simple cutting stool he shows here is proven by the regularity with which he uses it in the course of his work, and so we happily pass on Mr Sinnott's design here as a useful workhorse for readers to make up for themselves

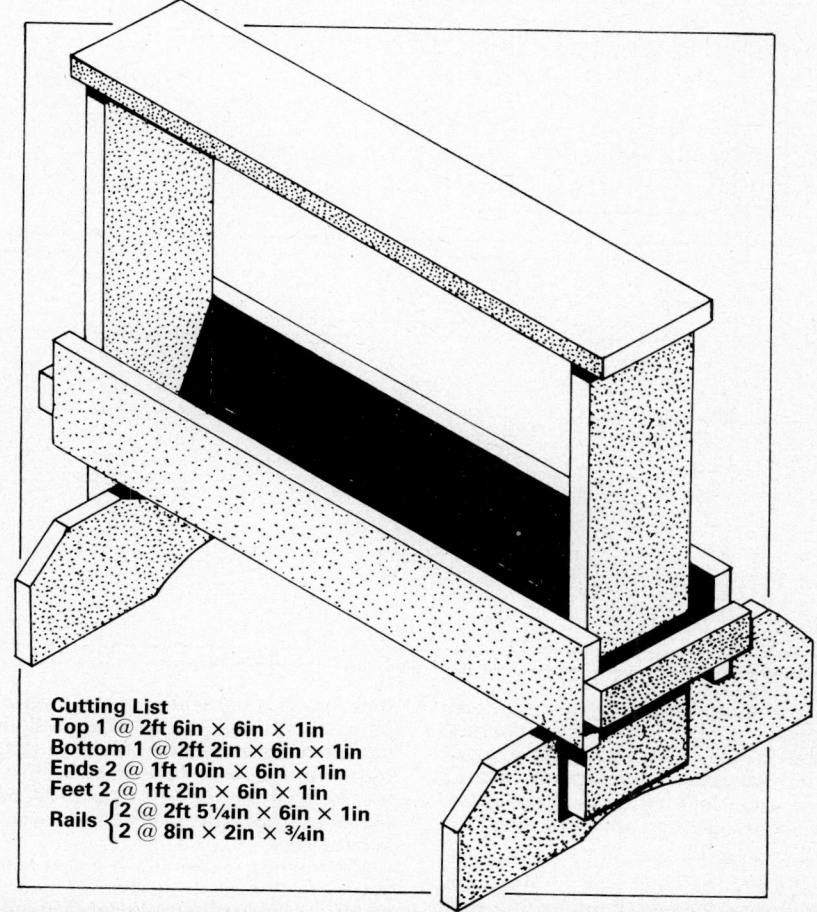

Cutting List
Top 1 @ 2ft 6in × 6in × 1in
Bottom 1 @ 2ft 2in × 6in × 1in
Ends 2 @ 1ft 10in × 6in × 1in
Feet 2 @ 1ft 2in × 6in × 1in
Rails { 2 @ 2ft 5¼in × 6in × 1in
{ 2 @ 8in × 2in × ¾in

WORKSHOP WAYS   by Bob Grant

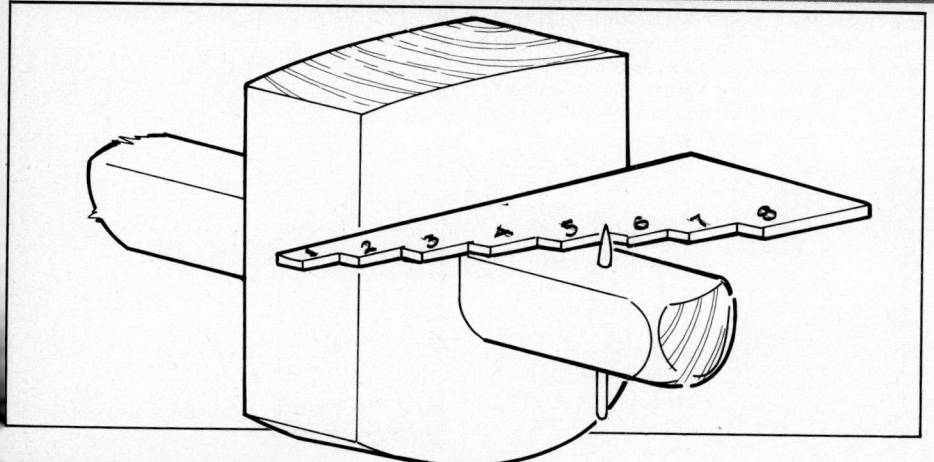

The setting of a gauge direct from a rule must always be open to error and for the smaller measures, that are constantly wanted, it is worthwhile making the gauge-setting device shown which ensures accuracy each time the gauge needs to be set. A piece of 10 SWG brass or mild steel should be accurately filed in steps to represent ⅛ths up to 1in (or in metric measures if you prefer). The graduations can be stamped or engraved on.

To avoid the risk of splitting wood when nailing near to the edges of boards, tap the point of the nail with a hammer so as to effectively blunt it. The nail when driven will crush its way through the wood fibres without splitting.

DOUBLE BEND

Bending solid timber is a workshop skill that often taxes the average woodworker's technique, but here Bill Gates shows how to set about two methods of doing the job without bending your patience as well

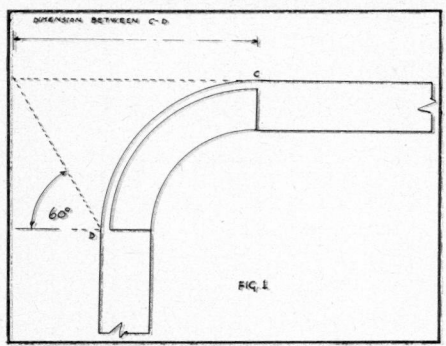

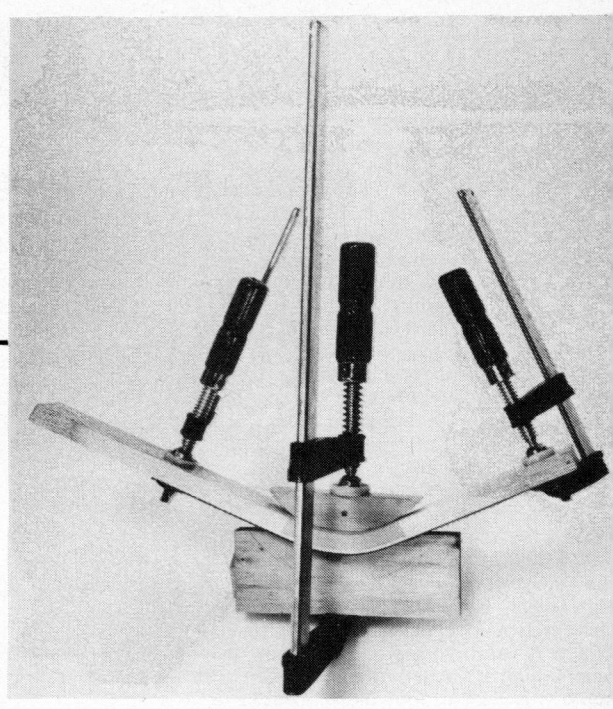

● *Right: forming the shape, sheet metal lightly cramped. Centre cramp pressing work into mould*

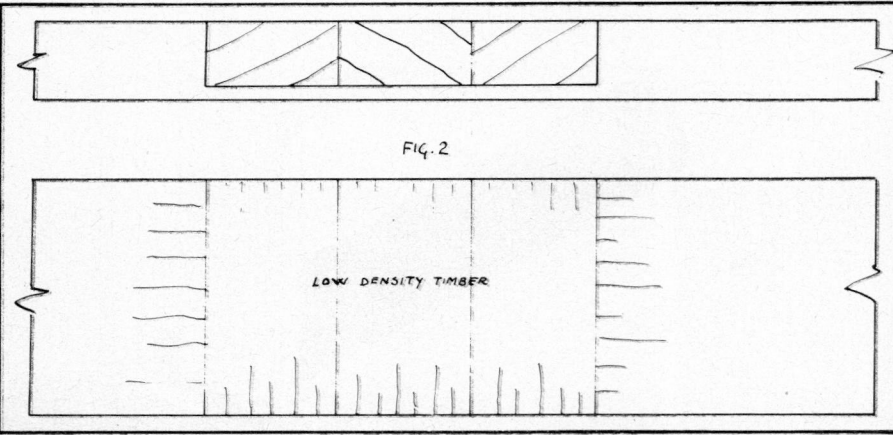

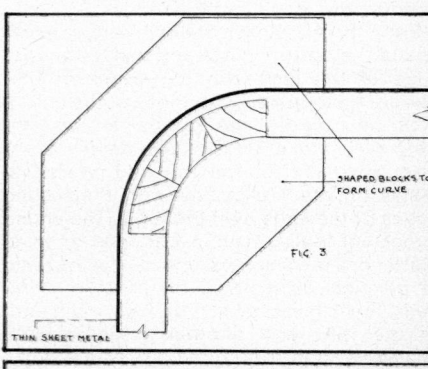

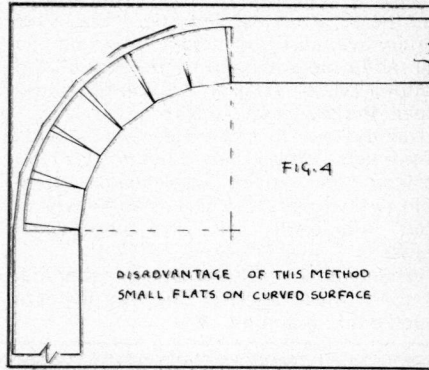

The method shown in Fig 1 and Fig 2 was developed by the Timber Development Association many years ago. It is possible to bend to quite small radii with the method using suitable infill timber such as balsa, cedar, obeche, gaboon or yellow pine.

Shown in Fig 1 is a method to determine geometrically the length of the quadrant, demonstrating the amount to be removed, leaving a thin veneer on the outer face. Fig 2 shows the recess infilled with cross grain timber. A low density timber that is compressible must be used for the infill.

Fig 3 shows the formers that are necessary to bend the timber to the required shape. To protect the outer face of the curve during the bending operation a piece of sheet metal is employed. To retain the shape of the curve after the cramps are

removed it is necessary either to face the inner curve with a veneer and screw a shaped block to the internal curve, or to fix the work in position, for instance, if this was a skirting or the base to a pedestal. When the inner curve is the face side then a veneer is necessary.

The method shown in Fig 4 dates back a long time. The result is, however, degraded by a series of flats and vertical stress marks where the saw cuts have been made. I would say that this method is only suitable for work which is not important.

Fig 5 shows the method of determining the number of saw cuts required so that they close on the inner curve. A thin lath equal in thickness to the work piece is cut as shown with the tenon saw that is to be used. The lath is placed on the drawing and gently bent until the saw cut closes.

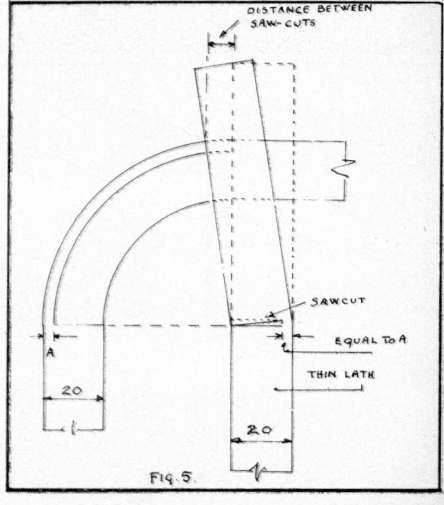

● *Left: cutting recess, the method I used was cutting on a bandsaw and finishing with a shoulder plane. It is essential that no cuts penetrate the thin veneer*

Who should pay the piper?

Ian Norbury, one of our more outstanding woodcarvers, has some controversial views about the effects of state sponsorship on the arts and crafts. In the spirit of free speech, we asked him to present his case for publication, and to explain why he sees the business of modern craftsmanship in terms of a regrettable class structure with incipient moral decay

Somebody once said that if a man made a better mousetrap than anyone else, the world would beat a path to his door. This does not appear to be true. These days, when we are hardened to seeing companies which make first class products go to the wall, it is apparent that there is a lot more than a good product necessary to succeed. The complexities of marketing, cash flow, management, public relations and so on, are virtually more important than the product.

The principles which apply to an industry also apply to the individual craftsman. A man can produce an article of superlative quality but without guidance in the harsh realities of the marketing side he is unlikely to succeed, as many know to their cost.

However, in a democratic free enterprise society like our own, it is the natural order of things that of all craftsmen working at a particular period of time some will succeed better than others and some will fall by the wayside for one reason or another. We all basically have the same opportunity to use our various talents.

This balance of nature has unfortunately been interfered with, by government sponsorship in the form of grants to selected craftsmen. The elite group who receive this patronage are selected by some mysterious process which is rapidly becoming a joke. It seems to me rather like going to Eton — one wouldn't relish wearing the silly clothes and being a fag, but you cannot ignore the advantages. No one likes to receive charity, and it's difficult to decide whether to pity the recipient for needing the money or envy them for being 'crafty' enough to get it.

However it is important to ask what is the effect of this situation on craftsmen in general? The first and most significant implication, logically, would be that since these happy few are the elite, then all others must be in some respect inferior craftsmen.

Secondly, it follows that these lesser craftsman will attempt to emulate the work of the elite in order to be admitted to the ranks.

Thirdly, one assumes that those already in receipt of government patronage will make stringent efforts to maintain the status quo and to remain an elite.

Fourthly, it follows that due to the hot-house climate of increased economic viability the product manufactured by the elite will become increasingly superior to that of the self-reliant craftsman.

One concludes, finally, that craftsmanship will be degraded by work that has to meet the approval of a committee rather than the buying public on the one hand, and imitations of it which are rejected by the buying public on the other.

Craftsmanship therefore acquires a kind of class structure, and the moral decay which goes with it.

These factors are becoming increasingly apparent if one observes the contemporary woodworking scene. State subsidised craftsmen tend to be regarded as trend setters and a guideline to quality. This is erroneous in many cases, as can be plainly seen by looking at the work, but since no private body is at this moment able to compete with the promotional facilities offered by the state, then it is very difficult to shake the unassailable position of the craftsman entrenched in it.

The popular assumption is that if a craftsman's work is not accepted by the establishment, then it's not good. This view has taken such a foothold that craftsmen have come to believe it themselves, and that they are in some way out of step with current trends. A look around a privately sponsored exhibition will reveal to the onlooker the gravitation towards the styles set by the elite.

In order to maintain their social distance, the elite tend to produce more and more outlandish work, squandering huge quanitities of exotic wood and countless man-hours on pieces that they do not even expect to sell. This is of course inconceivable for the professional who has to earn his living.

The result is that the bulk of craftsmen have to produce enormous quantities of bread-and -butter work in order to live and try to create the occasional exhibition piece which is the only way they can hope to improve their public image. However since even these pieces are rarely exhibited, the public at large tends to remain in ignorance of the large number of craftsmen ready and able to produce first class woodwork to their requirements, at reasonable prices. The public continues to believe that 'craftsmen' are a rare breed who manufacture outlandish creations at fabulous prices.

Why should the arts and crafts be subsidised by the state? Without government money many of them would fade away. Dozens of musicians, dancers, painters, and so on would be unemployed – but then thousands of working people in the real world are being dumped on the dole. The state did not subsidise their companies.

Surely if people wants to go to the ballet, they must be prepared to pay for it. If not, then let it go the way many other arts and crafts have gone. If craftsmen want public money, let them make something that the public will pay for voluntarily. ■

Right to the centre

Don Mayston of Woodbridge passes on a workshop tip that he discovered when faced with a turning problem

I occasionally turn batches of table legs from 4in square pine and in the past I have frequently had to drop the spindle speed due to vibration caused by unbalanced components. Examination of the corners of the blank during rotation indicated that this was caused by the blank not being centred properly. I had been following the conventional practice of marking diagonal pencil lines on the ends to find the centre, but this method always gives small errors, particularly if the corners are at all damaged.

Much improved results were obtained using a marking gauge to scribe four lines parallel to the sides but the lines were extremely difficult to see on the rough sawn timber.

The problem was eventually solved by removing the scribing blade from the marking gauge, drilling a ⁵⁄₃₂in diameter hole and fitting a ball pen refill. It is very easy to locate the centre in the middle of the parallel lines and the vibration problem has vanished.

The modified gauge also proved very successful for marking out cabinet making work, in fact the scriber has not been used since fitting the ball pen. ■

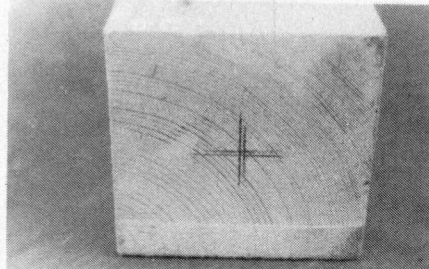

Whimsy in wood

Ivan Broadhead considers some unusual woodcarving cartoons to be seen in Beverley, North Humberside, and looks at the life and times of the woodworking man who was responsible for their creation

Cartoons and comedy have long been a feature of the British Press, but few have achieved the permanence of being carved in wood. However on the walls of two houses in North Bar Without at Beverley there are some carvings that reflect political progaganda and stage comedy of the 19th century.

They owe their existence to James Edward Elwell, who came from Birmingham in the 1850s and was apprenticed to a local cabinetmaker. He learned well and his skill became such that he and six assistants were entrusted with carving the oak chancel screen designed by Sir Gilbert Scott for Beverley Minster. Scott based his design on the 16th century choir stalls beyond, and although a fine stone screen had to make way for the new one, which was dedicated in 1880, it is an excellent example of Victorian Gothic and is generally regarded as Elwell's masterpiece.

Legend has it that Scott's patronage encouraged Elwell to start his own business in Beverley and at one time he is said to have employed 60 woodcarving craftsmen. Support for this belief comes from paintings by his son, Frederick, one of which shows James and a foreman studying architectural drawings about the time he and his men were working on screens and stalls for several churches. These included St Agnes at Kennington, Lincoln Cathedral, Tideswell in Derbyshire and Holy Trinity at Hull.

He also gained a commission for a major restoration of Driffield parish church. Apparently on one occasion after a visit from the Archbishop of York to discuss some piece of church work with Elwell, the bearded woodcarver set about clarifying his proposals for the clergyman. Taking a piece of chalk from his pocket, Elwell knelt on Beverley railway station and made rough drawings on the flagstones while the archbishop leaned over in complete absorption. They stayed in that posture it seems until the arrival of the train to convey His Grace back to York.

Frederick Elwell painted his father in several of his roles — mending ceramic treasures spread out before him; as the magistrate during a trial at Beverley's 17th century Guildhall; and as the benevolent mayor of the town in 1900/1.

Doubtless by then the political leanings of James were well stabilised, for he was a prominent Liberal during his early years but starting supporting the Tories as he progressed in business. The legacy of curious carvings he left for public entertainment were created about 1874.

Surprisingly perhaps, they were the work of the late W.J. Thornley and not Elwell himself. Two political scenes make amusing doorheads on Elwell's former house which also boasts John Bull, a Scotsman, and other figures on the pseudo-Tudor facade. The carving above the front door of the house portrays Disraeli who is depicted

as a 'Political Cheap Jack' talking to an agricultural audience. He is holding a small poster proclaiming Liberal opinions which he is ready to swallow and replace with the popular opinions represented on a larger manifesto in his left hand.

The other, which is above the entrance of what has become a hairdressing salon under part of the old house, shows 'The Grand Old Man', Gladstone, going shooting with Lord Roseberry and Sir William Harcourt, with four dogs representing the Labour, Radical, Nationalist, and Parnelite parties. The carving concerned the ever-controversial question of home rule for Ireland and asks 'Will they work?'.

The illustrations were based on some contemporary *Punch* cartoons but on a nearby house called Pinewood, once owned by Elwell, is another carved doorhead which expresses the craftsman's individual sense of humour and perpetuates Elwell's interest in the theatre, through which he developed a great friendship with the famous comedian J. C. Toole.

The panel illustrates the 'Doll's Eye-Maker' scene from 'The Cricket on the Hearth' in which Toole had recently taken the part of Caleb Plummer. The old toymaker, played by the comedian, is shown sitting at the table painting a wooden horse, whilst below is inscribed his well-remembered remark: 'We like to go as near to nature as we can for sixpence.' ■

THE POLITICAL CHEAP JACK

● Above: a damning comment on the policies of Disraeli. Below: 'We like to go as near nature as we can for sixpence'. Other page: Gladstone with political hounds straining at the leash, over the question 'Will they work?'

WE LIKE TO GO AS NEAR NATURE AS WE CAN FOR SIXPENCE

Pole lathe part two

In the March *Woodworker* we published a photograph of a 1/3rd scale working model pole lathe, built by a pupil at Cowley St John School in Oxford. We have since had many requests, from as far afield as Canada, for further details of its construction, so we asked Bob Grant to tell us more

As was mentioned in the original article, the idea for the pole lathe came from Aubrey Burstall's book *Simple Working Models of Historic Machines* (published by Edward Arnold Ltd). Actually, no dimensions or constructional details are essentially critical; part of the fun of making the thing was in deciding how to arrange and fix the parts.

The accompanying scale drawings show the lathe as it was built and these in conjunction with the following notes could serve as a guide to anyone wishing to make a similar machine. Starting at the top, the leaf spring is made up of three lengths of ash (for flexibility) tapering from a ½in square section to ¼in at their ends (see cutting list for precise sizes). They are lashed together and are contained by the locating boss which has an open mortice at the top to receive the spring. The bottom of this mortice is slightly rounded to give a good bearing when the spring is flexing. The boss is drilled to receive the pole which is glued in. The other end of the pole is drilled into the bed distance piece and although a good fit, it is not glued in; the pole can then be removed for carriage and storage

The bed and underframe are integral assemblies; the bed runners are held apart by the bed distance pieces and are fixed to them by screws and glue. The screws are pelleted in for neat appearance. These distance pieces are also bridle jointed and glued to the tops of the splayed legs. The A-frame formation of the legs is steadied by a lower frame rail which is through mortice and tenoned, wedged for extra strength. The back stretcher rail is similarly jointed. This in turn carries the plywood treadle board, fixed with a length of piano hinge.

The headstock blocks are adjustable along the bed of the lathe and the accompanying freehand sketch shows how the blocks are notched to ride over the bed runners and are pinched on to them by a mild steel plate pulled up on a bolt and wing nut. The bolt is anchored by a pin set through the block. The 'dead centre' at the headstock is held by a woodscrew locating in a 'dimple' drilled into the mandrel. The other stock carries a threaded mandrel with a length of studding run through it, one end of which is conically ground off at 60° and the other fitted with a locking ring and a handle that was made from cellulose acetate fluted rod – the same as seen on many screwdrivers – although a wooden handle would suit just as well. This assembly gave the lathe a fine adjustment after the initial spacing of the headstocks. The tool rest was a slotted bar of beech, bevelled along its top edge and pinched in position by a round-head screw and washer.

A backstay from the rear of the leaf spring to the machine bed is needed to counteract the plunging motion of the assembly and an early leather thong had to be replaced by ⅛in diameter wire anchored with a hook and eye, to prevent stretching. This was also something of a problem with the drive thong until it had fully stretched out.

To operate the lathe first fix the piece to be turned between the centres. Then with the spring at rest wrap the driving thong around the work and tie off so that the treadle board is well above its level position. Depressing the treadle with one foot will cause the work to revolve. This is the power stroke and cutting with the lathe tools can only happen on this forward stroke. The spring, of course, will return the work to its original position ready for the cycle to recommence. ■

MODEL POLE LATHE

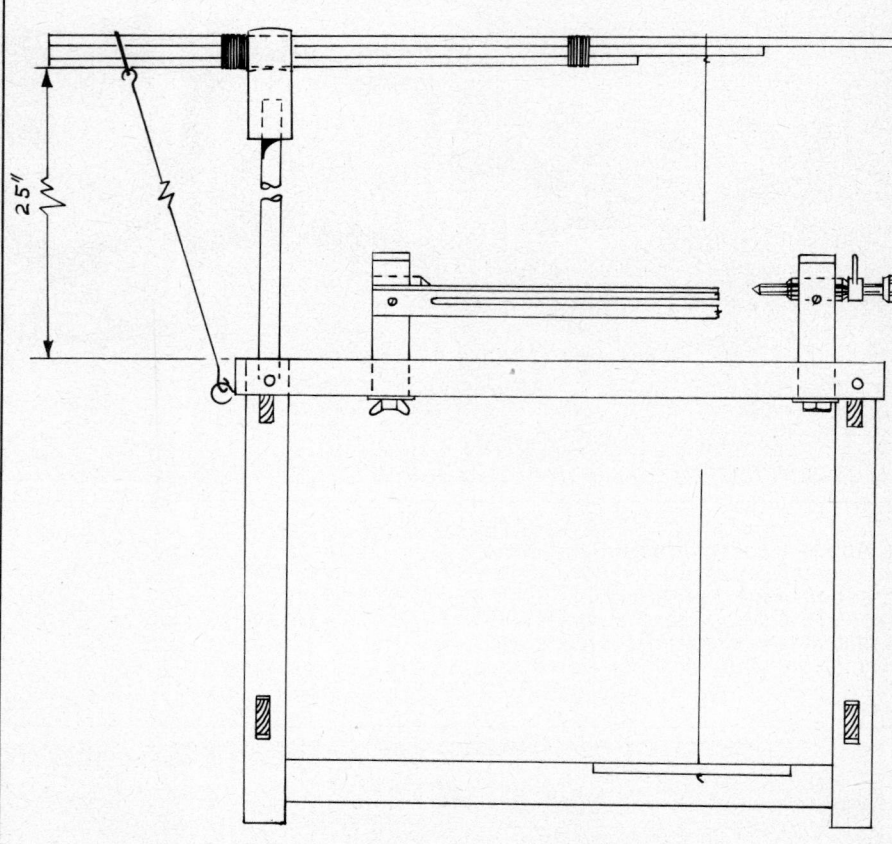

25"

PLAN VIEW—TOP ASSEMBLY REMOVED

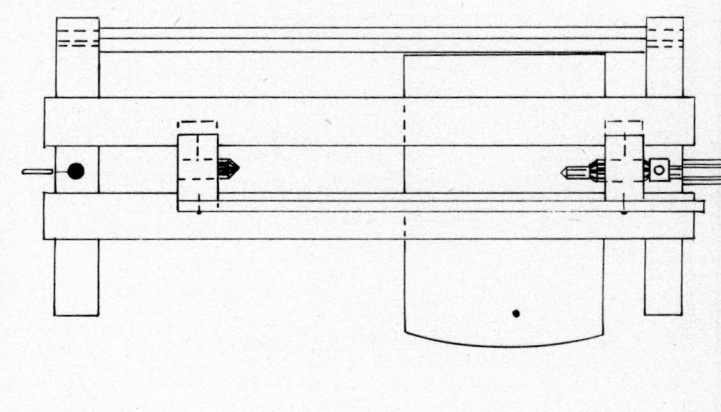

● *Pictured right: the model pole lathe made by David Thrower for his O Level design course work at Cowley St John School, as seen in March's* Woodworker. *(Picture: John Peacock).*

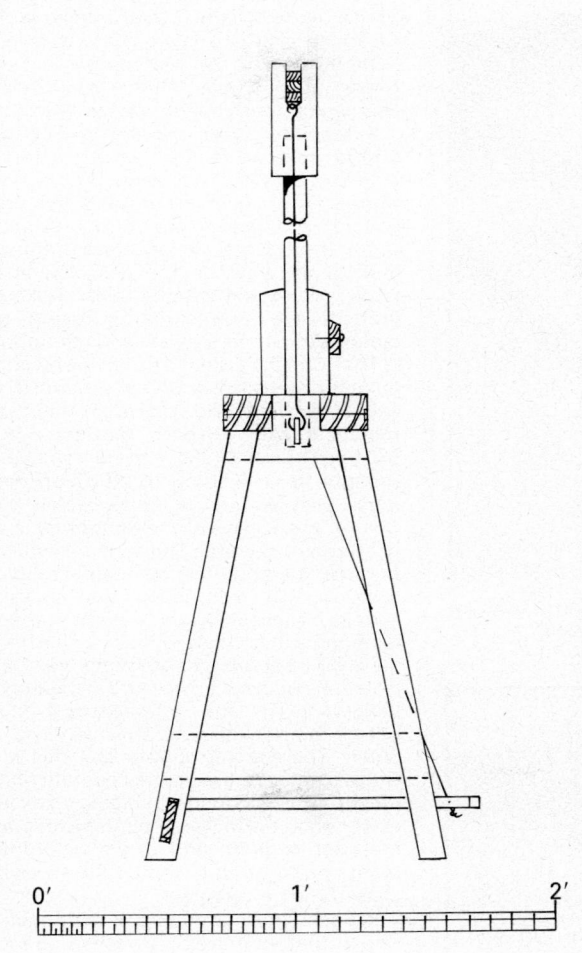

0'   1'   2'

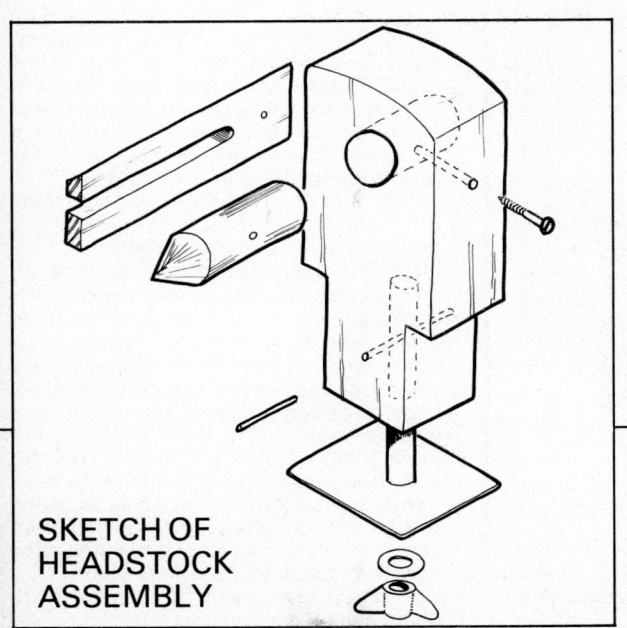

SKETCH OF HEADSTOCK ASSEMBLY

Pole Lathe

Cutting List. Net sizes given in inches

No.	Description		Length	Width	Thickness	Material
1	Top leaf spring	Taper	40	½	½	ASH
1	Middle leaf spring	in section	33	½	½	ASH
1	Bottom leaf spring		27	½	½	ASH
1	Spring locating boss		5	2	1¾	BEECH
1	Pole		25	1 dia	—	BEECH
2	Bed runners		30	2¼	1⅝	BEECH
2	Headstock blocks		7	2⅞	1⅝	BEECH
1	Tool rest		22	1½	¾	BEECH
2	Bed distance pieces		7	3	1⅝	BEECH
4	Legs		20½	1⅝	1⅛	PINE
2	Frame rails		12	1⅞	⅝	PINE
1	Stretcher rail		28½	1⅞	⅝	PINE
1	Treadle board		14	9	½	PLYWOOD

Leather thonging, lashings and wire backstay to suit. Two ⅜in Whitworth bolts or M10 equivalent, with ⅛in mild steel pinch plates, washers and wing nuts. Head and tailstock mandrels ex-1in diameter mild steel. Tailstock adjustable screw from ½in Whitworth studding.

Furniture in Context

Preview by Polly Curds of an exhibition at the
British Crafts Centre. You have until September 22 to find out more

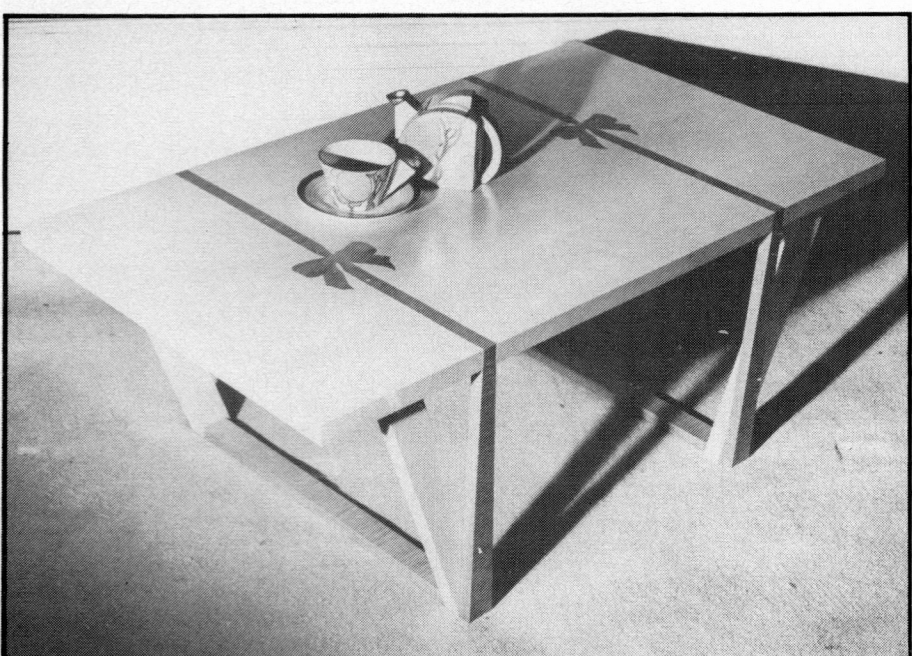

● *Coffee table in sycamore with dyed sycamore veneer inlay by Jakki Dehn. More
of Jakki's work can be seen at* Making it *14 July – 12 Sept, 12 Waterloo Place,
London*

● *Chest of drawers in solid English walnut with ebony and brass handles by Alan
Peters of Cullompton*

Confusion has reigned of late over the involvement and varying roles of the British Crafts Centre and the Crafts Council Gallery. An article by artist and art journalist Deanna Petherbridge in the March/April issue of *Crafts* (no 55) goes a long way towards clearing up these misunderstandings.

Karen Elder, Director of the British Crafts Centre, sees no conflict between the two galleries. Besides believing that there is room for more than one major British Crafts gallery in London, the Crafts Council's programme tends to concentrate more on individuals whereas the BCC has many large group exhibitions with unknown craftspeople and students taking part alongside the more established members. The British Crafts Centre receives an annual grant from the Crafts Council and exists to help and promote their own members who currently number around 850 (an increase of 200 in the last two years) brought up to 2,500 with 28 group members. Membership is non-selective. The Centre specialises in contemporary crafts not traditional crafts. The staff are available to recommend outlets for members' work, promote via exhibitions and one-man shows. Vanessa Swann (gallery manager) comments that furniture makers need exposure, they are often to be found working in isolation and need advice and exhibitions of their work. The latter not necessarily to sell but certainly to expose their work to the public. There are no storage facilities at the British Crafts Centre, it does not function as a shop, it is a London exhibition space in close contact with its membership of craftsmen and women and exists to promote them and to bring to the public an awareness of their existence.

It is with these thoughts in mind that the British Crafts Centre approached about 40 of their members who are working in wood — 40 furniture makers. Many have become familiar, almost household names already, many have already held exhibitions at the British Crafts Centre and elsewhere, but there are others whose work is less known, either because they have recently set up a workshop or are working in remote areas away from the so called 'mainstream'.

As a promotional body for the crafts, the British Crafts Centre is fully aware of the particular needs of these craftsmen — 'they often find due to the nature of furniture making, that they are unable to expand their market or even establish a reputation'. Joan Taylor who as exhibitions organiser has visited over 25 workshops, written letters and phoned all over the country says 'a new body of designer-makers is evolving that was not around 6-10 years ago'. Though there is only a relatively small market for exclusive hand-made furniture there is an increasing current trend towards batch production. One-off designers are therefore able to satisfy both their creative ambitions and their need for 'bread and butter'.

Furniture in context: 13 August — 22 September, has been arranged therefore to

● *Above: dining table and chairs in ash by Crowdys Wood Products Ltd of Clanfield, Oxon. Right: Music stand in English oak by David Gregson. Ebony pegs are used to adjust height and angle of support*

place contemporary furniture 'in context' by inviting about 20 makers to exhibit pieces of work, each item to be supported by working drawings, a written statement by the maker and photographs of their other work.

The exhibition divides itself neatly into three sections: 1 One-off or speculative work. 2 Commissions. 3 Multiple or batch production items.

These three sections make up the main content of the show, a fourth section covers British Crafts Centre members who all make furniture in wood including those not exhibiting whose work is covered by a photographic, slide and general information section of their output.

The show aims to increase public awareness of the availability of high quality designer-made furniture, often at competitive prices; to encourage a fruitful liaison between maker and public; to renew a collaboration between architects or interior designers and designer-craftsmen for unusual or important commissions — a collaboration that rarely occurs to specifiers or, when it does, the cost is often overestimated.

'An often encountered problem when attempting to exhibit commissioned furniture' says Joan Taylor 'is the problem of actually borrowing the piece for what can

be a lengthy period of time. Owners are very often reluctant to part with pieces that they see now as part of their home way of life'. Nevertheless, Joan has approached Ashley Cartwright, David Gregson, Alan Peters and Jakki Dehn for examples of their commissioned work.

'One-off' pieces include examples of work by Nick Partridge (I need the stimulus of a forthcoming exhibition to produce the incentive to make a one-off), Martin Grierson (I'd like to make a fireplace for exhibition), Paul Connell, Ian Heseltine, David Field, Michael Norris, (Michael made several pieces for Kirkham House) and Nigel Shelley.

Examples of batch production will probably centre around examples of work by Graham Peterkin (high chairs), Neville Neal (rush seated chairs), Richard La Trobe Bateman, Bim Burton and Jeremy Broun.

The exhibition is on until 22 September at the British Crafts Centre, 43 Earlham Street, Covent Garden, London WC2H 9LD, telephone 01-836 6993. Open Tuesday — Friday, 10 am — 5.30 pm, Saturday 10 am — 4 pm. The British Crafts Centre supports British crafts — go along and have a look, you'll see why and I guarantee if it's your first visit it won't be your last. ■

● *The Nobex jig, showing the three magnets that grip the saw blade. Pictured below, the device in action*

Gerald Dunn tests the Como Mini Drill (no385) with drill set no399D

It is a common fault in most hand-held electric motors and flexible drives, offered for small scale free-hand machining, to rotate much too fast. The tool tip overheats and the work-piece can be scorched, melted or heat fractured as a result. Such machines which have variable speed control are, as a rule, difficult to keep running at a constant slow speed.

Como Drills of Worth, near Deal in Kent have made a good effort to overcome this trouble with their outfit catalogued as the 399D mini drill set, by stepping down mains electricity supply via a transformer which delivers 12-volt direct current to the motor unit. The transformer is incorporated into the well made carrying box, along with its own integral safety fuse, speed control knob, and tell-tale lamp. This really does result in a reasonably steady rate of rotation without appreciable loss of torque but, as the makers point out in their instructions, this is, in fact, achieved by the current cutting in and out intermittently at a rapid rate. The consequence is a distinct pulsing of the drive force at the tool point at slow revs, and a visible strobing of the tell-tale lamp.

The mains transformer outfit does not exclude detachment of the power unit, after which it can be driven independently by a 12-volt battery. In this mode, of course, variable speed control is lost, and the motor revolves at a constant rate in the region of 1450rpm. Thus the motor and its tools can be used in off-site applications such as the motor car, caravan, or yacht. Indeed it is difficult to imagine any household in which this little power tool would not have many applications.

Nor can there be any workshop in which it would not have many uses. I used it for free-hand engraved lettering on brass plate, for intaglio cutting in glass, for brushing out the crevices of a deep-relief repoussé Indian silver bowl, and for polishing the decorative mouldings of a vintage motor car.

The drill's motor does not appear to have any means of ventilation and does become rather warm in the hand after a few minutes' continuous use. Also the finger grip could be much better. If the shell of the motor housing could be extended to form a comfortable pencil grip this would remove a principal fault. At present free hand

engraving is rather like trying to do fine caligraphy with a cucumber for a pen holder. Not impossible, but not easy.

The motor shaft ends in a small pin chuck with sundry collets to fit tool shanks of different sizes up to 2.5mm diameter, and there is a comprehensive catalogue of wheels, burrs, cutters, mops, brushes and bobs in carbon steel, tungsten carbide, diamond impregnate, stones and abrasive compounds of every kind.

All in all it is a well made, well styled, and useful little power tool with unlimited and yet limited applications – if you get my meaning. But it has to be borne in mind that wheels and brushes larger than about 3½ shaft diameters will almost certainly run eccentric at very high rates of rotation and set up severe vibration. Apart from rendering work impossible this could damage the tool, or more likely the power unit, and might well be dangerous if a composition wheel should fly apart, or a wire brush disintegrate under heavy centrifugal Gs.

Sensibly used with the delicacy of touch required in the kind of work for which this apparatus is obviously designed I am sure this miniature power tool fills a gap and will soon recover its cost, which is £40, inclusive of VAT. ■

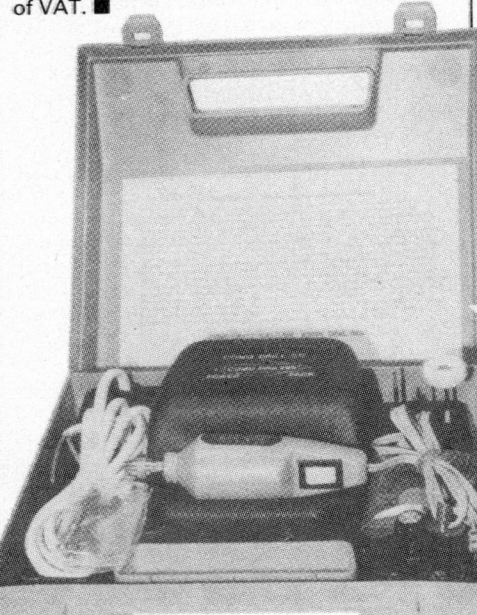

● *The Como Mini Drill in its case, complete with built-in transformer*

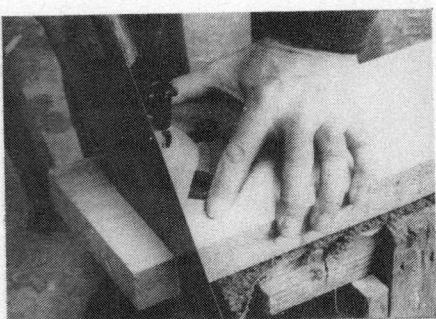

Bob Grant tests a Nobex Magnetic Saw Fixture

Nobex have recently brought on to the market a sawing aid that is available in this country from C. P. Monninger Ltd, Overbury Road, London N15 CRJ. It would be less than charitable to suggest that the designers of such aids have it in mind to cover up our various degrees of ineptitude when using hand tools and a more sympathetic view of their endeavours on our behalf is to increase both speed and accuracy if, of course, the thing actually works!

This latest device, although beautifully engineered and employing a clever idea of using permanent magnets to attract and hold the new blade set slightly proud of the magnets to create a running 'field' is nevertheless only partially successful.

Field trials revealed some operational faults (the team of investigators included school children and beginners to whom the jig might be orientated), the chief of which was the inherent danger of catching the saw teeth on the steel balls and knocking the set and sharpness off. One also hesitates to speculate what could happen to Teflon coated saw blades when used with this jig. In use, all operators found it somewhat difficult to hold: there are two stops at the back of the base casting but this does not help left-handed users, although the publicity sheet does suggest that the fixture can be held with a cramp. The calibrated fence, set at an angle, proved handy when cutting some rafters to correct bevel.

The jig is too big to take a tenon or dovetail saw, which is a pity because it could be put to better use on the bench for joinery work than on site carpentry with a handsaw.

Nevertheless, the item is handy and portable. ■

Your money's safe in timber

Arthur Jones looks at the current state of the world's timber markets, and concludes that to buy stocks now is a safe hedge against inflation

Inflation affects woodworkers just as much as anyone else, but in spite of the grumbles so often heard about the high cost of wood, this is a good time to remind woodworkers how lucky they are buying timber at today's prices. They should make the most of their good fortune, for no matter what happens to the rate of inflation over the rest of this year, it is reasonable to forecast that woodworkers will be paying more for their timber supplies by the turn of the year.

To put the issue in the right perspective it is best to look at the softwood market. Most woodworkers make use of softwood at some time, normally buying the best grades. So let us look at these prices. In the Russian softwood schedule for this year the price of top quality Kara Sea redwood was pitched at £110 per m³ for the unsorted grade, showing a reduction of some 8 per cent on the corresponding price for a year earlier. In fact, good softwood is currently selling for just a few pence more than the cost of two years ago when we deal in the quantities normally purchased by the woodworker. What other product can make a similar boast?

Not surprisingly, the overseas producers are desperately trying to push up their selling prices, but the demand among wood users in the UK is so sluggish that the importers are unwilling to pay more while competition for their orders is so keen. However, as sales are expected to edge up slowly this year and production overseas comes down closer to the reduced requirements of importers, it is certain that price will move quietly upwards.

In the hardwood market, while the same general assessment can be made, there are wide variations between species. For example, probably the most dramatic rise in price has taken place over the past year or so in Brazilian mahogany, which took a leap into fame a little earlier because of its low price when set against the very high price of the West African equivalent.

However, as always when demand rises, so did the price of Brazilian mahogany and even mushrooming mills in the south of Brazil to compete with the established firms in the north did little to halt the upward trend. Recently it has tailed off and there has

even been some weakness in the price of this wood.

Not long ago dollar hardwoods from North America were costly, but this trend was reversed when sterling became stronger, and several US woods are relatively attractive in price even though sterling has fallen, simply because the home demand in the States remains dismally poor. American oak (both red and white) is being attractively quoted on our market at a time when British oak sells at high rates. In the same way, American ash prices look good.

West African hardwoods are becoming a little cheaper, but these woods have been out of the market for a long time now because they had been priced out of use and there is uncertainty about the willingness of the authorities to allow market forces to settle the world rates for these valuable African woods much loved by the woodworker.

Much weakness has been seen in Far Eastern hardwoods like meranti, lauan and afrormosia, but some species, like ramin (which suffered a minor slump in value) are recovering a little. Beech and keruing have been among the best buys in recent months.

There are reports from time to time of more developing countries placing restrictions upon the export of logs, but sawn hardwood lumber shipments are unlikely to be affected greatly and there is no danger whatsoever to stocks in Britain from which the woodworker can select.

Individual countries and particular species can be affected by such factors as export regulations, lack of shipping space, internal conflicts or changes in world fashions in a single species. The hardwood trade has much in common with the rag trade.

In both softwood and hardwood most of the importers have now succeeded in bringing their stocks down to levels which do not force them into hasty sales to get money in the bank to meet their bills, which has removed some of the pressure leading to cheap offers. It also means that, while there is no question of any shortage, there can appear local supply difficulties, especially in hardwoods.

For the woodworker the best of the market in solid woods is probably now over. He must expect more problems in the immediate future getting precisely the sort of specification in the desired species which he desires, and must certainly expect to pay more for his wood. More searching will be needed, especially in hardwoods.

Turning now to the panel products, plywoods from the tropical suppliers are now coming to the stage where the non-duty imports under EEC regulations are being exhausted for this year, but this should make little difference to prices in the light of the level of demand experienced so far this year. Prices for most plywoods have been weak and they are still at low levels. Even in this dull state of the market there are still more overseas mills looking for an entry into the UK market, and we can expect to see larger supplies coming from South America.

Chipboards are now rising in price and this trend, albeit gradual, is likely to continue. The selling prices of chipboard have been so low for so long that it is a wonder more mills have not gone bankrupt. Here is another material which has failed utterly to keep pace with inflation.

MDF (medium density fibreboard) is really a competitor for solid wood rather than any other sheet material, and being among the newcomers to the panel products industry it is also one of the few to show increased sales, simply because it is new and starting from scratch.

Shortly there will be more MDF plants coming on stream with massive output potential and it is difficult to see how this material will avoid facing a surplus of output for the market demand. No doubt there is still plenty of untapped business for MDF, including among woodworkers, but the demand is certain to grow more slowly than the supply, which should keep prices down.

For the woodworker the timber market remains in a happy state, favouring the buyer at almost every turn. There are few difficulties to be seen in the months immediately ahead, apart from some modest increases in prices and increasingly fewer bargains. ■

WORKSHOP WAYS   by Bob Grant

To the beginner, the marking gauge has an innocent look about it and a simplicity of parts that belies an almost fiendish will to wander off in the grain of the wood when gauging to width. The trick of course is to tilt the gauge forwards so that the spur trails behind and generally behaves itself. A simple modification to tilt the gauge: re-set the pin at 45° as shown in the sketch. The gauge may now be used level and the spur will always be trailing.

□   □   □

Irritated by the continual clatter of the vice tommy bar as it descends and hits the poll? Simply wrap a stout rubber band under the knob of each end to ensure a quieter working day!

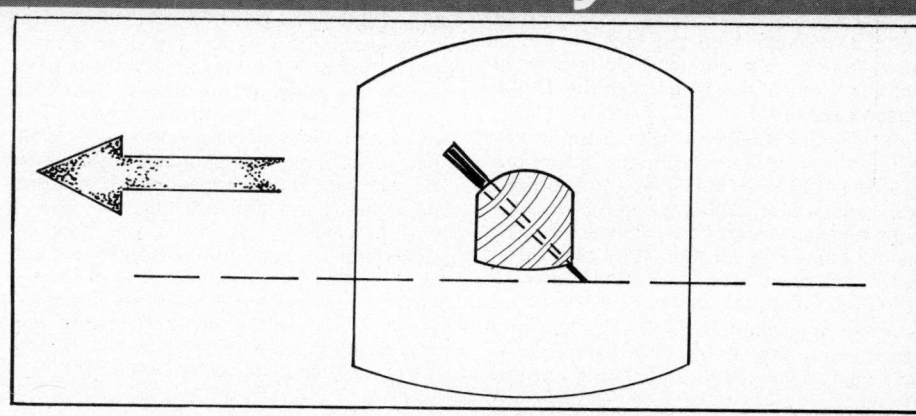

THE CRAFTSMAN IN HIS WORKSHOP: No2

Your handsaws should now be a joy to cut with, if you followed the advice given on sharpening them in Part 1 of Vic Taylor's series *The Craftsman in his Workshop* (June issue). Here, in Part 2, Vic tackles the question of keeping circular saws in business

Sharpening circular saws

Before dealing with the actual sharpening and setting of circular saws, it is a good idea to have a look at the various kinds you are likely to meet. The four types shown by no means exhaust the complete range of saws available, but they are the most popular.

The combination rip and cross-cut blade at (A) is intended for use in a saw bench and is more suitable for ripping than cross-cutting. The two principal features are the raker teeth and the gullets; the former is not meant to be a cutting tooth, but serves to keep the gap clear of dust and shavings as the saw rotates, while the gullets also help in the same task, and also assist in increasing the speed.

Another combination blade is shown at (B) and this one is likely to be found either in a saw bench or in a portable saw. It is happier working at ripping, but it can also cross-cut, although it gives a rough finish and is obviously labouring under difficulties. Again, it has the gullets which are a characteristic of circular rip saws, although they are not so pronounced as those in (A).

The radial-toothed cross-cut saw (C) is the best one for cross-cutting and will give you a nice clean finish, particularly on plywoods, hardboard, and the like. A peg-tooth cross-cut saw blade, such as (D), is often used in accessories which work off a power tool, and it is essentially a cross-cutting blade.

This is as good a place as any to point out that there is a fundamental difference between a portable saw, where you take the saw to the work, and a saw bench, where you take the work to the saw. As a result, the direction of rotation is opposite in each case, as illustrated at (E) and (G). The rotation in the portable saw (E) is anti-clockwise; on the saw bench (G), it is clockwise.

A consequence of this is that when you are cutting a plastic-faced board (or for that matter any board which has one show face) with a portable saw, the face should be downwards; the opposite obtains when cutting it on a saw bench, as the face is placed upwards.

Two more things to bear in mind: one should always start the motor before presenting the saw to the work; and another is that you should adjust the depth of cut to suit the thickness of the work so that the teeth just break through the underside if you are employing a portable saw, or through the upper side on a saw bench.

The first task before beginning the actual sharpening and setting is to 'range down' the tips of the teeth, and this is done to preserve the true circularity of the saw. The procedure is shown at (H) and you will need to make up a cradle from odd scrapwood into which you can fit a broken piece of emery stone or, better still, a piece of an old grinding wheel. Whichever you use, make sure it is held very firmly in the cradle, and this can be done by tightening down the cross piece on to the emery stone. The saw is then started up and the emery stone in its cradle is advanced up to just brush the tips of the teeth until the high teeth points are removed and all the points are bright. Do not overdo it or you could spoil the shape of the saw. Note that you can only range down a saw blade mounted in a saw bench, and it is most important that the guard should be in place.

When you have done all of this, make a test cut or two in a piece of scrapwood. At (L) you can see three test cuts, no1 being satisfactory, while that at 3 means that you will need to do a little more ranging down to achieve the square-ended cut as shown at no1. No2 shows how a correctly set cross-cut saw should cut.

The device shown at (F) is indispensable, and is known as a saw-sharpening vice, or a 'sawhorse'. Mine is double-ended and made from odd pieces of chipboard. One end is for 8in (203mm) saws, and the other end for 6in (153mm) saws; in each case the radius of the curve is from the centre of the saw blade to a point about ¼in (6mm) from the bottom of the deepest gullet, or tooth. In my case, the radii are 3⅛in and 2⅝in (80mm and 67mm) respectively, but you will make yours to suit your saws, of course.

Secure the saw by means of a bolt through the centre hole and tighten up the wing nut; then put the whole thing in your vice. But note that you'll need a piece of packing which is the same thickness as the saw blade at the bottom end of the saw horse (as illustrated), and a piece of cardboard will do for this.

Re-shaping the teeth is best done with a 6 or 7in (152 or 178mm) taper saw file applied across the gullet at right angles until each tooth point which has been topped becomes a point. When dealing with a gullet tooth saw, use a 6 or 8in (152 or 203mm) millsaw flat file with round edges, which will preserve the shape of the gullets.

Unfortunately, the pliers-type saw set described in Part 1 (June *Woodworker*) can only be used for the smaller sizes of circular saws, as generally the teeth are much too large. There are two ways of dealing with this problem, namely the gate saw-set (see K), and the anvil device shown at (M).

No doubt you can visualise the way the gate saw-set works from the illustration; the slots vary in width to suit the different gauges of saws. The alternative anvil method shown at (M) needs some explanation, although the principle should be clear enough. The saw blade is held down on to a collar by a nut and a bolt through the central hole in the blade. The bolt should be free to move sideways in a slot cut in the base – the length of the movement is governed by the sizes of the saw blades you are dealing with. The collar can be a piece of metal piping cut to a convenient length.

The anvil is a more difficult proposition, as it should (ideally) be machined from the solid and tapped to take the fixing screw. However, you could compromise by using a thick-walled piece of tubing with the edge filed to the setting angle; a piece of hardwood dowel jammed into the tube could provide an anchorage for the fixing screw.

At (J) you will see that the amount of set is a maximum of ¹⁄₆₄in (0.5mm) which should be applied by bending alternate teeth to the left and right equally. Note that the bending should only be applied to the top third of each tooth.

Final sharpening follows the same rules as outlined in Part 1, as crosscut and ripping circular saws can be regarded as equivalent to handsaws from this point of view. For a gullet tooth saw, file straight across the gullet with a second cut millsaw file; and file the teeth in the same direction as the set, making sure that you do not distort the shape of the tooth.

For crosscut teeth use a 6 or 7in (152 or 178mm) second cut taper sawfile at an angle of about 80 degrees to the face of the saw. It's best to go right round the saw at least twice so that you do not distort the shapes of the teeth by filing away too much at one pass. If you have done the job properly, the resulting trial cut should look like no2 (L).

'Briar' shape teeth, as illustrated in (B), need an extra filing across the tops of the teeth at an angle of 10 to 15 degrees on alternate teeth, as shown at (J).

In conclusion, do not worry too much if the set you have given is slightly more or less than that recommended, as the important thing is that the set should be consistent for all the teeth; the same remarks apply to the filing angles.

Please note that TCT (tungsten carbide tipped) saw blades cannot be sharpened or re-set by the methods described, and they need professional attention. ■

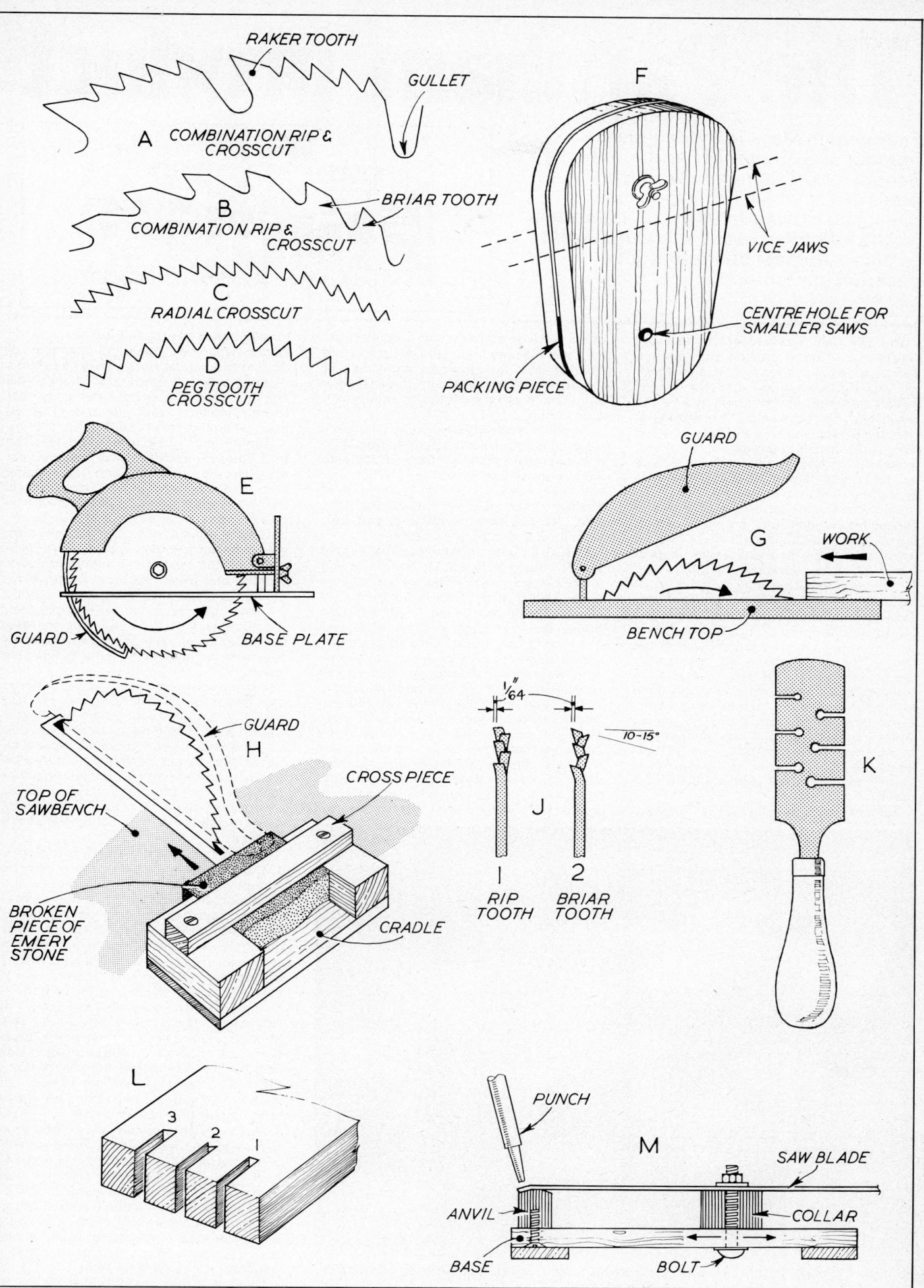

RAKER TOOTH

GULLET

A COMBINATION RIP & CROSSCUT

B COMBINATION RIP & CROSSCUT

BRIAR TOOTH

C RADIAL CROSSCUT

D PEG TOOTH CROSSCUT

F

VICE JAWS

CENTRE HOLE FOR SMALLER SAWS

PACKING PIECE

E

GUARD

BASE PLATE

GUARD

G

WORK

BENCH TOP

GUARD

H

CROSS PIECE

TOP OF SAWBENCH

BROKEN PIECE OF EMERY STONE

CRADLE

1/64"

10-15°

J

1 RIP TOOTH

2 BRIAR TOOTH

K

L

3 2 1

PUNCH

M

SAW BLADE

ANVIL

COLLAR

BASE

BOLT

The Parnham product

Each year in May, John Makepeace founder and mentor of Parnham House School for Craftsmen in Wood, holds a press day at which he introduces the latest batch of students and details plans for the following year. Polly Curds went to Dorset to meet this year's new designer craftsmen

PARNHAM HOUSE BEAMINSTER DORSET

The two year independent course designed to train some ten men and women a year in furniture design, making and woodworking of all kinds culminated last year (as it does this year) and will next year at the Royal Show at Stoneleigh, Warwickshire. Here the students exhibit and hopefully sell their work which consists of furniture, lights, signs, carvings and mechanical toys. As the course climax the show acts as a springboard into the real world.

John Makepeace can and does, pick and choose his commissions; his aims are high but he is no traditionalist. He attaches great importance to the theory of design, some of his students say 'too much, he ignores the fundamental fact that *their* furniture must be bought to use not to look at; functional aspects must not be sacrificed to design'. Makepeace believes design is a matter of personal attitudes. The second year of the course has an emphasis on open-ended design briefs, the first year to mastering techniques. Some students have only done a little rudimentary school woodwork, some have come from a college degree course, others from industry or management. They form a mixed age group (18-43 years this year) from mixed backgrounds and so spark off ideas and stimulate each other.

John Makepeace believes that Parnham

offers varied interests. Art, architecture, craft and industry join in the education and training of the country's craftsmen of tomorrow. His annual events give an insight at first hand into the youth and enthusiasm of the future.

Parnham is now five years old, this year's ten graduates are the third generation. Who will buy their work as they struggle to survive in remote workshops? What time will they have to use the principles of business management and selling they have learned, how much time can they actually spend making furniture?

One of this year's graduates, Nick Stening (ex St Albans School), utters a warning 'there's no success like a failure and a failure is no success at all'. Nick ran in the recent London marathon – he didn't fail there. One hopes that the chair and table he was finishing for the 'Royal' will also succeed.

Nick Searle would appear to have gone someway already towards success; he had no work on show – 'it's all been sold'.

Tony Portus will be joining two of Parnham's earlier graduates in September – Ian Heseltine and Declan O'Donaghue. Tony had a cabinet, desk, chair and fan-shaped screen at the Royal Show, the veneered table, chair and incised carving he exhibited at Parnham in May showed he has been learning his lessons well. He felt that the

time between school and his two years in Dorset was well spent as manager of Conran and Habitat stores. They gave him a maturity which is starting to show in his work; a confident open personality that complemented it well and should be an asset when it comes to selling.

'Timber is provided in our first year,' he said. This year seems to have been the year of ripple sycamore, Tony and David Archer both had similar jewellery boxes in it. Combined with rosewood they both worked on a spindle principle involving the mastery of turning skills. David came straight from school at Hertford and will set up a workshop for the next three years with Nick Stening and Ross Sharples. *Woodworker* intends to follow their progress and report on their successes and failures, their triumphs and their tribulations. In May, David had on show a dining chair with tall elegantly carved back in Foyha de Bolo, his jewellery box and a carved oak sign which proudly proclaimed 'David Archer designer and maker of quality furniture'. He had stayed up late the night before finishing a blanket chest. David hopes people will buy his furniture and use it; he wants to produce pieces that will last, look good but also be comfortable and part of a home. His philosophy 'cool, calm and can you collect it' was a just summing up of his furniture though I would substitute 'strong, subtle and shall I collect it.'

Ross Sharples, another Hertfordshire graduate 'designer and maker in wood' says he 'thought his only love was furniture and wood until he made an automaton parrot'. He has been pushed into an increasing awareness of the possibilities of other materials. Now he wants to explore the combined use of leather, fabrics and metals with wood. At £240 his parrot works out at nearly £4 a centimetre – a lot of bird. In contrast his low rocker 'be easy chair' in laminated English oak was a comfortable (though unusual seat) and eminently practical piece of work for those who like to stay near the ground and have both hands busy, (no chair arms to knock the elbows but excellent support for back and neck at any angle you wish). Nice one Ross.

Ripple sycamore, this time lined with cedar was featured by Nigel Worlidge in his chest of drawers. It came as no surprise to hear that before Parnham, Nigel was apprenticed to an antique restorer in Wiltshire and was also a student at the London College of Furniture. His chest of drawers was of the type produced as an apprentice piece by the craftsmen of history and a miniature gem in its own right.

Nigel had used sweet chestnut for an

● *Low 'jigsaw' table in oak and sycamore veneer by Charles Wheeler-Carmichael*

● *David's incised carving makes an attractive sign*

unusually shaped low stool on a flat bicon-cave principle. He had made an interesting feature of his jointing methods. Nigel hopes to travel to India and Japan on a Crafts Council advanced training scheme before settling down. He is very interested in unusual jointing and believes that seemingly complicated arrangements are all a matter of learning simple constructional techniques. Hopefully he can then use these skills to produce furniture that fits his cost-conscious ideals.

Incidentally, Nigel 'squeezes his tooth-paste from the top'.

Mark Burton had a chair in ash and willow and an ash dining chair on display. Nick Villeneuve from Kent, had chosen woven decoration for his screen and chairs. A chest showed an open fretwork ornamentation.

Charles Wheeler-Carmichael took three particular subjects at Radley College, geography, ancient history (because it's marvellous) and the Oxford board craft design and

● *Above: Ross Sharples' automaton parrot in a variety of materials. Left: Jewellery box in ripple sycamore by David Archer*

● *Triangular chair exhibited by Tony Portus*

● *Another example of work by Tony Portus, this time a low table making full use of the decorative characteristics to be featured with veneers*

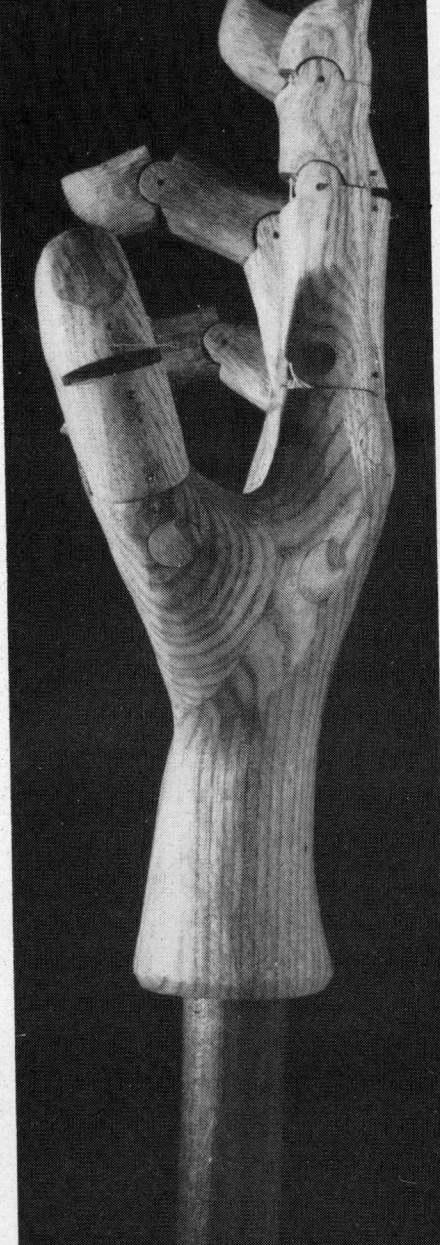

technology course. His sense of fun was eminently portrayed by his articulated hand – ash back-scratcher – and his design sense and craftsmanship by a low table in solid oak and sycamore veneer with red and blue veneers outlining the geometric jigsaw-like quality of its pattern. He too was making a chest, writing desk in yew and a screen.

'I shall be setting up in a workshop when I leave here,' said Charles. The *Daily Mail* for 11 May revealed that the workshop would be with Philip St Pier and Robert Senior (ex Parnham students) and the 10th student graduating this year – David, Viscount Linley.

'Would people buy his work just because it was made by Viscount Linley regardless of quality?' I asked. Viscount Linley was quick to reply that he certainly hoped people would buy his work, but would buy it because they liked it. 'If they buy it for my name it doesn't really matter,' he continued. 'The important thing is to sell and please someone; for whatever ulterior motive they started out with I think they will find they come to like my work when they have lived with it'. Why come to Parnham? 'I was selfish, I wanted to do it, I wanted to put myself first for a time'. Viscount Linley had a good beginning at Bedales, his A level project of a sand-blasted glass table showed an early feel for design and quality. He had sand-blasted the glass panels so that they shone with a blue sheen 'so that you can't see people's feet under the table'.

His work, too, showed fun – a mechanical wooden dog wagging its tail had all the elements of Sam Smith from the dog's expression to the fanatical tail waving produced by turning the handle. The Prescote Gallery have already exhibited his table and a screen he made was exhibited in London recently.

A prototype desk was taking shape on his table – still at planning stage; already the subject of much thought, when finished it would adapt to various angles and fold flat when not in use. A taxing design brief but one this young man was taking in his stride. It takes courage at any age to break away from a strong close-knit family, Viscount Linley has the strength of character to go it alone. He has the sense of duty and tradition behind him too; so he won't break entirely but will use the support not as a crutch but a lever and springboard into a successful future.

Lord Snowdon is 'delighted and excited about the whole thing' (*Daily Mail* 11 May). Viscount Linley is certain and sure about his future. The chest he had made he intends to keep to store his tools. His fingers are eternally busy – making little objects in his 'bored' and 'spare' time – boxes, photo-frames, lamps, pottery – he is exploring all avenues open to him. His irrelevancy, 'I dream things that never were and say 'why not?'.

The students' futures are to come and are uncertain. Parnham's immediate future is an atmosphere of seminars, exhibitions, evenings and commissions. The 'school' has now been copied by Japan, USA and Australia and will soon have parallels in West Germany and South Africa. Parallels in this country were announced in May – a second school for a new woodland industry.

John Makepeace has bought 330 acres of woodland from the Forestry Commission. One crop is a wasted resource he says. He believes in a large scale green timber project. In 1983 a new school will open for 24 students on a two-year course to produce independent artist craftsmen trained in ecology, forestry skills, design, marketing of timber and products from green timber. An exciting new prospect to look forward to; meanwhile we hope to enjoy the fruits of 10 exciting new designer craftsmen. ■

● *More work by David Archer. The drawers glided in and out effortlessly in a piece which featured its dovetail construction*

● *One couldn't resist this ash back scratcher by Charles Wheeler-Carmichael*

Letters

From: T. I. A. MacDougall, Sketty, Swansea
Dear Sir

Page 253 of your April issue, concerning ekki, reminds me that this species was included among imports of assorted West African hardwoods that we obtained shortly after the war. Machinery was then as difficult to come by as timber, and our current pride and joy was an old belt-driven Danckaert moulder restored and rescued from another mill. It worked its way through opepe, makore, utile and guarea, however, ekki proved to be the indigestible ingredient in the mixture, as one of the side-heads snapped. Looking back, only Billian from North Borneo rivalled it for intractability.

Ekki flooring blocks wore well, with some tendency to 'self-polishing', a trait that caused a Macassar ebony floor to be scrapped rather hurriedly on the 'Queen Mary', as passengers lost their footing in the cocktail bar before its wares had even been sampled.

Such a capacity prompts thoughts about wood finishing procedures, and the use of the term 'patina'. Frequently it seems to be used to describe plain common or garden dirt on antique furniture. Now it has been averred that a true patina will survive contact with boiling water; dirt washes away. It has also been noted that a handful of shavings will bring up a deep polish on a newly-turned bowl. Beech rollers handling cloth develop a mirror finish (Burma teak, greasy with a naturally high oleo-resin content, was discarded as duck-boards near a bandsaw, when we saw the shine that came up as passing traffic trod in sawdust). Perhaps patina development has something to do with the wood surface being burnished at low speeds to release part of the surface cell content as a natural varnish. It would be interesting to have some expert comment.

Reverting to the 'new' and lesser known woods, fascinating as these may be, surely it is time for a fresh appraisal of the riches so often squandered not far from the doorstep. Laburnum, mulberry, plum and even rhododendron species can produce results that rival the best of the exotics, given their 'year to the inch', and careful drying to about 10% m.c.

Yours faithfully **T. I. A. MacDougall**

From: Mark Kenning, Evesham
Dear Sir

I read with great interest the splendid and instructive article on locks by Charles Cliffe and Bill Gates in the April issue of *Woodworker* and feel that I must comment (constructively I trust) on some of the methods and points therein.

First may I point out what appears to be an inconsistency, even after re-reading the items several times. Page 258 centre column prefixed 'drawer lock (Fig 6)' it states for the keyhole 'bore a hole right through the drawer front. . .' yet page 261 photo 3 for a similar lock the advice is *not* to bore right through. By the run of the grain on the photo this could be a cupboard and not a drawer lock, but the question of whether to drill right through or not applies to both. Either method is correct. Personally I favour drilling right through because I believe that any fault due to the drilling would be more obvious.

My next comment concerns the statement, page 258 centre column prefixed 'cupboard lock (Fig 5)', and is to do with the measurement 'to pin'. It states 'This means obtaining a lock of such a size that the pin in the keyhole will be central in the door stile'. I would suggest that the other way round would be better. While it is possible to find small locks with different measurements to pin, it would be pure chance to find any to suit random stile widths, so that where the escutcheon has to be central than first get the locks and make the stile widths to suit. On flush doors of course, the above remarks do not apply.

Pages 260-261, photo and caption no 1, it states '. . . set a marking gauge to the centre of the lock pin'. In view of the fact that locks are – or should be – always set in a little from the edge (the face should be flush) to allow for a shaving or two to be removed if necessary, and it looks, better too, it is advisable to set the gauge a little beyond the centre to allow for this, say 1/16in. maximum. It is especially important where the flush escutcheon is used because of the very limited tolerance in this fitting. With the 'screw on' escutcheon plate there is a little more leeway, but it is still advisable to set the gauge beyond centre, for the reason that whereas one may get away with a small misalignment where the fixing holes are east and west, but where they are north and south it can happen (and it has) that the north screw hole in the plate will dome, if not directly, then almost into the hole in the wood, making it extremely difficult if not impossible to fix.

Photo 6, page 260, shows the bare steel of the hammer descending on to the escutcheon. I do hope that this has been done for clarity, although the caption to it on page 261 does not make this clear. The escutcheon should be hammered in via a block of waste wood otherwise some nasty half-moon bruises could result around it which could completely ruin the surface especially a veneered one.

Yours faithfully **M. Kenning.**

From: R. R. Gillies, Weybridge, Surrey
Dear Sir

The tool illustrated may interest readers. I use it for toothing surfaces to be veneered as an alternative to a toothing plane. It is simple to make, effective in use and can be made from any hardwood. The joints are screwed and glued, dimensions are not critical and can be scaled up if a larger tool is required.

The scraper itself is made from part of a hacksaw blade. These last a long time, so the tool is economical in use and there are no sharpening problems.

Only one component requires a little care in assembly, ie the wedge to its adjoining parts. An accurate fit ensures a tight grip on the scraper blade so that a thumb push tightening is sufficient: no hammering is necessary.

A word on the subject of veneering. Tooth the veneer as well as the ground: this point is not made clear in some textbooks but is essential for a sound glue joint.

Yours faithfully **R. R. Gillies**

From: E. Booth, Preston
Dear Sir

The table with the unusual butt joints shown on p230 of your April issue is very similar to some refectory tables made by 'Mouse' Thompson which are in current use in a London college hostel (London House, Mecklinburg Square). It is several months since I sat at one of these tables but I think that Thompson used five dowels to each board and there is no cleat at the end of the joints.

We have speculated on this joint and the best reason for this construction must be that the tables are usually moved by one person who takes hold of a corner and drags the table across the floor. Sine the tables must weigh about 150-200lb the ordinary tongued joint would not stand up to this use (abuse?) and some way of strengthening the joint is necessary. Gimson's butterflies would not be as strong as this dowelled joint, nor would it stay in position for many years if pulled about the floor by cleaners etc who lack any respect for the furniture they handle.

Thompson made many of these refectory tables: any of the works in N. Yorkshire could doubtless add a reason for the use of this joint. My own view is that it is necessary in a table of great weight which may be subjected to careless handling.

Yours faithfully **Ernest Preston**

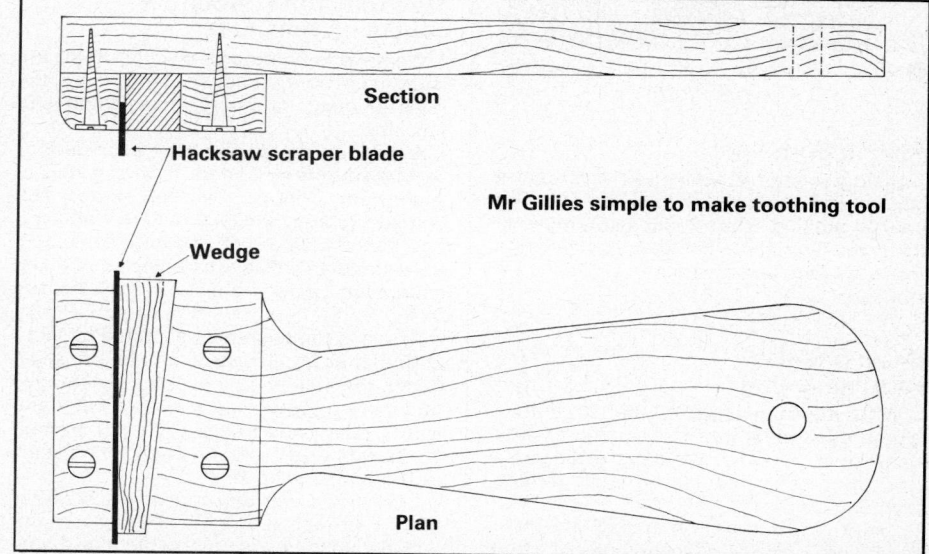

Section

Hacksaw scraper blade

Wedge

Mr Gillies simple to make toothing tool

Plan

Guild notes

Courses galore

The autumn and the long winter months creep up on us and now while the summer sun is shining is the time to plan what to do to occupy our minds and hands.

Why not take a course to improve skills, learn new ones or to just enjoy the company of other like-minded people, other woodworkers, other guild members?

With these thoughts in mind we have tried to arrange a varied programme for you.

Wood carving tuition

A course to suit beginners or more experienced students of all ages will be held at Bagley, Somerset (views from the studio over Glastonbury Tor and Wells Cathedral) from 23 October to 29 October. Tuition sessions are from 9am-1pm and from 2pm-6pm with appropriate coffee and tea breaks. Residential fee £115, non-residential fee £80. (Residential fee includes full board and tuition, non-residential fee includes lunch, evening meal and tuition).

The only tools needed for the course are some 3 in 1 oil and a wooden mallet, but if you have any carving tools or an oilstone they should also be brought.

Guild members will be very welcome on this course and should apply direct to the course organiser Zoë C. Gertner, Deans Cottage, Bagley, Wedmore, Somerset. (Phone 0934 712679).

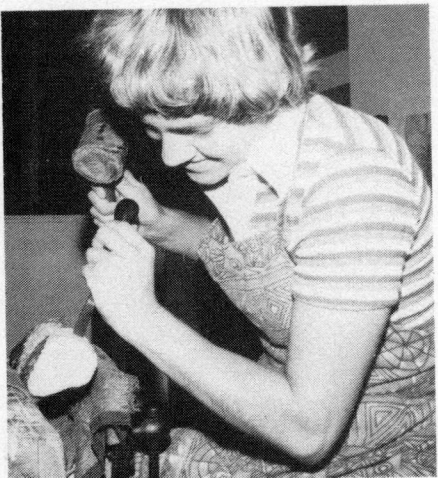

● *Zoë in action at her Somerset workshop*

Also in Somerset

Dillington House College & Arts Centre still have a few places available on a carving course running from 20-26 September at Ilminster, Somerset. Full details and forms from the Booking Secretary at Dillington House.

Basic one-day routing course

With the considerable interest that is being generated in routers and routing techniques in mind, we have arranged a one-day practical course on basic routing techniques.

The course aims to run through the most basic applications and techniques of using the router which is one of the most versatile and useful tools available to the professional or amateur woodworker of wood or wood products. It can be used for jobs as simple as bevelling the edge of a shelf and as complicated as making an accurate reproduction of a Chippendale chair. With the right accessory it can cut dovetails and staircase housing, carve letters, figures, turn table legs or chair arms on a lathe.

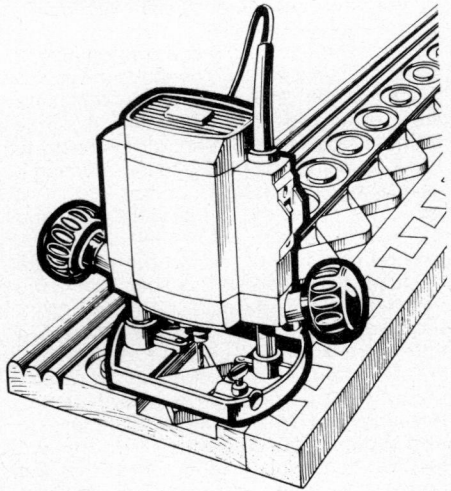

The course will be held on Saturday 30 October from 9.30am-5.30pm at the Trend Machinery Centre, Watford which is conveniently located for the main line station (Watford Junction), tube, and M1 (exit junction 5), has ample free parking facilities and for wives accompanying course-participants is near to the main Watford shopping centre.

Cost of the course is £25 inc VAT which includes, tea, coffee, buffet lunch and all tuition fees. Numbers of participants will be kept low so as to provide individual tuition and the full course programme will be published in our September issue.

We would like to take provisional bookings as soon as possible, to assess response. If response is high a second course could be run at a later date.

Two-day non-residential course on finishing

We have moved north of London for the latest in our courses aimed at improving the skills of guild members in polishing and finishing.

A two-day course has been arranged for guild members on 23 and 24 August 1982 at Aldenham School, Elstree, Herts. The course starts at 10.00am each day and will end about 4.30pm with an hour for lunch. Refreshments which are not included in the course fee can be obtained from a nearby pub.

As usual the course is restricted to six to permit individual instruction to be given under the following headings: materials, preparation of surfaces, staining (water and spirit), filling and making fillers, bodying-up, spiriting-off, acid and eggshell finishes, repolishing and waxing.

Cost of the two day course is £32.00 for each member inc VAT. This does not include lunch and is non-residential. Appli-cations should be sent as soon as possible, together with the remittance for the total of £32 to the guild administrator, PO Box 35 Bridge Street, Hemel Hempstead HP1 1EE. Aldenham School is situated between Radlett and Elstree and if necessary course members could be picked up from either main line station.

Courses in design and furniture making

The three pieces shown here require care in design as well as care in making. Do you need help with your designs? Would you like to be able to produce furniture of this quality on a short course?

● *Well designed chair by a Rycotewood student*

A three day course to attempt to give craftsmen a knowledge of and an ability to design through largely practical work has been arranged at Rycotewood College, Thame, Oxon on 1-3 September (and also/ or if sufficient response is achieved on 7-9 September at the same venue).

The course will consist of small lecture inputs prior to practical workshop projects to develop the craftsman's understanding and use of design when working with wood and to develop the sensitivity of detailing incorporating the basic principles of working.

A full programme of the course content will be published in the September issue (out 20 August). The cost is £69 inc VAT which covers full board and accommodation, morning coffee and afternoon tea, all lecture fees and practical instruction for the full 3 days.

Materials for the course will be available at cost, many varieties of timbers will be available for selection and naturally these will vary in price (a rosewood chair will be

● *Imaginative use of timbers lifts this design out of the ordinary. The chair below also shows evidence of design care producing an attractive finished article*

dearer than an ash or elm one for example!)

Rycotewood College has gained a reputation as one of the top three colleges in the country giving students a basic training in cabinetmaking skills, the relevant technolo-

gy, design skills, and projects which include commissioned furniture design and making, antique furniture restoration and industrial product model making. The college believes that the versatility of its graduates should ensure that whatever happens in the crafts world they will be able to adapt to changing needs.

Insurance

Remember our guild insurance cover runs from October to October each year. Premiums relate to a full year or any part thereof. The limit of £500 is still being offered at an unchanged premium of £5.00 per annum; alternative cover of £1,000 is also available at £12.50 per annum or part thereof.

Advance tickets
Woodworker Show

Advance tickets can be obtained from the Exhibitions Manager, PO Box 35, Bridge Street, Hemel Hempstead HP1 1EE. Guild members' admission charges are £1.75 for adults and £1.25 for juniors and senior citizens. Proof of guild membership will be required to obtain this discount.

Entry forms
Woodworker Show competitions

Competition entry forms can also be obtained from the exhibitions manager. They should be completed and returned by Friday, 3 September.

Exotics in the north

Woodworkers are often jealous of their timber suppliers and favourite merchants, since they have usually built up a good relationship whereby the merchant will ring and impart information upon what is available to his regular customer. Many timber merchants are finding now that there is a growing trend for individuals to make solid furniture as one-off pieces for their own pleasure and delight. This results in requests for small quantities of timber and too often disappointment.

Most of the timber suppliers who advertise in our pages make a point of being there to help just these people and we have recently had offers of timber from various regions of the country following the publication of requests.

Timber pools are an excellent idea for those people who like to dabble in small amounts or the occasional different wood for a small task, eg an inlay or stringing. They also provide a source of timber at an economical price in out of the way areas.

We have recently had a request from the Isle of Skye... more a plea. Where are the suppliers in Scotland, or even northern England who specialise in exotics? Can any guild member help on this one?

Timber visits

Guild members are reminded that several of the larger timber companies who advertise in *Woodworker* are delighted to show prospective buyers (big or small) around their premises during working hours. Companies who have said that they are happy to

participate include: E. C. Young Timber Merchants, Station Road, Market Bosworth, Leics; John Boddy & Son, Riverside Sawmills, Boroughbridge, N Yorks and Yorkshire Hardwoods Ltd, Pocklington Grange, Bielby Lane, Pocklington, York.

In the village hall

Matfield, consistant winner of the prettiest village in Kent is the venue for a demonstration of woodturning and light machining by Coronet Tools on 20 and 21 August. There is space available on a free basis to guild members to show their own goods provided they accept full responsibility for them. A British Legion collection box will be at hand for contributions. Interested members should contact Jack E. Durey, Leisure Craft in Wood, Ormonde, Maidstone Road, Matfield, Kent TN12 7JG at the earliest opportunity to reserve a space. (Phone Brenchley 2465).

Ties

Guild neckties are available in green with two narrow gold-coloured 'bandings' between which is the guild badge also gold-coloured. Ties are £3.50 each inclusive of VAT, postage and packing. Members requiring a tie should send a cheque or crossed postal order together with their guild number and address to the administrator at the usual *Woodworker* address.

Applications

For places on all the courses detailed on these pages and any other guild information write to:
Polly Curds
Guild Administrator
PO Box 35,
Bridge Street,
Hemel Hempstead, HP1 1EE
Please enclose a sae with all correspondence anticipating a reply.

A table for telly or telephone

The table that Harold King built to take his television set has now been promoted to service in the hall. But whatever its use, the table is of a pleasingly solid design and construction that will suit many purposes, and here Harold shares the secrets of its making

This small table was made some years ago to take a television set, but now that many TVs have their own stands, it has found a place in the hall as the telephone table.

Perhaps the design was a little in advance of its time when it was made and is therefore not out of place in a modern setting.

Mahogany was used simply because some rescued timber became available in the form of a large ⅞in thick drop-in leaf of a dining table, surplus to requirements. A local timber mill reduced it to ¾in strong to be finished ¾in thick while the mahogany for the rest was obtained from my favourite supplier. The bottom of the drawer carcase and the frame below it (to be ebonised later) are of agba for the sake of economy. The drawer sides and back were cut from some well seasoned oak ready to hand, although I

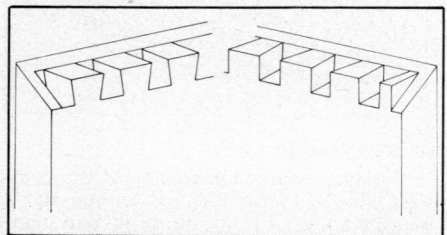

● Fig 2. Top corner joint of drawer carcase

now wish that I had used mahogany.

Being a firm believer in the correct joint for the job, secret mitre dovetails were used for the top corners of the drawer carcase but the bottom corners were lap dovetailed, the end grain being hidden. If speed and ease are important, all the joints could be lap

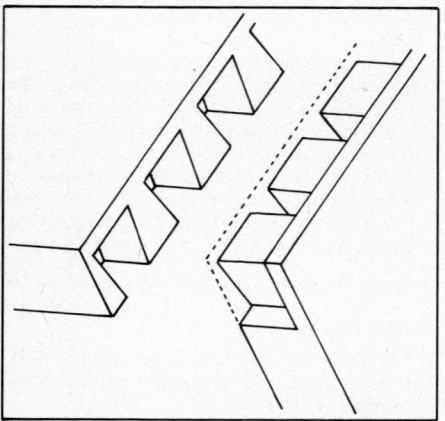

● Fig 3. Alternative top corner joint

dovetails, so long as the end grain at the top corners is kept to a minimum. Fig 3 shows both methods. Whichever is chosen, the pair of pins at each end of the row should be closer together than the rest. The front edge of the bottom is set back by ³⁄₁₆in to allow for a mahogany lipping. At the rear it finishes

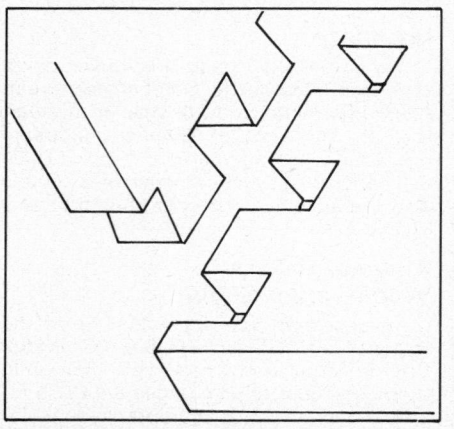

● Fig 4. Bottom corner joint of carcase

short by the thickness of the plywood back for which rebates are worked on top and ends. Accuracy in setting out and jointing with careful checks for squareness when gluing up are essential or difficulties will be experienced when it comes to drawer fitting. Having assembled the carcase, the lipping along the edge of the bottom can be fitted and the back, of mahogany veneered plywood, pinned in place with the veneer facing outwards.

The mid-frame, to be ebonised, is made from 1⅝ × ¾in material, mitred at the corners. An alternative would be to mortise and tenon it and mitre lipping around it. The frame is set in by ¾in at the front and ends but flush at the back. Holes were bored, about 1in from the inner edges to take 1¼in × 8 countersunk screws to fix it to the carcase. This method of joining the three parts together necessitates the use of rather

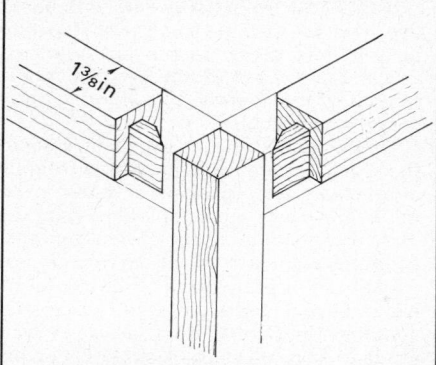

● Fig 5. Leg frame

heavy material for the leg frame rails. In consequence, joints between legs and rails are a little unusual as shown at Fig 5. The outer surface of the 1¼in square rails finish flush with the legs. Fig 7 shows how the leg frame is screwed to the mid-frame with 1½in × 8 screws.

The drawer front is ¾in thick while the

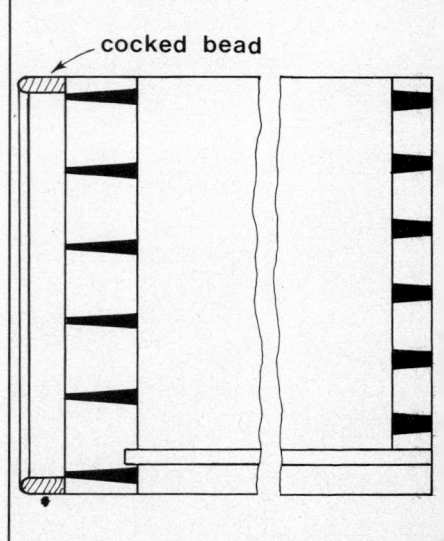

cocked bead

● Fig 6. Drawer details

sides and back are ⁵⁄₁₆in finish. The front was trimmed to fit snugly in its opening and a rebate ¼in wide and ⅛in deep was worked all round the front to take the cocked bead, shown at Fig 6, which protects the edges of veneer laid on the centre panel. After trimming the edges of the striped sapele veneer, a ⅛in wide semi-circular flute was worked at ½in from the edges of the panel. At the time that the table was made, small routers were few and far between so this was a tricky job and I regretted starting it. At this point the cocked bead was mitred round the front. The sides were trimmed to slide easily in the carcase and squared to length. Because of the bead, the dovetails are only ½in long. After they are set out, the position of the groove for the bottom can be arranged so as to miss the pins. The drawer back width was determined by the position of the groove, and dovetailed in the normal way. Mahogany veneered plywood, face up, forms the drawer bottom.

When cleaned up, a coat of matt polyurethane was applied as a sealer and then the grain filled. The rest of the finishing is a matter of choice, but further thin coats of the same material with light glasspapering between each would give a pleasing natural wood appearance. The table illustrated was finished with Rustin's plastic coating brought to a full gloss by burnishing, the mid-rail being treated with the black version of the coating. Some workers will, no doubt, prefer to use french polish. Whichever method is adopted, it should be completed before the three parts are screwed together. The last job was the fitting of two turned ivory knobs to the drawer. ■

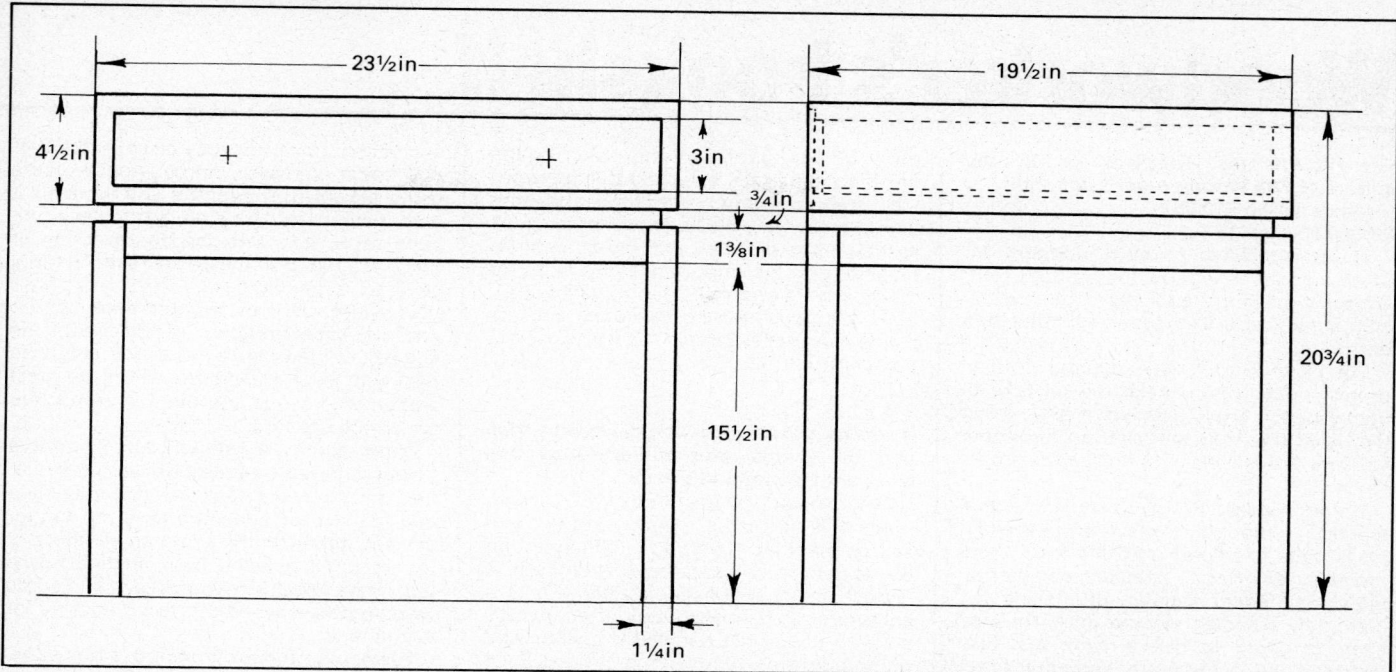

23½in

19½in

4½in

3in

¾in

1⅜in

20¾in

15½in

1¼in

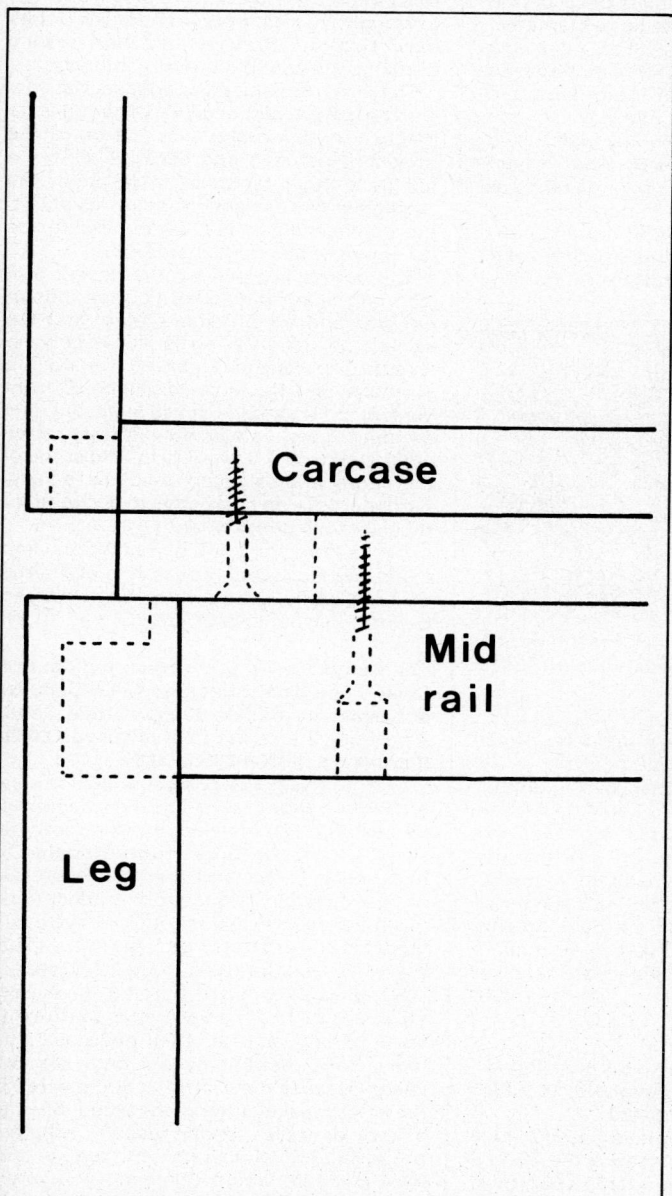

Carcase

Mid
rail

Leg

● Fig 7. Assembling the three units

Woodworker's bookshelf

101 Projects for Woodworkers, by the editors of *The Woodworker's Journal* (Stobart & Son £10.95)
ISBN 0 85422 0 18 5

There is always a ready demand for project books in woodworking, both from school workshops and from the kind of amateur whose skill is in making rather than designing.

But in spite of a well defined market, project books often make the mistake of going for too broad a range of projects, in the belief that they are catering for woodworkers of all levels of interest and competence.

Unfortunately, *101 Projects for Woodworkers,* although it has many excellent ideas, falls headlong into this trap. Commercially one has to consider whether an individual reader capable of making the extremely complex roll-top desk, for instance, is going to buy a book that also instructs him in the more elementary process of making a kitchen chopping board.

The potential buyer of a project book will first be looking for a quick subjective impression of whether it will provide the right sort of ideas for his particular taste and ability. And then he will want to know whether there are sufficient usable items in the book, as far as he is concerned, to justify spending the money.

I did the subjective test on *101 Projects* from my own point of view and came up with disappointing results. I looked carefully at the 101 projects and decided that just 13 of the designs offered were ideas I might conceivably use. Another browser with different priorities would choose quite different projects, obviously, but I think he would come to much the same conclusion as I did. To put it blandly, 13 out of 101 is not a high enough score to justify me spending £11 on the book.

In the school workshop and public library contexts, of course, where it will serve a wider range of taste and ability, this sort of project collection is ideal. Its excellent presentation and clear drawings will certainly recommend it to teachers, though they may feel, as I do, that the aesthetic standards of some of the articles to be made are a bit questionable. **C.D.**

Wood finishing and re-finishing by S. W. Gibbia, 3rd edition published by Van Nostrand Reinhold Co Ltd, Molly Millars Lane, Wokingham RG11 2PY at £12.70 (cloth) ISBN 0-442-24708-7.

Like its predecessors the third edition of S. W. Gibbia's book provides step-by-step techniques that even the inexperienced home craftsman can use to transform furniture pieces from old to 'new'. It includes information on how to bleach, fill, shellac, varnish, lacquer, rub and polish; how to select and use tools; how to antique, gold leaf, grain and distress furniture, repair loose parts, mix paints, remove oil stains and white spot, cover scratches and burns and prepare new wood for finishing.

Forty new illustrations, an expanded list of supplies and suppliers (all American) and a comprehensive glossary enhance the practicality of this latest edition.

The contents divide into five major sec-

tions; preparing for finishing; selecting the finishing materials; selecting the appropriate finish; painting, decorating and antiquing; preserving the finished surface; plus an appendix, glossary and index. Besides emphasising the importance and need for taking care of and refinishing quality furniture, this revision also describes and explains new processes and materials used in today's furniture. **P.C.**

A treasury of woodcarving designs by Alan and Gill Bridgewater published by Van Nostrand Reinhold at £16.95

One constant request from *Woodworker* readers is for ideas, plans, patterns and source material. Alan and Gill have found the answer for woodcarvers. Their book is almost all the publisher claims — it is a comprehensive source book of nearly 200 pp with over 1000 detailed drawings and photographs of woodcarving designs. Each is related to its cultural and historical period and arranged according to its fundamental form (lines, circles and twined, plant and animal forms). Style location is made easier by 'flip' page referencing — too large and dominant in my opinion when placed next to the well executed drawings which they unfortunately rather overshadow. Nevertheless the book is valuable, particularly as a pattern source manual. Pattern and ornamentation, design and motif dominate the pages; there is more here for the relief carver and those interested in surface

● *19th century Maori door lintel detail, pierced relief carved and incised, adze and knife work*

ornamentation than for those who prefer their carving in the round.

For my money, chapter five — animal forms — with its wealth of detail on African and Oceanian eyes, masks, idols and expressions, North American totems and Maori images and gods is alone an excellent reason for buying the book. Personal favourites in the rest of the book are the netsuke rat on page 85 (example of circle carving) and the French pedal harp detail on page 142 (plant form). **P.C.**

Plywood working for everybody by John G. Shea (Van Nostrand Reinhold at £8.45 paperback) ISBN 0 442 26429 1.

Almost two decades have passed since this book was first published in the US in a hardback edition. (Cloth edition 1963, third cloth impression 1969). This paperback edition is close to breaking the £10 barrier

and, at that price, can only be considered of any value to those home woodworkers using plywood in quantity and working it with machinery. There are particular problems associated with the handworking of this material but these are satisfactorily covered in many other books.

The description of plywood manufacture and its characteristics is excellent, the suggested plans for a workshop layout to deal with large sheet sizes will make most craftsmen envious and the use of machinery is well covered.

Three things are distinctly dated. Portable power tools have undergone a quiet revolution (sic) since the book was first published and the use of attachments is no longer advised either on the grounds of safety or for economic reasons. New single function tools have specific motor ratings and some work in new ways, routers and jigsaws for example.

Fastenings for the material, from adhesives and basic screw technology through to 'bought-in' plastic plugs and corner joints have become more refined and readily available outside the furniture industry.

The designs themselves appear relatively crude today, in part because plywood is no longer the best material for some of the projects illustrated and because we are a full generation removed in fashion. The 'swinging sixties' and 'savage seventies' have honed our visual awareness to the detriment of this particular book.

The author has divided the design projects into clearly defined categories, indoor, outdoor and for children's play, and the section on upholstering is still largely irrelevant. The finishes referred to are US products and the now familiar and convenient polyurethane finish gets but one mention — technology moves fast! Home craftsmen would do well to look to some of the more sophisticated medium density hardboards as an alternative to plywood for much of their sheet work.

For its time, the book is well written and copiously illustrated. Today it is of limited use — it really should have been revised before being published here. **D.W.**

The Woodcutter's Companion by Maurice Cohen, line illustrations by Mark Schultz, published by Rodale Press, Griffin Lane, Aylesbury, Bucks, at £4.25 (soft cover) £6.00 (hardback). ISBN 0-87857-328-3.

With domestic fuel costs soaring, the idea of burning wood as a fuel has begun to interest a great many people. Woodburning stoves have become quite popular — fashionable in fact, and importers of stoves of Scandinavian origin and manufacturers of similar devices in this country have been quick to take account of what promises to be a lucrative business over the next few years.

Supplies of logs for burning have also taken account of market trends and many seem to have adjusted their prices accordingly. Logs, bought by the bag, are not cheap because most of what you pay for is the empty space between the wood; buying a lorry or trailer load is usually a better proposition if you can get your logs in this way. But how about obtaining your own supplies? And if you can, how do you then go about converting the timber into sizes

Events

suitable for your stove?

This recent book from America tells how. *The Woodcutter's Companion* by Maurice Cohen is subtitled 'a guide to locating, cutting, transporting and storing your own firewood' and it does all this.

The author is obviously an enthusiast and he goes into a great deal of detail and personal philosophy about his chosen subject. He recommends woodcutting not only as an economic expedient but also as a good way of keeping mind and body in trim. There is a chapter on physical conditioning and body use, which is quite useful for – as I know from personal experience – woodcutting can be a very fatiguing form of exercise.

He also places a great deal of emphasis on safety, another important aspect. Saws and especially axes can be very dangerous implements if improperly used. His chapters on these and other tools include instructions on how to keep them sharp.

The book begins by discussing the places where someone living in a mainly urban environment might be most likely to obtain suitable wood. Trees felled on building sites, road schemes and so on; thinnings in park or forestry plantations and branches removed in pruning operations, storm damage, etc. The kinds of wood best for burning are also discussed.

Transport and storage matters include information on the use of block and tackle for lifting heavy loads with ease, the use of ropes and chains for hauling and the recommended ways of storing and drying wood ready for burning.

The use of both the saw and the axe for 'limbing' and 'bucking' – removing side branches and cutting up the trunk or stem into manageable logs – occupies two further chapters, with two more on cutting logs to stove length and how to split large logs into more handy sizes.

Mr Cohen advocates doing all this work by hand using hand tools. Only towards the end of his book does he mention chain saws. Hand saws and axes can be dangerous; chain saws are dangerous, is briefly what he believes. Their initial cost is high, as are their running and maintenance costs and they are noisy. 'You have to know more about this tool than where to point it after you pull the starter cord,' he says. And I agree.

The author does not recommend tree felling either, unless you are an expert. His book concentrates on the conversion of material already lying on the ground and the advice given is aimed specifically at the amateur and not the professional woodcutter. It should be noted that the book is also aimed at a predominantly North American readership and as a consequence has some shortcomings for the British reader.

But the general advice given and many of the sentiments expressed are truly transatlantic. 'The pleasures of woodcutting are many, but dangers are present too. Make caution your companion when you go to gather and cut wood, and you will be able to enjoy it all the more as it burns down to embers, warming you on a wintry day'.

And now I'm off to make toast on the glowing embers of my own wood fire. Lovely!   **J.H.**

Diary dates in London

British Craft Show to be held at Syon Park, London, 16-18 September, details from International Craft and Hobby Fair Ltd, 3 Rothesay Drive, Highcliffe, Christchurch, Dorset.

Antiques Fair at the Park Lane Hotel, London, 5-9 October, details from Marlowe Exhibitions Ltd, 57 Mill Lane, London NW6.

London International Building/Home Improvements Exhibition at Earls Court, London, 12-17 October, details from London Building Exhibitions Ltd, 11 Manchester Square, London W1M 5AB.

Woodworker Show at the Royal Horticultural Society Halls, London, 19-24 October, details from Model and Allied Publications Ltd, PO Box 35, Bridge Street, Hemel Hempstead, Herts HP1 1EE.

Kensington Antiques Fair at Kensington New Town Hall, London, 4-9 November, details from Cultural Exhibitions Ltd, 8 Meadrow, Godalming, Surrey GU7 2HN.

Indian Heritage

A major exhibition mounted as part of the Festival of India in room 45 at the Victoria and Albert Museum until 15 August. Admission £1.50p for children, students (with ID) OAP's and UB40 holders. The Indian Heritage covers court life and arts under Mughal rule. 24 June sees an important lecture at 6.30pm to complement this exhibition, entitled Crafts for the court it will be given by Robert Skelton in the lecture theatre on the first floor (off room 66).

Diary date in Denmark

Danish Furniture Trade Fair (MOBEL-MESSE) 19-22 August at Herning, details from A/S Herning Hallen, DK-7400, Herning.

Diary dates in France

European Furniture and Furnishing Industries Fair, 2-5 October, at Lyon, details from Foire International de Lyon, Palais des Congres, 69459 Lyon, Cedex 3.

Do-it-yourself exhibition, 30 October-11 November, at Paris, details from French Trade Exhibitions, 54 Conduit Street, London W1R 9SD.

Diary dates in USA

World Woodworking Exhibition, 18-22 August at Atlanta, details from Cahners Exposition Group, c/o Show Company International Division, 8687 Melrose Avenue, Los Angeles Ca90069.

International Woodworking Machinery and Furniture Supply Fair 11-14 September at Louisville, details from Show Manager, Suite 907, 8401 Connecticut Avenue, Chevy Chase, Maryland 20015.

At Cardiff

An exhibition of *Toys* by Sam Smith will be at the National Museum of Wales, Cathays Park until 31 July.

● *Carved and painted animals by Maggie Wareham recently on exhibition at the British Crafts Centre, 43 Earlham Street, London*

At Matfield

The village hall, Matfield, is booked for 20 and 21 August to provide accommodation for a demonstration of woodturning and light machining by Coronet Tools. There will be a large range of turnery on show from spinning wheels to barometers, plus wood carvings and a range of carving tools. There is still some space on a free basis if you wish to show your own goods. No entrance fee, simply a British Legion box. Further details contact: Jack Durey, Leisurecraft in wood, Ormonde, Maidstone Road, Matfield, Kent TN12 7TG.

Diary dates in Birmingham

International Woodworking Industries Exhibition (IWIE) 12-16 September at the N.E.C. Details from Andry Montgomery Ltd, 11 Manchester Square, London W1M 5AB.

International Furniture Show, 14-17 November, at the N.E.C. Details from BFM Exhibitions Ltd, 30 Harcourt Street, London W1H 2AA.

In store demonstrations

EME are having a series of in-store demonstrations throughout the country this year: 3/4 September at SouthWest Power Tools, Ferris Town, Truro; 13-19 September at the Southampton Boat Show, Southampton; 24/25 September at Euro Precision Tools, London Road, North End, Portsmouth; 1/2 October at Speedwell Tools, Meadow Street, Preston, Lancs; 8/9 October at Hoskins Ltd, 28 Portland Road, Worthing, W. Sussex; 15/16 October at Haslehursts Ltd, London Road, Derby; 19/24 October at the Woodworker Show, Royal Horticultural Halls, Westminster, London; 5/6 November at Fox Woodworking, Stebbings, Back Lane, Washbrook, Ipswich; 12/13 November at Gregory & Taylor, Worksop Road, Sheffield; 19/20 November at Asles Ltd, Broadway, Shifnal, Salop; 26/27 November at Peter Crisp Ltd, High Street, Rushden, Northants and 3/4 December at Brookers Tool Centre, Bucklersbury, Hitchin, Herts.

Offcuts

by Chris Dunn

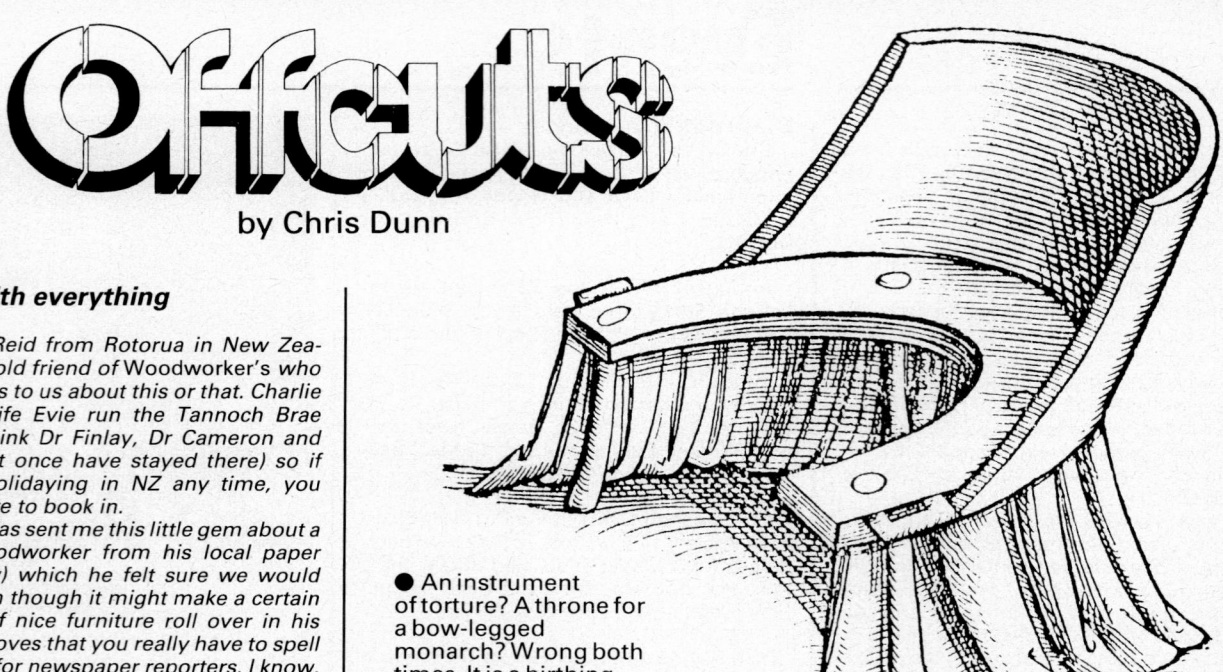

● An instrument of torture? A throne for a bow-legged monarch? Wrong both times. It is a birthing stool (see 'Mother of invention')

Chips with everything

Charlie Reid from Rotorua in New Zealand is an old friend of Woodworker's who often writes to us about this or that. Charlie and his wife Evie run the Tannoch Brae Motel (I think Dr Finlay, Dr Cameron and Janet must once have stayed there) so if you are holidaying in NZ any time, you know where to book in.

Charlie has sent me this little gem about a young woodworker from his local paper (see below) which he felt sure we would enjoy, even though it might make a certain designer of nice furniture roll over in his grave. It proves that you really have to spell things out for newspaper reporters. I know, because I woz wun wunce.

> Graeme Blair, 17, has an unusual hobby — he collects antique woodwork tools.
>
> Graeme — who has worked a year as an apprentice at a Rotorua cabinetmaking firm — uses some of his antique tools in his day to day employment.
>
> He has been interested in cabinetmaking since his early high-school years and has read up on the subject — including the lives of the famous Chip and Dale.

Mother of invention

Ladies and gentlemen. It is time for us to direct our thoughts to childbirth.

As you must be aware, there is much controversy about the general business of giving birth at the moment, and the avant garde of midwifery is pushing (if that is the right word) for changes in both attitude and method. It seems that giving birth in a horizontal position, the current custom in most maternity units, is not necessarily the best way. Taking the force of gravity into account, it is logical that standing up or sitting for the occasion makes some sense.

But you will also be aware that there is nothing new under the sun, so you won't be surprised when I tell you that the contrivance illustrated here, a chair designed for giving birth in a sitting position, is dated 1554. The drawing comes from Rueff's medieval textbook De Conceptu et Generatione Hominis, and I am indebted to Valerie Moyses of Warlingham in Surrey for sending it to me. She has good reason to send it, and if you have been wondering

what all this has to do with woodwork, the fog will now lift.

Come in Mrs Moyses: 'My husband has promised to make a copy of this medieval birth stool for me (and for any other mothers who would like to borrow it) and if it gets made it will probably end up in a local maternity hospital.'

Valerie Moyses, who is a medical librarian, tells me that she and her husband Dennis are thinking of having a third child soon, and her interest in contemporary gynaecological ideas has brought on thoughts of the birthing stool.

And this is where you come in.

'Could you please advise on construction?' asks Mrs Moyses. 'Would any of your readers or correspondents have any ideas on making a birthing stool?'

There are one or two designs around, including the tubular steel one used by the West London Hospital, but Mrs Moyses evidently favours wood as being a more sympathetic material.

The design brief she gives goes like this: 'It does not have to be identical to the one illustrated, but it does need to be very strong, to have stout straining handles and to have a somewhat sloping back. The curtains are not necessary.'

Any advice, drawings or helpful thoughts on the project should be sent to me (PO Box 35, Bridge Street, Hemel Hempstead) and I will pass them on to Mrs Moyses.

I don't think this is the last you will hear of the matter.

Robot regulations

We are advised by the Machine Tool Trades Association that they have recently issued a code of practice relating to the use of robots.

Now you may not have your own robot in the workshop, but if you do, I wouldn't like to have it on my conscience that I failed to inform you about the procedures for keep-

ing it under proper control. So if you choose to ignore this advice and your robot gets physical with you, be it on your own head.

Seriously though... as MTTA say, industrial robots are fast becoming an integral part of the manufacturing scene, and this publication is a timely piece of advice on the possible working dangers of a modern phenomenon.

Basic Principles for Safeguarding Industrial Robots is available from MTTA, 62 Bayswater Road, London W2 3PH, price £7 (inc post and packing).

Saw points

Now then. This chainsaw (Offcuts June). A number of readers have come up with the answer, and since they all provide the same explanation, I think we can take it that we now know most of what there is to know about the matter.

R. P. Stevens of Hornblotton, Shepton Mallet, was delighted to see the pictures of 'an old friend'. He bought one for 17/2d just after the war, and has regularly used it for felling, logging and pruning the orchard. 'One of its great benefits,' says Mr Stevens, 'is in pruning high branches. You simply shy a length of rope over the branch and then attach the ends of the rope to the rings on the saw.'

Hugh Blogg of Broadstairs tells me he has also used the saw and rope trick, adding that it works best with two people 'acting like bellringers'.

That brings me rather nicely to a letter from Bob Leavett of Tollesbury in Essex, who I happen to know is an accomplished bellringer as well as a woodworker, since Tollesbury is my home village too and you know how everybody knows everyone else's business in a village.

As for using the saw with ropes, Bob says: 'I can assure you that it is very tiring for one man to use.' He bought his just after the war and states, as do all the correspon-

Folding Saws Fig. 5074

Artillery Pattern
For cutting down trees

PRICE, 18/9 each

● This was the folding chainsaw that Buck and Hickman were advertising in their 1958 catalogue, sent to me by Mr Skilbeck (see 'Saw points')

dents, that they were sold off as wartime government surplus, having been issued to army units for field work such as clearing greenwood for gun cover and lorry shelter.

Mr Randolph from Corfe, Taunton, recalls using the saw during the war. 'I was with the Royal Artillery and saws like this were part of the equipment when we got our 25-pounders.' His verdict on its usefulness: 'Laborious but effective.'

Mr D. Skilbeck of Thornton-Cleveleys, Lancs, recalls seeing just such a saw before the war. Says he: 'My school woodwork master (circa 1937) possessed one, which he informed the class was of military issue.' Mr Skilbeck also sent me an extract from Buck and Hickman's 1958 catalogue which offered a similar folding saw for 18/9d.

Roy Roberts of Woodford Green tells me he has one bearing the WD arrow and the date 1942, but from both R. J. Smith of Skegness and Don Charman of Hythe in Kent we hear of such chainsaws dating back to the 14-18 war. Both report that theirs have leather pouches with wide belt loops, presumably to accommodate the military webbing belt. Also included with the earlier model, it seems, was a tooth-setting tool and a file.

All clear now?

Wheel dealings

Jack Donaldson's upright spinning wheel, shown in the May edition of 'Offcuts', created a deal of interest with much to-and-fro of letters from spinning wheel addicts who had something to say on the subject.

But both Jack and I are justly reprimanded by Mr Ernest Paris of Romford. Although Jack said he could find no example of an upright wheel anywhere, including the Science Museum, Mr Paris points out that his own half-size upright, based on an exhibit in the V and A Museum, has been in the Science Museum since early 1981. What is more, the wheel is that which won the Brian Bowman Cup at the 1979 Woodworker Show.

But in defence of Jack – and me – Mr Paris also points out that the wheel isn't necessarily on constant exhibition in the museum, though it can always be seen on formal request to the appropriate department.

By way of extending apology to Ernest Paris, let me advertise that his working model of a Tudor watermill is shortly to appear in the Science Museum's Power Technology Through The Ages exhibition.

Problems, problems

The forestry and woodworking industries of Latin America have their problems. Let us be more precise: they have 452 problems.

The figure comes from a recent publication with the somewhat biblical title of The Book of Problems which has been circulated as a consultative document by the organisers of Tecnoforest 82 as a run-up to their next symposium and exhibition, to be staged in Peru this November.

The project is a repeat of a successful previous venture for Tecnoforest 79, when a similar book of problems (they had 764 problems in 1979, so things are evidently getting better) yielded a large number of useful solutions to questions posed by various individuals and companies within the woodwork field in South America.

The 1982 version is being circulated among universities, technical institutes and machinery manufacturers worldwide, in an effort to connect up problems with technical minds which might know the answers.

The 452 problems run from forest management, harvesting, transport and saw milling through to the product end of the business, such as building in wood and the furniture trade.

I am sure the exercise will prove to be just as informative and helpful as the 1979 project. Some of the questions are highly technical, and many are relevant to woodworking industries worldwide. Others however are engagingly naive. Can you, for instance, throw some light on this one?

'At present what versatile equipment or machinery is available for the manufacture of toothpicks, and what criteria are employed for their selection?'

I'll leave you to think about that.

'Last one in the works'

It was the author Thomas Carlyle (1795-1881) who wrote 'without tools, man is nothing, with tools he is all'. Thus neatly summing up man's domination of his planet. Many of his hand tools assume a functional beauty like the famous Norris planes which have now become collector's items and a name to conjure with for tool enthusiasts everywhere.

The original firm of T. Norris appears to have manufactured planes from 1860-1940 when production ceased with the bombing of their London works. Sometime after the war Norris Planes & Tools Ltd started up production again as a subsidiary company of Aeronautical & General Instruments Ltd, based on Croydon Aerodrome at Purley, Surrey, albeit employing steel channel for the body of the plane and lacquered beech for the wooden parts in contrast to the pre-war practice of dovetailed steel or gunmetal body with rosewood inserts, though retaining the patent vertical and lateral adjustment and bronze lever cap.

The uniqueness of the plane illustrated here lies in the fact that it is probably the last Norris plane manufactured by a company bearing that name (there have been numerous and exquisite copies made of all the Norris range of planes). In 1958, C. W. Shute (see Woodworker, January 1982) who was crafts adviser to Oxford City Education Authority, was equipping a cabinetmaking shop for the Oxford College of Technology, housed in brand new premises overlooking the city on Headington Hill. He recalls ringing the Norris works at Purley and

Norristalgia is a pleasant diversion that often assails those who appreciate good tools. This Norris panel plane, pictured by John Peacock, is thought to be the 'last one in the works', and so has a special significance, as Bob Grant explains here

asking for details of their jack planes to be told that if he was prompt with his order he could have the last one in the works before it finally closed. The plane is 14½in long by 2¾in wide and would have been classed as a panel plane by Norris, they did not make a jack plane with its connotations of rough and imprecise work! The appeal of these

planes to a diminishing number of highly skilled cabinetmakers probably led to the firm's demise, although generations of cabinetmaking apprentices at Oxford, some trained by the author, have revelled in the superb working qualities of the plane which are not in the least part due to the rigidity of its blade which is some ³⁄₁₆in thick.

Woodworker, August 1982

553

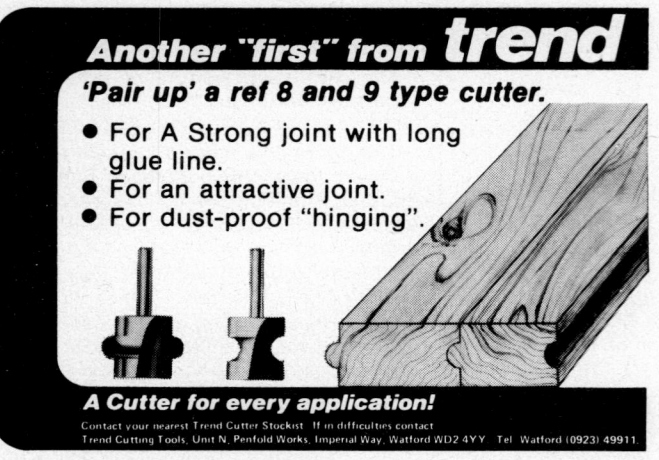
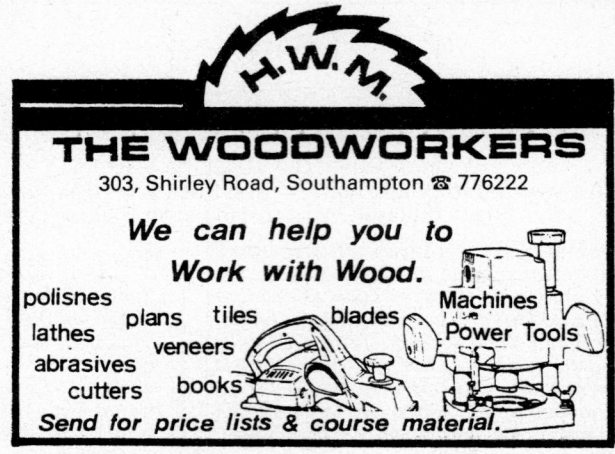
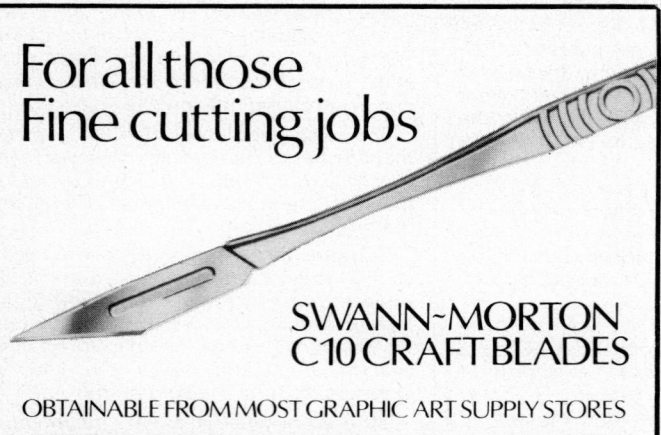
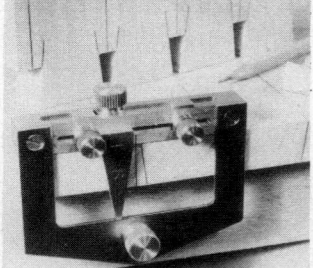

Woodworker Show

Despite its imitators, the Woodworker Show is still the premier event of its kind in the United Kingdom. As a showcase for the serious woodworker, the annual exhibition and gathering has proved that standards of British wood craftsmanship, amateur and professional, are second to none in the world, and we are proud to have been the instigators of such a revealing experiment. At this year's Woodworker Show, to be held at the Royal Horticultural Society's Halls in Greycoat Street, London, between 19 and 24 October, we are adding two new classes of competition, in recognition of technical developments in power tools on the one hand, and of the growing number of young professional craftspeople on the other

Two new classes for '82

1. ROUTOLOGY

Many thousands of hand routers are now being used both in urban and cottage industries. In the last decade this has escalated and indeed the router has become a must for any well-equipped workshop.

A new word has been coined, Routology, to imply routing technology. Great esteem is given to those able to produce beautiful things with hammer and chisel, but for the vast majority with less time and inclination to do things the hard way, the router is the most absorbing power tool of the 20th century.

However, in 25 years' study of the routing tool by the author, one thing stands out clearly: the hand router is still in its infancy. We know that the modern router will groove, mould, engrave, trim, drill, dovetail, slot and slit, but the accessories or devices to make them do it are often imprecise and limited. It is not just the quality of the existing accessories which needs attention, but the design factor. Therefore I feel that a fresh outlook is needed with an innovative frame of mind to further extend routing applications and efficiency. Manufacturers follow demand and it is almost unlimited. One good example is, how a Glasgow whisky distiller, who needed wooden shovels for mixing his grain, designed a jig to fit the Elu MOF 11 router motor for the purpose of machining a convex and concave shape for the business end of the shovel. A clear case of necessity being the mother of invention!

What can readers of *Woodworker* come up with, I wonder?

Here is the challenge...

This year a special class of exhibit is being introduced for the first time. Its purpose is to motivate the more ambitious router users to provide an exhibit showing new possibilities for this most versatile power tool. Furthermore, it is planned to publicise the best exhibits so as to provide up-to-date information for the thousands of other router users who are naturally eager to know how they can use their router to better advantage.

Some examples and suggestions for exhibitors

a) Improvements to standard routing accessories

b) Devices for setting the length and/or width of a router groove

c) Circular pattern or shaping device

d) A template making and/or measuring device

e) Jigs for drilling or dowel boring with the plunge router

f) Decorative edging and/or panelling device

g) Jig/template device for jointing, such as finger jointing, dowel jointing

h) Routing stand to accept hand router for stationary machining work

i) Copy routing machine incorporating the hand router

What the judges will be looking for...

- If an improved version of a standard router accessory, this should be well produced and a description provided showing the clear advantages together with, preferably, a working model supported by an example of finished work.

- If a novel attachment, a clear bold written description should be supplied, together with an illustration to show the method of working and the advantages. Once more a working model with a finished end product would be needed.

- If a novel jig or manufacturing device, a clear description will be required showing the various stages of setting up and putting it to use. Sketches and/or photographs would be helpful. End product required.

- If router is being adapted for use in a fixed position (above or below the table), the adjustments and/or accessories for it should be described clearly and supported by illustrations.

- If router is to be mounted on to another machine, such as a lathe, should it not be feasible to bring all the equipment to the show, clear photographs should be provided to support the claims of the exhibitor, together with written descriptive matter.

MOUNTING INSTRUCTIONS

Naturally, the size and shape of exhibits will vary extensively but so as to accommodate them and assess them in an orderly fashion, the following instructions should be observed:

NON FREE-STANDING EXHIBITS: Trestle tables will be provided for non-free standing exhibits. They should, if weight permits, be mounted on plywood panels approx 8-12mm thick, size in multiples 2in × 2in

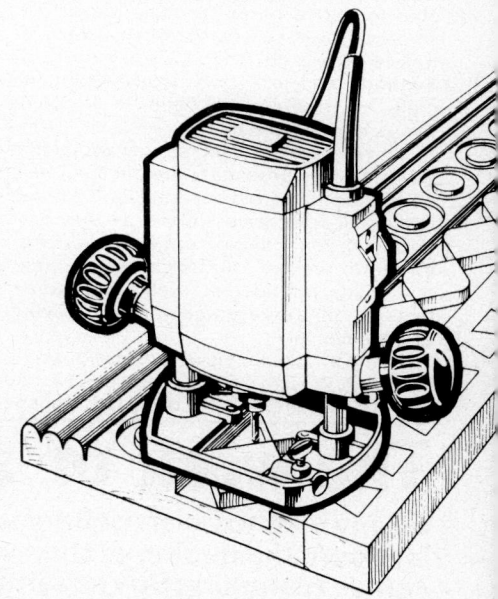

preferably, lengthwise. Illustrations and descriptive matter should also be mounted on such panels. Swing-out top hung leg(s) should be fitted to the rear of the panels to allow them to stand up safely on a table.

FREE-STANDING EXHIBITS: Floor standing exhibits should include a clip-on panel mounting, describing fully the operation and its advantages.

In judging, special consideration will be given to exhibitors who show originality and advantages in routing technology. It should be stressed that all exhibits should be supported by clear and concise instructions accompanied by a well-finished end-product.

PRIZES

Trend Cutting Tools Ltd, sponsors of this routing innovation class, are offering the following prizes:

1st Prize: A cup and a set of 50 router cutters (approx value £250)

2nd Prize: A set of 25 router cutters (approx value £100)

3rd Prize: A set of 15 router cutters (approx value £75).

Trend Cutting Tools gladly agree to give free advice to those exhibitors who require any extra information about cutters relative to their proposed exhibit. If necessary they would produce a special cutter for an exhibitor should it be thought the expenditure a worthwhile project. In this respect, please enquire direct to Mr J. H. Phillips of

Trend Cutting Tools, Unit N, Penfold Works, Imperial Way, Watford – Tel (0923) 49911.

Applications and entries should be sent in the normal way to the exhibition organisers.

2. YOUNG PROFESSIONAL

Woodworker has been a leader in the field of woodworking since 1901. It has always prided itself that it is read by the professional woodworker; both young and old being able to derive much from its pages. The so-called 'amateur' reader of *Woodworker* has always followed 'professional' methods and skills when developing his craft. He has always believed in doing things the right way.

Our recent readership survey showed us that many of our readers (nearly 30%) have taken the plunge and become 'professional' in the second sense of the word – they have elected to earn a living from woodworking – furniture makers, turners, carvers, marquetarians, horologists, joiners and carpenters are all represented in our growing readership.

It is with these 'new' professionals in mind that *Woodworker* is proud to have had the sponsorship of Rycotewood College (one of our leading colleges in design and furniture making) and Roger Buse (of Roger's, Hitchin, one of our leading tool specialists) in promoting this year a new competition class for the Woodworker Show.

Open to all professional craftsmen who have recently set up on their own, just finished at a furniture making college, or have worked as or with a craftsman for 5 years (the traditional apprenticeship period).

The subject is 'any piece of work to the craftsman's choice' within any of the woodworking disciplines. The prize for this class, which will be judged by some of Britain's top furniture makers and designers, including Alan Peters, is a challenge trophy and a boxed set of Japanese chisels.

The Woodworker Show attracts around 15,000 visitors a year. Where better for the young professional to launch his work and his name to the public. Though we cannot sell your work for you, it is possible that several worthwhile commissions can be found at such a large public exhibition in the heart of London. Entry forms available now from the Exhibitions Manager, Woodworker Show, PO Box 35, Bridge St, Hemel Hempstead HP1 1EE, to be returned by Friday 3 September.

The show catalogue usually contains black and white pictures of work entered for the various competition classes. Why not support your entry with a picture?

Competition coding

All the different competition categories within the Woodworker Show bear an identification/coding letter for ease of administration and recognition.

Classes used in previous years and again this year bear their now distinctive prefixes from WA1 (cabinetmaking) to WK2 (joinery). See pages 350/351 May issue *Woodworker.*

The new class for young professionals is prefixed WX.

The new class for routing innovations is prefixed WY and the new powered woodcarving class is WZ. Please use these codings where requested on the competition entry forms.

Following the custom of previous years no entry forms or codings are required for the special class of woodcarving (Ashley Iles/Woodworker) which this national maritime year takes as its theme Sea Dogs and Pirates.

Further information on this class can be obtained from page 353 of the May issue or direct from Polly Curds, Woodworker, PO Box 35, Bridge Street, Hemel Hempstead, HP1 1EE to whom completed entries should be sent between the dates Friday 3 September and Friday 1 October.

The work of art begins here

As any visit to an art gallery will demonstrate, painters often let down the quality of their work with poor jointing when it comes to making up canvas stretcher frames. Here Bill Gates shows how you can help your favourite artist off to a good start in producing a masterpiece

Here are two methods of joining the corners of a canvas stretcher frame. One is tenoned and mitred, and the other has square cut shoulders.

The canvas is fastened to the frame with staples, pulling it as tightly as possible. Wedges are then driven into the corners against the inner edges of the tenons, stretching the canvas to provide a taut surface.

Apart from stretcher frames, this is a good method of joining corners without using the wedges.

Fig 1: divide the thickness into five parts.
Fig 2: divide the thickness into four parts.

If plywood is used for the wedges the thickness of the tenons should equal the thickness of plywood, and a suitable gauge of plywood should be selected.

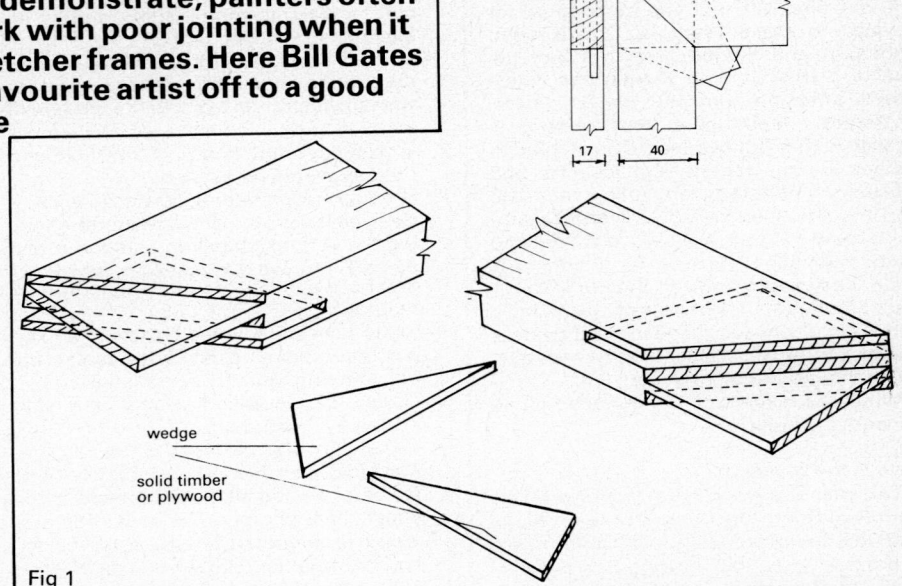

wedge

solid timber or plywood

Fig 1

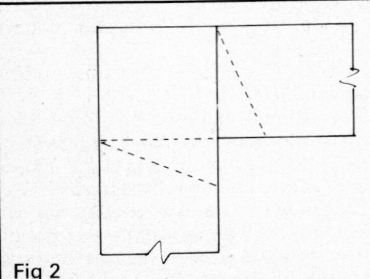

Fig 2

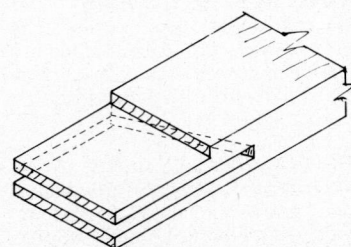

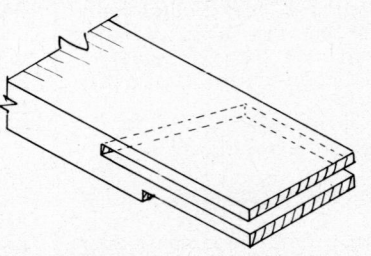

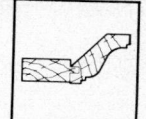

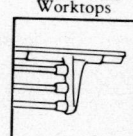

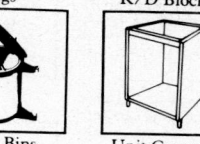
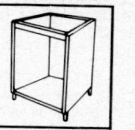

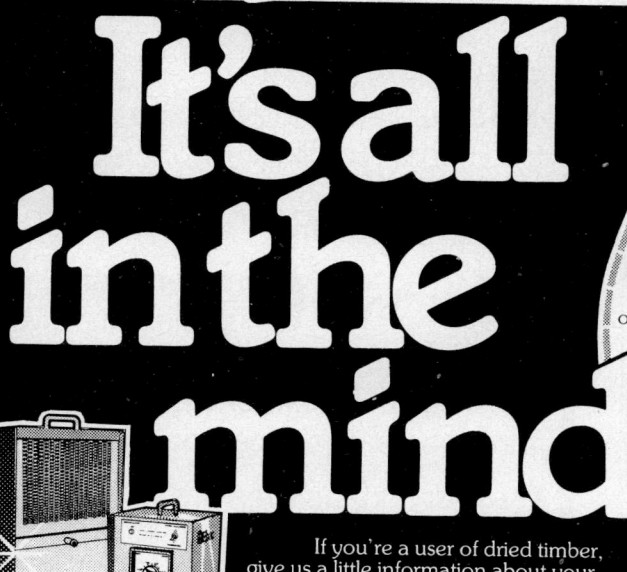

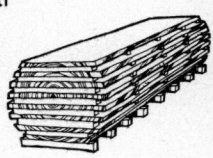

Especially aimed at the readers who require to buy and sell timber and allied materials. Make sure you reach the market.
Let Woodworker Wood Suppliers section work for you. Sizes available — Full Page £300. Half Page £160. Quarter Page £88. Eighth Page £50. Classified — Semi Display £4.00 per single column cm (Minimum £10.00). Lineage rate 20p per word (Minimum £3.00). Box Number £1.25 extra

For further details give Valerie Tester a ring on (0442) 41221 Ext. 262.

Rustic Woodslices

For House Signs, Wall Plaques, etc., seasoned hardwoods. Sawn obliquely with Bark on, up to 30" long **£2.00 each or three for £5.00. Post Free.**

A. CRACKNELL
2 ORFORD ROAD, BROMESWELL, WOODBRIDGE, SUFFOLK.

WOOD TURNERS SUPPLIES

Hardwood Blocks for bowls, lamps etc. cut from seasoned timbers — assortment of sizes and woods for £7.00 + £4.50 p&c to any UK mainland address.

TRADITIONAL DOORS, BIDDENDEN, ASHFORD, KENT

YORKSHIRE HARDWOODS

KILN DRIED HARDWOOD FOR CRAFTSMEN

We specialize in English Oak and can supply waney edged boards or dimensioned stock. We welcome enquiries for small quantities cut and machined to your exact requirements.

**Yorkshire Hardwoods Limited
Pocklington Grange,
Bielby Lane, Pocklington, York YO4 2NT**

☎ Pocklington
075 92-2870

CUT AND PLANED AS REQUIRED, WE SUPPLY
HARDWOODS
UTILE, MAHOGANY, IROKO, JAPANESE/ AMERICAN OAK. Also SOFTWOOD BOARD MATERIALS—MELAMINE CHIPBOARD—BLOCKBOARD
● **CUT TO SIZE IF REQUIRED.** *TRADE AND D.I.Y*—**NO JOB TOO SMALL**

PEARSON *TIMBER AND SERVICES LTD.*
38 RIVER ROAD, BARKING. Tel: 01-594 3074

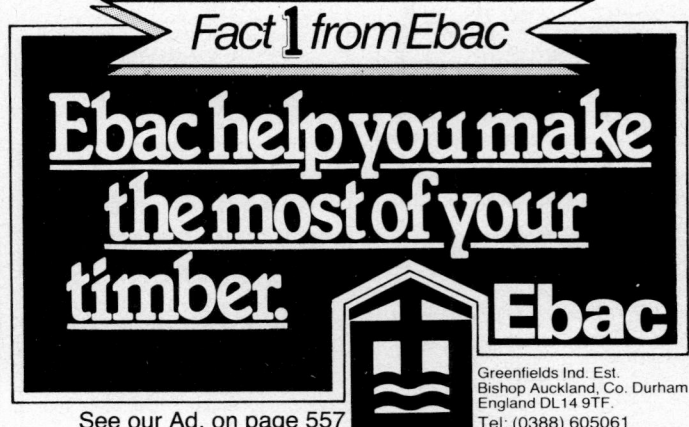

Fact 1 from Ebac

Ebac help you make the most of your timber. Ebac

See our Ad. on page 557

Greenfields Ind. Est.
Bishop Auckland, Co. Durham,
England DL14 9TF.
Tel: (0388) 605061

JOHN BODDY & SON (TIMBER) LTD.

offer

Direct from our Sawmill and Kilns

BRITISH HARDWOODS

As one of the few British Timber Merchants specialising in the production of kiln dried hardwoods in planking and dimension stock.

We invite craftsmen to inspect and select from our stock of over 30,000 cubic feet of kiln dried timber. Stored under cover.

APPLE, ASH, BEECH, CEDAR OF LEBANON, CHERRY, SWEET CHESTNUT, ELM, BURR ELM, LARCH, LIME, OAK, BURR OAK, PEAR, SYCAMORE, RIPPLE SYCAMORE, WALNUT and YEW.

available from stock in most thicknesses

*Please send for our Stock List or call and inspect
Open Monday to Friday 8 a.m. - 5 p.m.
Saturday 8 a.m. - 12 noon*

Riverside Sawmills,
Boroughbridge, YO5 9LJ, North Yorkshire.
Telephone (09012) 2370 Telex 57526

British Hardwoods
Kiln Dried—Air Dried—Fresh Sawn
Specialising in Kiln Dried Oak
Sawn to size and delivery arranged

For details and quotations apply to:

R.E. & R. Duffield & Sons Ltd.,
**The Boathouse, River View Road,
Ripon, N. YORKS.
Tel: (0765) 3667**

or our Sales Depot at:
**The Old Creamery, Currock Road,
CARLISLE. Tel: (0228) 46478**

MIDLAND FORESTRY LIMITED

TIMBER MERCHANTS AND CONTRACTORS

ENGLISH HARDWOOD

Oak plank T & T from £7.80 per cube
Ash plank T & T from £6.00 per cube
Elm plank T & T from £4.30 per cube
Other hardwood and softwood from £4.20. Odd mixed lots of hardwood approximately 10 cube lots at £50.00.

Wood turning blocks
Delivery within 70 miles
**Cleobury Lane, Earlswood,
Solihull, West Midlands.
Telephone: Earlswood 3195 or 3456**

R&S WOODCRAFTS

A service for the small user. First quality kiln dried hardwoods. American and Japanese Oak, Mahogany, Ash, Maple, Teak, Beech etc. *S.A.E. List.* **77 Lime Tree Avenue, Tile Hill, Coventry CV4 9EZ or telephone (0203) 461491 anytime.**

Continued Overleaf

Telephone Valerie Tester (0442) 41221 Ext 262 for further information regarding advertising in these columns.

Prices quoted are those prevailing at press date and are subject to alteration due to economic conditions.

Classified Advertisements

WORKSHOP EQUIPMENT

ADVERTISERS please note
FINAL COPY DATE for

OCTOBER ISSUE
(Published 17th September)
is **5th August**

NOVEMBER ISSUE
(Published 15th October)
is **3rd September**

EBAC TIMBER SEASONERS, Protimeter moisture meters, always good prices and advice from the man who pioneered small scale seasoning. John Arrowsmith, 74ª, Wilson Street, Darlington, Co. Durham BL3 6QZ. Tel: 0325 481970. T/C

WASHITA & ARKANSAS whetstones now readily available from importer. Large selection, SAE for list. C. Rufino, Manor House, South Clifton, Newark, Notts. T/C

FOR SALE Harrison Union Graduate short bed lathe complete £575.00 Belt sander, belts £70.00. Elu tool grinder £35.00. All under two years old. Chris Dryden Totnes 862567. Q

PLANERS 6″ × 9″, planers/thicknessers, 12″ × 7″, 9″ × 6″, 12″ × 7″, sawbenches, 10″ × 2″ combination woodworkers. British made. Particulars, send stamp. Dodd Machine Tools Ltd., South Woodham, Chelmsford. Telephone: (0245) 320 691 O-Z

CIRCULAR AND BAND SAW BLADES for all applications from: A.A. SMITH of Lancing Ltd., 63 Brighton Road, Shoreham, Sussex. Tel: 07917 61707 (24 hrs). P-Z

SET OF FOUR T.C.T. Grooving Router Cutters, ¼ inch, ⅜ inch, ½ inch, ⅝ inch diameters all ¼ inch shanks, only £25.99. T.C.T. and H.S.S. Cutters sharpened £1.25 each: Send cheque — Woodcutter Services, 88 Thornhill Road, Heaton Mersey, Stockport SK3 3DH. Telephone 061-432 4294. Q

MACHINERY. A comprehensive range of new/used machinery. Check our prices, eg. HMO 10″×5½″ planer/thicknesser £374. HF30; spindle moulder £365. 12″ tilt arbour sawbench 2hp motor £140. Shopsmith MK5 home workshop £897. Morso mitring machine £437, (including V.A.T.). Kity K-5. See these machines and Ryobi industrial small tools demonstrated at Woodman Woodworking Machinery Co. (Sign of the Axe), Little Malgraves Hall, Lower Dunton Road, Bulphan, Nr. Upminster, Essex. Tel: (0268) 415511 or (0702) 331729. I-U

K5 WOODWORKER with £100 accessories. New condition £550. Telephone 04215 67897.

CONVERTERS single to three phase to 10 h.p. bandsaws. 1 h.p. motors. H.A.B. Engineering, Fardons Industrial Estate, Glover Street, Bordesley, Birmingham 9. 021-772 2699. Q-T

MAKE A WOODTURNING LATHE easily, construction details and parts list, send SAE to: ORTAN LATHES, P.O. Box 46, Norwich NR7 8PB. M-R

CLASSIFIED
Telephone Valerie Tester
(0442) 41221 Ext. 262

5000
ELECTRIC MOTORS, FANS & BLOWERS
New & Used. Single & 3 Phase
ALWAYS IN STOCK
RING
(0742) 78088
FOR FREE STOCKLIST
Beatson & Co (Elec.) Ltd,
17-21 Mowbray St.,
Sheffield S3 8EN

WOOD TURNING LATHES

550mm between centres. 65mm centre height. Lever action tailstock. No.2 Morse tapers. Rear turning attachment takes 220mm dia. Various bed lengths available.
Prices from £80 + VAT
Send SAE for details

GREENFIELDS ENGINEERING

Building 3A, Site 1, Newport Road, High Ercall, Telford, TF6 6JA. Telephone High Ercall (0952) 770672

£££ OFF TREND
ROUTER CUTTERS
SAME DAY DESPATCH, POST FREE
FREE Cutter chart & price list on request.

AXMINSTER POWER TOOL CENTRE
CHARD ST., AXMINSTER, DEVON
TEL (0297) 33656 (after 6pm 33535)

AUSTINS OF WREXHAM LIMITED
POWER TOOLS AND MACHINERY CENTRE

Plas Acton, Wrexham, North Wales
Tel: 261095 and 262316. Evenings: 51186

Showroom or site demonstration of Sheppach, DeWalt, Elu Woodworking Machinery. Agents for Trend Router Cutters. Discs, drills, abrasives, hand tools at trade discounts. Repair workshop for all makes of power tools.

A·Pollard+Son LTD.

Come and browse through our huge stocks of machinery and tools.
● Ask for details of our prompt and low cost Mini Clipper delivery service

KITY UNITED KINGDOM K5 International Woodworker with Sawbench, Spindle Moulder, Planer/Thicknesser & Slot Mortiser. Full range in stock.

scheppach HMO ▶ 2HP 10″ × 6″ Planer/Thicknesser. HM2 Planer/Thicknesser also in stock.

Elu MOF 96 The professional Plunging Router 600 Watt Motor takes ¼″ shanked bits.

DeWALT DW125 Powershop, for Sawing, Grooving Sanding, Moulding etc. Dust Extractors, Planer/Thicknessers & Industrial R.A.S. also in stock.

◀ H.F.30 Spindle Moulder 2HP Motor. Shown with: Overhead Roller, Guard & Sliding Carriage. (Optional Extras)

mafell BIBEREX 12″. 2.3HP Sawbench with Rise & Fall, Mitre Guide, Fence and Tilting Arbor. Other Sawbenches in stock.

WABECO 1885 REMSCHEID GERMANY 1885

The professional 1 HP lathe 3 speed ● Heavy ● Strong ● Well engineered 33in. centres, 13in. swing **£333** INC.VAT (as illustrated)

Natural Sandstone wet grinder. Drill driven **£33** INC.VAT
Motorised **£90** INC.VAT

DIY Model **£149** INC.VAT

INCA 10½in. throat Bandsaw For Fretwork and Bandsanding 6in. depth of cut. Motorised **£289** INC.VAT Non-motorised **£189** INC.VAT

Dust Extractors, Lathes, Industrial R/A. Saws. Large stocks of Ironmongery & Handtools — Most accessories stocked. Open 6 days a week 8.30-5.30 Barclaycard, Access Business Established over 50 years.

A. POLLARD & SON LTD. 51 Queensway, Bletchley, Milton Keynes ☎ (0908) 75221

WADKIN TRADESMEN
SPECIAL LIMITED OFFER

Ring for best prices—
Tamworth (0827) 56188

MATTHEWS
MATTHEWS BROTHERS
(Woodworkers) Limited,
Kettlebrook Road, Kettlebrook,
Tamworth, Staffs.

Braywood Estates

Comprehensive range of **DeWALT** Accessories plus a super service for spare parts & on site servicing.

BRAYWOOD ESTATES LTD. FREEPOST, SLOUGH SL2 4BL
TELEPHONE : SLOUGH 0753 22567/70792

BANDSAW BLADES

Industrial quality long life blades for De Walt BS1310 & DW100. Kity. Burgess. B&D. Startrite 352. All widths & skips. Immediate despatch. Post paid. Write or phone for list.
AXMINSTER POWER TOOL CENTRE
Chard St., Axminster, Devon. Tel: Axminster (0297) 33656. (after 6pm 33535)

SCRU-DRILL

COMPLETE SET OF FOUR **£13.45** + 35p P&P

Top quality wood screw pilot drill and countersink adjusts to screw specification for fast accurate pilot holes in hard or soft wood for that professional finish.

Complete set will accommodate Nos 5 to 14 gauge screws in all popular lengths.

● Adjustable stop collar for counterbore depth or countersink
● Adjustable sleeve for screw body
● Adjustable pilot drill for screw thread

KELTEK PRODUCTS
St. Giles Mews, P.O. Box 5, Wadebridge, Cornwall PL27 7YZ. (S.A.E. Please for our complete range of exclusive products).

SHERWOOD WOOD TURNING LATHES

All cast iron constructed. 3¾″ CH 24″ or 36″ B.C. 3 or 4 speed, bowl turning up to 14″ dia. ball-bearing spindle c/w face plate, centres etc. Prices from **£75.29** inc. VAT.

Send stamp for leaflets and details of above and other low-priced machines and motors.

JAMES INNS (Engs),
Main St., Bulwell, Nottingham

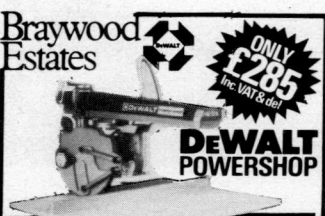
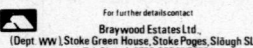

Prices quoted are those prevailing at press date and are subject to alteration due to economic conditions.

PLANS

BOAT PLANS. Canoes, dinghies, runabouts, cruisers. Sail and power. Full size patterns, fully detailed plans. Illustrated catalogue 30p. W.F. Harrison, (A) Crownest Road, Bingley, West Yorkshire. N-S

Rates
20p per word, minimum £3.00
Box nos. £1.25 extra.
Semi display s.c.c. £4.00
(min £10.00)

MAKE PINE FURNITURE FOR YOURSELF OR FOR PROFIT

Fully illustrated plans with step by step instructions for traditional designs in solid wood. Corner dresser, £1.75; Welsh dresser, £1.75; Refectory table and benches, £1.25; Refectory style coffee table, 75p; Beginners' guide to starting a profitable part-time or full-time furniture business, £1.50; Manual on working with solid wood, £1.00. **All six publications, £5.95 post paid.** Three-door Welsh dresser, £2.50; Bedside cabinet, £1.25; Two-door wall cupboard, £1.00; Wall shelf unit, 75p; Telephone seat, £1.50. **Complete set of 11 publications for £9.75.** Prices include postage. 'By return' service.

Read what our users say: "Your plans and literature contain a wealth of information." (Mr E.D., Notts.) "I am now in full-time business and have doubled my target." (Mr P.J., Yorks.) "All the plans . . . . were excellent. Let me know if you produce any more." (Mr T.E., N. Ireland.) "Very pleased indeed with the plans. A local shop is displaying my wares." (Mr F.C., Cornwall.)

L. GILMORE,
124, NORTH ROAD, BELFAST BT4 3DJ

BOOKS & PUBLICATIONS

MEDIEVAL BEASTS. How to carve for pleasure/profit. 20 designs for beginners and experienced woodcarvers. £3.50 post free. F. Oughton FRSA, 15 Princes Rd., Ealing, London W13. T/C

WOODCRAFT BOOKS — Carpentry, turning carving, etc., new and secondhand. Lists 20p. Bicester Bookshop, Stratton Audley Post Office, Bicester, Oxon. T/C

MAKE YOUR OWN wooden toys — Handbook — Make 45 different toys. £2.80 inc. T.P. Hall, 49 Thornleigh Road, Horfield, Bristol 7. N-S

PROFITABLE woodcarving and sculpture. New practical data-sheets profusely illustrated, part-time or full-time income for beginners and experienced carvers. £3.50 post free. Frederick Oughton, 15 Princes Road, Ealing, London W13. T/C

BOOKS AND PLANS. Send for our wide range of titles on all aspects of woodworking to H.W.M., The Woodworkers, 303 Shirley Rd., Shirley, Southampton. Tel: (0703) 776222. T/C

MARQUETRY FOR BEGINNERS, a 56-page instruction booklet complete with design. Available from the author, Ernie Ives, 63 Church Lane, Sproughton, Ipswich IP8 3AY. £1.20 post free. Q

HOBBIES

Prices quoted are those prevailing at press date and are subject to alteration due to economic conditions.

POPULAR CRAFTS does not.....
contain any horoscopes, advice on emotional problems,
have a cookery nook or a beauty consultant.
We do not have room for a fiction section and our fashions
are strictly practical.
We have never interviewed a TV personality or written
about a pop singer's peccadillos.
What we **DO** have are good factual features on all Popular
Crafts.
How to do them — how to make money from them — how
other people have made money from them.
Our Special Offers and Free Patterns are rather good too.
If you know someone who is a bit crafty get them to send 26p
in stamps to **Popular Crafts, P.O. Box 35, Hemel
Hempstead, HP1 1EE** and we will send them a free sample
copy so that they can see what they are missing.

Classified Advertisements

SHOP GUIDE SHOP GUIDE

The quickest and easiest method of reaching all Woodworkers is to advertise in SHOP GUIDE. Telephone **Valerie Tester (0442) 41221 Ext. 266. Rate: £8.00 per unit.** Minimum of 6 months.

Key: H — Hand tools, **P** — Power tools, **W** — Woodworking machinery up to £1000, **WM** — Woodworking machinery over £1000, **D** — Demonstration available on selected machines, **T** — Timber, **CS** — Cutting or sharpening services, **A** — Attachments, **BC** — Books/catalogues, * — Mail order.

AVON

BATH   Tel. Bath 64513
JOHN HALL TOOLS
RAILWAY STREET

Open: Monday-Saturday
9.00 a.m.-5.30 p.m.
H.P.W.WM.D.A.BC.

BRISTOL   Tel. (0272) 311510 ★
JOHN HALL TOOLS LIMITED
CLIFTON DOWN SHOPPING
CENTRE, WHITELADIES ROAD
Open: Monday-Saturday
9.00 a.m.-5.30 p.m.
H.P.W.WM.D.A.BC.

BRISTOL   Tel. 0272-633844 ★
ROBBINS LIMITED
THE WOODWORKER SHOP
MERRYWOOD MILLS, BEDMINSTER
Open: Mon-Fri 8.00 a.m.-5.00 p.m.
Saturday 8.30 a.m.-12.30 p.m.
H.P.T.CS.A.BC.

BRISTOL   Tel. 0272-629092 ★
TRYMWOOD SERVICES
2a DOWNS PARK EAST, (off
North View) WESTBURY PARK
Open: 8.30 a.m.-5.30 p.m. Mon. to
Fri. Closed for lunch 1-2 p.m.
P.W.WM.D.T.A.BC.

BRISTOL   Tel. 0272-667013 ★
V. H. WILLIS & CO. LTD
190-192 WEST STREET,
BEDMINSTER
Open: Mon-Fri 8.30 a.m.-5 p.m.
Saturday 9 a.m.-1 p.m.
H.P.W.WM.D.CS.A.BC.

BERKSHIRE

READING   Tel. Littlewick Green
DAVID HUNT (TOOL   2743
MERCHANTS) LTD ★
KNOWL HILL, NR. READING
Open: Monday-Saturday
9 a.m.-5.30 p.m.
H.P.W.D.A.BC.

READING   Tel. (0734) 586522 ★
SARJENT'S TOOL STORES
LTD.
44-52 OXFORD ROAD
Open: 8.30 a.m.-5.30 p.m.
Monday-Saturday
H.P.W.WM.D.A.BC.

READING   Tel. Reading 661511
WOKINGHAM TOOL CO. LTD
99 WOKINGHAM ROAD

Open: Mon-Sat 9am-5.30pm
Closed 1-2pm for lunch
H.P.W.WM.D.CS.A.BC.

BUCKINGHAMSHIRE

HIGH WYCOMBE   (0494) 22221
ISAAC LORD LTD
185 DESBOROUGH ROAD

Open: Mon-Fri 8.00 a.m.-5.00 p.m.
Saturday 8.00 a.m.-12.00 noon
H.P.W.D.A.

MILTON KEYNES   Tel. 0908
A. POLLARD & SON   75221
LTD.
51 QUEENSWAY, BLETCHLEY
Open: 8.30 a.m.-5.30 p.m.
Monday-Saturday
H.P.W.WM.D.A.BC.

CAMBRIDGESHIRE

CAMBRIDGE   Tel. 0223-353091
H. B. WOODWORKING
69 LENSFIELD ROAD

Open: 8.30 a.m.-5.30 p.m.
Monday-Friday
8.30 a.m.-1.00 p.m. Sat
P.W.WM.D.CS.BC.

CHESHIRE

CHESTER   Tel. 0244 42084 ★
ROBERT KELLY'S
19 NEWGATE ROW
GROSVENOR PRECINCT, CH1 1ER
Open: 9.00 a.m.-5.30 p.m.
Monday-Saturday
H.P.W.WM.D.CS.A.BC.

NANTWICH   Tel. Crewe 67010
ALAN HOLTHAM
THE OLD STORES TURNERY
WISTASON ROAD, WILLASTON
Open: Tues-Sat 9a.m.-5.30p.m.
Closed Monday
P.W.WM.D.T.C.CS.A.BC.

CLEVELAND

MIDDLESBROUGH   Tel. 0642-
WINTZ   460035/813650
INDUSTRIAL SUPPLIES ★
2 BESSEMER COURT
GRANGETOWN
Open: Mon-Fri 8.30 a.m.-5 p.m.
H.P.W.D.A.

CORNWALL

FALMOUTH   Tel. 0326-312915
WOODSTOCK
(HARDWOODS) S.W.,
ASHFIELD, PONSHARDEN,
Open: Mon-Fri 8.30 a.m.-5.30 p.m.
Sat 9 a.m.-1.00 p.m.
T.

HELSTON
SOUTH WEST
POWER TOOLS

Helston (03265) 4961
Truro (0872) 71671
Launceston (0566) 3555
H.P.W.WM.D.CS.A.

CORNWALL

NEWQUAY   Tel. 063 73 2516
CONWAY SUPPLIES
(NEWQUAY)   ★
70 FORE STREET
Open: Mon-Fri 9 a.m.-5.30 p.m.
Sat 9 a.m.-12.30 p.m.
H.P.W.WM.D.A.BC.

ST. AUSTELL   Tel. (0726) 65922
TOOLSERV   ★
TRURO ROAD

Open: 8 a.m.-5.30 p.m.
6 days
H.P.W.WM.D.CS.A.BC.

DERBYSHIRE

BUXTON   Tel. 0298-871636
CRAFT SUPPLIES   ★
THE MILL
MILLERSDALE
Open: Mon-Fri 9 a.m.-5 p.m.
Saturday 9 a.m.-1 p.m.
H.P.W.D.T.CS.A.BC.

DEVON

EXETER   Tel. 0392 73936
WRIDES TOOL CENTRE
147 FORE STREET

Open: 9.00 a.m.-5.30 p.m.
Wednesday 9.00 a.m.-1.00 p.m.
H.P.W.WM.A.

PLYMOUTH   Tel. 0752 330303 ★
WESTWARD BUILDING SERVICES
LTD., LISTER CLOSE, NEWNHAM
INDUSTRIAL ESTATE, PLYMPTON
Open: Mon-Fri 8 a.m.-5.30 p.m.
Sat 8.30 a.m.-12.30 p.m.
H.P.W.WM.D.A.BC.

PLYMOUTH   Tel. 0752-266179
JOHN WRIDE & CO (PLYMOUTH) LTD
146 CORNWALL STREET
Open: Monday to Saturday
9.00a.m.-5.30p.m.
Wed 9.00a.m.-1.00p.m.
H.P.W.WM.A.

DORSET

BOURNEMOUTH   Tel: 0202
MACHINE SALES & SERVICES   527780
(BOURNEMOUTH) LTD   527781
56 STROUDEN ROAD   ★

Open: Mon-Fri 8.15 a.m.-5 p.m.
H.P.W.WM.D.A.

WEYMOUTH   Tel: (0305) 787396
WEYMOUTH TOOL CENTRE   ★
30A ABBOTSBURY ROAD

Open: Monday to Saturday
8 a.m.-5.30 p.m.
H.P.W.WM.D.A.BC.

CO. DURHAM

BARNARD CASTLE   Tel: (0833)
WOODMEN   38442/31609
27 NEWGATE   ★

Open Monday-Saturday
9 a.m.-5.30 p.m.
P.W.WM.D.A.BC.

ESSEX

LEIGH ON SEA   Tel. (0702)
MARSHALL &   710404
PARSONS LTD   ★
1111 LONDON ROAD
Open: 8.30 am-5.30 pm Mon-Fri.
9.00 am-5.00 pm Sat.
H.P.W.WM.D.CS.A.

LEIGH ON SEA   Tel. (0702)
WEBBERS TOOLS   76503
204 ELM ROAD

Open: 9 am-5.30 pm
Monday to Saturday
H.P.W.

GLOUCESTERSHIRE

TEWKESBURY   Tel. 0684
TEWKESBURY SAW CO.   293092
LIMITED
TRADING ESTATE, NEWTOWN
Open: Mon-Fri 8.00 a.m.-5.00 p.m.
Saturday 9.30 a.m.-12.00 p.m.
P.W.WM.D.CS.

HAMPSHIRE

ALDERSHOT   Tel. 0252 28088
BURCH & HILLS LTD
BLACKWATER WAY TRADING
ESTATE
Open: Mon-Fri 8.30 a.m.-5.30 p.m.
Saturday 8.30 a.m.-12.00 p.m.
H.P.W.WM.D.A.BC.

PORTSMOUTH   Tel. 0705
EURO PRECISION TOOLS   67332
LTD
259/263 London Road, North End
Open: Mon-Fri 9 a.m.- 5.30 p.m.
Sat 9.00 a.m.-5.00 p.m.
H.P.W.D.A.BC.

SOUTHAMPTON   Tel. 0703
H.W.   776222
THE WOODWORKERS
303 SHIRLEY ROAD, SHIRLEY
Open: Tues-Fri 9.30 a.m.- 6 p.m.
Sat 9.30 a.m.-4.00 p.m.
H.P.W.WM.D.CS.A.BC.T.

HERTFORDSHIRE

WATFORD   Tel. 0923 48434
HOME CARE CENTRE
20 MARKET STREET
WATFORD, HERTS
Open 9.00 a.m.-5.30 p.m.
Mon.-Sat.
H.P.W.A.WM.BC.D.

SHOP GUIDE SHOP GUIDE

HERTFORDSHIRE

WATFORD   Tel. 0923 26052
J. SIMBLE & SONS LTD
76 QUEENS ROAD

Open 8.30 a.m.-5.30 p.m.
Mon-Sat. Closed Wednesday
H.P.W.WM.D.A.BC.

WATFORD   Tel. (0923) 49911
TREND MACHINERY & CUTTING
TOOLS LTD
UNIT N, PENFOLD WORKS
IMPERIAL WAY
Open: Mon-Fri 9 a.m.-5 p.m.
P.W.WM.D.CS.BC.

KENT

MATFIELD   Tel. Brenchley
LEISURECRAFT IN WOOD   (089272)
'ORMONDE', MAIDSTONE RD.   2465
TN12 7JG
Open: Mon-Sun
9 a.m.- 5.30 p.m.
W.WM.D.T.A.

SITTINGBOURNE   Tel.
B.T.S. (TOOLS),   Sittingbourne
Unit 25, SITTINGBOURNE   79551
INDUSTRIAL PARK   ★
Open: Monday - Friday
8.00 a.m. - 5.00 p.m.
H.P.W.BC.CS.

LANCASHIRE

LANCASTER   Tel. 0524 2886
LILE TOOL SHOP
43/45 NORTH ROAD
Open: Monday to Saturday
9.00 a.m.-5.30 p.m.
Wed 9.00 a.m.-12.30 p.m.
H.P.W.D.A.

PRESTON   Tel. (0772) 52951
SPEEDWELL TOOL CO.,   ★
62-68 MEADOW STREET
Open: Mon-Fri 8.30 a.m.-5.30 p.m.
Sat 8.30 a.m.-12.30 p.m.
H.P.W.WM.D.CS.A.BC.

LEICESTERSHIRE

COALVILLE   Tel. (0533) 415556
POOLE WOOD   (06077) 5777
MACHINERY
SERVICES LIMITED,
30 VALENTINE ROAD
Open: Mon-Fri 9 a.m.-5 p.m.
H.P.W.WM.D.A.BC.

LEICESTER   Tel. 0455 43254
ROY STARTIN LTD
134 WOOD STREET
EARL SHILTON
Open: Mon-Fri 8 a.m.-5.30 p.m.
Saturday 8.00 a.m.-1.30 p.m.
H.P.W.WM.D.T.A.

LINCOLNSHIRE

LINCOLN   Tel. 0522 30199/
WOODWISE LIMITED   39871 or
121 HIGH STREET   0522 68428
& 06077 2421/5777/5288
(after hours)   ★
Open: Mon-Sat 9 a.m.-5.30 p.m.
P.W.WM.D.A.BC.

LONDON

ACTON   Tel. 01-992 4835
A MILLS (ACTON) LTD   ★
32/36 CHURCHFIELD ROAD
W3 6ED
Open: Mon-Fri 9.00 a.m.-5.00 p.m.
Closed Saturday
H.P.W.WM.

HANWELL   Tel. 01-567 2922
G. D. CLEGG & SONS
83 Uxbridge Road, W7 3ST
Open: Monday to Friday
9.00 a.m.-6.00 p.m.
Saturday 9.00 a.m.-5.30 p.m.
H.P.W.WM.D.

KILBURN   Tel. 01-624 5146
W. THATCHER & SON LTD   ★
POWER TOOL CENTRE
AT THE TECHNICAL LEISURE CENTRE
1 THE GRANGEWAY, N.W.6.
Open: Mon-Sat 9 a.m.-5.30 p.m.
P.H.W.D.CS.A.BC.

LONDON   Tel. 01-636 7475
BUCK & RYAN LIMITED   ★
101 TOTTENHAM COURT ROAD
W1P 0DY
Open: Mon-Fri 8.30 a.m.-5.30 p.m.
Saturday 8.30 a.m.-1.00 p.m.
H.P.W.WM.D.A.

LONDON   Tel. 01-739 7126
CECIL W. TYZACK   ★
79-81 KINGSLAND ROAD
SHOREDITCH
Open: Mon-Fri 8.45 a.m.-5.15 p.m.
Saturday 9 a.m.-12 noon
H.P.W.WM.D.A.BC.

NORBURY   Tel: 01-679 6193
HERON TOOLS & HARDWARE LTD
437 STREATHAM HIGH ROAD
S.W.16
Open: Mon-Sat 8.30 a.m. - 6 p.m.
Wednesday 8.30 a.m. - 1 p.m.
H.P.W.A.

MERSEYSIDE

LIVERPOOL   Tel. 051-263 1359
TAYLOR BROS (LIVERPOOL) LTD
5/9 PRESCOTT STREET
Open: Monday to Friday
8.30 a.m.-5.30 p.m.
H.P.W.WM.D.A.BC.

MIDDLESEX

NORTH HARROW Tel. 01-863 2492
WILLIAMS TECHNICAL SERVICES   ★
36 STATION ROAD
Open: Mon-Fri 8 a.m.-5.30 p.m.
Wed 8 a.m.-1 p.m.,
Sat 9 a.m.-5.30 p.m.
H.P.W.WM.D.A.

HOUNSLOW Tel. 01-570 2103/5135
Q. R. TOOLS LTD
251-253 HANWORTH ROAD

Open: Mon-Fri 8.30 a.m.-5.30 p.m.
Sat 9 a.m.-1 p.m.
P.W.WM.D.CS.A.

NORFOLK

KINGS LYNN   Tel. (0553) 2443
WALKER & ANDERSON (Kings Lynn) LTD
WINDSOR ROAD, KINGS LYNN
Open: Monday to Saturday
7.45 a.m.-5.30 p.m.
Wednesday 1 p.m. Saturday 5.00 p.m.
H.P.W.WM.D.CS.A.

NORWICH   Tel. 0603 898695
NORFOLK SAW SERVICES
DOG LAND, HORSFORD
Open: Monday to Friday
8.00 a.m.-5.00 p.m.
Saturday 8.00 a.m.-12.00 p.m.
H.P.W.WM.D.CS.A.

NORWICH   Tel. 0603 400933
WESTGATES WOODWORKING   Tx.
MACHINERY, JUPITER ROAD   975412
OFF MILE CROSS LANE
Open: 9 a.m.-5 p.m. weekdays
9 a.m.-12 a.m. Sat.
P.W.WM.D.

NORTHAMPTONSHIRE

RUSHDEN   Tel. 093-34 56424
PETER CRISP LIMITED   ★
7 HIGH STREET
Open: Monday to Saturday
8.30 a.m.-5.30 p.m.
Thursday 8.30 a.m.-1.00 p.m.
H.P.W.D.BC.

NORTHUMBERLAND

BLYTH   Tel. (06706) 69279
ALLAN McNAIR WOODCRAFT   ★
69-71 PLESSEY ROAD

Open: Monday to Saturday
9 a.m.-5 p.m.
H.W.WM.D.T.CS.A.BC.

NOTTINGHAMSHIRE

NOTTINGHAM   Tel. (0602) 225979
POOLEWOOD   and 227929
EQUIPMENT LTD   (06077) 2421/5777
5a HOLLY LANE, CHILLWELL
Open: Mon-Fri 9 a.m.-5.30 p.m.
Sat. 9 a.m. to 12.30 p.m.
P.W.WM.D.CS.A.BC.

NOTTINGHAM   Tel. 0602 811889
THE WOODCUTTER
5 TUDOR SQUARE
WEST BRIDGFORD
Open: Tues-Sat 9 a.m.-5.30 p.m.
Fri 9 a.m.-7.30 p.m. Closed Mon.
H.P.W.WM.D.T.CS.A.

OXFORDSHIRE

BICESTER   Tel. (08692) 4156/
WOODMEN   3218/3219
104 CHURCHILL ROAD

Open: Monday-Saturday
9 a.m.-5.30 p.m.
P.W.WM.D.A.BC.

OXFORD   Tel. (0865) 45118/9
SARJENT'S TOOL   ★
STORES LTD
150 COWLEY ROAD
Open: Monday to Saturday
8.30 a.m.-5.30 p.m.
H.P.W.WM.D.A.BC.

SHROPSHIRE

TELFORD   Tel. Telford
ASLES LTD   (0952) 48054
VINEYARD ROAD
WELLINGTON
Open: Mon-Fri 8.30am-5.30pm
Saturday 8.30am-4.00pm
H.P.WM.D.A.

SOMERSET

TAUNTON   Tel. Taunton 79078
KEITH MITCHELL   ★
TOOLS AND EQUIPMENT
66 PRIORY BRIDGE ROAD
Open: Mon-Fri 8.30am-5.30pm
Saturday 9am-4pm
H.P.W.WM.D.CS.A.BC.

WESTON-SUPER-MARE   Tel.
JOHN TERRY   0934 21803
TOOL SALES   ★
36 ALFRED STREET
Open: Monday to Saturday
9am-5.30pm inclusive
H.P.W.WM.D.CS.A.

STAFFORDSHIRE

TAMWORTH   Tel. 0827-56188
MATTHEWS BROTHERS LTD
KETTLEBROOK ROAD
Open: Mon.-Sat. 8.30am-6.00pm
Demonstrations Sunday mornings
by appointment only
H.P.WM.D.T.CS.A.BC.

SUFFOLK

BURY ST. EDMUNDS   Tel.
TOOLS & THINGS   0284 62022
21 CHURCHGATE   ★

Open: Monday to Saturday
9.00 a.m.-5.30 p.m.
H.P.W.WM.D.A.BC.

IPSWICH   Tel. 0473 86216
FOX WOODWORKING   ★
'STEBBINGS' BACK LANE
WASHBROOK
Open: Tues. Fri. 9.00am-5.30pm
Sat. 9.00am-5pm

SURREY

CARSHALTON BEECHES   Tel.
SURREY WOOD   01-642 6636
MACHINE SALES LTD   ★
56A BANSTEAD ROAD
Open: Tues-Fri 9.30 a.m.-6.00 pm
Saturday 9.30 am-2.00 pm
P.W.WM.D.BC.CS.

CROYDON   Tel. 01-688 5513
L. H. TURTLE LTD   ★
6-12 PARK STREET

Open: Monday to Saturday
8.30 a.m.-5.30 p.m.
H.P.W.WM.D.A.

GUILDFORD   Tel. 0483 61125
MESSINGERS FOR TOOLS
14-18 CHERTSEY STREET
Open: Tuesday to Saturday
8.30 a.m.-5.30 p.m.
Closed all day Monday
H.P.W.D.BC.

SHOP GUIDE SHOP GUIDE

SUSSEX

BOGNOR REGIS   Tel: (0243) 863100
A. OLBY & SON (BOGNOR REGIS LTD)
"TOOLSHOP", BUILDER'S MERCHANT
HAWTHORN ROAD
  Open: Mon-Thurs 8 a.m.-5.15 p.m.
Fri 8 a.m.-8 p.m. Sat 8 a.m.-12.45 p.m.
H.P.W.WM.D.T.C.A.BC.

WORTHING   Tel. 0903 38739
W. HOSKING LTD (TOOLS &   ★
MACHINERY)
28 PORTLAND RD, BN11 1QN
  Open: Mon-Sat 8.30am-5.30pm
Wednesday 8.30am-1.00pm
H.P.W.WM.D.CS.A.BC.

WEST MIDLANDS

WEST BROMWICH   Tel: 021-
CONWAY SAW &   553 5461/2
SUPPLY LTD   ★
SWAN LANE
  Open: 8 a.m.-6 p.m. Mon-Fri
9 a.m.-1 p.m. Saturday
P.W.WM.D.CS.BC.

WILTSHIRE

SWINDON   Tel. (0793) 31361
SARJENT'S TOOL STORES LTD   ★
64 FLEET STREET

  Open: Monday to Saturday
8.30 a.m.-5.30 p.m.
H.P.W.WM.D.A.BC

YORKSHIRE

HALIFAX   Tel. 0422 43722/
TIMBERLITE LTD   884788/33575
WILLOWFIELDS ROAD   ★
WILLOWFIELD
  Open: Monday to Friday
Saturday 9.00 a.m.-5.00 p.m.
H.P.W.WM.D.CS.A.BC.

YORKSHIRE

HARROGATE   Tel. 0423 66245/
MULTI-TOOLS   55328   ★
158 KINGS ROAD

  Open: Monday to Saturday
8.30 a.m.-6.00 p.m.
H.P.W.WM.D.A.BC.

HUDDERSFIELD   Tel. (0484)
NEVILLE M. OLDHAM   641219/(0484)
UNIT 1 DAYLE ST. WORKS   42777
DAYLE STREET, LONGWOOD   ★
  Open: Mon-Fri 9.00am- 5.30pm
Saturday 9.30am-12.00pm
P.W.WM.D.A.BC.

LEEDS   Tel. 0532 574736
D. B. KEIGHLEY MACHINERY LTD   ★
VICKERS PLACE
STANNINGLEY
  Open: Mon-Fri 9am-5pm
Saturday 9am-1pm
P.W.WM.D.CS.A.BC.

LEEDS   Tel. 0532 790507
GEORGE SPENCE & SONS LTD
WELLINGTON ROAD   ★
  Open: Monday to Friday
8.30 a.m.-5.30 p.m.
Saturday 9.00 a.m.-5.00 p.m.
H.P.W.WM.D.T.A.

SHEFFIELD   Tel. 0742-441012
GREGORY & TAYLOR LTD
WORKSOP ROAD
  Open: 8.30 a.m.-5.30 p.m.
Monday-Friday
8.30 a.m.-12.30 p.m. Sat.
H.P.W.WM.D.

YORKSHIRE

SHEFFIELD   Tel. 0742-24659
GRAHAM OXLEY'S SHOWROOM
BRIDGE STREET   ★
  Open: Monday to Friday
9.00 a.m.-5.30 p.m.
Saturday 8.30 a.m.-12.30 p.m.
H.W.D.A.BC.

SCOTLAND

EDINBURGH   Tel. 031-337
SCOTSPAN   7788/665 3121
195 BALGREEN ROAD

  Open: Monday to Friday
9.00 a.m.-3.00 p.m.
P.W.WM.D.A.

GLASGOW   Tel. 041 429 4374/4444
THE SAW CENTRE   Telex: 777886
596-602 EGLINTON STREET   ★
G5 9RR
  Open: Mon.-Fri. 8 a.m.-5.30 p.m.
Saturday 9 a.m.-1 p.m.
H.P.W.WM.D.CS.A.

N. IRELAND

Co. ANTRIM   Tel. 0266 6384
GEORGE GARDINER
49 BALLYMONEY STREET
BALLYMENA
  Open: Mon-Fri 8.30am-5.30pm
Wednesday 8.30am-1.00pm
H.P.W.D.A.BC.

S. IRELAND

COUNTY KILKENNY   Tel.
WOODMEN   (0409) 5460
CASHEL HOUSE   ★
KELLS ROAD, KILKENNY

  Open: Monday to Saturday

WALES

BRITON FERRY   Tel. (0639)
WOODMEN   820803/4
49 NEATH ROAD   ★
  Open: Monday to Saturday
9.00 a.m.-5.30 p.m.
P.W.WM.D.A.BC.

CARDIFF   Tel. (0222) 373007
JOHN HALL TOOLS LIMITED   ★
22 CHURCHILL WAY
  Open: Monday to Saturday
9.00 a.m.-5.30 p.m.
H.P.W.WM.D.A.BC.

CARDIFF   Tel. (0222) 30831
F. W. MORGAN   & 25562
(CANTON) LTD., 129-133
COWBRIDGE RD EAST,
CANTON, CARDIFF
  Mon-Sat 8-5 Sun. 9.30-12.30
H.P.T.CS.A.BC.

CARDIFF   Tel. (0222) 36519/
WOODMEN   373793/35221
74-76 PARK ROAD
WHITCHURCH, CARDIFF

  Open: Monday to Saturday
9.00 a.m.-5.30 p.m.

CARMARTHEN   Tel. 0267 7219
DO-IT-YOURSELF SUPPLY
BLUE STREET, DYFED
  Open: Monday to Saturday
9.00 a.m.-5.30 p.m.
Thursday 9.00 a.m.-1.00 p.m.
H.P.W.WM.D.T.CS.A.BC.

YOU CAN BUY WITH CONFIDENCE FROM THE SHOPS IN THIS SHOP GUIDE

★*Shops offering a mail order service are denoted by an asterisk*

SWANSEA   Tel. (0792) 55680
SWANSEA TIMBER &   ★
PLYWOOD CO LTD
57-59 OXFORD STREET
  Open: Mon. to Fri. 9 am-5.30 pm
Sat. 9 am-1 pm
H.P.W.D.T.CS.A.BC.

Key: H — Hand tools, **P** — Power tools, **W** — Woodworking machinery up to £1000, **WM** — Woodworking machinery over £1000, **D** — Demonstration available on selected machines, **T** — Timber, **CS** — Cutting or sharpening services, **A** — Attachments, **BC** — Books/catalogues, ***** — Mail order.

Prices quoted are those prevailing at press date and are
subject to alteration due to economic conditions.

 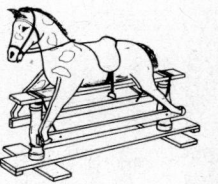  

Prices quoted are those prevailing at press date and are subject to alteration due to economic conditions.

Here's an easier way to construct cabinets with perfectly solid joints – the revolutionary **new** Elu Flat Dowel Jointing System.

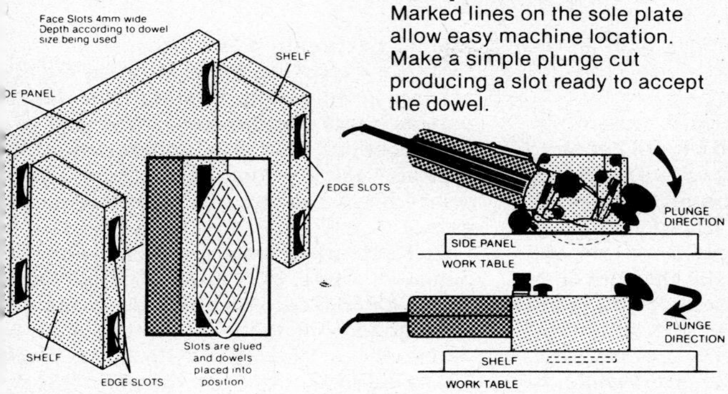

Face Slots 4mm wide
Depth according to dowel size being used

SIDE PANEL
SHELF
EDGE SLOTS
SHELF
EDGE SLOTS
Slots are glued and dowels placed into position

Simple to use

Marked lines on the sole plate allow easy machine location. Make a simple plunge cut producing a slot ready to accept the dowel.

SIDE PANEL
WORK TABLE
PLUNGE DIRECTION

SHELF
WORK TABLE
PLUNGE DIRECTION

How it works

The Elu Flat Dowels are manufactured from Hardwood (Beech) compressed into shape with the grain running diagonally thus providing the strength along its centre. When the dowel is fitted it absorbs the glue resulting in a solid joint. Slots allow the lining up of edges not possible with conventional round dowels.

Standard Equipment:

Steel Carrying Case
Super Hard TCT Grooving Blade
Parallel Guide
Saw Insert
Instruction Book
Special Mitre Guide

FREE!
Special Guide for slotting mitred edges

More information:

The ELU DS140 and Dowels are readily available from a nationwide network of over 200 authorised distributors. Contact us today for your free illustrated brochure and full list of Elu dealers.

Elu Machinery Ltd.,
310-312 Dallow Road,
LUTON,
Beds. LU1 1SS.
Tel: (0582) 425001
Telex: 825540 ELU G.

Elu INTERNATIONAL

Up a gum tree?

From: T. G. Holden, Witney, Oxon

I have a tree in my garden *Eucalyptus gunnii* which seems to have been killed by the winter's frosts. The trunk has a diameter of about eight inches. Is the wood likely to be of any use for cabinet purposes or turning? If so, how should I treat it. I can keep it in stick in a dry garage.

This is rather difficult to answer since the particular species is not thought of too highly as a wood producer. However, we will give an opinion. *Eucalyptus gunnii* is a native of Tasmania where it grows in the sub-alpine area and therefore, is considered quite hardy. Where it has been planted here, as a specimen tree, it has frequently shown itself to be capable of resisting very severe winter weather, in fact, to quote one report, 'It was badly frosted and grew up again in four separate stems joining at ground level. The girth of the main trunk is 20 feet, and the height is 55 feet approximately.' Again, H. J. Elwes, writing in 1912 speaks of a tree 'planted in an exposed situation, in light sandy soil – and is quite uninjured by wind or frost.' Since you say your tree 'seems' to have been killed, our first suggestion is to leave it for a couple of months and see if it recovers. So far as the wood of this species is concerned, it appears never to have been exploited in Tasmania; it may have a limited local use as firewood. This does not mean to say, however, that a sound bole of reasonable size grown here has no use. If you do cut down the tree, the wood must be dried slowly and carefully under restraint; in other words well weighted down. *Eucalyptus* wood generally, and there are many species, is refractory and in Australia, where the more commercial species of the genus are found, it is the practice to kiln dry the wood and then recondition it by a separate process. You cannot do this but what you should do is to decide on the actual sizes you want and cut these when the wood is green, in other words do not attempt to resaw the dried wood into other sizes. The wood tends to split so the ends of the green sections should be protected and not allowed to dry out too quickly. The wood is greyish-white and rather coarse-grained, not unlike plain oak. The well-known Tasmanian 'oak' is a eucalypt as you probably know, but a different species.

Is it of value?

From: L. Elkington, Doncaster, S. Yorks

I have recently felled a pear and a holly tree so I would be obliged if you could answer the following queries. The pear tree trunk is approx 18in diameter, 7ft long and in good condition, the holly approx 6in in diameter and 6ft long.

Is the timber of any use for furniture making eg table tops, drawer fronts, turned objects?

How should I proceed to season the trunks? I have no outbuildings in which to store it.

Has it any value as it is at the moment and therefore should I dispose of it rather than involve myself in seasoning it with all the attendant risks?

Both pear and holly wood is potentially valuable but the logs need careful handling because pear dries slowly with a tendency to warp and holly tends to split badly at the ends when dried in the round. The large diameter of the pear suggests the tree was over-mature and if this is the case not all of the wood is necessarily sound; you could check this visually on the end grain and physically by probing with a sharp tool. However, it will be quite impossible to season the pear log in its present dimensions and the ideal way would be to saw it lengthwise through the pith and then decide, on the strength of the quality revealed, into what other convenient sizes the wood could be reduced in order for it to be dried in the open air, in stick. If this is not practicable, then the log could be offered to a suitable buyer, but in the meantime, the log should be raised off the ground because with the advent of warmer weather, beetles and fungi could attack a log that was left lying directly on the ground or in wet grass.

Pear wood is pinkish-brown in colour, of smooth, even texture, and if large enough can be used for cabinets or occasional furniture, otherwise for carving, turnery and fancy goods. Holly is suitable for turnery, inlay, fancy articles and as a substitute for boxwood or, if stained black, as a substitute for ebony.

As mentioned, the wood does tend to split and it is generally desirable to saw the wood lengthwise and dry the half logs in the open air, in stick, with something heavy on top to keep the pieces flat. If you do not want to do that, then we suggest you place the log on end, in a shady outdoor spot, turning it periodically end for end. With reasonable air flow round the log, a year or so would bring it to condition but much depends on circumstances.

Matching furniture

From: E. G. Yates, Ollerton, Newark

I have been asked to make a dining table with a finish to match the reddish brown colour of reproduction mahogany furniture. I intend to use Brazilian mahogany for the construction. Can you tell me how to achieve the correct colour?

A certain amount of experimenting on waste wood from the job in hand is always advisable to ensure achieving the desired colour. Stains may be divided into three main categories: water, spirit and oil. Water stains are the simplest to use but they have the disadvantage of raising the grain. To avoid this the work should be damped with warm water prior to staining and allowed to dry. This swells the grain fibres which are then smoothed with fine garnet paper. When the stain is applied the fibres will swell to a lesser extent, if at all. The most popular water stain for mahogany is made by dissolving 2ozs bichromate of potash in a pint of water and is applied with a brush. Daylight and a free circulation of air are needed to enable the chemical action to take place.

Another pleasing stain is made by dissolving burnt sienna in stale beer. Polish houses supply bichromate of potash and burnt sienna. They also supply mahogany crystals which colour beech, deal, American whitewood, etc. to look like mahogany.

Spirit stains are made by dissolving one ounce of stain in a pint of methylated spirits. Bismark brown prepared in this way is a good mahogany stain and can be darkened by adding a little spirit black. These stains do not raise the grain but dry very quickly, so speedy application is essential.

Oil stains obtainable from polish houses are very good and if the mahogany stain is too red for your purpose it can be toned down by adding a little walnut stain.

Bandsaw wheel problems

From: C. W. Hicks, Carmarthen, Dyfed

I recently bought a second hand bandsaw which is in quite reasonable condition apart from the two wheels which ought to be re-rubbered. Is there any way I can do this myself?

I understand I could use cork strip glued to the wheels but I do not know how successful this would be and I should very much appreciate your comments.

A few years ago I had the same problem so can advise: that I received quotes ranging from £7-£10 per wheel for retyring 12in wheels. This set me back somewhat, so being a man of ingenuity (or so I am often told) I sought to find my own method.

I took one of the wheels to a local Rubber Stockist, M/S Rubber & Plastic Industries Ltd, 20, Broad St, Wolverhampton, West Midlands, and told them I wanted two bands of rubber 1¼in wide (width of my wheels) × ³⁄₁₆in thick × circumference of the wheel, and that the joint must be vulcanised. The rubber I chose to illustrate was about as hard, or nearly as hard as heels fitted to shoes.

In just a few seconds two strips of rubber were cut though the assistant informed me they did not vulcanise, my hopes were dashed, my idea would not work I thought. The strips were then cut to length, say about ½in less then the wheel circumference, to give a slightly stretched fit that is. A small bottle was produced and a smear of clear liquid applied to one surface, the two ends were brought together end and, 'hey presto', a joint almost as quick as that. That was my first encounter with 'instant glue'. I was astounded but overjoyed to say the least.

Having removed the old tyres I cleaned the wheel surfaces with coarse emery cloth, next was to fit the new tyres. I coated both the inner surface of the tyre and the cleaned wheel surface with Evo-Stick, but before putting on the new tyre I wrapped the wheel circumference with a strip of polythene which of course isolated the glued surfaces and allowed me to line up the tyre with the wheel. All that remained was to pull the polythene strip from between the wheel and the tyre.

Woodworker's Question Box

Write to: Question Box
Woodworker
PO Box 35
Bridge Street
Hemel Hempstead HP1 1EE

Timber advice
From: K. Richards, Welling, Kent

As a newcomer to *Woodworker* I would appreciate some advice. I am considering building some bedroom furniture eg wardrobes and chest of drawers in solid pine. Could you recommend the best type (fairly knot free) and tell me if it is available made up in board sizes eg 8 × 2ft, and the names of any local timber merchants who may supply it.

Woodworker is unable to recommend specific timber suppliers but many advertise within the pages of the magazine and you should find one relatively near to you. When you approach your selected merchant do tell him of the project you have in mind and seek his advice. It is possible he will allow you to select your own boards and thus you will be able to pick the best.

There are two species of pine that might suit your requirements though neither will be available in 24in widths and you will have to butt joint the boards to make up the required size. Parana pine is available in 12in wide boards up to 20ft in length. This timber is clean and easy to work, taking a good finish. However, it can prove unstable in conditions where temperature and humidity vary – such as partially heated bedrooms. Russian red pine is usually available in 9in and 11in widths with lengths up to 20ft.

Ask for joinery quality which will be generally knot free and clear of defects. It is a softer wood than parana pine but more reliable and stable. Russian pine is sometimes referred to by its point of export such as Kara Sea, Leningrad and Archangel and labelled as 'unsorted'.

Bending guitar ribs
From: M. Foden, Southport, Merseyside

I wonder if you could assist me with a query concerning the moisture content of timber. As I understand it, timber is 'air dried' to approx. 15-18% moisture content and 'kiln dried' to maybe 9-10% m.c. When these conditions have been achieved the cells which contained moisture have dried out and closed up. If the wood is subsequently wetted eg by immersing in water or leaving out in the rain, am I correct in assuming that the cells do not fill up with water again and that it is only the fibres of the wood that are wetted and these can be dried out again by the application of heat to revert to the original moisture content very quickly? These assumptions are based upon facts gleaned from a guitar construction manual. Mahogany or rosewood pieces are air dried and then kilned to a very low m.c. When required for use the timber is soaked in water to assist in bending the sides to shape. I can't believe that years of careful air and kiln drying are ruined by thoroughly saturating the timber for a couple of hours. Am I right in assuming that when the sides have been bent to shape they can be quickly dried out to their original low m.c.?

Your assumption regarding moisture in wood is reasonably correct: air dried wood is not ready for immediate use for wood goods to be installed in warm, dry rooms, so it must be dried further in a kiln or similar device. As you may know, the critical stage in seasoning is the fibre saturation point (FSP), that is when all the moisture has been removed from the cell cavities and only the walls are saturated. This is the point when wood begins to shrink and it occurs at a value of between 25 and 30 per cent moisture content. You will also appreciate that at this level, the wood has a degree of plasticity. If a kiln dried piece of wood is at say, 10 per cent m.c., it has lost some of its plasticity and if an attempt is made to bend it, it will tend to fracture on the tension side of the bend and buckle on the compression side. To restore plasticity to some degree, moisture must be put back into the wood to raise its m.c. back to near the FSP and this is usually best achieved by subjecting the wood to saturated steam or by placing the wood in warm, wet sand.

When the wood is now bent, the tension and compression areas are protected by straps in the former or jig. If you now apply this thinking to your reference to soaking the guitar ribs in water for a couple of hours it should be obvious that only the outer skin of the wood is likely to be thoroughly wetted, not the entire thickness, since dry wood takes a very long time to become thoroughly saturated. However, this could be sufficient to offset the fracturing and buckling tendencies when the wood was bent, and it would take less time to dry the wood out again. In the manufacture of a guitar, the ribs are not so critical in terms of tone as the belly and back. Accordingly they can be divorced, so to speak, from the main production techniques. Provided the wood is dry enough to be bonded to the blocks, the ribs can be produced in a variety of ways. They can be laminated from veneers directly in the jig, they can be dry bent from plywood routed out on the inner side and bent round the blocks; made from specially produced cross-grained plywood bent round the blocks with or without the use of saw kerfs, or they can be steam or otherwise bent from solid wood. There is no insuperable problem created if moisture is introduced into the rib making; it can be dried out afterwards. Steam bent ash tennis racket frames are easily dried so guitar ribs can be dried similarly.

Smelly not tasty
From: R. J. Farthing, Pontypool, Gwent

Having made a pine bread bin for my daughter in law and sealed it with polyurethane, she now complains that the bread smells and tastes of pine wood. Could you advise me on how to rectify this?

Pine is a highly resinous wood and will retain its distinctive smell for a considerable time, particularly when it has been made into a closed container such as a bread bin. Although it is not possible to entirely eliminate the smell, it can be reduced by washing much of the resin from the surface of the wood. A rag soaked in white spirit is wiped along the grain to thin the resin. This will remove some resin and will thin the remainder, driving it back into the wood fibres. Most pine furniture is sprayed with cellulose to give it a clear protective finish. This will probably give a better finish than a polyurethane varnish and if you obtain brushing cellulose from a polish supplier and add about 25% thinners it should brush on evenly.

Apple, pear and plum
From: A. Collis, Basildon, Essex

I have some fruit tree logs which have recently been felled. They are on average about 3ft in girth and consist of apple, pear and plum. Could you please tell me the best way to season these without a kiln, ready for hand woodcarving and when could I get to work using this timber?

Logs three feet in girth are about one foot in diameter, which means there is quite a lot of wood to dry per foot of length. You do not give their length or the number of logs, but you could think around several ways. You could stand each log on end, with its butt raised slightly off the ground and its top resting against something substantial, but this assumes that each log will have a reasonable air flow round each piece. If you did this, each log ought to be turned, end for end each week or fortnight in order to equalise the drying throughout the length and to reduce the tendency for the ends to open up.

Alternatively, you could stack the logs lengthwise, with good air spaces, but this would increase the tendency for end splits to develop so each end would need protecting by means of a water resistant seal eg bituminous paint, aluminium sealer, or proprietary end sealing compound. Under these conditions you would probably have to wait until this time next year before you could make any attempt to break into the wood and even then the centres would still be relatively wet. If it were possible and desirable to saw the logs lengthwise, through the pith, and you should note this is not necessarily dead centre, the drying time would not only be considerably shortened, end splitting would also be very much reduced. The half rounds would then be stacked, in stick.

Do not remove the bark from the logs whichever method you employ; when this cracks or peels it is one indicator that the wood is drying and, of course, it does slow down the drying through the outsides of the logs which is helpful. If you can get the wood drying quickly now, by the end of October you could try a couple of pieces in your workshop or wherever you want to do your carving. We do not know the air conditions of this area, but bearing in mind that you can carve dampish wood more easily than you can very dry wood, and the wood itself could lose quite a lot of excess moisture if carving took days or weeks rather than hours, it is not essential for the initial block to be more than air dry, say 16-18% m.c. This, of course, is a fairly tall order for thick stock to be that dry in the centres, but if drying is started off now, only by experiment will you know when the stock is ready.

Letters

From: Betty Norbury, White Knight Gallery, Cheltenham
Dear Sir

May I take advantage of your letters column to say a very sincere thank-you to all those people who have helped to make Masterclass '82 a very memorable occasion. Since I have returned to Cheltenham after the exhibition people have written or called to see me to say how much they enjoyed the speakers and the free exchange of knowledge and expertise given by the demonstrators. My thanks also to the exhibitors who brought their work from all corners of the country, and to the stewards who gave freely of their time to watch over these beautiful pieces, not forgetting the lady who arranged the flowers which enhanced them.

I hope they all feel they have contributed to a unique event and have benefited from the experience.

Yours faithfully, **Betty Norbury**

From: P. M. Vernon, Lytham St Annes, Lancs
Dear Sir

re Worksheet 10 New Series

With regard to the wall bracket described in the above published in your magazine dated March '82, I have to bring to your notice a number of points which electrically are potentially dangerous, and do not comply with the regulations for the electrical equipment of buildings.

(a) The brass lampholder should be earthed – regulation D1 to D6. If the case of the lampholder should become live a person touching the lampholder and an earthed object at the same time s ,y, solid floor, another earthed appliance or a radiator, they would receive a severe shock.

(b) The connections in the back of the bracket should be housed in a non combustible surround, regulation B78 and F10. All cables should terminate in a metal or plastic box.

(c) The fixing holes are in such a position that anybody drilling the wall for the fixings will pierce the cable feeding the point.

I enclose a sketch showing a modification which complies with the regulations.

Yours faithfully, **P. M. Vernon**
Electrical Contracting Engineer (retired).

From: W. A. Gidley, Tewkesbury, Glos
Dear Sir

Further to the subject of motor conversion (reply to C. J. Allen, April 1982). I would feel that it may be pertinent to point out a few engineering constraints upon the use of any electrical motor.

Many types of AC and DC machines are manufactured but for high power use two types predominate: 1. The squirrel cage induction motor, either three-phase or single-phase capacitor start motors. 2. The series-wound universal motor which has a commutator and brushes. This type of motor will operate from either AC or DC.

The induction motor is generally of sturdy construction, quiet in operation, and very reliable requiring little maintenance. This type of motor is most suitable for saws, lathes, pillar drills etc. The series-wound universal motor is small, noisy by comparison to the induction motor, but has high starting torque and can be made to operate

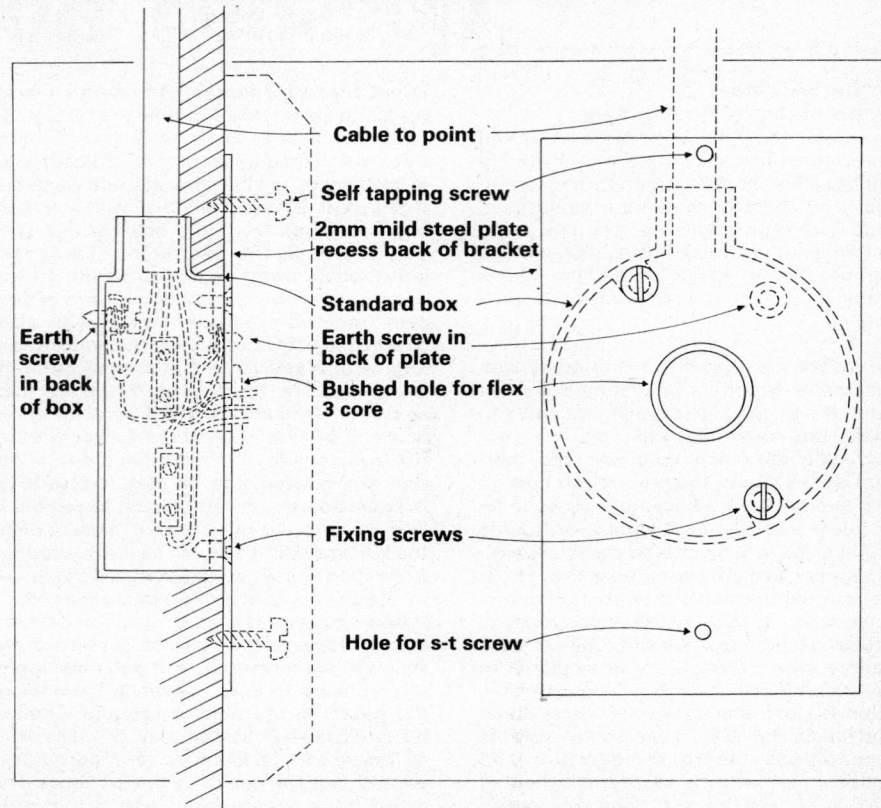

● *Modification to electrical connections for wall bracket worksheet 10 new series (see Mr Vernon's letter)*

at high rotational speeds. The brushes and commutator of this type of motor require regular inspection and maintenance. The universal motor is extensively used in portable power tools.

A crucial factor in the successful operation of any motor is the dissipation of the waste heat from the electrical windings. An efficiency of approximately 50% can be expected from a motor. It can be noted from advertisements that induction motors are rated for OUTPUT power whilst universal motors are rated by INPUT power.

C. J. Allen's motor sounds to be of the universal type both from the rating of 750 watts input power and the previous application. An efficiency of 50% indicates that 375 watts of heat are generated during operation. In vacuum cleaners the motor drives a large fan in whose draught the motor operates. Consequently a powerful torrent of air is used to cool the armature and starter windings. The armature can therefore be designed to be small and have little 'in hand' as far as heat dissipation is concerned. For this reason a fan must be included in the construction of the motor assembly. Also for safety reasons, the motor must be shrouded to electrically isolate the operator from the live brushes and commutator. This shrouding must be designed to maximise the cooling effects of the fan.

A guide to the maximum diameter of saw blade to use could be gleaned from hand-held power saw advertisements and data. These units employ universal motors.

In conclusion, there is no reason why the

motor cannot be used, however, the more suitable motor would be an induction motor of suitable output power (say ¾hp).

I hope that this information may be of some use.

Yours faithfully, **W. A. Gidley, BSc Electrical Engineering**

From: Geoffrey Luff, Bourgueil, France
Dear Sir

I was surprised to see your article in the April issue about the Welsh puzzle table belonging to Mr T. Charles-Edwards.

The joint is in fact a mortise and tenon joint and I come across it quite frequently in the restoration of table tops of early French tables of the Louis XIII period, in oak or cherry. But where I have seen it most is in the construction of 17th and 18th century doors. I remember one particular door which was so weather beaten that the wood had worn away leaving the joint apparent, the dowels still holding the oak inset in position. This door was an outside door of oak four centimetres thick and made up of six or seven vertical planks tongue and grooved together with the addition of these joints for each plank at the bottom, middle and top of the door.

As for the butterfly wood inlay this is probably one of the oldest ways of preventing two pieces of wood from separating and in the days before glue was used was very common. I have seen it on many 17th, 18th and 19th century pieces of furniture, especially table tops, chest tops and wardrobe door panels.

Yours faithfully, **Geoffrey Luff**

THE MAGAZINE FOR THE CRAFTSMAN

SEPTEMBER 1982 Vol 86 No 1066 ISSN 0043 776X

Front cover: Bench-top scene in Ralph Williams' Berkhamsted workshop. Story pp 586/7.

Editor	Chris Dunn
Deputy Editor	Polly Curds
Advertisement Manager	Glyn Crole-Rees

MEMBER OF THE AUDIT BUREAU OF CIRCULATIONS

SUBSCRIPTION DEPARTMENT: Remittances to MODEL AND ALLIED PUBLICATIONS, PO Box 35, Hemel Hempstead, Herts HP1 1EE. Price per copy 95p includes p&p. Subscription queries: Tel: Hemel Hempstead 51740. Subscription rate, including index, £11.90 per annum; overseas sterling £12.90; $29.00 US for overseas dollar subscribers. Second class postage paid in US at New York, New York. *Distribution* to North American hobby and craft stores, museums and bookshops by Bill Dean Books Ltd, 166-41 Powells Cove Boulevard, Post Office Box 69, Whitestone, New York 11357, USA. Tel: 1-212-767-6632. *Distribution* to news stand sales by Eastern News Distribution Inc, 111 Eight Avenue, New York, NY10011, USA Tel: 1-212-255-5620. (POSTMASTER: Send address changes to England).

WOODWORKER is printed in Great Britain by H. E. Warne Ltd, East Hill, St Austell, Cornwall PL25 4TN for the proprietor and publisher Model & Allied Publications Ltd (a member of the Argus Press Group). Trade sales by Argus Press Sales & Distribution Ltd, 12-18 Paul Street, London EC2A 4JS. WOODWORKER (ISSN 0043-776X) is published on the 3rd Friday of the month.

Model & Allied Publications Ltd

PO Box 35, Bridge Street, Hemel Hempstead, Herts HP1 1EE. Telephone: Hemel Hempstead (0442) 41221.

Show starters

There aren't many people around who are older than *Woodworker*, now in its 82nd year, but it may be significant that one of the woodwork world's most eminent figures, Charles Hayward, pre-dates the first issue of this magazine by a year or two.

As you will probably know, Charles Hayward edited *Woodworker* for more than a quarter of a century and its fine reputation among serious craftsmen is founded not least on its long partnership with a craftsman and writer of Mr Hayward's standing.

From his early life as an apprentice cabinetmaker in London, he rose to become the country's most prolific commentator on the craft of woodwork, both through his work as editor of *Woodworker* and his books on pretty well every aspect of the craft, which have become standard text books forming about half the total library of works on the subject.

So it is with great personal delight that, as a successor to Charles Hayward in the editor's chair here at *Woodworker,* I can announce that the man himself is to officially open this year's Woodworker Show for us, to be held in London from October 19-24.

But Charles Hayward is not the only big name to be involved with this year's show. Alan Peters, a former Edward Barnsley workshop apprentice who is now one of the top craftsmen among English furniture makers, is to take part as a judge in the new class for young professional woodworkers, while the turning classes will be assessed by Cecil Jordan as one of the judges, alongside another top name in the wood-turning field, Ray Key.

Many will know Richard Blizzard, who has popularised toymaking almost to the point of national hysteria, it seems, by his television appearances and books on his subject. Richard will be with us for the show, judging the toys and miniatures class, and other eminent names among the judges this year are John Sainsbury, Ian Norbury, Charlie Good, Ernie Ives and John Thompson.

I hope that you are looking forward to the Woodworker Show as much as I am. It is my first as editor of this magazine, and I expect the occasion to provide plenty of opportunity for meeting readers and hearing your comments and suggestions on how we can make *Woodworker* an even better read each month. Do make a point of calling in on the *Woodworker* stand. Either my deputy, Polly Curds, or myself will be on hand throughout the six days of the show, and a welcome is assured for anyone who cares to drop in.

Chris Dunn

September notes

Disc-belt sander

The Dremel model 738 disc-belt sander is now available through Microflame of Diss, Norfolk. Supplied with two 30in sanding belts and a 5in sanding disc, the 738 can be used for a variety of work from rough sanding hard wood and plastics to grinding metal or achieving a fine finish. To achieve angled sanding, the machine's sanding disc is equipped with a 45° tilting table and adjustable mitre gauge.

Mini plans

Makers of miniature furniture may be interested to know that a wide range of plans for one-twelfth scale furniture, designed by Ken and Margaret Varney, are available from MAP's plans service. Many classic designs from originals by the great furniture makers of the 18th century are included.

Further details from MAP Plans, PO Box 35, Bridge Street, Hemel Hempstead.

● *Quick action clamp for use in awkward places. See 'new clamp'*

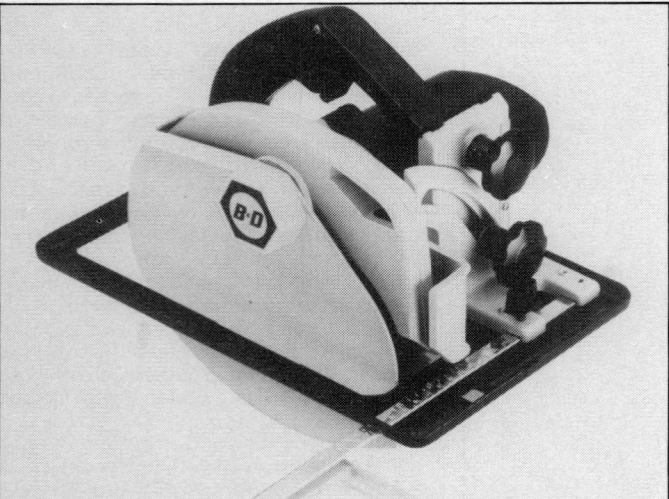

● *Circular saw from Black & Decker industrial tools. See 'new range'*

New range

Black & Decker have extended their industrial range of power tools by the addition of twelve new products. They are: industrial rotary hammer (22, 32 and 38mm), heavy duty morse taper drills (23 and 32mm), general duty drill (10mm variable speed), general duty percussion drills (13mm 2-speed and 13mm 2-speed variable), universal planer (82mm), bodygrip angle grinder (125mm), end handle angle grinder (125mm) and heavy duty circular saw (184mm).

T-square saw fence

Sumaco chose IWIE 82 to introduce the Biesemeyer T-square saw fence which it is claimed improves cutting productivity over conventional saw fence systems. Engaged to a guide rail only at the front of the table, the unit's fence can be moved to any desired distance from the blade and locked into position. A hairline pointer, secured to the fence, indexes against a scale on the guide rail to ensure accuracy up to $\frac{1}{64}$in. Components incorporate two L-shaped support brackets, guide rail, fence, shoe, clamping mechanism and indexing system.

Sumaco claim a single action handle locks the fence to give $\frac{1}{64}$in accuracy every time. Further details from the company at Suma House, Huddersfield Road, Elland, W. Yorks HX5 9AA (phone 0422 79811).

New clamp

A new patented quick-action clamp is now being marketed by Trend Machinery and Cutting Tools, Unit N, Penfold Works, Imperial Way, Watford, Herts. It has two useful features – speed of clamping and the ability to be used in remote and awkward corners.

To engage the clamp, the lower jaw is slid up the pillar to grip the workpiece lightly. A half turn of the lever handle on the upper jaw completes the tightening process, clamping the workpiece securely in position.

The patented feature of the clamp is the eccentric cam located in the upper jaw, which when actuated by means of the lever handle, exerts pressure on the workpiece to hold it tightly in position.

Clamps are available from stock in three sizes, with maximum openings from 150mm to 400mm and with a common maximum throat depth of 80mm. Prices are from £9.70 to £10.50 (plus VAT).

● *Win this challenge cup and replica trophy from Microflame UK. How? Enter this year's power tool carving competition at the Woodworker Show. Subject 'The Fox' open to your interpretation in any timber, longest overall dimension 9in*

Attention luthiers!

Musical instrument makers will probably be interested to hear about a quarterly publication entitled *International Luthiers News*. The aim of this magazine and newsletter, published by A. Highfield and Co, Rosewood House, Bridge Road, Downham Market, Norfolk, is to provide an information exchange and discussion forum for instrument makers both professional and amateur.

It is a non-profit-making venture run solely for the benefit of craftsmen who care about high standards.

Recent acquisition

The Victoria and Albert museum announce one of their latest acquisitions… an Austrian writing desk and chair designed by Koloman Moser in 1903 and made in the workshops of Caspar Hrazdil. This elaborate desk with its 'disappearing chair' is a fascinating mixture of Empire Revival and modern Austrian forms. Moser was one of the leading innovators of the Austrian Arts and Crafts movement; Hrazdil appears to have made mainly Empire and Biedermeier Revival pieces rather than the more advanced furniture of Moser and his associates in the Vienna Werkstätte group.

Treasures in wood

Historic pieces of carved woodwork will form part of a forthcoming exhibition at Gunnersbury Park Museum, Brentford. Due to open on December 11, it will run for seven weeks, and has been in preparation for more than a year.

Striking carvings from more than 20 countries, including Poland, will be shown, covering a span of several hundred years. There will also be some virtuoso examples of work by modern master carvers, including Walter Ritchie, who has executed commissions for many public buildings, and Ian Agrell, who carves decorative heads for stringed instruments.

Woodcarving Extravaganza – the title of the exhibition – will be one of the most unusual shows to be staged in the London area for many years. Among its highlights will be a collection of bizarre head-masks from Africa, most of them dating back to before 1850, English Jacobean grotesques, examples of German Gothic, a quartet of very early Indonesian rod puppets, and a number of historic carvings on loan from the British Museum and the Victoria and Albert Museum.

Winners all

The 30th national marquetry exhibition was held at Ipswich this year at the end of May and beginning of June. Membership of the society now stands at over 700 and it is recognised as a leading authority on the craft in all its aspects. It is a non-commercial organisation which exists solely to promote, foster and encourage interest in the craft. Fifteen local groups have now been set up throughout the country to provide meeting places for all those interested in practising the hobby. Active members of the Ipswich society (this year's hosts) range in age from 8-80. As in other group meetings experienced members give tuition to beginners and most groups also stage their own competitions and visit places and firms connected with marquetry.

This year's winners of the intergroup challenge shield were Bexley, second Bristol and third Redbridge. The Jack Byrne cup was awarded to A. G. Chalkley of Bexley (for the best piece of parquetry); the Walter Dolley award went to A. R. Reindorp (best entry from a non-group member); Mr Reindorp also gained the artistic merit award for his picture of Rye Harbour but the coveted prize of best in show — the rose bowl — went to R. G. Shellard of Bristol for his entry entitled long tailed tit. Other first places went to: J. T. Burrell (beginners); P. J. White (secondary); A. R. Reindorp (intermediate); Mrs D. I. Beecher (advanced); R. G. Shellard (premier); R. G. Shellard (miniatures) and J. J. Wilcox (applied).

The catalogue that accompanied the exhibition listed 372 entries. How many I wonder will we see at the Woodworker Show in October? Come on group secretaries, chivvy your members for another effort.

Routing slips

Apologies to all concerned, we got our feet and inches mixed up last month. Page 555 carried details of the new class for Routing Inventions to be added to this year's Woodworker Show classes. Unfortunately under *Mounting Instructions* in the paragraph dealing with non-free standing exhibits the fifth line was incorrect. It should read:-.....8-12mm thick, size in multiples 2ft × 2ft......

We also seem yet again to have mixed up the ISBN for Jim Phillip's book *Techniques of Routing*. Perhaps we can strike third time lucky? The copy in front of me at this moment has ISBN 7198 2840 6 boldly printed onto its pages.

● *This bureau made by Jeremy Higson was judged the best and most faithful copy of a classic item of furniture incorporating a high standard of craftsmanship, at the recent Maples exhibition of work by students at Rycotewood College. It won a prize of £500 for Jeremy in the Maples sponsored competition to encourage young designers*

Krenov moves

James Krenov has moved. Not his own house, but to another publishing house. His sought-after books, *A Cabinetmaker's Notebook* and *Fine Art of Cabinetmaking* have recently become unobtainable, but Van Nostrand Reinhold UK have just announced that these are now available again.

In addition to *Worker in Wood* and *The Impractical Cabinetmaker* Krenov's books make up a useful quartet of publications for the craftsman's library. All are now available from VNR, whose address is Molly Millars Lane, Wokingham, Berks.

Looking up

The British Woodworking Federation's latest state of trade enquiry, covering the first five months of 1982, reveals an improved trading pattern for 95 per cent of the woodworking manufacturing firms canvassed. And half of those member firms expect further improvement over the summer months.

Nevertheless, a number of companies stressed continuing trading difficulties, and were no less concerned about the short duration of many existing contracts as well as the general unpredictability of forward workload prospects.

The improvement in the industry's fortunes, compared with the very depressed levels of 1981, directly reflects the increased activity in new house-building. This, in turn, has reinforced the marked swing towards timber frame housing construction.

Demand for standard joinery in the private sector increased significantly, while in the public sector one third of the firms supplying standard joinery items also reported improved order books. Similarly, the demand for non-standard joinery has been much firmer.

Conversely, the majority of kitchen furniture manufacturers reported very quiet trading conditions during the first five months of the year, but they are hopeful that higher demand will come with the customary seasonal improvement of trade in the autumn.

More over ▶

September notes

Ornamental turners

Under the heading of 'ornamental bulletin' in the *June Notes* we slightly embarrassed the society by painting their bulletin in such glowing colours that many readers wrote to the secretary Phil Holden for a free sample copy.

Phil reminds us that they only print a limited number for members and if there are any to spare they have to be sold at £3.00 each to non-members.

He also tells us that Fred Howe of Hastings, one of the society's founder members and one of the foremost authorities on ornamental turning died in June. He will be missed by all who knew him.

Altendorf distributor

Interwood Ltd of Stafford Avenue, Hornchurch, Essex, has recently been appointed an official distributor for Altendorf's circular sizing saws. Twelve Interwood staff members sailed the North Sea in June on a trip to Altendorf's works in W. Germany to familiarise themselves with the product, and by all accounts they had a useful and enjoyable time.

Vee accurate

Accurate vee grooving can now be successfully accomplished on the range of Wadkin double end tenoning and profiling machines to a guaranteed depth of cut to within 0.05mm.

Operational accuracy is made possible by the introduction of a micro adjustable anvil. This unit is a screw adjustable support fitted to the chain beams and which incorporates a precision dial indicator that measures to within 0.05mm.

Down in price

Nice to hear of prices coming down, instead of the usual up. E. P. Barrus Ltd, have announced reductions in price on many items in their Shapecraft range of aids and power tool accessories.

The new price list, available from Barrus at Launton Road, Bicester, Oxon, shows reductions of up to 50p on items such as cutters for the hand shaper, fluted dowels and wire brushes.

The other news from Barrus is that they have recently landed a lucrative deal to supply their Supercraft range to Japan. This is the company's first export order to that country, and they sound confident that it is just the first of many.

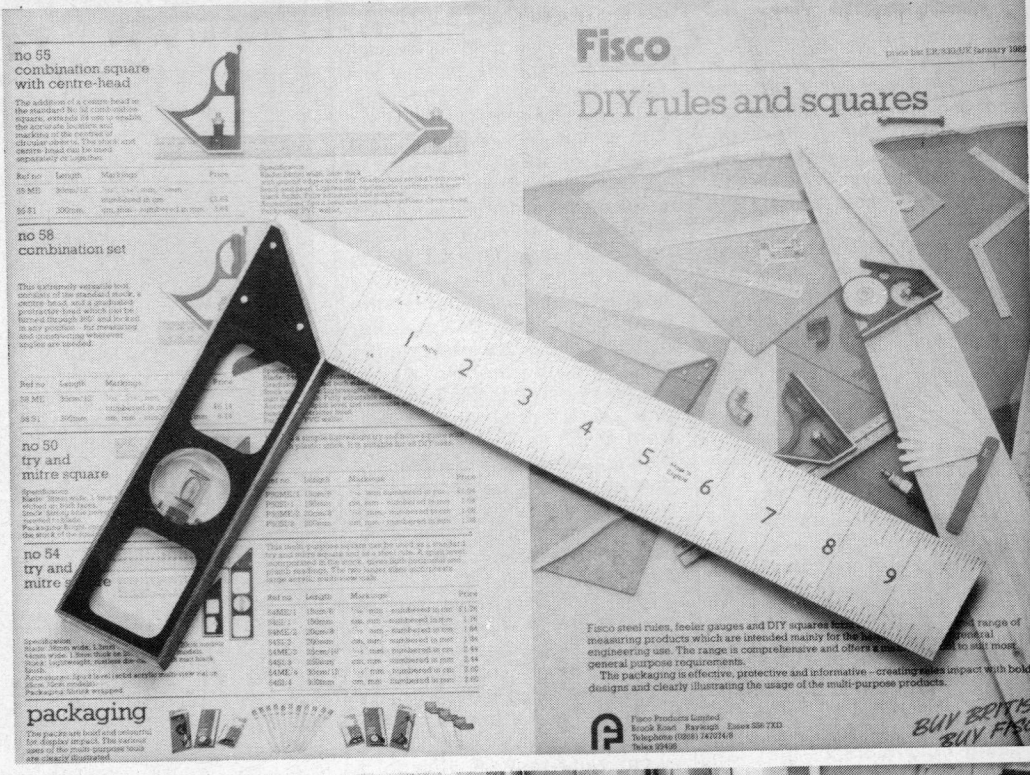

● *Combination squares from Fisco. See 'square deal' for more details*

Square deal

Two new products are featured in a new price list just issued by Fisco Products Limited of Rayleigh, Essex, for their range of steel rules, squares and feeler gauges.

The items are two multi-purpose squares in 25cm/10in and 30cm/12in sizes with a choice of metric and metric/English markings. As well as being accurate try and mitre squares their graduated blades allow them to be used as steel rules. A spirit level in the stock gives both horizontal and plumb readings by means of a large acrylic multi-view vial.

● *See 'hobby time'.*

Hobby time

New items featured in the latest *Hobby's annual* (no 13) include plans and/or kits for a Spanish doll's house, Victorian paddle steamer, pine clock, tug, toy train and a cabinet musical box. The 1983 annual costs 70p and is available from newsagents or direct from W. Hobby Ltd, Knight's Hill Square, London SE27 0HH.

Bending rules

Taking long measurements with a steel rule is often beset by one infuriating problem if you haven't anyone to hold the other end. You run the tape out, and it will stay rigid for just so many feet before, 'peeoing', the tape

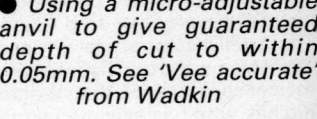

● *Using a micro-adjustable anvil to give guaranteed depth of cut to within 0.05mm. See 'Vee accurate' from Wadkin*

suddenly decides to buckle under its own weight.

This has evidently happened once too often to Fisco Products Ltd of Brook Road, Rayleigh, Essex, because they have now come out with a wider tape rule that promises to cover more distance before the 'peeoing' happens. They call it the Trimatic TW, a heavy duty tape with a 25mm wide blade. The width is said to give 'great elongation without kinking', especially useful for measuring room heights and so on, and the tape will run out to 8m in length.

Chair kits

Emperor Clock Company has introduced a pair of Queen Anne chair kits, the latest offerings in their full line of Queen Anne furniture. The splat back arm and side chairs are made in kiln-dried ¾in cherry. Kits come ready to assemble with pre-shaped cabriole legs and a pre-assembled back.

The Emperor Queen Anne furniture line includes a secretary, writing desk, commode table, end table and coffee table. For free information, write to Emperor Clock Company, Emperor Industrial Park, Fairope, Alabama, USA.

Punchy promotion

Henry Cooper OBE KSG will be appearing personally on the Cooper Tools stand at the International Hardware & Housewares Trades Fair, Olympia on Monday 6 September to launch a 10% discount off normal trade prices of selected Weller soldering irons and guns, Lufkin short tapes and Plumb hammers. Purchase of one of these products will entitle the purchaser to a special offer of a Henry Cooper sports bag for £4.75. New products in the Nicholson range will also be unwrapped at the HTF.

Database: Timber

The UK market for timber is analysed in one of the Database series of reports published by Marketing Strategies for Industry (UK) Ltd. The report studies a number of products including softwoods, hardwoods, particle boards, plywood and fibre boards. The bulk of the report contains a profile of the timber markets giving both historical data and projections. This 55pp report contains 17 tables and is available from 22 Wates Way, Mitcham CR4 4HR for £25.00.

Official Catalogue

The Italian Woodworking Machinery and Machine Tool Manufacturers Association (ACIMALL) is a nation-wide organisation aimed at distributing quality Italian woodworking tools the world over. 80 companies belong to the organisation accounting for a turnover of 85 per cent of the total national figure. Their official catalogue devotes two pages to each company, a classified product index (in 5 languages for easy reference) is included plus an alphabetical list of members. The 1982 edition is edition 10 of the catalogue and more information can be obtained from the association at Centro Commerciale Milanofiori, 1ª Strada, Palazzo F3, 20094 ASSAGO Milan.

Brisklathe for Marlin

The United States range of Marlin woodcarving machines are being handled by Brisklathe Ltd of Folkestone, Kent. Marlin state the kit or woodcarver package comes complete with letters for house signs, router and cutters plus a marketing plan for starting up your own sign business. Price of the package is high at £917 plus VAT. Brisklathe still manufactures their full range of engraving machines and all enquiries should be addressed to them at 108 Royal Military Avenue, Cheriton, Folkestone CT20 3EJ.

● *Business end of the Trimatic TW. See 'bending rules'*

● *Queen Anne side chair from the Emperor Clock Company. See 'chair kits'*

● *This decorated dovecote is a feature at the open air folk museum at Glentleiten in Bavaria south of Munich. It was spotted by David Askham who says it dates from 1854 and has decorated eaves, painted shuttered windows and balconies reflecting local domestic architecture. The inhabitants were away when the picture was taken.*

Guild notes

Courses in design and furniture making

The piece shown here requires care in design as well as care in making. Do you need help with your designs? Would you like to be able to produce furniture of this quality on a short course?

A three day course to attempt to give craftsmen a knowledge of and an ability to

● *Well designed chair by a Rycote-wood student*

design through largely practical work has been arranged at Rycotewood College, Thame, Oxon on 7-9 September.

The course will consist of small lecture inputs prior to practical workshop projects to develop the craftsman's understanding and use of design when working with wood and to develop the sensitivity of detailing incorporating the basic principles of working.

A full programme of the course content will be sent to course participants. Apologies that it has been delayed and is not printed here as promised. The cost is £69 inc VAT which covers full board and accommodation, morning coffee and afternoon tea, all lecture fees and practical instruction for the full 3 days.

Materials for the course will be available at cost, many varieties of timbers will be available for selection and naturally these will vary in price (a rosewood chair will be dearer than an ash or elm one for example!).

Rycotewood College has gained a reputation as one of the top three colleges in the country giving students a basic training in cabinetmaking skills, the relevant technology, design skills, and projects which include commissioned furniture design and making, antique furniture restoration and industrial product model making. The college believes that the versatility of its graduates should ensure that whatever happens in the crafts world they will be able to adapt to changing needs.

Basic one-day routing course

On our August pages we advised guild members of a one-day practical course on basic routing techniques to be run on Saturday 30 October. We promised a full course programme this issue and have been able to fulfil our promise.

Course duration: 9.30am-5.30pm, date 30 October 1982.

Course content:

1 Basic principles of the router
2 How to set up the router
3 Choice of cutters
4 Basic routing applications
5 Use of standard accessories
6 Home made accessories and devices for routing
7 Use of templates
8 Practical demonstrations and teach-in on routing techniques with emphasis on grooving, moulding, jointing, carving, dovetailing, trimming plastics and 'router lathe' work
9 Care and maintenance of both router and cutters
10 Question time and discussion

Breaks for refreshments and a mid-day buffet will occur at suitable points during the course.

Cost: Tuition fees, refreshments and mid-day buffet are all included in the cost of £25 (inc VAT).

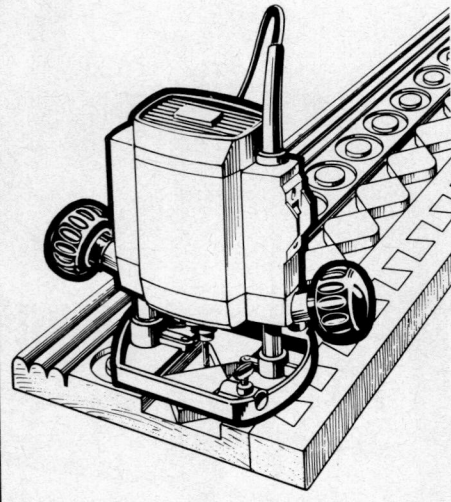

Venue: The Trend Machinery Centre, Watford, which is situated on the Penfold Works Estate. Nearest mainline/tube Watford Junction, by car, turn off the M1 at junction 5 into the A41. Full details can be supplied to course participants and those having difficulty reaching the venue can be collected from Watford and adjoining areas if necessary.

There will be a good participant/demonstrator ratio maintained at this course so that individual tuition can be given. For places and further information contact Polly Curds at the usual *Woodworker* address.

Insurance

Remember our guild insurance cover runs from October to October each year. Premiums relate to a full year or any part thereof. The limit of £500 is still being offered at an unchanged premium of £5.00 per annum; alternative cover of £1,000 is also available at £12.50 per annum or part thereof.

Two-day non-residential course on finishing

We have moved north of London for the latest in our courses aimed at improving the skills of guild members in polishing and finishing.

A two-day course has been arranged for guild members on 23 and 24 August 1982 at Aldenham School, Elstree, Herts. The course starts at 10.00am each day and will end about 4.30pm with an hour for lunch. Refreshments which are not included in the course fee can be obtained from a nearby pub.

As usual the course is restricted to six to permit individual instruction to be given under the following headings: materials, preparation of surfaces, staining (water and spirit), filling and making fillers, bodying-up, spiriting-off, acid and eggshell finishes, repolishing and waxing.

Cost of the two day course is £32.00 for each member inc VAT. This does not include lunch and is non-residential. Applications should be sent as soon as possible, together with the remittance for the total of £32 to the guild administrator, PO Box 35 Bridge Street, Hemel Hempstead HP1 1EE. Aldenham School is situated between Radlett and Elstree and if necessary course members could be picked up from either main line station.

Timber, timber

Following our *crie de coeur* in the last issue of Guild Notes for a supplier of exotic hardwoods north of Watford, we are delighted to have received in today's post a timber price list and note from Alan Holtham.

Alan is one of our regular advertisers in *Woodworker* and as a wood turner and forestry graduate knows what he is talking about when it comes to timber supplies. We had hesitated to say 'go to Alan' when the problem arose as we did not want to give him marketing difficulties, however he says: 'I am glad to send either by carrier or post, large, small or very small quantities'.

He has supplied a list with prices in pence per cubic inch or per kilo, and says he stocks a large selection of turning and carving blanks cut to size, but will be pleased to cut to individual requirements. Exotics are normally available in 1in., 2in. and 3in. thickness. Timber collected in plank form is eligible for a quantity discount and though customers are encouraged to make their own personal selection, carrier or post can be used at cost over longer distances.

I know I am well satisfied with the rosewood I bought from Alan at last year's Woodworker Show. His stock now includes black walnut, padauks, beefwood, bubinga, ebony, kingwood, pau bruna, purple heart, satinwood, shedua and tulipwood among others.

Alan can be found at The Old Stores Turnery, Willaston, Cheshire or on Crewe 67010.

Entry forms Woodworker Show competitions

Competition entry forms can also be obtained from the exhibitions manager. They should be completed and returned by Friday, 3 September.

Events

Advance tickets
Woodworker Show

Advance tickets can be obtained from the Exhibitions Manager, PO Box 35, Bridge Street, Hemel Hempstead HP1 1EE. Guild members' admission charges are £1.75 for adults and £1.25 for juniors and senior citizens. Proof of guild membership will be required to obtain this discount.

Courses galore

The autumn and the long winter months creep up on us and now while the summer sun is shining is the time to plan what to do to occupy our minds and hands.

Why not take a course to improve skills, learn new ones or to just enjoy the company of other like-minded people, other woodworkers, other guild members?

With these thoughts in mind we have tried to arrange a varied programme for you.

Ties

Guild neckties are available in green with two narrow gold-coloured 'bandings' between which is the guild badge also gold-coloured. Ties are £3.50 each inclusive of VAT, postage and packing. Members requiring a tie should send a cheque or crossed postal order together with their guild number and address to the administrator at the usual *Woodworker* address.

Applications

For places on all the courses detailed on these pages and any other guild information write to:
Polly Curds
Guild Administrator
PO Box 35,
Bridge Street,
Hemel Hempstead, HP1 1EE
Please enclose a sae with all correspondence anticipating a reply.

At Birmingham

Free demonstration of furniture restoration by Tom Thay, which will include wood available for sale, will be held on 4 September from 12 noon to 5 pm at Spock Woodcarvings, 810 Bristol Road, Birmingham B29 6NA

Making it

An exhibition in which David Poston, Pauline Solven and Janice Tchalenko review their careers in the crafts and introduce the work of 18 young makers. To be held until 12 September (Tuesday-Saturdays 10-5 pm, Thursdays until 7 pm and Sundays 2-5 pm, closed Mondays) admission free, at the Crafts Council Gallery, 12 Waterloo Place, Lower Regent Street, London.

British Crafts Show

The 1982 show will feature the work of over 150 craftspeople at Syon Park, Brentford, Middx from 16-19 September (Thursday-Sunday). Open from 10-6 pm (Sunday 5 pm) admission £1.50 for adults, 80p for children and OAPs. Outside demonstrations by besom maker, blacksmith, thatcher, hurdle maker, cooper, wheelwright and cane worker.

Paris Arts and Crafts

September 4-9 for the Arts and Crafts exhibitions in Paris, over 1000 exhibitors on 8 acres showing designs for table wear, furnishings, ceramics, ornaments, jewellery and lighting. Further details from French Trade Exhibitions, French Chamber of Commerce House, 54 Conduit Street, London W1R 9SD.

Design at Sea

Until 29 September at Parnham House, Beaminster, Dorset.

In London

At the Argenta Gallery, 82 Fulham Road until the 27 August, an exhibition of china, wood and jewellery. Further details phone 01-584 1841.

Furniture in context

At the British Crafts Centre, until 22 September. The Centre is in Earlham Street, Covent Garden, London. Exhibition covers commissioned, one-off and batch production of furniture.

Scotfair '82

Will be held from 5-7 October at the Royal Highland Exhibition Hall, Edinburgh, to include furniture, pottery, glassware, jewellery, textiles, knitwear, prints, food and perfumes. Further details from Scottish Development Agency, 102 Telford Road, Edinburgh EH4 2NP. Phone 031-343 1911.

Cotwall End Country Day

A country day out for all the family to be held at Cotwall End Nature Centre on Sunday, 5 September from 12 noon to 7pm. Admission 60p adults, 40p children and OAPs. Exhibition of country crafts including turning demonstrations and at least two woodcarving demonstrations. Come and see the Totem Poles special feature.

Woodworker Show

Woodworker Show at the Royal Horticultural Society Halls, London, 19-24 October, details from Model and Allied Publications Ltd, PO Box 35, Bridge Street, Hemel Hempstead, Herts HP1 1EE.

Clock weekend

Horological Solvents are having a special open weekend on Saturday and Sunday 11/12 September from 10-6pm at their premises in Proctor St, Bury, Lancs. There will be a collection of clocks, barometers, parts, books, tools and reproduction furniture handles for sale. Restoration products for woods and metals, demonstrations of wheel cutting, french polishing, dial painting are included. Phone 061-764 2741 for further details.

Lecture programme at the V & A

Monday 13 September at 3.00pm, Regency furniture by Sarah Bowles. Tuesday 14 September at 11.00am Victorian furniture by Geoffrey Opie. Wednesday 8 September Keyboard instruments at 11.00am and Stringed instruments at 3.00pm by Carole Patey, Charles Rennie Mackintosh – furniture at 12 noon by Geoffrey Opie. Wednesday 15 September at 3.00pm Japanned furniture by Jean Schofield. Thursday 2 September at 3.00pm Contemporary furniture by John Compton. Thursday 9 September at 11.00am Marcel Breuer and Isokon furniture by Geoffrey Opie. Thursday 16 September at 3.00pm Omega furniture by Geoffrey Opie. Saturday 11 September at 3.00pm Neo-classical furniture by Elizabeth Murdoch.

IWIE

International Woodworking Industries Exhibition at the National Exhibition Centre, Birmingham 12-16 September.

Trades Fair

International Hardware and Housewares Trades Fair, Olympia 6 September.

British Association Meeting

The British Association for the Advancement of Science hold their 144th annual meeting at the University of Liverpool this year from 6-10 September. Section Q/Forestry contains the themes of world forestry in Britain...the north-south interdependence; patterns, trends and forecasts of wood consumption to the year 2000; Britain's contribution to resource survey, management and investment in third world forest resources and a time to plant – the complementary need to expand intensive forestry programmes in developed and developing countries. Further information about the meeting can be obtained from the BAAS, Fortress House, 23 Savile Row, London W1X 1AB.

Karwei '83

The sixteenth annual exhibition for the diy trade will be staged in the Irene, Bernhard and Marijke halls on the Royal Netherlands Industries Fair site in Utrecht from 17-23 January 1983.

The Irene hall will be of interest to woodworkers since it will contain wood, kitchens, self assembly furniture. The Bernhard hall is the venue for locks and hinges, hand tools and workbenches.

The first four days of the exhibition are trade only, the final three are open to the general public.

584

Prices quoted are those prevailing at press date and are subject to alteration due to economic conditions.

Woodworker, September 1982

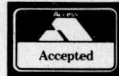

The bird man of Berkhamsted

Sydney Reynolds talks to Ralph Williams, a professional woodcarver best known for his outstanding carvings of birds

As a boy of seven Ralph Williams would pick up a piece of wood while walking home from school and whittle it into some shape to pass the time. Today he is a professional wood sculptor.

Forty-one year old Ralph, who lives in Berkhamsted, Herts, gave up eight years ago a safe but uncreative job with a chemical manufacturer, to become a full time woodcarver in spite of mortgage, growing family and rising cost of living. He said at the time that he had no excuse for not making a success of it.

Ralph Williams then took a job for a year at Tring Museum at £24 a week as an assistant scientific officer helping to unpack the skin collection of birds which has arrived from the Natural History Museum. The skins had been used for scientific research rather than for mounting and display.

'I signed the Official Secrets Act, learned a great deal about the structure of birds, and discovered how little I knew' he said.

Ralph has exhibited at the Berkhamsted Art Society show annually since 1966, about which time he came to the attention of Sir Peter Scott, director of the Wildfowl Trust at Slimbridge, Glos. The trust has sold some of his work, particularly ducks and geese.

● *Above: Ralph Williams, woodcarver. Right: Little owl in oak stands 15in high*

'Sir Peter encouraged me in the early days by showing an interest in my work and showing me around the Wildfowl Trust, which I visited for the first time through him in the 60s,' said Ralph.

In the 1970s A. L. Michael, former chairman of philatelists Stanley Gibbons, was patron to Ralph Williams for a couple of years. 'I was introduced to him at an exhibition,' Ralph said, 'he bought all my work apart from commissions for those years and encouraged me to develop intricate works in large pieces. He bought some 0 pieces in the two years before he retired to the south of France.'

Eric Hosking, the bird photographer, ornithologist and broadcaster, has also bought some of his work.

Ralph carves in walnut, lime, elm, oak, yew, plane and teak in that order of frequency. The works range in price from £50 to £300, some of which take up to 200 hours to complete. He now deals with Malcolm Innes and Partners, a wildlife and sporting art gallery in Walton Street, Chelsea, and since 1967 has shown at most of the exhibitions of the Society of Wildlife Artists.

In 1978 Ralph was elected a member of the Society, and he has also exhibited in other London galleries over the years. His work is in private collections in Britain, France and the United States. ■

Below: Goldcrest in walnut sitting in yew leaves. This 3in high carving sold for £60 recently. Right: Dove in lime, a 12in high carving that sold for £120

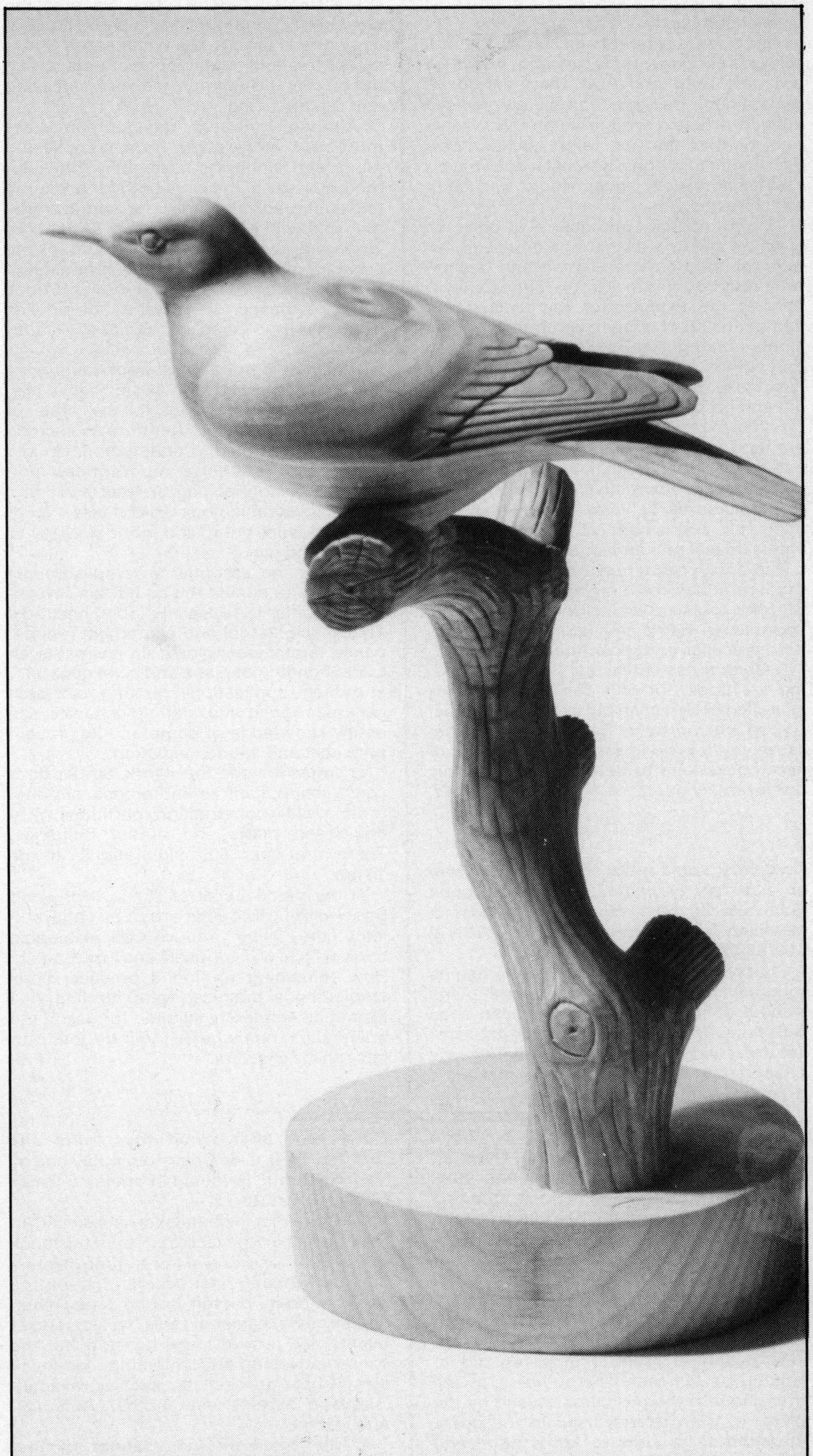

Woodworker's bookshelf

Woodworking Tools and how to use them by Jack Hill, published by David & Charles at £8.50 (hardback).

Correctly looked after and used, woodworking tools are a source not only of fine workmanship but also of great personal satisfaction for the craftsman.

This book is simply dedicated to the task of explaining how tools function, how they are best used and how they should be maintained. Being a completely revised version of a text written some thirty years ago most of the text refers to handtools used in the traditional way but it does have a new chapter on power tools and their attachments.

This traditional approach is, at once, its strength and its weakness. In an age of DIY aids' for the home craftsman and design-orientated studies in schools, almost inevitably at the expense of the teaching of workmanship, this book is refreshing in its single-mindedness. The late Alfred Morgan and author Jack Hill have indeed written a 'lucid text', but this new edition fails to take advantage of the new printing technology on offer to provide the photographs which are food and drink to today's 'reader'. The line drawings fail to fill the void and are not 'exceptionally instructive' as the publisher would have us believe. At best they are adequate and small; at worst they are vague, inaccurate and small.

The book covers new technology in that modern adhesives, chipboard screws and Surform tools are all included. It fails in its approach to metrication ignoring both standard practises and recommendations.

Despite these criticisms, I enjoyed reading the book not only for the memories rekindled of part of an old favourite of mine, (*Woodworking* by J. S. Chappell) but because it makes good sense. However, hardback books tend to be expensive and this one is no exception. **D. M. W.**

□ □ □

Carpentry, some tricks of the trade... from an old-style carpenter by Bob Syvanen published by East Woods Press, Fast & McMillan Publishers Inc at £7.95 (ISBN 0 914788 47 7).

Old style carpenter Bob Syvanen begins with advice on how to pick up a plank without doing yourself an injury and ends with a drawing of a shallow tray suitable for use in carrying building tools. In-between is a fascinating series of steps in making a large timber building.

The pages are heavily illustrated with over 400 clear and workmanlike drawings linked by a lively text devised by an experienced craftsman. I found the book fascinating, although the hand-written text is not easy to read, and it has filled me with enough confidence to replace my insubstantial garden shed in the near future! At each stage the advice given is sound and the 'tricks of the trade' vary in their magnitude from how to set nails without a punch and cutting batches of shingle in bulk, to the construction of scaffolding as an aid to working on the roof. The author is aware throughout of the problems caused by the nature of the material used in the open. Throughout, he aims to 'do it right' and mainly succeeds. **D.M.W.**

Site carpentry by C. K. Austin. A 'Building Trades Journal' book published by Northwood Publications Ltd. ISBN 7198 2730 2.

'Carpentry — the art of cutting, framing and joining timber, timbers connected by being framed together etc'. So runs the dictionary definition. 'In this book the term carpentry is used in the wider sense and is meant to apply to all woodworking carried out on site, including framework, carcasing and second fixing'.

'Although modern developments are more and more away from complicated joints and elaborate assemblies, the ultimate success of the work both for economy and quality still depends upon sound craftsmanship with a systematic approach to the work plus overall precision and first time accuracy in cutting, fitting and assembling.' So runs the first part of C. K. Austin's book which is based on a series of articles originally published in *Building Trades Journal*.

This then is not a 'new' book but it is so fundamental, solid and basic that it provides an overall guide to the craft of carpentry and should therefore as such be followed through and understood. On site carpenters, students, apprentices and building personnel, plus architects will find this an invaluable book which takes a lot of the hard work out of the job in an easy to understand way.

It gives the essential accomplishments necessary to enable the ambitious carpenter and joiner to tackle any job in his trade. These include tool and equipment maintenance, timber technology, simple maths, an understanding of plane and solid geometry and their applications (setting out arch centres, roofing etc), static mechanics, scientific knowledge of damp and its prevention, heat and sound insulation.

Chapters include formwork, timber floor construction, centres and arches, shoring, roofing, stair construction, partitions, windows and doors and timber buildings. There are over 600 illustrations in the 144pp.

At the modest cost of £5.95 Northwood Books and C. K. Austin are to be congratulated; they have produced an invaluable book which will be used and used again. How refreshing to find a practical book employing a practical spiro binding A 4 format so eminently suitable for use in the many situations where it will be found to 'give all the answers.' **P.C.**

□ □ □

Build your own wood toys, gifts and furniture by R. J. de Cristoforo published by Van Nostrand Reinhold (Popular Science Books) at £21.20.

I am sure that the publishers are sincere in their claims on the jacket cover of this book that the author is one of the all-time masters at woodworking instruction, one of the deans of do-it-yourself writing, a workshop genius and a master of tools. As a parade of talents this is awe inspiring stuff but the conservative and discriminating reader will by now have guessed that such extravagant language heralds yet another American publication.

In the tradition and manner of that country the book is typographically an

excellent publication but the contents d[o] not measure up to the promise of the cov[er] notes. It should be a success but a clos[e] inspection reveals a haphazard miscellan[y] of 70 projects for toys and furniture. [I] confess to being totally at a loss in efforts t[o] explain how table lamps made from biscu[it] tins and one gallon oil cans fit into th[e] scheme of things — yet there they are o[n] page 355.

The 44 ideas for toys are simple an[d] effective but the projects for furniture ar[e] crude in construction and lack visua[l] appeal.

A dangerously short treatise on using th[e] woodturning lathe is almost cavalier in i[ts] treatment of tools and techniques. Havin[g] introduced the subject, the author rapidl[y] closes it with but six spindle turning idea[s] and one faceplate job.

To my mind, books of this type are mos[t] useful for flipping through to look for idea[s]. But this one is very expensive at £21.20 an[d] many readers will cavil at such a high pric[e] for a handy catalogue. **R.W.C[.]**

□ □ □

Wooden toys by Didier Carpentier & Jo[e] Bachelet, a hobby craft book published b[y] E. P. Publishing Ltd at £2.45. ISBN 0 715[?] 0785 4.

Hobby horses have fascinated childre[n] since the days of ancient Greece. Man[y] other toys, almost as old are still bringin[g] joy to new generations. Tops still wobbl[e] unpredictably to a shuddering stop, acro[?] bats still whirl around based upon th[e] principle of the tension of a piece of cord. I[n] their introduction the authors state: 'Every[-] one has dreamt at one time or another, o[f] making one of these splendid wooden toys[,] from the rocking horse to little woode[n] puppets'. Wooden toys no matter ho[w] complicated their construction, have [a] naivety and charm which is hard to resist.

But with the majority of books on toys a[t] present on the bookshelves, resist is wha[t] the potential maker usually does. The boo[k] simply does not convey the appeal of the finished product.

This book however, immediately upo[n] opening its pages, stimulates and encour[-] ages both beginners (start with simple models, the lacing doll, a pair of stilts[)] enthusiasts (try jointed toys like the cove[r] illustration of a penny farthing) and the more advanced (steam rollers, rocking horses and garden slides). The cartoon cinema is an interesting project.

It is a slim volume (64pp) but is packed with a range of excellent toys (37 projects). It is very well illustrated with materials lists, line drawings and colour photographs on every page showing not only the main constructional details but also children and adults making and playing with the toys. This last so essential to give a good idea of scale. The book commences with useful lists of the necessary tools and their functions; suitable materials; constructional details and finishing. A large size, laminated paperback, excellent value at £2.45. Originally published in France under the title *Jouets en bois* translated by A. F. Hartley & P. Picot. **P.C.**

Chest of drawers

This chest of drawers has delightful proportions and offers useful accommodation. The main carcase is dovetailed and the front rails are crossbanded with oak veneer. The plinth is secured to the carcase with glued blocks. The drawers each have a cocked bead, set into a rebate and mitred at the corners, the drawer bottoms being held in grooved slips. The chest is made from dark oak but light oak, stained if necessary, could also be used.

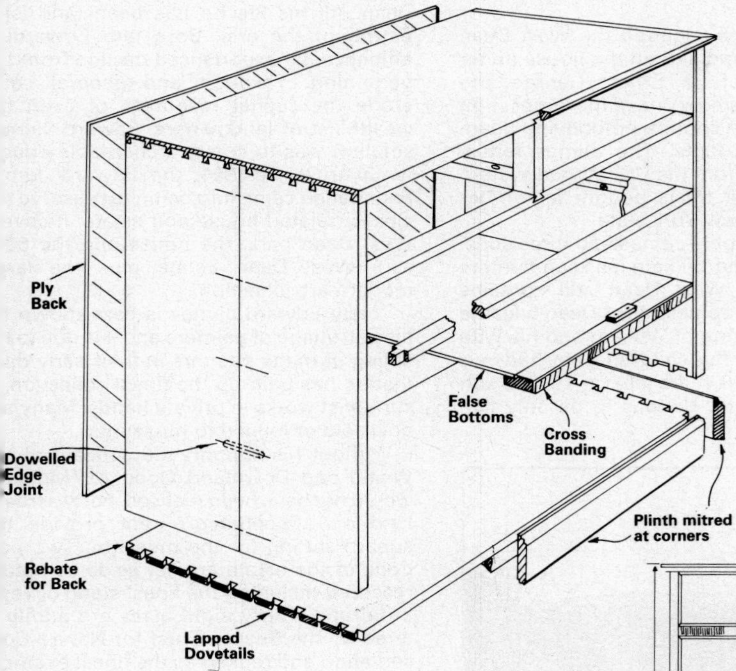

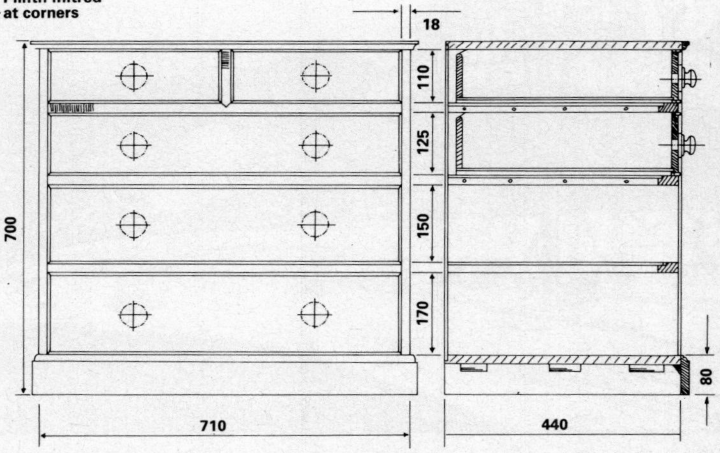

Ply Back

Dowelled Edge Joint

Rebate for Back

Lapped Dovetails

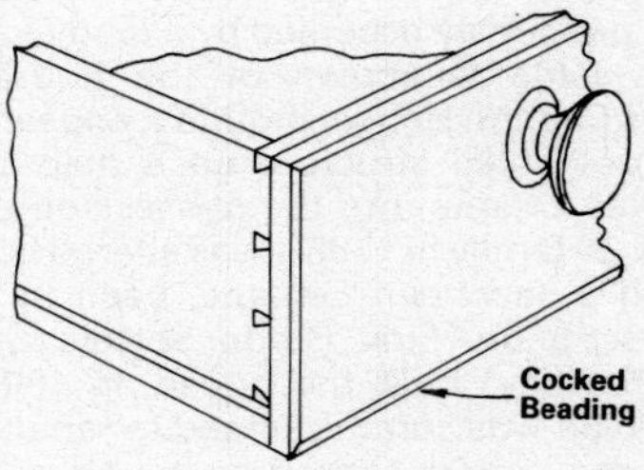

False Bottoms

Cross Banding

Plinth mitred at corners

Cocked Beading

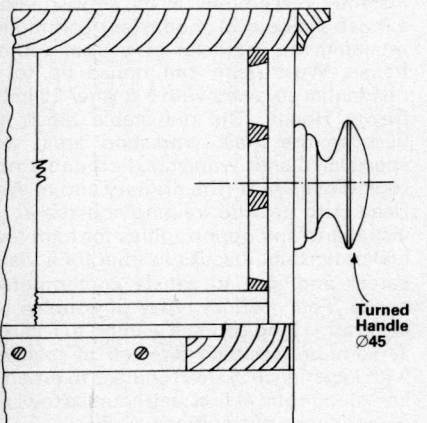

Turned Handle ⌀45

OAK CHEST OF DRAWERS CUTTING LIST					
	No	L	W	T	Material
CARCASE					
Top & Bottom	2	715	445	18	OAK
Sides	2	645	445	18	OAK
Back	1	715	645	4	PLY
False Bottoms	3	715	415	4	PLY
Plinth	1	1700	80	18	OAK
Front Rails	3	700	40	18	OAK
Drawer Rails	6	450	14	12	OAK
Top Moulding	1	1700	18	13	OAK
DRAWERS					
Top Sides	4	450	110	8	OAK
Fronts	2	330	110	18	OAK
Backs	2	330	105	8	OAK
2nd Sides	2	450	125	8	OAK
Front	1	680	125	18	OAK
Back	1	680	120	8	OAK
3rd Sides	2	450	150	8	OAK
Front	1	680	150	18	OAK
Back	1	680	145	8	OAK
4th Sides	2	450	170	8	OAK
Front	1	680	170	18	OAK
Back	1	680	165	8	OAK
Drawer Bottoms	4	675	450	6	PLY OAK-FACED
Drawer Cocked Beading	10	700	10	4	OAK

Oak veneer for cross-banding. Turned wooden handles ⌀45.

by Tony Lord

West Dean

In June Polly Curds visited West Dean College to see first hand the courses and opportunities offered

The earliest mention of West Dean (then named Earl's Court) was in 1086 as one of the manors under Singleton (Silleton) in the Domesday Book. The Jacobean manor house was built by John Lewkenor in 1622 on a site previously occupied by a medieval building. Little is known of the house, known as Cannon House, though it appears as a three-gabled structure on a map of 1623. After it came into the possession of the Peachey family in 1738 it was altered but remained a Jacobean E-shape, even in a 1774 description. First Baron Selsey (Sir James Peachey) built the house. In 1804 James Wyatt was commissioned to rebuild and enlarge – work carried on by his son Benjamin after James Wyatt died in 1813.

William James acquired the West Dean Estate in 1891 and altered the house under the direction of Sir Ernest George and Harold Peto. It is now one of the largest flint structures in the country embodying deep-mined Norfolk flints. The James family fortunes came from the US railroad system and huge forest tracts bought for timber production in New York state.

David and Sophia James had three sons, Frank, Arthur and William, all keen hunters and explorers. West Dean still contains many of their trophies. West Dean became the principal home of William and his wife Evelyn and their five children. They had four girls and then 18 years later in 1908, a son and heir, Edward. He was to be only five years old when his father died. The estate was held in trust. After Eton and Christ Church, Oxford, followed by a brief marriage to the ballet dancer Tilly Losch, Edward lived only spasmodically at West Dean. All his life he has been (and is) a patron of the arts. Born into Edwardian affluence, he experienced decline from the beginning. Taxation and general costs erode the capital resources of even the wealthiest of landowners. Edward James' solution was to create a charitable educational trust. In 1964, the Edward James Foundation came into being to preserve the closely related house and estate. It covers West Dean park, the house and the 600 acre West Dean Estate plus the large modern art collection.

Today Edward James is best known for his patronage of painters and it is due to his aiding of many painters in their early days that he has built up the finest collection of surrealist works in private hands. Many are now sold or loaned to museums.

Without his support the concept of the Weald and Downland Open Air Museum would not have been realised. Forty acres of land on a peppercorn rent provide the superb setting for the museum. Two portions of the estate are set aside as nature reserves, including the finest stand of yew in Europe. Thirty eight acres are administered by the Sussex Trust for Nature Conservation and ranked as the finest example of ancient woodland of oak standards and hazel coppice on chalk.

Not only materially but spiritually too the Foundation is the heir to Edward James.

Conversion of the mansion to a residential college has not altered the place too much, original furniture, carpets, pictures all have been left in place. One of the outstanding attractions of West Dean, and instantly discernible, is its atmosphere almost a medieval monastery community retaining the character of a great country house. West Dean can house up to 80 residential students with a further 20 in the Dower House. The old stable block has become the main workshop area, with specialised craft workshops around a now roofed over yard. The primary aim of West Dean is to provide training courses in the visual arts and opportunities for high level craftsmanship. It seeks to train for a viable career and also to satisfy contemporary needs. Four distinct types of courses are covered 1) long courses leading to a career 2) semi-professional directed at teachers with experience 3) short courses to broaden knowledge and 4) first step courses towards a wide range of traditional crafts.

The long courses directed towards conservation skills run from September to July and are run jointly with the Cultural and Educational Trust of BADA (British Antique Dealers' Association). There are three such – antique furniture restoration, antique clock restoration and antique pottery and porcelain restoration.

The restoration of antique furniture course is open to anyone over the age of 18 who can show that they are skilled with their hands in woodwork, are keenly interested in antiques and who have the necessary dedication and patience. Especially qualified for such a course are applicants with a high standard of training in cabinet making

● *West Dean Park engraved by Sarah van Niekerk who teaches wood engraving at the college*

● *Richard and Paul watch the ease with which Fred Lambert handles the draw knife during the country furniture making course in June*

Stanley Block, course tutor, stresses that the main course emphasis is 'training at the bench' where skills in restoration are acquired on antique period pieces. The course attempts to cover the history of furniture, science and properties (brasswork, metals, timbers, fungal and insect attacks, veneers, inlays and bandings), workshop technology, wood finishing (preparation and matching of stains, fillers, polishes), estimating (costing, materials, labour, insurance, VAT), gilding, lacquer work and painting of furniture, coupled with weekly furniture history lectures by BADA members.

These courses have gained an enviable reputation, both the Victoria & Albert museum and the National Trust support them and send objects for repair as do many antique dealers and country house owners. Payment for the repairs subsidises the course.

On the day that I visited the college students were involved in a variety of projects, one Dutch student, Peter, was restoring a cabinet that had once been painted, another Dutch student (female) had some intricate inlay work to match, Nigel was working on a clock case, John on a piece of French cabinetmaking, another student on a jardiniere. Only 'old' timber is used in a restoration and pieces which have been lost whether they be brasswork, fittings, mouldings, legs, finials, complete pieces or small areas are all made by the students. They are a continuing credit to the teaching by Stanley Block of both the techniques of restoration and the aesthetic and ethical aspects of the work.

Short courses extend over a weekend, five days or even longer. Tutors are practising craftsmen and women from all over the country. A wide range is available – of particular interest to *Woodworker* readers are the courses in mounting and framing pictures, caring for antique furniture (*not* to be confused with the year long study in restoration), wood carving, cane and rush seating, upholstery and cottage furniture making.

When I visited in June, five students were taking a five-day course in cottage furniture making with Fred Lambert. All had already taken two of Fred's other courses on the subject, one mainly an introduction to the subject but with a chair made by the student to one of Fred's designs to take home at the end; the second to make tools – mainly round planes; and now this third course to design and make their own chairs, stools, equipment and put to the test their previously gained experience and knowledge.

Fred describes the 'rounder' as a glorified pencil sharpener – to watch Fred use one was poetry in shavings. His classes are stimulating, informative and intensely practical. Through anecdotes, history, working models, tools, demonstrations and short lectures with even excursions into the evolution of the English language he imparts knowledge and skill accumulated over many years with the practised ease of a born craftsman and raconteur.

You could almost see the untrained boys rounding down the wood for the lathes in Worcester; the hay rakes being produced by the stail engine and the angling fraternity of Redditch waiting for their rods to be

turned thin from the trap. Caught in a cleft stick took on the old meaning as Fred expertly cleft an ash log and showed what could happen if you were not so expert. All he teaches has been practised for generations; when Fred presents it it is as fresh as if it was new technology only thought of yesterday. It all makes sense and falls into place as logically as (dare one say it) falling off a log! Young Farmers Club Booklet No 31 entitled *Tools and devices for coppice crafts* (by of course Fred Lambert) is an excellent book worth obtaining for around £1 from the Centre for Alternative Technology, Machynlleth, Powys. A small recompense if you can't attend a course yourself.

His students this June, Jane, Paul, Stephen, Richard and Charles showed after their previous visits an ease and familiarity with the man, the tools and the wood. I hope Dr Richard's grandchild appreciates the high chair; I am sure Charles Knight's craftshop – *Woodcraft* – at the Fort, Newhaven, will be the richer in quality furniture after the three courses. There are still some craft workshop premises available at Newhaven, incidentally, why not contact David Gee at Fort Newhaven Ltd. Present incumbents include a potter, a laceworker, a leather worker and others. All interested parties should be prepared to demonstrate their craft, not just be a shop. It is an educational venture for local school children interested in the various crafts as well as a workshop space for the craftsperson.

Many of the West Dean short courses are graded to cover different degrees of skill – if you want a beginner's course you can find it here, but if you need to advance already considerable skills again the opportunity affords itself and you will not be disappointed.

The courses for musical instrument making are a good example of this. We have written in *Woodworker* of the first ones planned for teachers making musical instruments easily used by school children eg the chordal dulcimer and the Nordic lyre. Then came the lute, harp, mandolin and spinet made by the more experienced craftsmen. At the end of a nine-day course the students give a concert on the instruments they have made. September 1982 sees the inception of a specialised apprenticeship in musical instrument making, starting with a three year training in plucked fretted instruments under resident maker Christopher Challen. The college anticipates starting bowed instruments in '83, brass and keyboard (including organ) workshops in the near future. The scheme will relate closely to the

● *A seventeenth century strong box being restored with care by a student on the one year course run in association with BADA*

old apprenticeship system with the emphasis on bench work and at least 15 instruments produced in the three years. An Early Music Summer School directed by James Tyler is planned for 1983.

There have been gardens at West Dean since 1622, the three cedars of Lebanon on the lawn by the main drive were planted in 1746. Many of the beech, limes, cedars, chestnuts and planes go back to the early 19th century. Exotic tree planting marked royal visits in the time of William James. Today there are over 30 acres of gardens, open to the public from April to September every afternoon except Saturdays. The estate, its 11 farms and 140 houses and cottages covers 6000 acres (reduced from the 8500 at William James's death in 1912 to pay death duties). The oldest cottage dates back to 1663 and some farm buildings still match the 1608 lease. The woodlands are legally 'dedicated' in perpetuity to the production of timber. Beech is the natural product of the South Downs, timber felled in 1977/8 was planted just after the Napoleonic Wars. Elms have been lost to Dutch elm disease and the drought of '76 and subsequent beech bark disease have taken a heavy toll.

The college is now self sufficient in heating fuel – the present system consumes firewood from the estate's own woodlands, processed through a chipping machine and automatically fed to the boilers. As a by-product of normal forestry practice the chips are a self renewing natural resource.

Forty two acres of arboretum are only half a mile away from the house. Not open to the general public it includes the tallest Lucombe oak in the country (124ft), Douglas firs imported as seeds by David Douglas in 1827, redwoods and spruce and other exotics.

Large numbers of students (*circa* 6000/year) visit West Dean, some come repeatedly, the college has links with students in Europe and America fostered over the years since 1971. Courses are open to anyone over school leaving age and run all the year (except the Christmas period of about 10 days). It is a friendly place with an atmosphere of ease but a place of professional learning and expertise. Want to learn more? Sae to the secretary, West Dean College, Chichester, W. Sussex PO18 0QZ will tell you all you want to know. New programmes are issued in August and February each year. ■

LONDON'S SIXTH

Woodworker Show '82

BIGGER THAN LAST YEARS — NOW IN TWO HALLS!

THE ROYAL HORTICULTURAL SOCIETY'S NEW & OLD HALLS VINCENT SQUARE & GREYCOAT STREET

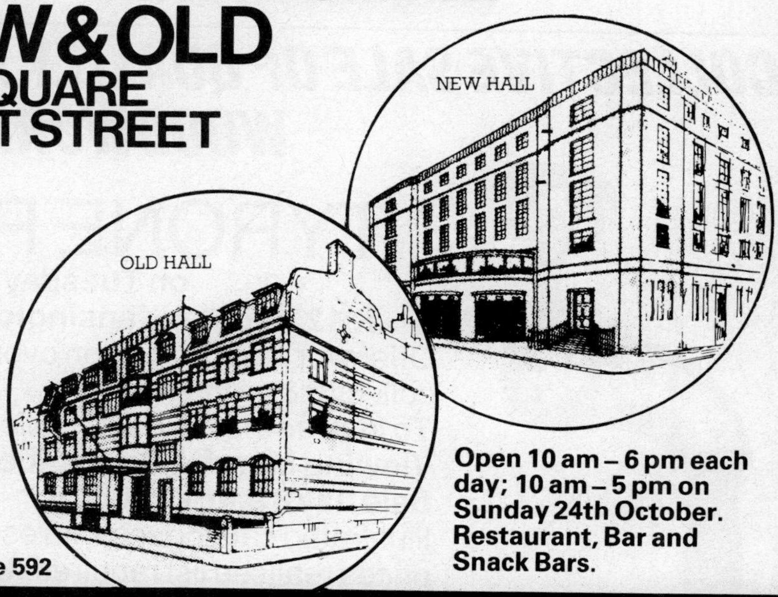

Such is the increasing popularity of the Woodworker Show, now in its 6th year, that this year the Show is to be staged in the attractive Old Hall as well as the New Hall. Tickets will be issued daily enabling visitors to pass from one hall to another and return later on the same day.

Both halls will display the competition exhibits in the many classes. There will be many more trade stands fulfilling every need of the amateur or professional craft woodworker.

The colleges and demonstration areas will be considerably expanded and so will the lecture programme.

Don't miss this year's super Woodworker Show.

For Advance Tickets see advertisement on page 592

NEW HALL

OLD HALL

Open 10 am – 6 pm each day; 10 am – 5 pm on Sunday 24th October. Restaurant, Bar and Snack Bars.

19th-24th OCTOBER 1982

Admission:
Adults £2.00
Children and OAPs £1.50
Advance booking details from the Organiser, Woodworker Show, 13/35 Bridge Street, Hemel Hempstead, Herts, HP1 1EE

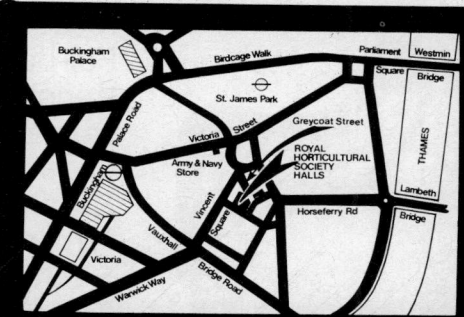

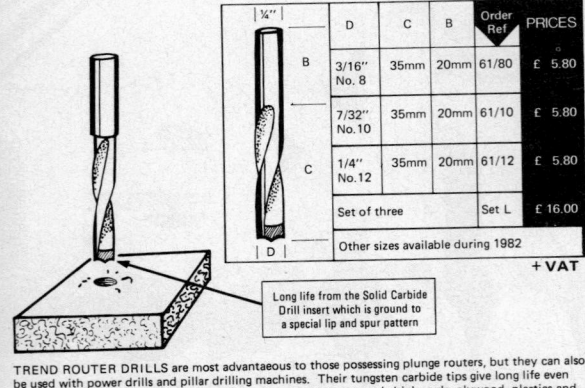
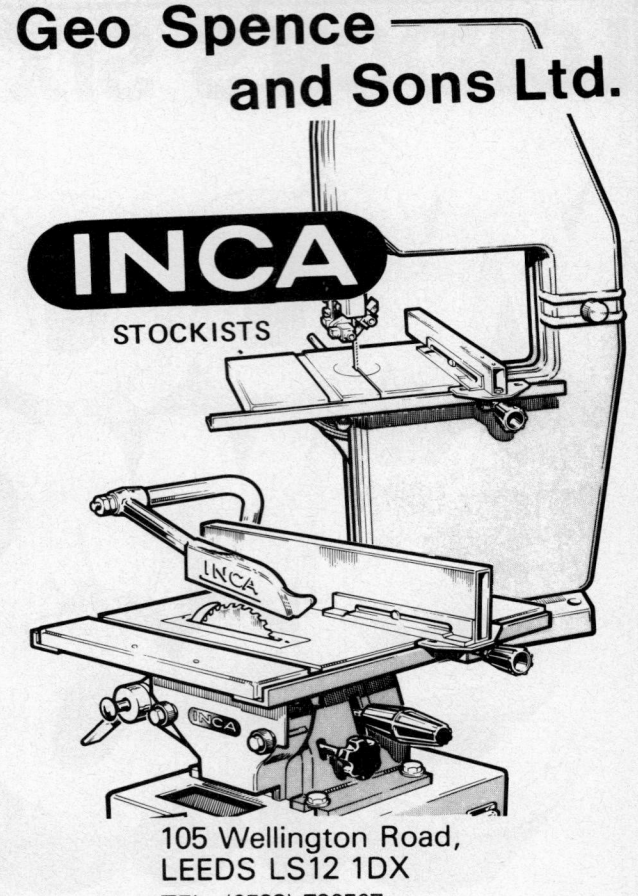
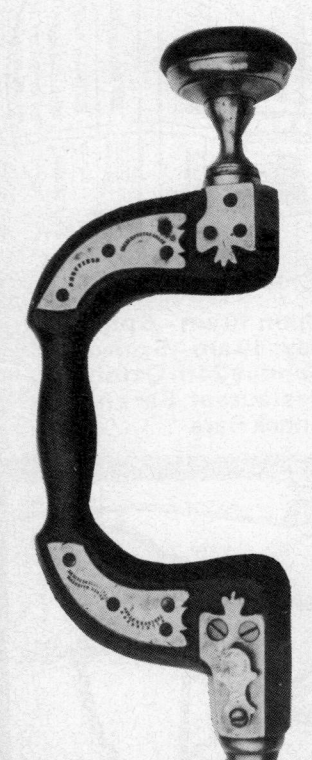

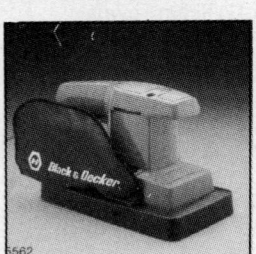
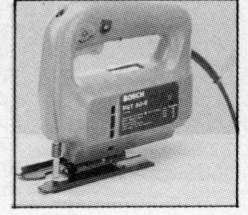
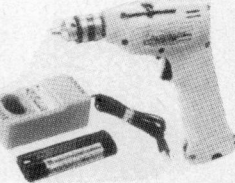

Wood on wheels

The wooden car is by no means a new concept, but as the pressed steel of today's car body shells deteriorates at such an alarming speed, the use of wood is once again an attractive possibility. Chris Dunn went to see a car designer who has developed a wooden car that might appeal to woodworking people

Woodworkers who have spent dreary hours trying to repair body rust on their cars, in the depressing knowledge that the scene is unalterably set for a Forth Bridge-style epic, may already have pondered the possibilities of wood as a more durable and dependable material for car bodies.

Certainly, when we heard of a motorcar designer who had developed a wooden vehicle called the Hustler in build-it-yourself kit form, it was clear that *Woodworker* ought to find out more on your behalf. After all, the idea of woodworking people driving round in wooden cars has an appealing logic.

The man behind the Hustler is William Towns, who has an impressive record as a

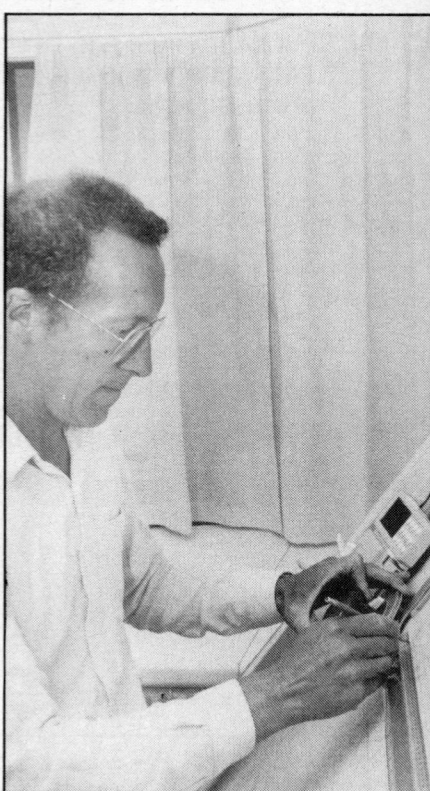

designer. From beginnings as a engineering apprentice with Rootes at Coventry in 1954, he has risen to become this country's best known freelance designer of car body shells. In 1966 he produced the classic DBS for Aston Martin, followed by its V8 version, then in 1976 the Lagonda and in 1980 the Bulldog.

Supercars are only part of William Towns' scope, however. He is also responsible for the nifty Elswich Envoy invalid car, for instance, as well as many prototype and experimental models of more humble runabouts, and others of his enterprises include the design of industrial equipment, furniture and boats. 'I do anything in three dimensions,' he told me with an air of

● *The Hustler in wood. The roof panels are designed to carry a load*

certainty that made it sound more like a motto than purely a statement of fact.

The wooden car is part of a range of Hustler kits that also come in fibreglass and steel and various degrees of perzazz besides, right up to the flared wheel arches and front-end spoilers of the Hustler Sprint. For £684 (inc VAT) the wooden Hustler kit supplies you with drawings, cutting layout, hardwood sections, assembly instructions, tinted glass in aluminium frames, plus all the fittings for lights, windows and so on.

Then you are on your own to buy three sheets each of 12mm and 18mm marine ply and some hardwood sections, and to start looking for good Mini parts to make up the rest. The Hustler is based on Mini front and rear subframes (there is also a six-wheeled version that requires a second rear subframe) complete with suspension and dampers, engine, gearbox, gearchange linkage, exhaust system, braking system, clutch, accelerator, heater, instruments, wiring, horn, wiper motor, screen washers, fuel tank, steering wheel, column and rack. Many of those who have bought Hustlers to date have in fact been owners of mechanically sound Minis which had lost the battle with body rust.

Mr Towns reckons that to build a wooden Hustler should cost less than £1,500 ready for the road, and he is similarly encouraging about the standard of skill required by the builder: 'You just need to be able to make a straight sawcut at 90 degrees, and to be able to measure accurately.'

So far William Towns has sold 11 wooden Hustlers and 36 of the steel and fibreglass kits. Customers seem well satisfied, and it certainly says something of the car's versatility that William and Elizabeth Towns find that the demonstration Hustler kept at their home near Moreton in Gloucestershire is constantly in demand for running their two children to and from school, shopping and so on. But the experience of driving round in a Hustler these last couple of years since the first one rolled off the production line leads Mr Towns to warn would-be buyers that they are doing the wrong thing if they wish to remain inconspicuous.

'People always react when you're driving along, or in town,' he said. 'You can never *not* get noticed. Most people automatically think that the car is powered by electric, which always drives us batty, and you also have to put up with those people who think they are being terribly original with little jokes like: Can you grow tomatoes in it?'

Anyone who wants further information should send sae to Interstyl (that's Mr Towns' company) at The Manor House, Stretton-on-Fosse, Moreton-in-Marsh, Gloucestershire. ∎

● *Left: William Towns at his drawing board. Right: Front end detail of the Hustler. Below: The wooden car from the rear, perhaps explaining why Mr Towns is so frequently asked: 'Can you grow tomatoes in it?'*

Shute's Jig

Bob Grant describes a clever idea for servicing planer knives devised by Dick Shute. John Peacock took the pictures

Woodworkers who have visited craft shows in recent years will no doubt be familiar with the Emco range of woodworking machines, usually being put through their paces by that most genial and expert of demonstrators, Dick Shute.

He possesses an Emco star machine of his own which, with its various accessories, can carry out some 16 separate woodworking operations. Now Dick has come up with a seventeenth idea of his own.

Maintenance of planer blades for light woodworking machines can be something of a problem with the 'down-time' lost whilst the blades are sent for professional servicing. Anyone wishing to service his own blades should find Dick's idea a good one and capable of adaptation to other universals or belt sanders.

Photo 1 shows the general configuration of the machine with its belt sanding attachment, while photo 2 shows a simple modification to the saw fence whereby a plate of ³⁄₁₆in aluminium is drilled and tapped to it. This modified fence can be brought right to the edge of the saw table so that the grinding jig, photo 3 can be dropped over it.

The plate now acts as a spine and, with the machine running, the jig is pushed up and down the belt (photo 4). To avoid wearing the abrasive belt excessively in one place, the jig can be moved over by laterally adjusting the fence. The accompanying sketch shows that there is clearance under the jig whilst the planer iron is brought into contact by adjusting it through its own slot holes.

The construction is simple and consists of two places of ½in plywood glued with a ³⁄₁₆in plywood sandwich piece above the aluminium plate. The angled block at the bottom of the jig is bevelled to give the desired grinding angle which is commonly 30°-35°. A partly worn medium grit belt has been found to give the best results and once ground the jig can be turned upside down in the bench vice and used to support the blade whilst it is dressed with an oilstone for the final honing. ∎

● *Photo 1 shows a general view of the machine*

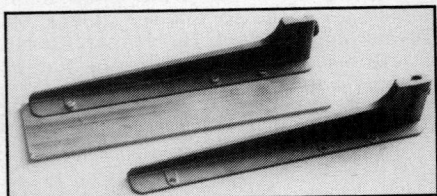

● *Photo 2 modification to saw fence*

● *Photo 3 grinding jig with modified fence*

● *Photo 4 jig moves up and down the belt*

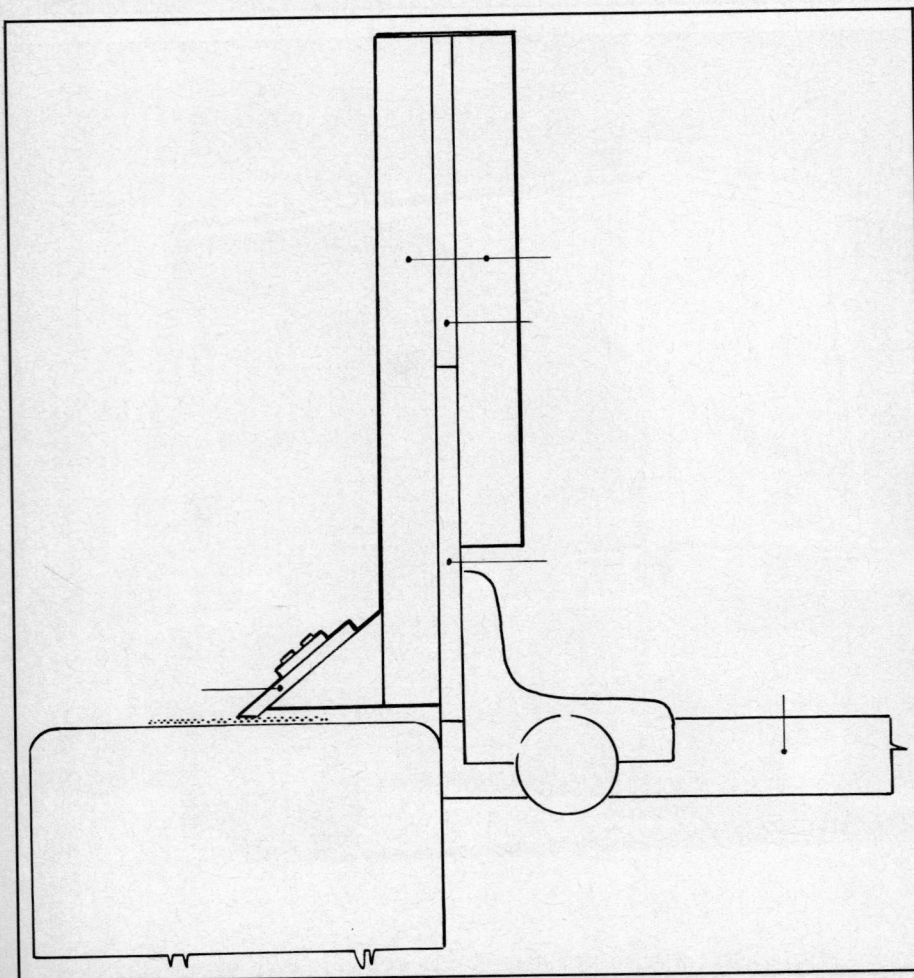

BERT MARSH
Woodturner

Bert Marsh took the turning classes by storm at last year's Woodworker Show. Harold King has been to see him in his Sussex home

Bert Marsh took the turning classes by storm at the 1981 Woodworker Show: four prizes, plus the Best of the Class award.

It all started when in 1946, Bert was apprenticed to a firm of cabinetmakers which specialised in making reproduction furniture. He soon became the top turner and developed a love of the process.

National Service took him to Malaya where he spent two years on active service in the RAF. Returning to cabinetmaking, he worked for several firms but found that furniture designs of the time did not involve turning. The lathe urge was such that he set up his own workshop at his home and turned for the sheer joy of it. At the same time, he experimented to see just what could be done with a sense of design, chunks of wood and a lathe. He also tried turning green timber and watching its change of shape as it dried.

Seventeen years ago he took up his present apointment at the Brighton College

of Art, later to become Brighton Polytechnic. His trade students study furniture design and making, timber science and woodworking machinery technology. Bert also has undergraduates for courses in wood, ceramics and plastics for BA degrees.

Bert, his wife and two sons live in a house on a hill top near Brighton, with magnificent views all round. The garage and workshop are cut into the hill and occupy the whole floor area of the house. The large workshop is well equipped with a Coronet Major lathe, band saw, pillar drill, radial saw and a grinder. The many cupboards are full of hand tools, jugs, turning blanks, chucks and

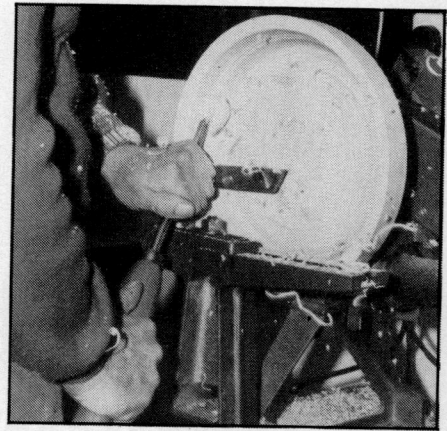

● *Chips fly from sycamore*

● *Above: a yew coopered bowl in rosewood with sycamore lines which won a second prize in segmental turning. Below: an American black walnut bowl made from six smaller bowls*

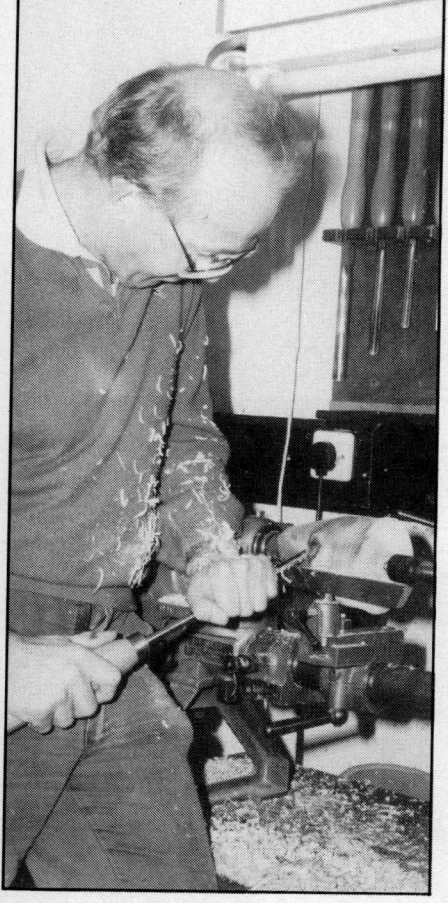

● *Bert starts to turn a bowl*

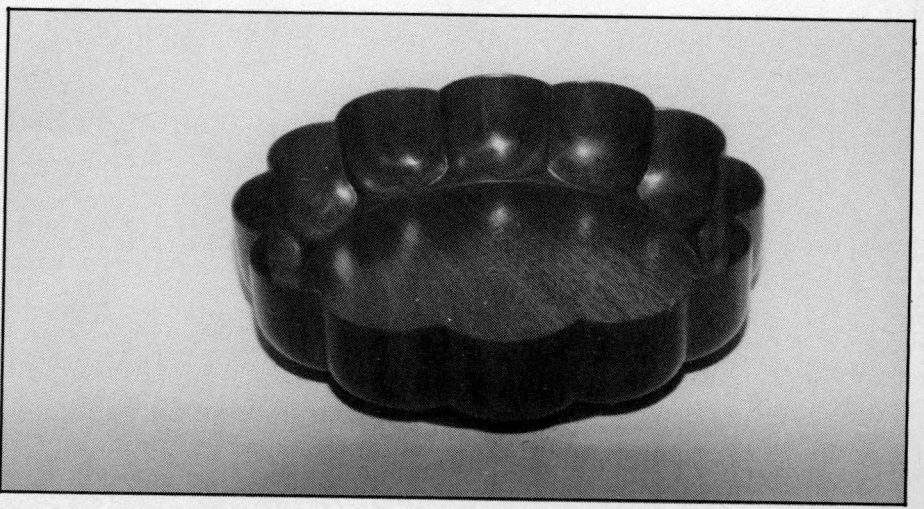

a number of home made gadgets. It is centrally heated. The brilliant lighting is by fluorescent tubes and a number of spotlight fittings.

To prove that all this is put to good use, Bert showed me an amazing collection of his turnery, some of which looked almost impossible to produce on a lathe. In view of the very high quality of his work, I was surprised the tool was being used straight from the grinder although a fine grit wheel was used.

Bert's advice to beginners is 'Sharp tools used with light pressure'. ∎

● *Right: Three examples of face plate turning by Bert Marsh. Back: a dish in American black walnut, front left: a bowl in Douglas fir showing a brushed grain and front right: a yew dish*

From antique shop to wheelwright's shop

Jocelyn Bailey records further doings from the village wheelwright's shop

I find my husband's old village wheelwrights' shop so interesting. Combined with his explanations and memories, the leisure moments that I can spend with him in the old shop are among the happiest of my life. Here are some recent notes and photographs.

Picture 1 shows Bert trimming the back of a felloe with a wheelwright's side-axe. Such axes belonging to his family were worn out years ago, and on a recent day trip to Hastings we were fortunate to find in an antique shop this right-handed side-axe which still has some tool-steel left in it. Soon Bert made a new handle for it, and it is already proving to be very useful indeed. The side-axe enables the user to shape wood carefully, rather than to just chop it.

Picture 2 shows a wooden spoke-shave which Bert was pleased to find on a stall at a Saturday market at the Maltings, Farnham, whilst on a day trip to meet our daughter there. Bert's old spoke-shave was really quite worn out — both the blade and the wooden part as seen at the top of the picture.

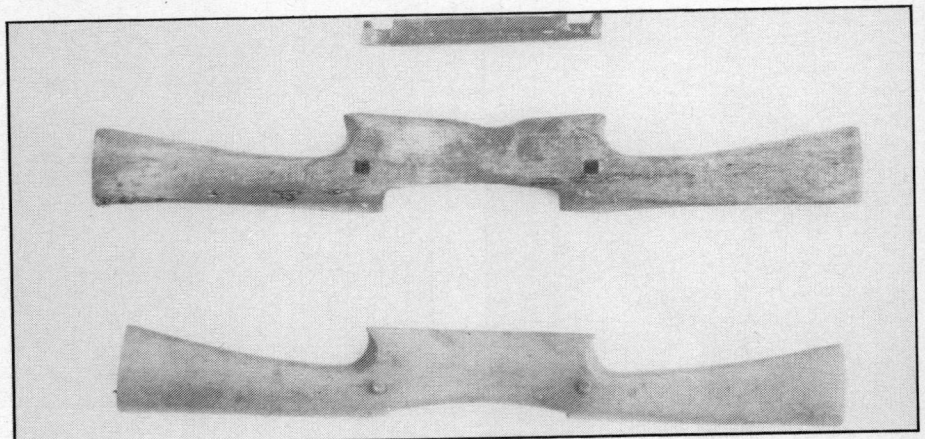

● *Right: (Picture 2) the old and the new spoke shaves for comparison*

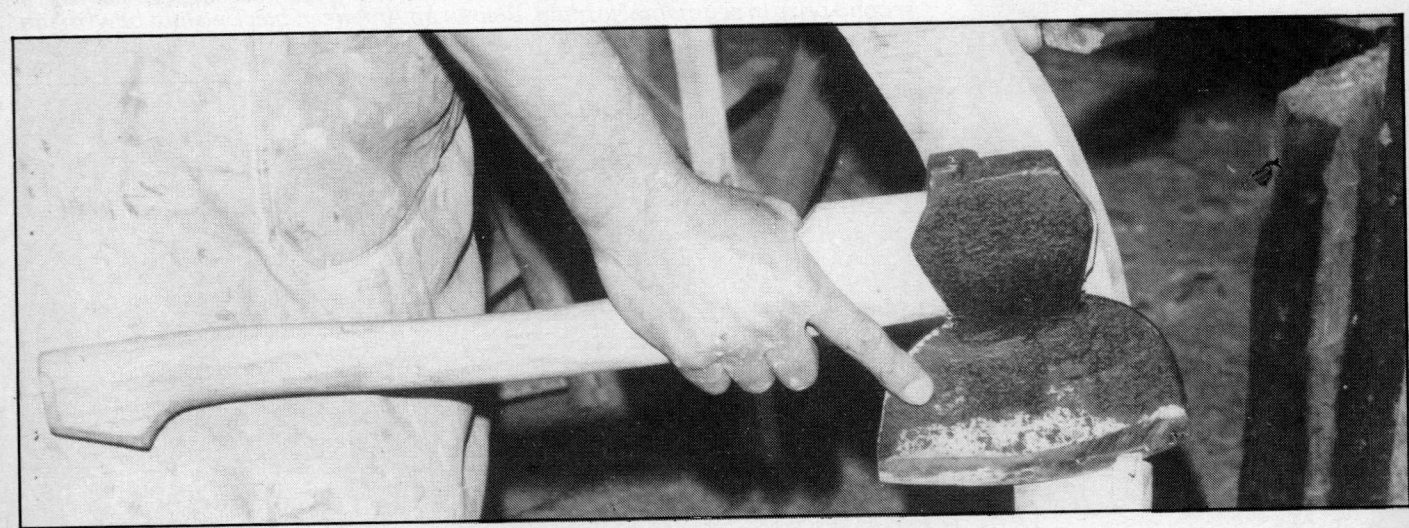

● *Above: (Picture 1) Bert trimming the back of a felloe with a wheelwright's side axe*

● *Above: (Picture 4) how the washer cutter is operated by means of a brace*

Our quest for replacement tools has only occurred fairly recently, partly owing to an increase in work on wooden wheels being wanted for both vehicle restoration and for general interest purposes.

Talking of tools, the wheelwright's brace has, of course, the larger 'sweep' to the shank, to help with the hard work of boring through seasoned hardwoods, and the bits have 'solid eyes' and are no longer obtainable, we fear.

In the maintenance of horsedrawn vehicles, leather washers often had to be made to renew the oilseal in the bearings of carriage type wheels. Leather as thick as that for soling shoes was used and Picture 4 shows how the washer cutter is operated by means of a brace.

In Bert's shop there is a rather old mechanical bandsaw with which he can cut out felloes, but how about it if he still had to use the old frame-saw, as posed in Picture 3? Or, worse still, hew them out with the adze as they were in even earlier times.

Today's DIY suppliers give us plenty of scope for textured finishes, but supposing we have a go with these old graining combs Picture 5). The hand-grained effect for paintwork must have once been a great favourite in the home, and was sometimes used on light horsedrawn vehicles, such as governess carts. ■

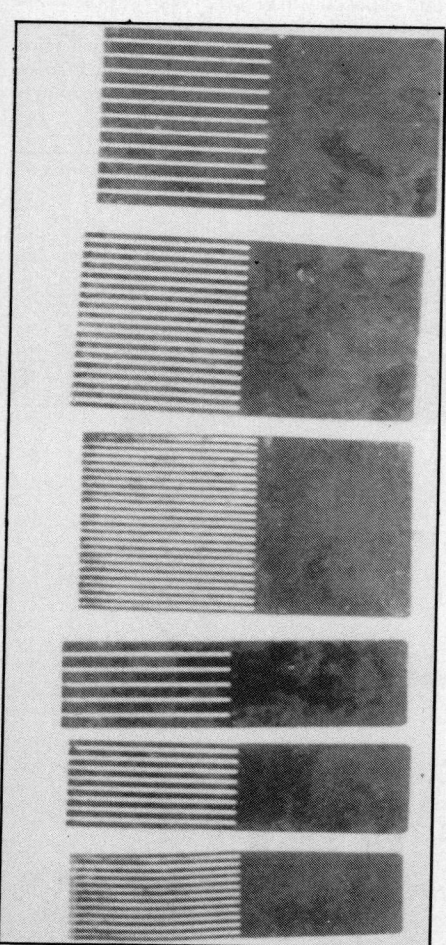

● *Right: (Picture 3) Bert using an old frame saw and above (Picture 5) a set of old graining combs used to produce that hand grained finish*

Wood and fire

Timber is an efficient burnable fuel, and yet it is not strictly speaking flammable. Here Bill Brown resolves the paradox

The question is often asked whether a timber frame house, or the addition of a timber extension to an existing brick built home, represents a fire hazard; the short answer is that it does not.

Wood is combustible but not strictly flammable, the seeming contradiction in terms being explained by their precise meaning; combustibility means a material is capable of burning, whereas flammability means it is easily set on fire. Wood is not easily set on fire, unless it is in a small section, like a match for example, and even that relies upon a chemically induced flame.

Wood used as a structural part of a building does not ignite in itself, although it might be encouraged to do so by arson. It is the contents of buildings that catch fire. In fairly recent years, one of the largest London fires involved the Crystal Palace, a building of glass and steel. In the case of the Great Fire of London it is true that the combustibility of the wood in the buildings helped to support the flames, but only because these were initiated and sustained by the flammable nature of other materials.

The Great Fire broke out on Sunday 2nd September, 1666 near the oven of Farynor, the king's baker, in Pudding Lane near London Bridge. A pile of wood faggots was stored by the oven, and flitches of bacon stood near. Fire engines were unknown, there had been a prolonged spell of dry weather, there was a strong north-east wind blowing, and the lane was one of the narrowest in the city. The houses had projecting upper storeys, and their woodwork was coated with pitch. Even under these conditions the fire spread slowly and took four days and nights before being controlled.

Wood is of course used as fuel, so what is so special about the use of wood as a structural material, apart from its high strength to weight ratio? The basic reason why it does not represent a serious fire hazard is its inherent ability to char under excessive heat, and because of this wood is generally better than steel or concrete when subjected to fire.

It is generally accepted that wood ignites when its surface temperature is raised to approximately 273°C. At this temperature wood ignites if there is an unlimited supply of oxygen; or, if the oxygen is controlled, it is the temperature at which gases begin to evolve from destructive distillation of the wood.

When subjected to extreme heat, wood decomposes with evolution of combustible gases and tarry substances, leaving behind a charcoal residue. This process is called pyrolysis. The speed with which combustion is initiated is dependent upon the rate of accumulation of heat at the surface of the wood. Several factors influence this rate: the size of the wood, the rate of heat loss from the surface to the interior, the presence of thin outstanding edges, and the rate at which heat is supplied to the surface of the wood. Small pieces with sharp projecting edges such as a match stick ignite readily because a relatively small quantity of heat is necessary to raise the temperature of the whole substance of the stick, particularly at the thin edges, to the ignition point.

Large pieces with rounded edges are much slower to catch fire because the conductance of heat into the interior keeps the surface below ignition temperature for some time. Wood has a low thermal conductivity and the pyrolysis reaction is accordingly prevented from spreading rapidly into the interior of a piece of wood.

Charcoal which forms on the surface until it reaches the glowing stage is an excellent heat insulating material; as it forms on the surface it slows pyrolysis still further. The rate of charring in untreated wood (without fire retardant coating) is slow, and this comes about because the temperature for about 6mm (¼in) ahead of the charring is only about 165°C, ie much lower than is required to sustain pyrolysis.

It is therefore possible to calculate the fire resistance of timber. A steady rate of charring of 0.64mm (0.025in) per minute, or about 38mm (1½in) per hour, has been established for softwoods, and accepted as generally applying to hardwoods, although in TRADA tests it was found that teak, jarrah and greenheart had charring rates about 62 per cent less than the values normally used, while those of oak, utile and keruing were even lower.

The behaviour of different materials in serious fire situations varies. Concrete and stone crack and disintegrate, steel rapidly begins to lose strength and to buckle, while at 550°C aluminium may lose half its strength. Timber will char and lose volume, but it will do so at a predictable rate, and while nothing can prevent its ultimate destruction in a bad fire, the collapse of a wood structure can often be delayed long enough for the fire to be brought under control.

The charring of wood can further be slowed down by the use of fire retardant chemicals which, by repelling oxygen, have an insulating effect. The use of intumescent paints is one way of denying oxygen to the wood. These do not ignite in a fire but swell and bubble on the surface of the wood. There is legislation within building regulations and local byelaws for wood in buildings to meet a particular requirement as to surface spread of flame.

There are clear or transparent flame retardant varnishes on the market, which can be applied by brush or spray to literally any wood based material to give a Class I Spread of Flame rating to all interior surfaces. These can be used in all situations and especially in wooden workshops where inflammable liquids may be stored or used. These varnishes are of the intumescing type, forming a microporous, dense insulating foam which reduces the transmission of heat to the under surface. ■

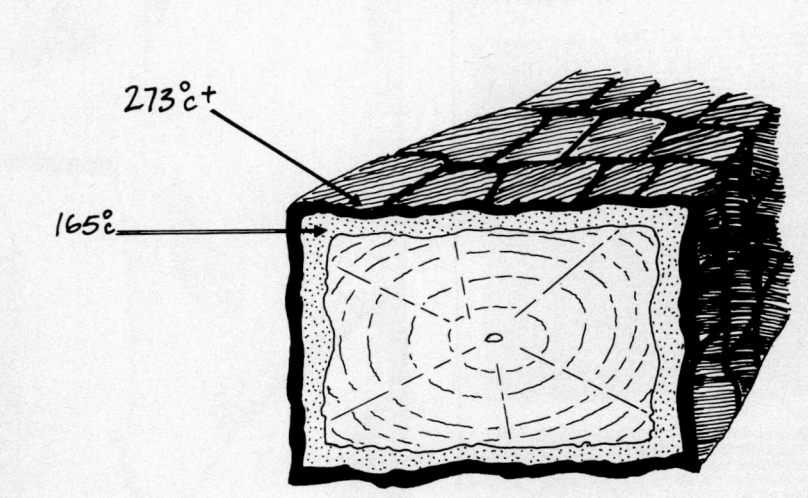

273°c+

165°c

When exposed to temperature of 273°C or higher, wood will ignite and char on the outside, but progression of pyrolysis into the wood is slowed to a predictable rate by a zone at a temperature of about 165°C in advance of the charring.

Woodturning from A to Z

Before the first cut is made, the cutters must be sharp — and kept sharp. In the fourth article in his guide to woodturning, Gordon Stokes goes back to the basics of good grinding and sharpening technique

AT THE SHARP END

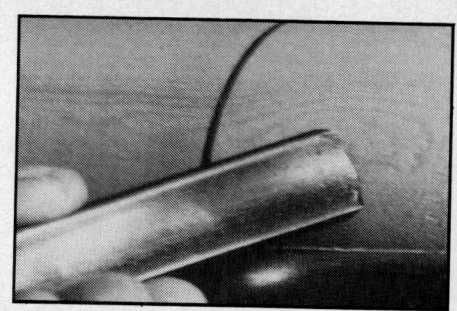

● *Heel of tool is placed on the wood first and the blade swung until the edge cuts when using a spindle gouge*

The subject this month is a very important one indeed, and I know that many people are bothered by their initial inability to master it. I refer to the actual procedures involved in the grinding and sharpening of the turning tools, backed up by the relevant facts concerning the shapes required on the ends of the blades.

It must be borne in mind that those who have recently taken up the craft, or who are about to do so, will need to practice their

● *Only the part of a chisel edge directly supported by the tool rest can be safely used in the smoothing cut*

tool grinding techniques just as much as the turning itself. For this purpose some scrap metal obtained from a local factory or small engineering firm will be very useful. Ideally some flat ferrous metal about 1in wide by ¼in thick will provide practice in grinding chisel bevels, and some tube about ¾in or 1in in diameter, which will need to be rolled back and forth as it is ground, will represent the gouges. Practising on expensive cutting tools is not a good idea!

The 'devil stone' should be used whenever there is any sign of a shine on the surface of the wheel. Note that it should also be used on a new grinding wheel, to remove the surface 'skin' which is formed in manufacture. These stones are rectangular in section, and extremely hard. Some of them contain dust which has been produced in the processing of industrial diamonds. The end of the stone is used, with the stone itself placed flat on the grinding rest and held horizontally. Firm, but not heavy, pressure is employed for some 15 to 20 seconds, which is usually sufficient. Make sure that no sign of glaze remains on the wheel.

One fact which surprises many people who watch me grinding my tools is that I

never rest them on the piece of metal which is provided on most grinders for just this purpose. If the tool is placed on this, it will not be possible to exercise the required high degree of control of the pressure between bevel and wheel, and burning of the tool edges will be a constant problem. Control of this pressure is one of the main secrets in the grinding process. It should be very light indeed if the temperature of the metal is not to be raised to an unacceptable level, and the 'off hand' method which I teach will be found to be the most satisfactory. I do steady my hand against the grinding rest, or some part of the grinder — but never the tools.

If the stone is clean and sharp, and the pressure is correctly controlled, there will be no need to use water to cool the tools.

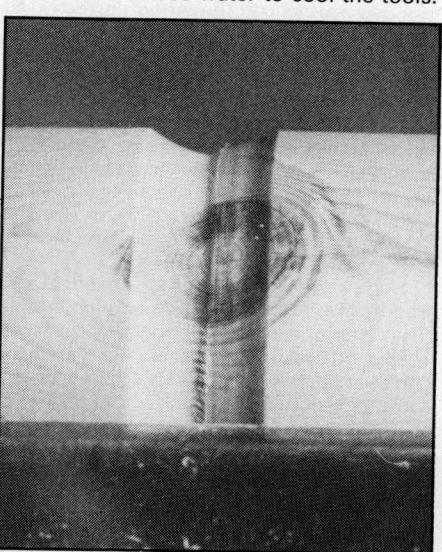

● *Avoid knots until you have some skill. Half inch spindle gouge used to commence cove shaping*

Plunging overheated blades into cold water is very bad practice, and should be avoided right from the outset.

The angle ground on a gouge or chisel provides a combination of strength and sharpness, so it will be seen that tools used on hard timbers will need steeper bevels than those used on the softer varieties. Here a mortise chisel and a firmer chisel can be compared. The former neds more strength, so it has a steeper angle. It is therefore obviously wrong to specify angles which should be ground on given types of tool, and those who know their subject will never do so.

As a general guide for the beginner, the width of the bevel on a gouge or chisel can

be about one third greater than the thickness of the material from which the tool is made. This will provide a satisfactory angle to be used while learning, and it allows for the fact that the thickness of tools can vary quite widely.

The angle by which a chisel is 'skewed' also has a direct relationship with the hardness or otherwise of the timbers on which it is to be used. Severe skew angles which produce fine points are good for soft timbers, but would quickly be overheated and blunted if used on really hard ones. Extremes of shape and bevel angle should be avoided during the learning period.

As for the grinding process itself, the biggest mistake made by beginners — apart from using too much pressure and so burning the tools — is in trying to place the bevels against the stone *correctly* at the commencement of the grinding. It is extremely difficult for an inexperienced person to put a tool on the stone exactly where it should be, and the usual result is a drastic shortening of the bevel angle. By far the best approach is to place the *heel* of the bevel against the stone, then bring the whole tool back down the stone, raising the handle slightly, until the edge is almost — but not quite — touching the surface. If the tool being ground is a gouge, it will now be rolled back and forth until sparks have been observed at all points along the cutting edge. In the case of a chisel, there is obviously no rolling, but if the tool is wider than the stone is must be moved slowly from side to side. A tool which is correctly shaped can be sharpened in about 15 seconds.

The 'burr' or wire edge which is produced in the grinding seems to worry some people, but it can be ignored. This is most certainly not the case with carving or

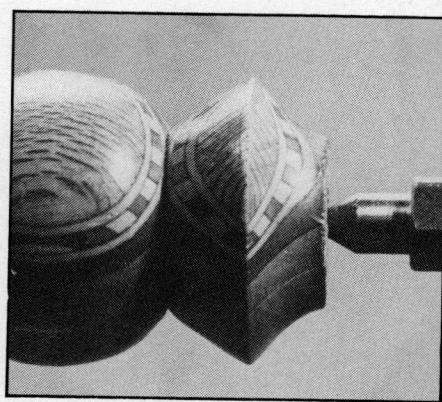

● *An infinite variety of patterns can be achieved in built up turning*

● Legs from old tables can be useful. Centred with extreme care they can be reshaped or skimmed to a new condition

Abrasive paper certainly has its uses, but it should be of a very fine grade, and should never be used to sand out rings or ridges produced by the tools. A fresh edge and a fine cut will do the job more quickly and efficiently. I never go below medium grade, and always use open coat garnet, which lasts a very long time, and does not clog. Good spindle work needs no abrasive paper, and certainly nothing coarser than grade 240 should be used. Where possible it is best to sand spindles along the grain while rotating the wood in the lathe slowly by hand. The fault which must at all costs be avoided is the production of scratches across the grain of spindles by sanding them with the lathe running. If the cutting techniques can be perfected there will be no need for this problem to arise. ■

general woodworking tools, but in this craft the burr is removed by the wood, the tools being virtually self honing in this respect.

Turning tools, as is the case with those used in other forms of woodwork, need to be sharpened when their edges are becoming dull, but since they do more work in a few minutes — in terms of shaving removal — than normal tools will do in an hour, the intervals between sharpenings can be very short. If the grinding is carried out correctly however, only a few thousandths of an inch of metal will be removed from the bevel surface, and very little time is taken up in the process, so that there is no excuse for continuing to work with dull edges. I would not expect more than about five minutes' work from the edge of a cutting tool in this craft.

Make sure that the bevel surface is smooth and continuous from heel to cutting edge, and does not consist of a series of facets, as it is likely to do if the tool is removed from the stone at intervals for inspection, or for immersion in water. Once the grinding has begun, I do not remove the tool from the stone until the job is finished.

Next month we will begin to try out the various tools which make up the set — so there is a month for the essential grinding practice!

Now a note or two on points which will be covered in more detail later. In woodturning the true master craftsman owes his status very largely to the fact that he — or she — has learned to control the depth of cut produced with the cutting tools (not scrapers) in the only manner which is entirely satisfactory. When used by craftsmen of this calibre the bevels of the chisels and gouges *always* rub the wood correctly, so that the surface finishes produced are remarkable in their smoothness, and little or no abrasive work is called for.

Eye protection is of paramount importance. During the initial learning period goggles of suitable quality, or better still an approved type of face visor, should be worn. I rely upon my spectacles to keep small chips out of my eyes, but those who do not wear them should take some form of precaution.

I rarely wear an overall or apron, but of course there is no objection to such things. The traditional woodworking apron is worn inside out by turners, to avoid the marsupial effect produced by the rapid filling of the large pocket with shavings.

● Good bead turning calls for constant practice

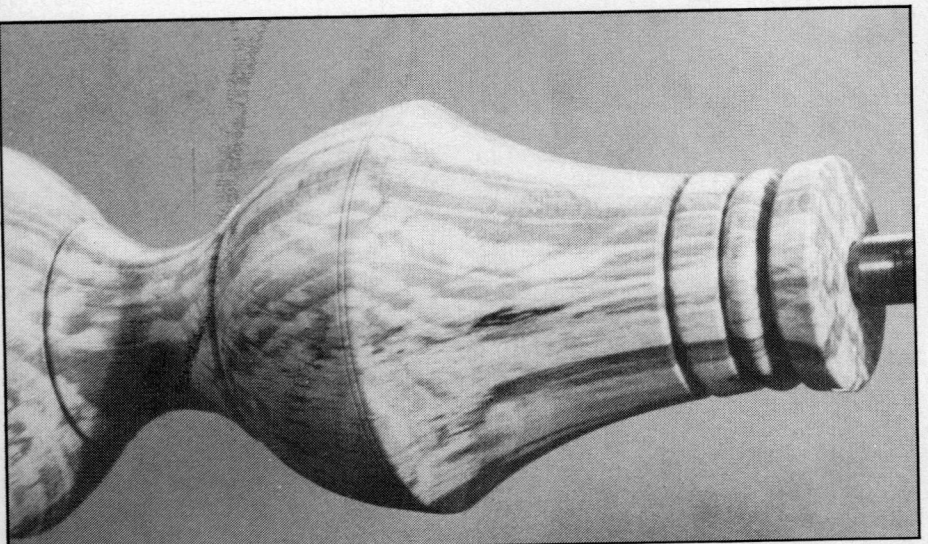

● Mottled beech stem for a table lamp turned as a ten min. demonstration, polished with no abrasive treatment

● Devil stone, essential for successful grinding, do not use a heavy metal dressing tool

Machine tools? Nu-tools!

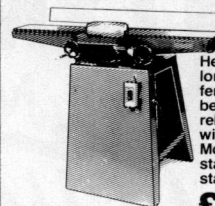

Symbolic Oak

by Polly Curds

In late June David Cooper (president of the British Home Grown Timber Merchants Association) officially opened the totally automated sawmill at Hartwell, Northants, with the ceremonial cutting of a magnificent oak log into boards ready for some lucky cabinetmaker. This sealed the addition of Midslade Sawmills to the company now known as Craftwoods.

The Mill at Hartwell was founded as E. Whatton & Sons Ltd in 1916 by Mr Eric Whatton. The three brothers Eric, Archie and Bob managed the mill until Bob died in April 1981: then in early 1982 John Baggs trading under the name Aird Associates purchased the assets of the company. John had been acting as a commission salesman since 1972; in 1975 he began to specialise in the growth area of marketing N American hardwoods to Europe. Recession loomed over the husband and wife team and in 1980 Aird Associates moved into exports from UK to USA and Europe. Sales of hardwoods in 1980 topped the £¼ million mark.

The object now as an importing company was to gain a foothold in the UK market – again primarily for US hardwoods. Business now thrived in the agency field, exports and imports (usually 15-20,000 cu ft in stock) were equally healthy. Two areas were lacking. One was filled in 1982 by the launch at Sherington, Bucks of Craftwoods. Billed as an up-market diy/craft outlet stocking over 50 species of hardwoods, veneers, turning squares and related products it became a success since it filled the needs of carvers, turners, sculptors and diy outlets wanting solid timber. Now with the signing over of the sawmill and the move of Craftwoods from Sherington to Hartwell (scheduled for early July) the company will

be able to consolidate, expand in any growth area as it presents itself and give a totally integrated business venture devoted to the hardwood industry.

When the mill is at full strength, Archie Whatton commented, it employs 17 men. He was delighted that work would continue

● *Some of the raw material that finds its way onto the timber stacks at Craftwoods perhaps? Obviously not the mighty oak though*

to be locally available for the men of the small Northants village. He will still be there too for consultation on home grown timbers, so too will John Baggs and David Tinegate. The latter has moved his family from the Yorkshire coast to the area that once was Rutland after an apprenticeship with Swedish firms in the Jonköping area.

Craftwoods, the Unique Woodworkers Store has been managed at Sherington by Steve Williams. Steve and his wife showed *Woodworker* around the premises principally to see at first hand the timber which is moving to Hartwell where it can be better presented to the public.

The Woodworker Show in October will be the place to see Craftwoods for yourselves on stand 94 in the Old Hall.

Craftwoods were one of the firms who responded to our pleas for Cuban mahogany and American black walnut. The latter they stock kiln dried (bubinga, lignum vitae, padauk and Indian rosewood are air dried, pear is freshsawn) to 10-12% m.c. by the square foot or as gun stock blanks. They have stocks of kiln dried American white ash in boards, wenge (panga panga), cherry, yew and rosewood. Stocks also include kiln dried African mahogany, lime, ebony, meranti, maple, tulipwood, teak, sapele and afrormosia. Discerning cabinetmakers might also like some of their supplies of kingwood.

Beside stocking hardwoods, they also supply logs and billets (laburnum, box, pear, apple, lilac, walnut, olive), ebony and rosewood fingerboards, turning and carving squares of teak, ebony, lignum vitae, mahogany, pau brauna, maple, red oak, ash and lemonwood: veneers (some nice birdseye maple and poplar burr among many others), veneer plys, panelling, mahogany doors, tools, books and finishing materials.

Banking on wood

George Mell recalls occasions when the world has used wooden coins — and even wooden cheques

One of the biggest cheques ever accepted by a bank was for one Canadian dollar only. What it lacked in monetary value it made up in size, for it was made out on a piece of wood 12 feet by four feet in payment of a government bill.

That is not the only instance of wooden money. In 1964 the Canadian Lumbermen's Association paid for a 10,000 square feet exhibition space at the World Fair in Montreal with a hand-carved wooden cheque 34in long. And in 1969 the Bank of Marin at Corte Madeira, accepted a cheque made out, for some unspecified reason, on a wooden door measuring 80in by 20in.

On many occasions when small change was scarce, municipalities and private traders have made their own coins, often from leather. During the siege of Leyden by the Spaniards in 1573-4 the Dutch exhausted their stocks of coins and made do with coins made from the leather bindings of old books.

But the first wooden coins appeared in Tenino, Washington, USA, during the great slump. Trade was at a standstill for lack of banknotes and coins, so the Chamber of Commerce started issuing wooden coins worth 25 cents, 50 cents, one dollar, five dollars and ten dollars, through the local bank. To prevent counterfeiting they were all signed by three of the bank's directors. About 5,000 25 cent coins were made and about 105 ten dollar coins. They were made of two rectangles of Sitka spruce with a piece of paper in between.

The town of Blaine made a similar issue in 1933, running to about 866,000 pieces.

News of these unusual currencies spread and orders poured in from all parts of the world, while other towns in Washington state copied them, often to commemorate some event.

Then other states took up the idea. In South Carolina, Columbia celebrated its Sesquicentennial with a wooden coin issue.

Atlanta thought the film *Gone With The Wind* a suitable occasion for more wooden money and went on to produce similar issues to commemorate the death of comedian Will Rogers and even one city's Hog Days.

As prosperity returned wooden coins were no longer needed, but a temporary shortage of coins in Wisconsin prompted the Bank of Monroe to remedy the deficiency with wooden coins, but the Treasury Department thought the issue should have a definite date of expiry and ordered the Secret Service to confiscate what wooden nickels were left.

An exhibition in Chicago saw another wooden issue, more as an advertising stunt than anything else, and in 1937 Portsmouth, Ohio, marked the 150th anniversary of the Northwest Territory with an issue of wooden rectangular nickels.

Collectors naturally sought out wooden coins and formed an Organisation of Wooden Money Collectors that soon had 500 members in the United States.

Tenino coins, being the first of their kind, are the most sought after, closely followed by those from Blaine and are classified as 'depression issues'. Less desirable are 'celebration issues', but even 'private advertising issues' are not to be despised.

As might be expected, wooden coins are rarely, if ever, seen in this country. ■

  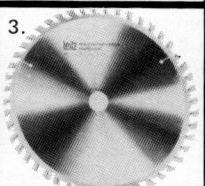
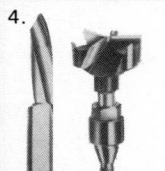  

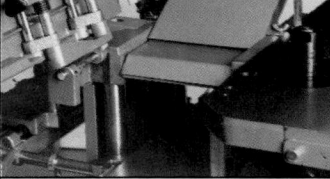

Sewing machine cabinet

One of the real show-stoppers of last year's Woodworker Show was Ray Petty's sewing machine cabinet. This complex piece of furniture employs some ingenious features of construction, and here Ray, who is a teacher of craft design and technology at Heathland School, Hounslow, explains how it is made

My sewing machine cabinet was made as a 'special exercise' at Shoreditch College of Education, now part of Brunel University, and for that reason there has been no corner cutting or use of inferior materials. In any case doing such things as lipping every edge prior to veneering provides a more hardwearing edge, and should eliminate chipped veneers on the corners and edges. I

used yew veneers and solid yew where appropriate, but any other timber could be used of course, and would probably be much easier to work. Yew can be rather difficult at times due to its interlocking grain, but it does make a large flat panel look much more interesting than a plainer timber.

The size of the cabinet was dictated by my own circumstances, as it lives in an alcove in my lounge. It could of course be made larger which would provide a larger working surface, though I am assured that it is amply big enough as it is. Two opening lids are provided so that there is access to the storage void at the back of the cabinet by lifting either opening flap, depending on which one you need to reach. The small right hand flap provides a handy place to put scissors, pins, and anything else which would otherwise clutter up the working surface. Going back briefly to veneers, when the flaps are opened the best effect is gained if the veneer runs right across the working surface. Also when the flaps are closed they should equally show continuity in the veneers, therefore when buying the veneers it is a good idea to buy two lengths, a long length for the opened out top, and a shorter length for the rest of the carcase.

No complicated stays or supports are provided for the flaps, the doors provide this function. This might seem hazardous at first glance, because if the flaps are opened without any support they will of course break, due to their weight. However when

the cabinet is in its alcove they cannot be fully opened. Also, in order to raise the sewing machine, the doors must be open in order to reach it, so even if the flaps are raised first the doors still need to be opened. So all is quite safe.

Shelves are hung from the insides of the doors. They are made of Perspex; plywood could be used but transparent Perspex means that the contents can be easily seen. The shelves hang on tracking but they could just as easily be permanently fixed.

I searched through the hardware stores and catalogues to try to find a stay which would lock the doors open, to prevent them being inadvertently closed when the flaps are resting on them. In the end I had to design a stay myself, which, can be made with hand tools, by the way. They are in fact optional; it is only if you have children that they are really necessary.

The sewing machine lifting mechanism was bought direct from the manufacturer, Turner Precision Engineering Ltd, Dovers Corner, New Road, Rainham, Essex, RM3 8QT. Whilst on the subject of the mechanism, it will accommodate a free arm sewing machine or the ordinary flat bed machine. Most sewing machine manufacturers seem to use the same plastic moulded plinth so the cabinet is pretty well universal.

CARCASE

Starting from the bottom and working up, the floor panel is first. I used two sheets of 9mm birch ply and laminated them together to achieve the required thickness of 18mm.

The material for the castor mounting blocks comes from the cutout for the operator's feet, so it is as well to cut this out in one piece. The top surface is veneered before final trimming, and to save materials this can be done with three strips, mitred where they join, which also gives the impression of long grain where the floor is narrow.

The rear plinth and castor mounting blocks are made up next, ready to be fixed to the floor panel before the back and sides are put on. I arranged the height of the castor mounting blocks so that the bottom edge of the plinth would just brush a carpet, thus the cabinet would look like a piece of furniture actually standing on its plinth. This depends on individual preference, and the thickness of the block also depends on the height of the castors; mine are 42mm.

The rear plinth is one of the few components made of solid wood, and so it is well worth cutting this and the front false plinth, which is attached to the doors, out of one length to get continuity of grain. It means putting aside two small pieces which will be part of the sides, but attached to the doors for use later. The joints at the rear are bare faced tongue-and-groove, with the tongue on the back piece. The castor mounting blocks are morticed into the back and sides. The front blocks can be left slightly oversize on the front, and in the case of the left hand one the inside face also, so that they can be trimmed flush with the edge of the floor panel after assembly. There is no edge treatment for the plywood floor panel, partly because when the cabinet is doubling as a piece of furniture it is hidden anyway, and also the effect of 40-plus plies on the blocks is in fact quite pleasing.

The rear plinth is dowelled on to the underside of the floor panel, but first the back, partition and sides are prepared with all their associated dowel holes ready to be assembled after the plinth has been attached.

I will not say very much about the

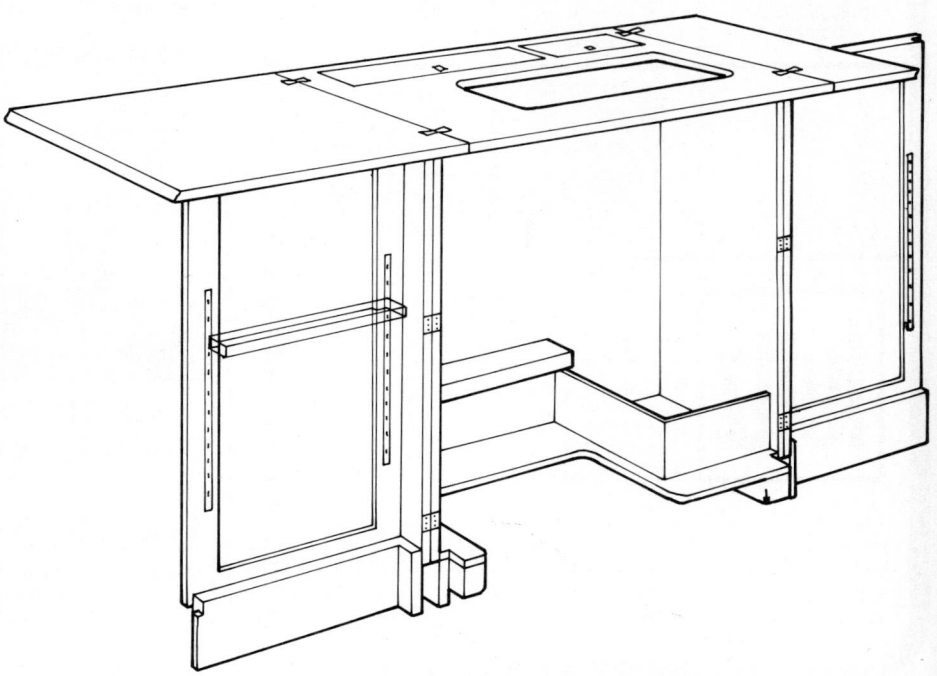

veneering as the method is usually dictated by circumstances. For instance, I was able to use a heated vacuum press which considerably speeded up the process. All the edges of the sheets which are veneered are lipped, for hidden edges I used utile simply because it was much easier to work than yew for no extra cost. For hidden surfaces in the storage void and the back panel I used a cheap mahogany balancing veneer. One thing is important at this stage; part of the sides are attached to the doors, so a narrow strip of veneer cut off the sheet used for the sides must be marked and put aside so that it will match the sides when the doors are hung. The inside face does not matter quite so much. It just depends on how much of a perfectionist you are.

Except for this forward planning, the construction of the sides, partition and back is quite straightforward, largely a veneering exercise in fact. A batten is glued and screwed to the back of the partition and on the front of the back panel, these will support the storage void floors. For the storage void divider, a housing joint is cut in the back of the partition and in the front of the back panel. The divider merely slides in, it need not be glued. The machine lifting mechanism support is glued and screwed on to the front of the partition also. The foot switch tray is fixed to the right hand side and the partition with housing joints, so these must also be cut before assembly.

Finally a rail is made which goes between the top front corners of the sides. This can be attached either with mortice and tenons or dowels, either way the joints are prepared now. If a door stay is going to be used the lower edge of the rail must be relieved to clear the moving parts of the stay. The exact position is difficult to determine until the stay can be offered up with the doors hung, therefore it is wise to only relieve enough to clear the connecting pins on the stay and not to try to let the whole stay in flush with the lower edge of the rail at this stage.

When all the dowel holes are drilled in the floor panel, sides, partition and back we can return to the rear plinth and attach it to the floor panel. When the glue has set the sides, partition and back can be assembled with the floor panel.

The foot switch tray is made from two pieces of yew, with a simple tongue-and-grooved joint on one corner. The ends are morticed into the side and the partition, while the bottom edge is screwed and glued to the floor panel. Rather large clamps are needed to assemble this component, and fairly slack joints are an advantage in this case, because neither of the joints can go straight into each other as they both start out of line when they are offered up.

The fixed top is a convenient part to make next, if only because it is easier to make the doors fit a complete carcase. The top might look needlessly complicated; why for instance could it not be made out of a sheet of plywood? There are three holes in the top, one for the sewing machine and two for the storage voids, and I wanted a solid edge round each of these. Also the front edge of the storage void holes is curved to allow the lids to open, which would be very difficult to do whilst working in a restricted gap.

The bulk of the material is utile with a yew

CUTTING LIST

NO	PART	MATERIAL	L	W	T
	Doors				
2	Hanging stile	Yew	647	50	20
1	LH Closing stile	Yew	647	60	20
2	Top rail	Yew	335	50	20
2	Lower rail	Yew	335	60	20
2	Panel	Ply	519	249	12
2	Part side	Yew	647	64	16
1	RH Closing stile	Yew	647	55	20
4	Lipping	Yew	279	15	12
4	Lipping	Yew	549	15	12
1	Cabinet top rail	Yew	708	50	20
	Foot switch tray				
1	Front	Yew	155	100	10
1	Side	Yew	278	100	10
1	Storage void partition	Ply	266	118	6
1	Storage void floor	Ply	238	96	6
1	Storage void floor	Ply	239	96	6
1	Storage void floor	Ply	225	96	6
1	Storage void lid	Lamin/B	411	99	18
1	Storage void lid	Lamin/B	159	99	18
2	Lipping	Yew	431	18	10
2	Lipping	Yew	179	18	10
4	Lipping	Yew	119	18	10
2	Rear castor mounting	Waste from Cabinet floor panel			
2	Front castor mounting				
	Front false plinth				
1	LH	Yew	359	100	16
1	RH	Yew	356	100	16
2	Side	Yew	50	100	16
	Rear plinth				
2	Side	Yew	414	70	16
1	Back	Yew/Utile	692	70	16
1	Floor panel	Ply	720	470	9
1	Floor panel	Ply	470	720	9
1	Partition	Lamin/B	698	619	16
1	Mechanism support	Utile	250	40	30
1	Back panel	Chip/B	698	619	12
2	Batten	Utile	708	10	10
4	Lipping	Utile	708	15	5
2	Lipping	Utile	647	15	5
2	Lipping	Utile	629	15	5
2	Side panel	Lamin/B	637	420	16
2	Lipping	Yew	647	16	5
2	Lipping	Utile	430	16	5
	Opening top				
1	LH flap	Lamin/B	520	490	18
1	RH flap	Lamin/B	520	238	18
4	Lipping	Yew	540	18	10
2	Lipping	Yew	510	18	10
2	Lipping	Yew	258	18	10
	Fixed top				
1	Centre section	Lamin/B	215	145	18
1	Centre section lipping	Utile	215	20	18
1	LH edge	Utile	520	50	18
1	RH edge	Utile	520	75	18
1	Front edge	Utile	640	122	18
1	Centre edge	Utile	640	63	18
1	Rear edge	Utile	640	25	18
1	Division	Utile	124	30	18
2	Lipping	Yew	760	18	10
2	Lipping	Yew	540	18	10
4	Shelf channel	Brass	456	12	1/16in
	Door stays				
2	Guide channel	Brass	145	20	1/16in
2	Lever arm	Brass	108	38	1/16in
2	Stay rod	Brass	166	16	1/16in
2	Connecting pins	Brass	10	∅12	
2	Connecting pins	Brass	7.5	∅12	
	Shelf, materials for one				
2	End	Perspex	41	25	3
1	Bottom	Perspex	296	40	3
1	Front	Perspex	302	28	3

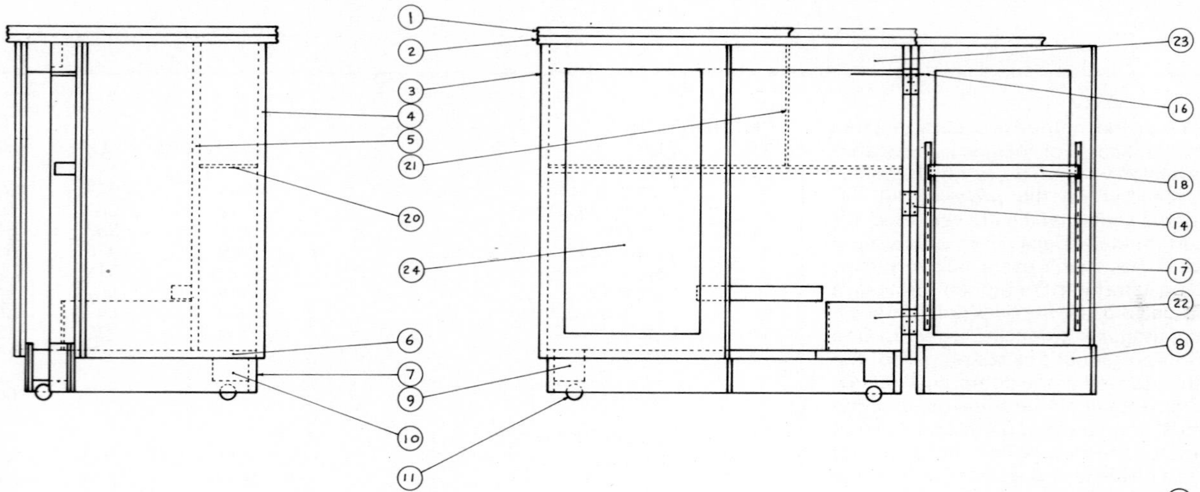

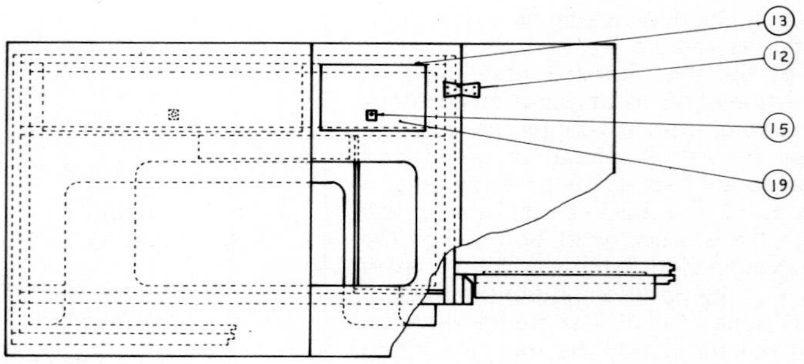

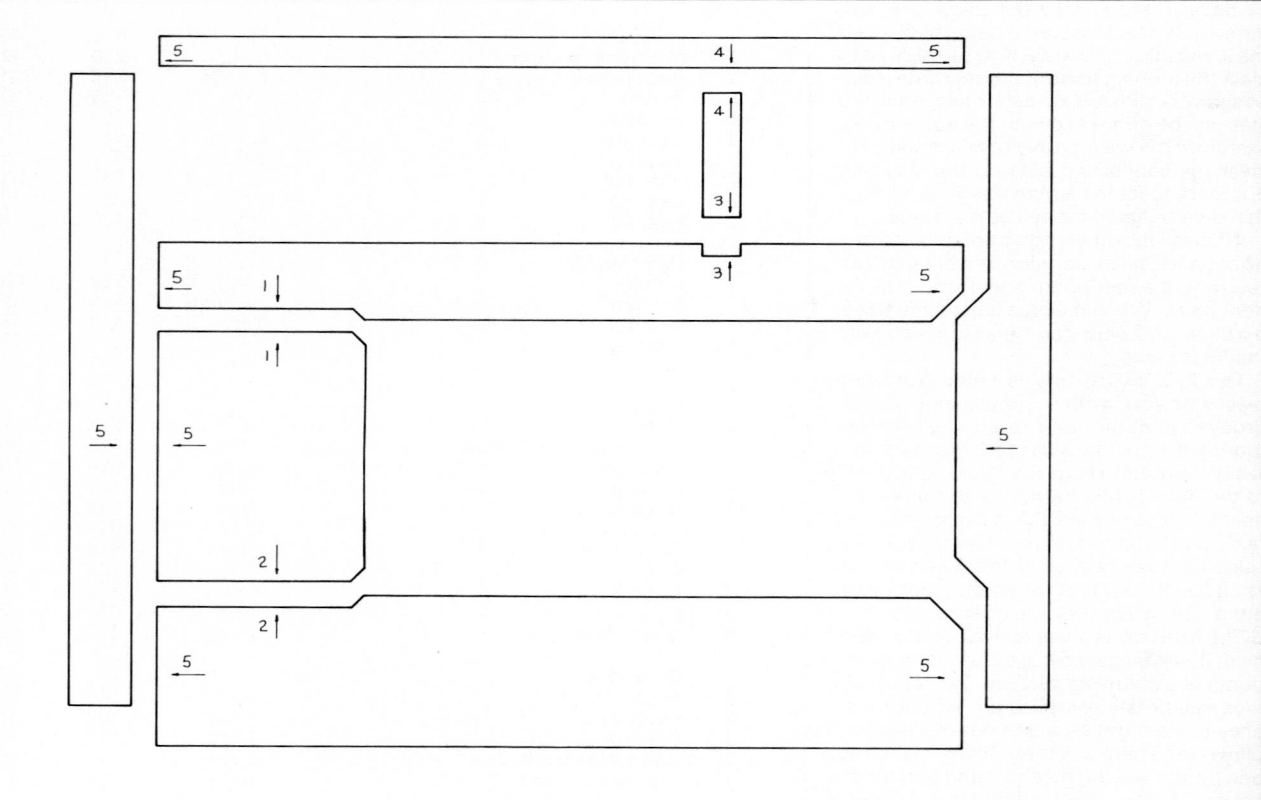

ITEM	PART	MATERIAL	NO	ITEM	PART	MATERIAL	NO
12	Counter flap hinge	Brass	4	24	Doors	Yew/Ply	2
11	Castors		4	23	Top rail	Yew	1
10	Rear castor mounting block	Ply	2	22	Foot switch tray	Yew	1
9	Front castor mounting block	Ply	2	21	Storage void partition	Ply	1
8	Front false plinth	Yew	1	20	Storage void floor	Ply	3
7	Rear plinth	Yew	1	19	Storage void lids	Laminboard	2
6	Floor panel	Ply	1	18	Shelf	Perspex	Max16
5	Partition	Chipboard	1	17	Shelf channel	Brass	4
4	Back panel	Chipboard	1	16	Door stay	Brass	2
3	Side panel	Laminboard	2	15	Ring pull	Brass	2
2	Fixed top	Utile/Laminboard	1	14	Draws butt hinge	Brass	6
1	Opening top flaps	Laminboard	1	13	Concealed Soss hinge	Brass	4

SEWING MACHINE CABINET
Assembly drawing
Scale 1:5   Projection ◁ ⦿

SEWING MACHINE CABINET
Fixed top – Order of assembly
Scale 1:2   Projection ◁ ⦿

lipping round the edge, and one small panel of laminated board. All the joints are dowelled, and as the finished item must be flat care must be taken to drill all the holes perfectly square into perfectly square edges. The top surface can be planed true after assembly of course, but this could be rather tedious.

Two points are important to note. Firstly, the position of the cut out for the sewing machine might vary for a different lifting mechanism so it would be advisable to purchase this early on and check. Secondly, the front edge of the storage void cut outs (ie the curved edge) should finish up halfway across the top edge of the partition, so as to provide a positive closing stop for the storage void lids, see Fig I.

The curved edge for the storage void lids to close against is worked first by planing a bevel, and then cutting the curve with a scratch stock. It is cut along the full length of the wood, then a square cut out is made for the short piece which divides the two storage voids, thus eliminating having to match the curved edge on the end of the short piece. The mortices for the boss hinges must be cut in the edge of the piece which runs along the back. Determine the exact distance from the top surface by experimenting with pieces of scrap first.

Assembly is in the order shown in the diagram. The outside edges are lipped with yew mitred at the corners. As to the method the best way is to put on two adjacent pieces, then the third and finally trim the fourth to fit and then glue it on. The finger grip moulding is worked with a scratch stock, which can be done now or after veneering. The edges of the machine cut out are shaped before veneering, using a

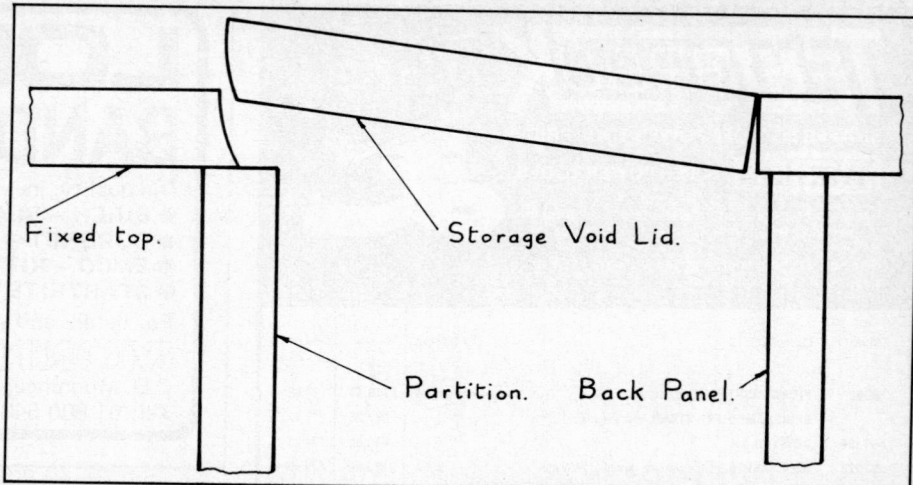

Fixed top.   Storage Void Lid.

Partition.   Back Panel.

spokeshave.

It would be best to make the storage void lids now and fix their position before veneering. I left them till later and spent a long time juggling about altering the mortices alternately filling and re-chopping before I got it right. The best way would be to make them too thick, by laminating thin plywood on to both sides of the laminated board, for instance, rather than using solid wood which might be unstable. Fix them in and plane the surface flush with the rest of the top, then remove them to veneer separately.

Foward planning needs to be carried out during veneering, because the storage void lids need to be veneered to match the rest of the top. It is not really possible to cut out of a sheet of veneer exact size pieces for the lids, either before or after fixing the veneer, so

the next leaf in a sheaf of veneers must be set aside to provide two pieces for the lids. These will not match absolutely correctly but they will give the illusion of coming out of the same sheet as the rest of the top. Clearly there are added complications if a join goes through the lids.

I mentioned continuity of the veneers in the introduction, and in order to achieve this it is necessary to make the opening flaps before the top can be veneered. The flaps are laminated board with a yew lipping. Only two corners of the lipping are mitred; the corners at the join in the flaps are simply butted, because an unsightly join would show where the meeting edges are shaped. The meeting edge is shaped by first planing a bevel on each piece, and finishing it with a scratch stock. Prepare three sheets of veneer; one to cover the entire working

(continued on p 616)

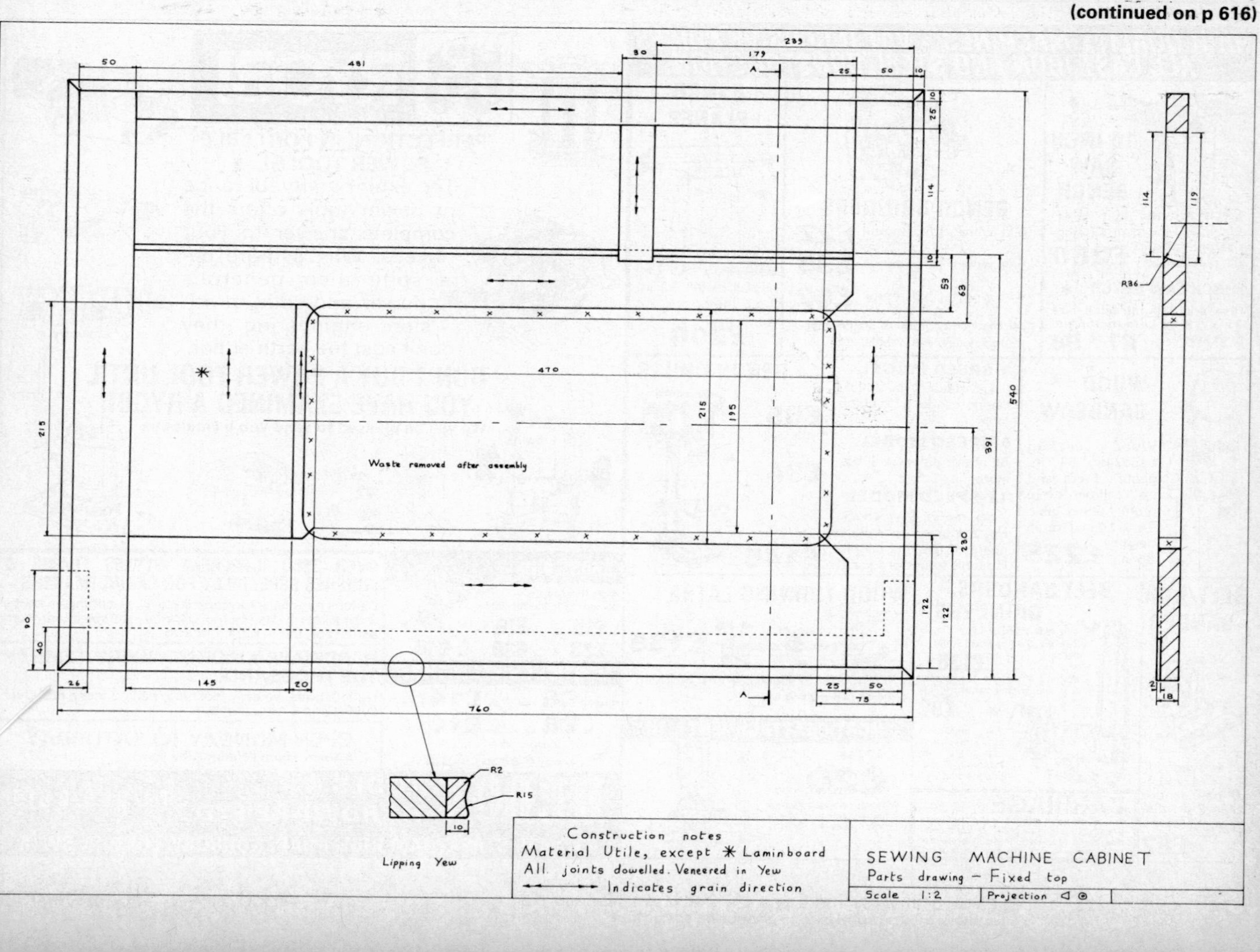

Waste removed after assembly

Lipping Yew

Construction notes
Material Utile, except ✳ Laminboard
All joints dowelled. Veneered in Yew
→ Indicates grain direction

SEWING MACHINE CABINET
Parts drawing – Fixed top
Scale 1:2   Projection

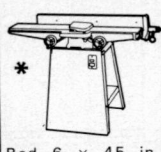

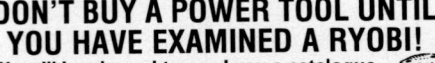

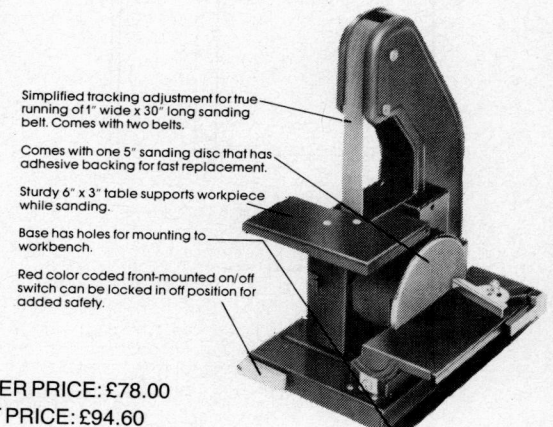

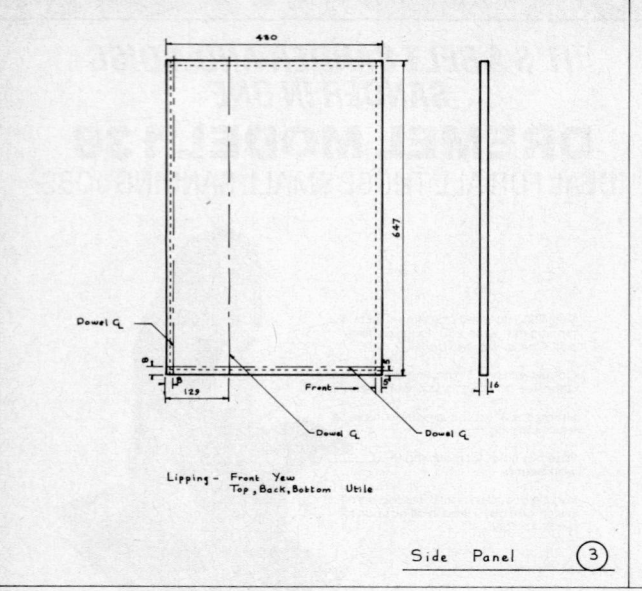

Lipping – Front View
Top, Back, Bottom Utile

Side Panel ③

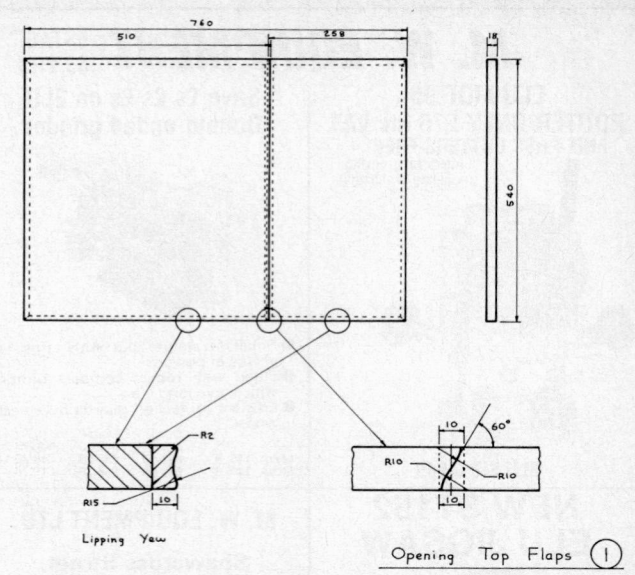

Lipping View

Opening Top Flaps ①

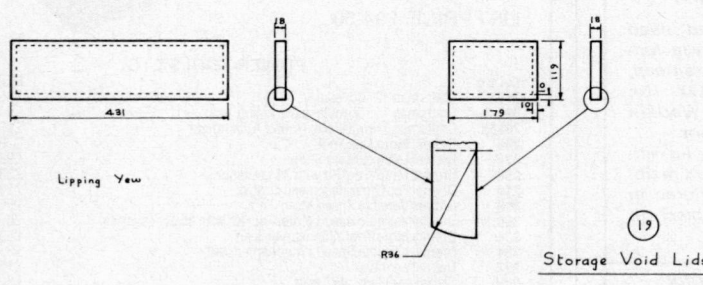

Lipping View

R36

Storage Void Lids ⑲

SEWING MACHINE CABINET
Parts drawing
Scale 1:5 | Projection ◁ ⊙

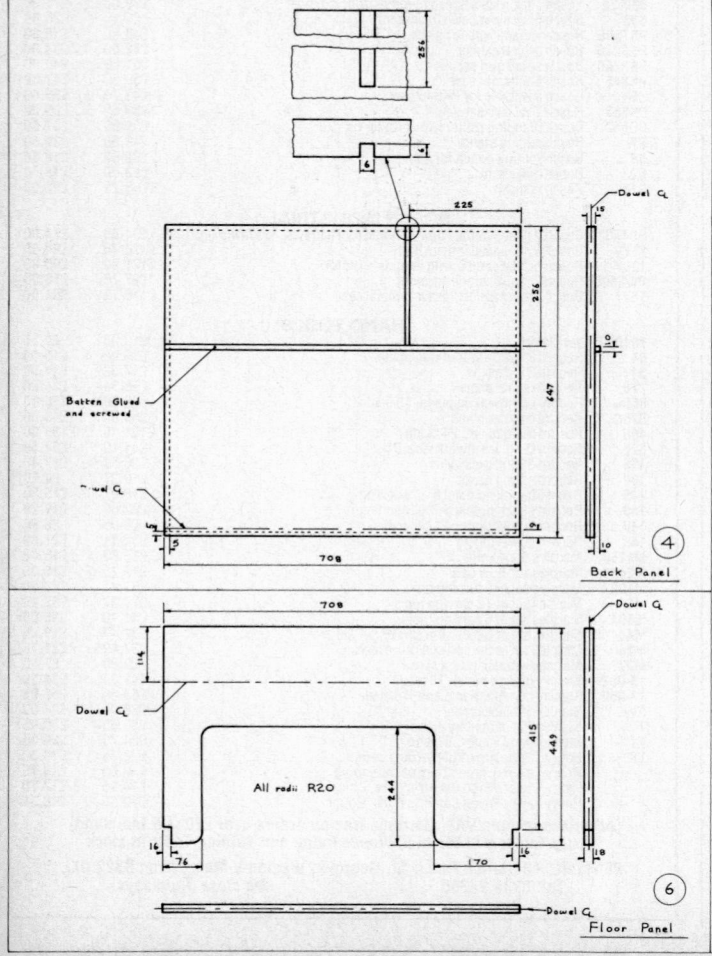

Batten Glued and screwed

Dowel C$_L$

Dowel C$_L$

Back Panel ④

Dowel C$_L$

All radii R20

Dowel C$_L$

Dowel C$_L$

Floor Panel ⑥

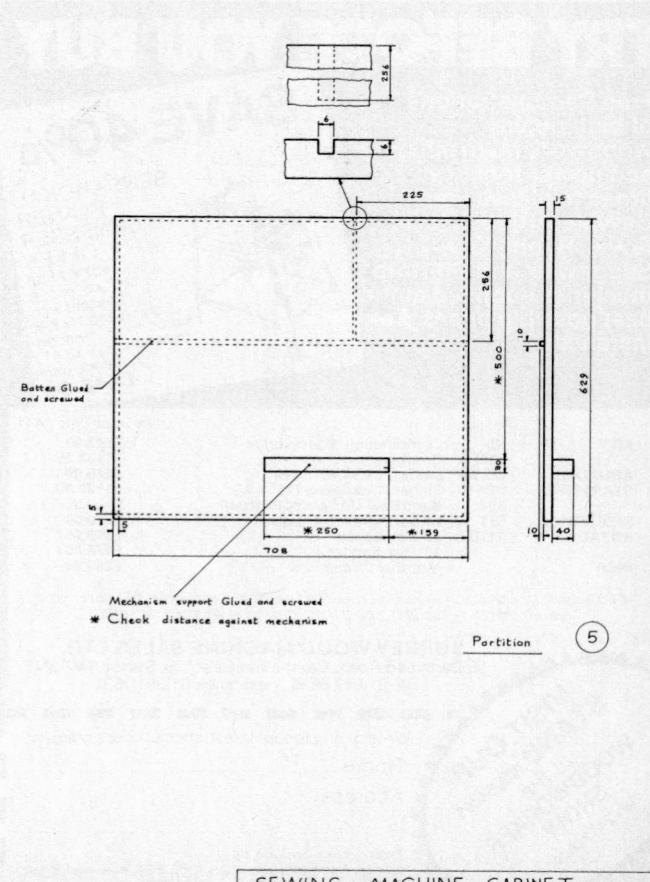

Batten Glued and screwed

Mechanism support Glued and screwed
* Check distance against mechanism

Partition ⑤

SEWING MACHINE CABINET
Parts drawing
Scale 1:5 | Projection ◁ ⊙

surface with the flaps open; one to cover just the flaps when they are closed; and one a cheap balancing veneer for the underside of the fixed top. Lay the fixed top and the flaps out and carefully cut the longest of the three sheets of veneer so that the middle section, over the fixed top, leaves the minimum amount of waste at the ends, and if necessary mark the sheets so that they cannot be put on the wrong way round. Close the flaps and make one cut in the short sheet of veneer, and again if necessary mark the sheets.

The top surface and underside of the fixed top are veneered without cutting the veneer to fit, it is then trimmed out of the cut outs after it has been glued down. If you can cut the veneer out of the storage void cut outs with a kerf of nil thickness then these pieces could be used for the lids, but I think it highly unlikely that it could be done without damaging the veneer in the process.

The top edges of the doors have a strip of felt on them to protect the flaps when they are opened, so the underside of the top needs relieving at the front and part way along the sides for a depth of 2mm to clear the felt strip.

It is best to let in the cabinet flap hinges on the bench before fixing the top to the carcase. This type of hinge is somewhat floppy in its closed position, but I chose these because I wanted them to be as hidden as possible when closed, without an unsightly knuckle showing.

The top is fixed to the carcase with brass screwplates, but slide the storage void divider into place first.

DOORS

Now that the carcase is assembled the doors can be made. They consist of a yew frame, grooved to take a flush panel which is veneered plywood with a wide yew lipping around the edges for working the tongues in. The joints are haunched mortice and tenon. Each door has part of the carcase sides, attached with a tongue-and-grooved joint to what would be the hanging stile; the part of the side then becomes the hanging stile.

Construction is the usual method. Chop the mortices first, then cut the tenons, and plough the grooves. The tongue-and-grooved joint can be prepared in what would be the hanging stiles, and the section of carcase sides. The side pieces can then be veneered, taking care to use the correct pieces of veneer and matching their position with the sides of the carcase. A small rebate 2mm × 2mm is cut on the front edge of the side pieces to give the appearance of a gap between the doors and the sides of the carcase. The panels are lipped and veneered next. The back faces should be cleaned up and polished before cutting them round the edges, so that the fit in the grooves is not loosened if a lot of cleaning up is needed. I decided to leave a 2mm gap around the edge of the panel so I accordingly left a step in the rebate, with a slight allowance for movement, to maintain this gap after clamping up.

I must now admit to a design fault. If a lock is fitted in the right hand door it will get in the way of the shelf channel, therefore before relieving the backs of the stiles for the channel check the size of the lock. What I had to do was make the channel for the right hand door in two parts so as to leave a gap for the lock. Once the channel recesses have been cut and the panels cleaned up and polished the doors are ready to be glued up. When the glue has set remove the horns from the stiles, clean up the back faces of the frames and fit the side pieces, these can then be trimmed to length with a final cleaning up of the top and bottom edges after the doors have been offered up to the carcase.

It will be necessary to fit a door stop under the top of the carcase, to which a bolt escutcheon can also be fitted. With this stop in place, the doors can be offered up and the top and bottom edges trimmed to fit, followed by cutting the rebates on the closing stiles. It is a good idea to actually hang the doors at this stage, obtain the required fit between them, and then remove them, because further work with a plane or router will be impossible once the false plinth has been fitted.

The false plinth is made using secret mitred dovetails on the corners and, as with doors, the rebates at the closing ends need to be cut to provide a finished fit before assembly, because afterwards the doors will be in the way of any further planing. The top section of each rebate will need to be removed in order to clear the opposite door, this will really need to be done after assembly when it can be seen exactly how much has to come off. The joints are glued up and the plinth is glued to the doors in one operation so that there are no gaps between the plinth and the doors. Trim the side pieces of the plinth, and relieve the top front corners to clear the doors and the doors are almost completed.

If the door frames are slightly proud of the panels, it simplifies cleaning up; all that is needed is a sheet of card or scrap veneer to prevent marking the panels. Yew can be

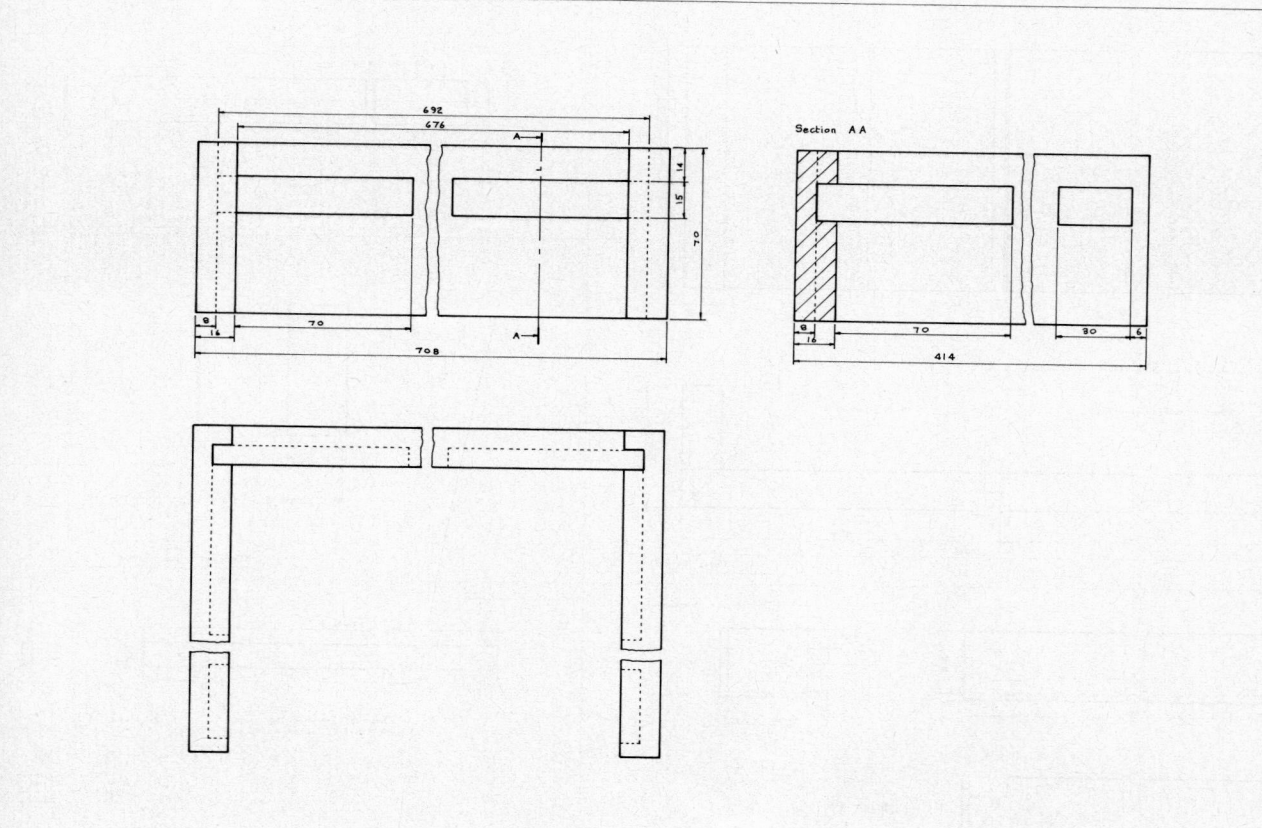

SEWING MACHINE CABINET
Parts drawing — Rear plinth
Scale 1:1   Projection ◁ ⊙

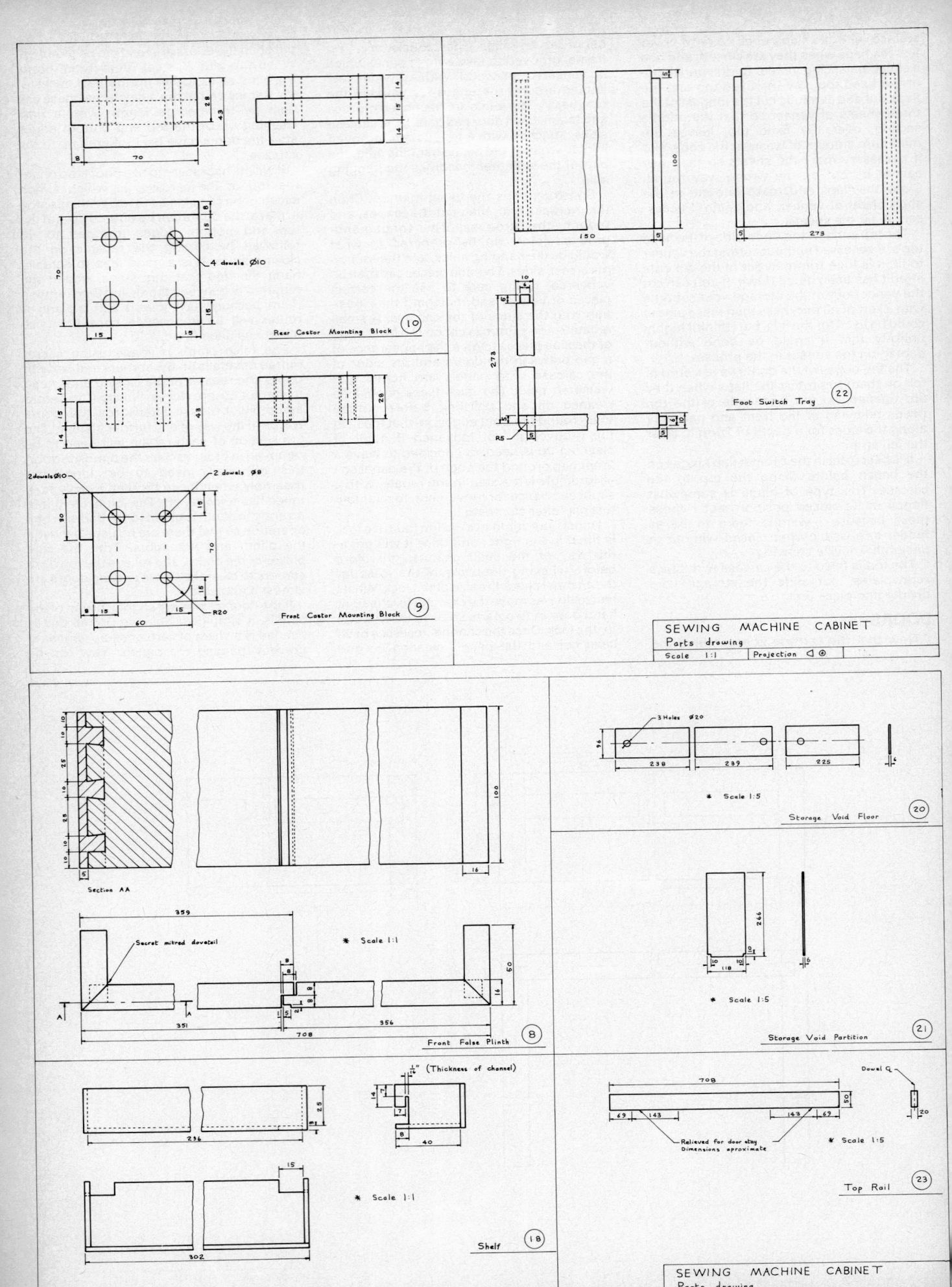

Rear Castor Mounting Block ⑩

4 dowels Ø10

Front Castor Mounting Block ⑨

2 dowels Ø10   2 dowels Ø8

R20

Foot Switch Tray ㉒

R5

SEWING MACHINE CABINET
Parts drawing
Scale 1:1   Projection ◁ ⊙

Section AA

Secret mitred dovetail

* Scale 1:1

Front False Plinth ⑧

3 Holes Ø20

* Scale 1:5

Storage Void Floor ⑳

* Scale 1:5

Storage Void Partition ㉑

1/16" (Thickness of channel)

* Scale 1:1

Shelf ⑱

Relieved for door stay
Dimensions approximate

* Scale 1:5

Dowel G

Top Rail ㉓

SEWING MACHINE CABINET
Parts drawing
Scale *   Projection ◁ ⊙

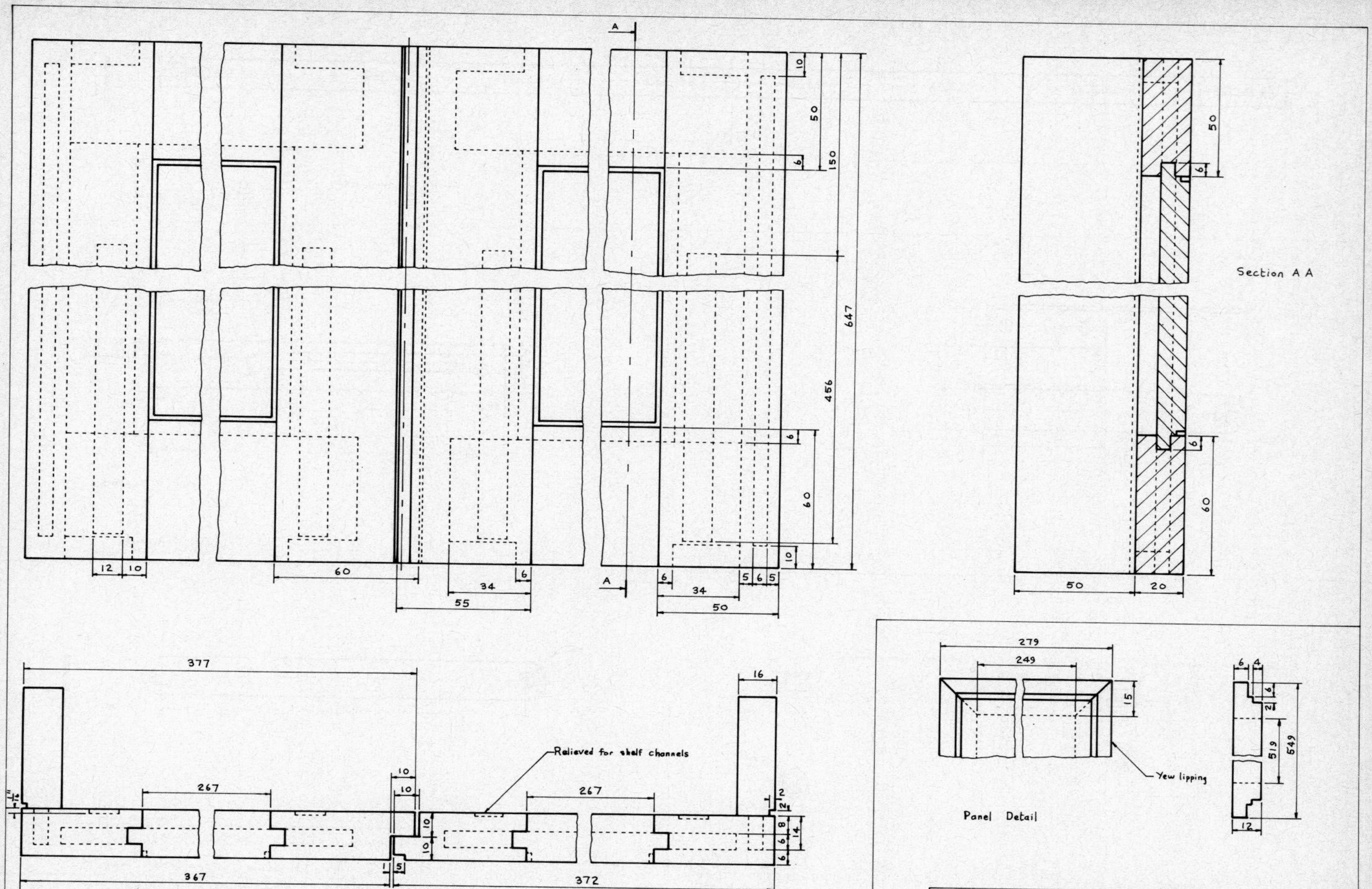

Section A A

Relieved for shelf channels

Panel Detail

Yew lipping

SEWING MACHINE CABINET
Parts drawing – Doors
Scale 1:1   Projection ◁ ⦿

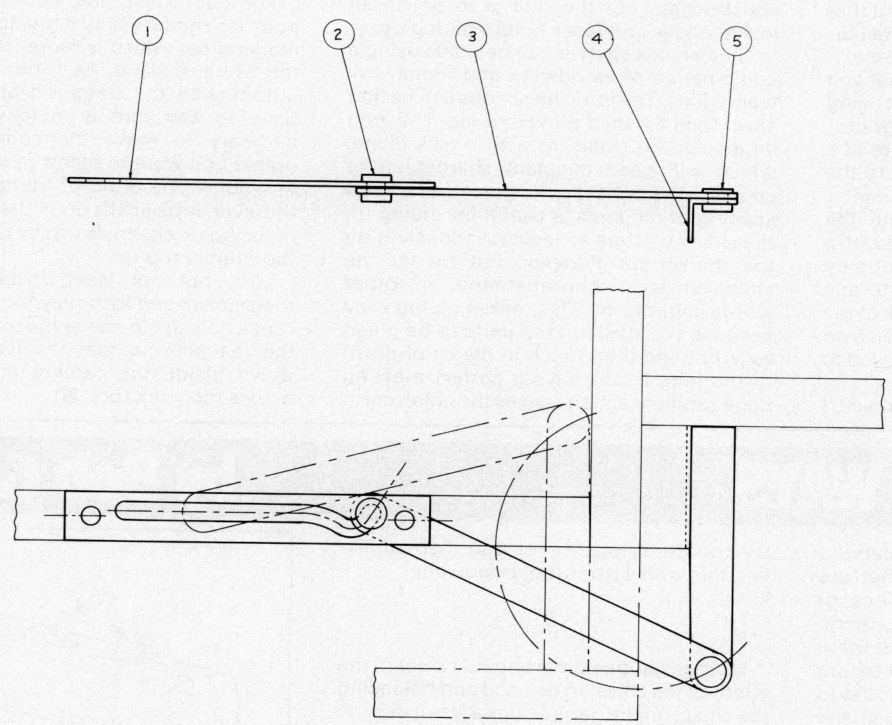

5	Connecting pin	Brass	2
4	Lever arm	Brass	2
3	Stay rod	Brass	2
2	Connecting pin	Brass	2
1	Guide channel	Brass	2
ITEM	PART	MATERIAL	NO

SEWING MACHINE CABINET
R.H. Door stay.   Assembly drawing
Scale 1:1   Projection ◁ ⦿

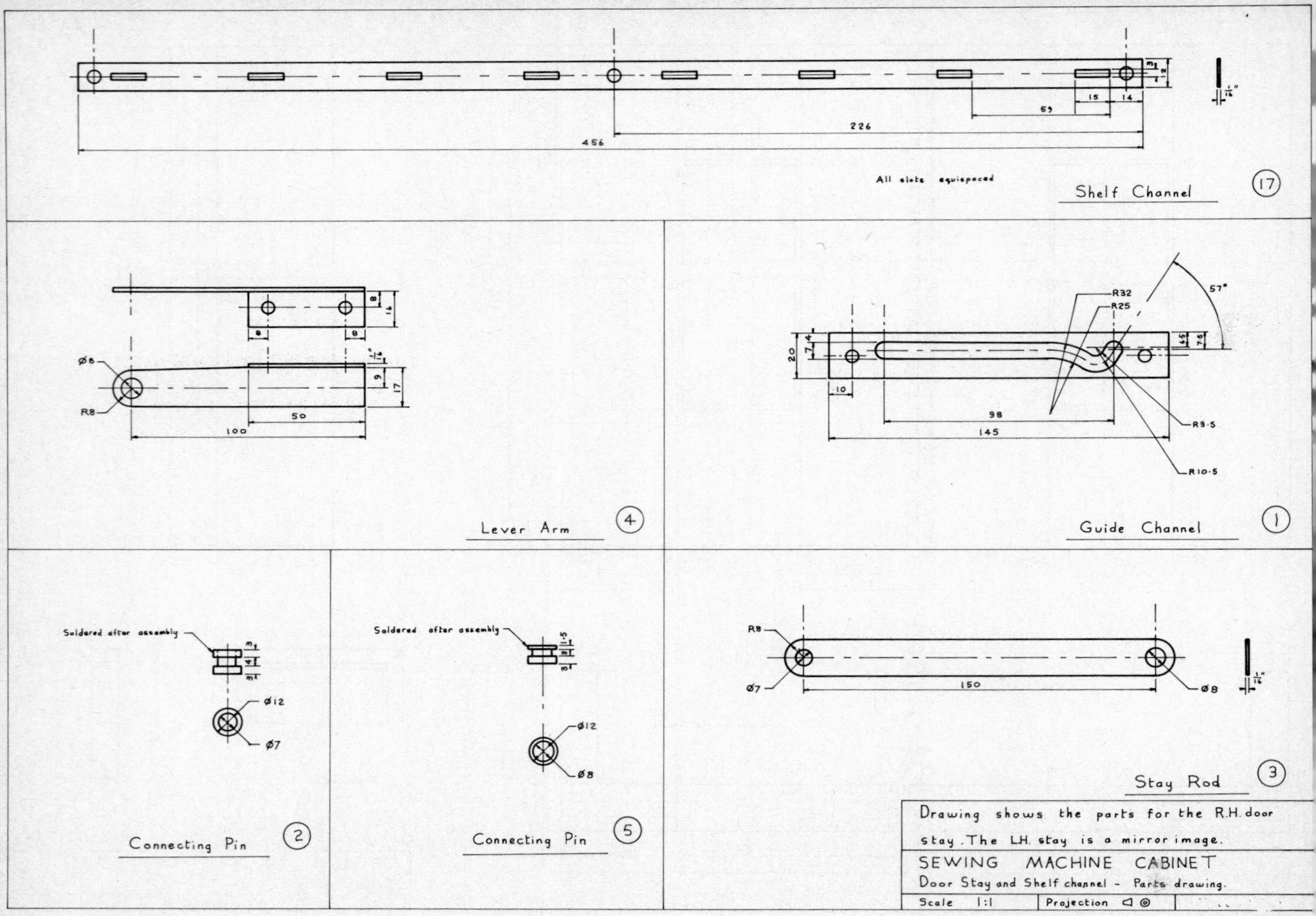

All slots equispaced

Shelf Channel (17)

Lever Arm (4)

Guide Channel (1)

Soldered after assembly

Connecting Pin (2)

Soldered after assembly

Connecting Pin (5)

Stay Rod (3)

Drawing shows the parts for the R.H. door
stay. The LH. stay is a mirror image.

SEWING MACHINE CABINET
Door Stay and Shelf channel - Parts drawing.

| Scale 1:1 | Projection ◁ ⊙ | |

very difficult to plane, even with a backed off plane iron, and to be honest I found that an orbital sander cleaned up my particular timber very quickly. So quickly in fact that it was behaving rather like a power planer and I had to be careful not to go too far, but using it I had no problem with tearing the grain.

All that remains with the doors is to fit a bolt to the left hand door and a lock to the right hand and then they can be rehung.

The storage void floors complete the woodwork, these are simply plywood with a finger hole bored in each one so that they can be lifted out. There is a large storage area underneath the floors at the back of the cabinet but it needs a full arm stretch to reach the bottom, which is why I decided to include a floor half way up.

The finish depends on personal choice, I

have made no mention of polishing during construction, but the rule is to polish all inside edges and faces before gluing up.

The Perspex shelves can be made using a combination of woodwork and metalwork techniques. The intricate shapes can be first sawn then finished off with a file. The long edges can be trued up with a jack plane, which will need constant sharpening of course. A simple jig to give the correct spacing of the ends is useful for gluing up the shelves. There are several adhesives on the market for Perspex, but by far the cheapest is trichloromethane, in other words chloroform. This makes gluing easy because you position the parts to be glued together and then touch in the chloroform to the join, if you have a perfect meeting edge capillary action causes the chloroform

to fill the join.

The door stays and shelf channels can both be made using hand tools. It is the marking out which is more important than the actual making. As I mentioned in the introduction the stays are optional, and I have to say that a metalwork lathe is necesary to make the connecting pins, unless you want to resort to unsightly nuts and bolts. The order of fitting is to mount the lever arms on the door, then the position of the guide channels can be determined on the cabinet top rail.

Last, but not least, install the lifting mechanism and fit the sewing machine to it. I cut a hole in the end of the plastic plinth on the machine so that the leads could go down inside the cabinet and not drape across the work top. ■

WORKSHOP WAYS by Bob Grant

From a 1904 manual on wood carving preventing rust on tools: 'Tools that are kept in a drawer may have a piece of newly-burnt lime placed amongst them. This lime takes up any moisture that there may be in the air, and so prevents it eating into the tools.' A more modern method is to place a bag of silica gel crystals in the drawer, these will do the same job as the lime.

□ □ □

An excellent and safe non-slip floor surface for work stations around machines can be made by spreading woodworker's adhe-

sive on the selected area and then sprinkling this with carborundum powder.

□ □ □

Mortise gauge points should be set to the width of the chisel to be used and balancing the chisel on the gauge points is not easy. A simple modification to the gauge will ensure accuracy each time. A fine file is used to remove half of each gauge point as shown in the sketch. The points can now be positively located against the mortise chisel selected and I have also found that the points scribe the wood in a better fashion too.

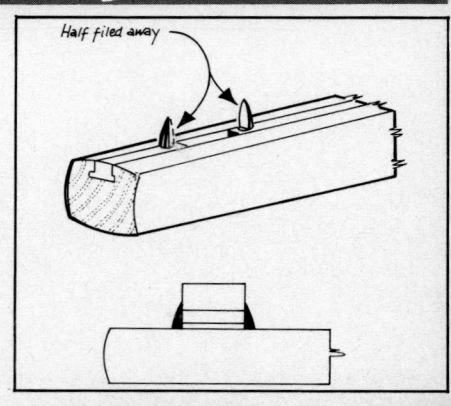

Half filed away

AEG HK45A Circular Saw
Outstanding Quality — Outstanding Value

only
£56.95
(inc. V.A.T.)

Once again AEG Power Tools break the price barrier to bring you a quality industrial circular saw at a DIY price. The HK45A circular saw has a blade diameter of 150mm (6″) and a powerful 710 watt motor. It comes complete with a Teflon coated TCT saw blade. The ideal saw for all those woodworking jobs around the home.

This is a special purchase from our factory in Germany and cannot be repeated at this special price. Contact your local AEG dealer now or write to: AEG-TELEFUNKEN (UK) LTD., Power Tools, 217 Bath Road, SLOUGH, Berkshire SL1 4AW

Please send me details of where I can see your HK45A Circular saw

Name

Address

ww

AEG
Electric Power Tools

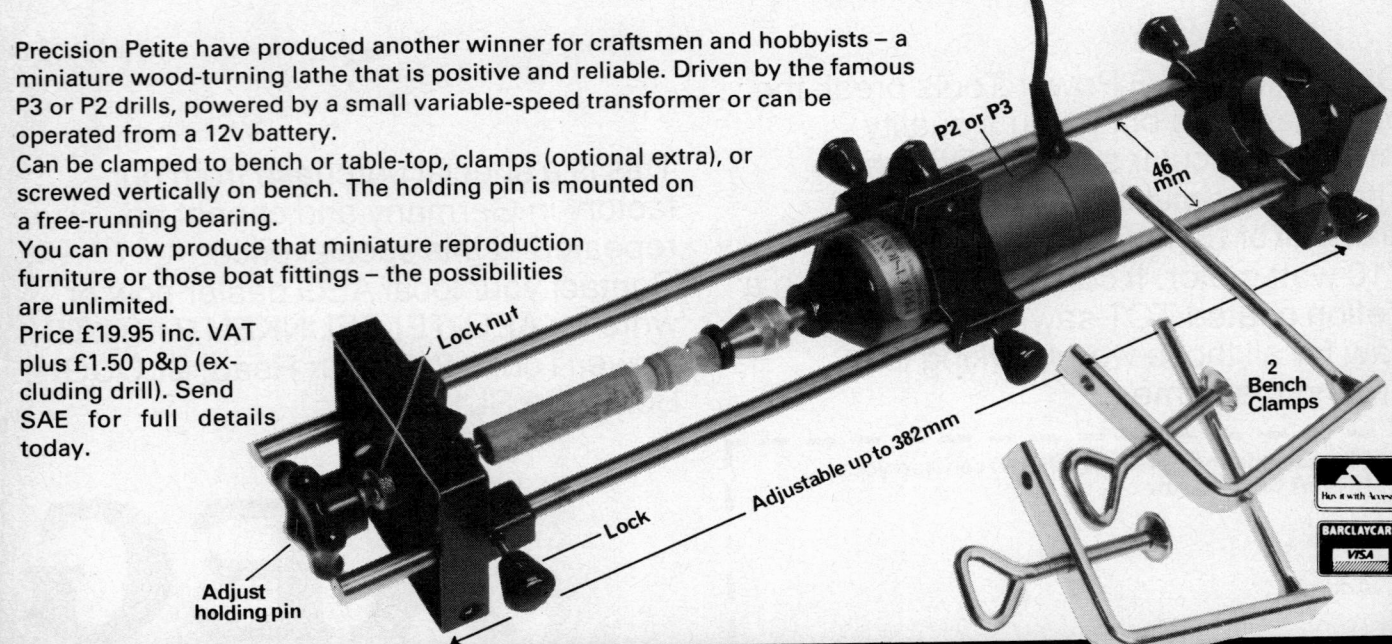
Prices quoted are those prevailing at press date and are
subject to alteration due to economic conditions.

Here's an easier way to construct cabinets with perfectly solid joints – the revolutionary new Elu Flat Dowel Jointing System.

Simple to use

Marked lines on the sole plate allow easy machine location. Make a simple plunge cut producing a slot ready to accept the dowel.

How it works

The Elu Flat Dowels are manufactured from Hardwood (Beech) compressed into shape with the grain running diagonally thus providing the strength along its centre. When the dowel is fitted it absorbs the glue resulting in a solid joint. Slots allow the lining up of edges not possible with conventional round dowels.

Standard Equipment:

- Steel Carrying Case
- Super Hard TCT Grooving Blade
- Parallel Guide
- Saw Insert
- Instruction Book
- Special Mitre Guide

FREE!
Special Guide for slotting mitred edges

More information:
The ELU DS140 and Dowels are readily available from a nationwide network of over 200 authorised distributors. Contact us today for your free illustrated brochure and full list of Elu dealers.

Elu Machinery Ltd.,
310-312 Dallow Road,
LUTON.
Beds. LU1 1SS.
Tel: (0582) 425001
Telex: 825540 ELU G.

Elu INTERNATIONAL

Miniature Turning Tools

This exciting set of six miniature turning tools – overall length 9″ (225mm) is now available to the discerning woodturner. You'll find these tools indispensible for fine work such as chess sets, lace bobbins etc. Boxed and available for only **£22.77** (inclusive of VAT).

Gordon Stokes the well known woodturner and author offers a free phone and advisory service. Full details in the catalogue supplement.

Send for our 12 page colour catalogue showing the full range of turning and carving tools (50p) refunded on order. For information on additional tools send for our free catalogue supplement. Available on request. Callers welcome. Weekends please 'phone.

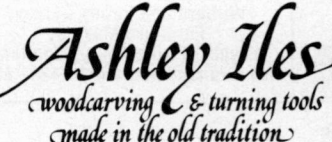

Ashley Iles
woodcarving & turning tools
made in the old tradition

Ashley Iles (Edge Tools) Ltd.,
East Kirkby, Spilsby,
Lincolnshire PE23 4DD.
Telephone (07903) 372

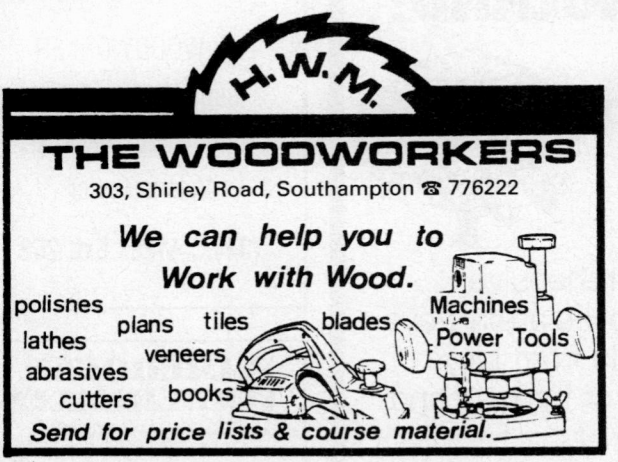

Wood Suppliers Wood Suppliers

ENGLISH TIMBERS

SEASONED HOMEGROWN AND IMPORTED HARDWOODS FOR THE CRAFTSMAN.
Please Contact:
P. Smith, Furniture Maker,
The Old Chapel,
Kirkburn,
Driffield.
E. Yorks.

Tel: 0377 89301

ADVERTISERS *please note*
FINAL COPY DATE for
NOVEMBER ISSUE
(Published 15th October)
is **3rd September**

DECEMBER ISSUE
(Published 19th November)
is **8th October**

HAVE ENGLISH YEW
(Will Haggle)

1000 cu ft — Come and choose from wide variety of sizes. Well Seasoned. Loads of Offcuts. Schools supplied.
Callers made welcome anytime.
"The more the cheaper"
W. Pearson, ASHLEY MOOR HALL, ORLETON, Nr. LUDLOW, SHROPSHIRE.
Tel: Yarpole 236

VENEERS
SHORT AND FULL LEAVES
In all popular timbers. Send S.A.E. for FREE price list or 55p for samples of 12 pieces 4″ × 3″ to:
ELLIOTT BROS
Four Winds, Moorwoods Lane, Dore
All letters to PO Box No. 6, Glossop, Derby. *Reg. No. 2064782*

VENEERS, all types. SAE List—S. Gould (Veneers), 342 Uxbridge Road, W12. Tel: 01-743 8561.
T/C

VENEERS AND MARQUETRY equipment, materials and books now in stock. Phone or send for details to: H.W.M., The Woodworkers, 303 Shirley Road, Shirley, Southampton. Tel: 0703 776222.
T/C

BEECH. Oak, Pitch-pine, Yew, Sycamore, various thicknesses, air and kiln dry. Ring Will Tyers (0468) 21292 (Nr. Lancaster).
P-U

CONVERT TIMBER YOURSELF, with a portable chain saw mill. Cuts a 36″ width 200 sq. ft. per hour. Keenest prices. Brochure, demonstration. Philip Cole, 16 Kings Lane, Flore, Northampton. Tel: Weedon 0327 40337 (evenings).
T/C

ALL BRITISH HARDWOODS. Kilned Oak £14 cu. ft. Open weekends/evenings. Select your own. Great Stour 470 Kent.
R-S

ENGLISH HARDWOODS. Oak Specialists, also Elm, Ash, Beech, Sycamore. Over 4,000 cu ft. Send for stock list to W. H. Mason & Son Ltd, The Sawmills, Wetmore Road, Burton-on-Trent, Staffs. Telephone 64651/2. Also imported hardwoods, softwoods and full machining facilities.
N-S

EXOTICWOODS. Boxwood, Ebony, Generolemonwood, Greenheart, Partridgewood, Lignum Vitae, Padauk, Rosewoods, Grande Pallisander. Many others. CHART Reading (0734) 695336 (evenings/Saturdays).
R

ACACIA, ASH, CHESTNUT, MAPLE, OAK, YEW, SYCAMORE, WALNUT.

Fresh Sawn, Air Dry or Kilned.
Send S.A.E. for Price List.
William and Penny Garvey, Furniture Makers, Leyhill, Payhembury, Honiton.
Tel: Broadhembury (040 484) 430.

WOOD VENEERS

Come and select your own from our extensive range of exotic timbers — from 0.6mm to 3 mm thick.
C. B. VENEERS LTD., River Pinn Works, Yiewsley High Street, West Drayton, Middx UB7 7TA.
Telephone: West Drayton (08954) 41986

Calling all Wood Suppliers —

Let WOODWORKER
supply the buyers.
Ring now to advertise
Valerie Tester

(0442) 41221 Ext. 262

MADE IN ENGLAND!

Wheelers Limited, established in 1860, traditional suppliers of English oak to the furniture industry.

Comprehensive supplies are always available from large stocks of through and through air dried material

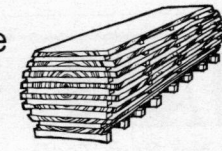

Fast drying facilities are also available, using a modern vacuum kiln.

Why not ring us to discuss your English oak requirements today?

≡S Wheelers Limited
CHILTON - SUDBURY - SUFFOLK CO10 6XH
Tel: 0787 73391 (9 lines) - Telex 987893

ENGLISH HARDWOODS

Air dried T & T Plank Walnut and Oak £12, Yew £8, Ash £6.50, S. Chestnut £7, Sycamore, Elm and Lime £5, Cherry £6, Beech & Hornbeam £5 per cu. ft. approx. prices, plus carriage and V.A.T.

Other timber prices on application

We welcome you to call and inspect our large stocks.

Enquiries: Harry Adcock, Saw Mills, Corby Glen, Grantham, Corby Glen 231.

LIMEHOUSE TIMBER SALES

TEAK MAHOGANY IROKO OAK
ETC ETC JOINERY SOFTWOODS

"TIMBERAMA" customer self-selection area with a wide variety of species and dimensions

MON-FRI: 9am-5pm
SAT: 9am-3pm
INTERESTING TIMBERS BOUGHT AND SOLD

a division of:
DAVEY AND COMPANY
5 GRENADE STREET
LONDON E14 8HL   01-987 1837

WOODWORKER, the magazine which leads the way. Don't wait advertise now for quick results. Telephone: Valerie Tester, Ext. 262 (0442) 41221.

CLASSIFIED
Telephone Valerie Tester
(0442) 41221 Ext. 262

Prices quoted are those prevailing at press date and are subject to alteration due to economic conditions.

Wood Suppliers

YORKSHIRE HARDWOODS

KILN DRIED HARDWOOD FOR CRAFTSMEN

We specialize in English Oak and can supply waney edged boards or dimensioned stock. We welcome enquiries for small quantities cut and machined to your exact requirements.

**Yorkshire Hardwoods Limited
Pocklington Grange,
Bielby Lane, Pocklington, York YO4 2NT**

☎ Pocklington
075 92-2870

VENEERS, inlay bandings, stringing and marquetry panels. Large selection. *Mail order and callers welcome. S.A.E. for list.*
**R. AARONSON (VENEERS) LTD
45 Redchurch St., London E2.
Tel: 01-739 3107**

R&S WOODCRAFTS

A service for the small user. First quality kiln dried hardwoods. American and Japanese Oak, Mahogany, Ash, Maple, Teak, Beech etc. *S.A.E. List.* **77 Lime Tree Avenue, Tile Hill, Coventry CV4 9EZ** or telephone **(0203) 461491** anytime.

Tree Work Services

WE SUPPLY HOME GROWN HARDWOODS IN THE ROUND, FRESH SAWN, OR DRIED.

SPECIES IN STOCK INCLUDE: Acacia, Apple, Ash, Beech, Cedar, Cherry, Chestnut, Elm, Holly, Holm Oak, Lacewood, Lime, Maple, Oak, Pear, Sycamore, Tree of Heaven, Tulip Tree, Walnut, Yew.
QUARTER SAWN AND STRAIGHT EDGED OAK SUPPLIED.
YOUR OWN TREES MILLED on site, to your specifications.

JOHN EMERY
THE 'OLD RECTORY, PILGRIMS WAY, CHEW STOKE, NR. BRISTOL.
TEL: CHEW MAGNA 3222

Fact 2 from Ebac

Ebac has a drying system to suit your needs. Ebac

See our ad on page 605

Greenfields Ind. Est. Bishop Auckland, Co. Durham, England DL14 9TF.
Tel: (0388) 605061

JOHN BODDY & SON (TIMBER) LTD.
offer
Direct from our Sawmill and Kilns

BRITISH HARDWOODS

As one of the few British Timber Merchants specialising in the production of kiln dried hardwoods in planking and dimension stock.

We invite craftsmen to inspect and select from our stock of over 30,000 cubic feet of kiln dried timber. Stored under cover.

APPLE, ASH, BEECH, CEDAR OF LEBANON, CHERRY, SWEET CHESTNUT, ELM, BURR ELM, LARCH, LIME, OAK, BURR OAK, PEAR, SYCAMORE, RIPPLE SYCAMORE, WALNUT and YEW.

available from stock in most thicknesses

*Please send for our Stock List or call and inspect
Open Monday to Friday 8 a.m. - 5 p.m.
Saturday 8 a.m. - 12 noon*

Riverside Sawmills,
Boroughbridge, YO5 9LJ, North Yorkshire.
Telephone (09012) 2370 Telex 57526

CRAFTWOODS

Good stocks of many hardwoods — Mahogany, Ash, Lime, Bubinga, Cherry, Lignum Vitae, Ebony, Meranti, Maple, Padauk, Pear, Oaks, Rosewood, Teak, Wenge, Sapele, Afrormosia.
Also Fingerboards, squares, veneers, panelling, carving kits, doors, plywood, tools, books. Logs and Billets for carving.
Send SAE for price list to
CRAFTWOODS,
Midslade Sawmills,
Forest Road, Hartwell, Northants. Tel: (0604) 862133
Callers Welcome

NORTH HEIGHAM SAWMILLS

Good, Kiln-Dried stocks of most Home-Grown timbers, and exotic, Imported Hardwoods.
Stocks include: Apple, ash, beech, blackwood, box, cedar, cherry, cocobolo, ebony, elm, holly, lemonwood, lignum, lime, mahogany, maple, oak, padauk, pear, plane, rosewood, satinwood, sycamore, walnut, yew, zelkova.
Please send S.A.E. for priced stock list to:
North Heigham Sawmills, Paddock St. (off Barker St.), NORWICH NR2 4TW. Tel: Norwich 22978.

TIMBERLINE

Suppliers of fine timbers for Musical Instrument Makers and craftsmen in wood.

Free catalogue: **1a Langton Road, Tunbridge Wells, Kent, England. Tel: 0892 42051 or 01 543 2434**

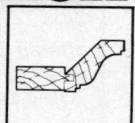
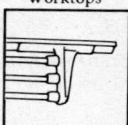
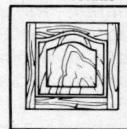

OFFCUTS

by Chris Dunn

The knight is named

You may recall that in Offcuts/May we showed a picture of Ian Norbury's outstandingly fine carving in lime of a skeleton in full armour astride a fiery horse. We asked you to send in your suggestions as to what the title of this sculpture should be.

Well you did, and we now have a winner.

Dr Barry Seward-Thompson, who lives in Geneva, Switzerland, offered The Boast of Heraldry as a worthy name for the knight. He was thinking along the lines of Gray's Elegy (learned folk these doctors) a stanza of which he quoted to back up his suggestion:

The Boast of Heraldry, the Pomp of Pow'r,
And all that Beauty, all that Wealth e'er gave,
Awaits alike th'inevitable hour.
The Paths of Glory lead but to the grave.

Ian Norbury thought that was e'er so good, adding: 'The line about the paths of glory is best in tune with my own idea, rather like Blake's rose carrying the seeds of its own destruction.' But while Ian had no doubt about the winner, he was also thoroughly delighted by the quality and thoughtfulness of so many of the entries you sent in.

Some, it must be said, played rather heavily on obvious puns, such as Dead of Knight (ouch!) and Knight Mare (ooof!) while the Battle of the Falklands prompted less playful suggestions such as Invincible, Hermes, and so on. Surprisingly, perhaps, only a single entry was inspired by Tolkien's Lord of the Rings, to wit Ringwraith.

Other readers took a more biblical point of view: '... behold a pale horse, and his name that sat on him was Death.' One such entry based on this quotation from Revelation 6/8 came from a nun of the Convent of Poor Clares at Arundel (Woodworker goes everywhere!) The Fourth Horseman of the Apocalypse was another popular choice – and even a Fifth Horseman.

Revelation 9/11 inspired the name Apollyon, offered by a gentleman who, I thought for a mistaken moment, had also suggested the name Amanda Girl. I blinked and then realised that Amanda Girl is the name of the boat aboard which he lives in Sandwich Marina. Meanwhile, back in the Old Testament, the name Ichabod ('The glory is departed') was also suggested, taken from Samuel 4/21.

The theme of evil was well worked over by many entrants: Malevolent Lord, Sir Death, Angel of Death, Satan's Champion, and the like, but among my favourites was one which displayed an utterly irreverent attitude: Skullerton. And the mind fairly boggled when my eye fell across the name Lambourne Bung, but that too turned out to be the name of someone's house (I kid you not).

We had many, many more suggestions, but Barry Seward-Thompson's Boast of Heraldry came out clear winner, and he receives the set of 12 carving tools which Roger Buse of Roger's Tools in Hitchin, Herts, so kindly and sportingly put up as a prize.

And I say cheers to all the many readers who took up the challenge to name the knight. I don't know who was more chuffed at your response, Ian Norbury or me.

Socket screw saga

I thought it was too good to be true. And it was. Not three days after the July Woodworker hit the streets, containing a snippet in Offcuts about socket-headed screws (you may remember), a press release from Rex Supply Company landed on my desk announcing: 'A big range of socket screws now available in small quantity packs.'

I telephoned Philip Hargreaves at Rex's north London address, thinking perhaps we had found our man, but it turned out that in all the huge range of socket-headed screws offered by that company, there is not a woodscrew to be had.

And so the search goes on.

Glue's company

During a recent week's hols in Chichester, I visited the Weald and Downland Open Air Museum at Singleton. This 35-acre site has been devoted to the preservation of old buildings which have been gathered from all parts of the country and re-erected as a permanent reminder of our architectural past.

I took a look at the Victorian Carpenter's Workshop, one of the exhibits, which is an interior that includes all the contemporary tools and devices used by the 19th century chippy. Unfortunately – but for obvious good reason – the visitor is contained behind a grill, to prevent itchy fingers from taking a closer working look at the tools on the bench.

A nostalgic scene, although I know that many of those tools' contemporaries are still working today. And as if to underline the enduring nature of these good hand

● There is an answer to every problem. Not always the right answer, but there is an answer to every problem. Bill Gates couldn't resist taking a picture of this crazy doorway in Canterbury, but if you think the chippy had some problems hanging that door, spare a tear for the glazier.

tools, the five-litre tin of Cascamite that somebody had inexplicably left on the bench did not look at all out of place.

Write of reply

A number of readers took exception to Ralph Fellows' contention in Woodworker/July that if you want to see real craftsmanship these days, you have to look to the amateur.

I thought at the time that this statement would prompt some stern rejoinders from readers wishing to dispute the point. However, while the response has been one of protest, every correspondent has adopted the line 'I'll leave it someone else to demolish Mr Fellows' statement about the amateur-versus-professional argument...'

So far everyone has been leaving it to everyone else. So would Someone Else now stand up and defend the position please.

Oak before ash

I have a bone to pick with oak trees, ash trees, and people who go round saying wise old country sayings. According to the lore of the jungle, if the oak comes into leaf before the ash, we can expect only 'a splash' of rain over the summer. Ash before oak and it's 'a soak' on the way.

Well, I have it on unimpeachable authority that the oak was way ahead of the ash in spring this year. Splash? Not on your life. Wimbledon was all but washed out, two Test matches got drowned, the British Open golfers are getting very wet, even as I write, and I don't think it is unfair to label this summer 'a soak' so far.

Furthermore, I am writing this on St Swithin's Day which, if wet, is said to herald 40 days of rain. It has been persisting with rain all day, but that isn't going to worry us, is it? Now that the oak-and-ash business has been disproved, who is going to fall for the one about St Swithin?

I also know that it is a fact of journalism that if you commit yourself to print with comments about the weather, it automatically does the opposite just to make a chump of you. So one way and another I confidently predict a fine and sunny summer, or what remains of it.

Just a little public service I like to render, you know.

Stoneleigh day-out

I was impressed by the recent Model Craft and Country Show at Stoneleigh, near Coventry. Where did all those people come from? Officially there were 25,000 who visited over the two days, but when I arrived on the Saturday morning I swear there were at least 50,000 milling about by shortly after breakfast time.

I was feeling a bit fazed, mind you, as my sister Mary got married the day before, and you know how there's nothing like a family wedding for sparking off a bit of a session.

But the remonstrances of an abused head were soon put to flight by such a variety of things to see. There was a bewildering array of crafts on display in the exhibition halls, offering practical demonstrations and artefacts ranging from the plain awful to the near-sublime, and everywhere you looked there were working models of pretty well everything that moves – or so it seemed – continuously strafed from above by model aircraft buzzing like wasps round a ripe

● Talk about changing your mind! Photographer David Askham spotted this example of natural indecision in an Oxford thoroughfare.

●

raspberry. It sort of brought out the ten-year-old in you.

I spent much time in the woodworking hall, and it was there that I met the inimitable Stan Thomas for the first time, surrounded by inquisitive visitors who clearly found his enthusiasm for woodwork quite irresistible. One of Stan's visitors even badgered him into promising a week's tuition later in the year, while another, a small boy, would just not let go of a plane that Stan had given him to try out.

It was good to talk to Jack Hill, another well known name to readers of this magazine, who was demonstrating his favourite subject – chairmaking – and also to Gordon Hall, whose knowledge of antique restoration is to be shared with Woodworker soon. Meanwhile woodcarver Alan Duncan was so busy answering visitors' questions that I couldn't even get a little word like Hello in edgeways.

They are doing the Model Craft and Country Show again next year – the Witsun weekend in fact – and I recommend a note in your diary to that effect. My own day out at Stoneleigh sure beat raw eggs in Worcestershire sauce. By the end of the day I quite felt like another wedding.

Orbital standing

A certain senior executive of a certain company which manufactures a certain orbital sanding machine tells me that he and his colleagues have developed an interesting cure for the ravages of being on your feet for long periods when manning exhibition stands.

Our man tells me that when the going gets tough, the sales team plug in the orbital sander and take it in turns to stand on the upturned pad. The effect is said to be most efficacious and rather cheaper than a massage, though an orbital sander might not be as nice to look at as a masseuse.

Bookshelf extra

Making picture frames in wood by Manly Banister. Published by Sterling Publishing Co Inc, New York, distributed in UK by Blandford Press. Hardback at £6.95 (ISBN 0 8069 5450 7) and paperback at £3.50 (ISBN 0 8069 7542 3).

A few years ago a visit to almost any exhibition of local art would have revealed the obvious contrast between the professionally made frame and that made by the artist. Quite simply, the professional had access to a wide range of routing and mitreing aids which always produced the perfect product. All that has changed.

There is a full range of framing materials available in retail outlets that require only corner jointing using fairly basic aids and care in cutting. These are ideal for one-off frames. However, many enthusiasts find that considerable demands can be made on their expertise by artists so that it is worthwhile to use power tools and to construct frames from the basic materials.

This book restricts itself to the making of frames in wood. A timely reminder in the age of the ready-cut and pre-packed aluminium extrusion that, whilst prints may look well in such light frames, most paintings require a more substantial support and definition.

It is a small paperback in the Home Craftsman Series which will be welcome in many a workshop. Not only does it deal with the obvious technicalities of frame making, it begins with advice on choosing the right type of frame for a particular work of art — quite the most crucial part of the whole exercise. Full chapters on mounting artwork and glazing follow and the book concludes with help in manufacturing round and oval frames and restoring existing ones.

The very clear drawings and photographs are complemented by an index and the geometry of complex frames is simple to follow. Adherents to the old Imperial measurements will find this American publication to their liking. 'Metricated' craftsmen will be incensed by the conversions used — the conversion chart adds further insult to injury but does not detract from the overall value of the book. **D.M.W.**

□ □ □

Marquetry for Beginners by Ernie Ives, 2nd edition, published by the author at £1.20 post free. (Available from 63 Church Lane, Sproughton, Ipswich IP8 3AY)

This booklet was first published by the Marquetry Society and was written to help beginners in marquetry choose their first tools and make a simple picture using the window method. Though the design is simple it covers a wide range of techniques and these form an excellent basic instruction manual to enable aspiring marquetarians to progress to more advanced pictures. The booklet gives step-by-step instruction through the stages from preparation to finishing, is illustrated by drawings and photographs and assumes the reader has no previous knowledge of the craft. The picture chosen for the exercise is the Fisherman's Harbour. **P.C.**

Classified Advertisements

WORKSHOP EQUIPMENT

EBAC TIMBER SEASONERS, Protimeter moisture meters, always good prices and advice from the man who pioneered small scale seasoning. John Arrowsmith, 74ª, Wilson Street, Darlington, Co. Durham BL3 6QZ. Tel: 0325 481970. T/C

MAKE A WOODTURNING LATHE easily, construction details and parts list, send SAE to: ORTAN LATHES, P.O. Box 46, Norwich NR7 8PB. M-R

MACHINERY. A comprehensive range of new/used machinery. Check our prices, e.g. HMO 10"×5½" planer/thicknesser £434. HF30; spindle moulder £365. 12" tilt arbour sawbench 2hp motor £140. Morso mitring machine £459, (including V.A.T.). Kity K-5. See these machines and Ryobi industrial small tools demonstrated at Woodman Woodworking Machinery Co. (Sign of the Axe), Little Malgraves Hall, Lower Dunton Road, Bulphan, Nr. Upminster, Essex. Tel: (0268) 415511 or (0702) 331729. I-U

CONVERTERS single to three phase to 10 h.p. bandsaws. 1 h.p. motors. H.A.B. Engineering, Fardons Industrial Estate, Glover Street, Bordesley, Birmingham 9. 021-772 2699. Q-T

PLANERS 6" × 9", planers/thicknessers, 12" × 7", 9" × 6", 12" × 7", sawbenches, 10" × 2" combination woodworkers. British made. Particulars, send stamp. Dodd Machine Tools Ltd., South Woodham, Chelmsford. Telephone: (0245) 320 691 O-Z

KITY K5 UNIVERSAL WOODWORKER, as new, complete with cutters, only £350. Telephone: (0733) 269481. Peterborough. R

CORONET IMP BANDSAW one year old, many spares blades, large circle cutting attachment. £220. Chesterfield 590015 evenings. R

CIRCULAR AND BAND SAW BLADES for all applications from: A.A. SMITH of Lancing Ltd., 63 Brighton Road, Shoreham, Sussex. Tel: 07917 61707 (24 hrs). P-Z

WASHITA & ARKANSAS whetstones now readily available from importer. Large selection, SAE for list. C. Rufino, Manor House, South Clifton, Newark, Notts. T/C

SALE CORONET ELF LATHE 36in bed as new, many extras including fifteen turning tools. Offers Tel: Honington 485. R

WOODCARVING tools

LARGEST STOCK IN EUROPE

Ashley Iles & Henry Taylor
Arkansas Bench & Slip Stones
Strops & Strop Paste
Bench Screws, Carvers' Vices

WOODTURNING tools

Complete range of
Henry Taylor & Ashley Iles
handled or unhandled

send 30p in stamps for illustrated catalogue

ALEC TIRANTI LTD
70 High St, Theale, Reading, Berks RG7 5AR
21 Goodge Place, London W1.

PETER CRISP OF RUSHDEN
THE CARPENTER'S SHOP

Hand Tools by leading makers. Stockists of:
- **Craftsmen, Coronet, Elu, Kity Woodworking Machinery**
- **Sorby Turning Chisels**
- **Taylor Carving Chisels**
- **Gomex T/Carbide Circular Saws**

High Street, Rushden, Northants.
Telephone:
093 34 56424-7

B/DECKER, SKIL, BOSCH, MAKITA TOOLS ALL IN STOCK

NEW LUTZ SAWBENCH NOW IN STOCK ONLY £165.00

BEST QUALITY TCT SAWS, 5" DIAMETER UP TO 36"
GUARANTEED PERFORMANCE
24 HOUR RETURN POST SHARPENING SERVICE.
PHONE OR WRITE TO MAYS HIGH SPEED SAWS LTD.,
NEW ROAD (Nr. CHANDLER CORNER), RAINHAM, ESSEX.
TEL. (04027) 55371/21331
(7 DAYS A WEEK)

TCT   ALLOY

SCRU-DRILL

COMPLETE SET OF FOUR
£13.45 + 35p P&P

Top quality wood screw pilot drill and countersink adjusts to screw specification for fast accurate pilot holes in hard or soft wood for that professional finish.

Complete set will accommodate Nos 5 to 14 gauge screws in all popular lengths.

- Adjustable stop collar for counterbore depth or countersink
- Adjustable sleeve for screw body
- Adjustable pilot drill for screw thread

KELTEK PRODUCTS
St. Giles Mews, P.O. Box 5, Wadebridge, Cornwall PL27 7YZ. (S.A.E. Please for our complete range of exclusive products).

WOODTURNERS SUPPLIES

Woodturning tools, Peppermills, Salt mills, Barometers, Thermometers, Lighters, Hourglasses, Eggtimers, Ceramic tiles and clock faces, Clock movements, Spinning wheel parts, Sealers & Polishes, etc. Fast and efficient mail order service + competitive prices. S.A.E. for lists.

ERIC TOMKINSON
86 Stockport Road, Cheadle, Cheshire, SK8 2AJ. Tel. 061-491 1726

Shop open Mon-Fri from 9am to 4pm, Sat 9am to 1pm.

Caber Sawbench 10" tilt arbor table size 26" × 23" h.p. 1.5 (also manufactured two wheel 12" bandsaw)

Send stamp for details

HUMBERSIDE TOOLS
89 Lambert St., Hull
Tel: 0482 43556

SHERWOOD WOOD TURNING LATHES

All cast iron constructed. 3¾" CH 24" or 36" B.C. 3 or 4 speed, bowl turning up to 14" dia. ball-bearing spindle c/w face plate, centres etc. Prices from **£75.29** inc. VAT.

Send stamp for leaflets and details of above and other low-priced machines and motors.

JAMES INNS (Engs),
Main St., Bulwell, Nottingham

Come and browse through our huge stocks of machinery and tools.
- Ask for details of our prompt and low cost Mini Clipper delivery service

A·Pollard+Son LTD.

KITY UNITED KINGDOM **K5** International Woodworker with Sawbench, Spindle Moulder, Planer/Thicknesser & Slot Mortiser. Full range in stock.

scheppach **HMO ▶** 2HP 10" × 6" Planer/Thicknesser. HM2 Planer/Thicknesser also in stock.

Elu **MOF 96** The professional Plunging Router 600 Watt Motor takes ½" shanked bits. **£59.50**

DeWALT DW125 Powershop, for Sawing, Grooving Sanding, Moulding etc. Dust Extractors, Planer/Thicknessers & Industrial R.A.S. also in stock.

◀ H.F.30 Spindle Moulder 2HP Motor. *Shown with:* Overhead Roller, Guard & Sliding Carriage. (Optional Extras)

mafell **BIBEREX** 12"..2.3HP Sawbench with Rise & Fall, Mitre Guide, Fence and Tilting Adjust. Other Sawbenches in stock.

REMSCHEID 1885 WABECO 1885 GERMANY Natural Sandstone wet grinder. Drill driven **£33** INC.VAT. Motorised **£90** INC.VAT

INCA 10½in. throat Bandsaw For Fretwork and Bandsanding 6in. depth of cut. Motorised **£289** INC.VAT Non-motorised **£189** INC.VAT

DIY Model **£149** INC.VAT

The professional 1 HP lathe 3 speed ● Heavy ● Strong ● Well engineered 33in. centres, 13in. swing **£333** INC.VAT (as illustrated)

Dust Extractors, Lathes, Industrial R/A. Saws. Large stocks of Ironmongery & Handtools — Most accessories stocked.
Open 6 days a week 8.30-5.30   Barclaycard, Access   Business Established over 50 years.

A. POLLARD & SON LTD. 51 Queensway, Bletchley, Milton Keynes ☎ (0908) 75221

5000 ELECTRIC MOTORS, FANS & BLOWERS

New & Used. Single & 3 Phase
ALWAYS IN STOCK
RING
(0742) 78088
FOR FREE STOCKLIST
Beatson & Co (Elec.) Ltd,
17-21 Mowbray St.,
Sheffield S3 8EN

BANDSAW BLADES

Industrial quality long life blades for De Walt BS1310 & DW100. Kity. Burgess. B&D. Startrite 352. All widths & skips. Immediate despatch. Post paid. Write or phone for list.
AXMINSTER POWER TOOL CENTRE
Chard St., Axminster, Devon. Tel: Axminster (0297) 33656. (after 6pm 33535)

630

Prices quoted are those prevailing at press date and are subject to alteration due to economic conditions.

Woodworker, September 198

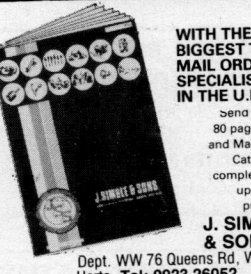
Prices quoted are those prevailing at press date and are subject to alteration due to economic conditions.

ONE DAY WOODTURNING COURSE: carefully designed, inexpensive. Trymwood, 2a Downs Park East, Westbury Park, Bristol. Telephone Bristol 629092. T/C

COURSES IN WOOD MACHINING AND WOODTURNING. Bookable by the hour—the most convenient and flexible way! all for £6.00 an hour (inc. VAT), H.W.M., The Woodworkers, 303 Shirley Rd., Shirley, Southampton. Tel: (0703) 776222. T/C

CRAFT HOLIDAYS AND COURSES in the Yorkshire Dales. Woodturning, Carving, Furnituremaking, Spinning, Silversmithing, Copper and Brasswork, Property Renovation. Professional tuition in well equipped workshops with full-board accommodation. SAE Rob and Jan Ellwood, Holroyd Mill, Micklethwaite, Bingley, W. Yorks. N-S

WOODTURNING day courses, or at £5.00 per hour, with Jack Durey. Enquire: Brenchley 2465 (Kent) T/C

BIRD CARVING TUITION. Two or three day course by internationally known wood sculptor. Comfortable accommodation available, close to Solent coast. Sae or phone for details: Derek George, West Lodge, Elizabeth Road, Stubbington, Hants PO14 2RF. Tel: Stubbington 2458. R

TWO-DAY Woodturning Course for beginners in mid-Norfolk village. Two students only. Accommodation available. SAE for details please. Doug Keeling, Church Lane, Beetley, Norfolk NR20 4AB. T/C

Thos. Harrison & Sons (Est. 1830)

WOODTURNING COURSES

★ Four days professional instruction
★ Discussion groups
★ Informal atmosphere
★ Farmhouse food and accommodation
★ Prices from £120
★ Beginners/advanced

For further details write or phone:
Mike Law, The Longhouse, Maxworthy Cross, North Petherwin, Launceston, North Cornwall. (056685) 322.

GORDON STOKES
Author of Modern Woodturning Beginner's Guide to Woodturning Woodturning for Pleasure, etc. etc
Will be pleased to send you full details of his intensive two day Woodturning and Woodcarving courses. Personal instruction based on thirty years experience. Don't struggle along the hard way. *Foolscap S.A.E. to:*
202 The Hollow, Bath, Avon BA2 1NG
Tel: Bath 22617

Australian Readers WOODTURNING
40 Years of woodturning experience available to you in a 2 day course. Basic or advanced. Personal tuition to your needs in a fully equipped workshop. Write for details:
PHILIP ELFORD 407 Peel St. N., Ballarat, Vic. 3350.

FURNITURE

3 and 1 Year Full Time Courses in Furniture Production and Making

Details: Head of School of Art and Design, Furniture and Timber, Buckinghamshire College of Higher Education, Queen Alexandra Road, High Wycombe, Bucks.

LEARN THE ART AND CRAFT OF RESTORING ANTIQUES AND DESIGNING AND MAKING YOUR OWN FURNITURE

Situated in a charming Norfolk village we offer professional tuition in courses of antique restoration, wood turning, machining, woodworking and finishing. Come to The Old Mill at Gayton for good food and comfortable accommodation in very pleasant surroundings.

WINDMILL ENTERPRISES

For full details send SAE to MR R Hirons, The Old Mill, Gayton, Norfolk. Tel: (055386) 613/717

Wood machining Course
A craftsman of forty years experience offers a unique two-day course to learn the basics of machine woodworking including spindle moulding and routing in his fully equipped modern workshop.
S.A.E. for details please to:
ROY SUTTON
14 St. Georges Avenue, Herne Bay, Kent CT6 8JU
Telephone: Herne Bay 3297 or Whitstable 272136 (evenings).

WOODTURNING COURSES
2 Day courses, mid-week or weekend. Expert personal tuition in modern well equipped workshop. Comfortable accommodation available in pleasant surroundings. SAE for details to
Cliff Willetts, Gables, Frisby On The Wreake, Melton Mowbray, Leics.

Rawdon Woodturners
Comprehensive courses geared to suit individual requirements offered in
Woodmachining
Woodturning
Take advantage of my 20 years of industrial and educational experience and realize the full potential of your machinery. Write or phone for details
Rawdon Woodturners
Peter Clark Woodcraft Ltd.,
Old Friends School, Low Green Rawdon, Nr Leeds, West Yorkshire
Tel: Leeds (0532) 676068 (evenings preferred)

Woodworking Machines of Switzerland LIMITED **SCHOOL OF WOODWORKING**

NEW ONE-DAY INTRODUCTORY COURSES

The Official INCA School of Woodworking is pleased to announce vacancies for Introductory One-Day Courses using the famous 'COMPACT UNIVERSAL SAW'.
These intensive courses are limited to 2 or 3 students each using a 'COMPACT' under the tuition of experienced instructors.
The cost of a one-day introductory course including lunch, refreshments and VAT is £35.
For full details of this and other woodworking courses using the finest INCA equipment and held in our purpose-built workshops, write now to:
Woodworking Machines of Switzerland Ltd., Inca House, Denbigh Road, Bletchley, Milton Keynes MK1 1PD. Telephone: Milton Keynes (0908) 641492.

EXHIBITIONS

WE'VE GOT SOMETHING UP OUR SLEEVE AT I.W.I.E. FOR YOU.

Visit Stand 4323, Hall 4
and we'll show you.

Michael Weinig (UK) Ltd.

Unit A 1
Watlington Industrial Estate
WATLINGTON, Oxfordshire OX9 5LU
Telephone (04 91 61) 31 31/2, Telex 8 49 128

WANTED

WANTED URGENTLY Norris planes, Mitre and low angle planes. Any gun metal planes. Ultamatum braces. Stanley planes up to £200 paid for No. 51/52 – 10¼ – 444. Top cash prices paid for all tools. R. Lowe, 45 Temple Hill, Whitwick, Nr. Leicester. Telephone Coalville (0530) 34581 evenings. R-T

GENUINE EBONY and Boxwood Stringing. Also "The Carver's Companion", by Peter Morton. Bridge, 2 Ashley Road, Southport, Merseyside. R

Make a Note

WOODWORKER SHOW

Royal Horticultural Society's
New & Old Halls,
London SW1
19-24 October 1982 inclusive

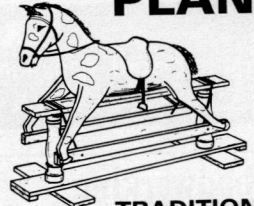

Prices quoted are those prevailing at press date and are subject to alteration due to economic conditions.

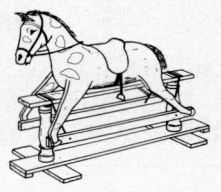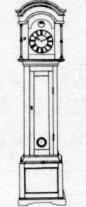

Classified Advertisements

From:

....

....

....

I enclose remittance value.......................to cover ....

Insertions under the heading:

WORKSHOP EQUIPMENT ☐	BOOKS & PUBLICATIONS ☐	
COURSES ☐	PLANS ☐	
CRAFT/ANTIQUE/SECOND-HAND TOOLS ☐	MATERIALS ☐	
	FOR SALE ☐	
WANTED ☐	SERVICES ☐	
MUSICAL INSTRUMENTS ☐	WOOD SUPPLIERS ☐	

To: **Valerie Tester WOODWORKER**

CLASSIFIED ADVERTISEMENT DEPT.
PO BOX 35, BRIDGE STREET,
HEMEL HEMPSTEAD, HERTS HP1 1EE

★ **Lineage rate 20p per word. Minimum charge £3.00**

★ **Semi display single column cm = £4.00 (Minimum £10.00)**

★ **Box numbers £1.25 extra**

Name and address if to appear must be paid for

BLOCK CAPITALS PLEASE

SHOP GUIDE SHOP GUIDE

The quickest and easiest method of reaching all Woodworkers is to advertise in SHOP GUIDE. Telephone **Valerie Tester (0442) 41221 Ext. 266. Rate: £8.00 per unit.** Minimum of 6 months.

Key: H — Hand tools, **P** — Power tools, **W** — Woodworking machinery up to £1000, **WM** — Woodworking machinery over £1000, **D** — Demonstration available on selected machines, **T** — Timber, **CS** — Cutting or sharpening services, **A** — Attachments, **BC** — Books/catalogues, *** — Mail order.

AVON

BATH   Tel. Bath 64513
JOHN HALL TOOLS   ★
RAILWAY STREET

Open: Monday-Saturday
9.00 a.m.-5.30 p.m.
H.P.W.WM.D.A.BC.

BRISTOL   Tel. (0272) 311510
JOHN HALL TOOLS LIMITED   ★
CLIFTON DOWN SHOPPING
CENTRE, WHITELADIES ROAD
Open: Monday-Saturday
9.00 a.m.-5.30 p.m.
H.P.W.WM.D.A.BC.

BRISTOL   Tel. 0272-633844
ROBBINS LIMITED   ★
THE WOODWORKER SHOP
MERRYWOOD MILLS, BEDMINSTER
Open: Mon-Fri 8.00 a.m.-5.00 p.m.
Saturday 8.30 a.m.-12.30 p.m.
H.P.T.CS.A.BC.

BRISTOL   Tel. 0272-629092
TRYMWOOD SERVICES   ★
2a DOWNS PARK EAST, (off
North View) WESTBURY PARK
Open: 8.30 a.m.-5.30 p.m. Mon. to
Fri. Closed for lunch 1-2 p.m.
P.W.WM.D.T.A.BC.

BRISTOL   Tel. 0272-667013
V. H. WILLIS & CO. LTD   ★
190-192 WEST STREET,
BEDMINSTER
Open: Mon-Fri 8.30 a.m.-5 p.m.
Saturday 9 a.m.-1 p.m.
H.P.W.WM.D.CS.A.BC.

BERKSHIRE

READING   Tel. Littlewick Green
DAVID HUNT (TOOL   2743
MERCHANTS) LTD   ★
KNOWL HILL, NR. READING
Open: Monday-Saturday
9 a.m.-5.30 p.m.
H.P.W.D.A.BC.

READING   Tel. (0734) 586522
SARJENT'S TOOL STORES   ★
LTD.
44-52 OXFORD ROAD
Open: 8.30 a.m.-5.30 p.m.
Monday-Saturday
H.P.W.WM.D.A.BC.

READING   Tel. Reading 661511
WOKINGHAM TOOL CO. LTD
99 WOKINGHAM ROAD

Open: Mon-Sat 9am-5.30pm
Closed 1-2pm for lunch
H.P.W.WM.D.CS.A.BC.

BUCKINGHAMSHIRE

HIGH WYCOMBE   (0494) 22221
ISAAC LORD LTD
185 DESBOROUGH ROAD

Open: Mon-Fri 8.00 a.m.-5.00 p.m.
Saturday 8.00 a.m.-12.00 noon
H.P.W.D.A.

MILTON KEYNES   Tel. 0908
A. POLLARD & SON   75221
LTD.   ★
51 QUEENSWAY, BLETCHLEY
Open: 8.30 a.m.-5.30 p.m.
Monday-Saturday
H.P.W.WM.D.A.BC.

CAMBRIDGESHIRE

CAMBRIDGE   Tel. 0223-353091
H. B. WOODWORKING
69 LENSFIELD ROAD
Open: 8.30 a.m.-5.30 p.m.
Monday-Friday
8.30 a.m.-1.00 p.m. Sat
P.W.WM.D.CS.BC.

CHESHIRE

CHESTER   Tel. 0244 42084
ROBERT KELLY'S   ★
19 NEWGATE ROW
GROSVENOR PRECINCT, CH1 1ER
Open: 9.00 a.m.-5.30 p.m.
Monday-Saturday
H.P.W.WM.D.CS.A.BC.

NANTWICH   Tel. Crewe 67010
ALAN HOLTHAM   ★
THE OLD STORES TURNERY
WISTASON ROAD, WILLASTON
Open: Tues-Sat 9a.m.-5.30p.m.
Closed Monday
P.W.WM.D.T.C.CS.A.BC.

CLEVELAND

MIDDLESBROUGH   Tel. 0642-
WINTZ   460035/813650
INDUSTRIAL SUPPLIES
2 BESSEMER COURT
GRANGETOWN
Open: Mon-Fri 8.30 a.m.-5 p.m.
H.P.W.D.A.

CORNWALL

FALMOUTH   Tel. 0326-312915
WOODSTOCK
(HARDWOODS) S.W.,
ASHFIELD, PONSHARDEN,
Open: Mon-Fri 8.30 a.m.-5.30 p.m.
Sat 9 a.m.-1.00 p.m.
T.

HELSTON
SOUTH WEST
POWER TOOLS
Helston (03265) 4961
Truro (0872) 71671
Launceston (0566) 3555
H.P.W.WM.D.CS.A.

CORNWALL

NEWQUAY   Tel. 063 73 2516
CONWAY SUPPLIES   ★
(NEWQUAY)
70 FORE STREET
Open: Mon-Fri 9 a.m.-5.30 p.m.
Sat 9 a.m.-12.30 p.m.
H.P.W.WM.D.A.BC.

ST. AUSTELL   Tel. (0726) 65922
TOOLSERV   ★
TRURO ROAD

Open: 8 a.m.-5.30 p.m.
6 days
H.P.W.WM.D.CS.A.BC.

DERBYSHIRE

BUXTON   Tel. 0298-871636
CRAFT SUPPLIES   ★
THE MILL
MILLERSDALE
Open: Mon-Fri 9 a.m.-5 p.m.
Saturday 9 a.m.-1 p.m.
H.P.W.D.T.CS.A.BC.

DEVON

EXETER   Tel. 0392 73936
WRIDES TOOL CENTRE
147 FORE STREET

Open: 9.00 a.m.-5.30 p.m.
Wednesday 9.00 a.m.-1.00 p.m.
H.P.W.WM.A.

PLYMOUTH   Tel. 0752 330303
WESTWARD BUILDING SERVICES   ★
LTD., LISTER CLOSE, NEWNHAM
INDUSTRIAL ESTATE, PLYMPTON
Open: Mon-Fri 8 a.m.-5.30 p.m.
Sat 8.30 a.m.-12.30 p.m.
H.P.W.WM.D.A.BC.

PLYMOUTH   Tel. 0752-266179
JOHN WRIDE & CO (PLYMOUTH) LTD
146 CORNWALL STREET
Open: Monday to Saturday
9.00a.m.-5.30p.m.
Wed 9.00a.m.-1.00p.m.
H.P.W.WM.A.

DORSET

BOURNEMOUTH   Tel: 0202
MACHINE SALES & SERVICES   527780
(BOURNEMOUTH) LTD   527781
56 STROUDEN ROAD   ★

Open: Mon-Fri 8.15 a.m.-5 p.m.
H.P.W.WM.D.A.

WEYMOUTH   Tel: (0305) 787396
WEYMOUTH TOOL CENTRE   ★
30A ABBOTSBURY ROAD

Open: Monday to Saturday
8 a.m.-5.30 p.m.
H.P.W.WM.D.A.BC

CO. DURHAM

BARNARD CASTLE   Tel: (0833)
WOODMEN   38442/31609
27 NEWGATE   ★

Open Monday-Saturday
9 a.m.-5.30 p.m.
P.W.WM.D.A.BC.

ESSEX

LEIGH ON SEA   Tel. (0702)
MARSHALL &   710404
PARSONS LTD   ★
1111 LONDON ROAD
Open: 8.30 am-5.30 pm Mon-Fri.
9.00 am-5.00 om Sat.
H.P.W.WM.D.CS.A.

LEIGH ON SEA   Tel. (0702)
WEBBERS TOOLS   76503
204 ELM ROAD

Open: 9 am-5.30 pm
Monday to Saturday
H.P.W.

GLOUCESTERSHIRE

TEWKESBURY   Tel. 0684
TEWKESBURY SAW CO.   293092
LIMITED
TRADING ESTATE, NEWTOWN
Open: Mon-Fri 8.00 a.m.-5.00 p.m.
Saturday 9.30 a.m.-12.00 p.m.
P.W.WM.D.CS.

HAMPSHIRE

ALDERSHOT   Tel. 0252 28088
BURCH & HILLS LTD
BLACKWATER WAY TRADING
ESTATE
Open: Mon-Fri 8.30 a.m.-5.30 p.m.
Saturday 8.30 a.m.-12.00 p.m.
H.P.W.WM.D.A.BC.

PORTSMOUTH   Tel. 0705
EURO PRECISION TOOLS   667332
LTD
259/263 London Road, North End
Open: Mon-Fri 9 a.m.- 5.30 p.m.
Sat 9.00 a.m.-1.00 p.m.
H.P.W.WM.D.A.BC.

SOUTHAMPTON   Tel. 0703
H.W.M.   776222
THE WOODWORKERS   ★
303 SHIRLEY ROAD, SHIRLEY
Open: Tues-Fri 9.30 a.m.- 6 p.m.
Sat 9.30 a.m.-4.00 p.m.
H.P.W.WM.D.CS.A.BC.T.

HERTFORDSHIRE

WATFORD   Tel. 0923 48434
HOME CARE CENTRE
20 MARKET STREET
WATFORD, HERTS

Open 9.00 a.m.-5.30 p.m.
Mon.-Sat.
H.P.W.A.WM.BC.D.

Prices quoted are those prevailing at press date and are
subject to alteration due to economic conditions.

SHOP GUIDE SHOP GUIDE

HERTFORDSHIRE

WATFORD Tel. 0923 26052
J. SIMBLE & SONS LTD
76 QUEENS ROAD

Open 8.30 a.m.-5.30 p.m.
Mon-Sat. Closed Wednesday
H.P.W.WM.D.A.BC.

WATFORD Tel. (0923) 49911
TREND MACHINERY & CUTTING
TOOLS LTD
UNIT N, PENFOLD WORKS
IMPERIAL WAY
Open: Mon-Fri 9 a.m.-5 p.m.
P.W.WM.D.CS.BC.

KENT

MATFIELD Tel. Brenchley
LEISURECRAFT IN WOOD (089272)
'ORMONDE', MAIDSTONE RD. 2465
TN12 7JG
Open: Mon-Sun
9 a.m.- 5.30 p.m.
W.WM.D.T.A.

SITTINGBOURNE Tel.
B.T.S. (TOOLS), Sittingbourne
Unit 25, SITTINGBOURNE 79551
INDUSTRIAL PARK ★
Open: Monday - Friday
8.00 a.m. - 5.00 p.m.
H.P.W.BC.CS.

LANCASHIRE

LANCASTER Tel. 0524 2886
LILE TOOL SHOP
43/45 NORTH ROAD
Open: Monday to Saturday
9.00 a.m.-5.30 p.m.
Wed 9.00 a.m.-12.30 p.m.
H.P.W.D.A.

PRESTON Tel. (0772) 52951
SPEEDWELL TOOL CO., ★
62-68 MEADOW STREET
Open: Mon-Fri 8.30 a.m.-5.30 p.m.
Sat 8.30 a.m.-12.30 p.m.
H.P.W.WM.D.CS.A.BC.

LEICESTERSHIRE

COALVILLE Tel. (0533) 415556
POOLE WOOD (06077) 5777
MACHINERY
SERVICES LIMITED,
30 VALENTINE ROAD
Open: Mon-Fri 9 a.m.-5 p.m.
H.P.W.WM.D.A.BC.

LEICESTER Tel. 0455 43254
ROY STARTIN LTD
134 WOOD STREET
EARL SHILTON
Open: Mon-Fri 8 a.m.-5.30 p.m.
Saturday 8.00 a.m.-1.30 p.m.
H.P.W.WM.D.T.A.

LINCOLNSHIRE

LINCOLN Tel. 0522 30199/
WOODWISE LIMITED 39871 or
121 HIGH STREET 0522 68428
& 06077 2421/5777/5288
(after hours) ★
Open: Mon-Sat 9 a.m.-5.30 p.m.
P.W.WM.D.A.BC.

LONDON

ACTON Tel. 01-992 4835
A MILLS (ACTON) LTD ★
32/36 CHURCHFIELD ROAD
W3 6ED
Open: Mon-Fri 9.00 a.m.-5.00 p.m.
Closed Saturday
H.P.W.WM.

HANWELL Tel. 01-567 2922
G. D. CLEGG & SONS
83 Uxbridge Road, W7 3ST
Open: Monday to Friday
9.00 a.m.-6.00 p.m.
Saturday 9.00 a.m.-5.30 p.m.
H.P.W.WM.D.

KILBURN Tel. 01-624 5146
W. THATCHER & SON LTD ★
POWER TOOL CENTRE
AT THE TECHNICAL LEISURE CENTRE
1 THE GRANGEWAY, N.W.6.
Open: Mon-Sat 9 a.m.-5.30 p.m.
P.H.W.D.CS.A.BC.

LONDON Tel. 01-636 7475
BUCK & RYAN LIMITED ★
101 TOTTENHAM COURT ROAD
W1P 0DY
Open: Mon-Fri 8.30 a.m.-5.30 p.m.
Saturday 8.30 a.m.-1.00 p.m.
H.P.W.WM.D.A.

LONDON Tel. 01-739 7126
CECIL W. TYZACK ★
79-81 KINGSLAND ROAD
SHOREDITCH
Open: Mon-Fri 8.45 a.m.-5.15 p.m.
Saturday 9 a.m.-12 noon
H.P.W.WM.D.A.BC.

NORBURY Tel: 01-679 6193
HERON TOOLS & HARDWARE LTD
437 STREATHAM HIGH ROAD
S.W.16
Open: Mon-Sat 8.30 a.m. - 6 p.m.
Wednesday 8.30 a.m. - 1 p.m.
H.P.W.A.

WOOLWICH Tel. 01-854 7767/8
A.D. Skillman & Sons Ltd.,
108-109 Woolwich High St.,
SE18 6DW
Open: Mon-Sat 8.30 a.m.-5.30 p.m.

H.P.W.CS.A.

MERSEYSIDE

LIVERPOOL Tel. 051-263 1359
TAYLOR BROS (LIVERPOOL) LTD
5/9 PRESCOTT STREET

Open: Monday to Friday
8.30 a.m.-5.30 p.m.
H.P.W.WM.D.A.BC.

MIDDLESEX

NORTH HARROW Tel. 01-863 2492
WILLIAMS TECHNICAL SERVICES ★
36 STATION ROAD
Open: Mon-Fri 8 a.m.-5.30 p.m.
Wed 8 a.m.-1 p.m.,
Sat 9 a.m.-5.30 p.m.
H.P.W.WM.D.A.

MIDDLESEX

HOUNSLOW Tel. 01-570 2103/5135
Q. R. TOOLS LTD
251-253 HANWORTH ROAD

Open: Mon-Fri 8.30 a.m.-5.30 p.m.
Sat 9 a.m.-1 p.m.
P.W.WM.D.CS.A.

NORFOLK

KINGS LYNN Tel. (0553) 2443
WALKER & ANDERSON (Kings Lynn) LTD
WINDSOR ROAD, KINGS LYNN
Open: Monday to Saturday
7.45 a.m.-5.30 p.m.
Wednesday 1 p.m. Saturday 5.00 p.m.
H.P.W.WM.D.CS.A.

NORWICH Tel. 0603 898695
NORFOLK SAW SERVICES
DOG LAND, HORSFORD
Open: Monday to Friday
8.00 a.m.-5.00 p.m.
Saturday 8.00 a.m.-12.00 p.m.
H.P.W.WM.D.CS.A.

NORWICH Tel. 0603 400933
WESTGATES WOODWORKING Tx.
MACHINERY, JUPITER ROAD 975412
OFF MILE CROSS LANE
Open: 9 a.m.-5 p.m. weekdays
9 a.m.-12 a.m. Sat.
P.W.WM.D.

NORTHAMPTONSHIRE

RUSHDEN Tel. 093-34 56424
PETER CRISP LIMITED ★
7 HIGH STREET
Open: Monday to Saturday
8.30 a.m.-5.30 p.m.
Thursday 8.30 a.m.-1.00 p.m.
H.P.W.D.BC.

NORTHUMBERLAND

BLYTH Tel. (06706) 69279
ALLAN McNAIR WOODCRAFT ★
69-71 PLESSEY ROAD

Open: Monday to Saturday
9 a.m.-5 p.m.
H.W.WM.D.T.CS.A.BC.

NOTTINGHAMSHIRE

NOTTINGHAM Tel. (0602) 225979
POOLEWOOD and 227929
EQUIPMENT LTD (06077) 2421/5777
5a HOLLY LANE, CHILLWELL
Open: Mon-Fri 9 a.m.-5.30 p.m.
Sat. 9 a.m. to 12.30 p.m.
P.W.WM.D.CS.A.BC.

NOTTINGHAM Tel. 0602 811889
THE WOODCUTTER
5 TUDOR SQUARE
WEST BRIDGFORD
Open: Tues-Sat 9 a.m.-5.30 p.m.
Fri 9 a.m.-7.30 p.m. Closed Mon.
H.P.W.WM.D.T.CS.A.

OXFORDSHIRE

BICESTER Tel. (08692) 4156/
WOODMEN 3218/3219
104 CHURCHILL ROAD

Open: Monday-Saturday
9 a.m.-5.30 p.m.
P.W.WM.D.A.BC.

OXFORDSHIRE

OXFORD Tel. (0865) 45118/9
SARJENT'S TOOL ★
STORES LTD
150 COWLEY ROAD
Open: Monday to Saturday
8.30 a.m.-5.30 p.m.
H.P.W.WM.D.A.BC.

SHROPSHIRE

TELFORD Tel. Telford
ASLES LTD (0952) 48054
VINEYARD ROAD
WELLINGTON
Open: Mon-Fri 8.30am-5.30pm
Saturday 8.30am-4.00pm
H.P.W.WM.D.A.

SOMERSET

TAUNTON Tel. Taunton 79078
KEITH MITCHELL ★
TOOLS AND EQUIPMENT
66 PRIORY BRIDGE ROAD
Open: Mon-Fri 8.30am-5.30pm
Saturday 9am-4pm
H.P.W.WM.D.CS.A.BC.

WESTON-SUPER-MARE Tel.
JOHN TERRY 0934 21803
TOOL SALES
36 ALFRED STREET
Open: Monday to Saturday
9am-5.30pm inclusive
H.P.W.WM.D.CS.A.

STAFFORDSHIRE

TAMWORTH Tel. 0827-56188
MATTHEWS BROTHERS LTD
KETTLEBROOK ROAD
Open: Mon.-Sat. 8.30am-6.00pm
Demonstrations Sunday mornings
by appointment only
H.P.W.WM.D.T.CS.A.BC.

SUFFOLK

BURY ST. EDMUNDS Tel.
TOOLS & THINGS 0284 62022
21 CHURCHGATE ★

Open: Monday to Saturday
9.00 a.m.-5.30 p.m.
H.P.W.WM.D.A.BC.

IPSWICH Tel. 0473 86216
FOX WOODWORKING ★
'STEBBINGS' BACK LANE
WASHBROOK
Open: Tues. Fri. 9.00am-5.30pm
Sat. 9.00am-5pm
H.P.W.WM.D.A.B.C.

SURREY

CARSHALTON BEECHES Tel.
SURREY WOOD 01-642 6636
MACHINE SALES LTD ★
56A BANSTEAD ROAD
Open: Tues-Fri 9.30 am-6.00 pm
Saturday 9.30 am-2.00 pm
P.W.WM.D.BC.CS.

CROYDON Tel. 01-688 5513
L. H. TURTLE LTD ★
6-12 PARK STREET

Open: Monday to Saturday
8.30 a.m.-5.30 p.m.
H.P.W.WM.D.A.

SHOP GUIDE SHOP GUIDE

SURREY

GUILDFORD Tel. 0483 61125
MESSINGERS FOR TOOLS
14-18 CHERTSEY STREET
Open: Tuesday to Saturday
8.30 a.m.-5.30 p.m.
Closed all day Monday
H.P.W.D.BC.

SUSSEX

BOGNOR REGIS Tel: (0243) 863100
A. OLBY & SON (BOGNOR REGIS LTD)
"TOOLSHOP", BUILDER'S MERCHANT
HAWTHORN ROAD
Open: Mon-Thurs 8a.m.-5.15p.m.
Fri 8a.m.-8p.m. Sat 8a.m.-12.45p.m.
H.P.W.WM.D.T.C.A.BC.

WORTHING Tel. 0903 38739
W. HOSKING LTD (TOOLS & ★
MACHINERY)
28 PORTLAND RD, BN11 1QN
Open: Mon-Sat 8.30am-5.30pm
Wednesday 8.30am-1.00pm
H.P.W.WM.D.CS.A.BC.

WEST MIDLANDS

WEST BROMWICH Tel: 021-
CONWAY SAW & 553 5461/2
SUPPLY LTD
SWAN LANE
Open: 8 a.m.-6 p.m. Mon-Fri
9 a.m.-1 p.m. Saturday
P.W.WM.D.CS.BC.

WILTSHIRE

SWINDON Tel. (0793) 31361
SARJENT'S TOOL STORES LTD ★
64 FLEET STREET
Open: Monday to Saturday
8.30 a.m.-5.30 p.m.
H.P.W.WM.D.A.BC

YORKSHIRE

HALIFAX Tel. 0422 43722/
TIMBERLITE LTD 884788/33575
WILLOWFIELDS ROAD ★
WILLOWFIELD
Open: Monday to Friday
Saturday 9.00 a.m.-5.00 p.m.
H.P.W.WM.D.CS.A.BC.

HARROGATE Tel. 0423 66245/
MULTI-TOOLS 55328 ★
158 KINGS ROAD
Open: Monday to Saturday
8.30 a.m.-6.00 p.m.
H.P.W.WM.D.A.BC.

HUDDERSFIELD Tel. (0484)
NEVILLE M. OLDHAM 641219/(0484)
UNIT 1 DAYLE ST. WORKS 42777
DAYLE STREET, LONGWOOD ★
Open: Mon-Fri 9.00am- 5.30pm
Saturday 9.30am-12.00pm
P.W.WM.D.A.BC.

LEEDS Tel. 0532 574736
D. B. KEIGHLEY MACHINERY LTD ★
VICKERS PLACE
STANNINGLEY
Open: Mon-Fri 9am-5pm
Saturday 9am-1pm
P.W.WM.D.CS.A.BC.

LEEDS Tel. 0532 790507
GEORGE SPENCE & SONS LTD
WELLINGTON ROAD ★
Open: Monday to Friday
8.30 a.m.-5.30 p.m.
Saturday 9.00 a.m.-5.00 p.m.
H.P.W.WM.D.T.A.

YORKSHIRE

SHEFFIELD Tel. 0742-441012
GREGORY & TAYLOR LTD
WORKSOP ROAD ★
Open: 8.30 a.m.-5.30 p.m.
Monday-Friday
8.30 a.m.-12.30 p.m. Sat.
H.P.W.WM.D.

SHEFFIELD Tel. 0742-24659
GRAHAM OXLEY'S SHOWROOM
BRIDGE STREET ★
Open: Monday to Friday
9.00 a.m.-5.30 p.m.
Saturday 8.30 a.m.-12.30 p.m.
H.W.D.A.BC.

SCOTLAND

GLASGOW Tel. 041 429 4374/4444
THE SAW CENTRE Telex: 777886
596-602 EGLINGTON STREET ★
G5 9RR
Open: Mon.-Fri. 8 a.m.-5.30 p.m.
Saturday 9 a.m.-1 p.m.
H.P.W.WM.D.CS.A.

N. IRELAND

Co. ANTRIM Tel. 0266 6384
GEORGE GARDINER
49 BALLYMONEY STREET
BALLYMENA
Open: Open: Mon-Fri 8.30am-5.30pm
Wednesday 8.30am-1.00pm
H.P.W.D.A.BC.

S. IRELAND

COUNTY KILKENNY Tel.
WOODMEN (0409) 5460
CASHEL HOUSE ★
KELLS ROAD, KILKENNY
Open: Monday to Saturday

WALES

BRITON FERRY Tel. (0639)
WOODMEN 820803/4
49 NEATH ROAD ★
Open: Monday to Saturday
9.00 a.m.-5.30 p.m.
P.W.WM.D.A.BC.

CARDIFF Tel. (0222) 373007
JOHN HALL TOOLS LIMITED ★
22 CHURCHILL WAY
Open: Monday to Saturday
9.00 a.m.-5.30 p.m.
H.P.W.WM.D.A.BC.

CARDIFF Tel. (0222) 30831
F. W. MORGAN & 25562
(CANTON) LTD., 129-133
COWBRIDGE RD EAST,
CANTON, CARDIFF
Mon-Sat 8-5 Sun. 9.30-12.30
H.P.T.CS.A.BC.

CARDIFF Tel. (0222) 36519/
WOODMEN 373793/35221
74-76 PARK ROAD
WHITCHURCH, CARDIFF
Open: Monday to Saturday
9.00 a.m.-5.30 p.m.

CARMARTHEN Tel. 0267 7219
DO-IT-YOURSELF SUPPLY
BLUE STREET, DYFED
Open: Monday to Saturday
9.00 a.m.-5.30 p.m.
Thursday 9.00 a.m.-1.00 p.m.
H.P.W.WM.D.T.CS.A.BC.

SWANSEA Tel. (0792) 55680
SWANSEA TIMBER & ★
PLYWOOD CO LTD
57-59 OXFORD STREET
Open: Mon. to Fri. 9 am-5.30 pm
Sat. 9 am-1 pm
H.P.W.D.T.CS.A.BC.

YOU CAN BUY WITH CONFIDENCE FROM THE SHOPS IN THIS SHOP GUIDE

★*Shops offering a mail order service are denoted by an asterisk*

Key: H — Hand tools, **P** — Power tools, **W** — Woodworking machinery up to £1000, **WM** — Woodworking machinery over £1000, **D** — Demonstration available on selected machines, **T** — Timber, **CS** — Cutting or sharpening services, **A** — Attachments, **BC** — Books/catalogues, ***** — Mail order.

£8.00 per Unit
Minimum of SIX insertions.
I enclose remittance of £48.00 ☐
I wish to be invoiced. ☐
Please tick as appropriate.

COUNTY ....

TOWN ....

NAME OF COMPANY/SHOP ....

....

ADDRESS ....

....

To: Valerie Tester
WOODWORKER MAGAZINE
P.O. Box 35,
13 Bridge Street, Hemel Hempstead,
HP1 1EE.

TELEPHONE No ....

DAYS AND HOURS OF BUSINESS

....

....

*TO DENOTE MAIL ORDER SERVICE AVAILABLE ☐

Prices quoted are those prevailing at press date and are
subject to alteration due to economic conditions.

 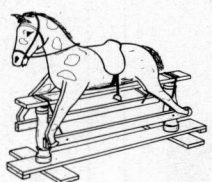 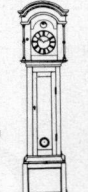 

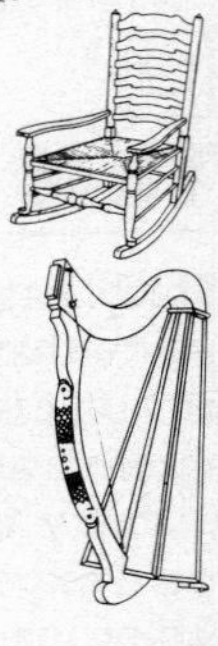

Hitachi can take it!

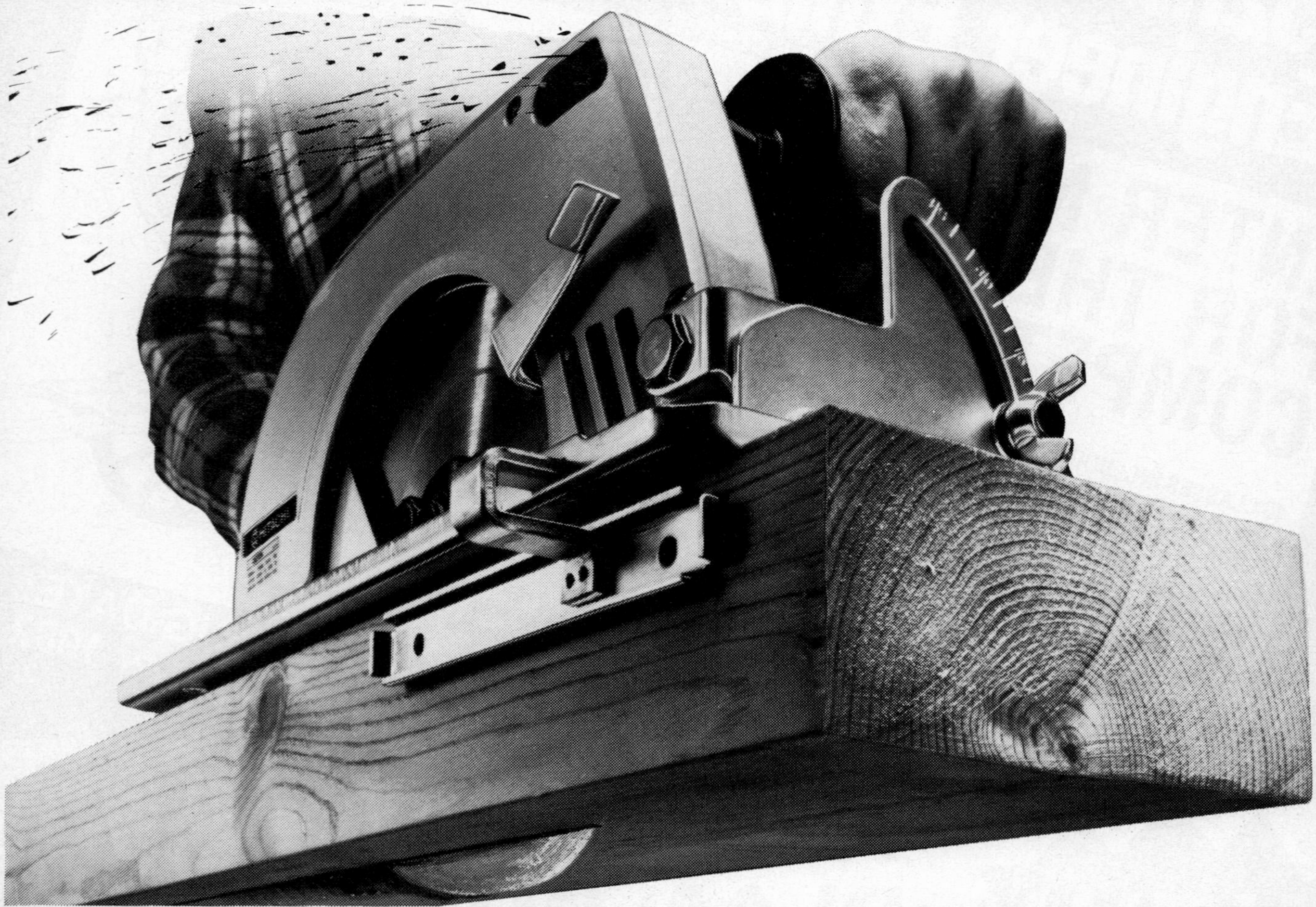

Compact, lightweight router with 3-stage turret. Capacity: Collet chuck ¼". Power input: 730 W. No-load speed: 24,000 rpm. Weight: 2.9 kg. (6.4 lbs.).

TR-8

2-speed belt sander with dust bag. Belts: 110mm x 620mm 4¼" x 24⅜". Power input: 950 W or 860 W. No-load speed: 300m/min (985 ft/min) or 350m/min (1,150 ft/min). Weight: 7.3 kg. (16.1 lbs.).

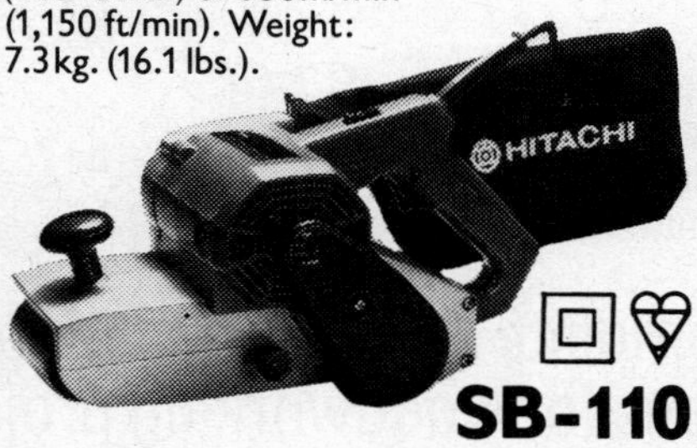

SB-110

Well-balanced rotary precision planer. Rabbeting 25mm (1"). Cutting width: 82mm (3¼"). Max. cutting depth: 3mm (⅛"). Power input: 620 W. No-load speed: 14,000 rpm. Weight: 2.8 kg. (6.2 lbs.).

FU-20

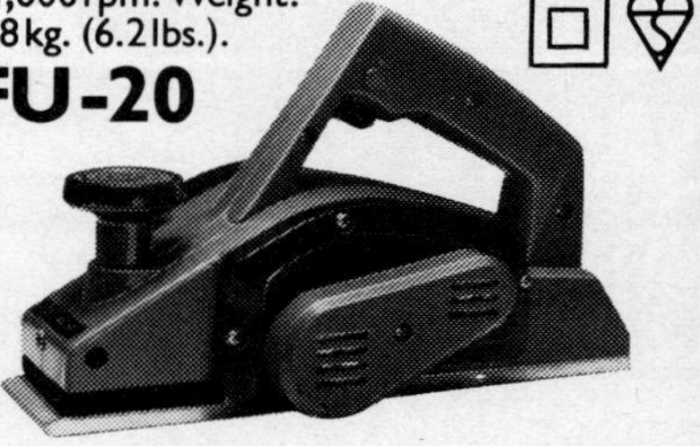

Hitachi has the power tool range with quality that shows, inside and out. Each unit is built from the highest grade materials and is precision engineered for reliability and superior performance– as you'd expect from one of the world's leading manufacturers. We have over 30 years' experience of producing electric motors for portable power tools and we know just how important quality and dependability are to the power tool user.

A wide range of circular saws is available, from 6"-9¼" capacity, for example our PSP-9: a 9¼" double-insulated circular saw with 84mm (3⁵⁄₁₆") cutting depth. Power input: 1,430/1,750 W. No-load speed: 3,900 rpm. Weight: 7.3 kg. (16.1 lbs.).

HITACHI
POWER TOOLS
easy to handle-hard to beat!

Prices quoted are those prevailing at press date and are subject to alteration due to economic conditions.

Masters of marquetry

Ernie Ives, editor of the Marquetarian, reviews the winning entries and reveals some of the secrets behind the pictures in this year's National which was held on his home ground at the Corn Exchange, Ipswich

About 400 exhibits were on show at the Marquetry Society's National Exhibition held this year in the Corn Exchange, Ipswich. The standard of the work was, as usual very high and the judges must have had a difficult task selecting the winners from the also rans.

● *Rye Harbour by Tony Rheindorp, which won first lace in the intermediate class and also took the artistic merit salver*

The rosebowl for the best in the show went to Richard Shellard, a disabled member from Wotton under Edge, Gloucestershire, for his picture *Long Tailed Tit*. Although Richard works from a wheelchair his fingers are nimble and his eyesight good to be able to fit in all the tiny slivers of veneer which made up much of the head and body of the bird. The whole picture only measures 7½ × 10ins and yet there must be hundreds of tiny pieces cut in to give the bird its fluffy feathery appearance. How is it done? Basically the technique is quite simple. An area is cut out to form a 'window' in the usual way and the opening covered with a piece of Sellotape. A pile of veneer slivers is then cut, all of different lengths, and each sliver is individually placed on the Sellotape until the window has been filled. A drop of glue rubbed into the surface holds all the pieces together and when this is dry the Sellotape is removed. Richard says that it is not really tedious as a lot of pieces can be put in in a short time.

The blackberries the bird is perching on are produced by another technique. First the whole berry is cut out and filled with a darkish veneer (some of the berries were shown in their red, unripe stage). From this, each little berry nodule is cut and filled with a lighter wood and then the highlight in each nodule is cut and fitted. An immaculate mirror finish helped to show these details up but one really needed a magnifying glass to appreciate the workmanship although the maker assures me that he doesn't use one.

● *Long tailed tit by Richard Shellard, first in the premier class and rosebowl winner*

A local artist, a non-marquetarian, is usually asked by the Marquetry Society to choose one picture from all those entered for the competition classes which he thinks shows the greatest artistic merit. This year Jack Haste, owner of an Ipswich art gallery, selected *Rye Harbour* by Tony Rheindorp of Basildon for this award. Tony's picture also gained a 1st in the Intermediate class and a salver for the best picture made by a non-group member. Mr Haste liked the picture because of its depth and atmosphere. Certainly just the right piece of olive ash had been found for the water as it really looked wet enough to swim in!

For pictures to be entered in Class 1 they must be one of the first four marquetry pictures ever made by the entrant. *Desert Salukis* by J. T. Burrell of St. Albans was a most difficult subject. It is not easy to get animals, particularly light coloured ones, looking alive and real, too often they are stiff and wooden but Mr. Burell's efforts were highly successful and gained him 1st place in this class.

The class for applied marquetry attracted a lot of interest, the winner being John Wilcox of Bury St. Edmunds with a tilting top table with *A Cotswold Lane in May* scene on the top. Running this a close second was a highly decorated guitar by H. Hulls of Altringham. On the front were butterflies, birds and flowers while inside the soundhole was a bull's head. The edges were herringbone veneered with silhouette leaves let in and the back had an overall parquetry design with some Spanish dancers in the centre panel. Truly a fine piece of work. I wouldn't have dared to let anyone try and play it.

This year there were special classes for children from Chantry High School, Ipswich. Marquetry is a popular club activity there mainly, with the girls. 11 years old Joanne Plumb ran away with all the prizes in one class. Her winning entry, *Summer Roses,* would tax the expertise of many an adult. ∎

● *Desert Salukis by J. T. Burrell. These beautiful dogs won a first prize in the beginners' class. Photography by Ernie Ives*

Letters

From: Miss R. Ricardo, Harrow, Middx
Dear Sir

Regarding your comments on 'Art or Craft?' I feel that I must reply to Mr N. O. Potter.

In 1948 I, in partnership with an ancient designer, designed a 'Knole Suite', and registered this design, which was most successful.

A few years later this design appeared 'exclusive design' by a certain designer, and won an award. We did not in any way appear indignant or upset about the award, and as the designer was a young man, wished him well.

It really was his idea, he had not in any way copied our design, owing to the fact that ours had lapsed, and entirely disappeared from view.

This young designer is no longer with us — as he lives in S. Africa, and again the Knole Suite has arrived at the recent N.F.S. Earls Court, and again has not in any way been copied by the designer.

It is an accepted fact that designers can have exactly the same ideas, years later, as in the case of fashions, furnishing accessories and the like. My own ideas crop up frequently, even registered ones, but I am aware that designers get exactly the same ideas, so therefore one must not, and does not become indignant as Mr N. O. Potter did.

Yours faithfully, **R. Ricardo.**

From: John Rowland, London N8
Dear Sir

I was interested and amused to read your editorial in the June issue of *Woodworker*. Two points struck me as being of particular interest: Ashley Iles' contention that woodcarving was craftsmanship with a very small amount of art content and, secondly, whether, as Mr Potter infers, it is playing the game to enter a work in an exhibition or competition which is a copy of some other person's creation.

I wonder if Mr Iles is now regretting his statement. He will most certainly have upset many of the great numbers of woodcarvers who practise their craft in this country. Whether carving 'in the round' or in relief, the nature of the craft and the material used demands great artistic finesse if a pleasing, harmonious result is to be obtained. As in music and painting, technique is merely a means to an end. Many uninspired works, on the other hand, can and have been executed with considerable technical expertise.

With respect to Mr Potter's grouse, I share his indignation. Surely the creations of other craftsmen are only to be copied as technical exercises, in order that we might learn something. Copies should be eschewed by the carver of integrity when we lay our art on the line in competition. As a regular reader of *Chip Chats*, magazine of the American National Woodcarvers Association, I have often noted winning entries in competitions held in that country which are carbon copies of the works of such masters as E. J. Tangerman and Harold Enlow. If such practices are to become acceptable, then perhaps Mr Iles' proposition that woodcarving is primarily craft and very little art may have some validity.

Finally, can I make a plea on behalf of those of us who seize upon the unexpected and unusual in the magazine, only to be frustrated by lack of details, illustrations, plans and follow-up addresses. The example that springs to mind is the unusual Welsh folk fiddle featured in a recent issue. Having devoured the article, I searched the remainder of the magazine for further information. Needless to say, I was disappointed. Please feature such articles more prominently and at greater length.

Yours faithfully, **John Rowland**

From: H. C. King, Addington, Surrey
Dear Sir

I am perplexed and worried. I set out to make a table with four legs but fortunately Mr N. O. Potter's tirade was noted just in time to prevent my being accused of plagiarism. Messrs Chippendale, Sheraton etc, ad infinitum, made tables with four and sometimes three legs so I hurriedly changed mine to a two legged one and felt much safer.

No sooner was work resumed than it struck me that the chisel being used was designed on the same principle as those used by the great masters. Even the mahogany on my bench was a copy of their material. What now?

The answer is simple — join a School of Art where we are told by Mr Potter that anything is permitted so long as it is in the name of art. Thank you for the tip.

Yours faithfully, **H. C. King**

Comments made by Mr N. O. Potter of Lindfield were quoted in the June issue's leader, under the heading of *Art of Craft?* Mr Potter has now sent us further thoughts on the subject, one of several letters we have received in response to the controversy.

From: N. O. Potter, Lindfield, W. Sussex
Dear Sir

What does the answer 'Yes' imply when given in response to the question 'Did you do this?' Or, more correctly I suppose, what does the question mean? If the subject is a newly decorated room, then the answer 'Yes' is quite correct. You thought up the colour scheme, you bought the paint, you put it on. If the scheme includes wallpaper, then everybody knows that whilst you hung it, you certainly didn't design it or print it. The same applies to buying material and making a dress.

When the question concerns individual works of art, such as an oil or water colour painting, a pencil drawing or a pen and ink sketch; a piece of pottery, a sculpture, some weaving or wood carving; then surely the question refers to total authorship? And if the subject is really a copy of an original, then the answer must be 'Yes, it's a copy of an original by etc', or 'Freely adapted from etc', 'Based on the original by etc', 'With acknowledgements etc'.

The copying of original works of art is an acknowledged means of discovering past methods of working, particularly in the case of oil paintings. The copying of pieces of furniture by Chippendale, Sheraton, Hepplewhite, Adam and others is an even more commonplace practice, because these masters very soon gave up making and concentrated on designing furniture for others to make. They cannot, however, be regarded in the same light as those who solely and individually create and produce artefacts.

Wherever you look today — in local potteries, artists' and sculptors' studios, small mills, stained-glass workshops, forges, individual woodworkers' workshops, craft centres, and so on — people are producing original works of art, and the worst of these is a thousand times better than the most meticulous copy.

To enter in a competition a woodcarving which is a copy without saying so, is to use the original artist's creativeness for your own reward and in doing so to also take an unfair advantage of the other competitors.

It is incomprehensible that anyone would copy another's painting and enter it for a painting competition as their own.

I do not think we should confuse art and craftsmanship with the ethics of copying, but I certainly would not agree with Ashley Iles' comment that woodcarving is 'craftsmanship with a small amount of art'. I think the mix is better balanced than that, if you exclude those employed on repetitive work and copying. Look at the wealth of creative woodcarvings in stately homes, institutions, public buildings, monasteries, cathedrals and the village church. Look at the carved screens, monk stalls and misericords, pulpits and pews; barge boards and fireplace surrounds; ecclesiastical figures and presentation caskets; coats of arms and heraldic devices. Like the local blacksmith, the local woodcarver developed and created his own designs and picture-forms. He was just as much artist as craftsman. The more I think about this the more I feel poor old Grinling Gibbons and his contemporary Carpenter, must be turning in their graves.

I wonder if Wheeler and Hayward, authors of that excellent book *Practical Woodcarving and Gilding*, consider that woodcarving is nearly all craftsmanship with just a little art? See the illustrations in this book of beautiful carving works. Although I'm a comparative newcomer to woodcarving, I've been an artist for as long as I remember and to me all these examples have a greater art than craft content.

When I look round our adult education class, I cannot find one of the 18 amateur woodcarvers copying someone else's work. All are working on original projects, all are designing, creating and finding ways of developing their talent. For Ashley Iles to evaluate woodcarving as mostly craftsmanship with just a little art is to deny woodcarvers acknowledgement of their creativity.

The more I think about this matter, the more other points come to mind, such as (1) Wheeler and Hayward in their book use the term woodcarving to describe all the forms they refer to: inscribed, relief and in the round. The term wood sculpture is not used at all. I assume that the former is generally understood to refer to all forms of woodcarving.

(2) With the availability today of powered modelling tools, I think a distinction should be made in competitions between entries carved entirely by hand and those carved by hand and machine.

(3) The suitability of judges: I do not mean this as any sort of reflection on the integrity of judges, but I do feel that if they are judging artefacts which combine art and craftsmanship, then they should have a good working knowledge of both. It takes a thoroughly experienced cabinetmaker to judge cabinet work, and in the woodcarving section the judges should be similarly qualified. Companies donating prizes should resist the temptation to be represented on the panel of judges (however standard the practice may be).

Yours faithfully, **N. O. Potter**

Our panel of experts
answer queries about
your workshop problems

Woodworker's Question Box

Write to: Question Box
Woodworker
PO Box 35
Bridge Street
Hemel Hempstead HP1 1EE

Floor finishing

From: R. Swift, Crewe, Cheshire

I have recently completed an oak floor with strip boarding in my dining room and ask your advice on the most suitable method of finishing. I wish to have a light oak finish and wonder if a spirit stain would be practical followed by a clear polyurethane. Alternatively would a teak oil give a durable surface?

We note that you wish to finish your oak floor a light colour and you have considered using a spirit stain. These are made by dissolving 1oz spirit soluble powder in 1pt of methylated spirits. Whilst they have the advantage of not raising the grain they dry so rapidly that we would not advise their use on such a large area as a floor. A water stain such as 2ozs bichromate of potash dissolved in a pint of water is suitable for oak but all water stains raise the grain. Consequently we would recommend the use of an oil stain which will not raise the grain and does not dry too quickly. Having let the stain dry overnight it can be varnished with an oil varnish which will be more suitable than polyurethane.

Oil stains and varnishes are obtainable from James Jackson & Co (London) Ltd. Major Works, 76/89 Alscot Rd., SE1 5SX.

We have seen oak floors polished by being regularly rubbed with raw linseed oil. This is a very durable finish which brings out the beauty of the grain. It does however have a darkening effect and consequently would not be entirely suitable for your purpose.

Split carvings

From: D. Smith, Boroughbridge, N. Yorks

I have recently started to carve wood in the round and have completed a carving of a barn owl (14in × 6in) in pear wood. This has split, no doubt due to the use of unseasoned wood. The carving is worth keeping so could you advise on how to fill in the cracks?

Provided that the pear wood is now completely seasoned it will not split further and any cracks which are filled will not reopen. There are several proprietary fillers sold in small tins which are available in various colours. Try to obtain a close match and with a palette knife press the stopping well into the crack. Allow it to harden before trimming off the surplus.

Another effective filler obtainable from polish supply houses is hard stopping or beaumontage. This also comes in a variety of colours and a stick of the correct colour should be selected and held directly above the crack. A hot steel knitting needle is held against the tip of the stopping to melt it. The blobs fall into and slightly overfill the crack. After a few minutes the stopping will be hard enough to trim to shape.

Although stopping takes polish well it cannot be stained and for this reason its colour must be the same as the finished work.

Timber samples

From: J. Disspain, New Malden, Surrey

Please could you identify the two samples of timber which I enclose?

I have examined the samples and would comment that the smaller of the two is a softwood, and I would say was Parana pine (*Araucaria angustifolia*), a popular timber from Brazil. In saying this, I am calling on my experience of handling the wood and knowing its appearance and not by anatomical expertise. It is essential for me to reiterate once again that without microscope and laboratory facilities it is highly impracticable to attempt positive identification of coniferous species because of their general primitive structure.

In this present case I have said the sample appears to be Parana pine, but the two main genera belonging to the Araucariceae, ie *Araucaria* and *Agathis* (various species of kauri), produce wood which by appearance is decidedly similar. Even by microscopic examination it is not always possible to separate the species and chemical tests are needed, eg the use of dilute caustic soda or potash in which to boil some tiny chips or an extract of ferric chloride by which to test the wood's reaction. It is probable the sample is as I have predicted, but it is guesswork. Similar remarks can be applied to hardwoods generally, but in a good many cases, macroscopic examination by means of a ×10 hand lens is satisfactory.

Accordingly, I would say your second sample is characteristic of West African abura (*Mitragyna ciliata*), an excellent wood for a good many end uses, but particularly for furniture, specialist shelving systems and similar. The rather plain nature of the wood allows it to be stained and polished to simulate other woods like walnut and mahogany.

Construct an 'open lot'

From: D. E. Pikett, Lincoln

I have been asked by a traveller to construct what he describes as an 'open lot' upon a nine foot dray, the chassis usually employed for this purpose. Having examined such a vehicle I believe the joinery, cabinet work, carving and turning involved are not outside my thirty years' amateur experience of these crafts and I am consequently looking forward to having a go.

However, short of following the Chinese tailor's technique there seems little chance of uncovering many hidden constructional details without outside help. I have, of course, noted the advertisement for plans of miniature horse-drawn vehicles in your magazine but wonder whether these would show traditional constructional methods. Tradition I gather is the name of the game! Hence any advice on where to look or whom to consult would be gratefully received.

Other more straightforward questions spring to mind.

1 The ash hoops or ribs spring from two side boards, each some 11ft × 1ft 4in × 1¼in. These says my traveller should be of parana pine. (On the vehicle I saw they were heavily

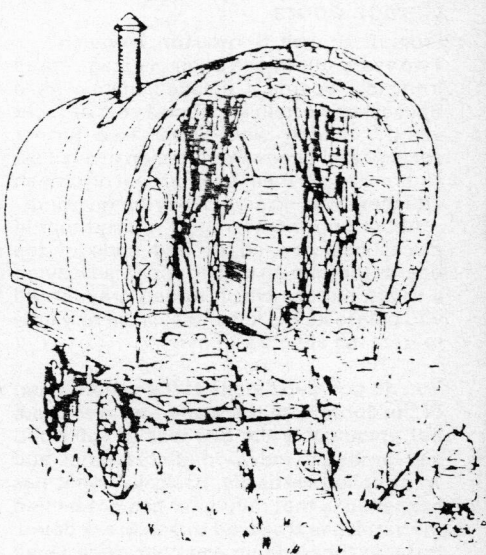

painted, one dare not draw one's penknife.) I wonder if you consider that wood suitable? Easy to carve I suppose but perhaps not very durable or stable.

2 The ash hoops: would green wood have to be used or could they be steamed? They are of approx 2in × ½in section.

3 Would you recommend a suitable mechanical router for the acres of low relief, rather than repetitive carving involved, maximum depth of ground no more than ½in? I have really no use for a professional, heavy duty machine.

4 If the painting is entrusted to me, will you recommend a durable substitute for gold leaf though of course tradition may demand the real thing?

Plans for an 'open lot' are in fact available from the Woodworker Plans Service, price £4.35 inc p&p. Although the plans are usually sold for modelmaking they do show the construction of the full size vehicles. Wheels, axles and springs would be difficult for the amateur builder but if Mr Pikett has been given a dray chassis then the hard work has been done.

1 Yes parana pine is best for the sides being much lighter than hardwood and very stable provided that it is not green when used. Old church pews would be an ideal source.

2 Yes the ash hoops should be steam bent.

3 As for carving, I would not recommend a lot of relief work on an open lot. Edges should be decorated with butterfly chamfers but otherwise most of the decoration consists of painting.

4 There is no adequate substitute for gold leaf, applied with gold size.

Whoops!

In the reply to Mr Tulloch's question (Teak finish p423 June *Woodworker*) the word stain has been omitted from paragraph two of the reply. This does tend to confuse the issue and we apologise. It should read. . . A suitable teak oil stain can be obtained from. . .

Woodworker's Question Box

Our panel of experts answer queries about your workshop problems

Write to: Question Box
Woodworker
PO Box 35
Bridge Street
Hemel Hempstead HP1 1EE

Garage doors

From: E. Stokell, Sprowston, Norwich

Two years ago I made a pair of garage doors from t&g boards. I finished them with a Ronseal spirit stain and then a coat of yacht varnish diluted with turps. Two further coats of yacht varnish were then given. Last summer I gave them another coat of varnish and there was no sign of anything wrong.

About two months ago I noticed that in places near the edges and ends of the boards the varnish had disappeared leaving a rough surface which turned grey. Could you please let me know the cause and how to treat the affected areas?

You do not give details of the construction of the doors or of the wood that was used, but presumably the t&g was of softwood and probably redwood (Scots pine) and was applied vertically. Basically, what has happened is that rainwater has got behind the varnish and caused this to break down. So far as the cladding was concerned, there would be two areas of vulnerability; one, the tongue within the groove, and two, the end grain at the base of the t&g boards. If the door was made up in the white, although the tongues would be hidden in the grooves rain water could still get in and the subsequent movement by swelling and shrinking across the faces of the boards would encourage minute checks to appear in the varnish film which would then tend to flake off. The end grain at the bottom of the doors would quickly absorb sufficient moisture with the same result.

Where boards are used like this on garage doors they are best applied diagonally because although there is still an element of end grain exposure, the ends are angled off so water is encouraged to be shed more rapidly. You will appreciate the extreme exposure of most garage doors to the elements.

On the Continent, where wooden garage doors are much more in evidence than here, hardwood is generally used, the panels are diagonal, and varnish is not used. The wood is finished off with an organic solvent preservative stain containing a water repellent and the life of the door is extended, the finish is attractive, generally a reddish or reddish-brown, and maintenance is reduced to a minimum; furthermore, as each additional maintenance coat of finish is applied, so does the water repellency increase and the matt finish take on a slight lustre.

Varnish does not preserve wood, but acts as a water shedder; the more efficient the varnish film, the worse it becomes should moisture find its way behind it. Accordingly, where a softwood is used, with a low natural durability factor, it is desirable to treat all the wood with a water repellent preservative before assembly, and if a varnish finish is insisted upon, the pre-treatment helps firstly by resisting long term decay, and secondly, the water repellent waxes and silicone help stabilise the wood against shrinking and swelling by resisting water absorption.

It is not possible to give you a treatment now that will be wholly effective. The simplest approach would be to sand back the damaged areas and revarnish, and if you can remove the doors without too much difficulty, try to seal the end grain of the wood at the base of the door. You will understand that wind blown rain does not generally penetrate past the base of an external door but tends to be held in the narrow air gap and persists there a lot longer than on the vertical surfaces. If a weather strip is placed at the bottom of the door, while this may help shed water off the door it will not prevent wind blown water gaining access. If you attempted to strip the varnish off the door, and Ronseal have brought out a new stripper which could cope with this, we do not think you could introduce a preservative because of the stain and sealing coat which, having penetrated the wood, would offer resistance to a preservative.

We feel that revarnishing on the lines suggested would be the best method, but we would make one final comment. The backs of the doors ought to be balanced by applying the same treatment as the fronts; if you have not done this then it is possible the build up of moisture affecting the finish has been exaggerated by moisture vapour getting to the wood from behind.

Timber sample from New Zealand

From: C. A. Reid, Rotorua, N.Z.

So that we can have some peace here, would you please identify the enclosed sample of wood?

I have asked six of my friends and have now got six different answers. Everything from mahogany to jarrah. One is a professional carpenter who swears it is blue gum, an Australian eucalypt, but I don't think so. Blue gum is so called after the colour of its bark not its timber. I thought it was rata (*Metrosideros robusta*) but the grain of rata is more open than the sample.

It was salvaged from the base of an old wardrobe I bought in a second hand shop. The robe was constructed of solid tawa apart from the base. As you will see this base is of two ¾in pieces glued together. Why cut them to ¾in and then glue them together again?

I have examined the sample and can well imagine the varying answers one would obtain from a cursory examination without recourse to some visual aid. This is especially applicable to many Australasian woods which not only look alike to the naked eye, but need a lot of time and expertise to separate them even under laboratory conditions; jarrah and karri for example, invariably require to be judged on the results of a burning splinter test. With regard to your sample, despite there being some five or six hundred *Eucalyptus* species, you can rule these out, the anatomy of your sample being different although typical of some other species of genera belonging to the same family to which the eucalypts belong, ie the Myrtaceae. I have broken down the possibles to two separate species, turpentine (*Syncarpia laurifolia*) and brush box (*Tristania conferta*), both of similar anatomy and general appearance.

There are two recognised tests for separating these woods; one by applying ferr chloride to the heartwood, when the solu tion turns black on *Syncarpia* and yellow brown to eventual brown on *Tristania*, an two, by burning a splinter of the wood i still air, and when the glowing ember ha subsided, examining the result, *Syncarp* giving a black charcoal, and *Tristania* white ash. I could not use the chemical tes but burning a match-like splinter gave definite ash. Accordingly, I would say you sample is characteristic of brush box. Wit regard to why two thin sections had bee glued together, it is only possible to hazar a guess. Brush box is not a furniture woo in the true sense, being more of a floorin and decking wood, and it is extreme refractory. It is possible that some machin rippings were available when the robe were being made, and in an effort to utilis these, and to help prevent warping durin the early stages of assembly, the section were glued together; the final weight of th robe holding the unit stable.

Damage to a pine top

From: G. T. Ingham, Colwyn Bay, N. Wale

My wife's favourite piece of furniture, a fi Welsh dresser has had an initial (P) carve into the top by a nephew who was stayin with us. It has been carved out with penknife and is about ⅛in deep. Pleas advise me as to the best way of treating and is it varnish or linseed oil finished at th moment?

'He that spareth his rod hateth his son: bu he that loveth him chasteneth him betime *Proverbs* 13.24.

It has been assumed that the pine Wels dresser has not been stained but has bee finished with linseed oil because of th labour involved and the fact that the oil ha a darkening effect. Varnish could have bee used but the probability is that a lacque was sprayed on. The knife will have le ridges on either side of the cut and thes will need to be levelled off with wire woo The whole of the top should be rubbe evenly matt in this way and then th scratch brought up level with either stic stopping or a tin of wood stopping of th appropriate colour. If stick stopping is use it is melted into the crack by holding against the end of a hot steel knittin needle until the crack is slightly overfille When hard the excess is sliced off flus with a wide chisel.

Finishing should follow the original finis which can be identified as follows:

From an inconspicuous part of the dres ser scrape off a little of the finish with chisel held almost upright. If a yellow shaving curls off then varnish was used; white powder, then the dresser was cellu losed. It is not necessary to have sprayin equipment to apply the cellulose. Bar-to lacquer, obtainable from polish houses, ca be applied either by brush or a polishin rubber made from wadding enclosed in clean white, preferably linen, handkerchie It will be advantageous to add about 25 pe cent to the cellulose whichever method i used.

THE MAGAZINE FOR THE CRAFTSMAN

OCTOBER 1982 Vol 86 No 1067 ISSN 0043 776X

Cover picture: an unfinished detail from a reproduction medieval chest in cleft ash, currently being made by Roger Champion, the 'carpenter of Singleton'. See page 654.

Editor	Chris Dunn
Deputy Editor	Polly Curds
Advertisement Manager	Glyn Crole-Rees

MEMBER OF THE AUDIT BUREAU OF CIRCULATIONS

SUBSCRIPTION DEPARTMENT: Remittances to MODEL AND ALLIED PUBLICATIONS, PO Box 35, Hemel Hempstead, Herts HP1 1EE. Price per copy 95p includes p&p. Subscription queries: Tel: Hemel Hempstead 51740. Subscription rate, including index, £11.90 per annum; overseas sterling £12.90; $29.00 US for overseas dollar subscribers. Second class postage paid in US at New York, New York. *Distribution* to North American hobby and craft stores, museums and bookshops by Bill Dean Books Ltd, 166-41 Powells Cove Boulevard, Post Office Box 69, Whitestone, New York 11357, USA. Tel: 1-212-767-6632. *Distribution* to news stand sales by Eastern News Distribution Inc, 111 Eight Avenue, New York, NY10011, USA Tel: 1-212-255-5620. (POSTMASTER: Send address changes to England).

WOODWORKER is printed in Great Britain by H. E. Warne Ltd, East Hill, St Austell, Cornwall PL25 4TN for the proprietor and publisher Model & Allied Publications Ltd (a member of the Argus Press Group). Trade sales by Argus Press Sales & Distribution Ltd, 12-18 Paul Street, London EC2A 4JS. WOODWORKER (ISSN 0043-776X) is published on the 3rd Friday of the month.

Model & Allied Publications Ltd

PO Box 35, Bridge Street, Hemel Hempstead, Herts HP1 1EE. Telephone: Hemel Hempstead (0442) 41221.

Beer, bacon, baccy and Woodworker

When the price of your magazine goes up, two things predictably happen. 1. You grumble. 2. The editor devotes his leader column to justifying the effects of inflation, rising costs of paper, increased production overheads and all that.

Well. The price of your magazine has gone up I'm afraid, and I hope you are not grumbling. For my part I am not going to tire you with a lecture on inflation, though if I really thought that *Woodworker* was only worth 70p a month, I surely would. If you *are* feeling the effects of paying an additional tenpence, you could make yourself feel better by taking the new cover price of 80p in context with prices generally, and it will suddenly look like pretty good value. Take the cost of a pint and a half at your local, for instance or three-quarters of a pound of bacon, or a packet of cigarettes. Beer, bacon and baccy are pretty soon dealt with, but your *Woodworker* stays with you for as long as you want it.

I have recently been reading, enjoying and learning from the very first edition of *Woodworker,* published in October 1901. It is still there to be useful after 81 years, but I doubt if anyone is still making use of a pound of bacon bought during the reign of Queen Victoria.

But there is no room for complacency. We strive to make your modern *Woodworker* even more indispensable.

And so to the Woodworker Show, which is almost upon us. It is going to be bigger and better than ever this year. The increasing success and demand for space in this premier event in the woodworking calendar has now obliged us to expand into two halls, providing the facilities to present an even better programme.

Since this is National Maritime Year (and Trafalgar Day also coincides with the show dates of 19-24 October, as it happens) we shall be leaning gently towards the nautical. For instance our carving competition, sponsored by Ashley Iles, has taken 'Sea Dogs and Pirates' as its theme this year, and also on the woodcarving front Mr William Ross, who so delighted visitors with his carvings and whittlings at last year's show, is to give continuous demonstrations of his craft throughout the week.

In addition to the myriad trade stands, where every significant name in the appropriate manufacturing and retail businesses will be represented, you will be able to see the exhibits stimulated by our many competition classes in all disciplines of woodworking, including two new classes.

Films, lectures and demonstrations will cover such subjects as miniature furniture, woodcarving, chairmaking, country crafts, coppicing and timber management, polishing, staining and finishing, setting up in business, timber technology and books for the woodworker.

It is going to be a great show in every sense, and we look forward to seeing all you readers of *Woodworker* there.

Chris Dunn

October notes

Spare parts purchased

West German edgebanding specialists, Heinrich Brandt, have purchased the Ney-Gozalon company, makers of a range of edgebanders and adhesive applicators previously known as Gerhard Ney Senior. Brandt will now manufacture this range at their new factory at Lemgo and the machines are to be marketed under the Brandt name.

A considerable number of spare parts and finished machines were purchased as part of the agreement. These are readily available through Brandt's sole UK agents, Jaydee (Machine Sales) Ltd of High Wycombe, who should be contacted for further details. Existing users of Gerhard Ney Senior machinery are requested to get in touch with Jaydee in order to establish spare part requirements.

Safety first from Husqvarna

Anyone buying a Husqvarna 50 Rancher or Husqvarna 61 chain saw in the next few months will get a helping hand towards the safe use of their saw, courtesy of the UK distributors, Hyett Adams, in the form of a free set of Nordtec safety helmet and safety gloves.

The safety helmet is approved for forestry work and features an integral visor and ear muffs, essential protection for eyes and an often overlooked area, ears. Nordtec protective gloves are made of thick, soft calfskin, with separate thumb and forefinger on the right hand to allow for throttle operation etc. The left glove is mitten-shaped with a ballistic nylon pad on the back which prevents injury occurring to the hand should it come into contact with the cutting chain. The set is worth a total of £32.71 including VAT and purchasers will be able to obtain the set on production of a voucher which is obtainable from dealers, in press advertisements and from Hyett Adams at Stonehouse.

The free safety set offer lasts until the end of February 1983.

Lathe from Tyme Machines

A new woodturning lathe, the Avon, has been introduced by Tyme Machines (Bristol) Ltd.

The Avon incorporates the best features of the 17 × 37 model from this company but offers more flexibility. The standard version has 24in between centres with the options of 36in or 48in. Diameter over the bed is 9in and over toolrest 6in.

The headstock can be rotated to 90° enabling bowls to be turned at the front of the machine, giving free chisel movement up to a maximum diameter of 18in or to 180° to give 21in diameter capacity.

The Avon comes complete with ¾hp motor, no volt overload switch, 5 speed poly-V drive allowing the operator to carry out most woodturning functions.

A full range of accessories is available for both the 17 × 37 and Avon lathes.

Hours change

G. K. Hadfield of Shepshed, Leicestershire inform us that they are altering their opening hours to satisfy the demands of customers. They are now joining the usual 9.00am to 5.00pm hours since these hours were specifically requested.

Finish and preserve

The range of Cover Plus Wood Preservatives and Finishes is available exclusively from the larger Woolworth and Woolco stores.

For the long term preservation of wood against the rigours of the elements, decay and insect attack, Cover Plus offers four different products. Teak Oil will replace oils that the atmosphere has dried out from naturally oily woods such as teak and aformosia, thus reducing the risk of the wood cracking, the silicone it contains will effectively repel water when used outdoors. Woodworm Killer, with its special spout dispenser to inject the liquid directly into the insect's bore holes is for immediate attack against all types of woodworm already present in the wood. Wood Treatment is a comprehensive remedy against wet and dry rot and all types of wood boring insects. It inhibits re-infestation by woodworm and death watch beetle at all stages of their life cycle. Wood Preservative is for use on all wood exposed to the elements, such as that used for cladding, sheds and fencing. Its powerful biocide fends off mildew, moulds and rot and its high wax content repels water while allowing the wood to 'breathe'. Wood Preservative is available in red cedar, medium and dark brown and ebony so that the wood's appearance is both decoratively improved and preserved.

Also available are various finishes including exterior hardwood finishes, Cover Plus clear varnish, yacht varnish, and

● *Nigel Baker, second year student at Shrewsbury made this chair in laminated sycamore and walnut.*

● *Bachelor's cabinet in white and olive ash with ebony handles by second year student Charles Anketell-Jones.*

● *These four pictures show a selection of work from the recently held college exhibition at Shrewsbury College of Arts and Technology. John Price, course tutor in furniture studies says the work reflects college practice in training students to design and make furniture rather than reproduce furniture from the past. The furniture reflects contemporary and traditional styles and it may not sell very well in the market place. Nevertheless the training students get in business studies hopefully makes them aware that the market may ultimately determine what furniture they make to earn a living.*

Above: second year student Richard Jones' sideboard in white ash with inlaid olive ash and steam bent handles. Below: an ash rocking chair made by first year student Simon Watson to his own design during the part of the course dealing with basic countrymade furniture.

polyurethane clear finish in gloss or satin for use on new timbers or as a protective coat for dyed or stained wood. Wood dyes and stains are included in the range.

New directory

The British Woodworking Federation has now published its 1982/83 Yearbook and Directory which contains the names, addresses and telephone numbers of some 700 member companies in England, Scotland and Wales and similar details of associate and affiliate members.

Intended as a guide for those who specify and use timber products in the building industry, the directory is divided into nine main categories.

The first six list the main sections of the BWF by product type — architectural and general; doors and doorsets; kitchen furniture; laminated structures and timber engineering; timber frame construction, and windows.

Where appropriate, these are further divided by sub-sectional headings showing the individual services offered by the member firm.

Published by Comprint Publications of 212-214 Lower High Street, Watford, Herts. (Watford 33231), copies of the BWF Yearbook and Directory are available free to members from the BWF, 82 New Cavendish Street, London W1M 8AD, and at £5 per copy (including post and packaging) to non-members.

Tooling for windows

Leicester Wood Technique announce a new tooling range for windows called Oppold. Designed for use on moulders, spindle moulders and tenoning machines. The new range is a complete system using segmented reversible knife components to produce all the profiles and joints necessary to complete a window frame and sash.

Each segment is interchangeable to enable profiles of differing shapes and sizes to be completed with the minimum amount of time and cost.

Constant cutting circle is the main feature of the new range, having reversible carbide knives, which give long life and consistent diameter for use on all types of machines including the latest computer controlled window lines.

Knife changing is simple with the use of carbide reversible knives. Each segment has a part number for ease of identification when setting.

All bore sizes are available to fit any machine. Further details and new catalogue available from: Leicester Wood Technique Ltd, Hothorpe House, Main Street, Theddingworth, Lutterworth, Leics LE17 6QY.

Sticky news

A four-page company newspaper has recently been issued by the Export Division of National Adhesives and Resins Ltd, Slough. According to export manager Basil Ford, the objective of *National Adhesives News* is to bring to the notice of industry some of the new techniques that are available from the National organisation.

Products covered in the first edition include a two-part water-based adhesive for producing flexible laminates; a special water-based adhesive for applying spray-on insulation; a sprayable neoprene used to bond panels for offshore accommodation modules; and a two-part thermosetting emulsion adhesive for customers in a wide range of wood-using industries.

It's the Gjerde-sagen

The Nor-Saw portable saw bench is new to the UK but it is not a new machine. Known in Norway as the Gjerde-sagen, its reputation for precision, versatility of application and mobility, together with durability, has made it a standard small workshop saw throughout Scandinavia.

It incorporates four major features in one machine: a 45 degree tilting arbor, the ability to fix the blade at any height — a useful feature for part depth ripping, notching and grooving — a revolving table which allows the blade to be rotated from the rip to the cross cut position, and a unique ability to feed the blade from below the table up through the wood for angle cutting — a major safety plus combined with the clear polycarbonate guard.

The machine is supplied as standard with an 8ft roller feed table, and shorter feed tables and roller take-off tables are available as extras. Ability to cut compound angles in addition to mitring, ripping and cross-cutting enables maximum use to be made of the machine to cope with a wide range of jobs.

Operated by one man, the Nor-Saw tackles jobs that would normally require two men, for instance, cutting sheet timber in seconds. Alternative blades are supplied for operating with other materials such as laminates.

Two models are available

October notes

offering 104mm and 150mm depth of cut, with a standard range of motors including 240 volt single phase, 110V single phase and 415 volt three phase. Other motors can be supplied to special order.

The Nor-Saw conforms to Woodworking Machine Regulations. Saws and a full range of spares are available from Norcem UK Limited, Old Bath Road, Twyford, Berkshire RG10 9PQ.

That's the spirit

A new range of spirit levels for the professional and home craftsman has been launched by Rabone Chesterman, the Birmingham based manufacturer of measuring equipment and hand tools.

Branded Artisan, the levels have an extruded aluminium box section body which gives strength and rigidity. Virtually unbreakable solid acrylic plumb and level vials are fitted. These are factory set and require no adjustment during the working life of the level. The vials also carry a five-year guarantee, full details are included with each level.

Artisan is finished with a powder coat spray paint making it an extremely hard-wearing and durable spirit level.

To satisfy most requirements seven different sizes are available.

Available now from tool shops, DIY superstores, hardware shops and departmental stores.

Ladders, steps and trestles

The British Standards Institution has published a revision of BS 1129 *Portable timber ladders, steps, trestles and lightweight stagings*, originally issued in 1966. It specifies requirements for materials, dimensions and workmanship for the following equipment: Single-section ladders, including builders' pole ladders and shelf ladders; extending ladders; standing step ladders, including swing-back steps, platform steps and ladder-backed steps; folding trestles and lightweight stagings.

The standard includes appendices giving the test requirements for slope of grain of the timber and for scarf joints, together with recommendations for the use, care and maintenance of the products covered by the specification. Since many of the accidents associated with ladders result from misuse, particularly overloading, the stan-

dard now requires the class and duty to be marked on the product.

The standard continues to specify particular species of timber and minimum dimensions of the sections which experience has proved to be satisfactory. All dimensions are expressed in metric units, but it has not been possible to rationalize many of the timber sections since commercially available timber is still prepared to sizes based on the inch.

Copies of BS 1129 may be obtained from the BSI Sales Department, 101 Pentonville Road, London N1 9ND. Price £13.00 (BSI subscribing members £6.50).

Modern adhesives in traditional craft

For many hundreds of years, High Wycombe has been one of the most important centres for the furniture industry, based upon the plentiful local supply of beech. Parker Knoll Furniture Ltd has been at Wycombe for some 60 years, the company having been founded in East London in 1870. At Wycombe, Parker Knoll combine the best of the old, in terms of quality and craftsmanship, with the best of the new, in terms of materials and equipment, including substantial use of Evo-Stik 9517 one part PVA adhesive.

Parker Knoll manufacture a range of 60 types of chair divided into four groups: traditional Queen Anne-style chairs and settees; modern upholstered; recliners and contract furniture. All frame-making is carried out at Wycombe, while final polishing and upholstery work is based at the company's factory at Chipping Norton in

Oxfordshire.

Evo-Stik 9517 is applied by hand as a cold-cure adhesive in assembling many of the timber frames, starting with many small sub-assemblies up to the side-assembly and cross-framing stage.

A smaller but vital use of the material is in radio frequency curing of the adhesive in bonding blocks together to form cabriole legs and other traditional chair legs. Radio frequency is used to save time both on machining and assembly, as the joints are cured sufficiently in 12 to 20 seconds for the assembly to be handled.

Circular saw launch

A new lightweight circular saw has just been launched by AEG — the HK 45A, designed for the professional user at a price

● *Evo-stik 9517 is applied by hand as a cold-cure adhesive in assembling many timber frames in the Parker Knoll making shop at High Wycombe (See Modern adhesives).*

of £56.95 inc. VAT. The machine is built to full industrial standards with a tungsten carbide-tipped blade and sturdy rip fence supplied as standard.

Clocks for Everyman
Pictured right:

Frank Scofield of Hegner Universal Saws (UK) Ltd, demonstrates the art of fretwork cutting on his company's Multicut-2 precision sawing machine at this year's Clocks for Everyman Exhibition at Kensington New Town Hall in London. The exhibition was well attended, despite the ASLEF rail strike, though this did affect the planned lecture programme — the first item on the programme, a lecture/demonstration by Charles Cliffe on wax polishing of oak cases, had to be cancelled because Mr Cliffe couldn't get to the exhibition. Among the exhibitors were companies selling wood-restoration products, for instance House of Harbru and Silverstrath, and Horological Solvents which had its new Curator range on show. Timecraft, Classic Clocks, Biddle & Mumford, Craft Supplies and Charles Greville were selling complete clock movements — ready to put into that case you've just built — and other companies were selling brassware and accessories — spandrels, finials, dials, bezels and so on — for case builders and restorers.

● *Frank Scofield demonstrating the art of fretwork cutting which has been the subject of letters to the editor in recent issues (See Clocks for Everyman).*

The HK45A circular saw from AEG (See Circular saw launch).

Popular Crafts Show

The Popular Crafts Show will be held at the New Kensington Town Hall from September 24-26. Open from 10am to 6pm daily with refreshments and parking available, admission for adults £1.50, children and OAPs £1.00. It offers a marvellous opportunity to find interesting and different craft work and see the craftsmen and women at work. Crafts covered will include hand turned wooden gift ware, patchwork and quilting, miniature furniture for dolls houses, jewellery, decorated eggs, etc. A good place to come to buy your Christmas presents and to get ideas for work of your own.

More from Makita

Additions to the Makita range include the 1000SB lightweight planer designed to be compact and easy to use. It has a powerful 210W motor and is particularly good for fast stock removal and achieving a fine finish in one pass, say the manufacturers. Accessories include sharpening holder assembly, blade gauge assembly, socket wrench, edge guide, dressing stone and removing pin.

The HP1300S pistol grip, variable speed hammer drill with a reversing facility which makes it ideal for use as a screwdriver. Delivering up to 29,700 blows per minute, it is ideal for working in any material from glazed tiles to concrete, masonry, plastic, wood and steel. It comes in a metal carrying case, with side-grip and a chuck key attached to the power lead.

Makita state lightweight handling, fine balance, plenty of power and push-button lubrication make the 5012B chain saw incredibly easy to use. Now they are making it even easier by offering a free sawhorse with every chain saw (while stocks last).

The rugged wooden saw-horse holds logs etc firm while the 5012B gets to work with its 300mm (11¾in.) chain — powered by the tried and tested Makita motor. At only 9½lbs handling is no problem and the comfortable grip, large hand protector and double insulation make sawing safe as well as speedy. Standard equipment includes a chain blade, oil supply, socket wrench, file and screwdriver.

● *Rugged wooden saw horse holds the logs, the 5012B does the work (See More from Makita).*

Guild notes

edited by Polly Curds

Admin. corner

Previous issues of Guild notes have started with me saying 'think about the long winter evenings, come and join us on a course'. Well though as I write this in early August no courses have actually taken place I am delighted so many of you responded. The polishing and finishing course will be run in a week's time at Aldenham with its full complement of participants. Early September will see at least a dozen guild members taking the design and furniture making course at Rycotewood. We will be seeing many of you I hope at the Woodworker Show in October and getting your thoughts and ideas for next year. But the routing course scheduled for 30 October has proved so popular that I am going to have to say 'first come first served' we are now over subscribed. The good news is that Trend have agreed to run more courses for us in the early months of next year and I will be contacting those of you on the waiting list as soon as possible with new dates.

I have just returned to the office after two weeks holiday in the sun of Greece. (My editor tells everyone I am now marinated in ouzo and retsina. . . not true.) In common with other guild members when they are on holiday I kept my eyes open for woodwork and woodworking crafts as usual this year. Perhaps I shall be receiving letters from some of you soon detailing what you saw. I hope so.

I holidayed on Corfu where olive seems to be the most popular timber and woodcarving quite common, though of course geared up to the tourist industry. George has a woodcarving workshop in the New Port, Corfu and has followed thirteen years of training since he was 'apprenticed' at the age of ten! He says he considers a ten year apprenticeship with an expert essential for the 'crafting of the olive.'

The wood is purchased after the olives are pruned and falls into three categories: the knots (karkinomas) are the best parts of the wood owing to their hardness and are usually used for salad bowls and similar objects, the other two categories are the trunk and branches.

Olive wood, George says must be stored for at least four years to allow for slow natural drying to ensure that the finished articles will not split. In fact George keeps his finished articles a further year 'just in case'.

From a purchase of 1000 kilograms of wood about 100 will be eventually used for finished articles. George says he takes up to two hours to determine whether a bowl will emerge from a piece of wood: for a large bowl he will use up to 50 kilograms of wood. Unlike the turners of this country and the States he does not use spalted or damaged, wormy or uninteresting timbers nor does he turn ultra thin bowls. He produces the solid tourist article designed to last in continual use.

In the Offcuts section of the August issue of *Woodworker* editor Chris Dunn pub-

lished a piece entitled 'mother of invention' sent in by a lady from Surrey and dealing with a medieval birth stool dated 1554.

Well, the village of Danilia was constructed by the Bouas family as a monument to the best traditions of Corfu. It is a village where craftsmen and women have workshops (including a wood carver) and at night it is the centre of traditional dancing and feasting but, most importantly from my point of view it has a museum.

After wandering through the rooms with the local industries and crafts represented by a reasonable collection of old tools, many of which were still in use on the island, one comes to a room that has furniture in it. I must admit I received some funny looks from other tourists, my own family and the security guard when instead of the usual museum quiet the air was rent with my 'Look, a birthing chair'. And there it was, dated 1853.

How does one explain to a gentleman who doesn't speak English, that you want to get nearer to the chair, even sit in it and look under it and all around it.

Well I managed, the ropes were taken away, the chair was revealed in all its glory, enormous in mahogany and red velvet, the back strengthened with butterfly-bow style joints, the arms, seat and legs massive in proportions. Alas I couldn't find out whether it had been a standard piece of household furniture (heaven forbid) or whether it had come from a doctor's house or hospital. However I left a very puzzled museum attendant wondering why the English lady who wasn't pregnant wished to try it out for size: he did obligingly turn the spotlight onto the chair for me. Perhaps he thought it was some quaint English custom that brought good luck? All I can say is it was very uncomfortable!

Advance tickets
Woodworker Show

Advance tickets can be obtained from the Exhibitions Manager, PO Box 35, Bridge Street, Hemel Hempstead HP1 1EE. Guild members' admission charges are £1.75 for adults and £1.25 for juniors and senior citizens. Proof of guild membership will be required to obtain this discount.

Letter from Australia

Robert Lamont has written to the guild recently to ask for membership and we are delighted to welcome another Australian member. Perhaps one day we will be able to visit all our members 'down under'. What a wonderful trip that would be. In the meantime we extend an invitation to any guild members from overseas to 'come and see us' in the *Woodworker* office if you are in Hemel Hempstead. We are always pleased to see you. A little advance warning of an impending visit would be nice.

Mr Lamont tells us he has been making Australian colonial furniture for the past five years and is now getting quite adept. Perhaps he would like to send some black and white photographs for us to see.

The timbers he uses are mainly old re cedar, silky oak, black bean, red bear brown beech and New South Wales rose wood. He makes me green with envy whe he states that he is virtually surrounded b untouched rainforest clad mountains an so the timbers are readily available. He als uses small quantities of Honduras mahc gany but he says the outlets are controlle by 'hungry importers' so he only uses ther for restoration work.

Where are you now?

It is always a pity to lose contact wit someone, a relative or friend, or a value guild member. We have done just that. we have lost contact with Duncan Cook c Hayle, Cornwall, guild member 1062 whos speciality is pine furniture. If you could ge in touch with us Duncan we can put you new address on our files.

Routing course

The routing course arranged for the 3 October is full, in fact it has become ove subscribed so we are pleased to be able t announce that we shall be fitting the dis appointed in early next year either on one c two dates to be announced later. We ar delighted with the response and wish t thank all members for their support.

Ties

Guild neckties are available in green wit two narrow gold-coloured 'bandings' be tween which is the guild badge also gold coloured. Ties are £3.50 each inclusive c VAT, postage and packing. Members re quiring a tie should send a cheque c crossed postal order together with the guild number and address to the admini trator at the usual *Woodworker* address.

When paint seals it in,

Bosch breaks it out.

Screws that have been painted over or become rusty are no joke. Try and get them out with a screwdriver and the chances are you won't.

Take a new Bosch 650-2 RLE Drill to them and they'll come out without a fight.

Because it's everything a reversible action hammer drill should be.

A powerful 650W motor drives three fully synchronised, mechanical gears (two forward and one reverse rotation).

The constant Electronic Control gets you through the hardest of materials with the minimum of effort.

The variable speed control, which takes you from 0-3400 rev/min, gives you precise, on-the-dot pilot drilling (useful for drilling through ceramic tiles).

And the robust lightweight body is ergonomically designed, fully insulated and suppressed.

So next time you've a job to do and you want to make it easy, you'll know the drill.

It's called the new Bosch 650-2 RLE.

BOSCH

The more professional D.I.Y. power tools.

2⅛" depth of cut circular saw, 6"x4" planer thicknesser, versatile spindle moulder (80 plus cutters available), power take-off for accessories, lever control slot mortiser, robust workbench, 1 h.p. motor, 2 year guarantee, £599.00 (+VAT £89.8.)

● Spindle moulder
6400 rpm shaft speed. 45mm (1¾")
vertical adjustment. Capable of taking
25mm (1") × 25mm (1") rebate in one
pass. Accepts both French moulding
profiles and "Whitehill" type blocks.

● Circular saw.
57mm (2¼") depth of cut. 2 speeds,
3750 for normal wood and 6200 rpm for
laminated boards. Complete with rip
fence, mitre guide, repeat cut length
stop, wobble washers for grooving,
tilting table 0.45°.

K5 power workshop
● Heavy alloy castings.
● Sealed for life bearings throughout
for maintenance free running.
● Distortion free bench table top
finished in tough polyurethane.
● Strong steel stand.
● All work surfaces are precision machined
and polished from a specially developed
drag resistant hard wearing alloy.
● Fully enclosed fan cooled
motor – stop any dust problems.
● All rotating cutting heads are dynamically
balanced for vibration free operation.

● Surface planer
700mm (27½") long × 200mm (8") wide
cast bed. Maximum planing width
150mm (6"). Adjustable 90°-45° fence
for bevel planing. Dynamically balanced
cutter block rotating at 11,400 cuts per
minute.

● Thickness planer
Fully automatic feed, 7.5m (24ft) per
minute. Maximum capacity 100mm (4")
deep, 150mm (6") wide. Calibrated scale.

● Slot mortiser. NEW IMPROVED!
Lever adjustment rise/fall table with
100mm (4") of movement. Maximum
bit diameter 12mm (½"). Produces an
accurate mortise, also horizontal boring
for perfect dowel joints.

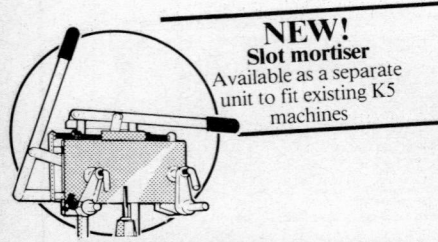

NEW!
Slot mortiser
Available as a separate
unit to fit existing K5
machines

KITY
UNITED KINGDOM

Now in Australia and South Africa.
Please write for details.

**The standard K5 power workshop
comes complete with...**
● **Circular saw.** Fully guarded with mitre guide and
repeat cut stop, rip fence, 180mm blade, grooving
washers.
● **Planer thicknesser.** Fully guarded, ground and set
planer knives, in dynamically balanced cutter
block.
● **Spindle moulder.** Fully guarded, with adjustable
tool insert, one french type cutter.
● **Slot mortiser.** Chuck, lever adjustable table and
one mortise bit.
● **1 H.P. motor.** Fan covered and dust sealed 240V
50HZ, will operate from a normal 13 amp socket.
● **Instruction manual.**
● **2 year guarantee.**
All units assembled and adjusted, stand complete
with legs and side panels, crated ready for delivery to
your door.

There are over 150 trained stockists and distrib
throughout the UK to provide a comprehensiv
after sales back up plus regular demonstration
test your K5 before you buy.

Write or phone *(24hr answer service)* for colou
leaflet and more information about K5.
Full Credit Terms available, ask your local dea
for details.

Please send me more information about

☐ K5   ☐ New Slot Mortise

Name ....

Address ....

Kity U.K., 6 Acorn Park, Charlestown, Shipley BD17 7SW. Tel: Bradford (0274) 597826.

Prices quoted are those prevailing at press date and are
subject to alteration due to economic conditions.

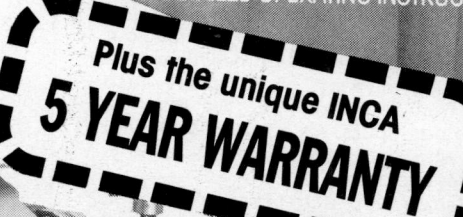
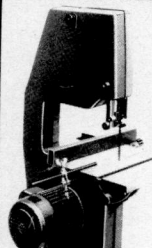

The carpenter of Singleton

The work of the Weald and Downland Open Air Museum at Singleton, West Sussex, has been attracting quite a bit of attention lately. *Woodworker's* editor, Chris Dunn, has been to Singleton to talk to Roger Champion, a woodworking man of skill and integrity, who has contributed much to the museum's success

Roger Champion is one of those happy people who is doing a job that he would not change for the world. Perhaps a clue to his satisfaction in life is that he doesn't look upon his work as 'a job'. 'It's more a way of life,' he told me over beer and sandwiches at his local Fox and Hounds.

Roger is estate carpenter to the Weald and Downland Open Air Museum at Singleton, West Sussex, a 35-acre site of uncommon natural beauty which is dedicated to the rescue and preservation of old buildings threatened by demolition. Conservation is not a philosophy that fits within the comfortable 9 am to 5 pm routine. 'You get more involved than that,' Roger said, trying to put his finger on why this museum, which is run largely by voluntary effort, elicits such loyalty from its workforce. 'We work all kinds of odd hours. It's good to work with people who are obviously so interested in what they are doing.'

Such an erratic pattern of working cannot, you would think, fit in with a calm domestic life, but fortunately for Roger his wife Heather works for the museum as conservation officer, and since she feels the same way as Roger about her job, all is harmony on the domestic front. As for the two labradors — well, they are quite happy just to fit in.

The principal facet of the museum carpenter's work is to patiently dismantle ancient timbers of a building on its original site and then to transport them to Singleton for safe storage until they can be rejoined when the building is reconstructed. As its name implies, the museum takes in all the Weald and Downlands as its catchment area — all of Sussex, most of Surrey, Kent and westwards into Hampshire.

The most recent addition to the museum is a house from the village of Walderton between Petersfield and Chichester. Staff painstakingly dismantled the house, which was derelict and due to be flattened for redevelopment, in the summer of 1980 (you may have seen a BBC 'Chronicle' programme about the project last March). What made this rescue all the more exciting was the discovery, within the house's flint and brick exterior, of the remains of a medieval timber framed house with an open hall.

The museum's director, Christopher Zeuner, who coordinated the project: 'The reconstruction had to be approached in a new way. The better preserved end of the house was rebuilt in its 17th century form; fortunately there was clear evidence for the missing features. The less well preserved end was reconstructed as a section through the building, demonstrating the medieval hall together with its soot-blackened rafters, exposed from the ground floor.'

The Walderton house, officially opened to the public in early July, was relatively easy in terms of accurate reconstruction. Other projects present a need for more imagination in rebuilding. Roger Champion: 'You often have to take liberties. For example, if

ou have no evidence how the original
taircase was, you have to make certain
ssumptions.'

However, it is policy not to try and make
uch imaginings look old by using re-
laimed timber. 'I like it to be obvious what
s original and what is new. Anyway, it is
ever possible to recreate the original
bsolutely faithfully.'

Naturally much of the dismantled timber
s found to be too far decayed to be
eusable, so replacements have to be made.
oger's workshop is not on the museum
ite but on the other side of the village. It is
omething of a museum piece in itself, as it
appens, a farmyard all set about with
arns and stables built of the characteristic
napped flint of West Sussex. The work-
hop is large, but surprisingly unmecha-
ised. The limit of Roger's machinery is a
0in power saw, a chainsaw, a lathe and a
ower drill. It is not that the carpenter has
ny strong feelings about modern methods.

have so little machinery quite simply
ecause the majority of timber I work with is
ist too big for the average machine.'

The yard is stocked with timber, in stick
nd in the round, most of which comes from
ne neighbouring West Dean estate. There
s a useful tie-up here. The local laird is
dward James (see article on West Dean in
Woodworker September) who now lives in
Mexico but still keeps a paternal eye on the
ld family seat and its environs. It was, in
act, Edward James who provided the land
t peppercorn rent for the Weald and
ownland Museum to be founded in 1967;
hus relations between West Dean and
ingleton, only a mile or twg apart, work
ntirely to mutual advantage. West Dean
ollege keeps itself warm on the brush-
vood and waste from the estate's felled
ees and Roger Champion gets the bulk
mber. It is oak in the main, with a certain
mount of ash besides, while both hazel
nd chestnut are available from the estate in
ufficient quantities for the making of wates.

'We used to be able to get elm,' Roger
aid, 'but the disease has killed off most of
hat. A diseased elm is still usable if felled
vhen it's green, but if it is allowed to stand it
oes doaty.'

Despite the reasonable quantities of tim-
er he holds in stock, Roger finds that he
as to use much of his wood still green. 'I
ist have to use what I can get,' says he,
earing in mind that I use oak in dimen-
ions that timber yards rarely stock.' He is
enerally able to keep his wood until the
najority of the sap has dried from it, but it is
sually far from well seasoned when used.
lot that Roger minds: 'Green oak works
uch more easily than dry. It cuts like
heddar cheese.'

Joints are inclined to shrink, of course,
ut as the shrinkage occurs across the grain
ather than along it, this is not necessarily a
ice in timber framed building work, so
oger assured me.

Aged 44, Roger is a quiet and thinking
erson who has seen enough of the world
o know that peace and satisfying work are
vorth more than all the excitement the
vorld can offer. As a youth in the late 1950s
e was apprenticed to what is now Philips
lectrical as a toolmaker, broken by two
ears' National Service in 1961/2. After

● *Above: the cupboard in oak which Roger Champion has made for the Walderton house. Below: the chest, built from wych elm. Note the scalloped endgrain on the chest's lid and the incised carving, copied from an example of the period*

demob he soon tired of toolmaking so he handed in his notice, oiled his bicylce, said goodbye to his mum and set off for Australia, intending to bogwheel all the way.

'I got as far as Afghanistan on the bike,' he recalls, 'but the going was getting too tough by then, so bike and I parted and I travelled on by bus, train and hitching.'

His travels took him through India, Thailand, Singapore and the Far East to Australia and New Zealand. In Australia the money was running out, so Roger worked at pulling weeds in cotton fields in the outback of north-west Oz for five months, earning the £800 ('a lot of money in those days!') he needed to get himself home. Cotton fields in Australia? 'The government had set up an experimental cotton-growing project, irrigating the bush by damming up a river. But the weeds grew as fast as the cotton, so I was hired to pick weeds.'

Roger made his way home and moved with his mother from Croydon to Midhurst, which is not far from Singleton. He took to making furniture for a living, but discovered that there were certain things about furniture making that he didn't like much: 'For one thing I found it difficult to get people to pay up for goods received, and of course everyone always wants everything in such a rush; for another thing I got sick of the retail trade taking more profit for selling my work than I got for making it.'

He heard about the Weald and Downland enterprise starting out, so he offered them his services, sometimes as a volunteer, sometimes as a paid part-timer. 'They paid me when there was any money available.'

Gradually he became more involved with the museum's preservation work over the years, and was finally taken on as full-time carpenter five years ago. Until recently he has been exclusively concerned with building structures, but a subtle shift in philosophy at the museum has now begun to involve him additionally in furnishing the museum's exhibits, as well as maintaining them.

'The museum has been concerned purely with buildings in terms of their fabric and structure until recently,' Roger said. 'The social aspect has tended to be left alone; but of course you can't really get away from the social aspect — buildings are the way they are simply *because* of social development.'

So the museum has been looking at possibilities of furnishing its buildings in a style contemporary to each. What got the ball into the air was the discovery, made during the routine archival search on the Walderton house, of an inventory listing its contents in 1634. This document, found in the records office at Chichester, provided only a sketch from which to work, listing household chattels and items of furniture but giving nothing away about their construction or style. Its other limitation in providing information was that it had been partially eaten by mice.

Nevertheless, the inventory told Roger enough to get him started on making furniture for the Walderton house. First, the research.

'The inventory lists only table, chair, and so on,' he said. 'We aren't told what they were like. So we had to look for appropriate examples to work from.'

Research took Roger to various sources in

● *Roger and chest in cleft ash. The tenons will finish up protruding by about an inch, decorated with a shallow ogee detail on their ends*

making a cupboard, an armchair, a chest, a table and a bench. The chair is a copy of one in Anne of Cleves' house in Lewes, Sussex (though probably rather more sophisticated than would have been found in the Walderton house, he says); the table is based upon a 17th century example in the V and A Museum, and the bench is an elongated version of one in Midhurst Parish Church. In making the chest (built from wych elm; the other pieces are of oak) he was able to copy one in his own museum's small collection of furniture, which is in store until a suitable space can be made to display it. They could have drawn on this collection to furnish the house, but it would have presented formidable security problems, so it was decided that replicas would be more practical.

Accurate copying of styles and techniques is difficult without taking originals apart to inspect jointing methods, so Roger had to work on logic for the most part. In certain instances he was able to look closely at jointing, and that came up with some surprises. Anne of Cleves' chair, for example, displayed an interesting feature to a design of mortice and tenon. The arm of the chair joins the rear stile at an angle of around seven degrees, but instead of tenon continuing along the line of the grain, parallel with the arm, it is cut at an angle to pass through its mortice at 90 degrees to the stile (see diagram).

● Above: Roger's copy of a chair in Anne of Cleves' house, which features the interesting mortice and tenon design shown left. Below: this crude linkage of wire loops forms a hinge in the lid of the chest shown on page 655

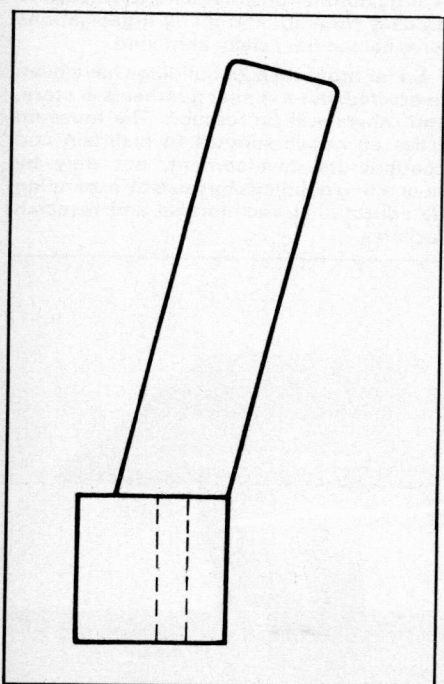

'I have no idea why it was done that way,' says Roger, 'but I went ahead and copied it for the sake of accuracy.'

In the matter of hinges and other metal fittings, Roger again copied contemporary examples, drawing on his experience as a toolmaker. The chest lid's hinges are simply a crude linkage of wire loops, while its lock, carefully copied from the original on the outside, conceals a modern mechanism.

Decoration of the period tended to be simple, dominated by an almost obsessive use of the ogee profile while endgrain was often finished with an attractive scallop. The

most taxing decorative problem was in copying the flourish of scrolls incised on the front of the chest.

Roger is currently working on another chest, in cleft ash with exposed tenons in a simple period style to befit Boar Hunt Cottage, an as yet unfurnished building dated c1500 which came from Wickham in Hants. For its design Roger has drawn on photographs of common styles of the period, plus a useful exploded diagram in the *Dictionary of English Furniture*.

'That kind of chest would have been made in oak usually,' Roger said. 'But I just happened to have ash available, so I used that, working in the general style rather than copying a particular example.'

When the present job of dismantling a cottage at Storrington is complete, followed by another similar job at Bexley, Roger will return to making more pieces of furniture for the Walderton house, whenever he can fit it in with maintenance work. The inventory lists a second chair and a bed, yet to be made.

He is always busy, but Roger is careful to ensure that pressure of work does not mean hurrying and cutting corners. He is painstaking and thoughtful, and the future of the museum is his primary consideration. He put it like this: 'I have seen the museum grow from nothing to what it is now, and that means a lot to me. I want to see it grow even more, but the greatest advantage I enjoy is working for an operation that isn't hide bound to making a profit. I am able always do things properly rather than the quick way. There is no commercial pressure.''

Nice work, as they say, if you can get it! ∎

● *Below: the table and bench in situ*

● Above: the reproduction period furnitue as seen by visitors to the Walderton house. On the facing page are the before and after pictures of the house. The interesting differences between the reconstructed building and the original amplify Roger Champion's comment that 'you often have to take liberties' in rebuilding.

The Walderton house is the most recent of the museum's exhibits, and the first flint and brick structure they have taken on.

The Weald and Downland Open Air Museum was launched in 1967 as a centre which could rescue threatened traditional buildings from south-east England, and to generate greater public interest in the buildings heritage of this part of the country. The museum's foundation coincided with a growing national concern about historic buildings and this general public interest has resulted in strong support for the museum from its inception.

The museum's central principle is that buildings should not be removed from their original sites unless there is no alternative.

Only when there is no future useful purpose for the building will the museum consider it for inclusion in the collection.

The aims of the museum have evolved over the years. Increasingly it is giving advice to people involved in conservation of buildings, and in addition to rescuing buildings, the museum is establishing a collection of artefacts representing the country crafts and industries, the building trades and agriculture.

The museum is a private, non-profit-making organisation, registered as a charity, receiving no regular grants or subsidies. A large number of volunteers contribute to its daily running, and many organisations have helped financially or in kind.

So far more than 25 buildings have been re-erected, but a similar number is in store, and others will be rescued. The museum relies on public support to maintain and continue its development, not only by re-erecting buildings but also by expanding its educational, recreational and research facilities.

What estate agents like to call 'a challenging renovation opportunity'. The Walderton house as it looked before its rescue, derelict and due for demolition. Below: the way that visitors to the Weald and Downland Museum see it today

JOY wood dye

a wide range of shades for a wide range of woods

The fast working flat, penetrating stain for new wood. Once dry it can be waxed, french polished or varnished for a truly professional finish. Available in Golden Oak, Light Oak, Mid Oak, Dark Oak, Jacobean Oak, Walnut, Teak, Mahogany and Ebony. To add a hardwearing gloss finish, use Joy Polyurethane Glaze.

Put some Joy into your work

quality products for Sticking Staining Polishing Painting

You'll find JOY products at all good stores, ironmongers, paint and DIY shops.

 is a registered trade mark

M. W. EQUIPMENT   ESTAB.* 61 YRS.

ELU MOF 96 ROUTER NOW ONLY £49.95 inc. VAT

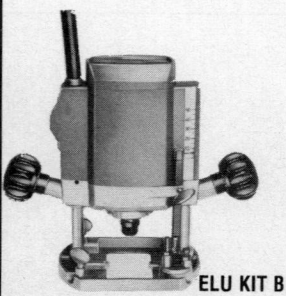

ELU KIT B £45

NEW ST152 ELU JIGSAW   £59

SPECIAL OFFER £59 (inc VAT & Post).
Complete with free plastic carrying case and three saw blades.
Two speed switch to adapt sawing speed to material, large saw baseplate tilts up to 45° to either side.
Pendulum movement four-way adjustment to give correct cutting action for all materials.

ELU Double-ended grinder

- Small in stature but with large reserves of power.
- Fitted with robust compact motors which give long life.
- Efficient protection guards over each wheel.

	Our price	Usual price	SAVE
MWA 146 5"	£37.00	£55.20	£18.20
MWA 147 6"	£47.00	£66.70	£19.70

M. W. EQUIPMENT LTD.

Shawcross Street, Stockport, Cheshire
Tel: 061-480 8481

Stockists of new and used woodworking machinery including; Elu, Skil, Bosch, Bursgreen, Multico, DeWalt, Startrite, S.C.M., Tradesmen, Adler, Hebor.
Prices shown are for cheque with order and include post (UK mainland only) and VAT. Offered in 220 volt only and subject to availability.

22 YEARS AN ELU STOCKIST, VISITORS VERY WELCOME—FULL SALES & REPAIR SERVICE OF OVER 600 MACHINES IN STOCK.

GLUE FIX 2000 FROM STEiNEL

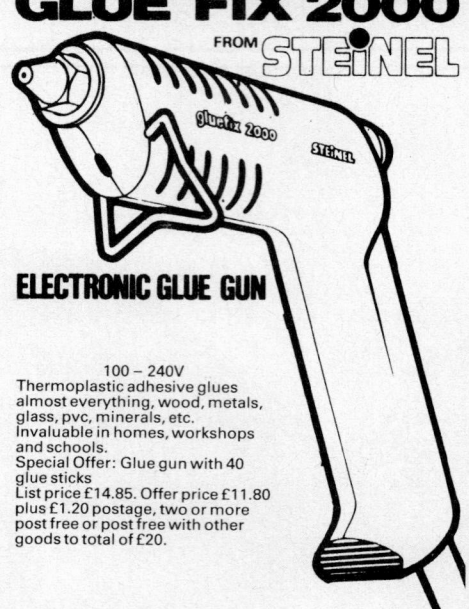

ELECTRONIC GLUE GUN

100 – 240V
Thermoplastic adhesive glues almost everything, wood, metals, glass, pvc, minerals, etc. Invaluable in homes, workshops and schools.
Special Offer: Glue gun with 40 glue sticks
List price £14.85. Offer price £11.80 plus £1.20 postage, two or more post free or post free with other goods to total of £20.

POWER TOOLS ETC

Cat No.		M.R.P.	Our Price
096-2	Craftsman 7½" circular saw, 2⅛hp	£94.45	£70.80
26269	Craftsman Trim-a-Form Router Attachment	£45.95	£33.00
238	Dremel Moto Flex Tool	£76.10	£63.95
577	Dremel DeLuxe Moto Shop	£98.40	£82.80
2509	Dremel Moto-Tool Kit with 35 accessories	£53.05	£44.50
215	Dremel Foot operated speed control	£29.15	£24.15
358	Dremel Variable Speed Moto-Tool	£55.35	£46.00
359	Dremel Variable Speed Moto-Tool Kit with 35 accessories	£69.20	£58.50
284	Dremel Moto Tool Woodcarver's Kit	£69.40	£58.65
384	Dremel Variable Speed Woodcarver's Kit	£84.00	£70.95
292	Dremel engraver	£15.75	£13.30
96H	Skil power plane, 480 watt	£80.39	£67.00
1474H	Skil ½" reversing hammer drill, 500 watt	£67.74	£55.00
574U	Skil 7¼" circular saw, 1000 watt	£62.10	£52.00
400-E	Bosch ½" variable speed hammer drill, 400 watt	£54.50	£42.50
450-2E	Bosch ½" variable speed hammer drill, 450 watt with kit	£88.80	£60.00
500-2E	Bosch ½" variable speed hammer drill, 500 watt	£79.00	£52.00
620-2E	Bosch ½" variable speed hammer drill, 620 watt	£92.00	£73.00
650-2RLE	Bosch ½" variable speed reversing hammer drill	£97.50	£77.00
S33	Bosch 6" circular saw attachment	£26.40	£21.00
PST50E	Bosch variable speed jigsaw	£48.50	£38.50
PSS230	Bosch orbital sander	£43.50	£34.50
PSP250	Bosch spray gun set	£55.00	£43.00
PKS46	Bosch 6" circular saw	£62.50	£49.00
S9	Bosch saw table for PKS46 saw	£46.00	£36.50
PKS65	Bosch 7½" circular saw	£93.00	£74.00
POF50	Bosch plunging router with 1 router bit	£59.50	£47.00
S7	Bosch milling stand	£52.00	£41.50
S8	Bosch routing bench for above	£24.00	£19.00
S2	Bosch drill stand	£24.00	£19.00
S18	Bosch lathe kit	£68.25	£54.50

BOSCH INDUSTRIAL

SB4502	Bosch 2 speed impact drill with free tool handy & 750 rawlplugs	£99.48	£79.00
1179	Bosch ½" 2 speed impact drill	£126.79	£100.00
1287-1	Bosch orbital sander with induction motor	£127.65	£101.00
PWS6000	Bosch 7" angle sander/grinder	£102.64	£81.00
1577	Bosch orbital action jigsaw in metal case	£116.15	£91.00

HAND TOOLS

781000	Jet Clamp	£10.98	£9.55
04	Record 2" blade smoothing plane	£19.90	£15.50
311	Record 3 in 1 plane	£37.52	£31.50
778	Record rebate plane	£28.34	£24.00
050C	Record combination plane, 18 blade	£65.50	£55.00
020C	Record circular plane	£56.93	£48.00
405	Record multi plane, 24 blade	£161.46	£136.00
52E	Record Q.R. woodwork vice, 7"	£44.19	£37.50
413	Record 3" drill press vice	£20.53	£17.40
130	Record cramp heads	£10.27	£8.60
145	Record bench holdfast 6⅞" opening	£18.07	£15.30
146	Record bench holdfast 7⅝" opening	£22.60	£19.20
140	Record corner cramp 2" capacity	£8.05	£6.80
148	Record dowelling jig	£32.11	£27.00
M1160	Marples draw knife	£17.83	£15.00
M2400	Marples 12" bow saw	£19.25	£16.25
M1002	Marples set of 8 turning tools	£51.41	£43.50
M60	Marples set of 12 carving tools	£73.37	£62.00
M60A	Marples set of 6 carving tools	£41.40	£35.00
M444/S5	Marples set of 5 blue chip chisels	£21.47	£18.20
M260	Marples set of 5 wood sculpture tools	£37.49	£31.75
M277	Marples wood carver's screw	£9.60	£7.60
13-052	Stanley plough plane, 10 blade	£41.35	£34.50
13-050	Stanley combination plane, 18 blade	£63.00	£52.95
5½	Stanley 15" jack plane	£28.99	£24.00
7	Stanley 22" jointer/try plane	£36.55	£30.95
71	Stanley hand router, 3 blade	£24.70	£20.50
TS	Henry Taylor superflute turning gouge	£22.35	£19.00
	Henry Taylor Wood Carver's Adze, Chisel	£14.95	£12.70
	Henry Taylor Wood Carver's Adze, Gouge	£19.55	£16.55

All prices include VAT. Carriage free on orders over £20 (UK Mainland)
Henry Taylor and Marples Woodcarving and Turning Tools in stock

BENMAIL, 48 Station Road, St. Georges, Weston-s-Mare, Avon BS22 0XL
Tel: 0934 24385   *We close Thursdays*

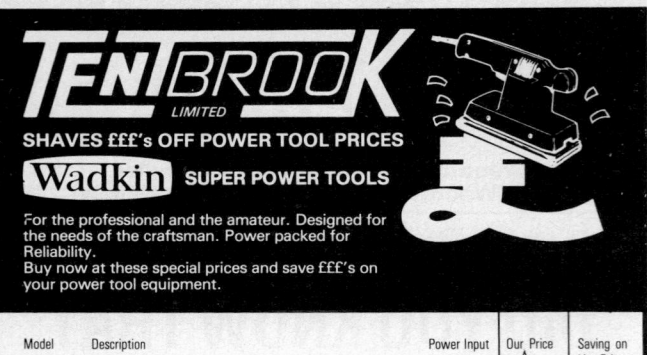

LONDON'S SIXTH

Woodworker Show '82

THE ROYAL HORTICULTURAL SOCIETY'S NEW & OLD HALLS VINCENT SQUARE & GREYCOAT STREET

Such is the increasing popularity of the Woodworker Show, now in its 6th year, that this year the Show is to be staged in the attractive Old Hall as well as the New Hall. Tickets will be issued daily enabling visitors to pass from one hall to another and return later on the same day.

Both halls will display the competition exhibits in the many classes. There will be many more trade stands fulfilling every need of the amateur or professional craft woodworker.

The colleges and demonstration areas will be considerably expanded and so will the lecture programme.

Don't miss this year's super Woodworker Show.

For Advance Tickets see advertisement on page 662

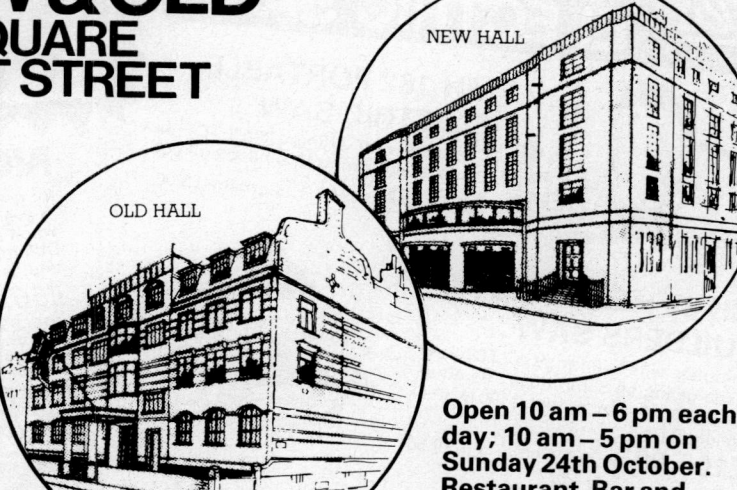

NEW HALL

OLD HALL

Open 10 am – 6 pm each day; 10 am – 5 pm on Sunday 24th October. Restaurant, Bar and Snack Bars.

19th–24th OCTOBER 1982

Admission:
Adults £2.00
Children and OAPs £1.50
Advance booking details from the Organiser, Woodworker Show, 13/35 Bridge Street, Hemel Hempstead, Herts, HP1 1EE

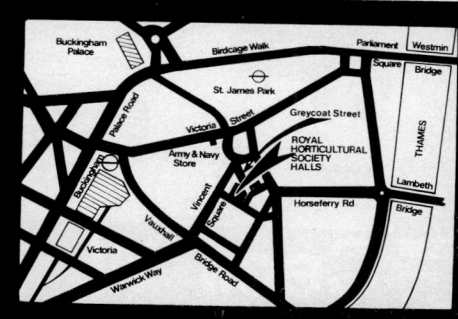

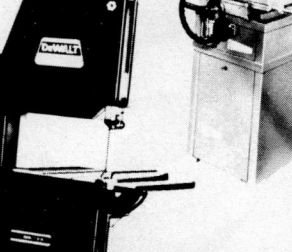

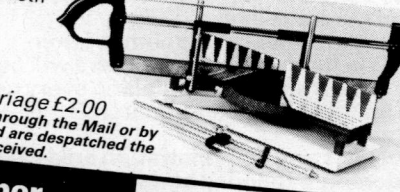

Chiseller's delight

Alan Thomas likes to keep a regular eye on the street markets around his south London home, where he has found neglected tools can often be picked up for a song and revived to useful effect. Here he relates the tale of a tenpenny Sorby firmer chisel that he brought back to life

For some reason I have never quite divined, stallholders in street markets are usually named John. Hardly ever a Douglas or Clive. And, to a man, their feathers are ruffled by gentle tones and clearly enunciated words. The successful punter must adopt local mannerisms and patois. My own technique is to rummage about disparagingly among the stock, hold up the object of my desire, look at space over its present owner's left shoulder, and mumble (but loudly) 'Wazziz, John?'

If the right note has been struck, back will come the right price. 'Two', or 'four'n'arf', or as the case may be. Should, however, the asked price be outrageously too high, the best plan, I find, is to drop said object back into the stock and walk on. There is always next week. Sometimes though a haggle is worth trying, in which case the dialogue takes on interest.

'Wazziz, John?'

'Five.'

'Give yer two'n'arf.' (While simultaneously counting out money. Never enter a transaction in which he has to give you change; for some psychological reason change puts the buyer into a disadvantageous position).

'Three.'

'Aw right.'

It was in this manner that I bought for tenpence a two-inch firmer chisel by Sorby. Not that it was a pretty thing; far from it. I think someone had used it for prising up paving stones. But with a blade still 5½in long it seemed worth the attempt to clean it up. There is also a certain scarcity value. It's not often you see a two-inch chisel for sale these days and, well, it's rather nice to rescue from oblivion things once treasured by someone.

The handle was a smashed oil-stained wreck, and it drove off easily enough. To my mind quite the best way of cleaning up things like chisels is with a flat, fairly freecutting stone and paraffin, with plenty of old rag for mopping up. As usual with the older carbon steels there were some small, deep rust pits, but on the whole it brightened up pretty well. Pitting can be a major snag; one such bargain turned out to be less so when it became all too clear that its pits were going to mar any cutting edge, with the result that they left their signature on every cut.

Only a rough suggestion of a bevel showed where the cutting edge of my new acquisition had once been, and herein lay a problem, for my grinding wheel is one of the double-ended baby sort, useful for touching up drills and the like but rather out of its class with a job like this. Soften down the chisel, file to shape, and reharden? Could do, but I don't like to interfere thus far with cutting tools. There is always a suspicion that the oldtimers might have known something we don't when it comes to obscure arts like tool hardening and tempering.

By way of a sighting shot I squared off the rounded, lopsided end by freehand grinding, and as a measure of how bad it was something like an eighth of an inch had to come off the worst side. My grinder, with its four-inch diameter wheels, originally had silly little pressed tin tool rests which I replaced with sensibly-sized and sturdy things made from bits of angle iron.

A tentative try at freehand grinding a new bevel soon showed that wasn't going to work, but then I hit on the notion of clamping a bit of flat metal bar to the chisel blade and using that as a guide, holding it against a tool rest and keeping the whole on the move across the wheel circumference. This, of course, produced a noticeably concave curve instead of a flat bevel, but fortunately wear has reduced slightly the diameter of one wheel and so, without having to move the clamped-on guide, two separate overlapping curves were ground.

It took time: probably at least an hour, with constant dippings in a jar of water to prevent overheating, and a final flatting and polishing on the side of a wheel. Of course, anyone belonging to a woodworking class or club would have access to a proper whet

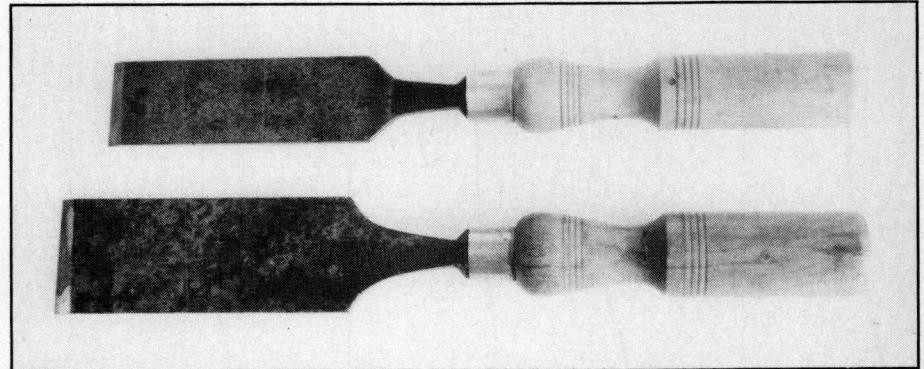

● A pair of tenpenny bargains. Obscured by rust and grime with their handles splintered, these 1½in and 2in firmer chisels once seemed almost useless

● So twisted and knotty were the blackthorn 'logs' that a great deal of apparent wastage was necessary to clean them up to final dimensions

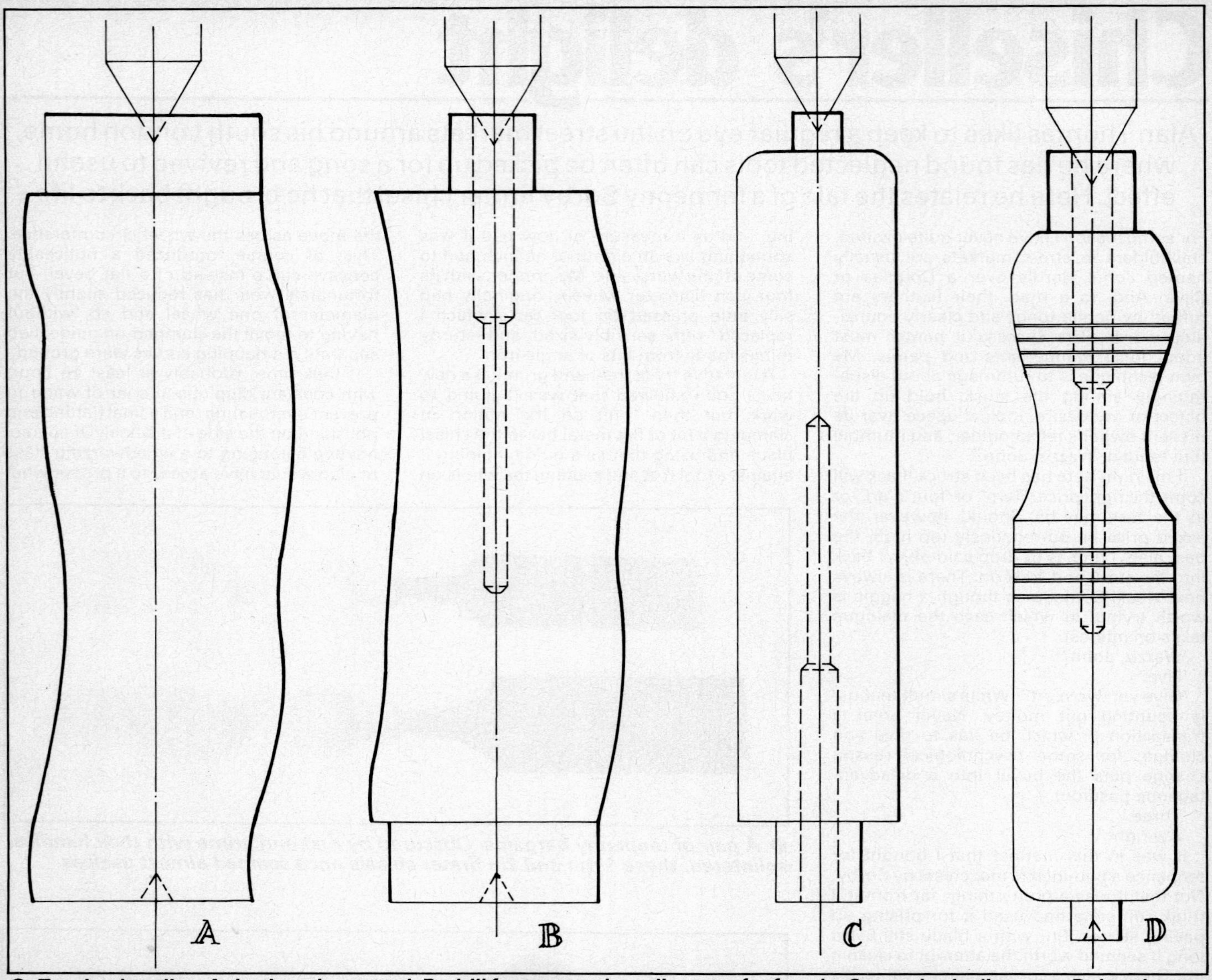

Turning handles. A: both ends centred. B: drill for tang, reduce diameter for ferrule. C: turn body diameter. D: hand-turn neck and knife cut decorations. Handles are 6in overall length, diameters between 26mm and 35mm in 1mm steps, for chisels from ⅛in to 2in

stone, preferably one of the big old fashioned sort with a water bath, but needs must when the Devil drives.

Next move — a handle. No mystery about that: all it needed was a lathe, and although mine is a metal-machining Myford, anything down to the Black and Decker drill in a benchstand will do perfectly well.

But my piece of wood had an interesting background. A couple of years ago, faced with a high and neglected thorn hedge, the only thing to do was to cut it down almost to ground level and let it sprout again into a more manageable form. As a result, apart from mountains of twigs (for it is a very long hedge) there were also some sizeable 'trunks', up to three inches in diameter, which it seemed a shame to burn.

The sawing down procedure had shown very clearly that the wood was both hard and close-grained, and also white, and after 12 months under the bench with the bark on had shown no tendency to split. What was there to lose?

An advantage of an engineering lathe showed itself in that the parallel slide movement in combination with an ordinary tool in the toolholder made it safe and easy to clean up the knotty, twisted, piece of wood, so twisted in fact that the centres had to be relocated at least twice in order to get the maximum diameter out of it.

My preference, having the equipment, is to turn such things between chuck and tailstock centre, so for me the procedure was to deeply centre each end, parallel turn much oversize one end, deeply drill for the chisel tang, turn the short parallel for a ferrule, turn parallel the whole length almost to size, hand-turn the waisted part, and knife in the decorative cuts. Then, having pressed on a shiny brass ferrule (a piece of tube), the blunt end could be finish-turned as far as the tool could go, leaving only a pip (with a centre in it) to be neatly removed with a sharp pocket knife. Personally I don't care for the time-honoured way of burning a hole for the chisel tang, so instead I use it like a reamer to taper the already drilled hole. When it has gone far enough, a few exploratory taps with a soft hammer will soon seat handle and blade.

For finish I used linseed oil, and I was amazed at how much that handle drank. For days its simply mopped up oil; indeed, that handle, I reckon, is now solid oil in a wooden matrix.

So are all the others, I fear. Inevitably that one new handle looked so handsome against the motley collection that disgraced all the others... that a whole new set, all uniform, just had to be made. ■

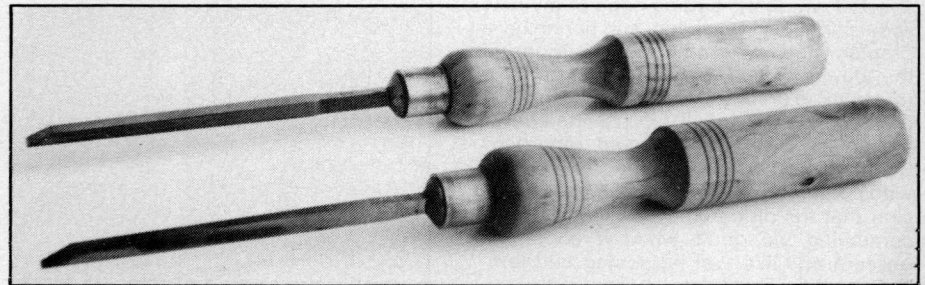

● **Home-made chisels, ⅛in and ¼in, blades made from scraps of silver steel and hardened**

THE CRAFTSMAN IN HIS WORKSHOP: No3

If you enjoyed Alan Thomas' tale on the previous pages about the rescue of a Sorby chisel, you can gather more tips about the care of good chisels and other sharp edged tools from The Craftsman In His Workshop

Keeping the sharp end sharp

by Vic Taylor

The logical and practical initial step is to explain and discuss the appliances used to sharpen these tools, and immediately we think of the two principal ones, which are the oilstone and the grinding wheel.

Dealing with oilstones first, there are two different types — the natural stones, and the industrial synthetic ones. The natural stones include the following, but it must be pointed out that they are becoming scarce and are very expensive.

1. The Arkansas. This comes from natural deposits of stone in the USA, and at best is almost pure quartz, and white in colour. It has no apparent grain, and as it is extremely hard it is used whenever a fine, keen edge is needed.

2. The Washita. Also an American stone. It is cheaper than the Arkansas, and is a medium grade stone, being softer and coarser. It sometimes has a tendency to harden up after a little use and become useless.

3. Turkey Stone. Unfortunately, these stones vary greatly in texture; the hardest ones can give a really good edge but softer ones can easily be grooved.

4. Charnwood Forest. Rarely seen these days; it gives a good edge but is slow in the cut.

Turning now to artificial (synthetic) stones, we find that in general they are made from carborundum, which is a factory-made compound. The stones are available in the three grades of coarse, medium and fine, and are comparable with the best natural stones. For our purposes, a 'combination' stone is probably best, as one side is coarse, and the other fine. In addition, it's a good idea to have a medium grade stone as well, as in some cases, tools have to be sharpened on the edge of the stone.

When you have got your oilstone, the first thing to do is to encase it in a wooden box, as oilstones shatter easily when dropped. Never use a vegetable oil (linseed, olive, or cooking oil) as a lubricant as they will quickly gum up the surface. A good lubricant is a mixture of two parts fine mineral oil (such as 'Three-in-One') and one part paraffin oil: employ it sparingly, and always

wipe the stone clean after use. If the stone shows signs of gumming up, brush it clean with a stiff brush and petrol; in bad cases, soak it in petrol for a day or two and then brush it clean.

Always try to employ the whole surface of the stone so that it does not become hollowed or bumpy; if this does happen, the stone will have to be re-surfaced, which is a laborious business, and calculated to make you more careful in the future!

To do it, first find a perfectly flat slab of stone, or a flat piece of marble, or a piece of good quality plate glass (which must be well supported on a flat surface, such as a pad of newspaper on the bench top). The stone is then rubbed flat in a figure-of-eight pattern, but you must of course, use a suitable grinding paste. For natural stones, silver sand and water is an effective lubricant, while silicon carbide grit (grade 60/90) does for artificial stones. You should be able to get the grit at gem craft shops, as it is used for tumble-polishing stones. When you have finished, wash the stone with soap

and water and let it dry before re-oiling.

In addition to your actual oilstones, try to collect a few assorted oilstone slips, as they are invaluable for sharpening various gouges and spokeshave blades, and you can see some of the different shapes available in Fig 1A.

GRINDSTONES

While oilstones are essential for applying the final cutting edges, you will also need a grinding wheel for grinding the cutting angle, and to remove any gashes from the edge. The old-fashioned sandstone wheel which was turned by hand, and revolved through a water bath, is now practically a museum piece. There is a modern version on the market made by Elektra which incorporates a wheel running in a water bath and a normal grinding wheel, both powered by electricity. The advantage of a wheel constantly cooled by water is one worth having as it avoids any likelihood of drawing the temper of the tool when it overheats.

Most of us, however, will have a powered grinding wheel which runs dry — in fact, you should never attempt to run it in water as it will turn soft. Keep a bucket of water handy and dip whatever tool you are sharpening into the water at frequent inter-

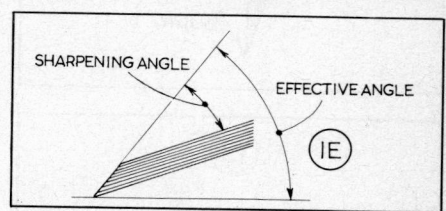

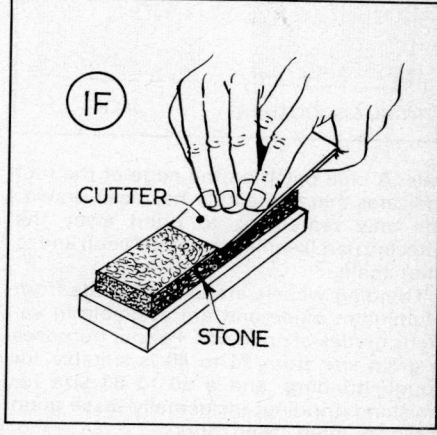

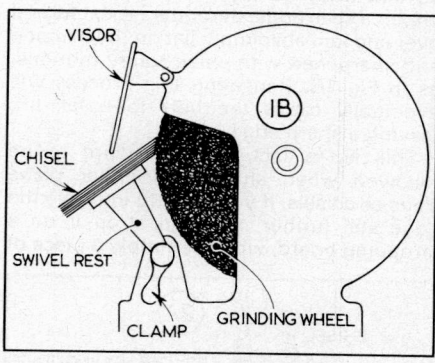

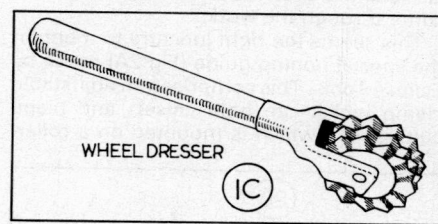

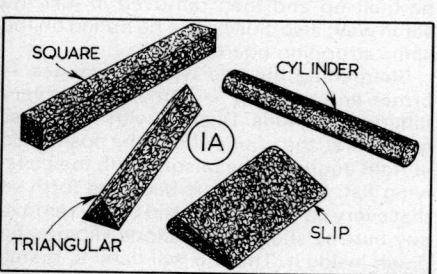

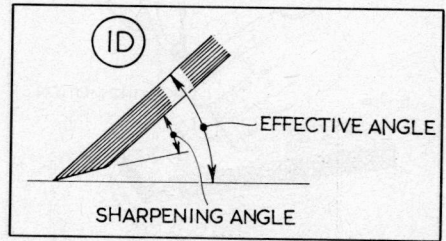

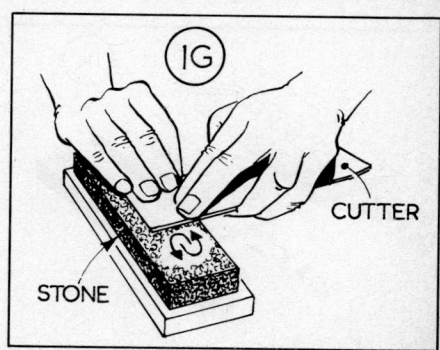

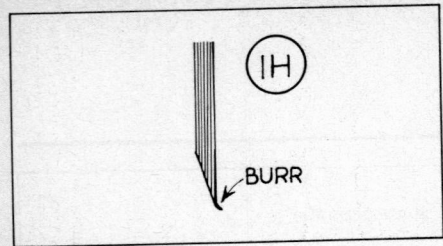

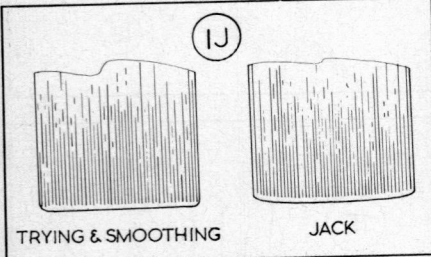

TRYING & SMOOTHING   JACK

vals. A blue patch on the edge of the tool indicates that the temper has been drawn; the only remedy is to grind away the affected part (keeping the metal cool) and to start again.

Grinding wheels are usually made from aluminium oxide and are available in various grades of grain size. For our purposes a grain size from 24 to 40 is suitable for rough grinding, and a 50 to 80 size for finishing grinding; incidentally these grain sizes are often called 'grits'.

One trouble you may have to contend with is the wheel becoming 'loaded' — this often happens because tools are pressed hard against the wheel and the metal particles are forced into the grains with the result that they no longer cut; grinding a lot of mild steel on a wheel intended for tool steel is a primary cause. Another problem is 'glazing' which occurs when the metal particles are not shed as the wheel revolves. The result is a wheel which rubs instead of grinding and soon overheats.

In both cases, the cutting surfaces will have to be restored by means of a 'wheel dresser'. This is shown at Fig 1C, and the tool is steadied on the tool rest of the grinder while the corrugated discs are held lightly but firmly against the wheel in order to scrape away the old, and expose the new particles.

Fig 1B shows the salient points to look for in any grinding wheel, and it is self-explanatory; in particular, note the visor which protects your eyes from flying particles and should always be used for this purpose.

SHARPENING PLANE IRONS

One important factor in discussing the angle at which plane irons should be ground is to appreciate that it is the front angle at the cutting edge which is the

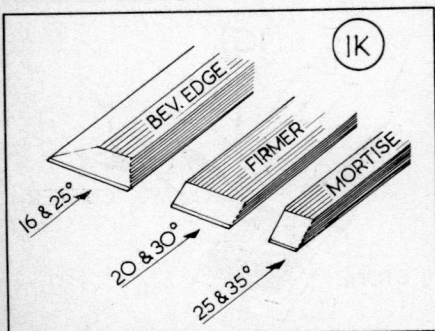

effective one, and (as shown in Figs 1D and 1E), this depends on the 'pitch' angle at which the cutter is mounted in the plane. Fig 1D relates to most bench planes and Fig 1E to most metal planes — you can see that the cutting bevel is opposite in each case.

The grinding angle for plane cutters is always 25 degrees and this is sharpened at the cutting edge to a higher angle of approximately 28 to 30 degrees. Figs 1F and 1G show how the cutter is sharpened by hand; in F the cutter is held with the bevel flat on the stone at first, then the hands are raised slightly to give the sharpening angle.

Sliding the cutter backwards and forwards on the oilstone causes a small burr to form and this is illustrated in Fig 1H. Some woodworkers prefer a loose circular motion, and Fig 1F shows that the cutter should be held firmly. To remove the burr and thus impart a keen edge, the cutter is next turned over and laid absolutely flat on the oilstone and sharpened with small rotary motions, as in Fig 1G. Repeating this process will eventually cause the burr to break off, leaving a sharp edge.

This is, in fact, the procedure to be followed when sharpening either plane irons or chisels. If you want to improve the edge still further, you can strop it on a stropping board, which is simply a piece of

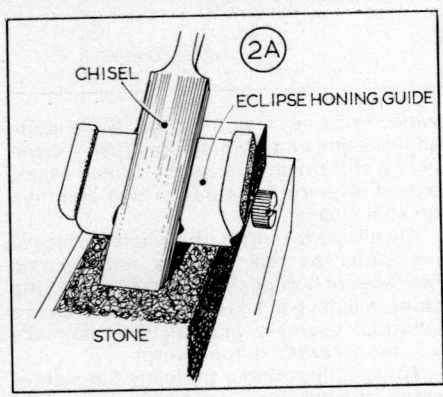

leather glued to a handy-sized wooden block. The leather should be dressed with a paste of fine emery powder and oil (although engineers' grinding paste makes a good substitute); draw the cutter along the strop several times with the bevel downwards, and then turn the cutter over and repeat.

Although it is not essential, it is a good idea to dub off the corners of trying and smoothing plane cutters as shown in Fig 1J to prevent them digging in; the edge of the jack plane is even more rounded to ease its cutter through the work.

This seems the right juncture to mention the special honing guide (Fig 2A) made by Eclipse Tools. This comprises an adjustable clamp which can hold chisels and plane cutters, and which is mounted on a roller.

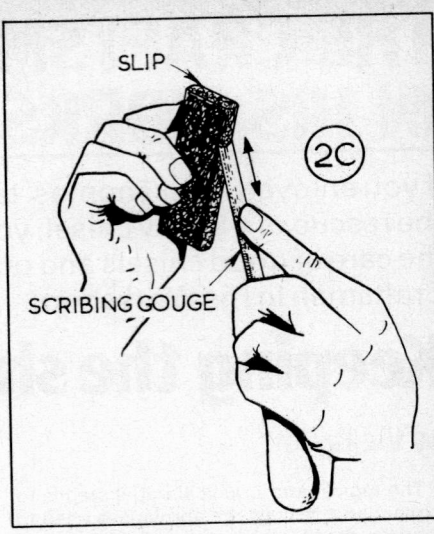

The amount by which the tool protrudes governs the angle at which it is sharpened, and the measurements are embossed on the side of the guide. The only reservation I have about it is that the roller has to run on the surface of the oilstone, which could result in excessive wear. To combat this I remove the oilstone from its box and butt it against a wooden block which is exactly the same height; this means that the roller runs mainly on the wood and not on the oilstone. To hold the stone and block against each other I clamp them between two bench stops, and I must say that the whole set-up yields first class results.

SHARPENING CHISELS AND GOUGES

Assuming that you use your chisels for a wide range of work, the grinding angle should be about 20 degrees, and the sharpening angle 30 degrees. However, if you like to use them for the purposes for which they were intended, then you will need to have different angles for each.

From Fig 1K, you will see that the bevelled edge chisel has a grinding angle of about 16 degrees and a sharpening angle of about 25 degrees. This low angle is necessary as the chisel is meant to make slicing cuts, and not to be struck with a mallet.

The firmer chisel, however, is intended to be used with a mallet, and to cut across the grain as well as with it. So, a more acute angle is called for as a shallow one would break off or jam in the wood, and the grinding angle is therefore about 20 degrees and the sharpening angle 30 degrees.

Lastly, we come to the mortise chisel which is almost invariably used with a mallet, and which employs a chopping action to cut cross-grained stuff. Here, an even more acute angle is needed to stand up to such robust treatment and the grinding and the sharpening could well be 25 and 35 degrees respectively.

Both the grinding and the sharpening techniques for chisels closely follow those outlined for plane cutters, and a burr should be built up and then removed in just the same way; also chisels can be honed on the same stropping board.

Sharpening the two types of gouges — firmer and scribing — demands two very different methods. Dealing with the firmer gouge first, the gouge should be positioned at right angles to the oilsone with the bevel lying flat, Fig 2B; rock it back and forth so that every part is treated, and finally remove any burr by sliding an oilstone slip up and down inside it. The slip will need to match

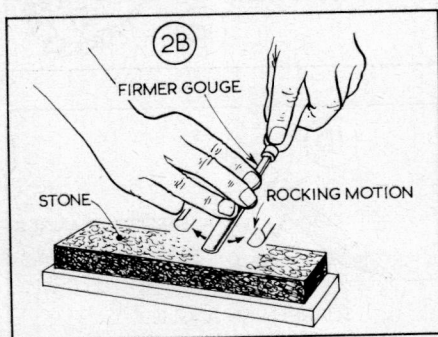

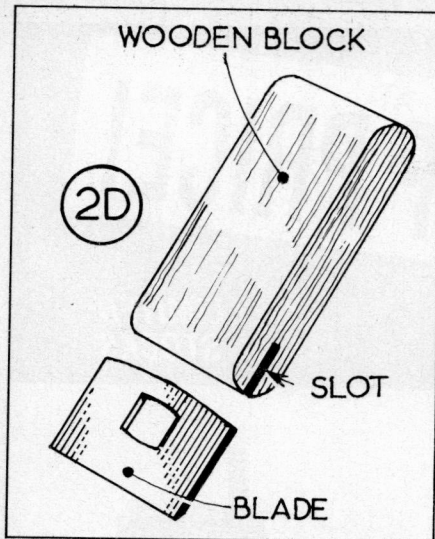

WOODEN BLOCK

2D

SLOT

BLADE

the inside curvature exactly, of course.

An oilstone slip will be needed for sharpening the scribing gouge, Fig 2C. The curve on the slip should be slightly less than that of the gouge; remove any burr by rocking the gouge backwards and forwards on the oilstone, with the bevel held flat.

SHARPENING SPOKESHAVES

There are two kinds of spokeshave — the metal one which has a small blade, and the wooden type which has a blade with a tang at each end.

The first kind is dealt with just as if it was a small plane cutter, and as it is so small it's worth making a wooden holder as shown in Fig 2D with a slot cut in it which accepts the blade as a push-fit.

Fig 2E shows the method of dealing with the other kind of blade by sharpening it on the edge of an oilstone; in both cases, any burr is removed by turning the blades over and rubbing them on the oilstone. ■

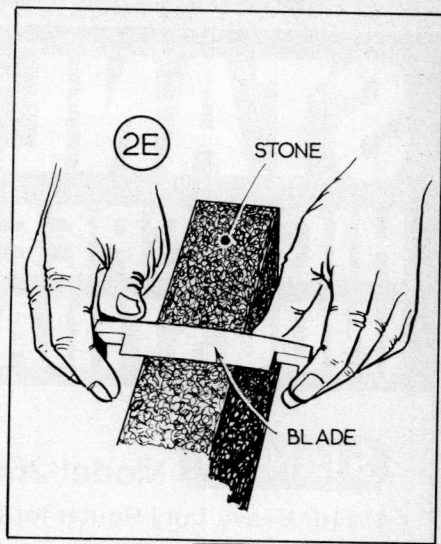

2E   STONE

BLADE

ON TEST

Hot weld glue gun

Chris Dunn takes a look at the hot weld adhesive gun made by Supergloy

A hot glue gun is a useful addition to any workshop's armoury. Although not applicable for every gluing job, such a tool comes usefully into its own when a quick weld is required.

The hot weld adhesive gun made by Supergloy, which I have been trying out, claims a wide range of applications, from fixing wood to masonry, bonding leather and repairing pottery to picture framing, fixing ceramic tiles, carpet laying and gluing metal to brick. Its accompanying leaflet says it 'bonds virtually everything', but while I wouldn't presume to argue with that, I don't think it would necessarily do the job *better* than the orthodox methods that apply individually to the range of its potential uses.

I used the gun for repair work on sash windows of the Georgian style which were badly damaged by wet rot and neglect, an ongoing job that I have found to be a laborious and time-consuming task, as the derelict which we fondly refer to as 'home' has nearly as many windows as a greenhouse. Each window has to be dismantled, cleaned and stripped before cutting out rotten sections and replacing good wood, prior to glazing and painting.

Not least of the problems is in faithfully copying the profile of a moulding plane that shaped the stiles and mullions 150 years ago — and that cannot be done until the glue joining new and original woodwork has thoroughly hardened. Using PVA glue, as I have in the past, the hardening process holds up further work for at least six hours, and since the Supergloy gun promised me a solid bond in less than two minutes, I put it to the test with some enthusiasm. And I was not disappointed.

The simple scarf joint is a difficult one to glue up, since cramping tends to produce the squeezed orange pip effect of one face on the other, and screwing to hold the joint is both laborious and, in the case of glazing bars which do not require additional strength, unnecessary. However, with the hot weld system I found I could simply hold the joint together under hand pressure while the glue went off. Three minutes later I had a workable bond.

Thus impressed, I then took the gun to a glazed earthenware plant pot which was in pieces, but here I encountered problems. Indeed, in this application the adhesive set too fast for its own good. In the time taken to run a bead of glue along the joint, put down the gun and take up the piece to be joined, the adhesive had already hardened sufficiently to prevent it squeezing out of the joint under hand pressure to make a tight fit. The glue certainly bonded with an impressive firmness, but tended to hold the pieces apart. Not such a success.

If, however, the broken pieces were heated to a reasonable temperature before gluing, the hardening process would probably be retarded sufficiently to prevent this, though I haven't been able to prove it as I haven't another broken pot to spare. Nevertheless, I suggest that Henkel Chemicals Ltd, who make the Supergloy gun, might usefully provide a leaflet to go with their product to cover such tips as this for the benefit of users.

The gun, which uses a fairly standard 11mm diameter stick of adhesive as raw ammunition, has a thermostatically controlled temperature regulator to maintain its operational heat of 206°C, which it will achieve in around four minutes from cold. Though I wouldn't expect the Supergloy hot weld adhesive gun to be applicable in every gluing instance, I would certainly commend it as a tool which will earn its keep in the workshop.

Recommended retail price £13.99 inc VAT. Ammunition £1.75 per 24 sticks. ■

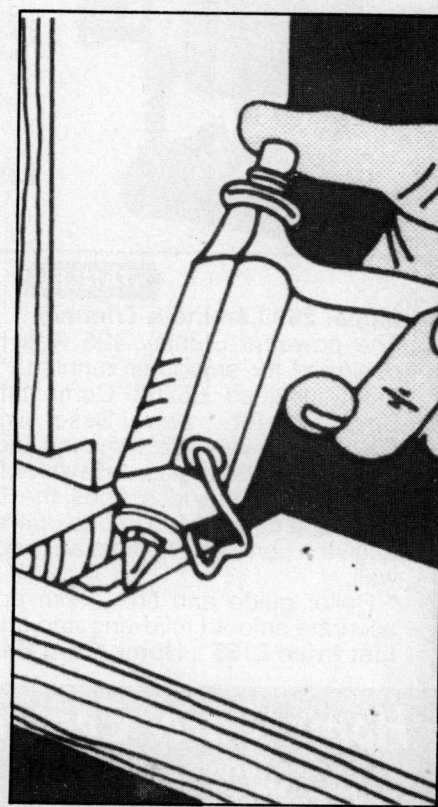

● *Hot glue at the press of the thumb*

Prices quoted are those prevailing at press date and are subject to alteration due to economic conditions.

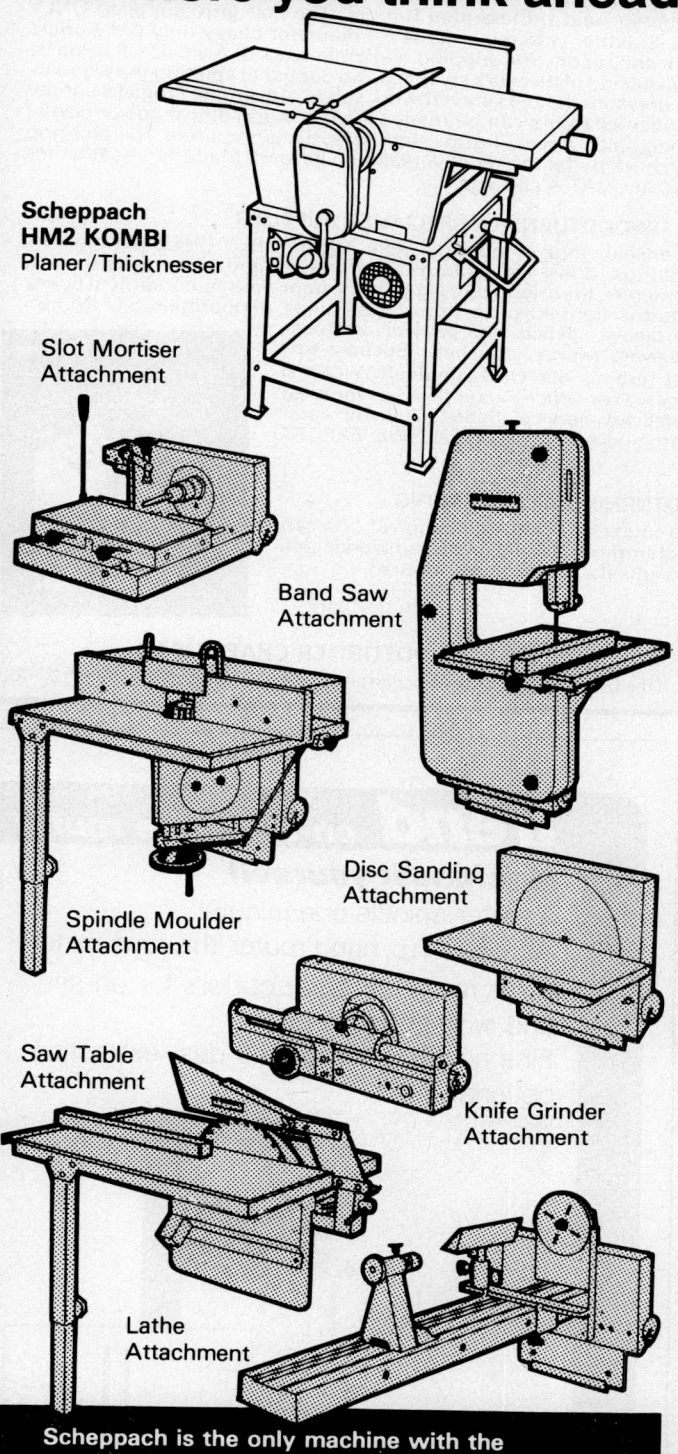

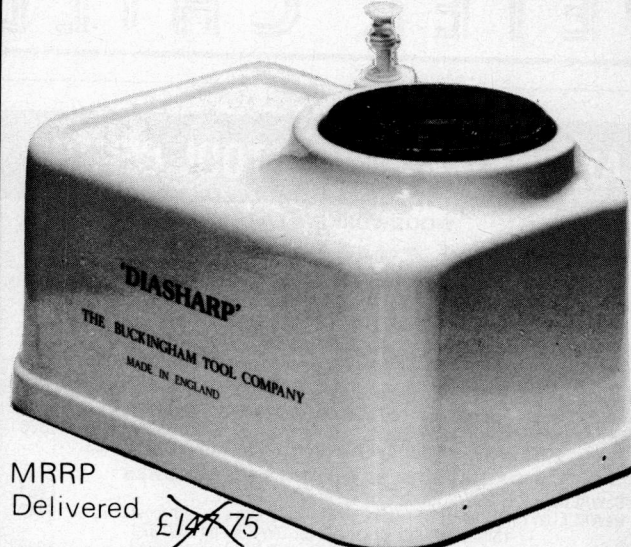

The Child Coil Grip Chuck

A COMBINATION CHUCK FOR HAND WOODTURNERS   *(copied but not improved on)*   *Patented*

This unique chuck is the outcome of many years experience by a professional woodturner and teacher, and the patented coil grip method together with the many extra modes of operation safely and neatly overcome the chucking problems encountered by amateur and professional turners. The coil grip, supplied ONLY WITH THIS CHUCK, together with the large (4½") diameter heavy duty body offers unbeatable strength and rigidity for gripping end grain work of ANY size. It grips by compression on the outside of the work so there is no danger of splitting the wood by excessive outward pressure. It holds staved work safely. An almost limitless variety of home-made wooden adaptors can be made which will grip any shape or size of work, internally, externally, dovetail grip, plain grip, or as required. The coil grip feature makes this chuck by far the most versatile of its kind. Made for most lathes (state model) £36.50 inc. VAT & carriage.

WOODTURNERS' SPECIALIST SUPPLIER

The most comprehensive range of tools available. The new ROY CHILD parting tool. Chucks, centres, fittings, drills. Flexicramps. Many types and sizes glass inserts, barometers, hygrometers, thermometers, eggtimers, hourglasses, condiment liners, 160 circular tile patterns, lighters, pens, flower vase tubes, peppermills, STAINLESS saltmills, knives, clocks, pencil sharpeners, ashtrays, clock dials. Abrasives, waxes, finishes. Speed-n-Eze, Rustins. WOOD for turning. MYFORD agents. ROY CHILD pyrography machines. Post Office Parcel Contract for most quick and direct delivery service. Send S.A.E. for catalogue, or $1.00 from overseas enquiries. We EXPORT worldwide.

WOODTURNING AND FINISHING

Two-day intensive course and personal tuition at 17th century Essex-Suffolk farmhouse. Fully equipped workshops. Maximum of two guests for any one course.

COIL GRIP ASSEMBLY

PETER CHILD

THE WOODTURNER CRAFTSMAN
The Old Hyde, Little Yeldham, Halstead, Essex. Tel. Gt. Yeldham (0787) 237291

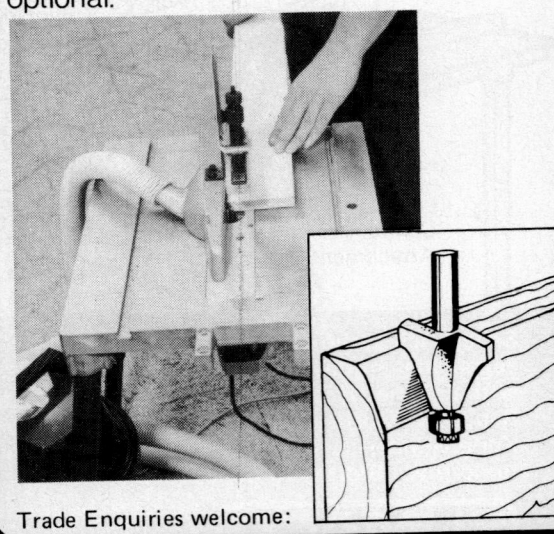

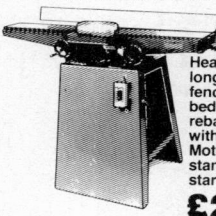

Automatic cash box

John Newton describes the construction of his ingenious cash box that automatically sorts coins, from 1p to £1, into their denominations. In addition to its obvious practical value, the cash box presents a fun element for children while offering a more serious and useful application for unsighted people

This cash box is very useful in the home, and will be appreciated by both sighted and blind persons. It measures approximately 12in long, 4⅛in deep and 8in high. It automatically sorts coins of different values and stores them in separate compartments.

It is designed to accommodate the following British coins, 50, 20, 10, 5, 2, 1 pence and £1, while the ha'penny piece has been omitted in anticipation of it being discontinued at some future date. In the meantime, any ha'penny coins inserted in the box will appear among the penny coins. The design could be modified to accommodate coins of other countries.

How it works

A coin which is placed in the slot at the top of the box rolls down an inclined track, whilst leaning against an inclined wall containing different sized apertures into one of which the coin falls and thence into one of seven compartments below.

Coins may be retrieved by raising the front sliding panel. To provide a finger-hold on this panel a dial thermometer or other adornment may be attached.

Construction

Start by making the base assembly (fig 3). This consists of four receptables A and three B (fig 1) and six partitions C (fig 2) glued together. By using ready-planed timber the sides of the receptacles will be exactly parallel and this is an essential requirement to ensure a satisfactory assembly. The widths of A and B need not be exactly 1⅜in and 1¾in as shown. It is better to accept the dimensions as received from the timber merchant as long as they are near those specified.

After completing the base assembly, its overall length should be measured so that parts F, R, S, and U can be later cut to suit.

The side panels P and Q (figs 9 and 10) are next screwed to the base assembly (fig 17). Note that these sides extend ¼in behind the rear of the base assembly, and are flush with the front and base.

The guide D, track E, support panel F, and spacer G (figs 4, 5, 6 and 7 respectively) should next be made. E and G should be made from 4mm plywood, as specified (⅛in material is not thick enough to provide clearance for the thickest coins).

The guide D has six holes for trapping all coins except the 50 pence coin which rolls off the end of the track instead of entering a hole. The height of each hole must be made exactly to the figures given in fig 4, and the bottoms of the holes must all be in line.

Parts D, E, F and G are glued together to form the sub-assembly (fig 8). E and G are sandwiched between D and F, the space between E and G forming a tunnel along which the coins will roll. The bottoms of the holes in D must be 1/32in above the track E as shown. This prevents the coins from slipping into the wrong holes.

The long slot shown at the left-hand end of fig 8 is cut through D and E coinciding

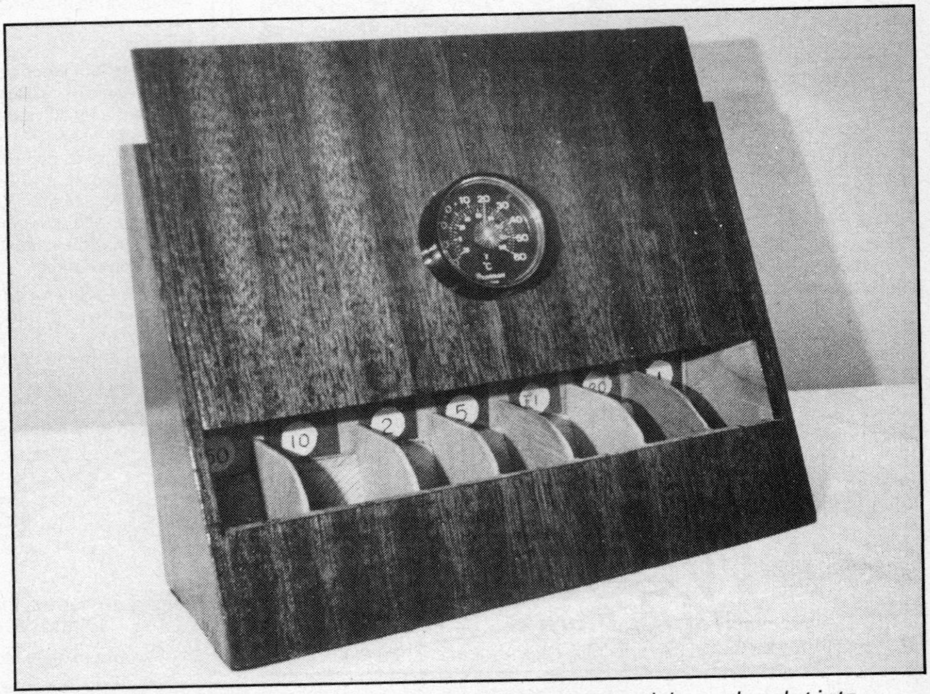

● *John Newton's finished cash box. It sorts coins entered through a slot into their denominations from 1p to £1.*

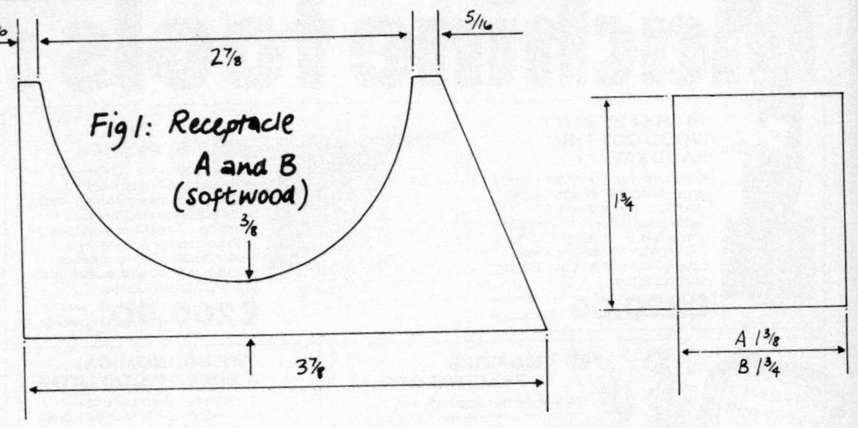

1/16
5/16
2⅞
Fig 1: Receptacle
A and B
(softwood)
⅜
3⅞
1¾
A 1⅜
B 1¾

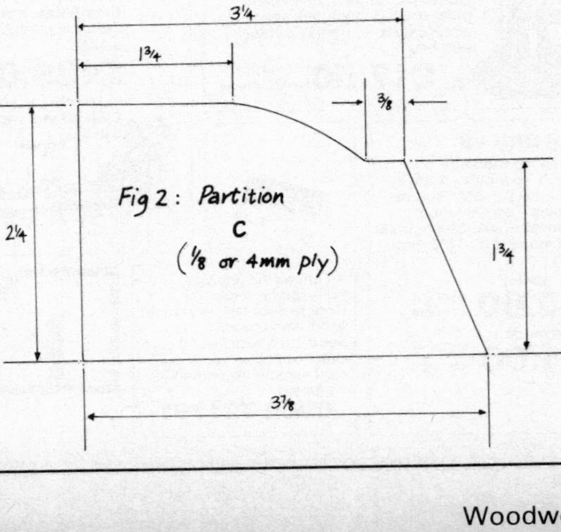

3¼
1¾
⅜
2¼
Fig 2: Partition
C
(⅛ or 4mm ply)
1¾
3⅞

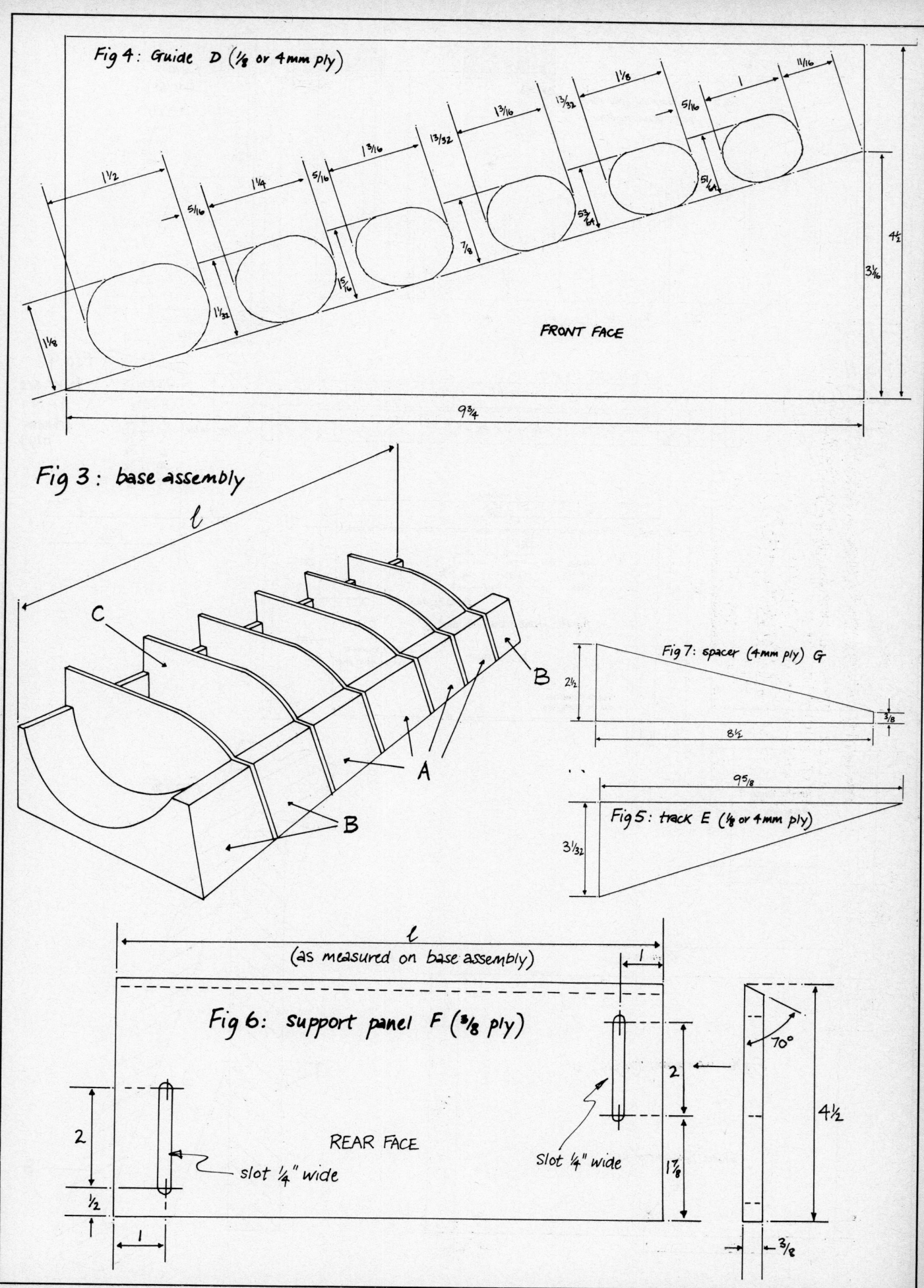

Fig 4: Guide D (⅛ or 4mm ply)

1½   5/16   1¼   5/16   1³/16   13/32   1³/16   13/32   1⅛   5/16   1   11/16

4½

3¹/16

FRONT FACE

1⅛   1¹/32   15/16   7/8   53/64   5/64   5/64

9¾

Fig 3: base assembly

ℓ

C

A

B

B

Fig 7: spacer (4mm ply) G

2½   8½   3/8

9⅝

Fig 5: track E (⅛ or 4mm ply)

3¹/32

Fig 6: support panel F (³/8 ply)

ℓ
(as measured on base assembly)

1

REAR FACE

2   slot ¼" wide

½

1

2   Slot ¼" wide

1⅞

70°

4½

3/8

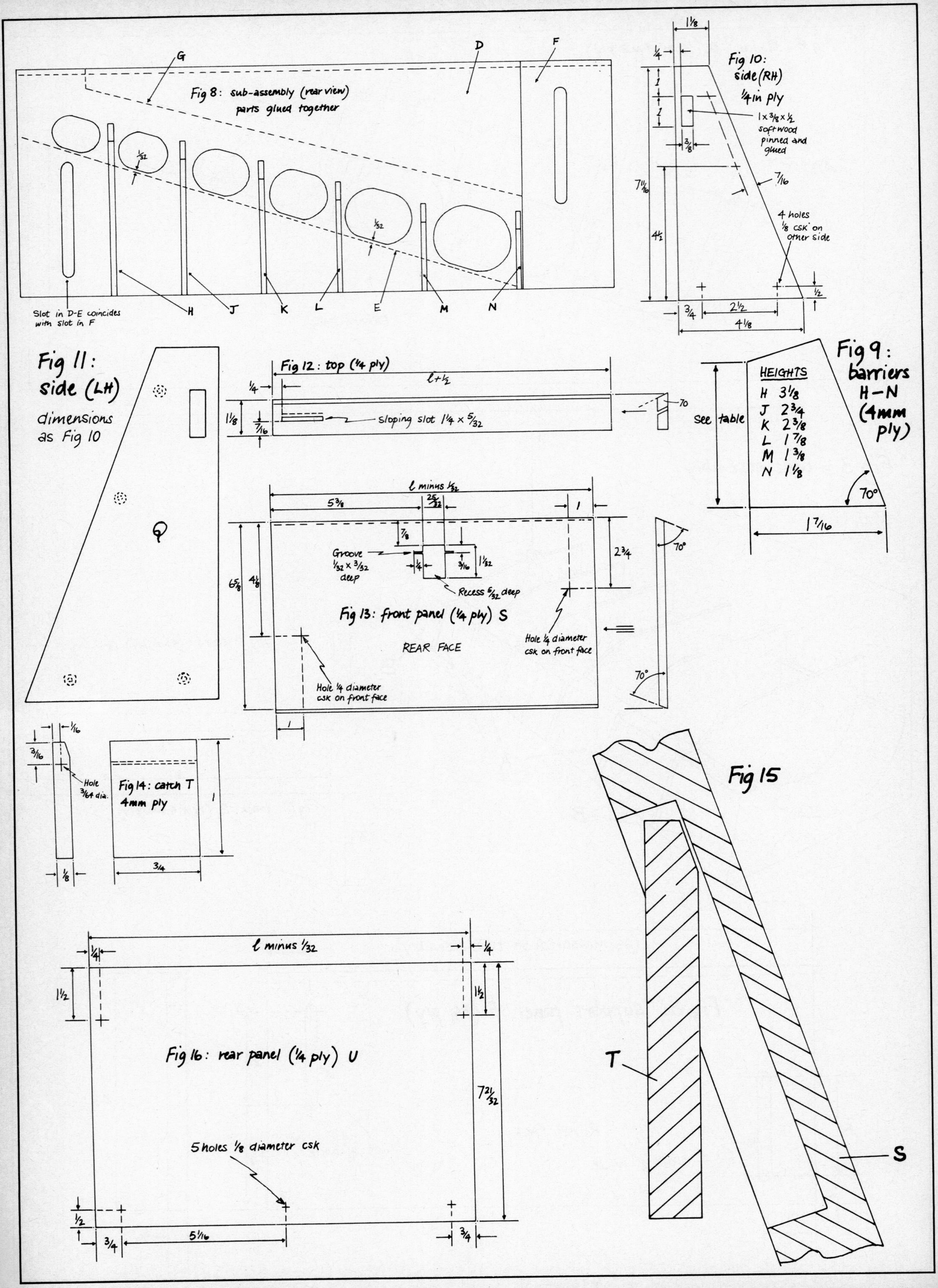
Fig 8: sub-assembly (rear view) parts glued together
G
D
F
1/32
1/32
Slot in D-E coincides with slot in F
H
J
K
L
E
M
N
Fig 10: side (RH) 1/4 in ply
1 1/8
1/4
1
1
1 x 3/8 x 1/2 softwood pinned and glued
3/8
7 11/16
7/16
4 1/2
4 holes 1/8 csk on other side
1/2
3/4
2 1/2
4 1/8
Fig 11: side (LH)
dimensions as Fig 10
Q
Fig 12: top (1/4 ply)
l + 1/2
1/4
1 1/8
7/16
sloping slot 1 1/4 x 5/32
70
Fig 9: barriers H–N (4mm ply)
see table
HEIGHTS
H 3 1/8
J 2 3/4
K 2 3/8
L 1 7/8
M 1 3/8
N 1 1/8
70°
1 7/16
l minus 1/32
5 3/8
25/32
1
7/8
Groove 1/32 x 3/32 deep
1/4
3/16
1 1/32
2 3/4
6 5/8
4 1/8
Recess 5/32 deep
Fig 13: front panel (1/4 ply) S
REAR FACE
Hole 1/4 diameter csk on front face
Hole 1/4 diameter csk on front face
70°
70°
1
1/16
3/16
Hole 3/64 dia.
Fig 14: catch T 4mm ply
1
1/8
3/4
Fig 15
T
S
l minus 1/32
1/4
1/4
1 1/2
1 1/2
Fig 16: rear panel (1/4 ply) U
7 21/32
5 holes 1/8 diameter csk
1/2
3/4
5 1/16
3/4

with the corresponding slot in F.

The barriers H to N shown in fig 8 should be omitted at this stage.

The front panel S (fig 13) should next be made. The recess in the rear face of this panel will conveniently be three-ply deep if the material used is five-ply. The sub-assembly fig 8, should now be fixed in place between the two side panels by four screws. Fig 17 shows the correct position of this assembly. The top chamfered edge of F should be in line with the top edges of the side panels. To ensure correct positioning, it is recommended that the unit be placed face down on a horizontal surface with the front panel S temporarily in position and the support panel F resting on it.

The top plate R (fig 12) can now be made and should be pinned and glued to F, P and Q. Check that the top edge of the front panel S is in line with the top surface of the top panel R when S is in the closed position.

The catch T (fig 14) should be made and fitted into the recess in the front panel, using a piece of steel wire (eg from a paper clip) as a pivot. The pivot should be a loose fit in the hole in the catch. The chamfer on the catch shown in fig 14 should be obtained by experiment such as to allow the catch to swing out just the right amount to hold the front panel open (see figs 15 and 17). A little glue on the ends of the pivots will secure it in place in the groove.

The two OBA screws should be inserted in the front panel and secured to it with a strong glue such as Araldite. The screw at the right-hand end (facing the front) should be 1½in long, the other 1⅛in long.

Place the front panel in position and secure with nuts and large plain washers, adjusting the nuts until the panel slides easily up and down.

The barriers H to N (fig 9) can now be glued to D as shown in figs 8 and 17; and the rear panel U (fig 15) fitted, with five screws.

Finally, wood veneer can be applied to front, top and sides, and polished. The optional dial-thermometer is attached last of all. ∎

PARTS LIST

4mm PLYWOOD
6mm (or ¼in) PLYWOOD (5-PLY)
10mm (or ⅜in) PLYWOOD
⅛in PLYWOOD (OPTIONAL)
2 × 1½in PSE
2 × 2in PSE
WOOD VENEER
No 4 WOODSCREWS ½in LG CSK
OBA (or 6mm) SCREWS 1½in & 1⅛in LG
CSK WITH NUTS & WASHERS
1/32" STEEL WIRE (PAPER CLIP)
DIAL THERMOMETER (OPTIONAL)

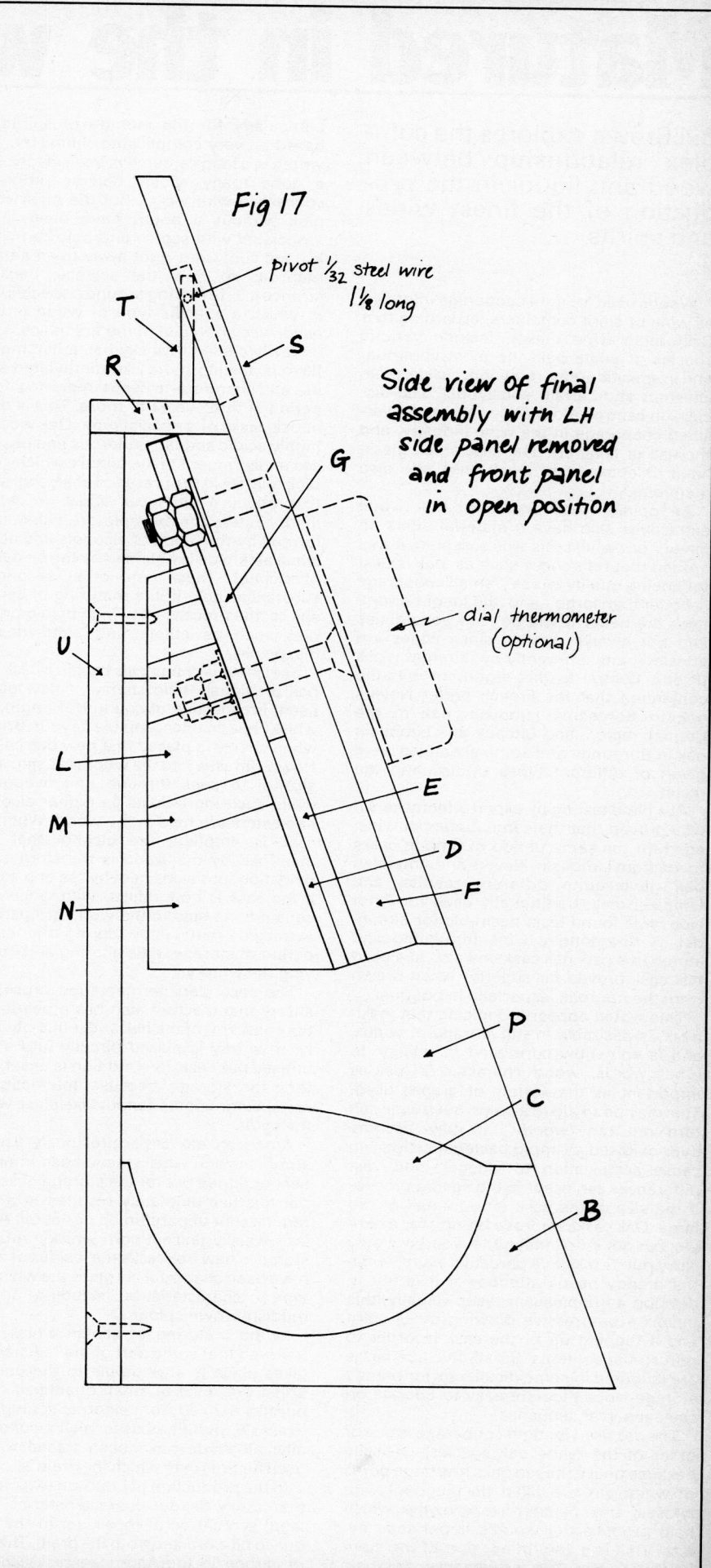

Fig 17

pivot ⅟32 steel wire 1⅛ long

Side view of final assembly with LH side panel removed and front panel in open position

dial thermometer (optional)

Matured in the wood

Bill Brown explores the complex relationship between wood and liquor in the production of the finest wines and spirits

Woods used for tight cooperage intended as wine or spirit containers, according to a Californian wine maker, include various species of white oak, the most common, and in specific areas, redwood, acacia, pine, chestnut and certain eucalyptus. The discussion centred around the values of diversified cooperage in the wine industry, and the use of concrete, stainless steel, glass-lined or epoxy-lined steel tanks was also mentioned.

An opinion was expressed that wood extractives also have a material effect on flavour but whilst this was accepted, it was argued that references such as 'oak is best for ageing quality wines', 'small cooperage is better than large'; and 'the longer a wine ages the better it will be', are generalities and not always correct, since wines are affected quite differently by different types of oak. Central to this argument was the contention that the French prefer Nevers oak in Bordeaux, Limousin oak in the Cognac region, and Citeaux and Limousin oak in Burgundy and some examples were given of different types of use and the result.

At a blind tasting by expert winemakers it was proved that the same Zinfandel wine, aged for the same period of time in casks made from Limousin, Nevers and American oak gave quite different results, and Limousin oak, traditionally used for Pinot Noir, was found least desirable for Zinfandel. A Chardonnay wine fermented and stored in a new oak cask and also in a used oak cask proved far superior when drawn from the new oak, especially in bouquet.

This would appear to indicate that 'oakiness' is desirable in the storage of wines, and is somehow correlated to quality. In other words, wood character is just as important as the variety of grapes used. This may be so, up to a point, but a wine can turn out too 'woody'; it may become over-oxidised, or rapid bacterial action can cause acetification to vinegar, and vast differences can occur in the ageing process if the size of the cask is too small or too large. Oak casks improve brandy for example, but not indefinitely; the wood will only carry out its task to a particular point, when the brandy needs attention if it is not to develop an unpleasant taste. Usually, this means a progressive drawing off of spirit and a topping up of the cask in order to refresh the contents. Small, five-litre casks are favoured in some distilleries for brandy storage since they are easy to operate on say a ten-year sequence.

The oak used for tight cooperage is one or other of the white oak species, basically because unlike the red oaks, the large pores of white oak are filled (ie plugged) with tyloses, tiny bladder-like growths which help produce the wood's impervious nature. This is a very minor part of the story however, and the preferences for oak, particularly for the storage of spirits, is based on very complicated chemistry. The writer, in a long career, has been involved in a good many widely diverse problems concerned with wood, but the most complex without a doubt have been those associated with scotch and bourbon whisky, and confesses right away to an amazement as to how the science, because science it is, revolving around a specific way in which a specific type of wood is best used, was arrived at in the first place.

Newly distilled whisky has a harsh acrid flavour, tasting more like methylated spirits, and therefore it needs maturing for a period of three years or more. This is done in oak casks of a special type. Oak wood is highly acidic and tanniniferous and possesses an astringent taste, factors which combine to react in the presence of alcohol so as to produce a beneficial effect on certain fluids. Esters for example are substances formed by the union of alcohols and acids, while aldehyde is obtained by the oxidation of alcohol. These, and other secondary substances help in the maturing of certain spirits, the process allowing volatile principles such as ethers and aldehydes to disappear.

Scotch whisky matures best in a cask that has previously held sherry; if new oak is used, irrespective of country of origin, the whisky has an unacceptable flavour. Briefly, when sherry is placed in a new oak cask, it slowly diffuses into the wood, causing ethyl alcohol to pass through and evaporate, while such ingredients as higher alcohols and esters are held in the wood. When the cask is emptied, the alcohol that was absorbed by the wood is transformed by oxidation into acids, aldehydes and esters. If the cask is now refilled with whisky the constituents held in the wood are partially extracted, particularly during the earlier period of storage, thus altering and improving the whisky.

The secondary fermentation process in sherry manufacture also has a bearing on the condition of the oak and, quite obviously, if whisky is placed directly into a new unused oak cask, its condition is unsatisfactory for storage because interaction of certain ingredients cannot take place within the spirit.

American oak casks previously used to store bourbon whisky have been imported here and tried out for the storage of scotch, but this has ultimately resulted in a taste reminiscent of paraffin oil or nut oil. American whisky (except corn whisky) must be stored in new oak casks the insides of which have been charred. This gives the whisky its typical characteristics including a deep reddish-brown colour.

In the maturing of scotch whisky it is believed that some part of the reaction that takes place is attributable to the unintentional presence of small quantities of impurities derived from external sources. For example, pyridine bases, allyl alcohol and allyl aldehyde have been traced to peat used for fires over which the grain is 'cured'.

In the production of bourbon (which lacks the smoky flavour characteristic of 'Highland' scotch) acrolein occurs in the spirit due to oil extracted from the grain. The layer of carbon in the American cask acts as a barrier to the reaction processes normal to the storage of scotch, and tends to absorb the oily tasting acrolein from the bourbon.

Wooden cooperage dates back to biblical and Roman times and while in recent years it has lost out to plastics in respect of some types of containers, it is not possible to engineer the complex chemistry of which wood is composed into an unnatural material. Accordingly, it would seem that wines and spirits matured in wood do have some special characteristics to commend them. ∎

Get a grip

Bill Gates looks at a versatile new design of clamp

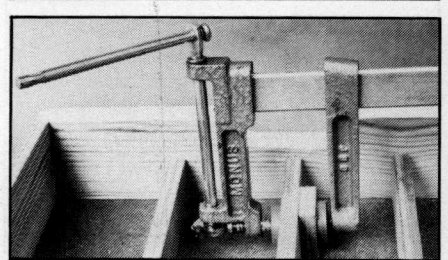

There are occasions when space is so restricted that holding parts together with standard clamps becomes extremely difficult. Recently I have acquired a Monus clamp designed to cope with such situations.

The pressure pad is operated with a cam via a spindle, which allows the turning movement to take place away from the face of the work. The pressure applied is sufficient to hold the parts together very securely. Another advantage is the long reach that facilitates holding parts some distance from the work face.

It is made in various sizes, marketed by Trend Machinery Tools. ∎

At the heart of a good job

ELEKTRA BECKUM

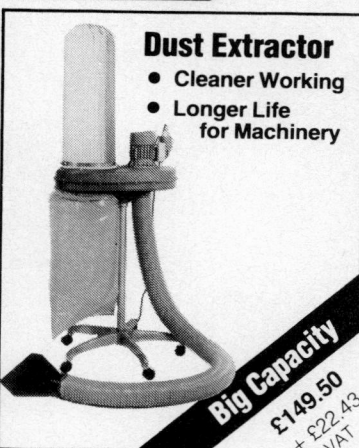

End of term

Rycotewood College, Thame, offers courses which educate versatile handcraftsmen and women with a strong design ability. One of the prime aims of the courses is to inculcate the highest standard of workmanship to produce top quality work. Another vital core of the course is design which is seen as being not only the aesthetic requirement of a particular piece, but an efficient organisational tool to enable craftsmen to produce technically correct and aesthetically pleasing work in an efficient manner. This can be summarised as developing a highly skilled craftsman with an educated 'thinking' eye.

The pictures here illustrate some of the end of term exhibition of college work which once again was also the subject of an exhibition at Maples, Tottenham Court Road, London. Maples sponsored two awards with the objective of giving support and encouragement to young designers and craftsmen who wish to set up their own business and compete with foreign imports.

The award for the best and most original design incorporating a high standard of craftsmanship went to mature student Alan Martin for his slatted-door sycamore cabinet and that for the best and most faithful copy of a classic item of furniture went to Jeremy Higson for his roll-top bureau.

● Jeremy Higson, winner of the Maples award for the best and most faithful copy of a classic item incorporating a high standard of workmanship, together with his winning piece

● Roanal van Asma also made this impressive tallboy in walnut veneer

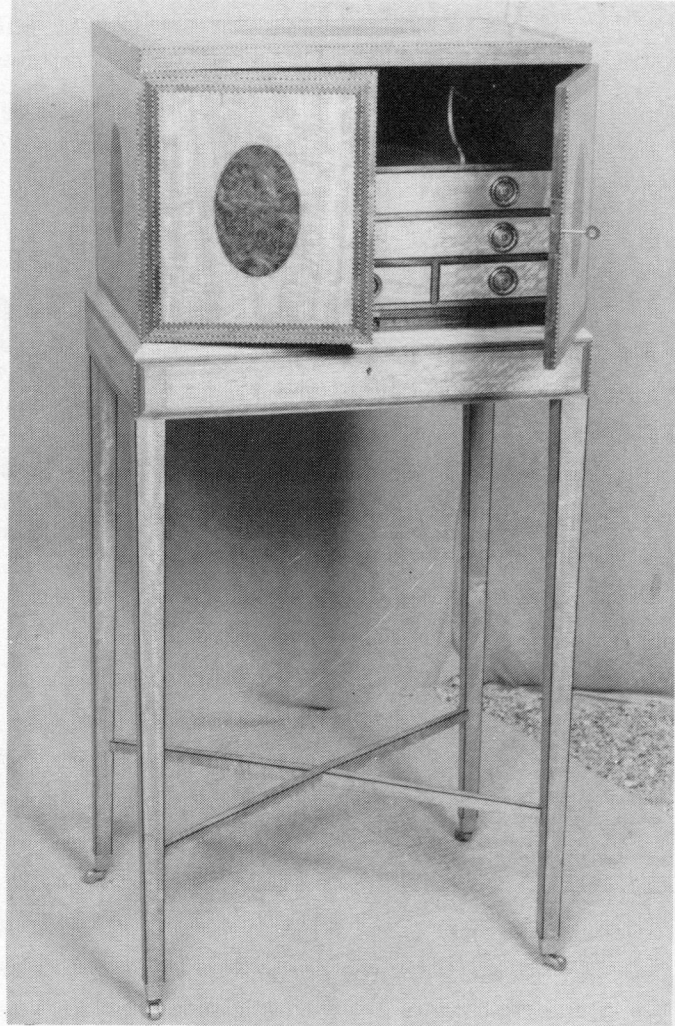

● Writing cabinet in satinwood veneer made by 19 year old Roanal C. van Asma from the Hague

● This clock in sycamore and rosewood was made by 19 year old Peter van der Burgh of Horsham

● Top: Dressing table and stool in cherry, the work of 26 year old Richard G. Henley from South Africa

● Above: Side table in birch and rosewood veneer, the work of South African Richard Henley

● Right: Eighteen year old Andrew Laker designed and made this set of occasional tables in burr elm and birdseye maple veneer

The world's timber trees

Bill Bond concludes his series on the timber trees of the world with a look at idigbo, greenheart and East African camphorwood

IDIGBO : 28

Terminalia ivorensis, Combretaceae

Continuing the series on the family Combretaceae it is appropriate to mention just one comparatively well known timber idigbo, also called emri or framire. This wood is somewhat variable both in colour and texture. The most characteristic feature is formed by a seasonal absence of vessels which gives a zone of plain tissue at intervals. Although not broad, these bands

of tissue are sufficiently impressive to provide quite a feature, particularly on flat-sawn surfaces.

As to the wood's variability, the best grades are pleasant to work but some material, probably from older trees, is soft and brittle and of little use for special work.

Other woods from the family are Indian silver greywood *Terminalia bialata* and Indian laurel *T. tomentosum* and afara or limba *T. superba.* The lighter coloured wood from the Indian species *T. bialata* may be met as white chuglam or white bombwe.

The family Lauraceae, occurring worldwide, chiefly tropical, consists of 40 genera and some one thousand species of trees and shrubs with evergreen leaves, many of which are noted for their aromatic qualities. The name laurel as applied to wood is another instance of a collective word which may mean almost anything. The cherry laurel, familiar in every shrubbery, is a member of the Rosaceae, related to apple and pear. The bay tree with its aromatic leaves used for flavouring is a genuine member of the Lauraceae. Indian laurel *Terminalia tomentosum* is unrelated, Chilean laurel, *Laurelia aromatica,* supplying Peruvian nutmegs as well as a good working wood, belongs to a related family, the Monimiaceae; and Ecuador laurel, *Cordia alliodora,* is a member of the forget-me-not and anchusa family, the Boraginaceae. Timber names are indeed confusing.

The fresh evergreen leaves of the Lauraceae have been looked up to and used as a symbol of victory since early times and

the family is of considerable economic importance for timbers, spices, perfumes, also the popular avocado pear and other edible fruits. The family supplies many valuable timbers but they are little known world-wide. The following are worthy of mention:- ranai (*Alseodaphne semicarpifolia*) from Sri Lanka, tawa (*Beilschmedia tawa*) from New Zealand, belian or Borneo ironwood (*Eusideroxylon zwaggeri*) used locally for shingles, sassafras (*Sassafras officinalis*) from North America, imbuya (*Phoebe porosa*) also known as Brazilian walnut, and the famous (infamous) Australian or Queensland walnut (*Endiandra palmerstonii*). The list should also include South African stinkwood (*Ocotea bullata*), a

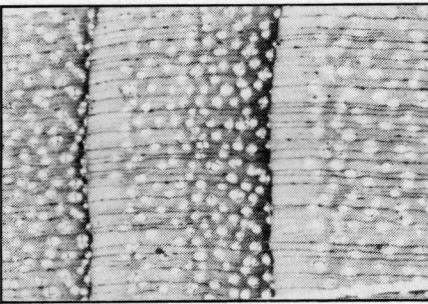

● **Cross section ×3.3**

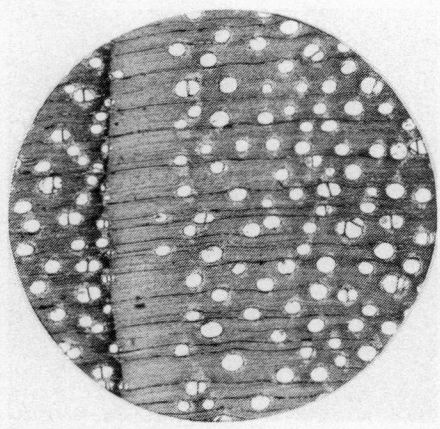

● **Cross section ×10**

rich brown wood much esteemed for furniture and fittings. As with the laurels, there appear to be several stinkwoods!

Such confusion must be halted somewhere and two woods only are described here, one very familiar, the other (unfortunately) less so.

GREENHEART : 29

Ocotea rodiaei, Ocotea — from a native name in the Caribbean, *rodiaei* — in honour of Dr Rodie, the first European discoverer of its anti-febrile properties. Lauraceae.

Greenheart has become almost a household word, not solely confined to the timber industry. It is such an outstanding wood and so useful in marine and other structures requiring great strength and durability, that everyone is more or less familiar with its

virtues. It is very resistant to fungal attack and to termites and marine borers. Massive pillars and piles are available to support sea groynes and piers and, at the other extreme, anglers in the past have praised its use in fishing rods cleft from pieces of very fine

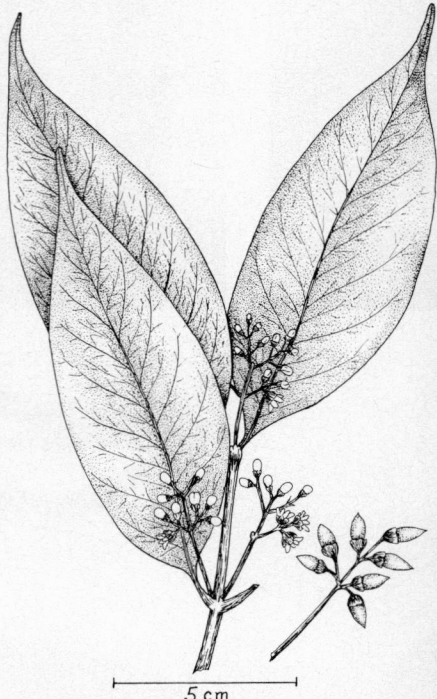

5 cm

dimensions. The elasticity of the wood was favoured for this specialised branch of manufacture until it gave place to modern carbon fibre.

The colour varies to some extent and may include dark, almost black, markings. It finishes to a very smooth surface, planed pieces are inconveniently slippery, and I remember the comment of a worker handling flooring strips from a four-cutter machine:- 'It nearly cut my neck in two.' Block and strip flooring panels, made for demonstration, showed off the wood to advantage.

Working qualities by hand, should anyone care to try it out for works of art and curios, are not too bad, provided one respects its weight and hardness, and the wood has rather a special interest should any off-cuts be available.

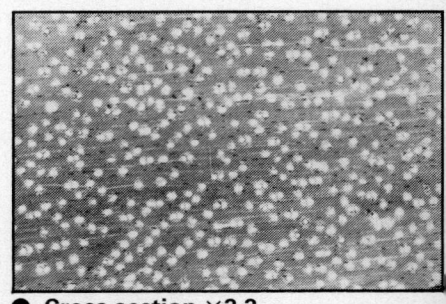

● **Cross section ×3.3**

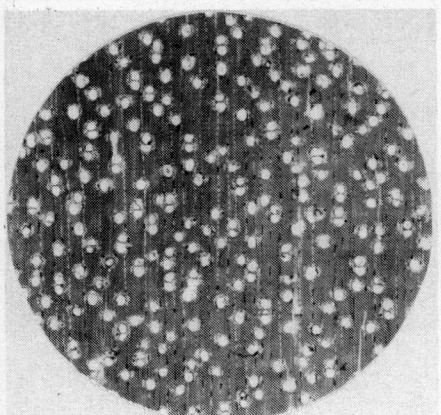

● Cross section ×10

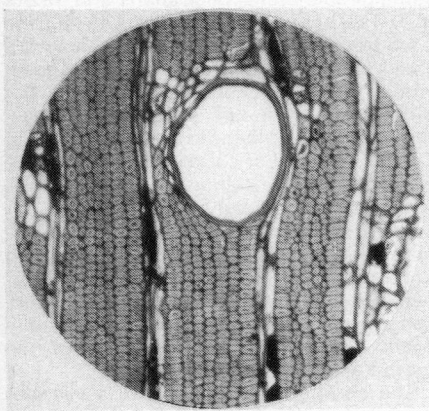

● Cross section ×100

The structure is seen from the photomicrographs to be very even. Parenchyma cells are mostly surrounding each vessel, that is more or less vasicentric and the rays are very fine. To illustrate the wood's great weight an illustration of higher magnification is included which shows the very thick-walled fibres.

EAST AFRICAN CAMPHORWOOD : 30

Ocotea usambarensis, usambarensis — from the Usambara mountains, East Africa. Lauraceae.

East African camphorwood is one of the pleasantest woods I have ever worked with. Should it appear on future international markets, the hand woodworker will have a treat in store. The scent is delightful and the crisp nature of the wood in chiselling across end-grain, for instance in cutting secret mitre dovetails, is a joy. In a more or less technical series it may be out of place to become sentimental about any particular wood; but these remarks are made with happy memories and I have often wished to possess a few feet of it. (Can wood and sentiment ever be separated?)

I seem to remember reading years ago that there is plenty of camphorwood, but much of it is difficult to extract. Only once have I met the wood since working with government material in the days of Empire, and this was when an evening class student brought some along. I tried to ascertain the source of supply but the replies were vague.

The above reference to its aromatic properties is not based on prolonged working.

The camphor-like odour noted when the timber is fresh disappears in due course.

The wood is of medium texture, very moderate in weight, rather variable in colour (yellow and greenish brown darkening on exposure). The sapwood is paler but not always clearly defined, there is a characteristic iridescence which is fascinating. Camphor as we know it is obtained from another tree *Cinnamomium camphora* of the same family, or from Sabah camphorwood *Dryobalanops* spp.

It must be one of the wiles of nature that such a good working wood should be related botanically to one of the very worst, Australian or Queensland walnut *Endiandra*

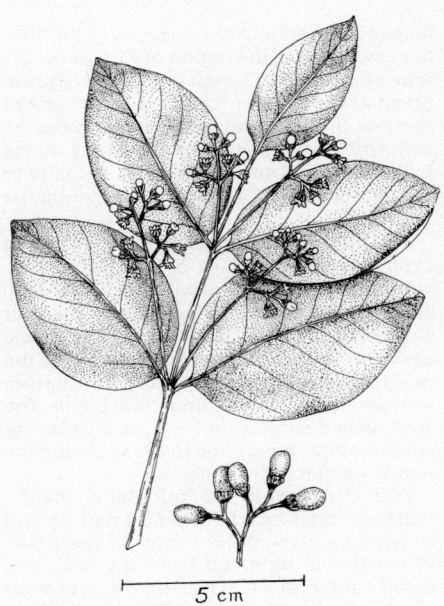

5 cm

remember a band-sawyer endeavouring to cut through a piece and the hot blue smoke nearly suffocated him. After ten minutes the saw was burnt and useless. (Before the days of TCT saw teeth!)

To round off this series, which could go on almost indefinitely, I have decided to mention one more family, the Sterculiaceae, named from *stercus* — Latin for dung. Some of the species of *Sterculia* bear flowers which smell like it!

This family includes the cocoa tree and various woods such as mankulang, ptery-

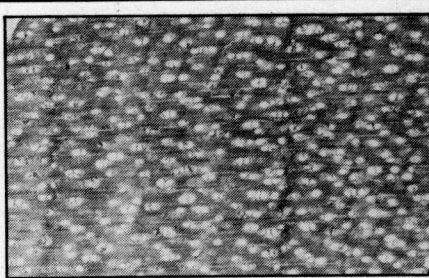

● Cross section ×3.3

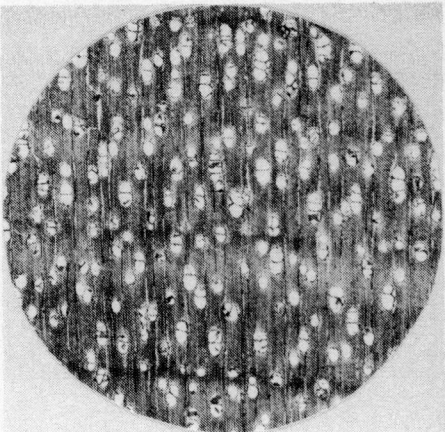

● Cross section ×10

gota, niangon and the red and yellow sterculias, familiar in the manufacture of plywood.

It also provides two well-known timbers which are distinctly different in character — obeche and mansonia. These two were formerly placed in separate families, Triplochitonaceae and Buettneriaceae respectively, but have recently been grouped with the sterculias. Both are quite distinctive; obeche is from a jungle giant in West Africa, noted for its large sizes and its light weight. The botanical name *Triplochiton scleroxylon* appears to be a misnomer, *scleros* — hard *xylon* — wood! The flower has an epicalyx of bracts, thus three protective elements — *triplo* — three, *chiton* — a coat of mail. Perhaps the specific name *scleroxylon* refers to the hard coating of the flower?

Mansonia has been compared with walnut, being of dark colour. This, however, soon fades in sunlight to a nondescript pale drab. ■

WORKSHOP WAYS   by Bob Grant

Dowels used to peg joints need to be grooved along their edges to allow excess glue to squeeze out. The dowel groover shown in the sketch is made from a suitable block of hardwood drilled out to receive the commoner sizes of rod. From either side and staggered in height are woodscrews with their points just protruding into the holes. The dowel lengths may be driven through with a hammer and wooden plug. Each length will be double grooved ready for use.

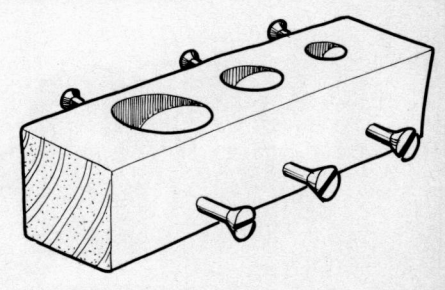

From the wood

Phil Sunderland describes
how a retired bowling wood
can be recycled to make a
businesslike
carver's mallet

● *Boring the hole for the shaft*

The ideal carver's mallet is a small, compact but heavy tool. Compact because it is often used in confined spaces, and heavy enough to give a positive blow to the chisel when cutting hard or problem timber. A hammer or metal headed mallet springs to mind at once as being the answer, but these would of course damage the handles of the chisels and gouges. A heavy timber must therefore be used, the heavier the better.

All heavier timbers however, such as boxwood, padauk, African blackwood, ebony and so on, fall into the category of exotic timbers, and therefore become both expensive and difficult to obtain. One exotic timber, however, I managed to obtain cheaply and easily. This was lignum vitae, which I found in a junk shop in the shape of an old bowling wood. It was not complete but that did not really matter as the bowl still had to be reduced, therefore removing any defects from the surface. Several cracks were visible along the grain but these turned out to be surface cracks.

Lignum vitae is an ideal timber for a mallet because it is one of the hardest and

heaviest timbers. After seasoning the timber can weigh in the region of 77lb per cubic foot, compared to beech which averages at about 45lb per cubic foot. It is in fact one of the few timbers that when fully seasoned will sink in water. It is an extremely dense oily timber and so causes quick damage to cutting edges. Constant resharpening is required.

The first stage in making the mallet is to centralise the bowl in a four-jaw chuck, supporting the free end with a revolving tail centre. It is possible to split away the four sides of the bowl if it is too big for the chuck, easily done with a chisel and a mallet as the grain of the bowl runs vertically, and lignum vitae splits well in the tangential plane. The split pieces should be kept, as later some small wedges have to be made to wedge the mallet head to the shaft.

With the bowl in the four-jaw chuck the tailstock end is faced off using a parting tool to within a ½in of the centre of the bowl. When this is removed from the lathe the small curved piece is broken off, revealing the flat faced-off surface. The small uncut piece in the centre of the flat surface should be ignored. The bowl is removed from the chuck and turned round and then, with the support of the tail centre again, faced off in a similar manner at the other end. I thought it wise to use the tailstock all the time, even though it was held firmly enough in the chuck, because if it was knocked off-centre the size of the mallet head would have to have been reduced.

A hole is then bored through the lignum stock. The size of the hole depends on the size of mallet required, as a bigger and heavier mallet requires a thicker shaft. A 1in hole I thought adequate for the largest mallet that could be obtained from a bowl,

but this is of course a personal choice as some people prefer thick shafts and others thin. The hole is bored without taking the bowl from the chuck. A flat bit in a Jacob's chuck, with the lathe running at full speed, works but puts a lot of stress on the thin flat bit. A 1 in twist drill produces the best results, as its size leads to stability in boring. The hole should of course be bored all the way through the lignum stock. It is then removed from the lathe.

Ash or hickory is ideal for the shaft, as both timbers are tough, have good bending properties and tend to act as shock absorbers between the head and the user's hand. Length, diameter and shape of the handle again depend on the preference of the maker, and the size of the mallet.

The shaft is first turned into a cylinder between centres. At the tailstock end a spigot should be turned down to the same diameter as the hole through the head, and left about ½in longer than required. I left the shaping of the handle until later as a great deal of strength and stability were required for the next process. The shaft is removed from the lathe and the head placed on the

● *The shaft, showing the spigot*

● *The bowl in the chuck, with one end parted off*

spigot. This must be an extremely good fit for the next process to work properly, which is to turn the head to the correct shape as it turns on the shaft between centres. If it is a sloppy fit, it can be tightened by cutting right angled slots in the shaft for about half the length of the spigot. As the tailstock tightens these sawcuts will open and therefore grip the head on to the shaft.

Light cuts are required with a sharp gouge, as heavy cuts may cause the head to slip round on the shaft and cause friction burns. The tools have to be kept sharp all the time as a blunt tool can also cause the head to slip on the shaft.

The head should be tapered slightly towards the shaft and the corners rounded off. Lignum vitae can be brought up to a good finish by working through the grades of glasspaper, particularly if the final glass-papering is done along the grain.

With the head completed, the shaft is then parted off at both ends to about ½in to be cleaned off later by hand.

Head and shaft are now ready to be joined. If slots are already in the shaft, as described earlier, these can be used for the wedges, but if not they will have to be cut now. Half the depth of the head is about right for the cut and wedges should be placed at right angles to each other, forcing the shaft on to the inside of the head.

A finish is not really required on the mallet as lignum vitae is very resistant to most things because of the oil it contains; but a coat of linseed oil could do no harm to either head or shaft.

By using this process I was able to make three sizes of mallet, ranging from 2lb 2oz to

● *ABOVE: the head and shaft ready to be turned together*
● *BELOW: mallet completed except for hand work*

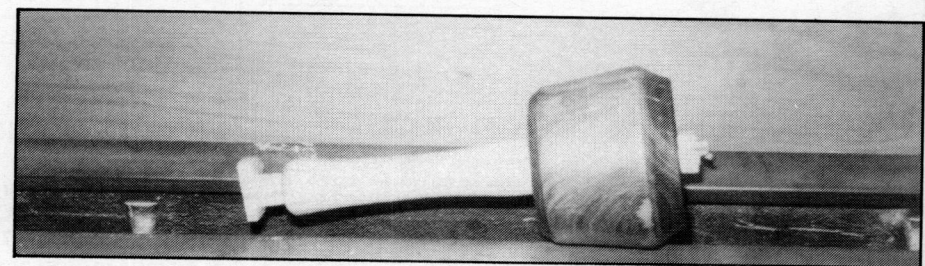

12oz. The small one was made from a rather badly damaged bowl with several deep cracks, but once these were turned out the centre was very solid.

Working in lignum vitae is very satisfying because despite its hardness it cuts very

easily, providing tools are kept sharp. Any pieces left after making the mallets such as the side pieces from the badly damaged bowl can quite easily be turned into key fobs or pendants, the denseness and colour of the timber being ideal for these articles. ■

Links in a chain

Charles Cliffe shows how to make a wooden chain

There is a certain fascination in solving puzzles and an even greater one in making puzzles for other people to solve. A chain constructed of wooden links is always a mystery — there must be a joint somewhere in the links, but why is it so hard to find? The straight answer is that there are no joints, and the chain is cut from the solid.

A piece of straight-grained timber is needed and this is planed truly to a square section of say 1½in square. Gauge the

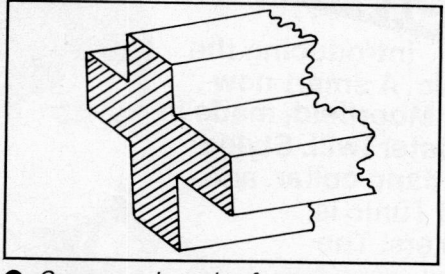

● *Corners rebated to form a cross*

length of the wood to about one third of its width and square the gauge marks across the ends as in Fig 1. The corners are then cut

away so that when viewed from the end the wood is in the shape of a cross (Fig 2). The links are then marked out on the tongues of the cross as in Fig 3 and the waste wood is chiselled away to form the ends of the links.

With a small drill, such as an Archimedean drill, vertical and diagonal holes are bored at A and B respectively. The blade of a fretsaw is threaded through holes A and the waste inside the links is sawn out. The waste between the links is carefully pared away with a sharp craft knife, the diagonal holes B facilitate this operation.

Once the links are separated, the square edges are rounded and glasspapered smooth. The chain is best left in the white so that it can readily be seen that the links are all solid and not joined. ■

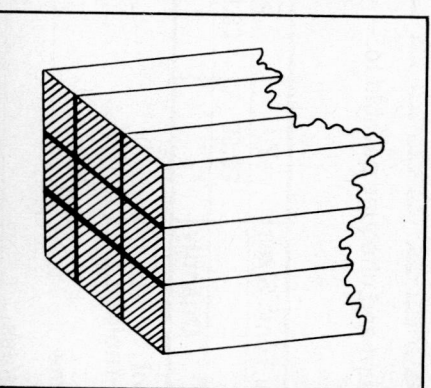

● *Square piece of wood gauged along length and across ends*

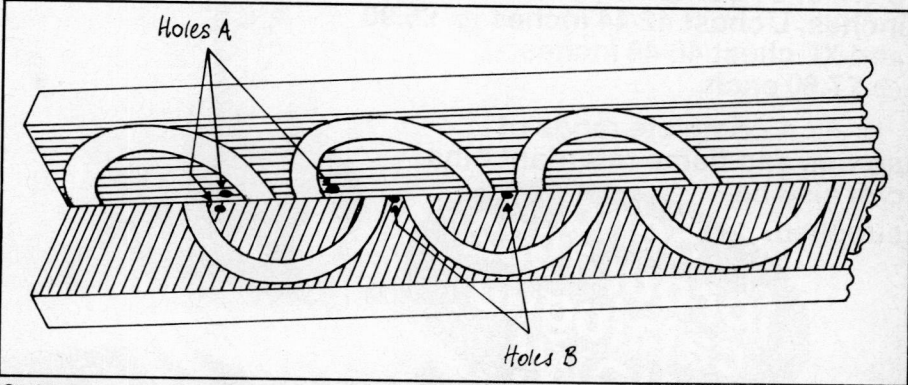

Holes A

Holes B

● *Links marked. Holes A drilled for fretsawing, holes B for paring*

The ELU MWA 149 will put a razor sharp edge on your Chisels and Plane Irons with the *added plus* - a highly useful Belt Linisher for little more than the cost of a conventional Grinder.

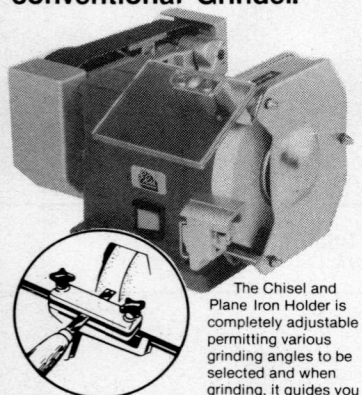

Pressure Plate Lowered
Allows the suppleness of the sanding belt to give on curved components.

The Chisel and Plane Iron Holder is completely adjustable permitting various grinding angles to be selected and when grinding, it guides you easily over the face of the stone.

The Grinder

The MWA 149 is equipped with a smooth and quiet induction type motor for production reliability and also accepts a wide variety of stones including white, green and G.P. in differing grit sizes.

The Linisher

This equipment provides the ability to effectively sand small components. There are 10 different grades of sanding belts available and the spring located roller controlled by a lever provides for quick belt changing. A leather Honing Belt is also available for putting a barber's edge on your Chisels and Plane Irons.

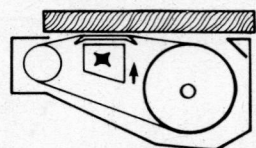

Pressure Plate Raised
Forces the belt rigid allowing the accurate sanding of flat surfaces.

More information:
The ELU MWA 149 Grinders are readily available from a nationwide network of over 200 authorised distributors. Contact us today for your free illustrated brochure and full list of ELU dealers.

ELU Machinery Ltd.,
310/312 Dallow Road,
LUTON, Beds.
LU1 1SS
Tel: (0582) 425001
Telex: 825540 ELU G

Elu INTERNATIONAL

PHOTOCOPY SERVICE

We are able to supply photocopies of articles from many past issues of WOODWORKER at a nominal cost of 15p a page (minimum 75p) plus 25p postage. Readers are asked to give month and year of the issue required to Mrs Anne Duncan at WOODWORKER office which is PO Box 35, Bridge Street, Hemel Hempstead HP1 1EE (0442 41221).

We cannot guarantee to supply photocopies from all past issues as unfortunately the office files of back-numbers are not complete.

Prices quoted are those prevailing at press date and are subject to alteration due to economic conditions.

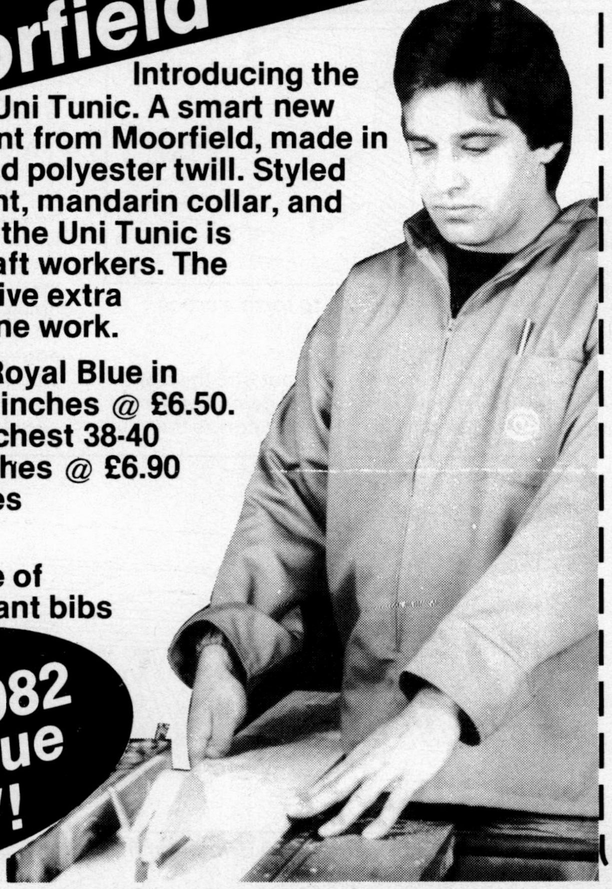

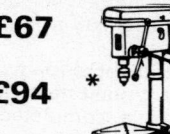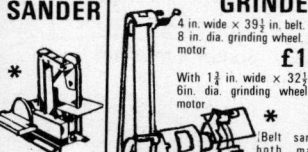

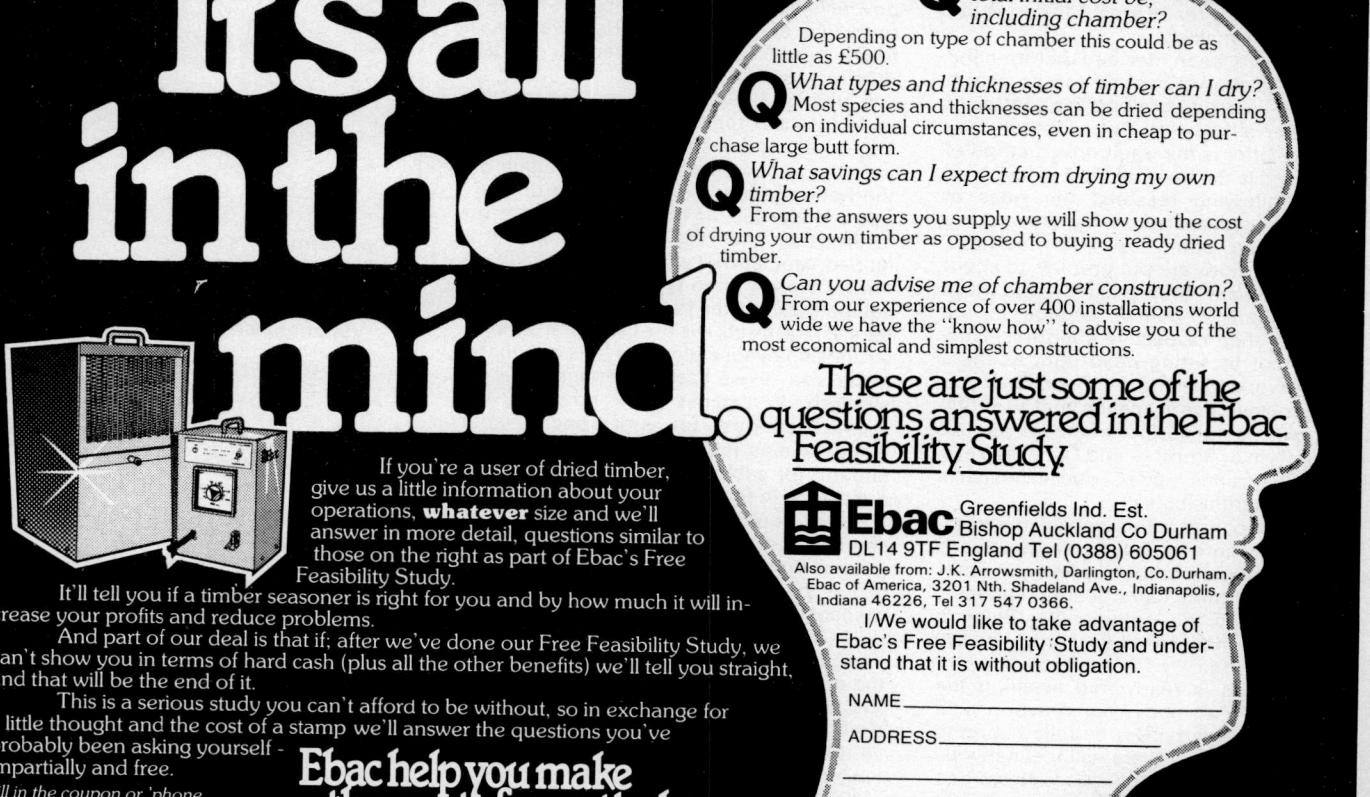

Making drawers the proper way

Stan Thomas explains the principles of good drawer making — illustrated with a few of his inimitable anecdotes along the way

'Assisting with making draws', wrote a fellow apprentice of mine (who was, hopefully, a better drawer maker than he was a speller!) upon his timesheet.

His 'draws' must have long since worn out, for this was back in the primeval dawn of 1936. I was a year senior to him — and far too superior for tea making — having climbed the stepladder up to the workshop on the cold morning of 4 November 1935. At the top of the steps we passed through a one-time shop door (it was a shopfitting establishment, so shop doors abounded.) They fed our combustion stove, and gave us at least some measure of psychological comfort through the winter months. But this was a half-glazed door, and across the glass, in great bold letters, was the word CAKE.

There were two snobby glue pots, which repeatedly boiled over and put out the gas; just above us were the bare, dusty rafters and slated roof, and there were enough mice to immortalise every poet in the world!

So the outward appearance of our door had a most unlikely association with what went on behind, but the men who climbed those steps each morning were among the very best hand craftsmen. (One of them had the charming idiosyncrasy of constantly licking the scotch glue off his hammer head!) Everything was done by hand, except morticing. My weekly pay was six shillings (30p). My weekly train fare was five shillings (25p) — so with the remaining shilling I could buy my tools!

However, I am really meant to be talking about drawer-making.

It will have been decided before-hand whether the drawers are to run on centre runners — ie grooves along the centres of the drawer sides — or upon bottom runners. The latter is the traditional method of course, and is the one I've always favoured for the following reasons: the sides of mass-produced, centrerunning drawers are usually about 9mm (⅜in) in thickness. Along these sides are put grooves to about half-depth — say 4mm (³⁄₁₆in) — and these grooves then of course engage in the runners of their respective apertures. Now they cannot be fitting dead tight as there must be working clearance. But even if you discount clearance it means that the total bearing (running) surface of the drawer is 2 × ³⁄₁₆in (⅜in or 9mm) — and I've even seen such drawer sides made of obechi, which is almost as hard as balsa!

Well now, compare this with the traditional method, where the full thickness of each drawer side, plus runners, takes the bearing. We have three extra bearing surfaces, or three times the running life. Being a traditionalist then, I shall deal only with the bottom running.

The carcase is ready and awaiting the drawers. Now a wooden construction such as our carcase can never be relied upon to be square all ways; there will inevitably be small discrepancies of squareness and dimension, in the drawer apertures. So each drawer front must be carefully planed to fit its respective place, then, on its *face* numbered for identification, with corresponding numbers upon the front rails of the apertures. The backs, which should be 25mm (1in) or so narrower than the fronts, can be cut and planned to suit their respective fronts, then numbered on their *back* faces. These numbers are to remain permanent for all future identification. This of course, is high-class hand cabinetmaking; as opposed to mass production.

So we have the fronts and backs ready; now the sides. An important point here, is their length. I have seen a completed cabinet (not mine!) with its drawers protruding 12mm (½in) or so. What a shattering experience it must be, after all the work, to discover that one's drawer sides were cut too long. Guard against this by cutting them 12mm or so shorter than the maximum permissible length. Widths of course should be as fronts.

Now let's look at the grooving of the sides and front; there is no groove in the back. There are two methods of doing this, according to personal preference. Fig 1 shows the joiner's usual method and the cabinetmaker's. But note in each the earlier-mentioned runners, which provide that all-important extra bearing. If the joiner's method is decided upon, the grooving is best done now at this early stage, for it facilitates the pin-marking of the back and the front lap dovetails can also be set out to suit the groove position.

In the trade, it was usual to pin together three pairs of sides, and to saw their dovetails all in one operation and this is a quick way of doing the job. However, most today would, I think, prefer to cut the drawers one at a time.

A pair of sides should be pinned with inside faces together, being carefully aligned along their *bottom* (groove) edges, then their ends planed square — again off the bottom edges. The joint for a drawer-front, is the lap dovetail; but we can go further than that. We can say that it is a lapped *cabinet-maker's* dovetail; for there are (or were!) three types of dovetail: the cabinetmaker's, the joiners and the carpenter's. Of the three, it is the carpenter's that is strongest because pins and tails are all the same size — we sacrifice appearance for strength. In cabinet work however, we sacrifice strength for appearance — but what remains is more than amply strong enough for cabinet work. The three joints are shown in Fig 2.

Having squared the ends, a cutting gauge should be set to side thickness, and a cut gauged right around the front ends, and just across the two faces of the back ends. Any marking gauge can be easily converted to dual marking/cutting, by inserting and wedging a strip of hacksaw blade through the opposite end of the stem from the pin. And in using a cutting gauge, the bevel of the knife must always be towards the waste, so that a good square cut is obtained into which the chisel will drop, as shown in Fig 3.

Now it may be assumed that anyone who is making a cabinet which is to have a

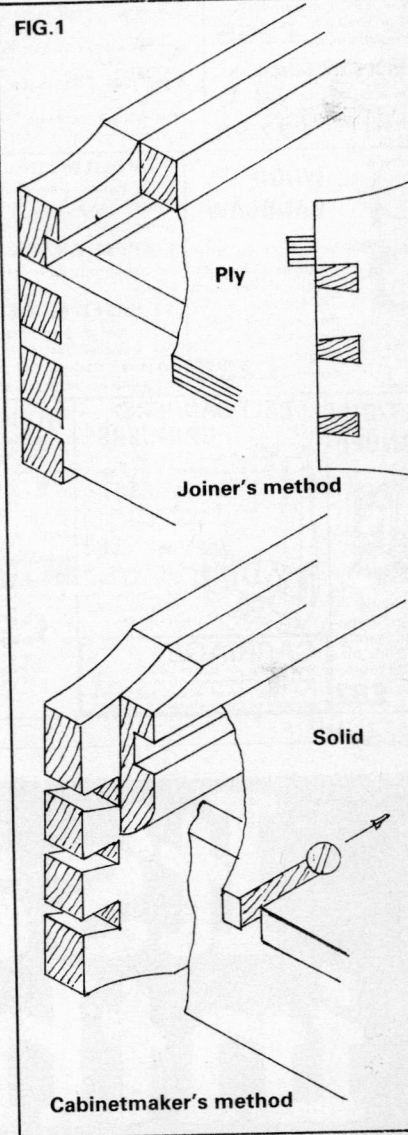

FIG.1

Ply

Joiner's method

Solid

Cabinetmaker's method

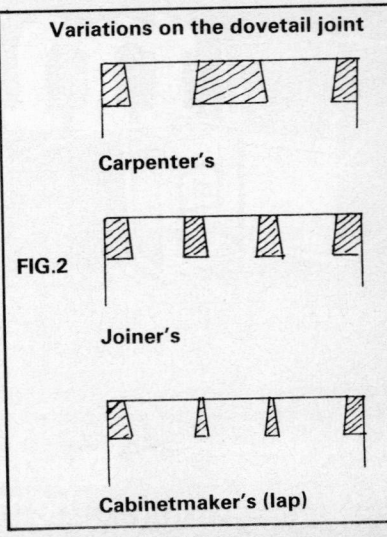

Variations on the dovetail joint

Carpenter's

FIG.2

Joiner's

Cabinetmaker's (lap)

number of drawers is already familiar with the lap dovetail. But setting-out methods do vary, and there are probably the few who are still a little hazy on procedure.

The pair of sides are placed vertically in the vice and lines squared across the ends, about 9mm (⅜in) from each edge. The intermediate space is divided into a number of equal parts, depending upon the number of tails required — obviously, the more the stronger. Upon these secondary lines the saw is placed for both right-hand, and left-hand, sawing (ie having sawn one splay, the saw is put into the same cut again for the opposite splay. Fig 4).

This is what produces the fine, elegant cabinetmaker's lap dovetail. Chopping and cutting away the waste is of course, common practice, but the multiple cutting-away shown in Fig 4 can only be done for these outside pieces. The intermediates must be done individually, *after* the pins have been marked by dropping the saw into each cut, and drawing it across the end of the member being marked.

In the sawing of the fronts, many people place the front vertically in the vice, and go down on their knees to do this inclined sawing. Instead, the timber should be placed *sideways* in the vice, and inclined at about 45°. The tail sockets can now be sawn comfortably, in the standing position. (Similarly, it is the practice of a novice to get up and kneel upon the bench for cutting a sheet of material. Either stand the sheet vertically — slightly inclined away — against the bench, or inclined across the bench. There is no need for the operator to get up upon the bench.)

So much for the front and two sides; now the back. Joiner's dovetails should be used for this. It is made narrower for two reasons: firstly, with the drawer glued up the bottom will have to slide in underneath it; secondly, the space along the back's top edge will allow the air to escape while the drawer is being closed. Without it, the closing of one drawer might cause another to open slightly. When marking the backs then, the bottom edge of the back must be kept in line with the top of the groove, as shown in Fig 1. And before assembly, all inner faces should of course be cleaned up and glasspapered.

Now we come to the bottoms: solid timber or ply? Well, it's mostly ply nowadays. This can be glued around the three grooves, then the runners glued into place. If of solid timber however, the grain *must* run parallel to the front, and it should protrude a little past the drawer back. Glue must be confined to the *front groove only;* it should also be fixed by the cabinet method (ie 'planted' grooves) for separate glued runners would impede its shrinkage movement, thus causing the bottom to split. And to further allow for shrinkage, the bottom should be fixed along the back, by slotted screws, see Fig 1. After glue-set, the final cleaning-up will give the required working clearance between drawer and carcase.

The only *outer* part of the drawer that may be glasspapered, is the front — its face, top edge and each end (across the lap 'tails). Similarly, painting or polishing should be confined to this — for any 'finish' would cause friction, while any glasspapering of

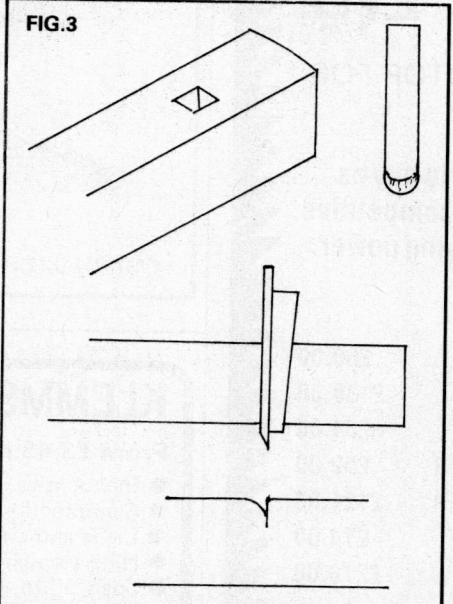

FIG.3

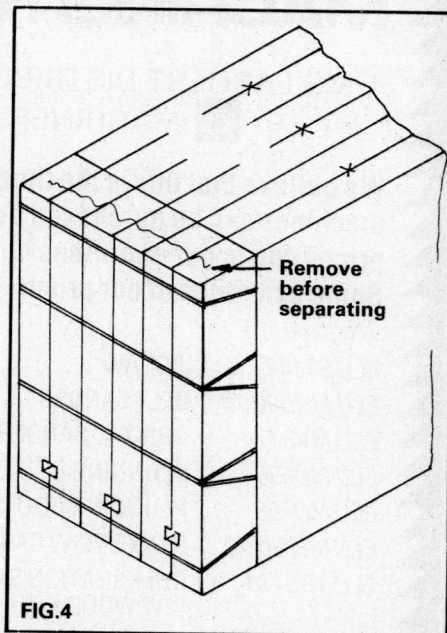

Remove before separating

FIG.4

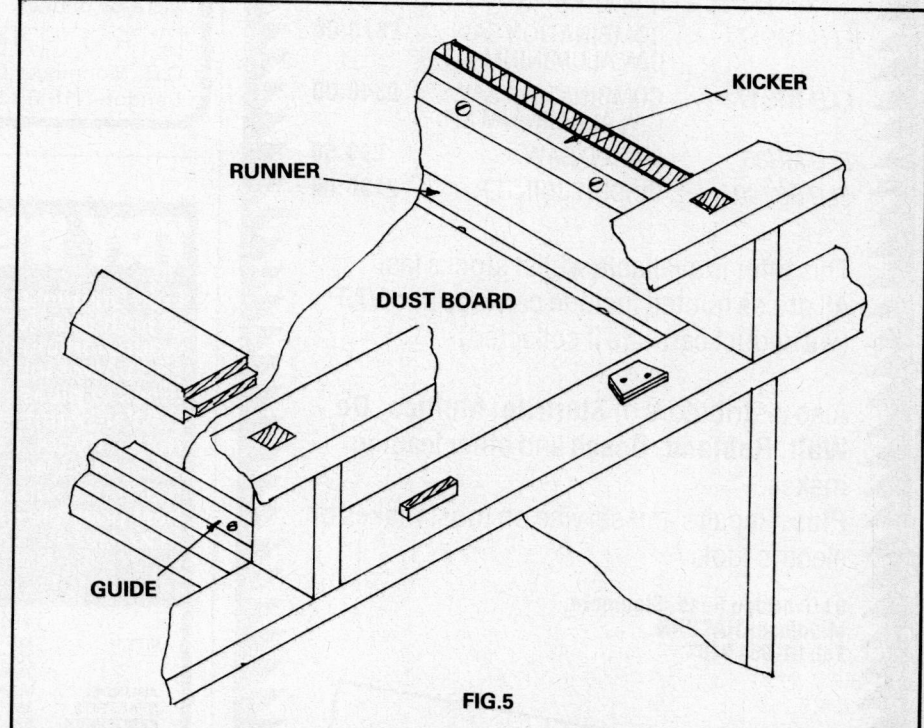

KICKER

RUNNER

DUST BOARD

GUIDE

FIG.5

the sides would produce abrasive surfaces.

Drawers should never be set to finish flush with the face of the carcase, but should be set back — say about 2mm. In this way a shadow is formed that hides the slight clearance gap around the front. Finally of course, all bearing surfaces should be well rubbed with candle wax. Stops can be either of ply, glued and tacked, or of end-grain bits of timber let into mortices. And for a really good job, 'dust boards' should be fitted (grooved all round) as Fig 5.

Drawers can be notorious swellers or shrinkers. Many years ago I was sent to a

house to try and do something to a lady's dressing table. They'd been away for a few weeks, and the house had been unoccupied — this was before we all became central-heating fanatics. Well, we'd had some damp weather, and the drawers in her dressing table had swollen tight. I failed to ease them — even by removing the back of the carcase, and trying to push them back. And, I was informed, most of her spare underwear was in those drawers!

But there was no more that I could do — not without damage to the piece. It was a long time before she finally retrieved her frillies! ■

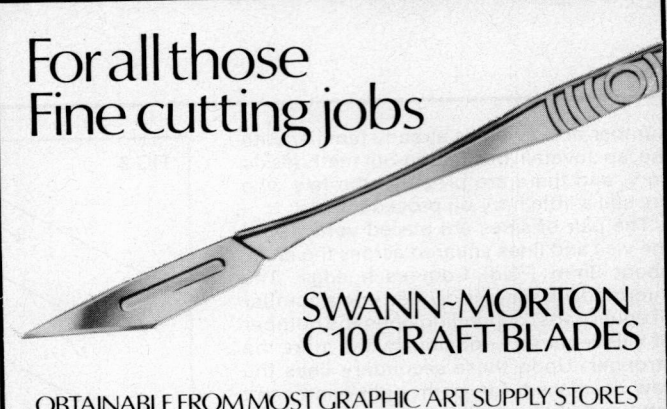
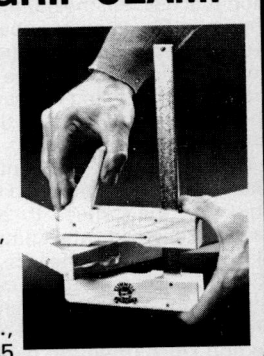

Prices quoted are those prevailing at press date and are subject to alteration due to economic conditions.

THE CLASSIC WORKBENCH FROM SJÖBERGS

Model BS 142, one
of a range to suit all needs.

Crafted in Sweden from selected beech, birch and pine by the world's leading suppliers of timberframe workbenches.

Precision machined for accuracy, kiln dried timber for stability, and constructed to give you long years of outstanding service.

Thoughtful design to a traditional concept offers you greater versatility, even from a wheelchair.

Send for our catalogue today and see for yourself the advantages which a Sjöbergs bench would offer you.

A letter or postcard will bring a speedy reply.

Scan Marketing Limited, Elstow Storage Depot, Kempston Hardwick, BEDFORD MK45 3NX Tel. 0234 741960 — 24 hour answering service

---

SARJENTS TOOLS

MASSIVE SALE
NOW ON
(Must end 2nd Oct.)

There are thousands of genuine unrepeatable bargains in our **biggest ever** clearance sale.

We recommend an early visit and browse around; however, for those unable to visit one of our branches a comprehensive postal sale list is available from: Sarjents Tools, Dept. S, Oxford Road, Reading.

All sale bargains offered on a first-come, first-served basis.

Access and Barclaycard welcome

44-52 Oxford Road, Reading (0734) 586522
62-64 Fleet Street, Swindon (0793) 31361
150 Cowley Road, Oxford (0865) 45118

SARJENTS TOOLS

Open 6 days a week
from 8.30 until 5.30

Prices liable to change without notice

Roger's Mail Order Catalogue

Still the best way to buy all your specialist tools through the post.

You may save money on petrol with other mail order catalogues but with Roger's Mail Catalogue you save on the price of the tools as well. With 160 pages showing over 1400 Specialist Woodcraft Tools at realistic prices all by top quality manufacturers, National and International, giving you the widest range of Specialist Woodcraft tools available through the post.

So why pay more for your tools through the post when Roger's Mail Order Catalogue can save you money.

Send for your Catalogue today and see what we offer. UK and Eire send £1.50 inc. p&p for overseas £3.00 in sterling.

Cost of catalogue refunded on your first order over £30.00.

Fill in your name and address and post the coupon back to us with your remittance.

Roger's Department W. 47, Walsworth Road, Hitchin. Hertfordshire SG4 9SU. Telephone: Hitchin (0462) 4177

Name:...

Address: ....

....

Roger's Department W
47, Walsworth Road, Hitchin.
Hertfordshire SG4 9SU
Telephone: Hitchin (0462) 4177

COMPLETE CLOCK KITS FROM UNDER £30

CLOCKMAKING HOLIDAYS

Now you can build a beautiful bracket, wall or long case clock at home, from our wide range of original designs.

Prices start at less than £30, including V.A.T., and the kits include:-

fully machined timber components

dial

movement

fittings

decorations

instructions and sandpaper

Buy direct from the manufacturer and get real value for money.

Combine a course in clock case making with a holiday in the breathtakingly beautiful High Peak National Park.

You can build yourself a clock under expert supervision in our brand new specialist workshop, set in a pretty village, and the rest of the family can enjoy the pleasures of walking, fishing, sightseeing, riding, cycling, sailing — a perfect holiday with something to show at the end of it!

We can offer packages including self-catering accommodation or hotel comfort: just state your preference and leave the rest to us.

For full details, send 1st class stamp to: Paul Eden Clocks (Dept WW), Buxton Road, Buxton, Derbyshire.

Hitachi: a cut above the rest

CS-280A

Specifications:
Bar size: 280mm (12")
Power input: 1,140 W
Power speed: 450 m/min. (1,475 ft/min.)

CS-350A

Specifications:
Bar size: 350mm (14")
Power input: 1,140 W
Chain speed: 450 m/min. (1,475 ft/min.)

Hitachi Power Tools (UK) Ltd., Unit 8,
Hampton Farm Industrial Estate, Bolney Way,
Feltham, Middlesex, TW13 6DB. Telephone: 01-894 1236.

HITACHI
POWER TOOLS

NOBELS WOODLATHE

*Available with
or without
legs*

* ★ 500 or 1,000 mm between centres, or any length to order
* ★ 400 mm turning diameter
* ★ 1 HP motor (Single phase)
* ★ 4 ideally stepped speeds
* ★ various attachments available
* ★ **VERY COMPETITIVE RATES**

Main U.K. & C.I. distributors

JOHN BLOM & SON

**Hallgate Holbeach
Spalding, Lincs.
Tel: 0406 23769**

*ALL TRADE ENQUIRIES
WELCOMED*

Here's an easier way to construct cabinets with perfectly solid joints – the revolutionary <u>new</u> Elu Flat Dowel Jointing System.

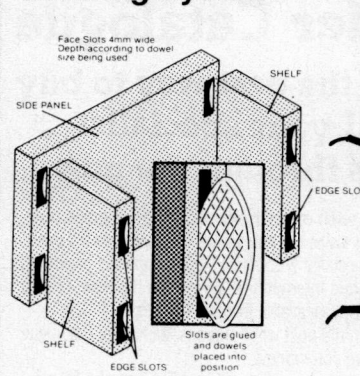

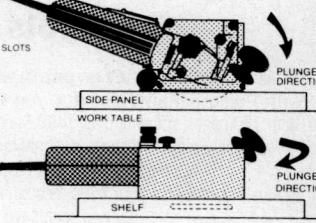

Simple to use

Marked lines on the sole plate allow easy machine location. Make a simple plunge cut producing a slot ready to accept the dowel.

How it works

The Elu Flat Dowels are manufactured from Hardwood (Beech) compressed into shape with the grain running diagonally thus providing the strength along its centre. When the dowel is fitted it absorbs the glue resulting in a solid joint. Slots allow the lining up of edges not possible with conventional round dowels.

Standard Equipment:

* *Steel Carrying Case
* *Super Hard TCT Grooving Blade
* *Parallel Guide
* *Saw Insert
* *Instruction Book
* *Special Mitre Guide

FREE!

Special Guide for slotting mitred edges

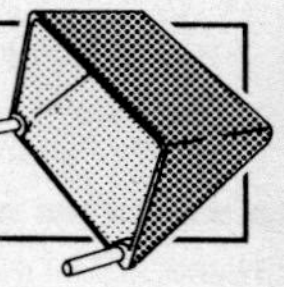

More information:
The ELU DS140 and Dowels are readily available from a nationwide network of over 200 authorised distributors. Contact us today for your free illustrated brochure and full list of Elu dealers.

Elu Machinery Ltd.,
310-312 Dallow Road,
LUTON,
Beds. LU1 1SS.
Tel: (0582) 425001
Telex: 825540 ELU G.

Model Engineer Exhibition

1-9 Jan `83
Open 10am-7pm
Late night Thurs.6th until 9pm

Wembley Conference Centre

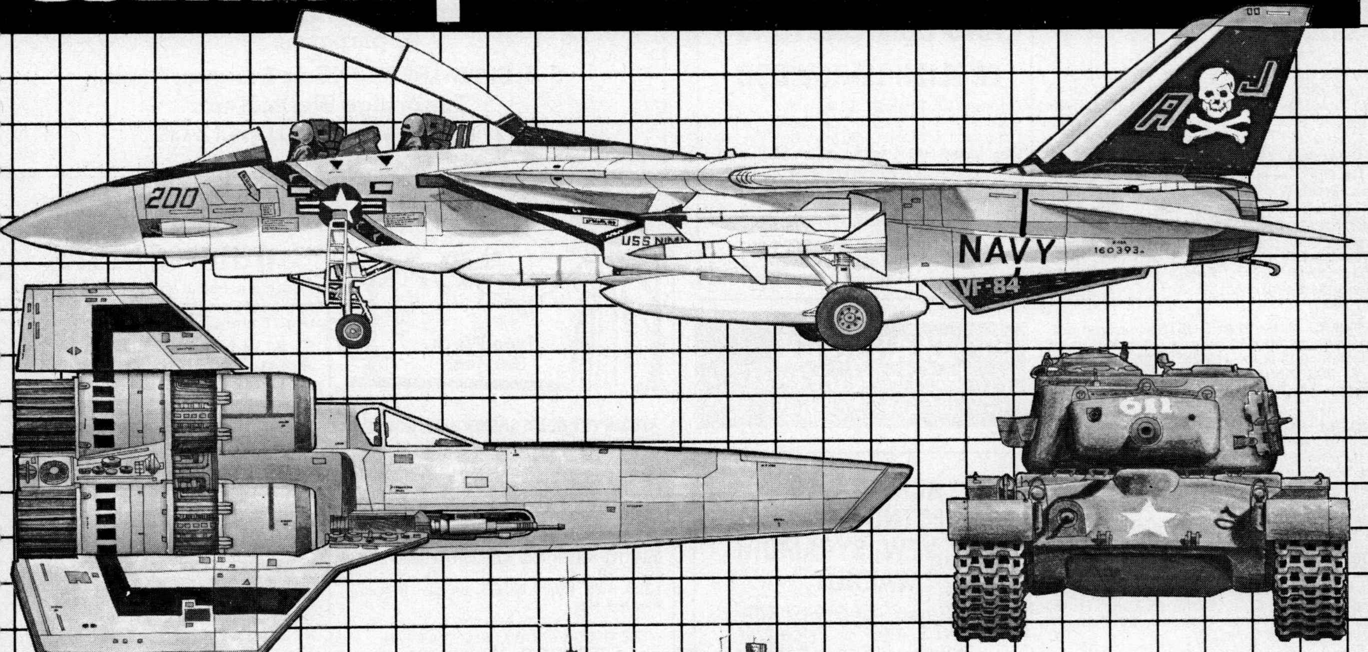

LECTURES AND FILMS • OVER 1000 MODELS • MODEL COMPETITIONS
TRADE STANDS • MODEL BOATS & CARS IN ACTION • MODEL TRAMWAY
WORKING MODEL RAILWAY • MODEL FLYING • STEAM TRAIN RIDES
To be opened by David Shepherd OBE • Adults £2. Children & OAP's £1.50

It is regretted that for safety reasons no prams or pushchairs can be admitted.However limited pram parking space is available.

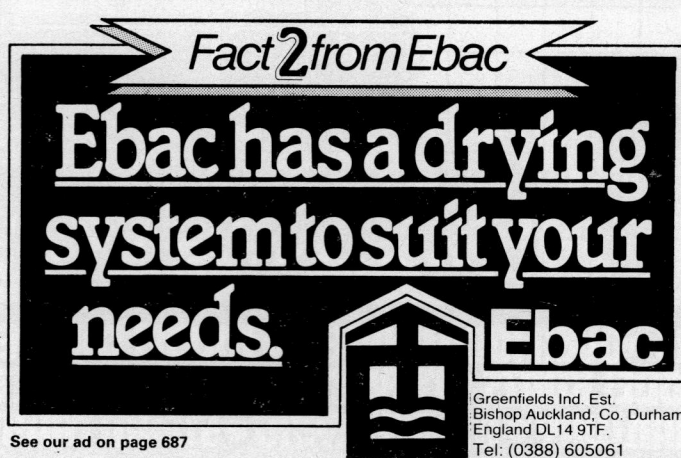

MADE IN ENGLAND!

Wheelers Limited, established in 1860, traditional suppliers of English oak to the furniture industry.

Comprehensive supplies are always available from large stocks of through and through air dried material

Fast drying facilities are also available, using a modern vacuum kiln.

Why not ring us to discuss your English oak requirements today?

Wheelers Limited
CHILTON - SUDBURY - SUFFOLK CO10 6XH
Tel: 0787 73391 (9 lines) - Telex: 987893

FOSS GLEN FORESTRY
Air Dried British Hardwoods

Burr Yew ● Burr Field Maple ● Bog Oak ● Mulberry ● Lacewood ● plus many other varieties.
For current catalogue ring.

MICHAEL GRIFFITH 024289 422
4 Kings Head Lane, Withington, Glos. GL54 4BD

Rustic Woodslices

For House Signs, Wall Plaques, etc., seasoned hardwoods. Sawn obliquely with Bark on, up to 30" long **£2.00 each or three for £5.00.** Post Free.
A. CRACKNELL
2 ORFORD ROAD, BROMESWELL, WOODBRIDGE, SUFFOLK.

LIMEHOUSE TIMBER SALES
TEAK MAHOGANY IROKO OAK ETC ETC JOINERY SOFTWOODS

"TIMBERAMA" customer self-selection area with a wide variety of species and dimensions

MON-FRI: 9am-5pm
SAT: 9am-3pm
INTERESTING TIMBERS BOUGHT AND SOLD

a division of:
DAVEY AND COMPANY
5 GRENADE STREET
LONDON E14 8HL   01-987 1837

CRAFTWOODS
Good stocks of many hardwoods, — Bubinga, Lime, Ebony, Maple, Rosewood, Wenge, Padauk, Oaks, Sycamore, Kingwood, Tulipwood, Lignum Vitae, Pau Brauna, Yew. Available in boards, slabs, squares and veneers.
Visit our sawmill and inspect and select from stock or send SAE for stock list to

CRAFTWOODS
Midslade Sawmills, Forest Road, Hartwell, Northants.
Tel: Northampton 862133

HEXHAMSHIRE HARDWOODS
Seasoned English hardwoods for Northeast England and Scotland. Hardwoods for Turning and Carving
Telephone: (After 4pm)
Slaley (043473) 585

R&S WOODCRAFTS
A service for the small user. First quality kiln dried hardwoods. American and Japanese Oak, Mahogany, Ash, Maple, Teak, Beech etc. *S.A.E. List,* **77 Lime Tree Avenue, Tile Hill, Coventry CV4 9EZ** or telephone **(0203) 461491** evenings and weekends only.

JOHN BODDY & SON (TIMBER) LTD.
offer
Direct from our Sawmill and Kilns

BRITISH HARDWOODS
As one of the few British Timber Merchants specialising in the production of kiln dried hardwoods in planking and dimension stock.

We invite craftsmen to inspect and select from our stock of over 30,000 cubic feet of kiln dried timber. Stored under cover.

APPLE, ASH, BEECH, CEDAR OF LEBANON, CHERRY, SWEET CHESTNUT, ELM, BURR ELM, LARCH, LIME, OAK, BURR OAK, PEAR, SYCAMORE, RIPPLE SYCAMORE, WALNUT and YEW.

available from stock in most thicknesses

Please send for our Stock List or call and inspect Open Monday to Friday 8 a.m. - 5 p.m. Saturday 8 a.m. - 12 noon

Riverside Sawmills,
Boroughbridge, YO5 9LJ, North Yorkshire.
Telephone (09012) 2370 Telex 57526

TIMBER
cut to your requirements
We cut and prepare to your cutting list

TEAK, OAK, ROSEWOOD, MAHOGANY, BEECH, BOXWOOD, etc. —VENEERS and PLYWOODS

We carry large stocks of dry hardwoods for cabinet and joinery trade. Turning done to your drawing. Brassware and cabinet fittings available.

Open all day Saturday — early closing Thursday.
Send S.A.E. with your cutting list for quote.

GENERAL WOODWORK SUPPLIES
Dept. W.W., 76-80 STOKE NEWINGTON HIGH STREET, LONDON N16   Phone: 01-254 6052

CLASSIFIED
Telephone Valerie Tester
(0442) 41221 Ext. 262

Continued Overleaf

YORKSHIRE HARDWOODS

KILN DRIED HARDWOOD FOR CRAFTSMEN

We specialize in English Oak and other Native hardwoods and can supply waney edged boards, dimensioned stock and blanks for turning and carving.

Yorkshire Hardwoods Limited
Pocklington Grange,
Bielby Lane, Pocklington, York YO4 2NT

Pocklington
075 92-2870

Earn £200 per hour drying timber with your own kiln...

My seasoners need so little attention that your time could hardly be better spent than by drying your own timber. Can you afford to invest a few hundred pounds in order to guarantee your work is stable in central heating and ensure that your English hardwoods will cost half as much for many years to come.

No need to keep large untidy stacks of timber slowly drying and spoiling for years and years — these machines work from green in a few weeks and cost only a few pence per cubic foot to run.

The smallest seasoner costs less than £340 and will dry enough timber to keep several people busy or make you some money selling surplus timber. It can live outside and does not usually need a box much larger than 8' × 4' × 4'. As I am the man who developed these machines, I hope that my information, prices, references etc., are second to none.
Write for details or ring me any time for answers to your questions completely without obligation.

JOHN ARROWSMITH

74 Wilson Street, Darlington,
Co. Durham DL3 6QZ. Tel: 0325 481970

VENEERS, inlay bandings, stringing and marquetry panels. Large selection. *Mail order and callers welcome. S.A.E. for list.*
R. AARONSON (VENEERS) LTD
45 Redchurch St., London E2.
Tel: 01-739 3107

HAVE ENGLISH YEW
(Will Haggle)

1000 cu ft — Come and choose from wide variety of sizes. Well Seasoned. Loads of Offcuts. Schools supplied.
Callers made welcome anytime.
"The more the cheaper"
W. Pearson, ASHLEY MOOR HALL,
ORLETON, Nr. LUDLOW, SHROPSHIRE.
Tel: Yarpole 236

WOODSTOCK (HARDWOODS) S.W.

HARDWOOD – *Ring us first*

Supplied to your cutting list or per cubic foot.
Both English and imported timbers.
ASHFIELD, PONSHARDEN, FALMOUTH, CORNWALL
Telephone: (0326) 312915

British Hardwoods

Kiln Dried—Air Dried—Fresh Sawn

Specialising in Kiln Dried Oak

Sawn to size and delivery arranged

For details and quotations apply to:

R.E. & R. Duffield & Sons Ltd.,

The Boathouse, River View Road,
Ripon, N. YORKS.
Tel: (0765) 3667

or our Sales Depot at:

The Old Creamery, Currock Road,
CARLISLE. Tel: (0228) 46478

ENGLISH HARDWOODS

Oak, Ash, Sycamore, Beech etc. Air & Kiln dried
All sizes in stock
HOGHTON TIMBER
HIGHER WALTON TRADING ESTATE
PRESTON, LANCS.
Tel: Preston 36193

VENEERS

SHORT AND FULL LEAVES
In all popular timbers. Send S.A.E. for FREE price list or 55p for samples of 12 pieces 4" × 3" to:
ELLIOTT BROS
Four Winds, Moorwoods Lane, Dore
All letters to PO Box No. 6, Glossop,
Derby. *Reg. No. 2064782*

Broughton—Head Timber Ltd

Unit 7,
W & G Estate, Challow,
Wantage, Oxon, OX12 9TF.

correspondence to:
2 Elizabeth Drive,
Wantage, Oxon, OX12 9YA.
Tel: 02357-67811

Kiln dried and air dried stocks including English and American Oak, English Ash, Cedar, Cherry, Apple, Pear, Plum, Lacewood, Chestnut, Walnut, Elm, Sycamore, Yew, Larch and Beech.
We specialise in small quantities.   Please telephone or send stamp for details

---

To:
Valerie Tester, Woodworker,
PO Box 35, Bridge Street,
Hemel Hempstead,
HP1 1EE

PLEASE NOTE
On lineage advertisements, copy to be submitted (pre-paid) with this form.

Full page £300 □ Half page £160 □ Quarter page £88 □ Eighth page £50 □
Semi-display £4·00 per single column cm (minimum £10·00)   Lineage rate
20p per word (minimum £3·00)   Series discounts available on request.
No. of insertions _____   Name _____
Address _____
Semi-display size _____ cms   Tel. No. _____

AEG Introduce a NEW Professional Woodworking System

The heart of our system is the motor, which drives the circular saw, the spindle moulder, the planer/thicknesser, the lathe and the band saw. We don't believe you should pay for motors you don't need. With the economical AEG MULTI Woodworking System you purchase just one motor that is interchangeable from one machine to another. AEG look after your power tool requirements and your pocket too!

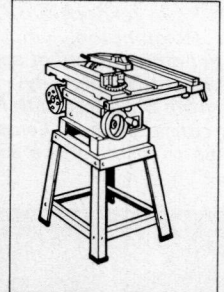

Circular Saw
Model No. SC25

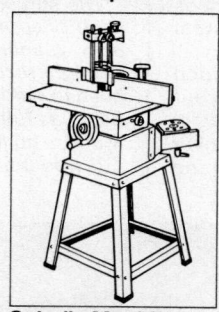

Spindle Moulder
Model No. T30N

Thicknesser
Model No. C260

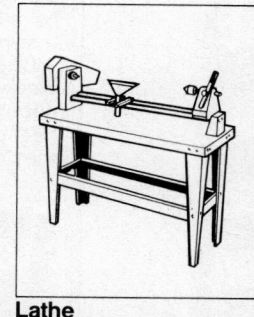

Lathe
Model No. TBJ

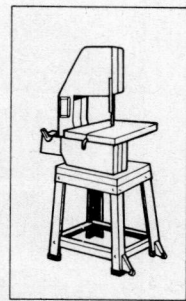

Band Saw
Model No. SR250

The AEG MULTI Woodworking System can be built up as you require it. Purchase your first machine (usually the planer/thicknesser or the circular saw) and the motor, and Hey Presto — you are on your way to owning a full professional woodworking system. You can then add to it at your leisure — it makes good sense!

Other machines in our Professional Woodworking programme include: The AEG UNIVERSAL range. The C2100 and C2600 machines will tackle all woodworking jobs on a unique operation selector system. Both described fully in our new Woodworking Programme brochure: For your own personal copy complete the coupon below and send to: AEG TELEFUNKEN (UK) LTD., Power Tools, 217, Bath Road, Slough, Berkshire, SL1 4AW.

Please send me details of your New Woodworking Programme.

Name_____

Address_____

_____

_____ W

AEG Electric Power Tools

OFFCUTS

by Chris Dunn

Tops to the bottomer

'Hello,' thought Graham Nichols when he spotted a photograph of a Gimson chair in the Woodworker Annual *for 1980. 'I know that chair.'*

So he wrote to me from his present home in Melbourne, Australia: 'From the picture I recognised the ladderback armchair by Ernest Gimson, now in the Victoria and Albert Museum, as being the one which I rush seated in June 1975. But the photograph is one taken before that time, still showing the old sea-grass seat which I removed.

'Because this is the only way work of mine, a humble bottomer, is capable of being shown among the high quality work of the kind which appears in your journal, I hope that one day the V&A will take a new picture of the Gimson chair.'

Well, Mr Nichols. Today's the day. Naturally I passed your letter on to the Department of Furniture and Fine Woodwork at the museum, and they responded by doing precisely as you suggested.

So it is with great pride that Offcuts can exclusively present 'The New Rush Seat' by top bottomer Graham Nichols, with grateful acknowledgements to the Victoria and Albert Museum.

And to E. Gimson, of course.

● *Ernest Gimson's ladderback armchair, with rush seat by Graham Nichols. Picture: V&A Museum, London*

Norristalgia

The piece in Offcuts/August about the last of the great Norris planes brought back some memories for A. W. Panario OBE, a Woodworker *reader from Worcester Park, Surrey, who used to work for T. Norris and Son before the war. Here is what he wrote to me:*

It was 1938 and I was 15 years old when I started work as a learner at the Chestnut Grove, New Malden, works of that great little firm. The last Norris had died a few years previously leaving the firm to be run by his widow. There were three master craftsmen: the boss, 'Rat' (Mr Ratcliff), 'Butch' (Tom Butcher) and another whose name now escapes me.

Demarcation of work was unknown; every man did every job — with distinction and dedication. There was a determined, almost fanatical attention to detail which, in my youthful innocence, I took to be the norm for British workmanship. Would that it were widespread today!

I recall the long days patiently fitting the dovetailed joints of the metal sides and face (that's when I learned to use a file) under the stern, exacting eye of Rat. Days at the great wet wheel grinding the bevels on the cutting irons (how my fingers ached!). Finishing the top edges of the metal sides with finer and finer abrasive paper; finally burnishing them. Getting the mirror finish on the big knurled brass clamping screws by hand turning. Working with beautiful rosewood and ebony.

One day I saw Butch fitting the rosewood block in a plane similar to the one in your photograph. Having shaped it to an exact fit, he slapped paint of no particular colour over the inside, unseen, surfaces. Seeing no useful purpose served by this, I asked him why he bothered to do it.

'Oh, we found some old paint and thought it would help to preserve it,' he replied. 'We build our planes to last.'

Sit vac

Eagle-eyed readers of our Classified pages will probably already have spotted that there is a job advertised which is of more than passing interest. The Edward Barnsley workshop and educational trust at Froxfield, Hants, is looking for 'someone with knowledge of the Gimson-Barnsley furniture tradition and with an interest in its development, who would join the workshop to work closely with the craftsmen, the Barnsleys and the trustees and to assist with the training of the apprentices, with a view to eventually taking full responsibility for the workshop and business'.

The starting salary is not terrific (but negotiable) as the trust admits, though 'it is hoped this would increase steadily along with the responsibility'. But I can't see that such an opportunity will be considered by candidates in terms of a fat salary. More a question of stepping into a place in the continuing history of English furniture.

Form an orderly queue now!

Re-turn of the screw

The subject of screws rears its socketed head once more . . . in response to Canadian reader G. Heighington, who was strongly recommending the use of socket headed woodscrews in Offcuts/July, I have heard as follows from Stewart Smith MIOB MBIM, a building consultant from Leicester.

'I was interested to discover the socket

● A problem not often covered in workshop tips is what to do with a persistent self-appointed apprentice who wants to 'help Daddy in the workshop'. Bob Ansell sent me this picture of 22-month-old James, which is both a delightful picture and a useful tip. 'I give him a kilo block of wax and some blunted old tools,' says Bob. 'It keeps him "me busy durking" for hours.' Just look at that concentration!

headed screw on a visit to Nova Scotia, but sadly disappointed in their use. In my opinion these screws are poorly made and of weak proportions and do not match the ordinary British standard woodscrew.

'My visit to Nova Scotia included the activity of equipping a workshop. Purchasing good hand tools was a problem, screwdrivers in particular. The square headed screwdrivers manufactured in packs for the square recessed screw were of poor quality.

'Might I suggest that the British standard woodscrew with the straight slot across it which has been evolved over a long period of time, is quite the best fixing for the purpose intended and, provided a normal screwdriver is used in the proper manner and with due care, there is no better fixing available.

'I proved this to my friends in Canada by a personal demonstration and straightforward comparison in front of their eyes and what is more I won my bet!'

I think that gives Round 2 to the British, don't you?

Back to the beginning

Shown above is the way your magazine announced itself with its very first issue in October 1901. I have been reading, with great delight, the early editions of Woodworker, and since there cannot be many readers today who were taking the magazine in 1901 it seems a fine idea to reproduce some snippets from those early days.

I have been heartily encouraged in discovering how little Woodworker's editorial philosophy has altered over 81 years.

Reproduced below are four small items from Woodworker Volume 1 Number 1 to give you a flavour of our past, and I fully intend to make a regular habit of dipping into the archives for future editions. There is a vast quantity of good material, including some marvellous constructional articles, that bears reprinting, so we shall be glancing back with more than just historical curiosity.

Here goes with October 1901...

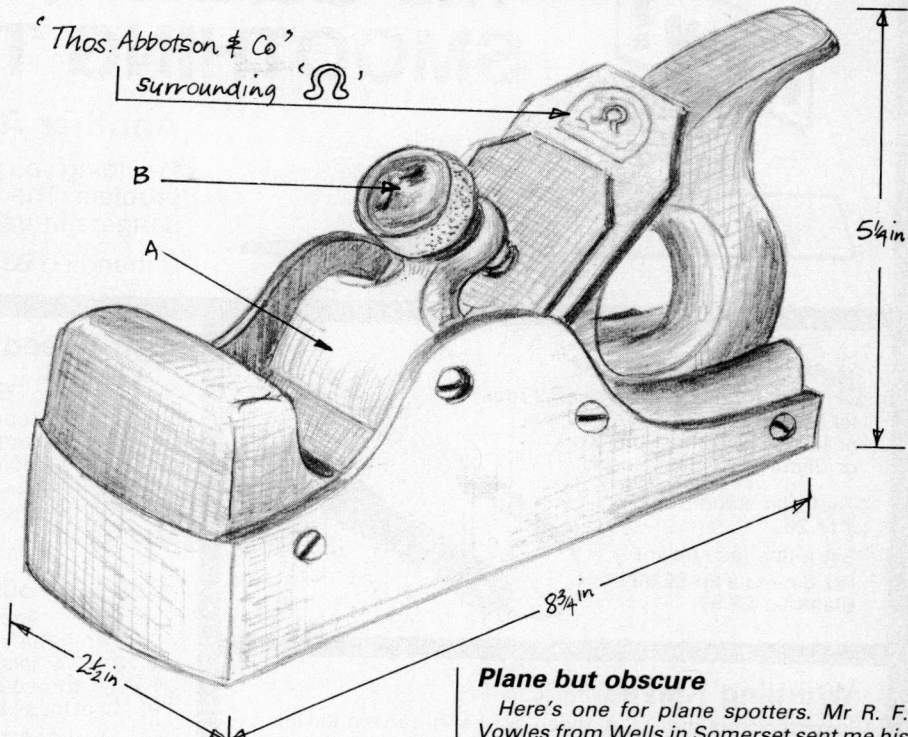

'Thos. Abbotson & Co' surrounding 'Ω'

B

A

5¼in

8¾in

2½in

Knight footnote

I received a charming note from Barry Seward-Thompson in Geneva, who was most delighted at having won the box of 12 carving tools from Roger's of Hitchin in our name-the-knight game. Though cabinet-making is more in his line, Barry threatens now to turn his hand to woodcarving. He suggests sending me photographs of his first attempt so that we can offer you another game, this time entitled What On Earth Is It?

Plane but obscure

Here's one for plane spotters. Mr R. F. Vowles from Wells in Somerset sent me his sketch of a plane with which he has been entrusted for sharpening and setting up.

Additional information supplied by Mr Vowles: 'It weighs 5½lbs and cuts quite well, though its sole has a slight bow across the width. The wood, which has the appearance of mahogany, is in good order and carries a good polish. Both the pressure plate A and the turn-screw B are of brass.'

But Mr Vowles wishes to know more. So if anybody can give more detail about Thos Abbotson or his plane, do please let me know and I will pass on any information to Mr V.

Fortunes in Furniture. That a very high value attaches to certain kinds of antique furniture is a well-known fact; but a set of chairs worth between 3000 and 4000 guineas is likely to be seldom met with. However, in a recent issue of a London morning newspaper an illustration of a chair belonging to such a set was given, and the writer of the accompanying description stated that a single chair of this kind would sell readily for £200. As another example of profitable dealing in antique furniture, it was mentioned that old-fashioned secrétaires could occasionally be bought in country districts for from £3 to £4 each, which, when re-sold in London, would fetch from £30 to £50. An interesting letter on the subject of antique furniture appears in "Our Readers' Views" column elsewhere in this issue.

About Exhibitions. The woodworker who desires to expand his ideas needs no other incentive to attend as many exhibitions of arts and crafts as possible; for it is by seeing what other workers are doing that he can best prevent his own efforts becoming concentrated in a special groove. But while the educational value of such exhibitions to the visitors is great, there is much to be gained by the competitors apart from any actual reward in the way of prizes or certificates. By setting his work against that of others the craftsman can gauge his own strength, and, what is equally important, he can realise his own failings. Knowledge is strength, and a knowledge of the weak points of one's work is the first step towards improvement.

* * *

A Giant Oak. An oak tree, having a trunk measuring 19 ft. in length by 21 ft. in girth, and weighing 20 tons, may fairly be regarded as a respectable member, even of this family of forest giants. Such were the proportions of the main trunk of "Thwaite's oak," a tree which for a long time past has been considered as one of the finest trees of this species in Norfolk. This tree was recently sold by auction at Tivetshall, where it grew, and realised over £90.

ON THE MARKET

[The Editor will be pleased to receive for review under this heading samples and particulars of new tools, apparatus, and materials for Woodworkers.]

An Instantaneous Cramp.

Every woodworker, who uses the ordinary G cramp, has experienced the annoyance of having to screw the bolt in or out, perhaps for its full length, and when this often occurs, a fair amount of time is necessarily lost in the operation. The object of a new patent clamp, which we here illustrate, is to obviate this trouble, the con-

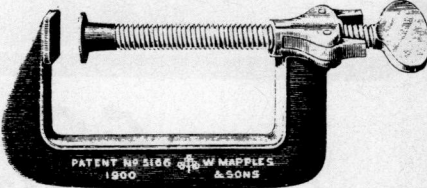

struction being such that, on pressing two wings when the bolt passes through the cramp, the thread is released, and the bolt can be instantaneously set to any required space. These cramps should appeal to joiners, cabinet-makers, and other woodworkers; and it is stated that they are strongly made, with T section malleable iron frames and bright steel screws. They can be obtained from any dealer in woodworkers' tools.

● *Facsimile reproductions, slightly reduced, from the pages of* Woodworker *Volume 1 Number 1, published in October 1901*

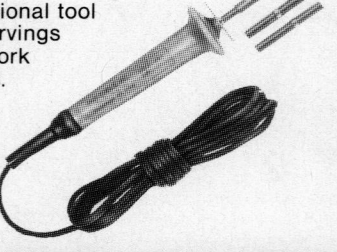

Classified Advertisements

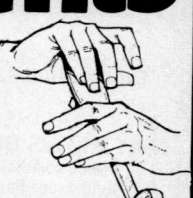

WORKSHOP EQUIPMENT

MACHINERY. A comprehensive range of new/used machinery. Check our prices, e.g. HMO 10"×5½" planer/thicknesser £434. HF30; spindle moulder £365. 12" tilt arbour sawbench 2hp motor £140. Morso mitring machine £459, (including V.A.T.). Kity K-5. See these machines and Ryobi industrial small tools demonstrated at Woodman Woodworking Machinery Co. (Sign of the Axe), Little Malgraves Hall, Lower Dunton Road, Bulphan, Nr. Upminster, Essex. Tel: (0268) 415511 or (0702) 331729. I-U

CIRCULAR AND BAND SAW BLADES for all applications from: A.A. SMITH of Lancing Ltd., 63 Brighton Road, Shoreham, Sussex. Tel: 07917 61707 (24 hrs). P-Z

PLANERS 6" × 9", planers/thicknessers, 12" × 7", 9" × 6", 12" × 7", sawbenches, 10" × 2" combination woodworkers. British made. Particulars, send stamp. Dodd Machine Tools Ltd., South Woodham, Chelmsford. Telephone: (0245) 320 691. O-Z

CONVERTERS single to three phase to 10 h.p. bandsaws. 1 h.p. motors. H.A.B. Engineering, Fardons Industrial Estate, Glover Street, Bordesley, Birmingham 9. 021-772 2699. Q-T

WASHITA & ARKANSAS whetstones now readily available from importer. Large selection, SAE for list. C. Rufino, Manor House, South Clifton, Newark, Notts. T-C

MARQUETRY SAW BLADES for Wood. Fine, medium, coarse. 20 for £2.50. Lea Blades, 16 Barclay, Hertford Heath, Herts. S

EBAC TIMBER SEASONERS, Protimeter moisture meters, always good prices and advice from the man who pioneered small scale seasoning. John Arrowsmith, 74ª, Wilson Street, Darlington, Co. Durham BL3 6QZ. Tel: 0325 481970. T-C

PARTNERSHIP ENDING, must sell Sperber Portable lumber mill, many accessories, little used. Cost over £1,300. Offers over £800. Cookesley Combination machine, heavy duty single or triple phase. Many cutters £550. Telephone: 01-263-9183 or 093-875-400 (Mid Wales) S

MAKE A WOODTURNING LATHE easily, construction details and parts list, send SAE to: ORTAN LATHES, PO Box 46, Norwich. NR7 8PB. S-X

OLD WOODWORK LATHE, wooden base, usual accessories, 30" between centres £200 ono. 10" Multico sawbench £70. Telephone Fulmer (02816) 2426. S

JOHN HALL WOODWORKING CENTRE

	JOHN HALL (inc. VAT)
DeWalt Dw125 Radial Saw	£265.00
Elektra TF100 Spindle Moulder with 6 Free Cutters & Block	£349.00
Elektra HC260 K Planer/Thicknesser with stand	£449.95
DeWalt DW50 Planer/Thicknesser	£430.00
DeWalt DW100 Mini Bandsaw	£115.00
DeWalt BS1310 12" Bandsaw	£237.50
Elektra Combi 2200 2.9H.P. Saw Bench	£139.50
Elekra Spa 1000 Dust Extractor	£155.00
Kity 7227 Spindle Moulder with Free Cutters	£419.95
Kity 7136 Planer/Thicknesser with stand	£449.95
Kity K5 Combination Machine	£642.85

Carriage £9.50 per unit (UK mainland only)
Bristol Clifton Down Shopping Centre, Whiteladies Road, Bristol. (0272) 741510
Bath 2, Railway Street. (0225) 64513
Cardiff 23, Churchill Way, Cardiff. (0222) 373007
Branches throughout the UK

BARCLAYCARD VISA

PETER CRISP OF RUSHDEN
THE CARPENTER'S SHOP

Hand Tools by leading makers.
Stockists of:
- **Craftsmen, Coronet, Elu, Kity Woodworking Machinery**
- **Sorby Turning Chisels**
- **Taylor Carving Chisels**
- **Gomex T/Carbide Circular Saws**

High Street, Rushden, Northants.
Telephone:
093 34 56424-7

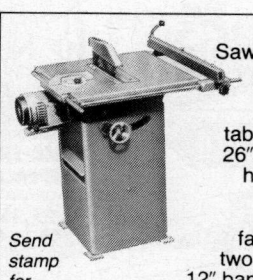

Caber Sawbench 10" tilt arbor table size 26" × 23" h.p. 1.5 (also manufactured two wheel 12" bandsaw)

Send stamp for details

HUMBERSIDE TOOLS
89 Lambert St., Hull
Tel: 0482 43556

SPECIAL!
ELU MOF 96 ROUTERS

600w Plunge base, ¼" collet. With FREE cutter chart & price list. £52 INC. VAT & Carr UK. (Eire £42.50) P/O, Cheque, VISA or ACCESS card no to:

AXMINSTER POWER TOOL CENTRE
Chard St., Axminster, Devon EX13 5DZ
Tel: (0297) 33656 (after 6pm 33535)

MULTICUT -2 SAW

The world's first universal precision saw, cuts 50mm wood, 10mm metals, plastics, rubber, etc. High performance, safe in use. Do not compare with standard fretsaws. Details 11½ stamp.

Hegner Universal Saws (U.K.) Ltd.
36 Gt. Eastern Road, Hockley, Essex.
Tel: Southend (0702) 205669

Demonstration:
Timecraft Clock Fair, 2nd-4th September International Press Centre, 76 Shoe Lane, London, EC4.
(Admission by invitation only. SAE for free ticket)
British Craft Show, 16th-18th September, Syon Park, Brentford, Middx.

WOOD TURNING LATHES

550mm between centres. 65mm centre height. Lever action tailstock. No.2 Morse tapers. Rear turning attachment takes 220mm dia. Various bed lengths available.
Prices from £80 + VAT
Send SAE for details

GREENFIELDS ENGINEERING

Building 3A, Site 1, Newport Road, High Ercall, Telford, TF6 6JA. Telephone High Ercall (0952) 770672

B/DECKER, SKIL, BOSCH, MAKITA TOOLS ALL IN STOCK

NEW LUTZ SAWBENCH NOW IN STOCK ONLY £165.00

BEST QUALITY TCT SAWS, 5" DIAMETER UP TO 36" GUARANTEED PERFORMANCE 24 HOUR RETURN POST SHARPENING SERVICE.
PHONE OR WRITE TO MAYS HIGH SPEED SAWS LTD. NEW ROAD (Nr. CHANDLER CORNER), RAINHAM, ESSEX. TEL. (04027) 55371/21331 (7 DAYS A WEEK)

TCT ALLOY

TOP QUALITY SHEFFIELD WOODTURNING TOOLS

A complete range of top quality Chisels and Gouges. Full size and long and strong.
EXAMPLES: FULL SIZE

1" gouge £4.25	½" skew £3.25
½" gouge £3.95	½" diamond £3.25
1" skew £3.95	½" round £3.25

S.A.E. for full price list
TOOLSHOP, 29 Walcot Street, Bath. Avon. Tel. Bath (0225) 61838

---

emcostar FOX WOODWORKING
Universal Woodworking Machine

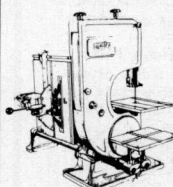

List price £557.75
Our price £460.00
both prices include VAT

Full range of light machines and accessories stocked: colour brochures available. Send 30p stamps for further information.

Fox Woodworking, Stebbings, Back Lane, Washbrook, Ipswich, Suffolk IP8 3JA
Telephone: 0473 86216

SCRU-DRILL

COMPLETE SET OF FOUR £13.45 + 35p P&P

Top quality wood screw pilot drill and countersink adjusts to screw specification for fast accurate pilot holes in hard or soft wood for that professional finish.

Complete set will accommodate Nos 5 to 14 gauge screws in all popular lengths.

Adjustable stop collar for counterbore depth or countersink

Adjustable sleeve for screw body

Adjustable pilot drill for screw thread

KELTEK PRODUCTS
St. Giles Mews, P.O. Box 5, Wadebridge, Cornwall PL27 7YZ. (S.A.E. Please for our complete range of exclusive products).

BOAT PLANS. Canoes, dinghies, runabouts, cruisers. Sail and power. Full size patterns, fully detailed plans. Illustrated catalogue 30p. W.F. Harrison, (A) Crownest Road, Bingley, West Yorkshire. N-S

PLANS

TRADITIONAL ROCKING HORSE

A traditional style rocking horse. The original of this design is called Dobbin and still sees active service after many years in a doctor's surgery. Rugged construction with some scope for carving. A design to please any child. Height to saddle 915mm (36").
Order Plan DB/52   Price £2.50 + 40p post & packing (overseas 85p)
WOODWORKER PLANS SERVICE
P.O. Box 35, Bridge Street, Hemel Hempstead, Herts. HP1 1EE.
Tel: 0442 41221

MAKE PINE FURNITURE FOR YOURSELF OR FOR PROFIT

Fully illustrated plans with step by step instructions for traditional designs in solid wood. Corner dresser, £1.75; Welsh dresser, £1.75; Refectory table and benches, £1.25; Refectory style coffee table, 75p; Beginner's guide to starting a profitable part-time or full-time furniture business, £1.50; Manual on working with solid wood, £1.00. Three-door Welsh dresser, £2.50; Bedside cabinet, £1.25; Two-door wall cupboard, £1.00; Wall shelf unit, 75p; Telephone seat, £1.50. **Complete set of 11 publications for £9.75. New plans** — Design for 3 garden seats plus garden table, **£3.50.** Prices include postage. 'By return' service.

Read what our users say: *"Your plans and literature contain a wealth of information."* (Mr E.D., Notts.)

"All the plans.... were excellent. Let me know if you produce any more." (Mr T.E., N. Ireland.) *"Very pleased indeed with the plans. A local shop is displaying my wares."* (Mr F.C., Cornwall.)

Trade inquiries invited
L. GILMORE,
124, NORTH ROAD, BELFAST BT4 3DJ

WOODWORKING PLANS

Build traditional style furniture with our illustrated plans, showing contruction details and full size details of mouldings and curves.
Welsh Dresser £2.95
Corner Display Cabinet £2.95
Rocking Chair £2.95
Grandfather Clock (left) £2.95
or with break arch dial £2.95
Four Poster Bed £2.95
Linen Chest £1.80
Extending Dining Table £1.80
Dining Chair £1.80
Refectory Table & Benches .. £1.25
Prices incl P&P. Send orders, or for details, to
Cullen and Ovenden (WW)
PO Box 76, Canterbury, Kent, CT1 2YB
Office — Latchmere House, Watling Street, Canterbury, Kent. Tel: (0227) 58505

TIMBER FRAME HOUSE PLANS

all £5.99 plus 50 pence postage

Toadstool plans are an easy to follow guide to building twelfth scale houses using the construction methods of the real thing. No power tools are needed — square and rectangular wood sections are laid out on full scale plans and glued. Choice of plans include Tudor, Farmhouse, American Gothic etc. Send £1.00 for our full list and catalogue of plans and kits to:

MINIMUS. Dept. W, 212 Waterhouse Moor, Harlow, Essex CM18 6BW Tel: 0279 25489 Mail Order

WOODTURNING COURSES in the Derbyshire craft village of Brailsford. Reg Slack formerly of Coronet and "Learn-a-Craft" offers ½, 1, 1½, 2 day courses. For details write or 'phone Reg Slack, Saracens Head Coaching House Yard, Brailsford, Derbyshire. (033528) 829 Evenings: (0283) 701662. STU.

ONE DAY WOODTURNING COURSE: carefully designed, inexpensive. Trymwood, 2a Downs Park East, Westbury Park, Bristol. Telephone Bristol 629092. T/C

TWO-DAY Woodturning Course for beginners in mid-Norfolk village. Two students only. Accommodation available. SAE for details please. Doug Keeling, Church Lane, Beetley, Norfolk NR20 4AB. T/C

WOODTURNING COURSE in Scottish borders. Two day professional tuition. For details SAE to Monteviot Woodcraft, Tower Workshop, Harestanes Mill, Jedburgh, Roxburghshire TD8 6UF. Telephone: 0450-87446 (Evenings) S-V

COURSES IN WOOD MACHINING AND WOODTURNING. Bookable by the hour—the most convenient and flexible way! all for £6.00 an hour (inc. VAT), H.W.M., The Woodworkers, 303 Shirley Rd., Shirley, Southampton. Tel: (0703) 776222. T/C

CRAFT HOLIDAYS AND COURSES in the Yorkshire Dales. Woodturning, Carving, Furnituremaking, Spinning, Silversmithing, Copper and Brasswork, Property Renovation. Professional tuition in well equipped workshops with full-board accommodation. SAE Rob and Jan Ellwood, Holroyd Mill, Micklethwaite, Bingley, W. Yorks. N-S

CABINET MAKING Bend the Ear of a top professional for two days in workshop surrounded by beautiful dales and wonderful ales. S.A.E. Middleham Furniture Company, Middleham, Leyburn, North Yorkshire DL8 4NP. Telephone: (0969) 22703. S

BIRD CARVING TUITION. Two day or three day course by internationally known wood sculptor. Comfortable accommodation available close to Solent coast. SAE or 'phone for details: Derek George, West Lodge, Elizabeth Road, Stubbington, Hants PO14 2RF. Tel: Stubbington 2458. S

WOODTURNING day courses, or at £5.00 per hour, with Jack Durey. Enquire: Brenchley 2465 (Kent). T/C

LEARN THE ART AND CRAFT OF RESTORING ANTIQUES AND DESIGNING AND MAKING YOUR OWN FURNITURE

Situated in a charming Norfolk village we offer professional tuition in courses of antique restoration, wood turning, machining, woodworking and finishing. Come to The Old Mill at Gayton for good food and comfortable accommodation in very pleasant surroundings.

WINDMILL ENTERPRISES

For full details send SAE to MR R Hirons, The Old Mill, Gayton, Norfolk. Tel: (055386) 613/717

Rawdon Woodturners

Comprehensive courses geared to suit individual requirements offered in
Woodmachining
Woodturning
Take advantage of my 20 years of industrial and educational experience and realize the full potential of your machinery. Write or phone for details

Rawdon Woodturners
Peter Clark Woodcraft Ltd.,
Old Friends School, Low Green Rawdon, Nr Leeds, West Yorkshire
Tel: Leeds (0532) 676068 (evenings preferred)

Wood machining Course

A craftsman of forty years experience offers a unique two-day course to learn the basics of machine woodworking including spindle moulding and routing in his fully equipped modern workshop.
S.A.E. for details please to:
ROY SUTTON
14 St. Georges Avenue,
Herne Bay, Kent CT6 8JU
Telephone: Herne Bay 3297 or Whitstable 272136 (evenings).

Australian Readers WOODTURNING

40 Years of woodturning experience available to you in a 2 day course. Basic or advanced. Personal tuition to your needs in a fully equipped workshop. Write for details:
PHILIP ELFORD 407 Peel St. N., Ballarat, Vic. 3350.

GORDON STOKES

Author of Modern Woodturning
Beginner's Guide to Woodturning
Woodturning for Pleasure, etc. etc
Will be pleased to send you full details of his intensive two day Woodturning and Woodcarving courses. Personal instruction based on thirty years experience. Don't struggle along the hard way. *Foolscap S.A.E. to:* 202 The Hollow, Bath, Avon BA2 1NG
Tel: Bath 22617

WOODTURNING COURSES

2 Day courses, mid-week or weekend. Expert personal tuition in modern well equipped workshop. Comfortable accommodation available in pleasant surroundings. SAE for details to
Cliff Willetts, Gables, Frisby On The Wreake, Melton Mowbray, Leics.

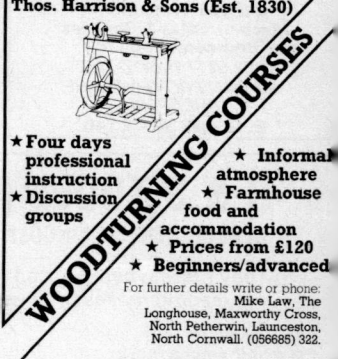

Thos. Harrison & Sons (Est. 1830)

WOODTURNING COURSES

★ Four days professional instruction
★ Discussion groups
★ Informal atmosphere
★ Farmhouse food and accommodation
★ Prices from £120
★ Beginners/advanced

For further details write or phone:
Mike Law, The Longhouse, Maxworthy Cross, North Petherwin, Launceston, North Cornwall. (056685) 322.

COURSES IN BASIC ANTIQUE RESTORATION

Bookings available for the 16th & 17th October in our workshops on the basic skills of restoring furniture Course includes laying and repairing veneers, staining distressing and french polishing.
For full details send 15½p stamp to
EDWIN TURNER, Home Farm, Gislingham, Eye, Suffolk. Tel: Mellis 280

MAKE YOUR OWN CLAVICHORD full size plans and instruction manual. SAE for details to: Early Keyboard Instruments, Morley Farm, Brancepeth, Durham DH7 8DS.   T/C

BUILD YOUR OWN HARPSICHORD
from a kit by Frank Hubbard.

All materials provided including comprehensive instruction manual and full scale drawing. Choose from spinets, virginals, harpsichords and forte-pianos. Free colour catalogue and price list on request. **Donald Mackinnon and Mimi Waitzman,** 11 Sprowston Road, Forest Gate, London E7 9AD. Tel: 01-519 1170.

Rates
20p per word, minimum £3.00
Box nos. £1.25 extra.
Semi display s.c.c. £4.00
(min £10.00)

Materials for the
Amateur and Professional
VIOLIN & GUITAR MAKER

Send S.A.E. 16p
plus 50p for either cat.
50p deductible
from purchase £5.00 or over

SYDNEY EVANS LTD.
45 Regent Place,
Birmingham, B1 3BN
Tel: (021) 233-1741

Harpsichord, spinet, clavichord kits for home or educational projects. Traditional materials are used, and no special skills are needed for kit assembly. Visitors are welcome. Residential keyboard instrument making course from 28th December to 6th January.

John Storrs Maker of Early Keyboard Instruments
Hunston Chichester West Sussex PO20 6NR England

TONEWOOD CATALOGUE
If you make, repair or restore any stringed instrument you will find our new free catalogue invaluable. We hold large stocks of selected materials for:
VIOLIN, VIOLA, 'CELLO, BASS, LUTE, GUITAR, BAROQUE VIOLS, ETC.
Callers welcome or return of post mail order service available. Open 10am - 4pm Tues/Sat.
A. HIGHFIELD & CO, Rosewood House, Bridge Road, Downham Market, Norfolk PE38 0AE.
Tel: Downham Mkt. 2614.

HARPSICHORD KITS
Unique new basic kit enables you to build a good harpsichord first time at half the price of a full kit.
SAE for details: **D. H. Bolton, Harpsichord Maker, 17 The Crescent, Linthorpe, Middlesbrough, Cleveland TS5 6SG.**

HARPS
I produce full size plans complete with instruction sheets for a wide range of harps as well as manufacturing all the hardware, strings etc needed for their construction. Additionally, complete kits including partly worked timber are available. For full illustrated details and price list please send large SAE (Overseas 3 irc's) to **Michael Saunders, Waterloo Cottages, Letton, Hereford, HR3 6DN. Tel: 05446 352**

MUSICAL INSTRUMENT
Makers and Repairer's supplies
Largest selection of tonewoods, parts and tools in the country. Callers or mail order welcome. Also Ebony offcuts, assorted sizes.
TOUCHSTONE TONEWOODS LTD.,
27 Lesbourne Rd., Reigate, Surrey RH2 7JS

EXHIBITIONS

Make a Note
WOODWORKER SHOW

Royal Horticultural Society's New & Old Halls, Westminster, London SW1.

19-24 October 1982 inclusive.

Telephone Valerie Tester (0442) 41221 Ext 262
for further information regarding
advertising in these columns.

Classified Advertisements

From:

....

....

....

I enclose remittance value...................to cover ....

Insertions under the heading:

☐ WORKSHOP EQUIPMENT   BOOKS & PUBLICATIONS ☐
☐ COURSES   PLANS ☐
☐ CRAFT/ANTIQUE/SECOND-   MATERIALS/FINISHES ☐
   HAND TOOLS   FOR SALE ☐
☐ WANTED   HIRE SERVICES ☐
☐ MUSICAL INSTRUMENTS   WOOD SUPPLIERS ☐
☐ GENERAL—(Classification of choice) ....
BLOCK CAPITALS PLEASE

To: Valerie Tester
WOODWORKER

CLASSIFIED ADVERTISEMENT DEPT.
PO BOX 35, BRIDGE STREET,
HEMEL HEMPSTEAD, HERTS HP1 1EE

★ **Lineage rate 20p per word. Minimum charge £3.00**

★ **Semi display single column cm = £4.00 (Minimum £10.00)**

★ **Box numbers £1.25 extra**

Name and address if to appear must be paid for

Prices quoted are those prevailing at press date and are subject to alteration due to economic conditions.

SHOP GUIDE SHOP GUIDE

The quickest and easiest method of reaching all Woodworkers is to advertise in SHOP GUIDE. Telephone **Valerie Tester (0442) 41221 Ext. 266. Rate: £8.00 per unit.** Minimum of 6 months.

Key: H — Hand tools, **P** — Power tools, **W** — Woodworking machinery up to £1000, **WM** — Woodworking machinery over £1000, **D** — Demonstration available on selected machines, **T** — Timber, **CS** — Cutting or sharpening services, **MF** — Material Finishes, **A** — Attachments, **BC** — Books/catalogues, * — Mail order.

AVON

BATH   Tel. Bath 64513
JOHN HALL TOOLS ★
RAILWAY STREET

Open: Monday-Saturday
9.00 a.m.-5.30 p.m.
H.P.W.WM.D.A.BC.

BRISTOL   Tel. (0272) 311510
JOHN HALL TOOLS LIMITED ★
CLIFTON DOWN SHOPPING
CENTRE, WHITELADIES ROAD
Open: Monday-Saturday
9.00 a.m.-5.30 p.m.
H.P.W.WM.D.A.BC.

BRISTOL   Tel. 0272-633844
ROBBINS LIMITED ★
THE WOODWORKER SHOP
MERRYWOOD MILLS, BEDMINSTER
Open: Mon-Fri 8.00 a.m.-5.00 p.m.
Saturday 8.30 a.m.-12.30 p.m.
H.P.T.CS.A.BC.

BRISTOL   Tel. 0272-629092
TRYMWOOD SERVICES ★
2a DOWNS PARK EAST, (off
North View) WESTBURY PARK
Open: 8.30 a.m.-5.30 p.m. Mon. to
Fri. Closed for lunch 1-2 p.m.
P.W.WM.D.T.A.BC.

BRISTOL   Tel. 0272-667013
W. H. WILLIS & CO. LTD ★
190-192 WEST STREET,
BEDMINSTER
Open: Mon-Fri 8.30 a.m.-5 p.m.
Saturday 9 a.m.-1 p.m.
H.P.W.WM.D.CS.A.BC.

BERKSHIRE

READING   Tel. Littlewick Green
DAVID HUNT (TOOL   2743
MERCHANTS) LTD
KNOWL HILL, NR. READING
Open: Monday-Saturday
9 a.m.-5.30 p.m.
H.P.W.D.A.BC.

READING   Tel. (0734) 586522
SARJENT'S TOOL STORES ★
LTD.
44-52 OXFORD ROAD
Open: 8.30 a.m.-5.30 p.m.
Monday-Saturday
H.P.W.WM.D.A.BC.

READING   Tel. Reading 661511
WOKINGHAM TOOL CO. LTD
99 WOKINGHAM ROAD

Open: Mon-Sat 9am-5.30pm
Closed 1-2pm for lunch
H.P.W.WM.D.CS.A.BC.

BUCKINGHAMSHIRE

HIGH WYCOMBE   (0494) 22221
ISAAC LORD LTD
185 DESBOROUGH ROAD

Open: Mon-Fri 8.00 a.m.-5.00 p.m.
Saturday 8.00 a.m.-12.00 noon
H.P.W.D.A.

MILTON KEYNES   Tel. 0908
A. POLLARD & SON   75221
LTD. ★
51 QUEENSWAY, BLETCHLEY
Open: 8.30 a.m.-5.30 p.m.
Monday-Saturday
H.P.W.WM.D.A.BC.

CAMBRIDGESHIRE

CAMBRIDGE   Tel. 0223-353091
H. B. WOODWORKING
69 LENSFIELD ROAD
Open: 8.30 a.m.-5.30 p.m.
Monday-Friday
8.30 a.m.-1.00 p.m. Sat
P.W.WM.D.CS.BC.

CHESHIRE

CHESTER   Tel. 0244 42084
ROBERT KELLY'S ★
19 NEWGATE ROW
GROSVENOR PRECINCT, CH1 1ER
Open: 9.00 a.m.-5.30 p.m.
Monday-Saturday
H.P.W.WM.D.CS.A.BC.

NANTWICH   Tel. Crewe 67010
ALAN HOLTHAM ★
THE OLD STORES TURNERY
WISTASON ROAD, WILLASTON
Open: Tues-Sat 9a.m.-5.30p.m.
Closed Monday
P.W.WM.D.T.C.CS.A.BC.

CLEVELAND

MIDDLESBROUGH   Tel. 0642-
WINTZ   460035/813650
INDUSTRIAL SUPPLIES ★
2 BESSEMER COURT
GRANGETOWN
Open: Mon-Fri 8.30 a.m.-5 p.m.
H.P.W.D.A.

CORNWALL

FALMOUTH   Tel. 0326-312915
WOODSTOCK
(HARDWOODS) S.W.,
ASHFIELD, PONSHARDEN,
Open: Mon-Fri 8.30 a.m.-5.30 p.m.
Sat 9 a.m.-1.00 p.m.
T.

HELSTON   Tel: Helston (03265) 4961
SOUTH WEST   Truro (0872) 71671
POWER TOOLS   Launceston
MONUMENT ROAD   (0566) 3555

H.P.W.WM.D.CS.A.

CORNWALL

NEWQUAY   Tel. 063 73 2516
CONWAY SUPPLIES ★
(NEWQUAY)
70 FORE STREET
Open: Mon-Fri 9 a.m.-5.30 p.m.
Sat 9 a.m.-12.30 p.m.
H.P.W.WM.D.A.BC.

ST. AUSTELL   Tel. (0726) 65922
TOOLSERV ★
TRURO ROAD

Open: 8 a.m.-5.30 p.m.
6 days
H.P.W.WM.D.CS.A.BC.

DERBYSHIRE

BUXTON   Tel. 0298-871636
CRAFT SUPPLIES ★
THE MILL
MILLERSDALE
Open: Mon-Fri 9 a.m.-5 p.m.
Saturday 9 a.m.-1 p.m.
H.P.W.D.T.CS.A.BC.

DEVON

EXETER   Tel. 0392 73936
WRIDES TOOL CENTRE
147 FORE STREET

Open: 9.00 a.m.-5.30 p.m.
Wednesday 9.00 a.m.-1.00 p.m.
H.P.W.WM.A.

PLYMOUTH   Tel. 0752 330303
WESTWARD BUILDING SERVICES ★
LTD., LISTER CLOSE, NEWNHAM
INDUSTRIAL ESTATE, PLYMPTON
Open: Mon-Fri 8 a.m.-5.30 p.m.
Sat 8.30 a.m.-12.30 p.m.
H.P.W.D.A.BC.

PLYMOUTH   Tel. 0752-266179
JOHN WRIDE & CO (PLYMOUTH) LTD
146 CORNWALL STREET
Open: Monday to Saturday
9.00a.m.-5.30p.m.
Wed 9.00a.m.-1.00p.m.
H.P.W.WM.A.

DORSET

BOURNEMOUTH   Tel: 0202
MACHINE SALES & SERVICES   527780
(BOURNEMOUTH) LTD   527781
56 STROUDEN ROAD ★

Open: Mon-Fri 8.15 a.m.-5 p.m.
H.P.W.WM.D.A.

WEYMOUTH   Tel: (0305) 787396
WEYMOUTH TOOL CENTRE
30A ABBOTSBURY ROAD

Open: Monday to Saturday
8 a.m.-5.30 p.m.
H.P.W.WM.D.A.BC

CO. DURHAM

BARNARD CASTLE   Tel: (0833)
WOODMEN   38442/31609
27 NEWGATE ★

Open Monday-Saturday
9 a.m.-5.30 p.m.
P.W.WM.D.A.BC.

ESSEX

LEIGH ON SEA   Tel. (0702)
MARSHALL &   710404
PARSONS LTD ★
1111 LONDON ROAD
Open: 8.30 am-5.30 pm Mon-Fri.
9.00 am-5.00 om Sat.
H.P.W.WM.D.CS.A.

LEIGH ON SEA   Tel. (0702)
WEBBERS TOOLS   76503
204 ELM ROAD

Open: 9 am-5.30 pm
Monday to Saturday
H.P.W.

GLOUCESTERSHIRE

TEWKESBURY   Tel. 0684
TEWKESBURY SAW CO.   293092
LIMITED
TRADING ESTATE, NEWTOWN
Open: Mon-Fri 8.00 a.m.-5.00 p.m.
Saturday 9.30 a.m.-12.00 p.m.
P.W.WM.D.CS.

HAMPSHIRE

ALDERSHOT   Tel. 0252 28088
BURCH & HILLS LTD
BLACKWATER WAY TRADING
ESTATE
Open: Mon-Fri 8.30 a.m.-5.30 p.m.
Saturday 8.30 a.m.-12.00 p.m.
H.P.W.WM.D.A.BC.

PORTSMOUTH   Tel. 0705
EURO PRECISION TOOLS   667332
LTD ★
259/263 London Road, North End
Open: Mon-Fri 9 a.m.- 5.30 p.m.
Sat 9.00 a.m.-1.00 p.m.
H.P.W.WM.D.A.BC.

SOUTHAMPTON   Tel. 0703
H.W.M.   776222
THE WOODWORKERS ★
303 SHIRLEY ROAD, SHIRLEY
Open: Tues-Fri 9.30 a.m.- 6 p.m.
Sat 9.30 a.m.-4.00 p.m.
H.P.W.WM.D.CS.A.BC.T.

HERTFORDSHIRE

WATFORD   Tel. 0923 48434
HOME CARE CENTRE
20 MARKET STREET
WATFORD, HERTS
Open 9.00 a.m.-5.30 p.m.
Mon.-Sat.
H.P.W.A.WM.BC.D.

HERTFORDSHIRE

WATFORD Tel. 0923 26052
J. SIMBLE & SONS LTD
76 QUEENS ROAD

Open 8.30 a.m.-5.30 p.m.
Mon-Sat. Closed Wednesday
H.P.W.WM.D.A.BC.

WATFORD Tel. (0923) 49911
TREND MACHINERY & CUTTING
TOOLS LTD
UNIT N, PENFOLD WORKS
IMPERIAL WAY
Open: Mon-Fri 9 a.m.-5 p.m.
P.W.WM.D.CS.BC.

KENT

LYDD Tel. (0679) 20107
LIBERON WAXES LTD., ★
6 PARK STREET
Open: Mon-Fri
10 a.m.-1 p.m. 2 p.m.- 5.30 p.m.
Saturday 10 a.m.- 1 p.m.
D. MF.

MATFIELD Tel. Brenchley
LEISURECRAFT IN WOOD (089272)
'ORMONDE', MAIDSTONE RD. 2465
TN12 7JG
Open: Mon-Sun
9 a.m.- 5.30 p.m.
W.WM.D.T.A.

SITTINGBOURNE Tel.
B.T.S. (TOOLS), Sittingbourne
Unit 25, SITTINGBOURNE 79551
INDUSTRIAL PARK ★
Open: Monday - Friday
8.00 a.m. - 5.00 p.m.
H.P.W.BC.CS.

LANCASHIRE

LANCASTER Tel. 0524 2886
LILE TOOL SHOP
43/45 NORTH ROAD
Open: Monday to Saturday
9.00 a.m.-5.30 p.m.
Wed 9.00 a.m.-12.30 p.m.
H.P.W.D.A.

PRESTON Tel. (0772) 52951
SPEEDWELL TOOL CO., ★
62-68 MEADOW STREET
Open: Mon-Fri 8.30 a.m.-5.30 p.m.
Sat 8.30 a.m.-12.30 p.m.
H.P.W.WM.D.CS.A.BC.

LEICESTERSHIRE

COALVILLE Tel. (0533) 415556
POOLE WOOD (06077) 5777
MACHINERY
SERVICES LIMITED,
30 VALENTINE ROAD
Open: Mon-Fri 9 a.m.-5 p.m.
H.P.W.WM.D.A.BC.

LEICESTER Tel. 0455 43254
ROY STARTIN LTD
134 WOOD STREET
EARL SHILTON
Open: Mon-Fri 8 a.m.-5.30 p.m.
Saturday 8.00 a.m.-1.30 p.m.
H.P.W.WM.D.T.A.

LINCOLNSHIRE

LINCOLN Tel. 0522 30199/
WOODWISE LIMITED 39871 or
121 HIGH STREET 0522 68428
& 06077 2421/5777/5288
(after hours) ★
Open: Mon-Sat 9 a.m.-5.30 p.m.
P.W.WM.D.A.BC.

LONDON

ACTON Tel. 01-992 4835
A MILLS (ACTON) LTD ★
32/36 CHURCHFIELD ROAD
W3 6ED
Open: Mon-Fri 9.00 a.m.-5.00 p.m.
Closed Saturday
H.P.W.WM.

HANWELL Tel. 01-567 2922
G. D. CLEGG & SONS
83 Uxbridge Road, W7 3ST
Open: Monday to Friday
9.00 a.m.-6.00 p.m.
Saturday 9.00 a.m.-5.30 p.m.
H.P.W.WM.D.

KILBURN Tel. 01-624 5146
W. THATCHER & SON LTD ★
POWER TOOL CENTRE
AT THE TECHNICAL LEISURE CENTRE
1 THE GRANGEWAY, N.W.6.
Open: Mon-Sat 9 a.m.-5.30 p.m.
P.H.W.D.CS.A.BC.

LONDON Tel. 01-636 7475
BUCK & RYAN LIMITED
101 TOTTENHAM COURT ROAD
W1P 0DY
Open: Mon-Fri 8.30 a.m.-5.30 p.m.
Saturday 8.30 a.m.-1.00 p.m.
H.P.W.WM.D.A.

LONDON Tel. 01-739 7126
CECIL W. TYZACK ★
79-81 KINGSLAND ROAD
SHOREDITCH
Open: Mon-Fri 8.45 a.m.-5.15 p.m.
Saturday 9 a.m.-12 noon
H.P.W.WM.D.A.BC.

NORBURY Tel: 01-679 6193
HERON TOOLS & HARDWARE LTD
437 STREATHAM HIGH ROAD
S.W.16
Open: Mon-Sat 8.30 a.m. - 6 p.m.
Wednesday 8.30 a.m. - 1 p.m.
H.P.W.A.

WOOLWICH Tel. 01-854 7767/8
A.D. Skillman & Sons Ltd.,
108-109 Woolwich High St.,
SE18 6DW
Open: Mon-Sat 8.30 a.m.-5.30 p.m.
H.P.W.CS.A.

MERSEYSIDE

LIVERPOOL Tel. 051-263 1359
TAYLOR BROS (LIVERPOOL) LTD
5/9 PRESCOTT STREET
Open: Monday to Friday
8.30 a.m.-5.30 p.m.
H.P.W.WM.D.A.BC.

MIDDLESEX

NORTH HARROW Tel. 01-863 2492
WILLIAMS TECHNICAL SERVICES ★
36 STATION ROAD
Open: Mon-Fri 8 a.m.-5.30 p.m.
Wed 8 a.m.-1 p.m.,
Sat 9 a.m.-5.30 p.m.
H.P.W.WM.D.A.

HOUNSLOW Tel. 01-570 2103/5135
Q. R. TOOLS LTD
251-253 HANWORTH ROAD
Open: Mon-Fri 8.30 a.m.-5.30 p.m.
Sat 9 a.m.-1 p.m.
P.W.WM.D.CS.A.

NORFOLK

KINGS LYNN Tel. (0553) 2443
WALKER & ANDERSON (Kings Lynn) LTD
WINDSOR ROAD, KINGS LYNN
Open: Monday to Saturday
7.45 a.m.-5.30 p.m.
Wednesday 1 p.m. Saturday 5.00 p.m.
H.P.W.WM.D.CS.A.

NORWICH Tel. 0603 898695
NORFOLK SAW SERVICES
DOG LAND, HORSFORD
Open: Monday to Friday
8.00 a.m.-5.00 p.m.
Saturday 8.00 a.m.-12.00 p.m.
H.P.W.WM.D.CS.A.

NORWICH Tel. 0603 400933
WESTGATES WOODWORKING Tx.
MACHINERY, JUPITER ROAD 975412
OFF MILE CROSS LANE
Open: 9 a.m.-5 p.m. weekdays
9 a.m.-12 a.m. Sat.
P.W.WM.D.

NORTHAMPTONSHIRE

RUSHDEN Tel. 093-34 56424
PETER CRISP LIMITED ★
7 HIGH STREET
Open: Monday to Saturday
8.30 a.m.-5.30 p.m.
Thursday 8.30 a.m.-1.00 p.m.
H.P.W.D.BC.

NORTHUMBERLAND

BLYTH Tel. (06706) 69279
ALLAN McNAIR WOODCRAFT ★
69-71 PLESSEY ROAD
Open: Monday to Saturday
9 a.m.-5 p.m.
H.W.WM.D.T.CS.A.BC.

NOTTINGHAMSHIRE

NOTTINGHAM Tel. (0602) 225979
POOLEWOOD and 227929
EQUIPMENT LTD (06077) 2421/5777
5a HOLLY LANE, CHILLWELL
Open: Mon-Fri 9 a.m.-5.30 p.m.
Sat. 9 a.m. to 12.30 p.m.
P.W.WM.D.CS.A.BC.

NOTTINGHAM Tel. 0602 811889
THE WOODCUTTER
5 TUDOR SQUARE
WEST BRIDGFORD
Open: Tues-Sat 9 a.m.-5.30 p.m.
Fri 9 a.m.-7.30 p.m. Closed Mon.
H.P.W.WM.D.T.CS.A.

OXFORDSHIRE

BICESTER Tel. (08692) 4156
WOODMEN 3218/3219
104 CHURCHILL ROAD
Open: Monday-Saturday
9 a.m.-5.30 p.m.
P.W.WM.D.A.BC.

OXFORD Tel. (0865) 45118/9
SARJENT'S TOOL ★
STORES LTD
150 COWLEY ROAD
Open: Monday to Saturday
8.30 a.m.-5.30 p.m.
H.P.W.WM.D.A.BC.

SHROPSHIRE

TELFORD Tel. Telford
ASLES LTD (0952) 48054
VINEYARD ROAD
WELLINGTON
Open: Mon-Fri 8.30am-5.30pm
Saturday 8.30am-4.00pm
H.P.WM.D.A.

SOMERSET

TAUNTON Tel. Taunton 79078
KEITH MITCHELL
TOOLS AND EQUIPMENT
66 PRIORY BRIDGE ROAD
Open: Mon-Fri 8.30am-5.30pm
Saturday 9am-4pm
H.P.W.WM.D.CS.A.BC.

WESTON-SUPER-MARE Tel.
JOHN TERRY 0934 21803
TOOL SALES ★
36 ALFRED STREET
Open: Monday to Saturday
9am-5.30pm inclusive
H.P.W.WM.D.CS.A.

STAFFORDSHIRE

TAMWORTH Tel. 0827-56188
MATTHEWS BROTHERS LTD
KETTLEBROOK ROAD
Open: Mon.-Sat. 8.30am-6.00pm
Demonstrations Sunday mornings
by appointment only
H.P.WM.D.T.CS.A.BC.

SUFFOLK

BURY ST. EDMUNDS Tel.
TOOLS & THINGS 0284 62022
21 CHURCHGATE ★
Open: Monday to Saturday
9.00 a.m.-5.30 p.m.
H.P.W.WM.D.A.BC.

IPSWICH Tel. 0473 86216
FOX WOODWORKING ★
'STEBBINGS' BACK LANE
WASHBROOK
Open: Tues. Fri. 9.00am-5.30pm
Sat. 9.00am-5pm
H.P.W.WM.D.A.B.C.

SURREY

CARSHALTON BEECHES Tel.
SURREY WOOD 01-642 6636
MACHINE SALES LTD ★
56A BANSTEAD ROAD
Open: Tues-Fri 9.30 am-6.00 pm
Saturday 9.30 am-2.00 pm
P.W.WM.D.BC.CS.

Prices quoted are those prevailing at press date and are
subject to alteration due to economic conditions.

SHOP GUIDE SHOP GUIDE

SURREY

CROYDON Tel. 01-688 5513
L. H. TURTLE LTD ★
6-12 PARK STREET

Open: Monday to Saturday
8.30 a.m.-5.30 p.m.
H.P.W.WM.D.A.

GUILDFORD Tel. 0483 61125
MESSINGERS FOR TOOLS
14-18 CHERTSEY STREET
Open: Tuesday to Saturday
8.30 a.m.-5.30 p.m.
Closed all day Monday
H.P.W.D.BC.

SUSSEX

BOGNOR REGIS Tel: (0243) 863100
A. OLBY & SON (BOGNOR REGIS LTD)
"TOOLSHOP", BUILDER'S MERCHANT
HAWTHORN ROAD
Open: Mon-Thurs 8 a.m.-5.15 p.m.
Fri 8 a.m.-8 p.m. Sat 8 a.m.-12.45 p.m.
H.P.W.WM.D.T.C.A.BC.

WORTHING Tel. 0903 38739
W. HOSKING LTD (TOOLS & ★
MACHINERY)
28 PORTLAND RD, BN11 1QN
Open: Mon-Sat 8.30am-5.30pm
Wednesday 8.30am-1.00pm
H.P.W.WM.D.CS.A.BC.

WEST MIDLANDS

WEST BROMWICH Tel: 021-
CONWAY SAW & 553 5461/2
SUPPLY LTD ★
SWAN LANE
Open: 8 a.m.-6 p.m. Mon-Fri
9 a.m.-1 p.m. Saturday
P.W.WM.D.CS.BC.

WILTSHIRE

SWINDON Tel. (0793) 31361
SARJENT'S TOOL STORES LTD ★
64 FLEET STREET

Open: Monday to Saturday
8.30 a.m.-5.30 p.m.
H.P.W.WM.D.A.BC

YORKSHIRE

HALIFAX Tel. 0422 43722/
TIMBERLITE LTD 884788/33575
WILLOWFIELDS ROAD ★
WILLOWFIELD
Open: Monday to Friday
Saturday 9.00 a.m.-5.00 p.m.
H.P.W.WM.D.CS.A.BC.

HARROGATE Tel. 0423 66245/
MULTI-TOOLS 55328 ★
158 KINGS ROAD

Open: Monday to Saturday
8.30 a.m.-6.00 p.m.
H.P.W.WM.D.A.BC.

HUDDERSFIELD Tel. (0484)
NEVILLE M. OLDHAM 641219/(0484)
UNIT 1 DAYLE ST. WORKS 42777
DAYLE STREET, LONGWOOD ★
Open: Mon-Fri 9.00am- 5.30pm
Saturday 9.30am-12.00pm
P.W.WM.D.A.BC.

LEEDS Tel. 0532 574736
D. B. KEIGHLEY MACHINERY LTD ★
VICKERS PLACE
STANNINGLEY
Open: Mon-Fri 9am-5pm
Saturday 9am-1pm
P.W.WM.D.CS.A.BC.

YORKSHIRE

LEEDS Tel. 0532 790507
GEORGE SPENCE & SONS LTD
WELLINGTON ROAD ★
Open: Monday to Friday
8.30 a.m.-5.30 p.m.
Saturday 9.00 a.m.-5.00 p.m.
H.P.W.WM.D.T.A.

SHEFFIELD Tel. 0742-441012
GREGORY & TAYLOR LTD
WORKSOP ROAD
Open: 8.30 a.m.-5.30 p.m.
Monday-Friday
8.30 a.m.-12.30 p.m. Sat.
H.P.W.WM.D.

SHEFFIELD Tel. 0742-24659
GRAHAM OXLEY'S SHOWROOM
BRIDGE STREET ★
Open: Monday to Friday
9.00 a.m.-5.30 p.m.
Saturday 8.30 a.m.-12.30 p.m.
H.W.D.A.BC.

SCOTLAND

GLASGOW Tel. 041 429 4374/4444
THE SAW CENTRE Telex: 777886
596-602 EGLINGTON STREET ★
G5 9RR
Open: Mon.-Fri. 8 a.m.-5.30 p.m.
Saturday 9 a.m.-1 p.m.
H.P.W.WM.D.CS.A.

N. IRELAND

Co. ANTRIM Tel. 0266 6384
GEORGE GARDINER
49 BALLYMONEY STREET
BALLYMENA
Open: Open: Mon-Fri 8.30am-5.30pm
Wednesday 8.30am-1.00pm
H.P.W.D.A.BC.

S. IRELAND

COUNTY KILKENNY Tel.
WOODMEN (0409) 5460
CASHEL HOUSE ★
KELLS ROAD, KILKENNY

Open: Monday to Saturday

WALES

BRITON FERRY Tel. (0639)
WOODMEN 820803/4
49 NEATH ROAD ★
Open: Monday to Saturday
9.00 a.m.-5.30 p.m.
P.W.WM.D.A.BC.

CARDIFF Tel. (0222) 373007
JOHN HALL TOOLS LIMITED ★
22 CHURCHILL WAY

Open: Monday to Saturday
9.00 a.m.-5.30 p.m.
H.P.W.WM.D.A.BC.

CARDIFF Tel. (0222) 30831
F. W. MORGAN & 25562
(CANTON) LTD., 129-133
COWBRIDGE RD EAST,
CANTON
Mon-Sat 8-5 Sun. 9.30-12.30
H.P.T.CS.A.BC.

CARDIFF Tel. (0222) 36519/
WOODMEN 373793/35221
74-76 PARK ROAD ★
WHITCHURCH

Open: Monday to Saturday
9.00 a.m.-5.30 p.m.

CARMARTHEN Tel. 0267 7219
DO-IT-YOURSELF SUPPLY
BLUE STREET, DYFED
Open: Monday to Saturday
9.00 a.m.-5.30 p.m.
Thursday 9.00 a.m.-1.00 p.m.
H.P.W.WM.D.T.CS.A.BC.

SWANSEA Tel. (0792) 55680
SWANSEA TIMBER & ★
PLYWOOD CO LTD
57-59 OXFORD STREET
Open: Mon. to Fri. 9 am-5.30 pm
Sat. 9 am-1 pm
H.P.W.D.T.CS.A.BC.

YOU CAN BUY WITH CONFIDENCE
FROM THE
SHOPS IN THIS SHOP GUIDE

★ Shops offering a mail order service are denoted by an asterisk

---

Key: H — Hand tools, **P** — Power tools, **W** — Woodworking machinery up to £1000, **WM** — Woodworking machinery over £1000, **D** — Demonstration available on selected machines, **T** — Timber, **CS** — Cutting or sharpening services, **MF** — Material Finishes, **A** — Attachments, **BC** — Books/catalogues, ***** — Mail order.

£8.00 per Unit
Minimum of SIX insertions.
I enclose remittance of £48.00 ☐
I wish to be invoiced. ☐
Please tick as appropriate.

COUNTY ....

TOWN ....

NAME OF COMPANY/SHOP ....

....

ADDRESS ....

....

To: Valerie Tester
WOODWORKER MAGAZINE
P.O. Box 35,
13 Bridge Street, Hemel Hempstead,
HP1 1EE.

TELEPHONE No ....

DAYS AND HOURS OF BUSINESS

....

....

***TO DENOTE MAIL ORDER SERVICE
AVAILABLE ☐**

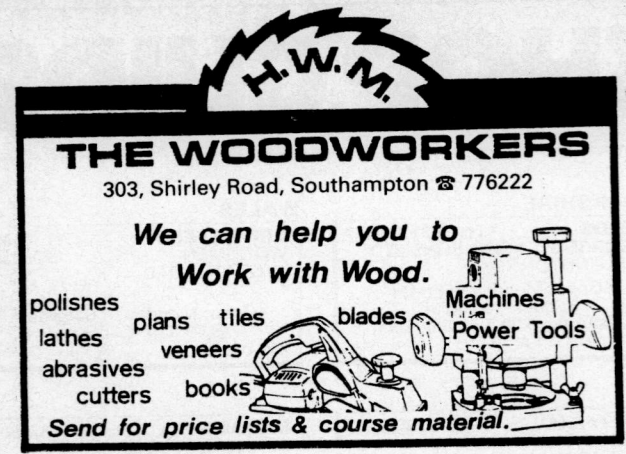

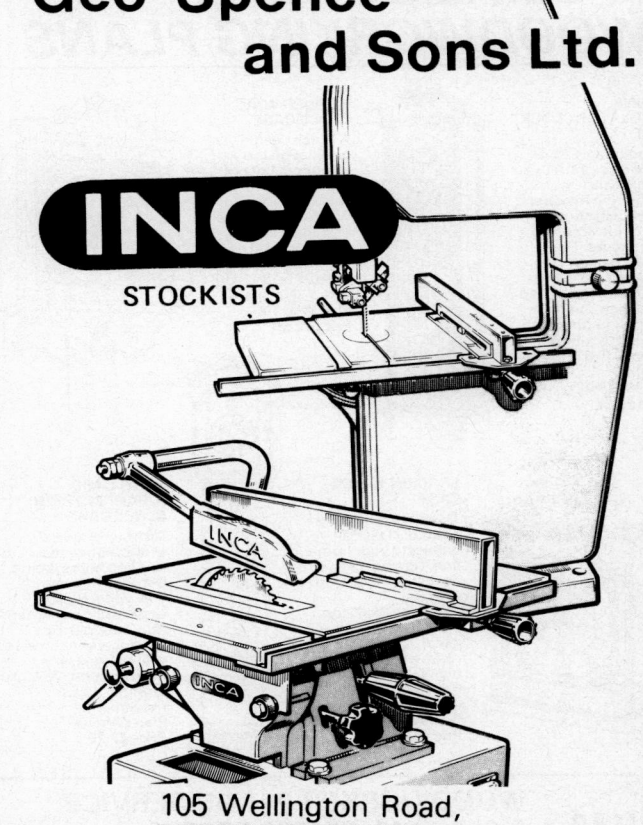

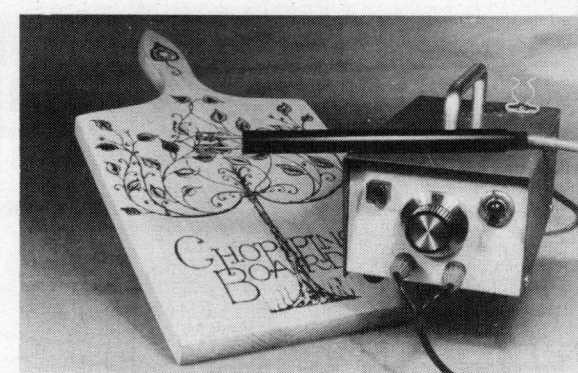
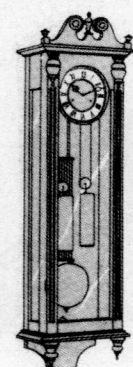

Our panel of experts
answer queries about
your workshop problems

Woodworker's Question Box

Write to: Question Box
Woodworker
PO Box 35
Bridge Street
Hemel Hempstead HP1 1EE

Leather desk inlays
From: R. R. Gillies, Weybridge, Surrey

I am interested in antique restoration, could you please offer advice on the fitting of leather tops to desk? The aspects I am interested in are: 1 The type of leather to be used. 2 How to 'antique' it. 3 The tools and gold leaf used for edgings and motifs and 4 sources of materials and tools.

With this subject one is tempted to say as with other very specialised craft work — leave it to the professional. The main reason for giving this advice is because the tools used are so very expensive, especially if you are not in the mass production market. If only one or two skivers are to be fitted then it is far cheaper to buy leather ready tooled and glue onto the job yourself, and in some cases it is less time consuming to get the job completed by a specialist firm.

However, if one wishes to carry out the work, leather skivers can be purchased mainly in sheep skin from various suppliers. Two names are J. Crisp & Son, Crispin Works, Hawley St, London NW1 and Messrs Woolnough Ltd, 23 Phipp St, London EC2.

The leather supplied by these companies is already antiqued (it is not possible to tan and antique leather unless you are in this specialised business) and can be bought in virtually any colour: antique gold, green and red being the most common. It must be realised that the skiver colour should complement the colour of the wood that it is to be set in.

Skivers are tooled, and usually embossed with a gold border of varying patterns. The brass rolls available for embossing can be purchased from Mackrell & Co Ltd, Witham, Essex but these are very expensive owing to the complicated nature of some of the patterns. The price range is between £50-£115 for these rolls, and obviously for a one-off job it does not pay to buy one. It is very unusual today for the tooling to be in gold leaf. Unless the item of furniture is extremely valuable, most companies use gold foil which is relatively inexpensive.

The leather is glued down onto the table or desk top with heavy-duty wall paper paste. Then it is under cut along the edges with a very sharp knife to make a neat finish.

Parana pine
From: Peter Bavington, Walthamstow, E17

Can you advise on the best method of finishing parana pine? I am constructing virginals in this wood and have been trying out various finishes on spare pieces. I have used Danish oil, polyurethane varnish, lacquer and white shellac but they all produce an unpleasant blotchy effect when the light strikes the finish at a certain angle. A pure wax finish seems to be free from this, but I would prefer to use a more durable finish if possible.

Parana pine has a brownish heartwood with a colour which ranges from a light shade to a very deep brown. The heart may also display prominent red streaks or patches while the sapwood is almost white.

Because brown predominates this wood is often stained a walnut colour and the procedure is:-

After glasspapering damp the wood with warm water to raise the grain. When dry, the wood is smoothed with worn, fine abrasive paper. The stain is made by simmering a teaspoonful of walnut crystals for ten minutes in a little more than a pint of water. When cool the stain should be filtered to remove any undissolved crystals and a dash of ammonia is added. Apply evenly with a brush and allow to dry overnight. Brush on two coats of button polish which may be thinned by adding up to 25% meths. This should be allowed to harden for four or five hours before being smoothed with fine garnet paper. After dusting off the work may be bodied and spirited off in the usual way. Should the colour appear too light when bodying, equal quantities of spirit black and Bismarck brown in small amounts may be added to the polish rubber. If there are some areas requiring additional colour this can be achieved by applying coloured polish with a mop. As soon as the required depth of colour is reached polishing with a clean rubber and ordinary button polish is resumed. The work is finally spirited off with a spirit rubber and methylated spirits.

When Mr H. R. Driffield of Taunton sent us a sketch of a box scraper that had come his way (*Woodworker*, July) our consultant, Bob Grant, was instantly able to identify it. However, his asurance that this tool was still available from Record Tools proved to be inaccurate, as both David Thomas of Bournemouth and F. Alderman of London NW1 wrote to tell us.

Over to you, Bob.

Perhaps I shall be excused for being so long in replying when I say that something of a nationwide search has been conducted on behalf of our two readers who want to get hold of the scraper.

In this I have been ably and diligently assisted by Mike Dean of Record Tools (now of course owned by Bahco) but all to no avail, I'm afraid. It is true that the item has been withdrawn from production — no doubt company mergers have led to rationalisation of product ranges — and of course I was unaware that this had happened when I wrote my original reply.

However, all is not lost!

Scrapers and scraper planes are still obtainable. They are listed and even illustrated in Messrs Sarjent's Tools current catalogue (44-52 Oxford Road, Reading, Berks) and in Roger's tool and book catalogue No 2 (47 Walworth Road, Hitchin, Herts).

If it was the passing reference to chair seat shaping that attracted the readers, then they may like to know that both catalogues show the special inshaves manufactured specifically for this job.

Gluing and varnishing teak
From: J. B. Davis, Truro, Cornwall

I wish to glue some teak. The adhesive I have used in the past has been GPX by CIBA, but I cannot obtain it locally. Is there another adhesive you would recommend?

Can you advise me also which varnish I can apply to teak for use outdoors?

If you particularly want to use the same adhesive, why not contact CIBA at Duxford, Cambridge, and obtain the name of your nearest stockist. Alternatively, Cascomite water-proof adhesive made by Borden Chemicals is in regular use in many furniture and woodworking establishments as are other cold setting adhesives based on urea, phenol, and resorcinol with formaldehyde. The UF types give a water-resistant glue line while PF and RF are more ambitious and give a boil-proof adhesion. Actually, any cold setting adhesive formulated for wood will, if used according to the manufacturer's instructions, give a good bond, the importance when using teak is that it may be awkward because of its greasy nature; therefore, the preparation of the wood is probably of more importance than the choice of adhesive.

In those instances where teak is found not to bond properly, if the quantity merits it, then the contact surfaces are wiped over with a rag soaked in a hydrocarbon solvent such as trichlorethylene or the less toxic trichloroethane to dissolve the chemical substances from the surface of the wood. In small amounts of wood, the use of white spirit or a detergent of the Teepol type will usually suffice to degrease the wood. It helps if, after degreasing, the adhesive is rubbed into the contact surfaces with a fairly stiff brush. Cramping or setting times ought to extended beyond that normally allowed.

With regard to varnishing teak that is to be exposed to the weather, the problem here is that long term durability of the film depends on regular (at least annual) maintenance of the original three or even four coats applied and this is liable to be forgotten when the surface looks reasonable. Once the surface film becomes cracked and moisture gets in, firstly there is discoloration and then patchy separation of the varnish film, and the better this was originally, the harder it now becomes to clean it up and make good.

The polyurethane varnishes give a really hard surface, but if they do fail then they are the most difficult to refurbish. Yacht varnish is excellent and since you ask the question this is the type we would recommend, but always with the proviso that it must be maintained properly. It was for the reasons given that finishes such as teak oil and other formulations were developed, but it really boils down to the fact that if the finish is too oily but does not craze or peel, then it tends to collect dust and become blackened in time. Much of course depends upon the exposure of the wood but if you consider say the mast of a small sailing boat, this is how you must regard your external teak.

Bookshelf

Home Working by Fred Sherlock, published by Newnes Technical Books in a Do-It-Yourself series (£3.95) ISBN 0.408 01121.1

The amazing growth over the years of the do-it-yourself movement has largely been attributed to factors of personal finance and economics. The parallel development of powered hand tools, principally the electric drill and its accessories, has done much to assist and advance the cause, as has also the steady stream of books and magazines devoted to the subject. Fred Sherlock's current work is one of this genre designed to encourage, explain and instruct. He has a lifetime's experience of working with wood and teaching others his skills, and I suspect that he has been too eager to reach an even wider audience by cramming his distilled knowledge and wisdom between the covers of this book. That he is a practical man is undoubted; I smiled at his reference to hemlock as being 'spiteful' as one who has also wrestled with this fractious wood.

Included are the almost ritual chapters on tools and techniques whilst a closing chapter outlines six projects to make, all pieces of furniture — one, interestingly enough in this year of the royal birth, a swinging crib.

In instructional books of this sort the illustrations play a very important part, far more so than the accompanying texts that are necessarily simplified; the classic case of one picture being worth at least 100 words. The diagrams in this book, although good, appear small and cramped on the page, but I very much liked the technique of using blue tint to emphasise and highlight relevant points. It would be nice to see the technique extended in future publications.

For the average and mature DIY enthusiast who has already discarded the philosphy of the bodge, this book should enable some creditable woodwork to be carried out around the home and garden.

R. W. G.

Chainsaw Lumbermaking by Will Malloff published by Taunton Press Inc, at $22.95 hardback ISBN 0-918804-12-4

There is no doubt Will Malloff knows his subject well; but since he has been a lumberjack in his native Canada for some thirty years, it should not be surprising he has developed some very special skills related to converting felled trees into commercial lumber. In producing this book he has drawn on his experience of felling trees ranging from giant redwoods to desert mesquite and in fact has produced a manual of on-site sawmilling based on his modified version of the standard chainsaw and his patented ripping chain.

There is a limited appeal of this type of timber production in countries such as Britain because we lack the type of forest land typical of countries like those in North and South America; nevertheless, there are many estates and plantations in the UK where either it is difficult or impossible to haul sizable trees from stump to sawmill, or it would be more convenient and economic to convert a tree where it fell, if only the right equipment were available. In circumstances such as these, this book is not only invaluable, it is indispensable.

The production of sawn planks by chainsaw is a relatively new method but since the standard chainsaw was developed primarily for cross cutting its adaptation to rip sawing imposes all sorts of responsibilities. The teeth must cut without premature blunting or burning and they must cut smoothly and without power loss due to drag; they must also be easily sharpened and maintained. Will Malloff has patented his own particular version and judging from the illustrations in the book the saw appears to work admirably.

No attempt has been made to use log examples which could be deemed easily sawn; on the contrary, and although the author does not mention it, it would seem that log shape, or type of grain is of no consequence; the saw will behave properly. On page 2 at the very beginning of the text is a series of photographs demonstrating the simplicity of the method of cutting, the equipment consisting of a modified chainsaw, a mill for adjusting the depth of cut, a guide board, for squaring the rounded outer slab, a hammer and three nails, the whole being carried easily by the operator. The refreshing thing I noted however, was that the log to be used for the purpose of photographing the sequence was one full of spiral grain and one which might have been expected to cause the saw to stall or jam because it was attempting to wander but was being held fast by the guide. That the saw chain appeared to stand up well was emphasised by a later section in the book devoted to explaining how very misshappen burls and natural bends were easily converted.

The book is divided into three parts: In the shop; In the field; and Speciality milling, where the saw is even shown doubling as a straight line edger. The text is concise and is backed by dozens of very good action photographs and the whole book reflects a lifetime of experience and expertise on the part of the author from his insistence on proper torquing of a new engine to making up a winch for easy operation of the saw through long, large logs in order to avoid the unpleasantness of inhaling engine fumes and the need for spitting out sawdust when the operator is in close proximity to the saw cut. There is however, so much of a highly specialised nature in this book that should commend it to landowners and agents with woodlands and plantations requiring regular exploitation who find normal sawmilling facilities unsuitable or inadequate.

W. H. B.

Letters

From: C. J. Joyce, 59 Blenheim Roa~
Birstall, Leicester
Dear Sir

I am a regular reader of your magazin~ and have found it to be very informative a~ helpful, in particular other readers' points ~ view and comments on your letter pag~ This has prompted me to ask if you wou~ kindly print a letter on my behalf asking a~ manufacturers or fitters in the door, wi~ dow or porch joinery industries if the~ would be interested in training a you~ person 19-20 in one of the above trade~ within the Leicestershire area.

After recently leaving the RAF on medic~ grounds, having a sound mechanical e~ gineering and woodworking backgroun~ find it hard to find suitable training. The~ are very limited opportunities with TOF~ training in this area.

Yours faithfully **C. J. Joyc~**

From: Stephen E. Schurman, 8577 Copl~
Court, Fair Oaks, California 95628.
Dear Sir

I am writing to you in hopes that you ma~ be able to help me locate old photograp~ (dated 1880-1930) depicting men worki~ around or with woodworking equipment.

I collect these photos, or copies I ca~ obtain, for my personal collection a~ display. If you have any information yo~ think may be of interest to me please let m~ know.

I would also be interested in any o~ receipts, invoices or paperwork from a~ woodworking companies and mills.

Yours faithfully **Stephen E. Schurma~**

● **Can anyone help Mr Schurman?**

From: C. Parker, Chingford E4
Dear Sir

I have been a regular reader of *Woodwo~ ker* for some time now, I look forward t~ each issue and with wonderment to th~ articles by Gordon Stokes, especially th~ 'expert' advice he gives to beginners.

My first recollection of woodturning wa~ as a small child in my father's workshop~ sitting on the lathe bed, watching him a~ work. A lathe bed in those days was tw~ lengths of 3in × 9in bolted to 3in × 9i~ uprights. The headstock and tailstock whic~ had a 7in throw, was usually set up on 3i~ blocks of wood so that one could turn a~ 18in wine table top if need be. Incidentally, ~ lathehead used to cost £7/10s including th~ four-step cone pulley. Always when th~ time came for me to go home, my fathe~ would turn me a wooden cup or goblet.

Ultimately, while still a schoolboy I bega~ to learn woodturning. As the East End o~ London had hundreds of master turners ~ had the opportunity to watch many of th~ really good turners of the time, who wer~ more than ready to pass on their knowledg~ to a young boy.

The first thing a would-be woodturne~ was taught was how to sandpaper turner~ of all kinds without destroying the crispnes~ of the design. Sorry Mr Stokes, but n~ French polisher would accept any turner~ that was not well sanded.

Every 'trade mill' had up to a dozen woodturners, all master men who rented a the and bench space. Every group of rners shared a common whetstone some in diameter and 6in thick, but each had own Washita or Arkansas oilstone for isels and a tin can with one or two pstones in paraffin, and so the second ing a would be turner was taught was now grind and hone gouges and chisels.

If Mr Stokes should hear a loud bumping ise, it is all those generations of wood rners 'turning' in their graves at the ought of the time they wasted honing ols with oilstones in a very, very competi- e business, when, as he has discovered, it as never necessary. Mr Stokes should ank his lucky stars. With beliefs like that would never have earned a living in ose days.

Mr Editor, please accept my congratula- ns on your excellent magazine. Long may flourish.

Yours faithfully **C. Parker**

om: W. Purcell, Mitcham Junction, rrey
ear Sir
I have been looking for years for a agazine giving a plan of an old fashioned ravan type cupboard bed. No one seems do them nowadays. Also I am no rpenter so I need some detailed guidance. ave made a fitted wardrobe and wish to fit single bed on one side, a dresser in the iddle and a single wardrobe on the other le. My problem is that I do not know how fit the bed and hinge it to make it look like wardrobe door. Any help would be preciated.

Yours faithfully **W. Purcell**

. Over to the readers of *Woodworker* for lp and advice.

om: R. Ward, Balsham, Cambridge
ear Sir
I have recently bought an old treadle lathe Stringer Bros, but unfortunately there is drive belt. Could you give me any formation as to the type required and here, if it is still possible, to get it? ternatively, what were the belts made of? uld I make one myself? This particular he was used in a forge by a blacksmith d I shall be grateful for any information d about treadle lathes and rhaps a clue as to its date.

Yours faithfully **Robert Ward**

om: A. F. Scofield, Hockley, Essex
ear Sir
read with interest the letter in the July oodworker from Mr R. Shann, concerning e difficulty he has experienced in making ternal cuts in 1½in oak.
Until a few years ago, the difficulty which experiences in sawing fine radii and ternal cutting in thick and hard timbers articularly internal cutting) was the bug- ar of all cabinetmakers. Often much dious and painstaking hand cutting and ishing was required to complete even the allest project.

During the last four years I have been demonstrating the Hegner universal saws, both the Multicut-2 and the commercial Polycut-3 models at all the major wood-working exhibitions, where we show that with these saws it is possible to cut hard-woods up to 2in thickness, to cut intricate external and internal shapes, with quick easy blade feeding for internal work, a minimum of blade breakage, often using fretsaw blades of good quality (which we also supply). The same machines will also cut metals, plastics, and other materials. I will gladly forward brochures and information on these saws.

Yours faithfully **A. F. Scofield**,
Hegner Universal Saws (UK) Ltd.

From: R. H. Wintin, Gt Dunmow, Essex
Dear Sir
Ref Mr R. Shann's letter in *Woodworker*, July p508. I would suggest that he tries a hand-held or machine fretsaw. I myself use hand-held fretsaws with spiral blades. If he tries nos 8-11 spiral blades he might have some success with 1½in oak.
I have no complaints with these types of blades.

Yours faithfully **R. H. Winton**

From: Alan M. Biggs, Swindon Village, Glos
Dear Sir
Some months ago I bought a dovetail marking gauge from Collett Engineering of Truro, Cornwall, that had been advertised in your magazine. When I received it I was delighted to find that it was superbly made and very accurate.
In use it is simplicity itself and far more durable than my wooden templates that I used to make and I have nothing but praise for this instrument, so well done to the makers, Collett Engineering. It's not often one has the chance to give out bouquets, is it? It's more often brickbats!

Yours faithfully **Alan M. Biggs**

From: H. Chart, Woodley, Berks
Dear Sir
I sympathise with Mr McQuire after hav-ing read his letter expressing difficulty in obtaining rosewood to make up a sixth matching chair (June p423). It seems tragic that substitute woods (which when col-oured down can be disappointingly unsym-pathetic) are having to be used nowadays as supplies of the 'real thing' are dwindling.
However, perhaps he (or other crafts-people having similar troubles) may take heart to know that I have some fine old stocks of rosewood available together with other traditionally known exotic woods in various sizes. SAE to H. Chart, 16 Walmer Road, Woodley, Reading, Berkshire or phone (0734) 695336.

Yours faithfully **H. Chart**

From: W. M. Thomas, Blackwood, Gwent
Dear Sir
Some years ago *Woodworker* published articles by Michael Gareth Llewellyn, now deceased. He wrote a book called *Sand in the glass* which now appears to be out of print. I do not know the publisher and local

book shops are unable to help me. Can any *Woodworker* reader trace this book or give me further details about it?

Yours faithfully **W. M. Thomas**

From: F. A. Sharman, Wolverhampton
Dear Sir
Permit me to be the one hundred and fifty-second reader to point out to you, the compiler of *July Notes* and Leonard Ball that, as the maximum size of parcel permit-ted by the Post Office is one where the greatest length of any side is not more than three feet, the maximum length of a thin moulding which can be sent by post is four feet.

Yours pythagorasly **Frank A. Sharman**

●**We make it 4.24 feet, but much depends on the thickness of the moulding, of course.**

From: M. J. Buckley-Golder, Cannock
Dear Sir
Ref. the letter from Mr Hicks on bandsaw wheel problems (*Woodworker*/August) I find that double sided adhesive tape is the perfect answer to bonding rubber tyres on to aluminium wheels.
The method I used was:
1. Lay the tape around the wheel, cut the tape neatly to form a butt joint. Do not remove outer layer of paper.
2. Fit the rubber strip around the tape, cut through the rubber where the ends overlap. Check to ensure a good butt joint, remove rubber.
3. Remove outer layer of paper, fit rubber strip, and it works.
I tyred six wheels by this method and have had no trouble at all. Six wheels? Oh, I forgot to mention I built two bandsaws, one for myself and one for my nephew, and they *both* cost less than the kit you see adver-tised.
Bandsaw blade 84in; throat 15in; depth of cut 7in.

Yours faithfully **M. J. Buckley-Golder**

From: W. H. Brown, Amersham, Bucks
Dear Sir
I would refer to the letter from Mr G. Stokes, published in July *Woodworker* in which he criticises a reply I gave to an inquirer under the Question Box heading in the February issue and with unnecessary flippancy suggests my reply was intended as a joke. Since I am the anonymous authority to whom he refers, and since the subject matter of both the inquiry and reply are of interest if not importance, I should be grateful for the opportunity to put the matter into perspective.
The question asked was whether a suit-able finish could be recommended for some proposed wooden goblets, the finish to be capable of resisting alcohol and stand up to washing in warm water. Although this was the direct question there was also the indirect aspect of the likely behaviour of the wood in this specific use, and while I only touched on the aspect of certain modern finishes and their high resistance to alcohol, it was fairly obvious to me that for the use in question, no finish could reasonably be expected to stand up long term to the

Letters

conditions imposed. Finishes of the type that stand up well to chemicals and hot plates are generally those which depend not only on polymerisation of the surface film, but good adhesion to the wood surface, and this is not so satisfactory where a high degree of end grain is present as is likely in the inside of a goblet bowl. In any case, a properly applied finish depends for its long term efficiency on regular maintenance of the film, for example, wine or tea spilt on a table top is generally wiped off fairly quickly, or a mark left by a hot plate removed and generally made good. Since a goblet in use as a drinking vessel is exposed to various chemicals in use and in cleaning and is likely to swell and contract because of washing and drying, it is unlikely that even the best of finishes would stand up well to the treatment and accordingly, it was not feasible to suggest one, but this part of the answer was governed to some extent by the general inadvisability of recommending wood (as a substance, not a material) for drinking vessels.

I did not say wood could not be used but I said "we are basically reticent to suggest a wooden goblet is an ideal vehicle from which to drink alcoholic beverages". I qualified this by referring to the chemistry of wood and the possibility of detrimental characteristics developing.

Your correspondent may well consider the above as "a new and shattering revelation", but I would refer him to the various Dermatology Departments of hospitals, where a proportion of patients whose ailments, often painful, have been attributed to contact with certain wood species and regard their problems as anything but humorous. He could pass his comments to High Wycombe General Hospital who care for the needs of the woodworking fraternity of the area, they are sure to be appreciated.

Over fifty years ago, in the late 1920s, a large company for whom I was then working, introduced a new timber into production; the wood was mansonia from west Africa, the intention being to use it as an alternative to walnut. Within hours of it being worked for the first time, practically the whole staff within close proximity to the sawmill became ill; personally, I felt as though I suddenly had influenza, but progressively, some extremely serious cases of dermatitis developed despite work on the wood being stopped after a couple of days. The Board of Trade had a say in temporarily banning the wood. I mention this ancient bit of history because Mr Stokes might like to know how that particular wood is regarded today, and I would refer him to FIRA NOTE 36: *Irritant Timbers* 1966 published by the Furniture Industries Research Association. From case histories they give the following:

Harmful effects Irritation of mucuous membrane, sneezing, nasal haemorrhage, eyes sore, eyes bloodshot, dizziness, dermatitis.

Severity Severity varied with individuals but can be quite high.

Frequency Quite frequent.

Remarks A cardiac glycoside and a quinone having irritant properties have been isolated.

Mansonia is not the only wood likely to have harmful properties and, of course, not everybody is allergic, but some of the other symptoms mentioned in this list include face swelling, bleeding from the ears, bronchial asthma, pains in the chest, irritation of nose and throat, drowsiness and severe vomiting.

I do not want to labour this point too much, but the lips and throat are sensitive parts of the human anatomy and I hold to the view that contact with some woods can be detrimental to health and there is adequate documentary evidence to support this view; accordingly, I concluded my reply to the inquirer by refusing to recommend wood for this specific use.

Wood of course has been used for centuries for kitchen utensils and this still obtains today, but we have learned to be selective and prefer woods with non-tainting properties where contact with foodstuffs is concerned, species like sycamore, birch, beech, poplar, etc. Unfortunately, these are not, as a rule, the types that are preferred by wood turners as decorative media, but even if they were, there is a difference between relatively short term food storage use, and long term food contact. Most people discard chipped china cups and cracked china plates for hygienic reasons and I can hardly believe they would be happy to use hardwood steak plates progressively scored by the use of serrated edged steak knives.

I would like to make one final point; many chemicals in wood are either directly soluble in alcohol or they undergo certain reactions in the presence of alcohol. In the identification of timbers, one of the tests for the separation of practically identical species is to place a few heartwood shavings in a solution of 97 per cent alcohol. When this is done and the mixture agitated for 20-30 seconds, a colour appears, perhaps orange-brown, brown, light or dark mauve or red indicating a specific type. It works well in identification techniques, but it is hardly likely to work wonders with a Château Moulin-Riche, Crus Exceptionnels, swirled lightly round a wooden goblet of doubtful condition, but then I suppose it is a matter of taste, literally.

It is possible that none of Mr Stokes' recipients of drinking goblets has suffered harm, if indeed they have actualy used them for drinking alcohol from, but a sufferer from heart disease or lung cancer attributed to cigarette smoking is in no position to say whose cigarettes caused the damage.

Yours faithfully **W. H. Brown**

From Sam Hamilton, Maghera, Co Derry
Dear Sir

Re query by R. Shann, July *Woodworker*. As a woodturner and repairer of antique furniture I have had problems similar to yours. After many trials with jigsaws and often finding a slip up near the final cuts, I was about to give up when I decided to enquire into what the *Multicut 2* could do. I finally decided to buy one and I find (for me) it does everything the manufacturers say. Furthermore, the cut you make whether inside or outside of your work requires very little sanding if any at all. I call it one of the best buys I ever made. I only give one small warning about this machine and that is that I found it takes a little time to get used to, and you may not do the best work first time round.

Yours faithfully **Sam Hamilton**

Events

Woodworker Show

Woodworker Show at the Royal Horticultural Society Halls, London, 19-24 October details from Model and Allied Publications Ltd, PO Box 35, Bridge Street, Hemel Hempstead, Herts HP1 1EE.

Furniture in context

At the British Crafts Centre, until 2 September. The Centre is in Earlham Street, Covent Garden, London. Exhibition covers commissioned, one-off and batch production of furniture.

Karwei '83

The sixteenth annual exhibition for the diy trade will be staged in the Irene, Bernhard and Marijke halls on the Royal Netherlands Industries Fair site in Utrecht from 17-23 January 1983.

The Irene hall will be of interest to woodworkers since it will contain wood kitchens, self assembly furniture. The Bernhard hall is the venue for locks and hinges, hand tools and workbenches.

The first four days of the exhibition are trade only, the final three are open to the general public.

Scotfair '82

Will be held from 5-7 October at the Royal Highland Exhibition Hall, Edinburgh, include furniture, pottery, glassware, jewellery, textiles, knitwear, prints, food and perfumes. Further details from Scottish Development Agency, 102 Telford Road, Edinburgh EH4 2NP. Phone 031-343 1911.

Don at Cardiff

An exhibition of work by Bristol woodturner Don White is currently on show at the National Museum of Wales in Cardiff. Closing date: 31 October.

Woodcarving Extravaganza

Historic pieces of carved woodwork will form part of an exhibition at Gunnersbury Park museum, Brentford. Opening on December, it will run for seven weeks and will also highlight bizarre masks from Africa and Jacobean grotesques. Further details from Frederick Oughton FRSA, The Civic Centre, Lampton Road, Hounslow TW3 4DN.

Ligna '83

The international trade fair for machinery and equipment for the wood industries will be held from 11-17 May 1983. The organisers say over 80 per cent of the 1981 exhibitors are set to return in 1983.

Ligna '83 will present forestry machinery, vehicles and equipment; machinery for working, treating and processing timber and wood materials in sawmills, planing mills and veneer works, panel and furniture factories; special purpose plastics machinery for the wood industry and auxiliary equipment; tools, abrasives, surface coating agents; chemical binders, solvents, glues and adhesives; environmental protection and industrial safety aspects, design engineering, energy generation and energy saving.

A programme of specialist conferences and seminars will support the exhibition.

Woodworker

The magazine for the craftsman
November 1982
Volume 86 Number 1068

EDITORIAL

Editor
Chris Dunn
Deputy Editor
Polly Curds
Design
Martin Streetly
Editorial Secretary
Ann Duncan
Contributors
W Bond FIWSc, W H Brown FIWSc,
D Cliffe, H W Gates, R W Grant DLC
RSA MSIAD, J Hill, A Lord, G Stokes,
J Taylor, S Thomas, H Turner.
Editorial Tel. *0442 41221*
Editorial Address:
*Woodworker, PO Box 35, Hemel
Hempstead, Herts HP1 1EE*
*All correspondence to be accompanied by a
stamped addressed envelope. No
responsibility can be accepted for the
loss/damage of unsolicited material. No
published material may be reproduced
without prior permission.*

ADVERTISEMENTS

Advertisement Manager
Glyn Crole-Rees
Tel: 0442 41221
*Woodworker reserves the right to refuse or
suspend advertisements without
explanation. The publishers can take no
responsibility for clerical or printing
errors/omissions or for the bona fides of
advertisers.*

SUBSCRIPTIONS

Tel: 0442 41221
UK Rate
£11.90 per annum (inc index)
Overseas Rate
£12.90/$29 per annum (inc index)

GUILD OF WOODWORKERS

Administrator
Polly Curds
Tel: 0442 41221
Guild Address: Guild of Woodworkers, PO
Box 35, Hemel Hempstead, Herts HP1 1EE

UK Trade Sales
Argus Press Sales & Distribution Ltd,
12-18 Paul Street, London EC2A 4JS
Tel: 01-247 8233
North American Distribution
(Trade) Eastern News Distributors Ltd,
66-41 Powells Cove Boulevard, PO Box 69,
Whitestone, New York 11357.
*Postmaster: Send address changes to
England.*
Printed in the UK by HE Warne Ltd,
East Hill, St Austell, Cornwall PL25 4TN

ABC
MEMBER OF THE AUDIT
BUREAU OF CIRCULATIONS

ISSN 0043 776X

© Model & Allied Publications Ltd 1982

Contents

On the cover: *Martin Streetly's drawing of
Fraser Budd who is a member of the
Somerset Guild of Craftsmen and head of
the technical and design department at
Ashton Park School, Blackmores Lane,
Bower Ashton, Bristol. Fraser trained at
Shoreditch College where he was
craftsman of the year. His work was on
show recently at the* Woodworkers of
Excellence *exhibition in Cheltenham and*
Masterclass *in Hitchin.*

Model & Allied Publications Ltd
P.O. Box 35, Bridge Street, Hemel
Hempstead HP1 1EE

Guild notes

Polishing and finishing course

Aldenham School, Elstree, was the setting for the latest in the series of courses the guild has been running on this subject. The course was held on 23 and 24 August to take advantage of the school premises during the holidays. Thank you to the bursar (Mr Moore) and Peter Gradwell (woodwork master) for their help in organising the running of the course. Both are guild members and we look forward to making their acquaintance again.

We also enjoyed meeting the other course members and hope they received the instruction they requested. Guild members came from London, Somerset, Essex, Bedford, Surrey and South Africa.

All I am sure will agree with me that Charles Cliffe knows his subject and the interplay of ideas and thoughts expressed during the short tea and coffee breaks were also of importance to complement the course content. Thank you Charles.

If you want to make Charles' acquaintence again this year he will be chief steward at the Woodworker Show and also will be lecturing and demonstrating wax polishing on the Saturday (23 October) at the Show.

Design course

The course on design and furniture making at Rycotewood College, Thame, took place on the 7-9 September and we were delighted to welcome guild members from as far afield as New Zealand, Trinidad, Dublin, Scotland, Cornwall, Northumberland, Derbyshire and many points nearer the south east corner of the country.

At this stage (10 September) I can only say thank you to the course organisers at the college, Chris Simpson and Hans Bromwich and Bob(?) in the workshops, Alex(?) and her staff in the kitchen and matron. Thankyou to all of you for your various roles in the course organisation. Also I hope that the course participants enjoyed their stay. I know we have some wrinkles to iron out, this was a first of its type and unlike a design brief where the models can be scrapped and altered at all stages this course had to be run with human guinea pigs, to find out exactly what is required, what support is needed and how to do it better next time.

Meanwhile photographs were taken and some notes were kept so I hope to produce a fuller report on a future guild page. Please keep in touch and let me know how you are getting on in your projects. I value your remarks and comments and I certainly enjoyed meeting you all.

Subscriptions

Would guild members note that those whose subscriptions are due should send their remittances to the administrator at the usual Woodworker address. Cheques or postal orders (£3.00 individual members, £6.00 trading craftsmen) should be made out to Model & Allied Publications Ltd and crossed.

I hope you will continue membership of the guild but if you do not wish to do so please return your indenture and personal identification card in accordance with the guild statutes.

● *The Three Horseshoes just down the road from the finishing and polishin course, Letchmore Heath (Study by Aldenham pupil)*

Woodworker Show

We are looking forward to meeting guild members on the Woodworker/Guild stand at the show this year. Remember your guild membership entitles you to a reduced fee for entry to the show. I hope many of you have also entered the competition classes. The show is an excellent London show case for your work and a chance to meet other woodworkers of like mind and inspiration.

Routing course

The routing course arranged for the 30 October is full, in fact it has become over subscribed so we are pleased to be able to announce that we shall be fitting the disappointed in early next year either on one or two dates to be announced later. We are delighted with the response and wish to thank all members for their support.

Jigsaw makers wanted

Mr K. Holmes of Trench Enterprises Ltd, Holmes Associates, Three Cow Green, Bacton, Stowmarket, Suffolk IP14 4HJ wishes to contact wooden jigsaw makers who cut hand puzzles rather than mass produce them. I do not know the exact nature of the proposition but if any readers are interested, why not contact Mr Holmes direct at the above address or phone him on (04492) 672734.

Windsor settee. . . the answer

On page 721 we picture a fine example of a Windsor two-seater and ask readers to determine the date.

It is a Windsor seat of the type made in the 18th century, but this one is the 1982 work of Hugh Loughborough of The Craftsman Solva, Dyfed. Hugh saw the seat pictured in a book on furniture in an Oxford garden setting and liked its proportions, hence the modern version.

Polly Curds
PO Box 35,
Bridge Street,
Hemel Hempstead, HP1 1EE
Please enclose a sae with all correspondence anticipating a reply.

OBITUARY
Fred Howe

Master craftsman Fred Howe, who die on June 16 at the age of 72, was worl famous for his skills in woodturning an lapidary.

His mind was ever active in thinking c new ideas, articles or sets and groups c things to create in a variety of materials. H transformed simple objects into maste pieces of ornamental turning, using the fu scope of the ornamental lathe.

Mr Howe was well known in Hastings an every year he opened his home during OI Town Week to show the public the object he had lovingly created during the year an to raise funds for the town's old people. Th front room of his house was crowded wit shining woodwork, ivory and stone. Ther were well over a thousand articles, includ ing a bowl of mixed fruits and vegetable carved in the appropriate natural woods chess sets, a wassail bowl and cups c lignum vitae and ivory, a case of butterflie created from slips of beach pebbles and table with inlays of various fish.

All his work is to be catalogued and it hoped to produce a photographic record i book form.

He will be missed by all members of th Society of Ornamental Turners which h formed with five members in 1948. It nov has a world-wide membership of more tha 250, many of whom have travelled far t meet him and see his collection and work shop.

He inspired all those who met him to g forward and create things to the best of thei ability and to emulate his high standard o design and finish. Fred was always ready t offer advice and help to all those who had feeling for turning and the materials i which he worked and loved.

Through his efforts to encourage the ar and science of ornamental turning he wa admitted as a Freeman of London in 195 and granted his livery to the Worshipfu Company of Turners in 1977. In the inter vening period he won numerous award and medals for his craftwork. **P. F**

November notes

Back number wanted
A telephone call to the *Woodworker* office recently brought a request from Mr Parker of Hull. Mr Parker needs a copy of *Woodworker* for December 1976 to complete his set for that year. Any reader who can help should contact the editorial office at the usual address and we will forward the copy to Mr Parker with any charges necessary.

Gypsy Museum
Reading the recent newsletter from the Model Horse Drawn Vehicles Club (no 58) I was interested to note a piece about a new gypsy museum. The small village of Selbourne in Hampshire now boasts a gypsy museum at Limes Yard. Founded by Peter Ingram the museum houses a fine collection of gypsy vans and waggons (together with household goods, clothing and examples of traditional arts and crafts). Until 1968 Mr Ingram travelled the road with his horse and van, making pegs, baskets and wooden flowers; he is now settled and restores vans, waggons and carts.

Change of address
Robert Longstaff, maker of folk and early instruments, toys, turning, timber and corn dollies has moved. His new address is Orchard View, Appleton Rd, Longworth, Abingdon, Oxon OX13 5EF.

Apart from finished instruments, kits and components for musical instruments Robert says he is increasing his stocks of air and kiln dried timbers for instrument making, turning, carving and modelling, either by mail order to a cutting list or by selection (by appointment only!).

Robert runs daily, weekend, and week-long courses in turning and instrument making. We hope to twist his arm a little and get him to arrange an instrument making course for guild members in 1983. Anyone interested?

Shute's Jig

On page 598 of the September issue of *Woodworker* we published *Shute's jig* which was described by Bob Grant and photographed by John Peacock. The annotations were omitted from the drawing and are therefore reproduced here. We are sorry for any inconvenience that this may have caused readers.

Plans wanted
Don Robinson is looking for plans or pictures of a horse-breakers cart. Anyone who can help can get in touch with Don via John Pearce (secretary) MHDV club, 4 Brentlea Crescent, Higher Heysham, Lancs LA3 2BT.

Make a Note
WOODWORKER SHOW

Royal Horticultural Society's New & Old Halls, Westminster, London SW1.

19-24 October 1982 inclusive.

● *On pages 754-759 of this issue we feature nursery furniture. This little chair by Jack Hill could easily fit into the nursery. It is a rush seated rocker based on a Fred Lambert design which Fred modelled on a chair said to have been used by John Bunyan*

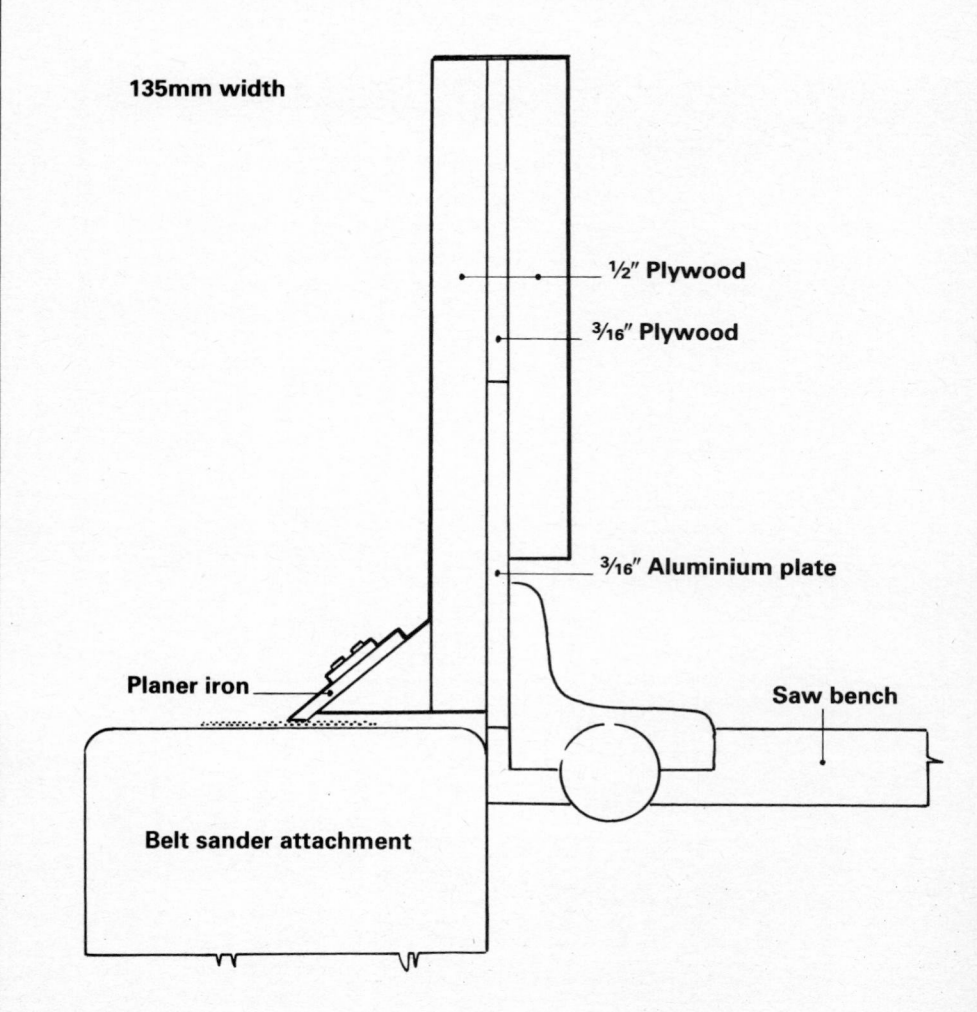

135mm width

½" Plywood

³/₁₆" Plywood

³/₁₆" Aluminium plate

Planer iron

Saw bench

Belt sander attachment

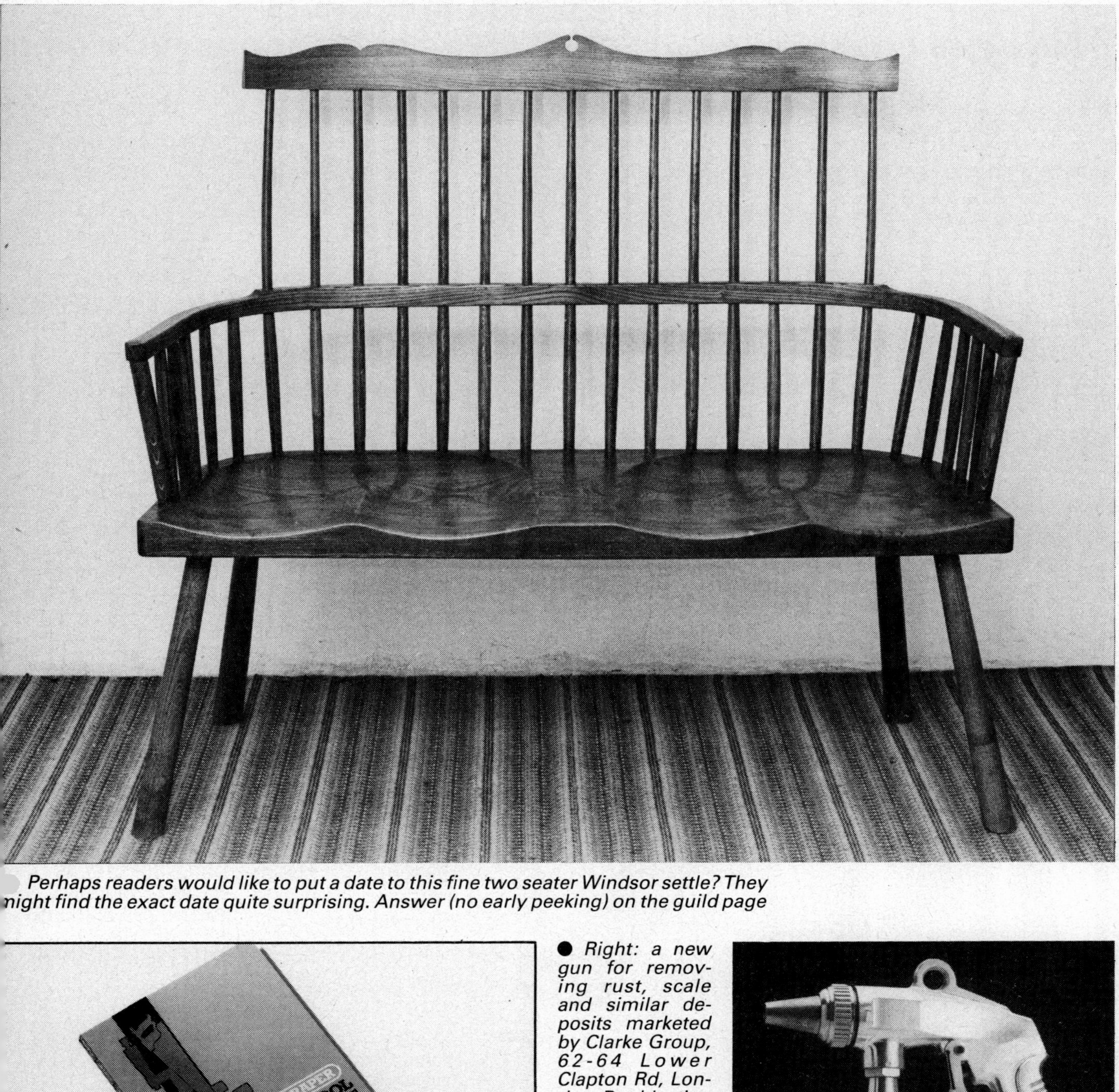

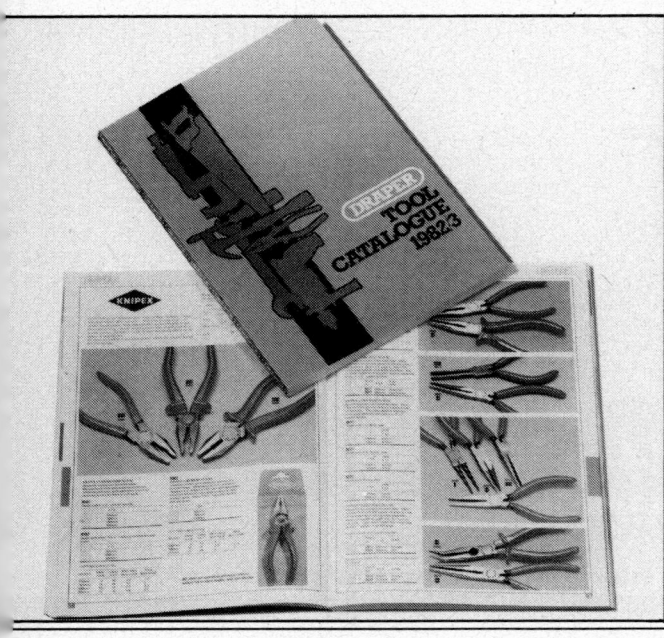

Perhaps readers would like to put a date to this fine two seater Windsor settle? They might find the exact date quite surprising. Answer (no early peeking) on the guild page

● Right: a new gun for removing rust, scale and similar deposits marketed by Clarke Group, 62-64 Lower Clapton Rd, London. Dry blasting is now widely used for renovation work. Left: Draper Tools comprehensive catalogue for hand tool buyers in full colour, cover price £6.50 now available from the company at Hursley Rd, Chandlers Ford, Eastleigh, Hants

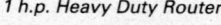

Prices quoted are those prevailing at press date and are subject to alteration due to economic conditions.

CECIL W. TYZACK [FAIR DEAL*] OFFERS
*SPECIAL PRICES BACKED BY FULL SPARES & SERVICING FACILITIES. VISIT STAND 45/46/47/48

TYZACK ROUTER CUTTERS
¼ inch shank
Made in U.S.A.

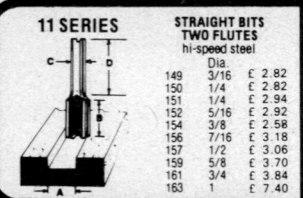

11 SERIES STRAIGHT BITS TWO FLUTES hi-speed steel

	Dia.	
149	3/16	£ 2.82
150	1/4	£ 2.82
151	1/4	£ 2.94
152	5/16	£ 2.92
154	3/8	£ 2.58
156	7/16	£ 3.18
157	1/2	£ 3.06
159	5/8	£ 3.70
161	3/4	£ 3.84
163	1	£ 7.40

21 SERIES STRAIGHT BITS SINGLE FLUTE SINGLE END hi-speed steel

	Dia.	
270	1/16	£ 1.52
271	1/8	£ 1.62
273	3/16	£ 1.58
274	3/16	£ 1.64
275	1/4	£ 1.75
282	1/8	£ 1.52
285	3/16	£ 1.48
288	1/4	£ 1.77

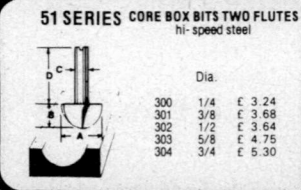

51 SERIES CORE BOX BITS TWO FLUTES hi-speed steel

	Dia.	
300	1/4	£ 3.24
301	3/8	£ 3.68
302	1/2	£ 3.64
303	5/8	£ 4.75
304	3/4	£ 5.30

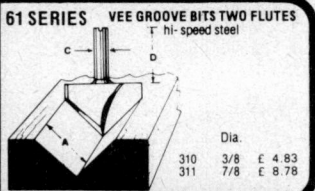

61 SERIES VEE GROOVE BITS TWO FLUTES hi-speed steel

	Dia.	
310	3/8	£ 4.83
311	7/8	£ 8.78

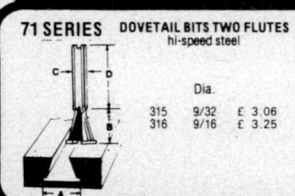

71 SERIES DOVETAIL BITS TWO FLUTES hi-speed steel

	Dia.	
315	9/32	£ 3.06
316	9/16	£ 3.25

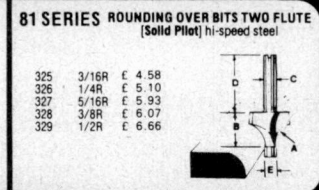

81 SERIES ROUNDING OVER BITS TWO FLUTE [Solid Pilot] hi-speed steel

325	3/16R	£ 4.58
326	1/4R	£ 5.10
327	5/16R	£ 5.93
328	3/8R	£ 6.07
329	1/2R	£ 6.66

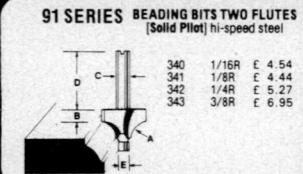

91 SERIES BEADING BITS TWO FLUTES [Solid Pilot] hi-speed steel

340	1/16R	£ 4.54
341	1/8R	£ 4.44
342	1/4R	£ 5.27
343	3/8R	£ 6.95

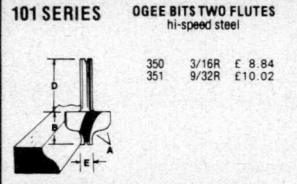

101 SERIES OGEE BITS TWO FLUTES hi-speed steel

350	3/16R	£ 8.84
351	9/32R	£10.02

111 SERIES ROMAN OGEE BITS TWO FLUTES [Solid Pilot] hi-speed steel

355	5/32R	£ 8.17
356	1/4R	£10.16

121 SERIES COVE BITS TWO FLUTES [Solid Pilot] hi-speed steel

360	3/16R	£ 5.82
361	1/4R	£ 4.34
362	3/6R	£ 5.33
363	1/2R	£ 5.88

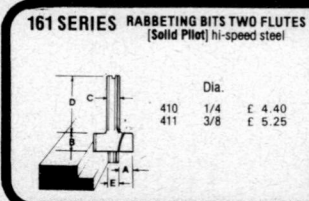

161 SERIES RABBETING BITS TWO FLUTES [Solid Pilot] hi-speed steel

	Dia.	
410	1/4	£ 4.40
411	3/8	£ 5.25

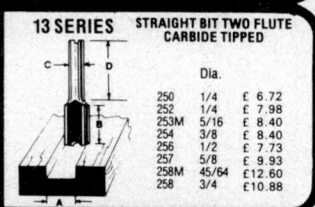

13 SERIES STRAIGHT BIT TWO FLUTE CARBIDE TIPPED

	Dia.	
250	1/4	£ 6.72
252	1/4	£ 7.98
253M	5/16	£ 8.40
254	3/8	£ 8.40
256	1/2	£ 7.73
257	5/8	£ 9.93
258M	45/64	£12.60
258	3/4	£10.88

The NEW Elu® TGS 171

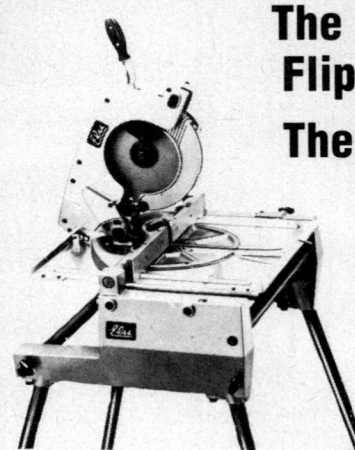

The Saw with the Flip-over Action:
The ELU TGS 171

Complete with TCT saw, Rip fence, Mitre fence.

For Aluminium

£245.00
inc. VAT, carr. £5.00
£17.00 Scotland

For Wood

£225.00
inc. VAT, carr. £5.00
£17.00 Scotland

Elu® PORTABLE ELECTRIC SAWS

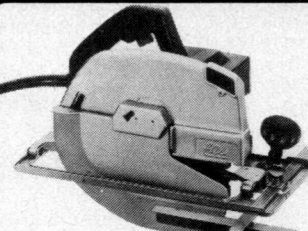

MH 182 PORTABLE ELECTRIC SAW
Complete with 215mm (8½") TCT Saw Blade giving 78mm (3⅛") depth of cut.
£78.00 (inc. VAT) Carriage £3.00

MH85 HEAVY DUTY BUILDER'S SAW
Complete with 240mm (9½") TCT Saw Blade giving an 85mm (3⅜") depth of cut at 90°. Power output 1100 watts. Weight 8.5 Kg.
£105.00 (inc. VAT) Carriage £3.50

ST 152 PENDULUM JIG SAW
Complete with three Saw Blades, 8mm spanner, 6mm Allen Key and carrying case.
£59.00 (inc. VAT) Carriage £2.50

Access

Cecil W. Tyzack LTD. TOOLS AND MACHINERY
79/81 Kingsland Rd., Shoreditch, E2 8AG Tel: 01-739 7126 & 2630

VISA

Prices quoted are those prevailing at press date and are subject to alteration due to economic conditions.

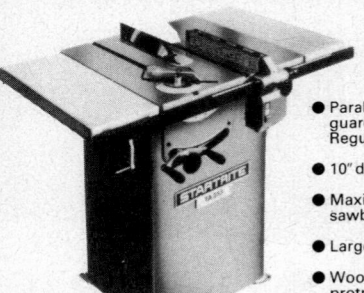

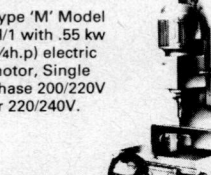

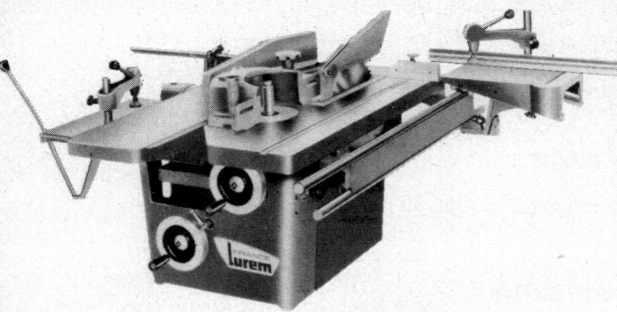

Hitachi: a cut above the rest

CS-280A
Specifications:
Bar size: 280mm (12")
Power input: 1,140W
Chain speed: 450 m/min. (1,475 ft/min.)

CS-350A
Specifications:
Bar size: 350mm (14")
Power input: 1,140W
Chain speed: 450 m/min. (1,475 ft/min.)

Hitachi Power Tools (UK) Ltd., Unit 8,
Hampton Farm Industrial Estate, Bolney Way,
Feltham, Middlesex, TW13 6DB. Telephone: 01-894 1236.

HITACHI POWER TOOLS

Oh!

That's the initial response we get from people when they discover how profitable and simple it is to dry their own timber.

Just think; you're completely independent of suppliers. No more timber that isn't dry enough by the time it reaches you.

Total control.

All we need to give you a Free Feasibility Study and answer questions similar to those on the right is a bit of information from you about your own particular operations.

And part of our deal is that if; after we've done our Free Feasibility Study, we can't show you the advantages in terms of hard cash (plus all the other benefits) we'll tell you straight, and that will be the end of it.

You'll get to know how much a timber seasoner will save you against your existing costs.

After that the decision is up to you

Um?

Q *What will the total initial cost be, including chamber?*
Depending on type of chamber this could be as little as £500.

Q *What types and thicknesses of timber can I dry?*
Most species and thicknesses can be dried depending on individual circumstances, even in cheap to purchase large butt form.

Q *What savings can I expect from drying my own timber?*
From the answers you supply we will show you the cost of drying your own timber as opposed to buying ready dried timber.

Q *Can you advise me of chamber construction?*
From our experience of over 400 installations world-wide we have the "know how" to advise you of the most economical and simplest constructions.

Q *What drying times can I expect?*
Other than your required finished quality this will be determined by the type and thickness of timber.

I See

The Ebac Feasibility Study

We offer our free study as a serious assessment of what a timber seasoner can do for your business.

Our questions are impartial and we guarantee an honest answer. The only thing you have to lose is a stamp. So send the coupon now, you're under no obligation whatsoever.

NAME _____

ADDRESS _____

_____

_____

BLM AD & DES 097

Ebac Greenfields Ind. Est.
Bishop Auckland,
Co. Durham DL14 9TF, England.
Tel:(0388) 605061. Tech. Enq. Direct Line
661991 Nick Greenwood.

Also available from: J.K. Arrowsmith, Darlington, Co.
Durham. Ebac of America, 3201 Nth. Shadeland Ave.,
Indianapolis, Indiana 46226, Tel 317 547 0366.

726

Prices quoted are those prevailing at press date and are subject to alteration due to economic conditions.

Woodworker, November 1982

Laminated woodwork

Stan Thomas, a cabinetmaker of many years' experience, discusses the various techniques that can be applied when laminating work is called for

There are two kinds of people to whom curved woodwork is a piece of cake: the experts and the uninitiated in any kind of woodwork.

The experts? Of course; but the others:
Well, I once overheard a remark from one of a group of people who were looking at some curved wall-panelling.

'Quite simple really. They just make flat panelling, then steam it and bend it!'

Well, I knew *that* wasn't true, for that particular panelling had just been completed in our workshop. I was just a few weeks into the trade, and very impressed by this, but couldn't for the life of me see the point in panelling the roof of the Severn Tunnel – for this is what I was told the panelling was for!

However, in doing such curved work, the curved members can either be cut out of solid by bandsaw or they can be laminated. Of the two, the latter is the better, for with cutting solid, short grains are produced, which are always a source of weakness. Also 'flowery' grain will occur upon the cut faces, and this is undesirable in the stiles or rails of panelling. It is the panels that should have the 'flowery', 'flame' or 'tangential' grain, and this will be enhanced if the surrounds are of plain straight grain. Incidentally, this 'flame' grain should always go upwards; it is aesthetically wrong to put it downwards (see Fig 1).

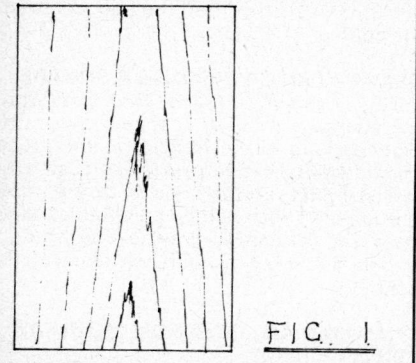
FIG. 1

In laminating the first thing to decide upon is the thickness of the laminations, and this is linked very closely with the radius of curve. Let's consider a chair back – say 375mm wide by 100mm deep, with 12mm of convex. For such a curve as this the pieces could be up to 5mm in thickness; but say the required convex is 50mm then the pieces should be no thicker than 3mm or so. These figures are all to some degree plus/minus of course, for some timbers (ash for example) *do* bend better than others. But they will serve as a guide.

For such a construction as this, a two-part former isn't necessary; one side of a piece of old timber – in this case 100mm by 75mm would be ideal – can be shaped, and the rest done with cramps by first cramping at centre, and then bringing in each end in turn. With the two end cramps tightened – with full-depth turning blocks (50mm by 5mm) – the centre cramp can, if required, now be removed (Fig 2).

A certain amount of spring-back must be allowed for, and this depends both upon the

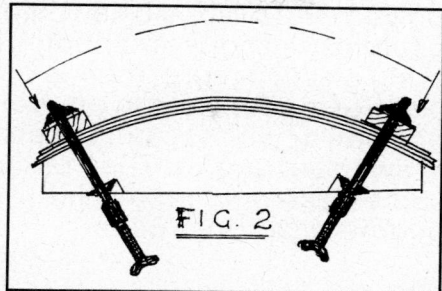
FIG. 2

nature of the timber and the curvature. Taking our chair back (of hardwood) the former for the 12mm curve would need to be brought in about 1.5mm at each end; for the 50mm curve 3mm would be about right. This means of course that the former would not be part of a true circle, but the job would spring back into circle. Is such accuracy necessary in a chair back? There are occasions, of course, when it is and this is why allowance for spring-back is mentioned here. Ordinarily, it can be ignored.

Now, it is important to get a square surface upon the curve of the former, and to achieve this the former should be laid upon a flat surface and the square used off this. The face upon which the *stock* of the square is placed should be equal to, or greater than, that which the blade is upon. To give an example: some years ago there appeared upon the cover of a woodworking magazine (not *Woodworker!*) an illustration of someone squaring the edge of what appeared to be a piece of 6in × ¾in. He had the stock of the square against the ¾in edge when it *should* have been upon the 6in face. The width of the material here is eight times the thickness; whatever small discrepancy of squareness there may be in the edge, will be increased by eight across the face. It could be only one hundredth of an inch out of square on the edge, but with the blade across the face, it would show eight hundredths. And this is what can happen at the ends of the former – trying to square 100mm off, say, 25mm. Former-squaring then, to be done off the flat surface, with the blade against the former and the stock always radial, for if the former is out of square at one end, then the finished job will be 'in winding'. (Fig 3).

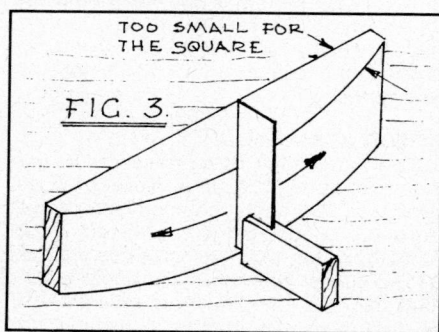
TOO SMALL FOR THE SQUARE
FIG. 3.

After that little digression, let's get to panelling in cabinet work.

The laminations for curved members should be arranged to form the grooves and moulds; a lot of laborious scratch-stock work will be thus saved (Fig 4). And in work

of this kind, the piece should be made longer than the finished length, so that the ends can be trimmed off – ends that would be outside the cramps, and consequently not bedding closely upon the former.

The timber for this work should be carefully examined (it should *always* be, anyway) and should there be any short grain or other defect, such pieces should be placed 'inside'. The two outer laminations must be of good straight grain, or a kinky curve could result. These two outer pieces should also be cleaned up of course, before bending, and the face of the former should be papered with newspaper, so that should

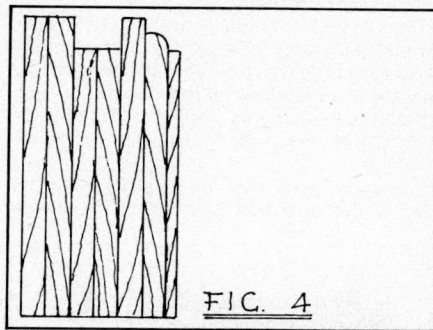
FIG. 4

any glue inadvertently get between the job and the former, it will not be damaged on removal.

Good gluing is vital, for upon this depends the satisfactory completion of the job. Some timbers do not take glue readily – teak, for example, on account of its greasy nature. It *can* be treated with a de-greasing agent, but to what effect is questionable. Pitch pine is another poor gluer, because of its resin content and this timber cannot even be de-greased. What happens in the event of glue failure is that the laminations slide one upon the other, and revert to straight. This process can be a slow one – up to a day or so after cramp removal. The laminations for these timbers then, should be made no more than half the usual thickness, so that upon bending, the strain is minimised. These are the only two, in my experience, to be poor gluers, but 'if in doubt, try out' with some waste pieces.

Assuming now, that a long straight something-or-other has to be curved at its ends only, it is not necessary to build up the

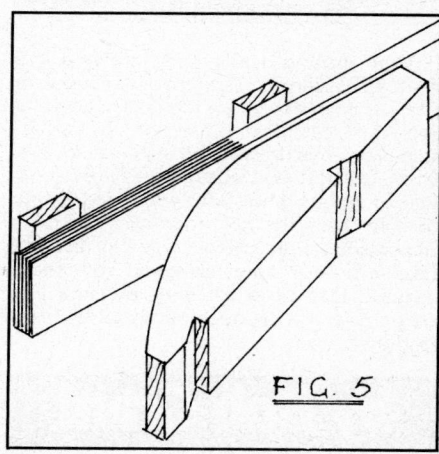
FIG. 5

whole piece with laminations. Saw cuts can be put through to the required distance, and these then feathered – ie slips of timber inserted into the cuts, and the whole then put upon the former (Fig 5). But if the cuts are done by circular saw, the ends of the cuts must be squared by hand. It would not do to leave the cuts circular, for distortion would again occur.

For small ornamental laminating – where the laminations may be of veneer thickness – a two-part former is of course necessary. The usual method is to run the former material through the bandsaw, and then place the job between the two-piece former so obtained. Theoretically, this is wrong of course, but it *will* work on most jobs, because the two halves of the former will 'give to shape' on cramping. If a curve is very sharp however, and the job rather thick (say 25mm) then, after bandsawing, one half of the former will have to be adjusted – the difference in radius being equal to the thickness of the job.

Back to bigger work – a double-curve arm for an easy chair, for example, with laminations of 4mm or so. This double curve again, can be produced by single former, using 'shaper and straights', but it is the shaper that should first be cramped, *then* the straights (Fig 6).

Lamination isn't limited to curved work of course. Besides straight lengths, flat widths

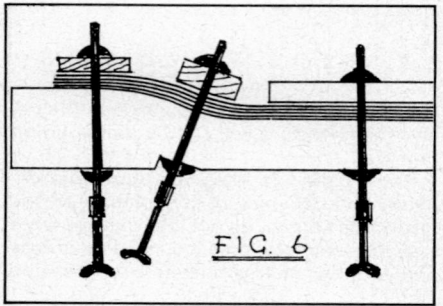

FIG. 6

can be built up, preferably by alternating the grain direction of each layer of laminations, thus producing a strong warp-free board – the principle of plywood of course.

Incidentally, has anyone, I wonder, ever *thought* of steaming and bending a panelling? It *might* work! ■

WORKSHOP WAYS

When making a workshop drawing it is often necessary to indicate a 'section' or artificial cut through an item. As a convention this cut line is shown by cross-hachured lines drawn with a 45° set square. To ensure that the hachure lines are evenly spaced, gauge a line with a marking gauge an ⅛in from the 45° edge of your clear plastic set square. When drawing hachure lines you need only move the set-square enough each time to bring the line just drawn over the gauge line to ensure a neat sectioned area.

by Bob Grant

Do you ever wish you had paid more attention during geometry lessons at school? There's nothing more likely to bring on such regret than to be confronted by a complicated piece of marking out in the workshop, such as constructing an octagon or working out the profiles of mouldings which meet at awkward angles. The Craftsman in his Workshop here jogs some classroom memories to provide a guide to the basics of geometrical construction

Woodworking geometry

Lack of space prevents this article from covering all the problems, which number several hundreds, so I have chosen only the ones that are commonest. For the same reason the simplest examples as, for instance, how to erect perpendiculars, or how to draw lines parallel to each other, have been omitted.

I have assumed that you have a protractor, a set of 30 degree and 60 degree set squares, and a pair of compasses. A word about the last-named item: ordinary draughtsman's compasses are often too small for our purposes as the greatest circle they can draw rarely exceeds about 8in (203mm). For circles larger than this, a draughtsman will use a beam compass, but these are expensive.

You can get over the difficulty by making up your own pair of compasses, comprising a pair of legs which are connected at one end of means of a small bolt and a wing nut, which will allow adjustment. One leg can have a pencil attached to it by a Jubilee clip, and the other can be fitted with a point such as a veneer pin.

BISECTING AN ANGLE

Now to get down to actual cases, the first example at Fig 1A is a piece of basic geometry. Although you can bisect (halve) an angle by using the protractor, it can sometimes be tricky for an angle such as 37½ degrees, where half the angle equals 18¾ degrees — a difficult number to read off accurately. The method I am about to describe does the job easily and precisely.

Suppose the angle is the one lettered as x, y,z. Then, using x as the centre and with any convenient radius, draw arcs cutting the arms of the angle at a and b. Next re-set the compasses at a smaller, suitable radius and

draw arcs with a and b as centres, so that the arcs intersect at c. Then the line xc bisects the angle.

DRAWING AN OCTAGON IN A SQUARE

This is shown at Fig1B. First of all draw the square a, b, c, d, and then put in the diagonals, ad and bc. Next put in the vertical and horizontal lines ef and gh, and using the intersection, j, of the lines as centre, draw the circle. At each point where the radiating lines cut the circle, draw a line at right angles, and this procedure will give you the octagon.

DRAWING AN OCTAGON AROUND A CIRCLE

See Fig1C. The method is the same as used for drawing an octagon in a square except that you do not need to draw the square at all.

DRAWING A HEXAGON OR AN OCTAGON IN A CIRCLE (ALTERNATIVE METHOD)

This describes how to draw, in Fig1D and E, a hexagon or an octagon in a circle using set squares only. Looking at D, the radius y is obtained by placing a 60 degree set square on the diameter wx and drawing a line. The following Fig1E shows how the next line vz, is marked by turning the set square over and repeating the process. The lines yz and zv can then be extended and where these lines cut the circle give the points for the corners of the hexagon. If you substitute a 45 degree set square, the result will be an octagon.

FINDING THE CIRCUMFERENCE OF A CIRCLE

The standard method for doing this is to measure the diameter of the circle and

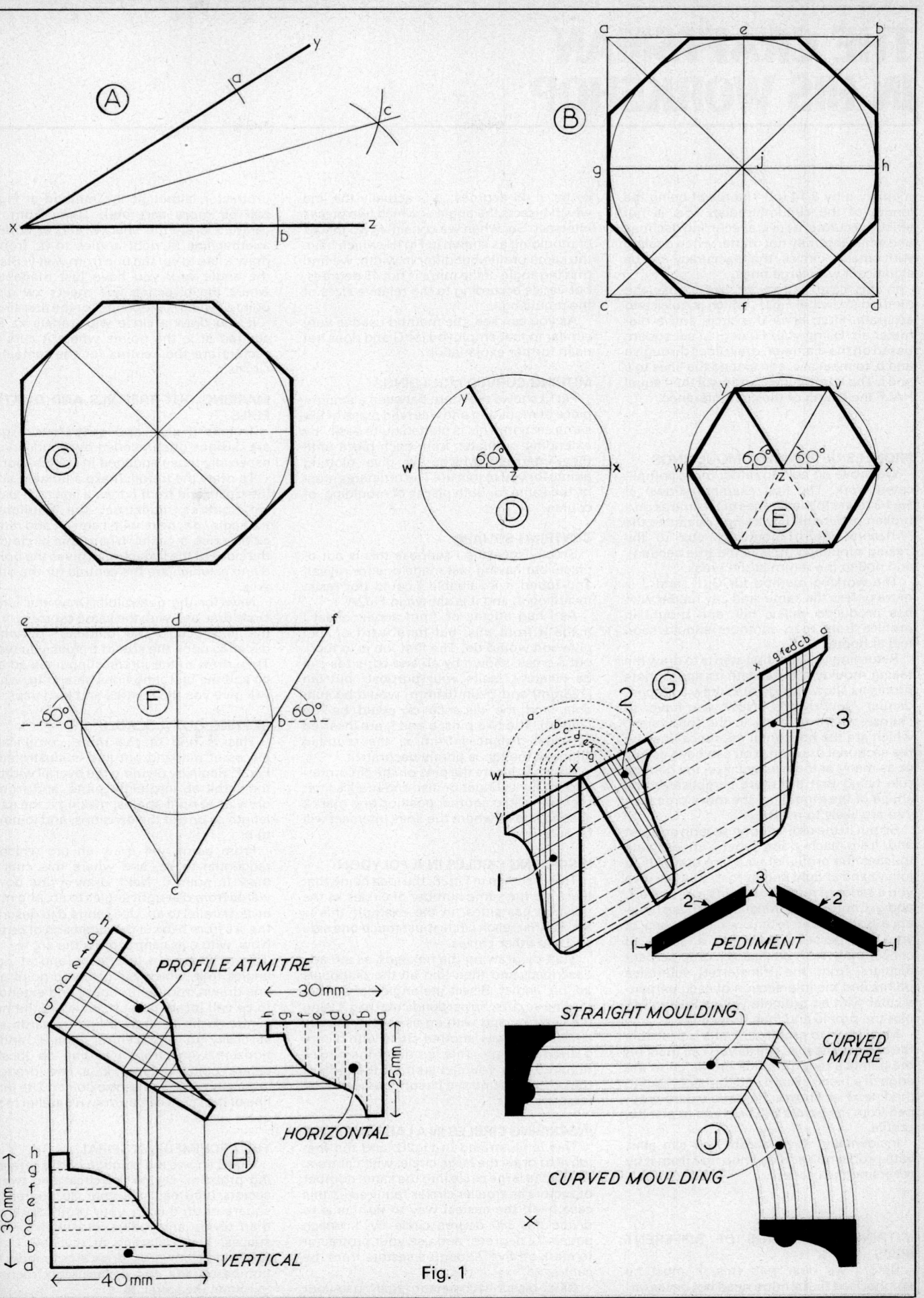

Ⓐ

Ⓑ

Ⓒ

Ⓓ

Ⓔ

Ⓕ

Ⓖ

2
3
2
2
PEDIMENT

Ⓗ
PROFILE AT MITRE
←— 30mm —→
25mm
HORIZONTAL
VERTICAL
30mm
←— 40mm —→

STRAIGHT MOULDING
CURVED MITRE
Ⓙ
CURVED MOULDING

Fig. 1

THE CRAFTSMAN IN HIS WORKSHOP

multiply it by 3.14 (pi), the result being the length of the circumference. This is not strictly accurate, as pi is a recurring decimal, and while this may not matter when dealing with smaller circles, the inaccuracy can be significant with large ones.

In this case you might like to use the method shown in Fig1F, which is quick and accurate. First, draw the circle and a diameter ab. Using your 60 degree set square based on the diameter, draw lines through a and b, to meet at c, and extend the lines to e and f. The line joining e and f will then equal HALF the length of the circumference.

PROFILES OF PEDIMENT MOULDINGS

We move on now to rather more complicated work. The first example shown at Fig1G refers to the profiles of the mitres on a broken pediment. Profile no1 relates to the horizontal return moulding, no2 to the 'raking moulding' (this is the true section), and no3 to the return at the break.

The working method for G, H, and J is more or less the same, and any reader who has produced valley, hill, and mountain profiles from map contours should soon feel at home!

Returning to G, the first step is to draw the raking moulding (no2) with its appropriate profile as shown; at point x, draw a perpendicular downwards. Now we have to choose where to draw in the 'ordinates', which are the horizontal reference lines on the sectional drawing. You can have as few or as many of them as you like, the general rule being that the more complicated the shape of the moulding, the more ordinates you are likely to need.

So put in the ordinates on section no2 first and from each point where an ordinate touches the profile draw a line upwards to join yz and at right angles to it; this will give you a series of reference points a, b, c, d, e, f, and g. Continue by transferring these reference points over to line wx by means of your compasses, describing a series of concentric arcs. From line wx, drop perpendiculars from the transferred reference points and the intersection of each perpendicular with an ordinate will enable you to plot the profile and then draw it in.

Moving on to profile no3, this is probably the easiest one to tackle as you can mark off the points a to g from no2 profile on to the edge of a piece of card and transfer them to the line xz as shown. Perpendiculars dropped from the points will help you to plot the profile.

Incidentally, if you wish, you can start with profile no1 and develop no2 from it by reversing the process.

MITRING MOULDINGS OF DIFFERENT SIZES

Before we deal with this, it must be emphasised that a mitre need not necessar-

ily be at 45 degrees; it is actually the line which bisects the angle at which two pieces intersect. So, when we consider two pieces of moulding as shown in Fig1H, which have the same profile but differ in width, we find that the angle of the mitre is not 45 degrees, but varies according to the relative sizes of the mouldings.

As you can see, the method used is very similar to that employed for G and does not need further explanation.

MITRING CURVED MOULDINGS

Fig1J shows the mitre between a straight piece of moulding and a curved piece of the same section. This is plotted quite easily by extending ordinates from each piece until they intersect, which will give plotting points for you to join up. The ordinates must be the same for both pieces of moulding, of course.

CENTRING SQUARE

Strictly speaking I suppose this is out of place, but having just made one for myself and found it invaluable I could not resist including it, and it is shown in Fig2A.

As I had offcuts of 2mm acrylic sheet I made it from this, but hardboard or thin plywood would do. The first job is to mark out a cross, shown by ab and cd; sizes can be whatever suits your purpose, but 5in (128mm) and 2½in (64mm) would be suitable, and the distance cx could be 1in (25mm). The two pins, e and f, are inserted at equal distances from x; the rounded shape at the top is purely decorative.

To use it, locate the pins on the circumference of the cylinder or disc and mark a line; then move it to another position and mark a second line — where the lines intersect will be centre.

INSCRIBING CIRCLES IN A POLYGON

This is shown in Fig2B, the idea being that there are the same number of circles as the polygon has sides; in the example this is six. Further, each circle must touch one side and two other circles.

Start by drawing the hexagon as already described, and then join all the diagonals ad, be, and cf. Bisect the angle daf so that the line ae cuts the perpendicular at g. Using the centre x and with xg as radius, draw a circle; next draw another circle with centre g and radius gy. This is one of the circles required, and you can step off the radii of the others around the circumference of the larger circle.

INSCRIBING CIRCLES IN A LARGER CIRCLE

This is illustrated in Fig2C, and the first job is to draw the large circle, with centre x. Divide the large circle into the same number of sectors as smaller circles required (in this case five); the easiest way to do this is to divide the 360 degree circle by 5, which equals 72 degrees, and use your protractor to mark off five 72 degree sectors from the centre, x.

Next, bisect each sector (again use your

protractor, although the method at Fig1A will be more accurate). Then, from the centre x draw the line xw and at w draw another line at right angles to it; from x draw a line to cut the one from w at y. Bisect the angle wyx you have just made and where the bisecting line meets xw gives point z, which is the centre for the first circle.

If you draw a circle with radius xz and centred at x, the points where it cuts the sectors are the centres for the remaining circles.

MARKING OUT TREFOILS AND QUATREFOILS

Trefoils (Fig2D) and quatrefoils (Fig2E) are designs often needed by woodcarvers, especially those engaged in church work.

To draw the trefoil, make a tangent ab to the circle, and from f draw a line to x. Using set squares, construct the equilateral trainagle cde; next, with centre x and radius cx describe a circle. Where this circle cuts the sides of the traingle cab gives the points d and e, which are the centres for the other arcs.

Now for the quatrefoil. Draw the larger circle first, and with the same centre x, draw the inner circle the diameter of which depends upon the size of trefoils you want. Then draw in the intersecting lines ad and bc and the bisecting lines eh and fg, which will give you the centres and the cusps.

SETTING OUT A SCROLL

This is one of the more complicated pieces of marking out and is illustrated in Fig2F. Begin by dividing the overall width of the scroll ab into eight parts, and from a draw ac at right angles, making it the same length as one of the divisions, and joining c to b.

From point no4 draw an arc which is tangential to bc, and where this cuts ab mark in point d. Next, draw a line downwards from d at right angles to ab, and mark in ce, parallel to ab. Use centre d to describe the arc from b to cut the extension of de at f. Now, with e as centre, draw the arc fc.

From f, draw a line to cb and at right angles to it, which will give you point g; a line drawn from d through g and extended to ce will locate point h, which is the next centre. From h, draw a line upwards and vertically to find centre point j, and a horizontal line from j to line dh locates centre point k. From k, a line dropped vertically gives you centre point l. The inner line of the scroll can be drawn parallel to the outer curve.

THE ARCHIMEDEAN SPIRAL

Fig2G shows the solution of this interesting problem. Divide the circle into twelve sectors (you can use your 30 degree set square to do this, or your protractor), and then divide any radius into twelve equal spaces. Then, starting at division 1 and working downwards, draw arcs to meet the numbered radii. Join up the points freehand to obtain the spiral. ∎

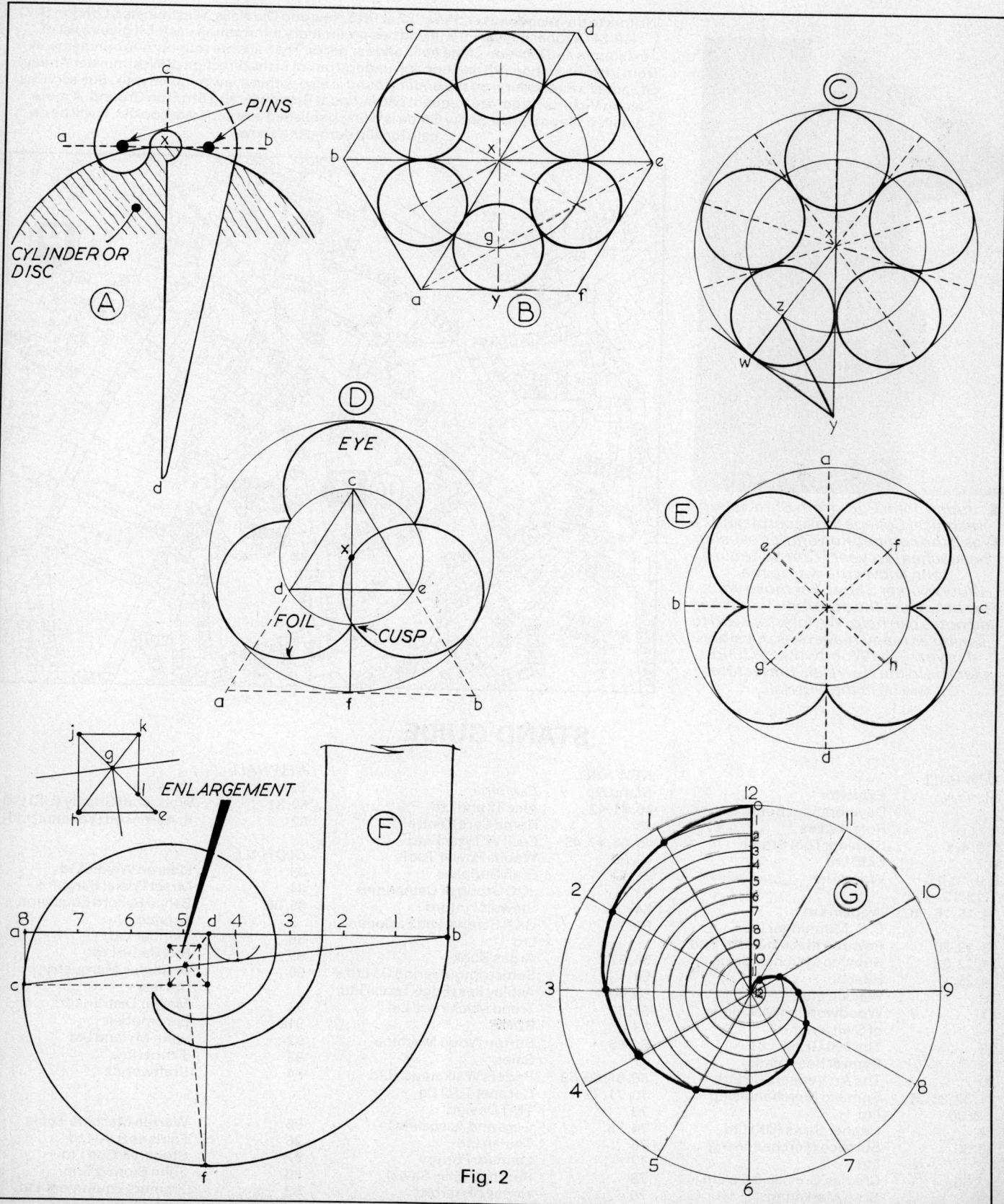

Fig. 2

Woodworker Show

ROYAL HORTICULTURAL SOCIETY'S NEW AND OLD HALLS
October 19th-24th 1982

● *Judge John Price from Shrewsbury Technical College looks perplexed. Was it the competition entries causing headaches last year? I am quite sure John knows the way to the Woodworker Show. For those who may be unsure the accompanying map and notes can help. We look forward to seeing as many readers as possible this year. The Woodworker/Guild stand is in the New Hall, the lectures will be in the Old Hall.*

Visitors to the Woodworker Show '82 at RHS New and Old Halls, Westminster, London SW1 (19-24 October inclusive) will find this preliminary information useful. It gives a list of exhibitors and location of the halls and car parks. The halls are roughly five minutes walk from Victoria station (BR and London underground) in the direction of Westminster Abbey. St James's Park station on the underground is also within a few minutes walk. Bus services along Victoria Street are frequent with stops at Broadway and Strutton Ground. A more detailed Woodworker Show Guide is being published as a separate booklet. It will be on sale for 40p during the show.

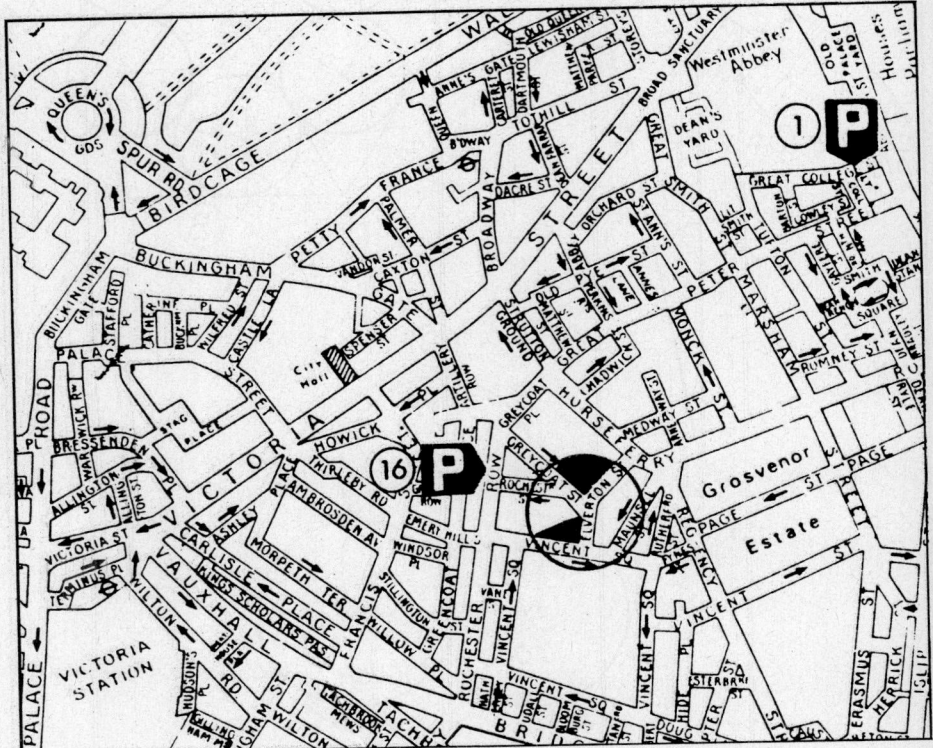

STAND GUIDE

NEW HALL Stand No	Exhibitor
1	Development Board for Rural Wales
2, 3, 4, 5	Sarjents Tool Stores
6, 7	EME Ltd
8, 9, 10, 11, 12, 13	Woodmen
14, 15, 16, 26	Wadkin Ltd
17	C. D. Monninger Ltd
18, 19, 20	Rawdon Machine Sales Ltd
21, 22, 23	Sumaco Merchandising
24, 25	Hitachi
26	Wadkin Ltd
27	Woodworking Machines of Switzerland
28	The 600 Group Ltd
29	Emm & Bee (Leeds)
30	The Art Veneers Co Ltd
31, 32, 33, 35, & 36	Sumaco Merchandising Ltd
34	Hegner Saws (UK) Ltd
35, 36	Sumaco Merchandising Ltd
37, 38	Charles Greville & Co Ltd
39	Scan Marketing

NEW HALL Stand No	Exhibitor
40, 41, 42	Alec Tiranti Ltd
43	Home Care Centre
45, 46, 47, 48	Cecil W Tyzack Ltd
49, 50	Webbs Power Tools
51, 52	Craft Supplies
53	JOC Group of Companies
54	Stewart Linford
55	GKN Screws and Fasteners Ltd
56, 57	Argus Books
58	Semco Engineering Co Ltd
59, 60	Ashley Iles (Edge Tools) Ltd
61, 62	Trend Machinery Ltd
63	RDMS
64, 65	Surrey Wood Machine Sales
66, 67, 68, 69	Rogers Walkareach Ltd
70, 71, 72	Coronet Tool Co
73	TMT Design
74, 75	Gera and Associates
76	Toulan Ltd
77	Lenham Pottery
78	Razedge (Ellis Saws)
79	House of Harbru

NEW HALL Stand No	Exhibitor
80, 81	Woodcraft Supply (UK) Ltd
82	R. Aaronson (Veneers) Ltd
OLD HALL	
83	Liberon Waxes Ltd
84	Direct Postal Bargains
85, 86	Bahco Record Education Service
88	Tamber Ltd
89	Brisklathe Ltd
90	St Albans Marquetry Society
91	Master Distributors
91a	Euromodels
92	John Myland Ltd
93	Timberline
94	Craftwoods
95	Warren Machine Tools
96	Fairlane (UK) Ltd
97	Stobart & Son Ltd
98	John Blom & Son
99	Framers Equipment Ltd

LONDON'S SIXTH

Woodworker Show '82

THE ROYAL HORTICULTURAL SOCIETY'S NEW & OLD HALLS VINCENT SQUARE & GREYCOAT STREET

Such is the increasing popularity of the Woodworker Show, now in its 6th year, that this year the Show is to be staged in the attractive Old Hall as well as the New Hall. Tickets will be issued daily enabling visitors to pass from one hall to another and return later on the same day.

Both halls will display the competition exhibits in the many classes. There will be many more trade stands fulfilling every need of the amateur or professional craft woodworker.

The colleges and demonstration areas will be considerably expanded and so will the lecture programme.

Don't miss this year's super Woodworker Show.

NEW HALL

OLD HALL

Open 10 am – 6 pm each day; 10 am – 5 pm on Sunday 24th October. Restaurant, Bar and Snack Bars.

19th–24th OCTOBER 1982

Admission:
Adults £2.00
Children and OAPs £1.50
Advance booking details from the Organiser, Woodworker Show, 13/35 Bridge Street, Hemel Hempstead, Herts, HP1 1EE

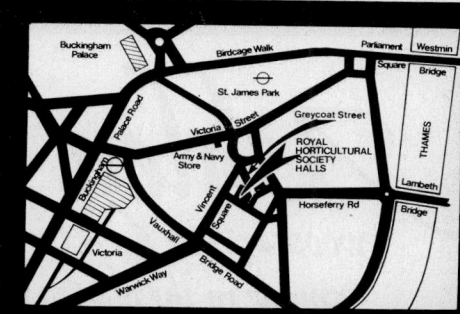

The Gordon Stokes SMOOTHING TOOL (Patent Pending)

Another Ashley Iles First!

Providing you with the answer to the skew chisel problem. The crank in the tang overcomes the dangers in using the top half of the edge.

Unhandled **£8.05** Handled **£9.75** width 1¼" size only

New! Woodburner

A unique professional tool for burning designs on carvings or turnery, signing your work or decorating love spoons.

Tool with standard tip **£17.25**

Extra tips (as shown)
No. 8 needle tip **£2.99**
Blank tip **£2.99**

Whittling Knives

Imported from the U.S.A. these are hand-carving knives. Two sets are available for light or heavy work. Both sets have a robust inter-changeable handle.

Set KB3
Handle (inter-changeable) with 6 blades for light duty work. **£7.94**

Set KLB3
Handle (inter-changeable) with 3 robust blades designed for heavy work. **£10.81**

High Speed Steel Turning Tools

Skew Chisel
Approx. 11" long. Standard pattern in 1" (25mm) size only.
Unhandled **£8.86**
Handled **£10.24**

Scraper
This useful tool, fashioned in High Speed Steel and designed by Gordon Stokes will give your bowl turning that professional touch in seconds.
Hand-ground – Black finish. **£5.75**

1" Roughing out Gouge
Approx. 11" long. The first time a gouge of this type has been forged and hand-ground in tough High Speed Steel.
Unhandled **£19.78** Handled **£21.16**

Ashley Iles All Bright Carving Tools

Colour Catalogue 50p

In conjunction with Ashley Iles Gordon Stokes offers a free phone or mail advisory service. Full details in the catalogue.

Courses of Tuition by Gordon Stokes
A step by step introduction to woodcarving from sharpening to finishing **£7.50** post free.

Woodturning Course – a solid introduction to woodturning based on 20 years experience. Vol. 1 **£7.50**, Vol. 2 **£7.50** both post free.

All Gordon Stokes books are listed in the new catalogue.

Ashley Iles
woodcarving & turning tools
made in the old tradition

Send 50p for our new enlarged colour catalogue (16 pages) showing the full range of carving and turning tools. Also list of stockists and carving and turning tutors. Callers and trade enquiries welcome.

Ashley Iles (Edge Tools) Ltd., East Kirkby, Spilsby Lincolnshire PE23 4DD. Telephone (07903) 372

All prices quoted are inclusive of VAT.

Full range of products can be seen on stands 59 & 60 at the Woodworker Show

INCA
TAKES IT OFF IN A BIG WAY

BIG NEW FEATURES ON THE INCA COMBINED JOINTER/PLANER AUTO FEED THICKNESSER

NOW INSTANT SPEED CONTROL

New Integral motor unit for more power, greater reliability positioned conveniently out of the users way.

FEATURES
- INSTANT SPEED CONTROL
- POWERFUL 1.5HP INTEGRAL MOTOR GIVING 2 SPEEDS—ONE SPEED FOR SOFT WOOD, ANOTHER FOR HARD WOOD
- DYNAMICALLY BALANCED SAFETY CUTTER HEAD WITH 2 CUTTERS
- NO ADJUSTMENT REQUIRED FOR CHANGE OVER FROM SURFACE PLANING TO AUTOMATIC THICKNESS PLANING
- TILTING FENCE FOR MITRE WORK UP TO 45° (BOTH WAYS)
- EFFICIENT ANTI-KICKBACK GUARD FOR THICKNESSING
- DETAILED OPERATING INSTRUCTIONS

Plus the unique INCA **5 YEAR WARRANTY**

INCA BANDSAW
Probably the finest bandsaw of its size available anywhere.
- Special blade tacking for accuracy.
- Sanding belt and fret saw options available.
- Fully motorised or unmotorised.
- INCA 5 YEAR WARRANTY

INCA COMPACT COMBINATION MACHINE
A truly versatile machine that lets you add accessories stage by stage for
- Moulding,
- Mortising,
- Tenoning,
- Sanding and many more functions. The INCA Compact comes complete with motor. INCA 5 YEAR WARRANTY. Available in the UK through 60 dealers.

Woodworking Machines of Switzerland LIMITED
Sole U.K. Agents for INCA Woodworking Machinery.

Please send me a FREE catalogue, price list and list of your distributors.

Name

Address

Woodworking Machines of Switzerland Ltd.,
Inca House, 49 Aylesbury Street,
Bletchley, Milton Keynes MK2 2BQ.
Telephone: Milton Keynes (0908) 641492.

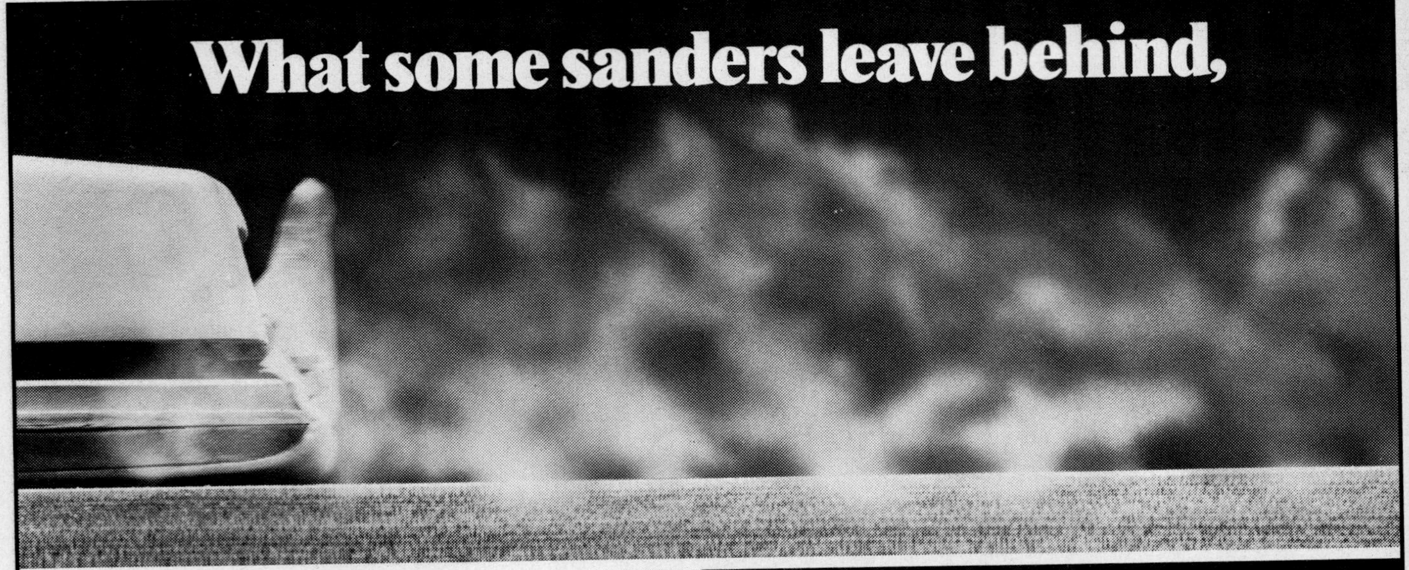

What some sanders leave behind,

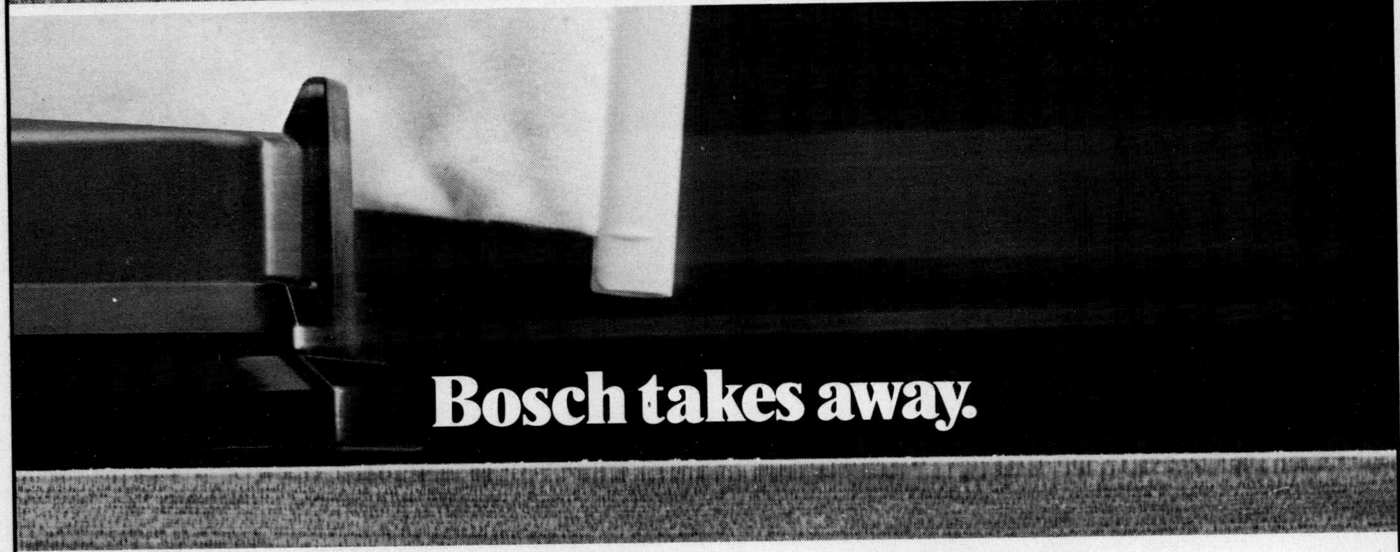

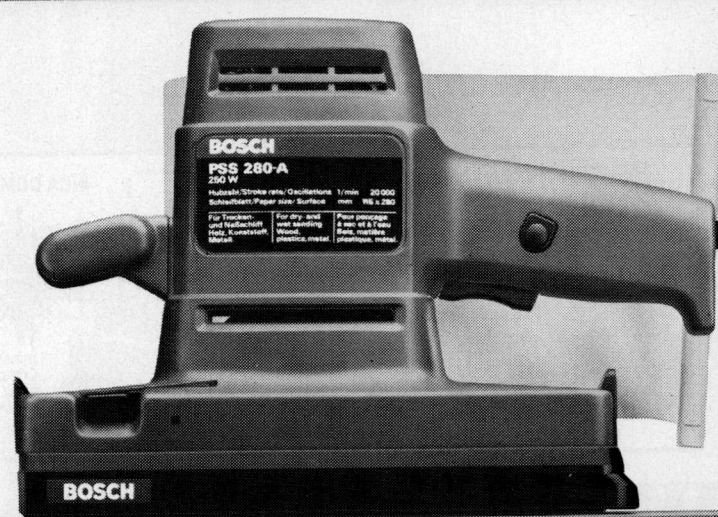

Bosch takes away.

Sanding down a surface can get up your nose. Quite literally.

Unless, of course, you use the Bosch PSS 280-A which comes fitted with a dust collection bag.

Thanks to the suction fan, which is integrated into the motor housing, dust is removed as you work. With the result that the sanding sheet lasts a lot longer.

It has a powerful 250 watt motor, delivering 10,000 rev/min.

A sheet holder designed for quick changes. And a large (114 mm x 227 mm) sanding pad.

Together, they enable you to complete the job quicker. And achieve a smoother, more even result.

While the sponge rubber pad provides just the right amount of elasticity for every kind of sanding job. Whether it's flat, or curved like the wing of a car, for instance.

What's more, it weighs in at only 2.9 kg with a well-designed, doubly-insulated body, a comfortable grip and a low-noise, low-vibration, suppressed motor.

So where some sanders can only leave dust behind, it's easy to see why the only thing the Bosch PSS 280-A leaves behind is the competition.

BOSCH
The more professional D.I.Y. power tools.

Storage and dining unit in pine

Bob Grant shows how he put restricted space to good use by combining a fold-away dining table with cupboards and shelving into a single pine unit. John Peacock took the pictures

Pressures on storage and eating space in a comparatively small room led to the design and construction of the unit featured here. The only available wall had a window in it and the sizes and proportions of the piece had to be designed around this feature. The other controlling factor was the need to keep to the standard table height of 2ft 5¼in.

The unit comprises cupboards with a fall flap table incorporated in the middle portion. This is supported on two gates, which fold away underneath, meeting in the middle when closed. Two shelving units with smaller cupboards stand on top of the assembly whilst the area between them and the existing window cill is blanked off with a loose cover board.

Anyone wishing to make a similar unit would need to adapt the design to the sizes of their room. Dimensions should be carefully checked; I found for instance that the window was not exactly in the middle of the wall and one of the shelving units had to be made ½in larger than the other. The accompanying scale drawings show the layout and detail of the whole piece, with some views sectioned for clarity, and these in conjunction with the cutting list will act as a reliable guide.

The whole design features the flush panel in solid wood, which was chosen because of the level surface needed for the table top. It is also possible to display matched panels enhanced with a decorative bead which runs down the side of each panel, effectively masking any shrinkage gaps. Detail A shows how the bead is worked deeper than the surface of the panel so that when the whole frame is flushed off no unsightly flats appear on the bead. The beads were worked with my Stanley 45 plane using a number 23 cutter (⅜in) for the cupboard and table units and a number 22 cutter (5⁄16in) for the beads on the shelving unit cupboard doors, this reducing the visual scale (the cupboard door handles were similarly reduced in size). The other main decorative feature was a 45° chamfer run on all edges with a portable router and pilot guided bit. The advantage of using the router is not only one of speed but of convenience too, because the chamfer can be worked after the job is assembled and glued up.

Conventional construction was employed throughout with carcass sides being lap dovetailed to tops; bottoms and shelves stopped housed with tenons brought through and wedged from the outside to tie the structure together. Further rigidity was gained by notching a tie-bar across the back of the whole cupboard unit. This was also used as a convenient location to plug the fixture to the wall. Mirror plates were fixed to the shelving units at their tops and were thus plugged to the wall, whilst their own weight keeps them standing firmly on the cupboard unit.

As the unit was planned to be a permanent fixture I removed the skirting board as an alternative to notching over; the wall

● *The middle cupboard of this attractive unit incorporates the fall flap table*

PINE UNIT. CUTTING LIST. NETT SIZES IN IMPERIAL
(inc. allowance for joints)

COMPONENT	No.	DESCRIPTION	L	W	T	MATERIAL
Unit carcass	1	Top	8' 9"	15"	7/8"	Joinery quality
	4	Sides	2' 5½"	15"	7/8"	pine or
	2	Bottoms	2' 6"	15"	7/8"	hardwood to
	2	Kick boards	2' 6"	3¼"	5/8"	suit
	1	Tie bar	8' 9"	3½"	7/8"	
	2	Shelves	29"	12¾"	7/8"	
Unit cupboard doors	8	Stiles	24¾"	2¼"	3/4"	"
	4	Bottom rails	12¾"	2⅞"	3/4"	
	4	Top rails	12¾"	2¼"	3/4"	
	4	Panels	20"	10½"	1/2"	
	4	Handles	2½"	3/4"	1/2"	
Table assembly	1	Top tie rail	4' 10½"	2½"	7/8"	
	1	Bottom tie rail	4' 10½"	2½"	7/8"	
	2	Gate stiles	28¾"	2"	7/8"	
	4	Gate rails	21"	2"	7/8"	
	2	Table top stiles	26"	2¼"	7/8"	"
	1	Table top rail	42"	2¼"	7/8"	
	1	Table bottom rail	42"	3"	7/8"	
	1	Table muntin	23½"	4"	7/8"	
	2	Panels	21"	18½"	1/2"	
Shelving units	4	Standards	5' 0"	7¾"	7/8"	
	2	Tops	30"	7¾"	7/8"	
	8	Shelves	30"	7¾"	7/8"	
	4	Feet	9"	3"	7/8"	
	2	Cupboard half-shelves	28½"	5"	3/4"	
Shelving cupboard doors	8	Stiles	14⅛"	2"	3/4"	"
	4	Top rails	12"	2"	3/4"	
Doors	4	Bottom rails	12"	2⅜"	3/4"	(see
	4	Panels	10¼"	10¾"	1/2"	ironmongery
	4	Handles	2⅜"	5/8"	1/2"	supplement)
Under Cill	1	Cover board	44½"	6½"	1/2"	

IRONMONGERY
4 mirror plates for fixing shelving units   4 pairs 1½in brass butt hinges for shelving cupboards   4 pairs 2in brass butt hinges for unit cupboards   3 1¼in brass back flaps for table top fixing   4 2in brass back flaps for table gates   4 magnetic catches for cupboards

serves as a back, although a ply back rebated in could be fixed if desired.

The pairs of cupboard doors employed a mortise and tenon frame with a groove worked round to take the ½in panels. The rebated shutting joint between the two had a bead worked down the shutting edge of the closing stile to match those on the panels, the right hand door opening first as being the natural way. The handles, as shown in detail B, are quarter ellipsi, hollowed out to form a grip and fixed by two screws from the back, positioned slightly above the centre line to counteract the tendency of the handles looking to be too low.

The door hinges were fixed on a visual line with the frame rails, again to present visual harmony, and were set back to the bottom of the chamfer line. The doors were held closed with magnetic catches. The upper shelves of the unit carry a groove at the back for plate display.

The table assembly consists of two gates hinged on to a top and bottom tie-bar set under the unit top. The scaled elevation and plan shows half of the table fall removed to show how the gates fold away behind the table fall, whilst detail C shows how the gate-bars are hinged to the tie-bar. The table top itself is a large framework with a central muntin which, like the doors, has a matching centre bead worked down it. This can be clearly seen in the photograph. The table edges are generously chamfered off and three back flap hinges are used to fix the top to the unit edge.

The finish used on the whole job was a special outside quality polish (No 0.004 from W. S. Jenkins and Co, 'Jeco' Works, Tariff Road, Tottenham, London) chosen because of its hard-wearing characteristics. Three coats were cut back with 0000 steel wool and then burnished to a pleasing sheen. In service this has proved to be extremely durable and serviceable. ■

● *Two gates support the fall flap table. The top is a large framework with a central muntin. Like the doors this has a centrally worked matching bead*

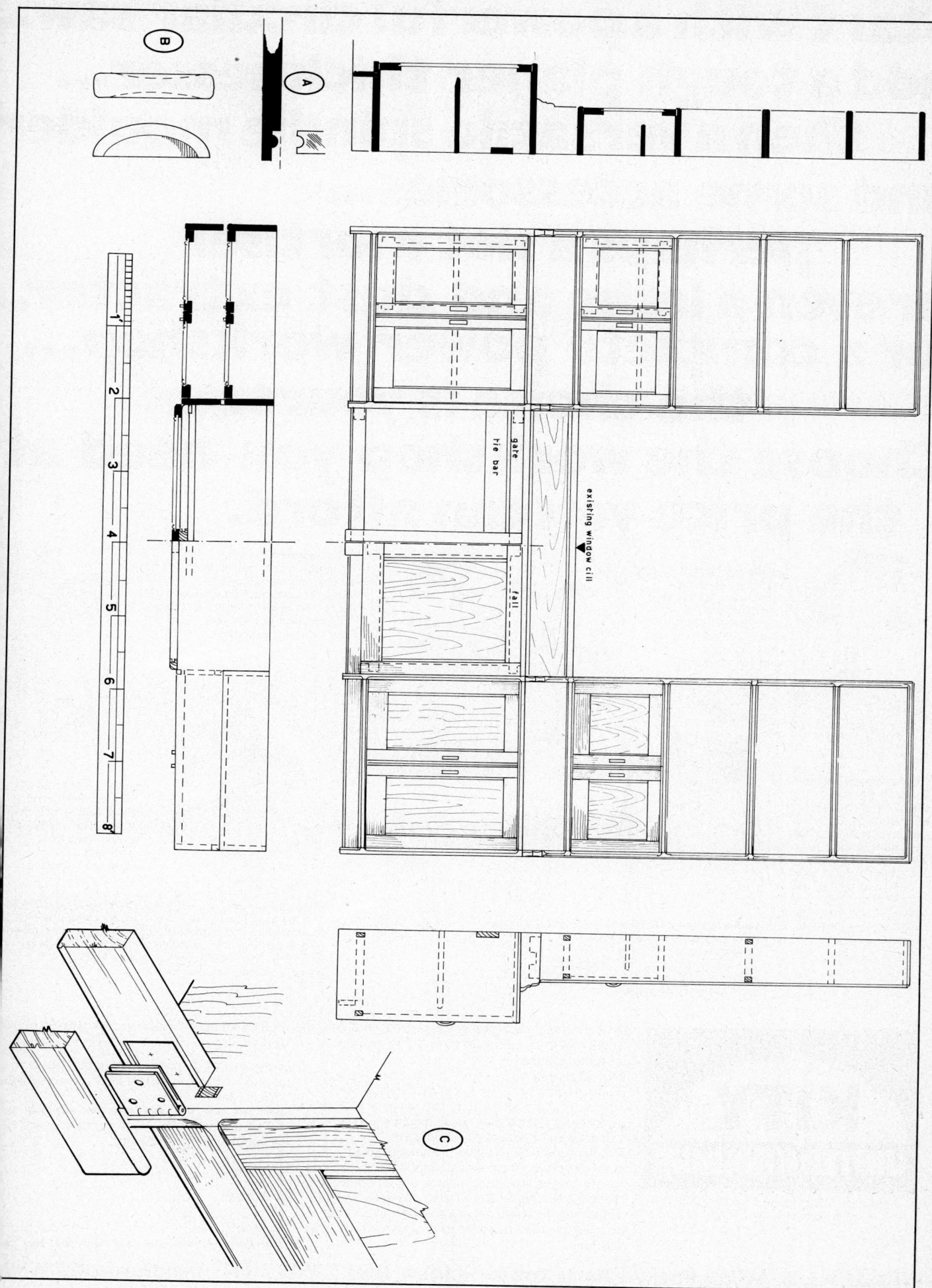

B

A

gate

tie bar

existing window cill

fall

C

Start with a powerful circular saw... add a tough planer thicknesser... then a versatile spindle moulder and some accessories... perhaps a slot mortiser or even a lathe and dust extractor. or a complete power workshop... the choice is yours. Choose the workshop you need at the price you can afford.

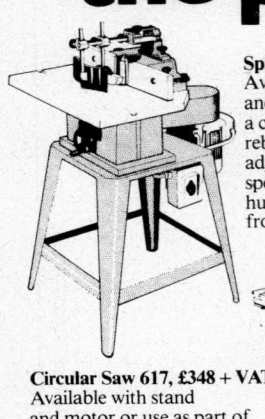

Spindle moulder 627, £440.00 + VAT
Available with stand and motor or use as part of a combination. 1¼" × 1¼" rebate, individually adjustable fences, cutting speed 7000 rpm, over one hundred cutters available from stock.

Circular Saw 617, £348 + VAT
Available with stand and motor or use as part of a combination.
Cast and machined, tilting work table, rise and fall arbor with hand wheel control, 3⅛" depth of cut, 2 speed — 3400 rpm and 7000 rpm, 1½ HP motor, mitre guide with repeat cut stop, guarded to comply with international standards.

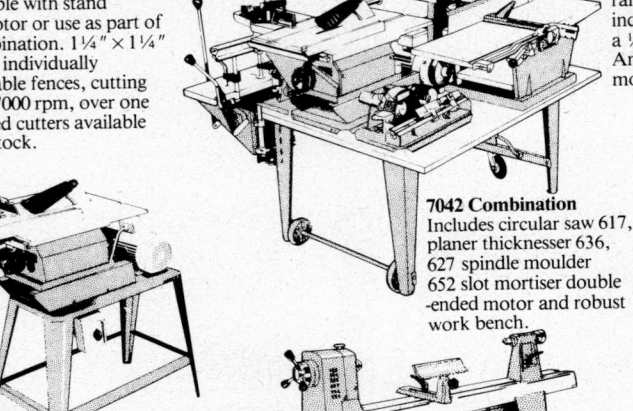

7042 Combination
Includes circular saw 617, planer thicknesser 636, 627 spindle moulder 652 slot mortiser double-ended motor and robust work bench.

Slot mortiser 652
The only machine in the Kity range not available as an independent unit. Will produce a ½" slot up to 5" long and 4" deep. An excellent machine for mortice joint production.

Band Saw 612, £388.50 +
All steel construction, 2 wheel band saw 5½" dept of cut, 11½" throat, will accept blades from ¼" fo tight turns to ⅞" for deep cutting and planking.

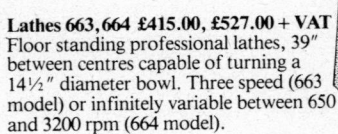

Lathes 663, 664 £415.00, £527.00 + VAT
Floor standing professional lathes, 39" between centres capable of turning a 14½" diameter bowl. Three speed (663 model) or infinitely variable between 650 and 3200 rpm (664 model).

Planer thicknesser 535, 635, 636, £428.00, £578.00, £604.50 +
Kity manufacture 3 models, a 6" × 4", 8" × 6" and 10" × 8". Each machine is available with stand and motor or can be used as part of a combination. Cast and machined table, twin knife dynamically balanced cutting block, power feed, fully guarded.

HIGHLIGHTS AT THE WOODWORKER SHOW.

Here is a selection of the very best tools and accessories to be found at the Woodworker Show. Not surprisingly, they are all from Sumaco — a name synonymous with quality and originality.

See them on Stands 21-22, 23, 33, 35-36

£38 — 70 PIECES

Maxi Clamp

Now there's a single answer to all your special clamping requirements — the all new, incredibly versatile Shopsmith Maxi Clamp lets you clamp in one, two, even three directions at once! It's fast too, because the quick-release knobs slide over the rod threads until they're where you want them. Then, a flick of the wrist locks them securely in place.

£55

Hirsh Saw Table

Gives a circular saw the accuracy of a saw bench. Use it also with your jig saw and router and get professional results with your power tools. Folds flat for easy storage.

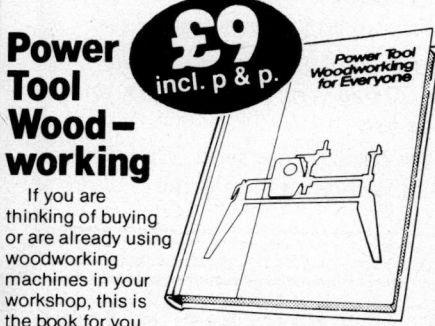

Power Tool Wood-working

£9 incl. p & p.

Power Tool Woodworking for Everyone

If you are thinking of buying or are already using woodworking machines in your workshop, this is the book for you.

'Power Tool Woodworking for Everyone' — a best seller in America for 30 years — superbly illustrates useful hints and ideas on how to get the very best from your equipment. 324 pages cover more than 150 different operations. It is a must for every woodworker.

Money back guarantee if not entirely satisfied.

£115

Supportable

At last! A material support system for every professional and enthusiastic home user. This handy portable table with adjustable legs allows one person to handle materials that would otherwise be impossible. Increase your safety, accuracy and efficiency with this sturdily constructed roller table.

*Folds flat when not in use.

£6·50

Nu-Life Abrasive Cleaner

Increase your efficiency in production, your quality of finish and your profits with the Nu-Life abrasive cleaner! This unique product removes all loaded material waste in seconds leaving your abrasives as good as new. Now available for the first time in the UK this tremendous aid to the woodworker is destined to become as popular here as it is in the States.

£78

Hirsh Saw Guide

Gives a circular saw the combined versatility of a radial arm saw and panel cutting sawbench. Now anyone can cut those 8' × 4' sheets. Use it also with your router.

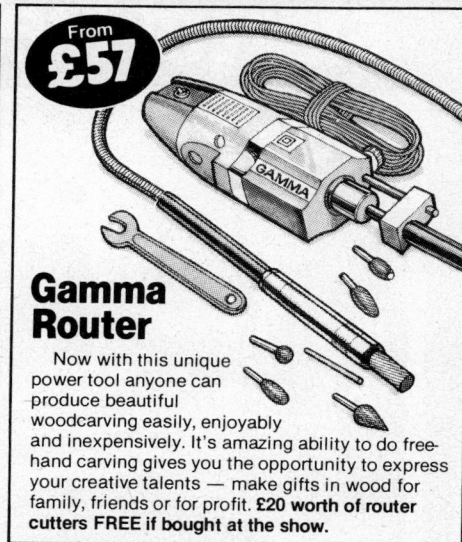

From £57

Gamma Router

Now with this unique power tool anyone can produce beautiful woodcarving easily, enjoyably and inexpensively. It's amazing ability to do free-hand carving gives you the opportunity to express your creative talents — make gifts in wood for family, friends or for profit. **£20 worth of router cutters FREE if bought at the show.**

From £17·50

Hempe Mitre Saws

There is a range of six Hempe Mitre Saws — for both DIY and professional workmen. Completely adjustable providing a perfect horizontal and vertical cut everytime.

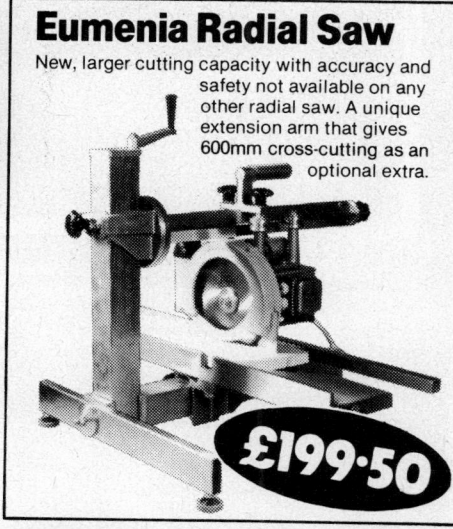

Eumenia Radial Saw

New, larger cutting capacity with accuracy and safety not available on any other radial saw. A unique extension arm that gives 600mm cross-cutting as an optional extra.

£199·50

SUMACO

For more information and ordering details contact Sumaco Machinery & Tools, Suma House, Huddersfield Road, Elland, West Yorkshire HX5 9AA. Telephone Elland (0422) 79811.

The ML8 for the man who wants to start at the top

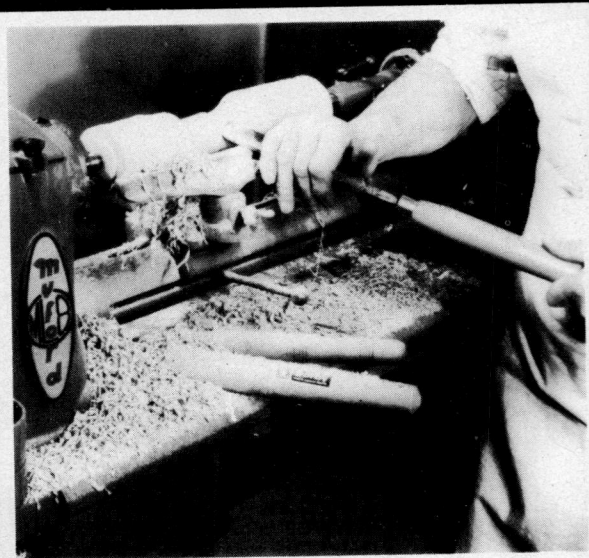

The Myford ML8 lathe has been designed and manufactured to meet the demanding standards of professional woodturners, pattern makers and training establishments throughout the world.

The longest bed model provides a full 42" between centres with an 8" swing over bed.

Being a professional tool it is accompanied by a full range of Myford accessories.

The ML8 is probably the finest quality lathe available in its price range.

For full details write for a copy of our latest brochure to Myford Ltd., Beeston, Nottingham NG9 1ER.
Tel: Nottingham (0602) 254222.

Myford Machine Tools

the choice of the craftsman

Prices quoted are those prevailing at press date and are subject to alteration due to economic conditions.

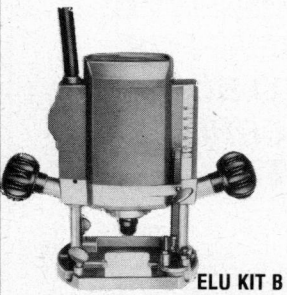

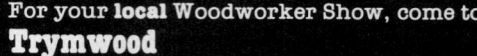

Bookshelf

Ernest Race by Hazel Conway published by the Design Council at £6.50 (available also by mail order from the Design Centre Bookshop, 28 Haymarket, London SW1Y 4SU at £6.50 plus £1.15 post and packing) ISBN 0 85072 128 8

The subject of this new book by Hazel Conway (principal lecturer in design history at Leicester Polytechnic) is Ernest Race FSIAD RDI 1913-1964. The book examines Race's contribution to design during the two decades after the war and discusses the nature of his design inspirations. It is a book full of nostalgia for someone like myself whose early furniture awareness began with the utility style and scope of the fifties.

Race himself is probably best known for the furniture he designed for the 1951 Festival of Britain, particularly the Antelope and Springbok chairs, though his career as interior designer of both textiles and furniture spanned the mid-1930s to the early 1960s.

● Ernest Race 1913-1964

Race's work as a furniture designer covered both domestic and contract areas, and his contribution to furniture design was recognised by gold and silver medals, design centre awards and various appointments and acclaim. He did not leave a wealth of documentation behind him and he wrote few articles for publication but many of the people with whom he worked and those he knew have contributed to the knowledge of the man that is contained in this book.

Hazel Conway traces Race, through his life, from his birth in Newcastle in 1913 via St Paul's School, London, the Bartlett School of Architecture, the lighting firm of Troughton and Young, his stay in India, the shop in Motcomb Street, the war, to the setting up of Ernest Race Ltd and the real start of his career as a professional furniture designer, following his involvement with Noel Jordan.

The design brief for the first Utility furniture was that it should be strong and serviceable, only hardwoods such as oak and mahogany were to be used for the main

● 1946 chair with plywood seat and chrome frame

structure and all joints were to be strongly mortised or pegged. Because plywood was unobtainable in the early years of the war, panels of veneered hardboard were specified. This book looks at the ideals, theories and economic elements as well as the forms of specific designs produced by Race, it understands the context of the period, it details Race's use of non-traditional materials, like aluminium and steel rod and also covers the highlights of his career. His simple, honest designs were ahead of his time, they were original and many are still popular even today. All of Race's designs were evolved within a tightly controlled budget, design and fashion are not synonymous, this book has attempted to look at his work in context so that an insight could be gained into the problems faced by the designer.

To a student of furniture design and history it is invaluable, to a child of the 50s it explains much of the environment and thinking of the time. **P.C.**

The Complete Home Guide to Furniture Finishing & Refinishing by Bernard Gladstone, published by Evans Bros Ltd at £3.25. ISBN 0 237 45647 8

Generally the major part of the text contains sound basic advice but this is surrounded by too many unnecessary words which can confuse and leave the reader in some doubt as to which method to choose for a particular purpose. It is possibly a minor point but the word *refinishing* does not appear to be correct, how is something that is finished, refinished? also the jocular idiom used in places detracts from the technical subject.

The book contains a reference section with illustrations of a few tools, I found very little information of value in this part, also the method shown to lift a piece of veneer from the side of a cabinet to repair an area in a more conspicuous place, using a chisel and a claw hammer to remove the veneer would be impossible to carry out successfully.

There are chapters on varnishes and special tools for the finisher, these are particularly well composed and contain excellent advice on the selection and care of brushes, their use and the application of enamels and varnish of various types.

To summarize the contents of the book which appears to be written for the amateur and DIY enthusiast, it gives useful information for those with very little experience, but

the text should be studied carefully before deciding which method described to adopt, and then to experiment with that system on a piece of furniture that is not important. It is a difficult book to make comments about, there is much to commend it, but like a good cine film it needs careful editing. **H.W.G.**

Working Green Wood with PEG by Patrick Spielman published by Sterling Publishing Co Inc., New York: Distributed in the United Kingdom by Blandford Press, Link House, West Street, Poole, Dorset, at £4.95 (softback)

Soon after World War II Dr Alfred Stamm carried out experimental work at the Forest Products Research Laboratory at Madison, Wisconsin, aimed at stabilising walnut gun stocks and he eventually discovered that polyethylene glycol of 1000 molecular weight (PEG 1000) did the job admirably. What happened was that the water in green walnut was replaced by a solid, inert enough to prevent or severely restrict shrinking or swelling tendencies, in other words, a 'bulking' agent was introduced into the wood.

Later, Harold Mitchell, who had assisted Dr Stamm in the initial work, continued the experiments, often at his own expense. Apart from some work carried out in Sweden, Stamm and Mitchell had proved a point, ie it was possible to apply the treatment successfully to wood, provided this was receptive and the most suitable woods are those with good natural permeability used in the fresh sawn condition ideally.

White oaks and some of the more dense tropical hardwoods are not permeable enough: however, this should not detract from the obvious advantages to be gained where the seasoning and stabilising of suitable woods are concerned. In preparing his book, Patrick Spielman has drawn on the already published results of Stamm and Mitchell and incorporated these with his own professional expertise as a woodworker and wood turner, so that while the introduction to the subject is perhaps well-known, the bulk of the text is a reflection of his personal experience in the use of PEG and this is invaluable to others who so far have no knowledge of its potential advantages.

Therefore, this book is not simply a work of reference, but is a very comprehensive guide to how to set about using the chemical, and indeed is the first book to do so, all other references being a few short articles, or test papers released generally to industry. Spielman has set out details of how to mix the solution, how to treat the wood, and how to finally dry it and finish it in wrought form, proceeding finally on how to make wall clocks, slab tables, picture holders, turned items etc, the whole text complemented by more than 200 drawings, and step by step photographs.

Splitting and checking of small diameter roundwood such as tree branches is invariably a problem if the wood is wanted for use in the round, and I was particularly impressed by the author's designs based on this type of material simply shaped out by sweeping cuts on a bandsaw of treated sections. This is an excellent little book which ought to find a place in the reference collection of all woodworkers. **W.H.B.**

Dressing the poles

The humble telegraph pole is an unremarkable feature of town and country landscapes, but there is quite a story to their manufacture, as Bill Gates here relates

Driving or walking in our towns and villages or rambling through the countryside, one gives little thought to the telegraph poles and poles carrying electricity cables. And yet they are everywhere. The majority of these are made from timber which, with deep preservative treatment, lasts for many years.

About 12 miles from Orpington in Kent is Belvedere, where Burt Boulton (Timber) Ltd have their factory site at Crabtree Wharf. It is here that many hundreds of poles for the telephone service and the electricity board are manufactured. The works of this long established company contain some very interesting old woodcutting machines, some designed and built by their own engineers, while others have been adapted to give better production.

'Dressing' the poles is a term used to describe the operation of preparing the log. Three men are required to handle and position the log on to a trolley system that

runs on a track. The pole is fed into the cutter blocks of the pole dressing machine by a power feed that rotates the log automatically as it travels through the machine, thus producing a pole that is circular in section. Another set of trolleys receives the finished pole which is moved along the track for stacking.

The poles are seasoned for five months to obtain a m.c. of 28 per cent; this is followed by preservative treatment. Redwood imported from Sweden and some home grown timber are the principal woods used for making the poles.

My first visit to this factory site with a group of building students was in the 1960s. At that time the timber came by boat and barge via the River Thames to be off-loaded by cranes. Now it is brought in by motor transport from the docks.

Vacuum/pressure impregnation is used for the preservative treatment, the timber to be treated is loaded on bogies which carry

the poles into the cylinder. The door is closed and fastened. By creating a vacuum inside the cylinder, air is withdrawn from the cells in the timber. Valves are then opened to allow the preservative to enter the cylinder, a sight glass indicating when the cylinder is full. The vacuum pump is stopped after closing the vacuum valve and the pressure pump started. A pressure of 200lb p.s.i. is built up, this is maintained until the gauge on the storage tank records that the timber has absorbed the required amount of preservative. The surplus liquid is returned to the storage tank by a transfer pump and a partial vacuum is applied to the cylinder to remove some of the excess moisture from the timber.

Two types of preservative are available creosote and tanalith, but the poles used by the electricity board and the telephone service in this country are treated with creosote. The average life of a pole is 50 years, though many last 80 years or more. A

Offcuts from the poles showing sapwood completely impregnated. The heartwood is resistant due to its greater density

● ABOVE: timber stacked in the round. BELOW: the loading truck which enters the cylinder carrying railway sleepers

● The incising machine which aids the penetration of preserving fluid

● Machine for drilling railway sleepers

● A pole after dressing. Wheels on the trolley allow the pole to rotate freely

number of the poles made in the factory are exported to China for the Chinese Light & Power Co. These are treated with tanalith preservative.

Railway sleepers are also produced in the factory, from either douglas fir or redwood.

The eight bolt holes in each sleeper are drilled in one operation on a machine that was made by the engineers in 1955. The bolts that hold the metal shoes to the sleeper are insulated from the shoes by bushes. Originally these were turned from

hardwood, but this has now been super seded by using moulded plastic bushes The bushes are tapered in their length t prevent movement and to provide a tigh vibration-free fixing. ∎

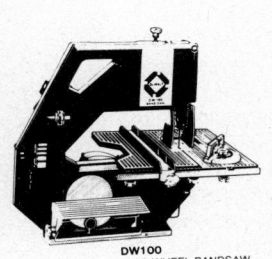
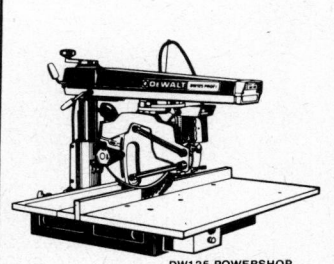

Here's an easier way to construct cabinets with perfectly solid joints – the revolutionary _new_ Elu Flat Dowel Jointing System.

Face Slots 4mm wide
Depth according to dowel
size being used.

SIDE PANEL

SHELF

EDGE SLOTS

SHELF

EDGE SLOTS

Slots are glued and dowels placed into position

Simple to use

Marked lines on the sole plate allow easy machine location. Make a simple plunge cut producing a slot ready to accept the dowel.

PLUNGE DIRECTION

SIDE PANEL

WORK TABLE

PLUNGE DIRECTION

SHELF

WORK TABLE

How it works

The Elu Flat Dowels are manufactured from Hardwood (Beech) compressed into shape with the grain running diagonally thus providing the strength along its centre. When the dowel is fitted it absorbs the glue resulting in a solid joint. Slots allow the lining up of edges not possible with conventional round dowels.

Standard Equipment:

* Steel Carrying Case
* Super Hard TCT Grooving Blade
* Parallel Guide
* Saw Insert
* Instruction Book
* Special Mitre Guide

FREE!
Special Guide for slotting mitred edges

More information:
The ELU DS140 and Dowels are readily available from a nationwide network of over 200 authorised distributors. Contact us today for your free illustrated brochure and full list of Elu dealers.

Elu Machinery Ltd.,
310-312 Dallow Road,
LUTON,
Beds. LU1 1SS.
Tel: (0582) 425001
Telex: 825540 ELU G.

Elu INTERNATIONAL

Simple smart tidy

£3.75
incl. postage
(Outside Europe overseas accelerated)
(Europe add 50p post) surface post add £1.25

Build up your WOODWORKER reference library and be sure of laying your hands quickly on your back issues of WOODWORKER by filing them in a TIDYBINDER, designed to hold 12 issues and smartly blocked with the WOODWORKER logo.

Send your Order now to:-
**MODEL & ALLIED PUBLICATIONS LTD.,
P. O. BOX 35, BRIDGE STREET, HEMEL HEMPSTEAD, HERTS, HP1 1EE.**

Order Form WOODWORKER

Please supply . . . binders for year(s) . . . . . I enclose £ . . .

Name _____

Address _____

_____

Date _____

Please charge my Access/Barclaycard* Account No

Delete as appropriate

BARCLAYCARD VISA

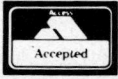

2¼" depth of cut circular saw, 6"x4" planer thicknesser, versatile spindle moulde (80 plus cutters available), power take-off for accessories, lever contro slot mortiser, robust workbench, 1 h.p. motor, 2 year guarantee, £599.00 (+VA £89.

● **Spindle moulder**
6400 rpm shaft speed. 45mm (1¾")
vertical adjustment. Capable of taking
25mm (1") × 25mm (1") rebate in one
pass. Accepts both French moulding
profiles and "Whitehill" type blocks.

● **Circular saw.**
57mm (2¼") depth of cut. 2 speeds,
3750 for normal wood and 6200 rpm for
laminated boards. Complete with rip
fence, mitre guide, repeat cut length
stop, wobble washers for grooving,
tilting table 0.45°.

● **Surface planer**
700mm (27½") long × 200mm (8") wide
cast bed. Maximum planing width
150mm (6"). Adjustable 90°-45° fence
for bevel planing. Dynamically balanced
cutter block rotating at 11,400 cuts per
minute.

● **Thickness planer**
Fully automatic feed, 7.5m (24ft) per
minute. Maximum capacity 100mm (4")
deep, 150mm (6") wide. Calibrated scale.

● **Slot mortiser. NEW IMPROVED!**
Lever adjustment rise/fall table with
100mm (4") of movement. Maximum
bit diameter 12mm (½"). Produces an
accurate mortise, also horizontal boring
for perfect dowel joints.

K5 power workshop
● Heavy alloy castings.
● Sealed for life bearings throughout
for maintenance free running.
● Distortion free bench table top
finished in tough polyurethane.
● Strong steel stand.
● All work surfaces are precision machined
and polished from a specially developed
drag resistant hard wearing alloy.
● Fully enclosed fan cooled
motor – stop any dust problems.
● All rotating cutting heads are dynamically
balanced for vibration free operation.

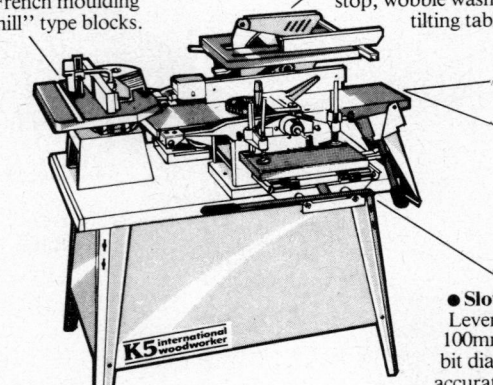

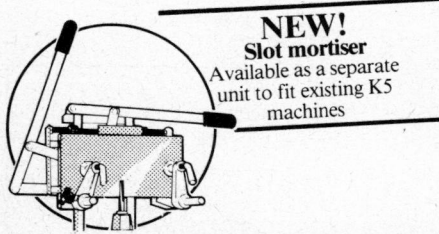

NEW!
Slot mortiser
Available as a separate
unit to fit existing K5
machines

KITY UNITED KINGDOM

Now in Australia and South Africa.
Please write for details.

The standard K5 power workshop comes complete with...
● **Circular saw.** Fully guarded with mitre guide and
repeat cut stop, rip fence, 180mm blade, grooving
washers.
● **Planer thicknesser.** Fully guarded, ground and set
planer knives, in dynamically balanced cutter
block.
● **Spindle moulder.** Fully guarded, with adjustable
tool insert, one french type cutter.
● **Slot mortiser.** Chuck, lever adjustable table and
one mortise bit.
● **1 H.P. motor.** Fan covered and dust sealed 240V
50HZ, will operate from a normal 13 amp socket.
● **Instruction manual.**
● **2 year guarantee.**
All units assembled and adjusted, stand complete
with legs and side panels, crated ready for delivery to
your door.

There are over 150 trained stockists and distri
throughout the UK to provide a comprehensi
after sales back up plus regular demonstratio
test your K5 before you buy.

Write or phone *(24hr answer service)* for colo
leaflet and more information about K5.
Full Credit Terms available, ask your local de
for details.

Please send me more information about

☐ K5   ☐ New Slot Morti

Name ....

Address ....

....

Kity U.K., 6 Acorn Park, Charlestown, Shipley BD17 7SW. Tel: Bradford (0274) 597826.

Prices quoted are those prevailing at press date and are
subject to alteration due to economic conditions.

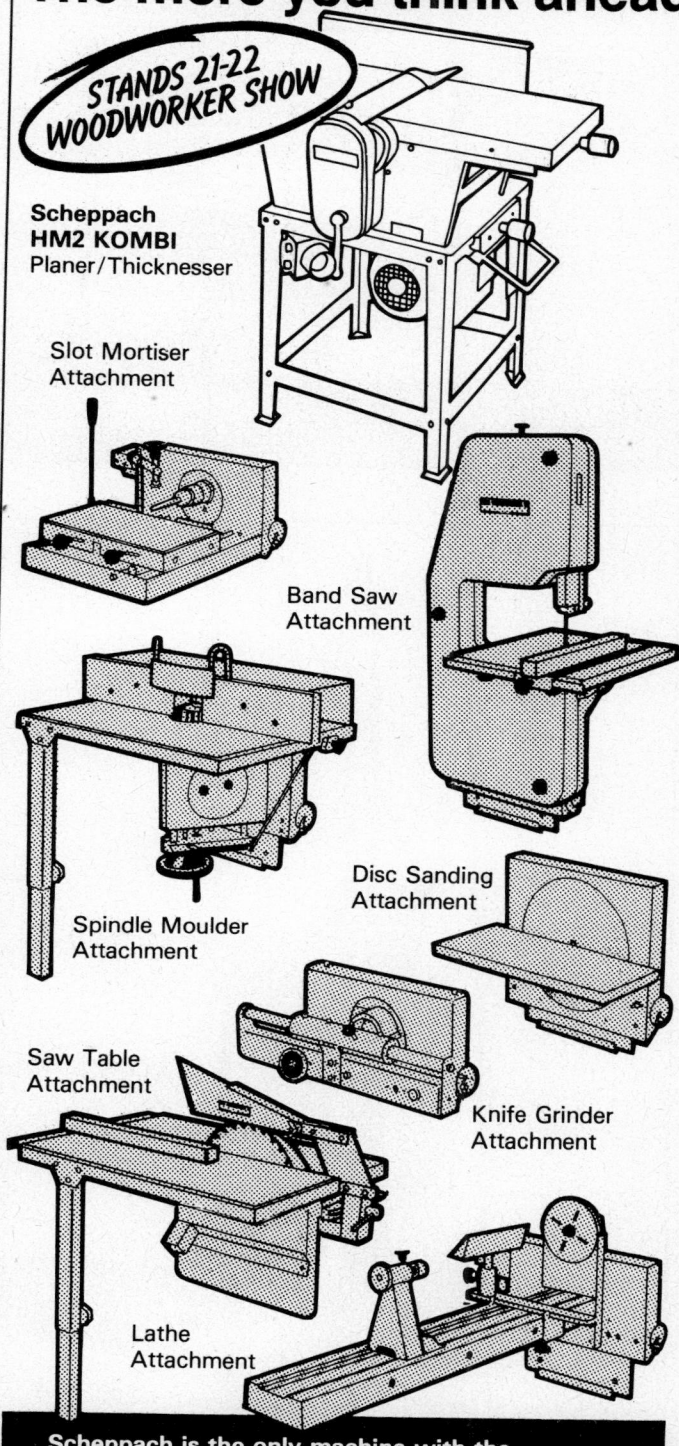

Children's furniture

To complement the constructional details of Harold King's child's chair we have gathered some examples of contemporary work and a short historical look at children's furniture and accessories of the past

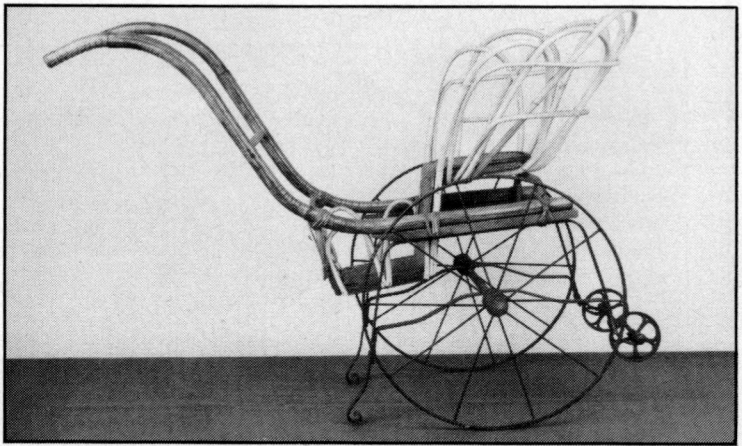

● *Swinging crib made by Bob Ansell which won the spindle turning section of the Woodworker Show two years ago*

● *Cane and wicker pushchair dated circa 1840 of English origin (Victoria & Albert Museum)*

● *A cradle in mahogany given to the Victoria & Albert Museum by Miss Ethel Woolmer. Dated early 19th century, the cradle measures 3ft 3in high, 3ft 1¾in long and 1ft 8in wide (Victoria & Albert Museum)*

A chair of her own

Harold King describes the construction of a small chair he made for a delighted little girl

Any young child takes great delight in having a miniature of an adult's everyday possession. I can still remember a little chair that just fitted me when I was three or four years old. What a pleasure it was to sit in it alongside my grandfather.

The example illustrated here is one I have just made for a very small girl. The making is interesting and is a useful way of using some of those odd bits of wood which are too small for most jobs yet are too good to discard. Every woodworker seems to have such a collection so that timber costs need not be a deterrent.

I used short ends of ⅝in thick Japanese oak but almost any of the cabinetmaking hardwoods would be suitable. As will be seen from the diagram, showing a side frame set out on 1in squares, it is wise to make a full-size one on card or plywood.

The mortise and tenon joints between legs and arm rests are unusual, the inner edges being at right angle to the arm rests and the outer edges in line with the legs. This is to avoid great difficulties when assembling the frames. As an aid to cutting the angled mortises, a jig was made in which to clamp the legs and arm rests. Four pieces of ½in scrap wood were used to tilt the work to the required angles. A collar, set screwed to a ⁷⁄₃₂in drill acted as a depth gauge.

Having prepared the legs and arm rests from ⅝in wood and the cross-rails from ½in stuff, a start was made on the cross-rails. These finish flush with the legs on the inside of the frame and are set in by ⅛in on the outside. Each angle was measured from the full-size set out with a protractor and an adjustable bevel set from that. The tenons are ⁷⁄₃₂in thick, with a ³⁄₁₆in shoulder on the top edge. With these joints completed, the legs and cross rails were glued up, using softwood angled pressure blocks on sash cramp pads. To prevent blocks slipping on the legs, pieces of ½in foam plastic were glued to the surfaces in contact with the legs using contact adhesive.

When set, the arm rests were laid in position and the shoulders of the tapered tenons marked. The arms were oversize in length, to be trimmed later. The appropriate block was used in the drilling jig to drill waste out of the mortises. Precise cutting of these joints, particularly the shoulders, is important. Cramping of the end frames is easy if a stout batten is placed along the top of the arm rests and another under the feet, and two sash cramps used. Later, the arm rest ends were finished in line with the legs and the top corners rounded off to a radius of ³⁄₈in. All outside corners had the sharpness taken off.

The seat and back frames are made from 1in × ⅝in material with stopped mortise and tenon joints. The front edges and corners of the former are rounded off and the same treatment given to the top edges and corners of the back frame. The back edge of the seat needed to be bevelled to give the back its slope when screwed to the seat.

The wooden surfaces were finished with three coats of polyurethane matt varnish,

● *Above the finished chair and below the drilling jig in operation*

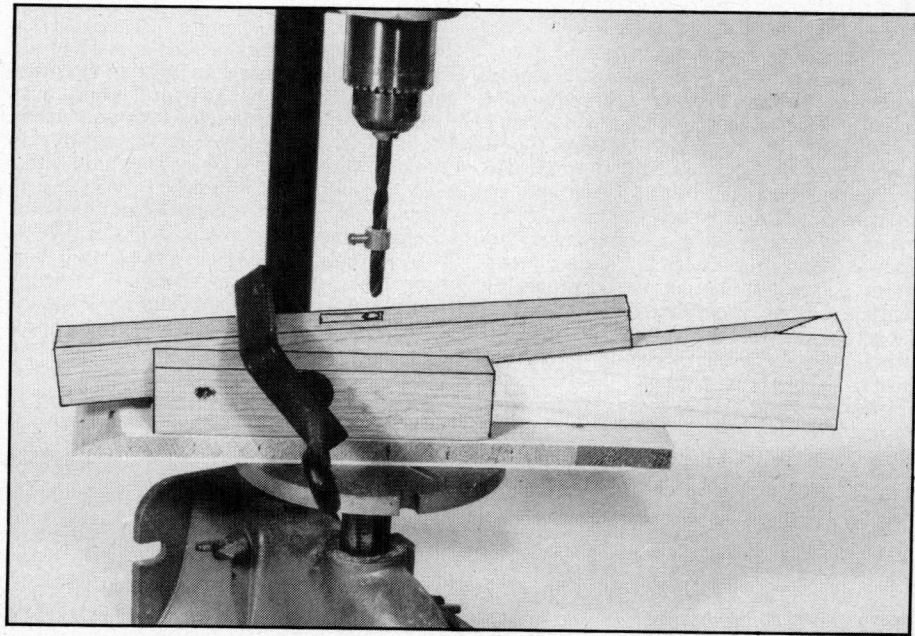

Children's furniture

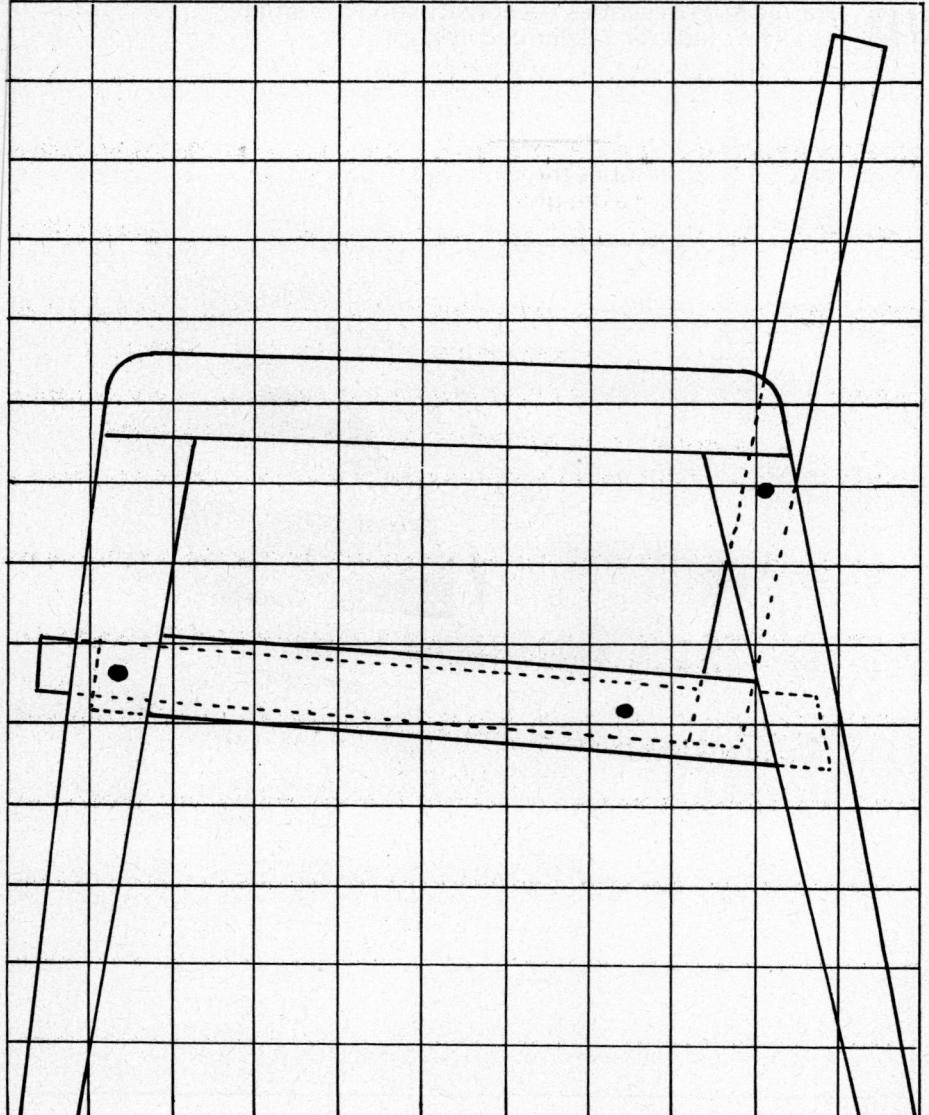

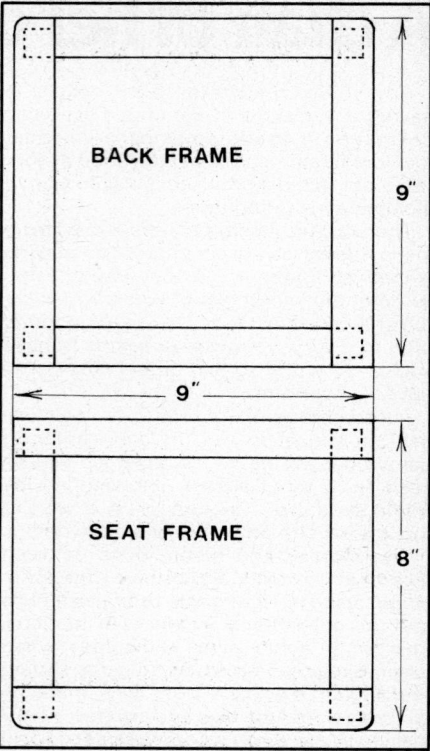

● Details of seat and back frames

● An end frame set out on one inch squares

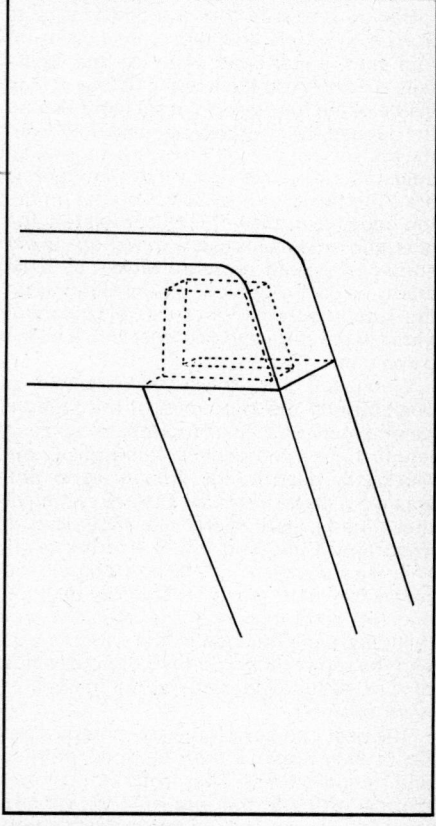

lightly rubbed down between coats.

For such a small chair, webbing would have been far too bulky. An alternative was to cut thin oak faced plywood ¼in less all round than the frames. They were glued and pinned to the backs of the frames. As few toddlers smoke, fire risk is minimal so that plastic foam could be used for padding. I had intended to do a simple pincushion seat and back but a wise and experienced mum suggested that in the interests of hygiene and in case of juvenile 'accidents', loose covers were essential. To solve the problem, pieces of ⅜in plywood were cut to give a gap of about 3/32in all round when in the frame openings. Cut away corners gave room for double thicknesses of the covers at their folded corners. The foam used was 1in thick, with a deep vee-groove cut along the centre of each edge with a very sharp craft knife. Contact adhesive was applied to the grooves which were then pinched together, giving a cushion shaped pad. The first cover was cotton material pulled tight and tacked to the back of the plywood. The removable covers were made to shape and fitted with a zip fastener down the back. Two ½in rnd screws through the ply backs of the frames hold the loose seat and back in position.

Assembly of the chair was by 1¼in × 6 chromed, raised head screws with screw cups. To make sure that the chair stands firmly, one end frame was fitted and only one screw put in the other. With the chair standing on a level surface with all legs in contact the other screw holes were marked through the end frame and starter holes bored for the screws.

All that remained to do was to witness the joy and gratitude of the small recipient.

● A leg to arm rest joint

● Opposite page: High chair in olive ash made by furniture designer Graham W. Peterkin of Hitchen

Children's furniture

● *Child's cradle in oak, carved, gilded and painted. The cradle was designed by Richard Norman Shaw (1831-1912) for one of the sons of Alfred Waterhouse. (Victoria & Albert Museum)*

● *Baby walker and doll from Nuremberg Doll's House, dated 1673, in the collection of the Bethnal Green Museum of Childhood. (Victoria & Albert Museum)*

Bookshelf extra ~ Nursery Furniture

Nursery Furniture by Edward Gelles, published by Constable & Co Ltd at £9.95 (hardback) ISBN 0 09 463990 6.

In recent years, good antique children's furniture and miniature furniture have become increasingly scarce and expensive, and such items are now highly prized by collectors.

With the considerable interest shown over the wedding of the Prince of Wales and the birth of his son, May of this year became an excellent month to introduce a book on nursery furniture. (In the Medallion *Collector's Series* edited by Gaby Goldscheider). Since the book covers miniature and dolls' house furniture as well as children's furniture it is a logical addition to the series which already includes books on dolls and children's china and to the Dover range of publications that Constable & Co distribute in the UK. These latter feature dolls' house paper, windows, floor coverings, furniture and buildings.

Edward Gelles book covers four centuries of children's furniture with an emphasis on English nursery furniture but also some fine American and European examples. Principal items are shown to be cradles and beds,

baby walkers and playpens, chairs, tables, coffers and chests, wardrobes and bureaux but ancillaries are also covered — rocking horses, dolls' houses, prams and push-chairs. Nearly 100 illustrations are included, most of the photographs being of museum pieces whose history is well documented. Many are on show at the Bethnal Green Museum of Childhood, London while others have changed hands in the auction rooms of Sotherby's, Christie's, Spink & Son, Phillip, Son & Neale or Mallett of Bond Street.

In his introduction Edward Gelles divides his book into four categories of nursery furniture 1) furniture made specifically for the use of children 2) furniture of adult size relegated to the nursery 3) miniature furniture ie for dolls or of a devotional nature (cradles for the Christ Child) and scale models and 4) dolls' house furniture. He grades his categories in size ½ adult, ⅛-½ and ¹⁄₁₆-½ size. Chairs are by far the most numerous and varied of extant children's antique furniture.

The book details the history of the nursery, rare in the medieval period but increasingly referred to from the 16th century onwards. Early cradles were made to accommodate babies to their third or fourth year. Until the time of Rousseau children

and their furniture were miniature copies of adults, even in play they were expected to follow adult roles as soon as possible. The nursery hey-day was in late Victorian and Edwardian times. Department stores started to design furniture, wall paper and pictures for children. The Bauhaus movement saw children's furniture suited to both psychological and physical needs.

For collectors of furniture the book details furniture styles and periods, the typical timber and the main designers of the day. And so the book progresses through the various categories of furniture with emphasis on antique wooden furniture but also mentioning basket-work, metal, papier mâché and synthetics. It ends with a short chapter of hints for collectors which contains addresses and the specialisations of (mainly) London dealers and auctioneers, an excellent bibliography, glossary and index and a list of collections to visit in Britain, USA and Europe.

Not only does the book contain a wealth of information, it is written in an easy relaxed style that makes it enjoyable to read. A little highly priced but well worth it, if only to save a lot of time researching the subject.

So much easier from an armchair!   **P.C.**

Jewellery cabinet

Polly Curds spotted Martin Raisbeck's work at the end of year exhibition at Buckinghamshire College of Further Education. Martin also took a foundation course at Harrogate College of Art and this autumn starts teaching woodwork and design at Chigwell School, Essex

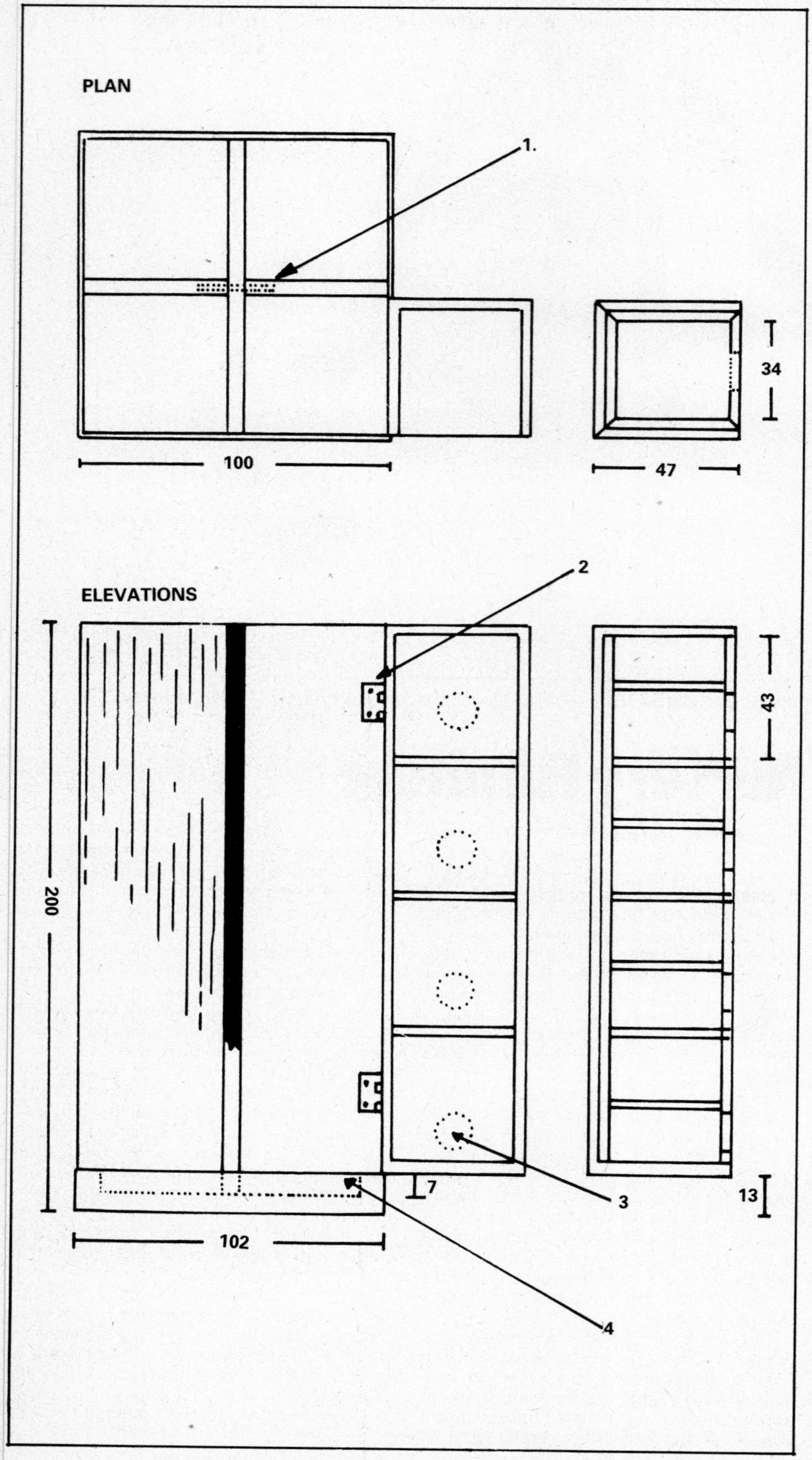

PLAN

1.

100

34

47

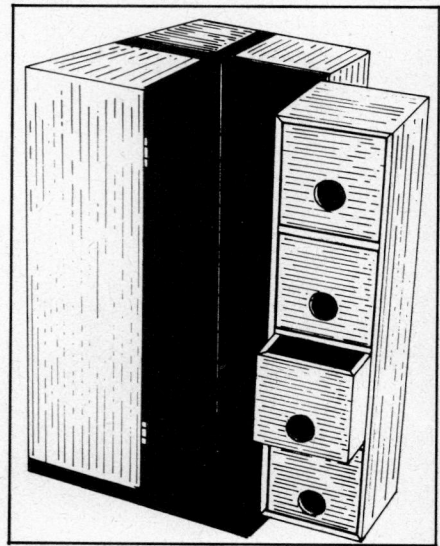

ELEVATIONS

2

200

102

7

3

4

43

13

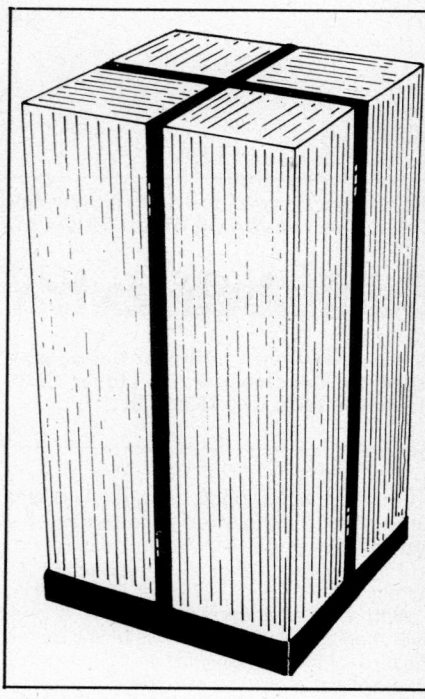

MATERIALS
3mm Sycamore
5mm Rosewood
13mm Rosewood base

NOTES
1. Loose tongue jointing
2. 13×16mm brass flap hinge
3. Finger pull, for opening the drawers
4. Stop housing with shoulder

Drawer bottoms are lined with material to protect the jewellery. Depth of the drawers decreases towards the top of the unit to allow smaller objects to be taken out with greater ease.

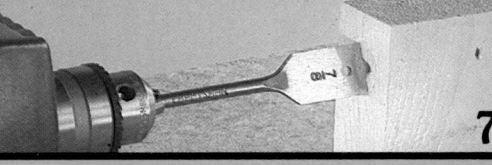

trend cutting tools

Sheet 2 — Shaping & Engraving Cutters

HSS / TC

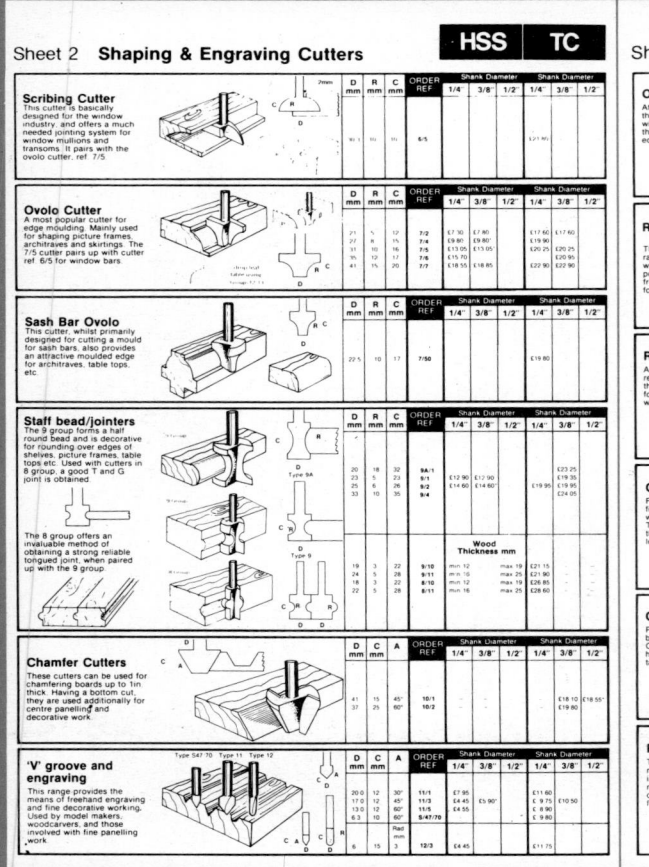

Scribing Cutter
This cutter is basically designed for the window industry, and offers a much needed jointing system for window mullions and transoms. It pairs with the ovolo cutter, ref. 7/5.

Ovolo Cutter
A most popular cutter for edge moulding. Mainly used for shaping picture frames, architraves and skirtings. The 7/5 cutter pairs up with cutter ref. 6/5 for window bars.

Sash Bar Ovolo
This cutter, whilst primarily designed for cutting a mould for sash bars, also provides an attractive moulded edge for architraves, table tops, etc.

Staff bead/jointers
The 9 group forms a half round bead and is decorative for rounding over edges of shelves, picture frames, table tops etc. Used with cutters in 8 group, a good T and G joint is obtained.

The 8 group offers an invaluable method of obtaining a strong reliable tongued joint, when paired up with the 9 group.

Chamfer Cutters
These cutters can be used for chamfering boards up to 1in thick. Having a bottom cut, they are used additionally for centre panelling and decorative work.

'V' groove and engraving
This range provides the means of freehand engraving and fine decorative working. Used by model makers, woodcarvers, and those involved with fine panelling work.

Sheet 3 — Edging Cutters with guide pins

HSS / TC

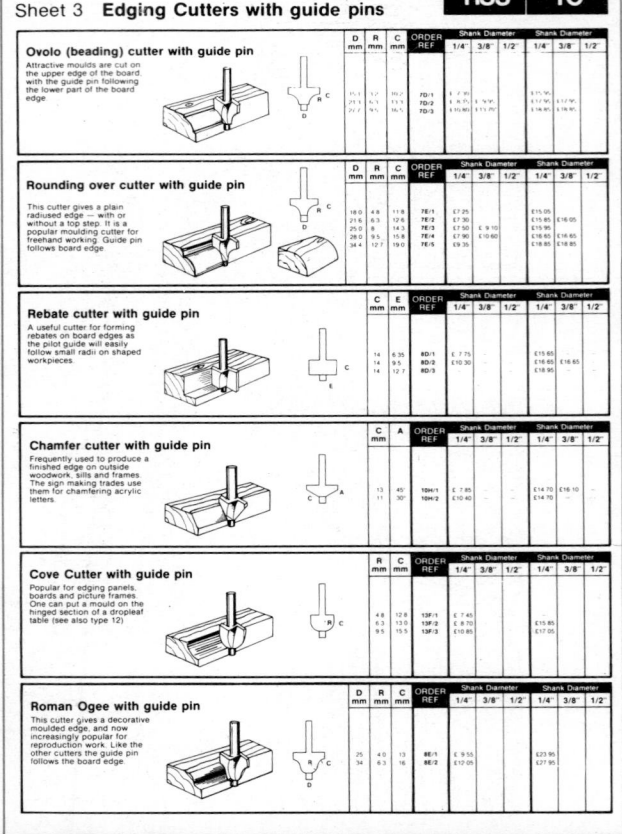

Ovolo (beading) cutter with guide pin
Attractive moulds are cut on the upper edge of the board, with the guide pin following the lower part of the board edge.

Rounding over cutter with guide pin
This cutter gives a plain radiused edge — with or without a top step. It is a popular moulding cutter for freehand working. Guide pin follows board edge.

Rebate cutter with guide pin
A useful cutter for forming rebates on board edges as the pilot guide will easily follow small radii on shaped workpieces.

Chamfer cutter with guide pin
Frequently used to produce a finished edge on outside woodwork, sills and frames. The sign making trades use them for chamfering acrylic letters.

Cove Cutter with guide pin
Popular for edging panels, boards and picture frames. One can put a mould on the hinged section of a dropleaf table (see also type 12).

Roman Ogee with guide pin
This cutter gives a decorative moulded edge, and now increasingly popular for reproduction work. Like the other cutters the guide pin follows the board edge.

Sheet 4 — Dovetail/Housing

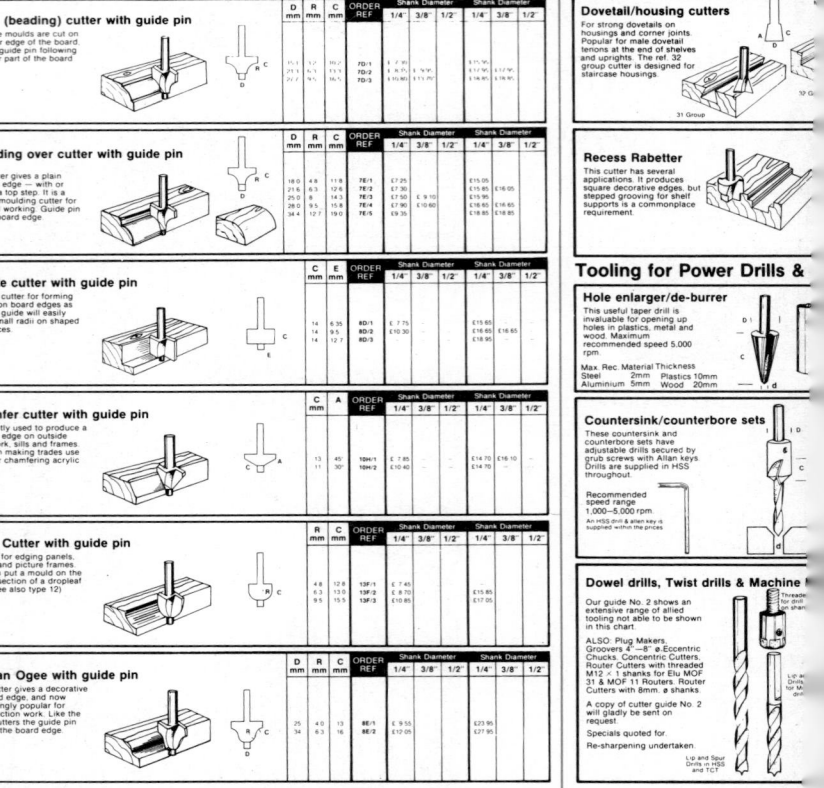

Dovetail/housing cutters
For strong dovetails on housings and corner joints. Popular for male dovetail tenons at the end of shelves and uprights. The ref. 32 group cutter is designed for staircase housings.

Recess Rabeter
This cutter has several applications. It produces square decorative edges, but stepped grooving for shelf supports is a commonplace requirement.

Tooling for Power Drills &

Hole enlarger/de-burrer
This useful taper drill is invaluable for opening up holes in plastics, metal and wood. Maximum recommended speed 5,000 rpm.
Max. Rec. Material Thickness
Steel 2mm, Plastics 10mm
Aluminium 5mm, Wood 20mm

Countersink/counterbore sets
These countersink and counterbore sets have adjustable drills secured by grub screws with Allan keys. Drills are supplied in HSS throughout.
Recommended speed range 1,000–5,000 rpm.
An HSS drill & Allen key is supplied within the prices.

Dowel drills, Twist drills & Machine
Our guide No. 2 shows an extensive range of allied tooling not able to be shown in this chart.
ALSO: Plug Makers, Groovers 4"–8" ø, Eccentric Chucks, Concentric Cutters, Router Cutters with threaded M12 × 1 shanks for Elu MOF 31 & MOF 11 Routers. Router Cutters with 8mm. ø shanks.
A copy of cutter guide No. 2 will gladly be sent on request.
Specials quoted for. Re-sharpening undertaken.

Sheet 8 — Shaping and Panelling Cutters

HSS / TC

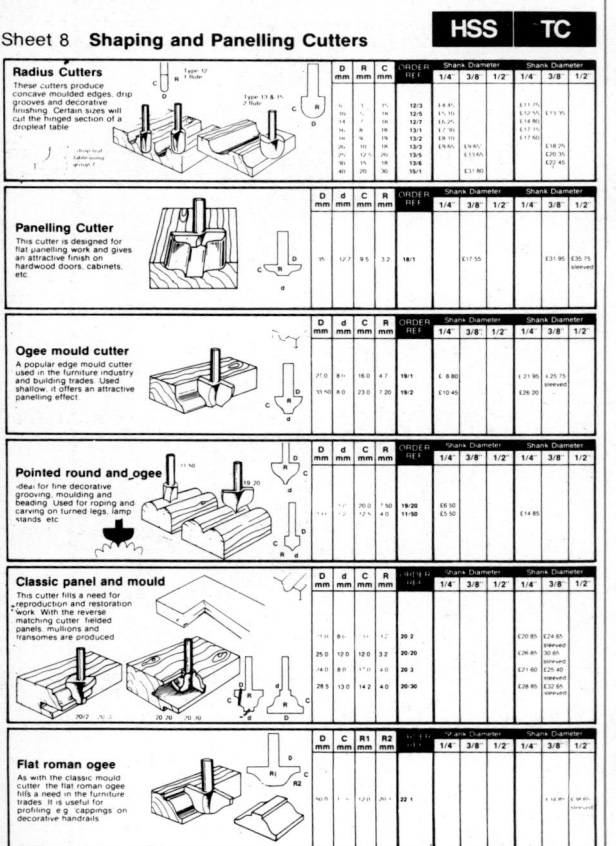

Radius Cutters
These cutters produce concave moulded edges, drip groove and decorative finishing. Certain sizes will cut the hinged section of a dropleaf table.

Panelling Cutter
This cutter is designed for flat panelling work and gives an attractive finish on hardwood doors, cabinets, etc.

Ogee mould cutter
A popular edge mould cutter used in the furniture industry and building trades. Shallow, it offers an attractive panelling effect.

Pointed round and ogee
Ideal for fine decorative grooving, moulding and beading. Used for roping and carving on turned legs, lamp stands etc.

Classic panel and mould
This cutter fills a need for reproduction and restoration work. With the reverse matching cutter folded panels, mullions and transomes are produced.

Flat roman ogee
As with the classic mould cutter the flat roman ogee fills a need in the furniture trades. It is useful for profiling e.g. cappings on decorative handrails.

Sheet 9 — Moulding/Edging Sets – Self Guiding

TC

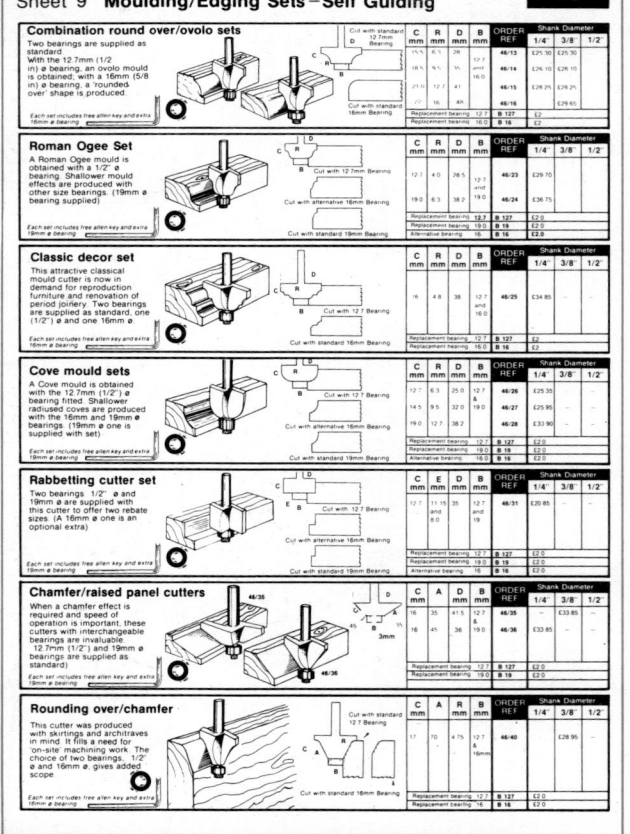

Combination round over/ovolo sets
Two bearings are supplied as standard. With the 12.7mm (1/2 in) ø bearing, an ovolo mould is obtained; with a 16mm (5/8 in) bearing, a 'rounded over' shape is produced.

Roman Ogee Set
A Roman Ogee mould is obtained with a 1/2" ø bearing. Shallower moulds are produced with other size bearings (19mm ø bearing supplied).

Classic decor set
This attractive classical mould cutter is now in demand for reproduction furniture and renovation of period joinery. Two bearings are supplied as standard, one (1/2") ø and one 16mm ø.

Cove mould sets
A Cove mould is obtained with the 12.7mm (1/2") bearing fitted. Shallower radiused coves are produced with the 16mm and 19mm bearings. (19mm ø one is supplied with set).

Rabbetting cutter set
Two bearings 1/2" ø and one are supplied with this cutter to offer two rebate sizes. (A 16mm ø one is an optional extra).

Chamfer/raised panel cutters
When a chamfer effect is required and speed of operation is important, these cutters with interchangeable bearings are invaluable. 12.7mm (1/2") and 19mm ø bearings are supplied as standard.

Rounding over/chamfer
This cutter was produced with skirtings and architraves in mind. It fills a need for 'on-site' machining work. The choice of two bearings, 1/2" ø and 16mm ø, gives added scope.

Sheet 10 — Universal Lamin

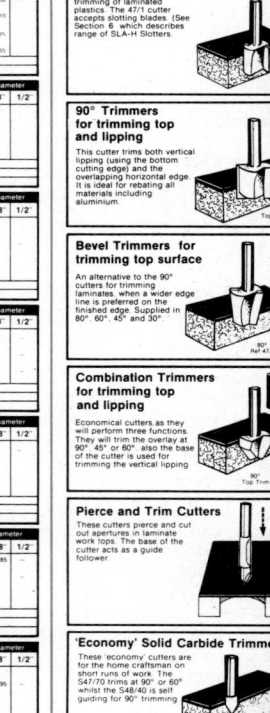

90° Trimmers for trimming top surface
Designed for the 90° trimming of laminated plastics. The 47/1 cutter accepts slotting blades. (See Section 6 which describes range of SLA-H Slotters.)

90° Trimmers for trimming top and lipping
This cutter trims both vertical lipping (using the bottom cutting edge) and the overlapping horizontal edge. It is ideal for rebating all materials including aluminium.

Bevel Trimmers for trimming top surface
An alternative to the 90° cutters for trimming laminates, when a wider edge line is preferred on the finished edge. Supplied in 80°, 60°, 45° and 30°.

Combination Trimmers for trimming top and lipping
Economical cutters, as they will perform three functions. They will trim the overlay at 90°, 45° or 60°, also the base of the cutter is used for trimming the vertical lipping.

Pierce and Trim Cutters
These cutters pierce and cut apertures in laminate work tops. The base of the cutter acts as a guide follower.

'Economy' Solid Carbide Trimmer
These 'economy' cutters are for the home craftsman on short runs of work. The S47/70 trims at 90° or 60° whilst the S48/40 is self guiding for 90° trimming.

HSS | TC

Sheet 5 Plunge Cut Tools for plunge routers & drill mc/s   **TC**

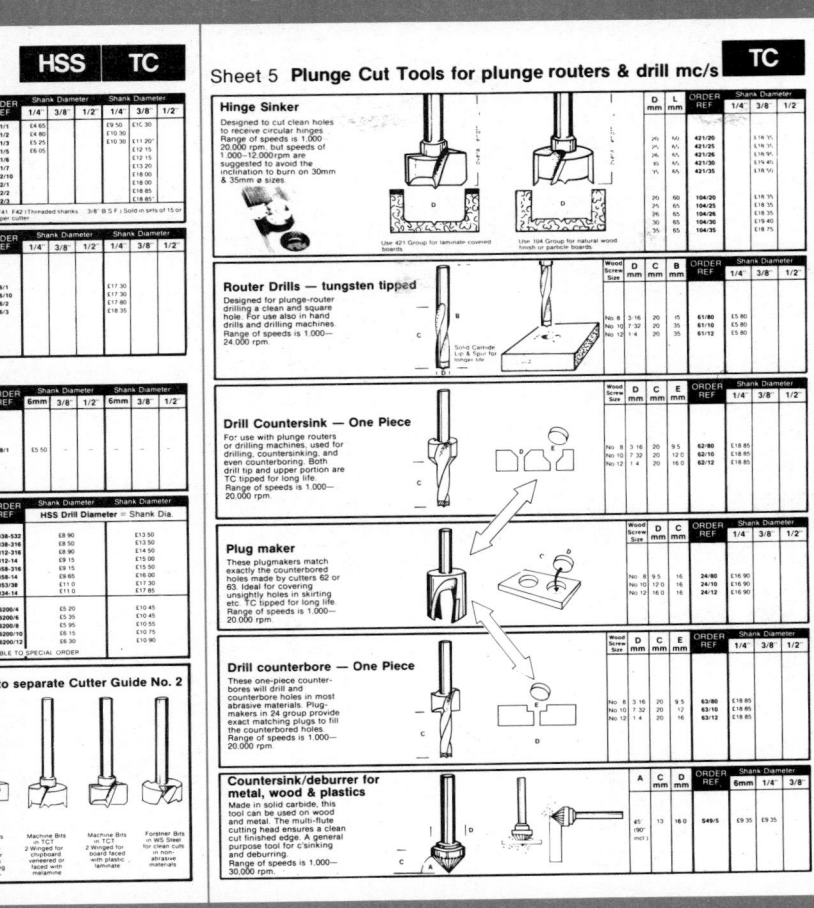

Hinge Sinker
Designed to cut clean holes to receive circular hinges. Range of speeds is 1,000-20,000 rpm. but speeds of 1,000-12,000 rpm are suggested to avoid the inclination to burn on 30mm & 35mm a sizes.

Use 421 Group for laminate covered boards. Use 104 Group for natural wood hough or particle boards.

Router Drills — tungsten tipped
Designed for plunge-router drilling a clean and square hole. For use also in hand drills and drilling machines. Range of speeds is 1,000-24,000 rpm.

Drill Countersink — One Piece
For use with plunge routers or drilling machines, used for drilling, countersinking, and even counterboring. Both drill tip and upper portion are TC tipped for long life. Range of speeds is 1,000-20,000 rpm.

Plug maker
These plugmakers match exactly the counterbored holes made by cutters 62 or 63. Ideal for covering unsightly holes in skirting etc. TC tipped for long life. Range of speeds is 1,000-20,000 rpm.

Drill counterbore — One Piece
These one-piece counterbores will drill and counterbore holes in most abrasive materials. Plugmakers in 24 group provide exact matching plugs to fill the counterbored holes. Range of speeds is 1,000-20,000 rpm.

Countersink/deburrer for metal, wood & plastics
Made in solid carbide, this tool can be used on wood and metal. The multi-flute cutting head ensures a clean cut finished edge. A general purpose tool for c'sinking and deburring. Range of speeds is 1,000-30,000 rpm.

Sheet 6 Slotters, Slitters and Groovers — on arbors   **Prices**

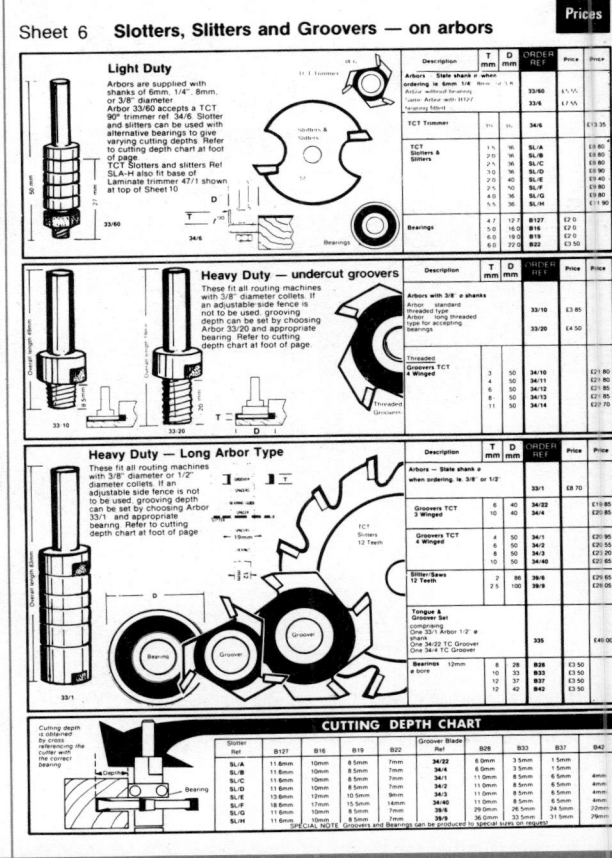

Light Duty
Arbors are supplied with shanks of 6mm, 1/4", 8mm, 3/8". Arbor 33/60 accepts a TCT 90° trimmer ref 34/6. Slotter and slitters can be used with alternative bearings to give varying cutting depths. Refer to cutting depth chart at foot of page. TCT Slotters and slitters Ref SLA-H also fit base of Laminate trimmer 47/1 shown at top of Sheet 10

Heavy Duty — undercut groovers
These fit all routing machines with 3/8" diameter collets. If an adjustable side fence is to be used, grooving depth can be set by choosing Arbor 33/20 and appropriate bearings. Refer to cutting depth chart at foot of page.

Heavy Duty — Long Arbor Type
These fit all routing machines with 3/8" diameter collets. If an adjustable side fence is not to be used, grooving depth can be set by choosing Arbor 33/1 and appropriate bearing. Refer to cutting depth chart at foot of page.

CUTTING DEPTH CHART

TC

Sheet 11 Universal Laminate Trimmers — self guiding   **TC**

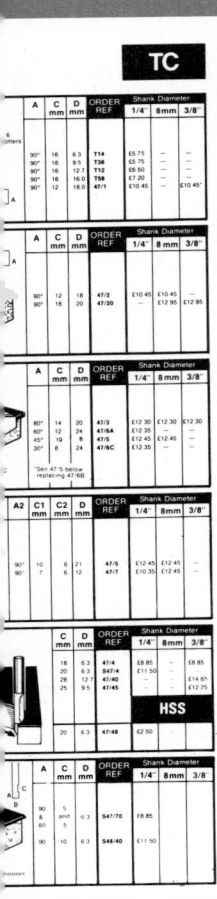

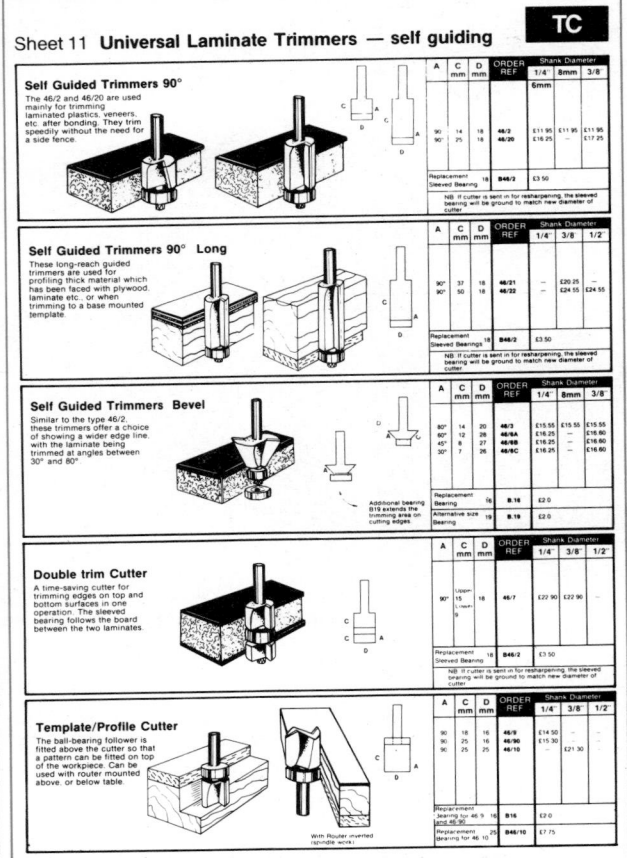

Self Guided Trimmers 90°
The 46/2 and 46/20 are used mainly for trimming laminated plastics, veneers, etc. after bonding. They trim speedily without the need for a side fence.

NB: If cutter is sent in for resharpening, the sleeved bearing will be ground to match new diameter of cutter

Self Guided Trimmers 90° Long
These long-reach guided trimmers are used for profiling thick material which has been faced with plywood, laminate etc. or when trimming to a base mounted template.

NB: If cutter is sent in for resharpening, the sleeved bearing will be ground to match new diameter of cutter

Self Guided Trimmers Bevel
Similar to the type 46/2, these trimmers offer a choice of showing a wider edge line, with the laminate being trimmed at angles between 30° and 80°.

Additional bearing B19 extends the trimming area on cutting edges

Double trim Cutter
A time-saving cutter for trimming edges on top and bottom surfaces in one operation. The sleeved bearing follows the board between the two laminates.

NB: If cutter is sent in for resharpening, the sleeved bearing will be ground to match new diameter of cutter

Template/Profile Cutter
The ball-bearing follower is fitted above the cutter so that a pattern can be fitted on top of the workpiece. Can be used with router mounted above, or below table.

With Router inverted (spindle work)

HSS

Sheet 12 Cutting Tools for Plastics & Metal   **HSS° | TC**

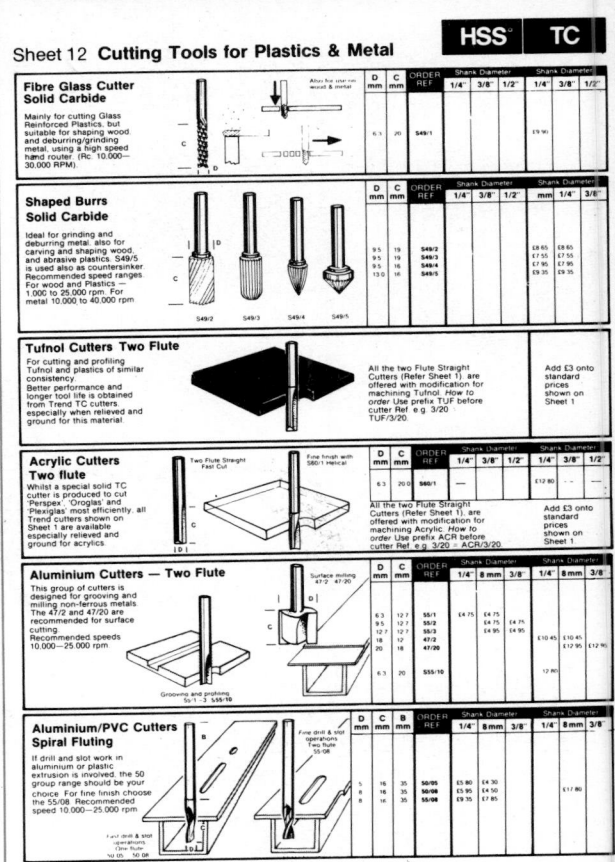

Fibre Glass Cutter Solid Carbide
Mainly for cutting Glass Reinforced Plastics, but suitable for shaping wood, and deburring/grinding metal, using a high speed hand router. (Rc 10,000-30,000 RPM).

Shaped Burrs Solid Carbide
Ideal for grinding and deburring metal, also for carving and shaping wood, and abrasive plastics. S49/5 is used also as countersinker. Recommended speed ranges. For wood and Plastics — 1,000 to 25,000 rpm. For metal 10,000 to 40,000 rpm.

Tufnol Cutters Two Flute
For cutting and profiling Tufnol and plastics of similar consistency. Better performance and longer tool life is obtained from Trend TC cutters, especially when relieved and ground for this material.

All the two Flute Straight Cutters (Refer Sheet 1) are offered with modification for machining Tufnol. How to order Use prefix TUF before cutter Ref e.g. 3/20 TUF/3/20. Add £3 onto standard prices shown on Sheet 1

Acrylic Cutters Two flute
Whilst a special solid TC cutter is produced to cut 'Perspex', 'Oroglas' and 'Plexiglas' most efficiently, all Trend cutters shown on Sheet 1 are available especially relieved and ground for acrylics.

All the two Flute Straight Cutters (Refer Sheet 1) are offered with modification for machining Acrylic. How to order Use prefix ACR before cutter Ref = ACR/3/20. Add £3 onto standard prices shown on Sheet 1

Aluminium Cutters — Two Flute
This group of cutters is designed for grooving and milling non-ferrous metals. The 47/2 and 47/20 are recommended for surface cutting. Recommended speeds 10,000-25,000 rpm

Aluminium/PVC Cutters Spiral Fluting
If drill and slot work in aluminium or plastic extrusion is involved, the 50 group range should be your choice. For fine finish choose the 55/08 and 50/08. Recommended speed 10,000-25,000 rpm

end Cutting Tools, Unit N, Penfold Works, Imperial Way, Watford WD2 4YY. ☎ (0923) 49911

Real Smooth
the Makita Range of Power Planers

A professional planer for every purpose - from the extra heavy duty model with its amazing 6⅛" wide blade down to its 3¼" cousin that makes spot work easy. *Send now for details.*

A tale of teak

What does teak, that most dependable of woods, have in common with the musical stage? Quite a lot, according to our timber expert Bill Brown, who here tells the tale of the King of Siam, Anna and teak

True teak, the product of *Tectona grandis*, is a wood renowned for its durability and stability in service, but it is outstanding in several other respects. At one time it was the only timber classed A1 at Lloyds, Kipling wrote poems in connection with the wood, a war was fought over it, and a famous musical has teak connections.

Teak is highly resistant to fire, both as wood and as a growing tree, in fact, it is said that forest fires improve the quality of young teak trees, and it is certainly true that fire aids the germination of teak seeds. The seeds are enclosed in a husk which needs to be removed in order to assist germination. A forest fire does this without harm to the seed so that new seedlings encourage natural regeneration.

Teak is highly resistant to termite (white ant) attack, and because of its short fibres tends to break under impact without splintering. It was for this reason it was used extensively for railway carriage construction and for backing armour plating in warships, thereby reducing accident potential damage to humans.

It is the only tropical hardwood tree that is commercially ring-girdled prior to felling, and the only one whose extraction from the forest developed around the use of elephants. It is said a well-trained animal could haul about 150 logs, each of about a ton, from forest to riverside each season.

Ring-girdling prevents the flow of sap from the roots to the crown of the tree and so allows excess moisture to evaporate through the leaves. In other words the tree partially seasons at stump, enabling the felled logs to float down river to the sawmills. Girdling is done by cutting into the bark with an axe, at about breast height, the cut going right through the sapwood and completely circling the hole. It is done annually, and girdled trees are allowed to stand for two or three years before felling.

I wonder how many people who have seen that delightful musical *The King And I* realise the element of truth that is in the story. Or the fact that Anna, the governess in the story, not only existed but represents a direct connection with the teak trade of London extending back from the present time to the mid-19th century, when Thailand was Siam.

The teak trade actually started in India and Burma, one of the principal British organisations being the Bombay Burma Trading Corporation Ltd, whose shipping mark BBTCL was literally the only one seen on teak when I was a boy. It was an extremely powerful company, but there was a fly in the ointment, so to speak. In fact there were two flies: the corrupt King Thebaw of Burma and the French consul of the time, one M. Haas, whose ambition it was to oust the British from Burma in connivance with the king. A treaty was negotiated between France and Burma under which the French would set up a state bank, take over the ruby mines, and exploit the teak forests of Upper Burma. In the event, the treaty signed by King Thebaw fell into British hands and the Foreign Secretary, Lord Salisbury, took appropriate action typical of the time: within a couple of months an expeditionary force was sent to Burma and the ensuing campaign led Kipling to write the poem *Mandalay*.

This Third Burmese War was quickly over and was probably the only war to be fought on behalf of the timber trade. The BBTCL eventually recovered and expanded, although a number of its staff were killed by the Burmese.

The best teak forests in Siam were in the territories of the Laos states of Upper Siam, and although independent, they acknowledged the King of Siam as suzerain. For many years Chinese merchants had exploited the teak from these forests, and one such organisation, Kim Sing Lee, sold out to BBTCL thus allowing them to get a toe-hold in Siam.

Anna Harriette Crawford was born in Caernarvon, north Wales, in 1834 and when she was six years old her parents sailed for India. Her father was an army captain whose regiment had been ordered to reinforce troops there in the face of impending war. A year later, her father was killed.

When Anna was 15, her mother married again but the stepfather and Anna did not get on and when she later met and fell in love with a young British army major, Thomas Louis Leonowens, there was much domestic strife culminating in Anna marrying her 'own Leon' in 1851. The break with her stepfather was now complete, but unfortunately the stepfather was the executor of the estate her father had left her, a fact that was to affect her later life.

Anna had an unfortunate marriage. She lost her first two children through illness very early. There were two other children, Avis, born in 1854 and Louis Thomas, born a year later. In 1857 the Indian Mutiny broke out and when it subsided Anna found she had not only lost her friends and relatives but also her fortune.

In 1856 Leon had been ordered to Singapore and there the family lived, but in 1858 Leon died from sunstroke brought on by carrying out a tiger hunt during the heat of the day – typical of mad dogs and Englishmen. Anna's stepfather had, in the meantime obtained possession of the old house in Caernarvon and now she had nothing beyond the two children.

To earn a living, Anna opened a school for officers' children and this came to the notice of Tan Kim Ching the Siamese consul in Singapore, who had been instructed by the King of Siam to secure an English governess for the royal children. After protracted negotiations Anna received a letter from the king himself offering her the job, and it is from this stage onwards that the basis of the play and film developed with, of course, a certain amount of poetic licence.

Among the pupils none attracted Anna so much as Prince Chulalongkorn and his sister Princess Chanthara Monthon. Both were exceptionally bright and being of about the same ages as Anna's children, became firm friends.

In 1867 Anna became ill and against the king's wishes went first to Ireland and then to New York to try to recuperate, taking Avis and Louis with her. A year later, King Somdetch Paraminder Maha Mongkut was dead and was succeeded by his son Prince Chulalongkorn. Anna never returned to Siam and although the king remembered her and Louis generously in his will, neither received the inheritance. The executors stopped it.

The new king was extremely progressive and pro-western; he had his sons educated at English public schools, abolished slavery, established telephone and telegraph services, constructed roads, hospitals and so on, and carried out reforms of law and taxation.

Louis Leonowens was by now very restless; he went to Australia, but in 1882 he returned to Siam where his friend the king made him an officer in the army. It was perhaps inevitable that Louis became a man of considerable influence with the king and eventually he set up in the teak trade as Leonowens and Company of Bangkok.

King Chulalongkorn died in 1910 and in more recent years, Leonowens became a subsidiary of a prominent firm of timber importers and are still represented in what is now an international group of timber companies based in London.

As an individual much caught up in the romanticism of timber and trees, I like to believe that it was Anna's work at the court of Siam that led to the young prince adopting western ideas and for providing the opportunity for young Louis to exploit the teak forests. As the song says, 'Getting to know you, getting to know all about you', which being interpreted could mean, 'It is not what you know, but who you know, that counts'. ■

Woodworkers of excellence

Mike Price reviews the recent Woodworkers of Excellence exhibition, held at the Queen's Hotel in Cheltenham. Pictures by Dave Johnson

In times when everyone is feeling cautious about how they spend their money, it should be very heartening for the craftsman to know that the public are still prepared to invest in fine woodwork, and that particular commodity was present in abundance at the White Knight Gallery's second exhibition.

Held in the Imperial Ballroom of the Queens Hotel, Cheltenham, there were more exhibits, and of a higher standard, than last year. The larger room, plus more effort on display, resulted in a civilised and comfortable atmosphere for the visitor.

The variety and range of the exhibits was amazing, as many visitors were heard to remark, including examples of furniture from many styles, in a bewildering array of woods and showing a uniformly high standard of craftsmanship. Indeed, it was fascinating to observe the equal dedication to technique, design and originality in a £4 lace bobbin, as in a £2,000 chest of drawers.

Prices varied widely, even for similar objects, but between the most expensive, Max Cooper's walnut marquetry clock at £3,090 and the cheapest, Toby Kaye's wooden eggs at £1.50, there were many beautiful objects to fit any pocket, as was proved by the steady flow of sales.

One thing that rapidly became obvious was the popularity of English yew with the buyers, in almost any shape or form; more pieces in yew were sold than all the others together. There must be something to be learned by exhibitors from that fact. ■

● ABOVE: Corner cupboard in pitch pine and rocking chair, both by Jeremy Broun. BELOW: marquetry dressing table and stool by Max Cooper

● ABOVE: desk in oak by John Sagar and chair in yew by Stewart Linford. LEFT: detail of marquetry work on clock by Max Cooper. BELOW: Red Rum in walnut by Ian Norbury

The ELU MWA 149 will put a razor sharp edge on your Chisels and Plane Irons with the *added plus* - a highly useful Belt Linisher for little more than the cost of a conventional Grinder.

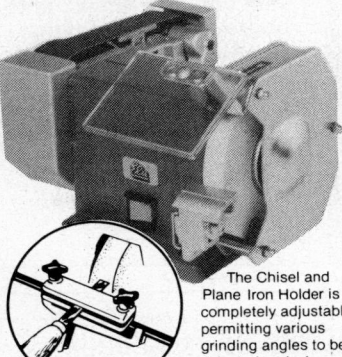

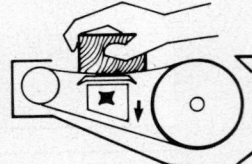

Pressure Plate Lowered
Allows the suppleness of the sanding belt to give on curved components.

The Chisel and Plane Iron Holder is completely adjustable permitting various grinding angles to be selected and when grinding, it guides you easily over the face of the stone.

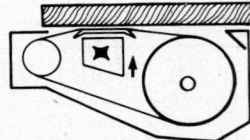

Pressure Plate Raised
Forces the belt rigid allowing the accurate sanding of flat surfaces.

The Grinder
The MWA 149 is equipped with a smooth and quiet induction type motor for production reliability and also accepts a wide variety of stones including white, green and G.P. in differing grit sizes.

The Linisher
This equipment provides the ability to effectively sand small components. There are 10 different grades of sanding belts available and the spring located roller controlled by a lever provides for quick belt changing. A leather Honing Belt is also available for putting that barber's edge on your Chisels and Plane Irons.

More information:
The ELU MWA 149 Grinders are readily available from a nationwide network of over 200 authorised distributors. Contact us today for your free illustrated brochure and full list of ELU dealers.

ELU Machinery Ltd.,
310/312 Dallow Road,
LUTON, Beds.
LU1 1SS
Tel: (0582) 425001
Telex: 825540 ELU G

CUTTERHEADS AND PROFILE CUTTERS
Multi-Profile Cutter
50 different profiles can be achieved with one cutterhead.
120mm diameter × 40mm wide × 30mm bore with 2 HSS teeth
Price £57.90, inc VAT.

REVERSIBLE KNIFE REBATING HEAD
With solid tungsten carbide replaceable knives. 100mm diameter × 30mm wide × 30mm bore.
Price £52.50 inc VAT.

Full details from:-

Leicester Wood Technique Ltd
Quality Tooling for the Woodworking Industry
Hothorpe House, Main St., Theddingworth, Lutterworth, Leicestershire LE17 6QY
Telephone: (0858) 880643 Telex: 342484

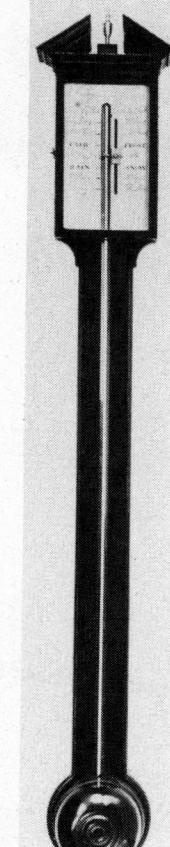
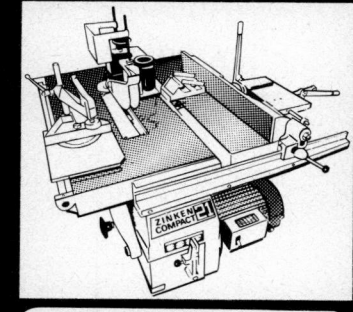

Primary project
Tombola drum

Richard Irving describes in words and drawings his design for a tombola or raffle drum

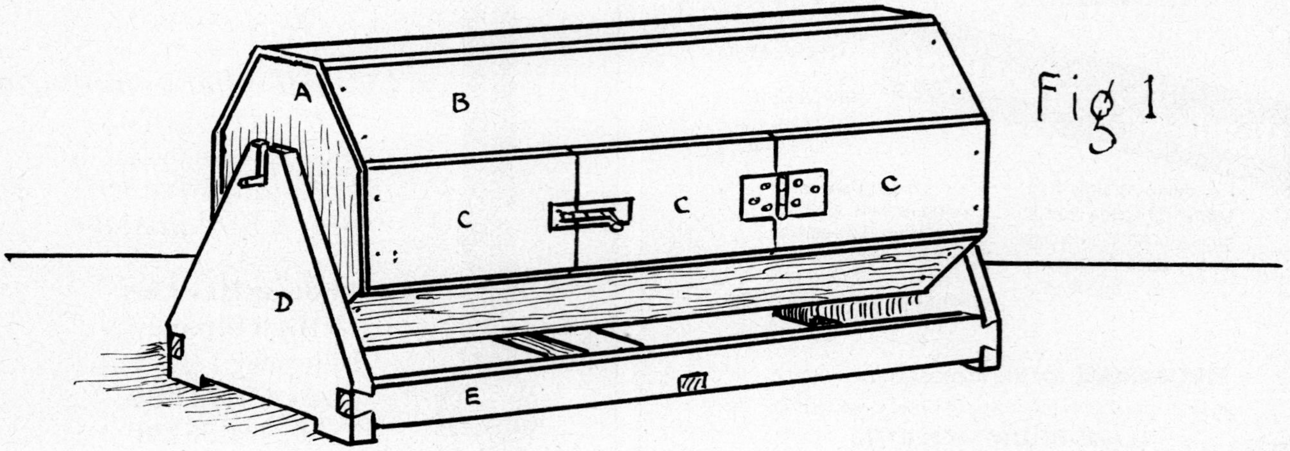

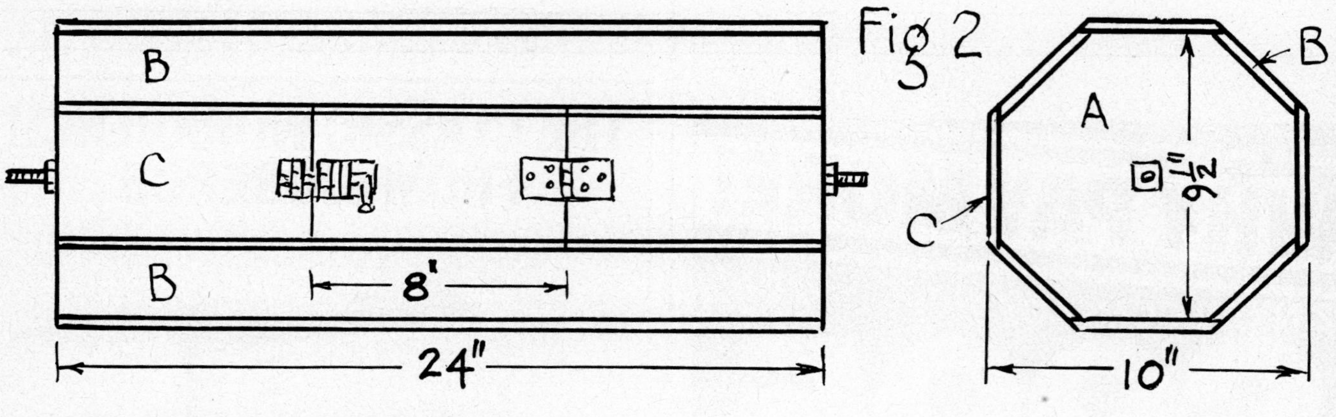

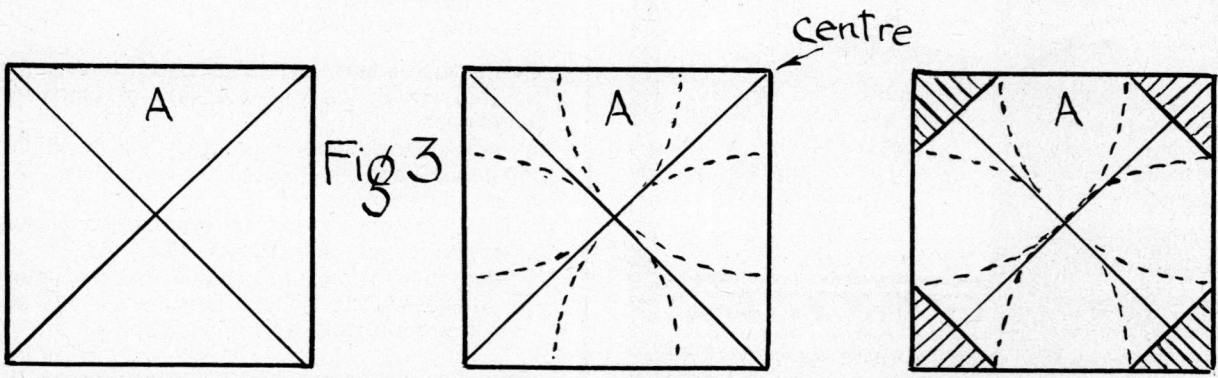

Fig 1

Fig 2

▲ *The position of the parts of the drum.*

Fig 3

Centre

▲ *Mark out the octagonal ends A. Saw off the waste corners. Plane the edges true.*

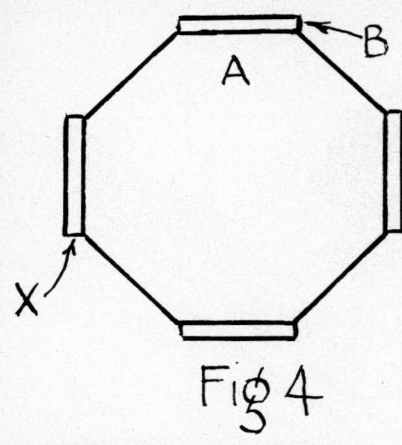

Fig 4

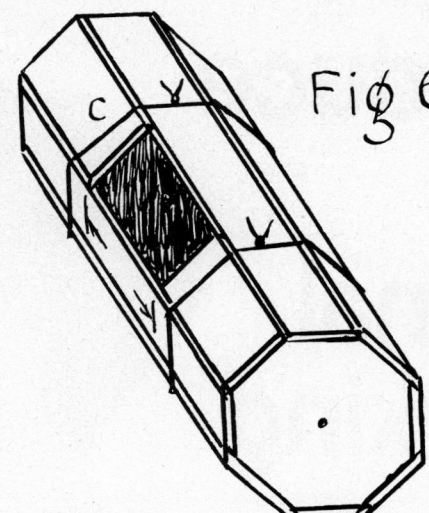

Fig 6

▲ *Glue and pin on the sides B. Leave for the glue to harden. Plane off the excess at the corners X.*

◀ *Bind stout string or masking tape tightly around the drum to exert pressure on the joints. When the glue has hardened, plane off the protruding corners.*

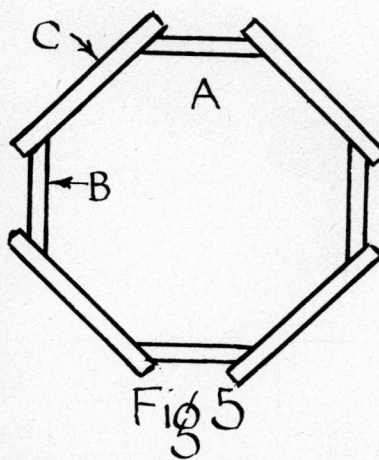

Fig 5

Fig 7

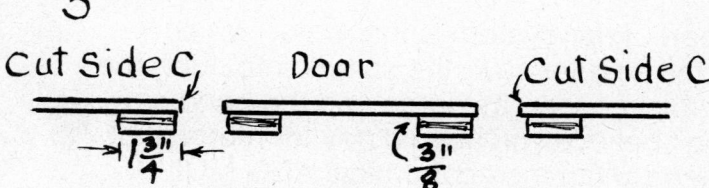

cut side C   Door   Cut Side C

Plywood Blocks G Inside

▲ *Cut one side (C) into three 8in long pieces, for the centre piece to make the door. Glue and pin three uncut sides (C) and the end pieces of the cut side onto the ends A and the edges of the sides B. Be particularly generous with the glue, so the surplus exudes inside to make strong joints.*

▲ *Glue and pin the screw blocks G under the cut side C and the door to give depth for ½in screws when fixing the fittings. Position the door. Screw on the hinge and the cupboard bolt. Plane the long edges of the door level with the sides C. Drill ¼in holes in the centre of the ends A. Insert the bolts from the inside of the drum and screw on the nuts tightly from the outside.*

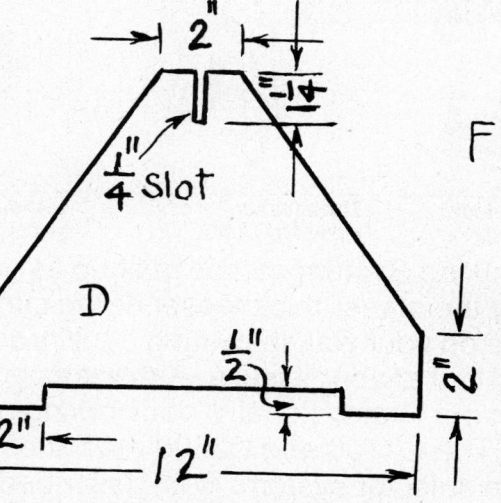

Fig 8

▲ *Saw the stand ends D to shape. Plane the edges smooth.*

TIMBER LIST

DRUM
A 2 ends 9½in × 9½in × ¾in blockboard
B 4 sides 24in × 4in × ¼in plywood
C 4 sides 24in × 4¾in × ¼in plywood

STAND
D 2 ends 12in × 9in × ⅝ or ¾in blockboard
E 2 rails 25⅝in × 1½in × ⅝in pine
F 1 cross rail 12in × 2in × ½in pine
G 4 screw blocks 3⅝in × 1¾in × ⅜in plywood

FITTINGS
2 1¾in × ¼in bolts threaded to the head, 2 nuts, 2 washers
1 1¾in cupboard bolt
1 1¼in back flap hinge

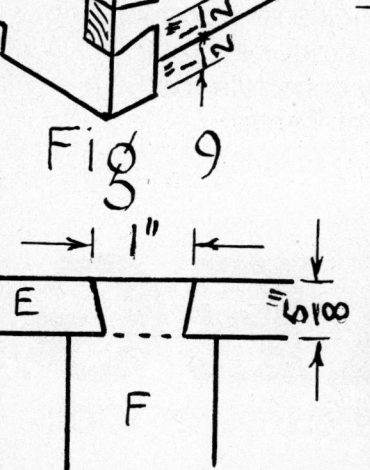

Fig 9

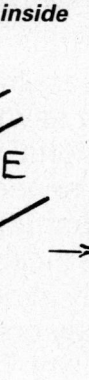

◀ *Use dovetail joints to secure the rails E to the ends D and secure the cross rail F under the rails E. Clean up all the parts and glue the stand together. Place the washers onto the drum bolts and drop into the stand slots whilst the glued joints are still soft. This ensures easy drum movement. Glue triangular blocks inside the corners of the stand for strength. Quick drying varnish makes a suitable finish for this piece.*

AEG Introduce a NEW Professional Woodworking System

The heart of our system is the motor, which drives the circular saw, the spindle moulder, the planer/thicknesser, the lathe and the band saw. We don't believe you should pay for motors you don't need. With the economical AEG MULTI Woodworking System you purchase just one motor that is interchangeable from one machine to another. AEG look after your power tool requirements and your pocket too!

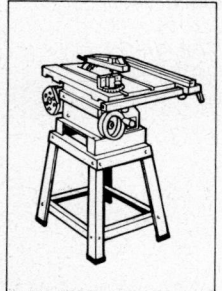

Circular Saw
Model No. SC25

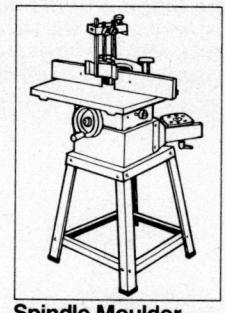

Spindle Moulder
Model No. T30N

Thicknesser
Model No. C260

Lathe
Model No. TBJ

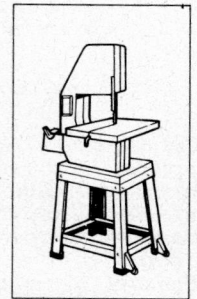

Band Saw
Model No. SR250

The AEG MULTI Woodworking System can be built up as you require it. Purchase your first machine (usually the planer/thicknesser or the circular saw) and the motor, and Hey Presto — you are on your way to owning a full professional woodworking system. You can then add to it at your leisure — it makes good sense!

Other machines in our Professional Woodworking programme include: The AEG UNIVERSAL range. The C2100 and C2600 machines will tackle all woodworking jobs on a unique operation selector system. Both described fully in our new Woodworking Programme brochure: For your own personal copy complete the coupon below and send to: AEG TELEFUNKEN (UK) LTD., Power Tools, 217, Bath Road, Slough, Berkshire, SL1 4AW.

Please send me details of your New Woodworking Programme.

Name_____

Address_____

_____

_____ W

AEG Electric Power Tools

Prices quoted are those prevailing at press date and are subject to alteration due to economic conditions.

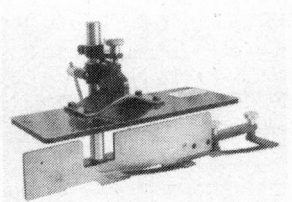

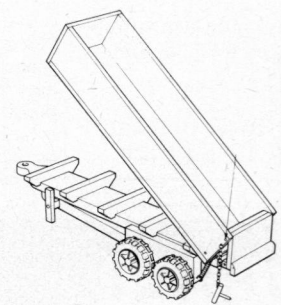
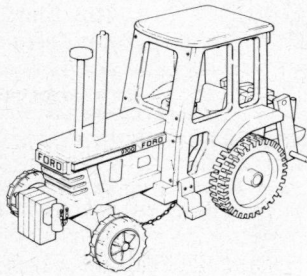

Prices quoted are those prevailing at press date and are subject to alteration due to economic conditions.

Woodturning from A to Z

In part five of his comprehensive guide to high quality woodturning, Gordon Stokes turns our attention to correct use of the grinding wheel

SKILL AT THE GRINDSTONE

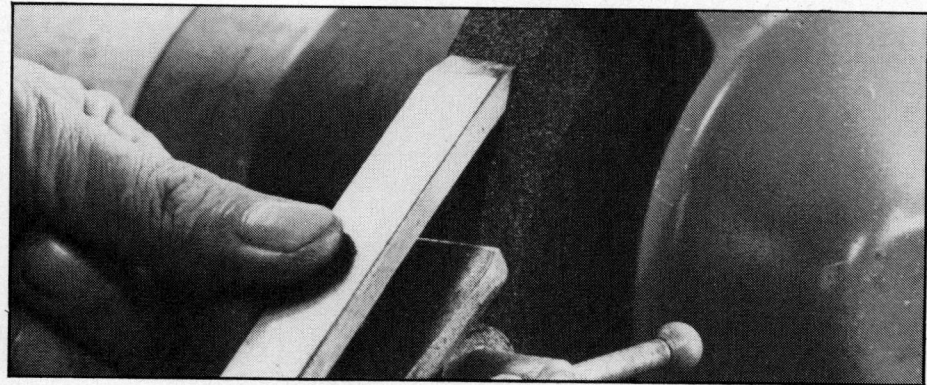

The content of this article will be of paramount importance to those who really wish to learn the craft, since incorrectly shaped or improperly sharpened tools will militate against the success of the student, and effectively prevent progress. We have already discussed the importance of the grinder in woodturning, together with the more significant points of the machine and its wheels, Now, before we can begin the turning itself, the grinding procedures must be examined.

It is not uncommon for beginners to purchase a grinding wheel and fit it to a home-made grinding machine. If the individual concerned happens to be an engineer, this is fine, but I would strongly advise others not to do it. Grindstones must be run within the speed limits laid down by the manufacturers, and if these are exceeded the situation becomes potentially dangerous. One must also note that a grindstone which is to be used for the sharpening of woodturning tools must run on top quality bearings – which are unlikely to be found in odd spindles purchased from the local tool shop. If the grinding of the tools is not to be made unnecessarily difficult, the bearings must have no significant side or end float, the stone must be truly circular, and it must be accurately centred on the spindle.

The stones must also be adequately guarded to protect the user if they should shatter in use, and to reduce the danger of small abrasive particles or slivers of metal flying into the eyes. Note that thick paper washers are always attached to both sides of these stones by the makers. These must on no account be removed, or the danger of the stone breaking will be greatly increased. The nut which holds the stone in place on the spindle should be pulled up firmly, but no more than that – do NOT overtighten it.

My aim in describing the shaping and sharpening of the turning tools is not to help beginners to 'manage', but to provide sufficient information to enable them, with practice, to take pride in the results of their grinding. There is a skill to be learned and developed, but success is well within the reach of a determined and reasonably intelligent student. Like many other things in life, once learned, this will never be forgotten.

In common with the lathe, the grinder should be positioned at a height which enables the user to work in comfort, which means without having to bend the knees or the back. Keen woodturners will spend quite a lot of time at the grinder, so things should be properly arranged at the outset.

It is important to remember that the exact angle which is ground on a tool is not in itself important. I do not know what angle I have on any of my tools, nor do I care, there being no way in which such knowledge could help my woodturning. It is the *shape* of the business end of a tool which is important. As we saw earlier, the grinding angle, whilst not critical, is related to the hardness of the wood to be cut. The aim must be to keep the tools on the grindstone throughout the grinding process without

● *From the top. Grinding a parting tool. Round nosed scraper being prepared. ¾in skew chisel used with light pressure on the stone. Slow side to side movement needed for 1¼in skew chisel.*

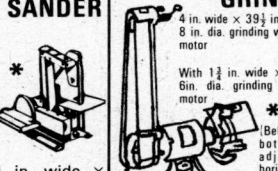
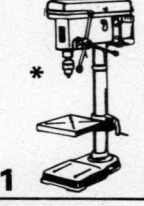

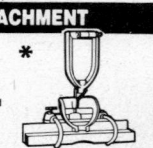
 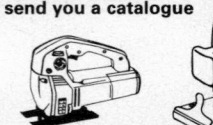

Prices quoted are those prevailing at press date and are subject to alteration due to economic conditions.

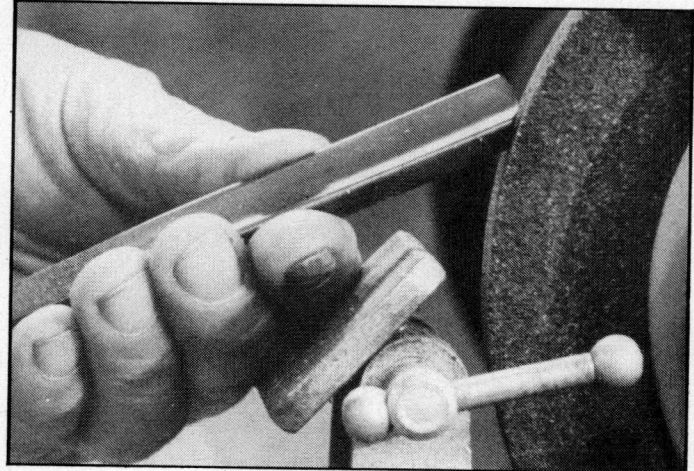

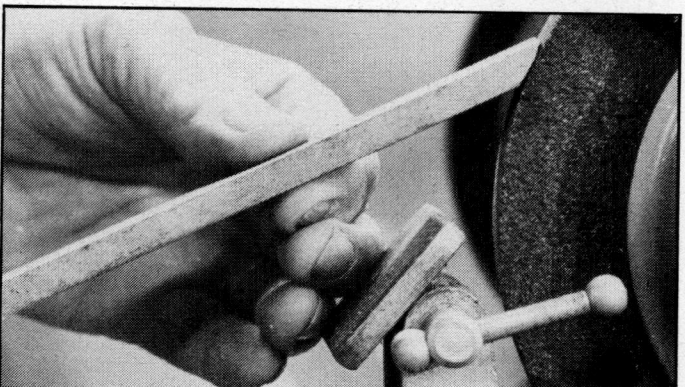

● *Left top. Slowly roll ½in spindle gouge. Below. Be careful not to burn the corners of the roughing gouge. Above top. Heavier roughing gouge, do not cool with water. Below. Scrapers must be capable of removing shavings.*

removing them, even momentarily, until the job is completed – and to control the pressure against the stone with great care so that the metal is not overheated. If the stone is kept sharp and clean, and the tools are not placed on the 'toolrest' of the grinder, this will not present any real problems.

Note that when spindle gouges, which have a slow curve or fingernail shape, are ground, the sparks will appear at the corners before they show at the centre. If the rolling action is gradually reduced from this point until the centre has shown sparks, the results will be satisfactory.

In the case of the square-ended gouges, the opposite applies. The sparks tend to appear at the centre of the cutting edge before they show at the corners, and if nothing is done about the situation, the edge will be eroded at the centre. The answer here is to lower the handle slightly at the centre of each roll, so that no further grinding takes place in this area. This knack can be acquired quite quickly.

It would be nice to have a grindstone which was wider than the widest chisel in the workshop, but such stones are expensive, and grinders suitable for them are beyond the pockets of most users. Fortunately a very wide stone is not essential, the problem being overcome by a slow side-to-side movement of the chisel.

If plenty of practice has been carried out on scrap metal, there should be no real problem in the shaping and sharpening of the turning tools, but in view of the supreme importance of the matter, I will run through it to make sure that there are no misunderstandings.

First a chisel, which most beginners will find easier to grind than a gouge. Most grinding wheels are at least ¾in wide, many are an inch or more, so the grinding of the ¾in skew chisel is quite straightforward. It should be placed fairly high up on the stone, so that the edge is well clear, and it is the heel of the bevel which makes the initial contact, the edge being square to the wheel rather than at an oblique angle across it. The tool is then drawn slowly down the stone, the handle being raised a little until the cutting edge is only just clear. If this position is maintained with constant but light pressure, sparks will appear at the cutting edge in a short while. The tool is then turned over, and the process is repeated. There should now be smooth bevels of equal width on each side.

Try a parting tool next, but remember that the smaller the tool, the greater the need for control in the pressure aspect of the matter to avoid burning. The procedure with a parting tool is the same as with a chisel, which is hardly surprising since a parting tool *is* a chisel. Try to produce identical bevels on each side – which may not be too easy at first.

The rolling movement which is required for the gouges will call for more practice, and can be tried out initially on a stationary wheel.

It should be noted that few professionals ever talk about gouges as such unless it is necessary to do so. To them all turning tools are chisels, though I have to remember to be specific when instructing. In fact, of course, a gouge is a chisel, which has been curled up to enable it to be used in certain situations without undesired portions of its edge contacting the wood. Unlike some of the carving gouges, woodturning gouges do not have a bevel on the inside – which is perhaps as well, since it would make the sharpening far more awkward. Do not overemphasise the curvature on the profile of the spindle gouges, which should have a slow curve – not a long pointed nose.

Newcomers are often enthusiastic about making handles for their tools. This is an easy project, and we will look at it when we reach that stage, but I find the handles which are supplied with new tools to be quite satisfactory – and I usually have quite enough jobs waiting to be started, without making more! Never make the mistake of thinking that a fancy home-made handle will work wonders for your woodturning, because it will not. Finally, make quite sure that all handles are tight. A loose handle on a turning tool can cause an accident.

The idea of rust on tools, and indeed on the lathe itself, seems to worry many people, but the problem can often be solved by being a little less fussy when clearing up the shavings. Leave plenty of them among the tools and around the lathe. Their hygroscopic action pulls great quantities of water out of the surrounding air. Also note that paraffin heaters, and some gas heaters, produce quite surprising quantities of water, and this can exacerbate the rust problem.

I have not gone into the full details of the tools yet, because the finer points can best be dealt with when we examine the basic cutting, and then move on into some exercises and simple projects. There are some things which must be explained, however, with particular reference to safety, so these will be covered next month when we start the lathe and begin the woodturning. ■

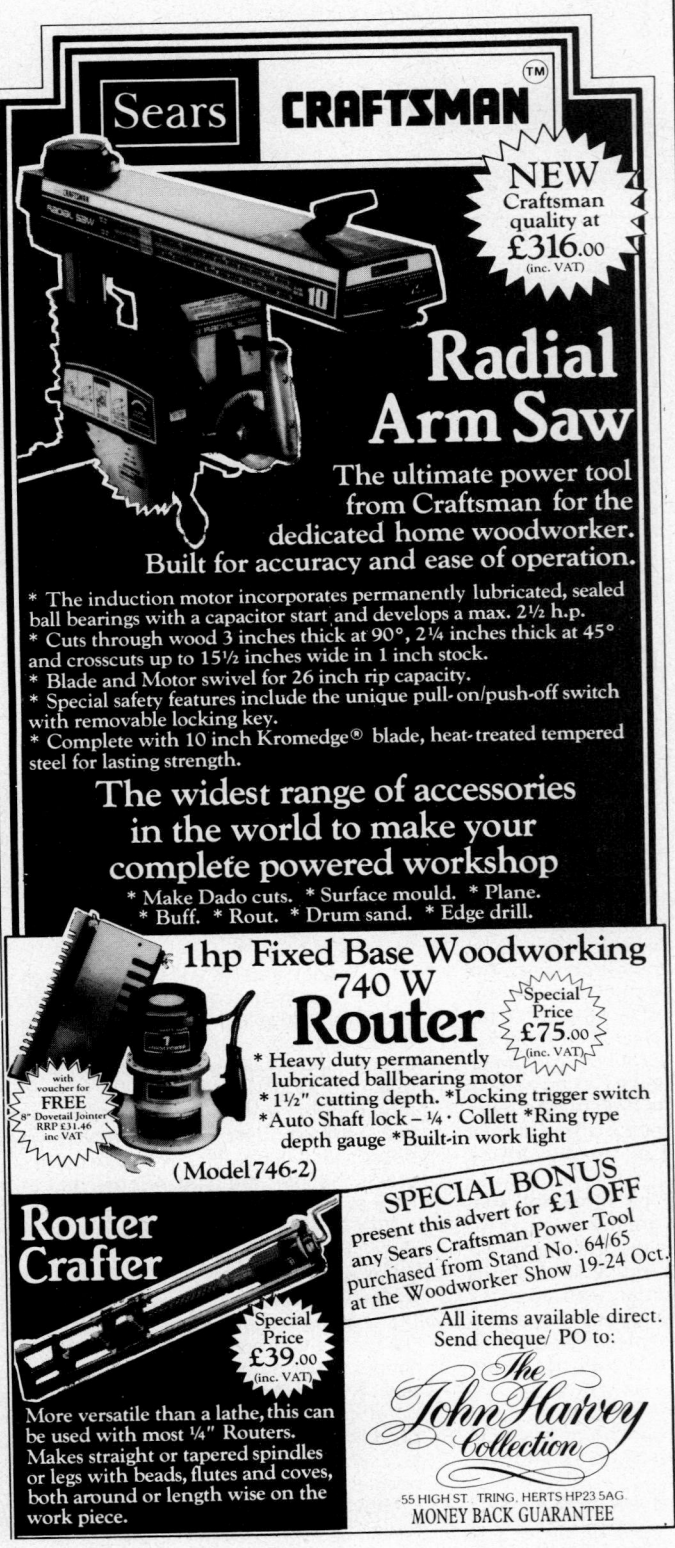
Prices quoted are those prevailing at press date and are subject to alteration due to economic conditions.

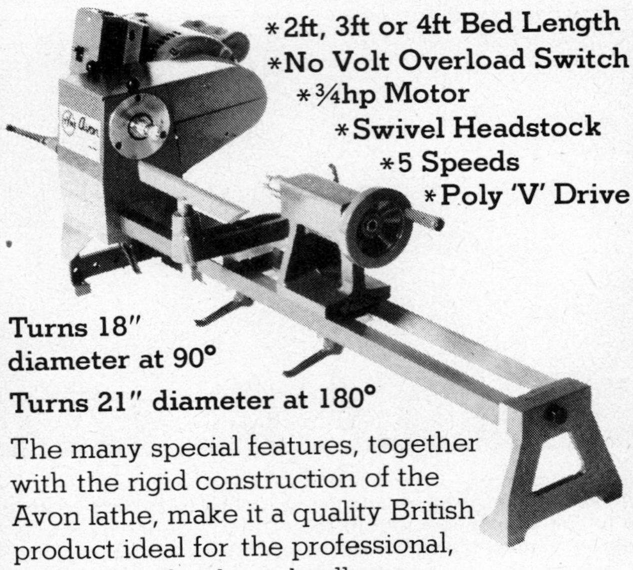

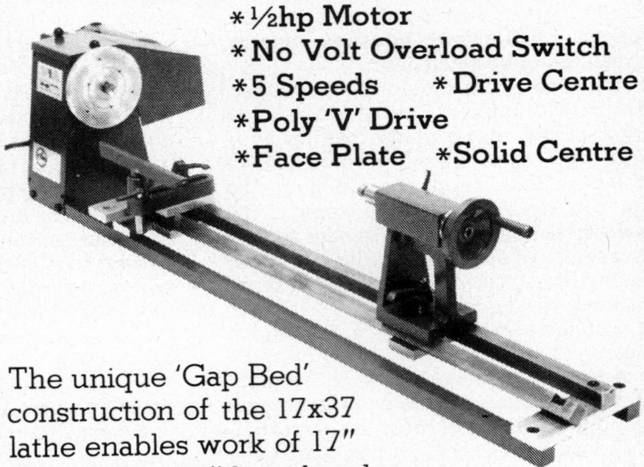

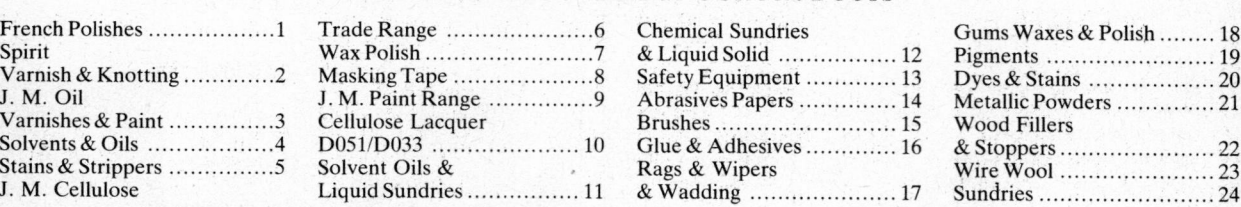
780

Prices quoted are those prevailing at press date and are subject to alteration due to economic conditions.

Woodworker, November 198

Model Engineer
Exhibition
1-9 Jan `83
Open 10am - 7pm
Late night Thurs. 6th until 9pm
Wembley Conference Centre

LECTURES AND FILMS • OVER 1000 MODELS • MODEL COMPETITIONS
TRADE STANDS • MODEL BOATS & CARS IN ACTION • MODEL TRAMWAY
WORKING MODEL RAILWAY • MODEL FLYING • STEAM TRAIN RIDES
To be opened by David Shepherd OBE • Adults £2. Children & OAP's £1.50

It is regretted that for safety reasons no prams or pushchairs can be admitted. However limited pram parking space is available.

52nd Model Engineer Exhibition

Wembley Conference Centre

**1st-9th January 1983
(including Sundays 2nd & 9th)
Late night Thursday 6th January — 9pm**

PLAN YOUR VISIT NOW

The Exhibition will open at 10.00 am each day (including Sundays) and will close at 7.00 pm except on Thursday 6th, when the Exhibition will remain open until 9.00 pm.

ADVANCE TICKETS

Advance tickets at the normal rate and advance party tickets at more favourable prices are available, valid for any day, direct from the Exhibition Manager, Model Engineer Exhibition at the following rates:

	ADULT	CHILD/O.A.P.
AT DOOR OR ADVANCE: for small parties less than 10	£2.00 each	£1.50 each
ADVANCE: for parties greater than 10	£1.50 each	£1.00 each

Teachers/Leaders of parties greater than 10: free ticket in the ratio of one per 10 in party.
Teachers/Leaders must remain with their parties while they are in the Exhibition.

Advance tickets are designed to help regular visitors avoid waiting in the long queues which form on well attended days, particularly at weekends. While it is not possible to guarantee that holders of advance tickets will not have to wait at the special 'Advance Ticket' position for a short while, these tickets take precedence over non-ticket holders. Please use the coupon below to apply for your tickets.

Also, please note that there are special British Rail fare rates, including admission, that are advertised in some MAP magazines. Trains to and from Marylebone, on the Princes Risborough line, stop regularly at Wembley Complex Station, three minutes walk from the Conference Centre. Car parking for the day, currently £1 but subject to increase, is available for thousands of cars at the rear of the Conference Centre.
Visitors should note that round-the-pole model flying takes place only on January 8th and 9th and that model car racing takes place on January 2nd, 3rd and 4th, and model car demonstrations on the 5th, 6th and 7th January.

PARTY AND ADVANCE BOOKING APPLICATION FORM

Please complete and return to:

The Exhibition Manager, Model Engineer Exhibition, Model & Allied Publications Ltd., P.O. Box 35, Hemel Hempstead, Herts.

Full Rate		**Party Rate**
.... Adults at £2.00 each	or	.... at £1.50 each
Child/O.A.P.'s at £1.50 each	or	.... at £1.00 each

(All admission charges include VAT)

TOTAL £ ....

I enclose cheque/PO for total amount stated above, payable to Model & Allied Publications Limited.
All applications must be accompanied by a stamped addressed envelope for return of tickets. Final date for receipt of applications for advance tickets 10th December 1982.

Please forward tickets to: *BLOCK CAPITALS PLEASE*

Name ....

Address ....

....

ww

GLUE FIX 2000
FROM STEINEL

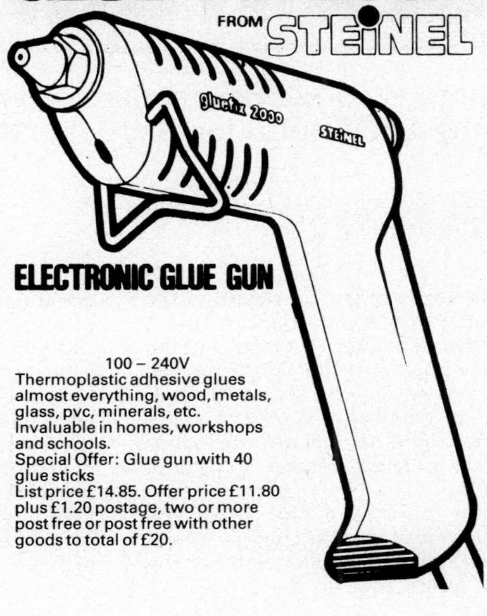

ELECTRONIC GLUE GUN

100 – 240V
Thermoplastic adhesive glues almost everything, wood, metals, glass, pvc, minerals, etc.
Invaluable in homes, workshops and schools.
Special Offer: Glue gun with 40 glue sticks
List price £14.85. Offer price £11.80 plus £1.20 postage, two or more post free or post free with other goods to total of £20.

POWER TOOLS ETC

Cat No.		M.R.P.	Our Price
096-2	Craftsman 7½" circular saw, 2⅛hp	£94.45	£70.80
26269	Craftsman Trim-a-Form Router Attachment	£45.95	£33.00
138	Dremel Disc/Belt sander	£94.60	£78.00
238	Dremel Moto Flex Tool	£76.10	£63.95
577	Dremel DeLuxe Moto Shop	£98.40	£82.80
2509	Dremel Moto-Tool Kit with 35 accessories	£53.05	£44.50
215	Dremel Foot operated speed control	£29.15	£24.15
358	Dremel Variable Speed Moto-Tool	£55.35	£46.00
359	Dremel Variable Speed Moto-Tool Kit with 35 accessories	£69.20	£58.50
284	Dremel Moto Tool Woodcarver's Kit	£69.40	£58.65
384	Dremel Variable Speed Woodcarver's Kit	£84.00	£70.95
292	Dremel engraver	£15.75	£13.30
96H	Skil power plane, 480 watt	£80.39	£67.00
1474H	Skil ½" reversing hammer drill, 500 watt	£67.74	£55.00
574U	Skil 7¼" circular saw, 1000 watt	£62.10	£52.00
400-E	Bosch ½" variable speed hammer drill, 400 watt	£54.50	£42.50
450-2E	Bosch ½" variable speed hammer drill, 450 watt with kit	£88.80	£60.00
500-2E	Bosch ½" variable speed hammer drill, 500 watt	£79.00	£62.00
620-2E	Bosch ½" variable speed hammer drill, 620 watt	£92.00	£73.00
650-2RLE	Bosch ½" variable speed reversing hammer drill	£97.50	£77.00
S33	Bosch 6" circular saw attachment	£26.40	£21.00
PST50E	Bosch variable speed jigsaw	£48.50	£38.50
PSS230	Bosch orbital sander	£43.50	£34.50
PSP250	Bosch spray gun set	£55.00	£43.00
PKS46	Bosch 6" circular saw	£62.50	£49.00
S9	Bosch saw table for PKS46 saw	£46.00	£36.50
PKS65	Bosch 7½" circular saw	£93.00	£74.00
POF50	Bosch plunging router with 1 router bit	£59.50	£47.00
S7	Bosch milling stand	£52.00	£41.50
S8	Bosch routing bench for above	£24.00	£19.00
S2	Bosch drill stand	£24.00	£19.00
S18	Bosch lathe kit	£68.25	£54.50

BOSCH INDUSTRIAL

SB4502	Bosch 2 speed impact drill with free tool handy & 750 rawlplugs	£99.48	£79.00
1179	Bosch ½" 2 speed impact drill	£126.79	£100.00
1287-1	Bosch orbital sander with induction motor	£127.65	£101.00
PWS6000	Bosch 7" angle sander/grinder	£102.64	£81.00
1577	Bosch orbital action jigsaw in metal case	£116.15	£91.00

HAND TOOLS

781000	Jet Clamp	£10.98	£9.55
04	Record 2" blade smoothing plane	£19.90	£15.50
311	Record 3 in 1 plane	£37.52	£31.50
778	Record rebate plane	£29.75	£24.50
044C	Record Plough Plane, 10 blade	£43.42	£34.00
050C	Record combination plane, 18 blade	£65.50	£55.00
020C	Record circular plane	£68.31	£57.00
405	Record multi lane, 24 blade	£161.46	£136.00
52D	Record QR woodwork vice with front dog	£46.13	£39.00
413	Record 3" drill press vice	£20.53	£17.40
130	Record cramp heads	£10.99	£9.25
146	Record bench holdfast 7⅝" opening	£19.33	£16.50
148	Record dowelling jig	£34.35	£28.00
M1160	Marples draw knife	£19.08	£16.00
M2400	Marples 12" bow saw	£20.60	£17.00
M1002	Marples set of 8 turning tools	£51.73	43.50
M60	Marples set of 12 carving tools	£68.60	£58.00
M60A	Marples set of 6 carving tools	£36.43	£31.00
M444/S5	Marples set of 5 blue chip chisels	£22.28	£18.00
M260	Marples set of 5 wood sculpture tools	£37.49	£31.75
M277	Marples wood carver's screw	£5.75	£4.90
13-052	Stanley plough plane, 10 blade	£41.35	£34.50
13-050	Stanley combination plane, 18 blade	£63.00	£52.95
5½	Stanley 15" jack plane	£28.99	£24.00
7	Stanley 22" jointer/try plane	£36.55	£30.95
71	Stanley hand router, 3 blade	£24.70	£20.50
TS	Henry Taylor superflute turning gouge	£22.35	£19.00
	Henry Taylor Wood Carver's Adze, Chisel	£14.95	£12.70
	Henry Taylor Wood Carver's Adze, Gouge	£19.55	£16.55

**All prices include VAT. Carriage free on orders over £20 (UK Mainland)
Henry Taylor and Marples Woodcarving and Turning Tools in stock**

**BENMAIL, 48 Station Road, St. Georges, Weston-s-Mare, Avon BS22 0XL
Tel: 0934 24385** *We close Thursdays*

Work from the schools

This month *Woodworker* focuses on two schools: the John Hampden School at High Wycombe and Tonbridge School in Kent

John Hampden

When the pupils enter the school in the second year they have the opportunity to take a woodwork course. At the end of the third year the pupils choose which subjects they wish to study for Ordinary level examinations. When woodwork is chosen, there are five time-tabled periods per week, four of which are practical lessons plus one theory lesson.

During the fourth and fifth years, the furniture produced by the pupils is not incorporated into the examination but the design and joints used in the process of construction will stand the pupils in good stead for such an examination.

Within the latter part of the fifth academic year the pupils' completed pieces of furniture are entered in a local Rotary Club competition which many of the schools in the High Wycombe area also enter. The competition started three years ago. In the previous years several of the local furniture manufacturers were invited to the school to judge the work produced by the pupils and to award appropriate prizes.

The judging of the Rotary Club competition this year took place in July. The John Hampden School achieved first places in two categories a second place and a third place. Robert Cross won first prize in the over-16 age-group with a feathered maple classical guitar. Adrian Heather won first prize in the under-16 age-group with a mahogany lyre sided sofa table. David Vitty won second prize in the under-14 age-group with a mahogany country cottage clock. Andrew Grace won third prize in the under-16 age-group with an African walnut desk and chair. ∎

● *Left, guitar in sycamore and mahogany by Robert Cross and right pine wall clock by S. Wright aged 13*

● Left, a shot gun cupboard in pine by Ian Smith and right, detail of a grandfather clock in English oak by Guy Mason

● A selection of table designs from Tonbridge, by left to right T. A. Sargeant, M. B. Robeson and D. C. Castle

Tonbridge

Tonbridge School in Kent is a boys' private school founded in 1553 by Sir Andrew Judde, Kt, Chartered by King Edward VI, the governing body being the Worshipful Company of Skinners. Each year the school celebrates 'Skinners' Day', and the pictures here show what the school's woodworkers, under the instruction of Mr P. E. Clay, were exhibiting on Skinners' Day this year.

The Technology Department consists of two full-time teachers, one teaching engineering and one teaching woodwork, and a part-time teacher of electronics. The courses offered to the students are constantly broadening to include work with other materials, and liaison with the Science Department helps create stimulating and interesting projects. In addition to the variety of projects undertaken by the students, the department places great value in maintaining high standards of craftsmanship and traditional methods of construction.

Students are timetabled for two 40-minute periods in their second year, and three in subsequent years, although being a boarding school, provides the opportunity to use the facility after school and at weekends. The photographs show a selection of work from the five years of the school, all projects being designed and made by the students.

The grandfather clock, made by Guy Mason, took 400 hours to complete. The timber used was English oak, which was fumed with ammonia and then french polished. The movement was purchased from Southern Watch and Clock, and help was given by Derek Roberts of Kent Clock Services in establishing case proportions in the design stages.

The gun cupboard was made by Ian Smith, a student with only two years' woodwork experience, who hopes to follow a career in farm management. The criteria for the design were that it should fulfil the regulations for shot gun cupboards (consequently, it is lined with 16-gauge steel covered with green felt) but also that it should be an attractive piece of furniture. With this in mind it has a door comprising of five raised and fielded panels, and the back was also panelled to complete the traditional appearance. ■

INTRODUCING THE NEW GENERATION
OF "ELECTRONIC" ELU POWER TOOL

MVS 156E NEW ELU ELECTRONIC VARIABLE SPEED ORBITAL SANDER WITH DUST BAG, MODERN DESIGN, SMOOTH AND COMFORTABLE TO USE, RUGGED 250 WATT MOTOR "SPECIAL FEATURES"

* "electronic" speed control 6000 - 24000 orbits per min, one machine to cope with all surfaces/materials. Efficient sanding of paint and varnish can now be achieved.
* the ingenious design allows dust to be drawn through ducts on the side of the base and holes in the sand paper.
* sanding sheet size 93 x 230 mm. No special sand paper is required as the machine is supplied with a template to punch the holes accurately in position.
* the design of this machine allows sanding right up into the corners as a hood is not required to aid the efficient dust extraction. **£49.99 inc VAT. Postage £2.00**

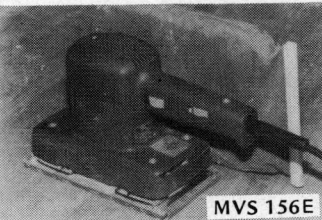
MVS 156E

MHB 157/10e

MHB 157. NEW ELU ELECTRONIC VARIABLE SPEED BELT SANDER WITH FRAME. THIS HAS GOT TO BE THE BEST 3" BELT SANDER AVAILABLE TODAY, A REAL THOROUGHBRED FROM THE ELU STABLES THIS NEW MACHINE IS SMOOTH AND COMFORTABLE IN USE, SUPERB ULTRA MODERN DESIGN, RUGGED 600 WATT MOTOR "SPECIAL FEATURES"

* dust collection bag situated at front of machine clear of hands
* compact design, weighs in at only 2.8 kg * one handed balance
* easy belt change * positive tracking system
* electronic variable speed control for the sanding of problem/ heat sensitive materials
* sanding frame enables micro adjustment of depth of cut essential when sanding veneered boards without the fear of ruining the work

MHB 157/10e "electronic" belt sander with dust extraction and sanding frame **£89.99 inc VAT. Postage £3.00**

"INVERSION STAND" available as an optional extra. This cleverly designed accessory allows the machine to be mounted either vertically or horizontally **£25.00 inc. VAT and postage**

3" belt for 157 belt sander pack of three either fine/medium/coarse **£2.99 inc. VAT. Postage 50 p**

*** OTHER ELU TOOLS AT BARGAIN PRICES ***
HALF PRICE BOOK OFFER
PURCHASE ANY ELU ROUTER AND BUY THE BOOK ON ROUTING, "TECHNIQUES OF ROUTING" BY JIM PHILLIPS FOR ONLY £2.87, INCLUDING POSTAGE ½ OUR RECENT ADVERTISED PRICE

MOF 96 Plunging Router 600 watts	£49.95
96 Router Accessory Kit	£42.00
Dovetail Jig with T/C Cutter for use with 96 Router	£42.00
Dovetail Jig with T/C ¼ in Shank Cutter for use with MOF 98 & 31 Routers	£50.95
MOF 98 Plunge Router 2.2 hp	£119.95
MOF 31 Plunge Router 1.7 hp	£99.95
MH 182 Saw with T/C blade 3" depth of cut. 1400 watt motor	£75.00
MH 85 Heavy Duty Saw 3¼" cut T/C blade 1600 watt motor	£107.00
ST 152 Pendulum Action Jig Saw *Free case while stocks last.* 450 watt	£67.00

All the above prices include VAT
Postage £2.50 per tool unless otherwise stated

 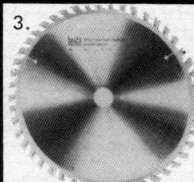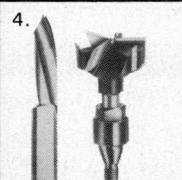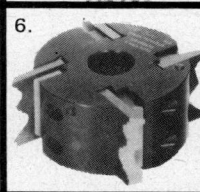

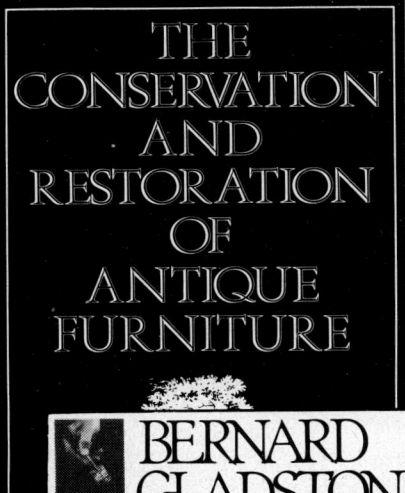

Wood Suppliers

ENGLISH HARDWOODS. Oak Specialists, also Elm, Ash, Beech, Sycamore. Over 4,000 cu.ft. Send for stock list to W. H. Mason & Son Ltd., The Sawmills, Wetmore Road, Burton-on-Trent, Staffs. Telephone 64651/2. Also imported hardwoods, softwoods and full machining facilities. T-V

BRITISH HARDWOODS KILNED, Beech, Sycamore, Elm, Lime, Pear, Apple, Ash, Cherry £10. Yew, Oak £14. Teak, Pine £6. Great Stour 470 Kent. S-T

FREE HAND WOODCRAFT. Small surplus of English hardwoods, surplus to requirements, for turnery, carving, etc. 2" thick. Walnut, Cherry, Spalted Beech (mottled), White Bean, Oak, Yew and Apple. Air or kiln dried, blanks supplied. Stock we don't keep – we will help you find. Westholme Farm, Goring Heath, Reading, Berks. Telephone: Checkendon (0941) 681337.

VENEERS AND MARQUETRY equipment, materials and books now in stock. Phone or send for details to: H.W.M., The Woodworkers, 303 Shirley Road, Shirley, Southampton. Tel: 0703 776222. T/C

CONVERT TIMBER YOURSELF, with a portable chain saw mill. Cuts a 36" width 200 sq. ft. per hour. Keenest prices. Brochure, demonstration. Philip Cole, 16 Kings Lane, Flore, Northampton. Tel: Weedon 0327 40337 (evenings) T/C

VENEERS, all types. SAE List—S. Gould (Veneers), 342 Uxbridge Road, W12. Tel: 01-743 8561. T/C

YEW, CHERRY, Black Walnut 1"-3" air dried. HINDON 237. Wiltshire. T-U

BEECH. Oak, Pitch-pine, Yew, Sycamore, various thicknesses, air and kiln dry. Ring Will Tyers (0468) 21292 (Nr. Lancaster). P-U

FOSS GLEN FORESTRY
Air Dried British Hardwoods

Burr Yew ● Burr Field
Maple ● Bog Oak ●
Mulberry ● Lacewood ●
plus many other varieties.
For current catalogue ring.

MICHAEL GRIFFITH 024289 422
4 Kings Head Lane, Withington, Glos.
GL54 4BD

Tree Work Services

WE SUPPLY HOME GROWN HARDWOODS IN THE ROUND, FRESH SAWN, OR DRIED.

SPECIES IN STOCK INCLUDE: Acacia, Apple, Ash, Beech, Cedar, Cherry, Chestnut, Elm, Holly, Holm Oak, Lacewood, Lime, Maple, Oak, Pear, Sycamore, Tree of Heaven, Tulip Tree, Walnut, Yew.

QUARTER SAWN AND STRAIGHT EDGED OAK SUPPLIED.
YOUR OWN TREES MILLED on site, to your specifications.

JOHN EMERY
THE OLD RECTORY, PILGRIMS WAY, CHEW STOKE, NR. BRISTOL.
TEL: CHEW MAGNA 3222

Fact 2 from Ebac

Ebac has a drying system to suit your needs. Ebac

Greenfields Ind. Est. Bishop Auckland, Co. Durham, England DL14 9TF.
Tel: (0388) 605061

See our ad on page 726

ENGLISH HARDWOODS
Oak, Ash, Sycamore, Beech etc. Air & Kiln dried
All sizes in stock
HOGHTON TIMBER
HIGHER WALTON TRADING ESTATE
PRESTON, LANCS.
Tel: Preston 36193

HAVE ENGLISH YEW
(Will Haggle)
1000 cu ft — Come and choose from wide variety of sizes. Well Seasoned. Loads of Offcuts. Schools supplied.
Callers made welcome anytime.
"The more the cheaper"
W. Pearson, ASHLEY MOOR HALL, ORLETON, Nr. LUDLOW, SHROPSHIRE.
Tel: Yarpole 236

WOODSTOCK (HARDWOODS) S.W.
HARDWOOD – Ring us first
Supplied to your cutting list or per cubic foot.
Both English and imported timbers.
ASHFIELD, PONSHARDEN, FALMOUTH, CORNWALL.
Telephone: (0326) 312915

CRAFTWOODS
Good stocks of many hardwoods, — Bubinga, Lime, Ebony, Maple, Rosewood, Wenge, Padauk, Oaks, Sycamore, Kingwood, Tulipwood, Lignum Vitae, Pau Brauna, Yew. Available in boards, slabs, squares and veneers.
Visit our sawmill and inspect and select from stock or send SAE for stock list to

CRAFTWOODS
Midslade Sawmills, Forest Road, Hartwell, Northants.
Tel: Northampton 862133

See us at the Woodworker Show
Stand 94.

VENEERS, inlay bandings, stringing and marquetry panels. Large selection.
Mail order and callers welcome. S.A.E. for list.
R. AARONSON (VENEERS) LTD
45 Redchurch St., London E2.
Tel: 01-739 3107

LIMEHOUSE TIMBER SALES
TEAK MAHOGANY IROKO OAK
ETC ETC JOINERY SOFTWOODS

"TIMBERAMA" customer self-selection area with a wide variety of species and dimensions

MON-FRI: 9am-5pm
SAT: 9am-3pm
INTERESTING TIMBERS BOUGHT
AND SOLD

a division of:
DAVEY AND COMPANY
5 GRENADE STREET
LONDON E14 8HL   01-987 1837

Hexhamshire Hardwoods

SEASONED ENGLISH HARDWOODS FOR THE CRAFTSMAN IN NORTH EAST ENGLAND & SCOTLAND

HARDWOODS FOR TURNING & CARVING

Telephone Slaley (043473) 585
any time

R&S WOODCRAFTS
A service for the small user. First quality kiln dried hardwoods. American and Japanese Oak, Mahogany, Ash, Maple, Teak, Beech etc. *S.A.E. List,* 77 Lime Tree Avenue, Tile Hill, Coventry CV4 9EZ or telephone (0203) 461491 evenings and weekends only.

CUT AND PLANED AS REQUIRED, WE SUPPLY
HARDWOODS
UTILE, MAHOGANY, IROKO, JAPANESE/ AMERICAN OAK. Also SOFTWOOD BOARD MATERIALS—MELAMINE CHIPBOARD—BLOCKBOARD
● **CUT TO SIZE IF REQUIRED.** *TRADE AND D.I.Y—NO JOB TOO SMALL*

PEARSON *TIMBER AND SERVICES LTD.*
38 RIVER ROAD, BARKING. Tel: 01-594 3074

ANY WOOD, ANY SIZE, ANY TIME
Cut, machined and turned to your cutting lists. For further information on range of service available telephone

Rustington (09064) 70374
C. J. DART Cabinet Makers, 6 Sea Lane, Rustington, West Sussex.

Rustic Woodslices
For House Signs, Wall Plaques, etc., seasoned hardwoods. Sawn obliquely with Bark on, up to 30" long **£2.00 each or three for £5.00. Post Free.**
A. CRACKNELL
2 ORFORD ROAD, BROMESWELL, WOODBRIDGE, SUFFOLK.

Nobex 303

The Nobex 303 mitre saw, tested by Chris Dunn

My quest for the perfect mitre joint has led me a dance over the years. I have tried many methods, from cutting freehand to a variety of gadgets and devices which have all made me unkept promises. So I cannot say the Nobex 303 mitre jig appeared to me on first sight as anything more than just one more gadget. However, now that I have worked with the Nobex 303 I can report that it has brought me nearer to the perfect mitre than any tool so far.

The 303 is labelled by Nobex as the 'baby brother' of their 202 mitre jig, which I have not personally tried but which was well reviewed by Bob Grant in last November's *Woodworker*.

The 303, as you will see from the picture, is a solidly constructed device, employing a right-angled table, a Sandvik tenon saw set in precisely engineered metal guides, which in turn are mounted on spindles that allow the sawblade to rock, rather than work in a fixed plane. This structure is mounted on a swivel that will go through 90 degrees. At various points there are notches into which the swivel automatically locks to provide right-angle and 45 degree cuts, as well as appropriate angles for octagon, hexagon and pentagon. A bonus is that the jig can be set up to any other angle you might need by aligning it against a protractor and locking the saw line in position by the use of a brake lever.

As it happened I needed to cut a large number of 45 degree angles for edging beads and trims to complete a sink unit and work surface. The prospect of doing the job by my previous methods had struck such gloom that these finishing jobs had been 'left until later', but with the Nobex ready for duty there was no longer any excuse for procrastination. And what joy! I sailed

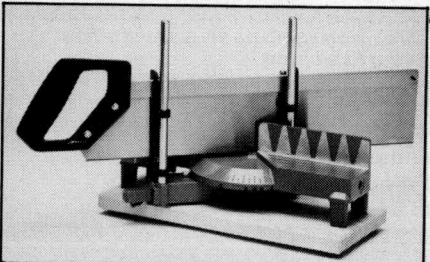

through the mitring work with unaccustomed pleasure.

The jig made quick, easy and accurate work of the beading, but where it really came into its own was in dealing with a 2¾in edging strip which had to make 45 degree joins. The 303 is the only jig I have used which offers such a depth of cut to make this sort of work possible. In fact it will cope with a maximum 3in depth, and I understand the 202 will go further still.

My experiments with polygons all pulled up tight under a webbing cramp, though the hexagon and pentagon were a bit touch-and-go due to unfortunate inaccuracies in the casting of the jig. In two of the angle settings the cog which engages to hold the sawcut in line was very sloppy in the notch, allowing an error of a couple of degrees, whereas the other seven settings were held perfectly rigid on course. This sudden lapse in production standards was disappointing in a tool that is otherwise extremely accurate. I hope the fault applies only to the particular one that I tested.

The Nobex 303 is making its official British debut at this year's Woodworker Show, and since you may well be reading this in time to take up my recommendation, I suggest you take a look at it on the Monninger stand at the show. If you are a fellow traveller in the quest for the perfect mitre, I think you will really enjoy the Nobex 303. I did.

● **The Nobex 303 costs £44.50 (inc VAT), and a length stop, offered as an optional extra, costs £6.20 (inc VAT).**

Woodplan

Woodplan wood finishing system by International Paints of Southampton. A workshop evaluation by Bob Grant

This new and total package comprises a timber preservative, woodstains, varnishes and the necessary thinners. It is claimed that the products are suitable for both interior and exterior use. They may be used separately or in a sequence that forms a complete wood finishing programme.

All of these substances are toxic and flammable and the usual precautions apply. The fumes from the varnishes are pungent and I found it helpful to have the workshop door open when using them, in volume application a respirator would be necessary.

The timber preservative contains biocides that are incorporated to give protection against dry and wet rot, woodworm and fungal attack. Application is by brush and two coats are recommended for maximum protection. A 24-hour drying period is needed before proceeding with any other finishing process.

The woodstains comprise pine, teak, light-, mid- and dark-oak effects plus a somewhat alarming green. The dark oak appeared rather severe but the colours are concentrated and may be thined out with white spirit. No woodfiller is included in the plan, possibly because these stains are thixotropic and are capable of laying an even coat on both close and open grained woods without patchiness or sinking. Application is simplicity itself, by brush or pad. I found that a pad made of cotton wool and

lint-free rag suited me best and I rejoiced in being able to apply a stain relieved from the tyranny of keeping a wet edge going. However, the penetration of the stains is not very deep and sanding with 400-grit silicon paper soon revealed bare patches. To be fair, very little of the grain is raised because of the jelly-like nature of the product. A second coat intensified the effect whilst maintaining the same hue.

As with all finishing techniques and processes, the basis of success is the thorough preparation of the bare surface and I took particular care with my various sample pieces to ensure that they were flat, smooth and dust free before experimenting with the varnishes. The satin and gloss varnishes may be used straight from the tin although on new work it is advisable to apply a first thinned coat using 10 per cent white spirit before working up to a full three-coat finish. The surfaces are touch dry within a couple of hours but rubbing down with 400-grit papers and re-coating needs a space of at least 16 hours. The varnishes were sufficiently viscous to flow out nicely under the brush which was cleaned out afterwards in white spirit. I was more than pleased with the quality of the finished results; the satin finish to my mind being preferable to the high gloss, both had flowed out evenly and needed no rubbing or burnishing.

The clear diamond varnish is a two-part polyurethane mixture which produces a tough mirror-like finish. Again, on new work a thinned coat is necessary before further full-strength coats are applied. The base and curing agents are mixed by volume and once brought together have a pot-life of about two hours. The finished result is an extremely clear and deep high gloss, akin to what I would call a 'piano finish'.

During a comparatively short test period it has obviously been impossible to gauge the long term effectiveness of the Woodplan range. Samples of the stains and finishes were left, like the Spartan children, to fend for themselves on my workshop roof. Over a number of weeks the samples were exposed to the vagaries of our English climate, including several thunder and hailstorms. I noticed no appreciable leaching of colours or deterioration of surface finish. However, time will tell. I shall leave them up there and see what happens.

The staining of wood seems to be enjoying something of a vogue at the moment and although the purist may harbour objections to such artificiality, including impermeable finishes, anybody who wants to indulge could do no better than use the Woodplan system. ■

Guidelines

Gerald Dunn takes a working look at a new gauged marking device, to be marketed by Pac Ltd of Hyde in Cheshire

Pac Ltd are introducing a simple marking gauge named Guidelines, embodied in a small sheet of stainless steel plate, bent at right angles along its centre line like a piece of angle iron, nicely engraved with both metric and imperial scales, and punched on both dihedrals with diagonal lines of small holes.

The idea is that a pencil point is to be inserted into an appropriate hole whilst the tool is run along the edge of the timber, thus scribing out the limit lines for, let's say, a mortice at any chosen distance off from the datum face. It may also be used indirectly as a mitre gauge but this requires two separate manipulations. A further possible application which the makers do not seem to have spotted is for pricking down the co-ordinates of compound geometric curves.

The trouble is that the holes are too small to admit any ordinary kind of pencil point. It might improve matters if the holes were countersunk but this would add appreciably to the cost. Alternatively you could forfeit the close spacing and settle for larger holes further apart. The difficulty of getting the pencil far enough through the holes to mark the wood underneath is aggravated by the small bending radius along the ariss. The diagram shows that unless the work piece itself is radiused either there is a gap between gauge and wood, or the distance off from the datum surface is incorrect (by an amount equal to the radius of the bend). Perhaps the inside corner could be relieved as indicated, disregarding of course the additional manufacturing cost. You could no doubt substitute a sharp metal scriber for the pencil but, as Bob Grant pointed out in the *Woodworker* August (p539) the grain of the wood does tend to take charge of the point and tram-line it off its proper course.

I suppose the most novel feature of the Guidelines is that you get several tools in one – a marking gauge, mitre gauge, curve plotter, set square, a compact measuring scale (who needs a stick of 12 inches to mark off ¾in on a 1½in surface?) and an accurate

straight edge of stainless steel, each one of which might cost you as much or more if you were setting up shop for the first time. For this reason I should think it would appeal to schools, to complete beginners, or to the domestic jobbing householder assembling a basic tool kit. I rather doubt if it would do much for the established workshop. It could at a pinch and for small scale work be used as a height gauge on a surface plate in the school metal shop.

It is quite an attractive looking little geometric gadget which feels nice in the hand and seems to possess that quality of impudent simplicity which is often the hall-mark of inspired design thinking. It is my guess that it was designed around one of those very thin clutch pencils which draughtsmen use, with half-millimetre leads. Or such was the only pencil in my possession which would fit through the holes. A very hard grade of lead (I used 6H) is necessary, otherwise the point snaps off too easily, and these very hard leads do not make a very visible line on wood (or on paper for that matter, because they are intended only for feint-line drawing). You still have to watch the grain snatch which, since it imposes a sideways force on the point, shears it off. Another handicap is that because the plate is opaque you cannot see your line until after it has been completed and the tool has been removed from the wood. Only then do you see that the lead broke off at the start of the line and you have literally 'drawn a blank'. The principle on which this tool works is often used in acrylic drawing-board aids through which you can see your line as it is drawn, as well as any other limit lines already on the drawing.

Experience would have to decide if it is

best to cause the tool to drag the penc along with it, or to use the pencil to prope the tool along the wood. I found both rathe difficult, but this could have been becaus of the pronounced burr left on the inne (sliding) surfaces by the press tool whic originally cut the steel. Naturally enoug this tried to grab the wood and rock the too along the edge in a series of jumps – penc point broke off every time. Of course th burr could be honed smooth – but think o the cost.

The prototype which I examined gave feeling that it had been made with a mor than ordinary quantum of love. For instanc it is engraved by hand operated pantograp and has several idiosyncratic errors an omissions – figures or letters just not quit completed. I expect in a full production ru this would be replaced by photo-etch calib rations, or stamping or moulding or some thing else which can be performed by numerically controlled machine withou any human help. Candidly, for my taste, it these little hidden indications of fallibilit which give hand made things that specia poignancy which is so much lacking i manufactured article nowadays.

But since Pac Ltd are not doing limite editions of works of fine art, the Guideline tool has to be evaluated on its performanc I cannot pretend it worked awfully well fo me but it is perfectly possible that man more bonus points would emerge fro longer acquaintance which were not caugh in the crude filter of a brief test. The mos unlikely tools often become a tradesman' favourite. I have a garden hoe, completel worn out, but for reasons I cannot explai my hand always selects it for every tillag operation. ■

Events

Woodworker Show

Woodworker Show at the Royal Horticultural Society Halls, London, 19-24 October, details from Model and Allied Publications Ltd, PO Box 35, Bridge Street, Hemel Hempstead, Herts HP1 1EE.

Winter Courses

Ten day residential courses in early keyboard instrument making are run at various times in Chichester by John Storrs. The next one will be from 28 December to 6 January. The course is limited to 10 participants who will stay in the Chichester Theological College in single study bedrooms. Cost of course is £200 which includes full board and tuition but not the cost of a kit. You can build a clavichord, spinet or harpsichord and there will be opportunities for music making, discussions and evening outings.

Craft market

Friday November 12 is the opening date for the eleventh Eastern Counties Craft Market, held at the Rhodes Centre, Bishop's Stortford. Open at 10am-6pm on the Friday and Saturday, 10am-5pm on the Sunday, admission 50p (under 14 – 20p), licensed bar and refreshments. The craft market provides a shop window for craftsmen who this year include woodcarver Martin Hazelwood; kitchen furniture designs from Wellingtonia Designs; coffee tables and mirrors from Redman and many others. Further details from Patricia Beswick, Thele, Great Amwell, Ware, Herts SG12 9RT.

Courses at West Dean

Some of the courses offered this winter at West Dean College are of interest to *Woodworker* readers. They include 22-24 October, Introduction to harpsichord making; 29-31 October, Upholstery for beginners; 7-12 November, Woodcarving; 28 November to 3 December, Rush and Willow basketry, cane or rush seating; 17-19 December, Woodcarving. Course fees booking form and full details from the college.

Hout '82

The 11th international trade fair for wood and woodworking machinery Hout '82 will be held in the Ahoy exhibition centre, Rotterdam, from 2-6 November. Products from more than 20 different countries will be represented and stands will feature wood products, wood finishing and accessories for the furniture industry as well as tools and machinery. There will be a large exhibit of tropical wood and semi-manufactured articles from various developing countries. Opening hours 10-5 daily plus 7-10pm on Thursday and Friday. Tickets and further information from: Interdex B.V., International Trade Exhibitions, Walenburgerweg 59 3039 AD Rotterdam, The Netherlands.

Ligna '83

The international trade fair for machinery and equipment for the wood industries will be held from 11-17 May 1983.

Karwei '83

The sixteenth annual exhibition for the diy trade will be staged in the Irene, Bernhard and Marijke halls on the Royal Netherlands Industries Fair site in Utrecht from 17-23 January 1983.

The Irene hall will be of interest to woodworkers since it will contain wood, kitchens, self assembly furniture. The Bernhard hall is the venue for locks and hinges, hand tools and workbenches.

The first four days of the exhibition are trade only, the final three are open to the general public.

One day seminar at Parnham

Timber as a structural medium is the subject of a one day seminar to be held at Parnham House on Saturday 16 October. The seminar will explore the properties of timber in structural use, the methods employed in the construction of aircraft, furniture, ships and buildings and the means of testing structural strength and design. The seminar starts at 10am with a series of speakers, after lunch there will be a general forum on structural problems. Delegates to the seminar are invited to submit in advance a brief written outline of a specific problem. Six or eight of these will be selected for discussion. Tickets for the day (inc. meals) £17.50 available from Brian James, Parnham House, Beaminster, Dorset DT3 3NA.

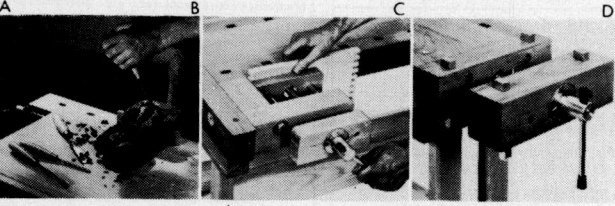

Classified Advertisements

Telephone Valerie Tester
(0442) 41221 Ex. 262

All classified Advertisements must be pre-paid.
Private and trade rate 20p per word (minimum £3.00). Box Numbers £1.25 extra. Display box rates s.c.c. £4.00 (min £10.00). All advertisements are inserted in the first available issue.
Box replies to be sent care of Advertisement Department, PO Box 35, Bridge Street, Hemel Hempstead, Herts, England HP1 1EE. There are no reimbursements for cancellations.

ADVERTISERS please note
FINAL COPY DATE for
JANUARY ISSUE
(Published 17th December)
is **4th November**
FEBRUARY ISSUE
(Published 21st January)
is **7th December**

CONVERTERS single to three phase to 10 h.p. bandsaws. 1 h.p. motors. H.A.B. Engineering, Fardons Industrial Estate, Glover Street, Bordesley, Birmingham 9. 021-772 2699. Q-T

MAKE A WOODTURNING LATHE easily, construction details and parts list, send SAE to: ORTAN LATHES, PO Box 46, Norwich NR7 8PB. S-X

MACHINERY. A comprehensive range of new/used machinery. Check our prices, e.g. HMO 10"×5½" planer/thicknesser £434. HF30; spindle moulder £365. 12" tilt arbour sawbench 2hp motor £140. Morso mitring machine £459, (including V.A.T.). Kity K-5. See these machines and Ryobi industrial small tools demonstrated at Woodman Woodworking Machinery Co. (Sign of the Axe), Little Malgraves Hall, Lower Dunton Road, Bulphan, Nr. Upminster, Essex. Tel: (0268) 415511 or (0702) 331729. I-U

PLANERS 6" × 9", planers/thicknessers, 12" × 7", 9" × 6", 12" × 7", sawbenches, 10" × 2" combination woodworkers. British made. Particulars, send stamp. Dodd Machine Tools Ltd., South Woodham, Chelmsford. Telephone: (0245) 320 691 O-Z

LUREM 260N Combination including accessories. 2 × 2 h.p. motors, single phase supply. BLC Lathe including accessories, tools and bench. 38" centres. 20" swing. ¾ h.p. single phase motor. Startrite 352 band saw, floor mounted with h.p. single phase motor. Telephone Aston Abbotts (0296 76) 471. Evenings. T.

EBAC TIMBER SEASONERS, Protimeter moisture meters, always good prices and advice from the man who pioneered small scale seasoning. John Arrowsmith, 74ª, Wilson Street, Darlington, Co. Durham BL3 6QZ. Tel: 0325 481970. T/C

SAW BLADES; Fretsaw, Marquetry, Coping. Send stamp for price list: Lea Blades, 16 Barclay, Hertford Heath, Hertford, Hert. T-U

DEWALT POWERSHOP 125 as new, complete with dado, head and T.C.T. blade. Offers around £300 01-863 9846. Also large pre-fab workshop for sale. T

CIRCULAR AND BAND SAW BLADES for all applications from: A.A. SMITH of Lancing Ltd., 63 Brighton Road, Shoreham, Sussex. Tel: 07917 61707 (24 hrs). P-Z

WASHITA & ARKANSAS whetstones now readily available from importer. Large selection, SAE for list. C. Rufino, Manor House, South Clifton, Newark, Notts. T/C

WANTED PLANER THICKNESSER 10" × 6". Approximately such as Kity 7136 or Electra 260K. Telephone Basingstoke 22068. T

WORKSHOP EQUIPMENT

B/DECKER, SKIL, BOSCH, MAKITA TOOLS ALL IN STOCK
NEW LUTZ SAWBENCH NOW IN STOCK ONLY £165.00
BEST QUALITY TCT SAWS, 5" DIAMETER UP TO 36"
GUARANTEED PERFORMANCE
24 HOUR RETURN POST SHARPENING SERVICE.
PHONE OR WRITE TO MAYS HIGH SPEED SAWS LTD. NEW ROAD (Nr. CHANDLER CORNER), RAINHAM, ESSEX. TEL. (04027) 55371/21331 (7 DAYS A WEEK)

TCT   ALLOY

WOOD TURNING LATHES
550mm between centres. 65mm centre height. Lever action tailstock. No.2 Morse tapers. Rear turning attachment takes 220mm dia. Various bed lengths available.
Prices from £80 + VAT
Send SAE for details

GREENFIELDS ENGINEERING
Building 3A, Site 1, Newport Road, High Ercall, Telford, TF6 6JA. Telephone High Ercall (0952) 770672

WOODTURNERS SUPPLIES
Woodturning tools, Peppermills, Salt mills, Barometers, Thermometers, Lighters, Hourglasses, Eggtimers, Ceramic tiles and clock faces, Clock movements, Spinning wheel plans, Sealers & Polishes, etc. Fast and efficient mail order service + competitive prices. S.A.E. for lists.

ERIC TOMKINSON
86 Stockport Road, Cheadle, Cheshire, SK8 2AJ. Tel. 061-491 1726
Shop open Mon-Fri from 9am to 4pm, Sat 9am to 1pm.

Braywood Estates
Comprehensive range of **DeWALT** Accessories plus a super service for spare parts & on site servicing.
BRAYWOOD ESTATES LTD. FREEPOST, SLOUGH SL2 4BL
TELEPHONE : SLOUGH 0753 22567/70792

20% DISCOUNT
on top quality hand tools. Record, Marples, Stanley etc. Send S.A.E. to:
RIVERSIDE CRAFT CENTRE
20 Beacon Buildings,
New Road,
Kendal, Cumbria

BURGESS BANDSAWS

IDEAL XMAS PRESENT

TWO SPEED MODEL BK2
3" CUTTING DEPTH
12" THROAT
FULLY GUARANTEED NEW MACHINES with full after sales service from our own workshop.
Price still held at
(LIST PRICE £133.92) **ONLY £84.95**
SPARE BLADES — **£2.58**; ADJUSTABLE FENCE — **£3.62**
when ordered with machine
Prices include V.A.T. Carriage and Insurance. Send cheque or P.O. to:

PEN TOOLS
EDGAR STREET HEREFORD 273018

20% OFF ROUTER CUTTERS ALL LEADING BRANDS
SAME DAY DESPATCH, POST FREE
FREE Cutter chart & price list on request.
P/O. Cheque, VISA or ACCESS card No. to:-
AXMINSTER POWER TOOL CENTRE
CHARD ST., AXMINSTER, DEVON
TEL (0297) 33656 (after 6pm 33535)

PETER GEE PRODUCTS FRETWORK MANUFACTURERS
Bench and Treadle machines and all Fretwork Tools and Blades etc available Ex Stock. Send S.A.E. for Illustrated Leaflet to: **Station Yard, Dereham, Norfolk. NR20 3AF. Tel. (0362) 5622.**

PETER CRISP OF RUSHDEN
THE CARPENTER'S SHOP
Hand Tools by leading makers. Stockists of:
- **Craftsmen, Coronet, Elu, Kity Woodworking Machinery**
- **Sorby Turning Chisels**
- **Taylor Carving Chisels**
- **Gomex T/Carbide Circular Saws**

High Street, Rushden, Northants. Telephone: 093 34 56424-7

AUSTINS OF WREXHAM LIMITED
POWER TOOLS
AND
MACHINERY CENTRE
Plas Acton, Wrexham, North Wales
Tel: 261095 and 262316. Evenings: 51186
Showroom or site demonstration of Sheppach, DeWalt, Elu Woodworking Machinery. Agents for Trend Router Cutters, Discs, drills, abrasives, hand tools at trade discounts. Repair workshop for all makes of power tools.

Braywood Estates

ONLY **£285** inc VAT & del.
DeWALT POWERSHOP

PLUS A FREE SET OF LEGS OR A T.C.T. BLADE

A superb woodworking machine.
With the DW125 Powershop you can make almost anything from a plain stool to a beautiful Welsh Dresser. Our offer does not end at the point of sale! We support you with an efficient After Sales Service.
Previous Rec. Retail Price inc. VAT and Delivery £547
Our price inc.VAT & Delivery £285
(UK Mainland)
Full range of DeWalt woodworking machines and accessories in stock all at discount prices.
All machines are new & current models with a 12 months guarantee

For further details contact
Braywood Estates Ltd. (Dept. WW), Stoke Green House, Stoke Poges, Slough SL2 4HN. Tel: Slough 0753 22567/70792

JOHN HALL
woodworking centre

DeWalt Radial Arm Saws

Cross cuts at any angle. It bevels, mitres and rips, and there is a whole range of accessories that turn it virtually into a complete workshop. It will cut grooves, housings, rebates and mouldings. It will grind, bore and jigsaw, and its accuracy is consistent. DW125 Radial Arm Saw.

£265.00 inc. VAT

Elektra

Elektra TF100 Spindle Moulder with 6 FREE Cutters and block	**£349.95**
Elektra HC260K Planer/Thicknesser with stand	**£449.95**
Elektra Combi 2200 Sawbench 2.9 h.p.	**£139.50**
Elektra SPA 1000 Dust Extractor	**£155.00**
Elektra 200/10/40W Compressor	**£285.00**

DeWalt

DeWalt 1370 Radial Saw with stand	**£465.00**
DeWalt BS1 310 Bandsaw	**£237.50**
DeWalt DW50 Planer/Thicknesser	**£430.00**
DeWalt DW100 Mini Bandsaw	**£115.00**

Kity

Kity K5 Combination machine	**£660.00**

Prices inc. VAT Carriage £9.50 UK mainland only

Tools of the Trade

Bristol Clifton Down Shopping Centre, Whiteladies Road, (0272) 741510

Bath 2, Railway Street. (0225) 64513

Cardiff Central Square. (0222) 396039

JOHN HALL woodworking centre

BARCLAYCARD
VISA

Buying and selling in the classified columns of WOODWORKER brings quick results. This space could have been yours for as little as £24.00. For further details ring Valeries Tester on (0442) 41221, Ext 266.

SHERWOOD WOOD TURNING LATHES

All cast iron constructed. 3¾" CH 24" or 36" B.C. 3 or 4 speed, bowl turning up to 14" dia. ball-bearing spindle c/w face plate, centres etc. Prices from **£75.29** inc. VAT.

Send stamp for leaflets and details of above and other low-priced machines and motors.

JAMES INNS (Engs),
Main St., Bulwell, Nottingham

5000
ELECTRIC MOTORS, FANS & BLOWERS

New & Used. Single & 3 Phase

ALWAYS IN STOCK

RING

(0742) 78088

FOR FREE STOCKLIST

Beatson & Co (Elec.) Ltd,
17-21 Mowbray St.,
Sheffield S3 8EN

WOODWORKING MACHINE

"In Store" Demonstration
Friday and Saturday 12th & 13th November 9am - 7pm
Sunday 14th November 9am - 1pm
On demonstration will be Multico, Wadkin Tradesmen, Coronet, DeWalt, Shopsmith, Sheppach, Elu and Bosch

MATTHEWS

Kettlebrook Road, Kettlebrook, Tamworth, Staffs.
Telephone: Tamworth (0827) 56188

---

emcostar
FOX WOODWORKING

Universal Woodworking Machine

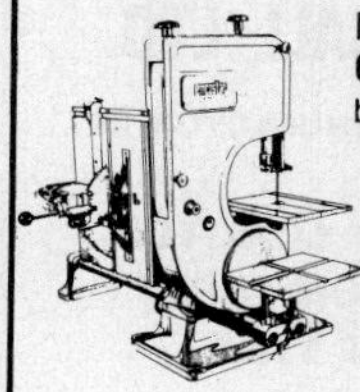

List price £557.75
Our price £460.00
both prices include VAT

Full range of light machines and accessories stocked: colour brochures available. Send 30p stamps for further information.

Emco & Startrite In Store Demonstrations 5th & 6th November

Fox Woodworking, Stebbings, Back Lane, Washbrook, Ipswich, Suffolk IP8 3JA
Telephone: 0473 86216

TOP QUALITY SHEFFIELD WOODTURNING TOOLS

A complete range of top quality Chisels and Gouges. Full size and long and strong.
EXAMPLES: FULL SIZE

1" gouge £4.25	½" skew £3.25
½" gouge £3.95	½" diamond £3.25
1" skew £3.95	½" round £3.25

S.A.E. for full price list
TOOLSHOP, 29 Walcot Street, Bath. Avon. Tel. Bath (0225) 61838

A·Pollard+Son LTD.

Come and browse through our huge stocks of machinery and tools.
● Ask for details of our prompt and low cost Mini Clipper delivery service

KITY UNITED KINGDOM K5 International Woodworker with Sawbench, Spindle Moulder, Planer/Thicknesser & Slot Mortiser. Full range in stock.

scheppach HMO▶ 2HP 10" × 6" Planer/Thicknesser. HM2 Planer/Thicknesser also in stock.

Elu MOF 96 The professional Plunging Router 600 Watt Motor takes ¼" shanked bits.

DeWALT DW125 Powershop, for Sawing, Grooving Sanding, Moulding etc. Dust Extractors, Planer/Thicknessers & Industrial R.A.S. also in stock.

◀ H.F.30 Spindle Moulder 2HP Motor. Shown with Overhead Roller, Guard & Sliding Carriage. (Optional Extras)

mafell BIBEREX 12". 2.3HP Sawbench with Rise & Fall, Mitre Guide, Fence and Tilting Arbor. Other Sawbenches in stock.

WABECO 1885 GERMANY

EXHIBITION & DEMONSTRATION
ELU · INCA · SHOPSMITH SCHEPPACH · KITY
WOODWORKING MACHINERY
Nov. 25, 26 & 27th

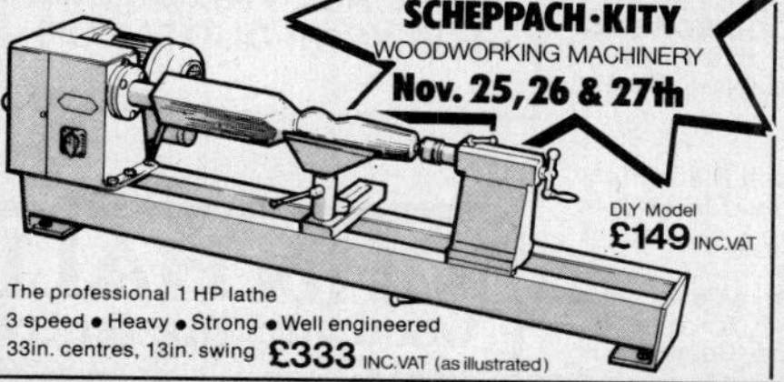

DIY Model **£149** INC.VAT

The professional 1 HP lathe 3 speed ● Heavy ● Strong ● Well engineered 33in. centres, 13in. swing **£333** INC.VAT (as illustrated)

INCA 10½in. throat Bandsaw For Fretwork and Bandsanding 6in. depth of cut. 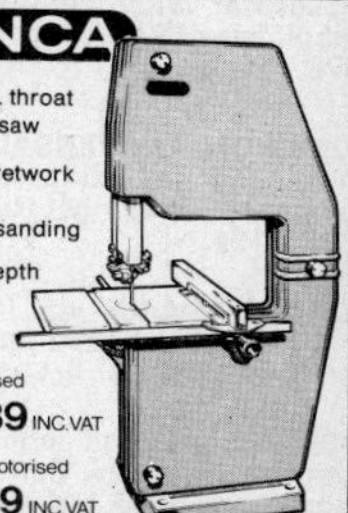
Motorised **£289** INC.VAT
Non-motorised **£189** INC.VAT

Dust Extractors, Lathes, Industrial R/A. Saws. Large stocks of Ironmongery & Handtools — Most accessories stocked.
Open 6 days a week 8.30-5.30 Barclaycard, Access Business Established over 50 years.

A. POLLARD & SON LTD. 51 Queensway, Bletchley, Milton Keynes ☎ (0908) 75221

FRETSAW KITS
NEW OFFER

Comprehensive kit contains:
Precision engineered spindles, bearings, clamps, pulleys, fastenings and tensioning assemblies, ready for home construction with full instructions. Mount, finish and motorise to your own standards.
Kit price **£24.85 + £1.50** p&p less baseboard and motor
Utilise your own motor Or suitable ex Equit Motors £9.00 + £1 p&p
For modelling or engineering in wood, plastic, laminates, metals and card
KIT PROJECTS, DEPT W, THE WORKSHOP, GT WASHBOURNE, GLOUCESTERSHIRE

BANDSAW BLADES

Industrial quality long life blades for De Walt BS1310 & DW100. Kity. Burgess. B&D. Startrite 352. All widths & skips. Immediate despatch. Post paid. Write or phone for list.
AXMINSTER POWER TOOL CENTRE
Chard St., Axminster, Devon. Tel: Axminster (0297) 33656. (after 6pm 33535)

CLASSIFIED

Telephone Valerie Tester
(0442) 41221 Ext. 262

POWER TOOL BARGAINS

New and ex-demonstration "SHOPMATE" power tools, some slightly marked but all in as new condition and guaranteed. All spares in stock with full after sales service and money back guarantee.

ORBITAL SANDER (very good tool)	£17.50
4" BELT SANDER (1.3HP Std belts)	£39.50
7¼" CIRCULAR SAW (1HP with blade and guide)	£27.95
7¼" CIRCULAR SAW (1.6HP powerful)	£37.95
⅜" BENCH PILLAR DRILL (variable speed)	£37.95
5" DOUBLE HEAD BENCH GRINDER	£25.00
6" DH BENCH GRINDER (1HP heavy duty)	£55.00
6" DISC SANDER/POLISHER (2 speed)	£25.00
2⅛" POWER PLANE (with guide nice tool)	£35.00
1HP ROUTER (by STANLEY std ¼" bits)	£30.00
ROUTER GUIDE (with vernier adjustment)	£7.50

All prices include VAT plus £2.50 p/p per tool. Illustrated cat 50p, refunded with order.
J D WOODWARD (power tool specialist) 6 Tilton Rd, Hinckley, Leics. Tel: 0455-613432.

SCRU-DRILL

COMPLETE SET OF FOUR **£13.45** + 35p P&P

Top quality wood screw pilot drill and countersink adjusts to screw specification for fast accurate pilot holes in hard or soft wood for that professional finish.

Complete set will accommodate Nos 5 to 14 gauge screws in all popular lengths.

Adjustable stop collar for counterbore depth or countersink

Adjustable sleeve for screw body

Adjustable pilot drill for screw thread

KELTEK PRODUCTS
St. Giles Mews, P.O. Box 5, Wadebridge, Cornwall PL27 7YZ. (S.A.E. Please for our complete range of exclusive products).

Phone Valerie Tester (0442) 41221 Ext. 262

RATES

20p per word, minimum £3.00. Box Nos £1.25 extra.
Semi-display s.c.c. £4.00 (min £10.00)

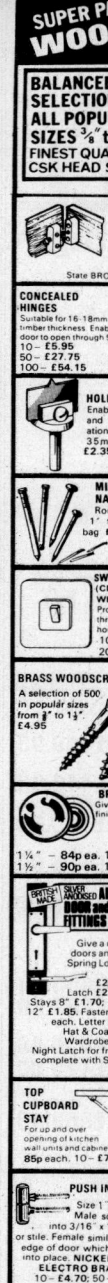

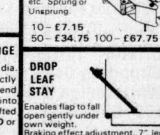

COURSES

COURSES IN WOOD MACHINING AND WOODTURNING. Bookable by the hour—the most convenient and flexible way! all for £6.00 an hour (inc. VAT), H.W.M., The Woodworkers, 303 Shirley Rd., Shirley, Southampton. Tel: (0703) 776222. T/C

WOODTURNING COURSES in the Derbyshire craft village of Brailsford. Reg Slack formerly of Coronet and "Learn-a-Craft" offers ½, 1, 1½, 2 day courses. For details write or 'phone Reg Slack, Saracens Head Coaching House Yard, Brailsford, Derbyshire. (033528) 829 Evenings: (0283) 701662. STU.

ONE DAY WOODTURNING COURSE: carefully designed, inexpensive. Trymwood, 2a Towns Park East, Westbury Park, Bristol. Telephone Bristol 629092. T/C

TWO-DAY Woodturning Course for beginners in mid-Norfolk village. Two students only. Accommodation available. SAE for details please. Doug Keeling, Church Lane, Feetley, Norfolk NR20 4AB. T/C

WOODTURNING day courses, or at £5.00 per hour, with Jack Durey. Enquire: Brenchley 465 (Kent). T/C

WOODTURNING COURSES in Scottish borders. Two day professional tuition. For details SAE to Monteviot Woodcraft. Tower Workshop, Harestanes Mill, Jedburgh, Roxburghshire TD8 6UF. Telephone: 0450-87446 (Evenings) S-V

WOOD MACHINING COURSE

A craftsman of forty years' experience offers a unique two-day course to learn the basics of machine woodworking including spindle moulding and routing in his fully equipped modern workshop. S.A.E. for details please to:
ROY SUTTON,
14 St. Georges Avenue,
Herne Bay, Kent CT6 8JU.
Tel: Herne Bay 3297 or
Whitstable 272136 (evenings)
Meet me on Stand 28 (Startrites) at:
WOODWORKER SHOW 1982
(19-24 October 1982)
Royal Horticultural New and Old
Halls, Westminster, London SW1

GORDON STOKES
Author of Modern Woodturning
Beginner's Guide to Woodturning, Woodturning for Pleasure, etc. etc
Will be pleased to send you full details of his intensive two day Woodturning and Woodcarving courses. Personal instruction based on thirty years experience. Don't struggle along the hard way. Foolscap S.A.E. to:
202 The Hollow, Bath, Avon BA2 1NG
Tel: Bath 22617

MAKE YOUR OWN CLAVICHORD full size plans and instruction manual. SAE for details to: Early Keyboard Instruments, Morley Farm, Brancepeth, Durham DH7 8DS. T/C

HARPS
I produce full size plans complete with instruction sheets for a wide range of harps as well as manufacturing all the hardware, strings etc needed for their construction. Additionally, complete kits including partly worked timber are available. For full illustrated details and price list please send large SAE (Overseas 3 irc's) to **Michael Saunders, Waterloo Cottages, Letton, Hereford, HR3 6DN. Tel: 05446 352**

HARP parts. Wrest pins, bridge pins, sharpening levers, all types of strings. Also Titebond glue and American Rock Maple timber.

KEMPSTER INSTRUMENTS
R.M.B. 799 Stirling
SOUTH AUSTRALIA 5153
Phone (08) 3882337

LEARN THE ART AND CRAFT OF RESTORING ANTIQUES AND DESIGNING AND MAKING YOUR OWN FURNITURE

Situated in a charming Norfolk village we offer professional tuition in courses of antique restoration, wood turning, machining, woodworking and finishing. Come to The Old Mill at Gayton for good food and comfortable accommodation in very pleasant surroundings.

WINDMILL ENTERPRISES
For full details send SAE to MR R Hirons, The Old Mill, Gayton, Norfolk. Tel: (055386) 613/717

FRENCH POLISHING COURSES

Enjoy an intensive four day traditional french polishing course in the informal atmosphere of our riverside home. We offer comfortable accommodation, good food, and professional tuition in this beautiful border countryside.
Now booking for 1983 spring and summer courses.
S.A.E. for details:

Colin Campbell

South Manse, New Castleton, Roxburghshire.
Telephone: Liddesdale (054 121) 206.

BIRD CARVING TUITION

Two or three day course by internationally known wood sculptor. Comfortable accommodation available, close to Solent Coast.
My students discover the excitement and delights of working with nature's most versatile material using man's simplest tool, the knife. Artistic and sensitive use is made of the grain patterns and natural colour of English woods, so that they harmonize symetrically with the finished sculpture.
SAE or phone for details
Derek George, West Lodge, 18 Elizabeth Rd., Stubbington, Fareham, Hants. PO14 2RF Tel: 03295 2458

MUSICAL INSTRUMENTS

Harpsichord, spinet, clavichord kits for home or educational projects. Traditional materials are used, and no special skills are needed for kit assembly. Visitors are welcome. Residential keyboard instrument making course from 28th December to 6th January.

John Storrs Maker of Early Keyboard Instruments
Hunston Chichester West Sussex PO20 6NR England

TONEWOOD CATALOGUE
If you make, repair or restore any stringed instrument you will find our new free catalogue invaluable. We hold large stocks of selected materials for:
VIOLIN, VIOLA, 'CELLO, BASS, LUTE, GUITAR, BAROQUE VIOLS, ETC.
Callers welcome or return of post mail order service available. Open 10am - 4pm Tues/Sat.
A. HIGHFIELD & CO, Rosewood House, Bridge Road, Downham Market, Norfolk PE38 0AE.
Tel: Downham Mkt. 2614.

BUILD YOUR OWN HARPSICHORD
from a kit by Frank Hubbard.
All materials provided including comprehensive instruction manual and full scale drawing. Choose from spinets, virginals, harpsichords and forte-pianos. Free colour catalogue and price list on request. **Donald Mackinnon and Mimi Waitzman,** 11 Sprowston Road, Forest Gate, London E7 9AD. Tel: 01-519 1170.

MUSICAL INSTRUMENT
Makers and Repairer's supplies
Largest selection of tonewoods, parts and tools in the country. Callers or mail order welcome. Also Ebony offcuts, assorted sizes.
TOUCHSTONE TONEWOODS LTD.,
27 Lesbourne Rd., Reigate, Surrey RH2 7JS

WOODTURNING COURSES
2 Day courses, mid-week or weekend. Expert personal tuition in modern well equipped workshop. Comfortable accommodation available in pleasant surroundings. SAE for details to Cliff Willetts, Gables, Frisby On The Wreake, Melton Mowbray, Leics.

Australian Readers WOODTURNING
40 Years of woodturning experience available to you in a 2 day course. Basic or advanced. Personal tuition to your needs in a fully equipped workshop. Write for details:
PHILIP ELFORD 407 Peel St. N., Ballarat, Vic. 3350.

Thos. Harrison & Sons (Est. 1830)

WOODTURNING COURSES
★ Four days professional instruction
★ Discussion groups
★ Informal atmosphere
★ Farmhouse food and accommodation
★ Prices from £120
★ Beginners/advanced
For further details write or phone:
Mike Law, The Longhouse, Maxworthy Cross, North Petherwin, Launceston, North Cornwall. (056685) 322.

COURSES IN BASIC ANTIQUE RESTORATION
Bookings available for the 16th & 17th October in our workshops on the basic skills of restoring furniture. Course includes laying and repairing veneers, staining distressing and french polishing.
For full details send 15½p stamp to EDWIN TURNER, Home Farm, Gislingham, Eye, Suffolk. Tel: Mellis 280

Rates
20p per word, minimum £3.00
Box nos. £1.25 extra.
Semi display s.c.c. £4.00
(min £10.00)

Materials for the Amateur and Professional VIOLIN & GUITAR MAKER
Send S.A.E. 16p plus 50p for either cat. 50p deductible from purchase £5.00 or over
SYDNEY EVANS LTD.
45 Regent Place,
Birmingham, B1 3BN
Tel: (021) 233-1741

HARPSICHORD KITS
Unique new basic kit enables you to build a good harpsichord first time at half the price of a full kit.
SAE for details: **D. H. Bolton, Harpsichord Maker, 17 The Crescent, Linthorpe, Middlesbrough, Cleveland TS5 6SG.**

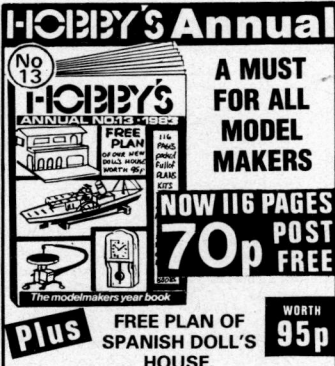

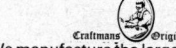

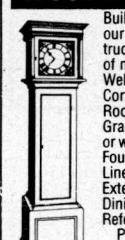

SHOP GUIDE SHOP GUIDE

The quickest and easiest method of reaching all Woodworkers is to advertise in SHOP GUIDE. Telephone **Valerie Tester (0442) 41221 Ext. 266. Rate: £8.00 per unit.** Minimum of 6 months.

Key: H — Hand tools, **P** — Power tools, **W** — Woodworking machinery up to £1000, **WM** — Woodworking machinery over £1000, **D** — Demonstration available on selected machines, **T** — Timber, **CS** — Cutting or sharpening services, **MF** — Material Finishes, **A** — Attachments, **BC** — Books/catalogues, * — Mail order.

AVON

BATH Tel. Bath 64513
JOHN HALL TOOLS *
RAILWAY STREET

Open: Monday-Saturday
9.00 a.m.-5.30 p.m.
H.P.W.WM.D.A.BC.

BRISTOL Tel. (0272) 311510
JOHN HALL TOOLS LIMITED *
CLIFTON DOWN SHOPPING
CENTRE, WHITELADIES ROAD
Open: Monday-Saturday
9.00 a.m.-5.30 p.m.
H.P.W.WM.D.A.BC.

BRISTOL Tel. 0272-633844
ROBBINS LIMITED *
THE WOODWORKER SHOP
MERRYWOOD MILLS, BEDMINSTER
Open: Mon-Fri 8.00 a.m.-5.00 p.m.
Saturday 8.30 a.m.-12.30 p.m.
H.P.T.CS.A.BC.

BRISTOL Tel. 0272-629092
TRYMWOOD SERVICES *
2a DOWNS PARK EAST, (off
North View) WESTBURY PARK
Open: 8.30 a.m.-5.30 p.m. Mon. to
Fri. Closed for lunch 1-2 p.m.
P.W.WM.D.T.A.BC.

BRISTOL Tel. 0272-667013
V. H. WILLIS & CO. LTD *
190-192 WEST STREET,
BEDMINSTER
Open: Mon-Fri 8.30 a.m.-5 p.m.
Saturday 9 a.m.-1 p.m.
H.P.W.WM.D.CS.A.BC.

BERKSHIRE

READING Tel. Littlewick Green
DAVID HUNT (TOOL 2743
MERCHANTS) LTD *
KNOWL HILL, NR. READING
Open: Monday-Saturday
9 a.m.-5.30 p.m.
H.P.W.D.A.BC.

READING Tel. (0734) 586522
SARJENT'S TOOL STORES *
LTD.
44-52 OXFORD ROAD
Open: 8.30 a.m.-5.30 p.m.
Monday-Saturday
H.P.W.WM.D.A.BC.

READING Tel. Reading 661511
WOKINGHAM TOOL CO. LTD
99 WOKINGHAM ROAD

Open: Mon-Sat 9am-5.30pm
Closed 1-2pm for lunch
H.P.W.WM.D.CS.A.BC.

BUCKINGHAMSHIRE

HIGH WYCOMBE (0494) 22221
ISAAC LORD LTD
185 DESBOROUGH ROAD

Open: Mon-Fri 8.00 a.m.-5.00 p.m.
Saturday 8.00 a.m.-12.00 noon
H.P.W.D.A.

MILTON KEYNES Tel. 0908
A. POLLARD & SON 75221
LTD.
51 QUEENSWAY, BLETCHLEY
Open: 8.30 a.m.-5.30 p.m.
Monday-Saturday
H.P.W.WM.D.A.BC.

CAMBRIDGESHIRE

CAMBRIDGE Tel. 0223-353091
H. B. WOODWORKING
69 LENSFIELD ROAD
Open: 8.30 a.m.-5.30 p.m.
Monday-Friday
8.30 a.m.-1.00 p.m. Sat
P.W.WM.D.CS.BC.

CHESHIRE

CHESTER Tel. 0244 42084
ROBERT KELLY'S *
19 NEWGATE ROW
GROSVENOR PRECINCT, CH1 1ER
Open: 9.00 a.m.-5.30 p.m.
Monday-Saturday
H.P.W.WM.D.CS.A.BC.

NANTWICH Tel. Crewe 67010
ALAN HOLTHAM *
THE OLD STORES TURNERY
WISTASON ROAD, WILLASTON
Open: Tues-Sat 9a.m.-5.30p.m.
Closed Monday
P.W.WM.D.T.C.CS.A.BC.

CLEVELAND

MIDDLESBROUGH Tel. 0642-
WINTZ 460035/813650
INDUSTRIAL SUPPLIES *
2 BESSEMER COURT
GRANGETOWN
Open: Mon-Fri 8.30 a.m.-5 p.m.
H.P.W.D.A.

CORNWALL

FALMOUTH Tel. 0326-312915
WOODSTOCK
(HARDWOODS) S.W.,
ASHFIELD, PONSHARDEN,
Open: Mon-Fri 8.30 a.m.-5.30 p.m.
Sat 9 a.m.-1.00 p.m.
T.

HELSTON Tel: Helston (03265) 4961
SOUTH WEST Truro (0872) 71671
POWER TOOLS Launceston
MONUMENT ROAD (0566) 3555

H.P.W.WM.D.CS.A.

CORNWALL

NEWQUAY Tel. 063 73 2516
CONWAY SUPPLIES *
(NEWQUAY)
70 FORE STREET
Open: Mon-Fri 9 a.m.-5.30 p.m.
Sat 9 a.m.-12.30 p.m.
H.P.W.WM.D.A.BC.

ST. AUSTELL Tel. (0726) 65922
TOOLSERV *
TRURO ROAD

Open: 8 a.m.-5.30 p.m.
6 days
H.P.W.WM.D.CS.A.BC.

DERBYSHIRE

BUXTON Tel. 0298-871636
CRAFT SUPPLIES *
THE MILL
MILLERSDALE
Open: Mon-Fri 9 a.m.-5 p.m.
Saturday 9 a.m.-1 p.m.
H.P.W.D.T.CS.A.BC.

DEVON

EXETER Tel. 0392 73936
WRIDES TOOL CENTRE
147 FORE STREET

Open: 9.00 a.m.-5.30 p.m.
Wednesday 9.00 a.m.-1.00 p.m.
H.P.W.WM.A.

PLYMOUTH Tel. 0752 330303
WESTWARD BUILDING SERVICES *
LTD., LISTER CLOSE, NEWNHAM
INDUSTRIAL ESTATE, PLYMPTON
Open: Mon-Fri 8 a.m.-5.30 p.m.
Sat 8.30 a.m.-12.30 p.m.
H.P.W.WM.D.A.BC.

PLYMOUTH Tel. 0752-266179
JOHN WRIDE & CO (PLYMOUTH) LTD
146 CORNWALL STREET
Open: Monday to Saturday
9.00a.m.-5.30p.m.
Wed 9.00a.m.-1.00p.m.
H.P.W.WM.A.

DORSET

BOURNEMOUTH Tel: 0202
MACHINE SALES & SERVICES 527780
(BOURNEMOUTH) LTD 527781
56 STROUDEN ROAD *

Open: Mon-Fri 8.15 a.m.-5 p.m.
H.P.W.WM.D.A.

WEYMOUTH Tel: (0305) 787396
WEYMOUTH TOOL CENTRE
30A ABBOTSBURY ROAD

Open: Monday to Saturday
8 a.m.-5.30 p.m.
H.P.W.WM.D.A.BC

CO. DURHAM

BARNARD CASTLE Tel: (0833)
WOODMEN 38442/31609
27 NEWGATE

Open Monday-Saturday
9 a.m.-5.30 p.m.
P.W.WM.D.A.BC.

ESSEX

LEIGH ON SEA Tel. (0702)
MARSHALL & 710404
PARSONS LTD
1111 LONDON ROAD
Open: 8.30 am-5.30 pm Mon-Fri.
9.00 am-5.00 om Sat.
H.P.W.WM.D.CS.A.

LEIGH ON SEA Tel. (0702)
WEBBERS TOOLS 76503
204 ELM ROAD

Open: 9 am-5.30 pm
Monday to Saturday
H.P.W.

GLOUCESTERSHIRE

TEWKESBURY Tel. 0684
TEWKESBURY SAW CO. 293092
LIMITED
TRADING ESTATE, NEWTOWN
Open: Mon-Fri 8.00 a.m.-5.00 p.m.
Saturday 9.30 a.m.-12.00 p.m.
P.W.WM.D.CS.

HAMPSHIRE

ALDERSHOT Tel. 0252 28088
BURCH & HILLS LTD
BLACKWATER WAY TRADING
ESTATE
Open: Mon-Fri 8.30 a.m.-5.30 p.m.
Saturday 8.30 a.m.-12.00 a.m.
H.P.W.WM.D.A.BC.

PORTSMOUTH Tel. 0705
EURO PRECISION TOOLS 667332
LTD *
259/263 London Road, North End
Open: Mon-Fri 9 a.m.- 5.30 p.m.
Sat 9.00 a.m.-1.00 p.m.
H.P.W.WM.D.A.BC.

SOUTHAMPTON Tel. 0703
H.W.M. 776222
THE WOODWORKERS *
303 SHIRLEY ROAD, SHIRLEY
Open: Tues-Fri 9.30 a.m.- 6 p.m.
Sat 9.30 a.m.-4.00 p.m.
H.P.W.WM.D.CS.A.BC.T.

HERTFORDSHIRE

WATFORD Tel. 0923 48434
HOME CARE CENTRE *
20 MARKET STREET
WATFORD, HERTS
Open 9.00 a.m.-5.30 p.m.
Mon.-Sat.
H.P.W.A.WM.BC.D.

Prices quoted are those prevailing at press date and are
subject to alteration due to economic conditions.

SHOP GUIDE SHOP GUIDE

HERTFORDSHIRE

WATFORD   Tel. 0923 26052
J. SIMBLE & SONS LTD
76 QUEENS ROAD

Open 8.30 a.m.-5.30 p.m.
Mon-Sat. Closed Wednesday
H.P.W.WM.D.A.BC.

WATFORD   Tel. (0923) 49911
TREND MACHINERY & CUTTING
TOOLS LTD
UNIT N, PENFOLD WORKS
IMPERIAL WAY
Open: Mon-Fri 9 a.m.-5 p.m.
P.W.WM.D.CS.BC.

KENT

LYDD   Tel. (0679) 20107
LIBERON WAXES LTD.,   ★
6 PARK STREET
Open: Mon-Fri
10 a.m.-1 p.m.   2 p.m.-5.30 p.m.
Saturday 10 a.m. - 1 p.m.
D. MF.

MATFIELD   Tel. Brenchley
LEISURECRAFT IN WOOD   (089272)
'ORMONDE', MAIDSTONE RD.   2465
TN12 7JG
Open: Mon-Sun
9 a.m.- 5.30 p.m.
W.WM.D.T.A.

LANCASHIRE

LANCASTER   Tel. 0524 2886
LILE TOOL SHOP
43/45 NORTH ROAD
Open: Monday to Saturday
9.00 a.m.-5.30 p.m.
Wed 9.00 a.m.-12.30 p.m.
H.P.W.D.A.

PRESTON   Tel. (0772) 52951
SPEEDWELL TOOL CO.,   ★
62-68 MEADOW STREET
Open: Mon-Fri 8.30 a.m.-5.30 p.m.
Sat 8.30 a.m.-12.30 p.m.
H.P.W.WM.D.CS.A.BC.

LEICESTERSHIRE

COALVILLE   Tel. (0533) 415556
POOLE WOOD   (06077) 5777
MACHINERY
SERVICES LIMITED,
30 VALENTINE ROAD
Open: Mon-Fri 9 a.m.-5 p.m.
P.W.WM.D.A.BC.

LEICESTER   Tel. 0455 43254
ROY STARTIN LTD
134 WOOD STREET
EARL SHILTON
Open: Mon-Fri 8 a.m.-5.30 p.m.
Saturday 8.00 a.m.-1.30 p.m.
H.P.W.WM.D.T.A.

LINCOLNSHIRE

LINCOLN   Tel. 0522 30199/
WOODWISE LIMITED   39871 or
121 HIGH STREET   0522 68428
& 06077 2421/5777/5288
(after hours)   ★
Open: Mon-Sat 9 a.m.-5.30 p.m.
P.W.WM.D.A.BC.

LONDON

ACTON   Tel. 01-992 4835
A MILLS (ACTON) LTD   ★
32/36 CHURCHFIELD ROAD
W3 6ED
Open: Mon-Fri 9.00 a.m.-5.00 p.m.
Closed Saturday
H.P.W.WM.

HANWELL   Tel. 01-567 2922
G. D. CLEGG & SONS
83 Uxbridge Road, W7 3ST
Open: Monday to Friday
9.00 a.m.-6.00 p.m.
Saturday 9.00 a.m.-5.30 p.m.
H.P.W.WM.D.

KILBURN   Tel. 01-624 5146
W. THATCHER & SON LTD   ★
POWER TOOL CENTRE
AT THE TECHNICAL LEISURE CENTRE
1 THE GRANGEWAY, N.W.6.
Open: Mon-Sat 9 a.m.-5.30 p.m.
P.H.W.D.CS.A.BC.

LONDON   Tel. 01-636 7475
BUCK & RYAN LIMITED
101 TOTTENHAM COURT ROAD
W1P 0DY
Open: Mon-Fri 8.30 a.m.-5.30 p.m.
Saturday 8.30 a.m.-1.00 p.m.
H.P.W.WM.D.A.

LONDON   Tel. 01-739 7126
CECIL W. TYZACK   ★
79-81 KINGSLAND ROAD
SHOREDITCH
Open: Mon-Fri 8.45 a.m.-5.15 p.m.
Saturday 9 a.m.-12 noon
H.P.W.WM.D.A.BC.

NORBURY   Tel: 01-679 6193
HERON TOOLS & HARDWARE LTD
437 STREATHAM HIGH ROAD
S.W.16
Open: Mon-Sat 8.30 a.m. - 6 p.m.
Wednesday 8.30 a.m. - 1 p.m.
H.P.W.A.

WOOLWICH   Tel. 01-854 7767/8
A.D. Skillman & Sons Ltd.,
108-109 Woolwich High St.,
SE18 6DW
Open: Mon-Sat 8.30 a.m.-5.30 p.m.

H.P.W.CS.A.

MERSEYSIDE

LIVERPOOL   Tel. 051-263 1359
TAYLOR BROS (LIVERPOOL) LTD
5/9 PRESCOTT STREET

Open: Monday to Friday
8.30 a.m.-5.30 p.m.
H.P.W.WM.D.A.BC.

MIDDLESEX

NORTH HARROW   Tel. 01-863 2492
WILLIAMS TECHNICAL SERVICES   ★
36 STATION ROAD
Open: Mon-Fri 8 a.m.-5.30 p.m.
Wed 8 a.m.-1 p.m.
Sat 9 a.m.-5.30 p.m.
H.P.W.WM.D.A.

MIDDLESEX

HOUNSLOW   Tel. 01-570 2103/5135
Q. R. TOOLS LTD
251-253 HANWORTH ROAD

Open: Mon-Fri 8.30 a.m.-5.30 p.m.
Sat 9 a.m.-1 p.m.
P.W.WM.D.CS.A.

NORFOLK

KINGS LYNN   Tel. (0553) 2443
WALKER & ANDERSON (Kings Lynn) LTD
WINDSOR ROAD, KINGS LYNN
Open: Monday to Saturday
7.45 a.m.-5.30 p.m.
Wednesday 1 p.m. Saturday 5.00 p.m.
H.P.W.WM.D.CS.A.

NORWICH   Tel. 0603 898695
NORFOLK SAW SERVICES
DOG LAND, HORSFORD
Open: Monday to Friday
8.00 a.m.-5.00 p.m.
Saturday 8.00 a.m.-12.00 p.m.
H.P.W.WM.D.CS.A.

NORWICH   Tel. 0603 400933
WESTGATES WOODWORKING   Tx.
MACHINERY, JUPITER ROAD   975412
OFF MILE CROSS LANE
Open: 9 a.m.-5 p.m. weekdays
9 a.m.-12.30 a.m. Sat.
P.W.WM.D.BC.

NORTHAMPTONSHIRE

RUSHDEN   Tel. 093-34 56424
PETER CRISP LIMITED   ★
7 HIGH STREET
Open: Monday to Saturday
8.30 a.m.-5.30 p.m.
Thursday 8.30 a.m.-1.00 p.m.
H.P.W.D.BC.

NORTHUMBERLAND

BLYTH   Tel. (06706) 69279
ALLAN McNAIR WOODCRAFT   ★
69-71 PLESSEY ROAD

Open: Monday to Saturday
9 a.m.-5 p.m.
H.W.WM.D.T.CS.A.BC.

NOTTINGHAMSHIRE

NOTTINGHAM   Tel. (0602) 225979
POOLEWOOD   and 227929
EQUIPMENT LTD   (06077) 2421/5777
5a HOLLY LANE, CHILLWELL
Open: Mon-Fri 9 a.m.-5.30 p.m.
Sat. 9 a.m. to 12.30 p.m.
P.W.WM.D.CS.A.BC.

NOTTINGHAM   Tel. 0602 811889
THE WOODCUTTER
5 TUDOR SQUARE
WEST BRIDGFORD
Open: Tues-Sat 9 a.m.-5.30 p.m.
Fri 9 a.m.-7.30 p.m. Closed Mon.
H.P.W.WM.D.T.CS.A.

OXFORDSHIRE

BICESTER   Tel. (08692) 4156/
WOODMEN   3218/3219
104 CHURCHILL ROAD

Open: Monday-Saturday
9 a.m.-5.30 p.m.
P.W.WM.D.A.BC.

OXFORDSHIRE

OXFORD   Tel. (0865) 45118/9
SARJENT'S TOOL   ★
STORES LTD
150 COWLEY ROAD
Open: Monday to Saturday
8.30 a.m.-5.30 p.m.
H.P.W.WM.D.A.BC.

SHROPSHIRE

TELFORD   Tel. Telford
ASLES LTD   (0952) 48054
VINEYARD ROAD
WELLINGTON
Open: Mon-Fri 8.30am-5.30pm
Saturday 8.30am-4.00pm
H.P.W.WM.D.CS.A.

SOMERSET

TAUNTON   Tel. Taunton 79078
KEITH MITCHELL
TOOLS AND EQUIPMENT
66 PRIORY BRIDGE ROAD
Open: Mon-Fri 8.30am-5.30pm
Saturday 9am-4pm
H.P.W.WM.D.CS.A.BC.

WESTON-SUPER-MARE   Tel.
JOHN TERRY   0934 21803
TOOL SALES   ★
36 ALFRED STREET
Open: Monday to Saturday
9am-5.30pm inclusive
H.P.W.WM.D.CS.A.

STAFFORDSHIRE

TAMWORTH   Tel. 0827-56188
MATTHEWS BROTHERS LTD
KETTLEBROOK ROAD
Open: Mon.-Sat. 8.30am-6.00pm
Demonstrations Sunday mornings
by appointment only
H.P.WM.D.T.CS.A.BC.

SUFFOLK

BURY ST. EDMUNDS   Tel.
TOOLS & THINGS   0284 62022
21 CHURCHGATE   ★

Open: Monday to Saturday
9.00 a.m.-5.30 p.m.
H.P.W.WM.D.A.BC.

IPSWICH   Tel. 0473 86216
FOX WOODWORKING   ★
'STEBBINGS' BACK LANE
WASHBROOK
Open: Tues. Fri. 9.00am-5.30pm
Sat. 9.00am-5pm
H.P.W.WM.D.A.B.C.

SURREY

CARSHALTON BEECHES   Tel.
SURREY WOOD   01-642 6636
MACHINE SALES LTD   ★
56A BANSTEAD ROAD
Open: Tues-Fri 9.30 am-6.00 pm
Saturday 9.30 am-2.00 pm
P.W.WM.D.BC.CS.

CROYDON   Tel. 01-688 5513
L. H. TURTLE   ★
6-12 PARK STREET

Open: Monday to Saturday
8.30 am-5.30 pm
H.P.W.WM.D.A.

SHOP GUIDE SHOP GUIDE

SURREY

GUILDFORD Tel. 0483 61125
MESSINGERS FOR TOOLS
14-18 CHERTSEY STREET
Open: Tuesday to Saturday
8.30 a.m.-5.30 p.m.
Closed all day Monday
H.P.W.D.BC.

SUSSEX

BOGNOR REGIS Tel. (0243) 863100
A. OLBY & SON (BOGNOR REGIS LTD)
"TOOLSHOP", BUILDER'S MERCHANT
HAWTHORN ROAD
Open: Mon-Thurs 8a.m.-5.15p.m.
Fri 8a.m.-8p.m. Sat 8a.m.-12.45p.m.
H.P.W.WM.D.T.C.A.BC.

WORTHING Tel. 0903 38739
W. HOSKING LTD (TOOLS &
MACHINERY) ★
28 PORTLAND RD, BN11 1QN
Open: Mon-Sat 8.30am-5.30pm
Wednesday 8.30am-1.00pm
H.P.W.WM.D.CS.A.BC.

WEST MIDLANDS

WEST BROMWICH Tel: 021-
CONWAY SAW & 553 5461/2
SUPPLY LTD ★
SWAN LANE
Open: 8 a.m.-6 p.m. Mon-Fri
9 a.m.-1 p.m. Saturday
P.W.WM.D.CS.BC.

WILTSHIRE

SWINDON Tel. (0793) 31361
SARJENT'S TOOL STORES LTD ★
64 FLEET STREET
Open: Monday to Saturday
8.30 a.m.-5.30 p.m.
H.P.W.WM.D.A.BC

YORKSHIRE

HALIFAX Tel. 0422 43722/
TIMBERLITE LTD 884788/33575
WILLOWFIELDS ROAD ★
WILLOWFIELD
Open: Monday to Friday
Saturday 9.00 a.m.-5.00 p.m.
H.P.W.WM.D.CS.A.BC.

HARROGATE Tel. 0423 66245/
MULTI-TOOLS 55328 ★
158 KINGS ROAD
Open: Monday to Saturday
8.30 a.m.-6.00 p.m.
H.P.W.WM.D.A.BC.

HUDDERSFIELD Tel. (0484)
NEVILLE M. OLDHAM 641219/(0484)
UNIT 1 DAYLE ST. WORKS 42777
DAYLE STREET, LONGWOOD ★
Open: Mon-Fri 9.00am- 5.30pm
Saturday 9.30am-12.00pm
P.W.WM.D.A.BC.

LEEDS Tel. 0532 574736
D. B. KEIGHLEY MACHINERY LTD ★
VICKERS PLACE
STANNINGLEY
Open: Mon-Fri 9am-5pm
Saturday 9am-1pm
P.W.WM.D.CS.A.BC.

LEEDS Tel. 0532 790507
GEORGE SPENCE & SONS LTD
WELLINGTON ROAD ★
Open: Monday to Friday
8.30 a.m.-5.30 p.m.
Saturday 9.00 a.m.-5.00 p.m.
H.P.W.WM.D.T.A.

YORKSHIRE

SHEFFIELD Tel. 0742-441012
GREGORY & TAYLOR LTD
WORKSOP ROAD
Open: 8.30 a.m.-5.30 p.m.
Monday-Friday
8.30 a.m.-12.30 p.m. Sat.
H.P.W.WM.D.

SHEFFIELD Tel. 0742-24659
GRAHAM OXLEY'S SHOWROOM
BRIDGE STREET ★
Open: Monday to Friday
9.00 a.m.-5.30 p.m.
Saturday 8.30 a.m.-12.30 p.m.
H.W.D.A.BC.

SCOTLAND

GLASGOW Tel. 041 429 4374/4444
THE SAW CENTRE Telex: 777886
596-602 EGLINGTON STREET ★
G5 9RR
Open: Mon.-Fri. 8 a.m.-5.30 p.m.
Saturday 9 a.m.-1 p.m.
H.P.W.WM.D.CS.A.

N. IRELAND

Co. ANTRIM Tel. 0266 6384
GEORGE GARDINER
49 BALLYMONEY STREET
BALLYMENA
Open: Open: Mon-Fri 8.30am-5.30pm
Wednesday 8.30am-1.00pm
H.P.W.D.A.BC.

S. IRELAND

COUNTY KILKENNY Tel.
WOODMEN (0409) 5460
CASHEL HOUSE ★
KELLS ROAD, KILKENNY
Open: Monday to Saturday

WALES

BRITON FERRY Tel. (0639)
WOODMEN 820803/
49 NEATH ROAD ★
Open: Monday to Saturday
9.00 a.m.-5.30 p.m.
P.W.WM.D.A.BC.

CARDIFF Tel. (0222) 37300
JOHN HALL TOOLS LIMITED
22 CHURCHILL WAY
Open: Monday to Saturday
9.00 a.m.-5.30 p.m.
H.P.W.WM.D.A.BC.

CARDIFF Tel. (0222) 3083
F. W. MORGAN & 2556
(CANTON) LTD., 129-133
COWBRIDGE RD EAST,
CANTON
Mon-Sat 8-5 Sun. 9.30-12.30
H.P.T.CS.A.BC.

CARDIFF Tel. (0222) 6158
WOODMEN
74-76 PARK ROAD
WHITCHURCH
Open: Monday to Saturday
9.00 a.m.-5.30 p.m.

CARMARTHEN Tel. 0267 72
DO-IT-YOURSELF SUPPLY
BLUE STREET, DYFED
Open: Monday to Saturday
9.00 a.m.-5.30 p.m.
Thursday 9.00 a.m.-1.00 p.m.
H.P.W.WM.D.T.CS.A.BC.

SWANSEA Tel. (0792) 556
SWANSEA TIMBER &
PLYWOOD CO LTD
57-59 OXFORD STREET
Open: Mon. to Fri. 9 am-5.30 p.m.
Sat. 9 am-1 pm
H.P.W.D.T.CS.A.BC.

YOU CAN BUY WITH CONFIDENCE FROM THE SHOPS IN THIS SHOP GUIDE

★Shops offering a mail order service are denoted by an asterisk

Key: H — Hand tools, **P** — Power tools, **W** — Woodworking machinery up to £1000, **WM** — Woodworking machinery over £1000, **D** — Demonstration available on selected machines, **T** — Timber, **CS** — Cutting or sharpening services, **MF** — Material Finishes, **A** — Attachments, **BC** — Books/catalogues, ***** — Mail order.

£8.00 per Unit
Minimum of SIX insertions.
I enclose remittance of £48.00 ☐
I wish to be invoiced. ☐
Please tick as appropriate.

COUNTY ....

TOWN ....

NAME OF COMPANY/SHOP ....

....

ADDRESS ....

....

To: Valerie Tester
WOODWORKER MAGAZINE
P.O. Box 35,
13 Bridge Street, Hemel Hempstead,
HP1 1EE.

TELEPHONE No ....

DAYS AND HOURS OF BUSINESS

....

....

*TO DENOTE MAIL ORDER SERVICE
AVAILABLE ☐

Prices quoted are those prevailing at press date and are
subject to alteration due to economic conditions.

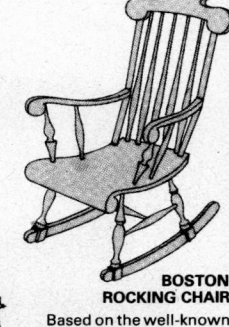
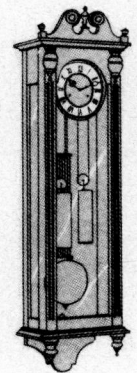

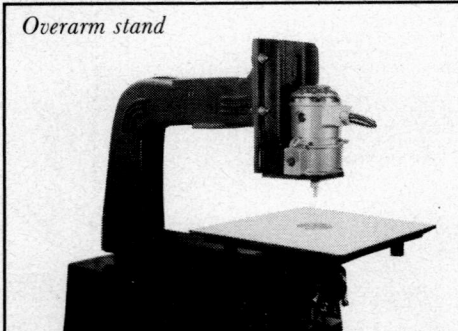

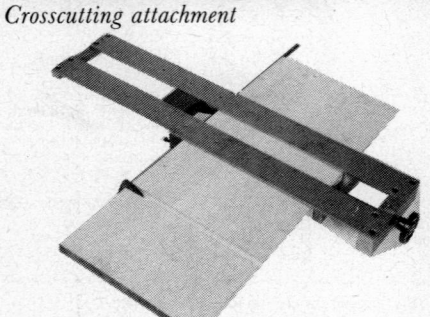